# Lecture Notes in Computer Science　　10072

Commenced Publication in 1973
Founding and Former Series Editors:
Gerhard Goos, Juris Hartmanis, and Jan van Leeuwen

More information about this series at http://www.springer.com/series/7412

George Bebis · Richard Boyle
Bahram Parvin · Darko Koracin
Fatih Porikli · Sandra Skaff
Alireza Entezari · Jianyuan Min
Daisuke Iwai · Amela Sadagic
Carlos Scheidegger · Tobias Isenberg (Eds.)

# Advances in Visual Computing

12th International Symposium, ISVC 2016
Las Vegas, NV, USA, December 12–14, 2016
Proceedings, Part I

Springer

Editors

George Bebis
University of Nevada
Reno, NV
USA

Richard Boyle
NASA Ames Research Center
Moffett Field, CA
USA

Bahram Parvin
Lawrence Berkeley National Laboratory
Berkeley, CA
USA

Darko Koracin
Desert Research Institute
Reno, NV
USA

Fatih Porikli
The Australian National University
O'Malley, ACT
Australia

Sandra Skaff
Pilot AI Labs
Redwood City, CA
USA

Alireza Entezari
University of Florida
Gainesville, FL
USA

Jianyuan Min
Google Inc.
Mountain View, CA
USA

Daisuke Iwai
Osaka University
Osaka
Japan

Amela Sadagic
The MOVES Institute
Monterey, CA
USA

Carlos Scheidegger
University of Arizona
Tucson, AZ
USA

Tobias Isenberg
Université Paris-Sud
Orsay
France

ISSN 0302-9743                    ISSN 1611-3349   (electronic)
Lecture Notes in Computer Science
ISBN 978-3-319-50834-4           ISBN 978-3-319-50835-1   (eBook)
DOI 10.1007/978-3-319-50835-1

Library of Congress Control Number: 2016959639

LNCS Sublibrary: SL6 – Image Processing, Computer Vision, Pattern Recognition, and Graphics

Printed on acid-free paper

This Springer imprint is published by Springer Nature
The registered company is Springer International Publishing AG
The registered company address is: Gewerbestrasse 11, 6330 Cham, Switzerland

# Preface

It is with great pleasure that we welcome you to the proceedings of the 12th International Symposium on Visual Computing (ISVC 2016), which was held in Las Vegas, Nevada, USA. ISVC provides a common umbrella for the four main areas of visual computing including vision, graphics, visualization, and virtual reality. The goal is to provide a forum for researchers, scientists, engineers, and practitioners throughout the world to present their latest research findings, ideas, developments, and applications in the broader area of visual computing.

This year, the program consisted of 15 oral sessions, one poster session, five special tracks, and six keynote presentations. The response to the call for papers was very good; we received over 220 submissions for the main symposium from which we accepted 80 papers for oral presentation and 34 papers for poster presentation. Special track papers were solicited separately through the Organizing and Program Committees of each track. A total of 25 papers were accepted for oral presentation in the special tracks.

All papers were reviewed with an emphasis on the potential to contribute to the state of the art in the field. Selection criteria included accuracy and originality of ideas, clarity and significance of results, and presentation quality. The review process was quite rigorous, involving two to three independent blind reviews followed by several days of discussion. During the discussion period we tried to correct anomalies and errors that might have existed in the initial reviews. Despite our efforts, we recognize that some papers worthy of inclusion may have not been included in the program. We offer our sincere apologies to authors whose contributions might have been overlooked.

We wish to thank everybody who submitted their work to ISVC 2016 for review. It was because of their contributions that we succeeded in having a technical program of high scientific quality. In particular, we would like to thank the ISVC 2016 area chairs, the organizing institutions (UNR, DRI, LBNL, and NASA Ames), the industrial sponsors (BAE Systems, Intel, Ford, Hewlett Packard, Mitsubishi Electric Research Labs, Toyota, General Electric), the international Program Committee, the special track organizers and their Program Committees, the keynote speakers, the reviewers, and especially the authors who contributed their work to the symposium. In particular, we would like to express our appreciation to MERL and Dr. Alan Sullivan for sponsoring the best paper award this year.

We sincerely hope that ISVC 2016 offered participants opportunities for professional growth.

October 2016

George Bebis
Richard Boyle
Bahram Parvin
Darko Koracin
Fatih Porikli
Sandra Skaff
Alireza Entezari
Jianyuan Min
Daisuke Iwai
Amela Sadagic
Carlos Scheidegger
Tobias Isenberg

# Organization

## Steering Committee

Bebis George     University of Nevada, Reno, USA
Boyle Richard     NASA Ames Research Center, USA
Parvin Bahram     Lawrence Berkeley National Laboratory, USA
Koracin Darko     Desert Research Institute, USA

## Area Chairs

### Computer Vision

Porikli Fatih     Australian National University, Australia
Skaff Sandra     Pilot AI Labs, USA

### Computer Graphics

Entezari Alireza     University of Florida, USA
Min Jianyuan     Google, USA

### Virtual Reality

Iwai Daisuke     Osaka University, Japan
Sadagic Amela     Naval Postgraduate School, USA

### Visualization

Scheidegger Carlos     University of Arizona, USA
Isenberg Tobias     Inria, France

### Publicity

Erol Ali     Eksperta Software, Turkey

### Local Arrangements

Morris Brendan     University of Nevada, Las Vegas, USA

### Special Tracks

Wang Junxian     Microsoft, USA

# Keynote Speakers

| | |
|---|---|
| James Regh | Georgia Institute of Technology, USA |
| Kristen Grauman | University of Texas at Austin, USA |
| James Klosowski | AT&T Research Labs, USA |
| Mubarak Shah | University of Central Florida, USA |
| Theisel Holger | University of Magdeburg, Germany |
| Daniel Keefe | University of Minnesota, USA |

# International Program Committee

## (Area 1) Computer Vision

| | |
|---|---|
| Abidi Besma | University of Tennessee at Knoxville, USA |
| Abou-Nasr Mahmoud | Ford Motor Company, USA |
| Aboutajdine Driss | National Center for Scientific and Technical Research, Morocco |
| Aggarwal J.K. | University of Texas, Austin, USA |
| Albu Branzan Alexandra | University of Victoria, Canada |
| Amayeh Gholamreza | Foveon, USA |
| Ambardekar Amol | Microsoft, USA |
| Angelopoulou Elli | University of Erlangen-Nuremberg, Germany |
| Agouris Peggy | George Mason University, USA |
| Argyros Antonis | University of Crete, Greece |
| Asari Vijayan | University of Dayton, USA |
| Athitsos Vassilis | University of Texas at Arlington, USA |
| Basu Anup | University of Alberta, Canada |
| Bekris Kostas | Rutgers University, USA |
| Bhatia Sanjiv | University of Missouri-St. Louis, USA |
| Bimber Oliver | Johannes Kepler University Linz, Austria |
| Bourbakis Nikolaos | Wright State University, USA |
| Brimkov Valentin | State University of New York, USA |
| Cavallaro Andrea | Queen Mary, University of London, UK |
| Charalampidis Dimitrios | University of New Orleans, USA |
| Chatzis Sotirios | Cyprus University of Technology, Cyprus |
| Chellappa Rama | University of Maryland, USA |
| Chen Yang | HRL Laboratories, USA |
| Cheng Hui | Sarnoff Corporation, USA |
| Cheng Shinko | HRL Labs, USA |
| Cui Jinshi | Peking University, China |
| Dagher Issam | University of Balamand, Lebanon |
| Darbon Jerome | CNRS-Ecole Normale Superieure de Cachan, France |
| Demirdjian David | Vecna Robotics, USA |
| Desai Alok | Brigham Young University, USA |
| Diamantas Sotirios | Athens Information Technology, Greece |
| Duan Ye | University of Missouri-Columbia, USA |

| Doulamis Anastasios | Technical University of Crete, Greece |
| Dowdall Jonathan | Google, USA |
| El-Ansari Mohamed | Ibn Zohr University, Morocco |
| El-Gammal Ahmed | University of New Jersey, USA |
| El Choubassi | Maha, Intel, USA |
| Eng How Lung | Institute for Infocomm Research, Singapore |
| Erol Ali | Eksperta Software, Turkey |
| Fan Guoliang | Oklahoma State University, USA |
| Fan Jialue | Northwestern University, USA |
| Ferri Francesc | Universitat de València, Spain |
| Ferzli Rony | Intel, USA |
| Ferryman James | University of Reading, UK |
| Foresti GianLuca | University of Udine, Italy |
| Fowlkes Charless | University of California, Irvine, USA |
| Fukui Kazuhiro | University of Tsukuba, Japan |
| Galata Aphrodite | The University of Manchester, UK |
| Georgescu Bogdan | Siemens, USA |
| Goh Wooi-Boon | Nanyang Technological University, Singapore |
| Ghouzali Sanna | King Saud University, Saudi Arabia |
| Guerra-Filho Gutemberg | Intel, USA |
| Guevara Angel Miguel | University of Porto, Portugal |
| Gustafson David | Kansas State University, USA |
| Hammoud Riad | BAE Systems, USA |
| Harville Michael | Hewlett Packard Labs, USA |
| He Xiangjian | University of Technology, Sydney, Australia |
| Heikkilä Janne | University of Oulu, Finland |
| Hongbin Zha | Peking University, China |
| Hou Zujun | Institute for Infocomm Research, Singapore |
| Hua Gang | IBM T.J. Watson Research Center, USA |
| Hua Gang | Stevens Institute, USA |
| Imiya Atsushi | Chiba University, Japan |
| Kamberov George | University of Alaska, USA |
| Kambhamettu Chandra | University of Delaware, USA |
| Kamberova Gerda | Hofstra University, USA |
| Kakadiaris Ioannis | University of Houston, USA |
| Kettebekov Sanzhar | Keane Inc., USA |
| Kimia Benjamin | Brown University, USA |
| Kisacanin Branislav | Texas Instruments, USA |
| Klette Reinhard | Auckland University of Technology, New Zeland |
| Kollias Stefanos | National Technical University of Athens, Greece |
| Komodakis Nikos | Ecole Centrale de Paris, France |
| Kosmopoulos Dimitrios | University of Patras, Greece |
| Kozintsev Igor | Intel, USA |
| Kuno Yoshinori | Saitama University, Japan |
| Kim Kyungnam | HRL Laboratories, USA |
| Latecki Longin Jan | Temple University, USA |

Lee D.J.                          Brigham Young University, USA
Levine Martin                     McGill University, Canada
Li Baoxin                         Arizona State University, USA
Li Chunming                       Vanderbilt University, USA
Li Xiaowei                        Google Inc., USA
Lim Ser N.                        GE Research, USA
Lisin Dima                        VidoeIQ, USA
Lee Seong-Whan                    Korea University, Korea
Li Shuo                           GE Healthcare, Canada
Lourakis Manolis                  ICS-FORTH, Greece
Loss Leandro                      Lawrence Berkeley National Lab, USA
Luo Gang                          Harvard University, USA
Ma Yunqian                        Honyewell Labs, USA
Maeder Anthony                    Flinders University, Adelaide, Australia
Makrogiannis Sokratis             Delaware State University, USA
Maltoni Davide                    University of Bologna, Italy
Maybank Steve                     Birkbeck College, UK
Medioni Gerard                    University of Southern California, USA
Melenchón Javier                  Universitat Oberta de Catalunya, Spain
Metaxas Dimitris                  Rutgers University, USA
Ming Wei                          Konica Minolta Laboratory, USA
Mirmehdi Majid                    Bristol University, UK
Morris Brendan                    University of Nevada, Las Vegas, USA
Mueller Klaus                     Stony Brook University, USA
Muhammad Ghulam                   King Saud University, Saudi Arabia
Mulligan Jeff                     NASA Ames Research Center, USA
Murray Don                        Point Grey Research, Canada
Nait-Charif Hammadi               Bournemouth University, UK
Nefian Ara                        NASA Ames Research Center, USA
Nguyen Quang Vinh                 University of Western Sydney, Australia
Nicolescu Mircea                  University of Nevada, Reno, USA
Nixon Mark                        University of Southampton, UK
Nolle Lars                        The Nottingham Trent University, UK
Ntalianis Klimis                  National Technical University of Athens, Greece
Or Siu Hang                       The Chinese University of Hong Kong, Hong Kong,
                                    SAR China
Papadourakis George               Technological Education Institute, Greece
Papanikolopoulos                  University of Minnesota, USA
  Nikolaos
Pati Peeta Basa                   CoreLogic, India
Patras Ioannis                    Queen Mary University, London, UK
Pavlidis Ioannis                  University of Houston, USA
Payandeh Shahram                  Simon Fraser University, Canada
Petrakis Euripides                Technical University of Crete, Greece
Peyronnet Sylvain                 LRI, University Paris-Sud, France
Pinhanez Claudio                  IBM Research, Brazil

| | |
|---|---|
| Piccardi Massimo | University of Technology, Australia |
| Pitas Ioannis | Aristotle University of Thessaloniki, Greece |
| Porikli Fatih | Australian National University, Australia |
| Prabhakar Salil | DigitalPersona Inc., USA |
| Prokhorov Danil | Toyota Research Institute, USA |
| Qian Gang | Arizona State University, USA |
| Raftopoulos Kostas | National Technical University of Athens, Greece |
| Regentova Emma | University of Nevada, Las Vegas, USA |
| Remagnino Paolo | Kingston University, UK |
| Ribeiro Eraldo | Florida Institute of Technology, USA |
| Robles-Kelly Antonio | National ICT Australia (NICTA), Australia |
| Ross Arun | Michigan State University, USA |
| Rziza Mohammed | Agdal Mohammed-V University, Morocco |
| Samal Ashok | University of Nebraska, USA |
| Samir Tamer | Allegion, USA |
| Sandberg Kristian | Computational Solutions, USA |
| Sarti Augusto | DEI Politecnico di Milano, Italy |
| Santhanam Anand | University of California, Los Angeles, USA |
| Savakis Andreas | Rochester Institute of Technology, USA |
| Schaefer Gerald | Loughborough University, UK |
| Scalzo Fabien | University of California at Los Angeles, USA |
| Scharcanski Jacob | UFRGS, Brazil |
| Shah Mubarak | University of Central Florida, USA |
| Shehata Mohamed | Memorial University of Newfoundland, Canada |
| Shi Pengcheng | Rochester Institute of Technology, USA |
| Shimada Nobutaka | Ritsumeikan University, Japan |
| Singh Rahul | San Francisco State University, USA |
| Skodras Athanassios | University of Patras, Greece |
| Skurikhin Alexei | Los Alamos National Laboratory, USA |
| Souvenir Richard | University of North Carolina - Charlotte, USA |
| Su Chung-Yen | National Taiwan Normal University, Taiwan (R.O.C.) |
| Sugihara Kokichi | University of Tokyo, Japan |
| Sun Chuan | University of Central Florida, USA |
| Sun Zehang | Apple, USA |
| Suryanarayan Poonam | Google, USA |
| Syeda-Mahmood Tanveer | IBM Almaden, USA |
| Tafti Ahmad | Marshfield Clinic Research Foundation, USA |
| Tan Kar Han | Hewlett Packard, USA |
| Tavakkoli Alireza | University of Houston - Victoria, USA |
| Tavares Joao | Universidade do Porto, Portugal |
| Teoh Eam Khwang | Nanyang Technological University, Singapore |
| Thiran Jean-Philippe | Swiss Federal Institute of Technology Lausanne (EPFL), Switzerland |
| Tistarelli Massimo | University of Sassari, Italy |
| Tong Yan | University of South Carolina, USA |

| | |
|---|---|
| Tsui T.J. | Chinese University of Hong Kong, Hong Kong, SAR China |
| Trucco Emanuele | University of Dundee, UK |
| Tubaro Stefano | DEIB Politecnico di Milano, Italy |
| Uhl Andreas | Salzburg University, Austria |
| Velastin Sergio | Kingston University London, UK |
| Veropoulos Kostantinos | GE Healthcare, Greece |
| Verri Alessandro | Università di Genova, Italy |
| Wang Junxian | Microsoft, USA |
| Wang Song | University of South Carolina, USA |
| Wang Yunhong | Beihang University, China |
| Webster Michael | University of Nevada, Reno, USA |
| Wolff Larry | Equinox Corporation, USA |
| Wong Kenneth | The University of Hong Kong, Hong Kong, SAR China |
| Xiang Tao | Queen Mary, University of London, UK |
| Xu Meihe | University of California at Los Angeles, USA |
| Yang Ming-Hsuan | University of California at Merced, USA |
| Yang Ruigang | University of Kentucky, USA |
| Yin Lijun | SUNY at Binghampton, USA |
| Yu Ting | GE Global Research, USA |
| Yu Zeyun | University of Wisconsin-Milwaukee, USA |
| Yuan Chunrong | Technische Hochschule Köln, Germany |
| Zabulis Xenophon | ICS-FORTH, Greece |
| Zervakis Michalis | Technical University of Crete, Greece |
| Zhang Dong | University of Central Florida, USA |
| Zhang Jian | Wake Forest University, USA |
| Zheng Yuanjie | University of Pennsylvania, USA |
| Zhang Yan | Delphi Corporation, USA |
| Ziou Djemel | University of Sherbrooke, Canada |

## (Area 2) Computer Graphics

| | |
|---|---|
| Abd Rahni Mt Piah | Universiti Sains Malaysia, Malaysia |
| Abram Greg | Texas Advanced Computing Center, USA |
| Adamo-Villani Nicoletta | Purdue University, USA |
| Agu Emmanuel | Worcester Polytechnic Institute, USA |
| Andres Eric | Laboratory XLIM-SIC, University of Poitiers, France |
| Artusi Alessandro | GiLab, Universitat de Girona, Spain |
| Baciu George | Hong Kong PolyU, Hong Kong, SAR China |
| Balcisoy Selim Saffet | Sabanci University, Turkey |
| Barneva Reneta | State University of New York, USA |
| Belyaev Alexander | Heriot-Watt University, UK |
| Benes Bedrich | Purdue University, USA |
| Bilalis Nicholas | Technical University of Crete, Greece |
| Bimber Oliver | Johannes Kepler University Linz, Austria |
| Bouatouch Kadi | University of Rennes I, IRISA, France |

| | |
|---|---|
| Julier Simon J. | University College London, UK |
| Kamberov George | Stevens Institute of Technology, USA |
| Klosowski James | AT&T Research Labs, USA |
| Ko Hyeong-Seok | Seoul National University, Korea |
| Lai Shuhua | Virginia State University, USA |
| Le Binh | Disney Research Pittsburgh, USA |
| Lewis R. Robert | Washington State University, USA |
| Li Bo | Samsung, USA |
| Li Frederick | University of Durham, UK |
| Li Xin | Louisiana State University, USA |
| Lindstrom Peter | Lawrence Livermore National Laboratory, USA |
| Linsen Lars | Jacobs University, Germany |
| Liu Feng | Portland State University, USA |
| Loviscach Joern | Fachhochschule Bielefeld (University of Applied Sciences), Germany |
| Magnor Marcus | TU Braunschweig, Germany |
| McGraw Tim | Purdue University, USA |
| Min Jianyuan | Google, USA |
| Meenakshisundaram Gopi | University of California-Irvine, USA |
| Mendoza Cesar | NaturalMotion Ltd., USA |
| Metaxas Dimitris | Rutgers University, USA |
| Mudur Sudhir | Concordia University, Canada |
| Musuvathy Suraj | Siemens, USA |
| Nait-Charif Hammadi | University of Dundee, UK |
| Nasri Ahmad | American University of Beirut, Lebanon |
| Noh Junyong | KAIST, Korea |
| Noma Tsukasa | Kyushu Institute of Technology, Japan |
| Okada Yoshihiro | Kyushu University, Japan |
| Olague Gustavo | CICESE Research Center, Mexico |
| Oliveira Manuel M. | Universidade Federal do Rio Grande do Sul, Brazil |
| Owen Charles | Michigan State University, USA |
| Ostromoukhov Victor M. | University of Montreal, Canada |
| Pascucci Valerio | University of Utah, USA |
| Patchett John | Los Alamons National Lab, USA |
| Peters Jorg | University of Florida, USA |
| Pronost Nicolas | Utrecht University, The Netherlands |
| Qin Hong | Stony Brook University, USA |
| Rautek Peter | Vienna University of Technology, Austria |
| Razdan Anshuman | Arizona State University, USA |
| Rosen Paul | University of Utah, USA |
| Rosenbaum Rene | University of California at Davis, USA |
| Rudomin Isaac | Barcelona Supercomputing Center, Spain |
| Rushmeier Holly | Yale University, USA |
| Saha Punam | University of Iowa, USA |

| | |
|---|---|
| Sander Pedro | The Hong Kong University of Science and Technology, Hong Kong, SAR China |
| Sapidis Nickolas | University of Western Macedonia, Greece |
| Sarfraz Muhammad | Kuwait University, Kuwait |
| Scateni Riccardo | University of Cagliari, Italy |
| Sequin Carlo | University of California-Berkeley, USA |
| Shead Timothy | Sandia National Laboratories, USA |
| Stamminger Marc | University of Erlangen-Nuremberg, Germany |
| Su Wen-Poh | Griffith University, Australia |
| Szumilas Lech | Research Institute for Automation and Measurements, Poland |
| Tan Kar Han | Hewlett Packard, USA |
| Tarini Marco | University dell'Insubria (Varese), Italy |
| Teschner Matthias | University of Freiburg, Germany |
| Tong Yiying | Michigan State University, USA |
| Umlauf Georg | HTWG Constance, Germany |
| Vanegas Carlos | University of California at Berkeley, USA |
| Wald Ingo | University of Utah, USA |
| Walter Marcelo | UFRGS, Brazil |
| Wimmer Michael | Technical University of Vienna, Austria |
| Wylie Brian | Sandia National Laboratory, USA |
| Wyman Chris | University of Calgary, Canada |
| Wyvill Brian | University of Iowa, USA |
| Yang Qing-Xiong | University of Illinois at Urbana, Champaign, USA |
| Yang Ruigang | University of Kentucky, USA |
| Ye Duan | University of Missouri-Columbia, USA |
| Yi Beifang | Salem State University, USA |
| Yin Lijun | Binghamton University, USA |
| Yoo Terry | National Institutes of Health, USA |
| Yuan Xiaoru | Peking University, China |
| Zhang Jian Jun | Bournemouth University, UK |
| Zeng Jianmin | Nanyang Technological University, Singapore |
| Zara Jiri | Czech Technical University in Prague, Czech Republic |
| Zeng Wei | Florida Institute of Technology, USA |
| Zordan Victor | University of California at Riverside, USA |

## (Area 3) Virtual Reality

| | |
|---|---|
| Alcaniz Mariano | Technical University of Valencia, Spain |
| Arns Laura | Purdue University, USA |
| Bacim Felipe | Virginia Tech, USA |
| Balcisoy Selim | Sabanci University, Turkey |
| Behringer Reinhold | Leeds Metropolitan University UK |
| Benes Bedrich | Purdue University, USA |
| Bilalis Nicholas | Technical University of Crete, Greece |
| Blach Roland | Fraunhofer Institute for Industrial Engineering, Germany |

| | |
|---|---|
| Blom Kristopher | University of Barcelona, Spain |
| Bogdanovych Anton | University of Western Sydney, Australia |
| Brady Rachael | Duke University, USA |
| Brega Jose Remo Ferreira | Universidade Estadual Paulista, Brazil |
| Brown Ross | Queensland University of Technology, Australia |
| Bues Matthias | Fraunhofer IAO in Stuttgart, Germany |
| Capin Tolga | Bilkent University, Turkey |
| Chen Jian | Brown University, USA |
| Cooper Matthew | University of Linköping, Sweden |
| Coquillart Sabine | Inria, France |
| Craig Alan | NCSA University of Illinois at Urbana-Champaign, USA |
| Cremer Jim | University of Iowa, USA |
| Edmunds Timothy | University of British Columbia, Canada |
| Encarnaio L. Miguel | ACT Inc., USA |
| Friedman Doron | IDC, Israel |
| Fuhrmann Anton | VRVis Research Center, Austria |
| Gregory Michelle | Pacific Northwest National Lab, USA |
| Gupta Satyandra K. | University of Maryland, USA |
| Haller Michael | FH Hagenberg, Austria |
| Hamza-Lup Felix | Armstrong Atlantic State University, USA |
| Herbelin Bruno | EPFL, Switzerland |
| Hinkenjann Andre | Bonn-Rhein-Sieg University of Applied Sciences, Germany |
| Hollerer Tobias | University of California at Santa Barbara, USA |
| Huang Jian | University of Tennessee at Knoxville, USA |
| Huang Zhiyong | Institute for Infocomm Research (I2R), Singapore |
| Jerald Jason | NextGen Interactions, USA |
| Julier Simon J. | University College London, UK |
| Johnsen Kyle | University of Georgia, USA |
| Jones Adam | Clemson University, USA |
| Kiyokawa Kiyoshi | Osaka University, Japan |
| Kohli Luv | InnerOptic, USA |
| Kopper Regis | Duke University, USA |
| Kozintsev Igor | Samsung, USA |
| Kuhlen Torsten | RWTH Aachen University, Germany |
| Laha Bireswar | Stanford University, USA |
| Lee Cha | University of California, Santa Barbara, USA |
| Liere Robert van | CWI, The Netherlands |
| Livingston A. Mark | Naval Research Laboratory, USA |
| Luo Xun | Qualcomm Research, USA |
| Malzbender Tom | Hewlett Packard Labs, USA |
| MacDonald Brendan | National Institute for Occupational Safety and Health, USA |
| Molineros Jose | Teledyne Scientific and Imaging, USA |
| Muller Stefan | University of Koblenz, Germany |

| | |
|---|---|
| Owen Charles | Michigan State University, USA |
| Paelke Volker | Bremen University of Applied Sciences, Germany |
| Peli Eli | Harvard University, USA |
| Pettifer Steve | The University of Manchester, UK |
| Pronost Nicolas | Utrecht University, The Netherlands |
| Pugmire Dave | Los Alamos National Lab, USA |
| Qian Gang | Arizona State University, USA |
| Rodello Ildeberto | University of San Paulo, Brazil |
| Sapidis Nickolas | University of Western Macedonia, Greece |
| Schulze Jurgen | University of California - San Diego, USA |
| Sherman Bill | Indiana University, USA |
| Singh Gurjot | Virginia Tech, USA |
| Slavik Pavel | Czech Technical University in Prague, Czech Republic |
| Steinicke Frank | University of Wurzburg, Germany |
| Suma Evan | University of Southern California, USA |
| Stamminger Marc | University of Erlangen-Nuremberg, Germany |
| Srikanth Manohar | Indian Institute of Science, India |
| Wald Ingo | University of Utah, USA |
| Wernert Eric | Indiana University, USA |
| Whitted Turner | TWI Research, UK |
| Wong Kin Hong | The Chinese University of Hong Kong, Hong Kong, SAR China |
| Yu Ka Chun | Denver Museum of Nature and Science, USA |
| Yuan Chunrong | Technische Hochschule Köln, Germany |
| Zachmann Gabriel | Clausthal University, Germany |
| Zara Jiri | Czech Technical University in Prague, Czech |
| Zhang Hui | Indiana University, USA |
| Zhao Ye | Kent State University, USA |

### (Area 4) Visualization

| | |
|---|---|
| Andrienko Gennady | Fraunhofer Institute IAIS, Germany |
| Apperley Mark | University of Waikato, New Zealand |
| Brady Rachael | Duke University, USA |
| Benes Bedrich | Purdue University, USA |
| Bilalis Nicholas | Technical University of Crete, Greece |
| Bonneau Georges-Pierre | Grenoble University, France |
| Bruckner Stefan | Vienna University of Technology, Austria |
| Brown Ross | Queensland University of Technology, Australia |
| Bihler Katja | VRVis Research Center, Austria |
| Burch Michael | University of Stuttgart, Germany |
| Callahan Steven | University of Utah, USA |
| Chatzis Sotirios | Cyprus University of Technology, Cyprus |
| Chen Jian | Brown University, USA |
| Chiang Yi-Jen | New York University, USA |
| Cooper Matthew | University of Linköping, Sweden |

| | |
|---|---|
| Chourasia Amit | University of California - San Diego, USA |
| Daniels Joel | University of Utah, USA |
| Dick Christian | Technical University of Munich, Germany |
| Duan Ye | University of Missouri-Columbia, USA |
| Dwyer Tim | Monash University, Australia |
| Entezari Alireza | University of Florida, USA |
| Ferreira Nivan | University of Arizona, USA |
| Frey Steffen | University of Stuttgart, Germany |
| Geist Robert | Clemson University, USA |
| Gotz David | University of North Carolina at Chapel Hill, USA |
| Grinstein Georges | University of Massachusetts Lowell, USA |
| Goebel Randy | University of Alberta, Canada |
| Gregory Michelle | Pacific Northwest National Lab, USA |
| Hadwiger Helmut Markus | KAUST, Saudi Arabia |
| Hagen Hans | Technical University of Kaiserslautern, Germany |
| Hamza-Lup Felix | Armstrong Atlantic State University, USA |
| Hochheiser Harry | University of Pittsburgh, USA |
| Hollerer Tobias | University of California at Santa Barbara, USA |
| Hong Lichan | University of Sydney, Australia |
| Hong Seokhee | Palo Alto Research Center, USA |
| Hotz Ingrid | Zuse Institute Berlin, Germany |
| Huang Zhiyong | Institute for Infocomm Research (I2R), Singapore |
| Jiang Ming | Lawrence Livermore National Laboratory, USA |
| Joshi Alark | University of San Francisco, USA |
| Julier Simon J. | University College London, UK |
| Klosowski James | AT&T Labs, USA |
| Koch Steffen | University of Stuttgart, Germany |
| Laramee Robert | Swansea University, UK |
| Lewis R. Robert | Washington State University, USA |
| Liere Robert van | CWI, The Netherlands |
| Lim Ik Soo | Bangor University, UK |
| Linsen Lars | Jacobs University, Germany |
| Liu Zhanping | Old Dominion University, USA |
| Maeder Anthony | Flinders University, Adelaide, Australia |
| Malpica Jose | Alcala University, Spain |
| Masutani Yoshitaka | Hiroshima City University, Japan |
| Matkovic Kresimir | VRVis Research Center, Austria |
| McCaffrey James | Microsoft Research/Volt VTE, USA |
| Melancon Guy | CNRS UMR 5800 LaBRI and Inria Bordeaux Sud-Ouest, France |
| Miksch Silvia | Vienna University of Technology, Austria |
| Monroe Laura | Los Alamos National Labs, USA |
| Morie Jacki | University of Southern California, USA |
| Moreland Kenneth | Sandia National Laboratories, USA |
| Mudur Sudhir | Concordia University, Canada |

| | |
|---|---|
| Museth Ken | Linköping University, Sweden |
| Paelke Volker | Bremen University of Applied Sciences, Germany |
| Papka Michael | Argonne National Laboratory, USA |
| Payandeh Shahram | Simon Fraser University, Canada |
| Peikert Ronald | Swiss Federal Institute of Technology Zurich, Switzerland |
| Pettifer Steve | The University of Manchester, UK |
| Pugmire Dave | Los Alamos National Lab, USA |
| Rabin Robert | University of Wisconsin at Madison, USA |
| Razdan Anshuman | Arizona State University, USA |
| Reina Guido | University of Stuttgart, Germany |
| Rhyne Theresa-Marie | North Carolina State University, USA |
| Rosenbaum Rene | University of California at Davis, USA |
| Sadlo Filip | Heidelberg University, Germany |
| Scheuermann Gerik | University of Leipzig, Germany |
| Shead Timothy | Sandia National Laboratories, USA |
| Sips Mike | Stanford University, USA |
| Slavik Pavel | Czech Technical University in Prague, Czech Republic |
| Thakur Sidharth | Intel, USA |
| Theisel Holger | University of Magdeburg, Germany |
| Thiele Olaf | University of Mannheim, Germany |
| Umlauf Georg | HTWG Constance, Germany |
| Viegas Fernanda | IBM, USA |
| Wald Ingo | University of Utah, USA |
| Wan Ming | Boeing Phantom Works, USA |
| Weiskopf Daniel | University of Stuttgart, Germany |
| Wernert Eric | Indiana University, USA |
| Wischgoll Thomas | Wright State University, USA |
| Wongsuphasawat Krist | Twitter Inc, USA |
| Wylie Brian | Sandia National Laboratory, USA |
| Wu Yin | Indiana University, USA |
| Xu Wei | Brookhaven National Lab, USA |
| Xu Weijia | University of Texas at Austin, USA |
| Yeasin Mohammed | Memphis University, USA |
| Yi Hong | University of North Carolina at Chapel Hill, USA |
| Yuan Xiaoru | Peking University, China |
| Zachmann Gabriel | Clausthal University, Germany |
| Zhang Hui | Indiana University, USA |
| Zhao Ye | Kent State University, USA |
| Zheng Ziyi | Stony Brook University, USA |
| Zhukov Leonid | Caltech, USA |

# Special Tracks

## 1. Computational Bioimaging Organizers

| | |
|---|---|
| Tavares João Manuel R.S. | University of Porto, Portugal |
| Natal Jorge Renato | University of Porto, Portugal |

## 2. 3D Surface Reconstruction, Mapping, and Visualization Organizers

| | |
|---|---|
| Nefian Ara | Carnegie Mellon University/NASA Ames Research Center, USA |
| Edwards Laurence | NASA Ames Research Center, USA |
| Huertas Andres | NASA Jet Propulsion Lab, USA |

## 3. Advancing Autonomy for Aerial Robotics Organizers

| | |
|---|---|
| Alexis Kostas | University of Nevada, Reno, USA |
| Chli Margarita | University of Edinburgh, UK |
| Garcia Carrillo Rodolfo Luis | University of Nevada, Reno, USA |
| Nikolakopoulos George | Lulea University of Technology, Sweden |
| Oettershagen Philipp | ETH Zurich, Switzerland |
| Oh Paul | University of Nevada, Las Vegas, USA |
| Papachristos Christos | University of Nevada, Reno, USA |

## 4. Computer Vision as a Service Organizers

| | |
|---|---|
| Yu Zeyun | University of Wisconsin-Milwaukee, USA |
| Arabnia Hamid | University of Georgia, USA |
| He Max | Marshfield Clinic Research Foundation, USA |
| Muller Henning | University of Applied Sciences Western, Switzerland |
| Tafti Ahmad | Marshfield Clinic Research Foundation, USA |

## 5. Visual Perception and Robotic Systems Organizers

| | |
|---|---|
| La Hung | University of Nevada, Reno, USA |
| Sheng Weihua | Oklahoma State University, USA |
| Fan Guoliang | Oklahoma State University, USA |
| Kuno Yoshinori | Saitama University, Japan |
| Ha Quang | University of Technology Sydney, Australia |
| Zhang Hao | Colorado School of Mines, USA |
| Horn Joachim | Helmut Schmidt University, Germany |

**Organizing Institutions and Sponsors**

# Contents – Part I

## Motion and Tracking

## Segmentation

## Pattern Recognition

## Visualization

## ST: 3D Mapping, Modeling and Surface Reconstruction

## ST: Advancing Autonomy for Aerial Robotics

## Medical Imaging

**Virtual Reality**

## ST: Computer Vision as a Service

## Biometrics

## ST: Visual Perception and Robotic Systems

# Contents – Part II

# ST: Computational Bioimaging

# Similarity Metric Learning for 2D to 3D Registration of Brain Vasculature

Alice Tang and Fabien Scalzo$^{(\boxtimes)}$

Neurovascular Imaging Research Core, Department of Neurology
and Computer Science, University of California,
Los Angeles (UCLA), Los Angeles, USA
fab@cs.ucla.edu

**Abstract.** 2D to 3D image registration techniques are useful in the treatment of neurological diseases such as stroke. Image registration can aid physicians and neurosurgeons in the visualization of the brain for treatment planning, provide 3D information during treatment, and enable serial comparisons. In the context of stroke, image registration is challenged by the occluded vessels and deformed anatomy due to the ischemic process. In this paper, we present an algorithm to register 2D digital subtraction angiography (DSA) with 3D magnetic resonance angiography (MRA) based upon local point cloud descriptors. The similarity between these local descriptors is learned using a machine learning algorithm, allowing flexibility in the matching process. In our experiments, the error rate of 2D/3D registration using our machine learning similarity metric (52.29) shows significant improvement when compared to a Euclidean metric (152.54). The proposed similarity metric is versatile and could be applied to a wide range of 2D/3D registration.

## 1 Introduction

During endovascular treatment for acute ischemic stroke, various images of the brain are taken at different time points before, during, and after intervention. While these images provide useful visual cues about the brain, the information obtained is often limited by the imaging technique used, thereby limiting the information available for treatment decisions. 2D-3D registration can partially address this problem by combining the advantage of 2D images with 3D ones; allowing 3D visualization of bodily structures during intervention by aligning pre-interventional 3D images (through CT, MRI, etc.) with realtime intra-interventional 2D images (e.g. fluoroscopy, DSA). Furthermore, registration also aids with comparisons of various images taken throughout the time frame, allowing further analysis of changes over time.

2D-3D coregistration has been widely used in the medical field for applications such as image-guided interventions and surgery [1] for treatments involving implants [2], spinal surgery [3], cancer therapy [4], and brain diseases. For treatment of neurovascular diseases, since 2D DSA is generally more efficiently used to visualize the vasculature during a procedure, corresponding 3D information

© Springer International Publishing AG 2016
G. Bebis et al. (Eds.): ISVC 2016, Part I, LNCS 10072, pp. 3–12, 2016.
DOI: 10.1007/978-3-319-50835-1_1

to those 2D images can provide surgeons insights about the positioning of surgical tools in relation to the target site during treatment [5]. In the context of stroke, 2D-3D registration is an especially challenging procedure as parts of the vasculature are missing or deformed, due to occlusions in the blood vessels. In this paper, we address these issues by presenting a 2D-3D registration algorithm that uses machine learning on local features.

Image registration can be defined as the process of finding the geometric transformation between two sets of images, which brings them to the same coordinate frame with the best possible spatial correspondence. Since manual registration can be time consuming and tedious, much work has been done on automatic ways to register medical images [6–8]. Previous works with feature-based methods use feature extraction to obtain matching geometries and correspondences [9], while intensity-based methods compare values in pixels [10]. Hybrid methods have also been employed that combine feature segmentation with pixelwise comparisons [11]. Recent methods also performed registration in different spaces, such as the Fourier space [12].

For algorithms that rely upon image match comparison, registration is performed by optimizing a similarity measure indicating the amount of correspondence between two images. Common similarity measures that have been employed include mutual information, cross correlation, entropy, and pattern intensity, among others. Recently, machine learning has gained much interest in the medical field, with its diverse use and predictive power [13]. By learning patterns of known matches, a machine learning model can be used to predict the correspondence between two images based for example on local features, often allowing greater flexibility.

With a similarity measure established, an iterative optimization procedure can be used to find the optimal parameters which maximize or minimize a cost function based upon the similarity measure. Numerous optimization procedures have been developed and are available in the literature such as Levenberg-Marquardt, Powell's method, downhill simplex, and gradient descent. Heuristic methods have also been used such as Monte Carlo random sampling, pattern search algorithm, and others.

This paper presents a registration algorithm that applies machine learning to learn the similarity of 2D and 3D local image features in a task dependent way, which can then be extended to predict the overall similarity of two images. By focusing on local image properties, the algorithm allows greater variations between the registered images. Optimization is performed with a heuristic search using the Nedler-Simplex method. We first outline the registration algorithm in Sect. 2, and then describe the optimization process and the accuracy of this algorithm in Sects. 3 and 4. Then, some discussion about the algorithm and comparisons with other algorithms are presented in Sect. 5.

## 2   Methods

**Image Dataset.** The dataset used in this study to evaluate our framework was collected from patients admitted at a comprehensive stroke center and diagnosed with symptoms of acute ischemic stroke. The use of this dataset was approved by the local Institutional Review Board (IRB). Inclusion criteria for this study included: (1) Final diagnosis of acute ischemic stroke, (2) last known well time within six hours at admission, (3) pre-interventional Magnetic Resonance Angiography (MRA) performed during the routine acute evaluation, (4) Digital Subtraction Angiography (DSA) of the brain performed at the end of a thrombectomy procedure. A total of 18 patients satisfied the above criteria and were included in this study. The patients had various success in revascularization. DSA images had a resolution of $1024 \times 1024$ pixels, while the resolution of MRA image varied across patients.

**Vessel Extraction and Groundtruth.** Blood vessels were detected on DSA with a Frangi filter [14]. This algorithm uses eigenvalues to compute the probability that a pixel contains a vessel by computing the similarity of a structure to an ideal tube. A simple threshold established with Otsu's method was used to create a binary mask and a cloud of 2000 points was extracted from each image. 3D MRA data was segmented semi-automatically using Osirix software to extract the major arteries of the brain. Similarly to the 2D DSA sampling, we extracted 2000 points from the segmented 3D image. The groundtruth was manually established between DSA and MRA images by a researcher in Neurology. An in-house software allowed the expert to rotate, scale, and shift the 3D MRA image volume to match the 2D DSA image. The result was a sequence of transformations that led to an ideal mapping between MRA and DSA that will later be used as groundtruth in our experiments.

**Registration Model.** The goal of 2D/3D registration is to find the transformation between the image coordinate system of the 3D image to a 2D image projection. The images are represented as point clouds and the transformation is assumed to be an affine transformation with constant scaling factor followed by a projection onto the $xy$ plane. Thus, we can represent our transformation $T : \mathbb{R}^3 \rightarrow \mathbb{R}^2$ as

$$T = A(r)S(s_x, s_y)PR_z(\theta_z)R_y(\theta_y)R_x(\theta_x) \tag{1}$$

where $R_x(\theta_x)$, $R_y(\theta_y)$ and $R_z(\theta_z)$ rotates a point respectively about $x$, $y$ and $z$ axis by $\theta_x$, $\theta_y$ and $\theta_z$, $P$ projects a point from $\mathbb{R}^3$ to $\mathbb{R}^2$ by taking the first two coordinates, $S(s_x, s_y)$ shifts a point by $(s_x, s_y)$, and $A(r)$ scales a point by a constant factor $r$. This decomposition simplifies the registration process as a search for a 6-parameter vector $\mathbf{p} = [\theta_x\ \theta_y\ \theta_z\ s_x\ s_y\ r]$ that optimally aligns the images. To find these transformation parameters, the 2D-3D registration algorithm utilizes a machine learning model to learn a similarity measure between points based upon their local neighborhood (Fig. 1).

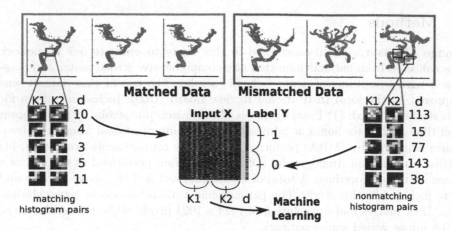

**Fig. 1.** Extraction of local input features from 2D DSA and 3D MRA to train the model. Local descriptors are local point cloud histograms. Pairs of point descriptors are sampled randomly from labeled matching and nonmatching transformations.

**Image Representation.** The 2D/3D images are represented as point clouds in their respective spaces. An erosion filter is applied to remove outliers. In this paper, we refer to the 2D point cloud as the Target image, and the 3D point cloud as the Source image. After a transformation is applied to the 3D point cloud, we refer to the transformed 3D image as the Transformed image. Note that the Transformed image is two dimensional (as it is projected to a 2D space).

With these representative sample of the Target and Transformed image, a local 2D histogram $H_i$ acts as a point descriptor to describe each point by its local neighborhood. The histogram can be created given parameters of histogram size, $h_s$, and number of bins, $h_b$, and is normalized by the total number of points in the histogram. Each histogram can be condensed and represented as a 1D array of size $1 \times h_b{}^2$. A collection of histograms for each point in an image can thus act as the image descriptor.

**Machine Learning Model.** We use Spectral Regression for Discriminant Analysis (SR-DA) [15] to find the parameters of a function that will output the likelihood of a match (i.e. similarity) between two points given the point distribution in their neighborhood. During image registration, the point correspondences are two presumed point matches computed by taking the closest neighbor point in the Target image for every sampled point in the Transformed image. The average of the similarities for a representative sample of point correspondences acts as the total similarity measure for the Target and Transformed image. For each iteration of the registration process, a transformation $\hat{T}$ obtained from the parameter vector **p** will be applied to the 3D Source image to obtain a 2D Transformed image. $N$ randomly sampled points in the Transformed image with point correspondences in the Target image will be used to construct the input feature matrix to be given to the machine learning model.

The input to the machine learning model can be represented as a matrix $X = (K_1 \; K_2 \; d)$. $K_1$ is the $N \times h_b{}^2$ matrix of point descriptors for the $N$ points, $\{p_1, p_2, ..., p_N\}$, that are sampled from the Transformed image. For each point in the Transformed image, $p_i$, the nearest neighbor point in the Target image, $q_i$, will be chosen by minimizing the distance between $p_i$ and $q_i$. $q_i$ will be taken as a point correspondence, that is, the point descriptor for $p_i$ is expected to be similar to the point descriptor for $q_i$. $K_2$ is then the $N \times h_b{}^2$ matrix where each row $i$ consists of the point descriptor of the nearest corresponding point to $p_i$ in the Target image. Lastly, $d$ is a $N \times 1$ vector consisting of the Euclidean distance between the two point correspondences for each row, that is, $d_i = \sqrt{(x_{pi} - x_{qi})^2 + (y_{pi} - y_{qi})^2}$. Therefore, $X$ is of size $N \times (2 \cdot h_b{}^2 + 1)$, where each row represent information of each corresponding point pairs. The similarity function is applied to each row of X, and the output can be represented as a vector $\hat{Y}$ in $\mathbb{R}^{N \times 1}$, where $\hat{Y}_i$ represents the probability of a match between $p_i$ and $q_i$. The average of all values of $\hat{Y}$ gives the similarity metric between the Target and Transformed image.

To train the model, we require representative pairs of matching and nonmatching points to construct the input feature matrix $X$ and a label vector $Y$ with entries 1 for the matching point pairs and 0 for the nonmatching point pairs. We use data augmentation to obtain the sample of matching point pairs by generating various transformations on the Source image by adding random variations to the groundtruth parameter vector, $\mathbf{p}_{gt}$. This allows the machine learning model to be robust. The matching point pairs are also thresholded by distance in order to improve the accuracy of training by removing points present as noise or extraneous vasculature. Nonmatching point pairs were generated by applying larger variations to the parameters of $\mathbf{p}_{gt}$. These samples are represented in a training matrix, $X$, with corresponding label vector $Y$.

$X$ is normalized column-wise and a Spectral Regression model is trained with $X$ and $Y$ and can then be used as a similarity function $F$ between two candidate matches. The constructed similarity function $F$ can be applied between point pairs in the Transformed and Target images, and the total similarity will be obtained: $\mathcal{SIM} = \hat{Y} = F(X)$.

**Registering a New Set of Images.** The goal of 2D-3D registration is to find $\hat{T}$, an estimated transformation, based upon finding the 6 parameter vector $\mathbf{p}$ that optimizes the similarity value. Although a higher similarity value generally indicates a greater chance of matching, the negative of the similarity will be taken as our cost function in order to frame the optimization as a minimization problem: $\mathcal{COST} = -\mathcal{SIM} = -F(X)$. An initial parameter must be given to start the optimization, which will then proceed by the Nedler-Mead Simplex algorithm [16] as an heuristic search method to iteratively test various points in the 6-parameter space to find the optimal transformation. Optimization is stopped when the similarity or parameters are within a tolerance interval, or when 50 iterations of the algorithm have been reached (Fig. 2).

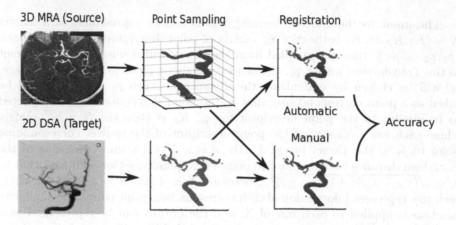

**Fig. 2.** Diagram representing the registration process. The accuracy of our algorithm is determined by comparing the computed and the manual transformations.

## 3   Experiments

**Parameter Optimization.** In order to find the optimal parameters for training and applying the machine learning model, cross-validation tests were performed to compute the accuracy of the model under different parameters, using the area under the curve (AUC) as the accuracy measure. These parameters include the number of training samples, the histogram size $h_s$, the number of bins per histogram $h_b$, the regularization parameter (alpha), and the similarity smoothing parameter (t) used in the machine learning model. For every set of parameters, k pairs of training images, $P_1, P_2, ..., P_k$, coupled with the corresponding groundtruth transformation vector, $\mathbf{p}_{gt,1}, \mathbf{p}_{gt,2}, ..., \mathbf{p}_{gt,k}$, were used for training and testing. For each set of training parameters, one image, $P_m$, was set aside while the rest were used to train the machine learning model and compute the similarity function. The similarity function was then applied to sampled point pairs in the excluded training image, $P_m$, to obtain prediction $\hat{Y}_{Pm}$. This process was repeated so that all k images are excluded once. The point pair predictions $\hat{Y}_{Pm}$ are then compared against known corresponding training labels $Y_{Pm}$ and the AUC value is computed as a measure of the accuracy of the set of training parameters. This process is repeated again for each set of training parameters and corresponding AUC value computed.

**Accuracy of Registration.** To determine the effectiveness of the learned similarity metric, the accuracy of the registration model was tested against another simple metric which corresponds to minimizing the Euclidean norm of the error between histograms of point correspondences. For both the learned similarity (ML similarity) and the Euclidean norm similarity (Eunorm similarity), the registration process was performed to obtain an estimated parameter vector, $\mathbf{p}_{ML}$ and $\mathbf{p}_{Eunorm}$, representing the predicted transformation.

Error in this algorithm was found by transforming the 3D Source image with the ground truth parameter $\mathbf{p}_{gt}$, then finding the distance between the same points transformed with the predicted parameters. The root mean square error was found for both the ML similarity and the Eunorm similarity as a measure of accuracy.

## 4  Results

Cross-validation was performed to evaluate and optimize the model such that the number of training point pairs, the number histogram bins, and the regularization parameter of the regression model were optimized at each iteration of the crossvalidation. The optimal parameters found for our data set: training sample size = 2000, alpha = .001, smoothing parameter t = 6, $h_b = 6$, $h_s = 400$.

18 samples of patient pre-interventional MRA scans and post-treatment DSA scans were used for the registration processes. For each Source image, the registration process was performed with both the machine learning model similarity and the Euclidean distance similarity. Initial parameters were same for both similarity measures and varied from groundtruth parameters within 60° about the x and y axis, 150° about the z-axis, 10% shift, and 15% scaling. Root mean square error was computed between the same points in the Source image transformed using the estimated parameters, and the groundtruth parameters. Manual visualizations show that the registration process using the machine learning model similarity failed to register 2 samples of images, while using the Euclidian norm similarity failed to register 12 samples of images. The root mean square error for the Euclidean similarity metric was $152.54 \pm 87.39$, while the proposed ML similarity metric led to an error of $52.29 \pm 64.69$.

## 5  Discussions

The use of machine learning for image registration has many advantages and allows greater adaptation for various applications. Although we focused on registration of MRA and DSA images in this paper, machine learning may be extended to compute the similarity function between images obtained from other modalities and acquisition parameters, provided enough training samples are available.

The disadvantage of this algorithm involves the need for training samples to exist in order to pre-train the machine learning model before the similarity function can be used for registration. The process to obtain optimal parameters for training and registration may also be challenging and time-consuming. Furthermore, the timing of registration using this algorithm varies from 1–10 min, which may be slow or adequate depending on the application.

Future experiments may involve testing machine learning applications for different image descriptor choices. Hybrid algorithms can be constructed by considering image features such as global histograms, gradient information, vessel shape, or transformations of the image in parameter or frequency space. It would also be advantageous to adapt the algorithm for a larger training sets in the future. Furthermore, since manual groundtruth parameters were also prone to error, it may be beneficial to obtain multiple manual registrations from various neurology researchers (Fig 3).

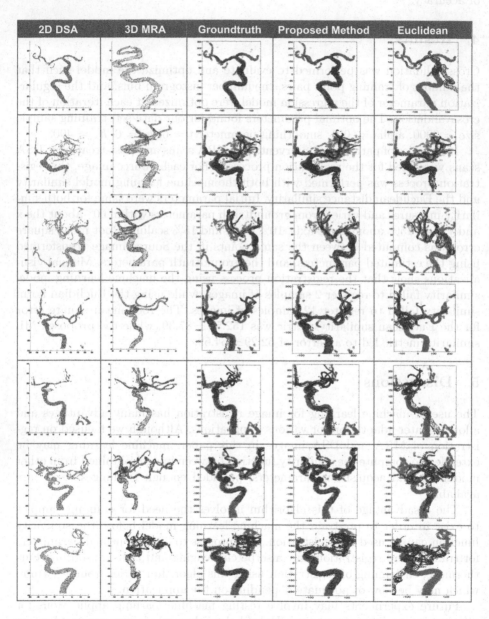

**Fig. 3.** Image panel illustrating the target 2D DSA, source 3D MRA, the groundtruth, and the result of the registration using ML and Euclidean norm metrics.

Despite these limitations, the proposed framework could be used to register perfusion angiography [17] maps to MRA, and compare/map Computational Fluid Dynamics (CFD) parameters extracted from DSA [18] with the ones computed from 3D MRA/CTA [19,20].

# 6   Conclusion

Given the outcome of our local similarity machine learning method, it is shown that using machine learning for future applications of 2D-3D registration can provide adaptability beyond what has been previously obtained. Machine learning models can be trained with different datasets, such as images obtained from other modalities and methods. Eventually, a database of trained models can be collected. These models then can be easily chosen, implemented, and rapidly used for registration purposes in future clinical or research settings. Overall, using machine learning in 3D-2D registration has the potential reach for far applications into the medical field.

**Acknowledgments.** Prof. Scalzo was partially supported by a AHA grant $16BGIA27760152$, a Spitzer grant, and received hardware donations from Gigabyte, Nvidia, and Intel. Alice Tang was partially supported by a UC Leads Fellowship.

# References

1. Holmes, D., Rettmann, M., Robb, R.: Visualization in image-guided interventions. In: Peters, T., Cleary, K. (eds.) Image-Guided Interventions: Technology and Applications, pp. 45–80. Springer, New York (2008)
2. Flood, P.D., Banks, S.A.: Automated registration of three-dimensional knee implant models to fluoroscopic images using lipschitzian optimization. IEEE Trans. Med. Imaging **PP**(99), 1 (2016). doi:10.1109/TMI.2016.2553111
3. Otake, Y., Wang, A.S., Stayman, J.W., Uneri, A., Kleinszig, G., Vogt, S., Khanna, A.J., Gokaslan, Z.L., Siewerdsen, J.H.: Robust 3D–2D image registration: application to spine interventions and vertebral labeling in the presence of anatomical deformation. Phys. Med. Biol. **58**, 8535–8553 (2013)
4. Fu, D., Kuduvalli, G.: A fast, accurate, and automatic 2D–3D image registration for image-guided cranial radiosurgery. Med. Phys. **35**(5), 2180–2194 (2008)
5. Markelj, P., Tomaevi, D., Likar, B., Pernu, F.: A review of 3D/2D registration methods for image-guided interventions. Med. Image Anal. **16**, 642–661 (2012)
6. Alves, R.S., Tavares, J.M.R.S.: Computer image registration techniques applied to nuclear medicine images. In: Tavares, J.M.R.S., Natal Jorge, R.M. (eds.) Computational and Experimental Biomedical Sciences: Methods and Applications. LNCVB, vol. 21, pp. 173–191. Springer, Heidelberg (2015). doi:10.1007/978-3-319-15799-3_13
7. Tavares, J.M.R.S.: Analysis of biomedical images based on automated methods of image registration. In: Bebis, G., et al. (eds.) ISVC 2014. LNCS, vol. 8887, pp. 21–30. Springer, Heidelberg (2014). doi:10.1007/978-3-319-14249-4_3
8. Oliveira, F.P., Tavares, J.M.R.: Medical image registration: a review. Comput. Methods Biomech. Biomed. Engin. **17**, 73–93 (2014)

9. Chen, X., Varley, M.R., Shark, L.K., Shentall, G.S., Kirby, M.C.: An extension of iterative closest point algorithm for 3D-2D registration for pre-treatment validation in radiotherapy. In: MedVis, pp. 3–8 (2006)

10. Birkfellner, W., Stock, M., Figl, M., Gendrin, C., Hummel, J., Dong, S., Kettenbach, J., Georg, D., Bergmann, H.: Stochastic rank correlation: a robust merit function for 2D/3D registration of image data obtained at different energies. Med. Phys. **36**, 3420–3428 (2009)

11. Vermandel, M., Betrouni, N., Gauvrit, J.Y., Pasquier, D., Vasseur, C., Rousseau, J.: Intrinsic 2D/3D registration based on a hybrid approach: use in the radiosurgical imaging process. Cell. Mol. Biol. **52**, 44–53 (2006)

12. Oliveira, F.P., Pataky, T.C., Tavares, J.M.R.: Registration of pedobarographic image data in the frequency domain. Comput. Methods Biomech. Biomed. Engin **13**, 731–740 (2010)

13. Khandelwal, P., Yavagal, D.R., Sacco, R.L.: Acute ischemic stroke intervention. J. Am. Coll. Cardiol. **67**, 2631–2644 (2016)

14. Frangi, A.F., Niessen, W.J., Vincken, K.L., Viergever, M.A.: Multiscale vessel enhancement filtering. In: Wells, W.M., Colchester, A., Delp, S. (eds.) MICCAI 1998. LNCS, vol. 1496, pp. 130–137. Springer, Heidelberg (1998). doi:10.1007/BFb0056195

15. Cai, D., He, X., Han, J.: Spectral regression for efficient regularized subspace learning. In: ICCV, pp. 1–8 (2007)

16. Lagarias, J.C., Reeds, J.A., Wright, M.H., Wright, P.E.: Convergence properties of the nelder-mead simplex method in low dimensions. SIAM J. Optim. **9**, 112–147 (1998)

17. Scalzo, F., Liebeskind, D.S.: Perfusion angiography in acute ischemic stroke. Comput. Math. Methods Med. **2014**, 1–14 (2016). doi:10.1155/2016/2478324. Article ID 2478324

18. Scalzo, F., Hao, Q., Walczak, A.M., Hu, X., Hoi, Y., Hoffmann, K.R., Liebeskind, D.S.: Computational hemodynamics in intracranial vessels reconstructed from biplane angiograms. In: Bebis, G., et al. (eds.) ISVC 2010. LNCS, vol. 6455, pp. 359–367. Springer, Heidelberg (2010). doi:10.1007/978-3-642-17277-9_37

19. Nam, H.S., Scalzo, F., Leng, X., Ip, H.L., Lee, H.S., Fan, F., Chen, X., Soo, Y., Miao, Z., Liu, L., Feldmann, E., Leung, T., Wong, K.S., Liebeskind, D.S.: Hemodynamic impact of systolic blood pressure and hematocrit calculated by computational fluid dynamics in patients with intracranial atherosclerosis. J. Neuroimaging **26**, 331–338 (2016)

20. Leng, X., Scalzo, F., Fong, A.K., Johnson, M., Ip, H.L., Soo, Y., Leung, T., Liu, L., Feldmann, E., Wong, K.S., Liebeskind, D.S.: Computational fluid dynamics of computed tomography angiography to detect the hemodynamic impact of intracranial atherosclerotic stenosis. Neurovascular Imaging **1**, 1 (2015)

# Automatic Optic Disk Segmentation in Presence of Disk Blurring

Samra Irshad[1(✉)], Xiaoxia Yin[2], Lucy Qing Li[3,4], and Umer Salman[5]

[1] The Superior College, University Campus, Lahore, Pakistan
sam.ershad@yahoo.com
[2] Centre for Applied Informatics, College of Engineering and Science,
Victoria University, Melbourne, Australia
xiaoxia.yin@vu.edu.au
[3] College of Engineering and Science, Victoria University, Melbourne, Australia
[4] EEC Bio-tech Co. Ltd., Guangzhou, China
[5] Hameed Latif Hospital, Lahore, Pakistan

**Abstract.** Fundus image analysis has emerged as a very useful tool to analyze the structure of retina for detection of different eye-related abnormalities. The detection of these abnormalities requires the segmentation of basic retinal structures including blood vessels and optic disk. The optic disk segmentation becomes a challenging task when the optic disk boundary is degraded due to some deviations including optic disk edema and papilledema. This paper focuses on the segmentation of optic disk in presence of disk blurring. The method proposed makes use of gradient extracted from line profiles that pass through optic disk margin. Initially the optic disk is enhanced using morphological operations and location of optic disk region is detected automatically using vessel density property. Finally, line profiles are extracted at different angles and their gradient is evaluated for the estimation of optic disk boundary. The proposed method has been applied on 28 images taken from Armed Forces Institute of Ophthalmology.

## 1 Introduction

Health surveys show approximately 40% of world population above the age of 25 has hypertension [1]. Systematic hypertension manifests ocular effects in retina, choroid and optic nerve [2]. The changes and abnormalities that are caused in retina due to hypertension can be detected and diagnosed by non-mydriatic retinal photography [2].

Computerized Automatic Diagnostic (CAD) systems are being developed for the past decade to detect different ocular diseases. These CAD systems not only alleviate the burden on ophthalmologists but also provide them with a second independent opinion. Majority of the systems which have been proposed for the detection of changes caused by hypertension like the quantification of blood vessels include the segmentation of the basic retinal structures like Optic Disk (OD) and retinal blood vessels as a preliminary step [3–6]. OD usually appears as a bright yellow circular structure from where the retinal vessels emerge, however this feature may vary across images significantly as shown in Fig. 1. Also, OD boundary is sometimes not clear enough due to

G. Bebis et al. (Eds.): ISVC 2016, Part I, LNCS 10072, pp. 13–23, 2016.
DOI: 10.1007/978-3-319-50835-1_2

other abnormalities like Optic Disk Edema and Papilledema, as shown in Fig. 2. These variations and other complications make the segmentation of OD difficult.

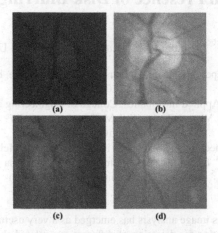

**Fig. 1.** Variations in appearance of OD: (a) Brownish OD image, (b) Whitish OD, (c) Reddish OD, (d) Yellowish OD. (Color figure online)

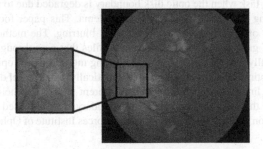

**Fig. 2.** Example of OD blurring

This paper presents a novel method for OD boundary segmentation in retinal fundus images with OD disk swelling. The proposed technique works correctly for images in which the OD boundary is blurred secondary to changes caused by malignant hypertension. The long-term high blood pressure can lead to raised intracranial pressure which is another reason for OD swelling [7–9]. Along with the obscured boundary, the color of OD also changes from bright to abnormally pale as shown in Fig. 2. This paper contains four sections. A review of previous methods is given in Sect. 2, Sect. 3 describes the proposed methodology, Sect. 4 shows experimental results followed by conclusion that is given in Sect. 5.

## 2   Related Work

The techniques which have been proposed so far segment the optic nerve head in absence of OD blurring. D. Marin et al. [10] presented a method for OD segmentation which includes the application of morphological operations followed by Hough transform. Circular Hough transform is also used in [11] for OD center approximation and grow cut algorithm for boundary segmentation. Another method presented in [12] used Principal Component Analysis (PCA) for detection of OD and active contour model is proposed for OD boundary segmentation. C. Wang et al. presented a work in which template matching is used to detect OD center followed by Level Set Method for boundary segmentation [13]. Region growing algorithm is used in [14] for segmentation of OD boundary. Recently a research is presented in [15], for detection of OD in presence of pathologies like exudates.

This paper contributes in correct detection and segmentation of OD in presence of retinal pathology i.e. OD blurring. OD blurring makes the identification and boundary segmentation of OD ambiguous because of its resultant effects.

## 3   Proposed Method

The proposed technique consists of four stages; Preprocessing, Vessel Segmentation, OD detection and Line profiles extraction followed by evaluation of maximum gradient along line profiles. In the first stage, preprocessing is applied on fundus image followed by segmentation of retinal vessels. In the second step, retinal vessels are segmented using Gabor Wavelet. In the third step, OD position is localized using Laplacian of Gaussian filter and highest vessel property of OD. Then, the center of detected OD region

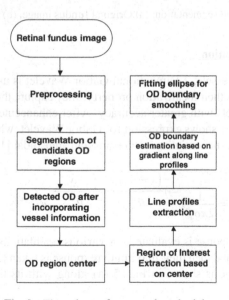

**Fig. 3.** Flow chart of proposed methodology

is found and based on that center; a region of interest is extracted containing the OD portion. Finally, line profiles are extracted at several orientations which pass through the OD region's center. The gradient along these profiles are recorded and the pixels with maximum gradient are marked. These pixels provide a basis for OD boundary detection and are used to fit an ellipse. The proposed methodology is tested on images gathered from AFIO, Pakistan. A comparison is also made with the ground truth OD masks. Figure 3 shows the flow diagram of proposed method. The steps adopted in the method are described in detail in this section.

### 3.1  Background Segmentation

In preprocessing, the fundus background is removed in order to suppress un-necessary pixels. The reason for this removal is that the dark background is not actually black. Background estimation is done using local mean and variance based method [16]. Then, thresholding and morphological operations are applied to create a binary mask. The original image along with background segmentation is shown in Fig. 4.

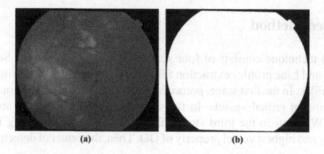

**Fig. 4.**  Background segmentation: (a) Original fundus image, (b) Background mask

### 3.2  Vessel Segmentation

For segmentation of vessels, 2-Dimentional Gabor Wavelet is used [17]. The purpose of using Gabor filter is their localization property, they capture the response of small as well large width vessels with greater accuracy. After enhancement, retinal vessels are thresholded. Equation 1 shows expression for Gabor Wavelet, which is simply a multiplication of complex exponential and 2-D Gaussian sinusoidal [18].

$$G(x, y) = \frac{1}{2\pi\sigma\beta} e^{-\pi[\frac{(x - x_0)^2}{\sigma^2} + \frac{(y - y_0)^2}{\beta^2}]} e^{i[\delta_0 x + \vartheta_0 y]} \tag{1}$$

Gabor Wavelet response is evaluated for various orientations spanning from 0° up to 179° at steps of 10° and then their maximum response is taken [17]. A Gabor Wavelet enhanced retinal image is shown in Fig. 5 (a) along with its thresholded version in Fig. 5 (b).

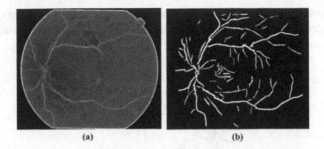

**Fig. 5.** Vessel segmentation: (a) Retinal vessel enhancement, (b) Segmented retinal vessel network

## 3.3 Localization of the Position of OD

In the proposed system, Laplacian of Gaussian (LoG) filter and highest vessel density property of OD is used to detect the location of OD [19]. Red channel of RGB image is selected and a circular-shaped inverted LoG filter is used to enhance the location of OD [19]. This template is particularly used because of circular structure of OD. Red channel of image and LoG filter is shown in Fig. 6 below. The Red channel has been selected because it provides the clear and discriminating visualization of OD.

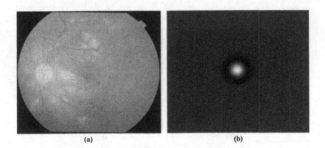

**Fig. 6.** Optic Disk detection: (a). Red channel of image (b). LoG filter. (Color figure online)

After the candidate circular regions have been enhanced using the LoG filter, they are binarized. The threshold that is used for this binarization is given in Eq. 2 [19]. $mLoG$ is the maximum value in LoG filtered image in Eq. 2.

$$T = 0.6 * mLoG \tag{2}$$

This threshold selects pixels having top 60% response from the LoG filtered image [19]. Preliminary experiment guided the selection of this threshold since it is optimal for all the images. Images in the dataset contain pathologies like exudates and cotton wool spots that have similarity in structural and color properties with OD, so the LoG filtered and subsequent thresholded image may contain more than one OD region. To overcome this issue, vessel density property is incorporated to separate out the OD region from the other segmented portions. A bounding box is drawn around these regions, and vessel density inside them is evaluated. The region with maximum vessel variation is selected. Figure 7 shows the complement of segmented vessel image with bounding box created around OD candidate regions.

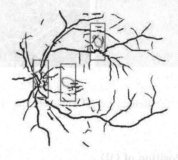

**Fig. 7.** Bounding boxes marked on candidate OD regions

Figure 8 shows the extracted candidate regions after thresholding with LoG filter and the OD region after incorporating vessel density characteristic. After determination of OD region, its center is evaluated and a sub-image containing OD is extracted. This sub-image is of dimensions 500 × 620 and is extracted by taking into account the center of OD region as shown in Fig. 9. This sub-image is used as input data for OD boundary estimation.

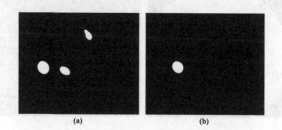

(a)                                    (b)

**Fig. 8.** Localization of OD region: (a). Segmented candidate OD regions (b). OD region after using vessel information

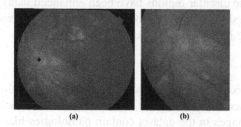

(a)                                    (b)

**Fig. 9.** Determination of ROI: (a). ROI marked in blue box and center of detected OD's region marked in black, (b). ROI region. (Color figure online)

### 3.4   Boundary Detection of OD by Variation Along Line Profile

In our dataset, the OD region has the most discriminating appearance in the red color plane, as mentioned before. However, in some sub-images, the fundus regions other than OD appears brighter due to intra-image variations and makes the appearance of OD as non-discriminating in red channel. Therefore, a mean threshold is chosen which determines the selection of color channel. If the mean threshold value of RGB sub-image is equal or greater than 130, blue color plane is selected as input image otherwise red component is chosen. Afterwards, the line segments of specific length are used to determine the pixels with highest gradient, which will lead to the evaluation of OD boundary. Radial line segments $l_i$ with the length of 120 are taken at several orientations and regular intervals i.e. from $\theta = 0°$ *to* 180° with the step of 10° that pass through the center of OD region. The length of the line segments is made such that it is long enough to capture the variation on OD boundary. The profiles across the line segments are evaluated and then their 1-D gradient is calculated. The absolute of this gradient is taken since the lowest negative value indicates the variation along the region of high intensity to low intensity and highest positive value of gradient indicates the variation of low to high intensity [20]. The location of these gradient values is obtained and marked.

The intensity inside the OD is not uniform due to the presence of vessel structures, therefore in some cases the gradient shows prominent variations not only at OD margins but also inside the OD region. To avoid this situation, the Euclidean distance is measured from the detected points to the center of region and the mean of all calculated distances is taken. If the distance from the coordinates of maximum variation point and center is less than mean value; the detected gradient point is discarded. After discarding the points that have less distance than the selected mean threshold, a boundary is traced that follows the retained gradient points. Moreover, as the blood vessel emerge from OD center and crosses the boundary, this vessel crossing characteristic will prevent the gradient-based method in tracing the smooth boundary. For this purpose, ellipse fitting is applied to the detected points in order to smooth the traced boundary [21]. Figure 10 (a) shows the selected component of RGB image with radial segments and detected points on OD boundary, (b) represents the ellipse fitted boundary and (c) shows the obtained binary mask. Figure 11 shows results of proposed methodology on two images. Note the OD boundary in colored

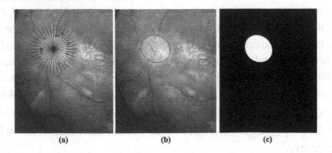

(a)                        (b)                        (c)

**Fig. 10.** OD detection: (a). Detected points of blurred OD margin, (b). Ellipse fitting to points, (c) resultant mask. (Color figure online)

image in the first row is blurred at temporal side, while in the second image; the vessels are twisted due to tortuosity which resulted in OD boundary distortion.

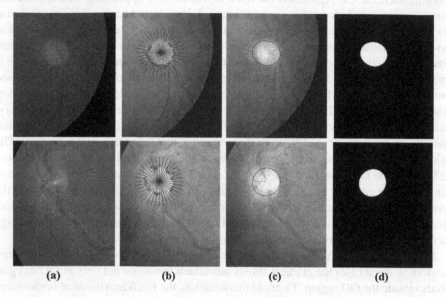

|     (a)     |     (b)     |     (c)     |     (d)     |

**Fig. 11.** Boundary segmentation of OD: (a). Colored sub-images (b). Selected channel for boundary segmentation with line segments and detected points superimposed, (c). Ellipse fitting to detected points, (d). Generated binary mask. (Color figure online)

## 4   Results

A dataset of 28 images is used for testing of proposed methodology. These images are of size 1504 × 1000, taken from Ophthalmology department of AFIO, Pakistan. The OD in these images has been annotated as 'blurring present' or 'not' by an experienced ophthalmologist. The OD boundary in the images has been annotated by our ophthalmologist and those annotations are then used as ground truth. Among the 28 images, 9 of them contain OD swelling.

In this paper, three performance measures are used for the performance evaluation of proposed method. Jaccard and Dice coefficients shown in Eqs. 3 and 4 are used to evaluate the OD boundary segmentation results whereas the third measure is the Euclidean distance between the center of OD obtained from the proposed method and ground truth masks is used to evaluate the localization of OD center [22]. Jaccard coefficient $(JC_{seg})$ is defined as the intersection divided by union of the OD segmentation resulted from the proposed system $(S_{test})$ and the ground truth segmentation $(S_{gt})$. While the Dice Coefficient $(DC_{seg})$ is about the size of the intersection of the OD boundary segmentation resulted from the proposed system $(S_{test})$ and the ground truth segmentation $(S_{gr})$ divided by their average size.

$$JC_{seg} = \frac{S_{test} \cap S_{gt}}{S_{test} \cup S_{gt}} \tag{3}$$

$$DC_{seg} = \frac{2.S_{test} \cap S_{gt}}{S_{test} + S_{gt}} \tag{4}$$

Table 1 shows the results of performance evaluation for OD boundary segmentation. The average values achieved for $JC_{seg}$, $DC_{seg}$ and distance between OD centers are 0.8331, 0.9078 and 6.44, respectively.

**Table 1.** Performance of evaluation parameters for 28 images

| Image no. | $(JC_{seg})$ | $(DC_{seg})$ | $(Dist)$ |
|---|---|---|---|
| 1 | 0.8539 | 0.9212 | 9.0554 |
| 2 | 0.8282 | 0.906 | 9.2195 |
| 3 | 0.854 | 0.9213 | 7 |
| 4 | 0.7836 | 0.8787 | 8.2462 |
| 5 | 0.695 | 0.82 | 2.2361 |
| 6 | 0.8365 | 0.9109 | 4.1231 |
| 7 | 0.9489 | 0.9738 | 2.8284 |
| 8 | 0.7172 | 0.8353 | 12.083 |
| 9 | 0.7377 | 0.8491 | 7.2801 |
| 10 | 0.9036 | 0.9493 | 2.8284 |
| 11 | 0.7896 | 0.8824 | 7.2111 |
| 12 | 0.8364 | 0.9109 | 7.2801 |
| 13 | 0.8565 | 0.9227 | 4 |
| 14 | 0.8041 | 0.8914 | 9.2195 |
| 15 | 0.8206 | 0.9015 | 10.6301 |
| 16 | 0.9046 | 0.9499 | 4.4721 |
| 17 | 0.829 | 0.9065 | 4 |
| 18 | 0.8478 | 0.9176 | 7.6158 |
| 19 | 0.7725 | 0.8716 | 4.4721 |
| 20 | 0.8788 | 0.9355 | 7.2111 |
| 21 | 0.8795 | 0.9359 | 5.6569 |
| 22 | 0.8166 | 0.899 | 10 |
| 23 | 0.8796 | 0.9359 | 5 |
| 24 | 0.7775 | 0.8748 | 8.0623 |
| 25 | 0.8139 | 0.8974 | 11.6619 |
| 26 | 0.9026 | 0.9488 | 1 |
| 27 | 0.8861 | 0.9396 | 3.1623 |
| 28 | 0.8743 | 0.9329 | 5 |

## 5    Conclusion

This paper presents an improved method for the segmentation of OD in colored retinal images with pathological degradations. A gradient based method is proposed for the OD boundary segmentation, which consists of maximum gradient pixels extraction followed by ellipse fitting. This technique provides accuracy for images with OD margin blurred. The algorithms which have been proposed so far [10–15] provide OD segmentation in normal images.

## References

1. World Health Organization: A Global Brief on Hypertension. World Health Organization, Geneva (2013)
2. Hyman, B.N., Moser, M.: Hypertension update. Surv. Ophthalmol. **41**, 79–89 (1996)
3. Agurto, C., Joshi, V., Nemeth, S., Soliz, P., Barriga, S.: Detection of hypertensive retinopathy using vessel measurements and textural features. In: 36th Annual International Conference of the IEEE EMBS. IEEE Press, Chicago (2014)
4. Yin, X., Ng, B.W.-H., He, J., Zhang, Y., Abbott, D.: Accurate image analysis of the retina using Hessian matrix and binarisation of thresholded entropy with application of texture mapping. PLoS ONE **9**(4), e95943 (2014)
5. Irshad, S., Usman Akram, M., Ayub, S., Ayaz, A.: Retinal blood vessels differentiation for calculation of arterio-venous ratio. In: Kamel, M., Campilho, A. (eds.) ICIAR 2015. LNCS, vol. 9164, pp. 411–418. Springer, Heidelberg (2015). doi:10.1007/978-3-319-20801-5_45
6. Irshad, S., Usman Akram, M.: Classification of retinal vessels into arteries and veins for detection of hypertensive retinopathy. In: IEEE 7th Cairo International Biomedical Engineering Conference (CIBEC). IEEE Press, Egypt (2014)
7. Auer, R.N., Sutherland, G.R.: Primary intracerebral hemorrhage: pathophysiology. Can. J. Neurol. Sci. **32**, S3–S12 (2005)
8. Sahni, R., Weinberger, J.: Management of intracerebral hemorrhage. J. Vasc. Health Risk Manag. **3**, 701 (2008)
9. Agarwal, S., Agarwal, A., Apple, D.J., Buratto, L., Alio, J.L.: Textbook of Ophthalmology, vol. 1, Jaypee Brothers Medical Publishers (2002)
10. Marin, D., Arias, M.E.G., Suero, A., Bravo, J.M.: Obtaining optic disc center and pixel region by automatic thresholding methods on morphologically processed fundus images. Comput. Meth. Programs Biomed. **118**, 173–185 (2015)
11. Abdullah, M., Fraz, M.M.: Application of grow cut algorithm for localization and extraction of optic disc in retinal images. In: 12th International Conference on High-Capacity Optical Networks and Emerging Technologies (HONET). IEEE Press (2015)
12. Mittapalli, P.S., Kande, G.B.: Segmentation of optic disk and optic cup from digital fundus images for the assessment of glaucoma. Biomed. Sig. Process. Control **24**, 34–46 (2016)
13. Wang, C., Kaba, D., Li, Y.: Level set segmentation of optic discs from retinal images. J. Med. Bioeng. **4**, 213–220 (2015)
14. Omid, S., Ghassabi, Z., Shanbehzadeh, J., Ostadzadeh, S.S.: Optic disc detection in high-resolution retinal fundus images by region growing. In: 8th International Conference on BioMedical Engineering and Informatics (BMEI). IEEE Press (2015)
15. Xiong, L., Li, H.: An approach to locate optic disc in retinal images with pathological changes. Comput. Med. Imaging Graph. **47**, 40–50 (2016)

16. Jamal, I., Akram, M.U., Tariq, A.: Retinal image preprocessing: background and noise segmentation. TELKOMNIKA **10**(3), 537–544 (2012)
17. Akram, M.U., Jamal, I., Tariq, A.: Blood vessel enhancement and segmentation for screening of diabetic retinopathy. TELKOMNIKA Indonesian J. Electr. Eng. **10**, 327–334 (2012)
18. Lee, T.S.: Image representation using 2D Gabor wavelets. IEEE Trans. Pattern Anal. Mach. Intell. **18**(10), 959–971 (1996)
19. Usman, A., Khitran, S.A., Usman Akram, M., Nadeem, Y.: A robust algorithm for optic disc segmentation from colored fundus images. In: Campilho, A., Kamel, M. (eds.) ICIAR 2014. LNCS, vol. 8815, pp. 303–310. Springer, Heidelberg (2014). doi:10.1007/978-3-319-11755-3_34
20. Gonzales, R.C., Woods, R.E.: Digital Image Processing, 3rd edn. Prentice-Hall, Upper Saddle River (2008)
21. Stojmenovic, M., Nayak, A.: Direct ellipse fitting and measuring based on shape boundaries. In: Mery, D., Rueda, L. (eds.) PSIVT 2007. LNCS, vol. 4872, pp. 221–235. Springer, Heidelberg (2007). doi:10.1007/978-3-540-77129-6_22
22. Nikravesh, M., Zadeh, L.A.: Soft Computing for Information Processing and Analysis. Springer-Verlag, Heidelberg (2005)

# An Object Splitting Model Using Higher-Order Active Contours for Single-Cell Segmentation

Jozsef Molnar[1], Csaba Molnar[1], and Peter Horvath[1,2(✉)]

[1] Synthetic and Systems Biology Unit,
Hungarian Academy of Sciences, Szeged, Hungary
horvath.peter@brc.mta.hu
[2] Institute for Molecular Medicine Finland (FIMM),
University of Helsinki, Helsinki, Finland

**Abstract.** Determining the number and morphology of individual cells on microscopy images is one of the most fundamental steps in quantitative biological image analysis. Cultured cells used in genetic perturbation and drug discovery experiments can pile up and nuclei can touch or even grow on top of each other. Similarly, in tissue sections cell nuclei can be very close and touch each other as well. This makes single cell nuclei detection extremely challenging using current segmentation methods, such as classical edge- and threshold-based methods that can only detect separate objects, and they fail to separate touching ones. The pipeline we present here can segment individual cell nuclei by splitting touching ones. The two-step approach merely based on energy minimization principles using an active contour framework. In a presegmentation phase we use a local region data term with strong edge tracking capability, while in the splitting phase we introduce a higher-order active contour model. This model prefers high curvature contour locations at the opposite side of joint objects grow "cutting arms" that evolve to one another until they split objects. Synthetic and real experiments show the strong segmentation and splitting ability of the proposed pipeline and that it outperforms currently used segmentation models.

## 1 Introduction

The development of an automated, reliable segmentation method for cellular images is often challenging due to touching or overlapping cell nuclei clumps. The segmentation of the individual cells is usually performed in two phases. In the presegmentation phase, the localization of the foreground objects or the region of interest (single cells or clumps of cells) is performed followed by the identification of the individual cells in the clumps during second phase. The presegmentation methods include simple intensity thresholding [8] (e.g. Otsu segmentation) variance measures [11]. Energy minimization methods, such as graph cut [1,20] or active contour models [2–4] are also used with high efficiency in this area [6]. In the second phase, cell nuclei clumps are separated into individuals. A big variety of methods were introduced to this area, usually utilizing a priori knowledge about the shape of individual objects.

© Springer International Publishing AG 2016
G. Bebis et al. (Eds.): ISVC 2016, Part I, LNCS 10072, pp. 24–34, 2016.
DOI: 10.1007/978-3-319-50835-1_3

A large family of such priors assume object ellipticity [9,12,16]. These priors are very effective for clusters of homogeneous objects, but can fail if the cluster is composed of diverse shapes. Other popular approaches prefer less specific priors and the separation of cell clusters mainly based on two underlying principles: either the localization of the individual cell centers [5,15,18,19,23] or the concavity analysis of shape boundaries [6,8]. In the former case, once cell centers are determined, effective methods such as repulsive active contours [19], voronoi tessellation [5,10], gradient flow back-tracking [15] or watershed [18] are used, however the accurate cell-center localization is still a challenging task. Methods based on the cluster boundary information include: the minimum model approach [22], graph cut [6,8] and rule based segmentation [13].

In this paper we present a cell segmentation framework merely based on energy minimization principles. The main components are the following (a) image normalization, using illumination correction [21], (b) presegmentation, using anisotrop local region active contour, (c) splitting of clumped objects using a novel higher order active contour model. The structure of the paper is as follows: in Sect. 2.2 we analyze the properties of the local region based active contour model, highlighting its strong edge tracking capability, in Sect. 2.3 we introduce a higher order functional designed for cluster splitting and in Sect. 3 we present our experimental results and compare with the most frequently used method in cell segmentation.

## 2    The components of the cell segmentation framework

In this section we introduce the model designed to efficiently segment foreground objects (cell clumps) and split them into simple, non-further-splittable parts. The presegmentation is performed by a *local-region active contour* (see Sect. 2.2) which effectively tracks object boundaries even if they are slightly overlap or touch each other. After this step, remaining objects have no longer edges to be tracked. A purely geometric splitting functional (see Sect. 2.3) is designed as a second step that splits these objects further by penalizing high curvature contour regions (see Fig. 3) and moving them towards each other until they cut.

### 2.1   Notations

The point set of the image plane is denoted by $\Omega$, parameterized by Cartesian image coordinates $x$ and $y$, $[x,y] \in \Omega \subset \mathbb{R}^2$. Contours are closed planar curves, given as vector valued function of a curve parameter $t$ such that: $\Omega \supset \mathbf{r}(t) = x(t)\mathbf{i} + y(t)\mathbf{j}$, where $\mathbf{i}$, $\mathbf{j}$ are the standard basis vectors and $\mathbf{k} \doteq \mathbf{i} \times \mathbf{j}$ is the unit normal vector of the image plane. The unit tangent vector of the contour is $\mathbf{t} \doteq \frac{\dot{\mathbf{r}}}{|\dot{\mathbf{r}}|}$, $\dot{\mathbf{r}} = \frac{d\mathbf{r}}{dt}$. The unit normal vector of the contour $\mathbf{n}$ is defined by the plane normal $\mathbf{k}$ as $\mathbf{n} = \mathbf{k} \times \mathbf{t}$. Note that assuming $\mathbf{i}, \mathbf{j}, \mathbf{k}$ are right-handed, contours that are parameterized counter-clockwise have normal vectors pointing inwards. Arclength of the curve is denoted by $s$. The coordinate differentials and differential operators are related with $ds = |\dot{\mathbf{r}}|\,dt$ and $\frac{d}{ds} = \frac{1}{|\dot{\mathbf{r}}|}\frac{d}{dt}$ respectively.

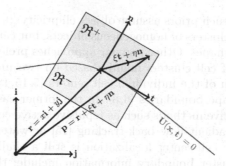

**Fig. 1.** Local regions are defined by the local Cartesian coordinate systems with the unit tangent and normal basis vectors. The data metric used for segmentation is the difference of the mean intensities of the regions distinguished by positive/negative local ordinate values.

The signed curvature of the contour is denoted by $\kappa$, defined with the help of the plane normal as $\frac{\ddot{\mathbf{r}} \cdot \mathbf{n}}{|\dot{\mathbf{r}}|^2}$.

## 2.2 The Local Region Active Contour

The presegmentation is performed by using a local-region active contour discussed in details in [17]. Here we summarize the theoretical background and the properties of this method.

The local region along the contour is defined by local Cartesian coordinate system. The functional $\oint \varPhi (\mathbf{r}, \mathbf{n}) \, ds$ contains the local coordinate system explicitly, represented by the unit normal vector of the contour. Note that the inclusion of either the unit normal or the unit tangent vector is equivalent, because in case of planar curves they are related by $\mathbf{n} = \mathbf{k} \times \mathbf{t}$. This functional was originally introduced in [7] for 3D reconstruction purpose. Applying this for image segmentation, requires the Lagrangian to be specialized. We use the difference of the mean image intensities given by local integrals

$$\varPhi (\mathbf{r}, \mathbf{n}) = \frac{1}{\|\mathfrak{R}\|} \left( \iint\limits_{\mathfrak{R}+} I(\mathbf{p}) \, dA - \iint\limits_{\mathfrak{R}-} I(\mathbf{p}) \, dA \right). \tag{1}$$

as introduced in [17], where the quantities are defined in Fig. 1. Using the local region active contour has the following advantages:

- its region-based nature does not require preliminary noise removal
- no smoothness term is required, the minimizing contour is not over-smoothed
- anisotropic: the gradient descent direction of the contour points depend on the image intensity distribution in the local regions

The last two properties explain the advantageous feature of the local-region active contours: they can track image edges even if the gaps between the foreground objects are very narrow (Fig. 2).

**Fig. 2.** Comparison of isotropic/anisotropic segmentation results: original image (left), isotropic segmentation (middle) and anisotropic segmentation (right).

## 2.3 The Split Functional

To design the split functional we are using an analogy from electrostatics. The variational formulation of the charge density distribution $\varrho(\mathbf{r})$ on a conductor can be characterized with the total potential energy of the system as: $\oint \oint \varrho(\mathbf{r}) \varrho(\mathbf{r}') l(d(\mathbf{r}, \mathbf{r}')) d\Omega d\Omega'$, where $d(\mathbf{r}, \mathbf{r}')$ is the Euclidean length between two points of the conductor, $l(d) = \frac{1}{|\mathbf{r} - \mathbf{r}'|}$. The minimizer of this system[1] is the equipotential distribution of the charge on the conductor surface. We will use this analogy with the following differences: (a) the problem is applied to planar curves; (b) the force acts between the contour points is attractive and anisotropic (explained later); (c) the "attractive charges" fixed to the contour points hence the contour evolves to reach the minimal energy.

First, we assume that the set of object that compose the clump of nuclei cannot be further segmented using the local-region active contour model due to missing edge information between the parts. The splitting functional should therefore be based on purely geometric information. Second, we reduce the set of contour points to a subset satisfying certain concavity and alignment criteria. We call it "feasible subset". The complement set of the "feasible subset" remains intact during the process. The feasible contour points are handled as weighted, oriented particle set. The associated orientation is defined by their normal vector $\mathbf{n}$, the weighs by their concavity as shown on Fig. 3. Within an energy minimization framework, the concavity is indicated by negative curvature $\kappa < 0$. The aliment of two oriented points (indexed by 1, 2) is defined by the relation of their orientations and relative position such that $a_{12} \doteq \mathbf{n}_1 \cdot \mathbf{e}_{12} + \mathbf{n}_2 \cdot \mathbf{e}_{21}$, where $\mathbf{e}_{12}$ is the unit normal vector pointing from point 1 to 2, and $\mathbf{e}_{21} = -\mathbf{e}_{12}$. Note that this definition of the alignment is symmetric, i.e. $a_{12} = a_{21}$. Now one can define the "anisotropic energy" for a pair of points as $U_{12} \doteq f(\kappa_2) f(\kappa_1) g(a_{12}) l(d_{12})$ with $d_{12}$ being the Euclidean distance between the points and $f, g, l$, are appropriately chosen functions discussed in the next subsection. Taking $f(\kappa(s))$ as the density of the potential source (the "attractive[2] charge") along the contour, the second-order functional:

$$-\oint \oint f(\kappa(s)) f(\kappa(s')) g(a(s, s')) l(d(s, s')) ds' ds \tag{2}$$

---

[1] Extended by the charge conservation principle.
[2] Hence the negative sign.

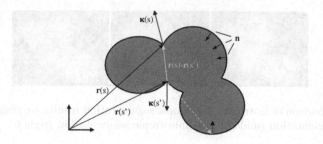

**Fig. 3.** Illustration of the object cutting method. Contour points connected by continuous line are well aligned, whilst points connected by dashed line are not.

represents the total energy of the contour. The integral is evaluated only on the feasible subset, defined as:

$$[\mathbf{r}\,(s)\mid \kappa\,(s) < -\varepsilon \wedge a\,(s, s') > \delta]. \tag{3}$$

Points out of the "feasible subset" do not contribute to the total energy. Note that the minimization of the negative of the simplified functional with $g \equiv 1$, $l \equiv 1$ would result in the convex hull of the initial contour. Functional (2) represents a geometric contour, the associated Euler-Lagrange equation has component only in the normal direction (see Appendix). We solve it iteratively via gradient descent, using the Level Set method.

## 2.4   The Roles of the Functions

The most important part of the Lagrangian (2) is the alignment function $g\,(a\,(s, s'))$. The appropriately designed function keeps the correct orientation (prevents biasing from the aligned direction) between the approaching tips of the "cutting arms" during the evolution process. It also guarantees the stability of the cutting arm preventing it from unexpected bifurcation. Note that we use the smooth version of the curvature for the same reasons. (The smoothing is done by simple averaging the curvatures of a small neighborhood.) The function in Fig. 4 left acts as potential barrier with minimum at the maximal alignment. The simplest splitting functional contains only the alignment function (this special form can be derived from the general functional setting the other constituent functions ($f$, $l$) identically constant one). This however, would represent a system with energy indiscriminate w.r.t. the distance between the points of the feasible subset.

To favor point pairs otherwise appropriate, the distance function $l\,(d\,(s, s'))$ is introduced in the functional (2) such that closer points exhibits bigger attractive force than further ones. The distance function may have limited scope as well.

The suitable function of the curvature can provide further stability for the "cutting arms" enforcing their tips to favor certain curvature value, thus make further bifurcations unlikely. This function can be chosen to be potential barrier. Its minimum value determines the curvature of the cutting tip, hence the width of the cutting arms (Fig. 4) as well.

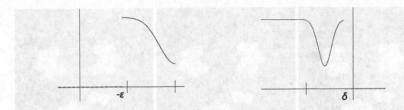

**Fig. 4.** The graphs of the Aligment (left) and the Curvature (right) functions. Both can be considered potential barriers. Points outside the feasible subset marked with dashed line.

## 3    Results

To demonstrate the segmentation ability of the proposed method we present quantitative results on synthetic images and qualitative results on real images of cancer cells.

The synthetic data was created using the SIMCEP simulation tool [14] designed to test and evaluate image analysis methods for fluorescent microscopy. 60 images were generated each containing 20 nuclei of a similar size and clustering into 3–5 clusters. A slight, maximum 5%, overlap was allowed between individual cells. The method was compared to CellProfiler using its IdentifyPrimaryObjects module with intensity- and shape-based clumped object splitting options [10]. To evaluate the segmentation quality of the proposed method and compare to others we used three metrics that was proposed earlier [16]. To analyze segmentation accuracy at object level we calculated precision and recall values. Precision is the ratio of true positives (TP) to the number of detected objects (Precision = TP/(TP + FP)), while recall (or sensitivity) is the proportion of the objects of interest is found (Recall = TP/(TP + FN)). Values close to 1 represent more accurate detection. First, a matching between the ground truth and the set of segmented objects was made. TP is the number of segmented objects with matching ground truth object, while FP is the number of segmented objects that have no matching ground truth object. FN is the number of ground truth objects that have no matching segmented object. The third metric was the Jaccard-index for pixel-level accuracy, a similarity measure between sets: $JI(A, B) = |A \cap B|/|A \cup B|$, for each matched pair. Figure 5 shows sample images of CellProfiler's intensity-based (Fig. 5 upper left) and shape-based (Fig. 5 middle) methods and results obtained using the proposed splitting model (Fig. 5 upper right).

Figure 6 represents results obtained using the proposed method on real images of cancer cell cultures. The method was able to successfully identify single cells in this highly complex environment.

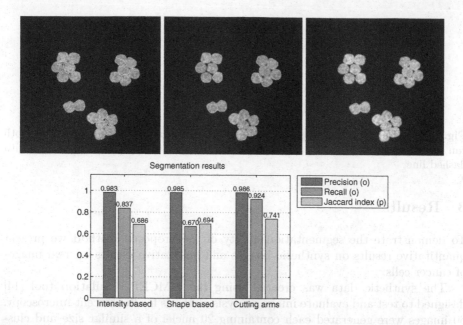

**Fig. 5.** Results on simulated data. Upper row: (left): intensity-based watershed method, (middle): shape-based watershed method; (right): result with the proposed method. Bottom plot: precision, recall and Jaccard-index statistics of the methods.

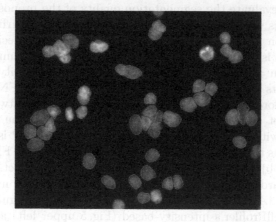

**Fig. 6.** Sample results on real microscopic image data of cancer cells.

## 4    Conclusion and Future Work

We presented a novel approach that successfully separates touching cells using intensity and cell clump geometry properties. The method first performs a segmentation based on local intensity differences, than closes contour arms opposite to each other. Experimental results show that the method outperforms currently used ones and has the potential to became the *de facto* cell segmentation tool for certain bioimage segmentation problems. Due to the active contour framework we used, it is possible to incorporate further shape prior information into the segmentation.

In the future, we will extend the model to 3D and provide a solution for the most recent cell segmentation challenges including cancer drug discovery in 3D environment or tissue analysis using deep imaging. The model will be implemented on GPU to speed up processes.

# Appendix

The derivation of the Euler-Lagrange equation associated to functional (2) is straightforward albeit long. Here we only provide the result. The notations used in the equations are the following: the point at contour parameter $t$ is designated by position vector $\mathbf{r}(t)$. The bound variable of the integrals is denoted by $\tau$, hence the invariant arc length: $ds = |\dot{\mathbf{r}}| \, d\tau$ (the derivatives of the position vector w.r.t. the contour parameter are denoted by dots: $\dot{\mathbf{r}}, \ddot{\mathbf{r}} \ldots$). The unit tangent and normal vectors of the contour are denoted by $\mathbf{e}, \mathbf{n}$, where $\mathbf{e} = \frac{\dot{\mathbf{r}}}{|\dot{\mathbf{r}}|}$. Using right handed coordinate system, they are related with $\mathbf{n} = \mathbf{k} \times \mathbf{e}$, where $\mathbf{k}$ is the normal of the image plane, hence the contour normals point inward. The (signed) curvature of the contour is given by $\kappa = \frac{\ddot{\mathbf{r}} \cdot \mathbf{n}}{|\dot{\mathbf{r}}|^2}$. The unit direction vector between points given by contour parameters $t$ and $\tau$ is denoted by $\mathbf{e}_{t\tau} = \frac{\mathbf{r}_\tau - \mathbf{r}_t}{d_{t\tau}}$, where $d_{t\tau} = |\mathbf{r}_\tau - \mathbf{r}_t|$ is their Euclidean distance. We also use the normal to this direction vector with definition $\mathbf{n}_{t\tau} = \mathbf{k} \times \mathbf{e}_{t\tau}$. The alignment between contour points is defined by $a_{t\tau} \doteq \mathbf{n}(t) \cdot \mathbf{e}_{t\tau} + \mathbf{n}(\tau) \cdot \mathbf{e}_{\tau t}$ ($\mathbf{e}_{\tau t} = -\mathbf{e}_{t\tau}$). $f, g, l$ are the appropriately chosen functions of the curvature, alignment and distance respectively, for their derivatives we use prime mark $f', f'' \ldots$ The first and second derivatives of the curvature w.r.t. the arc length are denoted by $\frac{d\kappa}{ds}, \frac{d^2\kappa}{ds^2}$. The curvature and its derivative are scalars. Note that the derivative w.r.t. the arc lenght of any scalar quantity $q$ can be calculated on the planar grid using the formula: $(\nabla q) \cdot \mathbf{e}$, where $\nabla$ is the gradient operator with components being the partial derivatives $\left( \frac{\partial}{\partial x}, \frac{\partial}{\partial y} \right)$ w.r.t. image coordinates $x, y$.

The formula: $A = \mathbf{e}_{t\tau} \cdot (\mathbf{e}(t) - \mathbf{e}(\tau))$, $B = \mathbf{e}_{t\tau} \cdot (\mathbf{n}(t) - \mathbf{n}(\tau))$, $C = \left[ \frac{l(d_{t\tau})}{d_{t\tau}} - l'(d_{t\tau}) \right]$, $D = \mathbf{e}_{t\tau} \cdot \mathbf{n}(t)$, $E = \mathbf{e}_{t\tau} \cdot \mathbf{e}(t)$, $F = \mathbf{n}(\tau) \cdot \mathbf{e}(t)$ are introduced to simplify the equation. The Euler-Lagrange equation associated to the half of (2) at point $t$ has the form $|\mathbf{r}(t)| Q\mathbf{n}(t) = \mathbf{0}$, where $Q$ is given by the following sum:

$$- \left[ f''' \left( \frac{d\kappa}{ds} \right)^2 + f'' \frac{d^2\kappa}{ds^2} \right] \oint g\left(a_{t\tau}\right) l\left(d_{t\tau}\right) f\left(\kappa\left(\tau\right)\right) ds$$

$$- 2f'' \frac{d\kappa}{ds} \oint g'\left(a_{t\tau}\right) l\left(d_{t\tau}\right) \frac{AD}{d_{t\tau}} f\left(\kappa\left(\tau\right)\right) ds$$

$$+ 2f'' \frac{d\kappa}{ds} \kappa \oint g'\left(a_{t\tau}\right) l\left(d_{t\tau}\right) E f\left(\kappa\left(\tau\right)\right) ds$$

$$+ 2f'' \frac{d\kappa}{ds} \oint g\left(a_{t\tau}\right) l'\left(d_{t\tau}\right) E f\left(\kappa\left(\tau\right)\right) ds$$

$$- f' \oint g''\left(a_{t\tau}\right) l\left(d_{t\tau}\right) \left[ \frac{\left(B - \kappa\left(t\right) d_{t\tau}\right) E + F}{d_{t\tau}} \right]^2 f\left(\kappa\left(\tau\right)\right) ds$$

$$+ f' \kappa \oint g'\left(a_{t\tau}\right) l\left(d_{t\tau}\right) \frac{AE - 2}{d_{t\tau}} f\left(\kappa\left(\tau\right)\right) ds$$

$$+ f' \kappa^2 \oint g'\left(a_{t\tau}\right) l\left(d_{t\tau}\right) D f\left(\kappa\left(\tau\right)\right) ds$$

$$+ f' \oint g'\left(a_{t\tau}\right) l\left(d_{t\tau}\right) \frac{BD^2}{d_{t\tau}^2} f\left(\kappa\left(\tau\right)\right) ds$$

$$- 2f' \oint g'\left(a_{t\tau}\right) \frac{ACDE}{d_{t\tau}} f\left(\kappa\left(\tau\right)\right) ds$$

$$+ 2f' \kappa \oint g'\left(a_{t\tau}\right) CE^2 f\left(\kappa\left(\tau\right)\right) ds$$

$$- f' \kappa^2 \oint g\left(a_{t\tau}\right) l\left(d_{t\tau}\right) f\left(\kappa\left(\tau\right)\right) ds$$

$$+ f' \kappa \oint g\left(a_{t\tau}\right) l'\left(d_{t\tau}\right) D f\left(\kappa\left(\tau\right)\right) ds$$

$$- f' \oint g\left(a_{t\tau}\right) l'\left(d_{t\tau}\right) \frac{D^2}{d_{t\tau}} f\left(\kappa\left(\tau\right)\right) ds$$

$$- f' \oint g\left(a_{t\tau}\right) l''\left(d_{t\tau}\right) E^2 f\left(\kappa\left(\tau\right)\right) ds$$

$$+ f \kappa \oint g''\left(a_{t\tau}\right) l\left(d_{t\tau}\right) E^2 f\left(\kappa\left(\tau\right)\right) ds$$

$$- f \oint g''\left(a_{t\tau}\right) l\left(d_{t\tau}\right) \frac{ADE}{d_{t\tau}} f\left(\kappa\left(\tau\right)\right) ds$$

$$- f \kappa \oint g'\left(a_{t\tau}\right) l\left(d_{t\tau}\right) D f\left(\kappa\left(\tau\right)\right) ds$$

$$- f \oint g'\left(a_{t\tau}\right) l\left(d_{t\tau}\right) \frac{D^2 - AE}{d_{t\tau}} f\left(\kappa\left(\tau\right)\right) ds$$

$$+ f \oint g'\left(a_{t\tau}\right) l'\left(d_{t\tau}\right) E^2 f\left(\kappa\left(\tau\right)\right) ds$$

$$+ f \oint g\left(a_{t\tau}\right) \left[\kappa\left(t\right) l\left(d_{t\tau}\right) + l'\left(d_{t\tau}\right) D\right] f\left(\kappa\left(\tau\right)\right) ds.$$

The factors outside the integrals are calculated at parameter $t$ (*i.e.* independent of the bound variable). Note that any factor depending only on parameter $t$, could be brought before the integrals, but would lead more complicated expression.

# References

1. Boykov, Y., Kolmogorov, V.: Computing geodesics and minimal surfaces via graph cuts. In: ICCV, pp. 26–33. IEEE (2003)
2. Caselles, V., Kimmel, R., Sapiro, G.: Geodesic active contours. IJCV **22**(1), 61–79 (1997)
3. Chan, T., Vese, L.: An active contour model without edges. In: Nielsen, M., Johansen, P., Olsen, O.F., Weickert, J. (eds.) Scale-Space 1999. LNCS, vol. 1682, pp. 141–151. Springer, Heidelberg (1999). doi:10.1007/3-540-48236-9_13
4. Chan, T., Vese, L.: A multiphase level set framework for image segmentation using the Mumford and Shah model. IJCV **50**(3), 271–293 (2002)
5. Chang, H., Yang, Q., Parvin, B.: Segmentation of heterogeneous blob objects through voting and level set formulation. Pattern Recogn. Lett. **28**(13), 1781–1787 (2007)
6. Daněk, O., Matula, P., Ortiz-de-Solórzano, C., Muñoz-Barrutia, A., Maška, M., Kozubek, M.: Segmentation of touching cell nuclei using a two-stage graph cut model. In: Salberg, A.-B., Hardeberg, J.Y., Jenssen, R. (eds.) SCIA 2009. LNCS, vol. 5575, pp. 410–419. Springer, Heidelberg (2009). doi:10.1007/978-3-642-02230-2_42
7. Faugeras, O., Keriven, R.: Variational principles, surface evolution, pdes, level set methods, and the stereo problem. Trans. Img. Proc. **7**(3), 336–344 (1998)
8. He, Y., Gong, H., Xiong, B., Xu, X., Li, A., Jiang, T., Sun, Q., Wang, S., Luo, Q., Chen, S.: iCut: an integrative cut algorithm enables accurate segmentation of touching cells. Sci. Rep., 5, (2015). Article no. 12089
9. Jiang, T., Yang, F.: An evolutionary tabu search for cell image segmentation. IEEE Trans. Syst. Man Cybern. Part B Cybern. **32**(5), 675–678 (2002)
10. Jones, T.R., Carpenter, A., Golland, P.: Voronoi-based segmentation of cells on image manifolds. In: Liu, Y., Jiang, T., Zhang, C. (eds.) CVBIA 2005. LNCS, vol. 3765, pp. 535–543. Springer, Heidelberg (2005). doi:10.1007/11569541_54
11. Kenong, W., Gauthier, D., Levine, M.D.: Live cell image segmentation. IEEE Trans. Biomed. Eng. **42**(1), 1–12 (1995)
12. Kothari, S., Chaudry, Q., Wang, M.D.: Automated cell counting and cluster segmentation using concavity detection and ellipse fitting techniques. In: IEEE ISBI, pp. 795–798. IEEE (2009)
13. Kumar, S., Ong, S.H., Ranganath, S., Ong, T.C., Chew, F.T.: A rule-based approach for robust clump splitting. Pattern Recogn. **39**(6), 1088–1098 (2006)
14. Lehmussola, A., Ruusuvuori, P., Selinummi, J., Huttunen, H., Yli-Harja, O.: Computational framework for simulating fluorescence microscope images with cell populations. IEEE Trans. Med. Imaging **26**(7), 1010–1016 (2007)
15. Li, G., Liu, T., Nie, J., Guo, L., Chen, J., Zhu, J., Xia, W., Mara, A., Holley, S., Wong, S.: Segmentation of touching cell nuclei using gradient flow tracking. J. Microsc. **231**(1), 47–58 (2008)
16. Molnar, C., Jermyn, I.H., Kato, Z., Rahkama, V., Östling, P., Mikkonen, P., Pietiäinen, V., Horvath, P.: Accurate morphology preserving segmentation of overlapping cells based on active contours. Sci. Rep. **6**, 1–10 (2016). Article no. 32412 EP

17. Molnar, J., Szucs, A.I., Molnar, C., Horvath, P.: Active contours for selective object segmentation. In: 2016 IEEE Winter Conference on Applications of Computer Vision (WACV), pp. 1–9 (2016)
18. Pinidiyaarachchi, A., Wählby, C.: Seeded watersheds for combined segmentation and tracking of cells. In: Roli, F., Vitulano, S. (eds.) ICIAP 2005. LNCS, vol. 3617, pp. 336–343. Springer, Heidelberg (2005). doi:10.1007/11553595_41
19. Qi, X., Xing, F., Foran, D.J., Yang, L.: Robust segmentation of overlapping cells in histopathology specimens using parallel seed detection and repulsive level set. IEEE Trans. Biomed. Eng. **59**(3), 754–765 (2012)
20. Shi, J., Malik, J.: Normalized cuts, image segmentation. IEEE Trans. Pattern Anal. Mach. Intell. **22**(8), 888–905 (2000)
21. Smith, K., Li, Y., Piccinini, F., Csucs, G., Balazs, C., Bevilacqua, A., Horvath, P.: CIDRE: an illumination-correction method for optical microscopy. Nature Methods **12**(5), 404–406 (2015)
22. Wienert, S., Heim, D., Saeger, K., Stenzinger, A., Beil, M., Hufnagl, P., Dietel, M., Denkert, C., Klauschen, F.: Detection and segmentation of cell nuclei in virtual microscopy images: a minimum-model approach. Sci. Rep. **2**, 503 (2012). 22787560
23. Yang, Q., Parvin, B.: Harmonic cut and regularized centroid transform for localization of subcellular structures. IEEE Trans. Biomed. Eng. **50**(4), 469–475 (2003)

# Tensor Voting Extraction of Vessel Centerlines from Cerebral Angiograms

Yu Ding[1], Mircea Nicolescu[2], Dan Farmer[2], Yao Wang[1], George Bebis[2], and Fabien Scalzo[1(✉)]

[1] Department of Neurology, University of California, Los Angeles (UCLA),
Los Angeles, USA
fab@cs.ucla.edu
[2] Department of Computer Science, University of Nevada, Reno (UNR),
Reno, USA

**Abstract.** The extraction of vessel centerlines from cerebral angiograms is a prerequisite for 2D-3D reconstruction and computational fluid dynamic (CFD) simulations. Many researchers have studied vessel segmentation and centerline extraction on retinal images while less attention and efforts have been devoted to cerebral angiography images. Since cerebral angiograms consist of vessels that are much noisier because of the possible patient movement, it is often a more challenging task compared to working on retinal images. In this study, we propose a multi-scale tensor voting framework to extract the vessel centerlines from cerebral angiograms. The developed framework is evaluated on a dataset of routinely acquired angiograms and reach an accuracy of 91.75% ± 5.07% during our experiments.

## 1 Introduction

Angiography or the imaging of the brain vasculature with X-ray is essential to the diagnosis and treatment of several neurovascular diseases. It provides a fast and accurate way to visualize blood vessels inside the brain. During an angiogram, X-ray images are obtained after injecting contrast dye inside a carotid artery. Although angiography is generally acquired in a 2D biplane mode, it is a useful diagnostic tool, mainly used by neurologists to find clots inside the blood vessels, stenosis, and aneurysms. It is generally combined with a background subtraction operation which reduces the artifacts created by the bones; such an imaging procedure is referred to as Digital Subtraction Angiography (DSA). Blood vessel segmentation is important for many clinical diagnostic tasks such as aneurysms, arteriosclerosis, arteriovenous malformations, vasculitis and tears in the lining of an artery. For some of these diagnostic tasks it is necessary to measure the vessel diameter, length, abnormal branching or bulging of the vessels.

Recently, several research efforts have focused on the study of hemodynamics of blood vessels in the brain using angiograms. For example, perfusion angiography [1] can be used to estimate the blood flow within major arteries of the brain.

G. Bebis et al. (Eds.): ISVC 2016, Part I, LNCS 10072, pp. 35–44, 2016.
DOI: 10.1007/978-3-319-50835-1_4

Other studies have investigated the 2D-3D reconstruction of the vessel for computational fluid dynamic simulations (CFD) [2]. Such simulations and analyses of blood flow are promising to establish imaging markers that are associated with outcome. Such information can play a major role in the personalization of treatment for several neurovascular diseases. However, the automatic extraction and quantification of blood vessel from angiograms in the brain is particularly challenging and beyond current methods. Manual vessel detection requires trained professionals and it becomes a tedious and reader dependent task when faced with a large number of X-ray images. For that reason, it is important to have an automatic blood vessel detection system. Automating blood vessel segmentation is itself a difficult task due to non-uniform illumination in the images and significant differences in the width of arteries and veins that often lead to an imprecise representation of the vasculature tree.

Several research studies have been done about vessel detection from angiograms while little work has been done on centerline extraction. In 1998, Frangi [3] proposed a multi-scale vessel enhancement filter and it is still in use in many studies nowadays. Staal [4] proposed a ridge-based vessel segmentation method that could reach an accuracy of 0.944 versus 0.947 for a second observer. Hooshyar [5] claimed his method of fuzzy ant colony algorithm could reach an accuracy of 0.933 versus 0.947 for a second observer. Sanjani [6] has combined different approaches before to examine the effect in 2013. Recently, a PSO-algorithm-based method was proposed by Sreejini [7]. In 2016, Christodoulidis implemented small retina segmentation using multi-scale tensor voting. It is worth noting that DSA images of brain vessels (considered in our study) may have much more noise because of the patients movement. In addition, the width of vessels in cerebral DSA images could change on a very large scale while retina vessels change little. Consequently, it is much harder to extract vessels or centerlines from DSA images of brains. In Egger's work [8], an efficient way to extract catheter centerlines was introduced. Sofka [9] presented an approach of retina vessel centerline in his work. Meanwhile, Yan Xu [10] and Puentes [11] have worked on coronary vessels.

Our work aims at extracting the centerlines of the vessels and remove the noise at the same time. Since tensor voting performs well on curve connection and noise removal [12–14], we adopt a multi-scale approach [15]. As for applying tensor voting on vessel centerlines, Risser [16] has used tensor voting in 3D. Leng [17] has proposed a rapid 2D centerline extraction method based on tensor voting, however, he did not focus on noise removal and his method is designed for retinal images. Compared with previous studies, this paper will present a multi-scale tensor voting framework extracting centerlines from cerebral angiograms based on the idea that vessels have a higher structure consistency than noise.

## 2   Methods

The diagram in Fig. 1 shows the pipeline of centerlines extraction from angiograms. We first implement a multi-scale filter on the raw image to capture vessels of different width. Then we extract the skeletons of vessels as well as noise. Next, in order to remove the noise and preserve the small vessels at the same time, a multiscale tensor voting framework is implemented since tensor voting has a great performance on curve connecting and noise removal [18]. The image is divided into segments and segments with low saliencies during scale changing are removed. After noise removal, the vessels are connected according to the saliency map.

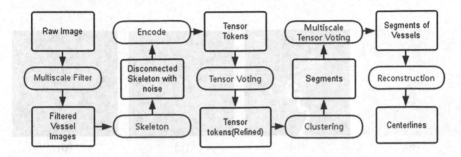

**Fig. 1.** Overall pipeline of our approach which involves image filtering, skeletonization, tensor voting, clustering and reconstruction.

## 2.1 Dataset

The dataset used to evaluate our framework originates from 19 patients treated at a University Medical Center for acute ischemic stroke. Source images were acquired using 2D DSA. Each run consists of a sequence of 20 frames. The orthogonal angiograms were acquired in an interleaved fashion; one frontal, one sagittal, and so on. The DSA scanning was performed on a Philips Allura Xper FD20® Biplane using a routine timed contrast-bolus passage technique. A manual injection of omnipaque 300 was performed at a dilution of 70% (30% saline) such that 10 cc of contrast was administered intravenously at an approximate rate of 5 cm$^3$/s. The median peak voltage output is 95 Kv. Image sizes were all 1024 × 1024 pixels but were acquired with a different field of view.

## 2.2 Pre-processing

**Multiscale Vessel Enhancement Filter.** We applied a multiscale vessel enhancement filter proposed by Frangi [3] to our raw images (Fig. 2) to delineate the vessels. Large scale filtering could remove most of the noise, however, it also filters out the small vessels while smaller scales accentuate the details and the noise at the same time. To account for this problem, we use a multi-scale approach and combine scales from 1 to 15 to allow for details to be preserved. We then select the maximum of these 15 scales for each pixel and set a threshold proportional to the one obtained by Otsu's method [19], to preserve as many details as possible. A binary image of the vessel image was extracted as shown in Fig. 2.

**Skeleton Extraction.** The binary image generated on the previous step was then processed with a skeleton extraction algorithm [20]. Because of the changing width of the main vessels and the existence of junctions, there are some additional branches in areas where vessel width changes and junctions are present. To remove these unwanted branches, we implement a high scale filter to the raw images to detect the main vessels where these unwanted branches always appear (Fig. 2).

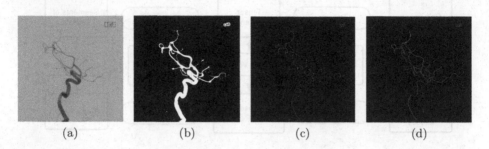

(a)　　　　　(b)　　　　　(c)　　　　　(d)

**Fig. 2.** The steps of our approach. (a) The raw image. (b) After applying the multi-scale filter on the raw image. (c) The skeleton extracted from the filtered image. (d) The saliency map generated after multi-scale tensor voting framework, which could be used to reconnect the vessels.

### 2.3   Multiscale Tensor Voting Framework

Following the pre-processing step, a multi-scale tensor voting framework was implemented in order to remove the noise and connect small vessels. This method works by having structurally salient features enforce each other in a neighborhood, while removing noise and preserving the details extracted in the previous step.

**Tensor Voting Framework.** In the tensor voting framework proposed by Medioni [21], each input token is encoded as a second order symmetric tensor to store its information according to the expression below:

$$T = \begin{pmatrix} a_{11} & a_{12} \\ a_{21} & a_{22} \end{pmatrix} = \lambda_1 e_1 e_1^T + \lambda_2 e_2 e_2^T . \tag{1}$$

where $\lambda_1$ and $\lambda_2$ are its eigenvalues and $e_1$ and $e_2$ are the corresponding eigenvectors, where $\lambda_1 \geqslant \lambda_2 \geqslant 0$. The tensor can also be decomposed into the form representing its stick and ball components:

$$T = (\lambda_1 - \lambda_2)e_1 e_1^T + \lambda_2(e_1 e_1^T + e_2 e_2^T) . \tag{2}$$

These two components represent two types of features: curves and points. $(\lambda_1 - \lambda_2)$ is the saliency of a curve feature while $e_1$ represents the normal curve orientation. Meanwhile, $\lambda_2$ is the saliency of a point feature. In addition, junction points usually have higher saliencies than noisy points, manifesting higher values of $\lambda_2$. Consequently, the saliency of the curves and the points represent the probabilities of local curves or sparse points, deciding the local pattern of the image. In the voting process, each token casts votes to the tokens in its neighborhood, where the neighborhood size is controlled by a scale parameter $\sigma$ set manually. Here we adopted a closed-form solution to tensor voting proposed by Wu [22]. Suppose we have two tokens $x_j$ and $x_i$, where $x_j$ is the voter and $x_i$ is the vote receiver. $r_{ij}$ is a unit vector pointing from token $x_j$ to $x_i$. The tensor vote at $x_i$ indicated by $T_j$ located at $x_j$ is given by the following expression:

$$S_{ij} = c_{ij} R_{ij} T_j R'_{ij}. \qquad (3)$$

where $c_{ij} = \exp(-\frac{\|x_i - x_j\|^2}{\sigma})$, $R_{ij} = I - 2 r_{ij} r_{ij}^T$, $R'_{ij} = (I - \frac{1}{2} r_{ij} r_{ij}^T) R_{ij}$ and I is an identity. And a structure-aware tensor $T_i$ can be assigned at each site $x_i$ by summing up all the $S_{ij}$ casted by $x_j$ under the chosen scale $\sigma$:

$$T_i = \sum_j S_{ij} . \qquad (4)$$

This tensor sum at token $x_i$ indicates the potential local feature of the token according to the saliencies of its two components as explained above. Here we set $T_j$ as an identity tensor before voting, assuming every input token has no prior orientation information.

**Grouping and Multi-scale Tensor Voting.** The skeleton we extracted after using the multi-scale filter consists of much noise and disconnected vessels. Since noise and small vessels are quite similar while small vessels have higher consistencies in their local structure, it is hard to set a single scale that could filter out noise without losing details. Considering the differences in sizes of vessels, here we adopt a multi-scale way to remove the noise and connect the vessels using tensor voting [23].

The only free parameter of tensor voting framework is $\sigma$, which controls the voting scale. When $\sigma$ is small, it preserves the local structures and details. As $\sigma$ grows, the results tend to retain only the global configurations, curves becoming smooth. Since we have both main vessels and small ones in our image and they adapt to different scales, we change the scale from a small value to a large one to fit all the vessels. As for noise, it is quite similar to small vessels, however it does not have a high consistency on local structures, so the saliency will decrease sharply compared to small vessels. Consequently, it is feasible to apply the multi-scale framework.

We first implement the single-scale tensor voting framework on the images after pre-processing. Then we segment the vessels into fragments according to the positions, curvatures and the $e_1$ of the tokens. The number of segments should be selected carefully since it influences both the processing time and the accuracy of the results. Since we have noise and small vessels that are fragments themselves, how meticulous we segment the main vessels matters the results. In our experiments we found that Large segments tend to losing details for the reason that they always have high saliencies. And small cuts may lose tokens near junctions because the saliencies near junctions would decrease. In practice, we apply large segment first and then small cuts in order to achieve a satisfying outcome.

After segmenting the vessels, we implement an iterative procedure of tensor voting: we change the scale from a small value to a large one and count how many times the saliency of each segment exceeds a certain threshold Ts. After every iteration, we remove the segments that have a low count of exceeding Ts and slightly increase the value of Ts. Since the saliency of segments would increase after removing the noise, a higher value of Ts is required after each iteration. After the multiscale tensor voting, we reconnect the vessels using the saliency map [24]. Figure 2 shows the saliency map after implementing the framework.

## 3  Experiments

Our experiments test whether the proposed multi-scale tensor voting framework could extract vascular centerlines from DSA images. For our experiments, we used 19 DSA images as input, and compared the results with the ground truth which was established manually by a neurologist. The filter scales range from 1 to 15 to capture as many vessels as possible. Then we extract the skeletons and refine them by the method illustrated above. Next, we input every pixel on the skeletons as a ball tensor into the single scale tensor voting framework. The skeletons are then segmented according to the coordinate, curvature and $e_1$ of the tokens. We implement the multi-scale tensor voting on these segments. Since both the scale and the number of segments influence the results, here we adopt a large scale range and a small segment number first for the purpose of removing most noise, and then use a small range and a more meticulous segmentation to erase little noise left near vessels. The two scale ranges we used in our experiments are 20 and 50, focusing on the local characteristics and general structures.

## 4  Results

The results of our experiments are shown in Fig. 3, and were evaluated by estimating the sensitivity (true positive rates) and specificity (true negative rates). We follow the formula below:

$$TPR = TP/P. \tag{5}$$

$$TNR = TN/N. \tag{6}$$

$$ACCURACY = (TP + TN)/(P + N). \tag{7}$$

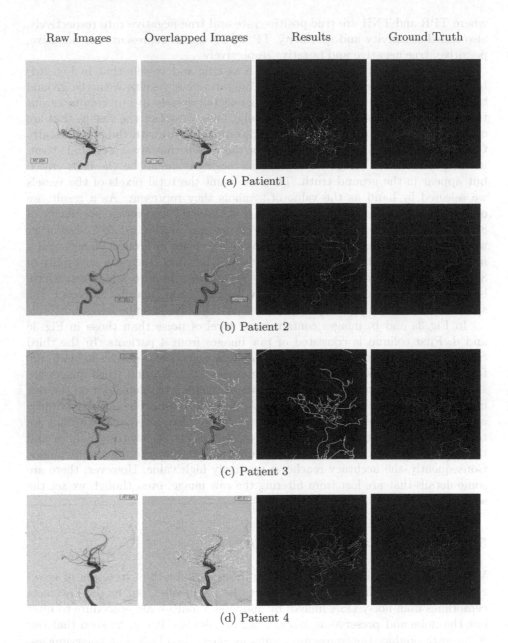

Raw Images          Overlapped Images          Results          Ground Truth

(a) Patient1

(b) Patient 2

(c) Patient 3

(d) Patient 4

**Fig. 3.** From left to right: raw images, raw images overlapped with centerlines, our results, ground truth. Results are annotated in the third column (black for true positive, yellow for false positive and red for false negative). Figures from the same row belong to a same patient. The first two rows are images with less noise while the last two rows are ones with much noise. The accuracy of four group of images (from top to bottom): 98.50%, 98.35%, 94.14% and 83.68%. (Color figure online)

where TPR and TNR are true positive rate and true negative rate respectively, also called sensitivity and specificity, TP, P, TN and N represent true possitive, possitive, true negative and negative respectively.

We select vessels in the ground truth as true and vessels that in Fig. 2(d) but not in the ground truth as false. Comparing our results with the ground truth, we select the vessels and the mis-selected vessels in our results as our true positive and false positive respectively. Then we select the vessels that are erased from step 3 to step 4 in Fig. 2 and compare them with the ground truth. Consequently, the true negative should be the vessels that are erased and absent in the ground truth image while the false negative should be the ones erased but appear in the ground truth. Then we count the total pixels of the vessels we selected by hand as the value of symbols they represent. As a result, we obtain an average sensitivity of 96.89% ± 1.91% and an average specificity of 82.19% ± 6.99%. Besides, our average accuracy was 91.75% ± 5.07%. For other works on retina images, they usually have a specificity of around 96.89% and a much lower sensitivity. For example, Christodoulidis has reached a sensitivity of 85.06% and a specificity of 95.82% [25]. The reason we have a high sensitivity is that we set the parameters empirically to avoid losing details. Moreover, the specificity is affected by the presence of scattered noise in some images.

In Fig. 3a and b, images contain lower level of noise than those in Fig. 3c and d. First column is consisted of raw images from 4 patients. In the third column of Fig. 3, we show the results and annotate the true negatives in black, the false positives in yellow and the false negatives in red. Ground truth images are shown in the right column. In addition, we overlapped the detection on the raw images to better illustrate the results in the second column. The positive samples and negative samples are selected from the skeleton extracted after filtering: we take the tokens that should be a part of the vessels as positive samples and take the rest of them as negative ones. Sample labeling was conducted manually. Consequently, the accuracy reaches a relatively high value. However, there are some details that are lost from filtering the raw image, even though we set the scale from 1 to 15.

## 5   Conclusion and Future Work

We proposed a multi-scale tensor voting framework for the extraction of vessel centerlines. Although small vessels tend to be fragmented, our method extracts centerlines from noisy DSA images by applying a multi-scale procedure to filter out the noise and preserve as much detail as possible. It can be seen that our framework produced encouraging results as shown in Fig. 3. For noisy images, we could remove most sparse noise while the noise with certain structure such as the shadow of skulls still remain. The reason why our method does not perform well on the last two patients (Fig. 3c and d) is that they all have noise consisting of long curves due to patient movement. These shadows of skulls have a higher consistency of structure than small vessels, so setting a high threshold to remove them will remove most of the vessels as well.

Other methods that process retinal images usually have an overall accuracy of around 95 % with sensitivity under 80% and specificity above 95%. In our results, we have an accuracy of 91.75%, a higher sensitivity of 96.89% and a lower specificity of 82.19%. In addition to being evaluated on a different dataset, our method focuses on noise removal. In our results, we concluded that our multi-scale tensor voting framework performs encouragingly on most cases, however it tends to fail when the noise has a structure similar to vessels. Note that this type of noise could be removed by using a co-registration method between the successive frames of the angiography prior to computing DSA.

**Acknowledgments.** Prof. Scalzo was partially supported by a AHA grant $16BGIA27760152$, a Spitzer grant, and received hardware donations from Gigabyte, Nvidia, and Intel.

# References

1. Scalzo, F., Liebeskind, D.S.: Perfusion angiography in acute ischemic stroke. Comput. Math. Meth. Med. **2016**(2), 1–14 (2016)
2. Scalzo, F., Hao, Q., Walczak, A.M., Hu, X., Hoi, Y., Hoffmann, K.R., Liebeskind, D.S.: Computational hemodynamics in intracranial vessels reconstructed from biplane angiograms. In: Bebis, G., et al. (eds.) ISVC 2010. LNCS, vol. 6455, pp. 359–367. Springer, Heidelberg (2010). doi:10.1007/978-3-642-17277-9_37
3. Frangi, A.F., Niessen, W.J., Vincken, K.L., Viergever, M.A.: Multiscale vessel enhancement filtering. In: Wells, W.M., Colchester, A., Delp, S. (eds.) MICCAI 1998. LNCS, vol. 1496, pp. 130–137. Springer, Heidelberg (1998). doi:10.1007/BFb0056195
4. Staal, J., Abràmoff, M.D., Niemeijer, M., Viergever, M.A., van Ginneken, B.: Ridge-based vessel segmentation in color images of the retina. IEEE Trans. Med. Imaging **23**, 501–509 (2004)
5. Hooshyar, S., Khayati, R.: Retina vessel detection using fuzzy ant colony algorithm. In: CRV, pp. 239–244 (2010)
6. Sanjani, S.S., Boin, J.B., Bergen, K.: Blood vessel segmentation in retinal fundus images (2013)
7. Sreejini, K., Govindan, V.: Improved multiscale matched filter for retina vessel segmentation using PSO algorithm. Egypt Inform. J. **16**, 253–260 (2015)
8. Egger, J., Mostarkic, Z., Großkopf, S., Freisleben, B.: A fast vessel centerline extraction algorithm for catheter simulation. In: CBMS, pp. 177–182 (2007)
9. Sofka, M., Stewart, C.V.: Retinal vessel centerline extraction using multiscale matched filters, confidence and edge measures. IEEE Trans. Med. Imaging **25**, 1531–1546 (2006)
10. Xu, Y., Zhang, H., Li, H., Hu, G.: An improved algorithm for vessel centerline tracking in coronary angiograms. Comput. Methods Programs Biomed. **88**, 131–143 (2007)
11. Puentes, J., Roux, C., Garreau, M., Coatrieux, J.L.: Dynamic feature extraction of coronary artery motion using dsa image sequences. IEEE Trans. Med. Imaging **17**, 857–871 (1998)
12. Tang, C.K., Medioni, G.: Curvature-augmented tensor voting for shape inference from noisy 3d data. IEEE Trans. Pattern Anal. Mach. Intell. **24**, 858–864 (2002)

13. Jia, J., Tang, C.K.: Inference of segmented color and texture description by tensor voting. IEEE Trans. Pattern Anal. Mach. Intell. **26**, 771–786 (2004)
14. Jia, J., Tang, C.K.: Image repairing: robust image synthesis by adaptive ND tensor voting. In: CVPR, vol. 1, pp. I–643 (2003)
15. Loss, L.A., Bebis, G., Parvin, B.: Iterative tensor voting for perceptual grouping of ill-defined curvilinear structures. IEEE Trans. Med. Imaging **30**, 1503–1513 (2011)
16. Risser, L., Plouraboué, F., Descombes, X.: Gap filling of 3-d microvascular networks by tensor voting. IEEE Trans. Med. Imaging **27**, 674–687 (2008)
17. Leng, Z., Korenberg, J.R., Roysam, B., Tasdizen, T.: A rapid 2-d centerline extraction method based on tensor voting. In: IEEE International Symposium on Biomedical Imaging: From Nano to Macro, pp. 1000–1003 (2011)
18. Medioni, G., Lee, M.S., Tang, C.K.: A computational framework for segmentation and grouping. Elsevier (2000)
19. Otsu, N.: A threshold selection method from gray-level histograms. Automatica **11**, 23–27 (1975)
20. Jain, A.K.: Fundamentals of Digital Image Processing. Prentice-Hall, Inc., Upper Saddle River (1989)
21. Medioni, G., Tang, C.K., Lee, M.S.: Tensor voting: theory and applications. In: Proceedings of RFIA, Paris, France, vol. 3 (2000)
22. Wu, T.P., Yeung, S.K., Jia, J., Tang, C.K., Medioni, G.: A closed-form solution to tensor voting: theory and applications. IEEE Trans. Pattern Anal. Mach. Intell. **34**, 1482–1495 (2012)
23. Loss, L., Bebis, G., Nicolescu, M., Skurikhin, A.: An iterative multi-scale tensor voting scheme for perceptual grouping of natural shapes in cluttered backgrounds. Comput. Vis. Image Underst. **113**, 126–149 (2009)
24. Deutsch, S., Medioni, G.: Intersecting manifolds: detection, segmentation, and labeling. In: AAAI, pp. 3445–3452 (2015)
25. Christodoulidis, A., Hurtut, T., Tahar, H.B., Cheriet, F.: A multi-scale tensor voting approach for small retinal vessel segmentation in high resolution fundus images. Comput. Med. Imaging Graph. **52**, 28–43 (2016)

# Stacked Autoencoders for Medical Image Search

S. Sharma[1], I. Umar[1], L. Ospina[1], D. Wong[1], and H.R. Tizhoosh[2](✉)

[1] Systems Design Engineering, University of Waterloo, Waterloo, Canada
[2] KIMIA Lab, University of Waterloo, Waterloo, Canada
tizhoosh@uwaterloo.ca

**Abstract.** Medical images can be a valuable resource for reliable information to support medical diagnosis. However, the large volume of medical images makes it challenging to retrieve relevant information given a particular scenario. To solve this challenge, content-based image retrieval (CBIR) attempts to characterize images (or image regions) with invariant content information in order to facilitate image search. This work presents a feature extraction technique for medical images using stacked autoencoders, which encode images to binary vectors. The technique is applied to the IRMA dataset, a collection of 14,410 x-ray images in order to demonstrate the ability of autoencoders to retrieve similar x-rays given test queries. Using IRMA dataset as a benchmark, it was found that stacked autoencoders gave excellent results with a retrieval error of 376 for 1,733 test images with a compression of 74.61%.

## 1 Introduction

Many physicians have experienced lawsuits due to perceived or actual medical malpractice and negligence in recent decades. Radiology, due to its diagnostic nature, has been one of most liable branches in medicine. Most claims and complaints deal with a correct diagnosis [11]. For instance, wrong interpretation of a malignant mass as a benign lesion accounts for approximately 45 % of radiologists' errors [8]. In addition, medical claims of misdiagnosis from medical images in Canada cost taxpayers over 8.3 million per year [2].

Radiologists do not have a reliable tool to cross-reference their initial diagnosis instantaneously. Receiving a second opinion on the diagnosis requires consulting a peer who must be pyhsically or virtually available, which is not always possible and constitutes an insurmountable financial and personal challenge for hospitals and clinics around the globe. Building a search engine for fast and accurate content-based image retrieval (CBIR) can potentially revolutionize diagnostic radiology and ultimately decrease both the number of patients affected by misdiagnosis and the number of costly claims against clinicians and hospitals. There are untapped petabytes of data already available in digital archives of hospitals – constantly growing –, that can be leveraged to reduce misdiagnosis through retrieving similar cases to exploit available knowledge from the past.

The challenge CBIR is that the image must be examined at the pixel level to quantify the similarity between images which is not an inherently quantitative

© Springer International Publishing AG 2016
G. Bebis et al. (Eds.): ISVC 2016, Part I, LNCS 10072, pp. 45–54, 2016.
DOI: 10.1007/978-3-319-50835-1_5

attribute, especially in medical imaging. Additionally, when dealing with "*big image data*", the computational costs of retrieval can become infeasible, if the image representation, i.e., image feature, is not chosen appropriately. Accuracy and speed of retrieval are understandably crucial in medical image applications. This paper looks at medical image search based on global image similarity. Single layered and stacked autoencoders are examined to search for similar images within the IRMA dataset that contains 14,410 x-ray images. Similarity is measured using the IRMA error score. The idea proposed is that given an input x-ray image, the system would search for the top $n = 3, 5, \ldots$ most similar images to display to the clinicians (ideally accompanied with other corresponding information such as biopsy reports, treatment plans, monitoring and follow-ups). This would allow practitioners to leverage the diagnosis, monitoring and treatment results of other patients with similar cases.

## 2    Background

The main idea proposed in this paper is feature extraction through the use of autoencoders. The main purpose of extracting features from x-ray images is to create a high-level description from low-level pixel values data. The accuracy of image retrieval is highly dependent on the quality of the features extracted. If the features do not represent the image content adequately, similar images cannot be retrieved.

Image search and retrieval has been studied over the past 20 years [7]. CBIR focuses on visual information as opposed to textual metadata, which is text-based search as we all know from daily Internet search when we type keywords to search for desired webpages [10]. However, implementing autoencoders as a feature extraction technique for x-rays has only been studied recently. CBIR is a valuable option for medical images. Text-based search may be limited for medical images due to insufficient text-based data or features, as well as lack of standardized software and procedure in clinical environments. Akgül et al. examine the various applications of CBIR towards medical imaging [1].

Feature extraction is the process of consolidating high signal information from the noisy input, in this case an image. These features are valuable in a model for training and retrieval. Some examples of visual features are color, shape, and texture, which can be extracted from low-level pixel information [6]. These visual features can range from low-level descriptors that are focused on a pixel or small group of pixels, to mid-level features that describe shapes, textures and colour, and finally to high-level features that describe the image and its components in rather general or abstract ways.

Tradition feature extractions have been extensively examined in computer vision. Using artificial neural networks to "represent" an image is rather a new development in computer vision. An autoencoder is a special type of neural network that automatically finds compressed encodings of images, while minimizing error. The compressed image can then be used to represent the image to search algorithms. A stacked autoencoder inputs the results from the previous autoencoder. Hinton et al. introduced the idea of using backpropagation networks to develop a complex unsupervised learning scheme [15]. The autoencoders were trained through Deep Belief Networks [15]. A denoising autoencoder can be trained on corrupted input versions in order to reduce the impact of future input noise [19]. Autoencoders have also been applied to mammograms for compression [17]. Ideas have been proposed to detect (and to ignore) irrelevant image blocks in each medical image class, by analyzing the error histogram of a autoencoder [5]. The purpose in such approaches is to reduce the dimensionality of features for image retrieval when dealing with a large number of images. The relevance of image blocks is directly proportional to the error of an autoencoder [5]. However, this approach only uses shallow autoencoders that mostly depend on features used to create the prediction model. On the other hand, the use of deep autoencoders allow to extract a better representation of the raw features of the image, therefore allowing to create a more accurate retrieval scheme. Some considerations in evaluating the suitability of autoencoders for this domain were the accuracy of retrieving similar images. Providing fast and accurate results to practitioners is necessary. Autoencoders may require longer training time dependent on the dimensionality of the problem, however this does not impact the retrieval time, once all images have been processed.

## 3   Proposed Approach

Fast and accurate CBIR is possible by extracting features from images that have the following two intuitive properties: two very similar images should produce two very similar feature vectors, and two very dissimilar images should produce two very different feature vectors. These two properties are especially critical for medical imaging where a region of interest needs to be analyzed (e.g., a tumour, an organ, a tissue type). A system is only valuable if it can return cases which contain regions similar to the selected region of interest.

Some CBIR solutions use local feature from feature descriptors such as SURF [18]. This technique creates many local feature descriptors for a given image and then combines all of them (up to a threshold) to create a pseudo-global image descriptor. This approach works well for general images but, as we verified in many preliminary experiments, fails in medical imaging, specifically for x-ray images. This could be due to x-rays not having many sharp or "good" features, e.g., corners, for the algorithms to use. To circumvent this problem, a global first approach is to be used to create one global feature descriptor (vector) for a given image. One such approach is to use autoencoders to generate a compressed feature vector.

Autoencoders, with $n/p/n$ architecture, encodes $n$ inputs into $p$ positions, and then decode $p$ positions back into $n$ outputs. By setting $p < n$, the autoencoder functions as a compressor to reduce the dimensionality. Such an autoencoder is basically a shallow neural network with some level of error to reconstruct the input signal from its minimalistic representation in the deepest layer.

While it is possible to use many visual features such as color, shape and texture as part of a feature extraction pipeline, we propose a very simple scheme.

We use the unprocessed pixel values as features into the autoencoder. The autoencoder, by virtue of its dimensionality reduction capability, will extract the complex anatomical features using the reconstruction error as its guide. We hypothesize that these features will satisfy the two properties mentioned above since the features are constructed relative to the training set, a claim that we seek to experimentally establish in following sections. The architecture can be deepened by creating an architecture of form $n/m/k/p/k/m/n$ (5 hidden layers) with $n < m < k < p$ by stacking multiple single layer autoencoders serially. Stacked autoencoders (SAE) can capture highly nonlinear mapping between input and output from the interactions between the many hidden layers and thousands of trainable weights.

## 4   Experiments

In this section, we describe the IRMA dataset, report the details of training and testing the stacked autoencoder, and finally analyze the results of image retrieval using autoencoders applied on IRMA dataset.

### 4.1   Image Data

Our goal is to provide the $n$ most similar image to an trained medical professional, the clinician, when she/he provides a query image. Images can be verified to be similar using many techniques such as RMS, and SSIM, however these metrics do not reflect medical domain information. To verify if two x-rays are indeed similar, the images would need to be shown to a medical professional. The IRMA data set contains images already annotated by medical professionals, which makes it a very useful benchmark dataset for retrieval purposes.

The IRMA dataset, supplied for the imageCLEF organization, had annotated codes were similar to domain expert knowledge [9,12–14]. This database has been used by many researchers and is comprised of preset test and training portions, which enable direct comparisons of metrics. The IRMA codes (manually created by several clinicians) contains information on technical, biological and diagnostic traits of the image in a structured manner: TTTT-DDD-AAA-BBB. Each section is hierarchical meaning there is a least significant bit and most significant digit (Table 1). Sample IRMA images are depicted in Fig. 1.

Table 1. Sections of the IRMA code

| T | Image modality and direction |
|---|---|
| D | Body orientation and anatomical code |
| A | Region of body examined |
| B | Biological system examined |

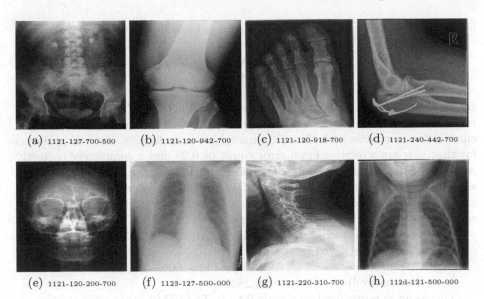

(a) 1121-127-700-500    (b) 1121-120-942-700    (c) 1121-120-918-700    (d) 1121-240-442-700

(e) 1121-120-200-700    (f) 1123-127-500-000    (g) 1121-220-310-700    (h) 112d-121-500-000

**Fig. 1.** Sample images with their IRMA codes TTTT-DDD-AAA-BBB.

As mentioned before, the objective of any CBIR system is to retrieve the most similar image from a dataset given an input (query) image. To build the database, each image in the training dataset is encoded using a trained Autoencoder. Processing the image through the autoencoder results in a compressed (encoded) feature vector that is assumed to "describe" the image content. This feature vector is created for all 12,998 x-ray images of IRMA dataset and stored. To retrieve an image, the query image is put through the trained autoencoder and a query feature vector is generated. The feature vector is then compared with all other indexed feature vectors to locate the most similar image. Various autoencoder specifications were tried, their results are stated in following sections.

**IRMA Error Score** – Let $I = \hat{l}_1, \hat{l}_2, \ldots, \hat{l}_i, \ldots, \hat{l}_I$ be the classified IRMA code (for one axis: T, D, A or B) of an image; where $l_i$ is set precisely for every position, and in $\hat{l}i$ is used when we 'don't know', marked by '*'. $I$ may be different for different images. If the classification at position $\hat{l}_i$ is wrong, then all succeeding decisions are wrong and, given a not-specified position, all succeeding decisions are considered to be not specified. if the correct code is unspecified and the predicted code is a wildcard, then no error is counted. In such cases, all remaining positions are regarded as not specified. Wrong (easy) decisions (i.e., fewer possible choices) are penalized for wrong difficult decisions (many possible choices at that node). A decision at position $l_i$ is correct by chance with a probability of $\frac{1}{b_i}$ if $b_i$ is the number of possible labels for position $i$. This assumes equal priors for each class at each position. Furthermore, wrong decisions at an early stage in the code (higher up in the hierarchy) are more penalized than wrong decisions at a later stage in the code (lower down on the hierarchy): i.e., $l_i$ is more important than $l_{i+1}$. Considering all these thoughts:

$$\text{IRMA Error} = \sum_{i=1}^{I} \frac{1}{b_i} \frac{1}{i} \delta(I_i, \hat{I}_i) \tag{1}$$

with $\delta(I_i, \hat{I}_i)$ being 0, 0.5 or 1 for agreement, 'don't know' and disagreement, respectively. In order to normalize the error, the maximal possible error is calculated for every axis such that a completely wrong decision (i.e., all positions for that axis are wrong) gets an error count of 0.25 and a completely correctly predicted axis has an error of 0. Therefore, an image with all positions in all axes being wrong has an error count of 1, and an image with all positions in all axes being correct has an error count of 0. Below a sample calculation of an error between a query and matched image:

IRMA code of Query Image:       $1111 - 223 - 555 - 777$
IRMA code of Retrieved Image:  $1111 - 010 - 555 - 778$
Digits Wrong:                           $0000 - 111 - 000 - 001$
Score (normalized):                    $0.2835$

The result is normalized on a scale 0 to 1. The IRMA error score is accumulated over the entire test set (1,734 images). The resulting number is the IRMa score reported in the results section. Since each IRMA error can range from 0 to 1, the sum of all error divided by the total possible error gives the error percentage for the test set.

## 4.2   Architecture of Autoencoder

We investigate both single layer autoencoders $n/p/n$ where $p \ll n$ and stacked autoencoders where the output of the previous autoencoder is fed to the next and so on. For the actual search we use the $k$-NN algorithm.

**Training single layer autoencoder** – We take 12,998 training x-ray images from the IRMA dataset. Each image is gray-scaled, and downscaled to $32 \times 32$ and normalized in $[0, 1]$. It is then fed to the input layer of the autoencoder as a column vector of size 1024. The encoding and decoding layers are trained to reconstruct the input vector (down sampled and vectorized image) by minimizing the reconstruction error measured by cross entropy using stochastic gradient descent. Note that we are using tied weights for encoding and decoding weights which has a regularization effect. We use sigmoid function for nonlinearity. Finally, we obtain the feature vector for each image by obtaining the latent representation from the hidden layer for each image.

**Training stacked autoencoder** – We obtain stacked autoencoders by serially arranging autoencoders such that the output of the first layer is fed as input to the second and so on (Fig. 2). Each autoencoder layer is trained greedily. Latent features from the first autoencoder are used as input to the second autoencoder layer. The process is repeated for all subsequent hidden layers. Finally, the latent feature vector from the last encoding layer acts as the final feature vector for the input image. We use Theano [3,4] and various python libraries to implement both the autoencoder and stacked autoencoder [16].

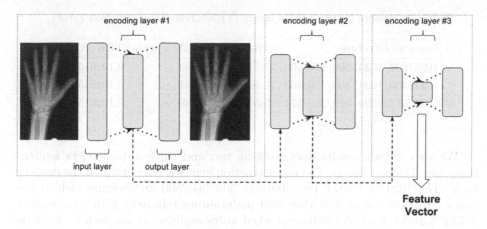

**Fig. 2.** Three hidden layers constructed via stacked autoencoders where the feature vector is extracted from the deepest layer.

### 4.3 Results

We report compression reduction, IRMA score and reconstruction error (root mean squared) for various AEs (autoencoders) and SAEs (stacked autoencoders).

We tried various configurations for a single layer autoencoder where $p < n$ as reported in Table 2. We used Euclidean distance to compare feature vectors between two images. The first hit (1-NN) IRMA score as well as the reconstruction error is reported on the test set. Interestingly, better reconstruction did not necessarily lead to lower IRMA score. For example, while the 1024/512/1024 configuration clearly had the lowest reconstruction error amongst the reported single layer architectures, it did not yield the lowest IRMA score. This implies that the features trained by minimizing the reconstruction error heuristic are clearly useful, we cannot easily predict the performance of the features on the test dataset from the reconstruction error alone. We note that the latent features produced significant compression while still maintaining low error. Each trial used the following settings: 30 epochs, a learning rate of 0.1, and a batch size of 20 for stochastic gradient descent.

**Table 2.** Results for an autoencoder with a single hidden layer (RMS captures the test reconstruction error).

| Architecture | % Reduction | IRMA score | RMS |
| --- | --- | --- | --- |
| 1024/225/1024 | 78.03 % | 407 | 0.104277 |
| 1024/512/1024 | 50 % | 405 | 0.091310 |
| 1024/150/1024 | 85.35 % | 393 | 0.114780 |
| 1024/275/1024 | 73.14 % | 388 | 0.100892 |

**Table 3.** Results for two hidden layers (TRE=Test Reconstruction Error).

| Layer architecture | % Reduction | IRMA score | TRE (RMS) |
|---|---|---|---|
| 1024/600/1024, 600/250/600 | 75.59 % | 393 | 0.102615 |
| 1024/400/1024, 400/250/400 | 75.59 % | 391 | 0.102615 |
| 1024/512/1024, 512/250/512 | 75.59 % | 389 | 0.102615 |

We also include results from stacking two and three autoencoders sequentially (see Tables 3 and 4). The reconstruction errors are reported on the deepest layer. The 1024/600/1024, 600/500/600, 500/260/500 architecture yielded the lowest IRMA score of 376 while still maintaining relatively high compression (74.61 % reduction). We believe stacked autoencoders, as opposed to a single layer autoencoder, produce a more useful higher-level representation from the lower-level representation output by the previous layer. To test for overfitting on the training data, the reconstruction error was calculated on the training set and compared to the testing images. For example, a triple stacked autoencoder 1024/600/1024, 600/500/600, 500/260/500, the error was 0.096200 and 0.101679, respectively. One can interpret the negligible difference in reconstruction errors as acceptable generalization. It should be noted that reconstruction error for stacked autoencoders is reported only for the first layer, and therefore the true reconstruction error is not simple to obtain. However, the differences in reconstruction for a simple non-stacked autoencoder (see Table 4) are also negligible.

**Table 4.** Results for three hidden layers (TRE=Test Reconstruction Error).

| Layer architecture | % Reduction | IRMA score | TRE (RMS) |
|---|---|---|---|
| 1024/600/1024, 600/400/600, 400/200/400 | 80.47 % | 400 | 0.111440 |
| 1024/600/1024, 600/500/600, 500/260/500 | 74.61 % | 376 | 0.101679 |

Observing the distribution of data in the IRMA training and testing images, we noticed that there exists both inter- and intra-statistical imbalances between the data sets. That is, the training set is severely imbalanced such that various classes are not represented normally. A histogram of image classes is shown in Fig. 3. Despite this problem, the trained autoencoders have a low IRMA score and exhibit negligible differences in reconstruction error (between training and test data). This can further compound the notion that there is no overfitting, hence the autoencoders are generalizing well.

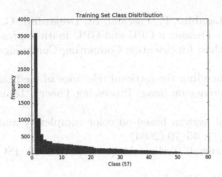
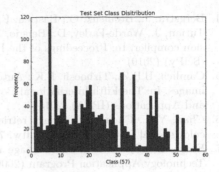

**Fig. 3.** Imbalance: class distribution of IRMA training (left) and test data (right).

## 5   Conclusions

Content-based image retrieval is a challenging problem for medical images. It is possible to analyze one image in a short amount of time and classify it in a medically meaningful way. However, given a new image, comparing it to the entire collection of medical images, to find the similar images, can be computationally expensive. Such a task requires a technique that searches through the big image data efficiently while still finding highly similar images. One method to reduce the dimensionality of the problem is to encode the images in a smaller, compact representation to enable faster image comparisons during the retrieval task. Such technology has clearly enormous potential in aiding domains such as diagnostic radiology and pathology. Due to the scarcity of text-based features associated with medical images directly embedded in medical image formats, i.e., in DICOM files, as well as the large quantity of images available, a search focused on visual features was explored in this paper. A global, content-based image retrieval technique was successfully applied to the application of medical images. The best performing feature extraction technique examined was an stacked autoencoder. Of the examined architectures, the most accurate setup consisted of three hidden layers with configurations 1024/600/1024, 600/500/600, and 500/260/500. On the IRMA dataset, with 14,410 x-ray images, the proposed approach achieved an IRMA score of 376 with a compression of 74.61 %.

## References

1. Akgül, C.B., Rubin, D.L., Napel, S., Beaulieu, C.F., Greenspan, H., Acar, B.: Content-based image retrieval in radiology: current status and future directions. J. Digit. Imaging **24**(2), 208–222 (2010)
2. Canadian Medical Protective Association: 2014 annual report of the Canadian medical protective association
3. Bastien, F., Lamblin, P., Pascanu, R., Bergstra, J., Goodfellow, I.J., Bergeron, A., Bouchard, N., Bengio, Y.: Theano: new features and speed improvements (2012)

4. Bergstra, J., Breuleux, O., Bastien, F., Lamblin, P., Pascanu, R., Desjardins, G., Turian, J., Warde-Farley, D., Bengio, Y.: Theano: a CPU and GPU math expression compiler. In: Proceedings of the Python for Scientific Computing Conference (SciPy) (2010)
5. Camlica, H.R.Z., Tizhoosh, F.K.: Autoencoding the retrieval relevance of medical images. In: The Fifth International Conference on Image Processing Theory, Tools and Applications (IPTA) (2015)
6. Chan, Y.K., Chen, C.Y.: Image retrieval system based on color complexity and color spatial features. J. Syst. Softw. **71**(1), 65–70 (2004)
7. Enser, P.G.B.: Content-based image retrieval. Technical report, JTAP-039, ISC Technology Application Program (2000)
8. Kundel, H.L., Nodine, C.F., Carmody, D.: Visual scanning, pattern recognition and decision-making in pulmonary nodule detection. Invest. Radiol. **13**(3), 175–181 (1978)
9. Idiap Research Institute: Error evaluation for ImageCLEF 2009 IRMA medical image annotation, December 2015
10. Joshi, M.D., Deshmukh, R.M., Hemke, K.N., Bhake, A., Wajgi, R.: Pictorial information retrieval. J. Doc. **51**(2), 126–170 (1995)
11. Kinsey, T.V., Horton, M.C., Lewis, T.E.: Interfacing the PACS and the HIS: results of a 5-year implementation. RSNA RadioGraphics
12. Lehmann, T.M., Deselaers, T., Schubert, H., Guld, M.O., Thies, C., Fischer, B., Spitzer, K.: The IRMA code for unique classification of medical images. In: SPIE Proceedings, vol. 5033, pp. 440–451. SPIE (2003)
13. Lehmann, T.M., Deselaers, T., Schubert, H., Guld, M.O., Thies, C., Fischer, B., Spitzer, K.: IRMA - a content-based approach to image retrieval in medical applications. IRMA Int. Conf. **5033**, 911–912 (2006)
14. Mueller, H., Clough, P., Deselares, T., Caputo, B.: ImageCLEF - Experimental Evaluation in Visual Information Retrieval. Springer, Heidelberg (2010)
15. Rumelhart, D.E., Hinton, G.E., Williams, R.J.: Learning internal representations by error propagation. Parallel Distributed Processing, vol. 1 (1986)
16. Sumanyu, S.: Source code for "stacked autoencoders" (2016). https://github.com/sumanyu/stacked-denoising-autoencoders
17. Tan, C.C., Eswaran, C.: Using autoencoders for mammogram compression. Syst. **35**(1), 49–58 (2011)
18. Velmurugan, K., Baboo, S.: Content-based image retrieval using surf and colour moments. Global J. Comput. Sci. Technol. **11**(10) (2011). ISSN: 0975-4172, Print ISSN: 0975-4350
19. Vincent, P., Larochelle, H., Bengio, Y., Manzagol, P.A.: Extracting and composing robust features with denoising autoencoders. In: International Conference on Machine Learning (2008)

# CutPointVis: An Interactive Exploration Tool for Cancer Biomarker Cutpoint Optimization

Lei Zhang$^{(\boxtimes)}$ and Ying Zhu

Department of Computer Science, Georgia State University, Atlanta,
GA 30303, USA
lzhang14@student.gsu.edu, yzhu@cs.gsu.edu

**Abstract.** In the field of medical and epidemiological research, it is a common practice to do a clinical or statistical dichotomization of a continuous variable. By dichotomizing a continuous variable, a researcher can build a eligibility criteria for potential studies, predict disease likelihood or predict treatment response. The dichotomization methods can be classified into data-depend methods and outcome-based methods. The data-dependent methods are considered to be arbitrary and lack of generics. While the outcome-based methods compute an optimal cut point which maximizes the statistical difference between two dichotomized groups. There is no standard software yet for an expedited cut point determination In this work, we present *CutPointVis*, a visualization platform for fast and convenient optimal cut point determination. Compared to existing research work, *CutPointVis* distinguishes itself with its real-time feature and better user interactivity. A case study is presented to demonstrate the usability of *CutPointVis*.

## 1 Introduction and Motivation

In biomedical research, a biomarker is used to identify or inspect a biological or pathological process or therapeutic responses [2]. Researchers tend to focus on continuous variables, while the prediction function of a variable can not easily be established. An illustrative example is that cancer biomarker research [12] is the process of identifying biomarkers with prognostic significance. A biomarker is often a continuous value, either percentile/score or an ordinary value. In order to predict the risk of subjects in a group, it is necessary to transform a continuous variable into a binary one, so that (1) The model is more interpretable to clinicians and (2) A clinical decision or a treatment can be made on each distinct group.

There are many methods/theories proposed to dichotomize a continuous variable. These methods fall into two main categories: data-oriented methods and outcome-oriented methods. The data-oriented methods dichotomize a continuous variable based on orders statistics, such as median or a percentile. However, the data-oriented methods are not reliable since the order statistics are

© Springer International Publishing AG 2016
G. Bebis et al. (Eds.): ISVC 2016, Part I, LNCS 10072, pp. 55–64, 2016.
DOI: 10.1007/978-3-319-50835-1_6

dataset-dependent. On the other hand, the outcome-oriented methods compute a cutpoint that has the most significant statistical relation with the outcome. Outcome-oriented methods are considered to be of a better dichotomization effect [9].

The outcome-oriented method proposed by Contal in [6] is a pervasive dichotomization solution. It calculates log rank test statistics (LRS) [11] at each event point (by using that risk point as threshold to split a given dataset into two groups) and determines an optimal cutpoint. Contals' method is computational intensive and it is not widely used until recently. Although a more efficient SAS macro [10] is proposed to calculate LRS, it is still relatively time-consuming. The reason is that the whole computation process may be carried out repeatedly with a small adjustment at each pass. A researcher is supposed to compare results of two different inputs (e.g. two Kaplan-Meier [8] curves based on two different cutpoints). To improve the efficiency in the state-of-art research practice, an intuitive and straightforward visualization research tool can expedite the research process and push towards a more systematic research practice.

In this paper, we present *CutPointVis*[1], an interactive visualization tool for cutpoint optimization. The goal of this work is twofold: (1) As the state-of-art biomarker research tends to overestimate its results and reduces its productivity [4], *CutPointVis* seeks to close the gap between biomarker research and its corresponding productivity. (2) *CutPointVis* seeks to provide a comprehensive and intuitive visualization research tool for biomarker research, which may exemplify future studies.

## 2    Related Work

As a pioneer work in cutpoint determination and visualization, X-Tile [5] focuses on dividing a dataset into three subsets. X-Tile precomputes the division results at each possible pair of cutpoints. After that, it populates a 2-D right-triangular grid for a researcher to choose a pair of cutpoints. At each cutpoint pair, the researcher can visualize the corresponding K-M plot and histogram analysis. Unlike X-Tile, *CutPointVis* focuses on dividing a dataset into two subsets. Furthermore, *CutPointVis* provides realtime interactivity: it does not precompute all the result before any user interaction, since the pre-computation may take too much computation resource, especially when a large dataset is given.

Cutoff Finder [4] provides static visualization of potential optimal dichotomization cutpoints. After loading a dataset, it computes an optimal cutpoint according to a user selected optimization method. Although Cutoff Finder optimizes the Cox Regression groups p-value, it does not allow flexibility or group stratification exploration. Therefore, with Cutoff Finder there is no way to identify other potential suboptimal cutpoints (which can be only slightly inferior

---

[1] A demonstrative example of CancerVis (CutPointVis) can be found at http://grid. cs.gsu.edu/~lzhang14/demo/biocancer1/main.html. Please be noted that since the system is still under development, the demonstrative example uses a given dataset for exploration use.

but lay on very different parts of the continuous biomarker spectrum) or identify stratification patterns (such as the high risk group survival with increasing threshold selection).

Besides aforementioned work, there is few research in visualization tool for cutpoint optimization. In this work, we focus on interactive visualization tool for Cox model optimization. We solve this problem by developing *CutPointVis*. Besides providing a fast and convenient graphical tool for biomarker optimization, *CutPointVis* offers interactivity for researchers to explore other context-dependent optimal cutpoints.

## 3   CancerVis Platform and CutPointVis Tool

As a comprehensive exploratory platform for cancer biomarker analysis, CancerVis [16] provides multiple views from different perspectives of a dataset. The views are synchronized so that a user can easily link the same data entry in multiple views.

Besides pure visualization features, CancerVis provides an interactive module, *CutPointVis*, which supports common data mining techniques in survival analysis for cancer biomarker research, such as visual assistance for determination of optimal cutpoint. As the interaction module of CancerVis, *CutPointVis* provides a full-fledged visual exploration support for data mining in survival analysis, which includes: (1) Realtime plot of Kaplan-Meier curve based on user selected cutpoints. (2) Displaying the log rank test statistics when stratifying for outcomes for multiple categorical classes (i.e. grade, stage, or lymph node status).

In the following parts of this section, we first briefly introduce the principle of cutpoint optimization in survival analysis (Log Rank Statistics), then we present the two aforementioned interaction features.

### 3.1   Cox Model for Optimal Cutpoint Determination

During cancer research, when a survival analysis is conducted, it is a common practice to dichotomizing a continuous covariate [1]. Compared to data dependent methods, a log rank test statistic based method [6] finds a statistically optimal solution [14]. However, due to relatively high computational cost, log rank test statistic based cut point determination method [6] has not been widely used until recently.

To conduct cutpoint determination on a given dataset $G$, a user first chooses the risk factor $R$ and the time-to-event variable $T$. $R$ is a continuous variable and $T$ is the time until the event happens. We use $t_{(1)} < t_{(2)} < ... < t_{(k)}$ to denote the ordered observed events of outcome variable $T$. We use $C$ to denote set of $K$ distinct values of the continuous variable $R$. Given a hypothetical point $P$ in $G$ where $R = p$, it divides the dataset into two groups, group with $R > p$ and group with $R <= p$. Let $d_{(i)}$ denote the number of events at time $t_{(i)}$, $r_{(i)}$ be the number of subjects at risk prior to time $t_{(i)}$. Let $d_{(i)}^{+}$ denote the number of events at time $t_{(i)}$ in group $R > p$ and $r_{(i)}^+$ be the number of subjects at risk prior to time $t_{(i)}$ in group $R > p$. The log rank statistic (LRS) of cutpoint $p$ can be computed as in [6]:

$$LRS(p) = \sum_{i=1}^{K} (d_i^+ - d_i \frac{r_i^+}{r_i}) \tag{1}$$

The optimal cutpoint $P_m$ is the point that maximizes the absolute value of LRS. Statistically, a stratification at $R = P_m$ maximizes the difference between two groups. This procedure is usually carried out by a scientific computation platform, such as a SAS macro or a Matlab program. Although the optimal point $P_m$ can be determined by manually reading literal LRS results or by an excel/SAS max function, it is not efficient or intuitive, as indicated in the spreadsheet on the right part of Fig. 1 (The left part is the LRS curve plotting provided by *CutPointVis*). Furthermore, as indicated in Fig. 2, besides theoretically optimal point, there are other suboptimal points that are worth investigating (black dots on the curve). These suboptimal points are not as likely to stand out when analyzing a simple text output.

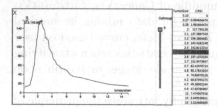
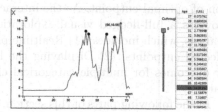

**Fig. 1.** Determining optimal LRS point by a figure (left) and by a spreadsheet (right)

**Fig. 2.** One optimal point and four sub-optimal points

## 3.2 Realtime K-M Plotting for Cutpoint Determination

According to Cox model, the optimal cutpoint $p_m$ is the point that maximizes the absolute value of LRS. However, as indicated in Fig. 2, besides the theoretically optimal cutpoint, there are other suboptimal cutpoints that are worth investigating (black dots on the curve). Furthermore, as stated in [10], "There is no single method or criterion to specify which criterion is best and thus the results of analyses from different categorization methods may be different".

To satisfy different criterions for cutpoint optimization practice in survival analysis, we developed *CutPointVis*, an interactive exploration tool for cutpoint analysis.

In this exploration tool, a researcher is able to select risk factor $R$, outcome variable $T$ and censoring indicator. Then a LRS curve can be plotted with the

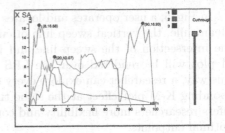

**Fig. 3.** Visualizing optimal LRS cutpoint (Color figure online)

**Fig. 4.** Visualizing optimal LRS cutpoint in different groups (Color figure online)

optimal cutpoint highlighted, as indicated in Fig. 3. From Fig. 3 we can see that the Cox optimal cutpoint is indicated with a red circle at $R = 11$.

Besides presenting optimal cutpoint for one group, *CutPointVis* provides a function to visualize optimal cutpoints for separate groups. A dataset can be split by a "Grouping" factor. Then the optimization can be applied to all the categories in the group, as indicated by Fig. 4. This plot represents the change in log likelihood when comparing patients above versus below the selected thresholds of the x-axis variable. The color of the lines indicate the grade (aka group) of the patients and the red dots show the value where optimal survival stratification is observed. We can interpret this data as clinical evidence in support of variable grade determined thresholds for cellular proliferative risks, with grade 3 patients showing highest risk in maximal Ki-67% while grade 1 and 2 show much better survival with minimal Ki-67%. We can also see that the ideal thresholds for grade 1 and 3 are not due to noise, and instead indicate real maximal survival stratification whereas for grade 2 the ideal threshold is a bit ambiguous because there exists multiple peaks at multiple Ki-67 values which show a similar log rank statistic. Also, using this type of data easily allows a biostatistician to identify if any threshold can be used regardless of grade to allow for suitable overall stratification (such as around 10 for the 3 grades).

As we stated before, due to different research contexts, Cox optimal cutpoint may not be an expected optimal cutpoint. To handle this flexibility, *CutPointVis* provides a feature for a researcher to further visually explore other potential optimal cutpoints.

A researcher may choose a different optimal cutpoint (other than Cox optimal cutpoint) due to many reasons, but in most of the cases a Kaplan-Meier estimator [3] would help the researcher to determine a context-dependent optimal cutpoint. Observing this fact, *CutPointVis* provides an interactive Kaplan-Meier plotting feature.

After a researcher has chosen variables $R$ and $T$ for survival analysis, a LRS plot will be presented as in Fig. 3 and the Cox optimal cutpoint (global maximum point) is tagged with a black dot. After that, as indicated by Fig. 5, the researcher can explore different cutpoints with the cursor.

In Fig. 5, a user operates and locates the cursor to any point of a LRS curve. Meanwhile, the vertical sweep line of cursor determines a cutpoint $P_c$ which is the intersection of the sweep line and LRS curve. Using $p_c$ as cutpoint, a K-M plot will be rendered over the LRS curve, the cutpoint is also labeled. In this way, a researcher can explore every single cutpoint, and visualize the corresponding K-M plot effect at the same time. We believe that realtime K-M plot offers researchers more flexibility and convenience to explore context-dependent optimal cutpoints.

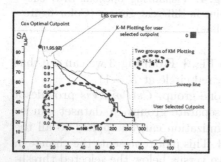
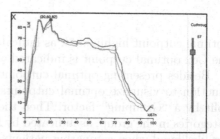

**Fig. 5.** Realtime KM plotting for optimal cutpoint determination

**Fig. 6.** Visualizing optimal LRS cutoff point with different cut-throughs

### 3.3   Realtime Visualization for Cut-Through Analysis

Cut-through analysis is another common data analysis practice in survival analysis. In cut-through analysis, a researcher assigns a cutpoint threshold $r_\delta$ for risk variable, and all the cases for those cases whose $R > r_\delta$ will be censored, no matter what their original censoring indicator values are. This operation might help to find a even better optimal cutpoint.

To conduct this analysis in pervasive software platforms, such as SAS, a researcher needs to modify the SAS macro and manually assign a threshold value, and then starts the time-consuming computation process. *CutPointVis* provides an alternative, visual approach. Figure 6 indicates the optimal cutpoint under the condition of cut-through analysis. Through GUI illustrated by Fig. 6, a research can use the sliding bar on the right side to locate any cut-through point. While a researcher is operating a dragging action on the sliding bar, a realtime plotting of LRS using that point as censoring threshold will be rendered.

From Fig. 6 we can see that, when the cut through threshold is set to 57, we find another optimal cutpoint at $R = 20$, while the previous optimal cutpoint is at $R = 11$. Moreover, to compare different cut-through thresholds, CancerVis provides a "memory" function. If a researcher is interested in a cut through threshold but wants to compare it with other cut through thresholds, he can double-click on the current curve to "memorize" it. All "memorized" curves are presented in grey dotted lines, as indicated in Fig. 6.

# 4    Verification and Case Study

## 4.1    Dataset and Workflow

In order to verify the usability of *CutPointVis*, in this section we conduct a case study to identify optimal hormone expression level thresholds which can most significantly stratify survival.

The datasets we use here are breast cancer mRNA datasets (GSE2034 and GSE7390), which are available online at the Gene Expression Omnibus (GEO) [7]. We choose probe 205225_at (estrogen receptor, ER) and 208305_at (progesterone receptor, PgR) as risk factors. In this study we separately analyzed ER (probe: 205225_at) and PR (probe: 208305_at) expression

There are 286 cases in GSE2034 and 198 cases in GSE7390. The analysis workflow can be descried as follows:

1. The researcher loads the dataset in cloud.[2]
2. The researcher chooses the biomarker variable, outcome variable and optional censoring variables.
3. A LRS plot will be generated. The researcher explores the LRS, either inspect K-M plot or check a cutthrough plot (both in realtime).
4. The researcher selects optimal cutpoint according to his own interpretation.

## 4.2    Exploration and Results

After loading GSE2034, we first choose an ER factor (205225_at in GSE2034) as risk factor and choose survival factor (time to relapse or last follow-up), choose relapse as censoring factor. The LRS plot can be illustrated in Fig. 7. We can see that besides the Cox optimal cutpoint, there is less likely to be another context-dependent optimal points.

In the next step we do cutthrough analysis. We slide the cutthrough threshold to 70 months (all those cases whose survival time over 70 will be censored)

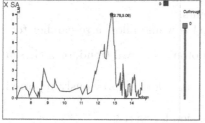
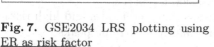
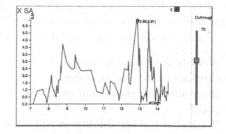

**Fig. 7.** GSE2034 LRS plotting using ER as risk factor

**Fig. 8.** GSE2034 LRS plotting using ER as risk factor with cut-through

[2] The *CutPointVis* tool is still under development. Users are not allowed to change dataset in the cloud yet. The current dataset for demo is extracted from gene expression series GSE2034.

and we have an updated LRS plot, which is illustrated in Fig. 8. From this figure we can see that besides the theoretical optimal cutpoint, there is another potential cutpoint which worth investigation. Due to the different research contexts, different researchers may conclude on different cutpoints. *CutPointVis* provides conveniences for a researcher to switch and compare between different conditions.

There are situations indicated in Fig. 2 where suboptimal cutpoint(s) that are also worth investigation. In the next step we use a PgR (20835_at) as risk factor and the LRS plot is illustrated in Fig. 9.

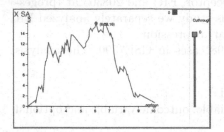
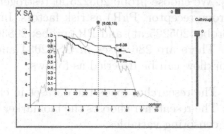

**Fig. 9.** GSE2034 LRS plotting using PgR as risk factor (Color figure online)

**Fig. 10.** GSE2034 LRS plotting using PgR as risk factor (KM plot at R = 6.08)

From this figure we can see that, although *CutPointVis* tagged the statistical optimal cutpoint with a red circle (where R = 6.08), but another suboptimal may be worth attention, which is the peak right beside the tagged red point. In this situation, a *CutPointVis* user can easily operate the cursor (the vertical sweep line) to both two points, compare the KM plot on-the-fly, then conclude on a context-dependent optimal cutpoint. The realtime KM plot at these two points are illustrated in Figs. 10 and 11. It should be noted that, although the nuance of KM plots between Figs. 10 and 11 is difficult to differentiate, the dynamic process of the KM plotting curve updates (when the cursor moves the cutpoint 6.08 to 6.79) can clearly tell a researcher the trend, such as if the gap is closing or growing. By this mode, *CutPointVis* provides the freedom for a researcher to conclude on his own version of optimal cutpoints.

As illustrated by this case study, *CutPointVis* would allow a researcher to:

- Identify if increasing hormones shows a monotonic survival trend, or if chosen thresholds are simply noise.
- Investigate all significant peaks to see if any are close to previously reported cutoffs.
- If ER/PR has bimodality at different expression levels [13]
- Potentially split cohorts into 3 survival groups (low, moderate, and high risk) based on hormone expression by identifying multiple extreme peaks

Thus due to the different research contexts, different researchers may conclude on different cutpoints. *CutPointVis* provides conveniences and the flexibility for a researcher to switch and compare between different conditions.

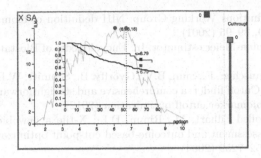

**Fig. 11.** GSE2034 LRS plotting using PgR as risk factor (KM plot at R = 6.79)

For example, in Fig. 9 multiple PR thresholds exist with very similar peaks (6.08 and 6.79), and if a researcher wanted to visually, real time, inspect the survival stratification when using these points using *CutPointVis* he could simply operate the vertical sweep line to both points. The realtime KM plot at these two points are illustrated in Figs. 10 and 11.

By the analysis of public datasets, we demonstrate that *CutPointVis* provides a fast and convenient tool for cutpoint optimization. We believe *CutPointVis* improves the efficiency of biomarker analysis in cancer research and promotes the productivity in cutpoint optimization.

## 5  Conclusion and Future Work

We introduced an interactive cutpoint optimization tool, *CutPointVis*. It helps a researcher to determine a context-dependent optimal cutpoint in a fast and convenient way. *CutPointVis* provides features for a researcher to visualize Kaplan-Meier plotting and cutthrough analysis in a realtime manner. By case studies of two public datasets, *CutPointVis* is demonstrated to improve the research quality and productivity in survival analysis of cancer biomarker.

Although the Cox model is the pervasive optimization method in state-of-art biomarker survival analysis, there are other methods that are also popular optimization models, such as survival. We plan to implement these optimization methods in *CutPointVis* to make it a more comprehensive analysis tool for biomarker analysis.

Furthermore, there are more interactions that can be conducted during an exploration process. For example, to visualize the cutpoint dichotomization quality, besides the KM plot, Nelson-Aalen [15] can also be used as an reference in some situations. We plan to integrate more assistant tools to help a researcher to visualize and conclude faster and more convenient.

## References

1. Altman, D.G., Lausen, B., Sauerbrei, W., Schumacher, M.: Dangers of using optimal cutpoints in the evaluation of prognostic factors. J. Natl. Cancer Inst. **86**(11), 829–835 (1994)

2. Biomarkers Definitions Working Group: NIH definition of biomarker. Clin. Pharmacol. Ther. **69**, 89–95 (2001)
3. Borgan, Ø.: Kaplan-Meier estimator. In: Encyclopedia of Biostatistics. Wiley, New York (2005)
4. Budczies, J., Klauschen, F., Sinn, B.V., Győrffy, B., Schmitt, W.D., Darb-Esfahani, S., Denkert, C.: Cutoff finder: a comprehensive and straightforward web application enabling rapid biomarker cutoff optimization (2012)
5. Camp, R.L., Dolled-Filhart, M., Rimm, D.L.: X-tile a new bio-informatics tool for biomarker assessment and outcome-based cut-point optimization. Clin. Cancer Res. **10**(21), 7252–7259 (2004)
6. Contal, C., O'Quigley, J.: An application of changepoint methods in studying the effect of age on survival in breast cancer. Comput. Stat. data Anal. **30**(3), 253–270 (1999)
7. Edgar, R., Domrachev, M., Lash, A.E.: Gene expression omnibus: NCBI gene expression and hybridization array data repository. Nucleic Acids Res. **30**(1), 207–210 (2002)
8. Kaplan, E.L., Meier, P.: Nonparametric estimation from incomplete observations. J. Am. Stat. Assoc. **53**(282), 457–481 (1958)
9. Kuo, Y.-F.: Statistical methods for determining single or multiple cupoints of risk factors in survival data analysis. Ph.D. thesis. The Ohio State University (1997)
10. Mandrekar, J., Mandrekar, S., Cha, S.: Cutpoint determination methods in survival analysis using SAS. In: Proceedings of the 28th SAS Users Group International Conference (SUGI), p. 261–28 (2003)
11. Mantel, N.: Evaluation of survival data and two new rank order statistics arising in its consideration. Cancer Chemother. Rep. **50**(3), 163–170 (1966). Part 1
12. Mishra, A., Verma, M.: Cancer biomarkers: are we ready for the prime time. Cancers **2**(1), 190–208 (2010)
13. Wang, J., Wen, S., Symmans, W.F., Pusztai, L., Coombes, K.R.: The bimodality index: a criterion for discovering and ranking bimodal signatures from cancer gene expression profiling data. Cancer Inf. **7**, 199 (2009)
14. Williams, B.A., et al.: Finding optimal cutpoints for continuous covariates with binary and time-to-event outcomes (2006)
15. Winnett, A., Sasieni, P.: Adjusted Nelson-Aalen estimates with retrospective matching. J. Am. Stat. Assoc. **97**(457), 245–256 (2002)
16. Zhang, L., Klimov, S., Zhu, Y.: Cancervis: an interactive exploratory tool for cancer biomarker analysis. In: 2015 IEEE International Conference on Bioinformatics and Biomedicine (BIBM), pp. 785–792. IEEE (2015)

# Computer Graphics

# Adding Turbulence Based on Low-Resolution Cascade Ratios

Masato Ishimuroya[✉] and Takashi Kanai

Graduate School of Arts and Sciences, The University of Tokyo, Tokyo, Japan
muroya@graco.c.u-tokyo.ac.jp

**Abstract.** In this paper we propose a novel method of adding turbulence to low-res. smoke simulation. We consider the physical properties of such low-res. simulation and add turbulence only to the appropriate position where the value of the energy cascade ratio is judged as physically correct. Our method can prevent noise in the whole region of fluid surfaces which appeared with previous methods. We also demonstrate that our method can be combined with a variety of existing methods such as wavelet turbulence and vorticity confinement.

## 1 Introduction

In grid-based fluid simulation, when the number of grid cells is large, the computational time drastically increases while more highly detailed fluids with small eddies are obtained. Therefore, various methods for procedually adding turbulence (or up-scaling resolutions) have been proposed to obtain detailed fluid appearances from low-res. simulation results. Generally, the resulting fluid motion of low-res. simulation added with high-frequency turbulences is totally different from that of naïve high-res. simulation, because information on high-frequency components in low-res. simulation is completely lost due to the Nyquist limit and numerical dissipation. On the other hand, the addition of turbulence is still an efficient approach for CG animation since the visual quality is often preferred over the numerical precision.

A serious issue with previous methods for adding turbulence is that the results are too noisy in appearance due to the distribution of small eddies to the whole surface of fluid. One reason is that these methods do not consider the physical properties of turbulence in low-res. simulation, and consequently noises are uniformly added to the whole region of a vector field.

In this paper, we consider such physical properties when adding turbulences during the fluid simulation for smoke. We specifically calculate the energy cascade ratio in the spatial frequency domain from the results of low-res. simulation. We then add a noise and an eddie to only the appropriate position where the value of such a ratio is judged as physically correct. Since we use only one parameter for this addition, the amount of detail can easily be controlled and thus the design process of fluid animation can be simplified. Our method for evaluating the energy cascade is easy to implement and can be combined with a variety of existing methods for adding turbulence.

© Springer International Publishing AG 2016
G. Bebis et al. (Eds.): ISVC 2016, Part I, LNCS 10072, pp. 67–76, 2016.
DOI: 10.1007/978-3-319-50835-1_7

## 2    Related Work

In grid-based fluid simulation, lots of adding turbulence methods have been proposed. We focus on two types of methods: One introduces eddies without changing the grid resolution, and the other adds high-frequency details by increasing the grid resolution.

In the former approach, Vorticity Confinement [1] introduces external forces that produce eddies into simulated fluid velocities. This method generates fine details that cannot be produced by the original simulation and can be applied not only for smoke simulation but also for water and explosion simulations using vortex particles [2]. However, the result looks too noisy due to the addition of eddies to the whole surface of fluid uniformly.

The latter approach is called up-resolution. This can inject highly detailed eddies which exceed the Nyquist frequency from low-resolution grids. Wavelet Turbulence [3] is a major method for this approach, which uses noise function and synthesizes high frequency noises to a coarse velocity field based on Kolmogorov's five-thirds law [4]. However, as for appearance performance, the result of adding turbulence is sometimes too noisy. The application of noise synthesis to liquid simulation [5], and a method for generating noises which have arbitrary spectral ratio and variance [6] have been proposed. All of these methods, however, do not consider the energy cascade of low-res simulation and still make the results noisy in appearance. To reduce the noisy appearance, an up-resolution approach based on data-driven techniques was proposed in [7]. This method applies the principal components analysis of coarse velocity field.

## 3    Our Approach

Our method for adding turbulence utilizes the physical property of turbulence, and the frequency ratio of the kinetic energy cascade from low-res simulation. By using this property, our method is able to add highly detailed noises or eddies.

We use the following notation in this paper. Non-bold italic characters denote scalars, such as $n$, $k$, and $w$. Bold characters denote a vector, such as $\mathbf{u}$ and $\mathbf{x}$. We attach a hat to denote a spectral component such as $\hat{\mathbf{u}}(\mathbf{x}, k)$. The common symbols used in this paper are shown in Table 1.

### 3.1    Kolmogorov's Law

In general, when a fluid flow rises vertically, the flow is first a simple laminar flow, and as time passes, large eddies collapse and change into small eddies, and then the flow becomes complex turbulences. In the spatial frequency domain, laminar flow has low frequency and turbulence has a higher one. **Energy cascade** is the relationship of energy between larger eddies and smaller eddies in frequency. More properties of typical turbulent flows are described in [8]. For a position $\mathbf{x}$ and a spectral band $k$, the kinetic energy $e$ is calculated by,

$$\hat{e}(\mathbf{x}, k) = \frac{1}{2}|\hat{\mathbf{u}}(\mathbf{x}, k)|^2. \tag{1}$$

**Table 1.** Common symbols used in this paper.

| Variable | Symbol | |
|---|---|---|
| Resolution | Low | High |
| Number of cells | $n^3$ | $N^3$ |
| Velocity | $\mathbf{u}$ | $\mathbf{U}$ |
| Position | $\mathbf{x}$ | $\mathbf{X}$ |
| Frequency band | $k$ | |
| Kinetic energy | $e$ | |
| Cascade ratio | $p$ | |

In turbulence, the kinetic energy follows Kolmogorov's five-thirds law [4],

$$\hat{e}(k) = C\epsilon^{\frac{2}{3}}k^{-\frac{5}{3}}, \tag{2}$$

where $C$ is a constant and $\epsilon$ is the dissipation rate.

## 3.2 Overview

Our algorithm consists of the following steps:

1. Compute the ratio of energy cascade (called **cascade ratio** hereafter) for each cell in low-res grid.
2. Compare cascade ratio and Kolmogorov's five-thirds law.
3. For each cell, apply the procedure of adding turbulence in the original method only if the cascade ratio follows the law.

The above method adds the turbulence to the appropriate positions of the velocity grid, thereby alleviating the noisy appearance of fluid.

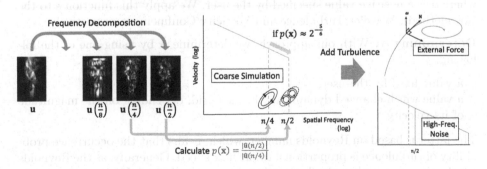

**Fig. 1.** Our algorithm overview. In low-res simulation on $n^3$ grid, eddies up to $\frac{n}{2}$ frequency can be represented. If the cascade ratio follows Kolmogorov's law $2^{-\frac{6}{5}}$, high-frequency noise or external forces to inject turbulences are synthesized.

## 3.3  Evaluation of Energy Cascade

**Calculating Cascade Ratio.** To evaluate the cascade ratio, we perform frequency decomposition of velocity field. According to Eqs. (1) and (2), the velocity ratio between frequency components for band $k$ and $2k$ can be expressed by,

$$\frac{|\hat{\mathbf{u}}(2k)|}{|\hat{\mathbf{u}}(k)|} = \frac{\sqrt{2\hat{e}(2k)}}{\sqrt{2\hat{e}(k)}} = \sqrt{2^{-\frac{5}{3}}} = 2^{-\frac{5}{6}}. \tag{3}$$

In a low-res grid with $n^3$ cells, the kinetic energy of flows which are developed and changed to turbulence should satisfy the following equation,

$$\frac{|\hat{\mathbf{u}}(\frac{n}{2})|}{|\hat{\mathbf{u}}(\frac{n}{4})|} = 2^{-\frac{5}{6}} \approx 0.56123. \tag{4}$$

We now define such a ratio $|\hat{\mathbf{u}}(n/2)|/|\hat{\mathbf{u}}(n/4)|$ as cascade ratio $p(n)$.

In our method, we decompose the low-res velocity field by using Wavelet Noise [9]. We then obtain two frequency components of velocity $\mathbf{u}$, $\hat{\mathbf{u}}(\frac{n}{2})$ in frequency band $[\frac{n}{4}, \frac{n}{2})$ and $\hat{\mathbf{u}}(\frac{n}{4})$ in $[\frac{n}{8}, \frac{n}{4})$. For each cell in the low-res grid, we calculate the ratio of their magnitudes from $\hat{\mathbf{u}}(\frac{n}{2})$ and $\hat{\mathbf{u}}(\frac{n}{4})$,

$$p(\mathbf{x}, n) = \frac{|\hat{\mathbf{u}}(\mathbf{x}, \frac{n}{2})|}{|\hat{\mathbf{u}}(\mathbf{x}, \frac{n}{4})|}. \tag{5}$$

From Eq. (4), we can say that if the velocity at position $\mathbf{x}$ contains turbulence, $p(\mathbf{x})/2^{-\frac{5}{6}} \approx 1$ is satisfied.

We now introduce a new function $s(\mathbf{x})$ in order to check whether the flow at position $\mathbf{x}$ is turbulence or not. The value of $s(\mathbf{x})$ can be determined by,

$$s(\mathbf{x}) = \begin{cases} 1 & \text{if } 1-\alpha < p(\mathbf{x})/2^{-\frac{5}{6}} < 1+\alpha, \\ 0 & \text{otherwise}, \end{cases} \tag{6}$$

where $\alpha$ is a positive value specified by the user. We apply this function $s$ to the two methods, Wavelet Turbulence and Vorticity Confinement respectively.

**Determining $\alpha$.** With our approach, we determine $\alpha$ by using one of the following,

– a value fixed by the user,
– a value which changed dynamically in each grid, depending on the magnitude of its velocity.

The latter is based on Reynolds number, which means that the occurrence probability of turbulence is proportional to the flow speed. Generally, as the Reynolds number becomes higher, the flow tends to be more turbulent. If we set parameters except the flow speed constant values, Reynolds number becomes proportional to the flow speed. Thus $\alpha$ can be determined by,

$$\alpha = \alpha' \frac{|\mathbf{u}(\mathbf{x})|}{|\bar{\mathbf{u}}|}, \tag{7}$$

where $\alpha'$ is a value fixed by the user, and $\bar{\mathbf{u}}$ is the average velocity in the scene. Because the value of $\alpha$ can affect the amount of turbulence, finding appropriate $\alpha$ for user desired results by trial and error is needed, According to the experiments, we found that $0.1 \leq \alpha \leq 0.2$ is good for suitable turbulence.

### 3.4   Application to Wavelet Turbulence

For Wavelet Turbulence, we create 3D noise textures in several different frequency bands by Wavelet Noise [9], and synthesize them to low-res velocity field with weighting for each band based on Eq. (2) like Perlin Noise [10]. In this method, the high frequency noise $\mathbf{y}(\mathbf{x})$ is defined by,

$$\mathbf{y}(\mathbf{x}) = \sum_{i=i_{min}}^{i_{max}} \mathbf{w}(2^i \mathbf{x}) 2^{-\frac{5}{6}(i-i_{min})}, \tag{8}$$

where $\mathbf{w}(\mathbf{x})$ is the curl of a noise texture which is divergence-free [11], and $(i_{min}, i_{max}) = (\log n, \log \frac{N}{2})$. The other variables are shown in Table 1. High frequency noise $\mathbf{y}$ is thought to be a cascade from the result of low-res simulation. Therefore, by weighting $\mathbf{y}(\mathbf{x})$ with the frequency component of kinetic energy $e$ for band $n/2$, the velocity $\mathbf{U}$ in high-res grid is calculated by,

$$\mathbf{U}(\mathbf{X}) = \text{Lerp}(\mathbf{u}, \mathbf{X}) + 2^{-\frac{5}{6}} \text{Lerp}\left(\hat{e}\left(\mathbf{x}, \frac{n}{2}\right), \mathbf{X}\right) \mathbf{y}(\mathbf{X}), \tag{9}$$

where Lerp is the linear interpolation operator for up-samplling. $\text{Lerp}(\mathbf{u}, \mathbf{X})$ and $\text{Lerp}(\hat{e}, \mathbf{X})$ are vector and scalar fields by linear interpolation from low resolution field $\mathbf{u}(\mathbf{x})$ and $\hat{e}(\mathbf{x})$ respectively to high resolution grid $\mathbf{X}$. The first term of the right side in Eq. (9), $\text{Lerp}(\mathbf{u}, \mathbf{X})$, is a simple mapping linearly interpolated from a coarse velocity field, and the second term is that of higher frequency eddies. With our approach, we consider not only the weight $\hat{e}(\mathbf{x}, n/2)$ but also the cascade ratio $p(\mathbf{x}, n)$. For this reason, we integrate the function $s(\mathbf{x})$ into Eq. (9),

$$\mathbf{U}(\mathbf{X}) = \text{Lerp}(\mathbf{u}, \mathbf{X}) + 2^{-\frac{5}{6}} \text{Lerp}(s(\mathbf{x}), \mathbf{X}) \text{Lerp}\left(\hat{e}\left(\mathbf{x}, \frac{n}{2}\right), \mathbf{X}\right) \mathbf{y}(\mathbf{X}). \tag{10}$$

According to Eq. (10), if the ratio follows Kolmogorov's law, we determine the flow to be turbulence and synthesize the noise texture based on the law (see Fig. 1). Otherwise, we simply apply linear interpolation to a low-res velocity field. Although noise field $\mathbf{y}$ is incompressible, the velocity field after synthesizing the noise violates incompressibility. This is because the weight of $\mathbf{y}$ differs depending on position $\mathbf{x}$, and this problem occurs at Eq. (9). However, the noise is small enough in magnitude and high frequency. Thus, it can be assumed that influence of compressibility is negligible in appearance.

We set $\mathbf{c}(\mathbf{x}) = (c_u(\mathbf{x}), c_v(\mathbf{x}), c_w(\mathbf{x}))$ for a set of texture coordinates. By advecting $\mathbf{c}(\mathbf{x})$ along with the low-res velocity field, the noise turbulence appears to advect with the flow.

## 3.5   Application to Vorticity Confinement

We also apply our method to Vorticity Confinement in low-res fluid simulation. For each frame of the simulation, we compute the cascade ratio from original simulation. In only places where the ratio follows the law, we add external forces to produce eddies. Our algorithm is shown in Algorithm 1. The difference between the previous method and ours is highlighted in red.

---

**Algorithm 1.** Vorticity confinement in consideration to the cascade ratio

1: Calculate $\mathbf{u}^n$, the fluid velocity at frame $n$
2: Vorticity $\boldsymbol{\omega} = \nabla \times \mathbf{u}^n$, $N = \frac{\nabla|\boldsymbol{\omega}|}{|\nabla|\boldsymbol{\omega}||}$
3: Calculate $s(\mathbf{x})$ from $\mathbf{u}^n$
4: $\mathbf{f}'_{vort} = \varepsilon h s(\mathbf{x}) (N \times \boldsymbol{\omega})$
5: $\mathbf{u}^{n+\frac{1}{2}} = \mathbf{u}^n + \mathbf{f}'_{vort}$
6: $\mathbf{u}^{n+1} = \mathbf{u}^{n+\frac{1}{2}} + \mathbf{f}_{ext} - (\mathbf{u} \cdot \nabla)\mathbf{u} + \frac{1}{\rho}\nabla p - \nu \nabla^2 \mathbf{u}$

---

Unlike the application to Wavelet Turbulence, this method cannot limit the frequency of eddies. So it does not guarantee that only high frequency eddies will be added. Although the behavior of flows can be drastically changed compared to that before adding eddies, this issue happens when simulating with low-res grid and we can modify the behavior in a short time. As for incompressibility, the velocity field can be kept divergence-free because we perform pressure projection after adding eddies. Since we add external forces only to turbulent flows, uniform noisy appearance can be alleviated.

## 4   Results and Discussion

Figures 2 and 3 show the results of up-resolution by Wavelet Turbulence and our method in a $48 \times 64 \times 48$ low-res grid. We implement our method and for comparison based on the source code of Wavelet Turbulence [12]. For low-res velocity fields, we simulated a smoke plume by heat buoyancy and we use the standard simulation framework proposed in [13] and MacCormack method [14] for advection. In our implementation, when computing a cascade ratio $p(\mathbf{x})$ we use the mean value of $|\hat{\mathbf{u}}(\mathbf{x}, k)|$ at a cell including position $\mathbf{x}$ and its surrounding cells instead of the frequency component only at a cell of $\mathbf{x}$. Figures 2 and 3 show the results of the 70th, 120th frames, respectively. In the result of the previous method (b), too much small noises appear compared to low-res simulation (a) which is undesirable. (c) and (d) are the results of our method. Compared to the original Wavelet Turbulence result (b), our method can synthesize noises to prevent the shape of smoke from changing in low-res simulation. In addition, compared to (b) in which high-frequency noises appear even in laminar flows on the lower part of fluid, such noises do not appear on the lower part of the fluid in our results (c) and (d). Figure 4 is another result of up-resolution. We used

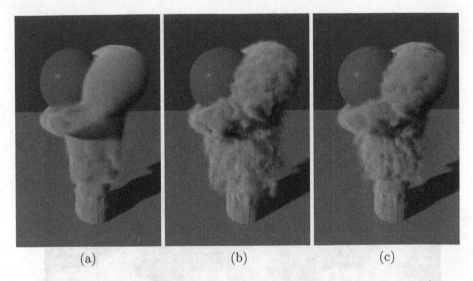

(a)                    (b)                    (c)

**Fig. 2.** Addition of turbulence for coarse grid simulations. The result of the $70^{\text{th}}$ frame is shown. (a) Linear interpolation. (b) Wavelet Turbulence. (c) Our method with $\alpha = 0.1$ everywhere.

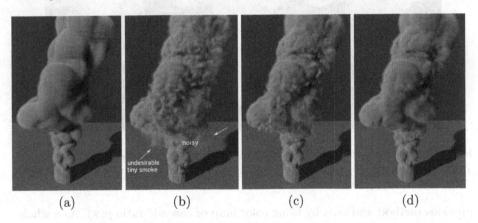

(a)                  (b)                  (c)                  (d)

**Fig. 3.** Addition of turbulence for coarse grid simulations. The result of the $135^{\text{th}}$ frame is shown. (a) Linear interpolation of coarse simulation. (b) Wavelet Turbulence. (c) Our method with $\alpha = 0.1$ everywhere. (d) Our method with $\alpha$ depending on the magnitude of velocity.

the IVOCK scheme [15] for $48 \times 64 \times 48$ low-res. simulation. As seen from the results, the same can be said for Figs. 2 and 3. These results indicate that noisy appearance can be controlled by our method.

Figure 5 shows simulation results using Vorticity Confinement with and without our cascade evaluation. It can be seen that larger eddies appear in our method. Figure 6 is an quantitative evaluation of the results between the

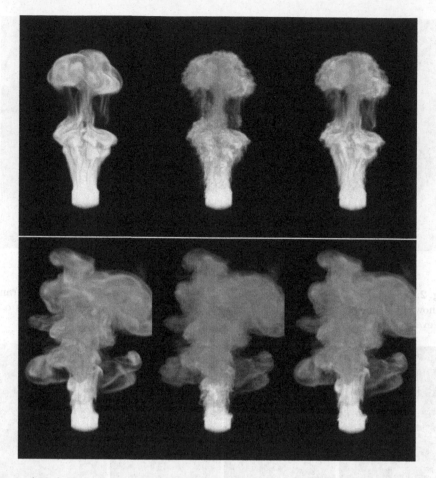

**Fig. 4.** Another result of smoke plume. Left: Linear interpolation. Middle: Wavelet Turbulence. Right: Our method with $\alpha = 0.2$ everywhere. The upper row is the result of the $104^{\text{th}}$ frame and the lower is that for $231^{\text{st}}$ frame.

previous method and ours by using color map of cascade ratio $p(\mathbf{x})$. As a whole, the ratio in our method is closer to the ideal ratio of turbulence model than that in the previous method, which shows higher ratio (more high-frequency eddies) than the ideal one.

**Limitation.** By taking the contraposition of Eq. (4) logically, at positions where the cascade ratio is out of range from its standard value $2^{-\frac{5}{6}}$, the flow is not turbulence. However, in the actual simulation, the cascade ratio may be affected not only by the physical properties considered in this paper but also by numerical errors in frequency decompositions, especially numerical diffusion in advection. Therefore the cascade ratios we compute can be different from correct values. Currently, we cannot identify the cause of the cascade ratio being out of range, and we will address these issues in future work.

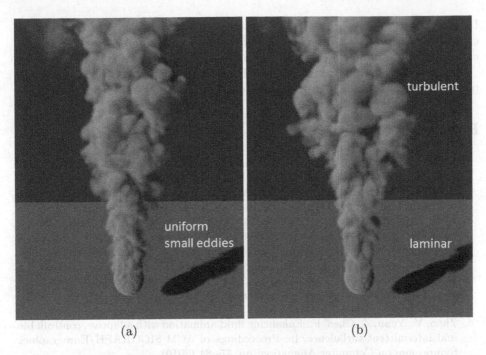

**Fig. 5.** (a) Vorticity Confinement. (b) Vorticity Confinement with our cascade evaluation.

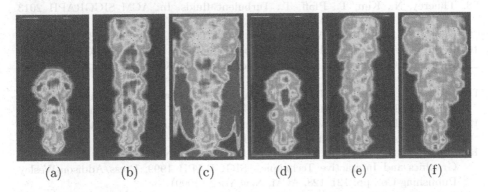

**Fig. 6.** Cascade ratios of Vorticity Confinement with and without our method. (a), (b) and (c) are the results of only Vorticity Confinement and (d), (e) and (f) are those from our method. In this figure, green pixels correspond to the ideal ratio of the turbulence model $p(\mathbf{x}) = 2^{-\frac{5}{6}}$, the red corresponds to higher ratios, and the blue to lower ones. (Color figure online)

# 5   Conclusion and Future Work

In this paper, we have proposed a method to apply the ratio of kinetic energy cascade to two methods for adding turbulence in smoke simulation. Our method can improve noise appearance and can make it more natural.

In future work, we hope to combine this cascade evaluation with other methods for adding turbulence and apply it to other types of fluids such as liquids.

# References

1.  Fedkiw, R., Stam, J., Jensen, H.W.: Visual simulation of smoke. In: Proceedings of SIGGRAPH 2001, pp. 15–22. ACM, New York (2001)
2.  Selle, A., Rasmussen, N., Fedkiw, R.: A vortex particle method for smoke, water and explosions. ACM Trans. Graph. **24**, 910–914 (2005)
3.  Kim, T., Thürey, N., James, D., Gross, M.: Wavelet turbulence for fluid simulation. ACM Trans. Graph. **27**, 50:1–50:6 (2008)
4.  Kolmogorov, A.N.: The local structure of turbulence in incompressible viscous fluid for very large reynolds' numbers. Dokl. Akad. Nauk SSSR. **30**, 301–305 (1941)
5.  Narain, R., Sewall, J., Carlson, M., Lin, M.C.: Fast animation of turbulence using energy transport and procedural synthesis. ACM Trans. Graph. **27**, 166:1–166:8 (2008)
6.  Zhao, Y., Yuan, Z., Chen, F.: Enhancing fluid animation with adaptive, controllable and intermittent turbulence. In: Proceedings of ACM SIGGRAPH/Eurographics Symposium on Computer Animation, pp. 75–84 (2010)
7.  Sato, S., Morita, T., Dobashi, Y., Yamamoto, T.: A data-driven approach for synthesizing high-resolution animation of fire. In: Proceedings of the Digital Production Symposium, DigiPro 2012, pp. 37–42. ACM, New York (2012)
8.  Thuerey, N., Kim, T., Pfaff, T.: Turbulent fluids. In: ACM SIGGRAPH 2013 Courses, SIGGRAPH 2013, pp. 6:1–6:1. ACM, New York (2013)
9.  Cook, R.L., DeRose, T.: Wavelet noise. ACM Trans. Graph. **24**, 803–811 (2005)
10. Perlin, K.: An image synthesizer. In: Proceedings of the 12th Annual Conference on Computer Graphics and Interactive Techniques, SIGGRAPH 1985, pp. 287–296. ACM, New York (1985)
11. Bridson, R., Houriham, J., Nordenstam, M.: Curl-noise for procedural fluid flow. In: ACM SIGGRAPH 2007 Papers, SIGGRAPH 2007. ACM, New York (2007)
12. Kim, T., Thürey, N.: Wavelet turbulence source code (2008). http://www.cs.cornell.edu/~tedkim/wturb/source.html
13. Stam, J.: Stable fluids. In: Proceedings of the 26th Annual Conference on Computer Graphics and Interactive Techniques, SIGGRAPH 1999, Press/Addison-Wesley Publishing Co., pp. 121–128. ACM, New York (1999)
14. Selle, A., Fedkiw, R., Kim, B., Liu, Y., Rossignac, J.: An unconditionally stable Maccormack method. J. Sci. Comput. **35**, 350–371 (2008)
15. Zhang, X., Bridson, R., Greif, C.: Restoring the missing vorticity in advection-projection fluid solvers. ACM Trans. Graph. **34**, 52:1–52:8 (2015)

# Creating Feasible Reflectance Data for Synthetic Optical Flow Datasets

Burkhard Güssefeld[✉], Katrin Honauer, and Daniel Kondermann

Heidelberg Collaboratory for Image Processing, University of Heidelberg,
Heidelberg, Germany
burkhard.guessefeld@iwr.uni-heidelberg.de

**Abstract.** Optical flow ground truth generated by computer graphics has many advantages. For example, we can systematically vary scene parameters to understand algorithm sensitivities. But is synthetic ground truth realistic enough? Appropriate material models have been established as one of the major challenges for the creation of synthetic datasets: previous research has shown that highly sophisticated reflectance field acquisition methods yield results, which various optical flow methods cannot distinguish from real scenes. However, such methods are costly both in acquisition and rendering time and thus infeasible for large datasets. In this paper we find the simplest reflectance models (RM) for different groups of materials which still provide sufficient accuracy for optical flow performance analysis. It turns out that a spatially varying Phong RM is sufficient for simple materials. Normal estimation combined with Anisotropic RM can handle even very complex materials.

## 1  Introduction

Creating accurate computer vision datasets with ground truth is a costly, challenging and time consuming task. Expensive measurement devices such as laser scanners and state-of-the-art camera systems are used to create large-scale, real-world datasets like KITTI [1] or HeiSt [2]. However, the accuracy of such ground truth is inherently limited due to measurement errors [2].

By contrast, synthetic datasets like MPI Sintel [3] and the UCL Ground Truth Optical Flow Dataset [4] are created with computer graphics and have nearly perfect ground truth. Another big advantage is that parameters, such as weather and lighting conditions, can easily be adjusted to create a large amount of varying sequences for different scenarios. However, the cost of synthetic datasets increases rapidly when trying to improve realism of the renderings.

Modeling material properties is a big challenge in computer graphics. It is considered to be the decisive factor for systematical differences between synthetic and real datasets [5,6]. A reflectance field measurement device such as the Dome II [7] can acquire highly accurate reflectance fields of materials that can be used for synthetic optical flow datasets [8]. However, such measurement devices are expensive, cannot always be used and reflectance field rendering is very time consuming.

© Springer International Publishing AG 2016
G. Bebis et al. (Eds.): ISVC 2016, Part I, LNCS 10072, pp. 77–90, 2016.
DOI: 10.1007/978-3-319-50835-1_8

In this paper, we investigate more feasible methods of describing material properties and examine their impact on optical flow algorithms. To this end, we analyze three different RM, each with and without normal estimation, for nine different material samples with respect to optical flow results, by comparing them with the state-of-the-art reflectance fields.

Our contribution is twofold. First, we show how to efficiently estimate normals and reflectance properties from high-dimensional BTF-Data. Second, we identify the most challenging reflectance effects for optical flow algorithms and evaluate our simulation of those critical effects.

## 2     Related Work

In this section we first illustrate the current work on the differences between real world and synthetic dataset. Material properties were identified as a major factor for creating sufficiently realistic synthetic datasets. Hence, we outline the currently available methods for modeling material properties in computer graphics.

### 2.1     Real Versus Synthetic Datasets

Ground truth datasets are often introduced together with performance analysis and benchmarking websites, but often without detailed analysis with respect to its accuracy and applicability to a given problem. Synthetic datasets are mostly used for computer vision performance analysis due to the availability of accurate ground truth.

One of the earliest synthetic dataset is the Yosemite sequence [9], which uses simple rendering techniques. Today, more sophisticated synthetic datasets are available, such as the grove and urban scenes of the Middlebury dataset [10], the naturalistic MPI-Sintel Dataset [3], and the stereo dataset by Martull [11]. Entire frameworks for generating optical flow data were published with the UCL Ground Truth Optical Flow Dataset [4] and the Haltakov dataset for generating automotive sequences with depth, flow and segmentation ground truth [12].

However, only few papers analyze how the systematic visual differences between synthetic and real-word datasets affect the performance of computer vision algorithms.

In 2008, Vaudrey et al. [5] studied the systematic differences between synthetic, laboratory and real-world scenes. They could show that in real scenes the brightness constancy assumption is violated more often and object boundaries are less distinguishable, both directly affecting the outcome of stereo and optical flow algorithms and how they rank. This difference is not being stressed enough by current synthetic datasets.

In [6], a laboratory scene was compared to the renderings of a computer graphics replica. It could be shown that the degree of realism of the illumination models has the highest impact on the outcome of optical flow algorithms.

Very simple scenes with isolated effects were used in [13]. Each effect was studied extensively but it remains unclear how such insights can be transferred to realistic renderings of complex scenes.

A recent work analyzing state-of-the-art reflectance field renderings and how they compare to real-world-sequences for optical flow performance analysis was carried out in [8]. The authors conclude that reflectance field renderings can be utilized for optical flow datasets and that the differences between flow fields on real versus synthetic scenes are minimal. This holds true even for complex, highly specular objects as long as the spatial and angular resolution is high enough to capture the reflectance of the object accurately.

## 2.2   Reflectance Modeling

Modeling the surface reflectance accurately is the decisive factor for synthetic datasets [5,6] and a challenging task in computer graphics. The physical reflectance is described by the *BRDF*, which was introduced by Fred Niodemus in [14]. It relates the radiance in an outgoing direction to the irradiance that is incident on a surface point. Determining this function is generally not possible, due to its high dimensionality. As such the BRDF is either sampled for many combinations of view and light directions or approximated by analytical models.

**Discrete Measurements.** A commonly used BRDF dataset with very dense measurements ($4M$ samples) is the MERL BRDF database [15].

A spatially varying alternative are the reflectance fields, which can be stored in an assembly of 2D-textures, the BTF 1999 [16]. Stationary measurement devices with multiple cameras and light sources are used to acquire such reflectance field [7]. While BTFs are less dense than the MERL data (22801 samples per texel), they provide a large spatial resolution. It could be shown that BTFs are sufficiently accurate for optical flow datasets [8] and learning problems [17].

Due to the large amount of reflectance data, compression algorithms have to be employed for further BTF processing. Hence, costly decompression algorithms are needed, leading to rendering times of several minutes per frame with a state-of-the-art ray tracer. Hence, rendering large datasets or complex scenes, as needed for many computer vision tasks, is not feasible. This is why we have to resort to faster analytical models to render synthetic datasets in realtime.

**Analytical Models.** Analytical models that approximate the BRDF, usually consist of a diffuse term, modeling lambertian material properties, and a view and light dependent specular term, modeling specular reflectance around the mirror direction and around grazing angles. Different specular terms exist.

The *Phong* model [18] uses a cosine lobe around the mirror direction to model specular reflectance. It assumes isotropic reflection, i.e. light is reflected in the same way in every surface direction.

However, real materials are often anisotropic: Cloth scatters light narrowly along the direction of the thread; wood, hair or brushed aluminum show similar behavior. The *Ward* model can model anisotropic reflectance with a gaussian specular lobe and independent lobe parameters along both surface directions [19].

The Cook-Torrance model [20] also incorporates a fresnel term that can simulate increased specular reflectance at low light and view angles.

## 3    Fitting Analytic Models to BTFs

To create synthetic datasets that can be rendered in realtime, we fitted different RM to a BTF Reference Dataset. In this section we first describe the BTF reflectance dataset that was chosen for our experiments. Then we describe the problems that arise when fitting analytical models to such data and propose a method to create satisfying results.

### 3.1    BTF Reference Dataset

The reflectance data from the BTF database Bonn [17] includes reflectance field measurements for 84 planar material samples. Each material sample includes a FMF encoded BTF for 151 view and light directions and surface geometry recorded with a structured light scanner. We chose a subset of seven material samples, covering each material category and a large variety of different reflectance properties: felt05, wood07, fabric07, leather01, stone06, wall02 and carpet02. We further used an aluminum and a copper BTF measured with the same dome setup. With this subset we cover almost diffuse reflectance (felt,carpet), strong specular reflections (aluminum, copper), anisotropic reflectance (fabric, leather, wood), fresnel effects (stone, leather, wood) and surface geometry significantly protruding from a flat reference surface (leather, carpet, felt, wall).

### 3.2    Challenges of BTF Fitting

While the surface geometry of the BTF samples is captured by a structured light scanner, it is limited to capture geometry on a macroscopic scale. Analytic models describe geometry on a microscopic scale via the surface roughness, which influences the shape of the specular lobe. On the mesoscopic texel scale of the BTF samples, we found that the surface normals differ from the flat surface normal assumption by up to 30°.

Additionally, BTFs with an angular resolution of roughly 15° are significantly sparser than the MERL BRDF data, which is mostly used in traditional BRDF-Fitting such as in [21]. Hence, outliers have a strong influence on the quality of the fits.

Both difficulties combined, result in spatially inconsistent fits when no additional constraints are applied. For example, the diffuse term can severely overcompensate for grazing effects at lower view and light angles while the specular term is almost non-existent, or the specular term can completely replace the diffuse term, even though lambertian reflectance is visible over all angles. Often both effects are present for a single material sample, creating spatially inconsistent appearance.

## 3.3   Fitting BTFs

The publicly available Ceres Solver (ceres-solver.org) was used to fit three analytical models to the BTF data: a physically plausible modified Phong model [22], a ward-duer model with a normalization fix for specular lobes and grazing angles [23] and a modified Cook-Torrance model [20] with an anisotropic microfacet distribution from Ashikhmin and Shirley [24].

All models consist of a lambertian diffuse term and a model specific specular lobe:

$$M(\mathbf{d}, \mathbf{s}, \mathbf{p}) = \mathbf{d}/\Pi + K(\mathbf{s}, \mathbf{p}) \qquad (1)$$

where $\mathbf{d}$ is the diffuse color vector, $\Pi$ the lambertian normalization factor, $K$ the reflectance model, $\mathbf{s}$ the specular color vector and $\mathbf{p}$ the vector of the model parameters. For the exact analytical form of each RM we refer to the original papers.

For each BTF Texel we constructed the objective function for the least square fit as the Mahalanobis-Distance:

$$E(\mathbf{d}, \mathbf{s}, \mathbf{p}) = \sqrt{\frac{1}{N} \sum (\cos \Theta_i \cos \Theta_o (A(\boldsymbol{\omega}_i, \boldsymbol{\omega}_o) - M(\boldsymbol{\omega}_i, \boldsymbol{\omega}_o, \mathbf{d}, \mathbf{s}, \mathbf{p})))^2} \qquad (2)$$

where $A$ is the apparent BRDF of a texel consisting of the measurements for each incident direction $\boldsymbol{\omega}_i$ and outgoing direction $\boldsymbol{\omega}_o$ and $\Theta_i$, $\Theta_o$ the corresponding elevation angles.

While [21] empirically chose a $\cos \Theta_o$ weighting to create visual pleasing fits of dense BRDF measurements, the uncertainty of the BTF measurements is inverse proportional to the solid angle of both the camera and the light. Thus our additional weighting with $\cos \Theta_i$ is mathematically motivated.

To accomodate for the challenges due to inaccuracies in the surface normals and the sparse measurements, several techniques were applied. First we used two specular lobes, as often multiple specular effects are present in real material [20, 21]. Second, a $\log(1 + \frac{s}{4})$ cauchy loss was used to reduce the impact of outliers present at low view and light angles, mostly caused by geometric inaccuracies. Third, the following two-step fitting process was used to make the fits spatially consistent:

1. Estimate $\mathbf{d}_0$ for $\Theta_i, \Theta_o < 45°$ with a single narrow specular lobe
2. Estimate M with $\mathbf{d} \in [\frac{2}{3}\mathbf{d}_0, \mathbf{d}_0]$ with narrow and broad specular lobe

By using specular lobe constraints (phong exponent $n \geq 6$) in the first step, we enforce that the lambertian reflectance is always modeled with the diffuse term and not the specular lobe. In the second step we create room for a broad specular lobe ($1 \leq n \leq 6$). We limited the reflectance amount to a maximum of one third of the initial diffuse estimate, a value that seemed to achieve best visual results. At the same time we set the maximum diffuse color to be the one observed for high view and light angles. This ensures that fresnel effects at grazing angles do not affect the diffuse term, but are modeled by the broad specular lobe. Additionally the narrow lobe is reestimated, to accomodate for the introduction of the second specular lobe.

## 3.4 Normal Estimation

To correct the geometric inaccuracies on the mesoscopic scale, we propose to estimate the surface normals in preprocessing step. It can be assumed that the highest reflectance is present along the perfect mirror direction, which is directly dependent on the surface normal. Extending ideas from Photometric Stereo [25], we build the normal estimation model for the objective function in 2 with a anisotropic cosine lobe around the perfect mirror direction:

$$M(\mathbf{d}, \mathbf{s}, \mathbf{n}) = \frac{\omega_i \cdot \mathbf{n} \, \omega_o \cdot \mathbf{n}}{\Theta_i \Theta_o} (\mathbf{d} + \mathbf{s} \sqrt{(n_u + 2) + (n_v + 2)} \mathbf{n} \cdot \mathbf{h}^{n_u \cos^2 + n_v \sin^2}) \quad (3)$$

where $\mathbf{h}$ is the half vector, $\mathbf{n}$ the surface normal and $n_u$ and $n_v$ the cosine exponents along each surface direction. The objective function was minimized for $\Theta_i, \Theta_o <= 60°$, so that fresnel effects did not influence the results.

The diffuse term conforms that of Photometric Stereo. The specular lobe is equivalent to an anisotropic phong model with a parametrized normal. The color normalization was removed, since physical plausibility of the color is not needed. A standard phong model was tested and can be used for isotropic material. The results do however differ for anisotropic material samples.

## 4    Experimental Setup

While the visual appearance of the BTF fits is an interesting indicator, we are more interested in finding the minimal model needed for Optical Flow datasets for varying material types. Optical Flow is sensitive to local brightness changes over time, such as moving specular highlights. However, it is robust towards color errors that are motion invariant, such as lambertian reflectance. Hence, we constructed our experimental workflow, described in Fig. 1, to create various kinds of motion variant effects that challenge the Optical Flow Algorithms.

First, we randomly sampled the geometry and camera-light setup in such a way that various critical effects occur. The heightmaps from the BTFs were modified by $1/f^4$ perlin noise [26], creating naturalistic deformations of the surface geometry. This allowed us to asses violations of the brightness constancy of varying sizes. The camera-light setup was sampled in such a way, that it recreates naturalistic camera and light motion centered around a stationary material sample.

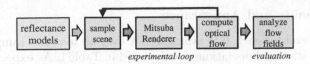

*experimental loop*                    *evaluation*

**Fig. 1.** Workflow describes how each image pair was created. The RM fits were applied to randomized scenes and rendered with Mitsuba. Optical flow was then computed on the renderings and the flow fields evaluated with respect to reflectance properties of the sample.

Second, the BTFs aswell as the RM fits were rendered with the open source, physics-based renderer "Mitsuba". The BTF rendering was done with a plugin supplied by the creators of the BTF database Bonn [17]. For the Cook-Torrance fits a new Mitsuba plugin was created. For the Phong and Ward fits we used the original plugin from Mitsuba.

As a last step Optical flow was computed and flow errors were analyzed with respect to normals, camera position and light position, enabling us to assess various reflectance effects. We computed optical flow using two algorithms: The *MDP-Flow2 Algorithm* by Xu et al. [27]; it is the best performing flow method on the Middlebury dataset, that is publicly available; and a multi-scale, non-linear version of the classical *Horn and Schunck algorithm* [28], which was implemented with the open source Charon framework [29]. Parameters for both methods were chosen to produce flow fields as accurate as possible. In order to draw meaningful conclusions with regard to the various reflectance effects, we computed endpoint error distributions with respect to the RM, materials, algorithms and scene geometries. We looked at the angle between the local surface normal and the view vector to assess fresnel effects close to $90°$. Furthermore, we investigated small angles between the view and the reflection vector to study the effects of specular effects.

# 5   Results

In this section we first analyze the quality and visual appearance of the BTF fits. Then we briefly report general insights from analyzing  750 million flow vectors computed by Horn and Schunck and mdp2-flow algorithms for 39 different scenes, that were generated with the workflow from Sect. 4. We used a **BTF** reference and the following analytical RM: **Ward**, Cook Torrance (**CT**) and **Phong** aswell as the corresponding RM with normal estimation **WardN**, **CTN** and **PhongN**. We further used nine material samples: carpet, copper, alu, fabric, felt, leather, stone, wall and wood. Subsequently, we show detailed results by analyzing specular highlights on the copper sample and complex surface geometry on the leather sample.

## 5.1   RM Quality and Appearance

The cost per texel for each RM averaged out over all material samples and the corresponding standard deviations are depicted in Table 1. As expected, the RM rank in the order of CT, Ward, Phong. Differences between CT and Ward are however marginal. Normal estimation reduces the cost by ~25% on average, with up to ~50% cost reduction for highly specular material samples and a minimum of ~10% cost reduction for almost diffuse material samples. The standard deviations equal ~0.6% − 1.1% of the measurents.

**Table 1.** Average cost per texel and standard deviation over all material types per RM. RM rank in order of CT, Ward, Phong. Normal estimation reduces avg. cost by roughly 25%.

|  | CTN | CT | WardN | Ward | PhongN | Phong |
|---|---|---|---|---|---|---|
| Cost | 6.74 | 10.43 | 7.39 | 11.02 | 14.84 | 17.50 |
| $\sqrt{cost/N}$ | 0.017 | 0.021 | 0.018 | 0.022 | 0.026 | 0.028 |

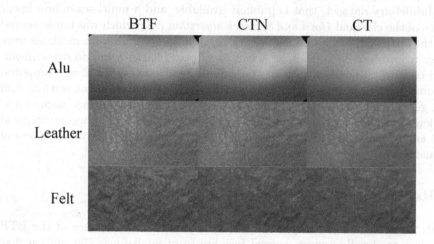

**Fig. 2.** For CT the specular highlight on the copper sample is slightly tilted to the right and the texture of the leather sample is blurred. Both effects are corrected with normal estimation. On the felt sample the appearance of both models seems almost identical.

Example videos for a reference scene and the parameter textures of each RM can be found online (https://hci.iwr.uni-heidelberg.de/bguessef). The RMs without normal estimation, examplary depicted for the CT model in Fig. 2, exhibit salient visual effects. For tilted rather planar material samples, such as the copper sample, we can observe the entire highlight being tilted in the opposite direction in comparison to the BTF Reference. For material samples with high frequencies in the surface normal, such as the leather sample, the texture of the material is blurred out. Both effects can be compensated with normal estimation.

However, layered material samples, such as the felt sample, can only be enhanced to a lesser degree by our normal estimation. This is possibly due to the fact, that each layer has a separate normal. However, such material types do usually not exhibit strong specular effects and thus do not challenge most optical flow algorithms.

## 5.2  Overall Reflectance Model Performance

Figure 3 depicts boxplots of the endpoint error distributions combined over all nine materials and 39 image pairs.

The errors of BTF reference are not distributed normally, but are heavy tailed. This indicates that few outliers are creating larger errors in the flow fields.

The CTN, WardN and PhongN exhibit similar mean errors for both Horn and Schunck and mdp2-flow, with slightly increased outliers for mdp2-flow and decreased outliers for Horn and Schunck, indicating that some difference remain.

CT, Ward and Phong exhibit significantly larger mean errors overall, likely due to inacurracies in the specular highlights and the loss of texture for complex material.

Overall, the error distributions give us a first indication, that synthetic datasets created with analytical models do not vastly differ from those created with BTFs.

## 5.3  Material Specific Properties

By inspecting error distributions for each material sample separately we get an indication which reflectance effects cause the highest errors in the flow fields.

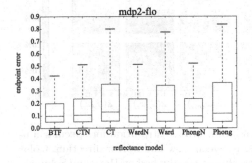
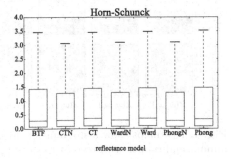

**Fig. 3.** Error distributions of both optical flow algorithms, combined over all 9 material samples and 39 image pairs. RMs with normal estimation have similar mean errors, yet different outliers depending on the optical flow algorithm. RMs without normal estimation exhibit significantly increased mean errors aswell as outliers, likely due to systematic differences in the appearance.

The almost diffuse carpet and felt materials exhibit very low quantile and mean errors and barely any outliers. As expected, they provide no challenge for flow algorithms and all RM perform similar.

Leather, stone and wood include fresnel effects at low grazing angles. However, the error distributions do exhibit only medium sized error values. By analyzing pixels for low grazing angles, we could identify fresnel effects to be mostly irrelevant for optical flow algorithms.

As expected, the copper, aluminum samples have the largest mean errors and the most outliers in the BTF reference flow fields. All three RMs have slightly larger errors, indicating that the highlights are too strong. The differences are mostly diminished when normal estimation is applied.

In the following sections we will more thoroughly analyze specular reflections and complex materials, with respect to the flow errors caused by each RM.

**Specular Effects.** In order to study the effect of specular reflections in more detail, we analyzed the aluminum and copper results. Specular effects occur at small angles between the view vector ($\omega_o$) and reflection vector ($\omega_r$). For each pixel, we computed the angle between $\omega_o$ and $\omega_r$ from the surface normals, world position and camera-light positions.

The endpoint error distributions with respect to that angle are depicted in Fig. 4. We compare the distributions of the BTF reference flow fields and the RM fits.

The heatmaps break down how the error sizes are distributed among the angle intervals, normalized per column by the total number of pixels which fall into the respective interval. In total, each heatmap shows the resulting errors of ~15 Mp. The differences between the heatmaps of the RMs and the BTF tell us how closely our models simulate the rendered input for the flow algorithms.

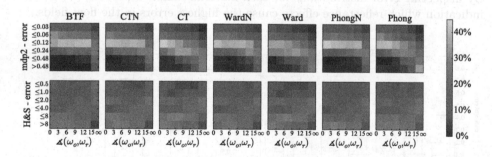

**Fig. 4.** Heatmaps show histograms of the endpoint error distribution for specular aluminum and copper with respect to the angle between view and mirror direction. Color encodes relative occurences. All RMs perform almost equally bad on Horn and Schunck. For the mdp2-flow algorithm errors are significantly increased for all angles above 6°, when no normal estimation is applied. (Color figure online)

For the mdp2-flow results of the BTF reference, we can observe that most errors fall into the interval $(0.06, 0.12]$. Errors increase slightly for larger angles.

The algorithm is mostly unaffected by the specular highlights, possibly due to strong adaptive regularization. In fact, higher errors occur when no specular highlight is present. We assume they are caused by the lack of texture when low light is reflected.

CTN, WardN and PhongN distributions are almost identical to BTF. Slightly larger errors are present for angles above $12°$. CT, Ward and Phong have increased error for angles above $6°$ indicating that specular highlights are slightly tilted and too strong.

For the Horn and Schunck method the BTF errors are much larger in total. In contrast to the mdp2-flow method, we observe higher errors for smaller angles. This is possibly due to less efficient regularization. The error distributions look almost identical for all RM, only a slightly decreased variance can be observed without normal estimation. This is possibly caused by a narrower specular lobe.

We conclude that all models with normal estimation are well-suited for optical flow evaluation on specular materials. The remaining differences to the BTF distribution lie within the optical flow accuracy limits. Using no normal estimation does produce sufficient results for the Horn and Schunck algorithm. However, the distributions differ for the mdp2-flow algorithms, affecting the ranking of the algorithms.

**Complex Materials.** To study materials with complex surface geometry and anisotropic reflectance, we analyzed the fabric and leather samples to greater detail. Similar as before we look at the angles between $(\omega_o)$ and $(\omega_r)$. The specular lobe is expected to be broader, thus we inspect larger angle intervals in the error heatmap from Fig. 5.

For the BTF Reference and the mdp2-flow algorithm most errors fall into the $(0.04, 0.08]$ and $(0.08, 0.16]$ intervals for all angles close to the mirror direction. For angles above $20°$ we observe slightly decreasing errors.

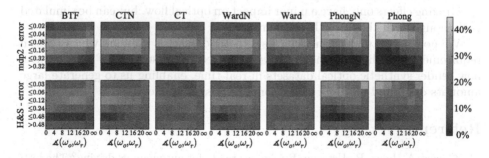

**Fig. 5.** Heatmaps of the fabric and leather samples as in Fig. 4. CT, CTN, Ward and WardN perform almost identical for mdp2-flow, with some minor differences without normal estimation. For Horn and Schunck increased errors occur without normal estimation, possibly caused by the loss of texture. Phong and PhongN cannot simulate anisotropy and thus perform poorly.

CTN and WardN exhibit almost identical distributions as BTF. Without normal estimation the errors are slightly decreased for small angles and slightly increased for larger angles. However, the differences are still within the accuracy of the algorithm. The PhongN and Phong model do however perform poorly. Errors are much larger overall, likely due to the non-existent anisotropic reflectance.

For Horn and Schunck CTN and WardN perform well again. CT and Ward have increased errors, possibly due to the loss of texture for the leather sample. PhongN and Phong perform poorly again.

We conclude that the Phong model is insufficient for complex and anisotropic materials. The CT and Ward models simulate BTF closely over all angles. Normal estimation further improves the simulation and is needed to not affect the ranking of the algorithms.

# 6  Conclusion

We studied three reflectance models that are commonly used in real-time computer graphics and their viability for synthetic optical flow dataset generation. We proposed methods to fit those models to BTF data and to estimate mesoscopic surface normals to further improve the quality of the fits.

We analyzed the flow fields, that were computed on the synthetic data, with respect to specular effects and geometric properties.

We could show that the choice of RMs can affect the ranking of algorithms, thus a basic RM accuracy must be met for each different material types.

For simple, mostly isotropic materials we could show that with our normal estimation method even a computationally cheap, spatially varying Phong fit is as good as the computationally expensive reflectance field rendering.

Highly specular materials affect optical flow the most and can also be simulated sufficiently well with a Phong fit and normal estimation.

For more complex anisotropic materials Cook-Torrance or Ward fits can be used with very high accuracy.

Grazing effects only have a minor impact on optical flow, but can be simulated well enough with the Cook-Torrance model.

We now better understand which synthetic dataset is fulfilling which realism requirements for different material types. Based on existing BTF data we can now render synthetic optical datasets in real-time, enabling us to generate large amounts of ground truth for many computervision applications.

# References

1. Geiger, A., Lenz, P., Urtasun, R.: Are we ready for autonomous driving? The kitti vision benchmark suite. In: Conference on Computer Vision and Pattern Recognition (CVPR) (2012)
2. Kondermann, D., Nair, R., Meister, S., Mischler, W., Güssefeld, B., Honauer, K., Hofmann, S., Brenner, C., Jähne, B.: Stereo ground truth with error bars. In: Cremers, D., Reid, I., Saito, H., Yang, M.-H. (eds.) ACCV 2014. LNCS, vol. 9007, pp. 595–610. Springer, Heidelberg (2015). doi:10.1007/978-3-319-16814-2_39

3. Butler, D.J., Wulff, J., Stanley, G.B., Black, M.J.: A naturalistic open source movie for optical flow evaluation. In: Fitzgibbon, A., Lazebnik, S., Perona, P., Sato, Y., Schmid, C. (eds.) ECCV 2012. LNCS, vol. 7577, pp. 611–625. Springer, Heidelberg (2012). doi:10.1007/978-3-642-33783-3_44

4. Mac Aodha, O., Humayun, A., Pollefeys, M., Brostow, G.J.: Learning a confidence measure for optical flow. IEEE Trans. Pattern Anal. Mach. Intell. **35**(5), 1107–1120 (2012)

5. Vaudrey, T., Rabe, C., Klette, R., Milburn, J.: Differences between stereo and motion behaviour on synthetic and real-world stereo sequences. In: Proceedings of the 23rd International Conference on Image and Vision Computing New Zealand (2008)

6. Meister, S., Kondermann, D.: Real versus realistically rendered scenes for optical flow evaluation. In: ITG Conference on Electronic Media Technology (2011)

7. Schwartz, C., Sarlette, R., Weinmann, M., Klein, R.: Dome II: a parallelized BTF acquisition system. In: Eurographics Workshop on Material Appearance Modeling: Issues and Acquisition, pp. 25–31. Eurographics Association (2013)

8. Güssefeld, B., Kondermann, D., Schwartz, C., Klein, R.: Are reflectance field renderings appropriate for optical flow evaluation? In: IEEE International Conference on Image Processing (ICIP), Paris, France. IEEE (2014)

9. Heeger, D.: Model for the extraction of image flow. J. Opt. Soc, Am. **4**, 1455–1471 (1987)

10. Baker, S., Scharstein, D., Lewis, J.P., Roth, S., Black, M.J., Szeliski, R.: A database and evaluation methodology for optical flow. Int. J. Comput. Vis. **92**, 1–31 (2011)

11. Martull, S., Peris, M., Fukui, K.: Realistic CG stereo image dataset with ground truth disparity maps. In: 2012 21st International Conference on Proceedings of The 3rd International Workshop on Benchmark Test Schemes for AR/MR Geometric Registration and Tracking Method (TrakMark2012). Pattern Recognition (ICPR) (2012)

12. Haltakov, V., Unger, C., Ilic, S.: Framework for generation of synthetic ground truth data for driver assistance applications. In: Weickert, J., Hein, M., Schiele, B. (eds.) GCPR 2013. LNCS, vol. 8142, pp. 323–332. Springer, Heidelberg (2013). doi:10.1007/978-3-642-40602-7_35

13. Haeusler, R., Kondermann, D.: Synthesizing real world stereo challenges. In: Weickert, J., Hein, M., Schiele, B. (eds.) GCPR 2013. LNCS, vol. 8142, pp. 164–173. Springer, Heidelberg (2013). doi:10.1007/978-3-642-40602-7_17

14. Nicodemus, F.E.: Directional reflectance and emissivity of an opaque surface. Appl. Opt. **4**, 767–775 (1965)

15. Matusik, W., Pfister, H., Brand, M., McMillan, L.: A data-driven reflectance model. ACM Trans. Graph. **22**, 759–769 (2003)

16. Dana, K.J., van Ginneken, B., Nayar, S.K., Koenderink, J.J.: Reflectance and texture of real-world surfaces. ACM Trans. Graph. **18**, 1–34 (1999)

17. Weinmann, M., Gall, J., Klein, R.: Material classification based on training data synthesized using a BTF database. In: Fleet, D., Pajdla, T., Schiele, B., Tuytelaars, T. (eds.) ECCV 2014. LNCS, vol. 8691, pp. 156–171. Springer, Heidelberg (2014). doi:10.1007/978-3-319-10578-9_11

18. Phong, B.T.: Illumination for computer generated pictures. Commun. ACM **18**, 311–317 (1975)

19. Ward, G.J.: Measuring and modeling anisotropic reflection. SIGGRAPH Comput. Graph. **26**, 265–272 (1992)

20. Cook, R.L., Torrance, K.E.: A reflectance model for computer graphics. ACM Trans. Graph. **1**, 7–24 (1982)

21. Ngan, A., Durand, F., Matusik, W.: Experimental analysis of BRDF models. In: Proceedings of the Eurographics Symposium on Rendering, pp. 117–226. Eurographics Association (2005)
22. Lafortune, E.P., Willems, Y.D.: Using the modified phong reflectance model for physically based rendering. Technical report (1994)
23. Geisler-Moroder, D., Dür, A.: A new ward BRDF model with bounded albedo. Comput. Graph. Forum **29**, 1391–1398 (2010)
24. Ashikhmin, M., Shirley, P.: An anisotropic phong BRDF model. J. Graph. Tools **5**, 25–32 (2000)
25. Prados, E., Faugeras, O.: Shape from shading. In: Paragios, N., Chen, Y., Faugeras, O. (eds.) Handbook of Mathematical Models in Computer Vision, pp. 375–388. Springer, New York (2006)
26. Hart, J.C.: Perlin noise pixel shaders. In: Proceedings of the ACM SIG-GRAPH/EUROGRAPHICS Workshop on Graphics Hardware, HWWS 2001, pp. 87–94. ACM, New York (2001)
27. Xu, L., Jia, J., Matsushita, Y.: Motion detail preserving optical flow estimation. IEEE Trans. Pattern Anal. Mach. Intell. **34**, 1744–1757 (2012)
28. Horn, D.K.P., Schunck, B.G.: Determining optical flow. Artif. Intell. **17**, 185–203 (1981)
29. Gottfried, J., Kondermann, D.: Charon suite software framework. Image Processing Online (IPOL) (2012)

# Automatic Web Page Coloring

Polina Volkova[✉], Soheila Abrishami, and Piyush Kumar

Florida State University, Tallahassee, FL 32306, USA
{volkova,abrisham,piyush}@cs.fsu.edu

**Abstract.** We present a new tool for automatic recoloring of web pages. Automatic application of different color palettes to web pages is essential for both professional and amateur web designers. However no existing recoloring tools provide full recoloring for web pages. To recolor web page entirely, we replace colors in .css, .html, and .svg files, and recolor images such as background and navigation elements. We create new color theme based on a color guide image provided by user. Evaluation shows a high level of satisfaction with the quality of palettes and results of recoloring. Our tool is available at http://chameleon.cs.fsu.edu/.

## 1 Introduction

Color is one of the most important components in web page design. The ability to automatically recolor a web page with a given color palette would be very valuable for web designers. Unfortunately the problem of automatic coloring of web pages has not been fully addressed. There exists a plethora of tools that can assist with web page coloring tasks such as palette selection, image recoloring, and image color adjustment. However, these tasks have to be performed separately. An automated web page recoloring tool should combine palette selection, web page and image recoloring. To the best of our knowledge, currently no tool provides this functionality.

The problem of web page recoloring has been partially addressed in research. Works on website recoloring for people with vision deficiencies [1,4] focus specifically on accessibility and cannot be used generically, because they do not ensure color harmony, do not allow users pick the colors, or provide full coloring. We found only one work that addresses a problem similar to ours, by Gu et al. [5]. Gu et al. presented a tool for redefining web page color scheme based on a mood board, using a genetic algorithm to generate assignment of palette colors to .css colors. Their work has several weaknesses, such as simplistic palette extraction method based on K-means, no image recoloring, and not adjusting size of new palette to match the variety of colors on the web page. We found patent applications for a website colorization system[1], and for recoloring images on a web page[2], which confirms that our problem is of practical interest but under researched.

---

[1] https://www.google.com/patents/US20090031213.
[2] https://www.google.com/patents/US8731289.

© Springer International Publishing AG 2016
G. Bebis et al. (Eds.): ISVC 2016, Part I, LNCS 10072, pp. 91–100, 2016.
DOI: 10.1007/978-3-319-50835-1_9

The goal of this paper was to create a web page recoloring method that fulfills the following objectives:

- *Esthetics*: give users a simple way to specify a harmonious color scheme.
- *Full coloring*: recolor web pages including images, keeping in mind that some images such as photos should not be recolored.
- *Consistency*: preserve color proportions and color variety of the original page.
- *Readability*: recolored web page should have proper contrast.
- *Availability*: the tool should be intuitive to use and publicly available.

To the best of our knowledge, our work is the first website coloring system that achieves the above goals simultaneously. Our contributions include a novel approach to palette extraction that combines human input and automation, and a method for palette expansion that preserves consistency of the color theme and ensures proper contrast. Our system works as follows: users submit their web page and a color guide image via a web interface. Based on the submitted image, a new color palette is created, and assignment for substituting colors in .css, .html, and .svg files is computed. Images such as logos, banners, and background tiles are recolored to reflect the new palette. Figure 1 gives an example of recoloring produced by our system. A survey conducted for evaluation shows that our palette extraction method outperforms other methods, and that recoloring results are rated well by users.

(a) Original web page  (b) Color guide image  (c) Recolored web page

**Fig. 1.** Web page recoloring example

**Notation.** Vectors are denoted by lower-case Roman letters. For a vector $p$, $p_i$ denotes its $i$th component. $i, j, k, l, m, n$ are positive integers. We reserve $w$ to denote weight and $d(\cdot)$ to denote Euclidean distance. Scalars are represented by lower-case Greek letters. Upper-case script letters are used for all other objects such as sets, images, and matchings. $LAB$ denotes LAB space and $RGB$ denotes RGB space. $\hat{x}$ denotes a weighted version of $x$, for instance if $x$ is a color, $x = \{\iota, \alpha, \beta\}$, where $\iota, \alpha, \beta$ are coordinates in LAB space, then $\hat{x} = \{\iota, \alpha, \beta, \ w\}$, where $0 \leq w < 1$ is weight. $\widehat{LAB}$ denotes LAB space with additional weight coordinate, as in $\hat{x} \in \widehat{LAB}$. We will use LAB space for all color manipulation, and K-means algorithm for all clustering tasks.

# 2  Automatic Web Page Recoloring

This section describes our approach to automatic recoloring of web pages. In Sect. 2.1 we introduce common color operations. Section 2.2 describes related work, and our method for automatic palette selection based on a guide image. Section 2.3 explains the steps of web page recoloring, which are color extraction from the web page, assignment of colors, and additional color generation. In Sect. 2.4 we describe images classification for recolorability, and explain our method for image recoloring. Figure 2 shows the organization of our system. Users submit a query consisting of an image and a web page URL. Query is queued and processed as described in Sects. 2.2, 2.3 and 2.4. Result is rendered and displayed to user.

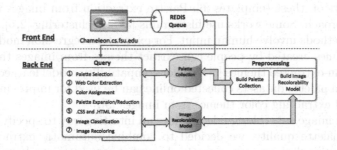

**Fig. 2.** System modules and data flow

## 2.1  Color Operations

**Summarizing Images.** To capture color characteristics of an image for comparison with other images, we summarize each image in a set of its cluster colors. Due to perceptual uniformity of LAB space, clustering works very well for grouping similar colors. Although it was pointed out that clustering is not a proper way to extract a palette from an image [6,9], it suits our purpose since we use it not to obtain the final palette, but rather as a fast and simple way to extract color features of an image.

We downscale an image for faster processing, represent it as an array of pixels in LAB space, and cluster it into $k$ clusters, $k = 5$. Clustering gives us centroid colors $\mathcal{C} = \{c_1, ..., c_k\} \in LAB$, and cluster weights $\mathcal{W}_c = \{w_1, ..., w_k\} \in \mathbb{R}$. As a result, an image is represented by $k$ weighted colors, $\hat{\mathcal{C}} = \{\hat{c}_1, ..., \hat{c}_k\} \in \widehat{LAB}$.

**Matching Two Sets of Colors.** The purpose of matching is to find best color-to-color assignment for all colors in two sets. It is useful for mapping to a new palette, and for evaluating image similarity.

Let $a, b$ be two colors $\in LAB$. *Perceptual Difference* $d(a, b)$ is a good measure of color similarity due to perceptual uniformity of LAB space. Adding weight, we get $d_\lambda^w(\hat{a}, \hat{b}) = \sqrt{d(a, b)^2 + \lambda(w_a - w_b)^2}$. In our context weight $w$ is color proportion. We experimented with coefficient $\lambda$ and found that $\lambda \approx 1$ works best for evaluating image similarity. Intuitively, color proportion is important but it is secondary to color information.

We use *Kuhn-Munkres* algorithm [8] with cost function $d(\cdot)$ to find minimum cost bipartite matching $\mathcal{M}^{\mathcal{A},\mathcal{B}}$ between two sets of colors $\mathcal{A} = \{a_1, ..., a_n\} \in LAB, \mathcal{B} = \{b_1, ..., b_n\} \in LAB, \mathcal{M}^{\mathcal{A},\mathcal{B}} = \{\langle a_i, b_j \rangle | a_i \in \mathcal{A}, b_j \in \mathcal{B}\}$. We use $d_\lambda^w(\cdot)$ to find weighted matching $\mathcal{M}^{\hat{\mathcal{A}},\hat{\mathcal{B}}}$ if weights are known.

## 2.2  Automatic Palette Selection from Image

Our goal is to give users an easy way to select a high-quality palette. Color theory states that color distribution templates can be used to create harmonious color themes [7]. However it has been shown that people do not prefer palettes based strictly on these templates [6]. Palette extraction from images is another popular approach. Some works use histograms [3] and clustering [2,5], but more advanced methods involve human input. For example, a regression model trained on color themes created by people can extract themes from images that closely match human-extracted themes [6]. A color compatibility model learned by linear regression on palette datasets collected online can be used for improving existing palettes and extracting color themes from images [9].

Using an image as a color guide provides an intuitive way to specify a palette. To ensure palette quality, we decided to combine automatic extraction with human expertise, because experiments show that artists create better palettes than extraction algorithms [9]. We will automatically select a palette generated by a professional color designer using a color guide image uploaded by user.

**Preprocessing.** Our approach requires a palette collection. We assembled a palette source[3] where each record consists of a palette created by a color expert, and an image on which the palette was based (Fig. 3d). We will use the palette for recoloring, and associated image for comparison with the user image. For each record, we retrieve palette colors $\mathcal{P} = \{p_1, ..., p_n\} \in LAB$, $|\mathcal{P}|$ can be different for different records. To compute weights for $p_i \in \mathcal{P}$, we cluster the image using

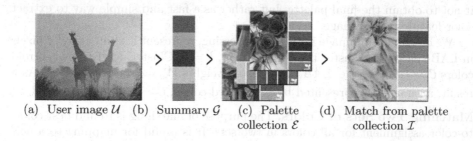

(a) User image $\mathcal{U}$  (b) Summary $\mathcal{G}$   (c) Palette        (d) Match from palette
                                              collection $\mathcal{E}$       collection $\mathcal{I}$

**Fig. 3.** Automatic palette selection example

---

[3] 4561 palettes obtained from color blog Design Seeds, http://design-seeds.com/.

$k = |\mathcal{P}|$ into $\mathcal{C} = \{c_1, ..., c_k\} \in LAB$ and $\mathcal{W_C} = \{w_1, ..., w_k\} \in \mathbb{R}$. Next we compute a matching $M^{\mathcal{P},\mathcal{C}} = \{\langle p_i, c_j \rangle | p_i \in \mathcal{P}, c_j \in \mathcal{C}\}$, and assign weights $w_j$ to palette colors $p_i$, $\mathcal{W_P} = \{w_j | \langle p_i, c_j \rangle \in M^{\mathcal{P},\mathcal{C}}\}$. Now we have a weighted palette $\hat{\mathcal{P}} = \{\hat{p}_1, ..., \hat{p}_n\} \in \widehat{LAB}$. Finally, we re-cluster the image with $k = 5$ to get summary $\hat{\mathcal{R}} = \{\hat{r}_1, ..., \hat{r}_5\} \in \widehat{LAB}$. $\hat{\mathcal{R}}$ and $\hat{\mathcal{P}}$ for all records comprise our palette collection $\mathcal{E} = \{\hat{\mathcal{R}}_i, \hat{\mathcal{P}}_i\}$. This data are stored in binary files and used in palette selection: $\hat{\mathcal{R}}_i$ for matching collection image to the user image, and $\hat{\mathcal{P}}_i$ as palette for recoloring.

**Automatic Palette Selection.** To automatically select a palette $\mathcal{T}$ that closely matches colors of a *guide image* $\mathcal{U}$, we find an image $\mathcal{I}$ in our collection that is most similar to $\mathcal{U}$, and retrieve its palette (Fig. 3). First we cluster $\mathcal{U}$ with $k = 5$ into $\hat{\mathcal{G}} = \{\hat{g}_1, ..., \hat{g}_5\} \in \widehat{LAB}$. Then we iterate through palette collection $\mathcal{E}$ to find a record $\{\hat{\mathcal{R}}_{i*}, \hat{\mathcal{P}}_{i*}\}$ such that bipartite matching cost between $\hat{\mathcal{G}}$ and $\hat{\mathcal{R}}_i^*$ is minimum. Finally, we retrieve the palette $\hat{\mathcal{T}} = \hat{\mathcal{P}}_{i*}$ to be used for recoloring the web page. We will refer to $\hat{\mathcal{T}}$ as *target palette*.

## 2.3  Automatic Web Page Coloring

To recolor webpage with palette colors $\mathcal{T}$, we need to extract all colors from web page, expand or shrink $\mathcal{T}$ to match the number of web page colors, map target palette colors to web page colors, and replace colors in .css, .html, and .svg files.

**Extracting Colors from Web Page.** We implemented our own color extraction for the following reasons. First, we encountered an issue of unused colors in the .css files. Web designers often reuse same .css files for multiple projects and do not remove unused styles. If we simply take all colors from .css files, we get many colors that do not actually appear on a web page (Fig. 4). This negatively affects speed and quality of recoloring. Cleaning up .css files turned out unreliable[4] or hard to automate[5]. Color extraction from website did not remove

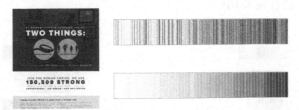

(a)  Web page screenshot   (b)  All colors from .css and .html (top),
colors used on web page (bottom)

**Fig. 4.** Color extraction from a web page.

---

[4] https://github.com/peterbe/mincss.

[5] https://chrome.google.com/webstore/detail/css-remove-and-combine/cdfmaaeapjm
acolkojefhfollmphonoh?hl=en-GB.

unused colors[6]. In addition, we needed to calculate color proportions, which is not provided by existing tools.

We solved the problem by discarding colors that do not appear in the screenshot of the web page. First, we find all hexadecimal, RGB, RGBA colors in .html, .css, and .svg files, and convert them to RGB format. Let's call this set $\mathcal{H} = \{h_1, ..., h_n\} \in RGB$. Then we take screenshot of the webpage without images. We extract all distinct colors from the screenshot and calculate their weights, getting $\mathcal{R} = \{r_1, ..., r_m\} \in RGB$, $\mathcal{W}_\mathcal{R} = \{w_1, ..., w_m\} \in \mathbb{R}$.

Next, we find mapping between colors in $\mathcal{H}$ and $\mathcal{R}$ to detect unused colors. Colors in $\mathcal{R}$ may slightly differ from corresponding colors in $\mathcal{H}$ due to image compression or use of gradients. We say that $\langle r_i, h_j \rangle$ is a match if $d(r_i, h_j) < \zeta$, where $\zeta = 20$ is a threshold derived experimentally. There can be multiple matches $r_i$ to the same $h_{j*}$. Let $\mathcal{X}_j$ be the set of indexes $i$ for $r_i$ matched to the same $h_{j*}$, then $w'_{j*} = \sum_{l \in \mathcal{X}_{j*}} w_l$. Now we have used colors $\mathcal{H}' = \{h_1, ..., h_l | h_j \in \langle r_i, h_j \rangle\} \subset \mathcal{H}$ and $\mathcal{W}_{\mathcal{H}'} = \{w'_1, ..., w'_l\} \in \mathbb{R}$. We convert all $h_j \in \mathcal{H}'$ to LAB, getting the set of weighted *web page colors* $\hat{S} = \{\hat{s}_1, ..., \hat{s}_l\} \in \widehat{LAB}$.

**Assigning Palette Colors to Web Elements.** To replace colors in files, we need to compute a mapping between old and new colors. As input to this step, we have two sets of colors: target palette $\hat{T}$ and web page colors $\hat{S}$. Most likely, $|\hat{T}| \neq |\hat{S}|$: $\hat{T}$ can be larger or smaller than $\hat{S}$. We need to expand or reduce palette $\hat{T}$ into a new palette $\hat{T}'$ of size $|\hat{S}|$.

Let $\mathcal{Q}$ denote the smaller palette, and $\mathcal{G}$ denote the larger palette. $\hat{Q} = \hat{T}$, $\hat{G} = \hat{S}$ if $|\hat{T}| < |\hat{S}|$, otherwise $\hat{Q} = \hat{S}$, $\hat{G} = \hat{T}$. Let $|\mathcal{Q}| = n$. First, we cluster $\mathcal{G}$ with $k = n$ to get $\mathcal{G}' = \{g'_1, ..., g'_k\} \in LAB$, $\mathcal{W}_{\mathcal{G}'} = \{w'_1, ..., w'_k\} \in \mathbb{R}$. We replace centroids $g'_i$ with actual palette colors $g_j \in \hat{G}$ such that $j = \arg\min_{i,j} d(g'_i, g_j)$ and keep $w'_i$. That gives us $\hat{G}' = \{\hat{g}_1, ..., \hat{g}_k\} \in \widehat{LAB}$. Now we can find a bipartite matching between two sets of colors of same size $n$: $\mathcal{M}^{\hat{G}', \hat{Q}} = \{\langle \hat{g}_j, \hat{q}_i \rangle \, | \hat{g}_j \in \hat{G}', \hat{q}_i \in \hat{Q}\}$. If $\hat{Q} = \hat{S}$, we can use $T' = \mathcal{G}'$ for recoloring (Fig. 5(a)). Otherwise, we need to expand palette $\mathcal{Q}$ (Fig. 5(b)).

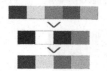

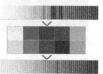

(a) Target palette $\mathcal{T}$ ($\mathcal{G}$) (top), web palette $\mathcal{S}$ ($\mathcal{Q}$) (center), reduced palette $\mathcal{T}'$ ($\mathcal{G}'$) (bottom)

(b) Web palette $\mathcal{S}$ ($\mathcal{G}$)(left), centroids $\mathcal{G}'$ matched to target palette $\mathcal{T}$ ($\mathcal{Q}$) (center), extended palette $\mathcal{T}'$ (right)

**Fig. 5.** Palette reduction (a) and extension (b)

---

[6] http://www.colorcombos.com/.

**Palette expansion.** We need to create suitable replacement colors for all colors on the web page, staying true to palette $\mathcal{T}$. It is critical to set the luminance of new colors correctly for the recolored web page to be legible. We could achieve same contrast as on the original web page by copying luminance of old colors to new colors, $\iota_t = \iota_s, \forall t \in \mathcal{T}', \forall s \in \mathcal{S}$. However this changes the appearance of colors, which may result in unpleasant palette, or a palette that does not represent user image well. A better solution is to preserve the original palette colors, and to shift $\iota$ for additional colors. This preserves contrast because new colors will be distributed similarly to the original colors, with respect to luminance.

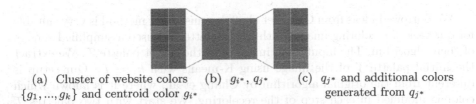

(a) Cluster of website colors $\{g_1, ..., g_k\}$ and centroid color $g_{i*}$    (b) $g_{i*}, q_{j*}$    (c) $q_{j*}$ and additional colors generated from $q_{j*}$

**Fig. 6.** Creating additional colors

Figure 6 demonstrates the process of creating additional colors on the example of one color. One of web colors $g_{i*} \in \mathcal{G}'$ represents a cluster of web colors $\{g_1, ..., g_k\} \in \mathcal{G}$ (Fig. 6a). $g_{i*}$ is matched to a target palette color $q_{j*} \in \hat{\mathcal{Q}}$ (Fig. 6b), $\langle g_{i*}, q_{j*} \rangle$ is added to final mapping $\mathcal{F}^{\mathcal{S},\mathcal{T}}$. We create new shades from $q_{j*}$ for the remaining web colors $g_i \in \{g_1, ..., g_k\}$ (Fig. 6c). We need to create $|\{g_1, ..., g_k\}| = m$ additional colors. Replacement color $q_i$ for $g_i$ starts with $q_i = q_{j*}$, but we set $\iota_{q_i} = \iota_{q_{j*}} + (\iota_{g_{i*}} - \iota_{g_i})$ for all $g_i \in \{g_1, ..., g_k\}$, where $\iota_x$ is the luminance of color $x \in LAB$. We check that $q_i$ is within the boundaries of LAB space and add $\langle g_i, q_i \rangle$ to $\mathcal{F}^{\mathcal{S},\mathcal{T}}$. Once we compute a replacement for each web page color, we convert colors in $\mathcal{F}^{\mathcal{S},\mathcal{T}}$ back to hexadecimal/RGB/RGBA format and substitute corresponding colors in .html, .css, and .svg files.

## 2.4  Image Classification and Recoloring

One of our objectives was to recolor images on a web page. However, not all images should be recolored. It makes sense to recolor images that contain few colors, e.g. text, logos, background tiles. Art and photographs are examples of images that should not be recolored (Fig. 7). To distinguish recolorable images, we use a decision tree trained on a sample set of images classified by hand. We pass only recolorable images to the image recoloring module.

**Image Recoloring** is a well-covered topic. Chang et al. [2] presented a tool for image color adjustment by editing palette extracted from an image. Reinhard et al. [10] gave a method for color correction that uses statistical analysis to transfer color characteristics from one image to another. Xia [11] extended the work of [10] by including saliency map into the color transfer formula.

(a)  Original webpage     (b)  Recolorable images (top) and     (c)  Recolored result
                               non-recolorable images (bottom)

**Fig. 7.** Image classification and recoloring

We borrowed ideas from Chang et al. [2] because their method is very suitable for our task of recoloring images with a set palette. We used a simplified version of their algorithm. The input is an image, and the target palette $\mathcal{T}$. We extract the initial palette $\mathcal{Y}$ of the image using K-means with $k = |\mathcal{T}|$. Our setup is different from the original algorithm by Chang et al., where it is known which color is modified in each step of the recoloring. We start with two palettes $\mathcal{T}$ and $\mathcal{Y}$, unknown order of recoloring, and unknown relation between colors of the palettes. We first perform matching to find the pairing of colors in the initial and target palettes $M^{\mathcal{T},\mathcal{Y}}$. Then, a sequential color transformation algorithm is used to recolor the image.

The transformation function $f(x)$ transforms a color $x \in LAB$ in the original image to a color $x' \in LAB$ in the recolored image. If $|\mathcal{Y}| = |\mathcal{T}| = 1$ we need one transformation function $x' = f(x)$ as $f(x) = (y - t) + x$. For $|\mathcal{T}| > 1$ we need $k$ transfer functions $f_i(x), i = 1 \ldots k$. In order to smooth the effect of the individual transfer functions $f_i(x)$ at $y_i$, the functions are blended with different weights. For weight calculation details refer to Section 3.5 of [2].

We treat background separately. The old background color $a \in \mathcal{S}$ is set to the color that appears most on the web page. The new background color $b \in \mathcal{T}'$ was calculated for $a$ per Sect. 2.3. Recoloring procedure takes $a, b$. If a certain percentage of pixels in the edges of the image passed for recoloring is of color $a$, we say that the image has background, and we replace all pixels of color $x \simeq a$ with $b$ (we allow for some color variance due to image compression). All other colors are replaced as described above.

## 3   Experiments

**Image Classification.** We assembled a sample set of images from Fortune 500 websites, labeled them by hand, and extracted the following features: number of colors, aspect ratio, size, grayscale or color, and histogram. Half of the sample set was used for training and half for testing. We experimented with multiple classifiers from Python package *sklearn*[7]. Classification works very well, all classifiers get above 90% of cases right (Table 1).

---

[7] http://scikit-learn.org/stable/.

**Table 1.** Classification precision on a test set of 1063 images (510 recolorable and 553 non-recolorable).

| Classifier | Decision tree | Random forest | SVM | KNN | Logistic regression | Naive Bayes |
|---|---|---|---|---|---|---|
| Precision | 1 | 0.99 | 0.96 | 0.93 | 0.93 | 0.91 |

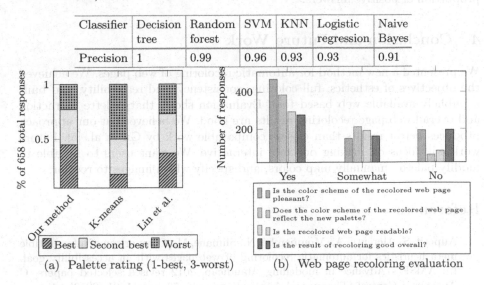

(a) Palette rating (1-best, 3-worst)    (b) Web page recoloring evaluation

**Fig. 8.** Survey results

**Palette and Recoloring Evaluation.** We conducted two surveys to confirm that our palette extraction method produces good palettes, and to evaluate the overall result of web page recoloring. For both surveys we collected responses from same 86 participants in the United States, who were not compensated. In order to evaluate the quality of palettes, we presented ten sets of three palettes, generated as follows. Ten images were picked at random from an art collection[8]. For each image, we extracted a palette using our method (Sect. 2.2), method by Lin et al. [6], and K-means. Resulting palettes were same size and rendered exactly same way. We asked to arrange palettes in order from best to worst. Initial ordering of palettes in the survey was randomized. Despite the fact that color scheme ratings are very subjective, the results are clear (Fig. 8(a)). Our palettes received more best ratings and fewer worst ratings than other palettes. We performed a Wilcoxon Rank-Sum test with Bonferroni correction on the pairs of ratings, showing that the results were significant ($p < .0001$ for our vs. K-means, $p < .005$ for our vs. Lin et al.). This is an encouraging validation of our palette extraction method.

To evaluate the quality of web page recoloring, we presented the participants with ten renderings of the original web page next to the web page recolored using a randomly chosen picture from an art collection (see footnote 8) and the new palette. We carefully selected representative websites for this experiment, aiming to cover typical web page types. We picked an information page, a forum-style page, and a blog; each with a light, medium, and dark color scheme, similar to [4]. The majority of respondents rated our recoloring positively (Figure 8(b)).

---

[8] Private digital art collection of 382 images.

For each question we found statistical significance at $p < .001$ using t-test on proportion of positive answers.

## 4   Conclusion and Future Work

We presented a new method for automatic recoloring of web pages. We achieved the objectives of esthetics, full coloring, consistency, and readability, and built a publicly available web based tool. Evaluation shows that palette extraction and overall web page recoloring results are good. We believe that our approach produces better results than closest comparable work by Gu et al. [5]. Future work will focus on making our tool interactive. We want users to be able to modify palette, manually map colors, and specify which images to recolor.

## References

1. Aupetit, S., Mereuta, A., Monmarché, N., Slimane, M.: Comparison of interruptible meta heuristics for automatic recoloring of web pages with an accessibility goal. In: AMSE - Advance in modelling, Handicap, 2012 revised selected papers. C Automatic Control (Theory and Applications), vol. 73, pp. 11–21 (2013)
2. Chang, H., Fried, O., Liu, Y., DiVerdi, S., Finkelstein, A.: Palette-based photo recoloring. ACM Trans. Graph. **34**(4), 139:1–139:11 (2015)
3. Delon, J., Desolneux, A., Lisani, J.L., Petro, A.B.: Automatic color palette. In: IEEE International Conference on Image Processing 2005, vol. 2, p. II-706-9, September 2005
4. Flatla, D.R., Reinecke, K., Gutwin, C., Gajos, K.Z.: SPRWeb: preserving subjective responses to website colour schemes through automatic recolouring. In: Proceedings of the SIGCHI Conference on Human Factors in Computing Systems, CHI 2013, NY, USA, pp. 2069–2078. ACM, New York (2013)
5. Gu, Z., Wu, Z., Yu, J., Lou, J.: A color schemer for webpage design using interactive mood board. In: Kurosu, M. (ed.) HCI 2013. LNCS, vol. 8004, pp. 555–564. Springer, Heidelberg (2013). doi:10.1007/978-3-642-39232-0_60
6. Lin, S., Hanrahan, P.: Modeling how people extract color themes from images. In: Proceedings of the SIGCHI Conference on Human Factors in Computing Systems, CHI 2013, NY, USA, pp. 3101–3110. ACM, New York (2013)
7. Matsuda, Y.: Color Design. Asakura Shoten, Tokyo (1995)
8. Munkres, J.: Algorithms for the assignment and transportation problems. J. Soc. Ind. Appl. Math. **5**(1), 32–38 (1957)
9. O'Donovan, P., Agarwala, A., Hertzmann, A.: Color compatibility from large datasets. ACM Trans. Graph. **30**(4), 63:1–63:12 (2011)
10. Reinhard, E., Adhikhmin, M., Gooch, B., Shirley, P.: Color transfer between images. IEEE Comput. Graph. Appl. **21**(5), 34–41 (2001)
11. Xia, J.: Saliency-guided color transfer between images. In: Bebis, G., et al. (eds.) ISVC 2013. LNCS, vol. 8033, pp. 468–475. Springer, Heidelberg (2013). doi:10.1007/978-3-642-41914-0_46

# Automatic Content-Aware Non-photorealistic Rendering of Images

Akshay Gadi Patil$^{(\boxtimes)}$ and Shanmuganathan Raman

Electrical Engineering, Indian Institute of Technology, Gandhinagar, India
{akshay.patil,shanmuga}@iitgn.ac.in

**Abstract.** Non-photorealistic rendering techniques work on image features and often manipulate a set of characteristics such as edges and texture to achieve a desired depiction of the scene. Most computational photography methods decompose an image using edge preserving filters and work on the resulting base and detail layers independently to achieve desired visual effects. We propose a new approach for content-aware non-photorealistic rendering of images where we manipulate the visually salient and non-salient regions separately. We propose a novel content-aware framework in order to render an image for applications such as detail exaggeration, artificial smoothing, and image abstraction. The processed regions of the image are blended seamlessly with the rest of the image for all these applications. We demonstrate that content awareness of the proposed method leads to automatic generation of non-photorealistic rendering of the same image for the different applications mentioned above.

## 1 Introduction

Non-photorealistic rendering of images have traditionally been done globally on the entire image grid. We would like to ask the question: can we achieve much better rendering of the given image if we deal with the image content in a content-aware manner? Content-aware processing has aided application such as re-targeting [1,2] and visual tracking [3]. We would like to explore the possibility of modern image filters with content-aware processing for more effective non-photorealistic rendering of images automatically. The challenge is to design a common pipeline for applications such as detail exaggeration, image abstraction and artificial blurring.

Consider an image which needs to be manipulated by an artist in a content-aware manner. She may want to alter certain aspects corresponding to the foreground region in the image without altering the other contents. She would like to alter it using certain image editing software according to her requirements and then use the resulting image for display purposes. To achieve this, she would have to manually select that portion of the image in the software every time. Further, the region needs to be manipulated using specific tools manually which is quite time consuming for multiple images. Instead, if the process of altering the foreground region with the desired manipulation is made automatic, then

© Springer International Publishing AG 2016
G. Bebis et al. (Eds.): ISVC 2016, Part I, LNCS 10072, pp. 101–112, 2016.
DOI: 10.1007/978-3-319-50835-1_10

such a problem can be addressed efficiently. The idea is to make image manipulation software to be content-aware with no human effort, thereby increasing the processing speed for large amount of images.

Recent advances in computational photography applications focus on filtering algorithms for image processing. The need for preserving the edges during the smoothing operation in an image led to the development of edge preserving filters. One such filter is the bilateral filter. Well known filters such as box filter, Gaussian filter, and Laplacian filter perform convolution across the edges in an image. However, edges across low texture variations, i.e., weaker edges, if smoothened will give a cartoon like appearance to the image which is known as image abstraction. Notable applications involving bilateral filter are high dynamic range compression [4], flash/no-flash fusion [5], tone management [6] and non-photorealistic relighting [7], to name a few.

In this paper, we present three new applications given below.

1. Content-aware detail exaggeration using guided filtering,
2. Detail exaggeration in salient region with defocused background, and
3. Independent abstraction of salient and non-salient regions in the image.

Zhang et al. in [8] presented a fast content-aware image resizing operator based on the image energy and dominant color descriptor using dynamic programming. We use guided filter for edge-aware processing of the images in this work [9,10] The reason behind using guided filter instead of the bilateral filter for detail exaggeration is that the edges are relatively better preserved across strong contrast changes and illumination transitions without the introduction of any halos. The user has the freedom to alter the "look" of the image. The image can be manipulated to give a non-photorealistic rendering by selective image abstraction using the bilateral filter. Instead of enhancing the detail in the entire photograph as mentioned in [6,7,11–14], we propose a new application of edge preserving filter aiming to exaggerate the detail only in the most salient region in the image and at the same time defocusing the non-salient region to give a more pronounced look of the salient region. In our case, we have used images which contain a salient foreground object and a background scene. We process only the foreground region and the background scene is left unaltered and vice-versa.

The main contributions of our work are listed below.

1. The proposed application is content-aware, i.e., this approach is well suited to manipulate the visibly significant regions in an image keeping all the other regions unaltered.
2. It is a novel *application* based framework based on edge preserving filtering, defocus blurring and stylization techniques that processes the brightness, contrast and texture information in a content-aware manner.
3. Since the method does not make use of any scale space pyramids and involves processing in the same scale, it is computationally less expensive.

We discuss the existing works, motivation leading to detail enhancement, defocusing approaches and image abstraction in Sect. 2. In Sect. 3, we describe the framework of our approach. We then present our results in Sect. 4 as a new application of edge preserving filters and image stylization, and rendering the manipulated image back in the original photograph using the state-of-the-art image compositing technique. We end the paper with conclusions and scope for future work in Sect. 5.

## 2  Related Work

We derive our motivation from a rich body of existing works on edge preserving filters and their applications to images such as detail enhancement [6,7,11–14], defocus blur [15], and image abstraction [16,17], all using different signal processing tools which are explained below.

Bae *et al.* in [6] described a method for spatial detail variation. The amount of high frequency detail (texture) and its spatial variation is manipulated using a new *textureness* map that performs an edge-preserving analysis. Fattal *et al.* in [7] showed detail enhancement in images photographed with a fixed viewpoint but in different lighting conditions. They performed multi-scale decomposition of the images, applied the bilateral filter on them and combined the shading information across all the input images. A new method for edge-preserving multi-scale decomposition was proposed by Farbman *et al.* in [12]. They incorporate weighted least squares (WLS) optimization framework instead of the base-detail decomposition technique based on bilateral filter which supposedly are limited in their ability to extract details at arbitrary scales. Fattal demonstrated edge-preserving smoothing and detail enhancement using a new edge avoiding wavelet basis as explained in [11]. A new scheme for edge based image coarsening is proposed in [18]. Here they construct a dimensionally reduced image space in which pixels are bound together according to the edge contents of the image using bilateral filter kernels. Gastal and Oliviera in [14] propose a transform for edge preserving filter based applications. Bhat *et al.* in [9] proposed a gradient domain optimisation framework for image and video processing which manipulates pixel differences (such as the first order image gradients) in addition to the pixel values of an image.

Blurring in an image can be caused due to many reasons. Lens abberations, diffraction, turbulence, camera shake, defocus and fast moving object are some of the causes. Defocus blurring operation is an image smoothing operation. When we capture a scene using a camera, focusing is achieved by adjusting the focal length of a camera. Once a scene is captured, the amount of defocus or blur can be controlled, irrespective of the camera parameter settings, by making use of convolution operation in the spatial domain as presented in [15]. The spatial domain approach involves convolution of the image with a fixed or a spatially varying kernel. The most commonly used blurring kernel filter is the Gaussian filter. Defocus has been used in applications involving depth estimation [15], video and image matting [19] and geometric shape estimation [20] with considerable success.

Image abstraction is the process of abstracting an image by suppressing the weaker edges while preserving the stronger ones iteratively. Decarlo and

Santella developed a method to distinguish important parts in an image by drawing bold lines [21]. But their approach needs user intervention and is computationally expensive for long video sequences containing many frames. Guastella and Valenti in [22] developed a method using wavelet transform that does not need user intervention. The wavelet edge detector maintains only the relevant information around a edge/contour and discards the irrelevant ones, thus obtaining image abstraction. Winnemoller in *et al.* proposed a real time video and image abstraction method that modified the contrast in the luminance and the color features in the image. Winnemoller proposed a new approach for stylistic depiction applications using the extended difference of Gaussians [17]. Image quantization after appropriately filtering the image would produce a good abstraction of the image since now the level of variations are fixed and any edges present after the filtering operation can take one of the quantized values [16]. Recently, Shen *et al.* in [23] make use of convolutional neural networks (CNNs) for content-aware image stylization technique through a supervised learning framework which is computationally expensive to train. They obtain the segmentation mask using CNNs whereas we use the saliency and Grabcut algorithm to do the same, which is much simpler.

Humans are smart to figure out the edges, illumination variations and flat regions in an image. Over the years our visual attention system has evolved to in its ability to predict the most relevant features of a scene where our eyes fixate in a fixed-time, free-viewing scenario [24]. Itti *et al.* in [25] proposed a model of saliency based visual attention that results in a saliency map which is robust to noise. Harel *et al.* in [24] proposed a new approach of visual attention fixation in an image based on Markov chain approach on graphs obtained by connecting pixels in an image and working on the similarity measure among the edges in the graph. The main aim of any saliency algorithm is to highlight the significant locations in an image that is informative according to some criterion, like the human fixation. Li *et al.* in [26] addresses the design bias problems of the existing saliency algorithms that create discomforting disconnections between fixations and salient object segmentation. In other words, a saliency map may include areas that do not constitute the salient object, yet we use such algorithms because they give us a measure of the content-awareness in a given image.

## 3   Proposed Methodology

The proposed approach involves the processing of salient region in an image which is directed towards three applications in this paper. The content-aware processing for non-photorealistic image rendering for these applications is a novel contribution. A similar technology is used in the *Smart Looks* plug-in in the Adobe Photoshop Elements 14 in a non context-aware manner [27]. We are not aware of the technology behind this plug-in. We provide a more simpler and comprehensive framework for not just one but three image processing tasks. The diagram in Fig. 1 explains our methodology of content-aware non-photorealistic rendering of images for the three applications mentioned in this paper.

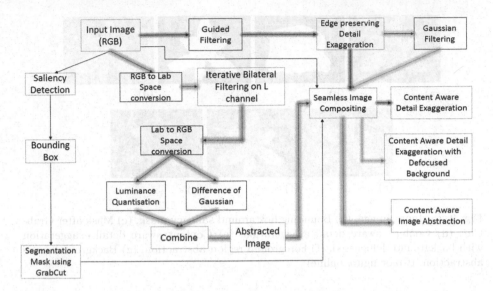

**Fig. 1.** Proposed approach. *The black line: flow for content-aware detail exaggeration, the blue line: flow for detail exaggeration with defocused background, and the brown line: flow for content-aware image abstraction.* (Color figure online)

### 3.1 Saliency Based Segmentation

As the title of our paper suggests, we aim to make our system content-aware. For this, we first find the salient region in the given image. We employed a graph based visual saliency method proposed by Harel *et al.* in [24]. This helps us in narrowing down to identify the most visually salient region in an image. The images used in our approach were collected from the salient object dataset provided by Li *et al.* in [26]. We obtain a binary mask from the saliency map using Otsu's threshold [28] as shown in Fig. 2(b) since saliency mask gives in a non-strict sense, two classes of pixels, one belonging to the foreground and the other belonging to the background because of which Otsu's algorithm can be applied. However, the saliency mask may include portions of the image on which a human eye fixates but it may not be a part of the most salient region in the image. Such regions are very tiny and appear as blobs in the binary mask. We find a bounding box around the binary mask corresponding to the salient region for each image automatically which is shown in red in Fig. 2(b). To remove the blobs of the binary mask which should not be present in the salient region and to ensure that the computer emulates the human perception to understand the

**Fig. 2.** (a) Input image, (b) Bounding box around saliency mask, (c) Mask after Grab-Cut, (d) Content aware detail exaggeration, (e) Content aware detail exaggeration with background defocussed, (f) Foreground region abstraction, (g) Background scene abstraction. (Color figure online)

visually meaningful parts in an image, we make use of GrabCut technique to accurately extract the salient region without any background contribution for further processing [29].

### 3.2    Content-Aware Processing and Compositing

The bounding box along with the input image of Fig. 2(a) is given to the GrabCut algorithm proposed by Rother *et al.* in [29] which extracts the complete salient region/object inside the bounding box. A mask of the object extracted using the GrabCut algorithm is shown in Fig. 2(c). The input to the GrabCut algorithm should be an image containing the foreground object within the bounding box irrespective of whether or not the object of interest needs to be processed or manipulated with respect to its contents.

**Content-Aware Detail Exaggeration.** We employ an edge preserving filtering approach taking cues from the existing literature as explained in the related work section. The edge preserving filter is used to get a structure and texture decomposition of the image without any halos. The input image is filtered using a guided filter as explained in [10]. Guided filter was proposed by He *et al.* in [10] where the output of the filtering operation is a local linear transform of the guidance image. The input image is enhanced with respect to the details present in it as can be seen from Fig. 2(d). It can be observed that the image has a similar feel as the original image with the details exaggerated. Fundamentally, detail exaggeration requires one to manipulate the gradients in the detail layer (which is the difference between the input image and the base layer) obtained from the guided filter. The modified gradients need to be re-integrated into the image to (a) prevent gradient reversal, (b) for the manipulations to take place, and (c) for the effects to be visible. The use of bilateral filter introduces halos along edges with strong illumination changes on either side of it because of gradient reversal in the reconstruction step. The detail exaggerated image is obtained by combining the boosted detail layer with the base layer. Unlike bilateral filter, the guided filter does not suffer from gradient reversal artifacts [10]. The input image of Fig. 2(a) along with the saliency mask in Fig. 2(c) and the detail exaggerated image is given as input to the image compositing algorithm proposed in [30] to get the content-aware detail exaggerated image as shown in Fig. 2(d).

**Content-Aware Detail Exaggeration with Defocused Background.** As we mentioned in the introduction section, we defocus the background and exaggerate only the salient region to give a more pronounced look of the enhanced image as could be seen from Fig. 2(e). As mentioned before, there are spatially variant and spatially invariant blurring kernels for defocus operation. We use a simple approach to defocus the image using a fixed size Gaussian kernel. Every pixel $(x, y)$ in the image is operated upon with a Gaussian filter $G_\sigma(x, y)$ of kernel $9 \times 9$ with a standard deviation 4 around the neighborhood of the pixel. The larger the value of $\sigma$, the larger is the blurring effect in the image. This filtering operation is given by Eq. 1 below:

$$\widehat{I}(x, y) = I(x, y) \otimes G_\sigma(x, y) \tag{1}$$

So the entire image is defocused. But we want only the background defocused. To achieve this, the defocus blurred image along with the mask in Fig. 2(c) and the image in Fig. 2(d) are given as input to the image compositing algorithm for a seamless compositing. We used the error tolerant image compositing algorithm proposed by Tao *et al.* in [30]. The output of this system is the content-aware detail exaggerated image with defocused background which is shown in Fig. 2(e).

**Content-Aware Image Abstraction.** Our next application is to show image abstraction in the salient and non-salient regions separately. We make use of the approach proposed in [16] for image abstraction. The input color image after conversion to *Lab* space is filtered using the bilateral filter. For the Gaussian filter, we used a spatial kernel with standard deviation 3 and a range kernel with a standard deviation 0.1. It is converted back to RGB space. Luminance values in the resulting image are quantized into 10 different levels and difference-of-Gaussian filter is applied on the resulting RGB image. These two images are then combined to get the abstracted image which gives a cartoon like appearance to the image as can be seen from Fig. 2(f) (foreground abstracted) and Fig. 2(g)(background abstracted). To get the abstraction of the visually important region, we again employ the GrabCut technique combined with error tolerant image compositing algorithm. The input image in its entirety is abstracted using the method described above. Mask obtained after the GrabCut technique, along with the input image and the abstracted image is given as the input to image compositing algorithm proposed in [30]. The result is that there is content-aware abstraction which can be seen from Fig. 2(f). If the binary mask obtained after the GrabCut algorithm is inverted, and the above mentioned operations are performed with this new mask, then the non salient region in the image is abstracted as could be seen from Fig. 2(g).

## 4    Results and Discussions

We present the results for a set of six images on the three different filtering applications mentioned in the application pipeline described in the previous section, which are presented from top row to the bottom row of Fig. 3. For every image, we show the content-aware processed images along with the original image. We show the results of the state-of-the-art global approaches for detail exaggeration and image abstraction in Fig. 3(b) and (c), respectively. We use them as standard benchmarks against which we would like to compare our results. As could be seen from Fig. 3(d), the images exaggerated using the guided filter approach [10] produce good exaggeration and this approach was selected from a set of other detail exaggeration methods based on minimal artifacts in the processed image. The background is defocused to give a more pronounced look of the detail exaggerated in the salient region. At the same time, the overall background and foreground illumination in the image is increased and has more contrast as seen in Fig. 3(d) column. Column (e) of Fig. 3 shows images where the salient region is abstracted and the non salient region is left unaltered. There is illumination and contrast change happening only in the foreground region when the salient region is abstracted. The level of abstraction can be controlled by applying the bilateral filter iteratively to suit the requirements from the user end. The last column of Fig. 3, i.e., Fig. 3(f) shows the results of abstraction on the background scene. The illumination in the foreground region as compared to the original image is reduced. The robustness of the error tolerant image compositing technique [30] ensures the seamless image compositing operation after the processing of the respective content-aware region. It also ensures that there is no background clutter effect and the halos do not appear during processing involved. Our approach is content-aware as it processes only the salient object in the image keeping the rest of the original image as it is. As can be observed from the results, the proposed method is able to achieve high quality rendering of images when compared to the other methods as evident from Fig. 3(b–f). The framework adapts itself to do different type of processing in the salient and non-salient regions of a given image which has resulted in a better non-photorealistic rendering of a given scene.

We performed the experiments in MATLAB environment on a laptop that runs Windows 8 with Intel core i5 (1.7 GHz) processor with 6 GB RAM. The time required for images of different resolution for all the three applications is given in the Table 1 below. Typical time required for an image of size $800 \times 533$ for content-aware detail exaggeration is 30 s, for content-aware detail exaggeration with defocused background is 37 s, for content-aware image abstraction for both salient and non-salient regions is 50 s each. Since we have designed our system to be content-aware, the kind of images our method is well suited for are the ones which contain a salient foreground region and a background scene.

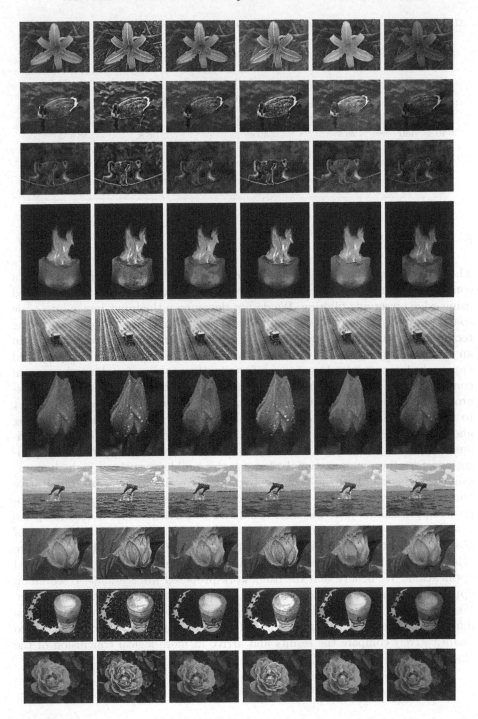

**Fig. 3.** Results: (a) Input image, (b) Global detail exaggeration [10], (c) Global image abstraction [17], (d) Detail exaggeration with defocused background, (e) Foreground region abstraction, and (f) Background scene abstraction.

**Table 1.** Processing times for the proposed applications on different image sizes.

| Image resolution | Content-aware detail exaggeration | Content-aware detail exaggeration with defocussed background | Salient region abstraction | Background scene abstraction |
|---|---|---|---|---|
| 800 × 533 | 30 s | 37 s | 50 s | 50 s |
| 640 × 480 | 24 s | 30 s | 38 s | 38 s |
| 400 × 300 | 17 s | 22 s | 30 s | 30 s |
| 320 × 400 | 18 s | 23 s | 30 s | 30 s |
| 300 × 400 | 15 s | 20 s | 26 s | 26 s |

# 5   Conclusions

The proposed approach manipulates the details and processes the image in a content-aware manner, i.e., only the most salient object in the image is processed using edge preserving filtering. We do not decompose the input image into scale space pyramids for any of the addressed applications. An image compositing technique is used which takes the mask corresponding to foreground object in an image which has to be composited on a background scene. The proposed approach does not introduce any artifacts in the process of making the system content-aware, be it content-aware detail exaggeration with defocused background or non salient image abstraction which inherently gives cartoon effect to the image. Such an application can be used for non-photorealistic rendering and can be extended to more applications requiring content awareness for various image manipulations. Future scope involves developing content-aware applications for other computational photography problems such as high dynamic range imaging and flash/no-flash photography. We aim to carry out qualitative analysis and image quality assessment of the results produced using the proposed approach. Subjective studies could also be carried out for determining the visual appeal of the abstracted images and thereby controlling the amount of abstraction suitable for non-photorealistic rendering. We also plan to explore other notions of content-aware processing other than saliency for the proposed applications. We believe that the framework proposed will stimulate research on applications of automatic content-aware non-photorealistic rendering of images. We would also like to develop a novel quality metric in order to compare the different non-photorealistic renderings of the same image. This would enable to quantitatively compare the results and arrive at more logical conclusion of the algorithms.

# References

1. Mansfield, A., Gehler, P., Gool, L., Rother, C.: Scene carving: scene consistent image retargeting. In: Daniilidis, K., Maragos, P., Paragios, N. (eds.) ECCV 2010. LNCS, vol. 6311, pp. 143–156. Springer, Heidelberg (2010). doi:10.1007/978-3-642-15549-9_11
2. Avidan, S., Shamir, A.: Seam carving for content-aware image resizing. ACM Trans. Graph. (TOG) **26**, 10 (2007). ACM
3. Yang, M., Wu, Y., Hua, G.: Context-aware visual tracking. IEEE Trans. Pattern Anal. Mach. Intell. **31**, 1195–1209 (2009)
4. Durand, F., Dorsey, J.: Fast bilateral filtering for the display of high-dynamic-range images. ACM Trans. Graph. (TOG) **21**, 257–266 (2002). ACM
5. Petschnigg, G., Szeliski, R., Agrawala, M., Cohen, M., Hoppe, H., Toyama, K.: Digital photography with flash and no-flash image pairs. ACM Trans. Graph. (TOG) **23**, 664–672 (2004). ACM
6. Bae, S., Paris, S., Durand, F.: Two-scale tone management for photographic look. ACM Trans. Graph. (TOG) **25**, 637–645 (2006). ACM
7. Fattal, R., Agrawala, M., Rusinkiewicz, S.: Multiscale shape and detail enhancement from multi-light image collections. ACM Trans. Graph. **26**, 51 (2007)
8. Dong, W.M., Bao, G.B., Zhang, X.P., Paul, J.C.: Fast multi-operator image resizing and evaluation. J. Comput. Sci. Technol. **27**, 121–134 (2012)
9. Bhat, P., Zitnick, C.L., Cohen, M., Curless, B.: Gradientshop: a gradient-domain optimization framework for image and video filtering. ACM Trans. Graph. (TOG) **29**, 10 (2010)
10. He, K., Sun, J., Tang, X.: Guided image filtering. IEEE Trans. Pattern Anal. Mach. Intell. **35**, 1397–1409 (2013)
11. Fattal, R.: Edge-avoiding wavelets and their applications. ACM Trans. Graph. (TOG) **28**, 22 (2009)
12. Farbman, Z., Fattal, R., Lischinski, D., Szeliski, R.: Edge-preserving decompositions for multi-scale tone and detail manipulation. ACM Trans. Graph. (TOG) **27**, 67 (2008). ACM
13. Paris, S., Hasinoff, S.W., Kautz, J.: Local laplacian filters: edge-aware image processing with a laplacian pyramid. ACM Trans. Graph. **30**, 68 (2011)
14. Gastal, E.S., Oliveira, M.M.: Domain transform for edge-aware image and video processing. ACM Trans. Graph. (TOG) **30**, 69 (2011). ACM
15. Subbarao, M., Surya, G.: Depth from defocus: a spatial domain approach. Int. J. Comput. Vis. **13**, 271–294 (1994)
16. Winnemöller, H., Olsen, S.C., Gooch, B.: Real-time video abstraction. ACM Trans. Graph. (TOG) **25**, 1221–1226 (2006). ACM
17. Winnemöller, H.: XDoG: advanced image stylization with eXtended difference-of-Gaussians. In: Proceedings of the ACM SIGGRAPH/Eurographics Symposium on Non-Photorealistic Animation and Rendering, pp. 147–156 (2011). ACM
18. Fattal, R., Carroll, R., Agrawala, M.: Edge-based image coarsening. ACM Trans. Graph. (TOG) **29**, 6 (2009)
19. McGuire, M., Matusik, W.: Defocus difference matting. In: ACM SIGGRAPH 2005 Sketches, p. 104. ACM (2005)
20. Favaro, P., Soatto, S.: A geometric approach to shape from defocus. IEEE Trans. Pattern Anal. Mach. Intell. **27**, 406–417 (2005)
21. DeCarlo, D., Santella, A.: Stylization and abstraction of photographs. ACM Trans. Graph. (TOG) **21**, 769–776 (2002). ACM

22. Guastella, D., Valenti, C.: Cartoon filter via adaptive abstraction. J. Vis. Commun. Image Represent. **36**, 149–158 (2016)

23. Shen, X., Hertzmann, A., Jia, J., Paris, S., Price, B., Shechtman, E., Sachs, I.: Automatic portrait segmentation for image stylization. In: Computer Graphics Forum, vol. 35, pp. 93–102. Wiley Online Library (2016)

24. Harel, J., Koch, C., Perona, P.: Graph-based visual saliency. In: Advances in neural information processing systems, pp. 545–552 (2006)

25. Itti, L., Koch, C., Niebur, E.: A model of saliency-based visual attention for rapid scene analysis. IEEE Trans. Pattern Anal. Mach. Intell. **20**(11), 1254–1259 (1998)

26. Li, Y., Hou, X., Koch, C., Rehg, J., Yuille, A.: The secrets of salient object segmentation. In: Proceedings of the IEEE Conference on Computer Vision and Pattern Recognition, pp. 280–287 (2014)

27. Adobe: Adobe Photoshop Elements 14 - Smart looks (2016). https://helpx.adobe.com/photoshop-elements/how-to/apply-effects-smart-looks.html/. Accessed 7 Apr 2016

28. Otsu, N.: A threshold selection method from gray-level histograms. Automatica **11**, 23–27 (1975)

29. Rother, C., Kolmogorov, V., Blake, A.: Grabcut: interactive foreground extraction using iterated graph cuts. ACM Trans. Graph. (TOG) **23**, 309–314 (2004). ACM

30. Tao, M.W., Johnson, M.K., Paris, S.: Error-tolerant image compositing. Int. J. Comput. Vis. **103**, 178–189 (2013)

# Improved Aircraft Recognition for Aerial Refueling Through Data Augmentation in Convolutional Neural Networks

Robert Mash$^{(\boxtimes)}$, Brett Borghetti, and John Pecarina

Department of Electrical and Computer Engineering,
The Air Force Institute of Technology, WPAFB, Dayton, OH 45433, USA
robert.mash@afit.edu

**Abstract.** As machine learning techniques increase in complexity, their hunger for more training data is ever-growing. Deep learning for image recognition is no exception. In some domains, training images are expensive or difficult to collect. When training image availability is limited, researchers naturally turn to synthetic methods of generating new imagery for training. We evaluate several methods of training data augmentation in the context of improving performance of a Convolutional Neural Network (CNN) in the domain of fine-grain aircraft classification. We conclude that randomly scaling training imagery significantly improves performance. Also, we find that drawing random occlusions on top of training images confers a similar improvement in our problem domain. Further, we find that these two effects seem to be approximately additive, with our results demonstrating a 45.7% reduction in test error over basic horizontal flipping and cropping.

## 1 Introduction

Training Data augmentation and simulation have become standard tools used for training practical deep neural networks in situations where there is not a very large amount of training data available. The popularity of Krizhevsky's Alexnet as a model Convolutional Neural Network (CNN) has led to adoption of his computationally simple Data Augmentation (DA) techniques as a default. Krizhevsky's strategy applies random horizontal flipping and randomly located fixed-size-cropping to each training image. As these amount to matrix indexing operations, they are computationally simple, but don't take full advantage of DA's potential. The negative consequence of using only simple DA techniques, is that for a given level of held out test set performance, practitioners tend to expand their network size to improve performance. The techniques we explore improve test set performance without increasing down stream network size and subsequent computational complexity.

In Related Work we discuss machine learning norms in data augmentation and simulation. In Problem Domain, automatic visual aircraft recognition is introduced in the Automatic Aerial Refueling (AAR) domain.

© Springer International Publishing AG 2016
G. Bebis et al. (Eds.): ISVC 2016, Part I, LNCS 10072, pp. 113–122, 2016.
DOI: 10.1007/978-3-319-50835-1_11

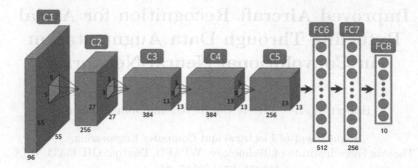

**Fig. 1.** Architecture of AfCaffe [1], an Alexnet [2] derivative. From left to right (input to output) five convolutional layers with Max Pooling after layers 1, 2, and 5, followed by a three layer fully connected classifier (layers 6–8). The number of neurons in the output layer is equal to the designed number of output classes.

In Methodology, the AfCaffe CNN from [1] is introduced in the AAR context and we detail several types of data augmentation. We conclude that significant performance improvements on held out test data can be made by applying these DA techniques individually or in combination. Using combinations of DA techniques, we demonstrate a 45.7% reduction in test set error on our aircraft recognition dataset. Also, we expect that due to the high cost of gathering aerial photography, AfCaffe may be further improved using simulated training data in the future.

## 2    Related Work

### 2.1    Training Data Augmentation

A critical tool for overcoming training data overfit with modern CNNs is data augmentation, the use of randomized data transformations to greatly expand the effective size of a training set. Data augmentation randomly applies certain types of label preserving transforms to training data. Typical transformations include random cropping, mirroring, rotations, occlusions, as well as affine and color transformations. The effect of which is to increase the size of a training data set by a large factor, beyond the capacity of an Artificial Neural Network (ANN) to memorize, or over-fit. The network is then forced to develop abstract feature detectors useful for recognizing patterns from general features.

Data augmentation normally includes randomly applied mirroring and random cropping as in [2–5]. When other methods of data augmentation are used, they are typically applied in addition to this baseline as in [6]. Here Dielman applies random rotations, scaling, and brightness jittering in addition to randomly applied mirroring to images of galaxies.

This is an example of a combination of data augmentation methods only suitable in certain domains. In this case of images of galaxies, which are often rotation invariant, unconstrained random rotations can be applied and the resulting image is still feasibly an image of a galaxy. Similarly, in the case of aerial refueling images as in Fig. 2, the refueling boom occludes the image of the approaching to-be-refueled aircraft. Consequently, randomly drawn occlusions are an appropriate data augmentation method in this domain and others as explored in [7]. Limited angle random rotations of non-rotation invariant objects can sometimes be effective as in [8,9]. However, others have cited null results as in [10].

## 2.2   Synthetic Training Data

A possible source of neural network training data are simulated images from the field of computer graphics as in [11]. Much work has been done in the sub-fields of vehicle and pedestrian detection as in [12–14]. Synthetic datasets enjoy several benefits over manually acquired photographic datasets. Instances of training data can be generated with total control over perspective, texture, lighting, range, orientation, etc. as in [15]. Further, in some fields of inquiry, real-world photography can be much more expensive to acquire than synthetic data. Lastly, training data labels can be generated with perfect accuracy, a particularly useful attribute when working in a continuous domain such as position and orientation regression.

## 2.3   Generative Networks

A new and burgeoning field is that of generative adversarial networks (GANs) [16] used to 'imagine' variations on a training image, based on the types of variations learned from real-world imagery. Two main types of have been developed, the Deep Convolutional GAN or DC-GAN [17] and the Laplacian - GAN or Lap-GAN [18]. For example, in a recent cross-over between these related fields Dosovitskiy in [19] trains a convolutional GAN to generate photorealistic images of many different never-seen-before chairs from previously rendered images of chairs from simulation.

# 3   Problem Domain

Consider a future scenario involving autonomous aerial refueling tanker aircraft operations. Visual identification of an aircraft by model is currently performed by trained aircrew. However, recent success in aircraft image recognition with AfCaffe in [1] motivates an approach wherein a CNN automatically identifies the model of an approaching aircraft "visually", in lieu of a human crew member.

In an autonomous refueling tanker, visual recognition of approaching aircraft is but one part of a greater collection of autonomous systems. For example, after recognizing the model of aircraft, the position and orientation of the aircraft must be continuously estimated in support of the tight formation flying required in the domain.

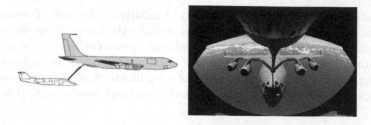

**Fig. 2.** (left) Refueling approach diagram [20] (right) Refueling approach camera perspective

## AAR Vision System Concept of Operations

During aerial refueling, an aircraft to be refueled approaches a tanker aircraft from below and behind in a predefined flight path resulting in the relative positions shown in Fig. 2. A refueling tanker equipped with an AAR vision system would have rear-facing cameras aligned with the aircraft approach vector. This would result in a forward perspective of an aircraft on refueling approach as shown in Fig. 2.

The refueling perspective imagery would then be down sampled as appropriate to match the input spatial and color dimensions of a previously trained CNN. Next, a forward pass of the CNN would be performed, the output of which is a probability mass function estimating the model of the approaching aircraft.

The aircraft model estimate could then be used for configuration of fuel transfer systems, formation flight systems, and generally improved situational awareness.

## 4    Methodology

### 4.1    Aircraft Recognition with the AfCaffe CNN

AfCaffe, as shown in Fig. 1, is a derivative of Alexnet which was originally designed to compete in the 1000 class ImageNet Large Scale Visual Recognition Challenge (ILSVRC) in [2]. The number of neurons in the output layer was reduced to ten, corresponding to ten models of US Air Force aircraft. Further, as AfCaffe only needs to recognize ten classes, the capacity of the Alexnet classifier design was optimized by reducing the number of neurons in the fully connected classifier. As seen in Fig. 3, eight variations of classifier hyper-parameters were evaluated with size 768 providing the best performance to capacity ratio. The convolutional portion of the network (layers 1–5) was retained from the Alexnet configuration. As AfCaffe has 7.8 million trainable parameters, it requires a large number of training examples in order to prevent overfitting to the training dataset.

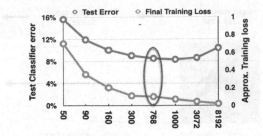

**Fig. 3.** Test and Training error vs. Classifier capacity from [1]

## 4.2 Training and Test Data

In order to train and evaluate AfCaffe, a body of imagery consisting of 76,426 images was sourced from the internet, primarily from Flickr groups and refueling sequences captured from YouTube videos. These data were selected to roughly evenly represent each aircraft class. Each image was given a numeric 1–10 label representing the class of aircraft captured in the image. Next, the dataset was randomly divided into two subsets, training and test. The training subset consisted of 61342 images (80%) and the test set 15084 (20%).

The training set input images are stored in a Lightning memory Mapped DataBase (LMDB) at $256 \times 256$ pixels with three 8-bit color channels. During neural network training, images are extracted from the LMDB and randomly transformed while preserving associated class labels. After transformation according to one or more of the following techniques, the images are applied to the input layer of the AfCaffe CNN which accepts images of resolution $227 \times 227$ with three 8-bit color channels.

## 4.3 Data Augmentation Techniques

Several types of DA are evaluated as shown in Fig. 4. They are described in detail as follows.

- Baseline: No data augmentation is performed on the input image. The input image is simply down sampled in order to match the $227 \times 227$ CNN input resolution.
- H+RC: The input image is flipped horizontally with probability = 1/2. This operation is followed by a fixed size crop randomly applied to the input image. The fixed crop size corresponds to the input dimensions of the CNN. Krizhevsky, et al. applied this technique with great success in [2]. Both the flipping and cropping operations amount to matrix indexing, which makes H + RC computationally inexpensive to perform during training.
- R360: The input image is rotated about its center by an angle randomly chosen from a uniform distribution ranging from 0° to 360°. As seen in Fig. 4, black triangular regions are left in the corners of the image after the rotation is performed. The resulting image is then re-sampled as appropriate to match the CNN input resolution.

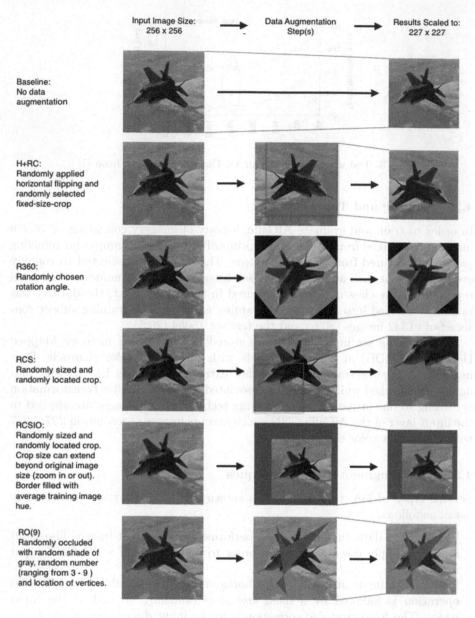

Input Image Size: → Data Augmentation → Results Scaled to:
256 x 256                Step(s)                227 x 227

Baseline:
No data
augmentation

H+RC:
Randomly applied
horizontal flipping and
randomly selected
fixed-size-crop

R360:
Randomly chosen
rotation angle.

RCS:
Randomly sized and
randomly located crop.

RCSIO:
Randomly sized and
randomly located crop.
Crop size can extend
beyond original image
size (zoom in or out).
Border filled with
average training image
hue.

RO(9)
Randomly occluded
with random shade of
gray, random number
(ranging from 3 - 9 )
and location of vertices.

**Fig. 4.** Data Augmentation Types

– <u>RCS:</u> A randomly sized and randomly located crop is taken from the input
image. The square crop dimension is randomly chosen from a uniform distribution ranging from 150 pixels to 256 pixels. The crop location is then
randomly selected from uniform distributions across the input image's x and

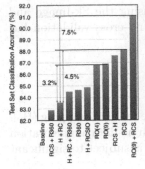

| Data Augmentation Type | Description Augmentation = Randomly Applied: | Final Training Set Loss | Test Set Classification Accy (%) | Test Set Classification Error(%) |
|---|---|---|---|---|
| Baseline | No Data Augmentation | 0.4 | 82.0 | 18.0 |
| RCS + R360 | Random Crop Size + Rotations | 0.41 | 82.9 | 17.1 |
| H + RC | Mirroring + Fixed Size Crop | 0.4 | 83.6 | 16.4 |
| H + RC + R360 | Mirroring + Fixed Size Crop + Rotations | 0.4 | 84.5 | 15.5 |
| R360 | Rotations | 0.4 | 84.6 | 15.4 |
| H + RCSIO | Mirroring + Random Crop Size with Zoom In and Out | 0.39 | 84.8 | 15.2 |
| RO(4) | 4 Vertex Polygonal Occlusions | 0.36 | 86.8 | 13.2 |
| RO(9) | 9 Vertex Polygonal Occlusions | 0.36 | 86.9 | 13.1 |
| RCS + H | Random Crop Size + Mirroring | 0.41 | 87.6 | 12.4 |
| RCS | Random Crop Size | 0.36 | 88.1 | 11.9 |
| RO(9) + RCS | 9 Vertex Polygonal Occlusions + Random Crop Size | 0.38 | 91.1 | 8.9 |

**Fig. 5.** Test set classification accuracy vs. data augmentation techniques. Training loss held constant at approximately 0.4.

y dimensions. The resulting crop is then re-sampled as appropriate to match the CNN input resolution. An example is shown in Fig. 4.

– RCSIO: The input image is scaled by a factor ranging from 0.39 to 1.13 randomly selected from a uniform distribution. Then a fixed size crop of $227 \times 227$ is taken from a location randomly selected from a uniform distribution on the resulting image. If the selected scale factor is less 1.0, the input image is effectively scaled down in size, resulting in a margin or border around the edges of the image as seen in Fig. 4. The resulting border is then filled with the mean training image hue to keep from shifting the mean of the training set. The scaled image is then re-sampled as appropriate to match the CNN input resolution.

– RO(n): Random occlusions are applied to the input image by first selecting a random number of vertices ranging from 3 to n, where n > 3. Locations for the selected number of vertices are then randomly selected from uniform distributions over the input image. The vertices are then used to draw an irregular polygon over the image as seen in Fig. 4 where the fill color is chosen as a randomly chosen shade of gray. The resulting image is then re-sampled as appropriate to match the CNN input resolution.

– Combinations: Various combinations of the approaches above are possible. H + RC + R360, RCS + R360, and RO(9) + R360 are implemented in this study. In each case, the transformations are performed in left-to-right reading order followed by resampling to match the CNN input resolution.

## 4.4 Implementation

The AfCaffe CNN was developed using the Caffe Deep Learning Framework from the Berkeley Vision and Learning Center. The following Caffe specific training parameters were used: base learning rate = 0.001, gamma = 0.1, stepsize = 7500, momentum = 0.9, weight decay = 0.0005, batchsize = 250.

Data augmentation techniques were implemented using the Sk-Image and OpenCV libraries in Python. Due to time constraints, no cross validation has been performed.

## 5 Results

As seen in Fig. 5, Krizhevsky style mirroring and fixed size random cropping (H + RC) provides some benefit over the baseline case on which no data augmentation is performed. This is not surprising, as the baseline case is subject to significant over-fitting of the training set.

Transitioning from a fixed crop size randomly selected from the original image to a randomly selected crop size (RCS) improves overall test set classification accuracy by 6% points over the baseline and 4–5 points over Krizhevsky's H + RC method. Conceptually, this is likely due to increasing scale invariance, as RCS applies the same training images to the CNN at various scales.

Additionally, in the aircraft recognition domain, random polygonal occlusions yield a similar improvement over the baseline and Krizhevsky's H + RC method as from random scaling. It's not clear if this is a domain specific improvement where some test aircraft images are occluded by a refueling boom as in Fig. 2. For example, Yilmaz concludes in [7] that random occlusion improves classification performance with Recurrent Neural Networks (RNNs), lending some credibility to the idea that randomly drawing occlusions on training images may improve the generalizing capability of ANNs. It may be that random occlusions contribute a drop-out like parameter regularization effect concentrated in regions of the image most represented by the probability distribution controlling the random occlusion generator.

Lastly, as detailed in Fig. 5, the greatest improvement in test set classification accuracy occurs when these two techniques are combined. Random occlusions (RO) and randomly selected crop size (RCS) seem to contribute almost independently to generalization as the total improvement over Krizhevsky's method is approximately additive.

## 6 Conclusions

Applying more computationally expensive DA techniques such as random crop scaling (RCS) and random occlusions (RO) to a training set improves CNN performance significantly over simpler DA methods as pioneered by Krizhevsky. By combining RCS and RO, we demonstrate a 45.7% reduction in test set classification error over Krizhevsky's method.

The primary benefit of more computationally expensive DA techniques is an increase in test set classification performance without an increase in network size and downstream computational complexity. The only cost of these DA techniques is an increase in training time, which is usually preferable to increasing the size of a network that is widely deployed to users after the training phase.

# 7  Future Work

It may be useful to further explore whether random occlusions as a DA technique is useful outside of specific domains with expected visual occlusions. If so, a comparison of the underlying mathematics to that of drop-out regularization may be in order.

Rotations and random occlusions should be modified to apply mean hue rather than black/gray as they inadvertently modify the training mean image. This change may well improve R360 and RO(n) performance significantly, as performance of CNNs is sensitive to normalization. Wang used a similar zero-pad fill technique in [10] and found no improvement with rotations. Further, a lesser extent of rotation may provide better results than unconstrained rotation as it may more closely match the operational domain of aircraft.

Lastly, as stated in Problem Domain, recognizing an approaching aircraft is not the only problem yet to be solved in the AAR domain. The problem of estimating the range and relative orientation of an approaching aircraft purely from visual cues is still open. We suspect that computer graphics techniques could be used to generate synthetic training imagery from the refueling perspective of an AAR tanker. Conceivably, the relative position and orientation of an approaching aircraft could be estimated using regression techniques.

**Acknowledgements.** This work was supported by the Air Force Research Lab's Sensors Directorate, Layered Sensing Exploitation Division. The views expressed in this work are those of the authors, and do not reflect the official policy or position of the United States Air Force, Department of Defense, or the U.S. Government. This document has been approved for public release.

# References

1. Mash, R., Becherer, N., Woolley, B.P., Pecarina, J.P.: toward aircraft recognition with convolutional neural networks. In: Proceedings of the 2016 IEEE National Avionics and Electronics Conference (2016)
2. Krizhevsky, A., Sutskever, I., Hinton, G.E.: ImageNet classification with deep convolutional neural networks. In: Advances in Neural Information Processing Systems, pp. 1–9 (2012)
3. Visin, F., Kastner, K., Cho, K., Matteucci, M., Courville, A., Bengio, Y.: ReNet: a recurrent neural network based alternative to convolutional networks, pp. 1–9. Arxiv (2015)
4. Karpathy, A., Toderici, G., Shetty, S., Leung, T., Sukthankar, R., Fei-Fei, L.: Large-scale video classification with convolutional neural networks. In: 2014 IEEE Conference on Computer Vision and Pattern Recognition (CVPR), pp. 1725–1732 (2014)
5. Simonyan, K., Zisserman, A.: Two-stream convolutional networks for action recognition in videos, pp. 1–11 (2014) arXiv preprint, arXiv:1406.2199
6. Dieleman, S., Willett, K., Dambre, J.: Rotation-invariant convolutional neural networks for galaxy morphology prediction. Mon. Not. R. Astron. Soc. **450**, 1441–1459 (2015)

7. Yilmaz, O.: Classification of occluded objects using fast recurrent processing (2015)
8. Malli, R.C., Aygun, M., Ekenel, H.K.: Apparent age estimation using ensemble of deep learning models (2016)
9. Chatfield, K., Simonyan, K., Vedaldi, A., Zisserman, A.: Return of the devil in the details: delving deep into convolutional nets. Brit. Mach. Vision Conf. **2014**, 1–11 (2014)
10. Wang, K.K.: Image classification with pyramid representation and rotated data augmentation on torch 7 (2015)
11. Pepik, B., Benenson, R., Ritschel, T., Schiele, B.: What is holding back convnets for detection? In: Gall, J., Gehler, P., Leibe, B. (eds.) GCPR 2015. LNCS, vol. 9358, pp. 517–528. Springer, Heidelberg (2015). doi:10.1007/978-3-319-24947-6_43
12. Rematas, K., Ritschel, T., Fritz, M., Tuytelaars, T.: Image-based synthesis and re-synthesis of viewpoints guided by 3D models. In: Proceedings of the IEEE Computer Society Conference on Computer Vision and Pattern Recognition, pp. 3898–3905 (2014)
13. Stark, M., Goesele, M., Schiele, B.: Back to the future: learning shape models from 3D CAD data. BMVC, pp. 1–11 (2010)
14. Xu, J., Vazquez, D., Lopez, A.M., Marin, J., Ponsa, D.: Learning a multiview part-based model in virtual world for pedestrian detection. In: Proceedings, IEEE Intelligent Vehicles Symposium, pp. 467–472 (2013)
15. Nykl, S., Mourning, C., Chelberg, D.: Interactive mesostructures with volumetric collisions. IEEE Trans. Vis. Comput. Graph. **20**, 970–982 (2014)
16. Goodfellow, I., Pouget-Abadie, J., Mirza, M.: Generative adversarial networks, pp. 1–9. arXiv preprint (2014)
17. Radford, A., Metz, L., Chintala, S.: Unsupervised representation learning with deep convolutional generative adversarial networks, pp. 1–15. arXiv (2015)
18. Denton, E., Chintala, S., Szlam, A., Fergus, R.: Deep generative image models using a Laplacian pyramid of adversarial networks, pp. 1–10. Arxiv (2015)
19. Dosovitskiy, A., Springenberg, J.T., Brox, T.: Learning-to-generate-chairs-with-convolutional-neural-networks. In: IEEE Conference on Computer Vision and Pattern Recognition, pp. 1538–1546 (2015)
20. Ross, S.M.: Formation flight control for aerial refueling. Master's thesis, pp. 1–280 (2006)

# Motion and Tracking

# Detecting Tracking Failures from Correlation Response Maps

Ryan Walsh and Henry Medeiros(✉)

Department of Electrical and Computer Engineering, Marquette University,
1551 W. Wisconsin Ave, Milwaukee, WI 53233, USA
{ryan.w.walsh,henry.medeiros}@marquette.edu

**Abstract.** Tracking methods based on correlation filters have gained popularity in recent years due to their robustness to rotations, occlusions, and other challenging aspects of visual tracking. Such methods generate a confidence or response map which is used to estimate the new location of the tracked target. By examining the features of this map, important details about the tracker status can be inferred and compensatory measures can be taken in order to minimize failures. We propose an algorithm that uses the mean and entropy of this response map to prevent bad target model updates caused by problems such as occlusions and motion blur as well as to determine the size of the target search area. Quantitative experiments demonstrate that our method improves success plots over a baseline tracker that does not incorporate our failure detection mechanism.

## 1 Introduction

Visual object tracking is an important aspect of computer vision. Much work has gone into designing methods to improve the robustness of visual trackers against a variety of challenging conditions. Some of these obstacles include partial and full occlusion, illumination variations and pose changes as well as deformation and blurring, all of which significantly alter the target's appearance. Recent developments, particularly with the popularization of correlation filters [1–3] and convolutional neural networks (CNN) [4,5], have vastly improved the robustness of these systems. However, most of these approaches do not address the long-term tracking problem in which a tracker must automatically detect whether it has lost track of the target and take remedial actions. Our work attempts to improve the long-term robustness of correlation filter-based trackers against temporary target losses caused by occlusion and motion blur. Although in this work we focus on the Correlation Filter with Convolutional Features algorithm (CF2) [4], a state-of-the art visual tracker, our method is applicable to any other approach that generates a confidence map of the target position at each image frame.

We propose a solution that attempts to preclude bad updates from occurring and gives the tracker a means of recovery from hard occlusions. Using the properties of the response map (see Fig. 1), we generate confidence scores from

© Springer International Publishing AG 2016
G. Bebis et al. (Eds.): ISVC 2016, Part I, LNCS 10072, pp. 125–135, 2016.
DOI: 10.1007/978-3-319-50835-1_12

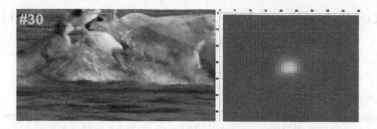

**Fig. 1.** Correlation filter tracker response map from CF2 over the OTB-2015 deer sequence

---

**Algorithm 1.** Proposed long-term tracking algorithm with failure detection

---
　　**Input:** Correlation filter response map
　　**Output:** Tracker state

1: **repeat**
2:　　Compute mean $\mu$ and entropy $s$ from response map according to Eqs. 1 and 2
3:　　Formulate confidence scores $D(\mu)$ and $D(s)$ according to Eqs. 3 and 4
4:　　Evaluate tracker state according to Fig. 3
5:　　Do tracker state operations according to Alg. 2
6: **until** End of video sequence

---

which we discriminate good frames from bad frames and enable or disable the target model update accordingly. We additionally use these confidence scores to readjust the search area within the image. This process is summarized in Algorithm 1. A significant observation that led to this approach was CF2's inability to handle partial occlusions without learning and having to unlearn the occluding object. While CF2 handles the majority of these events well, occlusions of extended duration hamper its performance. In certain circumstances, CF2 learns and begins to track the occluding object. By analyzing the mean and entropy of the response map over time, we were able to detect changes in the target's appearance and surroundings that may harm the tracker's ability. In addition, while CF2 is relatively insensitive to the size of target search area, dynamic variation of this parameter was critical to allow it to recover from temporary occlusions in which the position of the target changes significantly before and after the occlusion. Utilizing these concepts, our tracker is able to detect hard occlusions as well as significant appearance changes caused by motion blur.

## 2　Related Work

Tracking approaches based on correlation filters are often accompanied with modules to detect or mitigate tracker failures. One general approach to failure detection is to explore the consistency among multiple detectors with complementary characteristics. Multiple kernel correlation filters [2] and ensemble methods such as [6] are examples of such approaches applied to correlation filters. Deformable parts model approaches such as [7,8] also fall in this category.

Another effective failure detection mechanism is to analyze the temporal consistency along the target's trajectory. In [9], for example, the trajectory of the target is computed on a forward and on a backward pass, and the error between both trajectories is used to identify incorrect estimates. A similar approach is proposed in [10], where the distributions of a forward and a backward tracker are compared to determine reliable target features. In [11], Cordes et al. use temporal consistency to keep track of image features and improve scene structure reconstruction using bundle adjustment.

Methods that combine these two approaches are also very successful. The Multiple Experts using Entropy Minimization tracker (MEEM) [12] uses samples from several time instants to compute the cumulative confidence level of multiple classifiers and choose one among them to estimate the target position. The MULti-Store Tracker (MUSTer) [13] uses a keypoint-based approach for long term tracking and a correlation filter for short term tracking, and failures are detected according to the level of consistency among both trackers.

Finally, some approaches attempt to recognize abrupt variations in the target model to detect or avoid failures. In [14], the authors attempt to avoid tracking failures caused by motion blur by explicitly modeling the target appearance in the presence of blur of varying magnitudes and along multiple directions. Siena and Kumar [15] detect occlusions by monitoring color variations in the target model. While our approach may be considered to belong to this category, it differs from these methods in that it is the first to utilize the intrinsic characteristics of correlation filters to address tracking challenges.

## 3    Proposed Approach

In this section, we introduce the response map features utilized in our approach as well as the methods employed in the generation of our confidence scores. We also discuss how our proposed method handles target model learning and position update. Finally, we discuss the proposed search area scaling behavior.

### 3.1    Confidence Score Generation

Let $f_i$ be an $N \times M$ matrix representing the response map from the $i$th frame. The mean and the negative entropy of $f_i$ are given by

$$\mu_i = \sum_{x=1}^{N} \sum_{y=1}^{M} f_i^{(x,y)}, \tag{1}$$

$$s_i = \sum_{x=1}^{N} \sum_{y=1}^{M} f_i^{(x,y)} \log \left( f_i^{(x,y)} \right), \tag{2}$$

where $f_i^{(x,y)}$ corresponds to the $y$th element of the $x$th row of $f^i$. We then compute a moving weighted average over the last $N$ frames of the column vector $x_i = [\mu_i, s_i]^T$, which includes the mean and the entropy

$$W(x_i) = \frac{\sum_{i=1}^{N} x_i i}{\sum_{i=1}^{N} i}, \tag{3}$$

where $i$ is the frame number. Note that older frames are represented by lower values of $i$ and more recent frames by higher values. Our confidence score vector $D(x_i) = [D(\mu_i), D(s_i)]^T$ is given by the difference between the current value of $x_i$ and its moving average normalized by the mean of these two values:

$$D(x_i) = \frac{W(x_i) - x_i}{(W(x_i) + x_i)/2} \tag{4}$$

The state of the tracker can then be determined by comparing $D(\mu_i)$ and $D(s_i)$ with threshold values $\mu_t$, $s_{pt}$, $s_{ft}$ as explained in the next section.

### 3.2   Learning and Position Management

Depending on the value of confidence score $D(x_i)$, our method either (i) allows the tracker to operate normally, (ii) disables the target model learning mechanisms, or (iii) prevents the tracker from performing bounding box updates altogether. To do so, we designed a finite state machine that toggles state based upon thresholding confidence values. The finite state machine has three primary states: *Target Found*, *Partial Loss*, and *Full Loss*. In the *Target Found* state, the tracker has a high degree of confidence and it performs its normal operations. In the *Partial Loss* state, the tracker has lost enough confidence to assume that the target is sufficiently altered or occluded to disable learning. In the *Full Loss* state, the tracker has lost a severe amount of confidence, and hence the tracker avoids learning as well as updating the bounding box position. The state transitions conditions are expressed in Fig. 3.

The actions performed by our approach in each state are summarized in Algorithm 2. It is important to note that whenever the finite state machine is not in the *Target Found* state, the weighted averages are and corresponding confidence scores are not updated. Doing so prevents the expected mean and entropy from converging to the new values that the tracker should disregard. An example of our algorithm in action is shown in Fig. 2.

### 3.3   Search Area Scaling Behavior

The magnitude of the confidence score vector $D(x_i)$ is also used to determine the size of the search area $M_i$ at a given frame as follows

$$M_i = m_s \left[ \left( \frac{\sqrt{s_m \mu_m}}{2} \right) D(x_i)^T T \right] + m_o, \tag{5}$$

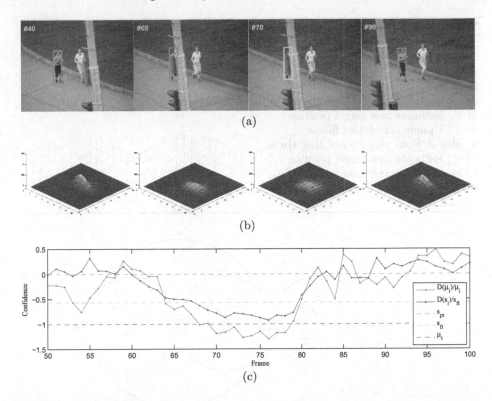

**Fig. 2.** Evolution of the confidence over the OTB-2015 *jogging-1* sequence. In (a), for each frame, a green bounding box shows the *Target Found* state and a yellow bounding box corresponds to a *Partial Loss* state (see Fig. 3 for a description of the states). In (b), the corresponding response maps are given. In (c) the confidence scores $D(\mu_i)$ and $D(s_i)$ are given as well as the corresponding thresholds $\mu_t$, $s_{pt}$, and $s_{ft}$ (Color figure online)

where $T = \left[\mu_t^{-1}, s_{ft}^{-1}\right]$, $\mu_m$ and $s_m$ are normalization constants such that the dot product $0 \leq D(x_i)^T T \leq 1$, and $m_s$ and $m_o$ specify the range of values desired for scaling the search window. That is, $m_o \leq M_i \leq m_o + m_s$. By multiplying the confidence vector by $T$, we make the search window size proportional to $D(\mu_i)/\mu_t$ and $D(s_i)/s_{ft}$. Since both thresholds are negative, the lower the confidence is with respect to its corresponding threshold, the larger the search window size.

## 4    Results

We evaluate our algorithm using two large and well known tracker benchmarks: OTB-2015 [16], and VOT2015 [17]. The OTB-2015 benchmark extends the traditional OTB-2013 benchmark [18] to 100 data sequences that are annotated with 11 attributes which represent challenging aspects of tracking. It benchmarks

**Algorithm 2.** Tracker state evaluation

---

**Input:** Mean weighted average, Entropy weighted average
**Output:** Tracker state

1: **if** State == *Target Found* **then**
2:      Update weighted averages of the mean $\mu$ and entropy $s$
3:      Estimate new target position
4:      Update correlation filters
5: **else if** State == *Partial Loss* **then**
6:      Estimate new target position
7: **else** state = *Full Loss*
8:      Update search area according to Eq. 5
9: **end if**

---

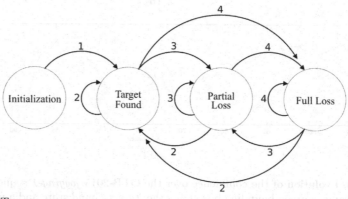

1. Always True
2. $D(\mu) > \mu_t \vee D(s) > s_{pt}$
3. $D(\mu) \leq \mu_t \wedge D(s) \leq s_{pt} \wedge D(s) > s_{ft}$
4. $D(\mu) \leq \mu_t \wedge D(s) \leq s_{pt} \wedge D(s) \leq s_{ft}$

**Fig. 3.** State transition diagram for the tracker. The number next to each arrow corresponds to the transition conditions described in the corresponding item below the figure

trackers against a one-pass evaluation (OPE), a spatial robustness evaluation (SRE), and a temporal robustness evaluation (TRE).[1] The VOT2015 benchmark contains 60 short sequences taken from popular and challenging datasets. Each frame of every sequence is annotated according to 5 attributes.

In OTB-2015, our method outperforms CF2 on a subset of attributes while maintaining reliability in the ones it does not. Improvements are most noticeable in sequences with low resolution and out of view portions. The four attributes in which our method shows improved performance are visualized in Figs. 4 and 5

---

[1] Because of implementation difficulties, our evaluation excludes the *redTeam* sequence and covers only 99 of the original 100 sequences.

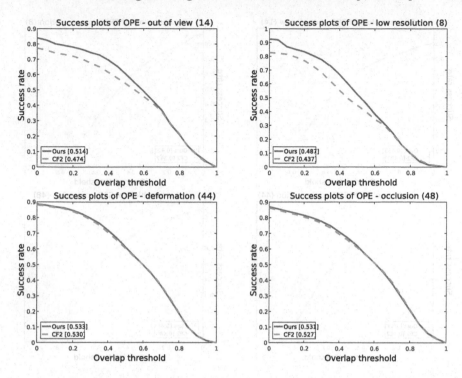

**Fig. 4.** OPE evaluation in the OTB-2015 dataset showing attributes in which our method outperforms the baseline tracker

for the OPE and SRE metrics. The improvement on the TRE metric was negligible (0.21%) and the corresponding graphs are omitted. The corresponding improvements in the overall dataset are modest, however, as sequences marked with low resolution and out of view attributes account for only 8% and 14% respectively of the entire benchmark. As a result, these gains are diluted in the overall results, as shown in Table 1.

We found that in the OTB evaluation, our method improves performance against several tracking challenges without negatively affecting the general performance of the tracker. Specifically, our tracker improves the SRE performance of most sequences and increases the chance that when the tracker loses track of the target, it will successfully recover later in the sequence. This performance gain is best shown in the *Biker, Bird1, Car1, Jogging-2,* and *Freeman1* sequences, where our scaling method helps prevents a target loss. These improvements extend to scenes where a quick occlusion or change in motion moves the target off track or blurs the target. Some of the sequences in which our method generated significant performance improvements are illustrated in Fig. 6.

In the VOT2015 evaluations, both methods perform similarly among most sequences, but our method shows slight reductions in accuracy, robustness, and expected overlap of 0.07, 0.01, and 0.008, respectively. We found,

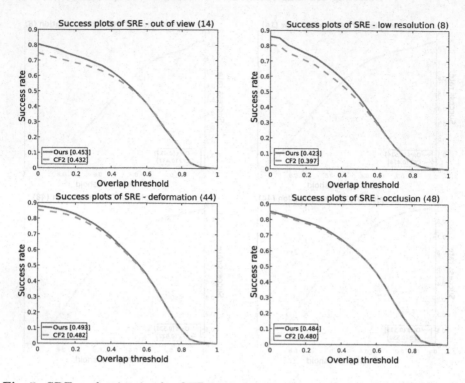

**Fig. 5.** SRE evaluation in the OTB-2015 dataset showing attributes in which our method outperforms the baseline tracker

**Table 1.** Relative overall performance change in the OTB-2015 dataset with respect to the baseline method. The modest gains are caused by the fact that the sequences in which our method shows the greatest performance improvements correspond to a small portion of the overall dataset

|           | OPE (%) | SRE (%) | TRE (%) |
|-----------|---------|---------|---------|
| Precision | 1.6     | 0.56    | 0.13    |
| Success   | 0.36    | 0.39    | -0.17   |

however, that these reductions are sometimes due to the evaluation method used by the VOT2015 testbench, which reinitializes trackers whenever a tracking failure occurs. In some sequences, these reinitializations penalize our method's ability to keep track of a target longer, even if with a lower accuracy. An example of this occurs in the *fish3* sequence where our tracker is able to track the target for the entire duration of the sequence, but with some drift towards the end. The baseline tracker fails early in the sequence and is accurately reinitialized with the ground truth allowing it to achieve a better precision score and essentially penalizing our tracker for not losing track of the target. We provide

**Fig. 6.** Select OTB-2015 sequences where our method significantly outperforms the baseline tracker in SRE and or TRE evaluation: From top to bottom, the sequences are *biker*, *bird1*, and *car1*. CF2 is represented by the green bounding box and our approach by the red one. Other sequences in which our tracker shows substantial performance improvement such as *faceOcc1*, *freeman1*, *jogging-2*, and *twinnings* and not shown here due to space constraints (Color figure online)

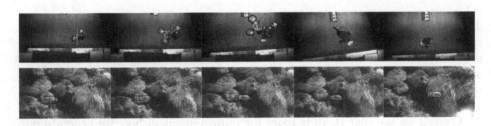

**Fig. 7.** Select VOT2015 sequences where our method outperforms the base tracker. From top to bottom, the sequences are *bmx* and *fish3*. CF2 is represented by the yellow bounding box, our approach by the red bounding box, and the ground truth by the black one (Color figure online)

relevant examples in Fig. 7, which illustrate highlights and instances where the benchmark made it difficult make divisive conclusions.

## 4.1 Failure Cases

In Fig. 8, we provide examples where our tracker performs worse than the baseline tracker. In the *Bolt2* sequence, low confidence scores in the initial frames cause the tracker's search space to grow until it finds a similar object nearby which it ultimately begins to track. For the *Singer1* sequence, a large bounding box, which includes a substantial portion of the background, coupled with

**Fig. 8.** Snapshots of the OTB and VOT sequences in which CF2 outperforms our method: The leftmost and the center sequences are OTB's *bolt2* and *singer1* sequences. CF2 is again the green bounding box and our approach is the red box. The leftmost figure corresponds to the VOT2015 *dinosaur* sequence where CF2 is shown in yellow, our method in red, and the groundtruth in black (Color figure online)

a scale change lowers our method's confidence and consequently causes it to expand its search space. The combination of these features spreads the convolution sampling thin and loses the target. In VOT2015's *dinosaur* sequence, the initial target also includes a significant portion of the background, and its clutter causes large swings in the response map. As a result, our method generates low confidence scores and consequently loses the target.

## 5    Conclusions

This work presents a failure detection module applied to a correlation filter tracker. This module utilizes the mean and entropy of the response map to generate confidence scores, which in turn, are used to scale the search space and control the learning behavior of the base tracker. Our results show that our method improves the base tracker's reliability with respect to blurry motion and abrupt occlusions.

Overall we see that there is room for improvement in how we generate our confidence scores. While the mean and the entropy are good indicators of tracking failures, additional metrics of the spread of the correlation maps, which are more robust to background clutter, are needed to address the issues discussed in Sect. 4.1. One possibility is to additionally weight our metrics by a radial function that makes it less susceptible to background clutter around the target.

## References

1. Chen, Z., Hong, Z., Tao, D.: An experimental survey on correlation filter-based tracking (2015). arXiv preprint arXiv:1509.05520
2. Tang, M., Feng, J.: Multi-kernel correlation filter for visual tracking. In: Proceedings of the IEEE International Conference on Computer Vision, pp. 3038–3046 (2015)
3. Danelljan, M., Hager, G., Shahbaz Khan, F., Felsberg, M.: Learning spatially regularized correlation filters for visual tracking. In: The IEEE International Conference on Computer Vision (ICCV) (2015)

4. Ma, C., Huang, J.B., Yang, X., Yang, M.H.: Hierarchical convolutional features for visual tracking. In: The IEEE International Conference on Computer Vision (ICCV) (2015)
5. Nam, H., Han, B.: Learning multi-domain convolutional neural networks for visual tracking (2015). arXiv preprint arXiv:1510.07945
6. Zhu, G., Wang, J., Lu, H.: Clustering based ensemble correlation tracking. Comput. Vis. Image Underst. (2016)
7. Lukežič, A., Čehovin, L., Kristan, M.: Deformable parts correlation filters for robust visual tracking (2016). arXiv preprint arXiv:1605.03720
8. Akin, O., Erdem, E., Erdem, A., Mikolajczyk, K.: Deformable part-based tracking by coupled global and local correlation filters. J. Vis. Commun. Image Represent. **38**, 763–774 (2016)
9. Kalal, Z., Mikolajczyk, K., Matas, J.: Forward-backward error: automatic detection of tracking failures. In: 2010 20th International Conference on Pattern Recognition (ICPR), pp. 2756–2759. IEEE (2010)
10. Biresaw, T.A., Alvarez, M.S., Regazzoni, C.S.: Online failure detection and correction for bayesian sparse feature-based object tracking. In: 2011 8th IEEE International Conference on Advanced Video and Signal-Based Surveillance (AVSS), pp. 320–324. IEEE (2011)
11. Cordes, K., Müller, O., Rosenhahn, B., Ostermann, J.: Feature trajectory retrieval with application to accurate structure and motion recovery. In: Bebis, G., et al. (eds.) ISVC 2011. LNCS, vol. 6938, pp. 156–167. Springer, Heidelberg (2011). doi:10.1007/978-3-642-24028-7_15
12. Zhang, J., Ma, S., Sclaroff, S.: MEEM: robust tracking via multiple experts using entropy minimization. In: Fleet, D., Pajdla, T., Schiele, B., Tuytelaars, T. (eds.) ECCV 2014. LNCS, vol. 8694, pp. 188–203. Springer, Heidelberg (2014). doi:10.1007/978-3-319-10599-4_13
13. Hong, Z., Chen, Z., Wang, C., Mei, X., Prokhorov, D., Tao, D.: Multi-store tracker (muster): a cognitive psychology inspired approach to object tracking. In: Proceedings of the IEEE Conference on Computer Vision and Pattern Recognition, pp. 749–758 (2015)
14. Wu, Y., Hu, J., Li, F., Cheng, E., Yu, J., Ling, H.: Kernel-based motion-blurred target tracking. In: Bebis, G., et al. (eds.) ISVC 2011. LNCS, vol. 6939, pp. 486–495. Springer, Heidelberg (2011). doi:10.1007/978-3-642-24031-7_49
15. Siena, S., Kumar, B.V.: Detecting occlusion from color information to improve visual tracking. In: 2016 IEEE International Conference on Acoustics, Speech and Signal Processing (ICASSP), pp. 1110–1114. IEEE (2016)
16. Wu, Y., Lim, J., Yang, M.H.: Object tracking benchmark. IEEE Trans. Pattern Anal. Mach. Intell. **37**, 1834–1848 (2015)
17. Kristan, M., Matas, J., Leonardis, A., Felsberg, M., Cehovin, L., Fernandez, G., Vojir, T., Hager, G., Nebehay, G., Pflugfelder, R.: The visual object tracking VOT2015 challenge results. In: Proceedings of the IEEE International Conference on Computer Vision Workshops, pp. 1–23 (2015)
18. Wu, Y., Lim, J., Yang, M.H.: Online object tracking: a benchmark. In: Proceedings of the IEEE Conference on Computer Vision and Pattern Recognition, pp. 2411–2418 (2013)

# Real-Time Multi-object Tracking with Occlusion and Stationary Objects Handling for Conveying Systems

Adel Benamara[1,2]([✉]), Serge Miguet[1,2], and Mihaela Scuturici[1,2]

[1] Université de Lyon, CNRS, Lyon, France
[2] Université Lyon 2, LIRIS, UMR5205, 69676 Lyon, France
{Adel.Benamara,serge.miguet,Mihaela.Scuturici}@univ-lyon2.fr

**Abstract.** Multiple object tracking has a broad range of applications ranging from video surveillance to robotics. In this work, we extend the application field to automated conveying systems. Inspired by tracking methods applied to video surveillance, we follow an on-line tracking-by-detection approach based on background subtraction. The logistics applications turn out to be a challenging scenario for existing methods. This challenge is twofold: First, conveyed objects tend to have a similar appearance, which makes the occlusion handling difficult. Second, they are often stationary, which make them hard to detect with background subtraction techniques. This work aims to improve the occlusion handling by using the order of the conveyed objects. Besides, to handle stationary objects, we propose a feedback loop from tracking to detection. Finally, we provide an evaluation of the proposed method on a real-world video.

## 1 Introduction

Multiple object tracking is a fundamental problem in computer vision; It plays a significant role in many applications, such as video surveillance, robot navigation, human-machine interaction, self-driving cars. Many studies in the recent years focus on tracking pedestrian, cars, bicycles. In this work, we investigate a novel application of multiple object tracking, which is automated conveyor systems. Automated conveyor systems play an important role in many industries, including postal services, packaging, automobile, aeronautics. The purpose of the conveying system is to transport material from one location to another. The controller of the conveying system needs to know the position of the conveyed objects to route them to the right location. Therefore, a robust real-time tracking system is required. Several tracking technologies have been used in the logistics industry, such as photo-electrical sensor network and RFID.

In this work, we follow an on-line tracking-by-detection approach that uses background subtraction techniques for object detection. We address the following problems:

**Complex occlusions management:** Some methods [5,6,9] introduce the notion of group in order to track collectively occluded and occluding objects

© Springer International Publishing AG 2016
G. Bebis et al. (Eds.): ISVC 2016, Part I, LNCS 10072, pp. 136–145, 2016.
DOI: 10.1007/978-3-319-50835-1_13

during occlusions. The model of each member of the group is used at the end of occlusion to achieve correct re-association. In these approaches object re-identification relies on appearance model (color and shape). However, in the logistics scenario, conveyed objects tend to have similar appearance both in color and size (e.g. parcels in the postal application). As a result, these methods fail to recover objects identity. Furthermore, conveyed objects are close to each other, which results in complex group aggregation as depicted in Fig. 1a. We propose to overcome this issue, an association scheme based on the ordering relation defined by conveyor pathways. In other words, we attempt to exploit the fact that conveyed objects travel serially along the conveyor routes.

**Stationary object detection:** This is a known issue of background subtraction methods [3,4]. The absorption of moving objects that become motionless is caused by the adaptation process of background subtraction techniques, where pixels of the stationary objects are progressively included to the background model as shown in Fig. 1b. In particular, in the logistics scenario, this issue has a dramatic effect on the tracking performance since conveyed objects may be stopped for certain periods of time for a routing purpose. In this paper, we propose a feedback loop from tracking to the detection module; the idea is to stop the adaptation process for regions that correspond to stationary objects. An idea was first presented in [8], we extend the original idea to several state-of-the-art background subtraction techniques [1,12], we show significant improvements of tracking results in real video sequence.

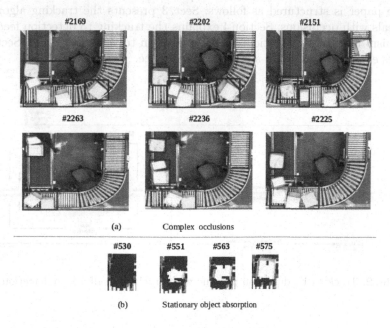

(a)    Complex occlusions

(b)    Stationary object absorption

**Fig. 1.** Examples of the addressed issues.

## 2    Overview of the Method

Figure 2 presents the overview of the pipeline. The proposed algorithm is a tracking-by-detection approach. Therefore, the pipeline is decomposed into two main modules: detection and tracking. The acquisition module grabs frames from the camera sensor and feeds sequentially the tracking pipeline with input frames. The first block of the detection module is background subtraction. This block extracts foreground mask by comparing the input frame to the background model. The morphology block removes noise and fills the holes present in the foreground mask. Erosion is first performed to remove noisy pixels, followed by dilation to fill the holes. Connected pixels are labeled using connected component analysis [11], the output of this block are called blobs (a blob is a set of 8-connected pixels). The blobs are filtered, blobs with small size are discarded. Features are extracted from the set of selected blobs, each blob is represented by its center coordinates, bounding box, and color histogram. The tracking module is decomposed into two blocks. The data association block detects associations between the tracked objects and detected blobs. Complex associations are first detected based on the overlapping criteria between objects and blobs. Blobs and objects who are not involved in a complex association are then matched using the Hungarian algorithm based on their centroid. Depending on the type of detected associations between blobs and objects, the tracking management block creates, suppress, associates, recovers objects after splits or merges objects into groups. The model of associated objects is also updated.

The paper is structured as follows: Sect. 3 presents the tracking algorithm that deals with occlusions. Section 4 explains the tracking to detection feedback mechanism used to stop static objects integration to the background. Section 5 presents extensive results on a real video sequence.

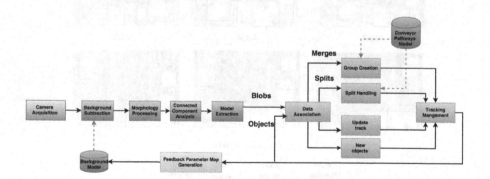

**Fig. 2.** Tracking-by-detection pipeline with tracking feedback to detection.

# 3    Tracking

## 3.1    Data Association

The aim of tracking is to maintain objects identity by resolving at each step the association between tracked and detected objects. In the ideal case, where individual detections are provided for each object in the scene, a greedy one-to-one association scheme would be sufficient to link detections reliably. However, in real situations, individual detection cannot be achieved for partial or total occlusions. Especially when a background subtraction technique is used, where a single pixel may connect two distinct blobs into a merged blob. Therefore, we perform data association in two steps. The first step detects complex situations that may result from merging and splitting blobs or in the presence of occlusions between objects. The second step considers only simple cases where individual objects are visible and can be matched with at most one blob.

## 3.2    Complexe Association

Complex association is based on the following observations:

- A blob $b_j$ with a large bounding box that overlaps simultaneously with smaller bounding box of several objects $M = \{o_1, o_2, ..., o_n\}$, with $n > 1$ corresponding to a **merged blob**.
- An object $o_i$ with a large bounding box that overlaps simultaneously with smaller bounding box of several blobs $S = \{b_1, b_2, ..., b_m\}$, with $m > 1$ corresponding to a **splitting object**.

The above observations are valid when the detection step is fast enough to observe a slow evolution of the objects bounding box (Fig. 3).

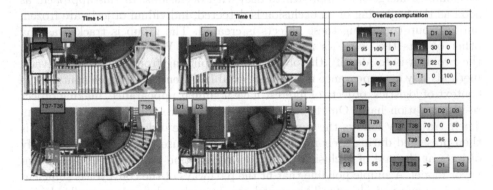

**Fig. 3.** Split and merge detection

## 3.3    Simple Association

For objects (denoted $\mathcal{O}$) and blobs (denoted $\mathcal{B}$) that are not involved in a complex assignment, detected blobs should be assigned to separate and visible objects based on spatial proximity. Hence, we define the cost $\phi_{ij}$ of assigning blob $j$ to object $i$ using the Euclidean distance as

$$\phi_{ij} = \begin{cases} \|b_j^c - o_i^c\| & \text{if } \|b_j^c - o_i^c\| < \tau_{max}, \\ \infty & \text{otherwise} \end{cases} \tag{1}$$

where $b_j^c$ and $o_i^c$ are respectively the centroid of blob $j$ and object $i$, $\tau_{max}$ is a distance threshold used to define the maximum allowed displacement of objects between two successive frames. In order to obtain the optimal assignment, we use Hungarian algorithm [7] for computing the assignment matrix $\mathbf{A}^* = [a_{ij}], a_{ij} \in \{0,1\}$, which minimizes the total assignment cost:

$$\begin{aligned} \mathbf{A}^* = \underset{\mathbf{A}}{\arg\min} \quad & \sum_{i=1}^{|\mathcal{O}|} \sum_{j=1}^{|\mathcal{B}|} a_{ij}\phi_{ij}, \\ \text{s.t.} \quad & \sum_{i=1}^{|\mathcal{O}|} a_{ij} = 1, \ \forall j \in \{1,\dots,|\mathcal{B}|\}, \\ & \sum_{j=1}^{|\mathcal{B}|} a_{ij} = 1, \ \forall i \in \{1,\dots,|\mathcal{O}|\}, \end{aligned} \tag{2}$$

Although the Hungarian algorithm is designed for square matrix ($|\mathcal{O}| = |\mathcal{B}|$), the algorithm can easily be extended for rectangular cost matrix by padding with impossible cost $\infty$.

## 3.4    Occlusion Handling with Ordering

We follow a merge-split approach to deal with occlusions. In this approach, as soon as the beginning of an occlusion is detected, individual objects are frozen, and a group containing these objects is created. The group is tracked as any other objects (i.e. with its model and attributes). When a split is detected, the problem is to identify the object that is splitting from the group. Several methods rely on appearance model to re-establish identities at each split. In the context of logistics, objects of interest have a similar appearance, making object re-identification hard. On the other hand, objects are conveyed in procession. Their trajectory follows the conveyor pathways. The ordering of the objects is then preserved during their routing. We propose to use this order to re-identify objects at the end of occlusion. The ordering relation is derived from the conveyor model. A simple polyline that fit the pathways of the conveyor is sufficient to order conveyed objects. This model can be either defined manually during a configuration step or by clustering objects trajectories in a training phase. Figure 4b illustrates the conveyor model used during the experiments.

In our method when a merge occurs, we maintain the object ordering inside the group using the conveyor model. When the group split into several blobs, we use Algorithm 1 to re-establish objects identity. The algorithm finds the group partition that maximizes the likelihood to the blobs involved in the split such as illustrated in Fig. 4a. Blobs are first sorted using the ordering relation. The algorithm processes the ordered objects and blobs sequentially. Let be $i$ the index of the current object and $j$ the index of the current blob. For each blob $b_j$, the algorithm tries to determine if the blob corresponds to a single object or several grouped objects using the area ratio as a clue. The algorithm constructs a new group $\mathcal{G}_j$ initialized with a single object $o_i$, if the area ratio match with the blob $b_j$, the algorithm moves to the next object and blob. Otherwise, the next objects are added to the candidate group until a match is found. Aside from the sort performed on the blobs, the complexity of the algorithm is $O(max(N, M))$, where $N$ is the number of objects member of the group and $M$ is the number of blobs detected in the split.

---

**Procedure 1.** Association based on order

**Input:** A group of ordered $N$ tracked objects $\mathcal{G} = \{o_1, o_2, \ldots, o_N\}$ that split into $M$ blobs $\mathcal{B} = \{b_1, b_2, \ldots, b_M\}$.

**Output:** Assignments pairs $< \mathcal{G}_j, b_j >$ where $\{\mathcal{G}_1, \ldots, \mathcal{G}_M\}$ is $M$ partition of $\mathcal{G}$.

```
 1: procedure RESOLVE–SPLIT
 2:     Sort(B)                                  ▷ sort the blobs using the ordering relation.
 3:     j = 1
 4:     i = 1
 5:     while i ≤ |G| and j ≤ |B| do
 6:         Gⱼ = {oᵢ}
 7:         while Match(Gⱼ, bⱼ) ≠ true and i + 1 ≤ |G| do
 8:             Gⱼ = Gⱼ ∪ {oᵢ₊₁}
 9:             i = i + 1
10:         end while
11:         j = j + 1
12:         i = i + 1
13:     end while
14: end procedure
15: function Match(Gⱼ, bⱼ)
16:     rGⱼ = area(Gⱼ)/area(G)               ▷ compute the contribution of Gⱼ to group G.
17:     rbⱼ = area(bⱼ)/area(B)               ▷ compute the contribution of bⱼ to blobs set B.
18:     if rGⱼ ≈ rbⱼ then
19:         return true
20:     else
21:         return false
22:     end if
23: end function
```

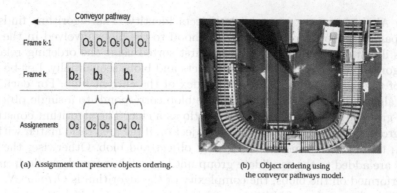

(a) Assignment that preserve objects ordering.    (b)  Object ordering using the conveyor pathways model.

**Fig. 4.** Occlusion handling with ordering

## 4   Feedback Framework

### 4.1   Feedback of the Parameter Map

In this section, we will describe the proposed feedback mechanism. We will first discuss background subtraction technique regarding the strategy they follow to update their background model. The update strategy can follow two schemes blind and conservative [1]. Conservative methods update their background model only with pixels classified as background. These methods can indefinitely detect stationary objects. However, pure conservative update scheme leads to everlasting foreground pixel in the case of misclassification. Conversely, blind methods update the background model with pixels whether they have been classified as background or foreground. These methods are not subject to the deadlock situation. However, blind methods are sensitive to slow moving objects.

We have modified the original methods in order to be able to selectively control the update parameters at pixel level rather than a global level. As shown in Table 1, the Gaussian mixture model (GMM) incorporates pixel samples with the learning rate $\alpha$. We zero out $\alpha$ for stationary objects pixels. ViBe is a conservative method uses a spatial update scheme to incorporate background information. This mechanism can cause the absorption of stationary objects. Therefore, we disable the neighborhood update process for stationary objects pixels. We also adapt the parameter of the method for stationary objects pixels. $\natural_{min}$ is the minimum number of samples of the background model close to the current pixel (the distance in the color space is under $R$), $\phi$ controls the frequency of the update process.

Stationary objects are detected using the speed estimation derived by the Kalman filter associated to each tracked object. An object is considered as stationary when its speed is less than a fixed threshold $v_{sta}$ for $c_{sta}$ successive frames.

**Table 1.** Background subtraction methods and parameters map generation. The $(x, y)$ subscript is left for ViBe in the first row, $M_{stationary}$ is a binary mask generated based on the union of the bounding boxes of objects detected as *Stationary*.

| Methods | Update strategy | Parameters map generation |
|---|---|---|
| ViBe [1] | Conservative | $(R, \natural, \phi) = \begin{cases} (R^{static}, \natural^{static}, \phi^{static}), & \text{if } (x,y) \in M_{static} \\ (R^{bg}, \natural^{bg}, \phi^{bg}), & \text{otherwise} \end{cases}$ |
| GMM [10, 12] | Blind | $\alpha(x, y) = \begin{cases} 0, & \text{if } (x,y) \in M_{static} \\ \alpha^{bg}, & \text{otherwise} \end{cases}$ |

## 5 Evaluation

In this section, we will discuss the evaluation protocol. We describe first the collected sequence and the methodology used to generate the ground truth dataset. We use a smart embedded camera to perform the video acquisition and the performance evaluation. The embedded platform includes a quad processor ARM Cortex-A9 running at 1 GHz with 1 GB of memory. The video was taken with an Omnivision OV5640 at a frame rate of 25 frames per second at VGA resolution $(640 \times 480)$. The video is 4 min and 9 s long (approximately 6231 frames). The annotated sequence contains 5419 frames. We use a dedicated tool for this task. Objects are manually annotated only on some keyframes by defining object's bounding box, the annotation between key frame is obtained by linear interpolation. The camera is mounted above a conveyor with a bird view angle. The camera capture only a portion of the conveyor system. We use 5 parcels in the experiments: 4 yellow boxes with similar color and size and one white rectangular parcel. The objects are circulating on the conveyor system in a loop. 22 objects are annotated in the whole sequence, including a human operator that manipulates a blocked parcel.

We use the CLEARMOT [2] metrics, particularly: the *Multiple Object Tracking Accuracy* (MOTA), *Multiple Object Tracking Precision* (MOTP), *False Positive* (FP), *Missed Object* (Miss), *ID Switch* (IDs). To measure the improvement of each contribution, we run the tracking pipeline with different settings. We execute the pipeline with the proposed tracking-to-detection feedback enabled and disabled for Vibe and GMM. In conjunction with the two possibles occlusion handling methods: ours with order and appearance as a baseline. For occlusion handling with appearance, we use a 2D histogram and quantize the H, V components of HSV color space using 3 and 2 bits respectively.

Quantitative results of our experiments are listed in Table 2. As expected GMM is more sensitive to stationary objects, the feedback loop demonstrates a significant improvement to lower missed objects (i.e. stationary objects). ViBe, on the other hand, is less sensitive to stationary objects due to the conservative update scheme. However, the inhibition of the spatial update mechanism with the feedback loop has also a significant effect in lowering missed objects. We achieve significant improvements with the proposed occlusion handling with ordering relation, we lower both id switches and missed objects in comparison to

**Table 2.** Tracking performance. MOTA (higher is better), MOTP (lower is better), FP false positive (lower is better), Miss (lower is better), IDS id switch (lower is better).

| Occlusion handling | Methods | MOTA [%] | MOTP [px] | FP | MISS | IDS |
|---|---|---|---|---|---|---|
| Appearance | ViBe | 80.4237 | 65.09 | 515 | 2223 | 34 |
| | ViBe + Feedback | 83.5805 | 60.98 | 566 | 1731 | 28 |
| | GMM | 61.9845 | 81.18 | 607 | 4737 | 39 |
| | GMM + Feedback | 84.7811 | 64.86 | 772 | 1357 | 26 |
| Order | ViBe | 86.815 | 67.13 | 742 | 1098 | 27 |
| | ViBe + Feedback | **88.6017** | **56.14** | 1577 | **23** | **14** |
| | GMM | 66.363 | 81.43 | **111** | 4043 | 37 |
| | GMM + Feedback | 82.3517 | 70.31 | 577 | 1897 | 25 |

the appearance method. Indeed, the lowering of id switches is explained by the presence of identical yellow boxes, which makes the appearance method fail to recover their identity reliably. On the other hand, the lowering of missed objects is explained by the ability of our method to handle complex occlusion situations, where a group splits into several smaller groups. In this situation, the appearance method can only handle blobs that correspond to individual objects, the blobs that correspond to more than one objects will not be matched and then generate misses.

## 6   Conclusion

We have proposed a multi-object tracker adapted for conveying systems. We have proposed an occlusion handling method that exploits the ordering of the object to reliably re-establish objects identity in complex occlusion situations. We have also addressed stationary objects detection with by introducing a feedback loop from tracking to detection. Our evaluations on real data demonstrate significant improvements of tracking results in logistics scenario compared to state-of-the-art approach for occlusion handling. In future works, we will extract the ordering relation by learning conveyed objects trajectories rather than relying on manual configuration.

## References

1. Barnich, O., van Droogenbroeck, M.: Vibe: a universal background subtraction algorithm for video sequences. IEEE Trans. Image Process. **20**(6), 1709–1724 (2011)
2. Bernardin, K., Stiefelhagen, R.: Evaluating multiple object tracking performance: the clear mot metrics. EURASIP J. Image Video Process. **2008**(1), 1–10 (2008)
3. Bouwmans, T.: Traditional and recent approaches in background modeling for foreground detection: an overview. Comput. Sci. Rev. **11**, 31–66 (2014)
4. Cuevas, C., Martínez, R., García, N.: Detection of stationary foreground objects: a survey. Comput. Vis. Image Underst. **152**, 41–57 (2016)

5. Di Lascio, R., Foggia, P., Percannella, G., Saggese, A., Vento, M.: A real time algorithm for people tracking using contextual reasoning. Comput. Vis. Image Underst. **117**(8), 892–908 (2013)
6. Dziri, A., Duranton, M., Chapuis, R.: Real-time multiple objects tracking on raspberry-pi-based smart embedded camera. J. Electron. Imaging **25**(4), 041005 (2016)
7. Munkres, J.: Algorithms for the assignment and transportation problems. J. Soc. Ind. Appl. Math. **5**(1), 32–38 (1957)
8. Pnevmatikakis, A., Polymenakos, L.: Kalman tracking with target feedback on adaptive background learning. In: Renals, S., Bengio, S., Fiscus, J.G. (eds.) MLMI 2006. LNCS, vol. 4299, pp. 114–122. Springer, Heidelberg (2006). doi:10.1007/11965152_10
9. Rogez, M., Robinault, L., Tougne, L.: A 3D tracker for ground-moving objects. In: Bebis, G., et al. (eds.) ISVC 2014. LNCS, vol. 8888, pp. 695–705. Springer, Heidelberg (2014). doi:10.1007/978-3-319-14364-4_67
10. Chris Stauffer, W., Grimson, E.L.: Adaptive background mixture models for real-time tracking. In: 1999 IEEE Computer Society Conference on Computer Vision and Pattern Recognition, vol. 2. IEEE (1999)
11. Suzuki, S., et al.: Topological structural analysis of digitized binary images by border following. Comput. Vis. Graph. Image Process. **30**(1), 32–46 (1985)
12. Zivkovic, Z.: Improved adaptive Gaussian mixture model for background subtraction. In: 2004 Proceedings of the 17th International Conference on Pattern Recognition, ICPR 2004, vol. 2, pp. 28–31. IEEE (2004)

# Fast, Deep Detection and Tracking of Birds and Nests

Qiaosong Wang, Christopher Rasmussen[⊠], and Chunbo Song

Department of Computer and Information Sciences,
University of Delaware, Newark, DE, USA
cer@cis.udel.edu

**Abstract.** We present a visual object detector based on a deep convolutional neural network that quickly outputs bounding box hypotheses without a separate proposal generation stage [1]. We modify the network for better performance, specialize it for a robotic application involving "bird" and "nest" categories (including the creation of a new dataset for the latter), and extend it to enforce temporal continuity for tracking. The system exhibits very competitive detection accuracy and speed, as well as robust, high-speed tracking on several difficult sequences.

## 1 Introduction

Visual object detection is a complex task which entails recognizing, localizing, and counting objects within an image. The human ability to rapidly detect natural objects in a scene has long been studied in neuroscience and cognitive psychology [2], but this task is particularly challenging for computers. Until recently, the best-performing detectors for objects such as people and cars used combinations of handcrafted image features such as histograms of oriented gradients [3,4].

Our motivation in this paper is not general object detection, but rather to rapidly and accurately detect and track *birds* and *bird nests* in forest scenes for a environmental robotic application. "Bird" is a category in the well-known PASCAL VOC dataset [5], a widely-used benchmark in visual category classification, detection, and segmentation. However, there is very little previous work on visual bird tracking or bird nest detection: [6] applies morphological analysis to analyze overhead images of poultry, [7] using saliency methods on visible-wavelength and infrared images to find ground nests in agricultural fields, and [8] uses shape analysis to find nests as outliers on power poles adjacent to high-speed rail.

In the last few years, standard detection pipelines have been dramatically outperformed by *deep learning* representations. Deep convolutional neural network (CNN) architectures such as [9,10] are able to generate high-level image representations that are effective for a variety of tasks. However, most CNN-based object detectors operate either in a sliding window fashion [11] or by generating object "proposals" separately [12,13] and then evaluating these hypotheses. These approaches can achieve good results on difficult detection benchmarks,

© Springer International Publishing AG 2016
G. Bebis et al. (Eds.): ISVC 2016, Part I, LNCS 10072, pp. 146–155, 2016.
DOI: 10.1007/978-3-319-50835-1_14

but are typically fairly slow and not well-suited to real-time deployment when compared to very fast and accurate special-purpose detectors (such as for pedestrians [14] and traffic signs [15]) built with other machine learning methods.

**Fig. 1.** Sample bird and nest detections from a test video sequence

More recently, it has been shown that current CNNs have sufficient power to represent geometric information for localizing objects, opening the possibility of building state-of-the-art object detectors that rely exclusively on CNNs free of proposal generation schemes [1,16,17]. In such approaches, the network is trained end-to-end to predict both the appearance and geometric information of an object. At test time, given an input image, the entire network is only evaluated once instead of evaluating at different locations and scales of the image, enabling a large speed-up.

Inspired by these examples, in Sect. 2 we build on the general-purpose "YOLO" detection network [1], which exhibits excellent accuracy and runs at up to 150 Hz by directly outputting detection bounding boxes with confidences. We improve upon the original network by making several modifications, and specialize it by training on only our two classes "bird" and "nest." To this end, we contribution a new dataset for nest detection, described in Sect. 4.1.

The speed of the detector permits it to be integrated into a real-time tracker. One advantage of a deep CNN tracker vs. most standard template-based trackers [18] is "automatic" initialization: because it has an *a priori* class concept, it can find the object(s) itself, and refind it/them if occlusions or mistracking occurs. There has been some recent work on applying deep learning techniques to visual tracking, or so-called "deep tracking" [19–21], but these are still relatively slow. In Sect. 3 we extend the baseline YOLO detector to improve the temporal smoothness of the localization estimate while retaining robustness to object appearance and pose changes.

## 2   Detection

We adapt the 24-layer YOLO network [1] for detection tasks, which we term
$YOLO_{B+N}$("YOLO Birds + Nests"). $YOLO_{B+N}$ has approximately the same
architecture as the GoogLeNet proposed by [10], except that the inception modules are replaced by $1 \times 1$ reduction layers + $3 \times 3$ convolutional layers. The full
network structure is shown in Fig. 2: it takes a raw input image, resizes it to
$448 \times 448$, and outputs the size and location of bounding boxes for all $C$ classes.

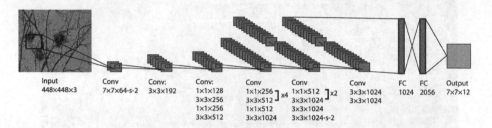

| Input | Conv | Conv: | Conv: | Conv | Conv | Conv | FC | FC | Output |
| 448×448×3 | 7×7×64-s-2 | 3×3×192 | 1×1×128 | 1×1×256 ⎤ | 1×1×512 ⎤ | 3×3×1024 | 1024 | 2056 | 7×7×12 |
| | | | 3×3×256 | 3×3×512 ⎟×4 | 3×3×1024 ⎟×2 | 3×3×1024 | | | |
| | | | 1×1×256 | 1×1×512 ⎦ | 3×3×1024 | | | | |
| | | | 3×3×512 | 3×3×1024 | 3×3×1024-s-2 | | | | |

**Fig. 2.** $YOLO_{B+N}$ detection pipeline (here $S = 7$, $B = 2$, and $C = 2$)

The resized input image is divided into an $S \times S$ grid of cells, each of which
contains information on $B$ hypothetical object bounding boxes. Each bounding
box is parametrized by a 5-D vector $[x, y, w, h, P(Obj)]$, where $P(Obj) = 1$
if the center of any ground-truth object bounding box is inside the cell and
$P(Obj) = 0$ otherwise. Each grid cell also includes a conditional class probability:
$Pr(c \mid Obj)$, where $c \in \{C\}$. Accordingly, the class-specific confidence is given
by: $P(c) = Pr(c \mid Obj)P(Obj)$. For each presented image, the output layer of
the network is an $S \times S \times (B * 5 + C)$ tensor. Non-maximal suppression is used
to remove duplicate detections, followed by thresholding on $P(c)$.

Our modifications are as follows. First, during the training stage, except
the final layer which uses a linear activation function $\phi$, all other layers in
$YOLO_{B+N}$ use *softplus* activation [22]: $\phi_{YOLO_{B+N}}(x) = ln(1 + e^x)$. This gives a
smoother approximation than the leaky activation function in the original implementation in [1]. Second, in [1] a term in the network loss function containing
the square roots of the bounding box width and height is used to address the fact
that small deviations in large boxes should weigh less than in small boxes. We
got better results using normalized coordinates to equally weigh errors between
large and small boxes:

$$\lambda_{coord} \sum_{i=0}^{S^2} \sum_{j=0}^{B} 1_{ij}^{obj} (\frac{w_i - \hat{w}_i}{\hat{w}_i})^2 + (\frac{h_i - \hat{h}_i}{\hat{h}_i})^2 \tag{1}$$

## 3   Tracking

A "naive" $YOLO_{B+N}$ tracker consists of running the detector on each successive
frame independently. As seen in Table 1, this approach surpasses a number of

recent trackers benchmarked in [18]. However, it still misses detections in isolated frames, and the localization is a little noisy, suggesting the introduction of a temporal filter.

We accomplish this by running $YOLO_{B+N}$ and a template-based tracker simultaneously, combining them to create a hybrid detector-tracker which we call **TrackYOLO$_{B+N}$**. For the single-object tracker here, we use the very fast kernelized correlation filter (KCF) [23] (coded as "CSK" in [18]), which maintains a trained linear classifier for all frames since last initialization. The two threads are combined as follows:

- When $YOLO_{B+N}$ first detects an object, KCF is initialized using the highest-probability detected bounding box
- Let $B^t_{YOLO_{B+N}}$ and $B^t_{KCF}$ denote the output bounding boxes at time $t$ of the base detector and the template tracker, respectively, where $B = [x, y, w, h]$
- Let $\Delta(t) = \|B^t_{YOLO_{B+N}} - B^t_{KCF}\|$ be a "disagreement" measure for each frame that $YOLO_{B+N}$ has at least one detection, and define a threshold $\epsilon = 0.5 \times \max(W/S, H/S)$ where $W \times H$ are the image dimensions and $S$ is the YOLO detection grid size
- If $\Delta(t) < \epsilon$, the hybrid tracking solution is a linear combination $B^t_{TrackYOLO_{B+N}} = \lambda_1 B^t_{YOLO_{B+N}} + \lambda_2 B^t_{KCF}$. Else, clear the training buffer of KCF and fall back to the detector $B^t_{TrackYOLO_{B+N}} = B^t_{YOLO_{B+N}}$
- Finally, if $YOLO_{B+N}$ does not detect an object, the template tracker alone is used: $B^t_{TrackYOLO_{B+N}} = B^t_{KCF}$.

## 4   Results

### 4.1   Data Sets

**Bird nests.** We collected 114 images from the web, each containing at least one nest from a variety of species, for a total of 169 nest instances[1]. A wide range of scales were included, from close-ups to very distant views, and image resolutions ranged from $500 \times 333$ pixels to $4000 \times 3000$. Some examples (with results overlaid) can be seen in Fig. 4(a).

**Birds.** We used the *bird* object category from the 2012 PASCAL VOC dataset [5], a widely-used benchmark in visual category classification, detection, and segmentation. VOC 2012 has 20 classes; there are 765 images containing birds in the *trainval* portion of the data, with 1,165 bird instances present. Samples are in Fig. 4(b).

**Tracking.** Neither birds nor nests are in standard tracking benchmarks [18], so we prepared several image sequences from YouTube videos; 3 are presented here. For each, we manually chose ground truth bounding boxes every 10 frames and linearly interpolated them to generate annotations for all frames. The first sequence has 540 frames at $1920 \times 1080$ resolution. It is taken from a ground-based

---

[1] Full nest dataset available here: http://nameless.cis.udel.edu/data/nests.

camera and the dominant motion is a zoom-in on a distant nest. The second sequence has 310 frames at $1280 \times 720$, and is from a drone flying around a tree containing a large bird nest. The third sequence has 564 frames at $854 \times 450$, and is a pan to follow a single bird flapping in front of a complex background. Samples from these sequences can be seen in Fig. 4(c)–(e).

### 4.2   Detection

We set the following parameters for $YOLO_{B+N}$ training: batch size = 64, momentum = 0.6, decay = 0.001, learning rate = 0.0001, iterations = 5,000. For robustness, we perform data perturbation during training via random scaling and translations of up to 30 % of the original image size and random adjustment of the exposure and saturation of the image by up to a factor of 2 in the HSV color space. Our model is pre-trained on the 1000-class ImageNet classification training set [9] and fine-tuned on the VOC 2012 trainval set containing only bird images and half of the nest dataset. For testing, detection threshold on P(c)= 0.2, and the correctness threshold on *Intersection over Union* (IoU) = 0.5.

Results are summarized in Table 1 in terms of mean Average Precision (mAP) [5] and time in seconds to process each image. For a baseline comparison (denoted "ImageNet-CNN"), we used the Caffe reference network [24] with approximately the same architecture as [9] and selective search to generate 4,000 object proposals per image. The network was trained and tested on the nest and bird data separately. mAP on both categories was quite low, and processing time very long. For a more competitive comparison, we refer to the PASCAL VOC 2012 detection task submissions [25]. At the time of submission, the leader using only PASCAL VOC data is "DenseBox", a VGG16-like CNN which performs end-to-end object detection [26]. DenseBox's mAP on the "bird" category is well below ours, and it is fairly slow and thus is not suitable for tracking.

**Table 1.** mAP %, time on detection, tracking datasets

|  | Nest | Bird | Ground nest | UAV nest | Flying bird | s / im |
|---|---|---|---|---|---|---|
| **YOLO$_{B+N}$** | 97.9 | 77.2 | 36.8 | 62.8 | 27.8 | 0.07 |
| ImageNet-CNN | 34.5 | 18.2 |  |  |  | 32.0 |
| DenseBox [26] |  | 28.8 |  |  |  | ≥ 2 |
| YOLO [1] |  | 57.7 |  |  |  | 0.07 |
| ResNet [27] |  | 84.8 |  |  |  | ≥ 2 |
| **TrackYOLO$_{B+N}$** |  |  | 63.8 | 45.6 | 77.4 | 0.07 |
| KCF ("CSK") [23] |  |  | 15.9 | 54.6 | 74.3 | 0.001 |
| CT [28] |  |  | 19.9 | 59.8 | 81.4 | 0.03 |
| SCM [29] |  |  | 17.5 | 6.0 | 75.3 | 9.61 |

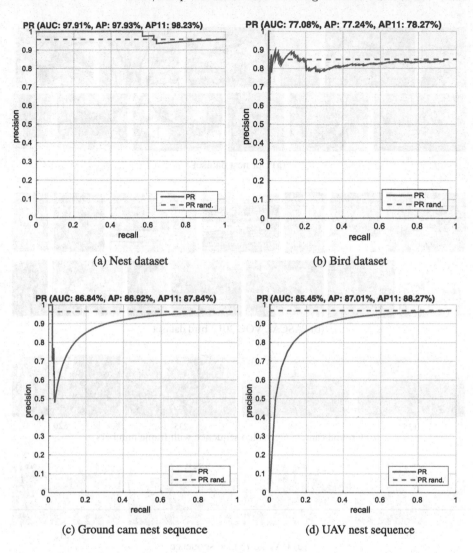

(a) Nest dataset    (b) Bird dataset

(c) Ground cam nest sequence    (d) UAV nest sequence

**Fig. 3.** Quantitative PR-curves for different datasets

When external training data is allowed, the current VOC 2012 detection leader is "ResNet", based on a residual network with a depth of over 100 layers [27]. Its "bird" mAP is the *only* submission higher than that of YOLO$_{B+N}$, but at a cost of considerably more processing time. However, this number is not directly comparable to ours. All of the detectors submitted to [25] are attempting a harder task in that they are trained for $C = 20$ classes rather than $C = 2$ as we do. To capture the difference in difficulty, we note the lower mAP for the original YOLO [1], also using external training data.

We were only able to directly compare ImageNet-CNN to YOLO$_{B+N}$on the "nest" category, but we obtained a higher mAP for it than *any* algorithm on any

(a) Our nest dataset

(b) PASCAL VOC 2012 bird dataset

125                    162                    235                    520
(c) Ground camera nest video sequence with frame numbers

10                     87                     210                    312
(d) UAV nest video sequence

5                      164                    318                    476
(e) Flying bird video sequence

**Fig. 4.** (a–b) Sample detection results of YOLO$_{B+N}$. (c)–(e) Sample tracking results, where blue bounding box is output of hybrid tracker TrackYOLO$_{B+N}$, yellow is naive tracker YOLO$_{B+N}$, and red is KCF [23] alone (initialized manually) (Color figure online)

other category in the VOC dataset. This may be because nests are rigid objects with relatively less appearance variation than other categories.

### 4.3 Tracking

Table 1 also shows tracking results for $YOLO_{B+N}$ and $TrackYOLO_{B+N}$ ($\epsilon = 60$ and $\lambda_1 = \lambda_2 = 0.5$) as compared to several trackers benchmarked in [18] (others were measured, but left out for space reasons). The comparison trackers and $TrackYOLO_{B+N}$ were started on the ground truth bounding box in the first frame, whereas $YOLO_{B+N}$ has to find the object by itself.

In all of the sequences, both YOLO-based trackers found and followed the object throughout the sequence, as seen in Fig. 4(c)–(e). We observe that the ground nest sequence was most difficult for the comparison trackers, most likely because of its extreme scale change. $TrackYOLO_{B+N}$ provided the most improvement on the flying bird sequence, because $YOLO_{B+N}$ did not reliably detect the bird in certain phases of its flapping cycle.

## 5 Conclusion

We have presented a deep CNN system specialized for bird and nest detection and tracking that exhibits excellent accuracy and speed. Current work focuses on incorporating scene context (sky/ground/tree segmentations) into the detection process, bringing more online learning into the tracking process without impacting speed severely, and extending the tracking to multi-object/class scenarios.

## References

1. Redmon, J., Divvala, S., Girshick, R., Farhadi, A.: You only look once: unified, real-time object detection. arXiv preprint arXiv:1506.02640 (2015)
2. Treisman, A., Gelade, G.: A feature-integration theory of attention. Cogn. Psychol. **12**, 97–136 (1980)
3. Dalal, N., Triggs, B.: Histograms of oriented gradients for human detection. In: Computer Vision and Pattern Recognition (CVPR) (2005)
4. Han, F., Shan, Y., Cekander, R., Sawhney, H., Kumar, R.: A twostage approach to people and vehicle detection with hog-based svm. In: Proceedings of the Performance Metrics for Intelligent Systems Workshop (2006)
5. Everingham, M., Van Gool, L., Williams, C., Winn, J., Zisserman, A.: The Pascal visual object classes (voc) challenge. Int. J. Comput. Vis. **88**, 303–338 (2010)
6. Sergeant, D., Boyle, R., Forbes, M.: Computer visual tracking of poultry. Comput. Electron. Agric. **21**, 1–18 (1998)
7. Steen, K., Therkildsen, O., Green, O., Karstoft, H.: Detection of bird nests during mechanical weeding by incremental background modeling and visual saliency. Sensors **15**(3), 5096–5111 (2015)
8. Wu, X., Yuan, P., Peng, Q., Ngo, C., He, J.: Detection of bird nests in overhead catenary system images for high-speed rail. Pattern Recogn. **51**, 242–254 (2016)

9.  Krizhevsky, A., Sutskever, I., Hinton, G.: Imagenet classification with deep convolutional neural networks. In: Advances in Neural Information Processing Systems (NIPS), pp. 1097–1105 (2012)
10. Szegedy, C., Liu, W., Jia, Y., Sermanet, P., Reed, S., Anguelov, D., Erhan, D., Vanhoucke, V., Rabinovich, A.: Going deeper with convolutions. In: Computer Vision and Pattern Recognition (CVPR) (2015)
11. Sermanet, P., Eigen, D., Zhang, X., Mathieu, M., Fergus, R., LeCun, Y.: Overfeat: Integrated recognition, localization and detection using convolutional networks. arXiv preprint arXiv:1312.6229 (2013)
12. Uijlings, J., van de Sande, K., Gevers, T., Smeulders, A.: Selective search for object recognition. Int. J. Comput. Vis. **104**, 154–171 (2013)
13. Zitnick, C.L., Dollár, P.: Edge boxes: locating object proposals from edges. In: Fleet, D., Pajdla, T., Schiele, B., Tuytelaars, T. (eds.) ECCV 2014. LNCS, vol. 8693, pp. 391–405. Springer, Heidelberg (2014). doi:10.1007/978-3-319-10602-1_26
14. Benenson, R., Mathias, M., Timofte, R., Gool, L.V.: Pedestrian detection at 100 frames per second. In: Computer Vision and Pattern Recognition (CVPR) (2012)
15. Mathias, M., Timofte, R., Benenson, R., Gool, L.V.: Traffic sign recognition how far are we from the solution? In: International Joint Conference on Neural Networks (2013)
16. Ren, S., He, K., Girshick, R., Sun, J.: Faster R-CNN: towards real-time object detection with region proposal networks. In: Advances in Neural Information Processing Systems (NIPS), pp. 91–99 (2015)
17. Lenc, K., Vedaldi, A.: R-CNN minus R. arXiv preprint arXiv:1506.06981 (2015)
18. Wu, Y., Lim, J., Yang, M.: Online object tracking: a benchmark. In: Computer Vision and Pattern Recognition (CVPR) (2013)
19. Wang, N., Yeung, D.: Learning a deep compact image representation for visual tracking. In: Advances in Neural Information Processing Systems (NIPS) (2013)
20. Li, H., Li, Y., Porikli, F.: Deeptrack: learning discriminative feature representations by convolutional neural networks for visual tracking. In: British Machine Vision Conference (BMVC) (2014)
21. Wang, L., Ouyang, W., Wang, X., Lu, H.: Visual tracking with fully convolutional networks. In: International Conference on Computer Vision (ICCV) (2015)
22. Dugas, C., Bengio, Y., Bélisle, F., Nadeau, C., Garcia, R.: Incorporating second-order functional knowledge for better option pricing. In: Advances in Neural Information Processing Systems (NIPS), pp. 472–478 (2001)
23. Henriques, J.F., Caseiro, R., Martins, P., Batista, J.: Exploiting the circulant structure of tracking-by-detection with kernels. In: Fitzgibbon, A., Lazebnik, S., Perona, P., Sato, Y., Schmid, C. (eds.) ECCV 2012. LNCS, vol. 7575, pp. 702–715. Springer, Heidelberg (2012). doi:10.1007/978-3-642-33765-9_50
24. Jia, Y., Shelhamer, E., Donahue, J., Karayev, S., Long, J., Girshick, R., Guadarrama, S., Darrell, T.: Caffe: convolutional architecture for fast feature embedding. In: Proceedings of the ACM International Conference on Multimedia, pp. 675–678. ACM (2014)
25. Pascal voc challenge performance evaluation and download server - detection, 31 January 2016. http://host.robots.ox.ac.uk:8080/leaderboard/displaylb.php?challengeid=11&compid=4
26. Huang, L., Yang, Y., Deng, Y., Yu, Y.: Densebox: unifying landmark localization with end to end object detection. arXiv preprint arXiv:1509.04874 (2015)
27. He, K., Zhang, X., Ren, R., Sun, J.: Deep residual learning for image recognition. arXiv preprint arXiv:1512.03385 (2015)

28. Zhang, K., Zhang, L., Yang, M.-H.: Real-time compressive tracking. In: Fitzgibbon, A., Lazebnik, S., Perona, P., Sato, Y., Schmid, C. (eds.) ECCV 2012. LNCS, vol. 7574, pp. 864–877. Springer, Heidelberg (2012). doi:10.1007/978-3-642-33712-3_62
29. Zhong, W., Lu, H., Yang, M.: Robust object tracking via sparsity-based collaborative model. In: Computer Vision and Pattern Recognition (CVPR) (2012)

# Camera Motion Estimation with Known Vertical Direction in Unstructured Environments

Jae-Hean Kim[(⊠)] and Jin Sung Choi

Content Research Division, Electronics and Telecommunication Research Institute,
218, Gajeong-Ro, Yuseongu, Daejeon 305-700, Republic of Korea
{gokjh,jin1025}@etri.re.kr

**Abstract.** We propose a novel approach to solve the problem of relative camera motion estimation with the information of known vertical direction in unstructured environments using the technique of 2D structure from motion (SFM). The information of vertical direction (gravity direction) can transform cameras into the camera of which vertical axis is parallel with the vertical direction. Moreover, feature point measurements can also be transformed into bearing angles and vertical coordinates with respect to this cameras. Then, 2D pose of the camera and 2D positions of point features can be estimated with 2D trifocal tensor method in closed form. After obtaining those estimates, the remained 1D information about camera and point features are estimated easily. The results of the experiments with simulated and real images are presented to demonstrate the feasibility of the proposed method. We also give the comparison between the proposed method and the state-of-the art method.

## 1 Introduction

The problems of solving a relative motion of moving camera in unstructured environments is a major field of computer vision. Robust and accurate solutions have very wide application to the area of AR and robotics. In the field of AR and robotics, computational efficiency is also critical issue. This paper propose a novel approach to solve the problem of relative camera motion estimation with the information of known vertical direction and 2D structure from motion (SFM) technique. We assume that the camera is calibrated. Since the information about vertical direction can reduce the dimension of the relative motion problem, the computational efficiency can be obtained. The remained variables to be estimated are angle of rotation with respect to the vertical direction and translational motion parameters.

There have been many researches to estimate the camera motion in unstructured environments using the prior information of vertical direction [1–4]. The vertical direction can be accurately determined with image measurements or inertial measurement unit (IMU). Vertical vanishing points can be detected by computer vision technique and gives vertical direction in the case of calibrated cameras. Most modern smartphone are equipped with IMU capable of delivering

© Springer International Publishing AG 2016
G. Bebis et al. (Eds.): ISVC 2016, Part I, LNCS 10072, pp. 156–166, 2016.
DOI: 10.1007/978-3-319-50835-1_15

the direction of gravity. Since the gyroscope measurements have drift effect, it is not reasonable to use a full rotation estimation from it for long-term pose estimation. Moreover, the compass sensor gives unreliable measurements. On the other hand, the vertical direction by measuring the gravity vector from the vanishing point or IMU does not have drift and gives relatively reliable estimates.

In this paper, we suggest a novel two-step approach using the prior information of vertical direction. The information of vertical direction can transform cameras into the camera of which y-axis is parallel with the vertical direction. This can be done by changing the normal direction of the image plane to be parallel to the ground plane and obtaining new image measurements by intersecting the ray of feature points and this new image plane. Consequently, the feature point measurements can be transformed into bearing angles and vertical coordinates with respect to this cameras. In this step, the problem can be reduced to 2D SFM problem. Then, 2D poses of the cameras and 2D positions of point features can be estimated with 2D trifocal tensor method in closed form [5]. After obtaining those estimates, the remained 1D information about camera and point features are estimated easily.

The proposed method is closely related to the method suggested in [4]. The formulation of this method is constructed in 3D space directly. The camera motion estimation problems with known vertical direction are formulated as Quadric Eigen Value Problems (QEPs). This formulation leads to increased robustness to image noise compared to the previous works [1]. In the experimental section, we give the comparison between the two methods. We show that the results from the two methods are comparable and that the proposed method is superior to [4] in some cases.

## 2   Transformation to Horizontal Camera

To solve the relative camera motion problem, we first perform the camera transformation. The vertical axis of the transformed camera is aligned with the vertical direction. From now on, we will call this new camera as a *horizontal camera*. The horizontal camera is a virtual camera that has a same origin position with the original camera and a frontal axis parallel with the ground plane (see Fig. 1). If the vertical direction can be represented with normal vector $\mathbf{v}$ with respect to the original camera coordinate system, then the rotation matrix $\mathbf{R_{ho}}$ between the original and horizontal camera can be represented as follows:

$$\mathbf{R_{ho}} = \left[ \mathbf{v} \times (\mathbf{x_o} \times \mathbf{v}) \ \mathbf{v} \ \mathbf{x_o} \times \mathbf{v} \right], \tag{1}$$

where $\mathbf{x_o}$ is the normal vector of the x-axis of the original camera. Equation (1) means that the y-axis of the horizontal camera is parallel to the vertical direction and the x-axis and y-axis of the horizontal camera is parallel to the ground plane. Let $\pi_o$ be the plane that is parallel with the ground plane and

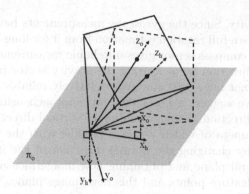

**Fig. 1.** Relation between the original camera (solid line) and the horizontal camera (dotted line). $\pi_o$ is the plane that is parallel with the ground plane and passes through the origin of the original camera.

passes through the origin of the original camera. The direction of the x-axis of the horizontal camera is determined by vertically projecting the x-axis of the original camera to $\pi_o$ as illustrated in Fig. 1.

According to the above definition of the horizontal camera, the image measurements should be transformed with respect to the horizontal camera. Since the camera is calibrated, the optical-ray vector for a feature point with respect to the original camera can be obtained by using inverse of internal camera matrix **K** and image measurement in pixel coordinate. Let this vector be $\mathbf{p}_o$. Then, the corresponding optical-ray vector with respect to the horizontal camera can be computed as follows:

$$\mathbf{p}_h = \mathbf{R_{ho}}^T \mathbf{p}_o. \qquad (2)$$

In the coordinate of horizontal camera, the direction of feature points can be represented with bearing and elevation angles with respect to the ground plane. If we omit the translational motion parameter $t_y$ of horizontal camera related to the up and down direction and the height parameter $Y$ of the feature points, these new cameras can be considered as the cameras having planar motion on the ground plane and the bearing measurements also can be considered as the image measurements of feature points on the ground plane. If we illustrate the new camera pose and the new feature position on the ground plane, the situation can be considered as a bird's-eye view of the original one as in Fig. 2. In this stage, the problem is reduced to 2D SFM problem. If we can first solve the 2D SFM problem, the remained 1D information $t_y$ about camera and the height parameter $Y$ of the feature points can be estimated easily by using the results from 2D SFM.

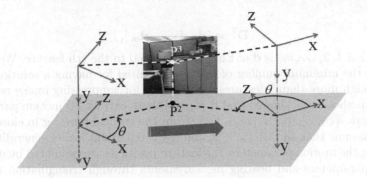

**Fig. 2.** The illustration of the first step of the proposed algorithm. Only the bearing measurements of feature points, $\theta$, are used in 2D SFM problem. The 2D positions of the features, $P^2$, are vertical projections of the 3D positions, $P^3$.

## 3   Closed Form Solution to 2D SFM

We can estimates 2D pose of cameras and 2D positions of point features simultaneously from the bearing only measurement of feature points with 2D trifocal tensor method in closed form.

Two different view positions of a camera are not sufficient to perform the SFM on 2D space. Since two lines on a plane always intersect at one point, two optical rays which correspond to the bearings of a 2D feature point observed at two different positions always satisfy correspondence constraint regardless of the motion parameters of a camera. However, some constraints exist on the motion parameters to satisfy that three optical rays of a feature point observed at three different positions intersect simultaneously. A relation between measured bearings and motion parameters of a camera are constrained by a nonlinear equation. This nonlinear relation can be represented linearly with 2D trifocal tensor $\mathbf{g}$, which is $6 \times 1$ matrix. Assuming that one feature point can be observed at three different positions, we have the following linear system [5]:

$$\mathbf{d}^T \mathbf{g} = 0, \tag{3}$$

where

$$\mathbf{d}^T = [\, \bar{x}_0 \bar{x}_1 \bar{z}_2 + \bar{z}_0 \bar{z}_1 \bar{z}_2, \ \bar{x}_0 \bar{x}_2 \bar{z}_1 + \bar{z}_0 \bar{z}_1 \bar{z}_2, \ \bar{x}_0 \bar{z}_1 \bar{z}_2 + \bar{x}_0 \bar{x}_1 \bar{x}_2,$$
$$\bar{z}_0 \bar{x}_1 \bar{x}_2 + \bar{z}_0 \bar{z}_1 \bar{z}_2, \ \bar{z}_0 \bar{x}_1 \bar{z}_2 + \bar{x}_0 \bar{x}_1 \bar{x}_2, \ \bar{z}_0 \bar{x}_2 \bar{z}_1 + \bar{x}_0 \bar{x}_1 \bar{x}_2 \,], \tag{4}$$

$[\bar{x}_i, \bar{z}_i] = [cos\theta_i, sin\theta_i]$, and $\theta_i$ is the bearing of the feature observed at $i$th position.

If $m$ feature points can be observed in three different positions, by stacking Eq. (3), we have the following linear system to solve:

$$\mathbf{D}\mathbf{g} = 0, \tag{5}$$

where
$$\mathbf{D}^T = [\mathbf{d}_1 \ \mathbf{d}_2 \ \dots \ \mathbf{d}_m], \tag{6}$$

and $\mathbf{d}_j$ $(j = 1, 2, \dots, m)$ is $\mathbf{d}$ of Eq. (4) associated to the $j$th feature. We can see that 5 is the minimum number of features required for having a solution of Eq. (6) although more than 5 features can be used for suppressing image noise.

The method in [5] showed that it is possible to extract 2D motion parameters of a camera, $\{\phi_1, \phi_2, t_{x1}, t_{z1}, t_{x2}, t_{z2}\}$, from the trifocal tensor $\mathbf{g}$ in closed form. We can assume that $\phi_0 = 0$, $t_{x0} = 0$, and $t_{y0} = 0$ without loss of generality. After obtaining the motion parameters, the feature positions are estimated by using the motion parameters and bearing measurements through triangulation method. All these parameters can be further refined by minimizing the angular error for the bearing measurements using Levenberg-Marquardt algorithm initialized with the estimation results obtained so far.

$$\min_{\phi_i, t_{xi}, t_{zi}, \mathbf{P}^{2j}} \sum_{i=0}^{2} \sum_{j=1}^{N} \| \tilde{\theta}_i^j - \hat{\theta}_i^j(\phi_i, t_{xi}, t_{zi}, \mathbf{P}^{2j}) \|^2, \tag{7}$$

where $\tilde{\theta}_i^j$ are the bearings measured from the cameras and $\hat{\theta}_i^j$ are the bearings synthesized with the estimated parameters. $N$ is the number of features. $\mathbf{P}^{2j}$ is the $j$th 2D feature point with respect to the first sensor coordinate system. This process is optional according to the time constraint.

It is also worthwhile noting that this method gives two candidate solutions. However, If the number of sensor position is four, the motion parameters of a camera that satisfy feature correspondences in 2D space are uniquely determined. However, the method proposed in [4] gives 4 candidate solutions.

## 4    Solution to the Remained 1D Parameters

From the method described in the previous section, the horizontal coordinates $\{X, Z\}$ of feature points can be obtained. The rotation matrix $\mathbf{R}$ and the horizontal coordinates $\{t_x, t_z\}$ of translational vectors are also can be determined for the horizontal cameras. The remained parameters are $Y$ of features and $t_y$ of translational vectors. In this section, it is explained how to compute these parameters.

The image measurement for $j$th feature at $i$th camera, $\{x_i^j, y_i^j\}$ can be represented as follows.

$$\begin{bmatrix} x_i^j \\ y_i^j \\ 1 \end{bmatrix} \cong \mathbf{R}_i \begin{bmatrix} X^j \\ Y^j \\ Z^j \end{bmatrix} + \begin{bmatrix} t_{xi} \\ t_{yi} \\ t_{zi} \end{bmatrix}, \tag{8}$$

where '$\cong$' indicates equality up to scale. By taking vector product of the two sides of Eq. (8), two independent homogeneous equations

$$\begin{bmatrix} x_i^j \mathbf{r}_{3i}^T - \mathbf{r}_{1i}^T & -1 & 0 & x_i^j \\ y_i^j \mathbf{r}_{3i}^T - \mathbf{r}_{2i}^T & 0 & -1 & y_i^j \end{bmatrix} \begin{bmatrix} \mathbf{X}^j \\ \mathbf{t}_i \end{bmatrix} = \mathbf{0} \tag{9}$$

are obtained, where $\mathbf{X}^j = \begin{bmatrix} X^j\ Y^j\ Z^j \end{bmatrix}^T$, $\mathbf{t}_i = \begin{bmatrix} t_{xi}\ t_{yi}\ t_{zi} \end{bmatrix}^T$, and $\mathbf{r}^T_{mi}$ means $m$th row of $\mathbf{R}_i$. Then, Eq. (9) can be rewritten as

$$\begin{bmatrix} x_i^j r_{32i} - r_{12i} & 0 \\ y_i^j r_{32i} - r_{22i} & -1 \end{bmatrix} \begin{bmatrix} Y^j \\ t_{yi} \end{bmatrix} = \begin{bmatrix} -(x_i^j \bar{\mathbf{r}}^T_{3i} - \bar{\mathbf{r}}^T_{1i})\bar{\mathbf{X}}^j + t_{xi} - x_i^j t_{zi} \\ -(y_i^j \bar{\mathbf{r}}^T_{3i} - \bar{\mathbf{r}}^T_{2i})\bar{\mathbf{X}}^j - y_i^j t_{zi} \end{bmatrix}, \qquad (10)$$

where $r_{mni}$ means $m \times n$ element of $\mathbf{R}_i$, $\bar{\mathbf{r}}^T_{mi} = \begin{bmatrix} r_{m1i}\ r_{m3i} \end{bmatrix}$, and $\bar{\mathbf{X}} = \begin{bmatrix} X^j\ Z^j \end{bmatrix}^T$. All the equations derived from Eq. (10) for all pairs of $i$th camera and $j$th feature point can be solved linearly to obtain $Y^j$ and $t_{yi}$. Since the world coordinate system can be set to be coincide with the first camera coordinate system without loss of generality, $t_{y0}$ can be set to be zero.

## 5    Simulated Experiment

To verify the feasibility of the algorithm, we performed synthetic experiment since a rigorous ground truth was available, while the relevant parameters were varied systematically. It is very difficult to obtain such a ground truth for real images. We assumed that a camera moved 1 m to side direction while looking at 18 feature points located about 1 m ahead of the camera. The features are distributed inside the volume of 1000 mm × 400 mm × 200 mm rectangular parallelepiped. Simulations were performed with synthetic 3000 × 2000 images, taken by three cameras located at different positions with the following intrinsic parameters: $(f_u, f_v, s, u_0, v_0,) = (3000, 3000, 0, 1500, 1000)$. We simulated the image noise and the noise of vertical direction estimate by adding Gaussian noise. The Gaussian noise of $N(0, n_p[\text{pixel}])$ and $N(0, n_v{}^\circ)$ are added for the measurements of imaged feature positions and vertical directions, respectively.

Figure 3(a) shows an example of camera transformation from original camera pose to horizontal camera pose for the simulated experiment. Overall results are shown in Fig. 3(b), when $(n_p, n_v) = (0.5, 0.25)$. The number of trials was 100 and the results are overlayed on the same coordinate system. Since the results are up to scale, we scaled the results for comparison so that the norm of the estimated translation vector of the last camera is equal to the norm of the ground-truth one. The estimated coordinate system of the first camera is aligned to be coincide with the ground truth.

Figure 4(a) shows the camera position error, when $n_p = \{0.1, \ldots, 0.9\}$ and $n_v = 0.25$. We compared our method with the method proposed in [4]. We refer to this method as *Sweeny*. Since *Sweeny* uses only 2 views, the measurements of the first and the third views are only used. We can see that the proposed method is better when the image noise is about under 0.5 pixels, whereas the method of [4] is stable against image noise. Figure 4(b) shows the camera position error, when $n_p = 0.5$ and $n_v = \{0.1, 0.25, 0.5\}$. It can be seen that the proposed method is stable against vertical direction noise. Although the method of [4] is better when vertical direction noise is about under 0.25°, the propose method gives better results for the noise level over 0.25°. Table 1 shows the error statistics, when $(n_p, n_v) = (0.5, 0.25)$. We can see that the results from the two methods are comparable.

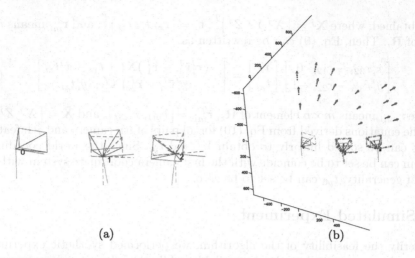

(a)                                                    (b)

**Fig. 3.** The graphical results of the simulated experiments. (a) Example of camera transformation from original camera pose (solid line) to horizontal camera pose (dotted line). (b) Overall simulation results. The number of trials was 100 and the results are overlayed. Pyramids represent the estimated camera pose. 'o' and '·' indicate the ground truth and estimated feature points, respectively.

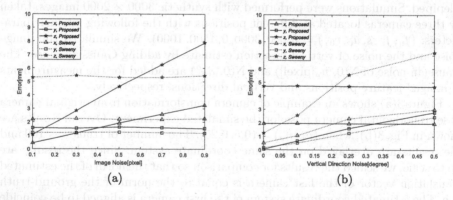

(a)                                                    (b)

**Fig. 4.** Camera position error for the simulated experiments. (a) Error for increasing the image noise, when $n_v = 0.25$. (b) Error for increasing the vertical direction noise, when $n_p = 0.5$.

Next, we performed simulated experiments when the features are distributed inside the volume of 1000 mm × 120 mm × 200 mm rectangular parallelepiped. The feature distribution along vertical direction was narrowed to be 30% relative to the previous experiment.

Figure 5(a) and (b) show the camera position error. Table 2 shows the error statistics, when $(n_p, n_v) = (0.5, 0.25)$. We can see that the performance of the proposed method is not almost changed. However, the performance of the method of [4] is degraded. The reason is that two view positions used in [4] are

**Table 1.** The quantitative evaluation of final camera position in the simulated experiments, when $(n_p, n_v) = (0.5, 0.25)$. $\rho$ represents the angle between truth and estimated rotation axis. $\psi$ represents rotation angle.

| Method | Error | $\rho(°)$ | $\psi(°)$ | $tx$(mm) | $ty$(mm) | $tz$(mm) | $RPE$(pixels) |
|--------|-------|-------|-------|-------|-------|-------|-------|
| Proposed | Mean | 0.188 | 1.316 | 2.087 | 1.555 | 5.019 | 1.629 |
|          | STD  | 0.091 | 0.998 | 1.504 | 1.099 | 3.601 | |
| *Sweeny* | Mean | 0.189 | 0.824 | 2.224 | 1.227 | 5.403 | 1.031 |
|          | STD  | 0.093 | 0.653 | 1.747 | 0.847 | 4.286 | |

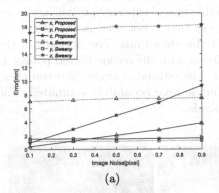 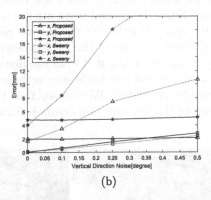

(a)                                    (b)

**Fig. 5.** Camera position error for the simulated experiments. The feature distribution along vertical direction was narrowed to be 30% relative to the previous experiment. (a) Error for increasing the image noise, when $n_v = 0.25$. (b) Error for increasing the vertical direction noise, when $n_p = 0.5$.

**Table 2.** The quantitative evaluation of final camera position with the same environment used in Table 1, but the feature distribution along vertical direction was narrowed to be 30% relative to the previous experiment.

| Method | Error | $\rho(°)$ | $\psi(°)$ | $tx$(mm) | $ty$(mm) | $tz$(mm) | $RPE$(pixels) |
|--------|-------|-------|-------|-------|-------|-------|-------|
| Proposed | Mean | 0.197 | 1.457 | 2.109 | 1.536 | 5.119 | 0.921 |
|          | STD  | 0.097 | 1.280 | 1.784 | 1.261 | 4.386 | |
| *Sweeny* | Mean | 0.197 | 3.085 | 8.382 | 1.201 | 20.337 | 1.112 |
|          | STD  | 0.098 | 2.164 | 5.748 | 0.857 | 14.014 | |

not sufficient to perform 2D SFM as explained in Sect. 3. As the feature distribution along vertical direction become narrow, 3D environment become similar to 2D environment. The results show that the proposed method is superior to the method of [4] in those situations, which can be met often in unstructured environments.

## 6   Real Image Experiment

Two experiments with real images were also performed to test the algorithms. The resolution of the images was 2736 × 1824. The intrinsic parameters of the camera were fixed and calibrated in advance.

Three captured images for the first real experiment are shown in Fig. 6. All line segments in the images were extracted automatically [6]. The vertical vanishing point were extracted using the intersection of the vertical lines extracted on the walls. The feature points were extracted from the intersections of the lines on the walls. Figure 7 shows the reconstructed feature points and the camera poses. Since the ground truth are not available in real experiments, the accuracy of the reconstruction for the known geometry that is not used in the algorithm is a useful measure of the performances of the algorithms. The normals of the two walls were computed from the plane-fitting with the reconstructed points. It was known that two walls were orthogonal. The estimated angles between these normals was 88.85°. We can see that the angle were accurately estimated. The mean of the re-projection errors is 0.234 pixels.

**Fig. 6.** Three captured images for the first real experiment.

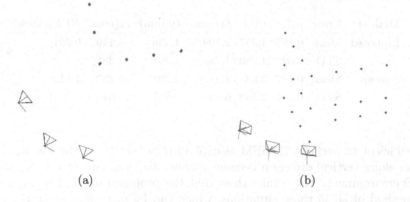

(a)                                    (b)

**Fig. 7.** Reconstructed feature points and camera poses for the first real experiment. (a) Top view. (b) Side view

Three captured images for the second real experiment are shown in Fig. 8. The vertical vanishing point were extracted using the intersection of the vertical lines extracted on the cabinet and the partitions. The feature points were extracted based on the Lucas-Kanade method [7]. Figure 9(a) and (b) show the reconstructed feature points and the camera poses. The mean of the re-projection errors is 0.634 pixels in this experiment. We can observe that the 2D features on the printer and the cabinet, denoted with 'A' and 'B' respectively in Fig. 9(c), are well geometrically reconstructed.

**Fig. 8.** Three captured images for the second real experiment.

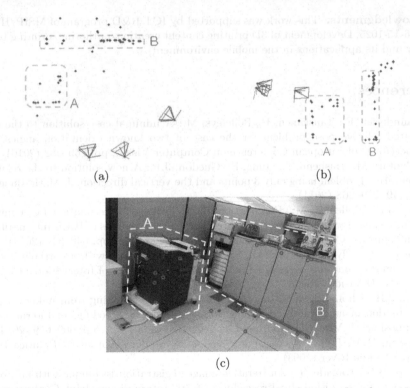

(a)                                          (b)

(c)

**Fig. 9.** Reconstructed feature points and camera poses for the second real experiment. The features on the printer and the cabinet are delineated by 'A' and 'B', respectively. (a) Top view. (b) Side view (c) 2D features (red 'o'). (Color figure online)

# 7　Conclusion

This paper propose a novel approach of solving the relative camera motion problem with the information of known vertical direction which can be obtained from image measurements or IMU sensor. We suggest a two-step approach using 2D SFM technique. The information of vertical direction can transform cameras into the camera of which vertical axis is parallel with the vertical direction. After this transformation, the problem can be reduced to 2D SFM problem. Then, 2D SFM was solved with 2D trifocal tensor method in closed form. After solving 2D SFM, the remained 1D information about camera and point features are estimated.

We presented experimental results with simulated and real images to demonstrate the feasibility of the proposed method. The proposed method was also compared with the state-of-the art technique [4]. We showed that the results from the two methods are comparable. However, the proposed method is more stable against vertical direction noise and superior when the feature distribution along the vertical direction is narrow. Our future research will include performing real experiments with smartphones equipped with an IMU sensor, which can be used to obtain vertical direction.

**Acknowledgments.** This work was supported by ICT R&D program of MSIP/IITP. [R0126-15-1025, Development of 3D printing content creation/authoring/printing technology and its applications in the mobile environment].

# References

1. Fraundorfer, F., Tanskanen, P., Pollefeys, M.: A minimal case solution to the calibrated relative pose problem for the case of two known orientation angles. In: Proceedings of European Conference on Computer Vision, pp. 269–282 (2010)
2. Kalantari, M., Hashemi, A., Jung, F., Guedon, J.P.: A new solution to the relative orientation problem using only 3 points and the vertical direction. J. Math. Imaging Vis. **39**, 259–268 (2011)
3. Lee, G.H., Pollefeys, M., Fraundorfer, F.: Relative pose estimation for a multi-camera system with known vertical direction. In: Proceedings of IEEE International Conference on Computer Vision and Pattern Recognition, pp. 540–547 (2014)
4. Sweeney, C., Flynn, J., Turk, M.: Solving for relative pose with a partially known rotation is a quadratic eigenvalue problem. In: Proceedings of International Conference on 3D Vision, Tokyo, Japan, pp. 483–490 (2014)
5. Kim, J.H., Choi, J.S.: Initial closed-form solution to mapping from unknown planar motion of an omni-directional vision sensor. In: Proceedings of International Symposium on Visual Computing, Las Vegas, Nevada, USA, pp. 609–619 (2014)
6. Forsyth, D.A., Ponce, J.: Computer Vision: A Modern Approach. Prentice Hall, Upper Saddle River (2003)
7. Lucas, B.D., Kanade, T.: An iterative image registration technique with an application to stereo vision. In: Proceedings of 7th International Joint Conference on Artificial Intelligence, Vancouver, British Columbia, pp. 674–679 (1981)

# A Multiple Object Tracking Evaluation Analysis Framework

Dao Huu Hung(✉), Do Anh Tuan, Nguyen Ngoc Khanh, Tran Duc Hien,
and Nguyen Hai Duong

FPT Japan Co. Ltd., 1-7-6-6F Shibakoen Park, Minato, Tokyo 105-0011, Japan
hungdh3@fsoft.com.vn

**Abstract.** Recently, CLEAR and trajectory-based evaluation protocols which generate particular scores such as MOTA and MOTP, etc., are often used in evaluating multiple object tracking (MOT) methods. These scores, indicating how good of tracking methods, seem to be good enough to compare their performances. However, we argue that it is insufficient since failure causes of tracking methods are not discovered. Understanding failure causes will definitely not only help improve their algorithms but also assess merits and demerits of algorithms explicitly. Thus this paper presents Tracking Evaluation Analysis (TEA) by answering the question: "why do tracking failures happen?" TEA comes out as an automatic solution, rather than a conventional way of manually analyzing tracking results, which are notorious for being time-consuming and tedious. In this preliminary version, we demonstrate the validity of TEA by comparing the performances of MOT methods, submitted to MOT 2015 Challenge, tested on TownCentre dataset.

## 1 Introduction

Multiple object tracking (MOT) has become a hot topic in recent years with dedication on two directions. One aims at maturing state-of-the-art methods [1–13]. The other endeavors to create challenge benchmarks and evaluation protocols [14–18] to assess and fairly compare performances. This paper devotes to the latter direction.

In computer vision research, benchmark datasets are critical to future development of methods. PETS2009 benchmark dataset [17] has become a standard in evaluating tracking methods. Since then, various benchmark datasets have been created to assess tracking methods in a variety of aspects, i.e., camera viewpoint, illumination, human density, and occlusion, etc. These datasets include TownCentre [3], Parking Lots [19], TUD Darmstadt [20], TUD Crossing [21], ETH-Person [22], and AFL datasets [23]. Some of them were created naturally by spotting real scenes in real life, or capturing real scenes with simulated activities. Their endeavors in creating and annotating the ground truths play vital roles in inspiring the future development of this field.

© Springer International Publishing AG 2016
G. Bebis et al. (Eds.): ISVC 2016, Part I, LNCS 10072, pp. 167–177, 2016.
DOI: 10.1007/978-3-319-50835-1_16

Along with benchmark creation and ground truth annotation, evaluation protocol is another important issue in evaluating computer vision algorithms. In general, evaluation protocols generate some particular scores, indicating how good of algorithms. These scores facilitate convenient ways of fairly comparing performances of algorithms. In MOT, CLEAR [14] and trajectory-based protocols [15] are commonly adopted in evaluation of state-of-the-art methods. It is noted that most MOT methods are tracking-by-detection paradigm which include a detector to localize objects of interest every frame and a tracker to link them temporally. The combination of these two protocols are used in MOT 2015 Challenge [18] by the following scores, False Positive (FP), False Negative (FN), Precision, Recall, and F.

All above scores characterize accuracy of the detector. It is not trivial to take them into account since detector accuracy has significant influence on tracking results. It is therefore recommended all trackers use same detection results when tested on same benchmark datasets for fair comparison [18].

In addition, the following scores characterize to tracking quality, such as MOT Accuracy (MOTA), MOT Precision (MOTP), False Alarm per Frame (FAF), Mostly Tracked (MT), Mostly Lost (ML), ID Switch (IDS), and Fragment (Frag).

Apparently, both CLEAR and trajectory-based evaluation protocols merely characterize the quality of tracking algorithms by single numbers. The major advantage of this evaluation is to provide a convenient way of comparing algorithms. However, the strengths and weaknesses of algorithms cannot be assessed explicitly since they may be concealed into single numbers such as MOTA and MOTP, etc. The evaluation protocols provide no hint or suggestion for further improvement of tracking algorithms.

Therefore, this paper proposes a method to analyze tracking evaluation results by discovering failure causes of tracking methods automatically. Since MOT methods are tracking-by-detection paradigms, we argue that tracking quality is purely characterized by the capability of maintaining ID temporally, given a fixed set of object detection results. Therefore hereafter, tracking failure causes and ID mismatches are used interchangeably without any confusion. We reveal that tracking failure causes can be characterized by 6 common mismatch categories, (1) receiving ID from a nearby person, (2) receiving ID from a nearby noise, (3) receiving ID from unmatched and existed ID, (4) suddenly receiving newly generated ID, (5) receiving newly generated ID due to not detected for a few frames, and (6) exchanging IDs between two people. In other word, this paper tries to answer the question: "why do tracking failures happen?"

This paper can be considered as a complementary extension of existing protocols which merely generate such above numbers for evaluation and comparison. We argue in this paper that by knowing why id switching events happen, it is straightforward to evaluate and compare performance of MOT methods more explicitly. For example, methods whose tracking failure causes are mostly due to receiving ID from a nearby noise, may use poorer people detectors than other methods. It also provides a direction to further accuracy improvement.

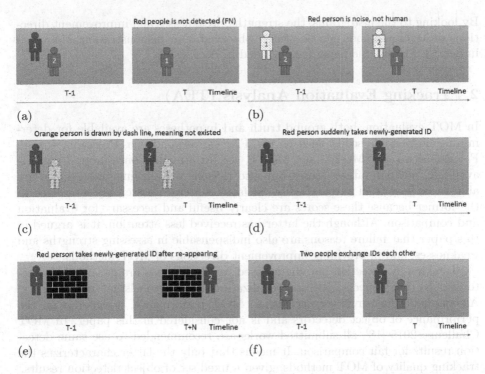

**Fig. 1.** Illustration of 6 common mismatch categories in which (a) Receive ID from a nearby person. (b) Receive ID from a nearby noise, (c) Receive ID from unmatched and existed ID. (d) Suddenly receive newly generated ID, (e) Receive newly generated ID due to not detected for a long time, and (f) Exchange ID between two people. The figure is best view in color.

For instance, a method whose most of tracking failure causes are exchanging IDs among people should focus on improving appearance models and/or motion models. In the future work, we are going to label challenges in some common datasets such as lighting variations, occlusion by human, and occlusion by objects, etc. When such datasets are available, our tracking evaluation analysis will become really valuable in understanding strengths and weaknesses of MOT method more explicitly.

This paper continues to be structured as the following. The Sect. 2 presents Tracking Evaluation Analysis (TEA), the main proposal of our paper by taking all possible causes of id switching events into account. We discuss why above 6 common categories are sufficient to represent common tracking failure causes. We demonstrate the merits of TEA by visualizing the histograms of tracking failure causes of several state-of-the-art methods most of which participated in MOT 2015 challenges, tested on TownCentre dataset (please see Fig. 2).[1]

---

[1] We do not consider all methods in MOT 2015 challenge and only test with Town-Centre dataset, because of space limitation.

By looking to the histograms, the strengths, weaknesses and improvement directions of MOT methods can be clearly observed. Our demonstration is devoted in Sect. 3. Finally, the paper is concluded in Sect. 4.

## 2  Tracking Evaluation Analysis (TEA)

In MOT evaluation, both ground truth and hypotheses are available for determining all possible scores such as FP, FN, Correspondence, Precision, Recall, F, mismatch rates, MOTA, and MOTP, etc. In principle, once ground truth is available, not only above scores but also reasons why having these scores are able to be generated automatically. So far the literature are only interested in the former because these scores are clearly useful and necessary for evaluation and comparison. Although the latter has received less attention, it is argued in this paper that failure reasons are also indispensable in assessing strengths and weaknesses, and in providing improvement directions of MOT methods.

Tracking-by-detection paradigm-based MOT methods are generally characterized by two aspects: position localization and id consistent maintenance. Although the former is very crucial to MOT performance, it depends on the performance of object detectors and is not considered in this paper. In MOT Challenge 2015 [18], all submitted works are recommended to use same detection results for fair comparison. It means that only the latter characterizes the tracking quality of MOT methods, given a fixed set of object detection results.

Common issues in id maintenance include people giving away ids or receiving ids. Answering the following questions, i.e. to whom a person gives away the id or from whom a person receives the new id, is the key to discover tracking failure causes. The latter question seems to be more important than the former one. A person can receive ID either from a nearby person, a noise (False Positive), or from unmatched and existed nearby ID. In MOT, a track (ID) which does not match with any hypothesis in the current frame will be deleted immediately or kept alive for a few frames. In the case of keeping unmatched tracks, hopefully they can match with true hypotheses again in few frames later since people who are not near the image borders cannot suddenly disappear. This strategy is usually employed to deal with short-term occlusion. That is why unmatched and existed ID must be taken into consideration. Moreover, people also can take newly generated ids. The final situation is about two people exchanging their ids. All common mismatch categories are discussed thoroughly in the following.

1. Mismatch category 1: Receiving ID from a nearby person
   Figure 1a shows a typical example of this mismatch category. At frame $T - 1$, two people are detected spatially near each other and assigned ID 1 and 2, respectively. But at frame $T$, only one person is detected and the other is not detected (FN). The detected person takes the id of the person who is not detected.

2. Mismatch category 2: Receiving ID from a nearby noise
   Figure 1b illustrates a typical situation of this mismatch category. At frame
   $T - 1$, one person and one noise source (FP) are spatially near each other.
   In principle, a noise is always assigned id. At frame $T$, the person receives id
   from the noise.[2]
3. Mismatch category 3: Receiving ID from unmatched and existed ID
   In MOT, a strategy of keeping an ID alive for a few frames has been generally adopted, even though the ID is not supported by any hypothesis. This
   strategy results in this kind of mismatch category which is demonstrated in
   Fig. 1c. At frame $T - 1$, a unmatched ID exists near a detected person. At
   frame $T$, the person takes the unmatched ID, instead of the previous id.[3]
4. Mismatch category 4: Suddenly receiving newly generated id
   For some certain reasons, a track suddenly does not match with any hypothesis in the current frame even though its true hypothesis is correctly located
   either near or far from its position in previous frame. As a result, the true
   hypothesis of this track become unmatched and is likely assigned a new id.
   From MOT evaluation viewpoint, the (ground truth) trajectory is suddenly
   fragmented by the newly generated id. This situation may happen due to
   missing-frame phenomena (the true hypothesis in current frame is located a
   little bit far from its position in previous frame), imperfect detection results,
   and sudden illumination changes (position of the true hypothesis in the current frame may be near its position in the previous frame), etc. as depicted
   in Fig. 1d.
5. Mismatch category 5: Receiving newly generated id due to not detected for
   a few frames
   This category is different from the fourth one in terms of the timing of receiving newly generated id. A ground truth trajectory is not explained by any
   hypothesis for a few frames, probably due to occlusion causing FN in $N$
   frames. When the person appears again in the current frame $T + N$, a new
   ID is likely generated. A scenario of this mismatch category is epitomized in
   Fig. 1e.
6. Mismatch category 6: Exchanging ids between two people
   It is very common that two people appear spatially near each other at frame
   $T - 1$ and their ids are exchanged at frame $T$, as shown in Fig. 1f. At the
   first glance, this category seems to be similar to the first one. Exchanging
   ids between two people also means both of them receives ids from a nearby
   person. The difference is that it happens under a condition of having presences
   of two people in the current frame. The first category takes place under a
   condition of observing only one person in the current frame. Therefore, only
   one person receives id from a nearby person. The other id is not supported by
   any hypothesis. We argue that sometimes the first mismatch category might
   not happen if both people were located correctly.

---

[2] It is trivial to consider the person giving id to the noise.
[3] It is also trivial to consider the unmatched track receiving id from a nearby person.

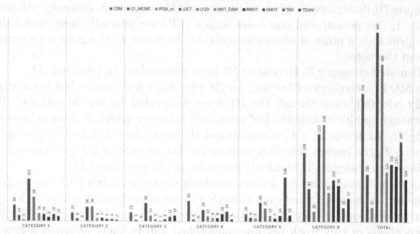

**Fig. 2.** Histogram of mismatch categories of state-of-the-art methods [4–13], tested on TownCentre dataset, whose results are submitted to MOT 2015 Challenge. The tracking results are publicly available in the website of MOT 2015 Challenge. The abbreviations of method names are identical to those in MOT 2015 Challenge. The figure is best view in color.

In summary, common tracking failures are classified into above 6 mismatched categories. As we mentioned in Sect. 1, TEA can be seen as a complementary extension of existing protocols. TEA not only generates scores, but also figures out the tracking failure causes which are visualized as histograms of mismatch categories. By looking at the histograms (please see Fig. 2), we are able to assess strengths and weaknesses of MOT methods and to realize an improvement direction.

Mismatch categories 1 and 2 indicates tracking failures induced by FN and FP, respectively. If the numbers of these mismatch categories are high, quality of detectors should be concerned. Mismatch category 3 are resulted from the tracking failures in previous frames. Mismatch category 4 may imply the existence of missing-frame phenomena, imperfect people detection results, and illumination variations, etc. Mismatch category 5 are mostly relevant to the robustness of MOT methods to occlusion. Finally, mismatch category 6 likely relate to the robustness to id switching among two people. A high number of mismatch category 6 likely indicates poor appearance and motion models or test scenarios containing many very-similar-appearance people. In summary, these mismatch categories are highly relevant to the robustnesses of MOT against various aspects. Statistics of these mismatch categories definitely reveal the strengths, weaknesses, and improvement directions of MOT methods. We will continue to highlight the merits of TEA in the next section.

**Table 1.** Scores generated by TEA when we evaluate tracking results of state-of-the-art methods, [4–13], tested on Town Centre dataset. The abbreviations of method names are identical with those in MOT 2015 Challenge. In the Table, GT is Ground Truths, Hypo is Hypotheses, FP is False Positive, Mis. is Mismatches, Corres. is Correspondence, and Prec. is Precision

| Methods | GT | Hypo | FP | Misses | Mis. | Corres. | MOTP | MOTA | Prec. | Recall | F |
|---------|----|------|----|--------|------|---------|------|------|-------|--------|---|
| CEM | 7145 | 4339 | 1577 | 4386 | 316 | 2762 | 0.5701 | 0.1216 | 0.6365 | 0.3865 | 0.481 |
| CF_MCMC | 7145 | 4336 | 330 | 3139 | 116 | 4006 | 0.6696 | 0.4982 | 0.9238 | 0.5606 | 0.6978 |
| JPDA_m | 7145 | 1845 | 47 | 5347 | 35 | 1798 | 0.6371 | 0.2401 | 0.9745 | 0.2516 | 0.4 |
| LDCT | 7145 | 6418 | 1136 | 1863 | 469 | 5282 | 0.6365 | 0.5146 | 0.8229 | 0.7392 | 0.7788 |
| LP2D | 7145 | 4416 | 811 | 3540 | 389 | 3605 | 0.5861 | 0.3365 | 0.8163 | 0.5045 | 0.6236 |
| MHT_DAM | 7145 | 3685 | 516 | 3976 | 122 | 3169 | 0.6646 | 0.3542 | 0.8599 | 0.4435 | 0.5852 |
| RMOT | 7145 | 2984 | 619 | 4780 | 141 | 2365 | 0.5696 | 0.2246 | 0.7925 | 0.331 | 0.4669 |
| SMOT | 7145 | 2609 | 983 | 5519 | 137 | 1626 | 0.5974 | 0.0708 | 0.6232 | 0.2275 | 0.3334 |
| TBD | 7145 | 2968 | 754 | 4931 | 197 | 2214 | 0.6063 | 0.1767 | 0.7459 | 0.3098 | 0.4378 |
| TDAM | 7145 | 4831 | 1150 | 3464 | 104 | 3681 | 0.6862 | 0.3396 | 0.7619 | 0.5151 | 0.6147 |

# 3    Experiments and Discussions

In this section, we carry out experiments to demonstrate the merits of TEA. Because of space limitation, only 2D tracking results of several state-of-the-art methods [4–13], tested on Town Centre dataset, which were submitted to MOT 2015 Challenge, are used. These tracking results are provided publicly on the website of MOT 2015 Challenge. Even though the original video in Town Centre dataset contains thousands of frames, from which only 450 frames are sampled for testing in MOT 2015 challenges. Our TEA program produces not only scores like existing protocols, as shown in Table 1 but also histograms of mismatch categories in Fig. 2. In addition, a text file containing in details about mismatch categories is also generated along with image evidences as shown in Fig. 3. In the following paragraph, we will discuss about strengths and weaknesses of these methods based on the histograms in Fig. 2.

For mismatch category 1, responses of all methods, except CEM, LDCT, and LP2D, are quite similar. The robustness of these methods to FN which suddenly happen when two people approaching each other should be questioned. They are also quite sensitive to the ids of nearby noise (the second category). The tracking errors accumulated in previous frames have considerable impact on CEM and LDCT. Ground truth trajectories suddenly fragmented by a newly generated id often occur in CEM, LECT, TBD, and SMOT. TBD, LDCT and LP2D seem to deal with long-term occlusion more poorly than the other methods, because of its high numbers of the fifth category. Exchanging ids between people takes place very frequently in all methods, particularly in LP2D, LDCT, and CEM.

In addition to taking methods submitted to MOT 2015 Challenge into consideration, we also obtain the tracking results of three other methods [3, 24, 25],

**Fig. 3.** An example of image evidence generated by TEA. The text in the top-left corner of the image (92-29)→(92-30) means that the ground truth trajectory number 92 gets rid of id of 29 in previous frame to take a newly generated id of 30 because severe occlusion may make a significant change in appearance. The blue rectangle representing ground truth and the yellow one showing hypothesis, enclose the person of interest. (Color figure online)

**Table 2.** Scores generated by TEA of three methods [3,24,25] are tested on TownCentre dataset.

|  | Benfold *et al.* [3] | Zhang *et al.* [24] | Benfold *et al.* [25] |
| --- | --- | --- | --- |
| Ground truths | 71460 | 71460 | 71395 |
| Hypotheses | 68787 | 64517 | 52558 |
| FP | 12326 | 9343 | 4351 |
| FN | 14999 | 16286 | 23188 |
| Mismatches | 317 | 501 | 105 |
| Correspondences | 56461 | 55174 | 48207 |
| MOTP | 0.79 | 0.74 | 0.8 |
| MOTA | 0.61 | 0.63 | 0.61 |
| Precision | 0.82 | 0.85 | 0.91 |
| Recall | 0.79 | 0.77 | 0.67 |
| F | 0.8 | 0.81 | 0.77 |

tested on whole video in Town Centre dataset, which are publicly available on websites of authors. The TEA outputs are described in Table 2, and Fig. 4.

Zhang *et al.* [24] proposed appearance model ensemble, updated online by detector responses. It seems that this idea can tackle well with id-exchanging category of two nearby similar-appearance people. However, Fig. 4 shows that updating templates regularly is not a good solution when the number of sixth category is higher than those of MCMCDA [3] and head feature-based tracking in Kalman filter framework [25]. Its performance against few-frame occlusion or

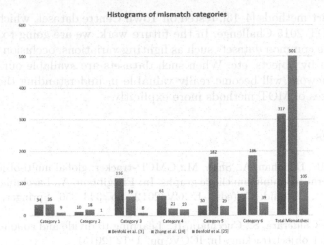

**Fig. 4.** Histograms of mismatch categories of [3, 24, 25], tested on whole video of Town Centre dataset. The figure is best view in color.

mis-detection (the fifth category) is also poorer than [3, 25]. The reason is because MCMCDA performs data association not only spatially but also temporally. However, only scale of detection, location and KLT motion are taken to calculate likelihood function in MCMCDA [3], MCMCDA may confuse current id with nearby unmatched and existed ids and may suddenly receive a new id (categories 3 and 4, respectively). Ensemble appearance models seem to deal with these two mismatch categories better than MCMCDA. Comparing [3, 24] with [25] seems to be subjective, because its number of hypotheses is significantly lower than those of [3, 24]. Many people who are not detected (FN) will affect the tracking performance. That is why it is recommended that MOT methods use same detection results for fair comparison [18]. For the same reason, comparing JPDA_m [6] and SMOT [5] with other methods are also quite subjective (please see Table 1).

## 4   Conclusions

We have presented a tracking evaluation analysis (TEA) for MOT evaluation. Although, TEA can be considered as a complementary extension of existing protocols, our research is driven by the needs of understanding tracking failure causes, which are the key to a better performance comparison and to provision of future improvement directions. Tracking failure causes are characterized by 6 common mismatch categories, receiving ID from a nearby person, receiving ID from a nearby noise, receiving ID from unmatched and existed ID, suddenly receiving newly generated id, receiving newly generated id because of not detected for few frames, and exchanging ids between two people. We have demonstrated the validity of TEA by preliminary experiments with tracking results of state-of-the-art methods [4–13], tested on Town Centre dataset, which were submitted to MOT 2015 Challenge. In the future work, we are going to label challenges in some common datasets such as lighting variations, occlusion by human, and occlusion by objects, etc. When such datasets are available our evaluation analysis framework will become really valuable in understanding the strengths and weaknesses of MOT methods more explicitly.

# References

1. Zamir, A.R., Dehghan, A., Shah, M.: GMCP-tracker: global multi-object tracking using generalized minimum clique graphs. In: Fitzgibbon, A., Lazebnik, S., Perona, P., Sato, Y., Schmid, C. (eds.) ECCV 2012, pp. 343–356. Springer, Heidelberg (2012)
2. Solera, F., Calderara, S., Cucchiara, R.: Learning to divide and conquer for online multi-target object tracking. In: ICCV, pp. 1–12 (2015)
3. Benfold, B., Reid, I.: Stable multi-target tracking in real-time surveillance video. In: CVPR, pp. 3457–3464 (2011)
4. Milan, A., Roth, S., Schindler, K.: Continuous energy minimization for multitarget tracking. PAMI **36**, 58–72 (2014)
5. Dicle, C., Camps, O., Sznaier, M.: The way they move: tracking multiple targets with similar appearance. In: ICCV, pp. 2304–2311 (2013)
6. Hamid Rezatofighi, S., Milan, A., Zhang, Z., Shi, Q., Dick, A., Reid, I.: Joint probabilistic data association revisited. In: ICCV, pp. 3047–3055 (2015)
7. Solera, F., Calderara, S., Cucchiara, R.: Learning to divide and conquer for online multi-target tracking. In: ICCV, pp. 4373–4381 (2015)
8. Kim, C., Li, F., Ciptadi, A., Rehg, J.M.: Multiple hypothesis tracking revisited. In: ICCV, pp. 4696–4704 (2015)
9. Yoon, J.H., Yang, M.H., Lim, J., Yoon, K.J.: Bayesian multi-object tracking using motion context from multiple objects. In: WACV, pp. 33–40 (2015)
10. Geiger, A., Lauer, M., Wojek, C., Stiller, C., Urtasun, R.: 3d traffic scene understanding from movable platforms. PAMI **36**, 1012–1025 (2014)
11. Yang, M., Jia, Y.: Temporal dynamic appearance modeling for online multi-person tracking. arXiv preprint arxiv:1510.02906 (2015)
12. Anonymous: CFMCMC (2015)
13. Leal-Taixé, L.: Linear programming on 2D image coordinates (LP2D) (2015)
14. Bernardin, K., Stiefelhagen, R.: Evaluating multiple object tracking performance: the clear mot metrics. J. Image Video Process. **1**, 1–10 (2008)
15. Li, Y., Huang, C., Nevatia, R.: Learning to associate: hybrid boosted multi-target tracker for crowded scene. In: CVPR, pp. 2953–2960 (2009)
16. Milan, A., Schindler, K., Roth, S.: Challenges of ground truth evaluation of multi-target tracking. In: CVPR, pp. 735–742 (2013)
17. Ferryman, J., Ellis, A.: Pets 2010: dataset and challenge. In: AVSS, pp. 143–150 (2010)
18. Leal-Taixé, L., Milan, A., Reid, I., Roth, S., Schindler, K.: Motchallenge 2015: towards a benchmark for multi-target tracking. arxiv:1504.01942 [cs] (2015)
19. Shu, G., Dehghan, A., Oreifej, O., Hand, E., Shah, M.: Part-based multiple-person tracking with partial occlusion handling. In: CVPR, pp. 1815–1821 (2012)
20. Andriluka, M., Roth, S., Schiele, B.: Monocular 3d pose estimation and tracking by detection. In: CVPR, pp. 623–630 (2010)

21. Andriluka, M., Roth, S., Schiele, B.: People-tracking-by-detection and people-detection-by-tracking. In: CVPR, pp. 1–8 (2008)
22. Ess, A., Leibe, B., Schindler, K., van Gool, L.: A mobile vision system for robust multi-person tracking. In: CVPR (2008)
23. Milan, A., Gade, R., Dick, A., Moeslund, T.B., Reid, I.: Improving global multi-target tracking with local updates. In: Agapito, L., Bronstein, M.M., Rother, C. (eds.) ECCV 2014. LNCS, vol. 8927, pp. 174–190. Springer, Heidelberg (2015). doi:10.1007/978-3-319-16199-0_13
24. Zhang, J., Presti, L.L., Sclaroff, S.: Online multi-person tracking by tracker hierarchy. In: AVSS, pp. 379–385 (2012)
25. Benfold, B., Reid, I.: Guiding visual surveillance by tracking human attention. In: BMVC, pp. 1–11 (2009)

# Segmentation

# Stereo-Image Normalization of Voluminous Objects Improves Textile Defect Recognition

Dirk Siegmund[✉], Arjan Kuijper, and Andreas Braun

Fraunhofer Institute for Computer Graphics Research (IGD),
Fraunhoferstrasse 5, 64283 Darmstadt, Germany
{dirk.siegmund,arjan.kuijper,andreas.braun}@igd.fraunhofer.de

**Abstract.** The visual detection of defects in textiles is an important application in the textile industry. Existing systems require textiles to be spread flat so they appear as 2D surfaces, in order to detect defects. In contrast, we show classification of textiles and textile feature extraction methods, which can be used when textiles are in inhomogeneous, voluminous shape. We present a novel approach on image normalization to be used in stain-defect recognition. The acquired database consist of images of piles of textiles, taken using stereo vision. The results show that a simple classifier using normalized images outperforms other approaches using machine learning in classification accuracy.

## 1 Introduction

Under the influence of increasing environmental awareness and cost reduction, has the use of reusable industry-textiles increased steadily. More than one billion cleaning textiles in Europe get nowadays leased and reused per year. Although, quality assurance of used textiles is still a mostly manually operated task. Compared to humans, automated systems can have several advantages, such as lower costs reliability and constancy. A lower price for cleaning may also encourage more companies to increasingly start using reusable textiles. If applied on clothing it can contribute to fulfill requirements like they exist in case of reflective clothing. Automatic fabric defect detection has therefore become one of the most relevant areas in this domain. Recent work in the field of textile inspection deals with continuous 2D textures. This is reasoned because manufacturer inspect their fabric mostly in production and usually during the furling process. Compared to that, cleaning industries handle textiles individually in an assembly-line workflow. Due to the sowing patterns and the high flow rates of textiles in quality assurance systems, an automatized mechanism has not yet been invented, though. In this paper we thus focus on an inspection of stains in a pile-like arrangement, where every item is dealt with separately on an assembly-line. The uneven surface, varying colors and weaving of different textile fibers are some of the challenges in this task. Textiles differ furthermore in the composition of fibers which includes cotton, linen, polyester or compositions. Most previous research in fabric classification was carried out on un-spread fabrics. The results can therefore be used as a baseline for further investigation. Textiles can show

© Springer International Publishing AG 2016
G. Bebis et al. (Eds.): ISVC 2016, Part I, LNCS 10072, pp. 181–192, 2016.
DOI: 10.1007/978-3-319-50835-1_17

different kinds of defects like stains, bonding, silicon relics, holes, enclosures, dropped stitches, press-offs or other defects as they are defined by the textile industry [1]. Because some textiles may have been washed more than one time, the fiber can also change its color and appearance (see Fig. 5). The voluminous shape, folds, edges and borders are some of the difficulties machine vision need to find a solution for. Especially folds, overlapping borders and ambient occlusion could have an negative impact on correct detection of stain defects using standard methods. The three dimensional (inhomogeneous) shapes of textiles tend to show fibers as nearer or further away. There are furthermore differences in stains between onlaying and absorbed color defects as shown in Fig. 1b and c. Shadows caused by folds and overlapping borders show different gradients but have a certain similarity to stains as shown in Fig. 1a.

**Fig. 1.** (a) Shadow (b) absorbed stain (c) on-laying stain.

In view of addressing the mentioned problems of the voluminous shape, we present in Sect. 3 a stereoscopic normalization approach that is evaluated in a recognition pipeline of stain defects. As we incorporate processing of CMOS-sensor images with depth channel information, shades and fold can be excluded from that texture. This approach is invariant to different fiber-weavings and fulfills the requirements of compatibility with different uniform colored textiles. As major advantage, the computational costs are low. In our experiments in Sect. 4 we implemented and integrated it with several object recognition techniques used in that field. The effectiveness of our method is shown in tests given in Sect. 5.

## 2   Related Work

A lot of research effort was spent on fabric web inspection of spread fabrics, carried out during manufacturing process. Most of them focused on defect detection and classification. Textiles can be categorized into uniform and different kinds of textured materials (uniform, random or patterned) [2]. Mishra et al. [3] distinguishes woven, knitted and dyeing/finishing defects which occur during spooning or weaving. For detection of defects on uniform textured fabrics, three defect-detection techniques exit: statistical, spectral and model-based [4]. Neural Networks (NN) AdaBoost [5] and Support Vector Machines (SVM) [6] are notable machine learning techniques that were used in a number of articles is that field. Some approaches on flat, and spread-out 2D surface achieve success rates in fabric defects detection higher than 90% [4,7,8]. Compared to that, humans achieve detection rates of only 60–75% [9]. Supervised learning strategies achieved a good performance using a counter-propagation NN, trained by a resilient back-propagation algorithm [10]. As several NN suffer from a high sensibility and require a lot of training image samples, we decided to use other machine learning techniques. In the work of Sun and Zhou [11], a threshold segmentation method was used to recognize defects in the fabric. An adoption of image-based features recognized oil stains and holes. The classification of the fabric defects was based on local features and training. In case of un-spread (inhomogeneous) textile classification, Siegmund et al. [12] proposed a textile fiber classification system using LBP-features and local-interest points. They evaluated the use of a pre-selection of image patches in order to reduce computational costs in the textile classification using SVM and AdaBoost. A problem which occurs in fabric classification is shadow, which impairs the classification quality. A normalization technique using color information to classify the physical nature of edges in images was presented in [13]. Parameter-free edge classifier for shadow-geometry can be calculated but hardly differentiates between stains and shadows. Kumar assumed in his work [2] that the image quality is highly affected by the type and level of illumination in industrial textile inspection. A comprehensive study of various lighting schemes for automated visual inspection was carried out in [14]. Their results on elimination of shadow and glare effects using back-lighting influenced the setting of the capturing environment in this work.

## 3   Normalization Approach Using Stereo-Vision

As discussed in the previous sections, competitive methods perform well on homogenous (spreaded-out) fabric, but lack in case of shadows caused by ambient occlusion, which look similar to stains. We propose a novel approach using a disparity map image for finding and normalizing these areas. It contains (1) the calculation of the disparity-map (see Sect. 3.1), (2) the recognition of folds (see Sect. 3.2), (3) the normalization of shadow around folds in these areas (see Sect. 3.3), (4) the definition of the fiber mean color (see Sect. 3.4) and (5) the shadow classification and normalization (see Sect. 3.5).

### 3.1   Calculation of Disparity Maps

A disparity map contains depth information from two dimensional images. Stereo geometric images without radial and tangential distortions on the same camera scan-lines with corresponding epipolar lines were used to create a disparity map. The intrinsic and extrinsic parameters were defined by using a calibration pattern and basic geometrical equations. The disparity $d$ is calculated as follows:

$$d = \frac{f \cdot b}{Z} = |x_1 - x_2| \tag{1}$$

**Fig. 2.** (a) Disparity map (b) background mask.

$x_1$ und $x_2$ are points on the image plane corresponding to a scene point in 3D, $b$ is the baseline (distance) of the cameras, $Z$ is the depth of a point and $f$ is the focal length of the cameras. Equation 1 shows that disparity values are inverse proportional to the depth of a point $Z$. The far points have low disparity and the close points have a high disparity. Furthermore, the disparity is proportional to the baseline $b$. A larger baseline results in a higher disparity. The image resolution used, allowed sufficient accurate disparity measurements. For the calculation of the disparity map, we use the non-parametric rank transform [15] and semi-global matching [15] was also used. These stereo matching methods outperformed local methods in terms of disparity map quality. We used simple median filtering to remove salt-and-pepper noise from the disparity map images.

## 3.2  Fold Recognition

The disparity map and the corresponding rectified image were used in the following process (see Figs. 2a and 5). We segmented the background using the chroma-keying method on the rectified image for masking. The morphological operators erosion and dilation were used to exclude smaller artifacts in the background from the foreground. The foreground and background separating mask was applied on the disparity image.

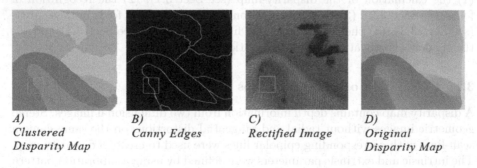

A)                    B)                    C)                    D)
Clustered             Canny Edges           Rectified Image       Original
Disparity Map                                                     Disparity Map

**Fig. 3.** Pipeline showing stain recognition and shadow reduction.

Folds are the only source of shadow in the image but not all folds can be seen as edges on the disparity map image. In deep and wide valley like folds (see Fig. 3C) of piled fabric inparticular, the shadow size is difficult to estimate. Some shadows also occur on fluent gradients along heights (see Fig. 3C). Edge detectors like Canny and Sobel are therefore not sufficient to detect shadow reliably. Other approaches discussed in literature either require a 3D mesh for shadow simulation or are too general to be applied on disparity maps. Instead the following method based on color quantization is proposed to detect shadowed folds in disparity maps. K-means clustering was used to reduce the number of colors in the image. Following the approach of Arthur and Vassilvitskii [16], centroid values were used for each color channel. These were applied to all pixels of a reshaped image array of $M \times 3$ size ($M = \#$ of pixels). After reshaping it back to the shape of the original image, that resulting image had a specified number of colors.

Experiments showed that the transitions of five colors within the defined range of false-colors (and their corresponding disparities) are highlighting edges with folds more accurately than by applying common edge detectors. To identify transitions that do not result in shadows:

(a) Their corresponding color in the rectified image was compared to the most common color of the textile (which is assumed to be not a defect) using the invariant color model c1c2c3 [17] which has shown good results in shadow identification [18].
(b) The difference in altitude within a certain region along a transition was defined and used for thresholding.

## 3.3 Normalization of Shadow Around Folds

The clustered disparity map $A$ (see Fig. 3A) is used to detect edges by applying the Canny edge detector on the color clustered disparity map. Borders in the resulting binary image $B$ (see Fig. 3B) have a line width of 1 pixel. The outer contour edge of the textile was removed from $B$ by calculating and subtracting the bit-wise conjunction of the inverted background mask (see Fig. 2b). Image $B$ containing the remaining edges of the disparity map was used as indicator of folds two times:

(a) To define the mean color of the fiber by using $B$ in pre-processing.
(b) To verify if regions along folds show shadow.

## 3.4 Definition of the Fiber Mean Color

For the definition of the mean fiber color representative, areas of the image need to be found and analyzed. Shadow and other defects interfere with the calculation of the mean fiber color. To reduce the negative impact of these, edges in the disparity map were used to exclude these areas extensively. Morphological operator dilate with a rectangle as structuring element and a factor of 12 was used to broaden the line in the binary image (see Fig. 3B). The pixels with positive color values in $B$ were removed in the corresponding rectified image (see Fig. 3C) by using inverted bit-wise conjunction (bit-wise and) between $B$ and the rectified image. Thus, the resulting image does not contain any edges. Then on that image k-mean color quantization was used to define the color which pccured most often $\delta$. It is assumed that the color value $\delta$ is the non defect color of the fabric.

## 3.5   Shadow Classification

In order to verify if regions along folds show shadow, image $B$ gets transformed into a vector of coordinates using topological structure analysis. By following the coordinates of the lines stepwise, square bounding boxes representing the region of interest $r$ (see Fig. 3A–C) with side length of $l$ were created using the line coordinate as the centerpoint. The coordinates of the line within $r$ were stored in a vector $v$.

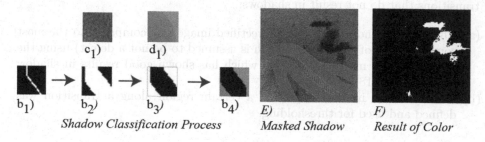

Shadow Classification Process    Masked Shadow    Result of Color

**Fig. 4.** E: Result of shadow-normalization, F: Result of color-range threshold, $b_1$–$b_4$: Pipeline to verify that a ROI shows a certain amount of depth and darkness in order to classify it as shadow.

The line coordinates $v$ were then used to extract Image $c_1$ from the rectified image (see Fig. 4$c_1$). The color $\alpha$ of the image $c_1$ was compared with the previously calculated color $\delta$ that occurred most often in the image. The deviation between the two colors needed to be higher than a threshold $\theta$ in order to classify $C_1$ a shadow.

$$\alpha < (\delta + \theta) \tag{2}$$

The difference in altitude within the region of interest $r$ of the fabric is a second requirement for shadow. The corresponding regions of $r$ were extracted from $B$ into a new matrice $b_1$ (see Fig. 4$b_1$). On this resulting binary image, the morphological operation dilation with a rectangle as a structure element and a factor of 3 was applied (see Fig. 4$b_2$). Then the image was inverted bit-wise so that two areas with positive binary values arose (illustrated in white color shown in Fig. 4$b_3$). These two areas represent both sides across a fold. The coordinates of the two areas of binary value 1 were now individually stored as vectors $a_1$ and $a_2$. The inverted edge mask image $b_3$ was then applied via the 'bitwise-and' operation on the corresponding region in the unclustered disparity map (see Fig. 4d$_1$). The difference between the mean color value of $a_1$ and $a_2$ $\eta$ (using the H channel of the HSV color space) represent the difference in altitude between both sides across the edge (see Fig. 4b$_4$).

$$\left\| \sum_i a_1 - \sum_i a_2 \right\| < \eta \tag{3}$$

Experiments showed that $\eta$ higher than 10 is adequate. In order to threshold stain defects in the rectified image, image $C$ was converted to gray-scale. The morphological operator dilate with a rectangle as structuring element and a factor of 12 were used to stretch the positive values in the binary image $B$. Positive values were then replaced by the mean color $\alpha$ and used as mask on image $C$ where pixel color values of $B$ are $\neq 0$ (see Fig. 4E).

## 4  Experiments

We tested our novel approach on an image database of woven cotton textiles and evaluated through our database with methods used in the state of the art.

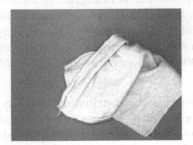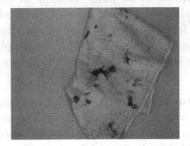

**Fig. 5.** (a) Textile after first washing (b) used textile with stains.

### 4.1  Capturing Environment and Database

In the image acquisition a whitebox with homogeneous illumination was used to guarantee a controlled image capturing process with reduced formation of shades. For image recording, two synchronized CMOS color cameras with a CMOS $1/1.8''$ sensor and a resolution of $1280 \times 1003$ pixels were used. The database contains $2 \times 606$ images of 174 different textiles with and without varying defects. Non-overlapping patches of images were used to reduce the complexity of the analyzed pattern.

These textile patterns contained different characteristics such as holes and stains and texture properties like: shadows, different kinds of edges, cuts, open ends, folds etc. The examined textiles were in clean and dry, but used condition, therefore fibers show different levels of brightness (see Fig. 5). Patches belonging to the background were rejected using their entropy value. Every patch was labeled manually by assigning them to the class 'stain' or 'other'. Images were captured from a top-view perspective, therefore, some stains might be hidden (e.g. if they are in a fold or on the bottom side). Iterations in which the textile is physically moved into a different position and then classified again could solve this problem.

## 4.2    Feature Extraction

Following features were used in the evaluation of the described application:

**LBP.** Local binary Patterns (LBP) features have shown their performance in previous work dealing with textile fiber classification tasks [12].

The used LBP type [19] is invariant against rotation and gray-scale and shows a relationship between pixel and its surrounding. It fulfills the requirements in aspects of computational costs compared to other scale-invariant LBP variants [20]. Experiments on a subset of the database showed that a radius of 3 and a block size of 32 pixels is ideal for the used database. A histogram of rotation-invariant binary patterns for blocks of 32 pixels was calculated and concatenated to a feature vector. To reduce the dimensionality of the feature vector, Principal Component Analysis (PCA) was applied to a subset of the data set. Experiments have shown that reducing the data set to 300components gives the best results.

**Color Histogram.** A color histogram represents the distribution of colors in an image. The optimal discretization of the colors into bins was calculated iteratively and evaluated with 4-fold cross validation. A histogram was calculated on the HSV color model for every channel and then concatenated with each other. The evaluation showed that the usage of 130 bins gives the best results for the data-set used.

**LBP+Color Histogram.** The histogram was calculated using 130 bins for each HSV channel, concatenated with each other and the LBP features vector.

**SIFT/SURF Bag of Words.** The local interest point descriptors SIFT and SURF [21] have shown in many applications their effectiveness as local feature detectors and descriptors for non-rigid 3D objects [22]. They are scale-invariant and robust against rotation, translation and changing lighting conditions. A set of interest points was extracted following the Bag of Words (BOW) approach of Siegmund et al. [12].

**SIFT/SURF BOW+Color Histogram.** As local interest points do not include any color information, a color histogram using 130 bins was computed and concatenated to the SIFT/SURF feature vector.

**Color Threshold.** Since stains defects on the given textiles contain other color than the fabric mean color, a simple binary threshold approach using a threshold on the gray-scale color value of each pixel was used. The amount of black pixels in each patch classifies them, instead of a machine learning classifier.

### 4.3   Classification

In the experiments using machine-learning, SVM and AdaBoost performed best among the classifiers: SVM, Random Forrest, AdaBoost and JRIP. Therefore, SVM with the SMO (Sequential Minimal Optimization) extension and AdaBoost were chosen in the experiments as classifiers. The SVM parameters were defined using a model, choosing the optimal parameters C, gamma, p, nu,

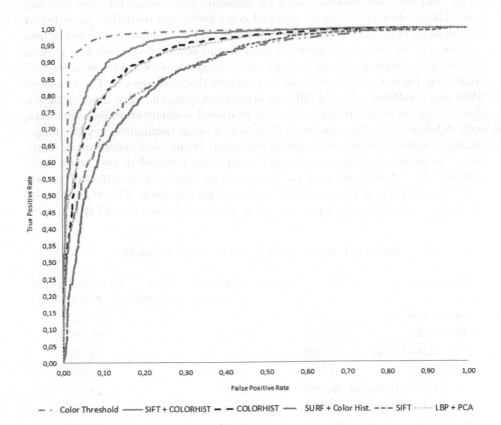

**Fig. 6.** ROC-curve showing results of classification with normalization and AdaBoost classifier.

coef0 and degree with cross-validation. The REAL boosting method was chosen for AdaBoost which utilizes confidence-rated predictions and was expected to work well with the categorical feature vectors. All features and classifiers were evaluated with-and without use of the proposed shadow normalization method. In the color threshold approach, a color range around the mean-color: $\alpha$ was specified to define the texture color. Pixels with a gray-scale color value higher or lower than the range where considered to be defects (see Fig. 4F).

## 5   Results

As shown in Table 1, almost random classification results were archived using LBP features with SVM and AdaBoost. This approach showed poor performance when distinguishing between stain characteristics and others regular texture properties like folds and shadow. In the feature extraction process of the LBP approach the selection of an adequate radius is furthermore error-prone, as the selection is very sensitive to the image quality. The local interest points SURF and SIFT are rotation and scale invariant but contain no color information. The combination with a extracted color-histogram tended to show better results in all approaches. The results indicate that local interest points features are not able to distinguish between shadow and stain defects (see Fig. 1). The results of the approach using a simple color-range threshold via gray-scale conversion on the not-normalized textiles confirms that assumption. The classifiers SVM and AdaBoost achieved different error-rates using the same input data. For the calculation of the results using the proposed normalization as input data, only AdaBoost training was used. The scores using normalized textile images as in-put showed better results for all examined feature and classification methods. The approach using color-range thresholding resulted in the lowest error rate of 5.68%. A proportion of positives that are correctly identified of 95,28% (TPR) and a FPR of 4% were achieved using this approach. The ROC (Receiving Operator Characteristic) curve in Fig. 6 shows the metrics TPR and FPR

**Table 1.** Equal error rates in stain defect recognition.

| Methodology | SVM w/o norm. | AdaBoost w/o norm. | Color      Th w/o norm. | Classification with norm. |
|---|---|---|---|---|
| Color histogram | 40.15% | 15.77% | - | 13.54% |
| LBP+PCA | 39.51% | 30.54% | - | 28.14% |
| LBP+PCA+ColorHist | 37.14% | 19.68% | - | 15.05% |
| SURF BOW | 32.56% | 20.11% | - | 25.32% |
| SURF BOW+ColorHist | 40.02% | 16.15% | - | 20.91% |
| SIFT BOW | 28.56% | 18.35% | - | 20.46% |
| SIFT BOW+ColorHist | 35.36% | 15.03% | - | 10.90% |
| Full image | - | - | 18.74% | 5.68% |

in relation to the threshold using the presented normalization technique and AdaBoost classifier. All approaches were evaluated using 4-fold cross validation. The Equal Error Rates (EER) per approach were defined by calculating the mean of all individual classifiers EERs.

# 6 Conclusion

We presented a novel approach for normalization of textiles arranged in piles, towards their classification regarding stain defects. Competitive approaches deployed on flat, and spread-out 2D textile surfaces were selected for an evaluation of this novel computer-vision application. The new database shows textiles in a pile-like arrangement, recorded with a stereo vision camera setup. For detection of stains in the textiles, machine learning as well as a color-range thresholding classifiers were used. We showed that all evaluated features have disadvantages when distinguishing between defect characteristics and regular textures of textiles arranged in piles. The presented normalization methods resulted in better classification results for all examined feature types. Nevertheless, best results were achieved using a simple color-range threshold on the normalized fabrics. We described underlying assumption in Sects. 3 and 5 and proved their relevance towards a robust classification of voluminous textiles. The novel approach uses stereo vision images to mask out image areas folds or shadow and will be evaluated in the classification of other inhomogeneous objects in future work.

# References

1. Hong Kong Productivity Council: Textile Handbook 2000. The Hong Kong Cotton Spinners Association (2000)
2. Kumar, A.: Computer-vision-based fabric defect detection: a survey. IEEE Trans. Ind. Electron. **55**, 348–363 (2008)
3. Mishra, D.: A survey-defect detection and classification for fabric texture defects in textile industry. Int. J. Comput. Sci. Inf. Secur. **13**, 48 (2015)
4. Ngan, H.Y., Pang, G.K., Yung, N.H.: Automated fabric defect detection–a review. Image Vision Comput. **29**, 442–458 (2011)
5. Borghese, N.A., Fomasi, M.: Automatic defect classification on a production line. Intell. Ind. Syst. **1**, 373–393 (2015)
6. Murino, V., Bicego, M., Rossi, I.A.: Statistical classification of raw textile defects. In: ICPR 2004, pp. 311–314 (2004)
7. Rebhi, A., Benmhammed, I., Abid, S., Fnaiech, F.: Fabric defect detection using local homogeneity analysis and neural network. J. Photonics **2015** (2015)
8. Abou-Taleb, H.A., Sallam, A.T.M.: On-line fabric defect detection and full control in a circular knitting machine. AUTEX Res. J. **8**, 21–29 (2008)
9. Schicktanz, K.: Automatic fault detection possibilities on nonwoven fabrics. Melliand Textilberichte **74**, 294–295 (1993)
10. Islam, M.A., Akhter, S., Mursalin, T.E., Amin, M.A.: A suitable neural network to detect textile defects. In: ICONIP 2006, pp. 430–438. Springer, Heidelberg (2006)

11. Sun, J., Zhou, Z.: Fabric defect detection based on computer vision. In: Deng, H., Miao, D., Lei, J., Wang, F.L. (eds.) AICI 2011. LNCS, vol. 7004, pp. 86–91. Springer, Heidelberg (2011). doi:10.1007/978-3-642-23896-3_11

12. Siegmund, D., Kaehm, O., Handtke, D.: Rapid classification of textile fabrics arranged in piles. In: Proceedings of the 13th International Conference on Signal Processing and Multimedia Applications, SIGMAP 2016, Lisbon, Portugal, 26–28 July 2016. SciTePress (2016)

13. Gevers, T., Stokman, H.: Classifying color edges in video into shadow-geometry, highlight, or material transitions. IEEE Trans. Multimedia 5, 237–243 (2003)

14. Batchelor, B.G.: Lighting and viewing techniques. In: Automated Visual Inspection (1985)

15. Hirschmüller, H.: Accurate and efficient stereo processing by semi-global matching and mutual information. In: IEEE Computer Society Conference on Computer Vision and Pattern Recognition, CVPR 2005. vol. 2, pp. 807–814. IEEE (2005)

16. Arthur, D., Vassilvitskii, S.: k-means++: the advantages of careful seeding. In: Proceedings of the Eighteenth Annual ACM-SIAM Symposium on Discrete Algorithms, pp. 1027–1035. Society for Industrial and Applied Mathematics (2007)

17. Gevers, T., Smeulders, A.W.: Color-based object recognition. Pattern Recogn. 32, 453–464 (1999)

18. Salvador, E., Cavallaro, A., Ebrahimi, T.: Shadow identification and classification using invariant color models. In: Proceedings of 2001 IEEE International Conference on Acoustics, Speech, and Signal Processing (ICASSP 2001), vol. 3, pp. 1545–1548. IEEE (2001)

19. Zhao, G., Pietikäinen, M.: Improving rotation invariance of the volume local binary pattern operator. In: MVA, pp. 327–330 (2007)

20. Li, Z., Liu, G., Yang, Y., You, J.: Scale- and rotation-invariant local binary pattern using scale-adaptive texton and subuniform-based circular shift. IEEE Trans. Image Process. 21, 2130–2140 (2012)

21. Bay, H., Tuytelaars, T., Gool, L.: SURF: Speeded Up Robust Features. In: Leonardis, A., Bischof, H., Pinz, A. (eds.) ECCV 2006. LNCS, vol. 3951, pp. 404–417. Springer, Heidelberg (2006). doi:10.1007/11744023_32

22. Zeng, K., Wu, N., Wang, L., Yen, K.K.: Local visual feature detection and description for non-rigid 3d objects. Adv. Image Video Process. 4, 01 (2016)

# Reliability-Based Local Features Aggregation
# for Image Segmentation

Fariba Zohrizadeh[✉], Mohsen Kheirandishfard, Kamran Ghasedidizaji,
and Farhad Kamangar

Department of Computer Science and Engineering,
University of Texas at Arlington, Arlington, TX, USA
fariba.zohrizadeh@uta.edu

**Abstract.** Local features are used for describing the visual information
in a local neighborhood of image pixels. Although using various types
of local features can provide complementary information about the pixels, effective integration of these features has remained as a challenging
issue. In this paper, we propose a novel segmentation algorithm which
aggregates the information obtained from different local features. Starting with an over-segmentation of the input image, local features are fed
into a factorization-based framework to construct multiple new representations. We then introduce a novel aggregation model to integrate
the new representations. Our proposed model jointly learns the reliability of representations and infers final representation. Final segmentation
is obtained by applying post-processing steps on the inferred final representation. Experimental results demonstrate the effectiveness of our
algorithm on the Berkeley Segmentation Dataset.

## 1 Introduction

Image segmentation is considered as an important low-level challenge in a diverse
fields of computer vision. It seeks to provide a segmentation layer by partitioning the input image into several non-overlapping coherent regions. The layer can
be used in a wide range of applications, such as object detection, scene understanding, and object recognition. Although several algorithms are proposed for
segmentation, their results are still not satisfactory to be used in high-level applications. It may due to the fact that lots of images inherently contain diverse and
ambiguous visual textures.

Most of the recent proposed algorithms are developed based on extracting
visual information from the local neighborhood of image pixels [1–5]. The local
information extracted at each single pixel is encoded as a feature vector corresponding to that pixel. Those pixels which have nearly similar visual properties
(feature vectors) are grouped together to shape larger structures. One of the
most powerful features for encoding the visual information of a locality is presented in [6] called Local Spectral Histogram (LSH) features. Yuan [1] adopted
the LSH features to develop an image segmentation algorithm based on Nonnegative Matrix Factorization (NMF).

© Springer International Publishing AG 2016
G. Bebis et al. (Eds.): ISVC 2016, Part I, LNCS 10072, pp. 193–202, 2016.
DOI: 10.1007/978-3-319-50835-1_18

Another category of algorithms are developed to provide a good segmentation by aggregating multiple segmentations of the local features. Li [4] presented a method called Segmentation by Aggregating Superpixels (SAS), which aggregates several segmentations resulted from two algorithms. Since various segmentations contain complementary information, the final result of SAS is improved in comparison with any primary segmentations. Despite the enhancement, an important point seems to be overlooked in SAS. This algorithm is mainly based on the assumption that all segmentation layers have contributed equally to shape the final segmentation. This assumption is not entirely reasonable due to the difference between the accuracy of segmentation layers.

In this paper, we employ multiple types of local features to acquire complementary information from various sources. Using the provided information makes our algorithm more robust to the ambiguity and diversity of image textures, which in turn leads to the improvement in final segmentation result. Given an over-segmentation layer of image, we extract multiple kinds of local features from each segment. The features are fed to a NMF-based framework to provide new representations. In order to aggregate the new representations into a single one, we introduce a novel aggregation model which is jointly optimized over the reliability of representations and the final representation. The final representation are then processed to shape final segmentation. The main contributions of our paper are summarized as follows:

1. We extract different kinds of local features and feed them into a NMF-based framework to shape new representations with the same size.
2. We propose an aggregation framework over the reliability of representations and the final representation. Given the new representations, our proposed algorithm jointly learns the reliability of representations and computes the final representation.
3. We perform an experiment on the Berkeley Segmentation Dataset to demonstrate the effect of our aggregation model on final segmentation result.

The rest of this paper is structured as follows: Sect. 2 briefly reviews the related works; Sect. 3 contains our method in details; Sect. 4 presents experimental results and discussion; Sect. 5 describes the conclusion of our algorithm.

## 2    Related Works

Recently, the initial step of most algorithms is to provide an over-segmentation layer of the input image. This layer is constructed by grouping the neighboring pixels which are nearly similar in terms of local visual properties. Mean Shift (MS) [7], Felzenszwalb and Huttenlocher's method (FelHut) [8], Watershed algorithm [9], Simple Linear Iterative Clustering (SLIC) [10], and Piotr Dollar algorithm [11] are among the most well-known algorithms for providing over-segmentation layer. Some segmentation algorithms are developed to merge the small segments of this layer and shape final segments. Liu [2] adopted watershed algorithm [9] over the gPb contour map [12] to obtain an over-segmentation layer. Then, Some cues are extracted from the small segments of training images to train a random forest classifier. Once the classifier is trained, it is applied on over-segmentation layer of the input image to merge the small segments and shape the final segmentation layer. Arbelaez [3] adopted a hierarchical tree for merging the similar segments to create larger segments. Fu [5] proposed Contour-guided Color Palettes (CCP) algorithm which uses contour and region cues to construct an over-segmentation layer. The small segments are merged throughout a pipeline to shape the final segments. SAS [4] adopted MS [7] and FelzHut [8] to provide multiple over-segmentation layers. These layers are effectively modeled using a bipartite graph over pixels and segments. Then, the spectral clustering algorithm is applied on the graph to determine final segments.

Our method is similar to SAS in the sense that the final segmentation is provided by aggregating the information obtained from various sources. Despite this similarity, our method differs from SAS in terms of two key aspects: developing the way of providing information and the method of aggregation.

## 3  Proposed Method

In this section, we explain our Reliability-based Local Feature Aggregation (RLFA) algorithm. The algorithm is mainly based on integrating the information obtained from different features. Since the various features do not necessarily have the same dimensions, it is not simple to integrate their information. To tackle this problem, we propose to use a NMF-based framework to provide the same size new representations for all features. The first part of this section describes the way of adopting NMF-based framework to construct the new representations. Given these representations, we propose an aggregation algorithm, which jointly learns the reliability of new features and infers the final representations. The details of our aggregation framework and the joint objective function are described in the second part of this section.

### 3.1  Providing New Representations

Given the input image $I$, an over-segmentation layer is constructed using [11]. Let $n$ be the number of segments and $l$ be the number of feature types. We define $l$ different feature matrices $\{X^v\}_{v=1}^l$ whose columns are the features extracted from the image segments. The dimension of these features are denoted as $\{d_i\}_{i=1}^l$ (e.g., $X^v \in R^{d_v \times n}$). The $v^{th}$ feature matrix can be modeled as:

$$X^v = D^v U^v + E^v \qquad (1)$$

where $D^v \in R^{d_v \times k}$ is a dictionary of features with $k$ words, $U^v \in R^{k \times n}$ indicates a new representation of segments features. The model error is defined as $E^v$ and $k$ is the dimension of new representation features.

We adopt a NMF-based objective function to compute the new representations of feature matrices $\{X^v\}_{v=1}^l$ as:

$$\min_{D^v, U^v} \|X^v - D^v U^v\|_F^2$$
$$s.t. \ D^v \geq 0, \ U^v \geq 0 \tag{2}$$

Using the Alternating Least Square (ALS) method presented in [13], this optimization problem will be solved for $v = 1, \ldots, l$ to compute new representations $\{U^v\}_{v=1}^l$. Despite the fact that the information extracted from different types of local features are highly correlated, the matrices $\{U^v\}_{v=1}^l$ are not similar to each other. This problem stems from the various order of rows in matrices $\{U^v\}_{v=1}^l$, which can be simply addressed by applying simple permutations on the rows. Once the rows of matrices $\{U^v\}_{v=1}^l$ are properly permuted, it can be seen the representations of the same segments are pretty close to each other. Given the assumption that these matrices contain complementary information about the segments, we propose to aggregate them into a single one which is more likely to be more informative than each one individually. Our aggregation strategy is described in the next part of this section.

The columns of $\{U^v\}_{v=1}^l$ are normalized to add up to 1 before applying any permutation which makes them appropriate for aggregation model.

### 3.2   Joint Learning of Aggregation Model

We propose a technique to aggregate all new representations $\{U^v\}_{v=1}^l$ into a final representation matrix $V \in R^{k \times n}$, which provides more accurate representation than any individual one. Let assume $V$ is modeled as a linear combination of matrices $\{U^v\}_{v=1}^l$. The coefficients of such linear combination are gathered into vector $w \in R^{l \times 1}$, called reliability of representations. To compute the final representation, we formulate our aggregation model as follows:

$$\min_{w, V} \left\| \sum_{i=1}^l w_i U^i - V \right\|_F^2 + \lambda Tr(VLV^T) \tag{3}$$
$$s.t. \ w \geq 0, \ \mathbf{1}^T w = 1$$

where $\mathbf{1}$ is a column vector of all ones, $\lambda$ is a regularization parameter, and $L$ indicates a Laplacian Matrix. The first term is adopted to penalize the objective function for violation of the linear model assumption. The Laplacian regularization term $Tr(VLV^T)$, is used to take account the effect of segments vicinity in the objective function. This term preserves the smoothness of $V$ with respect to matrix $L$. Note that the matrix $L$ is constructed over a graph $\mathcal{G}$ where nodes are segments and edges connect the neighboring segments. We propose to compute the edge weight between two neighboring segments $i$ and $j$ in graph $\mathcal{G}$ as follows:

$$A_{i,j} = e^{-(\frac{1}{l} \sum_{v=1}^l \frac{\|X_i^v - X_j^v\|^2}{\sigma_v}) - \frac{\|p_i - p_j\|^2}{\sigma_p}} \tag{4}$$

where $X_i^v$ is the $v^{th}$ feature type extracted from the $i^{th}$ segment and $p_i$ is the centroid of the $i^{th}$ segment. The parameters $\{\sigma_v\}_{v=1}^l, \sigma_p$ are used for controlling the importance of feature distances in Eq. 4. The Laplacian matrix $L$ is defined as $L = diag(A1) - A$, where $diag(.)$ builds a diagonal matrix formed by the elements of the input vector.

Since the objective function in Eq. 3 is non-convex, it is not easy to be solved directly. To address this problem, we propose to jointly optimize over $w$ and $V$. Two different steps of our algorithm are: (1) given fixed $w$, optimize over $V$ (2) given fixed $V$, optimize over $w$. These two steps are iteratively repeated until convergence is achieved.

**Given fixed $w$, optimize over $V$**: Given a $w$ which meets the constraints of Eq. 3, the objective function is reformulated as:

$$\min_V \|C - V\|_F^2 + \lambda Tr(VLV^T) \tag{5}$$

where $C = \sum_{i=1}^l w_i U^i$ is a constant matrix with respect to the variable $V$. As a consequence, Eq. 5 has closed-form solution $V^* = (\sum_{i=1}^l w_i U^i)(I + \lambda L)^{-1}$.

**Given fixed $V$, optimize over $w$**: Given computed $V$ from the last step, we reformulate the Eq. 3 as follows:

$$\min_w \|U_{total}w - v_{vec}\|_2^2 \tag{6}$$
$$s.t. \ w \geq 0, \ \mathbf{1}^T w = 1$$

which is efficiently solvable by standard techniques. Note that term $\lambda Tr(VLV^T)$ is eliminated because it would be constant with respect to the $w$. The $U_{total} \in R^{kn \times l}$ is a matrix whose columns are obtained by vectorizing the matrices $\{U^v\}_{v=1}^l$, and $v_{vec} \in R^{kn \times 1}$ is vectorized version of the matrix $V$.

The Eq. 6 minimizes a convex function with respect to variable $w$, subject to the probability simplex constraints. We employ the accelerated projected gradient algorithm presented in [14] to solve the optimization problem. The algorithm not only optimizes the objective function in an effective way, but also practically converges very fast in a few number of iterations.

Initializing $w$ with a vector of all $\frac{1}{l}$, the parameters $V$ and $w$ are updated until the convergence is obtained. Once the final representation $V$ is optimized, each segment is labeled to the index of the largest element of the corresponding column in $V$. In order to increase the performance of our result, the post-processing steps presented in [5] can be applied on the final segmentation.

## 4 Experiment

The proposed algorithm is applied on a benchmark image database to make a qualitative and quantitative comparison with state-of-the-art algorithms. The segmentation results are reported in Tables and Figures for a careful comparison.

RLFA adopts the algorithm presented in [11] to generate an over-segmentation layer with boundary-preserving and uniform segments. We extract LSH features from multiple layers of image to create different feature matrices. The feature matrices are constructed based on six sets of layers as follow: (1) color (includes color layers of CIE-LAB and $YC_bC_r$ color space); (2) gradient-based (contains convolved image with Laplacian of Gaussian filters and Gaussian derivatives); (3) soft segmentations (includes the first three principal components of soft segmentation layers presented in [15]); (4) texton (a texture-based layer presented in [16]); (5) combination of color and soft segmentations; (6) combination of color, gradient-based, soft segmentations, and texton. Once all types of features are extracted from the image pixels, a single feature vector is assigned to each segment which is computed by averaging the features of all pixels within that segment.

The parameter $\lambda$ in Eq. 3 controls the smoothness of the final segmentation result. Increasing the value of $\lambda$ will result in merging more segments, and vice versa. This parameter is set to 10 in all experiments. The parameters $\sigma_p$ and $\{\sigma_v\}_{v=1}^l$ in Eq. 4 are set as a fraction of total variations of feature distance and spatial distance in the image. The fractions are set to 0.6 and 1 for $\sigma_p$ and all $\{\sigma_v\}_{v=1}^l$, respectively.

We evaluate our segmentation result by performing an extensive experiment on Berkeley Segmentation DataSet (BSDS). The BSDS300 contains 300 natural images of size $321 \times 481$ captured from various scenes. Each image has in average five different groundtruths manually drawn by human in different levels of detail.

To perform a quantitative evaluation of our results, five measures have been adopted as follows: (1) Segmentation Covering (Cov) [17], which measures averaged matching between two segmentations of image; (2) Probabilistic Rand Index (PRI) [18], which measures the likelihood that a pair of pixels are consistently labeled in two segmentations; (3) Variation of Information (VoI) [19], which measures the relative entropy between two segmentations of image; (4) Global Consistency Error (GCE) [20], which measures the local refinement error at image pixels; (5) Boundary Error Displacement (BDE) [21], which measures the average displacement error of boundary pixels between two segmentations of image. Our final segmentation result and groundtruth are compared in terms of these five measures. Better segmentation result corresponds to the larger values of Cov and PRI, the smaller values of GCE, BDE, and VoI.

We compare our results with eight benchmark algorithms, NCut [22], MNCut [23], MS [7], FelzHut [8], MLSS [24], SAS [4], SDTV [25], gPb-UCM [3], CCP-2, CCP-LAS, and CCP-LAM [5]. The numbers are collected from [3–5,24].

The results of quantitative comparison are reported in Table 1. This table contains two separate sections depending on whether or not the method gets parameter $k$ as prior information for each image. To make a fair comparison, those segmentation algorithms which do not use any kind of prior information are gathered in the first section of Table 1. In this section, our algorithm is denoted as RLFA-C where C implies the parameter $k$ is set to a constant value for all images. This constant is set to 12 in our experiment. The second section of

Table 1 contains the result of those algorithms which have an image-dependent parameter. In this section, our proposed algorithm is denoted as RLFA-V where V implies the parameter $k$ is image-dependent and manually set for each image.

**Table 1.** Quantitative comparison of our method on the BSDS300. In each section of the table, the first two best of each column are colored with red and blue, respectively

| Algorithm | Cov | PRI | VoI | GCE | BDE |
|-----------|-----|-----|-----|-----|-----|
| NCut [22] | 0.44 | 0.7242 | 2.9061 | 0.2232 | 17.15 |
| MS [7] | 0.54 | 0.7958 | 1.9725 | 0.1888 | 14.41 |
| MNCut [23] | 0.44 | 0.7559 | 2.4701 | 0.1925 | 15.10 |
| FelzHut [8] | 0.51 | 0.7139 | 3.3949 | 0.1746 | 16.67 |
| SDTV [25] | 0.57 | 0.7758 | 1.8165 | 0.1768 | 16.24 |
| gPb-UCM [3] | 0.59 | 0.81 | 1.65 | N/A | N/A |
| CCP-2 [5] | 0.48 | 0.7932 | 2.7835 | 0.1077 | 11.17 |
| **RLFA-C** | 0.60 | 0.8148 | 1.7503 | 0.1827 | 11.763 |
| MLSS [24] | 0.53 | 0.8146 | 1.8545 | 0.1809 | 12.21 |
| SAS [4] | 0.62 | 0.8319 | 1.6849 | 0.1779 | 11.29 |
| CCP-LAM [5] | 0.68 | 0.8404 | 1.5715 | 0.1635 | 10.20 |
| CCP-LAS [5] | 0.68 | 0.8442 | 1.5871 | 0.1582 | 10.46 |
| **RLFA-V** | 0.68 | 0.8565 | 1.5094 | 0.1591 | 10.127 |

According to Table 1, RLFA-C is among the top two best in terms of four measures Cov, PRI, VoI, and BDE. Additionally, RLFA-V has achieved the best score in these four measures and the second best in GCE.

We perform an experiment on BSDS300 to demonstrate the effectiveness of our aggregation algorithm. The results are reported in Table 2. The first six rows of the table are labeled as Features-L1 through Features-L6. These are the segmentation layers obtained using each one of the representations. Given all representations, we average them into a new representation denoted as Features-Total. Note that the difference between the last two rows of Table 2 is that all representations are averaged (with the same weight) to shape the Features-Total, while RLFA-C optimizes the weights of the representations. Figure 1 shows the effect of our aggregation model in improving the accuracy of segmentation.

According to the Table 2, RLFA-C has improved the segmentation results in terms of Cov, PRI, and VoI, while it nearly preserves the score of GCE and BDE. The 7th row of Table 2 shows the accuracy is increased by integrating multiple segmentation layers. The last row indicates the superior result is obtained if we optimize the contribution weight of each layer in final segmentation result.

Figure 2 shows the segmentation provided using different algorithms to make a qualitative comparison. As it can be seen, different segmentation layers contain complementary information about the image pixels. RLFA-C effectively aggregates these sources of information to generate an accurate final segmentation result.

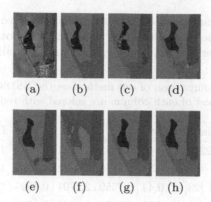

Fig. 1. Segmentation layers. (a) Input image. (b–g) segmentation layers provided using various representations. (h) RLFA-C

**Table 2.** Experiment on BSDS300 to show the effectiveness of RLFA on aggregating multiple representations

|                | Cov  | PRI    | VoI    | GCE     | BDE    |
|----------------|------|--------|--------|---------|--------|
| Features-L1    | 0.54 | 0.7978 | 2.1507 | 0.1795  | 11.206 |
| Features-L2    | 0.52 | 0.7896 | 2.2369 | 0.1990  | 11.879 |
| Features-L3    | 0.54 | 0.8000 | 2.1104 | 0.17092 | 11.142 |
| Features-L4    | 0.50 | 0.8007 | 2.5488 | 0.1691  | 11.023 |
| Features-L5    | 0.56 | 0.8032 | 2.0562 | 0.17355 | 11.182 |
| Features-L6    | 0.57 | 0.8054 | 1.9867 | 0.1922  | 11.622 |
| Features-Total | 0.58 | 0.8121 | 1.863  | 0.1821  | 11.505 |
| **RLFA-C**     | 0.60 | 0.8148 | 1.7503 | 0.1827  | 11.763 |

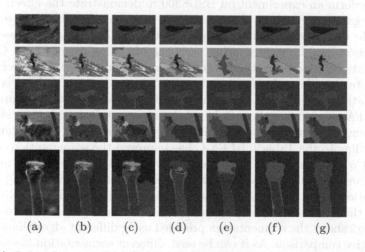

Fig. 2. (a) Original image; (b) MS [7]; (c) gPb-UCM [3]; (d) CCP-2 [5]; (e) SAS [4] (f) RLFA-C (g) RLFA-V

We have run the source codes released by the authors [3–5,7] to obtain these segmentations. Although the CCP-LAM and CCP-LAS algorithms achieve high scores according to Table 1, we did not find released source code for them.

## 5    Conclusion

We presented the Reliability-based Local Feature Aggregation (RLFA) algorithm for image segmentation. RLFA is mainly based on the fusion of information obtained from several sources. The Local Spectral Histogram (LSH) features extracted from various layers of input image are perceived as the sources of information. Since the LSH features of different dimensions are not generally comparable, they are converted into new representation which makes them more appropriate for aggregation. We proposed an objective function for aggregating these new representations into a single one called final representation, which is more likely to be informative than any individual representation. The objective function jointly learns the reliability of the new representations and infers the final representation. The final segmentation layer can be easily obtained using the computed final representation. The qualitative and quantitative comparisons have demonstrated that the RLFA algorithm is better than the state-of-the-art algorithms in terms of the segmentation accuracy.

## References

1. Yuan, J., Wang, D., Cheriyadat, A.M.: Factorization-based texture segmentation. IEEE Trans. Image Process. **24**, 3488–3497 (2015)
2. Liu, T., Seyedhosseini, M., Tasdizen, T.: Image segmentation using hierarchical merge tree. IEEE Trans. Image Process. **25**, 4596–4607 (2016)
3. Arbelaez, P., Maire, M., Fowlkes, C., Malik, J.: Contour detection and hierarchical image segmentation. IEEE Trans. Pattern Anal. Mach. Intell. **33**, 898–916 (2011)
4. Li, Z., Wu, X.M., Chang, S.F.: Segmentation using superpixels: a bipartite graph partitioning approach. In: 2012 IEEE Conference on Computer Vision and Pattern Recognition (CVPR), pp. 789–796. IEEE (2012)
5. Fu, X., Wang, C.Y., Chen, C., Wang, C., Jay Kuo, C.C.: Robust image segmentation using contour-guided color palettes. In: Proceedings of the IEEE International Conference on Computer Vision, pp. 1618–1625 (2015)
6. Liu, X., Wang, D.: Image and texture segmentation using local spectral histograms. IEEE Trans. Image Process. **15**, 3066–3077 (2006)
7. Comaniciu, D., Meer, P.: Mean shift: a robust approach toward feature space analysis. IEEE Trans. Pattern Anal. Mach. Intell. **24**, 603–619 (2002)
8. Felzenszwalb, P.F., Huttenlocher, D.P.: Efficient graph-based image segmentation. Int. J. Comput. Vis. **59**, 167–181 (2004)
9. Beucher, S., et al.: The watershed transformation applied to image segmentation. SCANNING MICROSCOPY-SUPPLEMENT, p. 299 (1992)
10. Achanta, R., Shaji, A., Smith, K., Lucchi, A., Fua, P., Susstrunk, S.: Slic superpixels compared to state-of-the-art superpixel methods. IEEE Trans. Pattern Anal. Mach. Intell. **34**, 2274–2282 (2012)

11. Dollár, P., Zitnick, C.L.: Structured forests for fast edge detection. In: Proceedings of the IEEE International Conference on Computer Vision, pp. 1841–1848 (2013)
12. Maire, M., Arbeláez, P., Fowlkes, C., Malik, J.: Using contours to detect and localize junctions in natural images. In: IEEE Conference on Computer Vision and Pattern Recognition, CVPR 2008, pp. 1–8. IEEE (2008)
13. Berry, M.W., Browne, M., Langville, A.N., Pauca, V.P., Plemmons, R.J.: Algorithms and applications for approximate nonnegative matrix factorization. Comput. Stat. Data Anal. **52**, 155–173 (2007)
14. Huang, J., Nie, F., Huang, H.: A new simplex sparse learning model to measure data similarity for clustering. In: Proceedings of the 24th International Conference on Artificial Intelligence, pp. 3569–3575. AAAI Press (2015)
15. Leordeanu, M., Sukthankar, R., Sminchisescu, C.: Generalized boundaries from multiple image interpretations. IEEE Trans. Pattern Anal. Mach. Intell. **36**, 1312–1324 (2014)
16. Malik, J., Belongie, S., Shi, J., Leung, T.: Textons, contours and regions: cue integration in image segmentation. In: The Proceedings of the Seventh IEEE International Conference on Computer Vision, 1999, vol. 2, pp. 918–925. IEEE (1999)
17. Malisiewicz, T., Efros, A.A.: Improving spatial support for objects via multiple segmentations (2007)
18. Rand, W.M.: Objective criteria for the evaluation of clustering methods. J. Am. Stat. Assoc. **66**, 846–850 (1971)
19. Meil, M.: Comparing clusterings: an axiomatic view. In: Proceedings of the 22nd international conference on Machine learning, pp. 577–584. ACM (2005)
20. Martin, D., Fowlkes, C., Tal, D., Malik, J.: A database of human segmented natural images and its application to evaluating segmentation algorithms and measuring ecological statistics. In: Proceedings of the Eighth IEEE International Conference on Computer Vision, ICCV 2001, vol. 2, pp. 416–423. IEEE (2001)
21. Freixenet, J., Muñoz, X., Raba, D., Martí, J., Cufí, X.: Yet another survey on image segmentation: region and boundary information integration. In: Heyden, A., Sparr, G., Nielsen, M., Johansen, P. (eds.) ECCV 2002. LNCS, vol. 2352, pp. 408–422. Springer, Heidelberg (2002). doi:10.1007/3-540-47977-5_27
22. Shi, J., Malik, J.: Normalized cuts and image segmentation. IEEE Trans. Pattern Anal. Mach. Intell. **22**, 888–905 (2000)
23. Cour, T., Benezit, F., Shi, J.: Spectral segmentation with multiscale graph decomposition. In: 2005 IEEE Computer Society Conference on Computer Vision and Pattern Recognition (CVPR 2005), vol. 2, pp. 1124–1131. IEEE (2005)
24. Kim, T.H., Lee, K.M., Lee, S.U.: Learning full pairwise affinities for spectral segmentation. IEEE Trans. Pattern Anal. Mach. Intell. **35**, 1690–1703 (2013)
25. Donoser, M., Urschler, M., Hirzer, M., Bischof, H.: Saliency driven total variation segmentation. In: 2009 IEEE 12th International Conference on Computer Vision, pp. 817–824. IEEE (2009)

# Chan-Vese Revisited: Relation to Otsu's Method and a Parameter-Free Non-PDE Solution via Morphological Framework

Arie Shaus[✉] and Eli Turkel

Department of Applied Mathematics, Tel Aviv University, Tel Aviv, Israel
ashaus@post.tau.ac.il

**Abstract.** Chan-Vese is an important and well-established segmentation method. However, it tends to be challenging to implement, including issues such as initialization problems and establishing the values of several free parameters. The paper presents a detailed analysis of Chan-Vese framework. It establishes a relation between the Otsu binarization method and the fidelity terms of Chan-Vese energy functional, allowing for intelligent initialization of the scheme. An alternative, fast, and parameter-free morphological segmentation technique is also suggested. Our experiments indicate the soundness of the proposed algorithm.

## 1 Introduction

Since its introduction at the beginning of this millennia, Chan-Vese (CV) segmentation [1] has become one of the most widely used algorithms in the field of Computer Vision. In fact, currently, with more than 8000 citations at Google Scholar, this method is almost twice as popular as the Mumford-Shah framework [2], upon which it is founded.

The power of CV technique lies within its ability to elegantly take into account the most important segmentation criteria. These include the length of the boundary curve between the segmented areas, the variance of gray-levels within each area, as well as the size of the "foreground" area. All these are handled within the scope of a single variational framework, leading to Euler-Lagrange equations, and thenceforth to numerical Gradient Descent PDE scheme. A straightforward extensions of this theme to vector-valued (e.g. RGB) images [3] (peculiarly published before [1]), as well as a multi-phase level set framework [4] were proposed by the same authors, based on the same natural formulation.

Nonetheless, CV segmentation presents its own share of challenges. Among these are several "free" parameters of the algorithm ($\mu$, $v$, $\lambda_1$, $\lambda_2$, $\varepsilon$, $h$, $\Delta t$; e.g. in experimental results of [1], $\mu$ ranges from $0.0000033 \times 255^2$ to $2 \times 255^2$!), its initialization problem, as well as the intricate and sometimes computationally-intensive PDE scheme, based upon re-calculating the level set function on each step (an approach advanced by Osher and Sethian [5]). Although some of these hindrances might be handled by heuristic approaches (e.g. random re-initializations, as proposed by [1]), these are ad-hoc solutions, which add an overhead to the algorithm's implementation – with no guaranteed and sometimes difficult to forecast outcome.

© Springer International Publishing AG 2016
G. Bebis et al. (Eds.): ISVC 2016, Part I, LNCS 10072, pp. 203–212, 2016.
DOI: 10.1007/978-3-319-50835-1_19

Various approaches to these issues have been proposed. The method in [6] initializes using a modification of Canny edge detector [7, 8] chooses an initial level set via Gradient Descent over a thresholding criteria, [9] substitutes the level set formulation with curve evolution driven by Gaussian smoothing, [10, 11] replace the energy functional with different ones working on a local level, while [12] suggests another adjustment to the functional, possessing convexity properties.

We propose a new approach: a combination of an initialization based on Otsu's binarization method [13] (proposed "heuristically" yet not justified in [14]), supplemented by a morphological non-PDE energy minimization framework. Indeed, morphological methods have been suggested in the past for minimization of energy functionals pertaining to Computer Vision in general [15–17] and CV in particular. Among the latter are: [18], replacing the energy minimization with three compound morphological operators; [19], taking into consideration some pre-computed morphological data; [20, 21], utilizing various structuring elements; [22], applying morphological filters *a-posteriori*; and [23], adjusting CV energy functional by morphological gradient difference (MGD) term. The citation statistics of [13–23] suggests such methods did not win wide acceptance, possibly due to their tendency to supplement one intricate solution with another.

The main contribution of the current article is an establishment of surprising relation between CV and Otsu's method, allowing for a simple initialization procedure. We also suggest a replacement of CV's PDE with a parameter-free morphological framework. The rest of the article is organized as follows: The CV algorithm is explained, and its individual components are analyzed. An alternative algorithm is provided and tested in different settings. We conclude with summary remarks and possible future research directions.

## 2   The Chan-Vese Algorithm

In their seminal paper [1], CV proposed the following segmentation energy functional:

$$
\begin{aligned}
F(c_1, c_2, C) = {} & \mu \cdot Length(C) + v \cdot Area(inside(C)) \\
& + \lambda_1 \int_{inside(C)} |u_0(x, y) - c_1|^2 dxdy + \lambda_2 \int_{outside(C)} |u_0(x, y) - c_2|^2 dxdy, \quad (1)
\end{aligned}
$$

where $u_0(x, y)$ is a given image; $c_1$, $c_2$ are constants; $C(s)$ is a parameterized curve partitioning the image domain $\Omega$ into disjoint *inside*(C) and *outside*(C) sets; while $\mu$, $v$, $\lambda_1$ and $\lambda_2$ are parameters. Equation 1 is closely related to the energy functional of Mumford and Shah [2], which can be written as:

$$
F^{MS}(u, C) = \mu \cdot Length(C) + \lambda \int_{\Omega} |u_0(x, y) - u(x, y)|^2 dxdy + \alpha \int_{\Omega \setminus C} |\nabla u(x, y)|^2 dxdy \quad (2)
$$

where $u(x, y)$ is the estimated image, and $\alpha$ is a parameter. Assuming $\alpha \to \infty$, a piece-wise-constant $u(x, y)$ is necessitated, eliminating the last term of $F^{MS}$. Assuming further that $u(x, y)$ has only two values, $c_1$ and $c_2$, and adding the area term, we arrive at CV functional (Eq. 1). Using the level set formulation $\phi$ (zero on $C$, positive on $inside(C)$ and negative on $outside(C)$), the Heaviside function $H$ and Dirac's function $\delta_0$:

$$H(z) = \begin{cases} 1 & 0 \le z \\ 0 & z < 0 \end{cases}, \quad \delta_0(z) = \frac{d}{dz} H(z), \tag{3}$$

Equation 1 can be reformulated in the following fashion:

$$F(c_1, c_2, \phi) = \mu \int_\Omega \delta_0(\phi(x,y)) |\nabla \phi(x,y)| dxdy + v \int_\Omega H(\phi(x,y)) dxdy$$
$$+ \lambda_1 \int_\Omega |u_0(x,y) - c_1|^2 H(\phi(x,y)) dxdy + \lambda_2 \int_\Omega |u_0(x,y) - c_2|^2 (1 - H(\phi(x,y))) dxdy \tag{4}$$

The first variation with respect to $c_1$ results in:

$$c_1(\phi) = \int_\Omega u_0(x,y) H(\phi(x,y)) dxdy \bigg/ \int_\Omega H(\phi(x,y)) dxdy, \tag{5}$$

while the first variation with respect to $c_2$ yields:

$$c_2(\phi) = \int_\Omega u_0(x,y)(1 - H(\phi(x,y))) dxdy \bigg/ \int_\Omega (1 - H(\phi(x,y))) dxdy. \tag{6}$$

On the other hand, the variation with respect to $\phi$ is less trivial. First, [1] presents an altered version of Eq. 4, introducing regularized $H_\varepsilon$ and $\delta_\varepsilon$ functions:

$$F_\varepsilon(c_1, c_2, \phi) = \mu \int_\Omega \delta_\varepsilon(\phi(x,y)) |\nabla \phi(x,y)| dxdy + v \int_\Omega H_\varepsilon(\phi(x,y)) dxdy$$
$$+ \lambda_1 \int_\Omega |u_0(x,y) - c_1|^2 H_\varepsilon(\phi(x,y)) dxdy + \lambda_2 \int_\Omega |u_0(x,y) - c_2|^2 (1 - H_\varepsilon(\phi(x,y))) dxdy \tag{7}$$

Next, an Euler–Lagrange equation for $\phi$ is derived and parameterized by an artificial time in the Gradient Descent direction:

$$\frac{\partial \phi}{\partial t} = \delta_\varepsilon(\phi) \left[ \mu \cdot div \left( \frac{\nabla \phi}{|\nabla \phi|} \right) - v - \lambda_1 (u_0 - c_1)^2 + \lambda_2 (u_0 - c_2)^2 \right]. \tag{8}$$

A numerical scheme for Eq. 8 is also suggested, for further details see [1].

## 3  From Chan-Vese to Alternative Solution

We now analyze the CV algorithm, and suggest its restatement in alternative terms. In particular, we prefer not to use the level set framework. Similarly to [1], we strive to achieve a partition of the image domain $\Omega$ into two disjoint sets of pixels, denoted herein as $A_1$ and $A_2$. Unlike [1], we have no prior assumptions and no limitations regarding their location within $u_0$. An additional preference would be to avoid a *regularized* version of the algorithm, which tends to smooth some of the image features (cf. the criticism of CV on Gaussian smoothing in [1]).

**Constants:** Already in [1], it was noted that Eqs. 5 and 6 represent the averages:

$$c_1(\phi) = average(u_0) \ in \ \{0 \leq \phi\}, \quad c_2(\phi) = average(u_0) \ in \ \{\phi < 0\}. \tag{9}$$

Our alternative (and symmetric) formulation retains the constants $c_1$ and $c_1$, associated respectively with $A_1$ and $A_2$, and calculates them in a similar fashion:

$$c_1 = average(u_0) \ on \ A_1, \quad c_2 = average(u_0) \ on \ A_2. \tag{10}$$

**Localization:** Equation 8 defines the evolution of the level set, and subsequently the sets *inside*$(C)$ and *outside*$(C)$. We substitute this scheme with its morphological counterpart. We first consider the multiplicand $\delta_\varepsilon(\phi)$, where $\delta_\varepsilon$ is a regularization of $\delta_0$. Since $\delta_0 \equiv 1$ at a zero-level $\{\phi = 0\}$, and $\delta_0 \equiv 0$ at $\{\phi \neq 0\}$, the term limits the evolution only to pixels belonging to $C$ (optionally including their immediate neighbors for $\delta_\varepsilon$). Agreeing with this strategy, we denote as "borderline" pixels the pixels of $A_1$ adjacent to at least one pixel in $A_2$, or vice versa.

**Curvature-driven evolution:** We next consider the first term of the second multiplicand of Eq. 8, $\mu \cdot div(\nabla\phi/|\nabla\phi|) - v - \lambda_1(u_0 - c_1)^2 + \lambda_2(u_0 - c_2)^2$. As explained in [4, 5], $\kappa = div(\nabla\phi/|\nabla\phi|)$ is the curvature at zero level, which induces a minimization of the curve's length. This theoretical construction may be supplemented by a low-level analysis. Assuming 4-connectivity (radius of 1 around the central pixel), and taking various symmetries into account, there exists only 5 possible neighborhoods of an $A_1$ borderline pixel (borderline pixels of $A_2$ admit similar analysis). These options are presented on Fig. 1. It can be seen, that given a non-negligible $\mu$, only Figs. 1a and b necessitate a re-assignment of the center pixel to $A_2$ - in both of these cases the radius of the osculating circle is $r = 1$, hence $\kappa = 1/r = 1$. Additionally, *ignoring the central pixel*, Figs. 1c and d present a symmetry between pixels assigned to $A_1$ and $A_2$, thus no re-assignment is needed (otherwise an oscillatory behavior is expected), while Fig. 1e presents a case of clear $A_1$ majority. The morphological operator perfectly representing such pixel assignment is the *median filter*. While the presented analysis represents a radius of 1 around the central pixel, if some kind of regularization is desired, a different median filter radius can be chosen (cf. [15, 20, 21] for the median filter in related contexts).

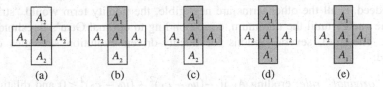

**Fig. 1.** Five options of neighborhood of an $A_1$ borderline pixel. Only $(a,b)$ require a re-assignment of the central pixel, due to a positive curvature.

**Area-driven evolution:** The next term to be analyzed within Eq. 8 is $-v$. If $0 < v$, this represents a constant reduction in the size of *inside*$(C)$, which is difficult to justify (unless a human operator fancies a specific result). If for some reason the initial sets *inside*$(C)$ and *outside*$(C)$ are switched, the dynamics is reversed, as *outside*$(C)$ is now expected to constantly grow, breaking the symmetry between the sets. Moreover, given images with small or zero curvature, and $\lambda_1$, $\lambda_1$ chosen to be small, the shrinking might continue until *inside*$(C)$ disappears completely! It seems that the dubious benefits of this term were understood by CV, since $v$ is mostly set to 0 in [1], and the term is no longer mentioned in [4]. We also advise against using this term, but in case it is desired, its morphological substitution would be an erosion in case of $0 < v$, and dilation in case of $v < 0$, with $A_1$ or $A_2$ chosen as a target.

**Fidelity-driven evolution:** The last terms to be considered within Eq. 8 are $-\lambda_1(u_0 - c_1)^2 + \lambda_2(u_0 - c_2)^2$, presenting a balance between reducing the size of *inside*$(C)$ due to its gray-levels variance, and its enlargement due to the variance of gray-levels within *outside*$(C)$. Reversing our steps shows these terms originate from

$$\lambda_1 \int_{inside(C)} |u_0(x,y) - c_1|^2 dxdy + \lambda_2 \int_{outside(C)} |u_0(x,y) - c_2|^2 dxdy \quad \text{in} \quad \text{Eq. 1,} \quad \text{or}$$

$\lambda_1 \int_{A_1} |u_0(x,y) - c_1|^2 dxdy + \lambda_2 \int_{A_2} |u_0(x,y) - c_2|^2 dxdy$ in our case. Using the recom-

mendation of $\lambda_1 = \lambda_2 = 1$ [1], this has a surprising relation to Otsu binarization method [13] (also cf. [14]). Otsu minimizes the thresholding quality criterion

$$\omega_1 \sigma_1^2 + \omega_2 \sigma_2^2, \quad \text{where} \quad \sigma_1^2 = \sum_{i=1}^{k} (i - \mu_1)^2 / \omega_1; \quad \sigma_2^2 = \sum_{i=k+1}^{L} (i - \mu_2)^2 / \omega_2; \quad \omega_1 = \sum_{i=1}^{k} p_i;$$

$\omega_2 = \sum_{i=k+1}^{L} p_i$ and $p_i$ represents the value of the gray-level $i \in [1, 2, \ldots, L]$ within the

normalized histogram of $u_0$. The image is thresholded by $k$ and partitioned into disjoint sets $A_1$ and $A_2$, respectively containing gray-levels $[1, \ldots, k]$ and $[k+1, \ldots, L]$. Thus,

$$\omega_1 \sigma_1^2 + \omega_2 \sigma_2^2 = \int_{A_1} |u_0(x,y) - c_1|^2 dxdy + \int_{A_2} |u_0(x,y) - c_2|^2 dxdy. \quad (11)$$

Equation 11 presents us with two opportunities. Firstly, it provides an excellent option for *initialization* of the algorithm, since Otsu's method efficiently handles the needed minimization of this energy functional, with only the curve length remaining to be optimized. Secondly, it offers an explanation of the inner machinery of the fidelity term. Indeed, if all the other terms are negligible, the fidelity term would "strive" to lower the energy until the minimum, corresponding to optimal Otsu's thresholding, is reached. Therefore, several options for fidelity-driven evolution strategies can be proposed:

1. *The "original" rule*: eroding $A_1$ if $-(u_0 - c_1)^2 + (u_0 - c_2)^2 < 0$ and dilating it if $-(u_0 - c_1)^2 + (u_0 - c_2)^2 > 0$.
2. *The "Otsu-aware" rule*: At initialization, $A_1$ and $A_2$ are associated with their "optimal" partitioning (calculated only once). Even if changes in $A_1$ and $A_2$ occur due to other terms, it is still possible to immediately recognize the "misattributed" borderline pixels, which need to be re-assigned.
3. *The "no-rule" rule* (our preference): Since the initialization already used Otsu's criterion in an optimal manner, it would be better to drop the fidelity from further consideration, allowing other factors to properly influence the calculations.

**Table 1.** Description of the algorithm, including various options

| Step | Recommendation | Additional options |
|------|----------------|--------------------|
| Initialization | Otsu's method in order to partition $u_0$ into $A_1$ and $A_2$ | |
| Evolution | Median filter with radius 1[a] on label ($A_1$ and $A_2$) map | Median filters with other radii[a] on label map, for regularization purposes |
| | No area term ($v = 0$) | If desired, dilation/erosion of $A_1$ or $A_2$ (and vice versa) |
| | No fidelity term ($\lambda_1 = \lambda_2 = 0$) | • Dilation/erosion depending on fidelity term <br> • Re-assigning "misattributed" Otsu borderline pixels |
| Stopping criterion | Convergence of $A_1$ and $A_2$ | |

[a] Please note, that due to certain challenges in implementing median filters utilizing Euclidean neighborhoods, a more convenient maximum norm is used in the experimental section below. E.g., radius 1 neighborhood now includes 9 and not 5 pixels.

**Proposed algorithm:** Our recommendations are summarized in Table 1.

## 4   Experimental Results

In the following experiments, a segmentation is demonstrated on non-trivial images, some of which resembling the ones used by [1]. Figure 2 presents an object with a smooth contour, Fig. 3 shows satellite image of Europe night-lights, Fig. 4 demonstrates a spiral art-work, while Fig. 5 represents a noisy inscription from the ancient biblical fort of Arad (for further details and analysis, see [24–26]). It can be observed that in general, the default or slightly regularized parameters produce high-quality segmentation, superior to

**Fig. 2.** Segmentation of an object of smooth contour: original image (*left*), vs. result with default setting (*center*), vs. result with radius = 11 (*right*)

**Fig. 3.** Segmentation of a satellite image of Europe night-lights: original image (*left*), vs. Otsu binarization (*center*), vs. result with the default setting (*right*). Image courtesy NASA/Goddard Space Flight Center Scientific Visualization Studio, public domain

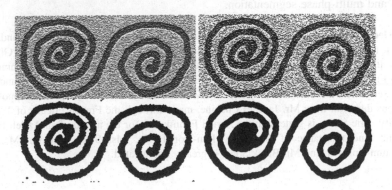

**Fig. 4.** Segmentation of a spiral art-work: original image (*upper left*), vs. Otsu binarization (*upper right*), vs. result with the default setting (*lower left*), vs. result with radius = 2 (*lower right*). Image courtesy José-Manuel Benito Álvarez, public domain

Otsu with no curvature evolution. We omit comparisons with the CV algorithm, due to the high dependence of its results on the various parameters in use, as explained above.

**Fig. 5.** Segmentation of an ancient and noisy inscription (Arad ostracon No. 1): original image (*upper left*), vs. Otsu binarization (*upper right*), vs. result with the default setting (*lower left*), vs. result with radius = 2 (*lower right*). Image courtesy Institute of Archaeology, Tel Aviv University and Israel Antiquities Authority

## 5 Summary and Future Directions

The paper presents a detailed analysis of the CV segmentation framework. Among the main novelties of the article are the surprising relation between the Otsu binarization method and the fidelity terms of CV energy functional (which may explain the results of [12], resembling binarization), allowing for intelligent initialization of the functional. This is accompanied by a suggestion of a very fast, parameter-free morphological framework, substituting the CV PDE-based segmentation method. The experimental results demonstrate the soundness of our approach. Future research direction may include further experiments, as well as the extension of our method into vector-valued images and multi-phase segmentation.

**Acknowledgements.** The research received initial funding from the Israel Science Foundation – F.I.R.S.T. (Bikura) Individual Grant no. 644/08, as well as the Israel Science Foundation Grant no. 1457/13. It was also funded by the European Research Council under the European Community's Seventh Framework Programme (FP7/2007-2013)/ERC grant agreement no. 229418, and by an Early Israel grant (New Horizons project), Tel Aviv University. This study was also supported by a generous donation from Mr. Jacques Chahine, made through the French Friends of Tel Aviv University. Arie Shaus is grateful to the Azrieli Foundation for the award of an Azrieli Fellowship. The kind assistance of Dr. Shirly Ben-Dor Evian, Ms. Sivan Einhorn, Ms. Shira Faigenbaum-Golovin, and Mr. Barak Sober is greatly appreciated.

## References

1. Chan, T.F., Vese, L.: Active contours without edges. IEEE Trans. Image Process. **10**(2), 266–277 (2001)
2. Mumford, D., Shah, J.: Optimal approximation by piecewise smooth functions and associated variational problems. Commun. Pure Appl. Math. **42**, 577–685 (1989)
3. Chan, T.F., Yezrielev Sandberg, B., Vese, L.: Active contours without edges for vector-valued images. J. Vis. Commun. Image Represent. **11**(2), 130–141 (2000)

4. Vese, L., Chan, T.F.: A multiphase level set framework for image segmentation using the Mumford and Shah model. Int. J. Comput. Vision **50**(3), 271–293 (2002)
5. Osher, S., Sethian, J.A.: Fronts propagating with curvature-dependent speed: algorithms based on Hamilton-Jacobi formulation. J. Comput. Phys. **79**, 12–49 (1988)
6. Xia, R., Liu, W., Zhao, J., Li, L.: An optimal initialization technique for improving the segmentation performance of Chan-Vese model. In: Proceedings of the IEEE International Conference on Automation and Logistics, pp. 411–415 (2007)
7. Canny, J.: A computational approach to edge detection. IEEE Trans. Pattern Anal. Mach. Intell. **8**(6), 679–697 (1986)
8. Solem, J.E., Overgaard, N.C., Heyden, A.: Initialization techniques for segmentation with the Chan-Vese model. In: 18th International Conference on Pattern Recognition, ICPR 2006, pp. 171–174 (2006)
9. Pan, Y., Birdwell, J.D., Djouadi, S.M.: Efficient implementation of the Chan-Vese models without solving PDEs. In: IEEE 8th Workshop on Multimedia Signal Processing, pp. 350–354 (2006)
10. Wang, X.F., Huang, D.F., Xu, H.: An efficient local Chan-Vese model for image segmentation. Pattern Recogn. **43**, 603–618 (2010)
11. Liu, S., Peng, Y.: A local region-based Chan-Vese model for image segmentation. Pattern Recogn. **45**(7), 2769–2779 (2012)
12. Brown, E.S., Chan, T.F., Bresson, X.: Completely convex formulation of the Chan-Vese image segmentation model. Int. J. Comput. Vision **98**(1), 103–121 (2012)
13. Otsu, N.: A threshold selection method from gray-level histograms. IEEE Trans. Syst. Man. Cybern. **9**(1), 62–66 (1979)
14. Xu, H., Wang, X.-F.: Automated segmentation using a fast implementation of the Chan-Vese models. In: Huang, D.-S., Wunsch, D.C., Levine, D.S., Jo, K.-H. (eds.) ICIC 2008. LNCS (LNAI), vol. 5227, pp. 1135–1141. Springer, Heidelberg (2008). doi:10.1007/978-3-540-85984-0_136
15. Catté, F., Dibos, F., Koepfler, G.: A morphological scheme for mean curvature motion and applications to anisotropic diffusion and motion of level sets. SIAM J. Numer. Anal. **32**(6), 1895–1909 (1995)
16. Álvarez, L., Baumela, L., Henríquez, P., Márquez-Neila, P.: Morphological snakes. In: Proceedings of the IEEE International Conference on Computer Vision and Pattern Recognition, CVPR 2010, pp. 2197–2202 (2010)
17. Welk, M., Breuß, M., Vogel, O.: Morphological amoebas are self-snakes. J. Math. Imaging Vis. **39**, 87–99 (2011)
18. Jalba, A.C., Roerdink, J.B.T.M.: An efficient morphological active surface model for volumetric image segmentation. In: Wilkinson, M.H.F., Roerdink, J.B.T.M. (eds.) ISMM 2009. LNCS, vol. 5720, pp. 193–204. Springer, Heidelberg (2009). doi:10.1007/978-3-642-03613-2_18
19. Anh, N.T.L., Kim, S.-H., Yang, H.-J.: Color image segmentation using a morphological gradient-based active contour model. Int. J. Innovative Comput. Inf. Control **9**(11), 4471–4484 (2013)
20. Fox, V.L., Milanova, M., Al-Ali, S.: A hybrid morphological active contour for natural images. Int. J. Comput. Sci. Eng. Appl. **3**(4), 1–13 (2013)
21. Fox, V.L., Milanova, M., Al-Ali, S.: A morphological multiphase active contour for vascular segmentation. Int. J. Bioinf. Biosci. **3**(3), 1–12 (2013)
22. Oliveira, R.B., Tavares, J.M.R.S., Marranghello, N., Pereira, A.S.: An approach to edge detection in images of skin lesions by Chan-Vese model. In: Proceedings of the 8th Doctoral Symposium in Informatics Engineering (2013)

23. Kishore, P.V.V., Prasad, C.R.: Train rolling stock segmentation with morphological differential gradient active contours. In: Proceedings of the International Conference on Advances in Computing, Communications and Informatics, ICACCI 2015, pp. 1174–1178 (2015)
24. Shaus, A., Turkel, E., Piasetzky, E.: Binarization of first temple period inscriptions: performance of existing algorithms and a new registration based scheme. In: 2012 International Conference on Frontiers in Handwriting Recognition, ICFHR 2012, pp. 645–650 (2012)
25. Shaus, A., Sober, B., Turkel, E., Piasetzky, E.: Improving binarization via sparse methods. In: Proceedings of the 16th International Graphonomics Society Conference, IGS 2013, pp. 163–166 (2013)
26. Faigenbaum-Golovin, S., Shaus, A., Sober, B., Levin, D., Na'aman, N., Sass, B., Turkel, E., Piasetzky, E., Finkelstein, I.: Algorithmic handwriting analysis of Judah's military correspondence sheds light on composition of biblical texts. Proc. Nat. Acad. Sci. **113** (17), 4664–4669 (2016)

# Image Enhancement by Volume Limitation in Binary Tomography

László Varga, Zoltán Ozsvár, and Péter Balázs[✉]

Department of Image Processing and Computer Graphics,
University of Szeged, Árpád tér 2., Szeged 6720, Hungary
{vargalg,ozsvar,pbalazs}@inf.u-szeged.hu

**Abstract.** We introduce two methods to limit the reconstruction volume in binary tomography. The first one can be used when the CT scanner is equipped with a laser distance measurement device which gives information of the outer boundary of the object to reconstruct. The second one uses dilated versions of a blueprint of the object under investigation. Such a blueprint is often available in non-destructive testing of industrial objects. By experiments we show that the proposed methods can enhance the quality of the reconstructed images.

**Keywords:** Binary tomography · Reconstruction · Volume limitation · Non-destructive testing

## 1 Introduction

Tomography [4,7] is a methodology of reconstructing the inner structure of objects. It is a set of tools for solving various problems from fields of medical radiology, industrial non-destructive testing, and crystallography, just to mention a few. In transmission tomography the goal is to reconstruct the structure of the object from transmitted projections. This is achieved by exposing the object of study to some type of radiation (e.g., X-ray, or neutron radiation), and measuring the intensity of the beams passing through the material. As the beams pass through the object, the material absorb a portion of the energy in a way characterising the density of the incident object pixels. Therefore, we can deduce the summed densities along the paths of the beams. This process is repeated from many directions, giving information along many beam paths which can be used to reconstruct (at least from the pure mathematical point of view) the density at any inner point of the object.

Although the reconstruction methods have a wide theoretical background, the acquisition of projections is also an important issue. In most cases the scanners use penetrating radiation, that on one hand damages the object of study

This research was supported by the OTKA grant of the National Scientific Research Fund. Project number: K112998. Project title: "Discrete Tomography from Incomplete and Uncertain Data: Modelling, Algorithms, and Applications".

© Springer International Publishing AG 2016
G. Bebis et al. (Eds.): ISVC 2016, Part I, LNCS 10072, pp. 213–222, 2016.
DOI: 10.1007/978-3-319-50835-1_20

(e.g., X-ray radiation can do harm to living tissue of human organs), and on another hand can be quite expensive to produce (e.g., neutron rays in industrial tomography). Therefore, there is always a strive to limit the number of projections. However, a highly accurate reconstruction can only be calculated from a sufficiently high amount of information which primarily arises from the projections. Thus, if we limit the projection count, we need additional knowledge, to achieve a good image quality.

Discrete tomography [5,6] assumes that the object of study consists only of a few known [3,8,10] or unknown [1,9,13] materials. In addition, the improvement of the results can be achieved by the adjustment of the projection directions [2,11]. In this paper, we propose the *limitation of the reconstructed volume* to improve the reconstruction quality. The lack of information in the projection set is augmented by reducing the search space of possible solutions. From the physical perspective, this can be reached by using the blueprint of the examined object or by equipping the scanner with extra measurement devices such as distance measurement lasers. Our aim is to investigate the pure outcome of this approach, regarding image quality. Nevertheless, we emphasize that the method to be presented here can be combined with the abovementioned advanced techniques exploiting also prior information of the image to reconstruct.

The paper is structured as follows. In Sect. 2 we provide a formulation of the mathematical background of our methodology. In Sect. 3 we describe two possible volume limitation techniques. Then, in Sect. 4 we outline an experimental set-up we used for validating the concept, and in Sect. 5 we summarize our results. Finally, Sect. 6 is for the conclusions.

## 2    Problem Formalism

Our formulation assumes that we want to reconstruct a 2-dimensional cross section of the object, represented by a 2D image of size $n \times n$. 3D images can be reconstructed by cleverly fusioning the 2D slices. We assume that rays belonging to the same projection are parallel. This parallel-beam geometry is typical, e.g., in synchrotron experiments. Thus, the projections can be represented by a set of parallel lines intersecting the image as illustrated in Fig. 1.

In this formulation, the reconstruction can be performed by solving a system of equations

$$\mathbf{Ax} = \mathbf{b}, \tag{1}$$

where $\mathbf{x} \in [0,1]^{n^2}$ is the vector of all $n^2$ unknown image pixels, $\mathbf{b}$ is the vector of all $m$ projection values, and $\mathbf{A}$ is a projection coefficient matrix of size $m \times n^2$ that describes the projection geometry by all $a_{ij}$ elements representing the intersection of the $i$-th projection line through the $j$-th pixel.

## 3    Volume Limitation

Our work is based on limiting the reconstructed volume to reduce the under-determinedness of the reconstruction. This is performed by creating a mask for

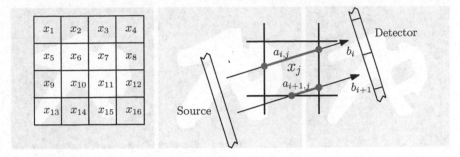

**Fig. 1.** Equation system-based representation of the parallel beam projection geometry on a discrete image.

the images, and pre-determining which pixels can correspond to the object of study, and which pixels must only contain the empty background. Depending on the application, the predetermination of non-object pixels can be based on shape priors of the object, or additional examinations, described below. Then, the reconstruction is carried out by removing the non-object variables from the equation system.

### 3.1  Known Objects with Small Misorientation

In non-destructive testing, it is a common task to reconstruct the structure of a known industrial specimen looking for small malformations (e.g., fractures or bubbles) in the material. If we have a blueprint of the object, its shape is almost perfectly known in advance. Therefore we can predict where the object pixels are likely to appear in the image. In the reconstruction we only have to take two issues into account. First, small malformations of the object can cause a slightly different boundary or interior compared to the blueprint. Second, the object can be misaligned in the scanner compared to the alignment of the blueprint, which can be described by a rigid-body transformation between the two.

Thus, having information about the approximate positioning and shape of the object, we only expect small distortions compared to the blueprint. These occur either on the boundary of the objects or inside the material, but for both cases a dilated version of the blueprint is satisfactory to obtain the positions of possible object pixels. The limit of the distance from the predicted object pixels can also be tuned to the application, if we can limit the size of the deformation of the object, and the level of misalignment. Therefore, we created the first set of masks by taking the rasterized blueprint of the objects, and performing a dilation with structuring elements of different sizes (see, e.g., Fig. 2b).

### 3.2  Laser Scanning the Outer Surface

Another approach for limiting the size of the reconstructed volume is to equip the transmission scanning device with a laser scanner. This small-distance measuring

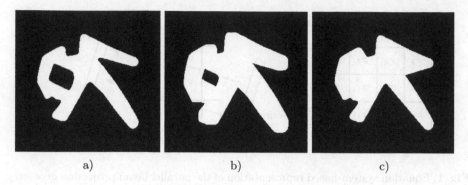

a)                    b)                    c)

**Fig. 2.** Example of the volume masks used for the reconstructions. A phantom object used for the experiments (a), a dilation of the blueprint with a disk of 5 pixel radius as structuring element (b), and a simulated laser scan (c).

device can be fixed, say, to the beam source. Such a device costs a few hundred dollars, and can be used to determine the hull of the object, limiting its volume. Therefore, the second set of masks was designed by simulating the scanning of the object.

The laser scanner setup was modelled based on a real scanning device rotating around the object of study, aiming to the center of rotation (that is the same as the center of rotation of the tomographic scanner). Along this circular orbit a ray is emitted towards the rotation center with an angular step of 0.1°. For each ray the closest object point is determined. If no object point is hit then we suppose the closest object point to be the intersection of the ray with the opposite side of the circle. Pixels covered by line segments defined by the source point of the rays and the corresponding closest points can be excluded from the reconstruction (they are surely background pixels). An example mask generated by this method is shown in Fig. 2c. Of course, this outer scanning procedure can be calculated with various device settings, and even with multiple laser scanners. This basic set-up was sufficient for our purposes.

## 4    Experimental Set-Up

In order, to study the effectiveness of our approach we conducted experiments on binary phantom images. We used the dataset of [12] that contained 23 images. After generating simulated projections of the phantoms we reconstructed them by the Simultaneous Iterative Reconstruction Technique (SIRT) [4] and also by the Discrete Algebraic Reconstruction Technique (DART) [3]. Due to space limitations we only report here on results obtained by SIRT. We observed similar trends in case of DART.

Our first aim was to determine if limiting the reconstructed volume can be beneficial regarding the quality of the reconstruction. If so, then such an extension of reconstruction methods could be used for improving the accuracy.

For this purpose we compared the reconstructed images to the original phantoms by the *Relative Mean Error* (*RME*) error measure given as

$$RME(\mathbf{x}^*, \hat{\mathbf{x}}) = \frac{\sum_i |x_i^* - \hat{x}_i|}{\sum_i \lceil x_i^* \rceil}, \tag{2}$$

where $\lceil . \rceil$ denotes the ceiling function, and $\mathbf{x}^*$ and $\hat{\mathbf{x}}$ stands for the original and the reconstructed image, respectively.

Our second goal was to study the effect of noise on the projections. It is known, that the projection values gathered from real scanners are usually affected by some type of noise, leading to imperfect reconstructions (showing up as misreconstructed pixels in the volume). In case of using a limited volume for the reconstruction one can note, that the effect of the noise is limited to a smaller set of pixels. This might lead to bigger distortions of the pixel values, and have a stronger unwanted effect as we reduce the volume size. For examining the phenomenon, we added Gaussian noise with zero mean and varying standard deviation to the data, and performed the reconstructions from the distorted projections.

In this experiment, we evaluated the results in two different ways. First we calculated the *RME* value of the reconstructions, and compared the statistics to the original noiseless reconstructions. Second, we calculated the pixel-based differences of the original, and each noise-affected reconstruction. The comparison was calculated by the average pixel difference

$$\frac{\sum_{i \in M} |x_i - y_i|}{\sum_{i \in M} 1}, \tag{3}$$

assuming that $M$ is the set of pixels inside the mask, and $\mathbf{x}$ and $\mathbf{y}$ are the reconstructions with and without the noise on the projections, respectively. This evaluation helped us to determine the level of change the noise can cause in the reconstruction, and also to compare the changes according to the size of the limited volume.

## 5   Results

The analysis of the results revealed, that the limitation of the reconstructed volume can indeed improve the accuracy of the reconstructions. In Table 1 one can find the average RME values of the reconstructions (calculated on the 23 test images), according to the number of projections, the size of the mask, and the amount of noise added to the reconstructions.

We can observe that regardless of the amount of noise added, or the number of projections, the reconstructed result was improved by the limitation of the reconstructed volume. In case of the dilatation-based limitation, the improvement was better with a smaller volume, with a strictly monotonous tendency. Examining the results of the laser-scanner generated masks we can also say, that smaller volumes lead to better reconstructions.

**Table 1.** *RME* values of the reconstructions with varying number of projections, volume limit sizes, and projection noise levels (standard deviation is given in the second row).

| 6 projections | | | | | | | | |
|---|---|---|---|---|---|---|---|---|
| Noise | 0.0 | 0.1 | 0.5 | 1.0 | 2.0 | 3.0 | 4.0 | 5.0 |
| Laser | 0.152 | 0.153 | 0.161 | 0.174 | 0.196 | 0.214 | 0.233 | 0.251 |
| Dil. 1 | 0.149 | 0.150 | 0.163 | 0.176 | 0.196 | 0.212 | 0.225 | 0.236 |
| Dil. 2 | 0.189 | 0.191 | 0.203 | 0.219 | 0.248 | 0.268 | 0.287 | 0.303 |
| Dil. 3 | 0.208 | 0.210 | 0.223 | 0.239 | 0.274 | 0.297 | 0.323 | 0.341 |
| Dil. 4 | 0.221 | 0.223 | 0.234 | 0.252 | 0.289 | 0.314 | 0.343 | 0.363 |
| Dil. 5 | 0.231 | 0.233 | 0.244 | 0.263 | 0.299 | 0.327 | 0.357 | 0.380 |
| Dil. 10 | 0.263 | 0.264 | 0.275 | 0.293 | 0.330 | 0.363 | 0.397 | 0.423 |
| Dil. 15 | 0.282 | 0.284 | 0.294 | 0.311 | 0.346 | 0.382 | 0.419 | 0.447 |
| Dil. 20 | 0.296 | 0.297 | 0.307 | 0.325 | 0.359 | 0.396 | 0.434 | 0.466 |
| Dil. 25 | 0.305 | 0.307 | 0.317 | 0.334 | 0.368 | 0.405 | 0.443 | 0.475 |
| Dil. 50 | 0.332 | 0.334 | 0.342 | 0.358 | 0.392 | 0.428 | 0.469 | 0.503 |
| No mask | 0.342 | 0.343 | 0.351 | 0.364 | 0.392 | 0.423 | 0.458 | 0.488 |

| 12 projections | | | | | | | | |
|---|---|---|---|---|---|---|---|---|
| Noise | 0.0 | 0.1 | 0.5 | 1.0 | 2.0 | 3.0 | 4.0 | 5.0 |
| Laser | 0.121 | 0.121 | 0.126 | 0.135 | 0.154 | 0.169 | 0.187 | 0.205 |
| Dil. 1 | 0.106 | 0.107 | 0.116 | 0.129 | 0.153 | 0.171 | 0.188 | 0.204 |
| Dil. 2 | 0.128 | 0.129 | 0.138 | 0.151 | 0.180 | 0.201 | 0.224 | 0.246 |
| Dil. 3 | 0.140 | 0.141 | 0.150 | 0.164 | 0.193 | 0.216 | 0.242 | 0.268 |
| Dil. 4 | 0.149 | 0.150 | 0.158 | 0.172 | 0.201 | 0.226 | 0.254 | 0.280 |
| Dil. 5 | 0.156 | 0.157 | 0.165 | 0.179 | 0.208 | 0.233 | 0.261 | 0.291 |
| Dil. 10 | 0.180 | 0.181 | 0.188 | 0.200 | 0.229 | 0.255 | 0.286 | 0.316 |
| Dil. 15 | 0.194 | 0.195 | 0.201 | 0.212 | 0.240 | 0.267 | 0.299 | 0.330 |
| Dil. 20 | 0.203 | 0.205 | 0.211 | 0.222 | 0.249 | 0.277 | 0.309 | 0.341 |
| Dil. 25 | 0.211 | 0.212 | 0.219 | 0.231 | 0.257 | 0.284 | 0.317 | 0.349 |
| Dil. 50 | 0.233 | 0.234 | 0.241 | 0.252 | 0.279 | 0.305 | 0.339 | 0.372 |
| No mask | 0.243 | 0.244 | 0.249 | 0.258 | 0.278 | 0.301 | 0.327 | 0.356 |

| 18 projections | | | | | | | | |
|---|---|---|---|---|---|---|---|---|
| Noise | 0.0 | 0.1 | 0.5 | 1.0 | 2.0 | 3.0 | 4.0 | 5.0 |
| Laser | 0.113 | 0.114 | 0.117 | 0.124 | 0.139 | 0.154 | 0.170 | 0.181 |
| Dil. 1 | 0.103 | 0.104 | 0.110 | 0.120 | 0.141 | 0.158 | 0.174 | 0.186 |
| Dil. 2 | 0.121 | 0.121 | 0.126 | 0.138 | 0.159 | 0.180 | 0.201 | 0.218 |
| Dil. 3 | 0.131 | 0.132 | 0.137 | 0.147 | 0.171 | 0.193 | 0.216 | 0.235 |
| Dil. 4 | 0.138 | 0.139 | 0.144 | 0.155 | 0.177 | 0.202 | 0.226 | 0.246 |
| Dil. 5 | 0.145 | 0.145 | 0.150 | 0.161 | 0.184 | 0.208 | 0.232 | 0.255 |
| Dil. 10 | 0.168 | 0.168 | 0.174 | 0.184 | 0.205 | 0.229 | 0.255 | 0.278 |
| Dil. 15 | 0.181 | 0.182 | 0.187 | 0.196 | 0.217 | 0.241 | 0.267 | 0.291 |
| Dil. 20 | 0.191 | 0.191 | 0.197 | 0.205 | 0.227 | 0.251 | 0.277 | 0.302 |
| Dil. 25 | 0.198 | 0.199 | 0.204 | 0.214 | 0.235 | 0.259 | 0.285 | 0.308 |
| Dil. 50 | 0.220 | 0.221 | 0.226 | 0.235 | 0.257 | 0.282 | 0.307 | 0.332 |
| No mask | 0.229 | 0.230 | 0.234 | 0.241 | 0.258 | 0.277 | 0.298 | 0.318 |

From the closer examination of the images we found that the outer boundary of the reconstructed object is nicer in the case of the laser scanning technique, while if the object contains holes the dilated masks can yield better image quality, especially in the interior of the object. An example can be seen in Fig. 3. This observation is in accordance with the method the mask is generated.

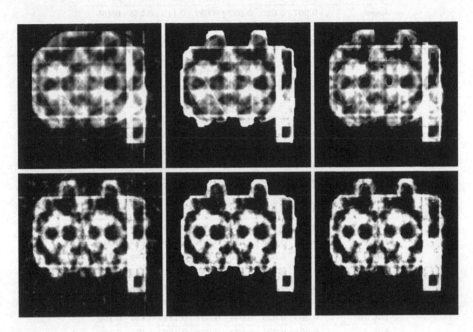

**Fig. 3.** Reconstruction from the noiseless data with different volume masks from 6 (top row) and 12 (bottom row) projections. Applied masks are from left to right: no mask; mask of laser scanner; and 5 pixel dilation of the blueprint, respectively.

We also compared the noiseless reconstructions to the noisy ones, to see the amount of change in the reconstruction according to the size of the reconstructed volume. Table 2 shows the numerical results of these comparisons while Fig. 4 presents some noisy reconstructions.

Based on these results we can deduce that the limitation of the reconstructed volume can amplify the effect of the projection noise. The reason of this is that the pixels of the reconstructed image absorb the noise, which results in small perturbation of the pixel values. If we limit the size of the reconstructed volume, then a smaller number of pixels have to absorb the same amount of noise. This is, however, limited to only a certain volume size in our experiments. Reconstructing the image without volume limitation, or with a small mask, practically worked the same. However, when we performed reconstructions with bigger masks, the effect of the noise became stronger. This phenomenon must be examined in more detail, in the further work.

**Table 2.** Absolute mean difference between the reconstructions from the noiseless and noisy data.

### 6 projections

| Noise | 0.0 | 0.1 | 0.5 | 1.0 | 2.0 | 3.0 | 4.0 | 5.0 |
|---|---|---|---|---|---|---|---|---|
| Laser | - | 0.007 | 0.029 | 0.052 | 0.087 | 0.112 | 0.135 | 0.155 |
| Dil. 1 | - | 0.012 | 0.050 | 0.079 | 0.115 | 0.137 | 0.154 | 0.168 |
| Dil. 2 | - | 0.011 | 0.049 | 0.083 | 0.128 | 0.156 | 0.179 | 0.198 |
| Dil. 3 | - | 0.011 | 0.048 | 0.082 | 0.133 | 0.164 | 0.191 | 0.212 |
| Dil. 4 | - | 0.010 | 0.046 | 0.081 | 0.134 | 0.167 | 0.196 | 0.219 |
| Dil. 5 | - | 0.010 | 0.045 | 0.080 | 0.133 | 0.167 | 0.198 | 0.222 |
| Dil. 10 | - | 0.008 | 0.040 | 0.074 | 0.127 | 0.166 | 0.199 | 0.225 |
| Dil. 15 | - | 0.008 | 0.037 | 0.069 | 0.120 | 0.162 | 0.196 | 0.224 |
| Dil. 20 | - | 0.007 | 0.035 | 0.066 | 0.117 | 0.158 | 0.193 | 0.223 |
| Dil. 25 | - | 0.007 | 0.034 | 0.064 | 0.113 | 0.155 | 0.190 | 0.219 |
| Dil. 50 | - | 0.006 | 0.029 | 0.054 | 0.102 | 0.142 | 0.176 | 0.208 |
| No mask | - | 0.005 | 0.026 | 0.050 | 0.093 | 0.131 | 0.164 | 0.194 |

### 12 projections

| Noise | 0.0 | 0.1 | 0.5 | 1.0 | 2.0 | 3.0 | 4.0 | 5.0 |
|---|---|---|---|---|---|---|---|---|
| Laser | - | 0.004 | 0.018 | 0.033 | 0.060 | 0.080 | 0.100 | 0.118 |
| Dil. 1 | - | 0.006 | 0.028 | 0.051 | 0.084 | 0.108 | 0.128 | 0.144 |
| Dil. 2 | - | 0.006 | 0.027 | 0.050 | 0.088 | 0.115 | 0.139 | 0.160 |
| Dil. 3 | - | 0.006 | 0.027 | 0.050 | 0.089 | 0.117 | 0.143 | 0.167 |
| Dil. 4 | - | 0.005 | 0.026 | 0.049 | 0.088 | 0.117 | 0.145 | 0.169 |
| Dil. 5 | - | 0.005 | 0.026 | 0.049 | 0.087 | 0.117 | 0.145 | 0.170 |
| Dil. 10 | - | 0.005 | 0.023 | 0.044 | 0.081 | 0.111 | 0.141 | 0.166 |
| Dil. 15 | - | 0.004 | 0.021 | 0.041 | 0.076 | 0.107 | 0.136 | 0.162 |
| Dil. 20 | - | 0.004 | 0.020 | 0.039 | 0.074 | 0.105 | 0.134 | 0.159 |
| Dil. 25 | - | 0.004 | 0.020 | 0.038 | 0.072 | 0.102 | 0.131 | 0.156 |
| Dil. 50 | - | 0.003 | 0.017 | 0.034 | 0.065 | 0.092 | 0.120 | 0.144 |
| No mask | - | 0.003 | 0.015 | 0.030 | 0.058 | 0.084 | 0.109 | 0.131 |

### 18 projections

| Noise | 0.0 | 0.1 | 0.5 | 1.0 | 2.0 | 3.0 | 4.0 | 5.0 |
|---|---|---|---|---|---|---|---|---|
| Laser | - | 0.003 | 0.013 | 0.025 | 0.046 | 0.065 | 0.084 | 0.097 |
| Dil. 1 | - | 0.004 | 0.021 | 0.040 | 0.070 | 0.093 | 0.111 | 0.126 |
| Dil. 2 | - | 0.004 | 0.020 | 0.039 | 0.070 | 0.095 | 0.118 | 0.136 |
| Dil. 3 | - | 0.004 | 0.019 | 0.038 | 0.070 | 0.096 | 0.120 | 0.139 |
| Dil. 4 | - | 0.004 | 0.019 | 0.037 | 0.068 | 0.096 | 0.120 | 0.141 |
| Dil. 5 | - | 0.004 | 0.018 | 0.036 | 0.067 | 0.095 | 0.119 | 0.142 |
| Dil. 10 | - | 0.003 | 0.017 | 0.033 | 0.062 | 0.089 | 0.114 | 0.136 |
| Dil. 15 | - | 0.003 | 0.015 | 0.030 | 0.058 | 0.085 | 0.109 | 0.131 |
| Dil. 20 | - | 0.003 | 0.015 | 0.029 | 0.056 | 0.083 | 0.106 | 0.128 |
| Dil. 25 | - | 0.003 | 0.014 | 0.029 | 0.055 | 0.080 | 0.103 | 0.124 |
| Dil. 50 | - | 0.002 | 0.012 | 0.024 | 0.049 | 0.072 | 0.093 | 0.113 |
| No mask | - | 0.002 | 0.011 | 0.022 | 0.043 | 0.063 | 0.083 | 0.102 |

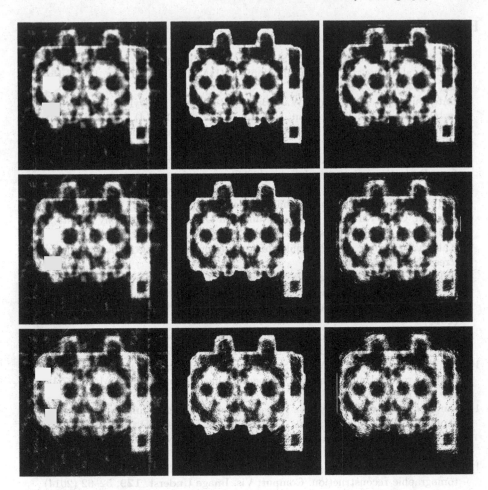

**Fig. 4.** Reconstructions with different volume limiting masks and different magnitudes of additive noise. Images from left to right were reconstructed with no mask, mask of the laser scanner and mask gained from 5 pixel dilation of the blueprint, respectively. Standard deviation of the added noise from top to bottom was 1, 3 and 5, respectively.

# 6    Conclusion

We proposed variants of a method to limit the reconstruction volume in binary tomography. By experiments on software phantoms we showed that this approach can enhance the quality of the reconstructed images, even if the projections are affected by noise. Although, here we only investigated binary images, we believe that our method can be applied in general for tomographic image reconstruction problems. A typical area where the presented approach can be introduced is industrial non-destructive testing.

# References

1. van Aarle, W., Batenburg, K.J., Sijbers, J.: Automatic parameter estimation for the discrete algebraic reconstruction technique (DART). IEEE Trans. Image Process. **21**(11), 4608–4621 (2012)
2. Batenburg, K.J., Palenstijn, W.J., Balázs, P., Sijbers, J.: Dynamic angle selection in binary tomography. Comput. Vis. Image Underst. **117**(4), 306–318 (2013)
3. Batenburg, K.J., Sijbers, J.: DART: a practical reconstruction algorithm for discrete tomography. IEEE Trans. Image Process. **20**, 2542–2553 (2011)
4. Herman, G.T.: Fundamentals of Computerized Tomography: Image Reconstruction from Projections. Springer, London (2009)
5. Herman, G.T., Kuba, A. (eds.): Discrete Tomography: Foundations, Algorithms, and Applications, 1st edn. Birkhäuser, Basel (1999)
6. Herman, G.T., Kuba, A. (eds.): Advances in Discrete Tomography and its Applications, 1st edn. Birkhäuser, Basel (2007)
7. Kak, A.C., Slaney, M.: Principles of Computerized Tomographic Imaging. IEEE Press, New York (1999)
8. Lukić, T.: Discrete tomography reconstruction based on the multi-well potential. In: Aggarwal, J., Barneva, R., Brimkov, V., Koroutchev, K., Korutcheva, E. (eds.) Combinatorial Image Analysis. LNCS, vol. 6636, pp. 335–345. Springer, Heidelberg (2011)
9. Nemeth, J.: Discrete tomography with unknown intensity levels using higher-order statistics. J. Math. Imaging Vis. **53**(3), 314–331 (2015)
10. Schüle, T., Schnörr, C., Weber, S., Hornegger, J.: Discrete tomography by convex-concave regularization and D.C. programming. Discrete Appl. Math. **151**(1–3), 229–243 (2005)
11. Varga, L., Balázs, P., Nagy, A.: Projection selection algorithms for discrete tomography. In: Blanc-Talon, J., Bone, D., Philips, W., Popescu, D., Scheunders, P. (eds.) Advanced Concepts for Intelligent Vision Systems. LNCS, vol. 6474, pp. 390–401. Springer, Heidelberg (2010)
12. Varga, L.G., Nyúl, L., Nagy, A., Balázs, P.: Local and global uncertainty in binary tomographic reconstruction. Comput. Vis. Image Underst. **129**, 52–62 (2014)
13. Zhuge, X., Palenstijn, W.J., Batenburg, K.J.: TVR-DART: a more robust algorithm for discrete tomography from limited projection data with automated gray value estimation. IEEE Trans. Image Process. **25**(1), 455–468 (2016)

# Resolution-Independent Superpixels Based on Convex Constrained Meshes Without Small Angles

Jeremy Forsythe[1,2]($\boxtimes$), Vitaliy Kurlin[3], and Andrew Fitzgibbon[4]

[1] Vienna University of Technology, Favoritenstr. 9-11/E186, 1040 Vienna, Austria
jforsythe@mail.cg.tuwien.ac.at

[2] Department of Mathematical Sciences, Durham University, Durham DH1 3LE, UK

[3] Computer Science Department, University of Liverpool, Liverpool L69 3BX, UK

[4] Microsoft Research, 21 Station Road, Cambridge CB1 2FB, UK

**Abstract.** The over-segmentation problem for images is studied in the new resolution-independent formulation when a large image is approximated by a small number of convex polygons with straight edges at subpixel precision. These polygonal superpixels are obtained by refining and extending subpixel edge segments to a full mesh of convex polygons without small angles and with approximation guarantees. Another novelty is the objective error difference between an original pixel-based image and the reconstructed image with a best constant color over each superpixel, which does not need human segmentations. The experiments on images from the Berkeley Segmentation Database show that new meshes are smaller and provide better approximations than the state-of-the-art.

## 1 Introduction: Motivations, Problem and Contributions

### 1.1 Spatially Continuous Model for Over-Segmentation of Images

Digital images are given by pixel values at discrete positions. Since images represent a spatially continuous world, the reconstruction problem should be solved in terms of functions defined over a *continuous image domain*, not over a discretization such as a regular grid. For example, grayscale values across a real image edge rarely drop from 255 (white) to 0 (black), but change gradually over 2–3 pixels, see details in [1, Fig. 1]. Hence a real edge between objects is often not along pixel boundaries and should be considered in the infinite family of line segments with any slope and endpoints having real coordinates. The first algorithm to output subpixel edges with theoretical guarantees is LSD [2].

The *over-segmentation problem* is to split an image into *superpixels* (larger than pixels and usually smaller than real objects) that have a nice shape and low variation of color. *Traditional superpixels* are formed by merging square-based pixels, e.g. by clustering. These superpixels often have irregular shapes

J. Forsythe—Supported by the Austrian Science Fund (FWF) project P24600-N23 at TU Wien.

G. Bebis et al. (Eds.): ISVC 2016, Part I, LNCS 10072, pp. 223–233, 2016.
DOI: 10.1007/978-3-319-50835-1_21

with zigzag boundaries and holes inside. The *resolution-independent* approach [1] models a superpixel as a convex polygon with straight edges and vertices at subpixel resolution. Such a polygonal mesh can be rendered at any higher resolution by choosing a best color for each polygon in the *reconstructed image*.

A resulting mesh with constant colors over all polygons can be used to substantially speed-up any higher level processing such as object detection or recognition. Figure 1 shows that only 231 convex polygons are enough to approximate the original $512 \times 512$ image with a small reconstruction error from Definition 1.

## 1.2    Energy Minimization for Resolution-Independent Superpixels

A real image is modeled as a function $I$ that is defined at any point of a continuous image domain $\Omega \subset \mathbb{R}^2$ and takes values in $\mathbb{R}$ (grayscale) or $\mathbb{R}^3$ (color images). We consider the function $I(\mathbf{x})$ taking the same color value at any point $\mathbf{x} \in \Omega$ within every square pixel $B_p$ considered as a continuous subset of $\Omega$. This function $I(\mathbf{x})$ defines a piecewise constant surface over the image domain $\Omega$.

**Fig. 1. Left:** $512 \times 512$ input. **Middle:** 275 Voronoi superpixels have nRMS $\approx 10.2\%$. **Right:** 246 superpixels based on a Convex Constrained Mesh have nRMS $\approx 4.48\%$.

**The reconstruction problem** is to find a latent image represented by a function $u(\mathbf{x})$ that minimizes the energy $E = \iint_{\Omega} \|I(\mathbf{x}) - u(\mathbf{x})\| d\mathbf{x} + R$, where $R$ is a regularizer that penalizes degenerate solutions or reflects an image prior.

The energy $E$ will be the reconstruction error from Definition 1. Usually $u(\mathbf{x})$ is simpler than $I(\mathbf{x})$ in a certain sense. In our case $u(\mathbf{x})$ will have constant values over geometric polygons (superpixels) that are much larger than original pixels. The regularizer will forbid small angles, because narrow triangles may not cover even one pixel, while large angles (even equal to $180°$) cause no difficulties.

So the reconstruction problem is to split a large image into a fixed number of polygons minimizing a difference between the original image function $I(\mathbf{x})$ over many pixels and the reconstructed image $u(\mathbf{x})$ over fewer convex polygons.

### 1.3 Contribution: Convex Constrained Mesh of Superpixels (CCM)

Here are the stages of the algorithm for resolution-independent superpixels.

**1.** The Line Segment Detector [2] finds line segments at subpixel resolution.

**2.** The LSD output is refined to resolve line intersections and small angles.

**3.** The resulting graph is extended to a triangulation without small angles.

**4.** Triangles are merged in convex polygons that also have no small angles.

**5.** The reconstructed image is obtained by finding the best constant color of any convex superpixel after minimizing the approximation error in Definition 1.

The input of the LSD and CCM algorithms above is a grayscale image. The Convex Constrained Mesh (CCM) built at Stage 4 is introduced in Definition 2 and has guarantees in Theorem 5 in terms of the following parameters.

- Min_Angle is the minimum angle between adjacent edges in a final mesh.
- Min_Distance is an approximation tolerance of LSD segments by CCM edges.

The default values are 3 pixels and $30°$ motivated by a similar angle bound in Shewchuk triangulations used at Stage 3. Here are the main contributions.

- The new concepts of the *reconstruction error* (a new quality measure for resolution-independent superpixels not relying on ground truth segmentations) and a *Convex Constrained Mesh* (CCM) are introduced in Definitions 1 and 2.
- The *LSD refinement* (Algorithm 3): disorganized line segments are converted into a planar graph well approximating the original LSD with guarantees.
- *Shewchuk's Triangle extension* (Algorithm 4): a triangulation is upgraded to a Convex Constrained Mesh without small angles as guaranteed by Theorem 5.
- The *experiments on BSD* [3] in Sect. 4 show that CCM have smaller sizes and reconstruction errors than other resolution-independent superpixels, also achieving similar benchmark results in comparison with traditional superpixels.

## 2 Pixel-Based and Resolution-Independent Superpixels

A pixel-based image is represented by a lattice $L$ whose nodes are in a 1–1 correspondence with all pixels, while all edges of $L$ represent adjacency relations between pixels. Usually each pixel is connected to its closest 4 or 8 neighbors.

The seminal *Normalized Cuts* algorithm by Shi and Malik [4] finds an optimal partition of $L$ into connected components, which minimizes an energy taking into account all nodes of $L$. The algorithm by Felzenszwalb and Huttenlocher [5] was faster, but sometimes produced superpixels of irregular sizes and shapes as found by Levinstein et al. [6]. The *Lattice Cut* algorithm by Moore et al. [7] guarantees that the final mesh of superpixels is regular like the original grid of pixels. The best quality in this category is achieved by the Entropy Rate Superpixels (ERS) of Lie et al. [8] minimizing the entropy rate of a random walk on a graph.

The *Simple Linear Iterative Clustering* (SLIC) algorithm by Achanta et al. [9] forms superpixels by $k$-means clustering in a 5-dimensional space using 3 colors and 2 coordinates per pixel. Because the search is restricted to a neighborhood of a given size, the complexity is $O(kmn)$, where $n$ and $m$ are the numbers of pixels and iterations. This gives an average time of 0.2 s per BSD500 image.

SEEDS (Superpixels Extracted via Energy-Driven Sampling) by Van den Bergh et al. [10] seems the first superpixel algorithm to use a *coarse-to-fine optimization*. The colors of all pixels within each fixed superpixel are put in bins, usually 5 bins for each color channel. Each superpixel has the associated sum of deviations of all bins from an average bin within the superpixel. This sum is maximal for a superpixel whose pixels have colors in one bin. SEEDS iteratively maximizes the sum of deviations by shrinking or expanding superpixels.

Almost all past superpixels have *no geometric or topological constraints*, only in a soft form of a regularizer [11]. If a final cluster of pixels in SLIC is disconnected or contains holes, post-processing is needed. TopoCut [12] by Chen et al. has a hard topological constraint in a related problem of image segmentation.

The *key limitation of pixel-based superpixels* is the fixed resolution of an original pixel grid. Resolution-independent superpixels are the next step in approximating images by polygons whose vertices have any subpixel precision.

The *only past resolution-independent superpixels* by Duan and Lafarge [13] and new CCM superpixels use constrained edges from the LSD algorithm of Grompone von Gioi et al. [2], which outputs thin rectangles such that the color substantially changes at their long middle lines, see Fig. 3. The parameters are a tolerance $\tau$ for angles between gradients and a threshold $\varepsilon$ for false alarms.

*Voronoi superpixels* [13] are obtained by splitting an image into Voronoi faces whose centers are chosen along LSD edges. The natural input would be a set of centers, however the algorithm first runs LSD [2] and then chooses centers on both sides of LSD edges. So the edges were soft constraints without proved guarantees yet. By Theorem 5 all given edges are a hard constraint for CCMs.

A *Shewchuk triangulation* is produced by the state-of-the-art Triangle software [14] that guarantees a lower bound (as large as 28°) for all angles. A Convex Constrained Mesh introduced in Definition 2 extends a Shewchuk triangulation to a mesh of convex polygons that also have no small angles by construction.

## 3   A Convex Constrained Mesh (CCM) with Guarantees

A superpixel in Definition 1 can be a union of square pixels or any polygon.

**Definition 1.** *Let an image $I$ have $n$ pixels, each pixel be the $1 \times 1$ square $B_p$ and have Intensity$(p) \in [0, 255]$. Let $I$ be split in superpixels $F_j$ (polygons or unions of pixels) with Color$(F_j) \in [0, 255]$, $j = 1, \ldots, s$. The Reconstruction Error is*

$$RE = \min \sum_{pixels\, p} \left( Intensity(p) - \sum_{j=1}^{s} Area(B_p \cap F_j)Color(F_j) \right)^2, \qquad (1a)$$

*where the minimum is over all $Color(F_j)$, $j = 1, \ldots, s$. The internal sum in $RE$ is small, because each square $B_p$ non-trivially intersects only few superpixels $F_j$, so the intersection $Area(B_p \cap F_j)$ is almost always 0 (when $B_p$ is outside $F_j$) or 1 (when $F_j$ covers $B_p$). For a fixed splitting $I = \cup_{j=1}^{s} F_j$, the function $RE$ quadratically depends on $Color(F_j)$, which are found from a linear system.*

$$\textit{The normalized Root Mean Square is } nRMS = \sqrt{\frac{RE}{n}} \cdot \frac{100\%}{255}. \qquad (1b)$$

*The reconstructed image is the superpixel mesh with all optimal $Color(F_j)$ minimizing $nRMS$. This colored mesh can be rendered at any resolution, see Fig. 2.*

In Definition 1 if a superpixel $F_j$ is a union of square pixels, then $Area(B_p \cap F_j)$ is always 0 or 1, so the optimal $Color(F_j)$ is the mean color of all pixels in $F_j$.

**Fig. 2. Left:** 589 Voronoi superpixels (mesh and reconstruction) have $nRMS \approx 9.22\%$. **Right:** 416 CCM superpixels (red mesh and reconstruction) have $nRMS \approx 6.32\%$ (Color figure online)

Another important motivation for the new CCM superpixels is in Fig. 2, where the reconstructed image from Definition 1 in the second picture is considered as the input for any higher level processing. Since boundaries of a Voronoi mesh may not well approximate constrained edges, the reconstructed image may miss long thin structures, such as legs of a camera tripod in Fig. 2.

**Definition 2.** *Let $G$ be a planar straight line graph with angles at least $\varphi \le 60°$. A Convex Constrained Mesh $CCM(G)$ is a piecewise linear complex such that (2a) $CCM(G)$ has convex polygons with angles $\ge$ Min_Angle $=$ $\arcsin\left(\frac{1}{\sqrt{2}} \sin \frac{\varphi}{2}\right)$;*

*(2b) the graph $G$ is covered by the edges of the Convex Constrained Mesh $CCM(G)$.*

Any Shewchuk triangulation is an example of a Convex Constrained Mesh. However, Definition 2 allows general meshes of any convex polygons without small angles. We build CCM by converting the LSD output in Algorithm 3 into a planar graph $G$ without self-intersections and then by extending $G$ into a polygonal mesh without small angles. All steps below are needed to satisfy main Theorem 5. Subsection 4.1 confirms that CCMs are smaller than past meshes.

**Algorithm 3.** *We convert disorganised line segments with self-intersections from the LSD output into a straight line graph as follows, see details in [15].*

*(3.1) When a segment* almost meets *another segment (within the offset parameter* Min_Distance = 3 *pixels), we extend the first one to a proper intersection.*

*(3.2) When two segments almost meet (endpoints within* Min_Distance*), we extend both to the intersection to avoid small angles/triangles in Algorithm 4.*

*(3.3) When segments meet, we insert their intersection as a vertex in the graph.*

**Algorithm 4.** *We extend a graph G from Algorithm 3, see details in [15].*

*(4.1) The Triangle [14] extends the constrained edges of the graph G to a triangulation that has more edges, no angles smaller than* Min_Angle = 30°.

*(4.2) We merge adjacent faces along their common edge e if the resulting face is still convex. If two new angles at the endpoints of e are almost convex, we try to perturb them within* Min_Distance *to guarantee convexity and no small angles.*

*(4.3) We collapse unconstrained edges if all constrained edges remain fixed.*

The steps above guarantee no small angles in CCM. Theorem 5 is proved in [15].

**Theorem 5.** *Let line segments* $S_1, \ldots, S_k$ *have m intersections. Algorithm 3 builds a* CCM *in time* $O((k + m) \log(k + m))$ *so that*

*(5a) any internal angle in a* CCM *face is not smaller than* Min_Angle*;*

*(5b) the union* $\cup_i S_i$ *is covered by the* Min_Distance*-offset of the CCM's edges.*

## 4    Experimental Comparisons and Conclusions

The sizes and reconstruction errors of the CCM and Voronoi superpixels are compared in Subsects. 4.1 and 4.2. Then two more superpixel algorithms SLIC [9] and SEEDS [10] are also included into BSD benchmarks in Subsect. 4.3.

### 4.1    Sizes of CCMs, Shewchuk's Triangulations and Voronoi Meshes

The first picture in Fig. 3 is the original LSD output. The second picture shows the graph $G$ obtained by the LSD refinement in Algorithm 3. The refined LSD output has more edges than the original LSD, because we include boundary edges of images and also intersection points, which become vertices of graphs.

We use $\phi = 30°$ for the LSD refinement, which leads to Min_Angle $\approx 10.5°$ in Shewchuk's Triangle [14]. We compare Shewchuk triangulations on the original LSD output and CCM on the refined LSD output in Fig. 3, where the 3rd picture shows a zoomed-in green box with many tiny triangles. The final picture in Fig. 3 contains only few faces after merge operations in Algorithm 4. The ratio of Shewchuk triangles to the number of faces in CCMs across BSD is 7.6.

The first step for Voronoi superpixels [13] is to post-process the LSD output when close and near parallel lines are removed, because the target application

**Fig. 3. Top left:** 259 LSD red middle segments in blue rectangles before the refinement in Algorithm 3. **Bottom left:** the refined LSD output (a graph $G$) with 294 edges. **Top middle:** Shewchuk triangulation $T(G)$ with 2260 triangles. **Bottom middle:** the Convex Constrained Mesh CCM$(G)$ with 416 faces. **Top right:** zoomed in green box with tiny triangles. **Bottom right:** zoomed in green box, all tiny triangles are merged. (Color figure online)

was satellite images of urban scenes with many straight edges of buildings. Then long thin structures such as legs of a camera tripod in Fig. 3 are represented only by one edge and may not be recognized in any further processing.

That is why the LSD refinement in Sect. 3 follows another approach and offers guarantees leading to Theorem 5. Table 1 displays the average ratios of face numbers over BSD images. Even when the parameter Eps_Radius of Voronoi superpixels is increased to 12, these ratios converge to a factor of about 3.25.

**Table 1.** Ratios of the face numbers for CCM and Voronoi meshes on the same LSD edges, averaged across BSD images [3]. The parameter Eps_Radius is in pixels.

| Eps_Radius of a superpixel | 4 | 5 | 6 | 7 | 8 | 9 | 10 | 11 | 12 |
|---|---|---|---|---|---|---|---|---|---|
| Mean $\dfrac{\text{Voronoi superpixels [13]}}{\text{number of faces in CCM}}$ | 8.91 | 6.21 | 4.86 | 4.03 | 3.96 | 3.43 | 3.27 | 3.27 | 3.26 |

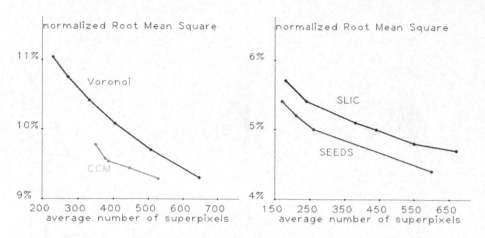

**Fig. 4.** The normalized Root Mean Squares in percents for Voronoi and CCM super-pixels (on the left), SLIC and SEEDS (on the right) averaged over BSD500 images.

**Fig. 5. Left:** 791 Voronoi superpixels (mesh and reconstruction) with $nRMS \approx 8.45\%$. **Right:** 791 CCM superpixels (red mesh and reconstruction) with $nRMS \approx 7.22\%$. (Color figure online)

## 4.2   Approximation Quality of the CCM and Past Superpixels

Since the aim of superpixels is to approximate a large image by a reconstructed image based on a smaller superpixel mesh, the important quality is the standard statistical error $nRMS$ over all pixels, which is introduced in Definition 1.

Figure 4 shows that the reconstructed images of CCM superpixels better approximate original images than Voronoi superpixels. Some convex polygons of CCMs are much larger than Voronoi superpixels, simply because the corresponding regions in images indeed have almost the same intensity, e.g. the sky. Hence taking the best constant color over each superpixel is reasonable.

Voronoi superpixels have similar sizes, because extra centers are added to empty regions using other non-LSD edges. Despite CCMs being obtained from only LSD edges without using colors, the reconstructions have smaller errors in comparison with Voronoi meshes containing more superpixels in Fig. 5.

Figure 4 confirms smaller approximation errors of CCM superpixels across all BSD500 images, where we used the same LSD parameters for CCM and Voronoi superpixels. For all superpixels, we computed optimal colors minimizing the reconstruction error and measured $nRMS$ in percents, see Definition 1.

Each BSD experiment outputs 500 pairs (number of faces, nRMS). We average each coordinate of these pairs and output a single dot per experiment. The first red dot at $(377.1, 9.626\%)$ in Fig. 4 means that CCMs have 377 faces and an approximation error of 9.6% on average. For a fixed image, the LSD algorithm outputs roughly the same number of edges for all reasonable parameters $\tau, \varepsilon$.

So smaller CCMs seem impossible, because all LSD edges are hard constraints, while all faces should be convex. To get larger CCMs, we stop merging faces in Algorithm 4 after getting a certain number of convex faces. The five experiments on Voronoi superpixels with Eps_Radius $= 7, 8, 9, 10, 11$ produced 5 dots along a decreasing curve. Figure 4 implies that Voronoi meshes require more superpixels (507.3 on average) to achieve the similar $nRMS = 9.696\%$.

### 4.3   Standard Benchmarks for CCM and Past Superpixels

The benchmarks BR and CUE are designed for pixel-based superpixels and use human segmentations from BSD [3], see details in [15]. We discretize CCM and Voronoi superpixels by drawing lines in OpenCV to detect boundary pixels. We put all pixels into one superpixel if their centers are in the same polygon.

It is unfair to compare discretized resolution-independent superpixels and pixel-based superpixels on benchmarks designed for the latter superpixels. CCM achieves smaller undersegmentation errors than SEEDS/SLIC and most importantly beats Voronoi superpixels on the objective $nRMS$ as well as on BR.

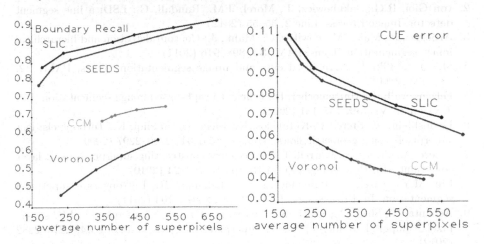

**Fig. 6. Left:** Boundary recall (BR). **Right:** Corrected undersegmentation error.

Pixel-based superpixels SLIC and SEEDS achieve better results on $nRMS$ and Boundary Recall (BR) in Fig. 6, because their superpixels can have irregular boundaries (of only horizontal and vertical edges). However, humans are more likely to sketch straight edges than boundaries consisting of short zigzags.

So irregular pixel-based superpixels are often split by straight ground truth boundaries. Resolution-independent superpixels are convex polygons with straight edges and are expected to have smaller undersegmentation errors in Fig. 6.

Since only a Windows demo is available for Voronoi superpixels [13], we couldn't directly compare the running times of resolution-independent superpixels. We worked on a different platform and confirm that the running time for the CCM on a laptop with 8G RAM is about 0.15 s across BSD500 images.

The key contribution is the new concept of a Convex Constrained Mesh (CCM), which extends any constrained line segments to a mesh of convex polygons without small angles. The paper focused on the quality of CCM superpixels, which seem ideal for detecting long thin structures in urban scenes, see Fig. 2.

- Theorem 5 guarantees the approximation quality and no small angles in CCMs, which also have smaller sizes on the same input in comparison with [13,14].

- The CCM outperforms the only past algorithm [13] for resolution-independent superpixels on BR (Boundary Recall) and the new error $nRMS$ in Fig. 4, and even outperforms pixel-based superpixels on the CUE benchmark in Fig. 6.

# References

1. Viola, F., Fitzgibbon, A., Cipolla, R.: A unifying resolution-independent formulation for early vision. In: Proceedings of CVPR, pp. 494–501 (2012)
2. von Gioi, R.G., Jakubowicz, J., Morel, J.M., Randall, G.: LSD: a line segment detector. Image Process. Line **2**, 35–55 (2012)
3. Arbelaez, P., Maire, M., Fowlkes, C., Malik, J.: Contour detection and hierarchical image segmentation. Trans. PAMI **33**, 898–916 (2011)
4. Shi, J., Malik, J.: Normalized cuts and image segmentation. Trans. PAMI **22**, 888–905 (2000)
5. Felzenszwalb, P., Huttenlocher, D.: Efficient graph-based image segmentation. Int. J. Comput. Vis. **59**, 167–181 (2004)
6. Levinshtein, A., Stere, A., Kutulakos, K., Fleet, D., Siddiqi, K.: Turbopixels: fast superpixels using geometric flows. Trans. PAMI **31**, 2290–2297 (2009)
7. Moore, A., Prince, S., Warrell, J.: Lattice cut - constructing superpixels using layer constraints. In: Proceedings of CVPR, pp. 2117–2124 (2010)
8. Liu, M.Y., Tuzel, O., Ramalingam, S., Chellappa, R.: Entropy rate superpixel segmentation. In: Proceedings of CVPR, pp. 2097–2104 (2011)
9. Achanta, R., Shaji, A., Smith, K., Lucchi, A., Fua, P., Süsstrunk, S.: SLIC superpixels compared to state-of-the-art superpixel methods. T-PAMI **34**, 2274–2282 (2012)
10. Van de Bergh, M., Boix, X., Roig, G., Van Gool, L.: Seeds: superpixels extracted via energy-driven sampling. Int. J. Comput. Vis. **111**, 298–314 (2015)
11. Veksler, O., Boykov, Y., Mehrani, P.: Superpixels and supervoxels in an energy optimization framework. In: Daniilidis, K., Maragos, P., Paragios, N. (eds.) ECCV 2010. LNCS, vol. 6315, pp. 211–224. Springer, Heidelberg (2010). doi:10.1007/978-3-642-15555-0_16

12. Chen, C., Freedman, D., Lampert, C.: Enforcing topological constraints in random field image segmentation. In: Proceedings of CVPR, pp. 2089–2096 (2011)
13. Duan, L., Lafarge, F.: Image partitioning into convex polygons. In: Proceedings of CVPR (Computer Vision and Pattern Recognition), pp. 3119–3127 (2015)
14. Shewchuk, J.R.: Delaunay refinement algorithms for triangular mesh generation. Comput. Geom. Theor. Appl. **22**, 21–74 (2002)
15. Forsythe, J., Kurlin, V., Fitzgibbon, A.: Resolution-independent superpixels based on convex constrained meshes (full version) (2016). http://kurlin.org

# Optimizing Intersection-Over-Union in Deep Neural Networks for Image Segmentation

Md Atiqur Rahman[✉] and Yang Wang

Department of Computer Science, University of Manitoba, Winnipeg, Canada
{atique,ywang}@cs.umanitoba.ca

**Abstract.** We consider the problem of learning deep neural networks (DNNs) for object category segmentation, where the goal is to label each pixel in an image as being part of a given object (foreground) or not (background). Deep neural networks are usually trained with simple loss functions (e.g., softmax loss). These loss functions are appropriate for standard classification problems where the performance is measured by the overall classification accuracy. For object category segmentation, the two classes (foreground and background) are very imbalanced. The intersection-over-union (IoU) is usually used to measure the performance of any object category segmentation method. In this paper, we propose an approach for directly optimizing this IoU measure in deep neural networks. Our experimental results on two object category segmentation datasets demonstrate that our approach outperforms DNNs trained with standard softmax loss.

## 1 Introduction

We consider the problem of object category segmentation using deep neural networks. The goal of object category segmentation is to label the pixels of a given image as being part of a given object (foreground) or not (background). In such a problem setting, the two classes (foreground and background) are often very imbalanced, as the majority of the pixels in an image usually belong to the background. Learning algorithms that are designed to optimize for overall accuracy may not be suitable in this problem setting, as they might end up predicting every pixel to be background in the worst case. For example, if 90% of the pixels belong to the background, a naive algorithm can achieve 90% overall classification accuracy simply by labeling every pixel as the background.

The standard performance measure that is commonly used for the object category segmentation problem is called intersection-over-union (IoU). Given an image, the IoU measure gives the similarity between the predicted region and the ground-truth region for an object present in the image, and is defined as the size of the intersection divided by the union of the two regions. The IoU measure can take into account of the class imbalance issue usually present in such a problem setting. For example, if a naive algorithm predicts every pixel of an image to be background, the IoU measure can effectively penalize for that, as

© Springer International Publishing AG 2016
G. Bebis et al. (Eds.): ISVC 2016, Part I, LNCS 10072, pp. 234–244, 2016.
DOI: 10.1007/978-3-319-50835-1_22

the intersection between the predicted and ground-truth regions would be zero, thereby producing an IoU count of zero.

Most deep learning based methods address the image segmentation problem using simple loss functions, such as, softmax loss which actually optimizes for overall accuracy. Therefore, they are subject to the problem mentioned above. We argue that directly optimizing the IoU loss is superior to the methods optimizing for simple loss functions. In this paper, we address the object category segmentation problem by directly optimizing the IoU measure in a deep learning framework. To this end, we incorporate the IoU loss in the learning objective of the deep network.

## 2 Related Work

Our proposed approach for object category segmentation overlaps with two directions of research – one involves direct optimization of application specific performance measures (in this case, IoU measure), and the other line of research focuses on image semantic segmentation using DNNs. Below we briefly present some of the works most related to our proposed approach.

**Direct loss optimization:** Application specific performance measure optimization has been studied so far mainly for learning linear models. For example, Joachims [1] proposed a multi-variate SVM formulation for optimizing a range of nonlinear performance measures including $F_1$-Score and ROC-area. Other SVM-based methods include [2,3] that proposed approaches to directly optimize the mean average precision (mAP) measure. Very recently, there have been a few deep models proposed to directly optimize some application specific measures (e.g., [4] and [5] for mAP, [6] for ROC-area).

Regarding direct optimization of the IoU measure, the first work to address this problem was proposed by Blaschko et al. [7] with an application to object detection and localization. Based on a structured output regression model, they used joint-kernel map and proposed a constraint generation technique to efficiently solve the optimization problem of structural SVM framework. Ranjbar et al. [8] used structured Markov Random Field (MRF) model in an attempt to directly optimize the IoU measure. Tarlow and Zemel [9] addressed the problem using highly efficient special-purpose message passing algorithms. Based on Bayesian decision theory, Nowozin [10] used a Conditional Random Field (CRF) model and proposed a greedy heuristic to maximize the value of Expected-Intersection-over-Expected-Union (EIoEU). Premachandran et al. [11], on the other hand, optimizes exact Expected-IoU. A recent work by Ahmed et al. [12] draws the best from both of these approaches. Based on the fact that the EIoEU is exact for a delta distribution, they take the idea of approximating EIoU from [11] by taking the average of EIoEU as computed in [10].

**Semantic segmentation using DNNs:** The semantic segmentation problem is similar to the object category segmentation problem, but requires labeling each pixel of an image as being part of one of several semantic object categories (e.g., cow, bus etc.), instead of just foreground or background. Recently, several approaches have been proposed for semantic segmentation that take advantage of high-level representation of images obtained from DNNs. For example, Hariharan et al. [13] used a CNN architecture that can simultaneously perform object detection and semantic segmentation. Long et al. [14] proposed a novel DNN architecture that turns a classification CNN (e.g., AlexNet [15]) into fully convolutional net by replacing the fully connected layers of the CNN with convolution layers. Our proposed approach is based on this approach, but optimizes for application specific performance measure of IoU, instead of overall accuracy. Very recently, some deep encoder-decoder based models (e.g., SegNet [16], TransferNet [17]) have been proposed that mark the state-of-the-art for image semantic segmentation.

# 3   Proposed Approach

In this paper, we consider the problem of object category segmentation. Given an object category, the goal is to label the pixels of an image as being part of objects belonging to the category (foreground) or not (background). To this end, we convert a classification CNN into a fully-convolutional net as proposed in [14], and then train the deep network end-to-end and pixel-to-pixel with an objective to directly optimize the intersection-over-union (IoU) performance measure. The architecture of the deep network as well as details of the IoU loss function are discussed in the following subsections.

## 3.1   Network Architecture and Workflow

Following the recent novel work for semantic segmentation by Long et al. [14], we start with a classification CNN called AlexNet [15], and replace the last two fully connected layers ($fc_6$ and $fc_7$) of AlexNet with $1 \times 1$ convolution layers ($C_6$ and $C_7$, respectively in Fig. 1) to convert the CNN into a fully-convolutional network (FCN). We then add a scoring layer ($C_8$) which is also a $1 \times 1$ convolution layer. The sub-sampled output out of the scoring layer is then passed to a deconvolution layer (DC) that performs bilinear interpolation at a stride of 32 and produces an output equal to the size of the original input to the network. Up to this point, everything remains the same as the original 32-stride version of the FCN called "FCN-32s" [14].

Once an output equal to the size of the input is produced, we pass it through a sigmoid layer to convert the scores into class probabilities representing the likelihood of the pixels being part of the object. From this point forward, the proposed approach differs from [14] which computes softmax loss on each pixel score and trains the whole network based on this loss. We argue that this is not the right approach for a task like object category segmentation, where the ratio of object to background pixels is very small. The softmax loss is closely tied to the overall classification accuracy. If the number of examples in each class are balanced, minimizing the softmax loss will give high overall classification accuracy.

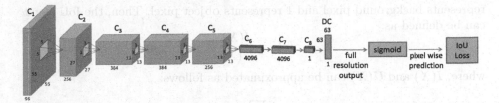

**Fig. 1.** Architecture of the proposed FCN. The first eight convolution layers ($C_1 - C_8$) and the deconvolution layer ($DC$) remain the same as the original FCN-32s proposed in [14]. For each layer, the number right at the bottom represents the depth, while the other two numbers represent the height and width of the layer output. The yellow boxes inside layers $C_1$ to $C_5$ represent the filters, while the numbers around them represent filter dimensions. The IoU loss layer at the end computes IoU loss on the full-resolution output representing object class probabilities of the pixels

For object category segmentation, the two classes are often very imbalanced, and therefore, the overall accuracy is not often a good performance measurement. For example, if 90% of the pixels belong to the background, a naive algorithm can achieve 90% overall classification accuracy simply by labeling every pixel as the background. In object category segmentation, the IoU score is often used as the standard performance measure, which takes into account of the class imbalance issue. Following this observation, instead of computing softmax loss, we pass the pixel probabilities out of the sigmoid layer to a loss layer that computes the IoU loss from the pixel probabilities and then train the whole FCN based on this loss. Figure 1 demonstrates the pipeline of the proposed approach.

### 3.2 Approximation to IoU and IoU Loss

The IoU score is a standard performance measure for the object category segmentation problem. Given a set of images, the IoU measure gives the similarity between the predicted region and the ground-truth region for an object present in the set of images and is defined by following equation.

$$IoU = \frac{TP}{FP + TP + FN} \tag{1}$$

where, $TP$, $FP$, and $FN$ denote the true positive, false positive and false negative counts, respectively.

From Eq. 1, we see that IoU score is a count based measure, whereas, the outputs of the proposed FCN are probability values representing likelihood of the pixels being part of the object. Therefore, we cannot accurately measure the IoU score directly from the output of the network. We propose to approximate the IoU score using the probability values. More formally, let $V = \{1, 2, \ldots, N\}$ be the set of all pixels of all the images in the training set, $X$ be the output of the network (out of the sigmoid layer) representing pixel probabilities over the set $V$, and $Y \in \{0, 1\}^V$ be the ground-truth assignment for the set $V$, where 0 represents background pixel and 1 represents object pixel. Then, the IoU count can be defined as:

$$IoU = \frac{I(X)}{U(X)} \tag{2}$$

where, $I(X)$ and $U(X)$ can be approximated as follows:

$$I(X) = \sum_{v \in V} X_v * Y_v \tag{3}$$

$$U(X) = \sum_{v \in V} (X_v + Y_v - X_v * Y_v) \tag{4}$$

Therefore, the IoU loss $L_{IoU}$ can be defined as follows:

$$L_{IoU} = 1 - IoU = 1 - \frac{I(X)}{U(X)} \tag{5}$$

We then incorporate the IoU loss $L_{IoU}$ into the objective function of the proposed FCN, which takes the following form:

$$\arg\min_w L_{IoU} = 1 - IoU \tag{6}$$

where, $w$ is the set of parameters of the deep network.

In order to obtain the optimal set of parameters $w$, Eq. 6 is solved using stochastic gradient descent. The gradient of the objective function with respect to the output of the network can then be written as follows:

$$\begin{aligned}
\frac{\partial L_{IoU}}{\partial X_v} &= -\frac{\partial}{\partial X_v} \left[ \frac{I(X)}{U(X)} \right] \\
&= \frac{-U(X) * \frac{\partial I(X)}{\partial X_v} + I(X) * \frac{\partial U(X)}{\partial X_v}}{U(X)^2} \\
&= \frac{-U(X) * Y_v + I(X) * (1 - Y_v)}{U(X)^2}
\end{aligned} \tag{7}$$

which can be further simplified as follows:

$$\frac{\partial L_{IoU}}{\partial X_v} = \begin{cases} -\frac{1}{U(X)} & \text{if } Y_v = 1 \\ \frac{I(X)}{U(X)^2} & \text{otherwise} \end{cases} \tag{8}$$

Once the gradients of the objective function with respect to the network output are computed, we can simply backpropagate the gradients using the chain rule of derivative in order to compute the derivatives of the objective function with respect to the network parameters $w$.

# 4    Experiments

We conducted training on individual object categories and learned segmentation models for each object category separately. In other words, when we train segmentation model for a particular object category, say dog, we assume pixels of all other categories as part of the background. During inference, we pass all test images through the learned models, one for each object category, and then segment the specific objects individually from the test images. In the following subsections, we describe the datasets and training setups used in the experiments, and also report and compare the experimental results of our approach and the baseline methods.

## 4.1    Experimental Setup

**Datasets.** To evaluate the proposed approach, we conducted experiments on three different datasets – PASCAL VOC 2010 [18] and PASCAL VOC 2011 [19] segmentation datasets, as well as the Cambridge-driving Labeled Video Database (CamVid) [20]. The PASCAL VOC is a highly challenging dataset containing images from 20 different object categories with the objects having severe variability in size, pose, illumination and occlusion. It also provides pixel-level annotations for the images. VOC 2010 includes 964 training and 964 validation images, while VOC 2011 includes 1,112 training and 1,111 validation images. We trained using 80% of the images in the training set, while the remaining 20% images were used for validation. We evaluated the different approaches on the dataset provided validation set.

CamVid is a road scene understanding dataset including over 10 min of high quality video footage and provides 701 high resolution images from 11 different object categories. It also provides pixel-level semantic segmentations for the images. Among the 701 images, 367 images were used for training, 233 for testing and the remaining 101 for validation.

**Baselines.** As a primary baseline, we compare our proposed approach to a method proposed in [14] that uses a fully convolutional net to address the semantic segmentation problem by optimizing for overall accuracy using softmax loss. We also perform comparison with [8] that tries to directly optimize the IoU measure based on an MRF model. For the rest of the paper, we refer to the proposed approach as $\text{FCN}_{IoU}$, the deep model optimizing for overall accuracy as $\text{FCN}_{acc}$, and the MRF-based model as $\text{MRF}_{IoU}$.

**Implementation Details.** We conducted training of the deep nets using stochastic gradient descent in mini batches. While preparing the mini batches, we made it sure that each batch contains at least one positive example (i.e., an image containing the object for which model is being trained). Training was initialized with pre-trained weights from AlexNet [15]. For PASCAL VOC, we

**Table 1.** Intersection-over-union (%) performance comparison for 6 different object categories on PASCAL VOC 2010 validation set

| Method | Aeroplane | Bus | Car | Horse | Person | TV/Monitor |
|---|---|---|---|---|---|---|
| MRF$_{IoU}$ | <20 | <30 | <30 | <10 | <25 | <15 |
| FCN$_{acc}$ | 71.07 | 72.85 | 71.67 | 60.46 | **75.42** | 64.03 |
| FCN$_{IoU}$ | **75.27** | **74.47** | **72.83** | **61.18** | 72.65 | **67.37** |

resized the training images to $375 \times 500$, while testing was done on the original images without resizing. On the other hand, for CamVid, all images were resized to $360 \times 480$. We used a fixed learning rate of $10^{-4}$, momentum of 0.99 and weight decay of 0.0005. We continued training until convergence and chose the model with the best IoU measure on the validation set. All the deep nets were implemented using a popular deep learning tool called MatConvNet [21].

### 4.2 Results on PASCAL VOC

For the PASCAL VOC 2010 dataset [18], Table 1 shows the results of the proposed approach and the baselines for 6 different object categories. Our proposed approach outperforms MRF$_{IoU}$ by huge margin on all 6 categories. This performance boost is simply due to the use of deep features learned automatically by the proposed approach FCN$_{IoU}$, whereas, MRF$_{IoU}$, being a shallow model, lacks this ability. Please note that we could not report the exact IoU values for MRF$_{IoU}$, since [8] reports the results using a bar chart without using the exact numbers.

While comparing the proposed approach FCN$_{IoU}$ to the primary baseline FCN$_{acc}$, we see that FCN$_{IoU}$ outperforms FCN$_{acc}$ in almost all categories. It is particularly noteworthy that the performance improvements are more significant

**Table 2.** Background to object pixel ratio in PASCAL VOC 2010 and VOC 2011 datasets

| Dataset | Aeroplane | Bicycle | Bird | Boat | Bottle | Bus | Car | Cat | Chair | Cow | Dining Table | Dog | Horse | Motorbike | Person | Potted Plant | Sheep | Sofa | Train | TV/Monitor |
|---|---|---|---|---|---|---|---|---|---|---|---|---|---|---|---|---|---|---|---|---|
| VOC 2010 | 152 | 319 | 107 | 142 | 150 | 64 | 66 | 40 | 97 | 152 | 82 | 75 | 117 | 91 | 25 | 182 | 111 | 99 | 85 | 104 |
| VOC 2011 | 153 | 341 | 100 | 158 | 152 | 60 | 68 | 41 | 94 | 160 | 82 | 71 | 127 | 86 | 23 | 176 | 115 | 88 | 76 | 113 |

**Table 3.** Intersection-over-union (%) performance comparison on PASCAL VOC 2011 validation set

| Method | Aeroplane | Bicycle | Bird | Boat | Bottle | Bus | Car | Cat | Chair | Cow | Dining Table | Dog | Horse | Motorbike | Person | Potted Plant | Sheep | Sofa | Train | TV/Monitor | Mean |
|---|---|---|---|---|---|---|---|---|---|---|---|---|---|---|---|---|---|---|---|---|---|
| $FCN_{acc}$ | 72.18 | 60.57 | 66.47 | 64.68 | **65.03** | 73.96 | 71.82 | 71.44 | 55.55 | **64.22** | 62.74 | **67.03** | 60.74 | 70.23 | **76.78** | 61.62 | 67.59 | 58.05 | 72.80 | 65.05 | 63.18 |
| $FCN_{IoU}$ | **75.07** | **62.00** | **67.45** | **67.64** | 65.00 | **75.37** | **72.87** | **71.94** | **56.01** | 64.13 | **63.91** | 65.71 | **60.92** | **70.90** | 73.61 | **63.78** | **68.83** | **58.56** | 72.66 | **66.81** | **63.82** |

for object categories (e.g., "Aeroplane", "TV/Monitor" etc.) where the ratio of the background to object pixels is very large as shown in Table 2.

Table 3 shows IoU comparison of the proposed approach $FCN_{IoU}$ and the primary baseline $FCN_{acc}$ on the PASCAL VOC 2011 [19] validation set. The other method does not report any result on this dataset. We see that $FCN_{IoU}$ performs better than $FCN_{acc}$ in most cases and also on average. Specifically, the performance improvements are more significant for object categories with a larger ratio of background to object pixels.

We also show some qualitative results of the proposed approach $FCN_{IoU}$ and the primary baseline $FCN_{acc}$ in Fig. 2. Since softmax loss is tied to overall classification accuracy, the $FCN_{acc}$ model tends to misclassify object pixels as background (i.e., false negative), as there exist more background pixels. In contrast, $FCN_{IoU}$ tends to recover some of the false negative errors made by $FCN_{acc}$, as it directly optimizes for IoU score. This observation is supported by the example segmentations as shown in the figure.

## 4.3 Results on CamVid

For the CamVid dataset [20], among the 11 object categories, we report results on 5, namely, "Road", "Building", "Column-Pole", "Sign-Symbol", and "Fence". We chose the "Road" and "Building" categories for their relatively lower ratio of

**Table 4.** Intersection-over-union (%) performance comparison for 5 different object categories on CamVid val (validation) and test set

| Method | Road | | Building | | Column-Pole | | Sign-Symbol | | Fence | |
|---|---|---|---|---|---|---|---|---|---|---|
| | val | test | val | test | val | test | val | test | val | test |
| $FCN_{acc}$ | 95.53 | 90.38 | 87.03 | 76.21 | 50.46 | 50.91 | 64.94 | 56.27 | 75.97 | 61.75 |
| $FCN_{IoU}$ | **95.58** | **90.69** | **88.30** | **76.72** | **53.48** | **52.79** | **67.78** | **57.78** | **80.68** | **62.23** |

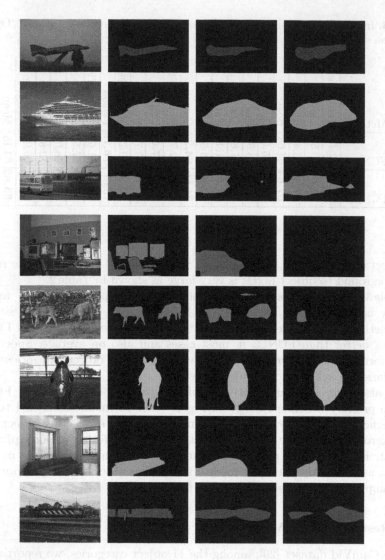

**Fig. 2.** Sample segmentations results on the PASCAL VOC 2011 validation set. Columns (left to right): original images, ground-truth segmentations, segmentations produced by FCN$_{IoU}$, and segmentations produced by FCN$_{acc}$

background to object pixels compared to other object categories in the dataset, while the other 3 categories were chosen for the opposite reason. We do this to investigate how the proposed approach performs as the ratio of background to object pixels varies. Table 4 reports IoU scores on the 5 object categories. The results show that FCN$_{IoU}$ outperforms FCN$_{acc}$ in all 5 categories. More importantly, performance improvements are more significant for smaller object categories (e.g., "Column-Pole", "Sing-Symbol", and "Fence") having higher class imbalance than those that are relatively balanced (e.g., "Road" and "Building").

We also show some qualitative results on the CamVid test set in Fig. 3. The results show that $FCN_{IoU}$ performs better than $FCN_{acc}$, specially for smaller object categories (e.g., Column-Pole) where there exists large imbalance in the number of object and background pixels.

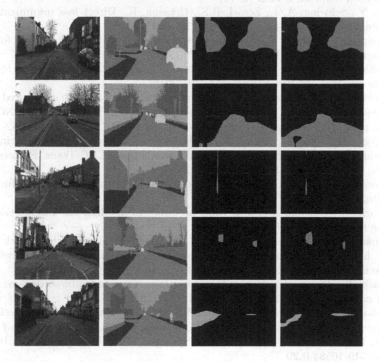

**Fig. 3.** Sample segmentation results on the CamVid test set. Rows (top to bottom): segmentations for "Building", "Road", "Column-Pole", "Sign-Symbol", and "Fence". Columns (left to right): original images, ground-truth segmentations, segmentations produced by $FCN_{IoU}$, and segmentations produced by $FCN_{acc}$

# 5 Conclusion

We have presented a new approach for direct optimization of the IoU measure in deep neural networks. We have applied our approach to the problem of object category segmentation. Our experimental results demonstrate that optimizing the IoU loss leads to better performance compared with traditional softmax loss commonly used for learning DNNs. In this paper, we have focused on binary segmentation problems. As for future work, we would like to extend our approach to directly handle multi-class image segmentation.

# References

1. Joachims, T.: A support vector method for multivariate performance measures. In: Proceedings of ICML (2005)
2. Yue, Y., Finley, T., Radlinski, F., Joachims, T.: A support vector method for optimizing average precision. In: Proceedings of SIGIR (2007)
3. Behl, A., Jawahar, C.V., Kumar, M.P.: Optimizing average precision using weakly supervised data. In: CVPR (2014)
4. Song, Y., Schwing, A.G., Zemel, R.S., Urtasun, R.: Direct loss minimization for training deep neural nets. CoRR abs/1511.06411 (2015)
5. Henderson, P., Ferrari, V.: End-to-end training of object class detectors for mean average precision. CoRR abs/1607.03476 (2016)
6. Rahman, M.A., Wang, Y.: Learning neural networks with ranking-based losses for action retrieval. In: Proceedings of CRV (2016)
7. Blaschko, M.B., Lampert, C.H.: Learning to localize objects with structured output regression. In: Forsyth, D., Torr, P., Zisserman, A. (eds.) ECCV 2008. LNCS, vol. 5302, pp. 2–15. Springer, Heidelberg (2008). doi:10.1007/978-3-540-88682-2_2
8. Ranjbar, M., Lan, T., Wang, Y., Robinovitch, S., Mori, G.: Optimizing non-decomposable loss functions in structured prediction. IEEE Trans. Pattern Anal. Mach. Intell. **35**(4), 911–924 (2013)
9. Tarlow, D., Zemel, R.S.: Structured output learning with high order loss functions. In: Proceedings of AISTATS (2012)
10. Nowozin, S.: Optimal decisions from probabilistic models: the intersection-over-union case. In: CVPR (2014)
11. Premachandran, V., Tarlow, D., Batra, D.: Empirical minimum bayes risk prediction: how to extract an extra few % performance from vision models with just three more parameters. In: CVPR (2014)
12. Ahmed, F., Tarlow, D., Batra, D.: Optimizing expected intersection-over-union with candidate-constrained CRFS. In: ICCV (2015)
13. Hariharan, B., Arbeláez, P., Girshick, R., Malik, J.: Simultaneous detection and segmentation. In: Fleet, D., Pajdla, T., Schiele, B., Tuytelaars, T. (eds.) ECCV 2014. LNCS, vol. 8695, pp. 297–312. Springer, Heidelberg (2014). doi:10.1007/978-3-319-10584-0_20
14. Long, J., Shelhamer, E., Darrell, T.: Fully convolutional networks for semantic segmentation. In: CVPR (2015)
15. Krizhevsky, A., Sutskever, I., Hinton, G.E.: Imagenet classification with deep convolutional neural networks. In: NIPS (2012)
16. Badrinarayanan, V., Kendall, A., Cipolla, R.: SegNet: a deep convolutional encoder-decoder architecture for image segmentation. arXiv preprint (2015). arXiv:1511.00561
17. Hong, S., Oh, J., Lee, H., Han, B.: Learning transferrable knowledge for semantic segmentation with deep convolutional neural network. CoRR abs/1512.07928 (2015)
18. Everingham, M., Van Gool, L., Williams, C.K.I., Winn, J., Zisserman, A.: The pascal VOC2010 challenge results (2010)
19. Everingham, M., Van Gool, L., Williams, C.K.I., Winn, J., Zisserman, A.: The pascal VOC2011 challenge results (2011)
20. Brostow, G.J., Fauqueur, J., Cipolla, R.: Semantic object classes in video: a high-definition ground truth database. Pattern Recogn. Lett. **20**(2), 88–97 (2009)
21. Vedaldi, A., Lenc, K.: Matconvnet - convolutional neural networks for matlab. In: Proceedings of ACM International Conference on Multimedia (2015)

# Pattern Recognition

# A Mobile Recognition System
# for Analog Energy Meter Scanning

Martin Cerman[1]($\boxtimes$), Gayane Shalunts[2], and Daniel Albertini[1]

[1] Anyline GmbH, Vienna, Austria
{mcerman,daniel}@anyline.io
[2] SAIL LABS Technology GmbH, Vienna, Austria
gayane.shalunts@sail-labs.com

**Abstract.** The work presents a mobile platform based system, scanning electricity, gas and water meters. The motivation is the automation of the manual procedure, increasing the reading accuracy and decreasing the human effort. The methodology comprises two stages - digits detection and Optical Character Recognition. The detection of digits is accomplished by a pipeline of operations. Optical Character Recognition is achieved, employing two different approaches - Tesseract OCR and Convolutional Neural Network. The performance evaluation on a vast number of images reports high precision for the algorithms of both stages. Furthermore, Convolutional Neural Network significantly outperforms the Tesseract OCR for all types of meters. The objective of functionality by the limited speed and data storage of mobile devices is also successfully met.

**Keywords:** Analog energy meter scanning · Water · Gas · Electricity meters · OCR · Tesseract · Convolutional Neural Network

## 1 Introduction

Electricity, gas and water meters are devices, measuring the amount of consumed electricity, gas and water correspondingly, to generate invoices for consumers. The usual procedure of reading of electric and gas meters is performed by a human operator, who goes from door to door, reads the number, writes it down and takes a picture as a proof. The operation is prone to errors at the reading step due to lack of attention and in the writing step due to illegible handwriting. To decrease the rate of errors another operator checks the proof image offline. The operation is costly in terms of human effort and time and has low efficiency. The automatic reading operation will reduce mistakes introduced by the human factor, save manpower, as well as provide real time data based on evidence. Realization of smartphone applications, reading electricity, gas and water meters, is motivated by the following factors: firstly, smartphones are widely used, secondly, their computational and image capabilities are being improved, thirdly fast networks allow as an alternative cloud based mobile applications, when data storage and computing resources of mobile devices are not sufficient [1].

© Springer International Publishing AG 2016
G. Bebis et al. (Eds.): ISVC 2016, Part I, LNCS 10072, pp. 247–256, 2016.
DOI: 10.1007/978-3-319-50835-1_23

Automatic reading of electricity, gas and water meters is still not widely applied. The recognition systems follow the typical workflow of image segmentation, feature extraction and object recognition [2]. The authors in [3] present an approach for gas meter reading from real world images. Their algorithm is a pipeline comprising five main steps. At the first and second steps, they localize the Region Of Interest (ROI) and segment the number contained, employing a method based on an ensemble of neural models. Thirdly, each digit of the number is separated. The next step detects the significant digits, since legally the decimal digits can be discarded. Here priori knowledge is exploited, assuming that non-significant digits are always located at the right side of the counter and they are surrounded by a red area, the shape of which is not standardized among different models. At the last step digit classification takes place using an SVM with a radial basis function. This is a classification task into 10 classes - one for each digit between 0 to 9.

The approach, proposed by [4], addresses reading of a single type of a watt meter, used in China. The gray-scale images of the meter observed have a gray shell, white digits and a black frame of the digital area. Based on this priori knowledge the first step of the approach obtains a binary image from the gray-scale image by means of simple thresholding. The second step segments the digital area, assuming it to have a fixed size and correct horizontal alignment. Here horizontal and vertical projections (the number of white pixels in each horizontal and vertical line respectively) reveal the bounding rows and columns of the segment of interest. The third step performs segmentation of characters, relying on the following assumptions: (1) The watt meter observed has 6 significant digits and a decimal digit, which can be discarded, (2) the size of the significant digits is fixed. The segmentation is then achieved by finding the minimums on the vertical projection, having a constant distance from each other. The final step of digits recognition employs a method based on the strokes of digital characters [5].

The method in [6] recognizes the characters of a specific type of an electric meter (M1A-T), utilized in Brasil. The algorithm comprises 3 major steps, processing input images of a fixed size and format. Firstly, the homomorphic filter is applied to reduce the effects of non-uniform illumination. Secondly, binarization and morphological operations are performed to obtain both the ROI and the separate digits. Thirdly, the segmented digits are classified by KNN algorithm.

The approach, introduced by [1], is more general, evaluated on 5 models of gas meters, which are employed by the major gas providor GDF Suez in France. The experiments are carried out by 16 smartphone models based on Android platform and 4 smartphone models based on iOS platform. To address the regions lacking internet connection, the computation is performed offline and takes maximum 3 s. The ROI is detected using a Haar cascade [7] and converted afterwards to HSV color format. By normalization of the V channel the image is divided into 2 sub-images, including the significant consumption part with black background and the insignificant decimal part with red background respectively. The sub-images are thresholded by Otsu method [8] and morphological operations are applied, obtaining the blobs to be passed to Optical Character Recognition (OCR). The final number is being validated based on the history of consumption.

The current work contributes a novel mobile digit recognition system for electricity, gas and water meters. The methodology is general, functioning for more than hundred models of meters. It is designed to operate in offline mode, employing the restricted resources of mobile devices. The implementation is realized on both Android and iOS platforms. The recognition of digits is accomplished in two stages - digit detection and OCR. The digit detection stage is a pipeline of filtering, histogram processing, thresholding and morphological operations. In the OCR stage two approaches are compared against each other - Tesseract OCR Engine [9] and Convolutional Neural Network (CNN) [10].

The paper is organized as follows: Sect. 2 clarifies the methodology of the recognition system. Section 3 gives details of our empirical dataset of real world images of electricity, gas and water meters. Section 4 presents the experimental setup, performance evaluation and results. And finally, Sect. 5 draws conclusions from the work presented.

## 2    A Double Stage Method for Reading Energy Meters

The method, proposed in the current work, solves the problem of automatic reading analog energy meters in two stages, namely digit detection and OCR. A pipeline of steps is constructed to effectively localize energy meter digits. The OCR stage focuses on the comparison of two different approaches - Tesseract OCR Engine [9], which is a well-established OCR library for desktop computers and mobile devices and a CNN [10] based approach. To make a fair comparison between Tesseract and a CNN based approaches, we will use binarized images of the localized digits as input to the neural network. The two stages of our methodology are described below.

### 2.1    Digit Detection

The requirements on the digit detection algorithm in the specific use-case of analog energy meter reading on a mobile device are challenging. On one hand, the algorithm should be resistant to different kinds of noise (camera noise, dirt on the meter, etc.), various lighting conditions and different kinds of blurring (bad camera focus, hand movement, etc.). On the other hand, it should be simple enough, to function by the restricted resources of mobile devices. Thus, the main problem in this stage is to find an efficient trade-off between accuracy and processing speed. The general digit detection algorithm can be summarized in the following steps:

1. Black and white background detection
2. Red decimal digit marker detection
3. Preprocessing (filtering, noise removal, overexposed reflection removal, histogram equalization)

4. Adaptive thresholding (Otsu's method [8], Sauvola thresholding [11])
5. Binarized image processing (Mathematical morphology, topology preserving thinning)
6. Connected component detection
7. Connected component filtering and digit extraction
8. Digit size normalization

The first two steps of the algorithm are optional and provide additional clues for a more specific processing of the image. Preprocessing of the image serves as an image enhancement step, to equalize unevenly lit displays, to remove noise (high ISO sensor sensitivity in dark rooms, dirty displays, etc.) and overexposed areas. After thresholding, small noisy blobs and holes in the digits are eliminated by morphological postprocessing of the binarized image. Digits are then detected by comparing features of connected components such as size, distance between components, the whereabouts of components on a line. Priori knowledge about the number of digits and additional clues from the first two steps are taken into consideration, to enhance the filtering of connected components. Finally, the detected digits are uniformly scaled, zero-padded at the border and passed further to the OCR engine.

One limitation of the current digit detection approach is, that after overexposed reflections are removed, the resulting connected components of digits may be split into several small components. Only the largest component is selected and passed to the OCR engine. This may lead to lower accuracy in the OCR stage, because incomplete digits may be interpreted as other numbers (e.g., 7 and 1, 8 and 3, etc.). Another limitation is, that if a digit in the middle of the line is discarded during filtering, no further OCR processing is performed. Finally, if an incorrect connected component is found and passed further to the CNN based OCR part, there will always be a result for this component, whereas the Tesseract OCR engine has a built-in check for such noisy blobs and discards them, if a component is not "similar" to a number.

### 2.2 Optical Character Recognition

In the second stage of our automatic meter reading method the connected components, found in the images, are classified based on a set of extracted features. The approaches, compared in this stage, use two completely different concepts to extract features. Tesseract OCR uses polygonal approximation of the connected components [9], whereas the CNN based approach hierarchically extracts features through self-learned filters.

**Tesseract OCR** was originally a PhD research project in Hewlett-Packard (HP) Labs, Bristol in 1987. It was maintained by HP until late 2005, when it was open-sourced. Google took over the development process since 2006. As described in [9], it is a very powerful OCR framework for printed text, which can not only classify text, but also perform text detection in binarized images, line fitting, as well as word recognition, jointed character chopping and broken character association.

The main idea of the extracted features of Tesseract OCR is, that the outline of each character can be approximated by a set of lines building up polygons. During training the segments of the polygons are collected and clustered, whereas during recognition a small set of features from an unseen character is extracted and matched in a many-to-one fashion to the clustered prototypes of the training data. The ability to handle damaged images of characters is the advantage of this approach. To make the classification process more efficient, a *class pruner* [9] selects only a small subset of candidate prototypes and only afterwards the similarity between the candidates and the unseen samples is computed. To train the Tesseract OCR Engine, we manually extracted and labeled 6150 images of digits and resized them to $38 \times 64$ pixels. While resizing the proportions of the digits were kept. All images had a small zero-padding of 2 pixels at the border. In total, a set of around 15 different fonts could be identified and grouped for training. Examples of training images are shown in Fig. 1.

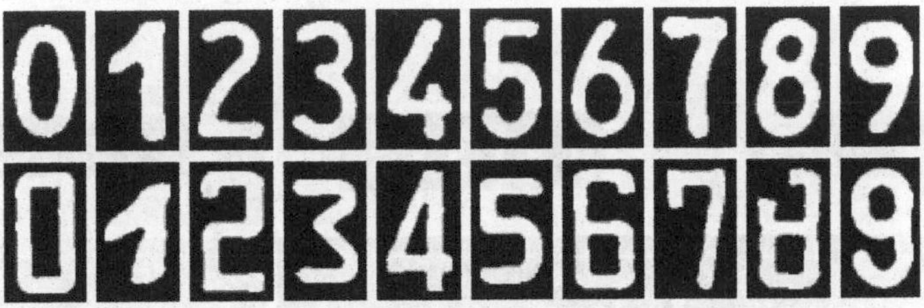

**Fig. 1.** Example images with different fonts for each digit pair, used to train the Tesseract OCR.

**CNNs** are a special type of feed-forward neural networks, which are inspired by the connectivity pattern, as it appears in the visual cortex of animals and humans. The idea of such networks dates back to the 1980s [12], however the major breakthrough was achieved 20 years later in a research paper by LeCun et al. [10], classifying handwritten characters. The main characteristics of a CNN is weight sharing within local receptive fields, which are replicated along the input image plane, as well as a successive sub-sampling of the resulting feature maps. These architectural ideas provide some degree of invariance of shift, scale, rotation and distortion, which are used to hierarchically extract visual features from an image. Afterwards a number of fully-connected layers act as a classifier.

For the training of the CNN we use the same 6150 binarized images of digits mentioned above, but with additional geometric transformations and mathematical morphology, to artificially increase the size of the training set to around 5.9 million images. The geometric transformations include small rotations and translations, perspective transformations and scaling so, that the digit is always fully displayed inside the image without cuts and there is at least a 2 pixel padding from each side. The same applies to the morphologically transformed images after performing erosion and dilation. Each image can have a maximum of 3 operations applied to it at the same time. This way the training set is artificially

**Fig. 2.** Images of electricity, gas and water meters with high variance of digit display area.

**Fig. 3.** Images with different problematic artifacts, such as blur, broken glass, color shifting, low contrast, shifted numbers, reflections, writing on the glass, dirt and water droplets, too bright or dark illumination.

enhanced, to counteract overfitting and to contain enough variation, potentially taking place during the meter scanning process.

## 3   The Empirical Dataset

The dataset used for the evaluation is a company internal collection of 1661 videos of electricity, gas and water meters. It includes data of more than 100 different types of meters, used predominantly in Europe, with a few exceptions recorded in India, Turkey, Brasil, USA and Colombia. Around half of the videos were taken on "meter farms" of large European energy providers and include brands such as Siemens, EMH, Uher, Landys+Gyr, AEG, Rossweiner, Reimer & Seidel, Danubia, DZG, Schlumberger and many more. The remaining videos were taken by employees of the energy providers in real life environments (households, cellars, etc.). Each video is 5 s long and has a resolution of 720p or 1080p. The records are made by 4 models of iOS and 18 models of Android devices, with and without built-in flash. Every 5th frame from each video is picked for the evaluation, resulting in 35 726 frames of electricity meters, 9701 frames of gas meters and 3921 frames of water meters. As there is no standard for the digit display area of the meters, the dataset has a high variance of different fonts, digit sizes and spacing, reflection properties of the background color and material, see-through properties of the housing. The color of the digits is also not unified and includes dark digits on bright background, as well as bright digits on dark background. The number of digits ranges from 4 to 7. A few samples of different digit display areas are displayed in Fig. 2. Other environmental and technical factors, that are well represented in the dataset, are different lighting conditions, caused by the placement of the meter (usually a badly lit cellar or cabinet) and flashlight of the mobile device, bad auto-focus of the device, broken see-through housing and vertically shifted numbers. Example images, exposed to these noisy factors, can be seen in Fig. 3.

## 4    Experimental Setup, Evaluation and Results

The two stages of our methodology are evaluated separately. The digit detection stage follows all the steps, listed in Sect. 2.1 and has an accuracy of 77.91% on correctly detecting all digits on gas meters, 82.5% – on electricity meters and 80.33% – on water meters. The average weighted detection accuracy on all meter types yields **81.42%** (Table 1).

**Table 1.** The accuracy of the digit detection algorithm.

| Meter type | Detected images | All images | Accuracy | Average accuracy |
|---|---|---|---|---|
| Gas | 7558 | 9701 | 77.91% | **81.42%** |
| Electricity | 29474 | 35726 | 82.5% | |
| Water | 3150 | 3921 | 80.33% | |

The evaluation of the OCR stage provides a comparison between the CNN and Tesseract OCR algorithms. The CNN is inspired by the LeNet-5 architecture [10], which originally consists of two convolutional layers with 6 and 16 feature maps and two fully-connected layers with 120 and 84 neurons. Since short computation time is a crucial requirement for mobile devices, we decided to reduce the input image size to $28 \times 28$ pixels, select $5 \times 5$ receptive fields followed by max-pooling [13] in the convolutional layers and keep only one fully-connected layer. The activation functions used in the network are all ReLU units [14] and the error function is the cross-entropy with an added L2-regularization term.

Training is performed using the Adam optimization method [15] in 40000 iterations with mini-batches of 300 samples, so that every image in the training set is seen at least twice by the CNN.

To search for a good trade-off between speed and accuracy, we started with 32 and 64 feature maps in the convolutional layers and 1024 neurons in the fully-connected layer. Afterwards the architecture of this network was iteratively simplified while classifying a set of 1000 images. These images were randomly selected from the electricity meter frames prior to classification and remained unchanged for each network architecture. Each network was trained 5 times and the best results were selected for comparison. The evaluation was performed on a Sony Xperia Z2 device, running Android L Version 5.1.1. In Table 2 **FM1** denotes the number of feature maps in the first convolutional layer, **FM2** – in the second layer and **FC** is the number of neurons in the fully-connected layer. The size of the network could be reduced from the initial CNN architecture to a network with 10 feature maps in each convolutional layer and 64 neurons in the fully-connected layer (Table 2). As observed in the top four rows of Table 2, this was achieved with almost no loss of accuracy, whereas the processing speed required was decreased more than twice in addition to a drastic reduction in space, needed to save the network. Further reduction in feature map and fully-connected neuron count induced an accuracy loss of around 5% (Table 2).

**Table 2.** Comparison of different CNN architectures on a set of 1000 randomly selected images from the electricity training set.

| Architecture (FM1/FM2/FC) | Accuracy | Network size | Speed |
|---|---|---|---|
| 32/64/1024 | 86.4% | 13.1 MB | 335 ms |
| 32/32/256 | 85.8% | 1.7 MB | 226 ms |
| 20/20/64 | 85.9% | 300 KB | 180 ms |
| 10/10/64 | 86.2% | 150 KB | 163 ms |
| 10/10/32 | 85% | 77 KB | 158 ms |
| 7/7/32 | 83.5% | 50 KB | 155 ms |
| 5/5/20 | 81.1% | 26 KB | 144 ms |

The comparison of classification accuracy by Tesseract OCR and CNN based algorithms is given in Table 3. Both classification algorithms score the lowest accuracy on the image dataset of gas meters, followed by water meters and electricity meters (Table 3). It is also obvious from Table 3, that the CNN algorithm considerably outperforms the Tesseract OCR for all types of meters. The average weighted accuracy of CNN yielded **97.34%**, whereas the Tesseract OCR falls behind with **85.76%** (Table 3).

The initial requirement of functionality on restricted mobile resources (speed and data storage) was successfully met. The experimental setup also achieved precise recognition on images with considerable visual artifacts. The CNN based

**Table 3.** Accuracy of the Tesseract OCR and CNN based classification for gas, electricity and water meters.

|           | Meter type  | Detected images | All images | Accuracy | Average accuracy |
|-----------|-------------|-----------------|------------|----------|------------------|
| Tesseract | Gas         | 6161            | 7558       | 81.51%   | **85.76%**       |
|           | Electricity | 25633           | 29474      | 86.96%   |                  |
|           | Water       | 2669            | 3150       | 84.73%   |                  |
| CNN       | Gas         | 7044            | 7558       | 93.2%    | **97.34%**       |
|           | Electricity | 29028           | 29474      | 98.48%   |                  |
|           | Water       | 3043            | 3150       | 96.6%    |                  |

**Fig. 4.** Images of gas and water meters with dirt and discolorations of digit display area. Notice the heavy embossing in the lower right water meter.

OCR approach brings a total improvement of almost 12% in comparison with the Tesseract OCR engine.

The lower classification rate of both OCR engines on the gas and water meters can be explained by the increased occurrence of dirt and discolorations due to the placement of the meters in the environment (Fig. 4). Very often industrial gas and water meters are located on the outside wall of buildings and are thus additionally exposed to natural factors, like weather and corrosion. The digits on water meters are also often heavily embossed, so that there are shadows next to the black digits. This leads to large malformed connected components, being falsely classified. Another problem of water meters is the curvature of the glass in front of the display area, increasing the occurance frequency of reflections in the images.

## 5 Conclusion

The work presented a mobile platform based method for automatic reading of electricity, gas and water meters. The proposed method consists of two main stages – digit detection and OCR. The digit detection is achieved by applying a sequence of operations on the input image. In the OCR stage two different approaches, namely Tesseract OCR and CNN, were taken and compared against each other. The evaluation on a big number of real world images reported high precision for both stages of digit detection and OCR. Further, the accuracy comparison of Tesseract OCR and CNN algorithms revealed, that CNN performs considerably better. The experimental setup also proved, that the system is fully functional on the restricted resources of mobile platforms. The method is general, since it is able to process data from more than 100 models of meters with a wide range of visual characteristics.

# References

1. Chouiten, M., Schaeffer, P.: Vision based mobile gas-meter reading. In: Proceedings of Scientific Cooperations International Workshops on Electrical and Computer Engineering Subfields, Istanbul, Turkey, pp. 94–97 (2014)
2. Nava-Ortiz, M., Gómez, W., Díaz-Pérez, A.: Digit recognition system for camera mobile phones. In: Proceedings of the 8th International Conference on Electrical Engineering Computing Science and Automatic Control (CCE), Merida City, Mexico, pp. 1–5. IEEE (2011)
3. Vanetti, M., Gallo, I., Nodari, A.: Gas meter reading from real world images using a multi-net system. Pattern Recogn. Lett. **34**, 519–526 (2013)
4. Shu, D., Ma, S., Jing, C.: Study of the automatic reading of watt meter based on image processing technology. In: Proceedings of the 2nd IEEE Conference on Industrial Electronics and Applications, Harbin, China, pp. 2214–2217 (2007)
5. Govindan, V.K., Shivaprasad, A.P.: Character recognition - a review. Pattern Recogn. **23**, 671–683 (1990)
6. Oliveira, D.M., Cruz, R.d.S., Bensebaa, K.: Automatic numeric characters recognition of kilowatt-hour meter. In: Proceedings of the 2009 Fifth International Conference on Signal Image Technology and Internet Based Systems, SITIS 2009, Washington, DC, pp. 107–111. IEEE Computer Society (2009)
7. Viola, P., Jones, M.: Rapid object detection using a boosted cascade of simple features. In: Proceedings of the IEEE Conference on Computer Vision and Pattern Recognition (CVPR), Kauai, Hawaii, USA, pp. 511–518 (2001)
8. Otsu, N.: A threshold selection method from gray-level histograms. IEEE Trans. Syst. Man Cybern. B Cybern. **9**, 62–66 (1979)
9. Smith, R.: An overview of the tesseract OCR engine. In: Proceedings of the IEEE International Conference on Document Analysis and Recognition (ICDAR), pp. 629–633 (2007)
10. LeCun, Y., Bottou, L., Bengio, Y., Haffner, P.: Gradient-based learning applied to document recognition. Proc. IEEE **86**, 2278–2324 (1998)
11. Sauvola, J., Pietikäinen, M.: Adaptive document image binarization. Pattern Recogn. **33**, 225–236 (2000)
12. Fukushima, K.: Neocognitron: a self-organizing neural network model for a mechanism of pattern recognition unaffected by shift in position. Biol. Cybern. **36**, 193–202 (1980)
13. Jarrett, K., Kavukcuoglu, K., Ranzato, M., LeCun, Y.: What is the best multistage architecture for object recognition? In: ICCV, pp. 2146–2153. IEEE (2009)
14. Nair, V., Hinton, G.E.: Rectified linear units improve restricted boltzmann machines. In: Proceedings of the 27th International Conference on Machine Learning (ICML-10), Omnipress, pp. 807–814 (2010)
15. Kingma, D.P., Ba, J.: Adam: a method for stochastic optimization. In: The International Conference on Learning Representations (ICLR) (2015)

# Towards Landmine Detection Using Ubiquitous Satellite Imaging

Sahar Elkazaz[1]([✉]), Mohamed E. Hussein[1,2], Ahmed El-Mahdy[1,2], and Hiroshi Ishikawa[3]

[1] Egypt-Japan University of Science and Technology (E-JUST), Alexandria, Egypt
sahar.elkazaz@ejust.edu.eg
[2] Alexandria University, Alexandria, Egypt
[3] Waseda University, Tokyo, Japan

**Abstract.** Despite the tremendous number of landmines worldwide, existing methods for landmine detection still suffer from high scanning costs and times. Utilizing ubiquitous thermal infrared satellite imaging might potentially be an alternative low-cost method, relying on processing big image data collected over decades. In this paper we study this alternative, focusing on assessing the utility of resolution enhancement using state-of-the art super-resolution algorithms in landmine detection. The major challenge is the relatively limited number of thermal satellite images available for a given location, which makes the possible magnification factor extremely low for landmine detection. To facilitate the study, we generate equivalent satellite images for various landmine distributions. We then estimate the detection accuracy from a naive landmine detector on the super-resolution images. While our proposed methodology might not be useful for anti-personal landmines, the experimental results show a promising detection rates for large anti-tank landmines.

## 1 Introduction

There exist millions of anti-tank and anti-personal landmines covering 100s of square km around the world in more than 70 countries [1]. They are mostly active with an average number of 10 casualties per day, four of which are children [1]. Such tremendous scale significantly complicates the landmine demining process, making the cost excessively high (global yearly donations reached $600 millions in 2015 [1]).

With the availability of big satellite imaging data, a new possibility to extract landmine information emerges, with almost no-cost. In particular, the US Global Survey (USGS) [2] provides a 40-years worth of global thermal images, freely accessible. While such coarse-resolution images are not directly usable for landmine detection, the large volume of images can potentially be used to enhance the resolution using super-resolution reconstruction algorithms, and hence allowing for landmine detection from the enhanced images.

M.E. Hussein and A. El-Mahdy—On-leave from Alexandria University.

G. Bebis et al. (Eds.): ISVC 2016, Part I, LNCS 10072, pp. 257–267, 2016.
DOI: 10.1007/978-3-319-50835-1_24

There exist many challenges beside the low spatial resolution of satellite images which increase the difficulty of the detection process such as the existence of corrupted images by having strip-lines caused by the failure of Landsat 7's Scan-Line Corrector in 2003 (SLC-OFF). Also, the satellite images are non-homogeneous, where each image was captured by a different satellite, carrying a different sensor, and at a different time of the day. The objects are pictured from different angles and different satellite orbits at different atmospheric conditions and cloud coverage levels. Additionally, there is the probability of a shift in object location due to non-linear land shape. Besides the challenges related to remote sensing data (satellite images), the soil where the landmines are buried might pose some limitations on infra-red (IR) landmine detection such as the following: the soil type (sand or clay) and the existence of vegetation, the soil water content where (the thermal signature is larger in moist soils than wet soils), the height, horizontal size, depth of the landmines [3]. Thus, IR based landmine detection techniques are useful only for arid climates with soil not covered by vegetation.

We focus on the spatial resolution problem in the satellite images, based on our belief that the low spatial resolution is the most fundamental challenge to start with before dealing with other issues. This paper conducts a simulation study to this problem to empirically assess the utility of the detection process from the available cost-free satellite images. The paper has the following contributions:

1. Constructing a simulation test bed to generate satellite-like low resolution images with the same landmine participation per pixel as typical landmine fields (considering only anti-tank (AT) landmines).
2. Evaluating state-of-the art super-resolution algorithms in terms of peak signal-to-noise ratio (PSNR) and mean square error (MSE), from the generated images, and detecting landmines using a threshold-based process (where an object covers only a fraction of a pixel).
3. Estimating the landmine detection accuracy for different landmine densities, and assessing the potential of using the ubiquitous thermal satellite images in the field of thermographic landmine detection.

The rest of this paper is organized as follows: Sect. 2 discusses related work. Section 3 explains our approach and the experimental setup. Section 4 presents the experimental results. Finally, Sect. 5 concludes the paper and discusses future work.

## 2    Related Work

This section overviews the related studies to landmine detection based on thermographics, followed by a brief summary of super-resolution image reconstruction techniques.

## 2.1   Thermographic Landmine Detection

The variety of landmine types and sizes leads to different landmine detection techniques [4], most of them consist of three parts: Ground sensing, processing collected signals, and decision making parts. For the ground sensing part, ground penetration radar (GPR), IR, and ultrasound (US) sensors are used [5]. For processing collected data and decision making parts, a set of image processing techniques are used for image preprocessing, such as noise reduction and filtering, segmentation and feature detection techniques [6]. The main concept of using IR techniques is based on the fact that landmines have different thermal properties than the surrounding materials, which are especially emphasized in dawns and sunsets, when extreme temperature changes occur. Experimental work based on IR thermographic landmine detection are surveyed in [6–8].

Many studies were done to increase the potential of landmine detection based on thermographic picturing; a model based on studying the time distribution of heating and cooling cycles of the soil with a buried landmine was proposed by Alberto and Mauro [9]. The authors have defined a mathematical model of soil with a buried landmine, aided by indoors experiments that studied heating and cooling cycles with reduced land volume and duration. The referenced data acquired in the laboratory were found to be comparable to realistic, on-field, tests by simply stretching the space and time scales.

Another study of the ground variation including motion of the landmines, as well as, changing landmine depths was proposed in [10]. In [11], the authors aim to enhance the detection accuracy by increasing the detection rate and reducing the false alarm rate in the detection process with different landmine depths. They suggest that the use of one sensor is insufficient for landmine detection and that a single sensor could result in a high false-alarm and low detection rates. They proposed a system that fuses the data from three sensors with different types: an infrared camera, a ground penetrating radar and a metal detector.

Our proposed approach augments related work in extending the scanning scale through improving IR image resolution; related work can then be applied on the enhanced images.

## 2.2   Super-Resolution Techniques

Generally, super-resolution (SR) reconstruction algorithms have three stages: (1) image registration stage, to estimate the relative motion between images; (2) interpolation to high resolution grid stage, to construct a high resolution image; and (3) restoration stage, to remove blur. Details for typical SR algorithms are elsewhere in the literature [12–16].

The performance of most super-resolution methods is affected by several factors; these include the observation conditions, which include how fine the Low Resolution (LR) images are, the number of available images, and the number of bits per single pixel. Another factor is the motion estimation process. The exact motion estimation between LR images is very hard to obtain. Some techniques use the Bayesian approach to solve this problem and estimate the transition and rotation parameters.

In general, prior image modelling is generally sought for constructing the high resolution image. Many image priors have been introduced in the literature and analyzed. Image estimation using non sparse Simultaneous Auto Regressive (SAR *Prior* models) [17] is known to over-smooth edge regions. Priors based on the *l1* norm of vertical and horizontal first order differences of image pixel values is introduced in [18]. In [19], the authors estimate the registration parameters based on Total Variational (TV) Bayesian analysis. Some methods tend to combine a set of prior models to obtain the most robust model: in [20], Villena *et al.* apply a combination of the sparse TV and *l1*, and the non-sparse SAR image prior models. The authors claim that this prior combinations utilize the ability of the sparse priors to recover image edges without over-smoothing inner regions, by combining them with a smoothness promoting prior model. We consider these different SR reconstruction techniques to assist the analytical part of our work.

## 3    Approach

This section introduces our methodology to assess the potential of using cost-free thermal satellite images to detect landmines. It explains how to construct satellite-like test images that simulate the real satellite images. We rely on well-known image processing algorithms to generate a realistic landmine field image, generate satellite-like LR images, reconstruct SR enhanced images from the LR ones, and finally generate landmine maps. Figure 2 illustrates our approach, which will be detailed in the following subsections.

### 3.1    Realistic Thermal Minefield Image Generation

This section explains our methodology of generating satellite-like LR images with varying landmine densities.

**Minefield Generation.** Our experiments rely on the minefield deployed in [21], where two groups of landmines were buried in the sand with 10 cm to 15 cm depths, for different time intervals, each containing one AT landmine and two AP landmines. We used the image of this minefield to generate a much larger field. First, the perspective distortion in the image was corrected such that after correction the landmine bounding boxes appear to be approximately squared with side lengths of 15 pixels. Then, a part of the background area was taken from the image and used as the seed to generate a large field of 6 k × 6 k pixels, using Efros and Leung's texture synthesis algorithm [22].

Finally, the images of the two AT landmines were placed at random locations in the background image to realistically generate our minefield (Fig. 1). Given that the bounding box of an actual AT landmine has the side length of 75 cm, the generated minefield in our experiments corresponds to an area of 300 m × 300 m. We refer to the generated large 6 k × 6 k pixels image as the High Resolution (HR) image.

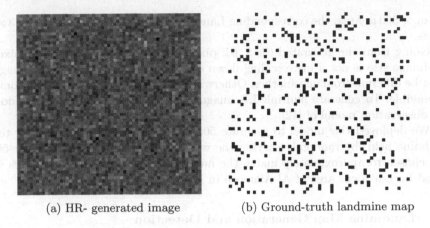

(a) HR- generated image          (b) Ground-truth landmine map

**Fig. 1.** Sample of the generated HR-images and corresponding landmine map

In order to obtain the ground-truth landmine locations in the generated minefield, the HR image is reduced in size by a factor of 15, such that a landmine occupies only one pixel of the reduced image. Then, the image is thresholded manually to detect all landmines locations.

Finally, the 6 k × 6 k pixels image is downscaled to 60 × 60 pixels, to be the input of the LR generation step. The choice of the size 60 × 60 is to match with the maximum magnification possible for the available satellite images, as will be clarified in Sect. 3.3.

**Varying Landmine Densities.** According to the International Mine Action Standards (IMAS) [23], a typical minefield could contain landmines with or without a pattern. A typical pattern of landmines (if a pattern is deployed) is to have both AT and AP landmines laid in clusters, with a 5–6 m between clusters along one direction and 10–100 m along the (roughly) orthogonal direction. Each cluster holds one AT landmine and three AP landmines. Accordingly, our generated minefield of 300 m × 300 m could contain approximately 150 to 1800 landmine clusters. We generate minefields of different landmine densities within this range. Precisely, considering only AT landmines, our generated minefields contain either 100, 200, 300, 400, 600, or 800 AT landmines. However, the landmines in our generated fields are placed in random locations without following a particular pattern.

### 3.2 LR Images Generation

The USGS provides thermal satellite images with resolutions of 60 m, 100 m, or 120 m per pixel, depending on the Landsat mission. In our evaluation, we assume a single intermediate spatial resolution of 100 m per pixel, and keep handling multiple spatial resolutions for future extensions. Thus, an area of 100 m × 100 m will be stored in 1 pixel. Given that our generated landmine field represents a

$300\,\mathrm{m} \times 300\,\mathrm{m}$ area, the corresponding Landsat-like LR images will be only $3 \times 3$ pixels.

Going from the generated $6\,\mathrm{k} \times 6\,\mathrm{k}$ pixels field to the reduced $3 \times 3$ pixels LR image size is not a mere scaling down operation. The generated LR images must be different from one another. Otherwise, enhancing the resolution becomes impossible. To generate multiple LR images from a single HR image, we adopt the observation model of [12].

We deployed this model to generate 500 different LR images, from our test landmine field, by randomly varying the warping parameters. The number 500 was chosen to approximately match the number of thermal Landsat images we found for our focus area of Al-Alameen in Egypt.

### 3.3   Landmine Map Generation and Detection

As illustrated in the right part of Fig. 2, this process contains three main steps: SR image reconstruction, feature extraction, and finally landmine detection, which are explained in detail below.

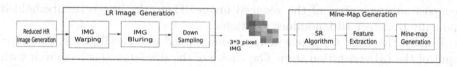

**Fig. 2.** The proposed evaluation pipeline: The left part illustrates the process of realistically generating LR images. The right part illustrates the process of landmine map generation

**SR Image Reconstruction.** Starting with only 500 LR images with a spatial resolution of $100\,\mathrm{m}$ per pixel, we could reconstruct a SR image with a spatial resolution $5\,\mathrm{m}$ per pixel. Considering the dimensions of our minefields, this magnification factor results in a SR image of $60 \times 60$ pixels. Thus, an AT landmine's participation in a pixel of the reconstructed SR image is only around $1.77\%$ (assuming a circularly shaped landmine with diameter $0.75\,\mathrm{m}$). This is considered a poor participation factor whose effect on the pixel intensity is hardly distinguishable from noise, except possibly for landmines with significantly different thermal energy reflections from their surrounding backgrounds.

**Feature Extraction.** The feature extraction stage is an important step for detecting landmines in thermal satellite images with high spatial resolution. This stage can be designed to make the thermal profile of landmines easily distinguishable from their surroundings. However, in our case, the landmine participation in a pixel is very low in the reconstructed SR image, which makes the landmine shape unrecognizable. Therefore, we just use the raw intensity values as features. It is worth noting that the soil surrounding landmines might appear either darker or lighter, depending on the time in the day in which the thermal images are taken [9]. However, in this paper, we consider only the case of day-time imaging, where landmines typically appear darker than their surroundings. Actually, all the images we found for our focus area of Al-Alameen in Egypt were taken between 7 and 8 am (local time).

**Landmine Detection.** As we explained above, we directly use the raw intensity values as features. Our detection algorithm simply applies a threshold to identify pixels containing landmines from those that do not. Particularly, pixels containing landmines are expected to be darker than their surroundings. We apply a threshold and report pixels below it as possible landmine locations.

## 4    Experimental Results

This section explores how far we could benefit from cost-less thermal satellite images in landmine detection. In particular, the following two experimental studies were conducted: (1) Comparing the quality of the reconstructed SR images using the state of the art super-resolution techniques in terms of Peak Signal to Noise Ratio (PSNR) and Mean Square Error (MSE), (2) Evaluating the accuracy of our simple detection methodology at different minefield densities.

### 4.1    Evaluation of SR Techniques

This section compares the reconstructed SR images using different super-resolution techniques. Figure 3 shows a sample of the resulting SR images (for

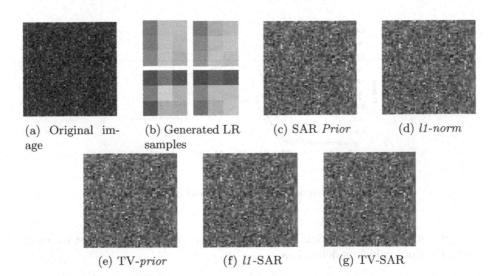

(a) Original image    (b) Generated LR samples    (c) SAR *Prior*    (d) *l1-norm*

(e) TV-*prior*    (f) *l1*-SAR    (g) TV-SAR

**Fig. 3.** SR image reconstruction using different SR enhancement algorithms.

**Table 1.** SR reconstruction quality measurements

| SR Techniques | PSNR | | MSE | |
|---|---|---|---|---|
| | 600 landmines | 800 landmines | 600 landmines | 800 landmines |
| TV | 28.3 | 26.8 | 0.0014 | 0.002 |
| L1 norm | 28.2 | 26.9 | 0.015 | 0.002 |
| SAR | 25.7 | 22.4 | 0.0031 | 0.006 |
| TV-SAR | 27.8 | 26.6 | 0.0016 | 0.0021 |
| L1-SAR | 27.9 | 26.4 | 0.0016 | 0.002 |

density of 600 landmines/image), reconstructed using different standard SR techniques, and Table 1 lists the reconstruction qualities, measured in PSNR and MSE, of the resulting images for minefield densities of 600 and 800 landmines per image. The best reconstruction quality is obtained by the TV Prior algorithm. However, even the best performing algorithm does not achieve a good PSNR value the results indicate a poor PSNR of the reconstructed SR images. In Sect. 4.2, we explore how far we could benefit from the low quality reconstructed images in landmine detection.

### 4.2 Detection Accuracy Assessment

This section discusses the ability of our proposed methodology to truly predict landmines, and compares our system's accuracy with the accuracy of a random guesser. The random guesser assumes that each location in the map has a 50% chance of containing a landmine and 50% chance of being free of landmines.

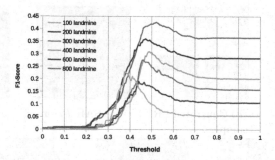

**Fig. 4.** F1-score at varies minefield densities

Figure 4 shows the detection accuracy of the proposed methodology, in terms the of F1-score, which is defined as:

$$F1score = \frac{2 \times \text{Precision} \times \text{Recall}}{\text{Precision} + \text{Recall}}$$

**Table 2.** Comparing proposed detector behavior with random guesser

| Minefield density | Proposed system | | Guesser |
|---|---|---|---|
| | Avg. | Max. | |
| 100 landmine | 0.084 | 0.229 | 0.053 |
| 200 landmine | 0.124 | 0.192 | 0.101 |
| 300 landmine | 0.180 | 0.276 | 0.147 |
| 400 landmine | 0.215 | 0.309 | 0.183 |
| 600 landmine | 0.296 | 0.360 | 0.248 |
| 800 landmine | 0.362 | 0.426 | 0.309 |

where

$$Precision = \frac{TP}{TP + FP}$$

and

$$Recall = \frac{TP}{TP + FN}.$$

where TP, FP, and FN represent the numbers of true positive, false positive, and false negative detection values at a given threshold level, respectively.

Table 2 lists the F1-score values at different landmine densities. Two F1-score values are reported for the system for each landmine density: one value represents the maximum F1-score, which corresponds to the best detection threshold; and the other value represents the average F1-Score over all possible thresholds, which corresponds to the case in which the best threshold is not known. The system consistently achieves better scores compared to the random guesser. This indicates that despite the low quality reconstruction and despite the low number of available images, the reconstructed images contain information about the buried landmines even if the best detection threshold is not known.

## 5   Conclusions

This paper represents an important step of indoors analysis for landmine detection. In contrast to other indoors analyses available in the literature, the presented study here is simulation-based, in which a realistic high resolution thermal image of a minefield was generated, from which many low resolution images were derived to represent freely-available thermal satellite images. A super-resolution image is then constructed from the low resolution images, and landmine detection was performed on it using a simple thresholding-based technique. The experimental results showed that the state of the art super-resolution algorithms did not produce high quality reconstructed image. Nevertheless, the simple landmine detector on the reconstructed images consistently performed better than a random guesser. Therefore, when more satellite images are available, better super-resolution algorithms are developed, and more sophisticated landmine detection algorithms are deployed, detecting landmines from free thermal satellite images can be a reality. While our results are not necessarily useful for AP landmines due to their small sizes, they are very promising for large AT landmines.

# References

1. International Campaign to Ban Landmines (ICBL): Country profile 2015. (www. the-monitor.org)
2. Wulder, M.A., Masek, J.G., Cohen, W.B., Loveland, T.R., Woodcock, C.E.: Opening the archive: how free data has enabled the science and monitoring promise of landsat. Remote Sens. Environ. **122**, 2–10 (2012)
3. Yin, Z., Collins, R.: Augmented Vision Perception in Infrared (2009)
4. Bello, R.: Literature review on landmines and detection methods. Front. Sci. **3**, 27–42 (2013)
5. Bruschini, C., Gros, B.: A survey of current sensor technology research for the detection of landmines. In: International Workshop on Sustainable Humanitarian Demining, vol. 6, pp. 18–27 (1997). Citeseer
6. Paik, J., Lee, C.P., Abidi, M.A.: Image processing-based mine detection techniques: a review. Subsurf. Sens. Technol. Appl. **3**, 153–202 (2002)
7. Schachne, M., Van Kempen, L., Milojevic, D., Sahli, H., Van Ham, P., Acheroy, M., Cornelis, J.: Mine detection by means of dynamic thermography: simulation and experiments. In: 2nd International Conference on the Detection of Abandoned Land Mines, IET, pp. 124–128 (1998)
8. Russell, K.L., McFee, J.E., Sirovyak, W.: Remote performance prediction for infrared imaging of buried mines. In: International Society for Optics and Photonics, AeroSense 1997, pp. 762–769 (1997)
9. Muscio, A., Corticelli, M.A.: Land mine detection by infrared thermography: reduction of size and duration of the experiments. IEEE Trans. Geosci. Remote Sens. **42**, 1955–1964 (2004)
10. Schavemaker, J.G., den Breejen, E., Cremer, F., Schutte, K., Benoist, K.W.: Depth fusion for anti-personnel landmine detection. In: International Society for Optics and Photonics Aerospace/Defense Sensing, Simulation, and Controls, pp. 1071–1081 (2001)
11. Milisavljevic, N., Bloch, I.: Sensor fusion in anti-personnel mine detection using a two-level belief function model. IEEE Trans. Syst. Man Cybern. Part C Appl. Rev. **33**, 269–283 (2003)
12. Park, S.C., Park, M.K., Kang, M.G.: Super-resolution image reconstruction: a technical overview. IEEE Signal Process. Mag. **20**, 21–36 (2003)
13. Shah, A., Gupta, S.: Image super resolution-a survey. In: 1st International Conference on Emerging Technology Trends in Electronics, Communication and Networking (ET2ECN), pp. 1–6 (2012)
14. Tian, J., Ma, K.K.: A survey on super-resolution imaging. SIViP **5**, 329–342 (2011)
15. Katsaggelos, A.K., Molina, R., Mateos, J.: Super resolution of images and video. Synth. Lect. Image, Video Multimedia Process. **1**, 1–134 (2007)
16. Chaudhuri, S.: Super-Resolution Imaging. Springer Science & Business Media, New York (2001)
17. Molina, R., Núñez, J., Cortijo, F.J., Mateos, J.: Image restoration in astronomy: a Bayesian perspective. IEEE Signal Process. Mag. **18**, 11–29 (2001)

18. Villena, S., Vega, M., Molina, R., Katsaggelos, A.K.: Bayesian super-resolution image reconstruction using an $l1$ prior. In: 6th International Symposium on Image and Signal Processing and Analysis (ISPA), pp. 152–157. IEEE (2009)
19. Babacan, S.D., Molina, R., Katsaggelos, A.K.: Variational bayesian super resolution. IEEE Trans. Image Process. **20**, 984–999 (2011)
20. Villena, S., Vega, M., Babacan, S.D., Molina, R., Katsaggelos, A.K.: Bayesian combination of sparse and non-sparse priors in image super resolution. Digital Sig. Process. **23**, 530–541 (2013)
21. Bruschini, C., Gros, B.: A survey of current sensor technology research for the detection of landmines. In: International Workshop on Sustainable Humanitarian Demining, vol. 6, pp. 18–27 (1997)
22. Efros, A.A., Freeman, W.T.: Image quilting for texture synthesis and transfer. In: 28th Annual Conference on Computer Graphics and Interactive Techniques, pp. 341–346. ACM (2001)
23. Keeley, R.: Understanding landmines and mine action (2003)

# Robustness of Rotation Invariant Descriptors for Texture Classification

Raissa Tavares Vieira[1]($\boxtimes$), Tamiris Trevisan Negri[1,2], and Adilson Gonzaga[1]

[1] Department of Electrical and Computer Engineering,
University of São Paulo, São Carlos, Brazil
raissa@ieee.org, tamirisnegri@usp.br, agonzaga@sc.usp.br
[2] Federal Institute of Education, Science and Technology of São Paulo,
Araraquara, Brazil

**Abstract.** In this paper, we present an evaluation of texture descriptors' robustness when interpolation methods are applied over rotated images. We propose a novel rotation invariant texture descriptor called Sampled Local Mapped Pattern Magnitude (SLMP_M) and we compare it with well-known published texture descriptors. The compared descriptors are the Completed Local Binary Pattern (CLBP), and two Discrete Fourier Transform (DFT)-based methods called the Local Ternary Pattern DFT and the Improved Local Ternary Pattern DFT. Experiments were performed on the Kylberg Sintorn Rotation Dataset, a database of natural textures that were rotated using hardware and computational procedures. Five interpolation methods were investigated: Lanczos, B-spline, Cubic, Linear and Nearest Neighbor with nine directions. Experimental results show that our proposed method makes a robust texture discrimination, overcoming traditional texture descriptors and works better in different interpolations.

## 1 Introduction

Texture description is an important task in many computer vision applications, such as segmentation, classification, object recognition and medical image analysis. Applications in real-world textures are the main challenges faced by texture descriptors. Changes in the scale, illumination, rotation and viewpoint conditions of the real scenes, affect significantly the descriptors performance.

In the precision agriculture, for example, images captured by drones are processed using texture analysis to provide information about plant health, soil condition, plant size and others. However, the acquired images could present the same texture pattern in different rotations, which makes the pattern recognition hard.

To address the problem of changes in the scenes rotation, many descriptors have been designed to extract rotation invariant features from the textures. In [1] is presented an extension of the multi-channel Gabor filters, which uses the Fourier magnitude of the texture energy measures to extract rotation invariant features. Han and Ma [2] also propose an invariant Gabor representation to

© Springer International Publishing AG 2016
G. Bebis et al. (Eds.): ISVC 2016, Part I, LNCS 10072, pp. 268–277, 2016.
DOI: 10.1007/978-3-319-50835-1_25

address this issue. Histogram of Gradients Magnitudes (HGM) of pixel intensities was proposed in [3] to extract orientation-neutral features. Rotation Invariant Local Parameter Histogram (RI-LPH) and Isotropic Local Parameter Histogram (I-LPH) were presented in [4] for classification of rotated textures.

Variations of the well-known texture descriptor Local Binary Pattern (LBP) were proposed to treat rotation invariance. In [5], the authors present a multiresolution approach to grayscale and rotation invariant texture classification based on Local Binary Patterns. Rotation Invariant Co-occurrence among adjacent Local Binary Patterns (RIC-LBP) was proposed for cell classification [6]. Local Binary Pattern Histogram Fourier features (LBP-HF) [7], which combines discrete Fourier transforms and LBP, and LBP variance (LBPV) [8], which computes the variance from a local region and accumulates it into the LBP histogram bin, were also proposed to rotation invariant texture classification.

The Completed Local Binary Pattern (CLBP) [9] is one of the most efficient descriptor to overcome the issue of rotated textures. In CLBP, a local region is represented by its center pixel and a Local Difference Sign-Magnitude Transform (LDSMT).

One common solution used by some researchers is rotating texture images through interpolation methods. Kylberg and Sintorn [10] have investigated the influence of interpolation methods on rotation invariance comparing several local binary patterns approaches: Local Binary Pattern Rotation Invariant (LBP$^{ri}$) [5], Improved Local Binary Pattern (ILBP) and Improved Local Binary Pattern Rotation Invariant (ILBP$^{ri}$) [11], Local Binary Pattern Discrete Fourier Transform-based method (LBP$^{DFT}$) and Improved Local Binary Pattern Discrete Fourier Transform-based method (ILBP$^{DFT}$) [12], Local Ternary Pattern Discrete Fourier Transform-based method (LTP$^{DFT}$) and Improved Local Ternary Pattern Discrete Fourier Transform-based method (ILTP$^{DFT}$) [10]. They concluded that the methods based on the ternary patterns and Fourier Transform has performed better than others, however, they are more computationally expensive than the basic LBP.

Computational cost is another issue of applications in real-world. Most of the computer vision systems designed for real scenes require real-time processing. Thus, texture descriptors which produce high accuracy with low computational cost are desirable.

New texture descriptors based on Local Mapped Patterns (LMP) have been proposed [13–15] aiming high performance and low execution time. They use a mapping function, to map the gray level differences between neighboring pixels to a histogram bin. The findings have shown that these descriptors based on LMP approach have presented good performance for object recognition and complex indoor scene classification.

In this paper, we introduce a new texture descriptor based on the LMP approach for classification of rotated textures. The proposed descriptor, named Sampled Local Mapped Pattern Magnitude (SLMP_M) considers the magnitude between neighboring pixels to extract rotation invariant features. We also compare five different interpolation methods to analyze their influence in the descriptors' performance.

The rest of the paper is structured as follows. In Sect. 2, we briefly describe the Local Mapped Pattern and its extension for circular neighborhoods. Section 3 describes the proposed method. In Sect. 4, we present the experimental evaluation and the results. Finally, we conclude the paper in Sect. 5.

## 2 Local Mapped Pattern

In this section, we present a brief explanation of the Local Mapped Pattern (LMP) approach and an extension of the methodology for circular neighborhoods.

### 2.1 LMP Descriptor

Vieira et al. [16] present a descriptor based on fuzzy numbers called Local Fuzzy Pattern (LFP). This method interprets the gray level values of a neighborhood as a fuzzy set and each gray level of a pixel as a fuzzy number. A membership function is used to describe the membership degree of the central pixel in a given neighborhood.

Local Mapped Pattern [13] is an evolution of LPF that allows the use of any mapping function, instead of fuzzy membership functions. Given the neighborhood of a pixel $v = W \times W$ its pattern can be mapped to a histogram bin $h_b$ by using the Eq. 1 where $f_g$ is the mapping function, $M(i)$ is a weighting matrix with pre-defined values for each pixel position within the neighborhood and $B$ is the number of histogram bins. This equation represents a weighted sum of each gray level difference, from each pixel of the neighborhood to the central pixel, mapped into the interval $[0,1]$ by a mapping function, rounding the values to the $B$ possible bins.

$$h_b = \text{round} \left( \frac{\sum_{i=1}^{v-1} f_{g_i} M(i)}{\sum_{i=1}^{v-1} M(i)} (B-1) \right), \qquad i = 1, \dots, (v-1). \qquad (1)$$

### 2.2 LMP Descriptor for Circular Neighborhoods

We can extend the LMP approach for circular neighborhoods by considering a neighborhood of a center pixel as a set of values within a circular symmetry radius. This methodology is called Sampled Local Mapped Pattern (SLMP). Thus, being $P$ the number of neighboring pixels, $g_p$ corresponds to gray level values of each pixel $P$, equally spaced in a circle of radius $R(R > 0)$, forming a set of circular symmetry. The central pixel $g_c$ is located at the coordinates $g_0 = (0,0)$ and the coordinates of each pixel $g_p$, $p = 0, \dots, (P-1)$ are given by $(-R sin(2\pi p/P), R cos(2\pi p/P))$.

The gray level values, not located in the exact center of each pixel, are estimated through bilinear interpolation. Each pattern defined by $P$ samples is mapped into a histogram bin $h_b$ defined by Eq. 2,

$$h_b = \text{round} \left( \frac{\sum_{p=1}^{P} f_{g(p)}}{P} (B-1) \right), \qquad (2)$$

where $f_{g(p)}$ is the Sigmoid mapping function defined by Eq. 3,

$$f_{g(p)} = \frac{1}{1 + \exp\left(\frac{-[g_p - g_c]}{\beta_1}\right)},$$ (3)

$\beta_1$ is the SLMP curve slope and $B$ is the number of histogram bins. The parameters $\beta_1$ and $B$ can be tuned according to the application, by an optimization method.

## 3 Sampled Local Mapped Pattern Magnitude

In this section, we propose a new descriptor for rotated texture analysis. The new model, called Sampled Local Mapped Pattern Magnitude (SLMP_M) combines SLMP descriptor with information related to the magnitude between neighboring pixels. The feature vector of the SLMP_M is built by concatenating a histogram provided by SLMP descriptor and a histogram with magnitude information. The magnitude information is also extracted from the texture by Eq. 2, but the mapping function is given by Eq. 4,

$$f_g(p) = \frac{1}{1 + \exp\frac{-(m_p - c)}{\beta_2}},$$ (4)

where $m_p = |g_c - g_p|$ is the magnitude of the differences between the central pixel $g_c$, $c$ is the mean value of $m_p$ calculated in the whole texture and $\beta_2$ is the SLMP_M curve slope.

## 4 Experiments

### 4.1 Experimental Setup

**Kylberg Sintorn Rotation Dataset.** To evaluate the effect of interpolation in classification process we used the generic textures from the Kylberg Sintorn Rotation Dataset [10] composed of 25 classes. The original images have the size of 2592 × 1728 pixels. Figure 1 shows an image sample of each class. All the captured images are divided into 100 samples with 122 × 122 pixels. The database includes texture images rotated by hardware, but also by software using five interpolation methods: Nearest Neighbor, Linear, Cubic, B-spline and Lanczos. For each texture class, an image was acquired in nine directions $\theta \in \{0°, 40°, 80°, 120°, 160°, 200°, 240°, 280°, 320°\}$. The texture images with a $0°$ orientation angle were used to interpolate the other eight directions using each of the five interpolation methods.

**Fig. 1.** Samples of 25 classes of Kylberg Sintorn Rotation Dataset.

**Classification Procedure.** The interpolation methods and the texture descriptors are evaluated by comparing the classification accuracy. The First Nearest Neighbor $(1 - NN)$ classifier with Euclidean distance metric are used to compare the feature vector of the test sample and training sample. To validate the trained classifier k-fold cross-validation with k = 10 is performed by randomly assigning each texture sample an index, thereby creating 10 disjoint subsets. The results of the classification of 10 cross-validation are combined into a single confusion matrix and classification average accuracy is calculated to perform the evaluation.

### 4.2 Experimental Results

**Methods in Comparison.** The following methods are investigated:

- Local Ternary Pattern Discrete Fourier Transform-based method ($\text{LTP}^{DFT}$) and Improved Local Ternary Pattern Discrete Fourier Transform-based method ($\text{ILTP}^{DFT}$) proposed by Kylberg and Sintorn [10].
- Completed Local Binary Pattern (CLBP) [9] which has shown great robustness in rotated texture classification and has three versions in its implementation (CLBP_S, CLBP_M, CLBP_C) and four combinations of those versions (CLBP_M/C, CLBP_S_M/C, CLBP_S/M e CLBP_S/M/C). In this work, we present the results for the combination CLBP_S/M/C that performed better.
- Sampled Local Mapped Pattern (SLMP) and the proposed method Sampled Local Mapped Pattern Magnitude (SLMP_M).

The tests performed in [10] evaluated the descriptors with the configuration radius $R = 1$ and the number of sampling points $P = 8$. It is because $P > 8$ for the tested descriptors generates a feature vector of high dimensionality. However, due to the parametric property of SLMP_M it is possible to increase the number of sampled points $P$ without a substantial increment in the vector dimension. Thus, we used $R = 2$ and $P = 16$ for our proposed descriptor. By using the same configuration to CLBP, it triples the feature vector's dimension to 648 elements, increasing its computational cost. Table 1 shows all the compared descriptors with their respective feature vectors' dimensions.

**Table 1.** Feature vectors' dimension.

| Descriptor | Dim. | Descriptor | Dim. |
|---|---|---|---|
| $LTP_{(8,1)}^{DFT}$ | 326 | $SLMP_{(8,1)}$ | 121 |
| $ILTP_{(8,1)}^{DFT}$ | 651 | $SLMP\_M_{(8,1)}$ | 211 |
| $CLBP\_S/M/C_{(8,1)}$ | 200 | $SLMP\_M_{(16,2)}$ | 229 |

Table 2 shows the tuned parameters by the Particle Swarm Optimization method for SLMP and SLMP_M descriptors.

**Table 2.** Optimized parameters to SLMP and SLMP_M.

| Descriptor | $\beta_1$ | $\beta_2$ | $B_1$ | $B_2$ |
|---|---|---|---|---|
| $SLMP_{(8,1)}$ | 0.8142 | – | 121 | – |
| $SLMP\_M_{(8,1)}$ | 0.5418 | 2.0579 | 83 | 128 |
| $SLMP\_M_{(16,2)}$ | 0.4974 | 1.8923 | 107 | 122 |

**Experimental Results on the Kylberg Sintorn Rotation Dataset.** In order to perform the evaluation of descriptors performance, the classifier 1-NN is trained with a set of images with $\theta = 0°$ followed by test in other directions. This test aims to evaluate which is the effect of each interpolation method in the recognition capability as well as to evaluate which of descriptor is more robust to image rotation. Tables 3, 4, 5, 6, 7 and 8 show the average accuracy over the eight considered angles, taking into account the compared texture descriptors.

By analyzing the robustness of each descriptor under each interpolation method, it is observed that the best performing results are due to the Lanczos and B-spline's methods. They have similar accuracies, even better than that gotten for textures rotated by hardware. This may, in some way, be explained by the fact that during rotations performed by hardware, the sensor noise is sampled repeatedly in different directions, while the interpolated images are generated from an image whose noise sensor is sampled only one time. Thus, the rotated set of images by interpolation are more homogeneous. This analysis is coherent with the conclusion of Kylberg and Sintorn performed by using other different descriptors.

**Table 3.** Average accuracy (%) for image rotation by *hardware*.

| Descriptor | 40° | 80° | 120° | 160° | 200° | 240° | 280° | 320° | Mean |
|---|---|---|---|---|---|---|---|---|---|
| $\text{LTP}^{DFT}_{(8,1)}$ | 84.1 | 91.1 | 86.3 | **96.1** | **93.5** | 89.3 | **97.5** | 88.5 | 90.8 |
| $\text{ILTP}^{DFT}_{(8,1)}$ | 87.9 | **94.8** | 86.4 | 94.1 | 90.5 | 85.1 | 91.1 | **93.6** | 90.4 |
| $\text{CLBP\_S/M/C}_{(8,1)}$ | 90.0 | 88.6 | 91.4 | 93.3 | 92.1 | 85.1 | 85.5 | 92.4 | 89.8 |
| $\text{SLMP}_{(8,1)}$ | **90.2** | 90.7 | 92.5 | 93.4 | 92.8 | 92.8 | 86.1 | 92.8 | **91.4** |
| $\text{SLMP\_M}_{(8,1)}$ | 88.9 | 88.6 | 90.1 | 91.6 | 89.6 | 90.2 | 82.9 | 90.9 | 89.1 |
| $\text{SLMP\_M}_{(16,2)}$ | 89.8 | 89.6 | 92.9 | 93.2 | 92.8 | **93.3** | 85.5 | 93.1 | 91.3 |

**Table 4.** Average accuracy (%) for *Lanczos* interpolation.

| Descriptor | 40° | 80° | 120° | 160° | 200° | 240° | 280° | 320° | Mean |
|---|---|---|---|---|---|---|---|---|---|
| $\text{LTP}^{DFT}_{(8,1)}$ | 92.8 | **97.9** | 93.6 | 97.1 | 95.5 | 95.6 | **97.8** | 94.2 | 95.6 |
| $\text{ILTP}^{DFT}_{(8,1)}$ | 92.6 | 97.7 | 87.8 | 93.5 | 89.9 | 85.7 | **97.8** | 94.1 | 92.4 |
| $\text{CLBP\_S/M/C}_{(8,1)}$ | 96.6 | 96.9 | 96.4 | 96.8 | 97.1 | 96.5 | 96.7 | 96.2 | 96.6 |
| $\text{SLMP}_{(8,1)}$ | 85.3 | 94.9 | 92.7 | 93.5 | 93.4 | 92.9 | 95.0 | 91.8 | 92.4 |
| $\text{SLMP\_M}_{(8,1)}$ | 95.9 | 97.4 | 95.9 | 96.3 | 96.7 | 95.7 | 96.9 | 95.4 | 96.3 |
| $\text{SLMP\_M}_{(16,2)}$ | **97.4** | 97.2 | **96.9** | **97.3** | **97.5** | **96.9** | 97.2 | **97.2** | **97.2** |

**Table 5.** Average accuracy (%) for *B-spline* interpolation.

| Descriptor | 40° | 80° | 120° | 160° | 200° | 240° | 280° | 320° | Mean |
|---|---|---|---|---|---|---|---|---|---|
| $\text{LTP}^{DFT}_{(8,1)}$ | 90.7 | 96.8 | 92.6 | 95.8 | 94.3 | 94.4 | 96.8 | 92.6 | 94.3 |
| $\text{ILTP}^{DFT}_{(8,1)}$ | 92.1 | 96.4 | 87.6 | 92.8 | 88.8 | 85.3 | **96.9** | 93.7 | 91.7 |
| $\text{CLBP\_S/M/C}_{(8,1)}$ | 95.4 | 95.7 | 94.9 | 95.7 | 95.9 | 95.2 | 95.5 | 94.8 | 95.4 |
| $\text{SLMP}_{(8,1)}$ | 88.4 | 91.3 | 85.5 | 89.8 | 89.5 | 89.1 | 91.0 | 87.6 | 89.0 |
| $\text{SLMP\_M}_{(8,1)}$ | 93.1 | 95.3 | 94.1 | 93.9 | 94.1 | 93.8 | 94.8 | 93.2 | 94.0 |
| $\text{SLMP\_M}_{(16,2)}$ | **96.9** | **96.7** | **96.5** | **96.9** | **97.1** | **96.3** | 96.2 | **96.7** | **96.7** |

**Table 6.** Average accuracy (%) for *Cubic* interpolation.

| Descriptor | 40° | 80° | 120° | 160° | 200° | 240° | 280° | 320° | Mean |
|---|---|---|---|---|---|---|---|---|---|
| $\text{LTP}^{DFT}_{(8,1)}$ | 77.1 | 83.9 | 80.9 | 82.7 | 81.8 | 83.5 | 84.6 | 78.7 | 81.6 |
| $\text{ILTP}^{DFT}_{(8,1)}$ | 84.4 | 87.5 | 81.1 | 84.1 | 80.1 | 77.8 | 88.1 | 84.6 | 83.5 |
| $\text{CLBP\_S/M/C}_{(8,1)}$ | 85.1 | 87.2 | 86.5 | 86.1 | 85.7 | 80.8 | 86.7 | 85.4 | 85.4 |
| $\text{SLMP}_{(8,1)}$ | 72.7 | 74.0 | 73.3 | 71.2 | 71.1 | 73.1 | 73.3 | 72.1 | 72.6 |
| $\text{SLMP\_M}_{(8,1)}$ | 81.8 | 82.6 | 81.2 | 80.4 | 80.4 | 82.1 | 81.7 | 80.4 | 81.3 |
| $\text{SLMP\_M}_{(16,2)}$ | **92.9** | **94.0** | **93.3** | **94.0** | **93.5** | **93.2** | **93.6** | **93.4** | **93.5** |

**Table 7.** Average accuracy (%) for *Linear* interpolation.

| Descriptor | 40° | 80° | 120° | 160° | 200° | 240° | 280° | 320° | Mean |
|---|---|---|---|---|---|---|---|---|---|
| $LTP^{DFT}_{(8,1)}$ | 41.0 | 48.7 | 49.8 | 46.3 | 45.5 | 49.9 | 47.9 | 39.9 | 46.1 |
| $ILTP^{DFT}_{(8,1)}$ | **64.3** | **66.6** | 65.6 | 59.7 | 60.6 | 62.2 | **67.3** | 65.0 | 63.9 |
| $CLBP\_S/M/C_{(8,1)}$ | 59.1 | 64.0 | 66.8 | 60.5 | 60.6 | 65.4 | 63.5 | 58.3 | 62.3 |
| $SLMP_{(8,1)}$ | 35.5 | 37.3 | 41.5 | 34.4 | 34.8 | 40.4 | 37.3 | 35.9 | 37.1 |
| $SLMP\_M_{(8,1)}$ | 38.8 | 41.0 | 46.4 | 37.8 | 38.7 | 44.8 | 40.9 | 36.8 | 35.5 |
| $SLMP\_M_{(16,2)}$ | 63.2 | 64.8 | **72.5** | **66.0** | **64.3** | **69.8** | 66.2 | 63.8 | **66.3** |

**Table 8.** Average accuracy (%) for *Nearest Neighbor* interpolation.

| Descriptor | 40° | 80° | 120° | 160° | 200° | 240° | 280° | 320° | Mean |
|---|---|---|---|---|---|---|---|---|---|
| $LTP^{DFT}_{(8,1)}$ | 20.3 | 79.2 | 22.1 | 37.2 | 38.0 | 22.4 | 76.8 | 20.4 | 39.6 |
| $ILTP^{DFT}_{(8,1)}$ | 43.9 | **95.6** | 47.6 | 60.4 | 60.6 | 46.5 | **92.6** | 44.5 | 61.5 |
| $CLBP\_S/M/C_{(8,1)}$ | 34.2 | 77.7 | 37.6 | 50.1 | 49.5 | 36.9 | 77.8 | 34.0 | 49.7 |
| $SLMP_{(8,1)}$ | 26.2 | 63.1 | 26.8 | 46.5 | 44.2 | 29.3 | 62.5 | 23.6 | 40.3 |
| $SLMP\_M_{(8,1)}$ | 32.9 | 80.5 | 40.8 | 57.5 | 59.3 | 37.4 | 81.1 | 31.6 | 52.6 |
| $SLMP\_M_{(16,2)}$ | **76.6** | 82.5 | **80.2** | **76.1** | **75.6** | **79.5** | 80.4 | **75.2** | **78.3** |

Another important observation is that, in spite of the general low accuracy, the Nearest Neighbor interpolation is relatively successful at the orientation of $\theta = 80°$. This is justified by the fact that rotations of a digital image performed at multiple angles of 90° are those with lower loss of information, and $\theta = 80°$ among the evaluated angles, is the closest to 90° orientation. Hence, the proposed descriptor $SLMP\_M_{(16,2)}$ is the more robust descriptor, among all compared ones, that captures texture information at all rotation angles, not only for multiple angles of 90°.

Moreover, the Linear interpolation is the poorest method for generating rotated texture images. It can be noted that the gray level structure of the micro texture of the considered neighborhood, suffers from a great loss of information. Under this interpolation method, all the compared texture descriptors have their worst performance.

## 5   Conclusions

In this work we have presented an extension of the study performed by Kylberg and Sintorn [10], including the evaluation of CLBP and we have proposed a new texture descriptor called SLMP_M. Based on our experiments the proposed SLMP_M was more robust to image rotation variation. By using the configuration $P = 16$ and $R = 2$ we obtained better accuracy than all the compared descriptors, surpassing the proposed by Kylberg and Sintorn and the CLBP. It is important to note that the last one is a texture descriptor widely used in the literature with excellent performance in rotated image recognition.

Regarding to image interpolation techniques, we conclude that the best performance were obtained by using Lanczos and B-spline's methods, even surpassing texture rotations performed by hardware. The Linear and Cubic's interpolations do not provide similar texture's structure for different angles, reducing all the compared texture descriptor's accuracies. Despite of this fact, it is still the most common interpolation method used by several image processing software.

Searching for a similar texture image within a database, in real computer vision applications, it is impossible to determine which is the angle that it was captured. Thus, the acquired image may be compared directly with the database, usually stored at an angle $\theta = 0°$, or rotated by an efficient algorithm, both in terms of accuracy and processing time, as Laczos or B-spline interpolations. Furthermore, our proposed texture descriptor called SLMP_M, is the most suitable to achieve higher classification efficiency, overcoming the CLBP and the descriptors proposed by Kylberg and Sintorn. The SLMP_M is faster to execute due to small feature vector and gets an excellent medium accuracy for rotated textures.

**Acknowledgements.** The authors would like to acknowledge the Sao Paulo Research Foundation (FAPESP) (Grant Process #2015/20812-5) and the Coordination for the Improvement of Higher Education Personnel (CAPES) for the financial support.

# References

1. Tan, T.N.: Rotation invariant texture features and their use in automatic script identification. IEEE Trans. Pattern Anal. Mach. Intell. **20**, 751–756 (1998)
2. Han, J., Ma, K.K.: Rotation-invariant and scale-invariant gabor features for texture image retrieval. Image Vis. Comput. **25**, 1474–1481 (2007)
3. Sharma, M., Ghosh, H.: Histogram of gradient magnitudes: a rotation invariant texture-descriptor. In: IEEE International Conference on Image Processing (ICIP), pp. 4614–4618 (2015)
4. Dharmagunawardhana, C., Mahmoodi, S., Bennett, M., Niranjan, M.: Rotation invariant texture descriptors based on gaussian markov random fields for classification. Pattern Recogn. Lett. **69**, 15–21 (2016)
5. Ojala, T., Pietikainen, M., Maenpaa, T.: Multiresolution gray-scale and rotation invariant texture classification with local binary patterns. IEEE Trans. Pattern Anal. Mach. Intell. **24**, 971–987 (2002)
6. Nosaka, R., Fukui, K.: Hep-2 cell classification using rotation invariant co-occurrence among local binary patterns. Pattern Recogn. **47**, 2428–2436 (2014)
7. Zhao, G., Ahonen, T., Matas, J., Pietikainen, M.: Rotation-invariant image and video description with local binary pattern features. IEEE Trans. Image Process. **21**, 1465–1477 (2012)
8. Guo, Z., Zhang, L., Zhang, D.: Rotation invariant texture classification using lbp variance (lbpv) with global matching. Pattern Recogn. **43**, 706–719 (2010)
9. Guo, Z., Zhang, L., Zhang, D.: A completed modeling of local binary pattern operator for texture classification. IEEE Trans. Image Process. **19**, 1657–1663 (2010)

10. Kylberg, G., Sintorn, I.M.: On the influence of interpolation method on rotation invariance in texture recognition. EURASIP J. Image Video Process. **2016**, 1–12 (2016)
11. Jin, H., Liu, Q., Lu, H., Tong, X.: Face detection using improved LBP under Bayesian framework. In: Third International Conference on Image and Graphics (ICIG 2004), pp. 306–309 (2004)
12. Fernández, A., Ghita, O., González, E., Bianconi, F., Whelan, P.F.: Evaluation of robustness against rotation of LBP, ccr and ILBP features in granite texture classification. Mach. Vis. Appl. **22**, 913–926 (2011)
13. Ferraz Jr., C.T., O.P., Gonzaga, A.: Feature description based on center-symmetric local mapped patterns. In: Proceedings of the 29th Annual ACM Symposium on Applied Computing, SAC 2014, pp. 39–44. ACM, New York (2014)
14. Ferraz, C., Pereira, O., Rosa, M.V., Gonzaga, A.: Object recognition based on bag of features and a new local pattern descriptor. Int. J. Pattern Recogn. Artif. Intell. **28** (2014). 1455010
15. Ferraz, C.T., Manzato, M.G., Gonzaga, A.: Complex indoor scene classification based on a new feature descriptor. In: Proceedings of the International Conference on Pattern Recognition Systems (ICPRS 2016) (2016)
16. Vieira, R.T., Oliveira Chierici, C.E., Ferraz, C.T., Gonzaga, A.: Local fuzzy pattern: a new way for micro-pattern analysis. In: Yin, H., Costa, J.A.F., Barreto, G. (eds.) IDEAL 2012. LNCS, vol. 7435, pp. 602–611. Springer, Heidelberg (2012). doi:10.1007/978-3-642-32639-4_73

# Feature Evaluation for Handwritten Character Recognition with Regressive and Generative Hidden Markov Models

Kalyan Ram Ayyalasomayajula$^{(\boxtimes)}$, Carl Nettelblad, and Anders Brun

Division of Scientific Computing, Center for Image Analysis,
Uppsala University, Uppsala, Sweden
{kalyan.ram,carl.nettelblad,anders.brun}@it.uu.se

**Abstract.** Hidden Markov Models constitute an established approach often employed for offline handwritten character recognition in digitized documents. The current work aims at evaluating a number of procedures frequently used to define features in the character recognition literature, within a common Hidden Markov Model framework. By separating model and feature structure, this should give a more clear indication of the relative advantage of different families of visual features used for character classification. The effects of model topologies and data normalization are also studied over two different handwritten datasets. The Hidden Markov Model framework is then used to generate images of handwritten characters, to give an accessible visual illustration of the power of different features.

## 1 Introduction

Transcription of digitized handwritten documents is an important task gaining a lot of attention from the image processing and pattern recognition research community. Degradation of documents over time, variation in writing styles, and inconsistent document background based on the medium, are but a few of the challenges encountered when working in this field, in particular for historical handwriting. One of the methods that has been successful in this area are the hidden Markov models (HMMs) [1]. Within natural language processing, these models were used for speech recognition early on. They are good at handling discrete as well as continuous sequences of data. Since text is often written along one direction, handling text as a sequence of characters that can be explained with a language model fits well within the HMM paradigm.

The process of training a HMM with a finite, discrete state space, depends on computing a matrix of *state transition probabilities* denoted by $\mathbf{A}$, a vector of *start probabilities* denoted by $\pi$, a matrix of state specific *emission probabilities* distributions denoted by $\mathbf{B}$. These are quantified using relevant training

---

This project is a part of q2b, From quill to bytes, an initiative sponsored by the "Swedish Research Council" Vetenskapsrådet (D.Nr 2012-5743) and Riksbankens Jubileumsfond (R.Nr NHS14-2068:1) and Uppsala university.

G. Bebis et al. (Eds.): ISVC 2016, Part I, LNCS 10072, pp. 278–287, 2016.
DOI: 10.1007/978-3-319-50835-1_26

examples. In the current context, we consider the Baum-Welch and Bakis algorithms. The Baum-Welch algorithm is an Expectation-Maximization procedure that tries to answer question of determining the $(\pi, \mathbf{A}, \mathbf{B})$ parameters for maximizing the HMM performance. However, there is an inherent directionality in Latin based text, which is exploited in the *left-right* topology using Bakis algorithm. Here the states move left to right but not the other way around. Further details on implementing HMMs can be found in [2].

As HMMs are efficient at handling sequential information, images are often processed using a sliding window. The sliding window approach can be used at word or character level to identify words or characters respectively [1]. In the current approach the content within each window is used to extract features, which are then labeled. By concatenating labels of successive sliding windows, a string is formed corresponding to the original image. An HMM-bank, containing multiple disjoint HMMs is trained on the labeled training sequences. A query image is then classified based on a scoring mechanism over all the HMMs in the bank. All hidden Markov models in the bank are applied. The model giving the most favorable overall likelihood is selected as the output. This setup provides an ideal testing environment to understand the strengths of different image features when used along with a sliding window HMM. A Support Vector Machine (SVM) classifier is also trained on the features under study, in order to provide a benchmark for comparison (Fig. 1(i)).

## 2   Architecture HMM Classifier

In order to evaluate various features we have used identical pre-processing and classification procedures for all feature sets tested. As shown in Fig. 1 each image is converted to a gray-scale image rescaled to $100 \times 100$ pixels (Fig. 1(a), (b)). Binarization is carried out for computing specific features such as background to foreground transitions. The image is then divided into overlapping patches allowing for about 50 % overlap over adjacent windows (can be stripes favored by Marti-Bunke type features or patch based Fig. 1(c), (d)). Features are then extracted on each patch independently. The features thus accumulated over the training data are then clustered using k-Means and a label is assigned to each patch as per the cluster to which it belongs. The experiments are repeated with and without whitening the feature vector to understand its behavior.

In the current context HMMs are primarily used as classifiers of labeled sequences. In transcription of documents in Latin based script one is likely to encounter alphabetic letters in both upper and lower case, so an individual class for each character in each case is defined. This architecture leads to an HMM-bank with 52 individual HMMs, one for each letter in upper and lower case. Virtual beginning and end states are introduced, denoted by *start* and *end*, respectively. Assuming the feature extraction step produces $n$ segments there will be $n + 2$ states in the HMMs. The classification of a query image is done by converting it to a query string using the labels obtained from the k-Means clustering. The query string is then passed to each character HMM in the bank

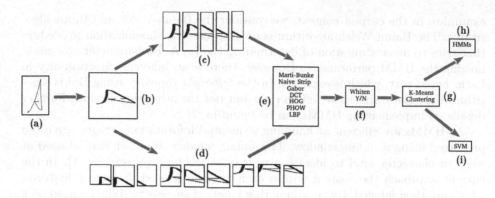

**Fig. 1.** An overview of the experimental setup with individual process blocks

and a likelihood score is returned. A decision based on the maximum score returned from HMM-bank results in the classification of the query image to a letter.

## 3    Feature Extraction

In the following section we provide a brief description of seven different feature extraction methods. They have all found previous use in character recognition. Some of these are unique to character recognition using HMMs, while others are widely known as generic feature extraction methods in image analysis and computer vision.

### 3.1    Naive Strip Features

Each image is binarized and then divided into vertical segments. Within each segment, connected components are identified. Three maximal components are picked based on the component length, $C_l$. These components are then identified as long, $\mathcal{L}$ if $C_l \geq n \cdot w_d$, short, $\mathcal{S}$ if $w_d \leq C_l < n \cdot w_d$, or none, $\mathcal{N}$ if $C_l < w_d$, where $w_d$ is the width of the segment and $n$ is a scale-factor. Each segment can thus be identified with a triplet formed by $\mathcal{L}, \mathcal{S}, \mathcal{N}$. There can be 10 combinations of these triplets that form the class labels for this feature.

### 3.2    Marti-Bunke Features

This is a nine-dimensional feature that is obtained for each vertical segment of the image. This feature captures rough shape, texture and span information of a character by computing some statistics and estimates over each segment. The shape information is based on computing the upper and lower contour position of the character in each segment, and the gradient of the upper and lower contours of the segment. The texture information is retained in the number of background-foreground transitions and by computing the number of foreground pixels between the upper and lower contour divided by the height of the contour. The character span is estimated by computing the mean, the center of gravity and the second order moment of the segment [3]. For efficient computation of these features binarized as well as gray-scale images are required. This feature is a compact representation of the shape information, but lacks a scale estimate that is required in differentiating the upper and lower case alphabet, for instance in the case of $x$, $o$, $c$ etc.

### 3.3  Gabor Features

The Gabor feature is built by dividing the gray-scale image into a grid. A complex Gaussian kernel is created with varying sigma at different angles between the real and imaginary part of the kernel (the argument of a complex number) [4]. The mean of the absolute value of the convolution output is used as a threshold. The count of instances that have exceeded this threshold in each grid at each scale and orientation is cascaded to form the overall feature vector [5]. In the current framework, the default settings used results in a forty-dimensional feature (5 scales × 8 orientations) per patch.

### 3.4  Discrete Cosine Transform Features

Each patch is then subjected to a discrete cosine transform (DCT) [6]. As most of the energy content of the image is contained in the low frequency, the coefficients are reordered by zig-zag scan in each patch. The most significant coefficients per patch can be picked up and cascaded to form the feature vector. In the default settings the 10 most significant coefficients are picked for each patch.

### 3.5  Histogram of Oriented Gradients Features

For each of the patch gradients are computed along various orientations [7,8]. A histogram over the computed gradients in the given patch is cascade into a feature vector. In the current setup this is a 31-dimensional vector per patch.

### 3.6  Pyramid Histogram of Visual Words Features

A PHOW feature is a bag of dense Scale Invariant Feature Transform (SIFT) features at various scales [9]. This is a 512-dimensional feature vector due to the accumulation of 128-dimensional SIFT features at 4 scales.

### 3.7  Local Binary Patterns Features

Within each selected patch the center pixel is compared against every other pixel in a 3 × 3 neighborhood. The pixelwise comparisons are encoded into a 8-dimensional vector of 0s and 1s depending on the gray scale value of the central pixel being higher or lower than the neighbor, respectively. The vector can thus be 128-dimensional, but is quantized into 58 possible patterns, i.e. a 58-dimensional vector averaging over the patch [10].

# 4    Experiments

All the experiments were conducted using two data sets as described below.

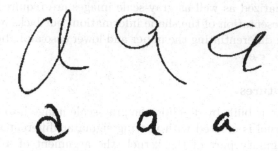

**Fig. 2.** Instances of 'a' based on UniPenn (first row), NIST (second row)

## 4.1    Data-Sets

**UJIPenchar2.** The UJIPenchar2 dataset of online handwritten characters [11] captures the stylus co-ordinates of 60 writers when writing two instances of each character in upper and lower case. This data-set has recorded information of 120 instances of each character as an (x, y)-coordinate trace of the pen. This on-line pen information is converted to offline images of characters using spline interpolation tracing the pen trajectory from captured coordinates. These images are subjected to morphological erosion with a $3 \times 3$ cross structuring element to create characters of varying stroke width. Then a series of affine transformations are applied to the resulting images such as clockwise and counter-clockwise rotation about the vertical axis by 10 degrees, skewing the image in horizontal and vertical direction and adding noise along the edges of the character. In total, there are 3600 instances of each letter, some of which are shown in Fig. 2.

**NIST-19.** The NIST[1] dataset consists of handwritten forms from 2100 different users provided with a form based handprint recognition system. About 1472 instances per lowercase character as shown in Fig. 2, were extracted from these forms using the underlying recognition system [12].

## 4.2    Evaluation

On each of the datasets a random sample of 1012 images is picked, of which 512 are used for training and 500 images are used for testing. The results reported

---

[1] The authors would like to thank Alicia Fornes and Computer Vision Center at Universitat Autonoma de Barcelona for their help in extracting the character images from the NIST data-set.

here are percentage of classification accuracy $\%accuracy = \frac{T_c}{N}$, where $T_c$ are images correctly labeled in the test set and $N$ total number of test images averaged over all the letters.

The experiments can be broadly classified into two classes. First, a regressive evaluation of classification accuracy of the HMM classifier trained on each of the features described previously is bench-marked against SVM using a polynomial kernel of degree three. The focus has been on not only understanding the classification capability of the features, but also capture the parameter settings that are well suited for each method, such as the effect of whitening, and k-Means clusters, which directly influence the number of labels at each state in the HMMs. These parameter settings are then used in the experiments where the HMMs are used as generative models for characters in order to further understand the ability of the features to capture the characteristics of the various handwritten characters. The results from the generative model are useful in visually interpreting the performance of features and also how spatial resolution affects the performance of HMMs.

## 4.3    Regression Tests

**Number of k-Means Clusters:** In state of the art HMMs for handwriting transcription labeling the feature vector is done through training Gaussian Mixture models. The features are used to train a mixture model with 4 distributions. This model is in turn used to initialize and train a mixture with 8 distributions and this procedure is repeated successively to obtain a model with either 16 or 32 distributions [13]. In a similar spirit we have clustered the features using k-Means with k = 5,10,...40 and found that going beyond k = 20 does not yield any significant improvement in classification accuracy but makes the HMM training slower due to more labels. The effect of moving from k = 10 to k = 20 is shown in Fig. 3. For all subsequent experiments k = 20 was used in the k-Means clustering step. When repeating the experiments a common initial seed is provided for the random number generator in k-Means initialization and for input sampling respectively. This is to ensure consistent training and testing files and consistency in k-Means centroids initialization, thus ensuring reproducible and comparable results.

**Topology and Whitening of Data:** Two transition matrix topologies were tested in these experiments, the *ergodic* and the *bakis* topologies. The classification accuracy for these topologies are mostly similar. The results with and without of data whitening on the two HMM topologies are shown in Table 1. The results from the HMM classifier are compared with SVM with a polynomial kernel of degree three, which is one of the top performing classifier on NIST digits dataset [14], with the entire image is used as input. This result is reported in Table 1. However, to make the comparison more fair, we also feed the SVM with feature data, in Table 2.

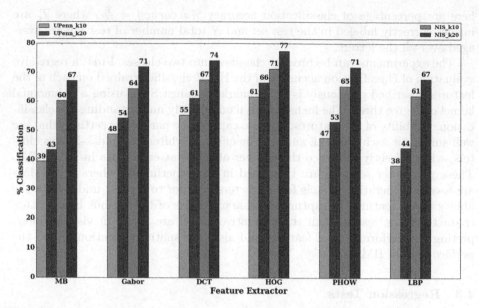

**Fig. 3.** Comparison of classification accuracy percentage of HMM classifier with k-Means Clustering with k = 10 and k = 20

**Table 1.** Classification accuracy percentages for HMM and SVM classifiers

| Feature | Ergodic | | Bakis | | Whitened |
| --- | --- | --- | --- | --- | --- |
| | UniPenn | NIST | UniPenn | NIST | |
| Naive-Strip | 12.9 | 26.13 | 12.92 | 25.49 | Yes |
| Marti-Bunke | 43.36 | 66.68 | 43.46 | 67.09 | |
| Gabor | 52.24 | 70.48 | 52.24 | 70.5 | |
| DCT | 59.37 | 72.82 | 60.89 | 73.76 | |
| HOG | 63.36 | 77.68 | 64.58 | 76.82 | |
| PHOW | 52.24 | 70.48 | 48.38 | 68.68 | |
| LBP | 42.37 | 65.82 | 41.56 | 65.76 | |
| Naive-Strip | 12.9 | 26.13 | 12.92 | 25.49 | No |
| Marti-Bunke | 37.68 | 65.47 | 38.2 | 66.0 | |
| Gabor | 54.24 | 71.99 | 54.23 | 71.93 | |
| DCT | 61.43 | 74.18 | 61.09 | 74.0 | |
| HOG | 65.16 | 79.66 | 66.48 | 77.32 | |
| PHOW | 55.94 | 72.38 | 53.03 | 71.86 | |
| LBP | 45.30 | 69.22 | 44.16 | 67.76 | |
| SVM poly. deg. 3 | 75.75 | 85.63 | - | - | - |

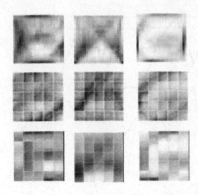

**Fig. 4.** Character instances of B, A, G from HMMs. top row: DCT + strip, middle row: DCT + patch, bottom row: MB + patch

**Table 2.** Comparison of features for patch vs. strip based sliding window approach

| Feature | UniPenn | NIST |
|---|---|---|
| HMM + MB + Strip | 43.46 | 67.09 |
| HMM + MB + Patch | 45.90 | 75.83 |
| HMM + DCT + Strip | 44.77 | 67.85 |
| HMM + DCT + Patch | 59.79 | 76.09 |
| SVM + MB + Strip | 59.56 | 82.23 |
| SVM + MB + Patch | 65.79 | 85.67 |
| SVM + DCT + Strip | 58.54 | 84.34 |
| SVM + DCT + Patch | 60.32 | 85.0 |

**Sliding Windows:** It is a common practice in word and character HMMs to apply the sliding window from left to right and feed the HMM with features from thin overlapping image stripes. In this paper, we extend this paradigm, also sweeping top-down and testing square shaped patches, and investigate whether the performance of the HMMs is improved. The size and step length of the sliding window in these cases are calculated such that length of the label sequence generated per image in both the methods are almost identical, thus no bias in introduced in the HMM training. Table 2 shows the comparison between Marti-Bunke and DCT. As the dimensionality of these features are nine and ten respectively, they are comparable.

### 4.4 Generative Tests

In the final experiments, we use the trained HMMs as generative models instead of classifiers. The results are synthesized instances of characters, which gives a glimpse of what a given HMM model is able to capture. It also enables us to make a qualitative comparison between features through the analysis of the emission matrix **B**. The most probable state transitions are generated from the transition matrix **A** and the label at each state is generated from the emission matrix **B**. The image corresponding to the label are generated from the k-Means cluster center of that label. This approach has two benefits. Firstly, it provides a qualitative way to visualize the results by showing the extent of variation in the writing of each character as captured by the features. Figure 4 helps in comparing the letters generated with strip and patch mode, by comparing top and middle rows, and also features from Marti-Bunke and DCT features by comparing the middle and bottom rows.

Secondly, the generative experiments helps to analyze the learning transfered to HMMs through the features. By construction, for an HMM with $N_s$ states its transition matrix **A** is square and diagonal dominant as we are forcing an

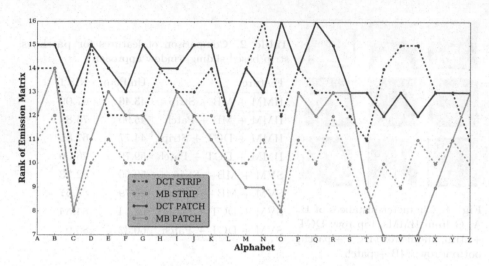

**Fig. 5.** Reduced rank of emission matrices over various character HMMs

inherent directionality through the way the image of the character is swept. The variation in the various handwritten characters are captured in the emission matrix $\mathbf{B}$, which is a rectangular matrix of size $N_s \times N_l$, where $N_l$ are number of emission labels at each state. In order to capture this variation efficiently, matrix $\mathbf{B}$ has to be of full rank. By performing a low rank approximation of $\mathbf{B}$, we can determine which feature is efficient. In the current experiment $N_s = 25$, $N_l = 20$. For an efficient feature, the rank for the low rank approximation of $\mathbf{B}$ needs to be as high as possible, i.e. as close to 20 as possible. Figure 5 shows these results in parallel coordinates [15] representation of the rank for Marti-Bunke and DCT features, respectively. In order to reduce the width of the graph, only the result for HMMs trained for upper case letters is provided.

## 5  Conclusions

The HMM performance of the ergodic and left-right topologies are almost identical over all the features. The Marti-Bunke features performs well when increasing the number of segments the image is split into. However, Marti-Bunke features suffers from performance issues when the sequence length get longer. Features that are able to encode the scaling information, such as HoG, Gabor and DCT, are able to outperform the other features such as Marti-Bunke and local binary patterns. This is particularly due to effectively handling the scaling that occurs over upper and lower case characters such as c,k,o,p,x. The best performing feature extraction appears to be HoG. DCT has only slightly worse performance than HoG, but is more compact (1/3 of the dimensionality). The results indicate that performance of character recognition HMMs could be improved, by moving from a strip based sliding window approach to a patch based. Finally, the SVM classifier, which processes all feature values in parallel rather than as a sequence, consistently beats HMM. This could indicate deficiencies in the state space and transition matrix structures, with their resulting simple one-dimensional interpretation, as well as in the k-Means dimensionality reduction.

# References

1. Plotz, T., Fink, G.A.: Markov models for offline handwriting recognition: a survey. Int. J. Doc. Anal. Rec. **12**, 269–298 (2009)
2. Rabiner, L.R.: A tutorial on hidden Markov models and selected applications in speech recognition. Proc. IEEE **70**, 257–286 (1989)
3. Marti, U., Bunke, H.: Using a statistical language model to improve the performance of an HMM-based cursive handwriting recognition systems. In: Hidden Markov Models: Applications in Computer Vision, pp. 65–90. World Scientic Publishing Co., Inc. (2002)
4. Chen, J., Huaigu Cao, R., Natarajan, P.: Gabor features for offline Arabic handwriting recognition. In: Proceedings of International Workshop on Document Analysis and System, IAPR, vol. 9, pp. 53–58 (2010)
5. Cheng-Lin Liu, M.K., Fujisawa., H.: Gabor feature extraction for character recognition: comparison with gradient feature. In: International Conference Document Analysis and Recognition, vol. 8, pp. 121–125. IEEE (2005)
6. Ahmed, N., Natarajan, T., Rao, K.: Discrete cosine transfom. IEEE Trans. Comput. **23**, 90–93 (1974)
7. Dalal, N., Triggs, B.: Histograms of oriented gradients for human detection. In: Proceedings CVPR (2005)
8. Felzenszwalb, P.F., Grishick, R.B., McAllister, D., Ramanan, D.: Object detection with discriminatively trained part based models. In: PAMI, vol. 32, pp. 1627–1645. IEEE (2009)
9. Bosch, A., Zisserman, A., Munoz, X.: Image classification using random forests and ferns. In: IEEE International Conference on Computer Vision (2007)
10. Ojala, T., M.P., Harwood, D.: Performance evaluation of texture measures with classification based on Kullback discrimination of distributions. In: Proceedings ICPR, vol. 1, pp. 582–585 (1994)
11. Llorens, D.: The UJIpenchars database: a pen-based database of isolated handwritten characters. In: Proceedings of International Conference on Language Resource and Evaluation, vol. 6, pp. 2647–2651. LREC (2008)
12. Grother, P.J.: NIST special database 19 handprinted forms and characters database, National Institute of Standards and Technology (1995)
13. Young, S., Odell, J., Ollason, D., Valtchev, V., Woodland, P.: The HTK Book: Hidden Markov Models Toolkit V2.1. Wiley, Hoboken (1997)
14. LeCun, Y., Bottou, L., Y.B., Haffner, P.: Gradient-based learning applied to document recognition. In: Proceedings of the IEEE, vol. 86, pp. 2278–2324. IEEE (1998)
15. Moustafa, R.: Parallel coordinate and parallel coordinate density plots. In: Interdisciplinary Reviews: Computational Statistics, vol. 3(2), pp. 134–148. Wiley (2011)

# DeTEC: Detection of Touching Elongated Cells in SEM Images

A. Memariani[1]([⊠]), C. Nikou[1], B.T. Endres[2], E. Bassères[2], K.W. Garey[2], and I.A. Kakadiaris[1]

[1] Computational Biomedicine Lab, Department of Computer Science,
University of Houston, Houston, TX, USA
{amemaria,cnikou,ikakadia}@central.uh.edu
[2] Department of Pharmacy Practice and Translational Research,
University of Houston, Houston, TX, USA
{btendres,ebassere,kgarey}@central.uh.edu

**Abstract.** A probabilistic framework using two random fields, DeTEC (Detection of Touching Elongated Cells) is proposed to detect cells in scanning electron microscopy images with inhomogeneous illumination. The first random field provides a binary segmentation of the image to superpixels that are candidates belonging to cells, and to superpixels that are part of the background, by imposing a prior on the smoothness of the texture features. The second random field selects the superpixels whose boundaries are more likely to form elongated cell walls by imposing a smoothness prior onto the orientations of the boundaries. The method is evaluated on a dataset of *Clostridium difficile* cell images and is compared to CellDetect.

## 1 Introduction

Cell detection is an important task in the analysis of microscopy images, with many applications such as cell counting, quantification of cell wall integrity, and deformation quantification. Despite the advances in scanning electron microscopy (SEM), the acquired cell images are often noisy with low contrast. In addition, inhomogeneously illuminated cells of various sizes may be touching, making the detection of micron scale cells a challenging task. Standard methods such as ellipse fitting and Hough transform [1] fail to detect cells in these types of images due to the their challenging nature.

Recent computer vision methods in cell detection fall into three categories. The first category assumes that cells differ significantly from their background. A machine learning algorithm such as random forests [2] assigns a score to pixels based on features extracted from a local neighborhood. Local extremum points of the scores represent the cell centroids [3–6]. Other approaches define the score based on the distance of each point to the nearest annotated cell centroid [2]. The second category includes methods that learn a mapping from global or local appearances to a real-value [7–9]. These methods are sensitive to the density of the cells in the image. Furthermore, their main focus is to count the number of

© Springer International Publishing AG 2016
G. Bebis et al. (Eds.): ISVC 2016, Part I, LNCS 10072, pp. 288–297, 2016.
DOI: 10.1007/978-3-319-50835-1_27

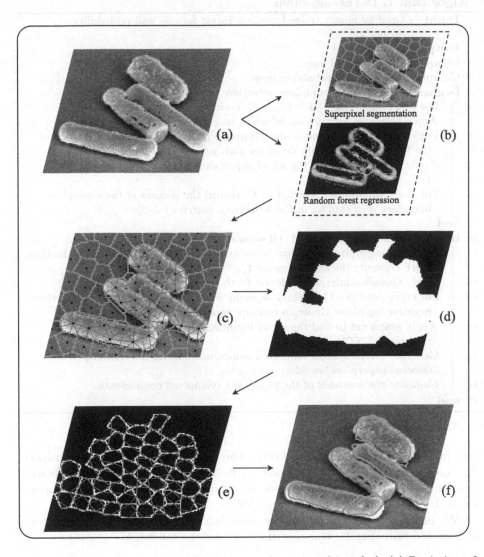

**Fig. 1.** Overview of the method (the figure is best viewed in color). (a) Depiction of a cell cluster in the original image. (b) Depiction of superpixel map (Top), and cell wall probabilities predicted by random forest regression (Bottom). (c) A random field defined over the superpixels provides potential cell regions (the nodes are represented by black dots and the edges by red lines). (d) Depiction of output superpixel area provided by the random field in (c). (e) A second random field defined over the remaining superpixel boundaries detects elongated cells (the nodes are represented by red dots and the edges by green lines). (f) Depiction of detected centroids (red), and cell walls (green). (Color figure online)

---

**Algorithm 1.** DeTEC algorithm.

---

**Input**  : Original image, trained random forest for cell wall probability estimation

**Output:** Cell centroids

1 Compute the superpixel map.

2 Compute the cell wall probability map.

3 **begin** First MRF: Cell candidate detection

4      For every superpixel $i$ ($i = 1, ..., n^1$), compute the feature vector $\mathbf{f}_i^1$.

5      Apply Gaussian mixture model on $\mathbf{f}^1$ to compute parameter set $\mathcal{T}$.

6      For every superpixel $i$ compute the unary potentials as the negative log of the Gaussian probability densities with parameter $\mathcal{T}$.

7      Apply graph cut to find the set of superpixel labels $\mathcal{L}^1$ that minimizes $E^1(\mathcal{L}^1)$.

8      For every superpixel $i$ selected in $\mathcal{L}^1$ record the indexes of the superpixel boundary segments $b_{ij}$ in the adjacency matrix, $j \in \mathcal{G}_i^1$.

9 **end**

10 **begin** Second MRF: Elongated cell separation

11      For every superpixel boundary segment $q$ ($q = 1, ..., n_2^2$), selected by the first MRF compute the feature vector $\mathbf{f}_q^2$.

12      Apply Gaussian mixture model on $\mathbf{f}^2$ to compute parameter set $\mathcal{O}$.

13      For every superpixel boundary segment $q$ compute unary potentials as the negative log of the Gaussian mixture model with parameter set $\mathcal{O}$.

14      Apply graph cut to find the set of boundary segment labels $\mathcal{L}^2$ that minimizes $E^2(\mathcal{L}^2)$.

15      Generate morphological connected components using the contours of the selected superpixel boundary segments.

16      Compute the centroids of the remaining connected components.

17 **end**

---

cells rather than the localization of cells. The third category are the region-based methods, where potential cell regions are first detected. Then, an optimization algorithm selects the best candidates based on statistical texture and appearances [10–15] or correlation clustering [16].

We propose a method capable of detecting touching and inhomogeneously illuminated cells (Fig. 1). Our contributions are the following:

- We propose two random fields, combining texture and shape information to detect elongated structures.
- We impose smoothness to the orientation between the segments of a contour to estimate the cell wall of elongated cells.
- We introduce a new dataset of *Clostridium difficile* cells obtained by SEM which is used for the evaluation of the method.

The rest of the paper is organized as follows: Sect. 2 describes DeTEC. Section 3 discusses the experimental results, including comparison with CellDetect [12].

## 2   Two Random Fields for Elongated Cell Detection

As a pre-processing stage, we apply a random forest regression to estimate the probability of a pixel belonging to a cell wall (Fig. 1(b), bottom). To train the random forest, we compute a feature vector containing a set of rotation invariant local binary patterns (LBP) [17], the response of the images to difference of Gaussians of varying width ratios, and to a vessel enhancement filter [18] (Fig. 1(b), bottom). Six images were manually annotated to provide the labels for training the random forest.

The next step involves developing a method based on two random fields: the first random field imposes texture smoothness while the second random field imposes smoothness on the continuity of superpixel boundary segments. At first, a cell image is divided into superpixels [19] and an MRF separates the cells from the background at superpixel level. However, a standard MRF may not separate clustered cells.

Cell walls have a key role in the detection of cells and the separation of adjacent cells. Every superpixel boundary segment has a likelihood of belonging to a cell wall. Moreover, neighboring superpixel boundary segments are more likely to have a small variance in orientation if they form an elongated cell wall. These two observations are key-issues in the proposed cell detection method.

**Cell Candidate Detection:** The first random field is imposed onto the superpixels adjacency graph (Fig. 1(c)). A graph cut provides a binary segmentation of superpixels with the following objective function:

$$E^1 = \sum_i u_i^1(\mathbf{f}_i^1 | \mathcal{L}^1, \mathcal{T}) + \sum_i \sum_{j \in \mathcal{G}_i^1} v_{i,j}^1(l_i^1, l_j^1), \tag{1}$$

where the first term is the sum of unary potentials $u_i^1$, consisting of a mixture of two Gaussians with parameter set $\mathcal{T} = \{\theta_0, \theta_1\}$, modeling the foreground and the background with superpixel label set $\mathcal{L}^1 = \{l_i^1 \in \{0, 1\} | i = 1, ..., n_s\}$. The feature vector $\mathbf{f}_i^1$ comprises a vector of orientation invariant LBPs, along with the mean, median, and standard deviation of pixels belonging to the $i^{\text{th}}$ superpixel. The second term is the pairwise potential where $\mathcal{G}_i^1$ is the set of superpixel neighbors of the $i^{\text{th}}$ superpixel.

In the standard MRF formulation, the pairwise term enforces the superpixels to have the same labels as their neighbors. However, when two cells are close to each other but not touching (e.g., they are separated by a small number of background pixels), the pairwise term forces the small background region between the two cells to be labeled as part of a cell. To avoid these false positives, we define a new pairwise penalty involving the probability of the boundary separating neighboring superpixels to be part of a cell wall [20,21]. Therefore, we define the pairwise potential between neighboring superpixel labels $l_i^1$ and $l_j^1$ by:

$$v_{i,j}^1(l_i^1, l_j^1) = \begin{cases} -\log(\pi_{ij}^1) \,, & \text{if } l_i^1 \neq l_j^1 \\ 0 \,, & \text{if } l_i^1 = l_j^1, \end{cases} \tag{2}$$

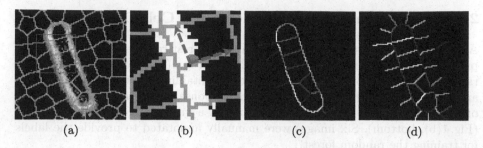

(a)                (b)                (c)                (d)

**Fig. 2.** (a) Depiction of the superpixel map (green) is overlaid onto the cell wall probability map. (b) Zoomed visualization of the area inside the red square in (a). The gray angle is between the largest connected component in the probability map (white) and the superpixel boundary segments (green). (c) The mean cell wall probabilities $\pi_{ij}^2$ of the image depicted in (a). (d) Depiction of the standard deviations of cell wall probabilities.(a) Depiction of the superpixel map (green) is overlaid onto the cell wall probability map. (b) Zoomed visualization of the area inside the red square in (a). The gray angle is between the largest connected component in the probability map (white) and the superpixel boundary segments (green). (c) The mean cell wall probabilities $\pi_{ij}^2$ of the image depicted in (a). (d) Depiction of the standard deviations of cell wall probabilities. (Color figure online)

where $\pi_{ij}^1$ is the probability indicating whether the boundary between the $i^{\text{th}}$ and $j^{\text{th}}$ superpixels is on a cell wall:

$$\pi_{ij}^1 = \frac{1}{|\mathcal{N}_{ij}|} \sum_{x \in \mathcal{N}_{ij}} p_x \cdot \cos \alpha_{ij}, \tag{3}$$

where $\mathcal{N}_{ij}$ is the set of all pixels at the border of the two superpixels indexed by $i$ and $j$, and $p_x$ is the probability of a pixel $x$ belonging to a cell wall. This value is obtained from the random forest (Fig. 1(b), bottom).

In Eq. (3) $\alpha_{ij}$ is the angle between the superpixel boundary component and the corresponding connected component in the probability map in a neighborhood around position $x$ (Fig. 2(b)). Thus, a superpixel boundary receives a high cell wall score when it is parallel to a real cell wall. If the boundary segment is more likely to be part of a cell wall, then the two touching superpixels are less likely to have the same labels.

This MRF model segments the cell regions from the background (Fig. 1(d)). However, when the cells are clumped together, every cluster of cells is segmented as one connected component. The second MRF takes the boundary segments of the cell superpixels and detects a set of boundary components that are more likely to form an elongated cell wall to detect elongated cells and separate the clustered cells. The second random field considers only the selected candidate superpixels. Therefore, the number of boundary segments in the second layer is much smaller than the total number of boundary segments in the original superpixel map.

**Elongated Cell Separation:** The second random field is defined over the superpixel boundary segments selected by the first random field. The objective of this step is to cluster these boundaries into two categories: boundaries that belong to elongated cell walls, and the rest of the boundaries. The energy function to be minimized is:

$$E^2 = \sum_q u_q^2(\mathbf{f}_q^2|\mathcal{L}^2,\mathcal{O}) + \sum_q \sum_{r\in\mathcal{G}_q^2} v_{q,r}^2(l_q^2,l_r^2). \tag{4}$$

The unary term represents the potential of the superpixel boundary component to be part of a cell wall. Similar to the first layer, $u_q^2$ is modeled by a Gaussian mixture model parameterized by $\mathcal{O}$ and $\mathcal{L}^2 = \{l_q^2 \in \{0,1\}|q = 1,...,n_2^2\}$. The feature vector $\mathbf{f}_q^2$ comprises the mean $\pi_{ij}^2$ (defined similarly as $\pi_{ij}^1$ in Eq. (3) and the standard deviation of the cell wall probabilities for the $q^{\text{th}}$ superpixel boundary components (Fig. 2). The second term models the pairwise potential enforcing the elongation of the $q^{\text{th}}$ boundary segment with respect to its neighbors in $\mathcal{G}_q^2$:

$$v_{q,r}^2(l_q^2,l_r^2) = \begin{cases} \cos\left(\beta_{qr}\right) & \text{if } l_q^2 \neq l_r^2 \\ 0 & \text{if } l_q^2 = l_r^2 \end{cases}, \tag{5}$$

where $\beta_{qr}$ is the angle between superpixel boundary segments $q$ and $r$, and is computed by taking the minimum angle between the estimated orientations of $q$ and $r$. When two adjacent boundary components have different orientations, they are less likely to have the same label. The extracted superpixel boundary components form the detected cell walls that separate the cell regions (Fig. 1(f)).

## 3   Experimental Results

To evaluate our method, we employed a dataset containing 7 *Clostridium difficile* cell images with a total of 78 cells acquired via SEM imaging with 10000X magnification and resolution of 411×712 pixels. The images have low cell densities but many cells are clustered together, making detection challenging. Furthermore, cells areas are highly inhomogeneously illuminated. This holds not only between cells but mainly for pixels belonging to the same cell (Fig. 4). In some cases, the cells are partially destroyed due to the biological treatment.

**Table 1.** Parameter settings used in DeTEC.

| Parameter(s) | Value(s) |
|---|---|
| DoG standard deviations | $\sigma_1 = 1$, and $\sigma_2 \in \{5,10\}$ |
| Vessel enhancement filter [18] parameters | Scale range $= [1,8]$, $\beta_1 = 0.5$, $\beta_2 = 15$, and Scale ratio $= 2$ |
| Distance from ground truth for true positives ($d$) | 20 pixels |

**Table 2.** Comparative results between DeTEC, CellDetect, and CellDetect*. In CellDetect*, a cluster of cells detected as one cell is considered a true positive.

| Method | Precision | Recall | F-score |
|---|---|---|---|
| CellDetect [12] | 0.53 | 0.27 | 0.36 |
| CellDetect* [12] | 0.95 | 0.57 | 0.71 |
| DeTEC | 0.69 | 0.93 | **0.79** |

Cell centroids are manually annotated to establish the ground truth. A centroid is considered to be detected if it lies within a distance $d$ from an annotated centroid. The distance is defined based on the length of the major axis of the smallest cell in the dataset. False positives are defined accordingly. We used the F-score for comparison.

Table 1 depicts the parameter settings for DeTEC. We compared the result with CellDetect [12], which is a supervised region-based cell detection method. CellDetect uses extremal regions [22] to detect candidate cell regions. Then, a statistical model of the cell appearance evaluates the selected extremal regions. The training and testing for CellDetect was based on a leave-one-out cross validation. In many cases, CellDetect fails to separate touching cells. Therefore, we considered two experiments for the comparison. The first experiment evaluates the detection of individual cells. The second experiment, which is strongly favorable to CellDetect, considers the attached cells as one object. In that case, detected clustered cells would be considered true positives even if CellDetect indicates the whole cluster as one cell.

Table 2 summarizes the performance of DeTEC against the two mentioned experiments. As may be observed, DeTEC achieves a higher F-score even in the case where detected clustered cells are considered as true positives for CellDetect. Accepting clustered cells improves the precision of CellDetect significantly. However, CellDetect fails to detect some cells due to the assumption of existing extremal regions that can represent the cells [15].

Figure 3 depicts representative examples of CellDetect and the DeTEC. The detected boundaries for an out-of-focus cell may not match the exact cell wall (Fig. 3(c)) since superpixel boundaries may not fit the cell wall line due to poor illumination. However, DeTEC could successfully estimate the centroid since we employed the cell wall probabilities from a small neighborhood around the superpixel boundaries.

DeTEC has a significantly higher F-score with respect to CellDetect [12]. This is also true for its precision and recall values. It seems that precision could have been better. However, this is due to the multiple cell centroids it detects in the case of overlapping cells or cells having undergone a biological treatment (3).

Finally, Fig. 4 depicts samples of detected inhomogeneously illuminated cells despite shadows and artifacts. Inhomogeneous illumination may cause the first random field to include the superpixels around the cells in the segmentation due to shadows and artifacts. However, the second random field examines whether the selected superpixel boundary segments are likely to form a cell wall with their neighbors, and eventually rejects them.

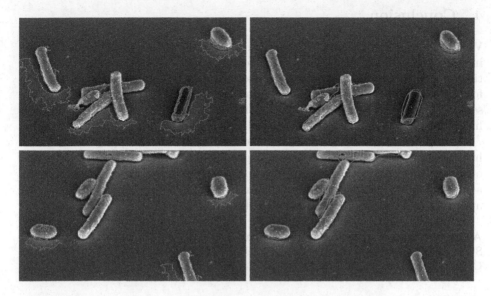

**Fig. 3.** Detected centroids and boundaries for CellDetect [12] (Left), and the DeTEC (Right). For DeTEC, annotated and detected centroids are shown in yellow and red, respectively. (Color figure online)

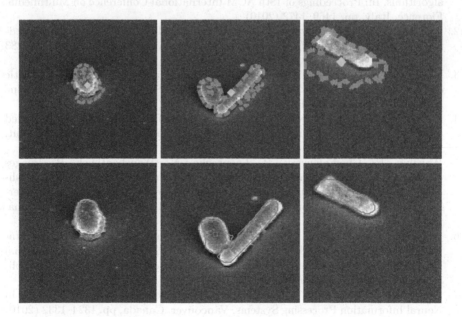

**Fig. 4.** Inhomogeneous illumination creates shadows on the cell surface and a bright area around the cell. Detected centroids for CellDetect [12] is shown (Top row). Detected and true centroids for DeTEC are shown as squares and circles, respectively (Bottom row).

# 4    Conclusion

We proposed a method with two random fields to detect elongated cells in SEM images that is robust for detecting inhomogeneously illuminated cells. The detection process is automatic, robust to inhomogeneous illumination, and suitable for the analysis of high-throughput microscopy images. The method successfully separates touching cells by estimating their cell walls. In general, our method has better overall performance than CellDetect.

In this work, we did not consider the case of cross-overlapping cells, which has been previously addressed by post-processing [6], deformable models [23], or watersheds [24]. Our detection method was implemented using a graph cut algorithm. However, the idea could be further extended to employ a supervised approach such as conditional random fields.

**Acknowledgments.** This work was supported in part by the Texas Department of State Health Services (Grant #2015-046620) and by the Hugh Roy and Lillie Cranz Cullen Endowment Fund.

# References

1. Vedaldi, A., Fulkerson, B.: VLFeat: an open and portable library of computer vision algorithms. In: Proceedings of 18th ACM International Conference on Multimedia, Florence, Italy, pp. 1469–1472 (2010)
2. Kainz, P.: You should use regression to detect cells. In: Proceedings of Medical Image Computing and Computer-Assisted Intervention, Munich, pp. 276–283 (2015)
3. Minaee, S., Fotouhi, M., Khalaj, B.: A geometric approach to fully automatic chromosome segmentation. In: Proceedings of IEEE Signal Processing in Medicine and Biology Symposium, Philadelphia, PA, pp. 1–6 (2014)
4. Wu, B., Nevatia, R.: Detection and segmentation of multiple, partially occluded objects by grouping, merging, assigning part detection responses. Int. J. Comput. Vision **82**, 185–204 (2009)
5. Wayalun, P., Chomphuwiset, P., Laopracha, N., Wanchanthuek, P.: Images enhancement of G-band chromosome using histogram equalization, OTSU thresholding, morphological dilation and flood fill techniques. In: Proceedings 8th International Conference on Computing and Networking Technology, Gueongju, China, pp. 163–168 (2012)
6. Saiyod, S., Wayalun, P.: A hybrid technique for overlapped chromosome segmentation of G-band mataspread images automatic. In: Proceedings of 4th International Conference on Digital Information and Communication Technology and its Applications, Bangkok, Thailand, pp. 400–404 (2014)
7. Lempitsky, V., Zisserman, A.: Learning to count objects in images. In: Advances in Neural Information Processing Systems, Vancouver, Canada, pp. 1324–1332 (2010)
8. Fiaschi, L., Koethe, U., Nair, R., Hamprecht, F.A.: Learning to count with regression forest and structured labels. In: Proceedings of 21st International Conference on Pattern Recognition, Tsukuba, Japan, pp. 2685–2688 (2012)
9. Foroughi, H., Ray, N., Zhang, H.: Robust people counting using sparse representation and random projection. Pattern Recogn. **48**, 3038–3052 (2015)

10. Daněk, O., Matula, P., Ortiz-de Solórzano, C., Muñoz-Barrutia, A., Maška, M., Kozubek, M.: Segmentation of touching cell nuclei using a two-stage graph cut model. In: Proceedings of Scandinavian Conference on Image Analysis, Oslo, Norway, pp. 410–419 (2009)
11. Keuper, M., Schmidt, T., Rodriguez-Franco, M., Schamel, W., Brox, T., Burkhardt, H., Ronneberger, O.: Hierarchical markov random fields for mast cell segmentation in electron microscopic recordings. In: Proceedings of IEEE International Symposium on Biomedical Imaging: From Nano to Macro, Chicago, pp. 973–978 (2011)
12. Arteta, C., Lempitsky, V., Noble, J.A., Zisserman, A.: Learning to detect cells using non-overlapping extremal regions. In: Proceedings of International Conference on Medical Image Computing and Computer-Assisted Intervention, Nice, France, pp. 348–356 (2012)
13. Arteta, C., Lempitsky, V., Noble, J.A., Zisserman, A.: Learning to detect partially overlapping instances. In: Proceedings of IEEE Conference on Computer Vision and Pattern Recognition, Portland, OR, pp. 3230–3237 (2013)
14. Santamaria-Pang, A., Rittscher, J., Gerdes, M., Padfield, D.: Cell segmentation and classification by hierarchical supervised shape ranking. In: Proceedings of IEEE International Symposium on Biomedical Imaging, Brooklyn, NY, pp. 1296–1299 (2015)
15. Arteta, C., Lempitsky, V., Noble, J.A., Zisserman, A.: Detecting overlapping instances in microscopy images using extremal region trees. Med. Image Anal. **27**, 3–16 (2016)
16. Zhang, C., Yarkony, J., Hamprecht, F.A.: Cell detection and segmentation using correlation clustering. In: Proceedings of Medical Image Computing and Computer-Assisted Intervention, Boston, MA, pp. 9–16 (2014)
17. Ojala, T., Pietikainen, M., Maenpaa, T.: Multiresolution gray-scale and rotation invariant texture classification with local binary patterns. IEEE Trans. Pattern Anal. Mach. Intell. **24**, 971–987 (2002)
18. Frangi, A.F., Niessen, W.J., Vincken, K.L., Viergever, M.A.: Multiscale vessel enhancement filtering. In: International Conference on Medical Image Computing and Computer-Assisted Intervention, Cambridge, MA, pp. 130–137 (1998)
19. Mori, G.: Guiding model search using segmentation. In: Proceedings of 10th IEEE International Conference on Computer Vision, Beijing, China, vol. 1, pp. 1417–1423 (2005)
20. Andres, B., Kappes, J.H., Beier, T., Kothe, U., Hamprecht, F.A.: Probabilistic image segmentation with closedness constraints. In: Proceedings of International Conference on Computer Vision, Barcelona, Spain, pp. 2611–2618 (2011)
21. Yarkony, J., Ihler, A., Fowlkes, C.C.: Fast planar correlation clustering for image segmentation. In: Proceedings of European Conference on Computer Vision, Florence, Italy, pp. 568–581 (2012)
22. Matas, J., Chum, O., Urban, M., Pajdla, T.: Robust wide-baseline stereo from maximally stable extremal regions. Image Vis. Comput. **22**, 761–767 (2004)
23. Plissiti, M.E., Nikou, C.: Overlapping cell nuclei segmentation using a spatially adaptive active physical model. IEEE Trans. Image Process. **21**, 4568–4580 (2012)
24. Karvelis, P., Likas, A., Fotiadis, D.I.: Identifying touching and overlapping chromosomes using the watershed transform and gradient paths. Pattern Recogn. Lett. **31**, 2474–2488 (2010)

# Object Detection Based on Image Blur Using Spatial-Domain Filtering with Haar-Like Features

Ryusuke Miyamoto[1]($\boxtimes$) and Shingo Kobayashi[2]

[1] Department of Computer Science, School of Science and Technology,
Meiji University, Kawasaki, Kanagawa 214-8571, Japan
miya@cs.meiji.ac.jp
[2] Department of Fundamental Science and Technology, Graduate School of Science
and Technology, Meiji University, Kawasaki, Kanagawa 214-8571, Japan
sin@cs.meiji.ac.jp

**Abstract.** In general, out-of-focus blur is considered to be disturbance that reduces the detection accuracy for object detection, and many researchers have tried to remove such noise. The authors proposed an object detection scheme that exploits information included in image blur. This scheme showed good accuracy for object detection, but it has a critical problem: huge computational cost is required owing to the DFT needed to evaluate image blur. This paper proposes a novel object detection scheme using the difference in image blur evaluated with simple spatial-domain filtering. Experimental results using synthetic images show that the scheme achieves perfect classification, though our previous scheme has about a 2.40% miss rate at 0.1 FPPI for circle detection. In addition to the improvement in accuracy, the processing speed becomes about 431 times faster than that of the old scheme.

## 1 Introduction

Image-based object detection and recognition are challenging problems in the field of image processing, and several schemes have been proposed to solve them. Haar-like features for face detection [1] and the histogram of oriented gradients (HOG) for human detection [2] are the most well known since the beginning of this research. One of the authors has also tackled this research field, enabling an improvement in processing speed [3–6] and detection accuracy [7]. Several schemes based on deep learning [8–10] have shown remarkable results in several competitions of image recognition [11,12]. However, a leading edge scheme [13] for object detection has shown better accuracy than deep learning. These results revealed that deep learning is not almighty and schemes need to be designed to treat detection and recognition targets appropriately.

For object detection, one of the most important cues to improve accuracy is an object boundary that represents the shape of a target object. Most existing schemes also use object boundaries as a visual cue, but it is difficult to evaluate

G. Bebis et al. (Eds.): ISVC 2016, Part I, LNCS 10072, pp. 298–308, 2016.
DOI: 10.1007/978-3-319-50835-1_28

them accurately if object detection needs to be performed in generic scenes that include cluttered background images. To improve accuracy of object detection, the authors have focused on image blur and proposed a novel scheme [14]. In the scheme, the difference in image blur corresponding to several image regions is used as a cue to construct weak classifiers though image blur tends to be removed for object detection and recognition. Also, several schemes have been proposed to remove it [15, 16] or to construct a classifier tolerant to it [17].

The object detection scheme proposed in [14] extends the Viola Jones scheme based on Haar-like features, where a discrete Fourier transform (DFT) is utilized in calculating weak classifiers to evaluate the difference in the image blur of rectangular features. The experimental results using artificially generated images and actual images including humans as detection targets show excellent classification accuracy. However, this scheme has a critical problem: the processing speed is too slow because of the computational amount of the DFT and its computation flow, which cannot utilize the integral images widely used in the field of object detection.

To solve this problem, we propose a novel scheme evaluating image blur using more simple operations to increase the speed of object detection based on image blur. The proposed scheme has the following two advantages: simple filtering in the spatial domain and computation flow that can utilize integral images. To show the feasibility of the proposed scheme, the authors evaluated the detection accuracy and the processing speed using artificially generated images that are used for evaluation in [14].

## 2    Object Detection Based on Image Blur with Haar-Like Features

This section describes our basic idea about object detection based on image blur. Then, it explains our previous proposal that evaluates image blur using a DFT with Haar-like features.

### 2.1    Basic Idea About Object Detection Based on Image Blur

Sharp in-focus images such as the upper row of Fig. 1 are utilized for detecting visual objects, which are obtained from a camera with a deep depth of field. In addition, our approach obtains blurred images as shown in the lower row of Fig. 1 by reducing the depth of field intentionally. In such images, the boundary between sharp and blurred regions corresponds to the contours of detection targets.

In some applications of object detection such as human detection or obstacle detection, objects should be found by evaluating object boundaries independently from a variety of textures of detection targets and background images. For example, one state-of-the-art scheme [18] has tried to improve the accuracy of human detection by designing weak classifiers considering the shapes

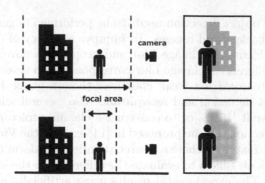

**Fig. 1.** Overview of object detection based on image blur.

of targets. Our proposal also aims to improve detection accuracy using object shapes that are easily obtained from the difference in image blur. However, the physical setting of a camera for a shallow depth of field reduces the available shooting range. Though our proposal has such limitations, we think they are not critical because some practical applications such as automotive and surveillance applications need only detect targets coming into previously defined areas.

## 2.2    Object Detection Based on Image Blur Using a DFT

A novel scheme that evaluates image blur using a DFT with Haar-like features in [14] was designed to achieve object detection based on image blur. In the scheme, feature extraction is performed with Haar-like features, as shown in Fig. 2. The feature extraction evaluates the difference in image blur between rectangular regions 1 and 2 included in a Haar-like feature using the DFT with *score*. After this calculation, $f$ is computed by subtracting *score* for region 1 and region 2. The order of this subtraction is shuffled in the training process. A final strong classifier using haar-like features as weak classifiers is constructed using Adaboost, which is the same process as the Viola Jones scheme [1] shown in Algorithm 1.

That is the summary of the previous scheme for object detection based on image blur. The details can be found in [14].

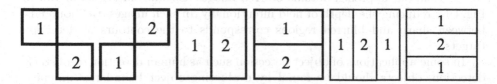

**Fig. 2.** Haar-like features used in the scheme [14].

---

**Algorithm 1.** AdaBoost algorithm

1: $w_{1,i} = \frac{1}{2m}$ where $m$ is the number of negative images.
2: **for** $t = 1, ..., T$ **do**
3:    $w_{t,i} \leftarrow \frac{w_{t,i}}{\sum_{j=1}^{n} w_{i,j}}$
4:    $\epsilon = \min_{f,p,\theta} \sum_i w_i |h(x_i, f, p, \theta) - y_i|$
5:    Define $h_t(x) = h(x, f_t, p_t, \theta_t)$ where $f_t, p_t,$ and $\theta_t$ are the minimizers od $\epsilon_t$.
6:    Update the weights: $w_{t+1,i} = w_{t,i} \beta^{1-e_i}$
7:    where $e_i = 0$ if example $x_i$ is classified correctly, $e_i = 1$ otherwise, and $\beta_t = \frac{\epsilon}{1-\epsilon}$
8: **end for**
9:    $\begin{cases} 1 \ \sum_{t=1}^{T} \alpha_t h_t(x) \geq \frac{1}{2} \sum_{t=1}^{T} \alpha_t \\ 0 \ otherwise \end{cases}$
10: where $\alpha_t = \log \frac{1}{\beta_t}$

---

# 3  Object Detection Based on Image Blur Using Spatial-Domain Filtering

This section details the proposed scheme. In the first subsection, feature extraction of our scheme is explained and the second subsection introduces how to apply integral image to it.

## 3.1  Feature Extraction Based on Spatial-Domain Filtering

Our scheme utilizes simple differential filtering in the spatial-domain so as to reduce the computational cost for evaluating image blur. The feature extraction proposed in this paper is composed of the following processes:

1. a sub-image extraction corresponding to Haar-like features,
2. calculation of *score* using differential filtering, and
3. calculation of $f$ based on *score* obtained from the previous process.

The 2nd process is detailed because it is the most significant operation in our scheme. In this process, differential filtering for vertical and horizontal directions is applied to rectangular features included in a Haar-like feature selected in the 1st step. This operation can be written using the following equations:

$$D_{\mathrm{h}}(i,j) = -I(i-1,j) + I(i+1,j), and \qquad (1)$$
$$D_{\mathrm{v}}(i,j) = -I(i,j-1) + I(i,j+1), \qquad (2)$$

where $I(i,j)$ means the luminance at $(i,j)$ in an image plane. To obtain *score*, the following operation is applied in addition to the aforementioned equation:

$$score = \sum_{i,j \in \mathrm{Rect}} \{|D_{\mathrm{h}}(i,j)| + |D_{\mathrm{v}}(i,j)|\} \qquad (3)$$

By using *score* obtained from each region of a Haar-like feature, $f$ is computed by the following equation:

$$f = score_k - score_l, \qquad (4)$$

where $(k, l)$ equals $(1, 2)$ or $(2, 1)$, which corresponds to the number used in Fig. 2.

## 3.2 How to Apply Integral Images

The previous scheme proposed in [14] applies the DFT for multiple rectangular regions of Haar-like features. Therefore, difficulty occurs in applying an integral image that is utilized in the Viola-Jones scheme to increase the speed of feature computation. However, an integral image can be applied to the our scheme because the calculation of *score* is composed of simple filtering in the spatial-domain represented by Eqs. 2 and 3. In our scheme, an integral image defined by the following equation is used to compute *score*:

$$II(i, j) = \sum \{|D_{\mathrm{h}}(x, y)| + |D_{\mathrm{v}}(x, y)|\}, \tag{5}$$

where, $(x, y)$ refers to two-dimensional coordinates in an input image.

If an integral image is generated by this equation, *score* surrounded by points $(x_0, y_0)$, $(x_1, y_1)$, $(x_2, y_2)$, and $(x_3, y_3)$ can be computed using the following equation:

$$II(x_3, y_3) - II(x_2, y_2)$$
$$-II(x_1, y_1) + II(x_0, y_0) \tag{6}$$

## 4 Evaluation

This section presents our evaluation of the proposed scheme using a dataset created by the authors with synthetic images.

### 4.1 Experimental Conditions

We had to define some parameters to construct classifiers using our scheme in actual cases. The detection accuracy was significantly affected by weak classifiers used to train a strong classifier. This evaluation trained a strong classifier by generating feature pools from six kinds of weak classifiers shown in Fig. 2 by changing their location and size randomly. Here, 400 and 1000 features were tested to evaluate the relationship between the number of a feature pool and the detection accuracy. A strong classifier was constructed using the Adaboost, where 100 weak classifiers were selected in the training process.

In a comparison of our scheme with other object detection schemes, the detection accuracies of the Viola-Jones scheme [1], the filtered channel features [13], and the DFT-based scheme [14] were also measured. The number of feature pools and the selected features were set to 1000 and 100, respectively, to train the Viola-Jones scheme. A feature pool of 3000 features was generated, and 200 decision trees were used as weak classifiers to train the filtered channel features.

The number of feature pools and selected features was set to 1000 and 100, respectively, for the DFT-based scheme.

The miss rate vs. false positive per image (FPPI), which is widely used criteria in the field of object detection, was measured as DET curves for the quantitative evaluation. Of course, an exhaustive search based on a sliding window was applied.

## 4.2   A Data Set Used for Evaluating Detection Accuracy

In this evaluation, we selected circles, stars, and squares as shapes of the detection targets, and three kinds of texture were mapped to them, as shown in Figs. 3, 4, and 5. The reason these detection targets had the same shape but different texture was that this experiment was conducted to show that the boundary information can be properly extracted from the difference in image blur independently from texture information. As background images for this evaluation, images with Gaussian blur instead of out-of-focus blur were generated from the INRIA dataset, whose resolution was 640 × 480. This approximation was suitable for our evaluation because the point spread function corresponding to out-of-focus blur could be represented using Gaussian distribution.

Test images were generated to evaluate FPPI, including several detection targets on a blurred background image. Here, the location and size of target objects were changed randomly to evaluate the detection accuracy of the proposed scheme properly.

## 4.3   Detection Accuracy

This subsection shows the accuracy of the detection for three kinds of objects, the shapes of which were circles, stars, and squares.

**Circle Detection.** This subsection shows the detection accuracy of circular objects. In this evaluation, positive samples were randomly selected from circle

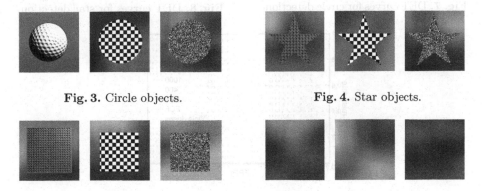

**Fig. 3.** Circle objects.                    **Fig. 4.** Star objects.

**Fig. 5.** Square objects.                    **Fig. 6.** Empty samples.

objects. Negative samples consisted of star objects, rectangle objects, and empty samples randomly selected from blurred images shown as Fig. 6. In addition, star and square objects treated as negative samples in this evaluation and some samples were also randomly selected from these objects. Figure 7 shows DET curves representing the miss rate vs. FPPI. The results showed that the proposed scheme had the best accuracy; perfect classification was achieved for all FPPI. The Viola-Jones scheme had a very bad miss rate for all FPPI. However, FCF had about an 8.41% miss rate in FPPI, which was much better than that of the Viola-Jones. With the DFT-based scheme, the miss rate became about 2.40% at 0.1 FPPI. These results show that the proposed scheme was the best.

**Star Detection.** Next, the accuracy for star detection is described. In this evaluation, a classifier was trained in the same way as with the circle detection, where positive samples consisted of only star objects and negative samples including circle objects instead of star objects. The DET curves of the proposed scheme, FCF, and Viola-Jones are plotted in Fig. 8. The results show that the miss rate became 0 for all FPPI using the DFT-based scheme and our scheme. Viola-Jones had a high miss rate for all FPPI, similar to the case of circle detection. However, the FCF had about a 10.5% miss rate at 0.1 FPPI, better than that of Viola-Jones. However, this score was not ideal for object detection. The

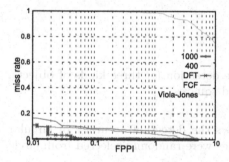

**Fig. 7.** DET curves for circle detection.

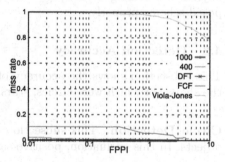

**Fig. 8.** DET curves for star detection.

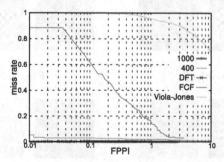

**Fig. 9.** DET curves for square detection.

results demonstrate, convincingly that even a state-of-the-art scheme could not work well in this simple experiment if feature extraction considering image blur was not utilized.

**Rectangle Detection.** Finally, the accuracy for square detection is shown in Fig. 9. In this evaluation, a classifier was trained in the same way as it was in the circle detection, where positive samples consisted of only square objects and negative samples including circle objects, star objects, and empty samples. The results were that squares were also detected perfectly using the DFT-based scheme and the proposed scheme. The DET curve of Viola-Jones was similar to the results of the circle and star detection. These results show that the Viola-Jones scheme didn't work well in this experiment. The detection accuracy using FCF worsened when the miss rate was about 62.6% at 0.1 FPPI. These results indicate that appropriate learning could not be performed for square detection even though accurate classifiers for circle and start detection were constructed.

### 4.4    Processing Speed

Next, the processing speed was evaluated. In this evaluation, the computation time per image was evaluated using all test images. These experiments were performed on a Linux PC with an Intel Corei7 4770 K CPU with 16 GB memory. Table 1 shows the computation speed of the DFT-based scheme, the proposed scheme with integral images, and the proposed scheme without integral images. The proposed scheme was much faster than the previous scheme using DFT even if integral images were not used. If integral images were utilized in the proposed scheme, the computation speed improved further. The computation time itself seemed too slow, but it could be improved by optimizing the implementation and faster schemes such as attentional cascade or soft-cascade.

**Table 1.** Processing speed

| Scheme | DFT [14] | wo int img | w int img |
|---|---|---|---|
| Time (seconds) | 1491 | 100.3 | 3.456 |

**Fig. 10.** Results of circle detection.

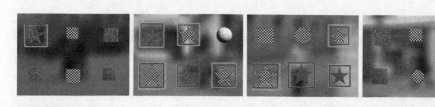

**Fig. 11.** Results of star detection.

**Fig. 12.** Results of square detection.

## 5  Conclusion

This paper proposed a novel scheme to resolve the defects of the scheme for object detection that uses DFT for feature extraction based on image blur proposed in [14]. The scheme extracts features using vertical and horizontal differential filtering for rectangular regions in Haar-like features and accumulation of their absolute values. A drastic improvement in processing speed can be expected because our scheme consists of simple operations in the spatial-domain;moreover, integral images can be applied to feature calculation.

The classification accuracy and the processing speed were evaluated with the same dataset as [14] to show the effectiveness of the proposed scheme. The results were that the classification accuracy improved: 0% miss rate for all FPPI using the proposed scheme even in the case of a 2.40% miss rate at 0.1 FPPI using the DFT-based scheme. The results show that our scheme had perfect classification in the experiment. In another evaluation, the processing speed became about 14.9 times faster than that of the DFT-based scheme. If integral images were used, it became about 431 times faster.

Experimental results showed that our scheme could achieve accurate object detection using image blur. However, it must be evaluated with a dataset including more complex objects to show its effectiveness with practical applications. Therefore, the authors will construct a novel dataset that simulates actual scenes using computer graphics. Finally, we want to evaluate our scheme with actual images obtained using generic cameras with a shallow depth of field. For a further increase in speed, we will apply a soft cascade structure trained with multiple instance pruning [19].

# References

1. Viola, P., Jones, M.: Rapid object detection using a boosted cascade of simple features. In: Proceedings of IEEE Conference on Computer Vision Pattern Recognition, vol. 1, pp. 511–518 (2001)
2. Dalal, N., Triggs, B.: Histograms of oriented gradients for human detection. In: Proceedings of IEEE Conference on Computer Vision Pattern Recognition, vol. 1, pp. 886–893 (2005)
3. Hiromoto, M., Sugano, H., Miyamoto, R.: Partially parallel architecture for AdaBoost-based detection with haar-like features. IEEE Trans. Circuits Syst. Video Technol. **19**, 41–52 (2009)
4. Hiromoto, M., Miyamoto, R.: Hardware architecture for high-accuracy real-time pedestrian detection with CoHOG features. In: Proceedings of IEEE International Conference on Computer Vision Workshops, pp. 894–899 (2009)
5. Yu, J., Miyamoto, R., Onoye, T.: Fast pedestrian detection using a soft-cascade of the CoHOG-based classifier: how to speed-up SVM classifiers based on multiple-instance pruning. IEEE Trans. Image Process. **22**, 4752–4761 (2013)
6. Miyamoto, R., Oki, T.: Soccer player detection with only color features selected using informed haar-like features. In: Blanc-Talon, J., Distante, C., Philips, W., Popescu, D., Scheunders, P. (eds.) ACIVS 2016. LNCS, vol. 10016, pp. 238–249. Springer, Heidelberg (2016). doi:10.1007/978-3-319-48680-2_22
7. Miyamoto, R., Jaehoon, Y., Onoye, T.: Normalized channel features for accurate pedestrian detection. In: Proceedings of IEEE ISCCSP, pp. 582–585 (2014)
8. Schmidhuber, J.: Multi-column deep neural networks for image classification. In: Proceedings of IEEE Conference on Computer Vision Pattern Recognition, pp. 3642–3649 (2012)
9. Erhan, D., Szegedy, C., Toshev, A., Anguelov, D.: Scalable object detection using deep neural networks. In: Proceedings of IEEE Conference on Computer Vision Pattern Recognition, pp. 2155–2162 (2014)
10. Yang, Y., Shu, G., Shah, M.: Semi-supervised learning of feature hierarchies for object detection in a video. In: Proceedings of IEEE Conference on Computer Vision Pattern Recognition, pp. 1650–1657 (2013)
11. Everingham, M., Van Gool, L., Williams, C.K.I., Winn, J., Zisserman, A.: The pascal visual object classes (VOC) challenge. Int. J. Comput. Vis. **88**, 303–338 (2010)
12. Deng, J., Dong, W., Socher, R., Li, L.J., Li, K., Fei-Fei, L.: ImageNet: a large-scale hierarchical image database. In: Proceedings IEEE Conference on Computer Vision Pattern Recognition, pp. 248–255 (2009)
13. Zhang, S., Benenson, R., Schiele, B.: Filtered channel features for pedestrian detection. In: Proceedings of IEEE Conference on Computer Vision Pattern Recognition, pp. 1751–1760 (2015)
14. Miyamoto, R., Kobayashi, S.: Object detection based on image blur evaluated by discrete Fourier transform and Haar-like features. IEICE Trans. Fundam. **E99-A**(11), 1990–1999 (2016)
15. Rhemann, C., Rother, C., Kohli, P., Gelautz, M.: A spatially varying PSF-based prior for alpha matting. In: Proceedings of IEEE Conference on Computer Vision Pattern Recognition, pp. 2149–2156 (2010)
16. Couzinie-Devy, F., Sun, J., Alahari, K., Ponce, J.: Learning to estimate and remove non-uniform image blur. In: Proceedings of IEEE Conference on Computer Vision Pattern Recognition, pp. 1075–1082 (2013)

17. Flusser, J., Suk, T., Boldys, J., Zitová, B.: Projection operators and moment invariants to image blurring. IEEE Trans. Pattern Anal. Mach. Intell. **37**, 786–802 (2015)
18. Zhang, S., Bauckhage, C., Cremers, A.: Informed haar-like features improve pedestrian detection. In: Proceedings of IEEE Conference on Computer Vision Pattern Recognition, pp. 947–954 (2014)
19. Zhang, C., Viola, P.A.: Multiple-instance pruning for learning efficient cascade detectors. In: Platt, J.C., Koller, D., Singer, Y., Roweis, S.T., (eds.) Advances in Neural Information Processing Systems 20. Curran Associates, Inc., pp. 1681–1688 (2008)

# Rare Class Oriented Scene Labeling Using CNN Incorporated Label Transfer

Liangjiang Yu and Guoliang Fan$^{(\boxtimes)}$

School of Electrical and Computer Engineering, Oklahoma State University,
Stillwater, OK 74078, USA
guoliang.fan@okstate.edu

**Abstract.** In natural scene images, rare class objects have low occurrence frequencies and limited spatial coverage, and they may be easily ignored during scene labeling. However, rare class objects are often more important to semantic labeling and image understanding compared to background areas. In this work, we present a rare class-oriented scene labeling framework (RCSL) that involves two new techniques pertaining to rare classes. First, scene assisted rare class retrieval is introduced in label transfer that is intended to enrich the retrieval set with scene-relevant rare classes. Second, a complementary rare class balanced CNN is incorporated to address the unbalanced training data issues, where rare classes are usually dominated by common ones in natural scene images. Furthermore, a superpixels-based re-segmentation was implemented to produce perceptually meaningful object boundaries. Experimental results demonstrate promising scene labeling performance of the proposed framework on the SIFTflow dataset both qualitatively and quantitatively, especially for rare class objects.

## 1 Introduction

Scene labeling is one of the most important problems of computer vision that pave the path to comprehensive scene understanding. It aims at assigning a semantic label to each pixel in an observed image, resulting in classification, semantic segmentation and recognition. In most natural scene images, unbalanced class distribution is often encountered, and rare class objects are easily ignored by most classifiers without careful consideration [1]. As a result, rare classes may be unintentionally and possibly neglected to achieve higher overall labeling accuracy [2] due to their temporal and spatial nature. However, in most scene understanding applications, rare class objects (human, boat, vehicle, etc.) are often important to object recognition/segmentation and visual understanding. We aim to develop a CNN-based rare class-oriented scene labeling framework for enhanced labeling performance, especially for rare classes. Our research is motivated by two main ideas to alleviate the unbalanced class distribution problems. First, we want to enhance the population of scene-specific rare classes in label transfer by selectively boosting the training data of rare classes pertaining to a specific scene in the retrieval set. Second, we improve detection and classification of rare classes by integrating a rare class balanced CNN in the original CNN framework to mitigate the unbalanced training data problem.

© Springer International Publishing AG 2016
G. Bebis et al. (Eds.): ISVC 2016, Part I, LNCS 10072, pp. 309–320, 2016.
DOI: 10.1007/978-3-319-50835-1_29

## 2    Related Work

In traditional scene understanding applications, either a single label [3], or a group of labels were allocated to a given image [4]. On the other hand, scene labeling provides not only object classification but also semantically meaningful scene segmentation, e.g., [5,6]. Recently, deep convolutional neural networks (CNN) [7] have successfully advanced scene labeling research by learning effective and discriminative high-level visual representations. In [8], a multi-scale CNN was developed to eliminate the needs for human engineered features. Such networks provide powerful representations not only for textures and shapes, but also for contextual information. A recurrent CNN was proposed in [9] to capture long-range pixel label dependencies rather than those over only small regions. Intra-layer recurrent connection was introduced in [10] that integrates contextual information in the 2D space explicitly.

Moreover, nonparametric methods [11–18] involving image retrieval and label transfer have achieved promising scene labeling performance. By doing so, irrelevant scenes in the training dataset may be skipped due to global contextual constraints, and the class likelihoods of superpixels can be specified by semantically transferring labels from retrieved images to the query image. The non-parametric label transfer method was incorporated into a parametric CNN framework in [19] where the local ambiguities from CNN models are alleviated by using global scene semantics, and scene-relevant class dependencies and priors are transfered by matching learned CNN features without additional training effort. To cope with rare class objects with unbalanced distribution, the retrieval set was expanded in [2] by explicitly adding superpixels of rare classes, and a global semantic context was developed to refine the retrieval and superpixel matching. Similarly, random sampling [19] was used to expand the retrieval set with extremely rare class objects. In [6], rare class representations were enhanced by merging classification costs of different contextual models. An ensemble of SVMs was designed in [1] where each SVM is trained for a single class.

Our research is motivated from two perspectives. First, we enhance the relevance of training data pertaining to scene-specific rare classes. Second, we increase the sensitivity and specificity of rare class classification by a second-round re-inference. Specifically, our research has three technical components:

- Rather than equally selecting all rare classes [2], we selectively add rare classes based on the global scene layout to reduce the class ambiguity and to simplify the inference process. This encourages scene-relevant class distribution in the retrieval set for more accurate rare class label transfer.
- A complementary rare class balanced CNN is proposed to mitigate the unbalanced training data problem with the focus on rare classes for re-inference. This additional CNN is implemented locally near the region of rare classes and embedded in the original CNN framework [19].
- A superpixels-based re-segmentation is adopted to produce perceptually meaningful object boundaries by taking advantage of CNN-based pixel labeling.

# 3   Overview of Proposed Methods

We present the proposed rare class-oriented scene labeling (RCSL) framework in Fig. 1. In this section, we first briefly introduce the baseline integration model in [19] (steps 1 and 2), followed by the proposed scene assisted image retrieval (steps 3, 4 and 5), and the complementary rare class balanced CNN (steps 6 and 7). Then the superpixels-based re-segmentation will be presented for perceptually meaningful object segmentation (step 8, RCSL-Seg).

## 3.1   Preliminary Work - Integration Model

Deep CNNs greatly reduce the needs of learning low-level features by providing higher-level discriminative representations. However, visually similar pixels/patches cause significant local ambiguities where insufficient contextual information has been considered during training. A lot of effort has been made to address this issue, such as augmenting the scale of context for pixel representation [8,9], and using graphical models to build pixel dependencies [13]. These methods are able to reduce local ambiguities to a certain degree, but they either cause negative effects on small objects (due to larger scales of context) [19], or introduce a computationally expensive optimization process (searching in the label space during prediction) [9].

In order to fully utilize global scene semantics to reduce local ambiguities, an integration of parametric and non-parametric models was proposed in [19], where

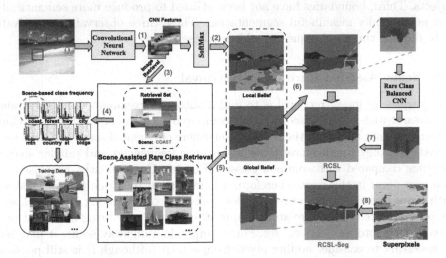

**Fig. 1.** Proposed RCSL and RCSL-Seg framework. (1) CNN features obtained by passing the input to the original CNN; (2) local belief computation [19]; (3) image exemplars retrieval using CNN features; (4) scene assisted rare class retrieval; (5) global belief computation; (6) rare class objects localization by combining global and local beliefs; (7) complementary local belief by rare class balanced CNN; (8) superpixels-based re-segmentation

not only CNN models were adopted for feature learning and local classification, but also a non-parametric label transfer method was incorporated to achieve enhanced classification robustness for locally indistinguishable pixels. This integration have three advantages. First, the global semantics helps to remove pixel level ambiguities by providing class dependencies globally from nearest exemplars in the training dataset. Second, discriminative features learned from CNN is used for global feature learning instead of human engineered low-level features. Third, a relatively small retrieval set is sufficient since a single input image usually contains limited number of objects compared to the whole training dataset. Specifically, the overall objective function is defined as follows,

$$E(\mathbf{X}, \mathbf{Y}) = -\sum_{i \in \mathbf{X}} (P_L(X_i, Y_j) + P_G(X_i, Y_j)) \tag{1}$$

where $\mathbf{X}$ is the observation image, $X_i$ is the $i$th pixel and $Y_j$ is the corresponding label ($j = 1, 2, \cdots, L$, and $L$ is the number of classes). $P_L(X_i, Y_j)$ is the pixel-wise local belief obtained by a learned CNN model evaluated on small image patches, and $P_G(X_i, Y_j)$ is the non-parametric global belief achieved by a weighted $K$-nearest neighbor ($K$NN) in a global feature space obtained through the CNN.

This integration model is able to mitigate the local ambiguities from pure CNN models by incorporating global scene context. But there are also several limitations. First, scene-relevant rare class objects may be missing during the image retrieval where only global scene semantics has been considered. Second, training the CNN using unbalanced data distribution tends to ignore rare class objects. Third, boundaries have not been utilized to produce more semantically and perceptually meaningful segmentation. These three observations motivate us to develop three techniques to address these issues.

### 3.2   Scene Assisted Rare Class Retrieval

The purpose of image retrieval is to find a subset of exemplars from the training dataset with a similar scene layout compared with the input. But rare class objects may not appear in the retrieval set where only global scene layout is preserved, and they usually have lower occurrence frequencies and smaller spatial coverage compared with common classes (Fig. 2a). Consequently, misclassification may occur in this case. Therefore, it is important to enrich the retrieval set with more rare classes. However, random selection [2, 19] among all rare classes introduces more inference-related computation, and it may bring irrelevant rare class objects into the retrieval set. For example, in a highway scene, it may not be necessary to consider adding pixels from a boat (although it is still possible to see a boat being towed by a truck on the highway). Also as shown in Table 1, humans appear most probably in the street scene, and cars are also more likely to appear in the street scene rather than in the natural forest. Scene information may play an important role for selecting rare class candidates. Hence, we fuse a scene assisted rare class retrieval method into the non-parametric model like the one in [19] for global label transfer, where scene information is incorporated

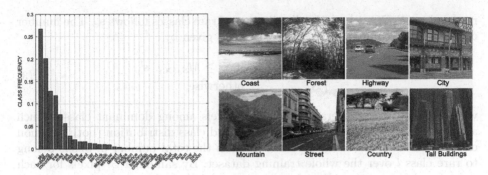

**Fig. 2.** The SIFTflow dataset [11] captured under 8 typical natural scenes. Left: unbalanced class distribution; right: 8 semantic natural scenes

**Table 1.** Selected class frequencies (%) under 8 scene categories [11]

|          | Coast  | Forest  | Highway | City | Mountain | Country | Street | Tall_buildings |
|----------|--------|---------|---------|------|----------|---------|--------|----------------|
| Car      | < 0.01 | 0.02    | 2.37    | 2.44 | < 0.01   | < 0.01  | **6.26** | 0.28         |
| Person   | 0.04   | 0.08    | 0.01    | 0.31 | 0.09     | 0.02    | **0.94** | 0.06         |
| Boat     | **0.13** | < 0.01 | 0      | 0.03 | 0        | 0.02    | 0.04   | 0.06           |
| Sidewalk | 0      | 0       | 0.44    | 3.24 | 0        | 0       | **4.32** | 0.25         |
| Road     | 0.04   | 0.19    | **36.08** | 8.56 | 0.23    | 0.51    | 24.52  | 0.76           |
| Field    | 0      | 0.07    | 1.42    | 0    | 0.16     | **19.05** | 0     | 0              |

to ensure the distribution of rare classes follows the same as they appear in the training dataset under each scene category.

Specifically, considering $C$ scene categories, we may obtain a $L_r \times 1$ occurrence frequency vector $\mathbf{f}_c$ of $L_r$ rare class objects under each scene. During scene assisted sampling, we obtain the ratio vector $\mathbf{s}_c$ as

$$\mathbf{s}_c = \frac{\mathbf{f}_c}{\sum \mathbf{f}_c}, \tag{2}$$

which provides the proportion of rare classes in the resulting retrieval set under scene $c$. Suppose we have a trained CNN model $\mathcal{M}$ using image patches from the training dataset $\mathbf{X} = [\mathbf{X}_1, \mathbf{X}_2, \cdots, \mathbf{X}_N]$ with ground truth labels $\mathbf{Y} = [\mathbf{Y}_1, \mathbf{Y}_2, \cdots, \mathbf{Y}_N]$, and $\mathbf{Y}_i \in \{1, 2, \cdots, L\}^{H \times W}$, where $H$ and $W$ are the image height and width, $N$ is the number of training images, $L$ is the number of classes. We compute feature tensors $\mathbf{F} \in \mathbb{R}^{H \times W \times T}$ for each training image by passing it to the truncated CNN (without the Softmax layer), and $T$ is determined by the output of the truncated CNN. Then global features $\mathbf{H} = [\mathbf{H}_1, \mathbf{H}_2, \cdots, \mathbf{H}_N]$ are obtained by averaging over the pooling regions [19]. Given a query image $\mathbf{X}_q$, similarly we can obtain CNN feature $\mathbf{H}_q$, and hence the retrieval set $\mathcal{S}_q(\mathbf{X})$ with $m$ exemplars by matching $\mathbf{H}$ and $\mathbf{H}_q$. The scene category $c$ could be obtained from the dominant scene in $\mathcal{S}_q(\mathbf{X})$. We introduce a scene assisted rare class retrieval set $\mathcal{B}_q(\mathbf{X})$, where the distribution of rare classes follows $\mathbf{s}_c$. The number of samples $S^l$ required for each rare class $l$ is given by

$$S^l = \begin{cases} M_{\mathcal{S}_q(\mathbf{X})} \cdot \mathbf{s}_c^l & \text{if } N_l \geq M_{\mathcal{S}_q(\mathbf{X})} \cdot \mathbf{s}_c^l, \\ N_l & \text{otherwise,} \end{cases} \tag{3}$$

where $M_{\mathcal{S}_q(\mathbf{X})}$ is the average number of pixels among dominant classes (such as sky, sea) in $\mathcal{S}_q(\mathbf{X})$. This ensures a balanced class distribution (both common classes and scene-relevant rare classes). $N_l$ is the total number of pixels belong to rare class $l$ over the whole training dataset. By sampling $S^l$ pixels for each rare class $l$ from the training dataset, we are able to obtain a new retrieval set $\mathcal{Z}_q(\mathbf{X}) = \mathcal{S}_q(\mathbf{X}) \cup \mathcal{B}_q(\mathbf{X})$. The scene assisted rare class retrieval is summarized in Algorithm 1. Similar to [19], the global belief $P_G(X_i, Y_j)$ could be obtained by statistical features in the retrieval set $\mathcal{Z}_q(\mathbf{X})$,

$$P_G(X_i, Y_j) = \frac{\sum_k D(X_i, X_k)\delta(Y(X_k) = Y_j)}{\sum_k D(X_i, X_k)}, \quad \forall X_k \in \mathcal{Z}_q(\mathbf{X}), \tag{4}$$

where $X_k$ is the $k$th nearest neighbor of pixel $X_i$ within $\mathcal{Z}_q(\mathbf{X})$ obtained by matching CNN features, $Y(X_k)$ is the ground truth label of pixel $X_k$ in the retrieval set, $\delta(True) = 1$ is an indicator function, and $L$ is the number of classes. $D(\cdot)$ gives the similarity of two pixels,

$$D(X_i, X_j) = \exp(-\alpha\|x_i - x_j\|)\exp(-\gamma\|z_i - z_j\|)\exp(-\beta\|b_i - b_j\|), \tag{5}$$

where $x_i$ is the CNN feature corresponding to pixel $X_i$, $z_i$ is the coordinate along the vertical direction of the image, $b_i$ is the size of the image blob where the pixel $X_i$ belong to (upon labeling using $\mathcal{M}$). This encourages a larger dissimilarity between rare and frequent classes. $\alpha$, $\gamma$ and $\beta$ control the trade-off among three terms based on empirical setting [19].

---

**Algorithm 1.** Scene Assisted Rare Class Retrieval

---

1: Input: CNN model $\mathcal{M}$ learned from unbalanced data, training images $[\mathbf{X}_1, \mathbf{X}_2, \cdots, \mathbf{X}_N]$ and their ground truth Labels $[\mathbf{Y}_1, \mathbf{Y}_2, \cdots, \mathbf{Y}_N]$
2: Input all training images $\mathbf{X}_{1:N}$ to $\mathcal{M}$, and acquire feature tensors $[\mathbf{F}_1, \mathbf{F}_2, \cdots, \mathbf{F}_N]$
3: Obtain global features $\mathbf{H} = [\mathbf{H}_1, \mathbf{H}_2, \cdots, \mathbf{H}_N]$ by average pooling
4: Based on the scene category $c \in \{1, 2, \cdots, C\}$ for all training images, compute $C \times L_r$ frequency matrix $\mathbf{f}$ for $L_r$ rare classes ($L_r < L$)
5: Given a query Image $\mathbf{X}_q$, similarly obtain CNN feature $\mathbf{H}_q$, and retrieve nearest exemplars $\mathcal{S}_q(\mathbf{X})$ from training images by matching $\mathbf{H}$ and $\mathbf{H}_q$
6: Assign the image category label $c$ for the query image based on $\mathcal{S}_q(\mathbf{X})$, and then Obtain $\mathbf{f}_c$ of rare classes from $\mathbf{f}$, and compute $\mathbf{s}_c$ by Equation (2)
7: Sample rare class image patches according to Equation (3) to obtain $\mathcal{B}_q(\mathbf{X})$
8: Final retrieval set for query image $\mathbf{X}_q$ is $\mathcal{Z}_q(\mathbf{X}) = \mathcal{S}_q(\mathbf{X}) \cup \mathcal{B}_q(\mathbf{X})$

---

## 3.3    Rare Class Balanced CNN

Training a comprehensive CNN is usually hard when facing unbalanced class distribution, and rare class objects tend to be dominated by common ones (i.e. insufficient training data available for rare classes). To address this issue, we develop a complementary CNN trained using data with balanced class distribution, which will be incorporated into the integration of original CNN and the scene-assisted rare class retrieval (as summarized in Algorithm 2). Specifically, the energy function $E_r(X_i, Y_j)$ evaluates the class likelihood of label $Y_j, j = \{1, \cdots, L\}$ only for rare class pixel $X_i$ in a query image $\mathbf{X}$,

$$E_r(X_i, Y_j) = -P_{Lr}(X_i, Y_j) \cdot \delta(Y(X_i) \in \mathcal{Y}_r), \tag{6}$$

where $\mathcal{Y}_r$ is a subset of $\{1, 2, \cdots, L\}$ that only contains rare class labels. $\delta(True) = 1$, $P_{Lr}$ is obtained by the rare class balanced CNN $\mathcal{M}_r$, and

$$Y(X_i) = \arg\min_{1, \cdots, L} E(X_i, Y_j), \tag{7}$$

where $E(X_i, Y_j)$ is the integration class likelihood obtained by

$$E(X_i, Y_j) = -(P_L(X_i, Y_i) + P_G(X_i, Y_j)), \tag{8}$$

where the local belief $P_L(X_i, Y_i)$ is computed by applying the CNN $\mathcal{M}$ [19], and the global belief $P_G(X_i, Y_i)$ is computed by Eq. (4). Since the training data contains significantly large number of pixels, only part of them is sampled to train $\mathcal{M}_r$. We first randomly sample patches of rare classes until they are equally distributed ($N_s$ samples), then all frequent classes are sampled to reach the same occurrence rate. Notice that unlike the class sampling in [20], the number of samples are largely reduced since $N_s$ is determined by the frequency of rare classes, and $\mathcal{M}_r$ is only applied near rare class objects to reduce ambiguities. Therefore, the final RCSL labeling $\mathbf{Y}$ can be computed pixel-by-pixel,

$$\mathbf{Y} = \cup_{i=1:N} Y_i, \tag{9}$$

---

**Algorithm 2.** Rare class-oriented scene labeling (RCSL)

---

1: Input: training images $[\mathbf{X}_1, \mathbf{X}_2, \cdots, \mathbf{X}_N]$. Ground Truth Labels $[\mathbf{Y}_1, \mathbf{Y}_2, \cdots, \mathbf{Y}_N]$
2: Train the CNN-Softmax $\mathcal{M}$ (learned from unbalanced data) and $\mathcal{M}_r$ (learned using rare-class balanced data)
3: **for** each testing image $\mathbf{X}_q$, $q = 1, \cdots, Q$ **do**
4:     find image retrieval set $\mathcal{Z}_q(\mathbf{X})$ as Algorithm 1
5:     **for** pixel $i = 1, \cdots, H \times W$ **do**
6:         compute local belief $P_L(X_i, Y_j)$ by $\mathcal{M}$, global belief $P_L(X_i, Y_j)$ as Equation (4)
7:         obtain $Y(X_i)$ as Equation (7)
8:         calculate $E_r(X_i, Y_j)$ as Equation (6) using $\mathcal{M}_r$
9:     **end for**
10:    obtain the labeling map $\mathbf{Y}_q$ of the input image $\mathbf{X}_q$ by Equation (9)
11: **end for**

---

where

$$Y_i = \arg \min_{1,\cdots,L} (E(X_i, Y_j) + E_r(X_i, Y_j)). \tag{10}$$

## 3.4  Superpixels-Based Re-segmentation

Image segmentation have been widely used [2] to provide perceptually meaningful contours that capture object boundaries effectively. During the CNN training, since only image patches are used without consideration of object contours, the resulting segmentation from RCSL tends to have smeared and rough boundaries, especially around rare classes due to the small size of objects. To address this issue, we develop a simple yet effective superpixels-based [21] re-segmentation method (RCSL-Seg) for better labeling accuracy and visualization.

Given an input image $\mathbf{X}$, we may be able to obtain a group of superpixels $R_p$, $p = 1, 2, \cdots, P$ by graph-based segmentation [21] and morphological processing, which divide an input image $\mathbf{X}$ into $P$ regions. Suppose each pixel $X_i \in R_p$ is labeled as $Y_i$ ($Y_i \in \{1, 2, \cdots, L\}$ and $L$ is the number of classes) based on the RCSL framework with scene assisted rare class retrieval, we further refine the final segmentation by evaluating the majority of labels in each superpixel $R_p$. The final label $Y_p'$ for each superpixel is given by

$$Y_p' = \arg \max_{j=1,\cdots,L} N_j^{(p)}, \tag{11}$$

where $N_j^{(p)}$ is the number of pixels labeled as $j$ in $R_p$. Thus, each superpixel could be labeled based on the RCSL framework for perceptually and semantically meaningful segmentation.

## 4  Experiments

The SIFTflow dataset [11] has been widely evaluated in many scene labeling work [2,19,20], which contains 2688 images captured under 8 natural scenes (Fig. 2b). Every image has $256 \times 256$ pixels, and each pixel is labeled as one of 33 semantic classes. The dataset has been split into 2488 training and 200 testing images equally distributed in each natural scene. We conduct two studies to demonstrate the promising performance of proposed methods quantitatively and qualitatively. First we will show the overall pixel accuracy (percentage of correctly labeled pixels) and class accuracy (average pixel accuracies per class). Second, both accuracies are evaluated for rare class objects only.

### 4.1  Overall Labeling Accuracy

We report the overall labeling accuracies of proposed methods and several recent research on the SIFTfow dataset in Table 2. Three versions of RCSL are evaluated, including RCSL-I (RCSL with rare class random sampling), RCSL-II

**Table 2.** Quantitative performance comparison on the SIFTflow dataset

|  | Pixel (%) | Class (%) |
|---|---|---|
| Multiscale ConvNet [8] | 67.9 | 45.9 |
| Multiscale [8] + cover (balanced frequencies) | 72.3 | 50.8 |
| Multiscale [8] + cover (natural frequencies) | 78.5 | 29.6 |
| CNN, Pinheiro et al. [9] | 76.5 | 30.0 |
| Recurrent CNN, Pinheiro et al. [9] | 77.7 | 29.8 |
| Superparsing Tighe et al. [17] | 76.9 | 29.4 |
| Eigen et al. [15] | 77.1 | 32.5 |
| Tighe et al. [18] | 78.6 | 39.2 |
| Singh et al. [16] | 79.2 | 33.8 |
| Gould et al. [22] | 78.4 | 25.7 |
| Yang et al. [2] | 79.8 | **48.7** |
| Integration model, Shuai et al. [19] | 79.8 | 39.1 |
| Integration model, Shuai et al. [20] | 81.0 | 44.6 |
| RCSL-I (random sampling) | 79.9 | 40.1 |
| RCSL-II (scene-specific sampling) | 80.8 | 41.2 |
| RCSL-Seg (with superpixels re-segmentation) | **81.6** | 47.5 |

(RCSL with scene assisted rare class retrieval), and RCSL-Seg (RCSL-II with superpixels-based re-segmentation).

As shown above, the proposed RCSL-II algorithm is able to achieve higher pixel and class accuracies compared with the baseline [19] and RCSL-I, which demonstrates the effectiveness of scene assisted retrieval and the complementary rare class balanced CNN for unbalanced class distribution problems. Compared with [19], RCSL-II and RCSL-Seg is able to achieve around 2% and 8%

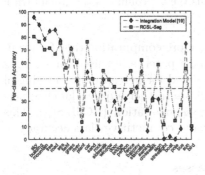

**Fig. 3.** Per-class accuracy of the baseline [19] and RCSL-Seg

**Table 3.** Quantitative comparison of rare classes on the SIFTflow dataset

|  | Pixel (%) | Class (%) |
|---|---|---|
| Tighe et al. [18] | 48.8 | 29.9 |
| Yang et al. [2] | 59.4 | 41.9 |
| Shuai et al. [19] | - | 30.7 |
| Shuai et al. [20] | - | 37.6 |
| RCSL-II | 61.3 | 39.2 |
| RCSL-Seg | **62.6** | **42.3** |

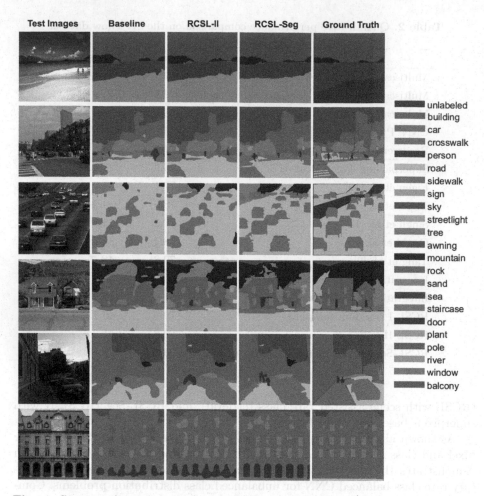

**Fig. 4.** Some qualitative examples of labeling results. The 1$^{st}$ column is the input images, the 2$^{nd}$ column is the baseline method in [19], the 3$^{rd}$ and the 4$^{th}$ columns are our proposed RCSL-II and RCSL-Seg results, while the 5$^{th}$ column is the ground truth

better overall class accuracy with roughly 20% more computation time for training and 10% more for testing. Since only image patches are used for learning and inference, where boundaries are not considered for perceptually meaningful segmentation, unlike pixel-level inference in [2], we further improve labeling performance of RCSL-II by superpixels-based re-segmentation (RCSL-Seg). This helps to achieve better overall pixel accuracy and competitive class accuracy.

### 4.2   Comparative Analysis on Rare Classes

We report pixel and class accuracies in Table 3 for rare class objects only (less than 5% frequency in the training dataset [2]).

Our proposed methods achieve higher class accuracy compared with several recent methods, which further demonstrate the robustness of proposed RCSL-II and RCSL-Seg methods on semantic labeling and segmentation. Moreover, per-class labeling accuracies are shown in Fig. 3, where the RCSL-Seg achieves significant improvement for rare classes compared to the baseline method. But performance on common classes, mainly in the background (sky, mountain, etc.), slightly drops, which occurs due to the fact that the additional rare class balanced CNN may have some over-fitting problem due to more rare class training data.

Some qualitative examples of proposed methods are shown in Fig. 4. We can see clearly that RCSL-II is able to correctly locate and label most rare class objects, and RCSL-Seg is able to preserve object contours with higher segmentation accuracy. For example in the RCSL-Seg result of the first image, human silhouettes are well recognized compared with those from RCSL-II and [19]. In the third image, vehicles tend to have more detailed boundaries, and in the sixth image, we are able to recognize almost all of the windows. Take a closer look at the second image, the person behind the rightmost car is detected even it is not labeled in the ground truth. Same situation happens to the streetlight appears right next to the building in the fifth image.

## 5    Conclusions and Future Work

We present a rare class-oriented scene labeling framework to address the unbalanced training data problems for rare class objects. Experimental results demonstrate effectiveness of the proposed framework for both pixel and class labeling accuracies on the SIFTflow dataset, especially for rare classes. In the future we may further investigate two issues. First, local ambiguities from CNN features can possibly result in inaccurate retrieval occasionally, so we will consider adding scene-level features to ensure accurate retrieval using global contextual information. Second, we want to study the possibility of directly incorporating super-pixels for CNN-based classification which may be more promising than merely using it for re-segmentation.

## References

1. Caesar, H., Uijlings, J., Ferrari, V.: Joint calibration for semantic segmentation. In: Proceedings of BMVC, pp. 29.1–29.13. BMVA Press (2015)
2. Yang, J., Price, B., Cohen, S., Yang, M.H.: Context driven scene parsing with attention to rare classes. In: Proceedings of CVPR, pp. 3294–3301 (2014)
3. Xiao, J., Hays, J., Ehinger, K.A., Oliva, A., Torralba, A.: Sun database: large-scale scene recognition from abbey to zoo. In: Proceedings of CVPR, pp. 3485–3492 (2010)
4. Li, J., Wang, J.Z.: Automatic linguistic indexing of pictures by a statistical modeling approach. IEEE Trans. PAMI **25**, 1075–1088 (2003)
5. Li, L.J., Socher, R., Fei-Fei, L.: Towards total scene understanding: classification, annotation and segmentation in an automatic framework. In: Proceedings of CVPR, pp. 2036–2043 (2009)

6. George, M.: Image parsing with a wide range of classes and scene-level context. In: Proceedings of CVPR, pp. 3622–3630 (2015)
7. LeCun, Y., Boser, B., Denker, J.S., Henderson, D., Howard, R.E., Hubbard, W., Jackel, L.D.: Backpropagation applied to handwritten zip code recognition. Neural Comput. 1, 541–551 (1989)
8. Farabet, C., Couprie, C., Najman, L., LeCun, Y.: Learning hierarchical features for scene labeling. IEEE Trans. PAMI 35, 1915–1929 (2013)
9. Pinheiro, P.H.O., Collobert, R.: Recurrent convolutional neural networks for scene labeling. In: Proceedings of ICML, pp. 82–90 (2014)
10. Liang, M., Hu, X., Zhang, B.: Convolutional neural networks with intra-layer recurrent connections for scene labeling. In: Advances in Neural Information Processing Systems 28. Curran Associates, Inc., pp. 937–945 (2015)
11. Liu, C., Yuen, J., Torralba, A.: Nonparametric scene parsing: label transfer via dense scene alignment. In: Proceedings of CVPR, pp. 1972–1979 (2009)
12. Liu, C., Yuen, J., Torralba, A.: Nonparametric scene parsing via label transfer. IEEE Trans. PAMI 33, 2368–2382 (2011)
13. Gould, S., Zhang, Y.: PatchMatchGraph: building a graph of dense patch correspondences for label transfer. In: Fitzgibbon, A., Lazebnik, S., Perona, P., Sato, Y., Schmid, C. (eds.) ECCV 2012. LNCS, vol. 7576, pp. 439–452. Springer, Heidelberg (2012). doi:10.1007/978-3-642-33715-4_32
14. Tung, F., Little, J.J.: CollageParsing: nonparametric scene parsing by adaptive overlapping windows. In: Fleet, D., Pajdla, T., Schiele, B., Tuytelaars, T. (eds.) ECCV 2014. LNCS, vol. 8694, pp. 511–525. Springer, Heidelberg (2014). doi:10.1007/978-3-319-10599-4_33
15. Eigen, D., Fergus, R.: Nonparametric image parsing using adaptive neighbor sets. In: Proceedings of CVPR, pp. 2799–2806 (2012)
16. Singh, G., Kosecka, J.: Nonparametric scene parsing with adaptive feature relevance and semantic context. In: Proceedings of CVPR, pp. 3151–3157 (2013)
17. Tighe, J., Lazebnik, S.: SuperParsing: scalable nonparametric image parsing with superpixels. In: Daniilidis, K., Maragos, P., Paragios, N. (eds.) ECCV 2010. LNCS, vol. 6315, pp. 352–365. Springer, Heidelberg (2010). doi:10.1007/978-3-642-15555-0_26
18. Tighe, J., Lazebnik, S.: Finding things: image parsing with regions and per-exemplar detectors. In: Proceedings of CVPR, pp. 3001–3008 (2013)
19. Shuai, B., Wang, G., Zuo, Z., Wang, B., Zhao, L.: Integrating parametric and non-parametric models for scene labeling. In: Proceedings of CVPR, pp. 4249–4258 (2015)
20. Shuai, B., Zuo, Z., Wang, G., Wang, B.: Scene parsing with integration of parametric and non-parametric models. IEEE Trans. Image Process. 25, 2379–2391 (2016)
21. Felzenszwalb, P.F., Huttenlocher, D.P.: Efficient graph-based image segmentation. IJCV 59, 167–181 (2004)
22. Gould, S., Zhao, J., He, X., Zhang, Y.: Superpixel graph label transfer with learned distance metric. In: Fleet, D., Pajdla, T., Schiele, B., Tuytelaars, T. (eds.) ECCV 2014. LNCS, vol. 8689, pp. 632–647. Springer, Heidelberg (2014). doi:10.1007/978-3-319-10590-1_41

# Pollen Grain Recognition Using Deep Learning

Amar Daood[1]($\boxtimes$), Eraldo Ribeiro[2], and Mark Bush[3]

[1] Department of Electrical and Computer Engineering,
Florida Institute of Technology, Melbourne, FL, USA
adaood2012@my.fit.edu
[2] Department of Computer Sciences and Cybersecurity,
Florida Institute of Technology, Melbourne, FL, USA
eribeiro@fit.edu
[3] Department of Biological Sciences,
Florida Institute of Technology, Melbourne, FL, USA

**Abstract.** Pollen identification helps forensic scientists solve elusive crimes, provides data for climate-change modelers, and even hints at potential sites for petroleum exploration. Despite its wide range of applications, most pollen identification is still done by time-consuming visual inspection by well-trained experts. Although partial automation is currently available, automatic pollen identification remains an open problem. Current pollen-classification methods use pre-designed features of texture and contours, which may not be sufficiently distinctive. Instead of using pre-designed features, our pollen-recognition method learns both features and classifier from training data under the deep-learning framework. To further enhance our network's classification ability, we use transfer learning to leverage knowledge from networks that have been pre-trained on large datasets of images. Our method achieved $\approx$94% classification rate on a dataset of 30 pollen types. These rates are among the highest obtained in this problem.

## 1 Introduction

The identification of pollen grains underpins the field of Palynology, which is the study of pollen grains, spores, and some types of diatoms [1]. Palynology is a valuable tool to many applications. For example, by analyzing fossil pollen found in soil extracted from the bottom of ancient lakes, ecologists can map past climate dated over thousands of years [2]. Because some pollen types may only exist in certain geographical locations, forensics scientists use pollen found in crime scenes to geolocate suspects [3]. Interestingly, pollen also helps the petroleum-exploration industry map potential oil fields [4].

In many palynology applications, scientists build statistical distributions of pollen species, a task done by trained operators who identify and count pollen grains seen under a microscope. Common identifying attributes used include shape, symmetry, size, and ornamentation [5,6]. Counting pollen can take months to complete, sometimes occupying operators for some 16 h a week.

© Springer International Publishing AG 2016
G. Bebis et al. (Eds.): ISVC 2016, Part I, LNCS 10072, pp. 321–330, 2016.
DOI: 10.1007/978-3-319-50835-1_30

This time-consuming step in palynology could be reduced from months to a few hours by an automated identification system [1].

There are three main groups of approaches to palynology automation. *Morphological* methods measure visual characteristics such as shape [2,7,8]. Treloar et al. [2] measured grain's roundness, perimeter, and area, which were input into a Fisher linear discriminant for classifying 12 types of pollen. Xie and OhEigeartaigh [9] measured 3-D geometrical features, radial and angular components from a voxel representation of pollen grains. They classified 5 types of pollen using support vector machine. Garcia et al. [8] used the changes along a grain's contour to train a Hidden Markov Model (HMM) for classification.

*Texture-based methods* use the grain's surface texture. Fernandez-Delgado et al. [10] classified 5 pollen types using measurements of gray-level co-occurrence matrix, neighborhood gray-level dependence statistics, entropy, and the mean. DaSilva et al. [11] transformed pollen images using wavelet coefficients representing the spatial frequency, and then calculated gray-level co-occurrence matrix to classify 7 pollen species.

*Hybrid methods* combine multiple characteristics. Ticay-Rivas et al. [12] classified 17 plant species based on geometrical features (i.e., area, convex area, and perimeter), Fourier descriptors, and color features. A multi-layer neural network was used as a classifier. Chica [13] also combined textures and morphological characteristics to detect 5 classes of bee pollen. The features included shape (i.e., area, perimeter, diameter) and texture (i.e., mean, standard deviation, the entropy of the gray-level histogram).

An alternative approach to using pre-designed features is to try to learn optimal features from training data. This approach can be implemented using convolutional neural networks (CNN), a class of pattern-classification methods known as deep learning [14]. Deep learning has been shown to successfully solve challenging classification tasks [15]. In this paper, we present a pollen-classification method that uses deep learning to classify 30 pollen types of two image modalities: light-microscopy (LM) and scanning electron microscopy (SEM). Figure 1 shows example images from our dataset.

## 2    Method

Our CNN has seven learned layers. The first six layers are convolutional layers and the final layer is a fully connected layer. The convolutional layers share the same architecture, where each convolutional layer includes a filters unit, a rectified Units (ReLUs), a pooling unit, and a local normalization unit. Network configuration, such as network depth and filters' size, determines computational speed. Although increasing the depth and filters size of CNN improves the recognition rate, it consumes more CPU and memory.

In our work, image resolution, network depth (i.e., number of layers), filters' size for each individual layer, and the training window size (i.e., number of images

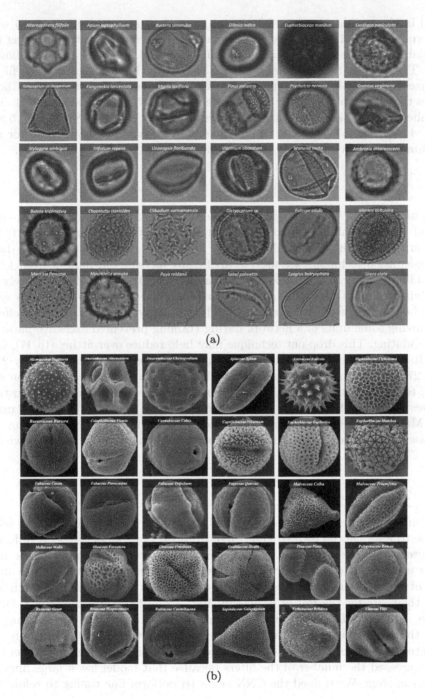

(a)

(b)

**Fig. 1.** One sample from each pollen type of our LM dataset. The dataset consists of some 1,000 images of 30 pollen types, provided by the our Paleoecology Laboratory. (a) LM dataset (b) SEM dataset.

used in the training process of each step to update networks parameters) were determined experimentally by maximizing the classification rate and using the available resources. For parameter initialization and learning rate, we followed [15]. The input of the first layer is $274 \times 274$ (i.e., the input image) with 50 filters of size $19 \times 19$. After the response is normalized and pooled, the second layer takes the output of the first layer and filters it with 75 filters of size $11 \times 11$. The number of filters and their size of the rest of layers are: 100, $8 \times 8$, 250, $5 \times 5$, 500, $4 \times 4$, 2000, $4 \times 4$, 30, $1 \times 1$. Stochastic gradient descent was used for the training process with window size of 25 images.

## 2.1  Training

The network has some 20 million parameters. Our dataset is small when compared to the number of learned parameters of the CNN. Training directly for all parameters using a small dataset may lead to over fitting. Therefore, a data-augmentation technique was used to artificially increase our dataset from 1,000 to 14,000 samples and 1,161 to 15,000 samples for LM and SEM respectively by applying different rotation transformations. Additionally, drop-out layers were attached to the last two layers by a 0.5 factor to reduce the over-fitting effect. Removing some units of a network during training prevented excessive parameter updating. This drop-out technique may help reduce over fitting [16,17]. Our results showed that data augmentation increased the classification rate by 24% and 27% for LM and SEM respectively. A zero-mean Gaussian distribution was used to initialize the weights in each layer. Biases were initialized with constant values of 1, and the learning rate equaled 0.001. We trained our network using the MatConvNet toolbox [18]. We trained our network for 60 epochs using our dataset, which took about three days to converge on a single machine with a core 7 processor and 16 G of memory.

## 2.2  Transfer Learning

We improved classification performance by adopting the transfer-learning technique to leverage the learned knowledge from previous models [19]. A different architecture is used to apply the transfer learning where the input of the first layer is $294 \times 294$ (i.e., the input image) with 50 filters of size $19 \times 19$. The number of filters of the second layer is 48, of size $11 \times 11$. The number of filters and their size for the rest of layers are: 100, $5 \times 5$, 250, $3 \times 3$, 256, $3 \times 3$, 2048, $6 \times 6$, 30, $1 \times 1$. The first two layers were initialized from the previous model and the rest of layer were initialized from ImageNet model [20]. Basically, we selected the size of the filter of these layers to match the ImageNet model but we decreased the number of the filters because that model has a large number of parameters. We trained the CNN again to perform fine tuning to refine the network parameters. Additionally, we increased our dataset from 1,060 to 25,000 samples and 1,161 to 28,000 samples for LM and SEM respectively using data augmentation by applying different rotation and scale transformations.

## 3 Results

By using transfer learning, we increased the recognition rate to nearly 90%. Figure 2 shows the misclassification error and the objective energy of our network during training. The error rate and the objective energy were computed at each epoch and visualized to monitor the network's convergence. Figure 3 shows the learned filters of the first layer of our networks. We also compared the performance of our network with the traditional approaches that used the pre-designed features. Results of this comparison are shown in Table 1. These approaches are based on pre-processing the pollen grain images (i.e., enhancement and segmentation), pre-defined feature extraction, and classification. We used the following features: histogram features (i.e., mean and variance of histogram), gray level statistics (i.e., mean, variance and entropy), geometrical features (i.e., area, perimeter, compactness, roundness, and aspect ratio based on minor and major axises), fractal dimension, gray level co-occurrence matrix (GLCM), moments invariant, Gabor features, histograms of oriented gradient (HOG) descriptors, and local binary pattern histogram (LBP). After we performed features extraction, we trained a support vector machine classifier based on these features.

We also compared our method with two approaches in the literature that combined multiple features: Marcos's method [21] and Silva's work [11]. Marcos combined gray-level co-occurrence Matrix, Gabor features, local binary patterns, and discrete moments features. Silva decomposed the pollen grain into four layers using wavelet transform and then gray-level co-occurrence matrix was computed to create features vectors using statistical measurements. Table 1 shows the classification rates.

To prove statistically that our CNN is significantly better than traditional approaches, we computed the P-value. Based on Table 1, we compared our results with the best method that combined histogram, gray level statistics, fractal dimension, and LBP. The P-value was $2.56 \times 10^{-4}$ and $9.76 \times 10^{-6}$ for both LM and SEM respectively, which means null the hypothesis can be rejected. Additionally, we computed the average of precision, recall, sensitivity, specificity, and F score [22], which are shown in Tables 2 and 3.

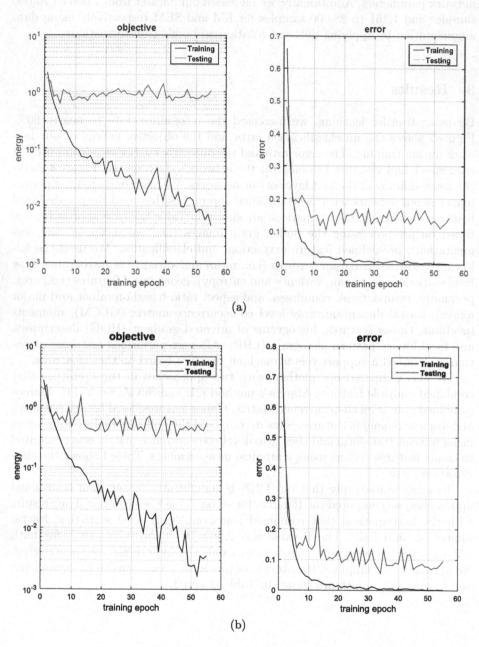

**Fig. 2.** Error and objective energy of the training process. At each iteration, feed forward technique is used to compute the objective function of the network, and the predictions of the training and testing samples to calculate the error rate. (a) LM dataset (b) SEM dataset.

(a)

(b)

**Fig. 3.** Learned filter of the first layer of CNNs. Basic features such as corners, edges, and blobs were learned. (a) LM dataset (b) SEM dataset.

**Table 1.** Classification rates

| Method | Classification rate of LM dataset | Classification rate of SEM datset |
|---|---|---|
| Histogram features, Gray level statistics | 70.97% | 61.20% |
| Geometrical features, fractal dimension | 71.97% | 60.59% |
| Gray level co-occurrence matrix | 51.34% | 48.24% |
| Moments invariants | 44.59% | 42.63% |
| Gabor features | 67.36% | 60.12% |
| HOG | 62.34% | 50.29% |
| LBP | 77.07% | 71.49% |
| Silva's Method | 67.36% | 59.55% |
| Marcos's Method | 78.92% | 74.96% |
| Histogram, Gray level statistics, fractal dimension, LBP | 80.19% | 78.11% |
| CNN | **84.47%** | **90.56%** |
| CNN (with transfer learning) | **89.95%** | **93.99%** |

**Table 2.** Evaluation measurements of LM dataset

| Method | Precision | Recall | Sensitivity | Specificity | F score |
|---|---|---|---|---|---|
| Features combination | 81.16% | 79.68% | 79.68% | 99.31% | 79.31% |
| CNN | **85.15%** | **84.28%** | **84.28%** | **99.48%** | **83.82%** |
| CNN (with transfer learning) | **92.04%** | **90.26%** | **90.26%** | **99.65%** | **89.13%** |

**Table 3.** Evaluation measurements of SEM dataset

| Method | Precision | Recall | sensitivity | specificity | F score |
|---|---|---|---|---|---|
| Features combination | 81.03% | 77.83% | 77.83% | 99.24% | 78.30% |
| CNN | **93.12%** | **90.45%** | **90.45%** | **99.70%** | **91.17%** |
| CNN (with transfer learning) | **95.00%** | **93.92%** | **93.92%** | **99.79%** | **94.05%** |

## 4    Conclusion and Future Work

In this paper, we proposed an approach to identify 30 types of pollen grain. The approach is implemented using a convolutional neural network. We trained a convolutional neural network to learn discriminating features such corners, blobs, and edges. The set of the learned features are used to classify the pollen grain images. Data augmentation and a drop-out techniques were used to reduce over fitting. Moreover, we adopted a transfer-learning technique to leverage learned features to improve classification rates. Experimental results showed that extracting features automatically using CNN has superior performance over the traditional techniques. Even though our approach offers promising classification rate, the training time of the convolutional neural networks becomes an issue especially when it runs on standard PCs. Increased processing speed can be achieved using parallel processing and GPU architectures.

# References

1. Flenley, J.: The problem of pollen recognition. In: Clowes, M.B., Penny, J.P. (eds.) Problems in Picture Interpretation, pp. 141–145. CSIRO, Canberra (1968)
2. Treloar, W.J., Taylor, G.E., Flenley, J.R.: Towards automation of palynology 1: analysis of pollen shape and ornamentation using simple geometric measures, derived from scanning electron microscope images. J. Quat. Sci. **19**, 745–754 (2004)
3. Mildenhall, D., Wiltshire, P., Bryant, V.: Forensic palynology: why do it and how it works. Foren. Sci. Int. **163**, 163–172 (2006). Forensic Palynology
4. Hopping, C.: Palynology and the oil industry. Rev. Palaeobot. Palynol. **2**, 23–48 (1967)
5. del Pozo-Banos, M., Ticay-Rivas, J.R., Alonso, J.B., Travieso, C.M.: Features extraction techniques for pollen grain classification. Neurocomputing **150**(Part B), 377–391 (2015)
6. Dell'Anna, R., Cristofori, A., Gottardini, E., Monti, F.: A critical presentation of innovative techniques for automated pollen identification in aerobiological monitoring networks. Pollen: Structure, Types and Effects, 273–288 (2010)
7. Travieso, C.M., Briceno, J.C., Ticay-Rivas, J.R., Alonso, J.B.: Pollen classification based on contour features. In: 2011 15th IEEE International Conference on Intelligent Engineering Systems (INES), pp. 17–21. IEEE (2011)
8. García, N.M., Chaves, V.A.E., Briceño, J.C., Travieso, C.M.: Pollen grains contour analysis on verification approach. In: Corchado, E., Snášel, V., Abraham, A., Woźniak, M., Graña, M., Cho, S.-B. (eds.) HAIS 2012. LNCS (LNAI), vol. 7208, pp. 521–532. Springer, Heidelberg (2012). doi:10.1007/978-3-642-28942-2_47
9. Xie, Y., OhEigeartaigh, M.: 3D discrete spherical Fourier descriptors based on surface curvature voxels for pollen classification. In: 2010 WASE International Conference on Information Engineering (ICIE), vol. 1, pp. 207–211. IEEE (2010)
10. Fernandez-Delgado, M., Carrion, P., Cernadas, E., Galvez, J.F.: Improved classification of pollen texture images using SVM and MLP (2003)
11. Da Silva, D.S., Quinta, L.N.B., Gonccalves, A.B., Pistori, H., Borth, M.R.: Application of wavelet transform in the classification of pollen grains. Afr. J. Agric. Res. **9**, 908–913 (2014)
12. Ticay-Rivas, J.R., Pozo-Baños, M., Travieso, C.M., Arroyo-Hernández, J., Pérez, S.T., Alonso, J.B., Mora-Mora, F.: Pollen classification based on geometrical descriptors and colour features using decorrelation stretching method. In: Iliadis, L., Maglogiannis, I., Papadopoulos, H. (eds.) AIAI/EANN -2011. IAICT, vol. 364, pp. 342–349. Springer, Heidelberg (2011). doi:10.1007/978-3-642-23960-1_41
13. Chica, M.: Authentication of bee pollen grains in bright-field microscopy by combining one-class classification techniques and image processing. Microsc. Res. Tech. **75**, 1475–1485 (2012)
14. Ngiam, J., Khosla, A., Kim, M., Nam, J., Lee, H., Ng, A.Y.: Multimodal deep learning. In: Proceedings of the 28th International Conference on Machine Learning, ICML 2011, June 28 – July 2 2011, Bellevue, Washington, USA, pp. 689–696 (2011)

15. Krizhevsky, A., Sutskever, I., Hinton, G.E.: ImageNet classification with deep convolutional neural networks. In Pereira, F., Burges, C., Bottou, L., Weinberger, K. (eds.) Advances in Neural Information Processing Systems 25, pp. 1097–1105. Curran Associates Inc. (2012)
16. Srivastava, N., Hinton, G., Krizhevsky, A., Sutskever, I., Salakhutdinov, R.: Dropout: a simple way to prevent neural networks from overfitting. J. Mach. Learn. Res. **15**, 1929–1958 (2014)
17. Ba, J., Frey, B.: Adaptive dropout for training deep neural networks. In: Advances in Neural Information Processing Systems, pp. 3084–3092 (2013)
18. Vedaldi, A., Lenc, K.: MatConvNet - convolutional neural networks for MATLAB. CoRR abs/1412.4564 (2014)
19. Yosinski, J., Clune, J., Bengio, Y., Lipson, H.: How transferable are features in deep neural networks? ArXiv e-prints (2014)
20. Chatfield, K., Simonyan, K., Vedaldi, A., Zisserman, A.: Return of the devil in the details: delving deep into convolutional nets. In: British Machine Vision Conference (2014)
21. Marcos, J.V., Nava, R., Cristobal, G., Redondo, R., Escalante-Ramirez, B., Bueno, G., Deniz, O., Gonzalez-Porto, A., Pardo, C., Chung, F., Rodriguez, T.: Automated pollen identification using microscopic imaging and texture analysis. Micron **68**, 36–46 (2015)
22. Sokolova, M., Lapalme, G.: A systematic analysis of performance measures for classification tasks. Inf. Process. Manage. **45**(4), 427–437 (2009). Elsevier

# Classifying Pollen Using Robust Sequence Alignment of Sparse Z-Stack Volumes

Amar Daood[1](✉), Eraldo Ribeiro[2], and Mark Bush[3]

[1] Department of Electrical and Computer Engineering,
Florida Institute of Technology Melbourne, Melbourne, FL, USA
adaood2012@my.fit.edu
[2] Department of Computer Sciences and Cybersecurity,
Florida Institute of Technology Melbourne, Melbourne, FL, USA
eribeiro@fit.edu
[3] Department of Biological Sciences, Florida Institute of Technology Melbourne,
Melbourne, FL, USA

**Abstract.** The identification of pollen grains is a task needed in many scientific and industrial applications, ranging from climate research to petroleum exploration. It is also a time-consuming task. To produce data, pollen experts spend hours, sometimes months, visually counting thousands of pollen grains from hundreds of images acquired by microscopes. Most current automation of pollen identification rely on single-focus images. While this type of image contains characteristic texture and shape, it lacks information about how these visual cues vary across the grain's surface. In this paper, we propose a method that recognizes pollen species from stacks of multi-focal images. Here, each pollen grain is represented by a multi-focal stack. Our method matches unknown stacks to pre-learned ones using the Longest-Common Sub-Sequence (LCSS) algorithm. The matching process relies on the variations of visual texture and contour that occur along the image stack, which are captured by a low-rank and sparse decomposition technique. We tested our method on 392 image stacks from 10 species of pollen grains. The proposed method achieves a remarkable recognition rate of 99.23%.

## 1 Introduction

The classification of pollen grains is the main data-collection task in many disciplines including ecology, forensic sciences, allergy control, and oil exploration [1]. In most of these applications, the task of counting and identifying pollen grains require pollen experts (i.e., palynologists) to spend hours looking at pollen under the microscope. Automation of pollen identification can reduce data-collection times from months to a few hours [2].

Since Flenley [2] suggested the automation of pollen identification as a means to increase research throughput in Palynology, a number of identification methods have been proposed to describe the visual appearance of pollen grains. For example, shape features such as roundness, perimeter, and area have been used

© Springer International Publishing AG 2016
G. Bebis et al. (Eds.): ISVC 2016, Part I, LNCS 10072, pp. 331–340, 2016.
DOI: 10.1007/978-3-319-50835-1_31

by [1,3]. Texture measurements such as gray-level co-occurrence matrix, Gabor features, and moment invariants were used by [4–6]. These methods work on images of pollen grains acquired under a single focal plane.

Instead of using isolated visual characteristics of a single focal plane, some methods combined multiple visual features extracted from multiple focal z-planes. Chica [7] identified five pollen classes by using shape and texture features from three focal images. The shape features were area, perimeter, diameter, and the texture features were mean, standard deviation, and the entropy of gray-level histograms. Lagerstrom et al. [8] extracted histogram statistics, moments, grey-level co-occurrence matrix, and Gabor features from nine focal planes to classify 15 types of pollen grains. Shape and texture features were also combined in [9] using gray-level co-occurrence matrix, Gabor features, local binary patterns, and moments to classify 15 pollen types.

Although the combination of visual features works well for pollen identification, the use of stacked multi-focal images is still underexploited. In this paper, we propose to classify pollen grains using multi-focal image sequences. We want to capture characteristic information of changes in visual appearance that occur on the grain's surface across multiple focal planes (i.e., z-stack). Our method commences by processing the entire z-stack volume using a low-rank and sparse decomposition [10] to extract the visual changes across focal planes. These changes will appear in the sparse component of the z-stack. From this sparse volume, we extract features from each one of its planes. Our feature-extraction method further decomposes each slice of the sparse volume into multiple concentric regions by clustering the gray-level intensity and their associated polar coordinates. Shape and texture features are then extracted from each layer. These features are used by a nearest-neighbor classifier that employs the Longest-Common Sub-Sequence (LCSS) algorithm to match the multifocal appearance descriptors. We tested our method on a dataset of 10 pollen types. The dataset has 392 z-stack sequences with 10 focal-planes for each sample. Figure 1 shows one sample z-stack for each pollen type in our dataset.

## 2   Method

Our method begins by processing the entire z-stack volume of the pollen grain using a low-rank and sparse decomposition. Then, we process each focal image inside the sparse volume to create multiple layers to represent the visual appearance of the pollen. Finally, we classify the pollen grain types using a sequence-alignment method which considers the multifocal volume as an image sequence. The sequence-matching algorithm computes the similarity between the appearance model of the entire volume for two pollen grains. Figure 2 shows a block diagram of the proposed method.

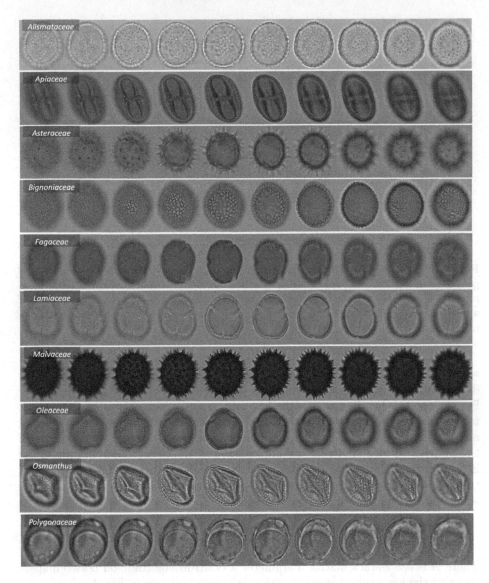

**Fig. 1.** Z-stacks from pollen types in our dataset. Dataset has 392 stacks of ten images of 10 pollen types. Images were provided by the Florida Tech's Paleoecology Laboratory.

## 2.1   Low Rank and Sparse Decomposition

The low-rank and sparse decomposition decomposes a matrix into two components: low-rank and sparse components. Given a data matrix $A \in R^{m \times n}$, it assumes the matrix $A$ can be decomposed as:

$$A = L + S, \tag{1}$$

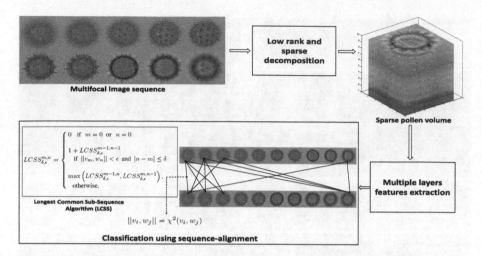

**Fig. 2.** Method overview. It takes multifocal image sequence as input. The sequence is processed using low-rank-sparse decomposition to create a sparse volume. Each focal plane of the sparse volume is represented by multiple features to create a sequence of appearance models. Finally, this sequence is matched to the known ones in a database using the LCSS alignment algorithm.

where $L \in R^{m \times n}$ is low-rank matrix and $S \in R^{m \times n}$ is the sparse matrix. This decomposition has been used widely to process sequential data such as videos. For pollen classification, we use the low-rank and sparse analysis on the z-stack to find regions of interest and decompose the entire volume to stationary and non-stationary pixels. We assume that changes in focus occurs only in regions of the pollen's surface, and that the information of the background and any noise is static inside the multifocal sequence. Our method uses the LRS library [11] that implements the robust principal component analysis (RPCA) [10]. RPCA solves the following optimization problem:

$$\min_{L,S} rank(L) + \lambda \|S\|_0 \quad \text{subject to } L + S = A, \tag{2}$$

where $A$ is the z-stack matrix. Parameter $\lambda$ controls the trade-off between sparsity and the low rank. A decomposition example is shown in Fig. 3.

As shown in Fig. 3, low rank and sparse decomposition separate z-stack pixels into two components. The low-rank component combines all z-stack frames into one image (Fig. 3b), essentially compressing the entire volume to a single focused plane. In contrast, the sparse component emphasizes the gray-level changes across the entire volume. The sparse volume helps recognition of the multi-focal stacks because it describes the changes across the stack planes. We use the sparse component to describe the characteristics of the pollen z-stacks.

Prior to extracting features, we apply low-rank-sparse decomposition to all z-stacks. With the sparse volumes at hand, we extract features from each individual focal plane. The feature-extraction process is described next.

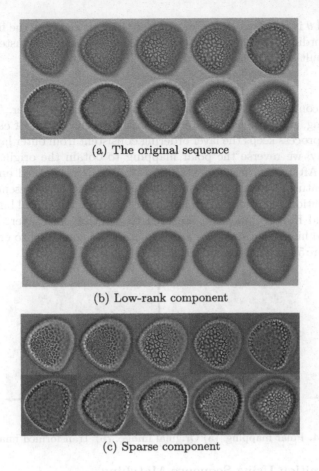

(a) The original sequence

(b) Low-rank component

(c) Sparse component

**Fig. 3.** Decomposing a pollen grain z-stack using RPCA.

## 2.2 Feature Extraction

We adopt a version of our previous work [12] to extract features from multiple concentric regions from pollen images. First, we normalize the image contrast using histogram equalization. Then, we decompose the image into multiple layers using clustering where each cluster represents a layer of pollen grain regions. The final set of regions is given by:

$$R = \{L_1, L_2, \ldots, L_d\}, \tag{3}$$

where d is the number of layers and L represents an individual layer of a image. We combine spatial information and intensity to perform the clustering process. Polar mapping is used to flattens the near-circular pollen region into a rectangular shape (Fig. 4). Each segmented pollen is represented by a distance-angle map $(r, \theta)$, where $r$ is the distance from boundary pixels to the grain's estimated centroid, and $\theta$ is the angle of vector $r$. After that, we combine the intensity and the polar coordinates to create vector $v = (r, \theta, i)$. Then, we cluster the pollen image into multiple regions where each layer is given by:

$$L_i = \{c_r, c_\theta, c_i, V_{r,\theta,i}\}, \tag{4}$$

where $V_{r,\theta,i}$ contains pixels and polar information of each layer. To keep the layers ordering, we reorder the layers according to the center of each layer $c_r$. This sorting process keeps the layer ordering consistent from outer layers to inner layers. Finally, we reverse the polar mapping to obtain the original Cartesian coordinates. After that, feature extraction process is performed on each layer. Extracting features for each layer individually improves the representation of the visual information. We adopt different types of features. The local binary pattern histogram and fractal dimension are used to describe each layer. In addition, gray level and histogram statistics are extracted and combined to create feature vectors. Figure 5 summarizes the method.

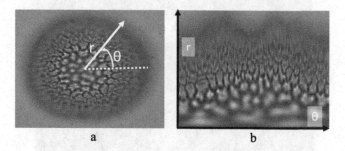

Fig. 4. Polar mapping. (a) Original image. (b) Transformed image.

## 2.3 Recognition Using Sequence Matching

We use a sequence-alignment method to measure the similarity between two sequences. This scheme considers the appearance variations in the sequence of multifocal pollen images rather than classifying the concatenated features blindly. We use the Longest Common Sub sequence (LCSS) matching scheme introduced in [13]. We define a distance measure between two sequences. Let $V = (v_1, \ldots, v_m)$ and $W = (w_1, \ldots, w_n)$ represent two multifocal image sequences for two different pollen grains. The measure used in the LCSS scheme can be defined for an integer $\delta$ and a real number $0 < \epsilon < 1$ as follows:

$$LCSS_{\delta,\epsilon}^{m,n} = \begin{cases} 0 \quad \text{if} \quad m = 0 \quad \text{or} \quad n = 0 \\[2mm] 1 + LCSS_{\delta,\epsilon}^{m-1,n-1} \\ \quad \text{if} \; ||v_m, w_n|| < \epsilon \; \text{and} \; |n - m| \leq \delta \\[2mm] \max\left(LCSS_{\delta,\epsilon}^{m-1,n}, LCSS_{\delta,\epsilon}^{m,n-1}\right), \\ \quad \text{otherwise.} \end{cases} \tag{5}$$

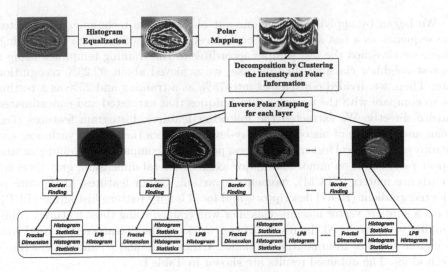

**Fig. 5.** Feature-extraction method. First, we use histogram equalization to enhance image contrast and then we apply a polar mapping to capture spatial information. A clustering process decomposes the image into concentric layers. Finally, we reserve the polar coordinates to obtain the original Cartesian coordinates of the layers. Feature vectors are extracted from each layer.

Here, $LCSS_{\delta,\epsilon}^{i,j} = LCSS_{\delta,\epsilon}((v_1,\ldots,v_i),(w_1,\ldots,w_j))$, and $||.,.||$ is the distance between points $v_m$ and $w_n$. The threshold $\epsilon$ controls the maximum distance between a pair of matched points, and $\delta$ controls the maximum number of consecutive unmatched points. The similarity between two sequences is given by:

$$D_{\delta,\epsilon}(V,W) = 1 - \frac{LCSS_{\delta,\epsilon}^{m,n}}{\min(m,n)}. \tag{6}$$

The distance between two focal slices as required by Eq. 5 is defined as:

$$||v_i,w_j|| = \chi^2(v_i,w_j), \tag{7}$$

where $\chi^2$ is the chi-square similarity. We create multifocal visual models for a set of known pollen grains. These models (templates) are stored to be compared with unknown sequences for identification. Formally, given templates $\{\widehat{V}_1,\ldots,\widehat{V}_M\}$, recognition of an unknown sequence $V$ is done by a nearest-neighbor classifier based on the similarity measure produced by the LCSS algorithm.

## 3    Results

We evaluated the effectiveness of the proposed method using two experiments. First, we used a leave-one-out classification technique then we divided our dataset into 75% as a training and 25% as a testing set.

We began by applying a leave-one-out classification technique. We selected one sequence as a test sample and considered the rest of our data for training. Then, we classified the test sample according to the training templates using a nearest-neighbor classifier. In this case, we achieved about 99.23% recognition rate. Then, we divided our dataset into 75% as a training and 25% as a testing set to compare with the traditional techniques that extracted and concatenated feature directly. We extracted the following features: histogram features (i.e., mean and variance of histogram), gray-level statistics (i.e., mean, variance, and entropy), geometrical features (i.e., area, perimeter, compactness, roundness, and aspect ratio based on minor and major axises), fractal dimension, gray level co-occurrence matrix (GLCM), moments invariant, Gabor features, histograms of oriented gradient (HOG) descriptors, and local binary pattern histogram (LBP). Then, a support vector machine classifier was trained using these features. Additionally, we reproduced the results of two works in the literature that used concatenated features from multifocal planes: Chica's Method [7] and Lagerstrom's Method [8]. The obtained results are shown in Table 1.

**Table 1.** Classification rates

| Method | Classification (%) |
| --- | --- |
| Histogram features, Gray level statistics | 81.92% |
| Geometrical features, fractal dimension | 80.12% |
| Gray level co-occurrence matrix | 73.44% |
| Moments invariants | 70.35% |
| Gabor features | 76.04% |
| HOG | 75.63% |
| LBP | 84.73% |
| Chica's Method | 86.18% |
| Lagerstrom's Method | 83.96% |
| Histogram, gray-level statistics, fractal dimension, LBP | 88.88% |
| Our proposed method | 98.66% |

To show the superiority of our method over traditional approaches, we compared the proposed method with a feature-combination method that combined histogram, gray-level statistics, fractal dimension, and LBP as features. This method achieved a 88.88% classification rate. After we applied a significance test, the P-value was $9.76 \times 10^{-4}$ which rejected the null hypothesis. Furthermore, we computed some classification metrics in Table 2 including the average of precision, recall, sensitivity, specificity, and F-score.

**Table 2.** Evaluation measurements

| Method | Precision | Recall | Sensitivity | Specificity | F score |
|---|---|---|---|---|---|
| Features combination | 89.77% | 89.07% | 89.07% | 98.75% | 88.98% |
| Our method | **99.09%** | **99.00%** | **99.00%** | **99.89%** | **99.03%** |

## 4  Conclusion and Future Work

We proposed a recognition algorithm to identify pollen grains using multifocal sequences of images. The main novelty in our algorithm is twofold. Firstly, we decomposed the pollen slice to create multiple layers by clustering intensity and polar information as an extra stage before performing features extraction. We captured the visual information of each slice by combining shape and texture features from each layer to build the appearance model. Secondly, instead of concatenating features from different focal-planes, we identified the pollen samples using sequence alignment technique to consider the sequence's effect in our recognition process. Additionally, our method does not require any specific set up of a focal length and thus it is applicable for other microscopic objects based on multifocal sequences. For future work, we plan to test our method on a larger number of species. We also plan to use the low-rank volume as a prior to pre-classify pollen into subgroups.

## References

1. Treloar, W.J., Taylor, G.E., Flenley, J.R.: Towards automation of palynology 1: analysis of pollen shape and ornamentation using simple geometric measures, derived from scanning electron microscope images. Quat. Sci. **19**, 745–754 (2004)
2. Flenley, J.: The problem of pollen recognition. In: Clowes M.B., Penny J.P. (eds.) Problems in Picture Interpretation, pp. 141–145. CSIRO (1968)
3. Boucher, A., Hidalgo, P., Thonnat, M., Belmonte, J., Galan, C., Bonton, P., Tomczak, R.: Development of a semi-automatic system for pollen recognition. Aerobiologia **18**, 195–201 (2002)
4. Fernandez-Delgado, M., Carrion, P., Cernadas, E., Galvez, J.F.: Improved classification of pollen texture images using SVM and MLP. In: 3rd IASTED International Conference Visualization, Imaging and Image Processing (2003)
5. Zhang, Y., Fountain, D., Hodgson, R., Flenley, J., Gunetileke, S.: Towards automation of palynology 3: pollen pattern recognition using Gabor transforms and digital moments. Quat. Sci. **19**(8), 763–768 (2004)
6. Li, P., Treloar, W.J., Flenley, J.R., Empson, L.: Towards automation of palynology 2: the use of texture measures and neural network analysis for automated identification of optical images of pollen grains. Quat. Sci. **19**, 755–762 (2004)
7. Chica, M.: Authentication of bee pollen grains in bright-field microscopy by combining one-class classification techniques and image processing. Microsc. Res. Tech. **75**, 1475–1485 (2012)
8. Lagerstrom, R., Arzhaeva, Y., Bischof, L., Haberle, S., Hopf, F., Lovell, D.: A comparison of classification algorithms within the classifynder pollen imaging system. In: International symposium on CMLS (2013)

9. Marcos, J.V., Nava, R., Cristobal, G., Redondo, R., Escalante-Ramirez, B., Bueno, G., Deniz, O., Gonzalez-Porto, A., Pardo, C., Chung, F., Rodriguez, T.: Automated pollen identification using microscopic imaging and texture analysis. Micron **68**, 36–46 (2015)

10. Wright, J., Ganesh, A., Rao, S., Peng, Y., Ma, Y.: Robust principal component analysis: exact recovery of corrupted low-rank matrices via convex optimization. In: NIPS, pp. 2080–2088 (2009)

11. Sobral, A., Bouwmans, T., Zahzah, E.h.: LRSlibrary: low-rank and sparse tools for background modeling and subtraction in videos. In: Robust Low-Rank and Sparse Matrix Decomposition: Applications in Image and Video Processing (2015)

12. Daood, A., Ribeiro, E., Bush, M.: Pollen grain recognition based on a multi-layer feature decomposition. In: FLAIRS-29 (2016)

13. Vlachos, M., Hadjieleftheriou, M., Gunopulos, D., Keogh, E.: Indexing multi-dimensional time-series with support for multiple distance measures. In: ACM SIGKDD, pp. 216–225 (2003)

# Complementary Keypoint Descriptors

Clark F. Olson$^{(\boxtimes)}$, Sam A. Hoover, Jordan L. Soltman, and Siqi Zhang

School of STEM, University of Washington, Bothell, USA
`cfolson@uw.edu`

**Abstract.** We examine the use of complementary descriptors for keypoint recognition in digital images. The descriptors combine multiple types of information, including shape, color, and texture. We first review several keypoint descriptors and propose new descriptors that use normalized brightness/color spatial histograms. Individual and combined descriptors are compared on a standard data set that varies blur, viewpoint, zoom, rotation, brightness, and compression. Results indicate that substantially improved results can be achieved without greatly increasing keypoint descriptor length, but that the best results combine information from complementary descriptors.

## 1 Introduction

We investigate the use of complementary descriptors for keypoint recognition. These keypoints combine multiple unrelated keypoint descriptors to form a longer descriptor that is better able to discriminate between correct and incorrect matches.

Historically, the most popular keypoint descriptors have used image gradients to encode shape information in the local region around keypoint. Lowe's SIFT descriptor [1] has been highly influential and has spawned many competing descriptors, including HOG [2], GLOH [3], SURF [4], BRIEF [5], and ORB [6]. These descriptors are based on pixel intensities (grayscale images).

Color has been incorporated into keypoint descriptors in several ways. One possibility is to run SIFT on each color channel in some color space and stack the results into a longer descriptor. Bosch et al. [7] use the HSV color space. Van de Sande et al. [8] additionally consider RGB and an opponent color space. However, these methods are still based on gradients and thus focus on shape, not color.

Less work has examined the use of color information directly. Van de Weijer and Schmid [9] use a hue histogram (without location information) stacked with the SIFT descriptor. Luke et al. [10] stack SIFT with a separate SIFT-like descriptor that replaces gradient orientation with pixel hue and gradient magnitude with pixel saturation. Olson and Zhang [11] instead use histograms of normalized colors in the grid cells of the keypoint neighborhood. Other color descriptors were considered by van de Sande et al. [8], but were found to have lower performance.

Texture descriptors have been developed by Lazebnik et al. [12]. Their descriptors are rotationally invariant based on the distance from the keypoint

© Springer International Publishing AG 2016
G. Bebis et al. (Eds.): ISVC 2016, Part I, LNCS 10072, pp. 341–352, 2016.
DOI: 10.1007/978-3-319-50835-1_32

center (and not the orientation). We consider additional descriptors that make use of the computed keypoint orientation in a manner similar to SIFT. Both techniques can be additionally extended to color images by stacking the descriptors for each color channel.

Given this rich set of descriptors that use differing image cues, we examine the use of combinations of descriptors in order to improve precision/recall performance. We use a straightforward method of combining the descriptors, concatenating the vectors and then taking the Euclidean distance between the concatenated vectors. In the context of multi-class object classification, Gehler and Nowozin [13] found that such simple methods yield equivalent results to more complicated combination methods, but with much faster results.

Previous work has combined descriptors in a similar fashion. Zhang et al. [14] concatenate the SPIN, SIFT, and RIFT descriptors to generate more effective combinations. Van de Sande et al. [8] found that even by combining a highly correlated set of descriptors (SIFT, OpponentSIFT, rgSIFT, C-SIFT, and RGB-SIFT), all of which rely on gradient (shape) information, a significant improvement in mean average precision is possible. In contrast, we combine highly differing descriptors using information from multiple modalities (shape, color, texture). Bo, Ren, and Fox [15] also concatenate their kernel descriptors for gradient, color, and shape into a single encompassing descriptor that outperforms the individual components.

Our experiments using the Oxford affine covariant regions data set [3,16] demonstrate techniques comparable and superior in performance to SIFT that do not use gradients and that combinations of descriptors outperform any single descriptor. The disadvantage of this technique is the additional computation time and space required. This yields a trade-off in selecting an appropriate descriptor/combination. Fortunately, much of the computation is parallelizable.

The next section describes the descriptors that we consider in this work. Section 3 describes the keypoint recognition process and metrics. Section 4 details our experiments and results. Finally, Sect. 5 gives our conclusions and observations.

## 2   Descriptors

We examine several keypoint descriptors that encode shape, texture, and color information.

### 2.1   SIFT

The Scale-Invariant Feature Transform (SIFT) descriptor was described by Lowe [1]. We use the OpenCV contributed implementation based on the code of Hess [17]. The technique generates histograms of the gradient orientation (weighted by the gradient magnitude) in a $4 \times 4$ grid around the keypoint center rotated to the keypoint orientation and scaled to the keypoint size. With eight magnitude bins, the SIFT technique yields a 128-dimensional descriptor for each keypoint. The SIFT descriptor and a variation called GLOH were found to be the best performing local descriptors by Mikolajczyk and Schmid [16] when compared to several grayscale descriptors.

## 2.2  RGB-SIFT

RGB-SIFT is the concatenation of the SIFT descriptors computed separately for three RGB channels, yielding a 384-dimensional descriptor. This descriptor was considered in the study by van de Sande, Gevers, and Snoek [8] and found to be among the top performers. Since normalization is performed separately on each channel, this descriptor is invariant not only to illumination intensity and shift, but also illumination color.

## 2.3  OpponentSIFT

OpponentSIFT is similar to RGB-SIFT, except that the color channels are first transformed into an opponent color space [8]:

$$\begin{bmatrix} O_1 \\ O_2 \\ O_3 \end{bmatrix} = \begin{bmatrix} (R-G)/\sqrt{2} \\ (R+G-2B)/\sqrt{6} \\ (R+G+B)/\sqrt{3} \end{bmatrix} \tag{1}$$

In order to prevent channels with little signal from becoming magnified, we first concatenate the channel descriptors and then normalize the values together. This yields significant improvements in our experiments.

Like RGB-SIFT, this yields a 384-dimensional descriptor and was one of the top performing descriptors in the study by van de Sande, Gevers, and Snoek [8].

## 2.4  SPIN and CSPIN

SPIN is a texture descriptor introduced by Lazebnik, Schmid, and Ponce [12]. Unlike other descriptors described here, it does not require the keypoint orientation; it is invariant to orientation based on its construction using concentric circular bins. We use 8 circular bins with 16 intensity bins each (unlike the $10 \times 10$ histogram in the original work) to yield a 128 dimensional descriptor. This circular descriptor is scaled to use the same image area as the other (square) descriptors.

CSPIN is our simple generalization of SPIN to color images by stacking the SPIN descriptors for each color channel.

## 2.5  HoNI: Histograms of Normalized Intensities

The HoNI descriptor uses the same rotated and scaled $4 \times 4$ grid as SIFT, but instead of gradient orientations, the histogram values are normalized image intensities. Like in the SIFT descriptor, the histogram votes are Gaussian-weighted according to their distance from the keypoint center and spread among spatially adjacent cells. The intensities are normalized such that average weighted intensity within the keypoint boundary is 127.5 and the standard deviation of the intensities is 64. This provides invariance to affine intensity changes (bias and gain). The intensity histograms have 8 buckets per grid cell, yielding a 128-dimensional descriptor. To our knowledge, this descriptor has not been previously studied, although it is similar to the SPIN descriptor [12] on a square grid and the HoNC descriptor [11] without color information.

Color HoNI (CHoNI) is an extension that stacks HoNI descriptors for each color channel.

## 2.6   HoNC: Histograms of Normalized Colors

Similar to HoNI, the HoNC descriptor [11] uses a $4 \times 4$ SIFT-like grid, but for each grid cell a simple 8-bin ($2 \times 2 \times 2$) color histogram is computed. The average color intensity is normalized to 127.5 (over all three color channels, not each channel separately) and the average standard deviation of the color channels is normalized to 48. This yields invariance to changes in illumination intensity, but not changes in illumination color. Since the color histograms have 8 buckets per grid cell, this also yields a 128-dimensional descriptor.

## 2.7   HoWH: Histograms of Weighted Hues

Luke, Keller, and Chamorro-Martinez [10] have suggested stacking the SIFT descriptor with a similar descriptor that replaces the gradient orientation and magnitude at each pixel with the hue and saturation. We consider here a version that is not (necessarily) stacked with the SIFT descriptor. Since hue is a circular value (like gradient orientation) and the saturation describes the strength of the hue (similar to gradient magnitude), a similarly structured descriptor results. This descriptor has the drawback that it will not work on grayscale images (or others with low saturation), since all grays have undefined hue. As suggested by van de Weijer and Schmid for their hue-based descriptor [9], when combining this descriptor with others, we weight it 60% as much as other descriptors, and this improves the performance.

## 2.8   CNN3: Deep Convolutional Descriptor

Simo-Serra et al. [18] developed a descriptor learned using a deep convolutional neural network. The input to the network is a $64 \times 64$ grayscale image patch. The network generates a 128-dimensional descriptor similar to SIFT and related descriptors. This descriptor was demonstrated to be superior to SIFT and recently developed competitors, including DAISY [19] and a state-of-the-art learned descriptor [20].

This technique doesn't fit clearly into the class of shape descriptors or texture descriptors, but it undoubtedly uses both shape and texture cues. While it is not invariant to any illumination changes (intensity, shift, or color), it is resilient to such changes and works well in practice. Interestingly, it generates descriptor vectors that are more correlated than the other methods (they have a smaller average angle between them). This is important when combining them with other methods. The vectors require lengthening for them to have equivalent weight in the combined score. We use an empirically determined scale factor of 5. This allows combinations of the descriptors to outperform individual descriptors.

## 2.9   Summary

In addition to the descriptors discussed below, we considered SURF [4], rgSIFT [8], and C-SIFT [8,21,22] descriptors. However, these performed poorly in our previous work [11] and are not included here.

Table 1 summarizes the characteristics of the descriptors. We classify SIFT, RGB-SIFT, and OpponentSIFT as shape descriptors, since they are primarily based on gradient orientations. We classify SPIN, CSPIN, HoNI, and CHoNI as texture descriptors, since they are based on spatial relationships of intensity or individual color channels. We classify HoWH and HoNC as color descriptors, since they do not separate the color channels in constructing the descriptor. CNN3 incorporates both shape and texture information.

# 3   Keypoint Recognition

In order to recognize keypoints between images, we first detect the keypoints in the images using the SURF keypoint detector [4]. We have found this detector to be fast and to generate good features for matching.[1] When the detector finds

Table 1. Characteristics of descriptors.

| Name | Size | Type | Illumination Invariance |
|------|------|------|-------------------------|
| SIFT | 128 | shape | intensity + shift |
| RGB-SIFT | 384 | shape (color) | intensity + shift + color |
| OpponentSIFT | 384 | shape (color) | intensity + shift |
| CNN3 | 128 | shape/texture | none |
| SPIN | 128 | texture | intensity + shift |
| CSPIN | 384 | texture (color) | intensity + shift + color |
| HoNI | 128 | texture | intensity + shift |
| CHoNI | 384 | texture (color) | intensity + shift + color |
| HoNC | 128 | color | intensity + shift |
| HoWH | 128 | color | intensity + shift |

---

[1] Note that this is the SURF keypoint detector, not the descriptor, which has not performed well in our experiments [11].

more than 1000 keypoints, only the top 1000 are retained for each image in order to maintain efficiency and relevance. Descriptors for each keypoint are constructed using the techniques described above. Individual descriptors may be used, but we also consider combinations of descriptors that are concatenated (i.e., stacked) into longer descriptors. When combined, each individual descriptor vector is scaled to have the same length, regardless of size (except as noted above for HoWH and CNN3).

The best match for each keypoint in the reference image is found in the target image using the Euclidean distance between the keypoint descriptors. Matches are considered correct if the projection of the keypoint location into the other image (using a known homography) lies within the computed size of the corresponding keypoint (and in reverse).

We measure the matching performance of each descriptor using the mean average precision as follows. The precision and recall are defined as:

$$\text{precision} = \frac{\text{\# correct matches detected}}{\text{\# total matches detected}} \tag{2}$$

$$\text{recall} = \frac{\text{\# correct matches detected}}{\text{\# keypoints possible to detect}} \tag{3}$$

In computing the recall, we exclude from the denominator those keypoints from the reference image that do not appear in the target image (because they have moved outside the boundaries of the image). We do not exclude keypoints that appear in the target image, but that are missed by the keypoint detector. As the threshold on descriptor distance varies, the number of matches changes and the precision versus recall can be plotted. The *average precision* is the average of the precision over the interval $r \in [0, 1]$ (the area under the curve). The *mean average precision* computes the mean over multiple plots. The maximum value is one and the minimum is zero. Figure 1 shows an example plot of precision versus recall for one image pair.

We ran experiments with each descriptor and many combinations of descriptors on the Oxford affine covariant regions data set[2] that models variations in viewpoint, rotation, zoom, lighting, blur, and compression. All six images (five pairs with the same reference image) of each of the eight data subsets were used. Some pairs are difficult to match, with no combination of descriptors achieving an average precision above 0.05. Others are straightforward, with most techniques performing well. This tends to compress the MAP differences between descriptors.

## 4    Results

We tested every possible combination of five (or less) descriptors from the set described in Sect. 2 using the process from Sect. 3. Table 2 shows the top performing combinations sorted first by the number of descriptors (or equivalently the descriptor norm) and then by the maximum average precision.

---

[2] http://www.robots.ox.ac.uk/~vgg/data/data-aff.html.

**Table 2.** Top descriptor combinations by number of descriptors (vector norm).

| Number | Descriptors | Size | MAP |
|---|---|---|---|
| 1 | CHoNI | 384 | .5330 |
| 1 | CNN3 | 128 | .5267 |
| 1 | OpponentSIFT | 384 | .5237 |
| 1 | RGBSIFT | 384 | .5185 |
| 1 | HoNI | 128 | .5139 |
| 1 | SIFT | 128 | .5136 |
| 1 | HoNC | 128 | .5043 |
| 1 | CSPIN | 384 | .4951 |
| 1 | SPIN | 128 | .4403 |
| 1 | HoWH | 128 | .3206 |
| 2 | CNN3+CHoNI | 512 | .5704 |
| 2 | CNN3+HoNC | 256 | .5668 |
| 2 | CNN3+CSPIN | 512 | .5650 |
| 2 | CHoNI+OpponentSIFT | 768 | .5621 |
| 2 | CNN3+HoNI | 256 | .5604 |
| 2 | CHoNI+RGBSIFT | 768 | .5599 |
| 2 | CHoNI+SIFT | 512 | .5589 |
| 2 | CNN3+OpponentSIFT | 512 | .5577 |
| 2 | HoNC+OpponentSIFT | 512 | .5550 |
| 2 | HoNI+OpponentSIFT | 512 | .5550 |
| 3 | CNN3+CHoNI+OpponentSIFT | 896 | .5781 |
| 3 | CNN3+CHoNI+HoWH | 640 | .5770 |
| 3 | CNN3+CHoNI+RGBSIFT | 896 | .5765 |
| 3 | CNN3+CHoNI+SIFT | 640 | .5758 |
| 3 | CNN3+HoNC+OpponentSIFT | 640 | .5733 |
| 3 | CNN3+CSPIN+OpponentSIFT | 896 | .5728 |
| 3 | CNN3+CSPIN+HoNC | 640 | .5727 |
| 3 | CNN3+HoNC+RGBSIFT | 640 | .5725 |
| 3 | CNN3+CHoNI+CSPIN | 896 | .5724 |
| 3 | CNN3+HoNI+OpponentSIFT | 640 | .5722 |
| 4 | CNN3+CHoNI+HoWH+OpponentSIFT | 1024 | .5848 |
| 4 | CNN3+CHoNI+HoWH+RGBSIFT | 1024 | .5842 |
| 4 | CNN3+CHoNI+HoWH+SIFT | 768 | .5839 |
| 4 | CNN3+CSPIN+HoWH+OpponentSIFT | 1024 | .5826 |
| 4 | CNN3+CSPIN+HoWH+RGBSIFT | 1024 | .5823 |
| 4 | CNN3+HoNI+HoWH+OpponentSIFT | 768 | .5818 |
| 4 | CNN3+CSPIN+HoWH+SIFT | 768 | .5813 |
| 4 | CNN3+HoNI+HoWH+RGBSIFT | 768 | .5810 |
| 4 | CNN3+CSPIN+HoNC+OpponentSIFT | 768 | .5804 |
| 5 | CNN3+CHoNI+HoWH+CSPIN+OpponentSIFT | 1408 | .5857 |
| 5 | CNN3+CHoNI+HoWH+CSPIN+RGBSIFT | 1408 | .5855 |
| 5 | CNN3+HoNC+HoWH+CSPIN+OpponentSIFT | 1152 | .5854 |
| 5 | CNN3+HoNC+HoWH+CSPIN+RGBSIFT | 1152 | .5854 |
| 5 | CNN3+HoNC+HoWH+CSPIN+SIFT | 896 | .5849 |

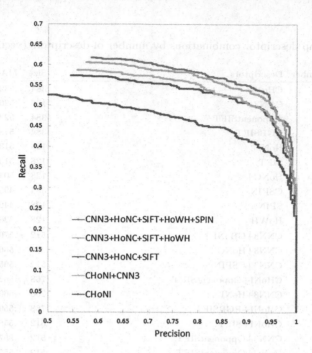

**Fig. 1.** Example precision/recall plot from the first pair of "bark" images in the Oxford data set.

For individual descriptors, three shape/texture descriptors that incorporate all color channels performed well, with CHoNI surpassing OpponentSIFT and RGB-SIFT. CNN3 was, by far, the strongest descriptor that did not include color information. SIFT is near the middle of these uncombined descriptors. Surprisingly, even a simple histogram of normalized intensities (HoNI) performed equivalently. It is clear that using SIFT as the only baseline for comparison to new descriptors is no longer sufficient to demonstrate the state-of-the-art.

Thirty-three pairs of descriptors (when stacked together) surpassed the best individual descriptor. The top three combined CNN3 with a descriptor that incorporates color. CHoNI also performed well when combined with the shape descriptors.

When triples of descriptors are considered, fifteen combinations surpassed the best pair. Most of these combine a descriptor from each type (shape, color, texture). All of the top performers combined CNN3, CHoNI, and another descriptor. CNN3 was included in the top twelve combinations.

Nineteen quadruples of descriptors surpassed the top triple. The top performers all combined CNN3, a shape-based descriptor, a color-based descriptor, and a texture-based descriptor. This demonstrates that the complementarity of the descriptors is important to improved keypoint recognition performance. While HoWH was a poor performer by itself, it is included in most of the top quadruples, indicating that it includes information that is not redundant with the other descriptors.

Only five quintuples were able to (barely) surpass the best performing quadruple. We have reached the limit of this set of descriptors. To improve performance beyond this point, we would require additional descriptors that incorporate information unused by the current set.

Another way of looking at the descriptor combinations is with respect to the number of elements in the descriptor vector (a minimum of 128 for the smallest vectors used in this work). Table 3 shows the results. The top five for each vector size are shown, unless fewer surpass previous (smaller) vectors. From

**Table 3.** Top performing descriptor combinations by number of elements (vector size).

| Size | Descriptors | Number | MAP |
|------|-------------|--------|-----|
| 128 | CNN3 | 1 | .5267 |
| 128 | HoNI | 1 | .5139 |
| 128 | SIFT | 1 | .5136 |
| 128 | HoNC | 1 | .5043 |
| 128 | SPIN | 1 | .4403 |
| 256 | CNN3+HoNC | 2 | .5658 |
| 256 | CNN3+HoNI | 2 | .5604 |
| 256 | HoNC+SIFT | 2 | .5522 |
| 256 | CNN3+SIFT | 2 | .5518 |
| 256 | HoNI+SIFT | 2 | .5506 |
| 384 | CNN3+HoNC+SIFT | 3 | .5715 |
| 384 | CNN3+HoNI+HoWH | 3 | .5711 |
| 384 | CNN3+HoNI+SIFT | 3 | .5694 |
| 384 | CNN3+HoNC+SPIN | 3 | .5684 |
| 384 | CNN3+HoWH+SIFT | 3 | .5675 |
| 512 | CNN3+HoWH+HoNI+SIFT | 4 | .5800 |
| 512 | CNN3+HoWH+HoNC+SIFT | 4 | .5779 |
| 512 | CNN3+HoWH+SPIN+SIFT | 4 | .5776 |
| 512 | CNN3+HoNC+SPIN+SIFT | 4 | .5763 |
| 512 | CNN3+HoWH+HoNC+SPIN | 4 | .5738 |
| 640 | CNN3+HoNC+HoWH+SPIN+SIFT | 5 | .5827 |
| 640 | CNN3+HoNI+HoWH+SPIN+SIFT | 5 | .5801 |
| 768 | CNN3+CHoNI+HoWH+SIFT | 4 | .5839 |
| 896 | CNN3+HoNC+HoWH+CSPIN+SIFT | 5 | .5849 |
| 1152 | CNN3+HoNC+HoWH+CSPIN+OpponentSIFT | 5 | .5854 |
| 1152 | CNN3+HoNC+HoWH+CSPIN+RGBSIFT | 5 | .5854 |
| 1408 | CNN3+CHoNI+HoWH+CSPIN+OpponentSIFT | 5 | .5857 |
| 1408 | CNN3+CHoNI+HoWH+CSPIN+RGBSIFT | 5 | .5855 |

**Fig. 2.** Matching examples. The top matches detected using CNN3+HoNC+SIFT on four example pairs. The top pair shows the 100 best matches. The other pairs show the 200 best matches.

this perspective, CNN3, HoNI, SIFT, and HoNC are the top short descriptors. Even at size 256 (shorter than RGBSIFT, OpponentSIFT, CHoNI and CSPIN), we are able to achieve significant improvements by combining CNN3 and/or SIFT with other short descriptors (CNN3+HoNC performs best).

At 384 elements, we improve noticeably on the longer single descriptors by combining three shorter descriptors. The top performers generally combine CNN3 with a color descriptor and a shape or texture descriptor (one exception combines CNN3 with both a shape and texture descriptor). Combining four short descriptors yields some additional gains (mostly CNN3 combined with a short descriptor of each type). Beyond that, the gains are even smaller, with the best overall descriptor (CNN3+CHoNI+HoWH+CSPIN+OpponentSIFT) besting the top 512-element vector only .5857 to .5800. This suggests that descriptors with size between 256 and 512 elements achieve the best trade-off between vector size (i.e., computation time) and performance.

Overall, CNN3 comes out a big winner, participating in most of the top combinations. The drawback to CNN3 is that it requires significantly higher computational expense when compared to SIFT or similar descriptors. A GPU implementation can improve this, but it is still not competitive with the speed of SIFT [18].

Figure 2 shows four examples of the use of a combination of descriptors. These examples combine CNN3, HoNC, and SIFT, which comprise the top performing descriptor with 384 elements. Despite changes in scale, perspective, and illumination, the descriptor combination finds a large number of correct matches, with very few mismatches.

## 5 Conclusions

We have demonstrated that improved recall/precision results can be achieved by stacking multiple keypoint descriptors. In particular, a combination of descriptors that use shape, color, and texture information significantly improve upon those that use a single modality (or even two). We believe that this will prove true not just for the descriptors studied here, but also more generally. This would imply that nearly every previously published descriptor could benefit through a combination with additional complementary descriptors.

**Acknowledgment.** This work was supported, in part, by a Worthington Distinguished Scholar award from the University of Washington Bothell.

## References

1. Lowe, D.G.: Distinctive image features from scale-invariant keypoints. Int. J. Comput. Vis. **60**, 91–110 (2004)
2. Dalal, N., Triggs, B.: Histograms of oriented gradients for human detection. In: Proceedings of the IEEE Conference on Computer Vision and Pattern Recognition, vol. 1, pp. 886–893 (2005)

3. Mikolajczyk, K., Schmid, C.: A performance evaluation of local descriptors. IEEE Trans. Pattern Anal. Mach. Intell. **27**, 1615–1630 (2005)
4. Bay, H., Ess, A., Tuytelaars, T., Van Gool, L.: SURF: speedup up robust features. Comput. Vis. Image Underst. **110**, 346–359 (2008)
5. Calonder, M., Lepetit, V., Strecha, C., Fua, P.: BRIEF: binary robust independent elementary features. In: Proceedings of the European Conference on Computer Vision, pp. 778–792 (2010)
6. Rublee, E., Rabaud, V., Konolige, K., Bradski, G.: ORB: an efficient alternative to SIFT or SURF. In: Proceedings of the International Conference on Computer Vision, pp. 2564–2571 (2011)
7. Bosch, A., Zisserman, A., Muñoz, X.: Scene classification using a hybrid generative/discriminative approach. IEEE Trans. Pattern Anal. Mach. Intell. **30**, 712–727 (2008)
8. van de Sande, K.E.A., Gevers, T., Snoek, C.G.M.: Evaluating color descriptors for object and scene recognition. IEEE Trans. Pattern Anal. Mach. Intell. **32**, 1582–1596 (2010)
9. van de Weijer, J., Schmid, C.: Coloring local feature extraction. In: Proceedings of the European Conference on Computer Vision, pp. 334–348 (2006)
10. Luke, R.H., Keller, J.M., Chamorro-Martinez, J.: Extending the scale invariant feature transform descriptor into the color domain. ICGST J. Graph. Vis. Image Process. **8**, 35–43 (2008)
11. Olson, C.F., Zhang, S.: Keypoint recognition with histograms of normalized colors. In: Proceedings of the 13th Conference on Computer and Robot Vision (2016)
12. Lazebnik, S., Schmid, C., Ponce, J.: A sparse texture representation using local affine regions. IEEE Trans. Pattern Anal. Mach. Intell. **27**, 1265–1278 (2005)
13. Gehler, P., Nowozin, S.: On feature combination for multiclass object recognition. In: Proceedings of the International Conference on Computer Vision, pp. 221–228 (2009)
14. Zhang, J., Marszalek, M., Lazebnik, S., Schmid, C.: Local features and kernels for classification of texture and object categories: a comprehensive study. Int. J. Comput. Vis. **73**, 213–238 (2007)
15. Bo, L., Ren, X., Fox, D.: Kernel descriptors for visual recognition. In: Advances in Neural Information Processing Systems 23, pp. 244–252 (2010)
16. Mikolajczyk, K., Tuytelaars, T., Schmid, C., Zisserman, A., Matas, J., Schaffalitzky, F., Kadir, T., Gool, L.V.: A comparison of affine region detectors. Int. J. Comput. Vis. **65**, 43–72 (2005)
17. Hess, R.: An open-source SIFT library. In: Proceedings of the 18th ACM International Conference on Multimedia, pp. 1493–1496 (2010)
18. Simo-Serra, E., Trulls, E., Ferraz, L., Kokkinos, I., Fua, P., Moreno-Noguer, F.: Discriminative learning of deep convolutional feature point descriptors. In: Proceedings of the International Conference on Computer Vision, pp. 118–126 (2015)
19. Tola, E., Lepetit, V., Fua, P.: DAISY: an efficient dense descriptor applied to wide-baseline stereo. IEEE Trans. Pattern Anal. Mach. Intell. **32**, 815–830 (2010)
20. Simonyan, K., Vedaldi, A., Zisserman, A.: Learning local feature descriptors using convex optimisation. IEEE Trans. Pattern Anal. Mach. Intell. **36**, 1573–1585 (2014)
21. Abdel-Hakim, A.E., Farag, A.A.: CSIFT: a SIFT descriptor with color invariant characteristics. In: Proceedings of the IEEE Conference on Computer Vision and Pattern Recognition, pp. 1978–1983 (2006)
22. Burghouts, G.J., Geusebroek, J.M.: Performance evaluation of local colour invariants. Comput. Vis. Image Underst. **113**, 48–62 (2009)

# Two Phase Classification for Early Hand Gesture Recognition in 3D Top View Data

Aditya Tewari[1,2]([✉]), Bertram Taetz[1], Frederic Grandidier[2],
and Didier Stricker[1]

[1] Augmented Vision, Technische Universität Kaiserslautern,
Kaiserslautern, Germany
aditya.tewari@dfki.de
[2] IEE S.A., Contern, Luxembourg

**Abstract.** This work classifies top-view hand-gestures observed by a Time of Flight (ToF) camera using Long Short-Term Memory (LSTM) architecture of neural networks. We demonstrate a performance improvement by a two-phase classification. Therefore we reduce the number of classes to be separated in each phase and combine the output probabilities. The modified system architecture achieves an average cross-validation accuracy of 90.75% on a 9-gesture dataset. This is demonstrated to be an improvement over the single all-class LSTM approach. The networks are trained to predict the class-label continuously during the sequence. A frame-based gesture prediction, using accumulated gesture probabilities per frame of the video sequence, is introduced. This eliminates the latency due to prediction of gesture at the end of the sequence as is usually the case with majority voting based methods.

**Keywords:** Driver assistance · Hand gesture · LSTM networks · Hand features · Neural networks

## 1 Introduction

The touch and tactile based systems in cars cause visual distraction which affects the attention while driving [1]. The work by [2] shows that simple and natural interactions with multimedia devices in cars improve the driver's safety. [3] has compared various in-vehicular interaction systems and reported that the gesture based interaction requires least eye contact. Work by [4] also shows that the performance of the driver can degrade sharply with small increase in the shift of attention. It can thus be argued that a robust, touch-sensor free gesture based interactions improve driver safety.

The vision based Hand Gesture Recognition (HGR) techniques can be distributed into two broad classes, static and dynamic. The first [5,6] only recognizes a static pose of a hand while the second uses the changing hand pose and hand

This work is supported by the National Research Fund, Luxembourg, under the AFR project 7019190.

G. Bebis et al. (Eds.): ISVC 2016, Part I, LNCS 10072, pp. 353–363, 2016.
DOI: 10.1007/978-3-319-50835-1_33

motion over frames in addition. The later scheme supports a potentially larger and more natural set of gestures. The primary challenge for an HGR system is the rapidly changing global illumination. Further, defining an optimal location for a camera that minimises the palm occlusion is a difficult task. It has been observed that an overhead location is best suited for such problems [7] because it minimises occlusion due to objects inside the car, however the self occlusion of the hand remains significant especially when a gesture is performed with vertically downward pointing palm. It is desirable to have a flexible system which can be modified to identify gestures which were not originally built into it. The problem of illumination is suppressed by the choice of sensor, on the other hand the problem of occlusion and flexibility require algorithmic solutions.

The early solutions for HGR used Finite State Machines (FSM) [8], a gesture was distributed into phases and a set of twelve gestures were classified. Inspired by the results on handwriting recognition [9] and speech analysis various adaptations of a Hidden Markov Model (HMM) have been used [10]. Another branch of solution includes neural networks and Recurrent Neural Networks (RNN) [11]. Most often, both the FSM and RNN strategies use the information of the instantaneous hand-pose for identifying gesture sequences.

The Long Short-Term Memory (LSTM) network [12,13] is a variation of the traditional RNNs and has been shown to outperform the traditional RNN. It has been extensively used for hand-writing and speech recognition tasks recently [14]. In contrast to the HMM where some prior experiments are required to identify the number of states, it is easier to construct an LSTM model. [15] have used LSTM for gesture identification and demonstrated that it performs better than HMM and SVM.

Location, orientation and velocity of the palm have been used as features for gesture recognition problems [16]. This work reaffirms that features like palm and finger positions along with their velocity are useful for gesture classification. A two-phase classification scheme using three LSTMs is introduced. It is demonstrated that distributing the learning in which one phase learns from the hand pose and the other learns from the direction of motion, simplifies the learning tasks.

An early-detection system which is capable of predicting gesture class while the gesture is being completed is introduced. This is an important requirement for an interaction system. To achieve this a one to one labelling scheme between the gesture frames and gesture class is used. Some sequences are sub-sampled for learning fast sequences. The proposed cumulative probability addition scheme for prediction also help stabilise the system response during discontinuous hand movements. The HGR with this LSTM architecture demonstrates an overall frame-wise accuracy of over 90.5%. We observed that, with an equal sized data the proposed two-phase early hand gesture recognition system outperforms a single all-class, but larger LSTM based system which provides accuracy of 86%.

Section 2 introduces the gestures used for the experiments and describes the data collection and feature extraction process along with the data augmentation method and the data distribution scheme for cross-validation. The overall system architecture, the prediction scheme and the cumulative probability method is described in Sect. 3. The analysis of the training process, test results and comparisons with single all-class network prediction is presented in the Sect. 4. Discussion on results and possible future directions are presented in the Sect. 5.

# 2 Gesture Data and Features

## 2.1 Gesture Definition

A hand-gesture is a sequence of frames of moving palm. It can involve motion of palm without change in the hand-pose or it could be defined as a sequence of hand-poses where the occurrence of the different hand-poses have a predictable, predetermined order. For this work the recorded hand-gestures include, 'Clicking', 'Swiping' in Left and Right direction and in Up and Down motion, 'Accepting', 'Declining', 'Drop' and 'Grabbing'. 'Clicking' involves a forward horizontal motion of the pointing finger. Hand motion in horizontal left-right direction is denoted as 'Swiping' in left and right direction. The swiping motion may be repeated more than once. Similarly vertical palm motion is denoted as vertical swiping. 'Accepting' is a motion of hand outwards from the screen (relative to the camera). 'Declining' is the motion of a hand into the screen. 'Grabbing' involves a transition of a spread hand with the palm facing vertically downwards to a position of joined fingers accompanied with some vertical motion. 'Drop' begins with joined fingers ending in a spread hand with a short downward motion.

## 2.2 Data Collection and Properties

The output frames from the camera have two channels, the depth and the amplitude. The amplitude value of the pixels are proportional to the reflectance of the surface and inversely proportional to the square of the distance values. The data is recorded with a frame rate of 25 Frames per second.

We use a Photonic Mixer Device (PMD) Nano sensor with a resolution of $120 \times 165$ pixel for recording data. This ToF based 3-D camera is attached to the rear-view mirror holder protection. Shown in Fig. 1. Thus the dataset is 3-D top view of hand gestures, it is used for hand pose recognition problem by [17]. The experiments for hand gesture recognition inside the car are conducted with seventeen participants. The data is recorded inside the car and each participant repeats nine gestures around the sat-nav screen of the car. Every participant repeats each gesture six to twelve times. Each frame of the sequence is marked with two labels. 'Accepting', 'Declining', 'Drop', 'Grabbing', 'Clicking', 'Horizontal', and 'Vertical' are used as the primary labels. Sequences marked as 'Horizontal' are marked with a secondary label 'Left' and 'Right', and those marked with 'Vertical' are marked with secondary labels 'Up' and 'Down'.

As the data is recorded inside a car it allows a combination of depth information with the information about the car environment. This information is utilised to extract the features for hand-shape, location and motion. Note that these features are explicitly utilized in the proposed approach and thus no comparison on a different dataset is shown.

(a) Camera behind    (b) Camera on
rear view mirror.        the mirror holder.

**Fig. 1.** The camera setup.

## 2.3   Training and Testing Strategy

Before training the network, the data was shuffled such that the frames from a complete gesture sequence stay together, while the gesture sequences were placed randomly. This shuffling was essential because the participant continuously repeated the same gesture multiple times during recording. Each frame of the gesture sequence is marked with the label for the entire sequence. This allows us to train the network in way such that it attempts at predicting the sequence-label from the start of the gesture.

The total number of available sequences for training the model are increased by sub-sampling approximately one-fifth of sequences in time. Equal proportion of sequences from each class of gesture are reduced to half duration. Such downsampling effectively creates sample-points on which the duration for completing a gesture is shorter than the average gesture sequence. The start and end of each sequence including the sub-sampled once are marked. Both training and testing phase of the algorithm use these sequence markers. Table 1 gives a description of the distribution of the data-samples over classes and the number of sub-sampled sequences created for each class.

For testing a leave-2 cross-validation was performed on the data. The data from the seventeen participants was distributed into eight sets of two participants and one set of one. Owing to an otherwise small test dataset a 9-fold cross-validation is done to report the average accuracy of the model. The sub-sampled sequences are separately divided into 9 groups and then used in training and testing accordingly.

**Table 1.** Number of gesture class samples in dataset

|              | Up  | Down | Left | Right | Click | Accept | Decline | Grab | Drop | Total |
|--------------|-----|------|------|-------|-------|--------|---------|------|------|-------|
| Data-points  | 220 | 226  | 247  | 247   | 160   | 188    | 194     | 172  | 160  | 1814  |
| Down-sampled | 44  | 45   | 49   | 49    | 32    | 47     | 48      | 34   | 32   | 380   |
| Total        | 264 | 271  | 296  | 296   | 192   | 235    | 228     | 204  | 192  | 2194  |

## 2.4  Segmentation and Feature Extraction

The palm region is segmented by creating a virtual cuboidal space in the region where we wish to observe the hand-gesture. The background was generated by recording a video in the car and keeping the consistent pixels. This 3-D background image was then removed from each incoming images of the video sequences. Furthermore, the palm pixel closest to screen is tracked. Hand region is segmented by assuming a real length of 18 cm, another threshold divides hand and finger and a Mahalanobis distance based K-mean clustering refines palm-finger segmentation. The hand palm centroid and finger-tip are estimated and tracked using Kalman filter. Features are further described in the Table 2. The features were centred and normalised such that the mean of each feature element over the training data was zero and the variance was unity.

**Table 2.** Description of features used for the experiments

| Type | Feature names | Description |
|------|---------------|-------------|
| Location | Finger coordinates | The X,Y,Z coordinates of the tracked pixel closest to the screen |
| | Hand coordinates | The X,Y,Z coordinates of the tracked palm centroid |
| | Finger azimuth | Polar angle of the principal component vector of the finger cluster of the palm |
| | Finger polar | Azimuth angle of the principal component vector of the finger cluster of the palm |
| Velocity | Finger Velocity | The X,Y,Z components of the tracked pixel closest to the screen |
| | Hand velocity | The X,Y,Z components of the tracked palm centroid |
| Shape | Concave depth | The maximum distance between convex hull and edge of the segmented palm region |
| | Convex ratio | The ratio of the size of the convex hull around the palm and the segmented palm region |
| | Active pixels | The number of pixels in the segmented palms provides an indication of palm-size |

# 3   System Architecture and LSTM Networks

A two-phase classification strategy is employed for classification. To this end, three neural network based systems are combined. The first network classifies the seven primary classes describing the nature of motion. The other two networks are trained to classify the direction of the motion, i.e. Up vs. Down and Left vs. Right. These networks are used in series with the first network. Various neural network architectures were trained and tested for the three classifiers, the network architectures which provided the best cross-validation results separately were used for the classification system. These networks are further described in detail.

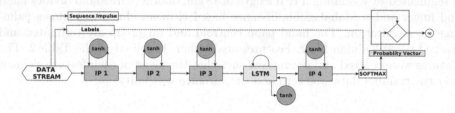

**Fig. 2.** LSTM network with the output decision unit.

Each network has an *LSTM layer* and several *fully connected dot product layers*. The input layer is connected to a dot product layer. Non-linearity is added to the network by using a *tanh activation function* with each fully connected layers. The network for the primary classifier has five layers apart from the input layer and the output *softmax layer*. The LSTM layer is placed as the fourth layer from the input. The output layer has seven output nodes, each node represents one gesture, see Fig. 2.

The binary classifier identifies the intended direction of the motion when the palm moves in horizontal or vertical direction. Since the swiping motion may be repeated more than once while completing the gesture the identification of the intended gesture is more sophisticated problem than merely identifying the direction of motion. The binary classifier LSTM network has *three hidden layers* along with the one LSTM layer. The output layers have two nodes and a softmax activation function. The connection weights and bias are independent of each other in all networks. The three networks are trained independently using the samples belonging to the corresponding classes from the same training dataset. The training uses the RPROP Algorithm for the optimisation process [18].

### 3.1   Prediction

The system is shown in Fig. 3, it can be broadly separated into a frame classification part Fig. 3a which produces a nine dimensional probability vector $\overrightarrow{p(t)}$ at time $t$, and an output probability combination part Fig. 3b which results in another nine dimensional probability vector $\overrightarrow{P(t)}$.

In the classification part of the system the primary classifier is connected with the two motion-direction classifiers, see Fig. 3. It provides a seven dimension probability vector, $\overrightarrow{p^1(t)}$. $\overrightarrow{p^1(t)}$ has five gesture probabilities $\overrightarrow{p(t)^g} = p(t)^{1-5}$

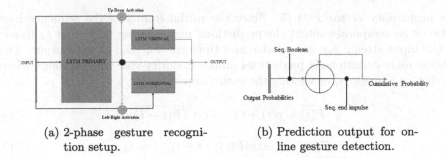

(a) 2-phase gesture recognition setup.

(b) Prediction output for online gesture detection.

**Fig. 3.** The system architecture and the cumulative probability addition scheme.

and probability for horizontal and vertical direction of motion $p(t)^h, p(t)^v$. On identifying vertical or horizontal swiping of the hand the vertical or horizontal motion classifier is activated with binary activation signals $A_v$ and $A_h$. The activated binary classifiers then detect the intended direction of the swiping gestures resulting in the two dimension probability vectors $\overrightarrow{p(t)^v}$ and $\overrightarrow{p(t)^h}$ for vertical and horizontal direction respectively. The output from these classifiers replace the motion probabilities in the primary classifier output, (1). The output probabilities from LSTM units are combined (2) to form a nine dimensional vector $\overrightarrow{p(t)}$ and are weighted by the there values in the primary probability vector, the resulting output vector is re-normalised to form a probability vector $\overrightarrow{p(\hat{t})}$, (3).

$$\overrightarrow{p(t)}'^k = \begin{cases} [\frac{p(t)^k}{2}, \frac{p(t)^k}{2}] & \text{if } A_k = 0. \\ \overrightarrow{p(t)^k} & \text{if } A_k = 1 \text{ where } k \in [v, h]. \end{cases} \tag{1}$$

$$\overrightarrow{p(t)} = [\frac{\sum_{j=1}^{5} p(t)^j}{5}.\overrightarrow{p(t)^g}; \; p(t)^v.\overrightarrow{p(t)}'^v; \; p(t)^h.\overrightarrow{p(t)}'^h]. \tag{2}$$

$$\overrightarrow{p(\hat{t})} = \overrightarrow{p(t)}/|\overrightarrow{p(t)}|. \tag{3}$$

The early predictions of the LSTM based system are stabilised by using a cumulative probability addition scheme Fig. 3b. The cumulative addition of the probability regularizes the estimates while making an early prediction. This adds robustness towards jerks, stops and change in hand direction, during the completion of the hand-gesture sequence. Also a strategy based on maximum-probability or majority decision approach predicts the gesture at the end of the sequence. The described method makes a probability estimation for the gesture at every frame.

The system output probability is given as $\overrightarrow{P(t)}$, (4). The sum is reset to zero whenever an end of sequence impulse is seen. $I_n$ is the impulse corresponding to the $n^{th}$ sequence. The impulse has a value 1 and the impulse time is given by $t_{I_n}$. The probability addition is initiated again with a sequence-begin impulse. The $n^{th}$ prediction $G_n$, corresponds to the index $i$ of the maximum value in the probability vector $\overrightarrow{P(t)}$ (5). Since the initial frames of the sequence have little or no temporal context the predictions made during these first $t_d$ frames of the input stream are not reliable and thus are not read at the output. This scheme allows continuous predictions unlike majority-vote like decisions where prediction is made after viewing the entire sequence.

$$\overrightarrow{P(t)} = \overrightarrow{p(\hat{t})} + (1 - I) \times (\overrightarrow{P(t - 1)}) \tag{4}$$

$$G_n = arg\max_i(\overrightarrow{P(t)}) : t - t_{I_{n-1}} > t_d \tag{5}$$

## 4   Results and Comparisons

This section describes the training progression of the three models and presents the performance of the entire system. As mentioned in the last sections the first few frames of the prediction made by the system are not considered for output, we also skipped these frames for the evaluation analysis. The output probabilities for sequences beyond the eighth frame of the gesture, which corresponds to a time-period of 0.3 s are considered for the analysis.

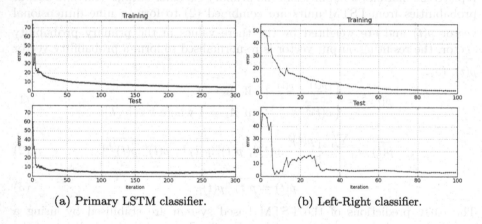

(a) Primary LSTM classifier.          (b) Left-Right classifier.

**Fig. 4.** Train-Test error progression.

The train-test error progression by learning epochs during a sample cross validation for primary phase of classification and the left-right binary classifiers are depicted in Fig. 4. The network was trained for 600 epochs and evaluation was conducted for every second epoch. The average misclassification rate for the given training was 5%. The misclassification rate for the test data at the end of the training was 7%, see Fig. 4a. Both up-down and left-right classifiers were trained as binary classifiers for 400 epochs. It is observed that the misclassification rate on training data after the completion of the training for the up-down motion classifier is 6%, and 1.5% for the left-right classifier. The misclassification rate for

**Table 3.** Confusion matrix proposed system.

| % | U | D | L | R | C | A | De | G | Dr |
|---|---|---|---|---|---|---|----|---|----|
| U | 84 | 4 | 2 | 0 | 8 | 2 | 0 | 0 | 0 |
| D | 4 | 85 | 0 | 0 | 0 | 0 | 8 | 0 | 3 |
| L | 0 | 0 | 92 | 1 | 0 | 0 | 3 | 3 | 1 |
| R | 0 | 0 | 0 | 93 | 0 | 0 | 3 | 4 | 0 |
| C | 0 | 0 | 0 | 0 | 96 | 0 | 4 | 0 | 0 |
| A | 8 | 4 | 0 | 0 | 1 | 82 | 4 | 1 | 0 |
| De | 3 | 7 | 0 | 0 | 0 | 4 | 84 | 2 | 0 |
| G | 4 | 0 | 0 | 0 | 0 | 5 | 0 | 89 | 2 |
| Dr | 1 | 4 | 0 | 0 | 0 | 0 | 4 | 0 | 91 |

**Table 4.** Confusion matrix single all-class LSTM

| % | U | D | L | R | C | A | De | G | Dr |
|---|---|---|---|---|---|---|----|---|----|
| U | 77 | 8 | 0 | 0 | 0 | 5 | 3 | 3 | 4 |
| D | 7 | 78 | 0 | 0 | 0 | 0 | 9 | 2 | 4 |
| L | 0 | 0 | 88 | 6 | 0 | 2 | 4 | 0 | 0 |
| R | 0 | 0 | 4 | 89 | 0 | 4 | 3 | 0 | 0 |
| C | 0 | 0 | 0 | 0 | 96 | 0 | 2 | 2 | 0 |
| A | 8 | 5 | 0 | 0 | 1 | 78 | 5 | 1 | 3 |
| De | 2 | 9 | 0 | 0 | 0 | 7 | 80 | 0 | 2 |
| G | 2 | 3 | 0 | 0 | 0 | 2 | 0 | 91 | 2 |
| Dr | 3 | 1 | 0 | 0 | 0 | 0 | 5 | 0 | 91 |

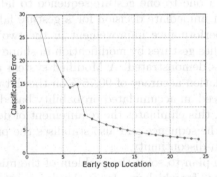

**Fig. 5.** Test error with early start location.

the test data is 8% and 3%, respectively. Figure 4b shows the left-right classifier error progression. On combining the three networks as the described system, the observed misclassification rate for the full system is 9.25%. The Table 3 shows the confusion matrix for the classification of the nine gesture classes in case of the architecture following the two level classification strategy.

In comparison with a larger all-class single LSTM, chosen after experiments on multiple LSTM models, the performance was considerably better. The improvement in the gestures where direction is important is large. In other gestures the performance improves in all classes apart from 'Drop' where accuracy remains the same and 'Grab' which has a small decrement. The performance of the compared LSTM model is shown in Table 4. Confusion matrices are calculated at each step of the 9-fold cross validation and the mean confusion matrix are reported.

# 5   Discussion and Conclusion

The performance of the system improves when decisions were taken after a longer delay from the beginning of the sequence. Figure 5 shows the accuracy performance when the latency period for the frame-wise prediction is changed. The decision after a longer latency gained from larger temporal context and is usually more accurate. Some gestures with similar shape and short motion were misclassified, which was reflected in the occasional misclassification of 'Accept' and 'Decline' as 'up', 'down', respectively. This explains the lower accuracy of the up-down gestures in the combined system even though the binary classification accuracy is high. The accumulated regularization of the system output also resulted in missing of fast-very short gestures.

## 5.1   Conclusion

This work presented a one to one gesture-sequence to label-sequence training procedure to make an immediate decision for a gesture label when the gesture sequence begins. A performance improvement in the two phase classification, when one phase classifies gestures by modification in shape and the other by the direction of motion, is demonstrated. A Modified system architecture achieves an average cross-validation accuracy of 90.75% on the dataset.

This work introduced an accumulated probability based solution for predicting gesture per frame, this eliminates the requirement of delaying the classification until the end of the sequence and also stabilises the prediction outcome to hand-jerks and motion-discontinuity.

As future work we plan to solve the problem of the misclassification of gestures with similar shapes for which we plan to develop more robust shape descriptors. Moreover, spotting of short intended motion of the palm might help in identifying the beginning of the sequences. The prediction performance for short gesture sequences is comparatively worse, using Bayesian filtering approaches with pose identification solutions may help improve this performance.

## References

1. Lansdown, T.C., Brook-Carter, N., Kersloot, T.: Distraction from multiple in-vehicle secondary tasks: vehicle performance and mental workload implications. Ergonomics **47**, 91–104 (2004)
2. Green, P.: Visual and task demands of driver information systems. Technical report (1999)
3. Jæger, M.G., Skov, M.B., Thomassen, N.G., et al.: You can touch, but you can't look: interacting with in-vehicle systems. In: Proceedings of the SIGCHI Conference on Human Factors in Computing Systems, pp. 1139–1148. ACM (2008)
4. Horrey, W.J.: Assessing the effects of in-vehicle tasks on driving performance. Ergonomics **19**, 4–7 (2011)
5. Freeman, W.T., Roth, M.: Orientation histograms for hand gesture recognition. In: International Workshop on Automatic Face and Gesture Recognition, vol. 12, pp. 296–301 (1995)

6. Liu, Y., Gan, Z., Sun, Y.: Static hand gesture recognition and its application based on support vector machines. In: Ninth ACIS International Conference on Software Engineering, Artificial Intelligence, Networking, and Parallel/Distributed Computing, SNPD 2008, pp. 517–521 (2008)
7. Alpern, M., Minardo, K.: Developing a car gesture interface for use as a secondary task. In: Extended Abstracts on Human Factors in Computing Systems, CHI EA 2003, pp. 932–933. ACM, New York (2003)
8. Davis, J., Shah, M.: Recognizing hand gestures. In: Eklundh, J.-O. (ed.) ECCV 1994. LNCS, vol. 800, pp. 331–340. Springer, Heidelberg (1994). doi:10.1007/3-540-57956-7_37
9. Hu, J., Brown, M.K., Turin, W.: Hmm based online handwriting recognition. IEEE Trans. Pattern Anal. Mach. Intell. **18**, 1039–1045 (1996)
10. Chen, F.S., Fu, C.M., Huang, C.L.: Hand gesture recognition using a real-time tracking method and hidden Markov models. Image Vis. Comput. **21**, 745–758 (2003)
11. Yang, J., Horie, R.: An improved computer interface comprising a recurrent neural network and a natural user interface. Image Vis. Comput. **60**, 1386–1395 (2015)
12. Hochreiter, S., Schmidhuber, J.: Long short-term memory. Neural Comput. **9**, 1735–1780 (1997)
13. Hochreiter, S.: The vanishing gradient problem during learning recurrent neural nets and problem solutions. Int. J. Uncertainty Fuzziness Knowl. Based Syst. **6**, 107–116 (1998)
14. Graves, A., Mohamed, A.R., Hinton, G.: Speech recognition with deep recurrent neural networks. In: 2013 IEEE International Conference on Acoustics, Speech and Signal Processing (ICASSP), pp. 6645–6649. IEEE (2013)
15. Neverova, N., Wolf, C., Paci, G., Sommavilla, G., Taylor, G.W., Nebout, F.: A multi-scale approach to gesture detection and recognition. In: 2013 IEEE International Conference on Computer Vision Workshops (ICCVW), pp. 484–491. IEEE (2013)
16. Yoon, H.S., Soh, J., Bae, Y.J., Yang, H.S.: Hand esture recognition using combined features of location, angle and velocity. Pattern Recogn. **34**, 1491–1501 (2001)
17. Tewari, A., Grandidier, F., Taetz, B., Stricker, D.: Adding model constraints to CNN for top view hand pose recognition in range images. In: Proceedings of the ICPRAM 2005, pp. 170–177 (2016)
18. Riedmiller, M., Braun, H.: A direct adaptive method for faster backpropagation learning: the RPROP algorithm. In: 1993 IEEE International Conference on Neural Networks, pp. 586–591. IEEE (1993)

# Visualization

# Adaptive Isosurface Reconstruction
# Using a Volumetric-Divergence-Based Metric

Cuilan Wang$^{(\boxtimes)}$ and Shuhua Lai

School of Science and Technology, Georgia Gwinnett College, Lawrenceville, USA
{cwang,slai}@ggc.edu

**Abstract.** This paper proposes a new adaptive isosurface extraction algorithm for 3D rectilinear volumetric datasets, with the intent of improving accuracy and maintaining topological correctness of the extracted isosurface against the trilinear interpolation isosurface while keeping the mesh triangle count from becoming excessive. The new algorithm first detects cubes where the extracted mesh has large error using a volumetric-divergence-based metric, which estimates the volume between the extracted mesh and the trilinear interpolation isosurface. Then, it adaptively subdivides those cubes to refine the mesh. A new strategy is developed to remove cracks in the mesh caused by neighboring cubes processed with different subdividing levels.

## 1 Introduction

Isosurface extraction is an important technique for visualizing volumetric datasets. Exploring surfaces of constant values helps to understand the structures of the volumetric data. Marching Cubes (MC) algorithm generates a triangular mesh representation of an isosurface from a scalar rectilinear volumetric dataset.

Over the years, many algorithms have been developed to improve the topological correctness and accuracy of MC [1]. Those algorithms are useful in the situations where the user needs to substantially zoom into the data or the data of low-resolution is viewed [2,3]. In those situations, improving the smoothness of the extracted isosurface and correctly representing the interior of cubes are necessary. Medical applications where thin specimens or internal small cavities need to be viewed require high quality isosurface rendering [3]. Generating isosurfaces for the manufacture purpose also needs highly accurate extracted isosurfaces to create fabricated surfaces that don't look coarse and "chunky" [4].

Trilinear interpolation is commonly used to model data variation within scalar rectilinear dataset cells. Therefore, the accuracy of the produced isosurface is usually determined by the closeness of the produced mesh and the isosurface given by trilinear interpolation. Volumetric divergence [5] measures the volume between the produced mesh and the trilinear interpolation isosurface. It is a natural and accurate metric to evaluate the accuracy of the produced isosurface.

To increase the accuracy of the extracted isosurface, an easy and straightforward way is to utilize a subdivision strategy similar to the one used in [6]. In this

© Springer International Publishing AG 2016
G. Bebis et al. (Eds.): ISVC 2016, Part I, LNCS 10072, pp. 367–378, 2016.
DOI: 10.1007/978-3-319-50835-1_34

strategy, first, each active cube (i.e., a cube that intersects the trilinear interpolation isosurface) is recursively subdivided into eight equal sized subcubes
until certain termination criteria are satisfied. Then, data are interpolated at
the subcube corners. Finally, MC is applied to extract the isosurface at the final
subcubes. In this paper, this method is called DC. As the subdivision degree
increases, the DC mesh becomes closer to the trilinear interpolation isosurface;
however, the number of triangles in the mesh also increases significantly.

In this paper, we proposed a new isosurface extraction algorithm, Multi-
Resolution Marching Cubes (MRMC), to increase the accuracy of the produced
isosurface and maintain its topological correctness, while keep the mesh triangle
count from becoming excessive. This algorithm uses a volumetric-divergence-
based metric to detect cubes where the extracted mesh has large error and
adaptively subdividing those cubes to refine the mesh. Also, MRMC is based
on Nielson's MC [7] to ensure the extracted isosurface is topologically correct.
In addition, a new strategy is developed to fix the cracks between neighboring
cubes processed with different subdivision levels.

## 2    Background and Related Work

### 2.1    The TVDP Metric

The volumetric divergence metric measures the volume between two closed surfaces to evaluate the closeness between them [5]. We denote the regions inside and
outside some surface $A$ as $A_{in}$ and $A_{out}$, respectively. The volumetric divergence
between two closed surfaces $A$ and $B$ is the volume of region $R_D$, defined as

$$R_D = (A_{in} \cap B_{out}) \cup (A_{out} \cap B_{in}). \tag{1}$$

A method was introduced in [5] to calculate the volumetric divergence (VD)
metric for a unit cube, which is the volume between the extracted and the trilinear interpolation isosurfaces inside the cube. Since the method requires recursively subdividing the cube into 8 subcubes until certain termination criteria are
satisfied and each subcube need to be processed to determine its contribution to
the volumetric divergence, the computational cost of the method is very high.

TVDP was designed to approximate the VD metric with much lower computational cost [8]. Since the volume between the extracted and trilinear interpolation isosurfaces is affected by both the area of the isosurface and the distance
between these two types of isosurfaces, TVDP uses the volume of a tetrahedron to approximately model the volume between the two. Figure 1 shows how
a tetrahedron is formed. In this figure, the triangle $\triangle P_1P_2P_3$ is the extracted
isosurface. The trilinear interpolation isosurface outline is shown in blue. $C$ is
the centroid of $\triangle P_1P_2P_3$. $M$ is the nearest intersection point of the trilinear
interpolation isosurface with the triangle normal line through $C$. Points $P_1$, $P_2$,
$P_3$, and $M$ form a tetrahedron. Since the extracted isosurface in a cube may
contain multiple triangles, the TVDP metric value is 2 times of the sum of the
volumes of all such tetrahedra in the cube. Here, 2 is a constant obtained from an
empirical study to match the TVDP metric values with the VD metric values [8].

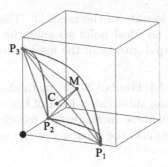

**Fig. 1.** Illustration of how a tetrahedron is formed in calculating the TVDP metric. (Color figure online)

## 2.2   Isosurface Extraction Algorithms

**Topological Correctness.** The original MC may produce an isosurface mesh that has "holes" due to its face ambiguity problem. One way to solve this topological problem is to use asymptotic decider (AD) [9]. Later, researchers recognized that the original MC also has internal ambiguity problem [10,11]. For example, the trilinear interpolation isosurface inside a cube may be in two separate pieces that separate two diagonal vertices with the same labelings or there may be a single "tunnel" piece that connects these two vertices. Nielson [7] proposed an improved version of MC that resolves both the face and the internal ambiguities of MC. He used the DeVella's necklace test to determine whether the isosurface inside the cube should have a tunnel or not.

**Accuracy.** Some approaches have been developed to improve the accuracy of the produced isosurface [3,4,12]. They usually generate an isosurface mesh with an increased triangle count in order to add more details to the produced isosurface.

Lopes and Brodlie [12] proposed a modification of MC, which not only has correct topology, but also improves the accuracy of the produced isosurface. This is achieved by adding a small number of key points in the cube interior to the mesh. Those points are critical to the surface definition. The accuracy level of this method is similar to that of DC with subdivision level 1 [13]. However, this method produces about 4 times as many triangles as MC does [12,13].

In the mesh refinement method of Cignoni et al. [3], the side midpoints and centroids of each mesh triangle are checked for their distances to the trilinear interpolation isosurface. If the distance exceeds the selected threshold, the point is moved to the true isosurface. The triangles are progressively split by inserting those moved points to the mesh. To move a point to the true isosurface, a sort of ray-tracing process is used and the point is gradually moved in the direction of the field gradient. However, this way of moving points may result in the mesh section partially contained in an adjacent cube. The gradient needs to be modified to maintain the locality of the mesh [3]. Therefore, in some cases the moved point may not be an ideal point to split the mesh. In addition, their method might lead to a rapid growth of the mesh triangle count.

**Adaptive Subdivision Methods.** Some methods have been developed to simplify meshes by adapting subdivision level of the volume data to the shape of the isosurface. Although these methods can reduce the mesh triangle count and achieve better performance, the accuracy of the mesh is usually decreased.

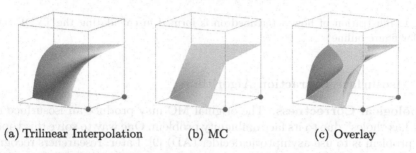

(a) Trilinear Interpolation        (b) MC        (c) Overlay

**Fig. 2.** An example of a very curved trilinear interpolation isosurface being well represented by the MC mesh isosurface inside a cube.

Some of those methods extend MC from uniform grids to adaptive grids [14–16]. In those methods, the subdivision of the cubes is driven by the flatness of the true isosurface, which is usually measured by curvature-based metrics. If the isosurface is not flat enough, the cube is subdivided. However, this subdivision criterion and curvature-based metrics have some drawbacks. First, for the trilinear interpolation isosurface, the surface curvatures can vary greatly at different surface points. If not enough isosurface points are sampled, the metric may not be accurate. Second, it is possible for the MC mesh isosurface to well represent a very curved true isosurface. In the example shown in Fig. 2, the true isosurface is obviously not very flat and the curvature metric value is also large. However, the MC mesh passes through the true isosurface at multiple locations, which shows that the MC mesh is close to the true isosurface. Here, the curvature metric fails to imply that the two isosurfaces are close, because it only considers the shape of the true isosurface, not both isosurfaces. On the other hand, the TVDP metric returns a small value for the volume between the two isosurfaces in the cube, which indicates that the two isosurfaces are close to each other.

Since cracks may occur between neighboring cubes with different subdivision levels, this class of methods require some crack fixing strategies. Shu et al. used polygons with the same shape of the cracks to patch the cracks [14]. However, the produced isosurface of their method is discontinuous in the region where cracks appear [14]. In the method of Kazhdan et al. [16], a polygonal mesh is formed by the extracted isoedges on cube faces. Then, an algorithm for computing a minimum area triangulation of a 3D polygon is used to transform the polygonal mesh into a triangular mesh. However, this way of generating the triangular mesh doesn't guarantee the topological correctness of the mesh inside the cube. The crack removing strategy of Westermann et al. is to split the coarse triangle by inserting its centroid and represent it as a fan of triangles [15]. However, their method has a restriction that the subdivision levels between two adjacent cubes can't be greater than one. Also, the inserted points usually are not on the trilinear interpolation isosurface, therefore, they may affect the mesh accuracy.

# 3    Multi-Resolution Marching Cubes Algorithm

There are two major steps in MRMC. In the first step, the multi-resolution isosurface mesh is extracted. Cubes where the mesh has large error are adaptively subdivided to refine the mesh. In the second step, cracks in the mesh caused by neighboring cubes processed with different subdividing levels are removed. Nielson's MC is used as the base method of MRMC. This makes the produced mesh topologically correct and having all mesh vertices lying on the trilinear interpolation isosurface. The following pseudocode summarizes these two steps (with $V$ the volumetric dataset, $threshold$ the user-selected accuracy threshold, and $maxSubdiv$ the maximum subdivision level of DC).

$\text{MRMC}(V, threshold, maxSubdiv)$

1    $\text{ExtractMultiResolutionMesh}(V, threshold, maxSubdiv)$
2    $\text{RemoveCracks}(V)$

## 3.1    Multi-Resolution Mesh Extraction

In MRMC, initially MC is applied to extract the mesh at each active cube. Then, cubes where the extracted mesh has low accuracy are adaptively subdivided and DC is applied to refine the mesh. Here, the accuracy of the extracted mesh is evaluated by the TVDP metric. This process terminates when the TVDP metric value is less than the user-selected threshold or the subdivision limit is reached.

In the following pseudocode for this step, $CubeData_{i,j,k}$ holds the corner values and locations of the cube $C_{i,j,k}$ ($i$, $j$, $k$ are the indexes of the cube in $x$, $y$, $z$ dimensions of the volumetric dataset). $MeshData_{i,j,k}$ stores the extracted mesh triangles in $C_{i,j,k}$. The $GetMCMesh$ and $GetDCMesh$ methods extract the MC and DC meshes at $C_{i,j,k}$, respectively.

$\text{ExtractMultiResolutionMesh}(V, threshold, maxSubdiv)$

1    **for each** active cube $C_{i,j,k}$ in $V$ **do**
2        $MeshData_{i,j,k} \leftarrow GetMCMesh(CubeData_{i,j,k})$
3        $metric \leftarrow CalculateTVDP(CubeData_{i,j,k}, MeshData_{i,j,k})$
4        $n \leftarrow 0$ //$n$ is the subdivision depth of DC
5        **while** ($metric > threshold$) and ($n < maxSubdiv$) **do**
6            $n \leftarrow n + 1$
7            $MeshData_{i,j,k} \leftarrow GetDCMesh(CubeData_{i,j,k}, n)$
8            $metric \leftarrow CalculateTVDP(CubeData_{i,j,k}, MeshData_{i,j,k})$

## 3.2    Solving the Crack Problem

In this paper, DC1 is denoted as DC with subdivision depth 1. Figure 3(a) shows an instance of the crack problem. In this figure, MC is applied to the left cube and DC1 is applied to the right cube. The intersection of the trilinear interpolation isosurface with a cube face is a hyperbola, which represents the isocontour of the bilinear interpolation on the face. Figure 4 shows the 2D view of the MC mesh edge (shown in orange), the DC1 mesh edges (shown in green), and isocontour hyperbola (shown in red) on the common face of the two cubes for this instance. DC1 evenly subdivides a cube into 8 subcubes and samples the isosurface points on subcubes edges. The polyline formed by DC1 edges in (b) better approximates the isocontour hyperbola than the MC edge in (a) due to DC1's increasing sampling resolution of isosurface points. Also, since the DC1 edges and the MC edge are different, there is a crack in the isosurface mesh.

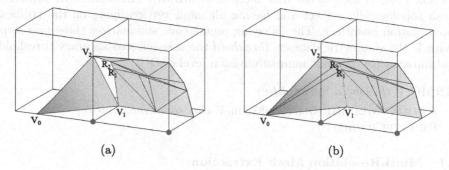

**Fig. 3.** (a) illustrates the crack problem. (b) shows that the crack in (a) is removed by using triangle fan $\{\triangle V_0 V_1 R_1, \triangle V_0 R_1 R_2, \triangle V_0 R_2 V_2\}$ to replace $\triangle V_0 V_1 V_2$.

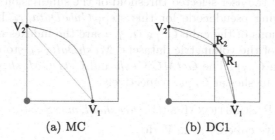

**Fig. 4.** (a) shows the overlay of the MC mesh edge and the isocontour hyperbola. (b) shows the overlay of the DC1 mesh edges and the isocontour hyperbola. (Color figure online)

MRMC can handle the general situation where adjacent cubes are processed with any two different subdivision levels. Its basic strategy to remove cracks is to replace any mesh triangle in a low resolution cube that has an edge on the common face of the two cubes, $f$, with a triangle fan. All triangles in the triangle fan share the vertex of the replaced triangle that is not on $f$. Their other vertices form edges that match the mesh edges of the high resolution cube on $f$. In the low resolution cube, the triangle fan increases the sampling rate of isosurface points on the common face, while keeps the original sampling rate at the rest of the cube. Figure 3(b) shows the crack in (a) is removed by this strategy.

If a cube has a lower subdivision level than multiple adjacent cubes of it, it may require that a mesh triangle is first replaced by a triangle fan, and then some triangles in the triangle fan are further replaced by other triangle fans. The following pseudocode summarizes the second major step of MRMC.

REMOVECRACKS($V$)
1   **for each** active cube $C_{i,j,k}$ in $V$ **do**
2       **for each** $C_{i,j,k}$'s adjacent cube, $C_{i',j',k'}$ **do**
3           **if** subdivision level of $C_{i,j,k}$ < subdivision level of $C_{i',j',k'}$
4               **if** $C_{i,j,k}$ and $C_{i',j',k'}$'s common face $f$ intersects isosurface
5                   **for each** triangle, $t$, in $MeshData_{i,j,k}$ **do**
6                       **if** $t$ has an edge on $f$
7                           generate the triangle fan, $t_f$, for $t$
8                           $MeshData_{i,j,k} \leftarrow MeshData_{i,j,k} - t + t_f$

Since MRMC is based on Nielson's MC, the mesh edges generated by MC or DC on a cube face are topologically correct in MRMC. This means that for each branch of the isocontour hyperbola intersected with the cube face, MC or DC generates one polyline with all vertices on this branch of hyperbola to approximate it inside the cube face (a line segment can be considered as a special polyline). Also, in DC the edges of the final subcubes form the grid lines where isosurface points are sampled. Let $C_l$ be the low resolution cube and $C_h$ be the high resolution cube between two adjacent cubes. Here, it is possible for the subdivision depth of $C_l$ be to greater than or equal to 1. Since the grid lines in $C_l$ is the subset of the grid lines in $C_h$, it is easy to prove that on the common face, every isoedge $e$ in $C_l$ is uniquely mapped to an iso-polyline $p_e$ in $C_h$ that shares the two ending vertices with $e$. If $e$ and $p_e$ are different, a triangle fan needs to be generated to match the edges of $p_e$ on the common face.

Next, given an isoedge $e$ in $C_l$, how to determine its corresponding polyline $p_e$ in $C_h$ is explained. Let the isocontour hyperbola segment between the two vertices of $e$ be $h$. Since each branch of hyperbola is a monotonic curve, the intersection points of $h$ and the grid lines can be sorted in order along one dimension of the cube face. Let this sorted set of intersection points be $S$. It is easy to prove that connecting every two adjacent points in $S$ forms the edges of $p_e$. Figure 5 shows an example of this process. Within the bounding box, the isocontour hyperbola intersects the grid lines parallel to $X$ and $Y$ axes at vertices $\{X_1, X_2, X_3\}$ and $\{Y_1, Y_2, Y_3\}$, respectively. Merging and sorting these two groups of vertices creates set $S$: $\{Y_1, Y_2, X_1, Y_3, X_2, X_3\}$. Connecting every two adjacent vertices in $S$ forms polyline $p_e$.

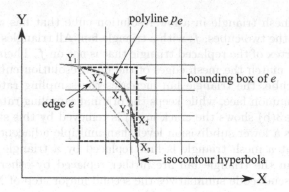

**Fig. 5.** Illustration of how to determine the corresponding polyline $p_e$ of edge $e$.

# 4    Experimental Results

## 4.1    Detecting Meshes Segments with Large Error

Next, the effectiveness of using the TVDP metric to detect cubes where the iso-surface mesh has large error is examined. Besides TVDP, we also tested MRMC with subdivision driven by a curvature metric. We call this method the curvature-based adaptive MC (CAMC). The curvature metric we used is similar to the one used in [15]. At each mesh vertex, $\frac{1}{4}(k_1^2 + k_2^2)$ is calculated, where $k_1$ and $k_2$ are the two principle curvatures of the isosurface at the point. Then, averaging those values of all mesh vertices in the cube yields the curvature metric value.

Results from testing a frog MRI-scan dataset with size $256 \times 256 \times 44$ and a lobster CT-scan dataset with size $301 \times 324 \times 56$ are shown in Figs. 6 and 7, respectively. In each figure, (b), (c), (d) and (e) show the zoomed-in views of the isosurfaces in the red box region in (a) extracted by MC, DC1, CAMC, and MRMC with the accuracy threshold (i.e., the TVDP metric threshold), $\varepsilon$, being 0.1. For each dataset, the curvature metric threshold in CAMC is set so that the CAMC mesh triangle count is close to the MRMC mesh triangle count. In both figures, there are obvious differences between the MC mesh and the DC1 mesh at the locations where the red arrows are pointing to. This indicates that the MC mesh has large error at those locations, since DC1 has much higher sampling resolution of isosurface points than MC. On the other hand, the MRMC mesh is close to the DC1 mesh at those locations. This shows that the TVDP metric successfully detects cubes where the mesh has large error and MRMC refines the mesh through subdividing those cubes. Results also show that CAMC fixes some large error mesh segments, but also misses some. This implies that the curvature metric is not as accurate as TVDP in detecting mesh segments with large error.

For each test case, the mesh triangle count and quantitative accuracy of the mesh measured by volumetric divergence (i.e., average VD per active cube) are summarized in Table 1. For both datasets, when $\varepsilon$ is 0.1 in MRMC, only about 3%-4% of active cubes are subdivided and the mesh triangle count is increased

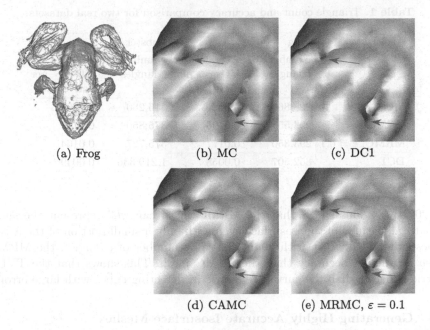

**Fig. 6.** Visual comparison of the meshes generated by MC, DC1, CAMC, and MRMC with $\varepsilon = 0.1$ for the frog dataset. (Color figure online)

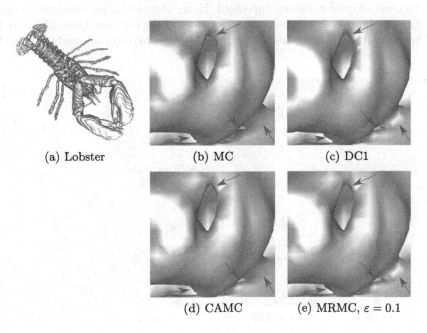

**Fig. 7.** Visual comparison of the meshes generated by MC, DC1, CAMC, and MRMC with $\varepsilon = 0.1$ for the lobster dataset. (Color figure online)

**Table 1.** Triangle count and accuracy comparison for two real datasets.

| Algorithm | Frog | | Lobster | |
|---|---|---|---|---|
| | Number of triangles | Average VD per active cube | Number of triangles | Average VD per active cube |
| MC | 228,868 | 0.0229 | 316,280 | 0.0200 |
| CAMC | 293,559 | 0.0196 | 375,850 | 0.0178 |
| MRMC, $\varepsilon = 0.1$ | 293,350 | 0.0177 | 375,727 | 0.0164 |
| DC1 | 852,507 | 0.0058 | 1,219,336 | 0.0049 |

by 20%-30%. This shows that the MRMC mesh can well represent the small structural features of the isosurface even with only a small portion of the active cubes subdivided. Also, with about the same number of triangles, the MRMC mesh has higher accuracy than the CAMC mesh. This shows that the TVDP metric is better than the curvature metric in detecting cubes with large error.

### 4.2 Generating Highly Accurate Isosurface Meshes

Another set of experiments was conducted to demonstrate that MRMC can generate highly accurate isosurface mesh. The accuracy of the mesh is controlled by the user-selected accuracy threshold. Here, the maximum subdivision depth of DC is 2. Figure 8 shows the zoomed-in views of the extracted isosurfaces in the red box region in Fig. 7(a). In this figure, subfigures (a), (b), (c), and (d) show the

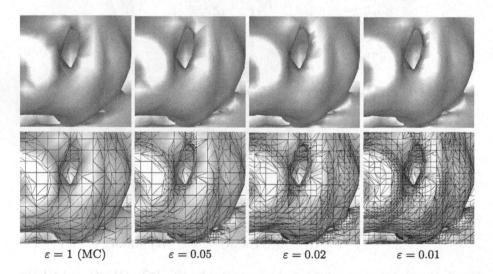

$\varepsilon = 1$ (MC)          $\varepsilon = 0.05$          $\varepsilon = 0.02$          $\varepsilon = 0.01$

**Fig. 8.** Visual comparison of the isosurfaces produced by MRMC with different accuracy thresholds ($\varepsilon$).

**Table 2.** Quantitative comparison of isosurfaces generated by MRMC with different accuracy thresholds ($\varepsilon$).

| $\varepsilon$ | Number of triangles | Average VD per active cube | Pecentage of MC cubes | Pecentage of DC1 cubes | Pecentage of DC2 cubes | Time (in seconds) |
|---|---|---|---|---|---|---|
| 1 | 316,280 | 0.0200 | 100% | 0.0% | 0.0% | 0.43 |
| 0.05 | 553,613 | 0.0117 | 90.4% | 9.3% | 0.3% | 0.98 |
| 0.02 | 1,054,910 | 0.0064 | 72.3% | 25.1% | 2.6% | 1.49 |
| 0.01 | 1,929,115 | 0.0037 | 57.3% | 30.2% | 12.5% | 2.51 |

isosurface meshes generated by MRMC with the accuracy threshold being 1.0, 0.05, 0.02, and 0.01, respectively. In each subfigure, the normal rendering of the isosurface is shown on the top and the mesh edges overlaid on the isosurface are shown on the bottom. The maximum volumetric divergence value for a unit cube is 1, which is the volume of the cube. Therefore, when the accuracy threshold is 1.0, no cube in the volumetric dataset needs to be divided. In this case, MC is used to extract isosurface mesh instead of MRMC. Figure 8 shows that as the accuracy threshold decreases, more and more areas of the isosurface mesh are refined, the MRMC mesh is gradually becoming smoother and closer to the true isosurface. It also shows that the MRMC mesh has multiple resolutions, which indicates that the mesh is adaptively refined.

Table 2 shows the mesh triangle count, average VD per active cube, percentages of cubes that are finally processed by MC, DC1, and DC2 (i.e., DC with subdivision depth 2), and isosurface extraction time for each test case. The results show that as the accuracy threshold decreases, more and more cubes are subdivided and the accuracy of the isosurface mesh increases.

## 5    Conclusion

This paper introduces a new algorithm for generating isosurface with high accuracy and correct topology in representing the trilinear interpolation isosurface, while keeping the mesh triangle count from becoming excessive. MRMC improves the accuracy of the extracted mesh by adaptively subdividing the cubes where the mesh has large error and refining the mesh with DC. The cubes with large error are detected by a volumetric-divergence-based metric. The cracks between neighboring cubes with different subdivision levels are repaired by a new crack removal method. In the future work, we will integrate view-dependent approaches to MRMC to speedup rendering for the applications where the mesh triangle count is a critical issue.

# References

1. Newman, T., Yi, H.: A survey of the marching cubes algorithm. Comput. Graph. **30**, 854–879 (2006)
2. Brodlie, K., Wood, J.: Recent advances in volume visualization. Comput. Graph. Forum **20**, 125–148 (2001)
3. Cignoni, P., Ganovelli, F., Montani, C., Scopigno, R.: Reconstruction of topologically correct and adaptive trilinear isosurfaces. Comput. Graph. **24**, 399–418 (2000)
4. Bailey, M.: Manufacturing isovolumes. In: Chen, M., Kaufman, A.E., Yagel, R. (eds.) Volume Graphics, pp. 79–93. Springer, London (2000)
5. Wang, C., Newman, T., Lee, J.: On accuracy of marching isosurfacing methods. In: Proceedings of the Eurographics/IEEE VGTC Workshop on Volume Graphics 2008, Los Angeles, pp. 49–56 (2008)
6. Cline, H., Lorensen, W., Ludke, S.: Two algorithms for the three-dimensional reconstruction of tomograms. Med. Phys. **15**, 320–327 (1988)
7. Nielson, G.: On marching cubes. IEEE Trans. Visual. Comput. Graphics 9 283–297 (2003)
8. Wang, C., Newman, T.: New metric for evaluating the accuracy of marching isosurfacing algorithms. In: Proceedings of the 2014 ACM Southeast Regional Conference, pp. 22:1–22:6, ACM, New York (2014)
9. Nielson, G., Hamaan, B.: The asymptotic decider: resolving the ambiguity in marching cubes. In: Visualization 1991, San Diego, pp. 83–91 (1991)
10. Natarajan, B.: On generating topologically consistent isosurfaces from uniform samples. Vis. Comput. **11**, 52–62 (1994)
11. Chernyaev, E.: Marching cubes 33: construction of topologically correct isosurfaces. Technical report CERN CN 95–17, CERN (1995)
12. Lopes, A., Brodlie, K.: Improving the robustness and accuracy of the marching cubes algorithm for isosurfacing. IEEE Trans. Visual. Comput. Graph. **9**, 16–29 (2003)
13. Wang, C.: New tomographic reconstruction and visualization techniques and applications to the plasmasphere. Ph.D. thesis, The University of Alabama in Huntsville (2009)
14. Shu, R., Zhou, C., Kankanhalli, M.: Adaptive marching cubes. Vis. Comput. **11**, 202–217 (1995)
15. Westermann, R., Kobbelt, L., Ertl, T.: Real-time exploration of regular volume data by adaptive reconstruction of iso-surfaces. Vis. Comput. **15**, 100–111 (1999)
16. Kazhdan, M., Klein, A., Dalal, K., Hoppe, H.: Unconstrained isosurface extraction on arbitrary octrees. In: Proceedings of the Fifth Eurographics Symposium on Geometry Processing, Barcelona, Spain, pp. 125–133 (2007)

# Large Image Collection Visualization Using Perception-Based Similarity with Color Features

Zeyuan Chen[✉] and Christopher G. Healey

Department of Computer Science, North Carolina State University, Raleigh, USA
zchen23@ncsu.edu

**Abstract.** This paper introduces the basic steps to build a similarity-based visualization tool for large image collections. We build the similarity metrics based on human perception. Psychophysical experiments have shown that human observers can recognize the gist of scenes within 100 milliseconds (ms) by comprehending the global properties of an image. Color also plays an important role in human rapid scene recognition. However, previous works often neglect color features. We propose new scene descriptors that preserve the information from coherent color regions, as well as the spatial layouts of scenes. Experiments show that our descriptors outperform existing state-of-the-art approaches. Given the similarity metrics, a hierarchical structure of an image collection can be built in a top-down manner. Representative images are chosen for image clusters and visualized using a force-directed graph.

## 1 Introduction

With the rapid development of cellphone cameras, storage devices and social media, capturing, saving and sharing images has become much more common. Because of this, the size of image collections is growing rapidly both in terms of absolute data size and the number of images being saved. For example, Flickr is reported to contain 5.26 billion public photos, with approximately 2 million photos uploaded each day in 2015 [1]. Instagram reports 95 million photos are being posted daily [2]. Even a personal gallery may contain many thousands of images. This makes it difficult or impossible for users to retrieve images or fully explore a large image collection by visual inspection. Therefore, we seek an effective exploration tool that allows users to interactively and efficiently browse and retrieve images from large collections in ways that keep the images organized. Although images are generally classified as object images or scene images, in this paper we focus on scene images.

Visualization is an effective way to communicate information through visual imagery. Currently, there are few examples of visualization tools for large image collections. Most exploration tools manage images using labels like dates, events, people and locations. Unfortunately, this method has numerous drawbacks. First, users usually do not provide detailed labels, which makes it difficult to retrieve images by keyword query when they are incomplete or unavailable. Second, many

© Springer International Publishing AG 2016
G. Bebis et al. (Eds.): ISVC 2016, Part I, LNCS 10072, pp. 379–390, 2016.
DOI: 10.1007/978-3-319-50835-1_35

words are ambiguous. For example, if a user searches on the label *apple*, it could be a fruit or a personal computer.

Recent works [3–5] have used similarity-based approaches to visualize large image collections. The images are grouped into clusters automatically based on their visual distances. There are two main issues: developing the metric of similarity between images, and visualizing clusters. First, the computational distances between images should be similar to their perceived difference. Many traditional computer vision approaches [6,7] describe images based on lower-level features (e.g. textures and edge-based structures). This can make them slow or inaccurate. We want to design similarity metrics by learning from human perception. Humans can understand the gist of a scene in a single glance, even if the image is blurred, which means people often recognize the categories of images as a whole without looking at significant amounts of low-level detail [8]. Recent works based on global features like the "gist" of Oliva and Torralba [9] and the spatial pyramid framework of Lazebnik et al. [10] have achieved great performance both in terms of accuracy and efficiency. Second, it is infeasible to display all the images in clusters at once, so it is crucial to find appropriate ways to visualize clusters.

In this paper, we present the following novel contributions: (1) a method to process scene descriptors in a way that preserves both color information and global scene properties; (2) an approach to construct highly compact scene descriptors; (3) an application of the Color Coherent Vector (CCV) model [20] to preserve coherent color region information, improving the performance of the scene descriptors; (4) and classification experiments on both small and large image datasets to statistically verify that our methods outperform existing state-of-the-art approaches.

## 2 Background

Human observers can understand a variety of visual information from an image and recognize its basic-level category within 100 ms [11]. Instead of relying entirely on computer vision techniques, there are potential advantages in learning from human observers' perceptual processing of images.

### 2.1 Human Perception of Scene Gist

The experimental work of Greene and Oliva [12] has shown that in the early perception stages, observers can comprehend global properties of a scene (such as the mean depth of the scene and whether it is navigable or not) more easily than classifying them into basic-level categories (e.g. mountains, rivers). This result supports the user study [13] in which seven global properties were chosen to represent scenes: openness, expansion, mean depth, temperature, transience, concealment and navigability. In the fast scene categorization task, the performance of human observers was indistinguishable from a Naive Bayes classifier whose input was rankings for the seven properties. These results suggest global properties are sufficient to represent the gist of a scene.

The role of color in rapid recognition of scene gist is significant. The experiments of Oliva and Schyns [11] have shown that color has an influence on recognition tasks when the color is related to the meaning or "diagnostic" of the scene categories. The experimental study of Castelhano and Henderson [14] demonstrated that gist activation is affected by color when the images are blurred. The study also showed the reason color expedites gist activation is not because it helps in the segmentation process, but because it is directly related to the scene's gist.

## 2.2    Scene-Centered Image Features

Many traditional scene recognition approaches are object-centered. They build hierarchical levels of features in a bottom-up manner [6,7]. The lower-level features (e.g. colors and textures) are grouped into higher-level ones (e.g. regions and objects). The semantic meanings of the scenes are inferred from the highest-level features.

However, recent scene-centered approaches [9,15,16] have shown that holistic representations of images can be built directly from low-level features. This is because there are regular and unique patterns of statistical distributions of features in different scene categories. The global properties of a "gist" descriptor [9] are estimated from a set of global feature templates that are effective to represent images.

Different from approaches based on the human perception of scene gist, related research [10,17,18] makes use of state-of-the-art computer vision techniques to build global features. Xiao et al. [17] identify several features as kernels including histogram of oriented gradients, scale-invariant feature transform (SIFT), color histograms, etc. The "all features" classifier that is based on a weighted sum of these kernels is reported to have higher precision than any individual feature during scene classification. Alternatively, the spatial pyramid framework [10] is a sophisticated method to summarize local features. Images are iteratively partitioned into sub-regions, and histograms of features are computed locally in each sub-region. Similar to the "gist" descriptor, this framework preserves the spatial layouts of features and is widely used in scene classification.

## 2.3    Color-Based Image Features

Color information plays an important role in scene recognition. A color histogram itself is not enough for complex recognition tasks, but color histograms with geometric information have achieved strong performance [19–21]. The CCV model [20] computes histograms for coherent and incoherent pixels separately. Pixels in large contiguous regions are considered coherent while the remaining pixels are incoherent.

## 2.4 Image Collection Visualization

After the image features are extracted, pairwise distances between images can be computed. The images are generally grouped into clusters using standard methods like $k$-means based on their pairwise distances. For example, Google Image Swirl [5] builds clusters of images based on visual similarity. An exemplar is chosen from each cluster as a representative. The exemplars are visualized using a balloon tree.

## 3  Similarity Metrics

There are two important findings we can harness from human perception. First, global properties are sufficient for scene recognition and scene descriptors can be built directly from low-level features. Second, color information helps scene recognition. State-of-the-art descriptors like "gist" [9] and histogram of oriented gradients with a spatial pyramid framework (denoted HOG) [10] have preserved the global features, but they only deal with grayscale images. There are many suggestions for color descriptors, such as RGB-SIFT [22] and HSV-SIFT [23]. They compute SIFT descriptors in different color channels separately, then stack the feature vectors together. However, the size of those descriptors are several times larger than the original ones, which makes them less efficient. In this paper,

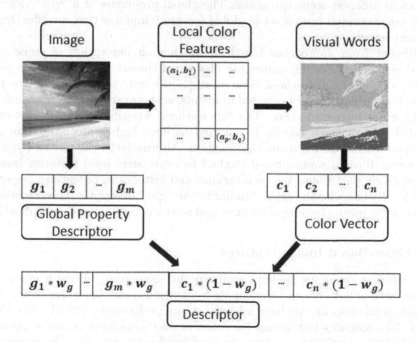

**Fig. 1.** Pipeline of our approach. $(a_i, b_i)$ is the color feature for each pixel. $(g_1, ..., g_m)$ is a global property descriptor. $(c_1, ..., c_n)$ is a color vector. $w_g$ is the weight of global property descriptor in feature combination

we will present novel approaches to build compact descriptors that preserve both color information and global properties.

The pipeline of our approach is shown in Fig. 1. The local color features are extracted densely and then are quantized into "visual words" using the bag-of-words model. An image is represented by a color vector computed from the frequencies of "visual words" in the spatial pyramid framework. The final descriptor of an image is the weighted combination of the color vector and a global property descriptor (e.g. "gist" or HOG). The details are discussed in the sections below.

## 3.1   Color Feature Extraction

In the experiments of Oliva and Schyns [24], the $(a, b)$ vector of $Lab$ color space is used to represent colors based on two important $Lab$ properties. First, the luminance $L$ is separated from the other two channels, so $(a, b)$ is invariant to changes of luminance in the scene. Second, $a$ and $b$ represent colors along two color-opponent dimensions. The human visual system processes colors along similar dimensions. Additionally, the Euclidian distance between two $(L, a, b)$ vectors is similar to their perceived color difference.

After converting an image from RGB space to $Lab$, each pixel is described by a $(L, a, b)$ vector. We discard $L$ for lightness change invariance and only use the $(a, b)$ vector as the color feature for each pixel.

## 3.2   Feature Quantization and Image Representation

The local color features are quantized to $n$ discrete colors using the bag-of-words models described in [25]. The local features are randomly sampled from the image collection and are then grouped into $n$ clusters using $k$-means. The $n$ cluster centers are called the "vocabulary". The "visual word", or the quantized values, of each pixel in the image is the index of its nearest center.

The CCV model [20] shows that splitting an image into coherent and incoherent regions contributes to the improvement of image retrieval accuracy, which matches the experimental results of Castelhano et al. [14] that shows color regions are related to human scene recognition. A pixel is coherent if it is in a color region whose size is greater than a threshold $T$. Given the total number of pixels in an image $N$, the normalized threshold $t$ is given by $t = \frac{T}{N}$.

In order to differentiate coherent and incoherent pixels in our approach, we update the visual word of each incoherent pixel using

$$VW_i = VW_i + n \tag{1}$$

Here, $VW_i$ is the visual word (which is a scalar value) of the $i$-th pixel in an image and $n$ is the length of the "vocabulary".

The spatial pyramid framework [10] is used to summarize the visual words. This framework divides images into sub-blocks at different levels and computes histograms within each sub-block. The histograms are stacked together with weights to generate a vector to describe the image. By applying Eq. 1, it is equivalent to stacking histograms of coherent and incoherent pixels together in each sub-block. Therefore, the coherent and incoherent information does not break the overall spatial layout of the spatial pyramid framework.

## 3.3 Feature Combination

In scene classification, the weighted combination of multiple kernels can generate better results if the weights are chosen properly. The weights of individual kernels of the "all features" descriptor of Xiao et al. [17] are proportional to the fourth power of their accuracy. Hou et al. [26] assigns higher weights to kernels with high accuracy. Past research has shown color features alone cannot achieve high accuracy. That is probably why color information is often neglected. However, the study of human perception [11,14] shows the importance of color in scene recognition. Instead of combining a large number of different features, we focus on combining color and global features.

The kernel combination method is designed for supervised learning, but we want to apply our approach to unsupervised clustering of images so that the image clusters can be constructed more flexibly. Let $G$ be a global feature descriptor and $C$ the computed color vector described in above sections. The descriptor $D$ of an image is the weighted concatenation of $G$ and $C$ as shown in this equation:

$$D = CAT(w_g * G, \ (1 - w_g) * C). \tag{2}$$

Here, $w_g$ is the weight of the global-property descriptor. Suppose $X$ and $Y$ are two sets of values (e.g. a collection of visual words) and $H_X$ and $H_Y$ are their histograms that both have $m$ bins. The histogram intersection kernel between $H_X$ and $H_Y$ is given by the *histogram intersection function* [27]:

$$K(H_X, H_Y) = \sum_{i=1}^{m} min(H_X(i), H_Y(i)). \tag{3}$$

Suppose $G$ is a descriptor built from histograms (e.g. HOG), and $K(G_X, G_Y)$ is a kernel of feature $G$. Let $K(C_X, C_Y)$ be a kernel of $C$, $K_{com}$ be the weighted combination of the kernel of $G$ (weighted by $w_g$) and $C$ (weighted by $w_c$), and $K_D$ be a kernel of $D$. Then $K_{com}$ is:

$$K_{com} = w_g * K(G_X, G_Y) + w_c * K(C_X, C_Y). \tag{4}$$

If $w_c = (1\text{-}w_g)$, $K_D$ is:

$$K_D = K(CAT(w_g * G_X, \ w_c * C_X), \ CAT(w_g * G_Y, \ w_c * C_Y)). \tag{5}$$

We can prove that $K_{com}$ equals $K_D$ given $w_c = (1\text{-}w_g)$, which illustrates that constructing the combined feature $D$ using Eq. 2 is equivalent to weighted kernel combination if $G$ is in the form of a histogram. A global feature descriptor like "gist" is not built directly from histograms, but it also summarizes low level features. Therefore, Eq. 2 works for other global feature descriptors like "gist" as well.

The descriptor $D$ is constructed in a very compact way since the vocabulary of $C$ is usually small. For instance, for a two-level HOG descriptor with a 200-word vocabulary and two-level color vector $C$ with an 8-word vocabulary, the length of the HOG descriptor is 1000 while the length of the $D$ vector is only 1080.

# 4  Experiments

We use scene classification experiments to evaluate the performance of our descriptors. Since the categories of images in the database are labeled by observers, the classification accuracy measures how different the similarity metrics are from human-perceived visual distances. The first part of the experiment is to find optimal values for $w_g$ (the weight of the global feature descriptor, denoted $w$ for simplicity) and $t$ (the normalized threshold to split coherent and incoherent pixels). The second goal is to compare our algorithms with other state-of-the-art approaches to scene classification. The "gist" [9] (denoted $gist$) and HOG [10] approaches are chosen for comparison.

There are two datasets used in the experiments. The first is the Eight Scene Categories (8-scene) Dataset [9] with 2,688 color images from eight outdoor scenes. The second is the SUN397 [17] Dataset with 108,604 color images from 397 categories including indoor, outdoor natural and outdoor man-made scenes. There are at least 100 images in each scene category in both datasets. The 1-vs.-all SVMs were trained using samples from those two datasets.

As described above, the descriptor $D$ could be constructed in multiple ways. First, the CCV model could be applied (denoted $ccv$) or not (denoted $noccv$). Second, the color vector $C$ could be combined with different global feature descriptors. There are four possible types of descriptors: $gist$-$ccv$, $gist$-$noccv$, HOG-$ccv$, and HOG-$noccv$.

## 4.1  Parameter Selection

The optimal parameters of the above four descriptors were computed from small sampled image sets of a database. For the 8-scene database, 50 training and 50 test images were randomly chosen from each category for each trial. There were 20 trials in total. The sample size was about 30% of the database. For SUN397, 10% of the images were uniformly selected to construct an image subset, then five training and five test images were randomly chosen for each category from the subset for each trial. Five trials were run. The size of samples for each trial was 3.65% of SUN397 database.

When the CCV model was not applied, $w$ was the only parameter. There were two parameters $w$ and $t$ when CCV was applied. As an example, in the 8-scene database, the classification accuracy of HOG-$ccv$ and HOG-$noccv$ with changes of $w$ and $t$ is shown Fig. 2.

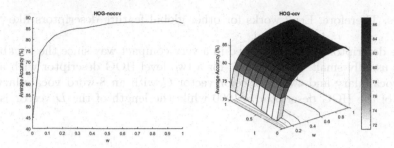

**Fig. 2.** The average accuracy of different descriptors with $w$ and $t$ changing from zero to one. Left: results of HOG-*noccv* descriptors. Right: results of HOG-*ccv*

**Table 1.** The optimal parameters for all descriptor in the 8-scene and SUN397 database

|        | gist-noccv | gist-ccv           | HOG-noccv | HOG-ccv            |
|--------|------------|--------------------|-----------|--------------------|
| 8-scene | w = 0.70   | w = 0.55, t = 0.95 | w = 0.95  | w = 0.90, t = 0.05 |
| SUN397 | w = 0.75   | w = 0.70, t = 0.95 | w = 0.80  | w = 0.70, t = 0.95 |

We simply chose the $w$ and $t$ associated with the highest average accuracy as their optimal values (shown in Table 1). In each case, the "slope" of the accuracy was small near the optimal values. This suggested the accuracy of descriptors was not sensitive to changes in $w$ or $t$.

### 4.2 Comparison with State-of-the-Art

The four combined descriptors were compared with *gist* and HOG respectively. Given the optimal values of $w$ and $t$, the experiments were run on the 8-scene database (50 trials) and the SUN397 database (10 trials). In each trial, 50 training and 50 test images were randomly selected from each category. All of the descriptors used the same training and test images.

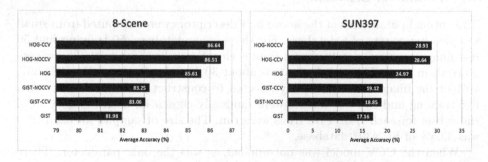

**Fig. 3.** The classification accuracy of different descriptors in 8-Scene and SUN 397 database

The average classification performances are shown in Fig. 3. For each database, we performed two groups of repeated measures one-way analysis of variance (ANOVA) and post-hoc tests to compare the accuracy of $G$ (HOG in group one and $gist$ in group two) with their combined descriptors $D$ (shown in Table 2, including F-values). In both 8-scene and SUN397 database, the combined descriptors $D$ were all significantly more accurate than the original global feature descriptors $G$ alone. Additionally, there were no significant differences between $G$-$ccv$ and $G$-$noccv$ in the 8-scene database, but $gist$-$ccv$ was significantly more accurate than the $gist$-$noccv$ while the accuracy of HOG-$noccv$ was significantly higher than HOG-$ccv$ in SUN397. This suggested that the CCV model worked well with gist-based descriptors (e.g. the "gist" [9]), but not so well with computer-vision-based descriptors (e.g. HOG [10]) in a large database. Moreover, we found that $gist$-$ccv$ performed consistently better than $gist$-$noccv$ for every trial in SUN397, which indicated that the color coherent information had a significant influence on the improvement of classification accuracy when combined with gist-based descriptors.

**Table 2.** The pairwise comparisons among the accuracy of state-of-the-art descriptors (i.e.$gist$ and HOG, denoted G) and the combined descriptors. The first two rows are the results on the 8-Scene database and the last two rows are on the SUN397 database

| Group | $G - G$-$ccv$ | $G - G$-$noccv$ | $G$-$ccv - G$-$noccv$ | F |
|---|---|---|---|---|
| HOG$_8$ | $-1.030$, $p < 0.01$ | $-0.900$, $p < 0.01$ | $0.130$, $p = 0.702$ | $F(2, 48) = 38.449$, $p < 0.01$ |
| $gist_8$ | $-1.080$, $p < 0.01$ | $-1.275$, $p < 0.01$ | $-0.195$, $p = 0.403$ | $F(2, 48) = 41.004$, $p < 0.01$ |
| HOG$_{397}$ | $-3.669$, $p < 0.01$ | $-3.962$, $p < 0.01$ | $-0.293$, $p < 0.01$ | $F(2, 8) = 1852.262$, $p < 0.01$ |
| $gist_{397}$ | $-1.967$, $p < 0.01$ | $-1.698$, $p < 0.01$ | $0.269$, $p < 0.01$ | $F(2, 8) = 435.452$, $p < 0.01$ |

## 5  Cluster Visualization

After the descriptors are computed for every images in a dataset, the images can be grouped into clusters using $k$-means. The visual distance between two images is defined by the distance of their descriptors. A tree structure of clusters is built in a top-down and breadth-first manner. Let $L_i$ be a set of clusters at the $i$-th level. Starting from the entire dataset ($L_0$), the dataset is divided into $k$ clusters ($L_1$). Every cluster in $L_i$ is split to construct $L_{i+1}$. A cluster cannot be split once its size is smaller than a certain threshold. The process terminates when there are no more clusters to split. The number $k$ of $k$-means clustering is determined using the gap statistic method [28] or set by a user.

One image is chosen from each cluster to represent it. The selected image should be as similar to all other images as possible. The distances of every pair of images are computed, and the image with the smallest average distance from all other images is chosen as the representative.

0 ——⊟—— Max

**Fig. 4.** The visualization of clusters at level one. The Dataset is the 8-scene database

To achieve intuitive and aesthetic visualization results, the distances of images should be preserved and occlusions should be avoided if possible. To achieve this, a force-directed graph is employed. The visualization of clusters at level one of the 8-scene database is shown in Fig. 4. The on-screen Euclidean distance represents the visual differences between images: farther apart for larger dissimilarities. The overall distribution of images is uniform and relatively symmetric.

If the users want to see the details of a cluster, they can expand (or "zoom into") it. Then, only the representative images of the sub-clusters of the expanded cluster will be shown. A slider bar on the top of the screen shows the current level of the clusters being displayed.

## 6 Conclusion

We have introduced the basic steps for constructing a similarity-based large image collection visualization system based on gist-based similarity metrics. Inspired by the exceptional ability of humans to perceive scenes, we designed global feature descriptors that exploit color information. Our descriptors preserve the information from coherent color regions, as well as the spatial layouts of scenes. The color features are combined with sophisticated global property features in a compact way. Parameter selection experiments were run on small sampled images sets to find optimal parameters for our descriptors. The experimental results showed that our descriptors are insensitive to changes in those parameters. Follow-on similarity experiments identified our approaches as achieving significantly improved precision over state-of-the-art algorithms like "gist" [9] and HOG with spatial pyramid framework [10].

We have also introduced methods to build hierarchical structures for image collections given our similarity metrics, and have shown how to use these hierarchies to visualize image clusters using force-directed graphs.

We note that a single image may not be able to represent clusters with large variance. It is better to synthesize representative images that are in accordance with the users' impressions of clusters. This is left for future work.

# References

1. Michel, F.: How many public photos are uploaded to flickr every day, month, year? (2015). https://www.flickr.com/photos/franckmichel/6855169886. Accessed 5 August 2016
2. https://www.instagram.com/press/ (2016). Accessed 5 August 2016
3. Nguyen, G.P., Worring, M.: Interactive access to large image collections using similarity-based visualization. J. Vis. Lang. Comput. **19**, 203–224 (2008)
4. Yang, J., Fan, J., Hubball, D., Gao, Y., Luo, H., Ribarsky, W., Ward, M.: Semantic image browser: bridging information visualization with automated intelligent image analysis. In: 2006 IEEE Symposium on Visual Analytics Science and Technology, pp. 191–198. IEEE (2006)
5. Jing, Y., Rowley, H., Wang, J., Tsai, D., Rosenberg, C., Covell, M.: Google image swirl: a large-scale content-based image visualization system. In: Proceedings of the 21st International Conference Companion on World Wide Web, pp. 539–540. ACM (2012)
6. Barnard, K., Forsyth, D.: Learning the semantics of words and pictures. In: Proceedings of the Eighth IEEE International Conference on Computer Vision, ICCV 2001, vol. 2, pp. 408–415. IEEE (2001)
7. Carson, C., Belongie, S., Greenspan, H., Malik, J.: Blobworld: image segmentation using expectation-maximization and its application to image querying. IEEE Trans. Pattern Anal. Mach. Intell. **24**, 1026–1038 (2002)
8. Schyns, P.G., Oliva, A.: From blobs to boundary edges: evidence for time-and spatial-scale-dependent scene recognition. Psychol. Sci. **5**, 195–200 (1994)
9. Oliva, A., Torralba, A.: Modeling the shape of the scene: a holistic representation of the spatial envelope. Int. J. Comput. Vis. **42**, 145–175 (2001)
10. Lazebnik, S., Schmid, C., Ponce, J.: Beyond bags of features: spatial pyramid matching for recognizing natural scene categories. In: 2006 IEEE Computer Society Conference on Computer Vision and Pattern Recognition, vol. 2, pp. 2169–2178. IEEE (2006)
11. Oliva, A.: Gist of the scene. Neurobiol. Atten. **696**, 251–258 (2005)
12. Greene, M.R., Oliva, A.: The briefest of glances the time course of natural scene understanding. Psychol. Sci. **20**, 464–472 (2009)
13. Greene, M.R., Oliva, A.: Recognition of natural scenes from global properties: seeing the forest without representing the trees. Cogn. Psychol. **58**, 137–176 (2009)
14. Castelhano, M.S., Henderson, J.M.: The influence of color on the perception of scene gist. J. Exp. Psychol. Hum. Percept. Perform. **34**, 660 (2008)

15. Torralba, A., Oliva, A.: Statistics of natural image categories. Netw. Comput. Neural Syst. **14**, 391–412 (2003)
16. Oliva, A., Torralba, A.: Building the gist of a scene: the role of global image features in recognition. Prog. Brain Re. **155**, 23–36 (2006)
17. Xiao, J., Hays, J., Ehinger, K.A., Oliva, A., Torralba, A.: Sun database: large-scale scene recognition from abbey to zoo. In: 2010 IEEE conference on Computer vision and pattern recognition (CVPR), pp. 3485–3492. IEEE (2010)
18. Zhou, B., Lapedriza, A., Xiao, J., Torralba, A., Oliva, A.: Learning deep features for scene recognition using places database. In: Advances in Neural Information Processing Systems, pp. 487–495 (2014)
19. Chang, P., Krumm, J.: Object recognition with color cooccurrence histograms. In: IEEE Computer Society Conference on Computer Vision and Pattern Recognition, vol. 2. IEEE (1999)
20. Pass, G., Zabih, R.: Histogram refinement for content-based image retrieval. In: Proceedings 3rd IEEE Workshop on Applications of Computer Vision, WACV 1996, pp. 96–102. IEEE (1996)
21. Huang, J., Kumar, S.R., Mitra, M., Zhu, W.J., Zabih, R.: Image indexing using color correlograms. In: Proceedings of the 1997 IEEE Computer Society Conference on Computer Vision and Pattern Recognition, pp. 762–768. IEEE (1997)
22. Van De Sande, K.E., Gevers, T., Snoek, C.G.: Evaluating color descriptors for object and scene recognition. IEEE Trans. Pattern Anal. Mach. Intell. **32**, 1582–1596 (2010)
23. Bosch, A., Zisserman, A., Muoz, X.: Scene classification using a hybrid generative/discriminative approach. IEEE Trans. Pattern Anal. Mach. Intell. **30**, 712–727 (2008)
24. Oliva, A., Schyns, P.G.: Diagnostic colors mediate scene recognition. Cogn. Psychol. **41**, 176–210 (2000)
25. Yang, J., Jiang, Y.G., Hauptmann, A.G., Ngo, C.W.: Evaluating bag-of-visual-words representations in scene classification. In: Proceedings of the International Workshop on Workshop on Multimedia Information Retrieval, pp. 197–206. ACM (2007)
26. Hou, J., Gao, H., Xia, Q., Qi, N.: Feature combination and the knn framework in object classification. IEEE Trans. Neural Netw. Learn. Syst. **27**, 1368–1378 (2016)
27. Swain, M.J., Ballard, D.H.: Color indexing. Int. J. Comput. Vis. **7**, 11–32 (1991)
28. Tibshirani, R., Walther, G., Hastie, T.: Estimating the number of clusters in a data set via the gap statistic. J. Roy. Stat. Soc. Ser. B (Stat. Methodol.) **63**, 411–423 (2001)

# Chasing Rainbows: A Color-Theoretic Framework for Improving and Preserving Bad Colormaps

Robert Sisneros[1]([✉]), Mohammad Raji[2], Mark W. Van Moer[1], and David Bock[1]

[1] National Center for Supercomputing Applications, Urbana, IL 61801, USA
sisneros@illinois.edu
[2] University of Tennessee at Knoxville, Knoxville, TN 37996, USA

**Abstract.** The scientific visualization community increasingly questions the use of rainbow colormaps. This is not unfounded as significant problems are readily seen in a luminance plot of the rainbow colormap. Many good, generally applicable colormaps are proposed as direct replacements for the rainbow. However, there are still many who choose rainbows and like them. Would a colormap with perfect luminance and the chromaticity of a rainbow find a wider audience? This was our motivation in studying the range of chromatic effects arising from luminance corrections. Consequently we developed a framework for adjusting colormaps to various degrees which produces favorable results on a wide range of colormaps. In this work we will detail this framework and demonstrate its effectiveness on several colormaps.

## 1 Introduction

A rapidly increasing contingent advocates using alternatives to the rainbow colormap for scientific visualization. The wealth of accessible content advising the discontinuation of using the rainbow are strongly supported by sound theory and conclusive examples. There is an active community of scientists and artists utilizing color theory providing alternative colormaps and usage examples. Nonetheless, this is juxtaposed with the fact that rainbow variants are still prevalent. This suggests a practical method for generating colormaps for scientific visualization might have more to gain from the rainbow than a list of things to avoid.

Scientific visualization is a field rooted in computer graphics with deep ties to data analysis. As such the field's combination of scientists, developers, and practitioners represent a diverse community with a wide range of priorities. These priorities are not always well-aligned as is evident in the use of color. Principles of aesthetics and graphic design dictate judicious use of a few colors which combine harmoniously in a colormap with a uniform luminance gradient. This is routinely at odds with data-centric desires to maximize the ability to categorize, compare, and discern among data elements, tasks often utilizing a large number of discernible hues. The purpose of this work is to help bridge the gap between these conflicting practices.

G. Bebis et al. (Eds.): ISVC 2016, Part I, LNCS 10072, pp. 391–402, 2016.
DOI: 10.1007/978-3-319-50835-1_36

Our method is a gradual, perceptual correction for colormap improvement. Specifically we leverage color theory including a perceptually uniform color space along with the best practices of colormap design to explore, for a given input colormap, the range of possibilities between correcting it to strictly adhere to these practices and simply making improvements while maintaining the chromatic integrity of the original. The critical component for a good colormap is an appropriate luminance. A correction of luminance alone is likely sufficient to make a good colormap out of a bad one. In a perceptually uniform space (we use CIELUV) the optimal color is readily identifiable as Euclidean distances relate to perceptual differences; the problem is that such a color is likely impossible with a physical light source. Additionally, "appropriate" luminance is situation dependent, e.g. the luminance of a standard colormap is notably varied from that of a divergent colormap. However, those luminance mappings best for common scenarios are generally agreed upon. With any of these luminance functions as a guideline for the ideal luminance, we consider the original colormap as the guideline for ideal chromaticity.

In summary, given a luminance function and a colormap to correct, the framework employs an algorithm weighted toward either perfect luminance or preserved chromaticity. In the former case, at the ideal luminance we find the color with chromaticity nearest to that of the original. In the latter, we find the nearest luminance to the ideal where there is a visible color with chromaticity identical to the original. The intuitive nature of the approach belies subtle implementation considerations. The potential to significantly augment the availability of good, diverse colormaps represents the obvious benefit of such a system. We will demonstrate various adjustments of a rainbow colormap, the results of maximizing correction on a large set of colormaps, as well as the capability of using alternate luminance functions.

In the remainder of this paper we discuss related works in Sect. 2 and provide the motivating background in Sect. 3. We outline our framework and demonstrate its use in Sects. 4 and 5, respectively and conclude in Sect. 6.

## 2   Related Works

Different works have investigated issues with the rainbow colormap [1, 2] in great detail. A lack of intuitive hue ordering and nonuniform perceptual change are only two of the major issues which cause obscurity and misguide the viewer [2,3]. As a countermeasure, some works have studied and presented elements of useful colormaps. Trumbo et al. presented several principles (order, separation, rows and columns and diagonal) as ideal properties for a color scale. Through visual experiments, Rogowitz et al. suggested that luminance monotonically changes in good colormaps [4].

Ware [5] determined that spectral colormaps were suited for distinguishing quantities while grayscale colormaps were suited for distinguishing form. He proposed constructing colormaps which spiral through increasing luminance within a color space in order to combine the benefits of both. Additional spiral color sequence methods include the Linear Optimized Color Scale (LOCS) by Levkowitz [6] and cubehelix by Green [7]. A similar approach was taken by van der Walt [8] in proposing a new default colormap for Matplotlib. Brewer proposed the ColorBrewer tool with different hand-crafted colormaps which can be used for different types of tasks [9]. Wijffelaars et al. presented an algorithm to generate ColorBrewer-like colormaps automatically [10]. Lee et al. [11] presented an alternative optimization algorithm for categorical colormaps. Moreland used a custom color space to create suitable divergent colormaps for scientific purposes [12]. Recently Samsel et al. presented an asymmetrical divergent colormap with a wide perceptual range for high resolution oceanic data [13].

While many alternative colormaps have been suggested, the community has been reluctant to accept a new default colormap or disregards the usage of any proposed new default. This has led to some works correcting the rainbow colormap manually and providing alternative defaults such as the normalized rainbow colormap [14].

Despite all of these works, the rainbow colormap is still widely used through different fields including scientific visualization. We believe that the rainbow colormap and other common and suboptimal colormaps are chosen by users for a reason and moving away from this bad practice must happen progressively to be effective.

## 3 Motivation

Figure 1 contains a compelling illustration of the poor aesthetics of the rainbow colormap in opposition to Matplotlib's default perceptual colormap (Viridis) [15]. However, people still use the rainbow for visualizing scientific data. Indeed, spatial variations of data are highlighted through a colormap's hue and saturation [1]. Nevertheless, the apparent first rule for a good colormap is that it be aesthetically pleasing. To evaluate what a good and pleasing colormap is we must first discuss how our eyes see and the role of color in vision.

### 3.1 Luminance

We see because of the relative presence or absence of light. We distinguish visual information from relative differences in luminance. Specifically, we are able to distinguish shape and edges by juxtaposition of different light tones. Edges emerge as what is dark abuts with what is light. Shape and dimension emerge from shades of luminance. Given the important dependence of luminance with sight, we even accept a monochromatic representation of reality, as with black and white photographs. Contrast provides primary meaning and information while color is secondary.

### 3.2 Chromaticity

Chromaticity is the information about the saturation and hue of a color. Although secondary to luminance in distinguishing visual information, chromaticity serves many purposes. Gradual changes in an image cannot be picked

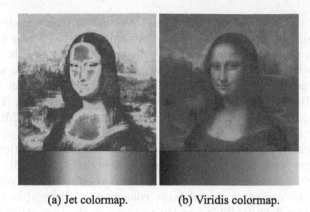

(a) Jet colormap.          (b) Viridis colormap.

**Fig. 1.** Typical example illustrating the aesthetics of a good (b) vs. a bad (a) colormap. (Color figure online)

up by only luminance while chromaticity is a stronger cue of low frequency values in an image [16]. Hue and saturation are also key components of aesthetics.

### 3.3   Good and Bad Colormaps

Even with the absence of ordered luminance, the rainbow colormap is still widely used. We believe that its dominant use is related to the following factors:

**Variety:** The many chromatic changes of the rainbow, while associated with creating false boundaries, do show structures in low frequency data.

**Aesthetics:** Many people find the vivid colors aesthetic.

**Prevalence:** Over the years, the scientific community has associated blue with lower and red with higher data values. Since this association has been consistently used, the rainbow has become conventional.

Based on the literature and the reasons behind choosing bad colormaps, we summarize four principles to be addressed in defining a good colormap:

**Order:** The colors should follow a perceptual order which is natural and intuitive for viewers to see. In this regard, luminance is known as the strongest cue of order.

**Monotonic luminance:** Luminance should change monotonically in order to avoid creating unreal boundaries.

**Perceptual uniformity:** The observed distance between two equal-sized segments of the colormap should be proportional to the distance between those points in the data.

**Chromaticity change:** The effects of chromaticity change must be taken into account. Although the grayscale colormap is ideal for high spatial frequency data, low spatial frequency values can be best visualized with changes in chromaticity.

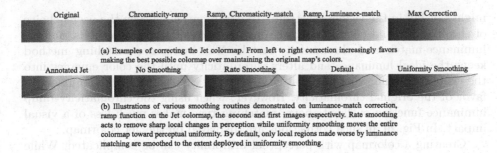

(a) Examples of correcting the Jet colormap. From left to right correction increasingly favors making the best possible colormap over maintaining the original map's colors.

(b) Illustrations of various smoothing routines demonstrated on luminance-match correction, ramp function on the Jet colormap, the second and first images respectively. Rate smoothing acts to remove sharp local changes in perception while uniformity smoothing moves the entire colormap toward perceptual uniformity. By default, only local regions made worse by luminance matching are smoothed to the extent deployed in uniformity smoothing.

**Fig. 2.** Examples of various correction capabilities and smoothing techniques used in our framework. (Color figure online)

## 4 Color Map Correction Framework

The basis of our correction framework is to define an ideal luminance ramp and then update the chromaticity or luminance values based on the other. In the following we describe the two main steps of our colormap correction framework and describe the smoothing routines that are applied after correction.

### 4.1 Luminance Functions

We define ideal luminance via a *luminance function*. The correction process is independent of these ramps so different types of colormaps, not just those with increasing luminance, are possible targets (see Sect. 5.3 for a luminance function alternate to those described here).

As the default, based on the first three principles above, we define the ideal luminance as a monotonically increasing ramp from 0 to 100 in the CIELUV color space. In this context the grayscale colormap with its linear luminance ramp is ideal. However, as discussed in Sect. 3, the grayscale colormap is not preferable over those with color for scientific visualization. We therefore offer a slight variation on the default we refer to as the chromaticity ramp. For this luminance function, the range across which we monotonically increase luminance is now from $[First_{min}, Last_{max}]$ where $First_{min} \geq 0$ is the minimum luminance for which the chromaticity of the left of edge of the original colormap and similarly $Last_{max} <= 100$ is set from the original colormap's right edge. We will demonstrate these and an alternate function (described in Sect. 5).

### 4.2 Correcting Chromaticity and Luminance

Depending on the type of data, chromaticity variations can help show subtle changes and provide aesthetic value. We believe this to be one of the reasons certain colormaps are chosen over gradient colormaps. However, one cannot simply change the luminance values of a colormap to an ideal luminance ramp to get the best of both worlds. There is an inevitable trade-off as the resulting colors might not fall in the visible spectrum. To compromise between the user's choice of chromaticity and ideal luminance, our method defines two methods, namely luminance-match and chromaticity-match. The luminance matching method keeps the ideal luminance and alters chromaticity until the color emerges into the visible spectrum while chromaticity matching changes the ideal luminance in favor of the original chromaticity. However, when using the chromaticity-ramp luminance function outlined above, matching type makes much less of a visual impact. In Fig. 2a all such corrections are displayed on the Jet colormap.

Creating a colormap with perceptual uniformity can be complicated. While utilizing a color space which is perceptually uniform (e.g. CIELUV) makes this possible, the significant impact luminance has on perception coupled with the nonlinear relationship between it and chromaticity creates difficulties. For example, in the CIELUV color space, the $u$ and $v$ components that define chromaticity are also functions of luminance $(L)$. Therefore to change chromaticity independently of luminance we convert $u$ and $v$ to the $u'$ and $v'$ coordinates of the uniform chromaticity diagram [17]. The relationship between the two is

$$u' = \frac{u}{13L} + u'_n$$
$$v' = \frac{v}{13L} + v'_n \tag{1}$$

where $u'_n$ and $v'_n$ are the chromaticity coordinates of a standard white point. In this work we use the standard illuminant C ($u'_n = 0.2009$, $v'_n = 0.4610$).

The luminance matching method is applied to every color of the original colormap. Algorithm 1 shows the luminance matching process. The arguments $L$, $U$ and $V$ refer to the Luv components of the original color while $L_{new}$ represents the new intended luminance. The algorithm starts by updating the $U$ and $V$ components with the new luminance since they are both functions of luminance as well as $U'$ and $V'$. It then finds the magnitude and normals that point to the standard white point from the current $U'$ and $V'$ in the chromaticity diagram. The algorithm then progressively updates $U'$ and $V'$ by a factor of a small number ($\epsilon$) until the color becomes visible. The reason behind moving the chromaticity components towards the white component is that in the CIELUV and CIELAB color systems the closer we are to the white component, chances of color visibility increases. At the white point itself, all luminance values result in valid grayscale colors. In our work, visibility of a color is determined by converting the color to RGB space and checking if the values are in the visible spectrum or not.

Luminance matching forces the ideal luminance ramp on the colormap. On the other side of the spectrum we have provided chromaticity matching that favors the original chromaticity over ideal luminance. To do this we used a similar method to Algorithm 1 but with some differences. In every iteration of chromaticity matching, if the color is not valid, the ideal luminance is updated and moved towards the original luminance. Figure 2a shows an example of chromaticity matching versus luminance matching on the Jet colormap. We can see how the chromaticity-matched result is more similar to the original colormap.

**Algorithm 1.** Set new luminance and update chromaticity until the color becomes visible

1: **procedure** LUMINANCEMATCH(L, U, V, $L_{new}$)

2:     $U \leftarrow U/L \times L_{new}$

3:     $V \leftarrow V/L \times L_{new}$

4:     $U' \leftarrow U'_n + U/(13L_{new})$

5:     $V' \leftarrow V'_n + V/(13L_{new})$

6:     $magnitude \leftarrow \sqrt{(U'_n - U')^2 + (V'_n - V')^2}$

7:     $U_{norm} \leftarrow (U'_n - U')/magnitude$

8:     $V_{norm} \leftarrow (V'_n - V')/magnitude$

9:     $color \leftarrow (L_{new}, U, V)$

10:    **while** $color$ is not visible **do**

11:        $U' \leftarrow U' + U_{norm} \times \epsilon \times magnitude$

12:        $V' \leftarrow V' + V_{norm} \times \epsilon \times magnitude$

13:        $color \leftarrow (L_{new}, (U' - U'_n) \times 13L_{new}, (V' - V'_n) \times 13L_{new})$

14:    **return** $color$

### 4.3 Smoothing

The images in Fig. 2b detail the full range of smoothing deployed in our framework. In each of these two curves are added to the colormap. The lighter is the luminance of the colormap and the darker is the distance in CIELUV of each color in the colormap to the left edge of the colormap. The first image shows these on our representative colormap to correct, Jet. The second image shows how luminance-first correction may create sharp perceptual changes; this is luminance-match correction of the luminance ramp.

The final three images show our different smoothing strategies applied to the second image, each of which accomplishes smoothing on sections of colormaps via interpolation through the CIELUV space. For *Rate* smoothing, the difference in perceptual change from each color in the colormap to both the previous and following colors of the map. Sections of the map for which the difference of these two values is greater than the average such distance are interpolated between the two colors that sandwich this reason, i.e. for the two colors for which this does not hold. This technique is similarly applied for each smoothing routine, what differentiates them is sections are selected. Rate smoothing acts to simply smooth any sharp perceptual changes and is always used as a final step in our framework.

The most disruptive smoothing, the final image of Fig. 2b, more directly smooths the colormap toward perceptual uniformity. In this case, the metric for selection is a range where the sum of perceptual difference between each color and its neighbors (rather than difference, as in rate smoothing) is above the average across the colormap. By default, the image between rate and uniformity smoothing, the same metric as uniformity smoothing is used, but only for ranges of the colormap where the sum of perceptual change is worse than in the original colormap. That is we believe luminance correction improves a colormap to the extent that color-based perceptual changes that are not worse than those found in the original colormap are an acceptable cost for incorporating the chromaticity of the original.

## 5    Results

### 5.1    Jet, Corrected

By applying representative matches of both chromaticity- and luminance-ramp functions to the Jet colormap, we can create the chromaticity-based and luminance-based versions shown in Fig. 3. We can see that the fully corrected colormap shows no artificial boundary but is very different from the original Jet colormap. The chromaticity-based colormap although less perceptually correct shows a good compromise between the original and the ideal and has a high perceptual change similar to the original. The chromaticity-based colormap also performs better than the luminance-based colormap in the low frequency test case because of the high change in chromaticity. However, the hurricane rendering shows that the luminance-based map performs better on high frequency data and faithfully exposes fine details.

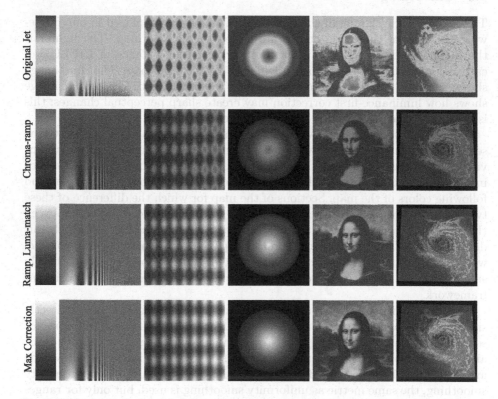

**Fig. 3.** The original Jet colormap along with the three types of corrections. (Color figure online)

## 5.2  All Things Corrected

In order to evaluate the generality of our approach we applied our colormap correction algorithm with maximum correction to all 67 Matplotlib colormaps. Figure 4 shows eighteen of the results. In the case of the "Accent" colormap,

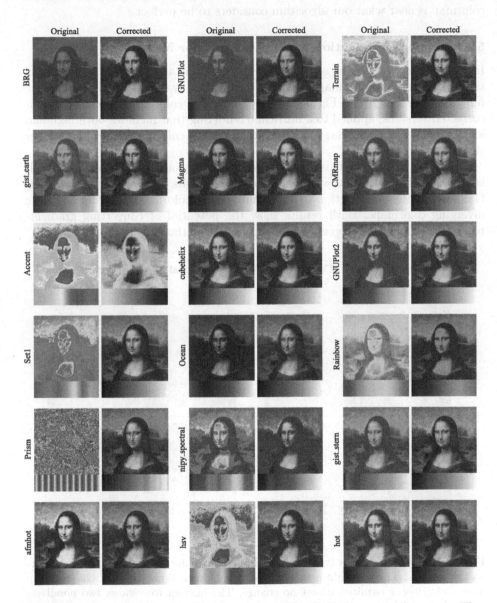

**Fig. 4.** Eighteen of the Matplotlib colormaps along with their corrected versions. The correction method used was matchLuminance using a luminance ramp. (Color figure online)

the luminance ramp was automatically set to [100, 0] based on the original colormap's luminance. In almost all cases the corrected colormaps are significantly better and more faithful to the data than the originals. In the case of Matplotlib's "Magma" colormap, we can see that apart from setting the low and high luminance values to 0 and 100, little has changed, showing that the original colormap is near what our algorithm considers to be perfect.

### 5.3   Luminance Function for Diverging Color Maps

In this section we look at some of the results of an alternate luminance function. For divergent colormaps, a Gaussian function was used as the luminance function. The first row of Fig. 5 shows two divergent colormaps, along with their corrected versions, applied to a hurricane rendering that includes both high and low frequency areas. Similar to Magma, the RdYlGn colormap from ColorBrewer shows almost no change.

Diverging colormaps have recently become more common in scientific visualization [18]. The bottom row of Fig. 5 shows the results of forcefully applying the Gaussian luminance function to two nondivergent colormaps in order to create diverging colormaps. Both results show the potential of converting gradient-based colormaps to divergent versions using our method.

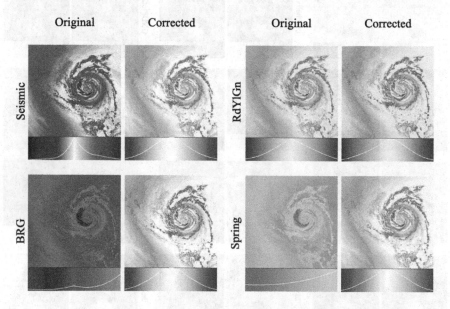

**Fig. 5.** The first row shows two divergent Matplotlib colormaps along with their corrected versions. The top-right example shows that the well-known RdYlGn colormap from ColorBrewer requires almost no change. The bottom row shows two nondivergent colormaps that are forcefully diverged using a Gaussian function as the alternate luminance function. (Color figure online)

# 6    Conclusion and Future Work

In this work we have proposed a color-theoretic approach which we believe to be generally applicable for creating useful and aesthetic colormaps using well-worn colormaps as inspiration. This work is also rich in potential for future directions. First, a user study or perceptual evaluation would help qualify the effectiveness of our approach in improving the perception of or understanding of scientific data. Moreover at even this early stage we have applied multiple corrections to a large set of colormaps. Each application offers the opportunity to visualize and conceptualize a quantifiable relationship between a colormap before and after correction. Such insights are invaluable for iterative improvement (indeed, we found guidance in the creation of luminance functions) but also represent a step toward addressing the dissonance between visualization and graphic design.

# References

1. Rogowitz, B.E., Treinish, L.A.: Data visualization: the end of the rainbow. IEEE Spectr. **35**, 52–59 (1998)
2. Borland, D., Taylor, R.M.: Rainbow color map (still) considered harmful. IEEE Comput. Graph. Appl. **27**, 14–17 (2007)
3. Ware, C.: Information Visualization: Perception for Design. Elsevier, Amsterdam (2012)
4. Rogowitz, B.E., Kalvin, A.D.: The "which blair project": a quick visual method for evaluating perceptual color maps. In: Proceedings of Visualization, VIS 2001, pp. 183–556. IEEE (2001)
5. Ware, C.: Color sequences for univariate maps: theory, experiments and principles. IEEE Comput. Graph. Appl. **8**, 41–49 (1988)
6. Levkowitz, H.: Color Theory and Modeling for Computer Graphics, Visualization and Mutlimedia Applications. Kluwer Academid Publishers, Norwell (1997)
7. Green, D.A.: A colour scheme for the display of astronomical intensity images. Bull. Astron. Soc. India **39**, 289–295 (2011)
8. van der Walt, S., Smith, N.: A better default colormap for Matplotlib. In: SciPy 2015, Austin, TX, 6–12 July 2015 (2015)
9. Brewer, C.A., Hatchard, G.W., Harrower, M.A.: Colorbrewer in print: a catalog of color schemes for maps. Cartogr. Geogr. Inf. Sci. **30**, 5–32 (2003)
10. Wijffelaars, M., Vliegen, R., Van Wijk, J.J., Van Der Linden, E.J.: Generating color palettes using intuitive parameters. In: Computer Graphics Forum, vol. 27, pp. 743–750. Wiley Online Library (2008)
11. Lee, S., Sips, M., Seidel, H.P.: Perceptually driven visibility optimization for categorical data visualization. IEEE Trans. Vis. Comput. Graph. **19**, 1746–1757 (2013)
12. Moreland, K.: Diverging color maps for scientific visualization. In: Bebis, G., Boyle, R., Parvin, B., Koracin, D., Kuno, Y., Wang, J., Pajarola, R., Lindstrom, P., Hinkenjann, A., Encarnação, M.L., Silva, C.T., Coming, D. (eds.) ISVC 2009. LNCS, vol. 5876, pp. 92–103. Springer, Heidelberg (2009). doi:10.1007/978-3-642-10520-3_9
13. Samsel, F., Petersen, M., Geld, T., Abram, G., Wendelberger, J., Ahrens, J.: Colormaps that improve perception of high-resolution ocean data. In: Proceedings of the 33rd Annual ACM Conference Extended Abstracts on Human Factors in Computing Systems, pp. 703–710. ACM (2015)

14. Gresh, D.: Self-corrected perceptual colormaps (2010)
15. Garnier, S.: viridis: Matplotlib default color map. R package version 0.2 (2015)
16. Rogowitz, B.E., Treinish, L.A., Bryson, S., et al.: How not to lie with visualization. Comput. Phys. **10**, 268–273 (1996)
17. Robertson, A.R.: The CIE 1976: color-difference formulae. Color Res. Appl. **2**, 7–11 (1977)
18. Zhou, L., Hansen, C.: A survey of colormaps in visualization (2015)

# Interpolation-Based Extraction of Representative Isosurfaces

Oliver Fernandes[✉], Steffen Frey, and Thomas Ertl

VISUS Visualization Research Institute, University of Stuttgart, Stuttgart, Germany
`oliver.fernandes@visus.uni-stuttgart.de`

**Abstract.** We propose a novel technique for the automatic, similarity-based selection of representative surfaces. While our technique can be applied to any set of manifolds, we particularly focus on isosurfaces from volume data. We select representatives from sets of surfaces stemming from varying isovalues or time-dependent data. For selection, our approach interpolates between surfaces using a minimum cost flow solver, and determines whether the interpolate adequately represents the actual surface in-between. For this, we employ the Hausdorff distance as an intuitive measure of the similarity of two components. In contrast to popular contour tree-based approaches which are limited to changes in topology, our approach also accounts for geometric deviations. For interactive visualization, we employ a combination of surface renderings and a graph view that depicts the selected surfaces and their relation. We finally demonstrate the applicability and utility of our approach by means of several data sets from different areas.

## 1 Introduction

The visual analysis of surfaces is an important task in many different domains, including a variety of medical applications and engineering. While the approach presented in this paper can deal with arbitrary surface representations, in the following, we mainly focus our discussion on isosurfaces generated from volume data. This data can be obtained through measurements via scanners (e.g. medical CTs, but also material testing for industrial applications), or simulations. Additionally, data may be static or time-dependent. While three dimensional scalar fields represent a common data type in scientific visualization, the complexity of these data sets increases steadily with their size. A default tool used to examine them is the generation of isosurfaces for a given threshold value. However, selecting threshold values showing the interesting features of the data set is aggravated by several problems. With the infinite possibilities of thresholds to choose from, manually identifying the more interesting isosurfaces can be very tedious.

In the following, we discuss our approach to determine characteristic isosurfaces based on transportation-based interpolation. We review related work in Sect. 2, and give on overview on our approach in Sect. 3. In particular, we contribute the following:

© Springer International Publishing AG 2016
G. Bebis et al. (Eds.): ISVC 2016, Part I, LNCS 10072, pp. 403–413, 2016.
DOI: 10.1007/978-3-319-50835-1_37

- our approach to determine interpolated surfaces and their similarity w.r.t. a reference (Sect. 4)
- the matching of similar surfaces across time or isolevels (Sect. 5)
- determining characteristic surfaces on the basis of the similarity between interpolate and reference (Sect. 6)

We evaluate our approach, and discuss its merits and limitations in Sect. 7. We finally conclude our work in Sect. 8.

## 2    Related Work

**Isosurface Extraction and Rendering.** For uniform grids based on trilinear interpolation, classical Marching Cubes (MC) [1] and variants are the most popular to explicitly extract isosurfaces, and are used as a basis for isosurfaces in this paper. Other approaches use Voronoi diagrams [2], advancing front techniques [3], and meshing from point clouds [4]. An overview on quad meshing techniques is given by Bommes et al. [5]. Theisel [6] represents the contours of a piecewise trilinear scalar field as trimmed surfaces of triangular rational cubic Bézier patches. For isosurface extraction from higher-order data, quad mesh generation techniques [7], contouring [8], and approximate isocontouring [9] have been proposed. Approaches for rendering implicit surfaces include BlobTrees [10] and raytracing with both interval and affine arithmetic [11].

**Isosurface Selection.** A prominent approach for selecting characteristic representatives is the contour tree, which can be used to track the evolution of the topology of isosurfaces. A good overview of methods generating the graph is given by Biasotti et al. [12], and many improvements have been made towards efficiently employing the contour tree in arbitrary dimensions, e.g. Carr et al. [13]. Another approach is collecting statistical information on the scalar field [14,15], and selecting thresholds based on these results.

**Isosurface Similarity and Morphing.** Several methods for comparing surfaces for their similarity and consequentially morphing them have been proposed. With the Hausdorff distance being very intuitive and generally applicable, and in addition fast to compute [16], it is a choice similarity metric for two comparing two surfaces. The method in Bruckner et al. [17] enables automatic selection of isosurfaces based on an entropy similarity metric. It is noteworthy to mention, that while [17] generally takes a similar approach, our method differs as we do not necessarily require an underlying continuous representation as a scalar field. Unlike their entropy-based similarity metric (which requires an continuously defined/interpolated data set), our approach, based solely on the Hausdorff distance metric, works on arbitrary point cloud sets, including ones derived e.g. from analytically defined and higher order surfaces. The goal of the technique proposed by Wei et al. in [18] is to verify that a set of isosurfaces are sufficient to represent the entire scalar field. This is complementary to our technique, and may be used to set up the input set to our method.

# 3   Overview

In this work, we propose a novel technique for the automatic, similarity-based selection of representative surfaces, chosen from a set of surfaces constructed by varying a generating parameter like threshold value or time. Note that this 'base' set is acquired from a different source, e.g. using an isovalue threshold sweep, or employing complementary algorithms as mentioned in Sect. 2. We rely on two different similarity metrics in this work (Sect. 4): (1) the Hausdorff distance for fast computation, and (2) the scalable Minimum Cost Flow (MCF) Distance, which in addition to similarity also yields an surface interpolation scheme, used in the refinement step later on. First, our approach uses a low-accuracy, high-speed variant of the MCF Distance to do a comparison between connected components for consecutive thresholds. This establishes a set of so-called paths approximating the evolution of individual components similar to a contour tree (Sect. 5). In the refinement step, a component's change along a path is examined, by first calculating a linear interpolation between the first and the last component of a path using the MCF Interpolation. All components of the path are then compared to their appropriately evaluated interpolate using the fast and accurate Hausdorff distance. Provided the similarity distance exceeds a user-defined threshold, the path is subdivided at the deviating (and therefore representative) surface, and the sub-paths are retested.

# 4   Distances and Interpolation Between Isosurfaces

To decide if two arbitrary surfaces are similar, several metrics with different properties can be employed. In our approach we use two different schemes, Hausdorff distance and Minimum Cost Flow (MCF) Distance. We also employ a point cloud interpolation, which maps samples of a surface to samples of a different surface, invoking a MCF solver. In this section, we give a short overview of employed metrics and how the MCF Distance calculation yields an interpolation for two point clouds.

**Hausdorff Distance.** As mentioned earlier, we calculate the Hausdorff distance between surfaces, which is the supremum of the pairwise shortest distance from all points of one surface compared to the other. The mathematical definition also works on arbitrary point sets. One can easily see that taking a subset of points from the surfaces and calculating the Hausdorff distance for these will yield a good approximation for the surfaces themselves, while a uniform sampling with density based on largest surface area ensures a reasonable accuracy. Another important trait of the Hausdorff distance is that no further information is required, rendering it applicable for arbitrary geometry.

**Minimum Cost Flow Distance.** In this paragraph, we first explain the MCF problem, and then how it maps to a similarity function. Given two sets of nodes, sources and targets, weighted edges between sources and targets are established. A quantity $Q$ is defined on all nodes, while the sources get positive values, the targets gets negative ones. The sum of $Q$ over both the source and target set must be exactly zero. The problem is now to move the quantity along the given edges, so that each node has zero quantity after the procedure. Depending on the edges available, this problem can be usually be solved in numerous ways. An additional condition can be imposed by requiring the so-called cost $C$ to be minimal. $C$ can be calculated by multiplying the weight of an edge with the amount of quantity moved across this edge, and summing this up for all edges participating in the solution. This severely reduces the number of possible solutions, very often the global minimum of $C$ is unique.

The solution and it's cost $C$ of a MCF problem can be mapped to a distance function between two point sets $A$ and $B$ using the following rules:

- Without limiting the generality of the mapping we declare the points in $A$ to be the sources, and the points in $B$ to be the targets.
- By connecting a point from $A$ with a point from $B$ we define an edge, and set its weight (i.e. cost) to the Euclidean distance between the points. This is done for all possible pairings.
- Each source node gets the quantity 1, each target receives -1.
- To fulfill the prerequisite of having a sum of exactly zero, the necessary amount of quantity (either positive or negative) gets distributed randomly to the set with less nodes (points).

Unlike the Hausdorff distance, the MCF distance additionally yields a direct point to point assignment, which is also useful for interpolation.

**Minimum Cost Flow Interpolation.** Executing the MCF algorithm will yield an assignment for each point of the set containing fewer points, to one or more points of the set containing more points. Per definition, all edges will be transporting exactly none or one unit (since both sets initially receive only 1 unit, either negative or positive). The assignments defined are simply the edges transporting a unit of the quantity. The Hausdorff distance definition may be used in a similar way, by assigning each point its closest neighbor of the other set. This will however introduce a heavy bias for certain points, e.g. the protruding peaks of a surface, since there is no limit on how many points are allowed to be mapped, which is avoided by the MCF solution.

## 5    Determining Component Evolution

As a preliminary similarity association, a coarse pre-matching is applied to connected components of consecutive isolevels, with the goal of associating a component $c_s \in C^s$ for an isolevel $\rho_i$ to it's most similar candidate $c_t \in C^t$ for $\rho_{i+1}$. Performing this for all components at all isolevels will yield something similar to a contour tree, but based solely on point geometry (as opposed to topology). The matching of components for consecutive isolevels is done by executing the following two steps.

**Determine Component Similarity.** The first step is performed by comparing the connected components with each other. For each component $c_s, s \in 1 \ldots n$

and $c_t, t \in 1 \ldots m$, where $n, m$ denotes the number of components in $\rho_i, \rho_{i+1}$ respectively, the surface is sampled uniformly (with respect to the surface area), but fairly coarse. All resulting point clouds of $C^s$ are compared pairwise to all point clouds associated with $C^t$, and the MCF distance metric (as explained in Subsect. 4) is applied, with the calculated distance $d$ resembling a (coarse) measure for their similarity.

**Find Best Association.** If the connected components are interpreted as nodes of a graph $G$, the pairs $(c_s, c_t)$ can be interpreted as directed edges, with $d$ being an associated edge value, and the direction being defined by increasing $\rho$. The first $k$ edges, ordered by similarity $d$, are then added to the graph $G$, where $k = \max(n, m)$, while any edges containing a node already part of an edge in $G$ are skipped. This leaves at the most one associating edge for each component in $\rho_i$ and $\rho_{i+1}$. This is repeated for all isolevels $\rho_{\min} < \rho_i < \rho_{\max}$, and the graph $G$ is defined containing all connected components of all isolevels as nodes, and edges connecting each node to their most similar component at the previous and next isolevel. The sub-graphs defined by a set of nodes which are connected by a series of edges will be called path $P$. Components which have exactly one edge, or none (i.e. the first and the last component $c_f, c_l$ of a path), can be considered as candidates for representative surfaces. The resulting graph has some similarities to a contour tree, but additionally also has a few advantages. It already gives an impression of the similarity (determined as $d$) between components on a path $P$, which, in a contour tree, would simply be represented on a single edge. The above procedure will already yield representative surfaces similar to a contour tree. Even though this step will cover all correct matches for components, it might produce false positives. This can happen since the algorithm always picks a best match, even if there aren't any "true" matches left. In addition, a slight change of geometry on each increase of $\rho_i$ can easily accumulate to a significant change of geometry from the first to the last node of a path. Hence a more accurate scheme is needed to augment this fast but coarse pre-selection.

# 6    Refining Selection of Characteristic Isosurfaces

Even though the information gathered in the first step described in Sect. 5 already yields a significant set of representative surfaces (by choosing the first and last components of established paths), potentially interesting candidates could be missed within a path, and false connections might still be in there. Since the first and last nodes of a path $P$ are already marked as representative components, the intermediate nodes now need to be examined. To find other potential candidates $c_o \in P$, which differ significantly from both the first or last component, a linear interpolation scheme is executed and Hausdorff similarity metric applied. The following scheme is iterated on each path $P$ to find further candidates.

**Determine Similarity by Interpolation.** More specifically, to determine if an original surface $c_o$ shows enough similarity to both the first and last component

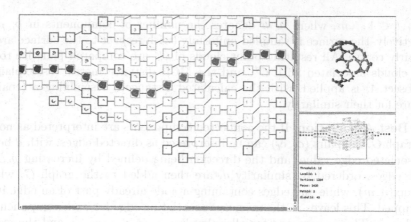

**Fig. 1.** Screen capture of the interactive graph tool. The main view shows the graph in detail with the nodes showing renders of the appropriate component. The top right view shows a detailed render of a selected node, while the lower shows statistical of a node or path. The overview window to the middle right assists in navigating the graph. (Color figure online)

$c_f$ and $c_l$ in a path $P$, a linear interpolation is performed between point clouds derived from $c_f$ and $c_l$ as explained in Sect. 4. The employed point clouds are again uniformly distributed samples, but unlike in Sect. 5, the resampling here is fairly dense (with respect to surface areas of $c_f$ and $c_l$), to ensure a reasonably accurate interpolation between the point clouds of the components.

The linear interpolation $c_i$ is then evaluated at an interpolation parameter $t$ based on the square root $a$ of the surface areas of $c_f, c_l$ and $c_o$ using $t = (a_o - a_f)/(a_l - a_f)$. This ensures that, if a surface changes exactly linear, it will also be perfectly interpolated by $c_i$.

Conversely, the Hausdorff distance $d_{oi}$ between original component $c_o$ and interpolated component $c_i$ is a measure for geometrical deviations from $c_l, c_f$, which might change the visual appearance of the component significantly.

**Subdivide Paths.** If any of the comparisons $d_{oi}$ for the interpolated component $c_i$ to the corresponding original component $c_o$ yields a difference greater than a user-defined threshold $\epsilon$, the deviation is considered significant, and the path needs to be subdivided. To reach a meaningful subdivision, the tested sub-path is increased incrementally. This means, a sub-path starting at the first $c_{f'} = c_f$ and ending two nodes along the path, at $c_{l'} = c_{f+2}$, is defined. If all nodes $c_i$ between $c_{f'}$ and $c_{l'}$ fulfill the interpolation similarity as defined above, a node is added to the sub-path, $l' = l' + 1$, and the entire sub-path is retested. If the test fails at any given intermediate node $c_i$, the path is subdivided at the current $l'$. The procedure is reiterated and sub-path now starts on the first unsuccessfully added node, setting $c_{f'} = c_{l'}$, and $c_{l'} = c_{l'+2}$. The algorithm completes when $l' \geq l$, i.e. the current sub-path's end surpasses path $P$'s end. The nodes $c_{f'}, c_{l'}$ of each sub-path are added to the characteristic set $S$. Note that per construction,

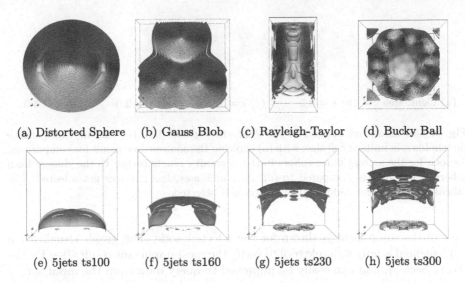

(a) Distorted Sphere    (b) Gauss Blob    (c) Rayleigh-Taylor    (d) Bucky Ball

(e) 5jets ts100    (f) 5jets ts160    (g) 5jets ts230    (h) 5jets ts300

**Fig. 2.** Images giving an impression for the input data sets. (a) A radially increasing scalar field, with an added distortion in $x$ direction. (b) Three gauss functions of varying intensity summed up to produce the scalar field. (c) Time step 14 of the Rayleigh-Taylor data set. (d) The C60 molecule in a scalar data field representation. (e)–(h) A fixed threshold generates surfaces for various time steps of the 5jets data set.

all nodes on the sub-paths can be approximated by linear interpolation from the characteristic nodes (within the error of $\epsilon$).

## 7    Results

To demonstrate the usability of the approach, we applied the technique to several data sets. Data set size range from $64^3$ to $128 \times 128 \times 256$. An impression of the input data sets is given in Fig. 2. The renderings are clipped to better see the contours for a subset of the isosurfaces. In all data sets for which the threshold value is varied, it ranges from minimum to maximum scalar value of the corresponding data set (except for *Bucky Ball*, see below), on 30–32 intervals. For the *5jets* data set, every tenth time step was used from time step 100 to 300. All calculations were performed on a Intel(R) Core(TM) i7-2600K CPU @ 3.40 GHz. For each data set, we give a render of the complete set of selected isosurface components (Fig. 4), clipped to better show the results. Below the renderings of all data sets the graph $G$ is drawn, showing components as square nodes, sorted by isovalue from left to right, and longer paths closer to the center on the vertical axis. Components selected by the algorithm are highlighted in red. Edges show the preliminary paths established. The graph is also interactive, and may be used to acquire additional information about components and paths, as seen in Fig. 1. For this, paths can be selected, and while selected nodes are highlighted with a blue outline, associated data is displayed on the right. A detail

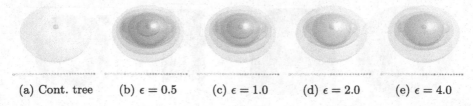

(a) Cont. tree    (b) $\epsilon = 0.5$    (c) $\epsilon = 1.0$    (d) $\epsilon = 2.0$    (e) $\epsilon = 4.0$

**Fig. 3.** Our algorithm applied to the *Distorted Sphere* data set for varying distance thresholds $\epsilon$, in units of cell size, with (a) showing the contour tree result for comparison. As seen for the second inner sphere in (b), a small $\epsilon$ reacts earlier to the change from spherical to elliptical compared to (c). As $\epsilon$ increases, less surfaces get selected. The salient surface in the middle range always gets selected.

view of the component is shown for the selected node. The graph visualization implemented is only a simple tool to verify the most important results (see Future Work, Sect. 8), and can easily be improved to query data from the input set.

**Distorted Sphere.** This data set, shown in Fig. 3, is the first synthetic data set, and serves to give an impression of how the user-defined Hausdorff distance error $\epsilon$ affects the selection of isosurfaces. As is to be expected, fewer isolevels are selected for increasing $\epsilon$. Obviously the technique selects more isosurfaces characteristic to the data set than the contour tree, which would simply be two nodes for maximum/minimum isovalue, missing the salient surface in between.

**Gauss Blob.** Figure 4a shows the second synthetic data set. This data set highlights how the algorithm handles changes in the contour tree. As can be easily be discerned from the graph, the first step creates the "contour tree", encoded in the node connections. Even though the algorithm does not show the actual merging (like a contour tree would), it successfully determines all involved components as characteristic, as well as selecting a few additional isovalues, since they differ enough from the surfaces associated with topology changes.

**Rayleigh-Taylor.** To get a clear view of the results obtained for the Rayleigh-Taylor instability, the surfaces have been rendered opaque, and a clipping plane was introduced. Comparing Fig. 4(c) with the input (see Fig. 2(c)) one can see that many cluttering surfaces have been removed. However, the most distinct features are still visible, as well a few supporting isolevels selected by our algorithm. The corresponding graph can be used to further investigate the selected surfaces.

**5jets.** Being a time series of isosurfaces, intersecting surfaces may occur, which however get handled by the algorithm directly. Since the myriad of surfaces would severely hinder exploration due to occlusion, we have picked a component (i.e. an edge in the contour tree) in the interactive graph and show its evolution over several isolevels (Fig. 4d), in terms of the surfaces selected by our algorithm. The corresponding path is shown on the graph below.

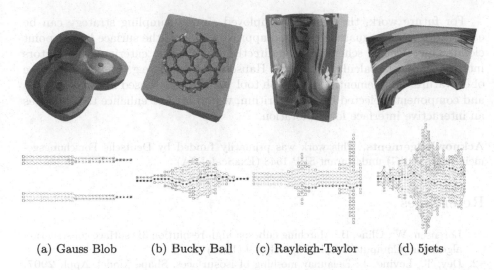

|          (a) Gauss Blob | (b) Bucky Ball | (c) Rayleigh-Taylor | (d) 5jets |

**Fig. 4.** Isosurfaces selected by our algorithm for the respective data sets, including the generated graph. For the time series data in (d), a contour tree edge is chosen (blue path in graph) and the isosurfaces selected by the scheme are shown. The Gauss example (a) includes a contour tree (lower graph) for comparison. (Color figure online)

**Bucky Ball.** For this dataset, a sub-range of thresholds was chosen as input, where the main feature of the data set disintegrates into smaller components. As can be seen in Fig. 4b, the boundary regions form a path dominating the graph. The splitting of the main feature components, as well as the evolution of the sub components can be easily extracted from the graph. Note that most selections are topology changes, correctly identified as characteristic surfaces.

## 8    Conclusion

We proposed a novel technique for automatically selecting a set of representative surfaces according to a minimum cost flow-based similarity metric. While our approach works for arbitrary sets of surfaces, we focussed on isosurfaces in the context of this paper. Here, we changed either the threshold value for a fixed time, or the time was varied for a fixed threshold. We demonstrated that our technique enabled a detailed selection of representative isosurfaces, based on the changes in geometry, as the isosurface threshold is varied. To achieve this, connected components of isosurfaces with increasing threshold are matched using a similarity measure derived from the cost of matching points of the surface with a minimum cost flow algorithm. However, even though geometrical changes accumulate over several steps, the individual distances cannot be simply added. We remedy this by interpolating a component's surface over a threshold range, employing the minimum cost flow algorithm again to obtain the interpolation. Based on the Hausdorff distance of the interpolated surface to the original, additional threshold values are added to the representative set.

For future work, the currently employed simple sampling strategy can be easily improved, to guarantee a good approximation of the surface by the point cloud. The selection scheme can be directly improved by entering other factors into the similarity calculation besides Hausdorff distance, e.g. employing change of curvature. Supplementing the graph tool with a query-based filtering of paths and components selected by the algorithm, would further enhance the utility as an interactive interface for exploration.

**Acknowledgements.** This work was primarily funded by Deutsche Forschungsgemeinschaft (DFG) under grant SPP 1648 (ExaScaleFSA).

# References

1. Lorensen, W., Cline, H.: Marching cubes: a high resolution 3D surface construction algorithm. Comput. Graph. **21**, 163–169 (1987)
2. Dey, T., Levine, J.: Delaunay meshing of isosurfaces. Shape Model. Appl. **2007**, 241–250 (2007)
3. Schreiner, J., Scheidegger, C., Silva, C.: High-quality extraction of isosurfaces from regular and irregular grids. TVCG **12**, 1205–1212 (2006)
4. Scheidegger, C.E., Fleishman, S., Silva, C.T.: Triangulating point set surfaces with bounded error. In: EG symposium on Geometry processing (2005)
5. Bommes, D., Lévy, B., Pietroni, N., Puppo, E., Silva, C., Tarini, M., Zorin, D.: Quad meshing. In: Eurographics, The Eurographics Association, pp. 159–182 (2012)
6. Theisel, H.: Exact isosurfaces for marching cubes. Comput. Graph. Forum **21**, 19–32 (2002)
7. Remacle, J.F., Henrotte, F., Baudouin, T., Geuzaine, C., Béchet, E., Mouton, T., Marchandise, E.: A frontal Delaunay quad mesh generator. In: 20th Meshing Roundtable, pp. 455–472 (2012)
8. Wiley, D.F., Childs, H.R., Gregorski, B.F., Hamann, B., Joy, K.I.: Contouring curved quadratic elements. In: VisSym, p. 1 (2003)
9. Pagot, C.A., Vollrath, J., Sadlo, F., Weiskopf, D., Ertl, T., Comba, J.: Interactive isocontouring of high-order surfaces. In: Scientific Visualization (2011)
10. Shirazian, P., Wyvill, B., Duprat, J.L.: Polygonization of implicit surfaces on multi-core architectures with SIMD instructions. In: EGPGV, pp. 89–98 (2012)
11. Knoll, A., Hijazi, Y., Kensler, A., Schott, M., Hansen, C.D., Hagen, H.: Fast ray tracing of arbitrary implicit surfaces. CGF **28**, 26–40 (2009)
12. Biasotti, S., De Floriani, L., Falcidieno, B., Frosini, P., Giorgi, D., Landi, C., Papaleo, L., Spagnuolo, M.: Describing shapes by geometrical-topological properties of real functions. ACM Comput. Surv. **40**, 12:1–12:87 (2008)
13. Carr, H., Snoeyink, J., van de Panne, M.: Flexible isosurfaces: simplifying and displaying scalar topology using the contour tree. CGTA **43**, 42–58 (2010)
14. Khoury, M., Wenger, R.: On the fractal dimension of isosurfaces. IEEE Trans. Vis. Comput. Graph. **16**, 1198–1205 (2010)
15. Tenginakai, S., Lee, J., Machiraju, R.: Salient iso-surface detection with model-independent statistical signatures. In: IEEE Visualization (2001)

16. Tang, M., Lee, M., Kim, Y.J.: Interactive Hausdorff distance computation for general polygonal models. ACM Trans. Graph. **28**, 74:1–74:9 (2009)
17. Bruckner, S., Möller, T.: Isosurface similarity maps. Comput. Graph. Forum **29**, 773–782 (2010). EuroVis 2010 best paper award
18. Wei, T.H., Lee, T.Y., Shen, H.W.: Evaluating isosurfaces with level-set-based information maps. Comput. Graph. Forum **32**, 1–10 (2013)

# Image-Based Post-processing for Realistic Real-Time Rendering of Scenes in the Presence of Fluid Simulations and Image-Based Lighting

Julian Puhl[1], Martin Knuth[2], and Arjan Kuijper[1,2](✉)

[1] Technische Universität Darmstadt, Darmstadt, Germany
[2] Fraunhofer IGD, Darmstadt, Germany
arjan.kuijper@igd.fraunhofer.de

**Abstract.** For real-time fluid simulation currently two methods are available: grid-based simulation and particle-based simulation. They both approximate the simulation of a fluid and have in common that they do not directly generate a visually pleasant surface. Due to time constraints, the subsequent generation of the fluid surface may not consume much time. What is usually generated is an approximate surface, which consists of many individual mesh elements and has no optical properties of a fluid. The visualization of a fluid in image space may contain different detail densities depending on the distance between observer and the fluid. Therefore, filters need to be applied in order to smooth these details to a consistent surface. Many approaches use strong filters in this step, which results in a too smooth surface. To this surface then noise is added in order to give it a rough appearance. To avoid this ad-hoc approach we present a post-processing approach of the direct visualization of the simulation data via image processing applications by both smoothing filters and an image pyramid. Our presented approach based on an image pyramid provides access to various levels of detail. These are used as a controllable low pass filter. Thus, different amounts of smoothing can be selected depending on the distance to the viewer, granting a better surface reconstruction.

## 1 Introduction and Motivation

For real-time simulation of fluids one has the choice between simulation of the cells of a grid-based approach or simulation of particles to mimic the fluid behavior [1,2]. Both approaches have in common that they do not create a smooth surface but only an approximate one. It is rough, consists of many individual elements and also has no nice optical properties of a fluid, see e.g. Youtube videos ID U3acQ5dDKEs and BIjj3Qcmbf4. In real-time simulation and visualization, the subsequent generation of the surface cannot be time consuming [3].

For this reason we tackle the post-processing of the simulation data via (fast) image processing. We analyze the application of smoothing filters as well as an image pyramid as a tunable low pass filter. The advantage of the image pyramid is its simultaneous availability of several details levels to choose from.

© Springer International Publishing AG 2016
G. Bebis et al. (Eds.): ISVC 2016, Part I, LNCS 10072, pp. 414–425, 2016.
DOI: 10.1007/978-3-319-50835-1_38

**Fig. 1.** A scene rendered with our proposed method.

This allows it to be used as a dynamically adjustable filter dependent on the current scene state. This is necessary, since in the post-processing step surfaces near the viewer require larger filter kernels then the ones farther away. Thus, if not properly handled either too many details of the single simulation elements are visible, or the contours are lost and the surface appears too smooth with no details anymore. An often found approach found in literature uses the latter and adds noise later on in order to artificially roughen the surface's optical appearance. When the surface is generated, distance and normal vector information exist and can be used for normal lighting approaches. We overcome these problems and ad-hoc approaches by our real-time multi-scale post-processing method. Our approach provides access to various levels of detail which are used as a controllable low-pass filter. We are therefore able to select different amounts of smoothing, depending on the distance to the viewer and therefore granting a better surface reconstruction. An example of the visual results is given in Fig. 1. More details of our approach can be found in [4].

## 2   Related Work and Theoretical Background

To generate a fluid-like appearance from fluid simulation data in real time, several approaches exist. In [5] the authors smooth the surface in screen-space and are investigating an alternative to Gaussian and Bilateral filters. The authors of [6] generate a surface from a point cloud utilizing a modified Marching squares variant. Macklin et al. [7] used an alternative simulation algorithm. This is combined with real-time rendering based on the methods of Van der Laan et al. [5] and Yu and Turk [8]. A real-time approach to simulation and display of fluids is presented by Goswami et al. [9] utilizing CUDA. Non of them achieve nice-looking real-time results for larger data sets, though.

In a Bilateral Filter, smoothing is performed while taking edges into account. The filter uses two functions; one of them is used for the smoothing, and the other one for calculating the distance. Usually, a Gaussian function with parameter $\sigma^2 = 2$ can be chosen for the standard deviation [10] for both. The result is a smoothed image of which the edges are preserved.

Image-Based Lighting is based on the idea of having the light-source far away and surrounding a local, small scene [11]. The small scene is approximated to a point in the center of the light-source. This allows one to store lighting information inside an environment map, since the same direction will always hit the same spot on the map [12]. Thus, effects such as reflection and refraction can be implemented with very little computational effort: the incoming beam is accordingly reflected or refracted before it returns a color value. The technique goes back to Paul Debevec's rendering with natural light that uses a so called light-probe, to generate 360° panoramic images and using them for static lighting [13]. The information is thus derived from the recording instead of from multiple simulated light sources [14].

If a scene is rendered with conventional hardware by current rasterization methods (via DirectX, OpenGL, etc.), depth information is stored in the depth buffer (or Z-buffer) of the graphics card. Its values are scaled from the viewer from zero to one (maximum depth) and nonlinear, i.e. the distance between the individual values becomes always higher on a linear scale, the greater the distance to the viewer is. The reason for this is the perspective projection: the distance is linear in the case of orthogonal projection. Since objects in the distance are far smaller, the precision loss is rather negligible than at short distances to the observer. In addition, the area between two planes, the near and far clipping plane, is scaled. These are located in the viewer's space perpendicular to the $z$-axis. Only the $z$-coordinates of the planes are freely selectable. Anything that is out of range is not rendered. By appropriate choice of the limits, the precision can be adapted to suit the application [15].

## 3    Our Approach

The goal of this work is to derive a good looking surface of the fluid in screen space in real-time. Our approach consists of three steps: First we render the fluid as particles in the screen buffer [16,17]. The resulting depth values are then smoothed with our approach. We finally construct the surface based on these smoothed depth values. Smoothing the depth values melts the single particles into one volumetric continuum As it blurs the boundaries of each single particle. The quality of the result is highly dependent on the amount of low-pass filtering (i.e.: blurring). Additionally, the scene can be viewed from different angles and distances. Therefore, it is necessary to control the degree of filtering depending on the current view of the scene. Note that we do also real-time rendering! To achieve this, we use an image pyramid of the depth values. In contrast to classical mipmapping, we additionally introduce a low pass filtering to each reduction step. Since the filter type influences the result, we compare different filter variants.

### 3.1    Generation of the Depth Values

First, the individual particles are rendered in order to extract their depth values. Due to perspective projection, and the resulting non-linear scaled values in the

Depth-buffer, we normalize the Z-coordinates from the view space by the distance to the clip plane far away: $z_{norm} = z/z_{far}$. This normalization is necessary to obtain linearity. Otherwise the results of the filtering afterward are wrong.

## 3.2   Construction of the Image Pyramid

Based on these depth values the image pyramid is build. For generating the individual stages, the image of the previous stage must be reduced by a factor 2 and then smoothed. Basically, four pixels of the source image will be merged into one pixel of the target image with halve the size. Clearly, different approaches are possible. For the arithmetic mean value, the average value of the four pixels is taken. However, since edges should not be affected, edge pixels must be ignored. For the median value, the four pixels are sorted based on their value and the center value is taken. If the number of values is even, the arithmetic mean of the two middle ones is taken used. Here, we deal with this case. For this reason, we evaluate various variants in addition to the arithmetic mean: First, the larger or smaller value is chosen, called Median$_H$ or Median$_V$ respectively. Second, depending on the difference between the two values, either the arithmetic mean is calculated or the larger or smaller value is used, called Median$_{DH}$ or Median$_{DV}$, respectively.

The size of the interpolation filter can introduce artifacts on boundaries of the fluid. To avoid these artifacts, either the boundaries need to be expanded or the filter needs to be adapted. If this is not done properly, different parts of the scene are mixed in the filter process (for example background and fluid). This has to be taken care of, not only in the smoothing phase, but also for the subsequent interpolation for all points related to boundaries. Since the GPUs have built-in trilinear and bilateral filters, we use them for fast interpolation. The smoothing filters are used with extended boundaries, where we investigate the effect of zero, one, and two pixel extended boundaries.

A proper smoothing of the depth values can be done with a wide range of filters. For the evaluation we focused on the most popular Gaussian and bilateral filters. As filter core sizes we used $3 \times 3$ and $5 \times 5$ [18,19]. In order to respect borders while using a Gaussian filter we dynamically adjust the filter's core size [20]. This way blending between background and fluid is prevented. The single filter sizes are combined using weighted blending. The so-modified filter we call Gauss$_M$. The bilateral filtering automatically takes into account boundaries between different parts of the scene. This is especially the case here, since the change from foreground to background results in a sudden change in the depth values. In order to prevent filtering of non-fluid parts of the scene additional modifications are required. Thus, both filters have to be adjusted so that the background is not smoothed, otherwise it modifies values close to the boundaries of the fluid in the foreground, yielding minimal different depth levels. It could therefore no longer be recognized as background in the following stages.

## 3.3   Reconstruction of the Surface

After construction of the smoothing filter, an image pyramid can be computed. With the availability of the image pyramid we can now reconstruct the surface of the fluid by upscaling the appropriate level in the pyramid. Depending on the resolution of the screen and the particle size we may also have to select between two adjacent levels in the pyramid and use interpolation to obtain a smooth surface. We then compute the 3D coordinates and the normal vectors that are needed for the illumination. With an appropriate *up-scaling* method, we can reduce artifacts caused by the interpolation. The GPU itself supports nearest neighbor sampling and trilinear interpolation [15]. Additionally we investigate bicubic interpolation to get an smoother reconstruction.

Now the *3D position* of a point on the surface can be simply found by multiplying the so-called eye vector with the current surface depth value. This vector is formed by the ray starting from the center of the camera and running through the current pixel towards the end plane. Multiplying the direction vector with the fluids' depth value of the pixel, we obtain the corresponding coordinates.

In the next step the *surface normals* are derived by evaluation of neighboring pixel positions [21]. There are different ways to combine the gradient values into a normal vector by using the various available pixel difference schemes (left, right, center, ..., [20,22]). The discrete Total Variation [18,23] option is to compare left and right difference and take the smallest value in order to avoid smoothing over boundaries/edges. This approach can be changed to use the distance to the viewer and threshold values in order to control when something is an edge. This way we can even implement a control mechanism to switch between different gradient construction methods, for example a smoothing one and a edge pronouncing one. A good candidate for a threshold value is the particle radius. The normal is then simply generated by using the gradients along both two axes and the cross product.

After the surface has been generated, it needs to be *illuminated*. Since we have an image of the surface, this can be basically done the same way as it is done in Deferred Shading in common computer games. However, we have to take into account that a fluid is usually transparent and we need to take into account reflection, refraction, and other phenomena created when light interacts with a fluid. As an application example of this we used water, but this can be changed by adjusting the constants. We model the fluid's absorption using the Lambert-Beer law [15]: $T = e^{-\alpha l}$. Here, $T$ denotes the transmittance of light, $l$ is the depth of the fluid and $\alpha$ is the absorption constant for a particular wavelength. For water, commonly used values for this constant are $(5, 1, 0.1)$ for red, green, and blue. Since the depth of the fluid is needed for each pixel, it must be stored separately. Reflection and refraction of the fluid is approximated by only targeting the environment map used for image based lighting of the scene. The reflection and refraction properties of a fluid vary based on the angle of incidence. Here we use the approach of Schlick [15], a standard for shading fluids in real-time graphics:

$$R(\theta) = R_0 + (1 - R_0)(1 - \cos\theta)^5, \ R_0 = \left(\frac{n_1 - n_2}{n_1 + n_2}\right)^2,$$

where $\theta$ is the angle between the viewing direction $V$ and half-angle direction $H$, which is located in the middle between gaze and the light direction $L$. Consequently, $\cos\theta = H \cdot V$. Furthermore, $n_1$ and $n_2$ denote the refractive indices of the two media. In the transition from air to water we have $R_0 = [(1 - 1,33)/(1 + 1.33))]^2 \approx 0.02$. Since an image-based lighting is used, there is no direct light direction. Instead, the light reflected at the surface of the viewing direction is taken and inverted. For the vector $H$, this results in $H = V + L = V - V_{refl}$.

The reflection of the cube map arises from the fact that $C_{refl} = C_{Cuberefl}(\theta)$. The fractional part is absorbed by the water per wavelength until it is no longer visible. Approaching this behavior using linear interpolation and the Lambert-Beer's law gives the formula

$$C_{trans} = dC_{refl}C_{lambeer} + (1 - d) \cdot C_{lambeer}(d),$$

where $d$ corresponds to the water depth. Combining both components yields $C = C_{trans} + C_{refl}$ as a formula for the color of each pixel.

### 3.4  In-Depth Curve

To select the right level of detail dependent on the distance to the viewer, we use a non-linear function to steer between the amount of details. For such functions typically logarithmic or the $n^{th}$ root function $x^{1/n}$, is suitable (cf. gamma correction in monitors).

## 4  Implementation

For implementation we used OpenGL in conjunction with shaders written in GLSL. While rendering, the main work is done within fragment shaders since most of the work done is image based. For storing intermediate data of the screen images we used frame buffer objects. Fluid simulation data was generated from a sample of NVIDIA's CUDA SDK[1], but every fluid simulation generating particles should work.

The *depth image* of the fluid's particles are generated by rendering billboards [24] into a depth image. This way the particles have a spherical appearance but do not introduce much additional rendering overhead. The billboards are rendered using instancing [14]. This way only the particles' positions need to be send to the GPU. While a vertex shader sets up the vertex and texture coordinates of the single billboards, a fragment shader is used to convert the billboards into small spheres. The texture coordinates for each billboard range from (0.0) to (1.1) allowing interpolation of the billboard's square. To achieve this, we first transform the texture coordinate for a currently rasterized pixel to the range $-1$ to 1. This is then inserted into the equation of a unit sphere, where $x, y$ is given by the transformed texture coordinate and $z$ is open. Resolving to $z$ either tells

---

[1]  http://docs.nvidia.com/cuda/cuda-samples/#particles.

us the $z$ value on the sphere or that the pixel is not on the sphere of the current particle. In the latter case the calculation is discarded. Otherwise the $z$ value leads to the new depth value. This is done by scaling $z$ by the particle's radius and adding the depth of the particle's position.

The thickness is computed in an analogous way. However, here the $z$ values are used to add up the thickness of the single particles in a buffer. This gives an approximation of the fluid's thickness under a given pixel. From these two images, image pyramids for the subsequent filtering are calculated. The image pyramid is computed manually on the GPU in order to add the custom filter stages discussed in the previous section after each minification.

For reading from the image pyramid we used two approaches. First, the build-in trilinear hardware interpolation for textures with mipmaps. Second, bicubic interpolation done in a shader based on the closest mipmap levels. Since in OpenGL the highest level of detail of the pyramid is referenced with zero and the lowest number of pyramid levels depends on the image resolution, it is necessary to scale the look-up values accordingly. We start with the depth value stored in the up-most level. Its depth value is then used to calculate the mipmap level:

$$S_{n,f}(x) = \left(1 - (f \cdot x)^{1/n}\right) \cdot S_{max}$$

The initial selection can also be chosen to be in lower levels of the mipmap pyramid in order reduce artefacts for non-overlapping particles. The gradients for the normal reconstruction are then computed using the horizontal and vertical neighbors of a pixel and the corresponding eye-vectors in world space. Based on the smoothed normals, the fluid is then rendered using image-based lighting. For background removal, the image in the highest level of the image pyramid is used for masking.

# 5    Results

In this section we briefly show the most important results on the topics that we discussed before. More details of our approach can be found in [4].

We first compared the different methods for reconstruction of the **normal vectors**. Since the way the pyramid levels are formed plays a role, different approaches are evaluated. Due to interpolation, problems arise at the edges. The objective is to obtain normal vectors that follow the edges and do not take intermediate values. Figure 2 illustrates the problem. When we compare the generation of normal vectors with edge detection at a reduced image with $Median_{DV}$ and the generation with simple gradients and linear reduction of the image, the difference between the two images shows the edges quite clearly. If we generate the normal vectors with edge detection based on the with $Median_{DV}$ reduced image and with bicubic interpolation as smoothing, we create new edges and other artifacts, as illustrated in Fig. 3. For this reason, this type of normal generation appears to be unsuitable because one has to interpolate. The same holds for dynamic selection generation. The variant that uses only the neighbors for the generation, gives rise to a greater margin. Consequently, the simple gradient for generating the normal remains. Since the bilinear interpolation introduces additional artifacts, bicubic interpolation remains as a better option. Therefore, if not otherwise stated, all images in the following are rendered with *linear reduction*, *simple gradients* and *bicubic interpolation*.

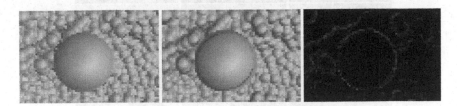

**Fig. 2.** Left: Edge detection with reduction and the normal generation; Middle: Linear reduction and simple gradient for the generation of normal vectors; Right: Difference between the two images. A distinct edge is visible.

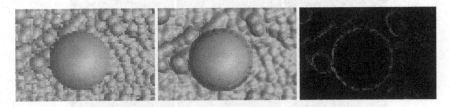

**Fig. 3.** Edge detection with reduction and normal generation; Left: No interpolation; Middle: Bicubic interpolation; Right: Difference between the two images. A distinct edge and other artifacts are visible.

Experiments showed that for the modified Gaussian filter with a core size of $5 \times 5$ no **boundary extension** is required. With a size of $3 \times 3$ a simple boundary (one pixel) extension is necessary. The bilateral filter requires for bilinear interpolation a single margin expansion, and for bicubic interpolation a two-pixel margin expansion.

Regarding the **smoothing filter**, other experiments showed that the edge boundaries are blurred when using the Gaussian filtering, while a bilateral filtering expectedly yields better results on the edges. The difference between $3 \times 3$ and $5 \times 5$ core size is visibly not very clear. Using bicubic interpolation, the particles become sharper, though [4].

The parameter $n$ in the **detailed curves** has a distinct influence on the image sharpness. The best compromise between too much and too little sharpness appears to be in the range $n \in [3..3, 5]$. Here, since the depth values are scaled by a factor of 10 and seven steps are used, the value is tunable for other cases

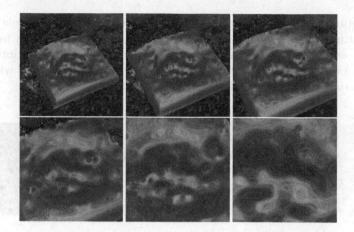

**Fig. 4.** Various distances to the surface at different detail curves with the equation $S_{2,f=10}(x) = (1 - \sqrt[v]{f \star x}) \star 7$ and $Z_{Far} = 10000$.

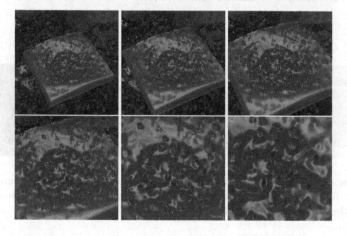

**Fig. 5.** Various distances to the surface at different detail curves with the equation $S_{3.5,f=10}(x) = (1 - \sqrt[v]{f \star x}) \star 7$ and $Z_{Far} = 10000$.

– which is no problem since we achieve a real-time performance. See Figs. 4, 5 and 6, as well as [4].

To measure the **performance** we set up a scene that covers an entire screen with a resolution of $1920 \times 1080$, The number of images per second of the different rendering options was computed. As a graphics card an AMD Radeon R270x was used. Table 1 shows the results for 65,536 and 262,144 particles. The type of reduction is negligible and was therefore omitted.

It can be seen that the calculation of the fluid depth is relatively time-consuming albeit still real-time. The most time-consuming part is due to the blending, because every time values must be read from memory and written again. The linear bicubic interpolation is less computationally expensive, but

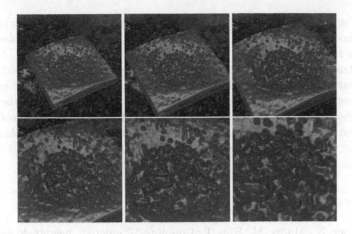

**Fig. 6.** Various distances to the surface at different detail curves with the equation $S_{5.5, f=10}(x) = (1 - \sqrt[n]{f \star x}) \star 7$ and $Z_{Far} = 10000$.

**Table 1.** Frames per second with 65536 (left) and 262144 (right) particles for Trilinear & Linear-Bicubic pixel interpolation; Notation: With/without calculated liquid depth

| Kernel | 65536 particles | | 262144 particles | |
|---|---|---|---|---|
| | Trilinear | Linear bicubic | Trilinear | Linear bicubic |
| 3 × 3 Gauss | 44/56 | 32/37 | 32/45 | 24/32 |
| 5 × 5 Gauss | 41/55 | 32/35 | 28/41 | 24/32 |
| 3 × 3 Bilateral | 42/50 | 32/36 | 32/44 | 24/32 |
| 5 × 5 Bilateral | 40/48 | 30/34 | 28/44 | 24/32 |

still consumes some time. The core size has little influence, as well as the nature of the filtering. It is also apparent that a quadrupling of the number of particles does not quarter the frame rate.

## 6    Conclusions

We investigated the post-processing of the direct visualization of the simulation data via image processing applications of (i) smoothing filters as well as (ii) an image pyramid. The reason for this, is that for real-time simulation a fluids currently the two available methods (grid-based simulation and particle-based simulation) both approximate the simulation of a fluid and do not directly generate a visual pleasant surface. Due to time constraints the subsequent generated surface is usually an approximation, which is uneven, consists of many individual elements, and also has no optical properties of a liquid.

We exploited the fact that if the visualization of a fluid in image space contains differing detail densities they depend of the distance between observer and the fluid. We therefore introduced filters in order to smooth these details to a consistent surface. Ad-hoc approaches use strong filters in this step which result in a too smooth surface, which must then later on be treated with noise in order to give it a rough appearance.

In contrast, our presented approach based on an image pyramid provides access to various levels of detail. These are used as a controllable low pass filter. Now, different amounts of smoothing can be selected depending on the distance to the viewer granting a better surface reconstruction. The visible most pleasing combination was obtained for a rendering with linear reduction, simple gradients and bicubic interpolation. Most important, results are obtained at real-time frame rates.

# References

1. Chentanez, N., Müller, M., Kim, T.: Coupling 3D eulerian, heightfield and particle methods for interactive simulation of large scale liquid phenomena. IEEE Trans. Vis. Comput. Graph. **21**, 1116–1128 (2015)
2. Liu, W., Ribeiro, E.: A higher-order model for fluid motion estimation. In: Kamel, M., Campilho, A. (eds.) ICIAR 2011, Part I. LNCS, vol. 6753, pp. 325–334. Springer, Heidelberg (2011). doi:10.1007/978-3-642-21593-3_33
3. Bender, J., Müller, M., Otaduy, M.A., Teschner, M., Macklin, M.: A survey on position-based simulation methods in computer graphics. Comput. Graph. Forum **33**, 228–251 (2014)
4. Puhl, J.: Materialsysteme für das realistische echtzeit-rendering von szenen in anwesenheit von flüssigkeitssimulationen und image-based lighting. Technical report, TU Darmstadt (2014)
5. van der Laan, W.J., Green, S., Sainz, M.: Screen space fluid rendering with curvature flow. In: Proceedings of the 2009 Symposium on Interactive 3D Graphics, SI3D 2009, 27 February – 1 March, 2009, Boston, Massachusetts, USA, pp. 91–98 (2009)
6. Müller, M., Schirm, S., Duthaler, S.: Screen space meshes. In: Proceedings of the 2007 ACM SIGGRAPH/Eurographics Symposium on Computer Animation, SCA 2007, pp. 9–15. Eurographics Association, Aire-la-Ville (2007)
7. Macklin, M., Müller, M.: Position based fluids. ACM Trans. Graph. **32**, 104:1–104:12 (2013)
8. Yu, J., Turk, G.: Reconstructing surfaces of particle-based fluids using anisotropic kernels. ACM Trans. Graph. **32**, 5 (2013)
9. Goswami, P., Schlegel, P., Solenthaler, B., Pajarola, R.: Interactive SPH simulation and rendering on the GPU. In: Proceedings of the 2010 Eurographics/ACM SIGGRAPH Symposium on Computer Animation, SCA 2010, pp. 55–64 (2010)
10. Kornprobst, P., Tumblin, J., Durand, F.: Bilateral filtering: theory and applications. Found. Trends Comput. Graph. Vis. **4**, 1–74 (2009)
11. Wong, T.: Image-based lighting. In: Ikeuchi, K. (ed.) Computer Vision, A Reference Guide, pp. 387–390. Springer, Heidelberg (2014)
12. Knuth, M., Altenhofen, C., Kuijper, A., Bender, J.: Efficient self-shadowing using image-based lighting on glossy surfaces. In: Vision, Modeling and Visualization, VMV 2014, pp. 159–166 (2014)
13. Reinhard, E., Ward, G., Pattanaik, S.N., Debevec, P.E., Heidrich, W.: High Dynamic Range Imaging - Acquisition, Display, and Image-Based Lighting, 2nd edn. Academic Press, Orlando (2010)

14. Shreiner, D., Sellers, G., Kessenich, J., Licea-Kaneand, B.: OpenGL Programming Guide: The Official Guide to Learning OpenGL, Versions 4.3, 8th edn. Addison-Wesley Professional, Upper Saddle River (2013)

15. Akenine-Möller, T., Haines, E., Hoffman, N.: Real-Time Rendering, 3rd edn. A.K. Peters Ltd., Natick (2008)

16. Schmitt, N., Knuth, M., Bender, J., Kuijper, A.: Multilevel cloth simulation using GPU surface sampling. In: Proceedings of 10th Workshop on Virtual Reality Interactions and Physical Simulations, VRIPHYS 2013, Lille, France, pp. 1–10 (2013)

17. Bauer, F., Knuth, M., Kuijper, A., Bender, J.: Screen-space ambient occlusion using a-buffer techniques. In: 2013 International Conference on Computer-Aided Design and Computer Graphics, CAD/Graphics 2013, November 16–18, 2013, Guangzhou, China, pp. 140–147 (2013)

18. Kuijper, A.: P-laplacian driven image processing. In: Proceedings of the International Conference on Image Processing, ICIP 2007, September 16–19, 2007, San Antonio, Texas, USA, pp. 257–260 (2007)

19. Kuijper, A., Florack, L.: Understanding and modeling the evolution of critical points under Gaussian blurring. In: Heyden, A., Sparr, G., Nielsen, M., Johansen, P. (eds.) ECCV 2002. LNCS, vol. 2350, pp. 143–157. Springer, Heidelberg (2002). doi:10.1007/3-540-47969-4_10

20. Kuijper, A.: Geometrical PDEs based on second-order derivatives of gauge coordinates in image processing. Image Vis. Comput. **27**, 1023–1034 (2009)

21. Julià, C., Sappa, A.D., Lumbreras, F., Serrat, J., López, A.: Recovery of surface normals and reflectance from different lighting conditions. In: Campilho, A., Kamel, M. (eds.) ICIAR 2008. LNCS, vol. 5112, pp. 315–325. Springer, Heidelberg (2008). doi:10.1007/978-3-540-69812-8_31

22. Aubert, G., Kornprobst, P.: Mathematical Problems in Image Processing: Partial Differential Equations and the Calculus of Variations. Applied Mathematical Sciences, vol. 147, 2nd edn. Springer, Heidelberg (2006)

23. Rudin, L.I., Osher, S., Fatemi, E.: Nonlinear total variation based noise removal algorithms. Physica D **60**, 259–268 (1992)

24. Germann, M., Hornung, A., Keiser, R., Ziegler, R., Würmlin, S., Gross, M.: Articulated billboards for video-based rendering. Comput. Graph. Forum (Proc. Eurographics) **29**, 585–594 (2010)

# A Bioplausible Model for Explaining Café Wall Illusion: Foveal vs. Peripheral Resolution

Nasim Nematzadeh[✉] and David M.W. Powers

CSEM, Flinders University, Adelaide, Australia
{nasim.nematzadeh,david.powers}@flinders.edu.au

**Abstract.** Optical illusions highlight sensitivities and limitations of human visual processing and studying them leads to insights about perception that can potentially help computer vision match or exceed human performance. Geometric illusions are a subclass of illusions in which orientations and angles are distorted and misperceived. In this paper, a quantifiable prediction is presented of the degree of tilt for the Café Wall pattern, a typical geometric illusion, in which the mortar between the tiles seems to converge and diverge. Our study employs a bioplausible model of ON-center retinal processing, using an analytic processing pipeline to measure, quantitatively, the angle of tilt content in the model. The model also predicts different perceived tilts in different areas of the fovea and periphery as the eye saccades to different parts of the image. This variation is verified and quantified in simulations using two different sampling methods. Several sampling sizes and aspect ratios, modeling variant foveal views, are investigated across multiple scales in order to provide confidence intervals around the predicted tilts, and to contrast local tilt detection with a global average across the whole Café Wall image.

## 1 Introduction

Optical illusions are one source of evidence about vision, and do not necessarily occur in a computer vision model, but should be apparent in a vision model that claims to represent the way human vision works, or a vision system that tries to identify the same patterns and features that a human would. There are many levels of processing involved between eye and cortex before the final perception of a visual scene. The visual processing starts in the retina where the visual signal from the photoreceptors is passed to bipolar cells and then to retinal ganglion cells (RGCs) whose axons carry the visual signal to the cortex. There are also two types of interneuron cells called horizontal and amacrine cells, providing lateral interaction with other neurons.

New physiological findings about the retina have significantly extended our understanding of RGCs and their functionality. A comprehensive study about retinal circuitry and coding reported the existence of a diverse range of RGC types [1] within the retina, each with their specific encoding role. The neural mechanism of retinal multiscale encoding is supported by variations of RF type and size in relation to distance from the

© Springer International Publishing AG 2016
G. Bebis et al. (Eds.): ISVC 2016, Part I, LNCS 10072, pp. 426–438, 2016.
DOI: 10.1007/978-3-319-50835-1_39

fovea, as well as intra-retinal circuitry. It is noteworthy that some retinal cells have an orientation selectivity property similar to the cortical cells [1, 2].

The highly directional effect in many geometric illusions, and in Café Wall in particular, might tend to direct explanations toward physiological interpretations of orientation detectors in the cortex. We are going to show how tilt in Café Wall illusion specifically, and in tile illusions generally, can emerge earlier still as the result of processing by simple cells. The reason for the tilt perception in the Café Wall pattern is often claimed to be the emergence of slanted line segments along the mortar lines in a local view, which leads to a perception of alternating converging and diverging mortar lines at a more global level [3–5]. There are also putative low level explanations for the illusion such as 'brightness assimilation and contrast' [6] and 'band-pass spatial frequency' [3, 4]; and high level explanations such as 'Border locking' [7] and 'phenomenal model' [8]. Other descriptive explanations and psychophysical experiments on the stimulus can be found in [7–9], but give little consideration to the underlying neurological mechanisms involved in the emergence of tilt illusion. Superficially, these theories might seem to explain the illusion at different levels of processing, but at a deeper level they have common features as underlying neural mechanisms, including *lateral inhibition* [10–12] of *retinal* and/or *cortical cells*.

The center–surround organization in retinal ganglion cells (GCs) is thought to be mainly due to *lateral inhibition (LI)* at the first synaptic level in the outer retina [10, 11], where activated cells inhibit the activations of nearby cells. It is reported that spatial tuning properties of retinal ganglion cells (*RGCs*) are also sharpened by this mechanism (LI), originating at both the outer and inner plexiform layers [12]. This is a biological convolution with the effect of edge enhancement [12]. The contrast sensitivity of RGCs based on a circular center and surround organization for the retinal RFs [13, 14] is implemented in our model.

The intentional and unintentional eye movements while we look at the scene (pattern), notably overt saccades and gaze shifts, allow the high resolution fovea to rapidly scan the field of vision for pertinent information. Therefore different parts of the visual scene are processed at different scales at different times.

The model we are using here is an ON-center receptive field (RF), or classical receptive field (CRF) model implementing retinal GCs responses [5]. It is based on the well-known Difference of Gaussian (DoG) and is explored here to explain the emergence of tilt in the Café Wall illusion, providing quantitative measurements of tilt angle in the pattern, and explaining how incorporation of different foveal points during saccade lead to different tilt or bulge phenomena due to their perception at different scales and their integration into a multiscale edge map. Although related models for explaining Café Wall stimulus have been proposed by others [3, 4], only our earlier work has quantified the degree of tilt by computational analysis [15, 16], where similar tilts are highlighted by both ON-center and OFF-center receptive fields. We also offer a systematic multiple scale analysis of the model outputs that is missing in earlier studies, although the effects of scale are illustrated in [4, 5].

In Part 2 of this paper we formalize a simple Difference of Gaussian model as a basic bioplausible model of lateral inhibition. Part 3 introduce the entire modeling and analysis pipeline used in our experiments and the range of parameters we will use in our analysis. In Part 4, we then proceed to present results for two experiments, for investigation of local 'cropped' samples based on two methods of sampling (*Systematic* and *Random*), simulating foveal locus only (Exp1), and investigation of the Gestalt pattern, simulating peripheral awareness across the entire image (Exp2).

## 2    Difference of Gaussian Model and Formal Descriptions

Physiological evidence [1, 2] show a diverse range of RGCs with different sizes in the retina, and cells of different type and eccentricity (the distance from the fovea) that suggest a multiscale encoding [17] of the visual scene in the retina. The history of the receptive field models back to Kuffler's demonstration of roughly concentric excitatory center and inhibitory surround [18]. Later, Rodieck and Stone [13] and Enroth-Cugell and Robson [14] showed that the signals from the center and surround regions of photo-receptor outputs can be modelled by two concentric Gaussians with the different radii.

A feature representation for the image is explained here which is interpretable as the image edge map using the DoG model which clearly reflects the perceived tilt in the pattern (Fig. 2). The DoG output of the retinal GCs model with the centre and surround organization for a 2D image such as $I$, is calculated as:

$$\Gamma_{\sigma,s\sigma}(x,y) = I * \frac{1}{2\pi\sigma^2} e^{-(x^2+y^2)/(2\sigma^2)} - I * \frac{1}{2\pi s^2\sigma^2} e^{-(x^2+y^2)/(2s^2\sigma^2)} \tag{1}$$

$$s = \sigma_{surround} / \sigma_{center} = \sigma_s / \sigma_c \tag{2}$$

where the distances from the origin in the horizontal and vertical axes are characterized by x and y respectively, and $\sigma$ shows the sigma of the centre Gaussian. The sigma of the surround Gaussian is represents by $s\sigma$ in (1), which we refer to it as $\sigma_s$. Parameter $s$ is referred to as the *surround ratio* given in (2). It has shown that for modeling the RFs of retinal GCs, DoG is a good approximation of Laplacian of Gaussian (LoG) when the centre-surround ratio is $s \approx 1.6$ ($\approx \varphi$, the Golden Ratio) [19]. Increasing $s$ leads to more surround suppression result, covering a wider area while its height declines. For convenience, in the experimental runs in this paper $s = 2$ is chosen and other commonly used values like $1.6 \approx \varphi$ show little difference.

As a further practical matter, the DoG model is only applied within a window of a size chosen so that the value of both Gaussians is insignificant outside the window (less than 5 % for the surround Gaussian). So we control windowSize as large windows have high computational cost. The *windowSize* is determined by $h$ (*window ratio*) parameter defined as below:

$$windowSize = h \times \sigma_c + 1 \tag{3}$$

Parameter $h$ determines how much of the center and surround Gaussians are included in the filter, and we use $h = 8$ in this paper (two standard deviations of surround).

# 3    Model and Processing Pipeline

The DoG transformation creates a bioplausible image/pattern representation (edge map) inducing the tilted line segments in the pattern. Then quantitative measurement of tilt angles in the edge map let us to compare them with the tilt perceived by a human observer. For this we embed the DoG model in a processing pipeline involving multiple standard image processing transformations to find the predicted tilt in our computational model (Fig. 1).

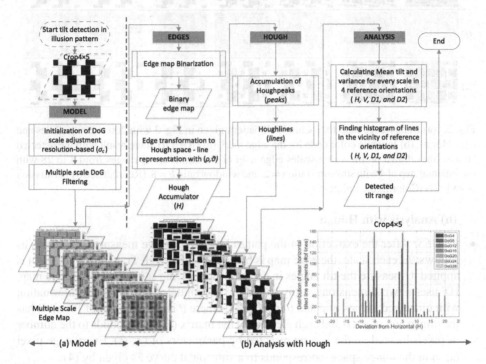

**Fig. 1.** Flowchart of the model and analytical tilt processing. (Reproduced by permission from [22])

## (a) MODEL

The most fundamental parameter in the model is the diameter of the center Gaussian ($\sigma_c$), which is highly correlated with characteristics of the pattern elements. So, to extract the tilted line segments along the mortar lines, the output of the MODEL for a cropped section of a Café Wall pattern with $200 \times 200$ px Tiles ($T$) and 8 px Mortar ($M$) is shown in Fig. 2(a, b) in a binary form as well as false colored using jetwhite[1] color map. Based on the fixed parameters of *surround ratio* and *window ratio*, relative to $\sigma_c$, and the pattern characteristics, a range of 0.5 M to 3.5 M, with incremental step of 0.5 M, is as an illustrative range for $\sigma_c$. So the output of the MODEL is an edge map representation for the pattern with multiple scales of DoG. Now we move on to explore how to measure the slope of the detected tilts in the edge map.

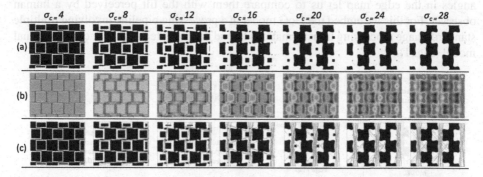

**Fig. 2.** (a) Binary edge map for a Café Wall pattern given in Fig. 3 with $200 \times 200$ px Tiles and 8 px Mortar. (b) Jetwhite color code for the edge map. (c) HOUGH stage result with the detected Hough lines drawn on the seven scales edge map of the stimulus. $\sigma_c$ ranges from 4 to 28 with incremental step of 4 with surround ratio $s = 2$, and window ratio $h = 8$. (Reproduced by permission from [22]) (Color figure online)

### (b) Analysis with Hough

- *EDGES:* After the extraction of the pattern's edge map, we measured tilt angles as follows: At each scale, the edge map is binarised and Hough Transform (HT) [20] is applied to measure the tilt angles in detected slanted line segments in the edge map. HT uses a two-dimensional array called the accumulator to store lines information with quantized values of $\rho$ and $\theta$ in its cells, where $\theta$ is in the range of $[0, \pi)$. It has the dimension of $\rho \times \theta$ and each element of the matrix $(H)$ corresponds to the number of pixels located on the line represented by parameters of $(\rho_i, \theta_i)$. Every edge pixel $(x, y)$ in the image space, corresponds to a sinusoidal curve as given by (4):

$$\rho = x.\cos\theta + y.\sin\theta \tag{4}$$

  where $\rho$ represents the distance between the line passing through the edge point with a specific $\theta$ and the origin, and $\theta$ is the counter-clockwise angle between the normal vector $(\rho)$ and the x-axis. So, the output of the *EDGES* is $H$ matrix, representing the edge map in Hough space.
- *HOUGH:* Inside $H$-matrix we now have all possible lines that could pass through every edge point in the edge map, but we are more interested in the detection of tilt inducing line segments inside the Café Wall pattern. Two MATLAB functions called *Houghpeaks* and *Houghlines* have been used here for this reason.
  The '*Houghpeaks*' function finds the peaks in the Hough accumulator matrix $(H)$. The local maxima in the accumulator show the most likely lines that can be extracted. It has parameters of *NumPeaks*, *Threshold*, and *NHoodSize* each indicating maximum

number of lines to be detected, threshold value for searching $H$ for the peaks, and the neighborhood suppression size which set to zero after the peak is identified. The *'Houghlines'* function, however, extracts line segments associated with a particular bin in a Hough accumulator. It has parameters of *FillGap*, and *MinLength* standing for the maximum gap allowed between two line segments associated with the same Hough bin, which result in merging them to a single line segment, and the minimum length for merged lines to be kept, respectively.

Figure 2(c) illustrates a sample output of the *HOUGH* analysis stage on the same crop section of the Café Wall $9 \times 14$ - T200-M8 (Fig. 3). Detected line segments are shown in green, displayed on a binarized edge map with DoG scales ranges from 4 to 28. Blue lines indicate the longest detected line segment. As shown in Fig. 2(c) in fine scales, near horizontal lines are detected and by increasing the scale, the mortar lines are disappeared, and the near horizontal tilts are replaced by zigzag vertical lines joining similar colored tiles [5, 15, 16].

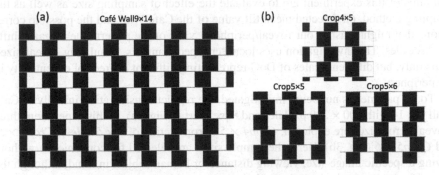

**Fig. 3.** (a) Café Wall stimulus with $200 \times 200$ px Tiles, and 8 px Mortar. (b) Three "foveal" sample sizes explored. (CropH × W is H × W Tiles)

- *ANALYSIS:* We have considered four reference orientations including horizontal ($H$), vertical ($V$), positive diagonal ($+45°$, $D1$), and negative diagonal ($-45°$, $D2$), and an interval of $[-22.5°, 22.5°)$ around them to cover the whole space. In this stage the information from *HOUGH* are saved inside four matrices based on how close they are to one of these reference orientations for tilt analysis. The statistical analysis of the detected lines in the neighborhood of each reference orientation is the output of this stage.

# 4    Experimental Results

In this section, we discuss two sample experiments that correspond to local and global tilt and foveal/peripheral view of the pattern, and compare them.

Our visual perception of tilt is affected by our fixation on the pattern. When we fixate on a part of the pattern, the tilt in a region around fixation point weakens, but the peripheral tilts still exist. It seems that the peripheral tilt recognition has a greater effect on our final perception of the pattern compared to the foveal/local tilt perception. This is because peripheral/global understanding provides a wholistic impression of the visual field, and can be linked to a Gestalt (psychology) percept of tilt induction.

From a biological point of view in the fovea the acuity is high due to high density and small size receptors. As eccentricity increases, the acuity declines with increasing RF sizes and nearest neighbor distances. The first model for foveal retinal vision was proposed by Lindeberg and Florack [17] and our model is inspired by it. Since our vision is scale-invariant, so what is sent to the brain is a stack of images or a scale-space, not a single image. The Lindeberg and Florack's model is based on simultaneous sampling of the image at all scales, and we generate the edge map in a similar way. One of the main advantages of a scale-space model is that the result is not very sensitive to specific characteristics of the pattern elements.

## 4.1   Experiment 1

The aims of this experiment are to evaluate the effect of sampling size as well as the sampling method, on detected mean tilt value of the Café Wall and the possible correlations that might exist to our foveal/peripheral view of the pattern due to gaze shifts and saccades. The investigation uses local 'cropped' samples, simulating foveal-sized locus only, but different scales of DoG representing different degrees of eccentricity in the periphery.

To fix parameters not being investigated, we restrict consideration initially to Café Wall $9 \times 14$ with $200 \times 200$ px Tiles and 8 px Mortar (Fig. 3a). In this experiment three "foveal" crop sizes are explored, $Crop4 \times 5$ (Crop section of $4 \times 5$ Tiles), $Crop5 \times 5$, and $Crop5 \times 6$ (Fig. 3b). Here, the sample sizes are selected for convenience without having a specific image size, viewing distance or human subject in mind, although the size of foveal image can be estimated given these.

We have applied two sampling methods. The first method is called 'Systematic Cropping' [15] in which for each specified crop window size, 50 samples are taken from Café Wall $9 \times 14$ in which for the first sample, the top left corner is selected randomly from the pattern and for the rest of the samples, the cropping window shifts horizontally to the right with an offset of 4 pixels in each step. We have a total shift of a Tile size (200 px) at the end. In the second method which called 'Random Cropping', for each specified crop window size, all 50 samples are taken from randomly selected location (top-left corner of cropped window) with the only consideration of the crop borders to stay inside the pattern.

For the edge map representation of the samples based on the DoG model, the $\sigma_c$ parameter is chosen in the range of 0.5 M to 3.5 M with incremental step of 0.5 M, since coarser scales exceeding the Tile size, result in a very distorted edge pattern. The parameters of *houghpeaks* and *houghlines* functions should be selected properly to detect the slanted line segments in the pattern in lower scales. E.g. *FillGap* should assign a value to fill small gaps between line segments located on the edge map to detect near horizontal tilted lines, and *MinLength* should be larger than *TileSize* to avoid the detection of the outlines of the tiles. These parameters have been chosen empirically based on these intuitions and the pattern's attributes, and kept constant for this experiment. $NumPeaks = 100$, $Threshold = 3$, $FillGap = 40$, and $MinLength = 450$.

Figure 4(a, b) shows the results of mean tilt for each sample set in box plot representation, for the two sampling methods and the four reference orientations of Horizontal (*H*), Vertical (*V*), and Diagonal (*D1, D2*), at the seven DoG scales of the edge map. As Fig. 4 indicates, the *'Random Cropping'* method provides us with more stable tilt results across different crop window shapes compared to the *'Systematic'* sampling method. Also the Random Sampling is a more standard statistical approach, but the systematic version is closer to the bias of our saccades and gaze shifts toward interest points. In the first four scales of both sampling methods in Fig. 4 (a, b), only horizontal and vertical lines are detected and the horizontal tilted line segments, inducing the tilt effect, appear in these scales. (Only at *Crop5 × 5* do we have a few samples with border effect that have *D2* components-only 4/50 samples). Among these four scales, DoG8 detects the horizontal tilt in a nearly stable range around 7° in all samples (it apparently correlates with the Mortar size). As the scale increases from 20 onwards, there are no near horizontal lines detected, but more vertical and diagonal lines are extracted. This is due to disappearing of the mortar lines and the enlargement of the outlines of the tiles by increasing $\sigma_c$, which results in more line detection in the coarse scales of the edge map. For Horizontal mean tilt deviation, as the scale of the DoG model increases, the mean tilt value is also increases, although it is nearly 8° for DoG8 and 12. However, in the

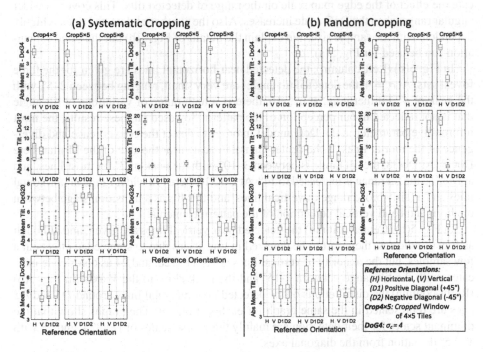

**Fig. 4.** Mean tilt for the three "foveal" sample sizes explored, the four reference orientations of (*H, V, D1, D2*), and the two sampling approaches of (a) Systematic and (b) Random methods explained in Sect. 4.1. The parameters are: The DoG scales ($\sigma_c$ = 4, 8, 12, 16, 20, 24, 28), $s = 2$, $h = 8$, with *NumPeaks* = 100, *Threshold* = 3, *FillGap* = 40, and *MinLength* = 450. (Reproduced by permission from [22])

finest scale (DoG4) the horizontal tilt angle is quite small (3.5°) compared to DoG8. This suggests why the tilt effect in the pattern is much weaker when we fixate on the pattern, since similarly in the fovea the acuity is high because of high density and small size receptors. For vertical deviation, the mean tilt jumps a little bit after the first few scales (8, 12) and nearly stays around 5° to 6° from V orientation (axis). The diagonal mean tilt deviation is mainly around 4° and 5° from D1, and D2 axis which can be seen after DoG20.

Comparing the results of the detected tilts at a given scale shows slight differences across sample sets, and this is expected because of random sampling and the fixed parameters of *houghpeaks* and *houghlines* that are not optimized for each scale and sampling size, and kept constant here for the consistency of the higher level analysis/ model. The tilt detection results are sensible when compared to our angular tilt perception of the pattern, while the computational cost of the model and tilt analysis is reasonable. But more accuracy may be achieved by optimizing parameters.

Figure 5(a, b) shows the distribution of lines near each reference orientation (H, V, D1, D2) for the three foveal sampling sets and the two sampling methods at the seven DoG scales. The results of near diagonal tilted lines have been graphed together for fairer representation. Figure 5(a, b) shows that the detected tilt result in (b) is more normally distributed around reference orientations compared to (a). All the graphs indicate the effect of the edge map scale on the range of detected tilts. This covers a wider angular range when the DoG scale increases. Also the number of detected lines is highly dependent with the sample size. We explain the details of Fig. 5(b) but the same explanation can be used for Fig. 5(a).

In Fig. 5(b) (Left-column), the detected near horizontal lines are given for the three foveal sets. At $\sigma_c = 4$, the detected tilt angles are very small, ranging between 2–5°, with the peak of 4°. Furthermore, at $\sigma_c = 16$, there is a high range of variations of tilt angle that is not reflected in our perception of the pattern. So based on these results, the most informative parameter in the DoG model in order to detect the convergence and divergence of the mortar lines, is the center Gaussian scale near the size of the Mortar, here DoG8. At DoG8, the tilt range is between 3–10° with the peak of 7° for most lines, and at DoG12 the tilt range is increased to 14°. At DoG16 there is a wider range of horizontal lines and a fairly broad range of vertical lines, and this fits as a transition stage between the horizontal and vertical perception of the pattern elements.

In Fig. 5(b) (Center-column) the detected near vertical lines are given, and although as Fig. 4 indicates, they start to be detected in fine scales due to some edge effects in a few samples, but the majority of vertical lines are at DoG20, and 24 as color code indicates, with the tilt range between 2-15° and the peak close to the V axis. In Fig. 5(b) (Right-column) the distributions of the detected near diagonal lines around D1 and D2 axes are represented in the same graph for each sample set. The graphs show that the dominant scales for their detection are mainly the coarse scales of DoG24, and 28 with 1–2.5° deviation from the diagonal axes.

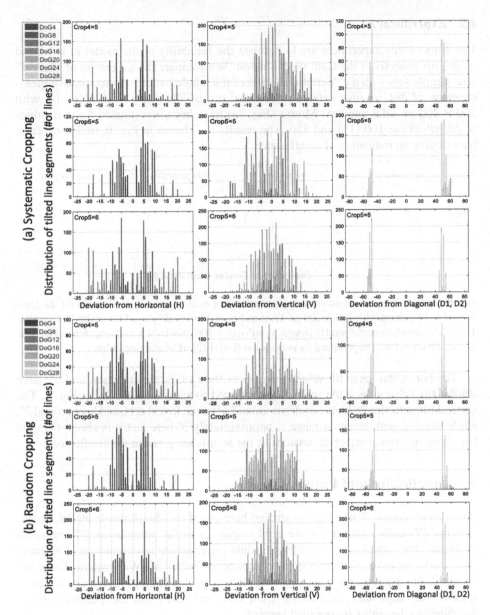

**Fig. 5.** The distribution of near Horizontal (Left Column), near Vertical (Center Column), and near Diagonal (Right Column) detected line segments for the three "foveal" sample sets, with the two sampling methods (a) Systematic, and (b) Random cropping, at the seven DoG scales of $\sigma_c = 4, 8, 12, 16, 20, 24, 28$, and fixed parameters for *houghpeaks* and *houghlines*, the same as Fig. 4. (Reproduced by permission from [22])

## 4.2    Experiment 2

The aims of this experiment are to confirm the reliability of the model in local and global tilt analysis of the Café Wall illusion. We compare the tilt results of "foveal" size sample sets with the "peripheral" tilts of the whole pattern. A quantitative measurement of tilt in four reference orientations of the Café Wall 9 × 14 with 200 × 200 px Tiles and 8 px Mortar (Fig. 3a) have been investigated for two values of *NumPeaks* = 100 [15] and 520. The results are shown in Fig. 6, including error bars to give an indication of significance.

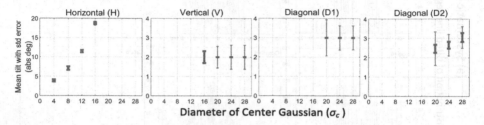

**Fig. 6.** Mean tilt and standard error arround reference orientations (*H, V, D1, D2*) for the Café Wall 9 × 14 pattern with 200 × 200 px Tiles and 8 px Mortar, displayed for seven DoG scales. Thick blue errorbars correspond to Hough *NumPeaks* = 100 as in Expt 1, and long thin red wiskers to *NumPeaks* = 520. (Reproduced by permission from [22]) (Color figure online)

The horizontal mean tilt value increases as the DoG scale increases, and we have similar tilt value around the scale of 8 compared to sample set results in Fig. 4. The vertical tilt detection in higher scales is around 5° in the foveal sets, and here around 2°, while the diagonal deviation range is approximately 3° here and it is about 4° in the foveal sample sets. Further discussions of the results are given in the conclusions.

## 5    Conclusions and Future Work

The optical illusion "Café Wall" is studied here based on a bioplausible model, implementing ON-cells retinal receptive field responses to the stimulus as Difference of Gaussian. The model generates a bioplausible intermediate representation at multiple scales (edge maps) that reflects the emergence of tilt in the Café Wall pattern. These can be fused into a multiscale edge map that allows for detection of features at different scales, with edge/scale information from both the fovea and the periphery being combined in the cortex for our final percept.

Based on the model used here, we have shown that although the perceptual effect in the pattern is highly directional, the lateral inhibition in the retinal/cortical simple cells, is capable of predicting the tilt in the pattern, although for the discrimination of the angle of tilt, further processing by orientation selective cells in the retina/cortex might be needed. An image processing pipeline is exploited here for a quantitative measurement of tilt angle using Hough space. The results for the three foveal sample sets and the two sampling approaches are then compared with the whole Café Wall pattern, whereby random sampling method shows more reliable tilt results.

Our quantified predicted tilt results nicely reflect and support the effects that a viewer of a Café Wall pattern notices, in which the tilts seem larger in their peripheral vision than at their focal point: coarse scales DoGs corresponding to the lower resolution of the periphery gives rise to larger perceived angles in both experiments. Also when the mortar lines start to fade, the results show the zigzag vertical patterns or eventually diagonal patterns similar to the brightness illusions that correspond to viewing from greater distances. One of the reasons for the slight tilt difference in the global versus local tilt analysis is due to the fixed parameter values such as *NumPeaks*, which is kept constant across the foveal samples and the global image. Figure 6 illustrates global analysis with a larger value of *NumPeaks* but this does not change the mean tilts significantly although it does substantially increase the variance.

No psychophysical tests have been performed to confirm the predictions implicit in our results, and this is one of our future research priorities, relating the tile, mortar and DoG size to visual angle and make specific predictions for the effect at different distances and viewing sizes. A non-CRFs (nCRF) extension of the model [21] might also facilitate the directionality evaluation of the tilt in tile illusions.

# References

1. Field, G.D., Chichilnisky, E.J.: Information processing in the primate retina: circuitry and coding. Ann. Rev. Neurosci. **30**, 1–30 (2007)
2. Gollisch, T., Meister, M.: Eye smarter than scientists believed: neural computations in circuits of the retina. Neuron **65**(2), 150–164 (2010)
3. Morgan, M.J., Moulden, B.: The Münsterberg figure and twisted cords. Vis. Res. **26**(11), 1793–1800 (1986)
4. Earle, D.C., Maskell, S.J.: Fraser cords and reversal of the Café Wall illusion. Perception **22**(4), 383–390 (1993)
5. Nematzadeh, N., Lewis, T.W., Powers, D.M.W.: Bioplausible multiscale filtering in retinal to cortical processing as a model of computer vision. In: ICAART2015-International Conference on Agents and Artificial Intelligence, SCITEPRESS (2015)
6. Jameson, D., Hurvich, L.M.: Essay concerning color constancy. Ann. Rev. Psychol. **40**(1), 1–24 (1989)
7. Gregory, R.L., Heard, P.: Border locking and the Café Wall illusion. Perception **8**(4), 365–380 (1979)
8. Kitaoka, A., Pinna, B., Brelstaff, G.: Contrast polarities determine the direction of Café Wall tilts. Perception **33**(1), 11–20 (2004)
9. McCourt, M.E.: Brightness induction and the Café Wall illusion. Perception **12**(2), 131–142 (1983)
10. Ratliff, F., Knight, B., Graham, N.: On tuning and amplification by lateral inhibition. Proc. Nat. Acad. Sci. **62**(3), 733–740 (1969)
11. Cook, P.B., McReynolds, J.S.: Lateral inhibition in the inner retina is important for spatial tuning of Ganglion cells. Nat. Neurosci. **1**(8), 714–719 (1998)
12. Huang, J.Y., Protti, D.A.: The impact of inhibitory mechanisms in the inner retina on spatial tuning of RGCs. Scientific reports 6 (2016)

13. Rodieck, R.W., Stone, J.: Analysis of receptive fields of cat retinal ganglion cells. J. Neurophysiol. **28**(5), 833–849 (1965)
14. Enroth-Cugell, C., Robson, J.G.: The contrast sensitivity of retinal Ganglion cells of the cat. J. Physiol. **187**(3), 517–552 (1966)
15. Nematzadeh, N., Powers, D.M.W.: A quantitative analysis of tilt in the Café Wall illusion: a bioplausible model for foveal and peripheral vision. In: DICTA (2016)
16. Nematzadeh, N., Powers, D.M.W., Trent, L.: Quantitative analysis of a bioplausible model of misperception of slope in the Café Wall illusion. In: Workshop on Interpretation and Visualization of Deep Neural Nets (WINVIZNN), ACCV (2016)
17. Lindeberg, T., Florack, L.: Foveal scale-space and the linear increase of receptive field size as a function of eccentricity (1994)
18. Kuffler, S.W.: Neurons in the retina: organization, inhibition and excitation problems. In: Cold Spring Harbor Symposia on Quantitative Biology, vol. 17, pp. 281–292. Cold Spring Harbor Laboratory Press (1952)
19. Marr, D., Hildreth, E.: Theory of edge detection. Proc. Roy. Soc. London B: Biol. Sci. **207**(1167), 1187–1217 (1980)
20. Illingworth, J., Kittler, J.: A survey of the Hough transform. Comput. Vis. Graph. Imag. Process. **44**(1), 87–116 (1988)
21. Passaglia, C.L., Enroth-Cugell, C., Troy, J.B.: Effects of remote stimulation on the mean firing rate of cat retinal Ganglion cells. J. Neurosci. **21**(15), 5794–5803 (2001)
22. Nematzadeh, N.: A neurophysiological model for geometric visual illusions. Ph.D. thesis, Flinders University (in preparation)

# Automated Reconstruction of Neurovascular Networks in Knife-Edge Scanning Microscope Rat Brain Nissl Data Set

Wookyung An$^{(\boxtimes)}$ and Yoonsuck Choe

Department of Computer Science and Engineering,
Texas A&M University, College Station, TX 77843-3112, USA
{aqualiquid,choe}@tamu.edu

**Abstract.** Analyzing mammalian brain image can help to understand the interaction between cerebral blood flow and its surrounding tissue. However, extracting the geometry of the vasculature and the cells is difficult because of the complexity of the brain. In this paper, we propose an approach for reconstructing the neurovascular networks from Knife-Edge Scanning Microscope (KESM) rat Nissl data set. The proposed method includes the following steps. First, we enhanced the raw image data using homomorphic filtering, fast Fourier transform, and anisotropic diffusion. Next, we initially extracted the vessel cross section from the image using dynamic global thresholding. Subsequently, we computed local properties of the connected components to remove various sources of noise. Finally, the proposed method connected small and large discontinuities in the vascular traces. To validate the performance of the proposed method, we compared reconstruction results of the proposed method with an existing method (Lim's method [1,2]). The comparison results show that the proposed method outperforms the previous method: faster and robust to noise.

## 1 Introduction

The relationship between cerebral blood flow and neuronal activity plays an important role in understanding brain diseases [3]. For example, in Alzheimer disease, cerebral vascular reactivity is decreased resulting in vascular dysfunction [4]. In ischemic stroke, oxygen free radicals are generated between the microvessels and the brain tissues resulting in cell damage [5]. These studies show that investigating neurovascular networks can lead to a breakthrough in understanding macro and microcirculation and their influences on brain disorders. To analyze neurovascular networks, Knife-Edge Scanning Microscope (KESM) enables us to image whole-brain that stained in Golgi (neuronal morphology), Nissl (somata), and India ink (vasculature) at submicrometer voxel resolution [6]. In particular, Nissl stain labels the nucleic acid contents of the cells, including endoplasmic reticulum, ribosomes, and the cell nuclei [7], whereas the vessels remain unstained. Through the KESM Nissl data, we can see the relationships between somatic cells and microvascular networks. However, KESM Nissl data

© Springer International Publishing AG 2016
G. Bebis et al. (Eds.): ISVC 2016, Part I, LNCS 10072, pp. 439–448, 2016.
DOI: 10.1007/978-3-319-50835-1_40

set has several challenging issues to be resolved to reconstruct the microvascular networks: uneven illumination artifacts, high-frequency streaks due to nick on the knife and ribbon boundary, and some noise due to chatter. These artifacts degrade the quality of the image resulting in erroneous vascular reconstruction. In this paper, we aim to reconstruct neurovascular networks from KESM rat Nissl data by applying a novel automated method. Our method provides fast and accurate reconstruction results, offering accurate analysis on its anatomical statistic. In the following, we will describe the KESM, the proposed method, and the comparison results.

## 2    Knife-Edge Scanning Microscope

KESM is a high-throughput imaging method providing a high-resolution image, and bridges the gaps between high resolution imaging technique with a small volume (e.g. EM provides nano-scale voxel resolution [8]) and low resolution imaging technique with a large whole-brain volume (e.g. MRI approaches at most 156 μm voxel resolution [9]). Figure 1(a) illustrates the major components of the KESM [10,11].

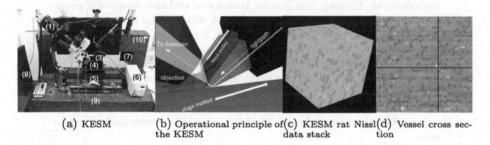

(a) KESM       (b) Operational principle of (c) KESM rat Nissl (d) Vessel cross sec-
               the KESM                   data stack        tion

**Fig. 1.** (a) shows the KESM: (1) high-speed line-scan camera, (2) microscope objective, (3) diamond knife assembly and light collimator, (4) specimen tank, (5) three-axis precision air-bearing stage, (6) white-light microscope illuminator, (7) water pump for the removal of sectioned tissue, (8) PC server for stage control and image acquisition, (9) granite base, and (10) granite bridge. (b) shows the operational principle of the KESM. Adapted from [6]. (c) shows a KESM rat Nissl data stack (200 voxels × 200 voxels × 200 voxels volume with voxel size 0.6 μm.) (d) shows vessel cross sections (the bright spots).

The imaging principle of the KESM is illustrated in Fig. 1(b). The specimen is affixed on the positioning stage, and then the stage with the specimen is moved toward the diamond knife to generate 1 μm-thick sections. At the time of sectioning the specimen, line-scan imaging is done near the top of the diamond knife at the edge, from which a high-resolution image is generated from each cut tissue. The resolution of the voxel is 0.6 μm × 0.7 μm laterally, and 1.0 μm axially. The number of coronal sections of the KESM rat Nissl brain is 968 (cortical tissue that is about 2 mm thick) sagittal sections.

# 3  Methods

## 3.1  Subsampling and Image Enhancement

Before we start to process the rat Nissl data set, we utilized image subsampling (down to 50%) to reduce the computational overhead because the size of the KESM Nissl data set is large: the whole-brain data set is approximately 2 TB, uncompressed. Subsequently, we manually triaged damaged images (e.g. long streaks and large smear) from the Nissl data set since the damaged image could lead to the generation of error-prone results. The number of triaged images are 8, which is 0.82% among the data set. We also need to correct the inconsistent illumination artifacts that are caused by variable cutting speed and tilt in the diamond knife surface relative to the optical axis. This misalignment led to a reduction in illumination across parts or the entirely of the image. To correct such illumination artifacts, we applied a homomorphic filter [12]. The basic model of homomorphic filtering is as follows:

$$I(x, y) = L(x, y) \ R(x, y)$$

where $I(x, y)$ is a 2D image, $L(x, y)$ is scene illumination across the image, and $R(x, y)$ is the image reflectance. The key task of homomorphic filtering is to remove the illumination $L(x, y)$, but to preserves the reflectance component $R(x, y)$. The reflectance $R(x, y)$ and illumination $L(x, y)$ can be separable by the log function:

$$ln(I(x, y)) = ln(L(x, y)) + ln(R(x, y))$$

Since the illumination of the image $L(x, y)$ typically resides in the low-frequency domain, high-pass filter is used to remove the log domain of $L$. Therefore, only the reflectance $R(x, y)$ is remained.

As mentioned in the Sect. 1, the KESM rat Nissl data set exhibits dark periodic noise patterns due to nick on the diamond knife and ribbon boundary. We used fast Fourier transform (FFT) [12] to eliminate high-contrast streak in the 3D volume. The pipeline of the periodic pattern reduction is as follows: (1) We computed 2D Fourier space $F(u, v)$ from the spatial domain of the image $f(x, y)$ (size $M \times N$) corresponding to each coordinate $F(u, v)$.

$$F(u, v) = \frac{1}{MN} \sum_{x=0}^{M-1} \sum_{y=0}^{N-1} f(x, y) \cdot e^{-j2\pi(\frac{ux}{M} + \frac{vy}{N})}$$

where $j = \sqrt{-1}$, $x = 0,1,2,...,(M-1)$ and $y = 0,1,2,...,(N-1)$.

(2) To remove the vertical and horizontal peaks in the frequency domain, we created Fourier notch filter $H(u, v)$ and multiplied $F(u, v)$ by $H(u, v)$ (Fig. 2):

$$G(u, v) = F(u, v) * H(u, v).$$

(3) We took inverse FFT to restore the image in the spatial domain $g(x, y)$.

$$g(x, y) = \frac{1}{MN} \sum_{u=0}^{M-1} \sum_{v=0}^{N-1} G(u, v) \cdot e^{j2\pi(\frac{ux}{M} + \frac{vy}{N})}$$

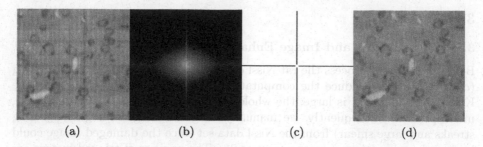

(a)     (b)     (c)     (d)

**Fig. 2.** (a) shows the raw image. (b) shows the Fourier spectrum of (a). (c) shows the notch filter $H(u, v)$. (d) shows the denoised result.

Subsequently, we applied anisotropic diffusion [13] to suppress the image noise without removing significant details such as edges and lines.

### 3.2 Thresholding

We utilized dynamic global thresholding method to extract high contrast object from the image stack. Global thresholding is fast but determining the global threshold value is difficult because each image in the KESM Nissl data has the uneven illumination artifacts across the image and the imaging errors. However, we found that most vessel cross sections were likely to be located around the local maxima of the image intensity histogram, and the local maxima were mostly located above the mean pixel value of the image. Additionally, the image histogram was skewed to the left. For these reasons, we dynamically calculated a mean value of each image as a threshold value. Furthermore, we put a standard deviation of each image into the thresholding model to reduce excessive removal of noise. The following model is the dynamic global thresholding value, $T$.

$$T(k) = m_k + |s_k|$$

where $k$ is the current image layer, $m_k$ is the mean value of the $k$-th layer, and $s_k$ is a standard deviation of the $k$-th layer. As a result, all possible vessel cross sections could be segmented by the proposed global thresholding approach since we loosened the threshold value.

### 3.3 Connected Component Analysis

After the thresholding step, all subsequent images are stacked to render a 3D volume. To eliminate noisy results among all detected foreground, we detected vessel cross sections among the initially thresholded 3D volume. Note that we identified the vessel cross sections in the 3D context instead of in the 2D context since there is no clear difference between vessel cross sections and noise objects in the 2D context.

Previously, Lim applied a simple heuristic, called the guidance map: $min(I_x, I_y)$, where $I_x$ and $I_y$ are axially two aligned images [1]. This method only considers the previous and the subsequent image, not the whole 3D context. Therefore, Lim's method cannot accurately distinguish the entire connected component (CC) as noise or vascular segment. To overcome this issue, we implemented a simple, yet intuitive method to remove the noise in 3D context. Our proposed method goes through the following steps: (1) The proposed method measures centerline length along the axial direction of each connected component in the 3D volume. (2) If the CC is longer than the threshold, the CC will remain. Otherwise, the CC will be eliminated. Note that the threshold value of axial length is empirically determined in advance. In this paper, we used 30 (i.e., the number of layers) as a threshold value. However, some connected components (CCs), those that are shorter than the threshold, seem to be vascular segments in the 3D context. This is a common problem with thresholding-based segmentation when the image has low contrast. Thus, we should connect such disconnected vascular segments before applying this noise removal method.

There were two types of discontinuities present in the volume: small discontinuity and large discontinuity. We defined small discontinuity as one or two missing vessel cross sections along the axial direction between two CCs. We defined large discontinuity as more than three missing vessel cross sections along the axial direction between two CCs, and upper bound of the discontinuity was empirically set to 30.

**Table 1.** Example of connecting small discontinuity.

|  (a)  |  (b)  |  (c)  |

To connect the small disconnected segments, the proposed method is designed to detect small discontinuities in each of the four consecutive images, and connect the disconnected segments if the discontinuity of axial length is less than three. The basic idea of the approach is as follows (Table 1): (1) Let the four consecutive images be $L_{n-1}$, $L_n$, $L_{n+1}$, and $L_{n+2}$, where $n$ is a positive integer ($n$=2, 3, 4, ...). (2) If $L_{n-1}$ has a blob or more than one blob, the proposed method renders a bounding box, $B_{n-1}$, around the detected blob from $L_{n-1}$. (3) Also, the proposed method renders the bounding boxes for $L_n$, $L_{n+1}$, and $L_{n+2}$, respectively, with the same size and coordinate of $B_{n-1}$ from $L_{n-1}$. (4) If $B_n$ or $B_{n+1}$ is empty, the empty one will be replaced with the bounding box that is generated by $B_{n-1} \cup B_{n+1}$ or $B_n \cup B_{n+2}$ (Table 1(a)). (5) If $B_n$ and $B_{n+1}$ are empty, $B_n$ and $B_{n+1}$ will be replaced with a new bounding box that is generated by $B_{n-1} \cup B_{n+2}$ (Table 1(b)). (6) If $B_{n+2}$ is empty, the proposed method will not fill in $B_{n+2}$ because it is the last one among the four consecutive bounding boxes (Table 1(c)).

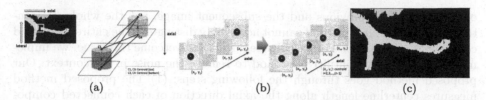

(a)                            (b)                            (c)

**Fig. 3.** (a) shows an example of large discontinuity (sagittal view). (b) shows finding the minimum Euclidean distance between the CCs. If there is a discrepancy between the initial centroid that are extracted from the 2D images and the predicted centroids (e.g. $(x_2, y_2)$, $(x_3, y_3)$, ..., $(x_{n-1}, y_{n-1})$), the bounding box of the predicted blob will be shifted. The location of the bounding box will be automatically adjusted once it reaches the end of the CC. (c) shows a sagittal view of the 3D volume where two components are successfully connected by the proposed method.

As shown in Fig. 3(a), there is a large gap in the 3D volume along the axial direction. To connect the large disconnected segments, the proposed method measures the minimum Euclidean distance between the CCs in the 3D volume. Initially, the proposed method extracted two centroids from the top and the bottom of the bounding box of the $n$-th CC, where $n$ is a positive integer ($n = 1$, 2, 3, ...), and sequentially stores the centroid information to the list. Note that a centroid is defined as a center of the smallest rectangular window containing the vessel cross section. The idea of the distance measuring between the CCs is as follows (Fig. 3(a)): The Euclidean distance between two points $C1 = (x, y, z)$ and $C2 = (a, b, c)$ in space is defined as $d(C1, C2) = \sqrt{(x - a)^2 + (y - b)^2 + (z - c)^2}$. The basic idea of the approach is as follows: (1) Let the top of the centroid on the left side be C1, and the bottom of the centroid on the left side be C2. (2) Let the top of the centroid on the right side be C3, and the bottom of the centroid on the left side be C4. (3) In this case, the minimum Euclidean distance between the CCs is $d(C1, C4)$. Note that if the centroids are not in the same CC, the proposed method will calculate the Euclidean distance between the centroids. Otherwise, the distance between the centroids in the same CC will be disregarded. (4) Each minimum Euclidean distance between the CCs and the index of the CCs are stored in a list. Note that duplicated distances, such as $d(C1, C3)$ and $d(C3, C1)$ were removed. (5) Finally, the proposed method examines the minimum Euclidean distance of the discontinuity that is stored in the list. If the distance of the discontinuity is within the threshold value, then the proposed method will connect the discontinuity (Fig. 3(c)).

## 4    Results and Analysis

Throughout the procedure, we reconstructed microvasculatures in the KESM rat Nissl data set (Fig. 4). To quantify the performance of the proposed method, we compared the 3D reconstruction results of the proposed method against Lim's method from the same KESM rat Nissl data set (somatosensory cortex). In the first part, we compared the results on a small volume (200 voxels × 200 voxels × 200 voxels) and then compared the results on a large volume (2200 voxels × 2600 voxels × 960 voxels).

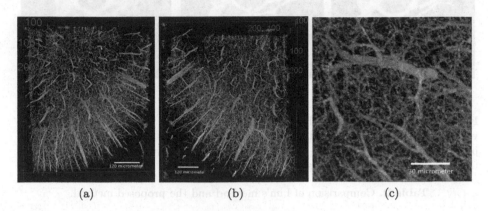

(a)                            (b)                            (c)

**Fig. 4.** Reconstructed volume visualization of the KESM rat Nissl data. (a) shows anterior view, (b) shows posterior view, and (c) shows close up view.

In a small volume, we generated 200 ground truth images with a local window (200 pixels × 200 pixels) by a human (other than the authors). Then, the reconstructed volume of the ground truth and the reconstructed volume generated by Lim's method were compared. Finally, we estimated each reconstructed result by calculating precision, recall, and F-score. In detail, precision indicates the portion of true positive (TP) among all objects labeled as vessels cross sections, and recall indicates how many of the true vessel cross sections in the ground truth are detected. F-score is a harmonic mean of precision and recall. The measurement can be described as follows: every two-dimensional image and the corresponding human segmentation of ground truth were superimposed on each other. If there is an intersection of the blob in the superimposed image, the blob is labeled and counted.

As shown in Fig. 5, the volume reconstructed by Lim's method has a number of discontinuities, whereas the processed volume from the proposed method does not have many discontinuities. Also, we found that some vasculatures were disconnected from each other in Lim's method, while the topology of the vasculature in the proposed method was more likely to be preserved. The results are summarized in Table 2. The proposed method shows superior performance on all measures compared to that of Lim's method.

We further conducted a quantitative comparison in a large-scale volume (2200 voxels × 2600 voxels × 960 voxels) to verify the performance of the proposed result. Different quantitative analysis method should be utilized to compare the results because it is difficult to manually generate ground truth by a human in case of the large data set. In this paper, we assumed that a small size of the CC is a noise due to imaging error and the extracted CC has integrity if the

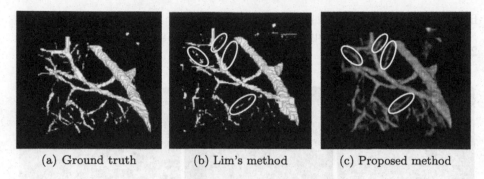

(a) Ground truth　　　　(b) Lim's method　　　　(c) Proposed method

**Fig. 5.** (a) shows the stack of the ground truth images (200 voxels × 200 voxels × 200 voxels). (b) and (c) show the stack of the generated images by Lim's method and the proposed method, respectively. (b) has frequent discontinuities (white ellipse) but (c) they are connected (white ellipse).

**Table 2.** Comparision of Lim's method and the proposed method.

|  | Lim's method | Proposed method |
|---|---|---|
| Precision | 69.64% | 77.52% |
| Recall | 83.29% | 99.38% |
| F-score | 75.85% | 87.09% |

centerline of the CC is long. With this assumption, we measured the centerline length and the number of voxel of each extracted CC to observe the error rate in the volume.

In order to quantify the difference between the two distributions, we measured the centerline length and plot the results as a histogram. Let $L$ be the centerline length in the CC. As shown in Fig. 6(a), Lim's method produces a large number of CCs with centerline length equal to 1 pixel (i.e., $L \leq 1$). On the other hand, the proposed method produces only a few such CCs. This indicates Lim's method produces a large number of small discontinuities, while the proposed method produces fewer small discontinuities compared to Lim's method. Furthermore, the proportion of CCs with long centerline ($L > 8.5$) in the volume that was generated by the proposed method is higher than that in Lim's method. This is because the proposed method connects the small and the large discontinuities while extracting the vasculature. Moreover, we measured the processing times between the two methods with five different voxels (Fig. 6(b)). The results show that the proposed method is approximately nine times faster (linearly) than Lim's method. The hardware used for the experiments had an Intel Core i7-4790K Quad-Core (4.0 GHz) processor, HDD 1 TB 64 MB Cache SATA 6.0 Gb/s, and 16 GB DDR3 RAM. All experiments were tested under Windows 10 Enterprise (64-bit) and Matlab 2016a.

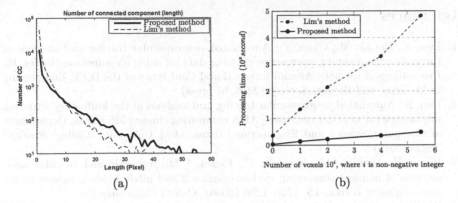

(a)                                                              (b)

**Fig. 6.** (a) is a log scale histogram that indicates the number of CCs in each volume as a function of CC length. The $X$-axis represents the centerline length of CC, and the $Y$-axis represents the number of CC in the volume (log scale). (b) shows the speed comparison between Lim's method and the proposed method.

## 5   Conclusion

In this paper, we proposed a novel method to extract the vessel cross sections accurately and reconstruct 3D geometry of the vascular networks. This method provides an automated process to reconstruct the large-scale vascular network in the brain. Additionally, the proposed method enhances the image quality through a couple of noise removal and correction heuristics, which make the proposed method robust to noise. In sum, we pre-processed the data set by triaging corrupted image, removing the periodic noise patterns, and correcting illumination artifacts. Next, we initially segmented the vessel cross section using dynamic global thresholding. After that, we applied a couple of heuristics to remove the noise due to chatter, and corrected the image errors by connecting the discontinuous CCs in the microvascular networks. To validate the proposed method, we compared the results with the volume processed by a previous method. The comparison results indicate that the proposed method is more robust to noise and nine times faster than the previous method. We expect that the proposed method will provide insights into analyzing microvascular networks in various types of mammalian brain.

**Acknowledgments.** Part of this research was funded by National Science Foundation, under grants #0905041, #1208174, and #1256086. This paper is largely based on the first author's master's thesis [14]. Lim's method's results were obtained from original Matlab code.

# References

1. Lim, S., Nowak, M., Choe, Y.: Automated neurovascular tracing and analysis of the knife-edge scanning microscope rat nissl data set using a computing cluster. In: Proceedings of the 38th Annual International Conference of the IEEE Engineering in Medicine and Biology Society (2016, in press)
2. Lim, S.: Automated neurovascular tracing and analysis of the knife-edge scanning microscope rat nissl data set using ADA computing cluster. MS thesis, Department of Computer Science and Engineering, Texas A&M University, College Station, Texas (2015)
3. Wang, H., Hitron, I.M., Iadecola, C., Pickel, V.M.: Synaptic and vascular associations of neurons containing cyclooxygenase-2 and nitric oxide synthase in rat somatosensory cortex. **15**, 1250–1260 (2005). Oxford University Press
4. Wells, J.A., Holmes, H.E., O'Callaghan, J.M., Colgan, N., Ismail, O., Fisher, E.M., Siow, B., Murray, T.K., Schwarz, A.J., O'Neill, M.J.: Increased cerebral vascular reactivity in the tau expressing rTg4510 mouse: evidence against the role of tau pathology to impair vascular health in Alzheimer's disease. J. Cereb. Blood Flow Metab. **35**, 359–362 (2015)
5. Girouard, H., Iadecola, C.: Neurovascular coupling in the normal brain and in hypertension, stroke, and Alzheimer disease. Am. Physiol. Soc. **100**, 328–335 (2006)
6. Choe, Y., Mayerich, D., Kwon, J., Miller, D.E., Chung, J.R., Sung, C., Keyser, J., Abbott, L.C.: Knife-edge scanning microscopy for connectomics research. In: The 2011 International Joint Conference on Neural Networks (IJCNN), pp. 2258–2265. IEEE press (2011)
7. Kádár, A., Wittmann, G., Liposits, Z., Fekete, C.: Improved method for combination of immunocytochemistry and nissl staining. **184**, 115–118 (2009). Elsevier
8. De Jonge, N., Peckys, D.B., Kremers, G., Piston, D.: Electron microscopy of whole cells in liquid with nanometer resolution. Natl. Acad. Sci. **106**, 2159–2164 (2009)
9. Roebroeck, A., Galuske, R., Formisano, E., Chiry, O., Bratzke, H., Ronen, I., Kim, D.s., Goebel, R.: High-resolution diffusion tensor imaging and tractography of the human optic chiasm at 9.4 T. **39**, 157–168 (2008). Elsevier
10. Mayerich, D., Abbott, L., McCormick, B.: Knife-edge scanning microscopy for imaging and reconstruction of three-dimensional anatomical structures of the mouse brain. Library **231**, 134–143 (2008). Wiley Online
11. Chung, J.R., Sung, C., Mayerich, D., Kwon, J., Miller, D.E., Huffman, T., Keyser, J., Abbott, L.C., Choe, Y.: Multiscale exploration of mouse brain microstructures using the knife-edge scanning microscope brain atlas. **5**, 84–100 (2011). Program No. 516.3
12. Gonzalez, R.C., Woods, R.E.: Digital Image Processing. Pearson, New York City (2002)
13. Perona, P., Malik, J.: Scale space and edge detection for visual scene analysis. In: Proceedings of IEEE Computer Society Workshop on Computer Vision, pp. 16–22 (1987)
14. An, W.: Automated reconstruction of neurovascular networks in knife-edge scanning microscope mouse and rat brain nissl stained data sets. MS thesis, Department of Computer Science and Engineering, Texas A&M University, College Station, Texas (2016)

# Spatiotemporal LOD-Blending for Artifact Reduction in Multi-resolution Volume Rendering

Sebastian Thiele, Carl-Feofan Matthes$^{(\boxtimes)}$, and Bernd Froehlich

Bauhaus-Universität Weimar, Weimar, Germany
carl-feofan.matthes@uni-weimar.de

**Abstract.** High-quality raycasting of multi-resolution volumetric datasets benefits from a well-informed working set selection that accounts for occlusions as well as output sensitivity. In this work, we suggest a feedback mechanism that provides a fine-grained level-of-detail selection for restricted working sets. To mitigate multi-resolution artifacts, our rendering solution combines spatial and temporal level-of-detail blending to provide smooth transitions between adjacent bricks of differing levels of detail and during working set adjustments. We also show how the sampling along rays needs to be adapted to produce a consistent result. Our implementation demonstrates that our spatiotemporal blending in combination with consistent sampling significantly reduces visual artifacts.

## 1 Introduction

The visualization of massive models exceeding the size of internal memories requires out-of-core multi-resolution rendering algorithms, designed to effectively reduce the amount of data loaded and considered during rendering [1]. However, out-of-core rendering systems frequently compromise the visual quality of the rendering result [2].

We present a set of novel methods developed for high-quality ray-guided real-time out-of-core visualization of large volumetric data sets. Disturbing popping artifacts during working set changes and salient discontinuities at brick boundaries are mitigated by a spatiotemporal interpolation scheme, which combines trilinear interpolation with spatial and temporal level-of-detail blending. Since our blending approach requires a restricted working set, we add two conditions for split and collapse operations during level-of-detail selection. Frequently, ray-guided feedback mechanisms are employed to inform the working set selection process and optimize resource utilization [3,4]. During raycasting, we accumulate feedback information for visible bricks of the working set and derive priorities to inform our level-of-detail selection scheme.

Our main contributions are:

- an efficient blending approach that combines spatial and temporal level-of-detail blending to overcome the most salient multi-resolution artifacts,
- a consistent adaptive sampling technique that avoids oversampling as well as abrupt changes of the sampling stepsize, and

G. Bebis et al. (Eds.): ISVC 2016, Part I, LNCS 10072, pp. 449–461, 2016.
DOI: 10.1007/978-3-319-50835-1_41

- a low-overhead level-of-detail feedback mechanism and an efficient priority distribution scheme to guide the working set selection process.

We integrated all proposed techniques into a multi-resolution volume raycasting framework and demonstrate the improved rendering quality of our approach.

## 2   Related Work

Multi-resolution volume rendering is a well-researched field and in this paper we limit our discussion to the work most closely related to our contributions. Beyer et al. [5] provide an overview of state-of-the-art volume rendering.

Multi-resolution approaches for the visualization of large volumetric datasets display the volume at locally varying levels of detail (LOD) and employ an octree representation of the dataset to store the working set in a texture atlas [1,3,6]. The *working set* is the result of a level-of-detail selection process and constitutes the set of bricks available during rendering. A brick consists of a fixed number of voxels (e.g. $64^3$) and serves as the paging unit. The leaf-level of the working set is also referred to as the *cut*. Commonly, view-dependent LOD cut updates are incrementally performed using a greedy-style split-and-collapse algorithm similar to [7], maximizing the data reuse by exploiting frame-to-frame coherence. In our work, the working set is *restricted* by adjacency relationships between bricks and we demonstrate how two conceptually simple conditions suffice to maintain a restricted working set on a frame-to-frame basis.

Ideally, a feedback mechanism is used to gather information about required data bricks directly during rendering. This is central to the output sensitivity of the system and greatly facilitates a restriction of the working set to the bricks actually visible. Crassin et al. [3] use render targets to keep track of brick utilization and store a single bit to indicate whether a given brick should be split. Hadwiger et al. [8] store feedback information in form of cache misses and usage statistics atomically in a set of feedback-tiles shared with other rays through screen-space partitioning directly during rendering. Fogal et al. [4] implement a lock-free set datastructure to store cache misses. However, the feedback generated in previous systems is limited to binary information about whether bricks should be split or collapsed and does not involve per-brick priorities gathered during sampling. To provide a fine-grained prioritization during working set selection, we store level-of-detail differences in our feedback table and provide a priority distribution algorithm connecting the feedback mechanism with a split-and-collapse working set selection strategy.

There are a number of artifacts commonly arising in multi-resolution volume raycasting systems. Carmona et al. [2] observe that visible *boundary artifacts* between bricks of differing levels of detail can be reduced through *spatial level-of-detail blending* with the parent brick towards boundaries of coarser neighboring bricks. Ljung et al. [9] interpolate boundary voxels between adjacent bricks, leaving the boundary discontinuity between bricks quite noticeable. Furthermore, frame-to-frame working set adjustments in out-of-core scenarios often cause *popping artifacts* during split and collapse operations. We introduce a novel *spatiotemporal level-of-detail blending* algorithm by generalizing the work of Carmona et al. [2], who employ a binary weight at each vertex. In this work, we introduce continuous spatiotemporal weights which are updated on a frame-to-frame basis to provide for both animated transitions during working-set changes and gradual transitions across adjacent bricks of differing LODs.

Commonly, the sampling density is adapted to match the brick resolution, e.g. [1]. However, in order to obtain a consistent rendering result in our approach, we incorporate additional considerations into the computation of the sampling density such as spatial and temporal blending as well as the ideal level-of-detail.

## 3  Direct Level-of-Detail Feedback

Performance and resource utilization benefit from a well-informed LOD selection that accounts for occlusions and output sensitivity. Volume rendering techniques that incorporate per-brick information gathered during sampling to drive the LOD selection process are referred to as *ray-guided* [4].

Our out-of-core multi-resolution volume rendering framework [10] is able to interactively handle massive volumetric datasets in the terabyte range. Figure 1 illustrates our basic system architecture. Similar to [1], our out-of-core data management system is based on a two-level cache hierarchy and consists of three main components: The brick cache, the brick atlas and the level-of-detail feedback mechanism.

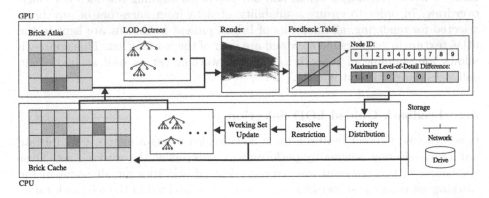

**Fig. 1.** This Figure depicts a high-level overview of our system. Each time a ray begins sampling a brick during rendering, the difference between the ideal level of detail at the sampling position and the level of detail actually available is stored in a feedback table. Next, we distribute derived priorities for the entire working set from the subset of bricks for which the priority was obtained through the feedback mechanism. During the resolve restriction step, we guarantee a restricted working set every frame and implement the adjacency constraint through forced split-operations. The actual working set update controls asynchronous data-delivery from external storage.

## 3.1   Feedback Table

During rendering, we populate a feedback table of brick usage statistics that is shared across all rays and transferred from graphics memory to main memory in order to guide our LOD selection process. Before rendering, we reserve a feedback entry for each brick present in the working set. In order to converge on the best possible working set for rendering, we store the maximum level-of-detail difference required by all rays that sample a brick in the feedback table. Similar to [8], we index the location of feedback information based on the corresponding brick id which allows for direct feedback accumulation without an additional histogram compaction step.

We initialize all entries in our feedback table $P$ with $-\infty$. Whenever a ray begins sampling a brick, we atomically store the maximum of all differences of the depth of brick $N$ to the optimal LOD at the given sampling position in the feedback table:

$$P_N = \max \{LOD_{actual}(N, R) - LOD_{ideal}(N, R) \mid R \in \mathscr{R}\} \qquad (1)$$

where $\mathscr{R}$ is the set of rays that sample brick $N$. We also keep a record of the number of rays that have sampled each brick to augment our working set selection prioritization.

We opt to serialize the layout of our level-of-detail octree in graphics memory instead of using an index texture, because at raycasting time we stop traversing the working set as soon as the ideal level-of-detail is reached. This guarantees that we never oversample bricks and our restricted working set does not cause overdraw. In order to ensure availability of data from ancestors of any brick selected for rendering, all ancestors of bricks present in the cut are kept in the atlas texture in graphics memory and are part of the working set. This approach allows for sampling of inner bricks of the working set as well as immediate collapses during the cut update.

## 3.2   Feedback-Guided LOD Selection

Given the most recent feedback table downloaded to main memory, we initiate our LOD selection scheme by performing a sweep over the working set. Over the course of this traversal, we compute derived priorities for all nodes in the working set from the subset of known priorities contained in the feedback table.

First, we obtain priority $P_N$ corresponding to node $N$ from the feedback table. We define $P_N$ to be the maximum of $LOD_{actual}(N, R) - LOD_{ideal}(N, R)$ for all rays $R$ that sample brick $N$ (Sect. 3.1). Note that $P_N$ is positive for nodes that are too coarse and zero if the LOD of $N$ is ideal. If there is no priority for node $N$ available in the feedback table, then $P_N = -\infty$. Next, we traverse the entire working set top-down breadth-first and propagate priorities from the feedback table (cmp. algorithm in Fig. 2(a)). During the bottom-up traversal, we store the corresponding value of $P_N$ of each node $N$.

After the priority distribution, the priority $P_A$ for any given node $A$ is larger than $P_N$ for ancestors of $N$, and smaller than $P_N$ for descendants of $N$ (Fig. 2(b)). Over the course of the LOD selection process, nodes in the leaf level of the working set for which $P_N < 0$ are queued for collapse because their LOD is considered too fine by all rays. In contrast, any nodes at the leaf level of the working set for which $P_N > 0$ are candidates for splitting as their LOD is considered too coarse by some rays. Nodes that are occluded or outside of the viewing-frustum receive a negative priority and are therefore subject to collapse.

During the split-and-collapse working set update, split operations are performed in accordance with the per-brick priorities established above. If two bricks have equal priority, then we consider the number of rays that sampled the bricks in question to augment our prioritization. Thus, we achieve a fine-grained prioritization during the LOD selection, which is used to adhere to global memory constraints and memory transfer budgets. Our priorities are suitable for the prioritization of the out-of-core data delivery queue in external memory scenarios as well.

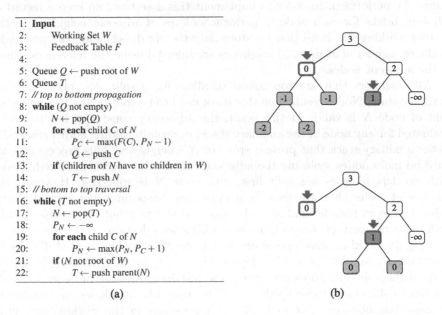

```
 1: Input
 2:     Working Set W
 3:     Feedback Table F
 4:
 5: Queue Q ← push root of W
 6: Queue T
 7: // top to bottom propagation
 8: while (Q not empty)
 9:     N ← pop(Q)
10:     for each child C of N
11:         PC ← max(F(C), PN − 1)
12:         Q ← push C
13:     if (children of N have no children in W)
14:         T ← push N
15: // bottom to top traversal
16: while (T not empty)
17:     N ← pop(T)
18:     PN ← −∞
19:     for each child C of N
20:         PN ← max(PN, PC + 1)
21:     if (N not root of W)
22:         T ← push parent(N)
```

(a)                                              (b)

**Fig. 2.** (a): Priority propagation algorithm. (b): Illustration of the propagation of priorities across the working set in our approach, depicted as a binary tree. Feedback information is obtained for two nodes marked with arrows. The resulting propagated priorities after the working set traversal are shown on top. Over the course of the working set update, nodes with negative priority are collapsed and nodes with a positive priority are split. The updated working set is shown below.

## 4  Spatiotemporal Level-of-Detail Blending

Abrupt changes in resolutions between adjacent bricks cause salient discontinuities that domain experts considered distracting. We mitigate these cross-block artifacts using an approach that extends the one described in [2] where bricks are gradually interpolated with data from their parent in the octree as rays are sampled towards the boundary of coarser neighbors. Disturbing popping artifacts during working set changes remain visible in [2] and we generalize their binary spatial weights to continuous spatiotemporal weights to provide for visually pleasing transitions over time during working set adjustments. In this approach, the working set selected for rendering is restricted such that the difference with respect to the LOD between adjacent bricks does not exceed one level.

## 4.1   Restricted Working Set Selection

To maintain a restricted working set throughout LOD selection, we include additional conditions for split and collapse operations. The adjacency constraint dictates that node $N$ can be split only if $(\text{depth}(N) - \text{depth}(B_i)) < 1$ holds for all its neighbors $B_i$. As long as there are neighbors that are too coarse, the split cannot be performed. In order to implement this assertion, we keep a record of adjacent bricks for each node to perform lookups of adjacent neighbors in the current working set. Note that we store only the six direct neighbors per node, as the remainder of at most 26 neighbors are inferred using the references stored in the adjacent nodes.

All neighbors that are too coarse to allow for a split are collected in an auxiliary stack. Nodes residing on this stack need to be split before the restricted split of node $N$ is valid. At this point, the adjacency constraint has to be re-evaluated for any node in the auxiliary stack, eventually adding additional nodes to the auxiliary stack that prevent splits of $N$'s neighbors. This process repeats until no more nodes violating the adjacency constraint are encountered. Nodes with no dependencies are split first, and node $N$ is split last. However, the number of nodes that are split on a per-frame basis must not exceed a predefined memory transfer budget and occasionally, it may not be possible to split node $N$ in the current iteration of the working set selection.

Priority-based collapse operations of a node $N$ are only executed if all of its neighbors $B_i$ fulfill $(\text{depth}(N) - \text{depth}(B_i)) \geq -1$. In contrast to split operations, if there are neighbors preventing the restricted collapse of node $N$, we do not force collapses of these neighbors. This approach introduces an asymmetry or hysteresis between split and collapse operations in the working set selection which stabilizes the working set and significantly reduces flickering between states.

In our implementation, we restrict the entire working set. In theory, bricks that are occluded or outside the viewing-frustum do not have to be subjected to restriction. However, as soon as previously occluded bricks become visible or move into the viewing frustum, not having restricted them before causes noticeable artifacts.

## 4.2   Temporal Level-of-Detail Blending

Our renderer animates transitions between LODs during split and collapse operations. We associate a *primary temporal weight* $t_N$ with each node in the hierarchy, indicating the interpolation between the parent and the node itself. During split operations, we gradually increase $t_N$ over time from 0.0 to 1.0 at which point the node is fully visible. Similarly, we decrease $t_N$ during collapse operations. All nodes for which $t_N > 0.0$ are part of the working set. Furthermore, we guarantee that the outcome of any temporal transitions pending do not invalidate the restriction of our working set.

## 4.3   Spatial Level-of-Detail Blending

Carmona et al. [2] use one bit at each vertex of a brick to indicate whether any adjacent brick is coarser than the brick in question. During rendering, they consider eight vertex bits for any given sampling position to determine the influence of the parent of the brick being sampled. If at least one adjacent brick is coarser than brick $N$, samples taken from brick $N$ and its parent in the LOD hierarchy are linearly interpolated to obtain the final sample and provide for smooth transitions between bricks of differing levels of detail (Fig. 3(a)).

In our work, we generalize the binary weight at each vertex to a continuous *spatiotemporal weight* that is used to adapt gradually between the brick being sampled and its parent (Fig. 3(b)). The spatiotemporal weight indicates the minimum time step of all nodes of equal depth adjacent to the corresponding vertex. As soon as any brick adjacent to the vertex is coarser than the brick in question, we set the corresponding spatiotemporal weight to zero. Otherwise, the spatiotemporal weight $s_v$ of vertex $v$ for brick $N$ is given by $s_v = \min(t_{B_i})$, $i < 8$

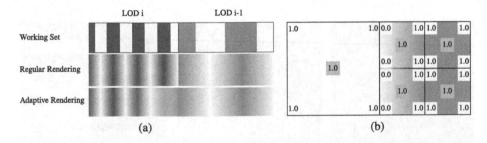

(a)                                           (b)

**Fig. 3.** (a): Illustration of spatial level-of-detail blending. The working set (top) contains bricks of differing level of detail. A regular rendering of these bricks comes with salient boundary artifacts (middle). An adaptive rendering strategy provides for higher visual fidelity in theses cases (bottom). (b): This Figure illustrates spatiotemporal blending for a quadtree along with the configuration of spatiotemporal weights $s_v$ shown in white squares and primary temporal weights $t_N$ in blue squares. When the right brick is split all weights are initialized to zero, indicating that samples are taken from the parent brick only. Over time, we increase the weights, gradually adding to the influence of the child bricks. (Color figure online)

where $t_{B_i}$ represent the primary temporal weights of all bricks of equal depth sharing vertex $v$. Whenever a node in the working set is split or collapsed, the spatiotemporal weights of all affected neighbors need to be updated accordingly. This ensures that temporal transitions of bricks during working set adjustments correctly composite with spatial blending between bricks of differing levels of detail and provides for visually continuous results regardless of the LOD chosen for rendering and ongoing temporal transitions.

## 5   Adaptive Sampling for Spatiotemporal Blending

In general, sampling the volume at a constant stepsize may cause severe oversampling or undersampling because it is not view-dependent and does not account for local changes in level-of-detail. In our experience, abrupt changes of the stepsize during sampling may cause visible artifacts. Therefore, we believe that an artifact-optimized adaptive sampling strategy must avoid abrupt changes in the sampling stepsize. Consequently, we consider a number of influences to compute an adaptive stepsize at a given sampling position. These influences include the level of detail of the brick being sampled as well as the ideal continuous level of detail at the sampling position. To adapt the sampling density along rays to our spatiotemporal LOD-blending approach, we also incorporate temporal and spatial LOD blend weights in our adaptive stepsize computation. Our particular transfer function (transparency highest in the middle of the transfer function domain) requires the use of the Gauss filter approach for appearance preserving LOD rendering as suggested in [11]. However, this technique cannot be easily combined with pre-integrated volume rendering since it already uses a 2D transfer function lookup. For this reason, we use adaptive sampling in combination with opacity correction.

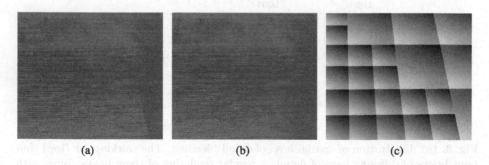

(a)                    (b)                    (c)

**Fig. 4.** Cross-brick artifacts along the boundary between bricks of differing LODs without LOD blending and adaptive sampling (a). Our spatiotemporal LOD blending and the adaptive sampling scheme provide for smooth, almost imperceptible transitions in these cases by gradually increasing the influence of the parent brick towards the boundary of coarser neighbors (b). The current working set configuration is shown in (c).

For perspective projections, the ideal level of detail decreases as the distance between the sampling position and the view point increases. To avoid oversampling or undersampling, the level of detail should be related to the footprint of the pixel at the sampling location, e.g. the diameter of the pyramid created by the pixel and viewpoint at the sampling location. Since the edge length of voxels increases by a factor of two between octree levels, however, voxels with an ideal edge length of $v_{ideal}$ do not usually exist in our octree. We can assume that the smallest voxels have an edge length of one and thus, we define the fractional ideal $LOD_{ideal} = MaxOctreeDepth - log_2(v_{ideal})$. For consistency reasons, we set the sampling distance along a ray to $v_{ideal}$ for a voxel to pixel size ratio of 1:1. In case the brick of the ideal level of detail is not present in the working set, we adapt the sampling stepsize to the available brick being sampled (Fig. 5(b)), which is usually the highest LOD available in the current working set.

In addition, we incorporate spatiotemporal LOD-blending as indicated by the corresponding blend weights into our stepsize computation since the stepsize along a ray should be consistent with the fractional LOD required for spatiotemporal blending. Each brick comes with eight spatiotemporal weights as well as one primary weight, which are used to transition between the stepsizes required for the brick being sampled and its parent brick. During a temporal transition, we trilinearly interpolate all eight spatiotemporal weights of the brick being sampled to determine the influence of the parent brick at the current sampling position. In essence, the result of the trilinear interpolation of spatiotemporal weights is used to increase the sampling stepsize smoothly as we sample the ray towards the boundary of a coarser neighbor. Starting from the sampling density required by the brick being sampled, we gradually increase the sampling stepsize up to the sampling density required by the parent brick (Fig. 5(c)). The primary temporal weight $t_N$ of any adjacent brick factors into the computation of the

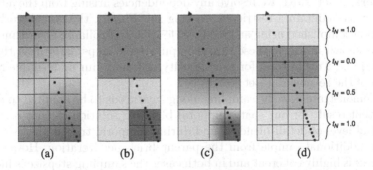

(a)          (b)          (c)          (d)

**Fig. 5.** Our adaptive sampling strategy considers four influences: the ideal LOD at the sampling position (a), the actual LOD available in graphics memory (b), the spatial blending between bricks of differing LODs (c) and the primary temporal blendweights for animated transitions during working set adjustments (d). In these illustrations, the color red corresponds to the highest, green to the lowest level of detail and the viewpoint is assumed to reside in the lower right corner. (Color figure online)

spatiotemporal weight of a vertex (Sect. 4.3). Therefore, any pending temporal transitions correctly blend into the resulting stepsize and require no extra handling.

As a result, we need to consider three cases with respect to the current sampling position and the stepsize computation. First, if there is spatial or temporal blending active for the current brick being sampled, we compute the stepsize from the fractional LOD that corresponds to the interpolated blend weight at the current sampling location. Second, if the available LOD is coarser than the ideal LOD, then we use the sampling stepsize that corresponds to available LOD. Finally, if the ideal LOD is available, which requires that $\lceil LOD_{ideal} \rceil$ is in the working set, we can use the corresponding stepsize and interpolate appropriately between the corresponding bricks based on the fractional part of $LOD_{ideal}$. As evident from Fig. 4, artifacts along brick boundaries are mitigated using this scheme.

# 6    Results and Discussion

The evaluation was conducted on an *Intel Xeon* CPU with 6 cores at 3.5 GHz, 128 GB main memory along with a *Nvidia GTX Titan X* graphics card with 12 GB video memory. Large datasets in the oil and gas domain are mostly confidential. Fortunately, we received permission to use a seismic dataset from an oil field located in New Zealand for publications. The dataset is $5989 \times 3933 \times 1501$ voxels in size and was processed using a bricksize of $64^3$ voxels. Given an octree depth of 7, its total size is 87.3 GB and contains 16 bit Gaussian coefficients per voxel as contributed in [11] to overcome inconsistency artifacts during prefiltering and down-sampling of the dataset.

Our working set generation consists of three steps. Over the course of the priority propagation, we determine a priority for every brick currently residing in the working set. Next, we resolve any dependencies arising from the adjacency constraint to maintain a restricted working set. Finally, the actual working set update is accomplished using an greedy-style split-and-collapse algorithm similar to [7]. As shown in Fig. 6, these three computational steps perform in the range between 4 and 8 ms in total for the majority of frames during a simple rotation scenario of the seismic dataset.

We demonstrate how the sampling along rays needs to be adapted to produce a consistent result for our spatiotemporal blending solution as shown in Fig. 7. For spatial level-of-detail blending and during temporal transitions, we need to take one additional sample from the parent brick per iteration. However, this data access is highly coherent and in both cases the sampling stepsize is increased in accordance to the influence of the parent brick, resulting in a limited overall sampling overhead in the range of 10 to 20% in our experience (Fig. 6). This is also consistent with what was reported by Carmona et al. [2] who performed only spatial blending between LODs.

It is conceivable to prevent cross-block boundary artifacts by trilinearly interpolating voxels within a certain neighborhood of the boundary with multiple

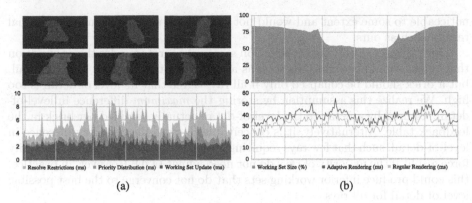

(a)  (b)

**Fig. 6.** These plots illustrate the performance of our system in a simple rotation scenario at a display resolution of $1920 \times 1080$. The seismic dataset rotates once about the y-axis as depicted in the top rows (a). The stacked area chart shows the duration of the individual algorithmic steps of the per-frame working set update in milliseconds. The memory consumption of our working set over time is depicted in the area chart in (b). The bottom graph shows the raycasting time in milliseconds for both regular state-of-the-art volume raycasting as well as our adaptive spatiotemporal rendering scheme.

ancestors in arbitrary, non-restricted working set configurations. However, data-based working set selection metrics frequently deliver large differences in level-of-detail adjacent to homogenous regions in the volume. If the working set is not restricted, then it is not obvious how to sample efficiently at decreasing density over multiple bricks and multiple levels of ancestry towards the boundary of a coarser neighbor. Limiting the transition to one brick only in this case is not advisable either, since it leaves the boundary between the bricks in question

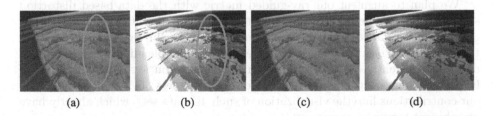

(a)  (b)  (c)  (d)

**Fig. 7.** Visualization of per-pixel iteration count during sampling of the seismic dataset. The state-of-the-art sampling approach without spatiotemporal blending shown in (a) and (b) requires a considerable number of sampling operations and produces salient artifacts (marked blue) on the boundaries between adjacent bricks of differing levels of detail. Our adaptive sampling solution requires fewer sampling operations (d) and and in combination with spatiotemporal blending it results in smooth transitions across brick boundaries (c). The intensity in (b) and (d) corresponds to the number of iterations where the color white indicates a number of iterations exceeding 1024. (Color figure online)

noticeable to some extent and would not provide for similarly convincing visual results such as ours.

Our ray-guided working set selection strategy operates under the assumption that bricks should be refined as soon as any ray requires a higher level of detail, but a brick should be collapsed only if all rays agree that its level of detail is too high. We realize this assumption by storing the *maximum* difference in level-of-detail required by any ray to the level-of-detail actually sampled per brick in the feedback table. Alternatively, it is conceivable to store the *average* difference in level-of-detail, such that few rays requiring a high level of detail do not necessarily force a split if the majority of rays do not need a finer LOD. However, in practice, this could produce inferior working sets that do not converge to the best possible level of detail for all rays.

## 7    Conclusion and Future Work

Our main contribution is a ray-guided artifact-optimized volume rendering scheme and an efficient level-of-detail feedback mechanism to guide the working set selection. We generalized the work of Carmona et al. [2] from static spatial LOD blending to dynamic spatiotemporal LOD blending to provide visually pleasing transitions between adjacent bricks of differing levels of detail as well as animated transitions over time during working set adjustments. For the reduction of sampling artifacts in multi-resolution rendering, we demonstrated a consistent adaptive sampling technique that accounts for spatiotemporal blending and avoids oversampling as well as abrupt changes of the sampling stepsize. In addition, we provide implementation details for a priority-distribution algorithm, connecting the feedback generated during raycasting with a split-and-collapse working set selection strategy. Our feedback-scheme allows occluded parts of the scene and bricks outside the frustum to collapse automatically and optimizes memory utilization in a straightforward manner.

We plan to augment our ray-guided metric with the data-based distortion suggested by Ljung et al. [12] to focus on volume regions with the highest information density. Of course, it is straightforward to use our algorithm in conjunction with quadtrees to achieve spatiotemporal LOD-blending for large image datasets. Currently, we are working on a visualization system for a series of large 3D volumes captured over time. However, it is less obvious how to include our contributions into the visualization of such 4D data sets, which already have an inherent temporal component.

**Acknowledgments.** We thank Rhadamés Carmona for early discussions of the spatiotemporal blending approach and Christopher Lux for providing the out-of-core volume rendering framework which we used to implement the techniques presented in this paper. This work was supported in part by the German Federal Ministry of Education and Research (BMBF) under grant 03IPT704X (project Big Data Analytics) and by the VRGeo Consortium. The seismic data set shown in this work is courtesy of Crown Minerals and the New Zealand Ministry of Economic Development (www.crownminerals.govt.nz).

# References

1. Gobbetti, E., Marton, F., Guitián, J.A.I.: A single-pass GPU ray casting framework for interactive out-of-core rendering of massive volumetric datasets. Vis. Comput. **24**, 797–806 (2008)
2. Carmona, R., Rodríguez, G., Fröhlich, B.: Reducing artifacts between adjacent bricks in multi-resolution volume rendering. In: Bebis, G., Boyle, R., Parvin, B., Koracin, D., Kuno, Y., Wang, J., Wang, J.-X., Wang, J., Pajarola, R., Lindstrom, P., Hinkenjann, A., Encarnação, M.L., Silva, C.T., Coming, D. (eds.) ISVC 2009. LNCS, vol. 5875, pp. 644–655. Springer, Heidelberg (2009). doi:10.1007/978-3-642-10331-5_60
3. Crassin, C., Neyret, F., Lefebvre, S., Eisemann, E.: Gigavoxels: ray-guided streaming for efficient and detailed voxel rendering. In: ACM SIGGRAPH Symposium on Interactive 3D Graphics and Games (I3D), pp. 15–22. ACM (2009)
4. Fogal, T., Schiewe, A., Krüger, J.: An analysis of scalable GPU-based ray-guided volume rendering. In: 2013 IEEE Symposium on Large-Scale Data Analysis and Visualization (LDAV), pp. 43–51. IEEE (2013)
5. Beyer, J., Hadwiger, M., Pfister, H.: State-of-the-art in GPU-based large-scale volume visualization. Comput. Graph. Forum **34**, 13–37 (2015)
6. Engel, K.: CERA-TVR: a framework for interactive high-quality teravoxel volume visualization on standard PCs. In: 2011 IEEE Symposium on Large Data Analysis and Visualization (LDAV), pp. 123–124. IEEE (2011)
7. Carmona, R., Fröhlich, B.: Error-controlled real-time cut updates for multi-resolution volume rendering. Comput. Graph. **35**, 931–944 (2011)
8. Hadwiger, M., Beyer, J., Jeong, W.K., Pfister, H.: Interactive volume exploration of petascale microscopy data streams using a visualization-driven virtual memory approach. IEEE Trans. Visual. Comput. Graph. **18**, 2285–2294 (2012)
9. Ljung, P., Lundström, C., Ynnerman, A.: Multiresolution interblock interpolation in direct volume rendering. In: Proceedings of EUROGRAPHICS/IEEE-VGTC Symposium on Visualization and Graphics 2006, pp. 256–266 (2006)
10. Lux, C., Fröhlich, B.: GPU-based ray casting of multiple multi-resolution volume datasets. In: Bebis, G., Boyle, R., Parvin, B., Koracin, D., Kuno, Y., Wang, J., Pajarola, R., Lindstrom, P., Hinkenjann, A., Encarnação, M.L., Silva, C.T., Coming, D. (eds.) ISVC 2009. LNCS, vol. 5876, pp. 104–116. Springer, Heidelberg (2009). doi:10.1007/978-3-642-10520-3_10
11. Younesy, H., Möller, T., Carr, H.: Improving the quality of multi-resolution volume rendering. In: Eurographics/IEEE-VGTC Symposium on Visualization 2006, ISVC, vol. 2, pp. 251–258 (2006)
12. Ljung, P., Lundstrom, C., Ynnerman, A., Museth, K.: Transfer function based adaptive decompression for volume rendering of large medical data sets. In: 2004 IEEE Symposium on Volume Visualization and Graphics, pp. 25–32. IEEE (2004)

# Visual Analytics Using Graph Sampling and Summarization on Multitouch Displays

Nicholas G. Lipari[✉], Christoph W. Borst, and Mehmet Engin Tozal

School of Computing and Informatics, University of Louisiana at Lafayette,
Lafayette, LA 70504, USA
{nlipari,cxb9999,metozal}@louisiana.edu

**Abstract.** Private industry datasets and public records contain more information than any algorithm can efficiently process or any person can reasonably interpret. This is a basic problem faced by researchers in visual analytics. Graph visualizations (a common large dataset representation) can organize relationships and entities in a visually accessible manner. Our work applies graph sampling and summarization to the interactive visualization of complex networks. We implemented several unbiased sampling techniques to facilitate large scale graph analysis. Moreover, we show biased sampling techniques can improve visualization by emphasizing key graph nodes. We combine algorithmic processing with human interpretations by allowing users to adjust sampling parameters, inspect sample graph visualizations, and compare sample distributions. Summarization also reduces graph complexity. By adjusting rendered graph density, users can navigate and maintain constant on-screen density.

## 1 Introduction

We are studying the combination of complex network analysis with multitouch interaction and visualization. A complex network is a class of graphs with non-trivial topological structures [1]. Researchers have studied these networks across different fields of science and engineering such as economics, biology, computer science, and physics. Examples include human disease networks [2], citation networks [3], online social networks [4], and Internet topology maps [5]. Disease networks represent diseases as graph nodes and connect nodes by links if they tend to co-occur in patient diagnostic records. Medical professionals study these graphs to discover the relations between multiple diseases. Nodes in citation networks denote academic publications, and a directed link between two nodes represents one paper referencing another. Citation networks reveal the important papers in a scientific domain and how authors reference those papers. Similarly, Internet topology maps at the autonomous system (AS) level encode such systems as nodes and their relations as edges. Network engineers and researchers use AS graphs to understand the Internet's dynamics and evolution.

Studying large-scale complex systems is often challenging. Storing an entire graph in memory, processing to extract useful information, and visualizing for decision making are resource and time consuming tasks [1]. Moreover, accommodating human-computer

© Springer International Publishing AG 2016
G. Bebis et al. (Eds.): ISVC 2016, Part I, LNCS 10072, pp. 462–471, 2016.
DOI: 10.1007/978-3-319-50835-1_42

interaction for cognitive analysis is difficult due to visually dense graph layouts, relatively few high importance nodes, and lack of good interaction techniques.

Graph sampling is a useful approach that provides the ability to select important components and relations of a large-scale source graph. As seen in Fig. 1, an otherwise densely crowded graph with no discernible structure (Fig. 1a) can be sampled to reveal examples of paths and neighborhoods (Fig. 1b) that were not immediately visible. Within some margin of error and for certain graph topologies [6], sampling can also preserve individual structural characteristics (e.g., degree distribution, path length distribution), select smaller and representative subgraphs from the source graph, and simplify challenges related to interaction and understanding.

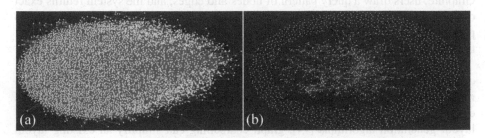

**Fig. 1.** Generic example of network dataset. (a) No meaningful information can be obtained from the complete graph. (b) A random path sampling exposes visible structure within the graph and allows more complex analysis to be conducted

In this study, we have increased the feasibility of large graph visualization and analysis by integrating several graph sampling and summarization routines into a multitouch graph analytics application. Sampling occurs as an offline or disk-based operation, not requiring the source graph to be loaded into memory. The sampling algorithms provide either biased or unbiased results, allowing users to quickly find nodes with high importance or estimate large-scale graph properties, respectively. Users can interactively adjust sampling parameters (e.g., percent of nodes from the source graph), highlight a range of nodes based on a centrality metric or structural characteristic, and control the on-screen graph density.

We begin by reviewing the relevant literature on graph sampling and visualization. Our system overview appears next, including organization and communication descriptions. We then detail the sampling, visualization, and summarization components. Last, we demonstrate the utility of our approach with an example use case by interactive visual analysis of a human disease co-occurrence dataset [2] consisting of 16,459 diseases labeled by their ICD-9 codes and 6,088,553 edges among them.

## 2  Related Work

The visual analytics field has produced several works on graph analysis. GraphViz [7] and Network Repository [8] are among those combining graph sampling with visual analytics. A web-based graph analytics system uses edge sampling with a sample and hold strategy to support streaming graphs. The sampling algorithm used in [7, 8] maintains a small amount of state and samples over the streaming graph.

A multi-touch interaction survey by Ingram et al. [9] reviewed multiple methods of selection and interaction, as well as multiple analogies for manipulating virtual objects. The authors suggest a framework centering around interaction feedback, physics-based virtual object movements, and an understanding of prior experience of users. Touch-Wave [10] and TouchViz [11] allow users to manually interact with time-series data in chart form. TouchWave attempts to improve the legibility of chart data, the ability to make comparisons, and the scalability to interpret dense datasets. Graphite [12] and Apolo [13] emphasize more micro-scale visualizations of graphs or networks. In Graphite, users draw a query pattern of nodes and edges, and the system returns exact or approximate subgraphs matches within a larger network. Our work allows users to participate in the sample creation process via touch interactions and presents visualizations such as graph diagrams and statistical plots.

The main form of graph rendering for the above solutions has been node-link diagrams. Hu [14] discusses several fundamental diagram layouts. Physics-based models arrange nodes according to some process found in nature (e.g., spring forces and electrically charged particles) [15]. While also used to improve the performance of layout generation algorithms [14], graph coarsening can simplify an existing layout based on topology and geometry. A common coarsening method collapses edges incident on less important nodes and requires summaries to be precomputed [16]. Another greedy approach to graph simplification [17] forms supernodes by examining neighbor lists and grouping the nearest matches between all pairs of nodes. Our work includes a summarization method that uses edge collapsing similar to [16] and arranges items in heaps as suggested by [17]. Unlike these, however, we compute summaries dynamically by storing collapsed graph components in a second heap.

Graph sampling has a wide range of applications [6], such as extracting key components of a graph, estimating structural properties of a graph, and visualizing large-scale graphs. Three classical examples of graph sampling are node sampling, edge sampling, and exploration based (traversal-based) sampling [18]. Node sampling and edge sampling involve selecting nodes and edges according to some predefined distributions. Traversal-based sampling approaches start from one or more initial nodes and sample the graph by expanding toward the neighbors of the current nodes. Many traversal-based sampling approaches use well-known graph exploration algorithms including Breadth-First Search, Depth-First Search, and Random Walk.

## 3 System Overview

Before detailing the sampling and visualization contributions of our research, we give an overview of our framework's organization and internal communication. To assist users in navigating through datasets and finding structure from noise, we developed a graph analytics system wherein users interactively explore large, dense graph datasets while requesting different samples and analysis. As illustrated in Fig. 2, our solution is separated into two main components: an analytics server and a visualization station, with an inter-process communication protocol using a message-passing approach.

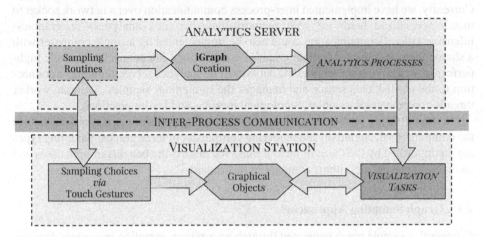

**Fig. 2.** Analytics Server, Visualization Station, and component communication. Users interact with touch gestures to select sampling algorithms and parameters. Sampled graphs are stored in an igraph object on the Analytics Server. Users may also perform various visualization tasks, which spawn corresponding analytics processes. The Visualization Station renders the results as graphical objects (e.g., node-link diagrams and ECDF plots)

The analytics server is responsible for reading graphs from a data store (e.g., SQLite, MongoDB, Neo4j), sampling graphs, and computing topology metrics. The igraph software suite [19] stores sampled datasets, manages graph metadata (e.g., node labels and positions), computes centrality measures, and generates graph layouts. Several different sampling techniques can reduce the source dataset as users tune the sampling parameters (e.g., percentage of nodes or edges) for best visualization and analysis of the resulting graph. The sampling routines operate in worker threads and communicate progress to the visualization station.

The visualization station renders graph objects, presents analytics results in forms understandable to users, and processes touch input from users. Interactions (touch inputs or mouse clicks) may be visualization specific, such as navigation gestures, or require communication to and from the analytics server. The system interprets these actions and issues requests to the analytics server. In a common sequence of actions, a user specifies a dataset choice and sampling type, which the station sends to the analytics server. Upon sample completion, the visualization station receives and stores the sample's topological information (e.g., node degree and sorted neighbor lists) and graph layouts in a form efficient for rendering.

# 4   Methods

Currently, we have implemented inter-process communication over a network socket to match specialized hardware with memory-intensive (i.e., analytics) or graphics-intensive tasks. Communication could also be implemented on a single computer with a shared memory object. Multiple graphics workstations can connect to a single high-performance analytics server over the network. The analytics server maintains a connection to the on-disk data source and manages the in-memory samples. Separate worker threads compute graph samples, topological metrics, and layout positions.

In the following section, we present how sampling and summarization can reduce the computational, cognitive, and rendering complexity of large graphs. Sampling types are distinguished by their bias or lack of bias. We discuss the benefits of both cases and show how selected algorithms compare in this regard.

## 4.1   Graph Sampling Approaches

In general, a sample graph generated through an arbitrary sampling procedure does not preserve all characteristic (degree, betweenness, and clustering coefficient) distributions of the population graph. As a result, one needs to align the sampling procedure with respect to the characteristic to be preserved. In recent years, researchers have proposed several solutions, e.g., [20], to construct randomly uniform sample graphs. These unbiased sampling strategies are effective for various characteristic estimation problems. On the other hand, biased sampling techniques may be useful for analysis and visualization purposes. To illustrate, biased sampling is a cost effective solution to extract nodes, edges, or paths similar to each other in terms of a centrality measure in a graph. Similarly, visualizing a graph obtained through a biased sampling allows users to focus on important nodes, edges, or paths in the graph.

We implemented several disk-based sampling algorithms including random node sampling, induced random edge sampling, random path sampling, random walk, and Metropolis-Hastings sampling. Random node sampling generates a sample graph by selecting a number of vertices with equal probability from a population graph. This technique is effective in estimating local properties of nodes in a population graph. Similarly, induced random edge sampling generates a sample graph by randomly selecting edges and the endpoint nodes (induced nodes) from a population graph. Induced edge sampling has bias towards high degree nodes. Those nodes have more edges to be sampled compared to low degree nodes. Ideally, random path sampling generates a sample graph by selecting paths at random among all possible shortest paths in a graph. However, generating all shortest sample paths in a graph is a costly operation. We approximated random path sampling by randomly selecting a source and a destination node in the population graph and computing the shortest path(s) between them. This technique produces good estimations for path-based node properties, e.g., betweenness. Random walk sampling generates a sample graph by first selecting seed nodes and randomly selecting an edge toward one neighbor at each step. This approach is also biased toward high degree nodes. Metropolis-Hastings sampling removes the bias in random walk sampling by reweighting the neighbor selection procedure to reduce transitions toward high degree neighbors.

## 4.2   Visualization and Interaction

A visual analytics system for large graphs should create meaningful graph representations and draw a user's attention to important features. The system should also mitigate the impact of graph scale on visual performance. We designed and implemented the multitouch visualization station (Fig. 3) in order to provide interactive graph analysis to users. The basic navigation and selection tasks follow standard, intuitive gestures such as tap to select and pinch to zoom. Aside from these, we have tested several multi-touch interactions to improve the exploration of graphs. Our application-specific interactions include sampling algorithm selection, adjustment of sample size, Empirical Cumulative Distribution (ECDF) plot management, ECDF range selection, and interactive summarization, all accessed through a touch interface.

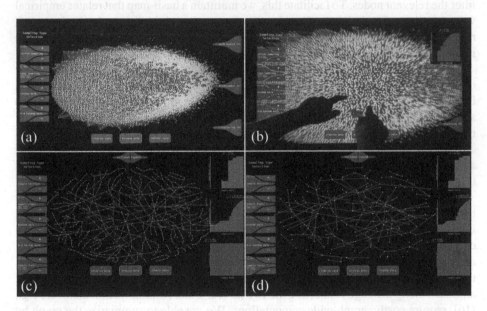

**Fig. 3.** Graph sample creation. (a) Graph with one percent of edges. The sample has approximately 10,000 nodes and 60,000 edges. Sampling parameter can also be adjusted up (+) and down (-) by a constant ratio. (b) Two-finger navigation allows users to narrow the scope of graph to be rendered. (c) Path sampling with 731 nodes and 723 edges, also described by ECDFs to the right. (d) The path-sampled graph after two summarization levels

Graph sampling controls allow users to interact with the analytics server and achieve the most appropriate sample for their needs. For example, to achieve a sample graph with high betweenness nodes (which roughly are the nodes appearing on many paths), users can select a path sampling or walk-based sampling algorithm with bias towards high-betweenness nodes. The sampling thread updates progress percentage and estimated time during execution.

When the sampling algorithm completes, the visualization station receives the node and edge lists from the analytics server. We currently support two graph-rendering methods: pre-rendered and direct-rendered. The pre-rendered method creates a high-resolution texture of the graph drawing to allow faster redraw and interaction rates. We primarily choose the rendering method based on node and edge counts; graph samples are pre-rendered when the number of graphical objects would cause rendering rates below real-time interaction constraints (about 60 fps). Except, when users update graph summarization (discussed below), we direct-render intermediate layouts and reevaluate the rendering method choice with the summarized graph.

ECDFs objectively reflect the structure and connectivity in the graph sample. Users can analyze the sampled graphs by their centrality metric distribution. We aggregate per-node metrics from igraph and render an empirical CDF plot (Fig. 3b–d, right). A two-finger pinch gesture on the plot can specify a range of plot values to highlight or filter the relevant nodes. To facilitate this, we maintain a hash-map that relates empirical values to lists of node labels. The visualization station highlights nodes in the range, rendering a label above each node's location. The analytics server can create a subgraph induced by these vertices.

Summarization is a related but alternative method to reduce the size and complexity of graphs. While a sample graph is a subset of the population graph, a summary graph is a transformation of the population. That is, the nodes or edges of a sample graph also appear in the population graph, whereas the nodes and edges in a summary graph may not appear in the population. We implemented a summarization approach based on concepts from [16, 17]. Users can simplify the graph by removing unimportant nodes and edges, reducing visual clutter, dynamically updating the graph based on interactions (e.g., pinch to zoom), and maintaining a constant visual density during navigation.

Users adjust two parameters to contract or expand nodes with respect to their neighbors. A user-defined threshold metric (e.g., node degree) is directly updated by touch input, and the zoom level (i.e., scale) is extracted from the navigation interactions. To choose the graph nodes that will collapse into others, we compare each node's metric against the product of these two parameters. We collapse all (source) nodes below the threshold onto the neighbor (sink) with the largest metric value. Node movement animates along the edge connecting the two nodes. Other summarization methods, e.g., [16], require costly, graph-wide computations. We are able to summarize the graph by only visiting the nodes and edges that the routine will update. To maintain interactive rates, the routine uses two heaps to determine which nodes to collapse or expand, based on changes of the threshold.

Nodes move back and forth between collapsed and visible heaps based on the current setting of the threshold and scale (zoom) parameters. Two animation steps translate nodes and edges in the collapse and expand queues. Once the animations complete, we update the heaps based on the summarized graph's topology. Through summarization, users can interactively remove less important nodes and reduce the clutter caused by unneeded edges. By controlling summarization with two parameters, the graph can be explored with a given density regardless of navigation choices. The algorithm is currently implemented in our application and does not suffer any large slowdowns for even dense graphs such as Fig. 3a.

## 5 Use Case Example

We now provide an example of our visual analytics system with a large dataset from the medical field. We have used several real world datasets for visualization, including a citation network [3] and a disease co-occurrence graph [2], as well as synthetic graphs (e.g., Erdos-Renyi, Albert-Barabasi, Watts-Strogatz) [21] for metric distribution comparison. Rendering these large graphs as node-link diagrams and performing analytics tasks can tax even the most advanced workstation.

The disease co-occurrence graph [2] being manipulated in Fig. 3a contains approximately 10,000 nodes and 60,000 edges (a one percent edge sample). Our analytics and visualization modules mediate the impact that large datasets have on the system's responsiveness. Figure 3b demonstrates that, even after scaling and navigating the graph, nodes are still tightly clustered and individual edges cannot be distinguished. Due to the sample's topology, automatic layout generation also fails to reveal patterns within the graph. We are unable to see any apparent structure such as the most highly connected nodes or distinct paths of nodes connected by edges.

The path-sampling used in Fig. 3c is biased towards high betweenness nodes (middle ECDF plot), known to be of relative importance in many datasets. The sampling also produces a coarse approximation of the larger graph's degree ECDF (upper-right plot within Fig. 3c). The resulting graph has about 750 nodes and edges, and the smaller graph size allows fast estimation of betweenness centrality. The automatic layout contains readily visible hubs and paths, placing branching structures and long paths throughout the graph with minimal overlap. The shorter, isolated paths surround the graph's border without occluding other structures.

Figure 3d shows how summarization further simplifies the sampled graph by collapsing low degree nodes onto their largest neighbors. After two levels of summarization (i.e., collapsing nodes with degree two and lower), a clearer image appears of the important nodes in the sample. Long paths with no branches are simplified to single edges, larger connected components are more clearly linked by paths, and we emphasize those nodes containing collapsed neighbors with an increase in size. Users can visit and expand the collapsed neighborhoods by navigating and adjusting scale. Users can more clearly understand where the changes to the graph occur with this gradual visual feedback.

## 6 Conclusion and Future Work

Among our contributions to graph visualization and interaction, we have demonstrated how biased and unbiased sampling simplify finding information about a dense graph dataset. With biased sampling, users can visualize nodes with similar centrality metric values, such as nodes with high betweenness. Unbiased sampling allows us to find large-scale graph properties more quickly without requiring the entire graph be loaded into memory or waiting a prohibitive amount of time. Some metrics require visiting every node in the graph (degree distribution), while others require the measurement of all paths in the graph (betweenness). By producing an unbiased sample with Metropolis-Hastings Random Walk, we can more efficiently estimate the degree distribution of the population graph.

Summarization further reduces clutter in graph renderings, maintaining a constant on-screen density. The graph visualization can temporarily hide nodes of low importance, based on user interactions (threshold and scale). With the combination of sampling and summarization, users can attain a clearer understanding of their data and request more detailed analysis.

We plan to incorporate other interactive visualization methods and provide users with greater control of the various sampling methods. Users will be able to access summaries and detailed subgraphs to help understand analytics results. Users will specify an area of the sample and request further analysis from the original dataset (e.g., several random walks or paths starting at the area of interest). To help bring the user's attention to these areas of interest, we will perform a highlighting of subgraphs based on topology metrics. Instead of manually selecting ECDF regions and performing time-consuming search tasks, we can highlight nodes based on the biases of the selected sampling method or similarities to nodes and subgraphs the user has selected. Finally, we plan to extend the sampling and analytics modules by introducing additional sampling techniques and centrality measures, respectively.

**Acknowledgments.** This research was funded by the Center for Visual and Decision Informatics (CVDI), an Industry/University Cooperative Research Center of the National Science Foundation, members from an Industry Advisory Board, and University matching funds. Information about CVDI can be found at nsfcvdi.org. We thank Dr. Raju Gottumukkala, Sivarama K. Venna, and Maryam H. Beisafar for earlier Analytics Server work.

# References

1. Cohen, R., Havlin, S.: Complex Networks: Structure, Robustness and Function, 1st edn. Cambridge University Press, New York (2010)
2. Hidalgo, C.A., Blumm, N., Barabási, A.-L., Christakis, N.A.: A dynamic network approach for the study of human phenotypes. PLoS Comput. Biol. **5**, e1000353 (2009). doi:10.1371/journal.pcbi.1000353
3. Gehrke, J., Ginsparg, P., Kleinberg, J.: Overview of the: KDD Cup. ACM SIGKDD Explor. 5(2003), 149–151 (2003)
4. Jiang, J., Wilson, C., Wang, X., Sha, W., Huang, P., Dai, Y., Zhao, B.Y.: Understanding latent interactions in online social networks. ACM Trans. Web **7**, 18 (2013)
5. Tozal, M.E.: The internet: a system of interconnected autonomous systems. In: Rassa, B. (ed.) Proceedings of the 11th Annual IEEE Systems Conference, Orlando, FL pp. 1–8 (2016)
6. Cem, E., Tozal, M.E., Sarac, K.: Impact of sampling design in estimation of graph characteristics. In: Wang, Y., Xu, K. (eds.) Proceedings of the 32nd International Performance Computing and Communications Conference (IPCCC), San Diego, CA, pp. 1–10 (2013)

7. Ahmed, N.K., Rossi, R.A.: Interactive visual graph analytics on the web. In: Hamilton, C. (ed.) Proceedings of the International 9th AAAI Conference on Web and Social Media, Oxford, UK, pp. 566–569 (2015)

8. Rossi, R.A., Ahmed, N.K.: An interactive data repository with visual analytics. ACM SIGKDD Explor. Newslett. **17**, 37–41 (2015)

9. Ingram, A., Wang, X., Ribarsky, W.: Towards the establishment of a framework for intuitive multi-touch interaction design. In: Tortora, G., Levialdi, S., Tucci, M. (eds.) Proceedings of the International Working Conference on Advanced Visual Interfaces, Capri Island, Italy, pp. 66–73 (2012)

10. Baur, D., Lee, B., Carpendale, S.: TouchWave: kinetic multi-touch manipulation for hierarchical stacked graphs. In: Shaer, O., Shen, C. (eds.) Proceedings of the ACM International Conference on Interactive Tabletops and Surfaces, Cambridge, MA, pp. 255–264 (2012)

11. Drucker, S.M., Fisher, D., Sadana, R., Herron, J., Schraefel, M.: TouchViz: a case study comparing two interfaces for data analytics on tablets. In: Mackay, W.E. (ed.) Proceedings of the SIGCHI Conference on Human Factors in Computing Systems, Paris, France, pp. 2301–2310 (2013)

12. Chau, D.H., Faloutsos, C., Tong, H., Hong, J., Gallagher, B., Eliassi-Rad, T.: GRAPHITE: a visual query system for large graphs. In: Wu, X. (ed.) Proceedings of the IEEE International Conference on Data Mining Workshops, Las Vegas, NV, pp. 963–966 (2008)

13. Chau, D.H., Kittur, A., Hong, J., Faloutsos, C.: Apolo: making sense of large network data by combining rich user interaction and machine learning. In: Tan, D. (ed.) Proceedings of the SIGCHI Conference on Human Factors in Computing Systems, Vancouver, BC, pp. 167–176 (2011)

14. Hu, Y.: Algorithms for visualizing large networks. In: Naumann, U., Schenk, O. (eds.) Combinatorial Scientific Computing, 1st edn., pp. 525–545. Chapman and Hall/CRC, Berkeley (2012)

15. Eades, P.: A heuristic for graph drawing. Congressus numerantium **42**, 146–160 (1984)

16. Hendrickson, B., Leland, R.W.: A multi-level algorithm for partitioning graphs. In: Karin, S. (ed.) Proceedings of the ACM/IEEE Conference on Supercomputing, San Diego, CA (1995). Article 28

17. Navlakha, S., Rastogi, R., Shrivastava, N.: Graph summarization with bounded error. In: Lakshmanan, L., Ng, R.T., Shasha, D. (eds.) Proceedings of the ACM SIGMOD International Conference on Management of Data, Vancouver, BC, pp. 419–432 (2008)

18. Hu, P., Lau, W.C.: A survey and taxonomy of graph sampling, CoRR 1308.5865 (2013)

19. Csardi, G., Nepusz, T.: The igraph software package for complex network research. Int. J. Complex Syst. **1695**, 1–9 (2006)

20. Kurant, M., Markopoulou, A., Thiran, P.: Towards unbiased BFS sampling. IEEE J. Sel. Area Commun. **29**, 1799–1809 (2011)

21. Albert, R., Barabási, A.-L.: Statistical mechanics of complex networks. Rev. Mod. Phys. **74**, 47–97 (2002)

# Evaluation of Collaborative Actions to Inform Design of a Remote Interactive Collaboration Framework for Immersive Data Visualizations

Rajiv Khadka[1](✉), Nikhil Shetty[1], Eric T. Whiting[2], and Amy Banic[2]

[1] University of Wyoming, Laramie, USA
{rkhadka,nikhil.shetty}@uwyo.edu
[2] Idaho National Laboratory, Idaho Falls, USA
eric.whiting@inl.gov, abanic@cs.uwyo.edu

**Abstract.** Data visualization and interaction is an important part of understanding and analyzing complex data. Immersive display systems provide benefits to exploration. In this paper, we present a user study to analyze co-located tasks and behaviors during a collaboration task. Results from this study helped us to identify patterns in co-located collaborative interaction to be able to better design remote collaborative environments. We discuss the challenges while interacting with data in an immersive data visualization environment and our design of a remote interactive collaboration framework for analysis and workflow of data visualizations. The goal of this framework is to preserve the benefits of physically co-located collaboration actions and add the benefits of virtual components that do not conform to real world restrictions.

## 1 Introduction

Collaborative virtual environments (CVEs) can be valuable in sharing 3-dimensional (3-D) spatial information among collaborators in multiple locations using a variety of display and interactive environments types. An immersive environment uses a combination of stereoscopic displays, tracking, and interaction to increase the sense of 'being' in that environment. A shared immersive workspace will allow collaborators in geographically separated regions to exchange knowledge, ideas and information in real-time [2, 9]. CVEs can be invaluable when it comes to data visualization with multiple people drawing insights from the same data sources and sharing insight with one another. There are many benefits to using these types of environments when they are spatially and physically in the same CVE. However, there are difficulties in providing realistic user experience and spatial awareness to the collaborators when their physical space is being shared in the immersive environment for data visualization. Also, scientific workflow is no longer defined by a single type of display [8]. There is a lack of methods permitting scientists' workflow and collaborative tasks across multiple platforms and contexts. Collaborations in such environments have the potential to enhance analytical capabilities, user workflow, and scientific discovery. Each collaborator should be able to navigate, interact, view and manipulate data in shared or individual immersive (full/semi) 3D environment. This becomes a

© Springer International Publishing AG 2016
G. Bebis et al. (Eds.): ISVC 2016, Part I, LNCS 10072, pp. 472–481, 2016.
DOI: 10.1007/978-3-319-50835-1_43

strong platform for learning, understanding and evaluating complex data. Although there are quantitative and qualitative benefits for the visualization process, solutions still do not facilitate dynamic workflows which allow ways to support collaborative needs ranging from desktop to mobile or to high-end immersive displays. While this has technically been achieved in the discipline specific academic circles, it is relatively uncharted in the common use of CAVEs and visualization communities, due to complexity such as differing hardware arrangements, lack of standards, and various protocol options [3, 4]. The work on the supportive interactive tools will add to the state-of-the-art. While these tools have been identified independently, rarely have they been tested in actual real-world data visualization and network situations. In this paper, we present a user study on task-analysis and behavioral patterns in co-located collaborative interaction, current challenges for collaboration in a 3D immersive virtual environment, and the design of a remote interactive collaboration framework for analysis and workflow of data visualizations. This work has applicability specifically for scientific 3D visualizations of 2D or 3D data, 3D structural modeling, and visualizations of any other 3D spatial data. Our goal is to investigate the physical actions, spatial relationships, and behavioral patterns that are important and should be preserved when developing remote collaborative virtual environments. Our work has the potential to provide efficient mechanisms and interaction tools to replicate the benefits from co-located collaboration (Fig. 1).

**Fig. 1.** Example CAVE collaborative usage in a visualization of 3D spatial data

## 2   Background and Related Work

In a workflow, face-to-face interaction is a natural way to initiate collaborative work [5]. Interaction methods have been designed to support pointing and communicative gestures to communicate more naturally and clearly but is more suitable for small scale virtual model environments. This initial work is a great start to what is still unknown about these environments when working with data visualizations. In a previous study, researchers explored the use of virtual user representations in local and remote users were face-to-face, side-by-side or decoupled [5]. They found that this type of representation allowed for mutual understanding even in the remote user case. In more recent work, researchers developed an architecture for providing some basic collaborative interactions which include: shared view as face-to-face, side-by-side, or decoupled; video avatar sharing; and teleporting to user's location in a virtual environment [10]. The initial work in this area is promising for collaborative virtual environments. However, again this has yet to be accomplished in data visualization environments, which have added complexities of user functionality, need for higher precision, complexity of data and rendering architecture, as well as fostering shared analytical tools and workflow [7]. Furthermore, little is understood about what should be preserved from physically located environments to enhance collaboration across virtual environments. There is less understood about how much should be preserved across heterogeneous systems, from immersive to non-immersive systems. The following describes the existing immersive visualization applications which support some collaboration capabilities. Little is known about how these environments should be designed to replicate the benefits of co-located collaboration. COVISE is known as Collaborative Visualization and Simulation Environment [i]. COVISE has been developed to integrate supercomputer-based simulation, high performance visualization computing and post processing in a collaborative environment. COVISE uses a menu driven user interface to collaborate among multiple collaborators. It is easy to add new modules to add a new functionality. Virtual Reality User Interface (VRUI) [11] provides an API called VRUI Tele-Collaboration which facilitates to connect multiple immersive or non-immersive VRUI environments by mapping them into a shared 3D space and sharing toolkits and an application state between them. It provides an infrastructure to develop new applications for large multivariate data sets. VRUI provides an application independent communication support plugin such as low-latency transmission of audio, 2D or 3D video avatars. VRUI applications work with an intermediate tool layer that expresses interaction with input devices at a higher semantic level [12]. Immersive Para-View is an open-source, multiplatform visualization application, built on Visualization Toolkit (VTK) [11]. It provides an effective and efficient computation models to process and analyze large datasets. Users create a visualization pipeline locally or remotely and interact with data via mouse/keyboard using different user interaction capabilities. It helps to easily migrate the visualization data sets from desktop PCs to immersive environments. It supports collaboration among multiple collaborators using a web platform. It is an open source visualization system that utilizes immersive technologies to analyze data. It supports hardware-accelerated parallel rendering to achieve interactive rendering [13].

## 3    Experimental Study 'In the Wild'

We conducted a study to investigate how users collaborate for data exploration and analysis in the same physical environment, or co-located space, using an immersive display. We collected data on participants performing tasks (specific to each participant group) of exploring an immersive visualization environment while collaborating with other participants in the same space. The data resulting from this study informed our design of a remote interactive collaboration framework. This study was designed to help us to understand how participants interact and collaborate in the same physical space. This understanding has helped us to better design interaction techniques to support these collaboration styles when connected remotely.

### 3.1 Experimental Conditions and Data Collected

Our study used an ethnographic approach, collecting qualitative and quantitative data on their interactions as the participants completed their normal tasks in the collaborative virtual environment. Interaction tasks included navigation, scaling of the environment, and selection of menus and widgets provided by the specific application used. Our goal was to observe spontaneous physical performance as it was naturally occurring in the co-located environment. Our between-subject's conditions were the type of participants (novice vs expert) and the data set types used for the exploration task. Novice participants were presented with random data sets for the experimental session. Expert participants were presented with the data sets related to their field of work. Participants then used the interaction tools for exploring and other analytic tasks provided in the visualization applications (COVISE, VRUI, or Paraview) corresponding to the data sets. We used direct observation and video recording to gather data during the experimental session. Participants' experience, feedback, and suggestions were collected and analyzed. All data collected was used to reveal the frequency of occurrence of specific collaboration behaviors and actions.

### 3.2 Apparatus and Data Sets Used

A four-walled display CAVE Automatic Virtual Environment was used by participants to complete an exploration task in an immersive visualization environment. The dimensions consisted of $10 \times 10 \times 7.5$-foot cube which uses rear projection to display computer graphics on three walls and front projection on the floor. Each participant wore stereoscopic glasses for immersion. For each group of participants, at least one participant's head position and orientation were tracked. A wireless "wand" device's position and orientation were tracked in 3-dimensions, for navigation and selection tasks, as well as control of analytical tools. Scientific datasets were used for the application used during the experimental session which included Lidar [15], Computer Tomography (CT) and 3-dimensional CAD. Both ground-based and airborne Lidar device was used to collect the data points appropriately. LIDAR device uses a laser scanner which scans data points between 20,000 to 150,000 points per second. The data produced is in a 'point cloud' format, which is a 3-dimensional array of points, each having x, y and z positions relative to a chosen coordinate system. Each Lidar application used for the experimental session consists of millions of points. Lidar data was used for landscapes and architecture applications. CT data was used for medical imaging data application and 3-dimensional CAD data was used for training purposes.

### 3.3 Procedure

Participants provided information about their familiarity with immersive visualizations and their technical background or level of expertise before starting the experiment. Participants were assigned to a dataset and visualization application accordingly. Novices were provided with a brief introduction and training in the CAVE and visualization environment. Each experimental session lasted approximately 30–60 min, which varied based on participants' goals and data they were exploring. Interaction tasks, such as navigating, scaling, selecting, were completed in short durations of about 5 min or less. Since we were testing 'in the wild', the overall tasks were brought by the participants rather than assigning tasks to participants. These tasks for expert users ranged from exploring data, showing another collaborator the result of an analysis, or preparing for a later meeting to demonstrate activities. Tasks for novice users ranged from working with scientists to understand results, exploration, and demonstration. In between interactions, participants were engaging with each other, looking at the content on the screen, or discussing aspects. Datasets were displayed and interacted using COVISE, VRUI, and Paraview. Each application used point cloud data with millions of points. Actions and observations were logged and video recorded. After the experimental session, we debriefed participants about their experience and feedback regarding the usage of the virtual environment for large datasets.

# 4   Results and Discussion

The user study was conducted at Idaho National Laboratory. The user study included 367 participants in groups of 4 to 10 participants per group. Participants ranged from novices to expert users. There were 267 males and 165 females. Participants' ages ranged from 14 to 70 with a median of 32. Our analysis of the data collected describes the collaborative behaviors, human-human interactions, and human-VE interactions exhibited by the participants in a co-located immersive space while interacting with data visualizations. We calculated the frequency of different human-VE interaction techniques participants used while collaborating with other participants while interacting with data visualizations in the immersive environment. The frequency of interactions was categorized by task type: expressions (N = 145), Selection (N = 876), Navigation (N = 59), and Other Interactions (N = 89). Most participants used selection methods to interact with the data being displayed in the virtual environment. Participants were attempting to select a specific section of data using their natural hand gestures. Participants (N = 35) expressed a need for gesture recognition for interaction and others (N = 40) expressed a need for availability of using multiple application while working in the immersive space. Participants were also using their expressions or words to interact with other collaborators during the experiment. Navigation was used the least frequent. Collaborative actions which supported collaboration were broken down into most frequent and specific actions used. Figure 2 shows the selective collaborative actions that participants used while interacting. Most the participants were trying to grab and touch data being displayed in the application. The next most frequently used communicative gestures were those which included pointing at a specific area of the data in which they were interested to communicate an idea or show an issue to the other participant(s). At times participants touched walls of the CAVE to be more precise in the pointing gesture. This key result shows that spatial relationships between users and each other, users and data, and users and the display are essential for communication and task completion for collaboration. Additionally, collaborative actions were revealed were ego-centric. As such, for a remote collaborative virtual environment, relationships not only between the user and the data should be preserved. Preservation of spatial relationships between the user and their own co-located display, as well as those with the other users, should occur.

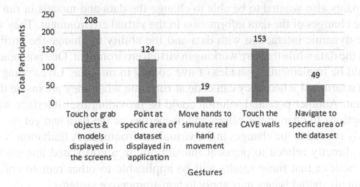

**Fig. 2.**  Frequency of specific collaborative actions used

In Fig. 3, we present the important feedback and suggestions provided by the technical experts during participation:

- 64% of participants who were expert users wanted the effects of change in data at run-time while working in the virtual environment. Example comment: "If I had a facility of changing the value of data at the run time while working in virtual space and view the changes, it would be more helpful for my research work".
- 24% of the participants who were expert users wanted to manipulate the data dynamically while being immersed. Example comment: "Making the VR system from static to dynamic environment would change and enhance the working ability of collaborators".
- 44% of the participants who were expert users wanted to have the haptic feedback while they were working with the objects and models in the virtual environment. Example comment: "I have depth perception of the objects and models but I cannot

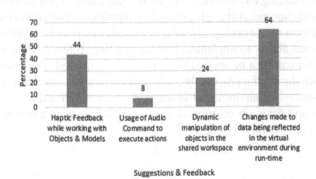

**Fig. 3.**  Expert feedback during collaboration

sense or feel anything while I am navigating or selecting an object or model in the environment".

- 8% of the technical participant wished to complete actions using voice.

Participants also wanted to be able to change the data and models in run time and analyze the changes of the data information in the virtual environment. They wanted to have more dynamic interaction with data and the ability to change the attributes and features of the data while they are working in virtual environment. One potential solution to this could be implementing an idea of live coding in run time. Live coding provides users with a terminal where they can code at run time when they are inside the virtual environment. Another potential solution could be providing user interface where they have the options to change the values and properties of the data and get the feedback immediately related to the changes in the virtual environment. A limitation is that these results are directly related to physical interactions in a co-located immersive space. While we believe that these results will be applicable to other remote collaborative systems, not all spatial issues may apply to non-immersive systems.

## 5    Design of Remote Immersive Collaboration Framework

In this section, we present our design of a remote interactive collaboration framework.

### 5.1    Workflow

Based on the users' suggestions and feedback we identified two features to enhance workflow. The first ability is to be able to specify data flow pipeline within an immersive data visualization. Users should be able to specify numerous visualization pipelines and look at different informational representations of the same data. For example, users could subsample the data using a subsample filter and examine only a part of the data. Each algorithm is represented by a proxy where the actual algorithm is applied on the data in parallel in the background. This process and capability help in constructing data-parallel workflow and apply different algorithms while simultaneously utilizing a HPC backend. The second feature is the ability to do live coding (as defined in Sect. 4) in such environments. A live coding environment will enable the users to add newer functionality into the system at runtime. Although a data-flow pipeline, construction pipeline can be considered as a form of live coding that we are emphasizing is a much lower level ability. This process is the ability to implement and inject newer filters into the system on the fly. The new filter can then be applied to the pipeline as needed. The system will never be brought down during the process. We will thus introduce a mechanism which helps create a workspace-like environment inside an immersive visualization environment which goes beyond basic observation of data, enabling users to experiment with data from within the environment itself.

## 5.2   Selection, Manipulation, and Navigation

Based on data from our user study, using communicative gestures and natural interactions is the most effective method to communicate during collaboration. Using natural interactions will allow the researchers, scientists, and remote participants to collaborate better. Spatial relationships of these pointing and expressive gestures between users, between users and data, and between users and the display, need to be preserved and rescaled to map appropriately to the physical space of each individual collaborator. Representations can be enhanced through visual interaction history trails to better illustrate the physical body to data visualization relationship. We preserve these relationships by providing cues in the environment of each participant's view and pointing gestures. Collaborators working in immersive data visualization environments who participated in this study have expressed that they want to share their navigated view along a specific path to other collaborators. We introduce an interaction technique where collaborators can share views of pre-set navigation paths. This sharing of view point with the remote collaborators will help them to have more active and productive discussions, without wasting time in the exploration phase of navigation. This allows the collaborators to explore different aspects of the visualization at the same time, having individual view control, and share their individual views without losing context. In addition, this technique of sharing view perspective of navigation can help remote collaborators to explore in natural ways, such as bending over or looking under an area, when they are unable to work in a same shared virtual environment. Other researchers have integrated the support of awareness of how views are linked and can use these views to work collaboratively or independently [14].

## 5.3   Portability

There is a need to bridge the gap between the remote collaborative virtual environments using immersive and non-immersive environment together [6]. For instance, one of the collaborators might be using 3D immersive environment, CAVE, and the other collaborators might be using a desktop while working together. There is a need for collaboration tools which can be accessed in both immersive and non-immersive environment. This will provide an effective medium to communicate between the collaborators. Interaction should be able to provide non-immersive users with the benefits of immersive interaction while collaborating or off-line. Navigation should be designed to explore outside of the immersive environment. Selection should be designed to separate out the areas which are defined by depth. Scale should be communicated to non-immersive users in other low-cost ways, such as projecting on the wall to provide relative size assessments. This helps to exchange information and discussion among the collaborators when in different types of immersive systems.

## 5.4   Visual and Audio

While working with the remote collaborative virtual environment in immersive data visualization, sense of presence between collaborators can be preserved better through

3-dimensional video avatars. However, current implementations do not necessarily preserve all the relationships between the user and data as they would appear to be in the physical space of the immersive display. This relationship should be preserved when providing these representations. This method will help to increase the user experience of the collaborators in immersive visualization while working with their large multivariate datasets. Audio can be used as an effective tool for communicating commands and executing actions. Use of audio as interaction techniques will help to increase the level of user experience collaborators experiences while working in an immersive virtual environment. Spatial audio should be preserved across the immersive visualization environments to facilitate collaborative communication. Spatial audio helps with the challenge of multiple collaborators talking in a CVE.

# 6    Summary and Conclusion

In this paper, we presented our results on a ethnographic study which identified patterns in co-located collaborative interaction, the current challenges faced during the collaboration in a 3D immersive virtual environment, and our design of a remote interactive collaboration framework for analysis and workflow of data visualizations. We found that participants used their natural behavior to navigate, manipulate, view and change the data displayed in the virtual environment. There is a need for the ability is to be able to specify data flow pipeline within an immersive data visualization and to do live coding in such environments in a collaborative way. Live coding is defined as tools that facilitate programmable actions within the immersive environment. This does not necessarily mean to make coding immersive, but rather provide the capability using the appropriate hardware and interaction techniques. Spatial relationships between users and data, users, and users with the display technology are important and need to be preserved across remote environments among collaborators, whether those environments are immersive or not. Navigation paths and representations need to be preserved. Preservation of interaction, gestures, communication mechanisms, and spatial relationships should be adapted across multiple platforms. Also, spatial audio and video should preserve relationships across the multiple viewing and data scaling environments for effective collaboration. Our goal was to investigate what the physical actions, spatial relationships, and behavioral patterns that are important that should be preserved when developing remote collaborative virtual environments. Our work has the potential to provide efficient mechanisms and tools that will allow users to overcome these challenges, provide interaction support which enabling the same benefits as co-located collaboration. Our work may have an impact in other areas where remote collaborative virtual environments are used.

**Acknowledgements.** We thank the Idaho National Laboratory for funding and use of equipment for conducting the experiment. We also thank all participants who contributed this study.

# References

1. Beck, S., Kunert, A., Kulik, A., Froehlich, B.: Immersive group-to-group telepresence. IEEE Vis. Comput. Graph. **19**(4), 616–625 (2013)
2. Bente, G., Rüggenberg, S., Krämer, N.C., Eschenburg, F.: Avatar-mediated networking: increasing social presence and interpersonal trust in net-based collaborations. Hum. Commun. Res. **34**(2), 287–288 (2008)
3. Billinghurst, M., Poupyrev, I., Kato, H., May, R.: Mixing realities in shared space: an augmented reality interface for collaborative computing. In: Multimedia and Expo, ICME 2000, vol. 3, pp. 1641–1644 (2000)
4. Churchill, E.F., Snowdon, D.N., Munro, A.J.: Collaborative virtual environments: digital places and spaces for interaction. Educ. Technol. Soc. **5**(4), 43–54 (2002)
5. Cioc, A., Djorgovski, S.G., Donalek, C., Lawler, E., Sauer, F., Longo, G.: Data visualization using immersive virtual reality tools. In: American Astronomical Society Meeting Abstracts, vol. 221 (2013)
6. Donalek, C., Djorgovski, S.G., Davidoff, S., et al.: Immersive and collaborative data visualization using virtual reality platforms (2014)
7. Isenberg, P., Elmqvist, N., Scholtz, J., Cernea, D., Ma, K., Hagen, H.: Collaborative visualization: definition, challenges, and research agenda. Inf. Vis. **10**, 310–326 (2011)
8. Johnson, C.R., Moorhead, R., Munzner, T., Pfister, H., Rheingans, P., Yoo, T.S.: NIH-NSF visualization research challenges report. IEEE Press (2006)
9. Lascara, C.M., Wheless, G.H., Patterson, D.C.R., Johnson, A., Leigh, J., Kapoor, A.: TeleImmersive virtual environments for collaborative knowledge discovery. In: Advanced Simulation Technologies Conference (1999)
10. Martin, P., Tseu, A., Férey, N., Touraine, D., Bourdot, P.: A hardware and software architecture to deal with multimodal and collaborative interactions in multiuser virtual reality environments. In: IS&T/SPIE Electronic Imaging. International Society for Optics and Photonics (2014)
11. Kreylos, O.: Environment-independent VR development. In: Bebis, G., et al. (eds.) ISVC 2008. LNCS, vol. 5358, pp. 901–912. Springer, Heidelberg (2008). doi:10.1007/978-3-540-89639-5_86
12. Rantzau, K.F.D.: COVISE in the cube: an environment for analyzing large and complex simulation data
13. Shetty, N., Chaudhary, A., Coming, D., Sherman, W.R., O'Leary, P., Whiting, E.T., Su, S.: Immersive paraview: a community-based, immersive, universal scientific visualization application. In: IEEE VR, pp. 239–240 (2011)
14. Tobiasz, M., Isenberg, P., Carpendale, S.: Lark: coordinating co-located collaboration with information visualization. IEEE Trans. Vis. Comput. Graph. **15**(6), 1065–1072 (2009)
15. Kreylos, O., Bawden, G.W., Kellogg, L.H.: Immersive visualization and analysis of LiDAR data. In: Bebis, G., et al. (eds.) ISVC 2008. LNCS, vol. 5358, pp. 846–855. Springer, Heidelberg (2008). doi:10.1007/978-3-540-89639-5_81

# ST: 3D Mapping, Modeling and Surface Reconstruction

# An Efficient Algorithm for Feature-Based 3D Point Cloud Correspondence Search

Zili Yi$^{(\boxtimes)}$, Yang Li, and Minglun Gong

Department of Computer Science, Memorial University of Newfoundland,
St. John's, NL A1B 3X5, Canada
yz7241@mun.ca

**Abstract.** Searching correspondences between 3D point Clouds is computationally expensive for two reasons: the complexity of geometric-based feature extraction operations and the large search space. To tackle this challenging problem, we propose a novel and efficient 3D point cloud matching algorithm. Our algorithm is inspired by PatchMatch [1], which is designed for correspondence search between 2D images. However, PatchMatch relies on the natural scanline order of 2D images to propagate good solutions across the images, whereas such an order does not exist for 3D point clouds. Hence, unlike PatchMatch which conducts search at different pixels sequentially under the scanline order, our algorithm searches the best correspondences for different 3D points in parallel using a variant of the Artificial Bee Colony (ABC) [2] algorithm and propagates good solutions found at one point to its k-nearest neighbors. In addition, noticed that correspondences found using geometric-based features extracted at individual points alone can be prone to noise, we add a novel smooth term to the objective function. Experiments on multiple datasets show that the new smooth term can effectively suppress matching noises and the ABC-based parallel search can significantly reduce the computational time compared to brute-force search.

## 1   Introduction

As a versatile representation for geometric models, 3D point clouds can be captured by laser scanners, estimated from stereo matching, or sampled from 3D surface models. The point set correspondence problem is to find the optimal matching between the two sets of points. It plays an important role in a number of applications, such as building statistical shape models [3–6], estimating 3D object movements [4, 7–9], smoothly interpolating the key frames in cartoon animations [4], morphing between shapes of disparate objects [10], and recognizing/classifying 3D objects [11, 12]. These applications all involve finding the optimal correspondence between closely related but disparate objects or shapes.

When there are only rigid transformations between the two point clouds, computationally efficient methods such as Iterative Closest Point (ICP) and Robust Point Matching (RPM) can be applied, which seek to search the transformation and correspondence iteratively. However, non-rigid deformations across matching surfaces (e.g., elastic deformation) widely exist in real world applications.

© Springer International Publishing AG 2016
G. Bebis et al. (Eds.): ISVC 2016, Part I, LNCS 10072, pp. 485–496, 2016.
DOI: 10.1007/978-3-319-50835-1_44

Although efforts have been made to adapt ICP or RPM for non-rigid correspondence [13–15], the deformations are approximated to be articulated rigid, rather than fully non-rigid.

Non-rigid deformations can be handled by finding pointwise correspondences between the point clouds, which is a computationally expensive task because of the large search space and the complexity of 3D feature descriptor computation. The difficulty is further enhanced due to presence of noise and the possibility of distinct points having very similar geometric features. The presence of noise, which might result from the process of point set acquisition or feature extraction, means that visually corresponding points may differ a lot in the feature space. On the other hand, 3D points from semantically different parts, such as left and right arms of a human model, can have almost identical features. The introduction of additional constraint such as isometric consistency can effectively solve these issues [16,17].

Previous feature-based correspondence methods use hierarchical searching strategy [18] or course-to-fine process [19] to accelerate the searching process. Nevertheless, they entail expensive computation of local features at multiple levels, making them unsuitable for dense correspondence search of large 3D point clouds. In addition, introducing the smoothness term that enforces isometric consistency makes the pointwise correspondence results dependent upon each other and turns the problem into a combinatorial optimization problem. Under this scenario, an efficient heuristic optimization method is needed.

Motivated by the success of PatchMatch [1] on finding correspondences among 2D pixels, we propose a 3D feature-based point matching algorithm, which takes advantage of randomized search and solution propagation among neighboring points. Given two 3D point clouds, one as source and the other as target, the algorithm searches for the optimal correspondences between the two under an objective function that considers both similarity in geometric feature space and smoothness among neighboring matches. However, PatchMatch relies on the natural scanline order of 2D images to search and propagate good solutions across the images. Since such an order does not exist for 3D point clouds, our algorithm conducts searches at different 3D points in a parallel manner and propagates good solutions through k-nearest neighbors. In particular, a swarm intelligence algorithm, the Artificial Bee Colony (ABC) [2], is used to search for the best match at each point. Good matches found at a given point are propagated to its k-nearest neighboring points, which can greatly accelerate the convergence. The method proposed in [20] employs a similar propagation scheme to accelerate the searching process. However, the absence of randomized search in [20] limits its capability to fully explore the solution space and find a global optimal solution.

The main contributions of this work are as follows:

– A new feature-based 3D point matching algorithm based on a variant of the ABC algorithm is proposed to randomly search for the optimal match at each point and propagates the good matches to neighboring points.

– We propose an novel objective function that dynamically balances between the feature similarity and isometric consistency, and guides the optimization to a smooth and optimal solution.

## 2   Related Work

### 2.1   Geometric-Based Point Feature Extractions

Numerous approaches have been proposed for extracting feature descriptors for a given point based on geometric properties of points in its local neighborhood. The evaluation carried out by Alexandre [21,22] finds that Signature of Histograms of OrienTations [23], Point Feature Histograms [24], Fast Point Feature Histogram [25], 3D deep descriptor [26] and Unique Shape Context (USC) [27] stand out in tasks such as category recognition and object recognition.

For the correspondence search problem that we try to solve, the desired feature descriptor should uniquely represent the geometric pattern around the given point and be informative enough to distinguish the pattern from others. The USC approach proposed by [27] first finds a unique local reference frame (LRF) at the query point, then encodes the statistical histogram of point densities within a spherical grid surrounding the point. It is chosen in our implementation, although other types of feature descriptors can be easily adopted in the proposed framework as well.

### 2.2   Nearest Neighbor Search

Feature-based point cloud match comes at expense of large search space and higher dimensional feature descriptors. Previous acceleration techniques for nearest neighbor search generally involve binary space partitioning tree structures such as TSVQ [28], kd-trees [29], and VP-trees [30], each of which supports both exact and approximate search. Another thread is to use dimensionality reduction methods such as Primary Component Analysis [31] for acceleration.

In image editing/synthesis domain, PatchMatch (PM) [1] and Generalized PatchMatch (GPM) [32] are widely used for approximate nearest neighbor search, making use of the neighborhood coherency which naturally exists among 2D image patches. In specific, PM alternatively conducts randomized search and propagation along scanlines for better match in coherent areas [1]. GPM extends PM for $k$-nearest neighbors searches, and enables searching across scales and rotations [32]. The neighborhood coherence in correspondence also exists for 3D point clouds. However, there lacks a natural ordering along which good matches can be propagated and hence PM and GPM cannot be applied. Our method utilizes a variant of the ABC algorithm to perform both population-based searching at individual points and match propagation among neighboring points.

## 2.3   Artificial Bee Colony

Artificial Bee Colony (ABC) is an optimization algorithm based on the intelligent behavior of honey bee swarm. Karaboga et al. proposed this algorithm and tested its performances on multiple optimization problems [2,33,34]. The results show ABC outperforms or is equal to other popular swarm intelligence and population based algorithms in avoiding being trapped in local minima.

In our approach, a bee colony is setup at each 3D point to search for the best correspondences. An additional type of bees is also introduced to facilitate communication between different bee colonies, which allows good matches being propagated along neighboring 3d points.

## 3   Feature-Based Point Correspondence Search

The feature-based point cloud correspondence problem is described as follows: Given the source $(S)$ and target $(T)$ point clouds, we search for the optimal correspondence mapping $M : S \mapsto T$ that maps each point $\mathbf{p} \in S$ to a point $M(\mathbf{p}) \in T$ so that the following energy function is minimized:

$$\mathbf{E} = \sum_{\mathbf{p} \in S} \left( (1 - \alpha)\mathbf{E}^{geo}(\mathbf{p}, M(\mathbf{p})) + \alpha \mathbf{E}^{smo}(\mathbf{p}) \right) \tag{1}$$

where $\alpha$ is referred to as smoothness coefficient, a parameter balancing between the geometry term ($\mathbf{E}^{geo}$) and the smoothness term ($\mathbf{E}^{smo}$).

The geometry term examines the similarity between point $\mathbf{p}$ and its correspondence $M(\mathbf{p})$ in feature space:

$$\mathbf{E}^{geo}(\mathbf{p}, M(\mathbf{p})) = \|USC(\mathbf{p}) - USC(M(\mathbf{p}))\|, \tag{2}$$

where $USC(\cdot)$ is the USC feature vector extracted at a given point and $\| \cdot \|$ computes the $L^2$ norm.

The smooth term measures the correspondence smoothness among $\mathbf{p}$ and its neighbors, and is computed as:

$$\mathbf{E}^{smo}(\mathbf{p}) = \sum_{\mathbf{q} \in \Omega_{\mathbf{p}}} \left| \|M(\mathbf{q}) - M(\mathbf{p})\| - \|\mathbf{q} - \mathbf{p}\| \right|, \tag{3}$$

where $\Omega_{\mathbf{p}}$ is a set containing the $k$ nearest neighbors of $\mathbf{p}$ in $S$.

As shown in Fig. 1, the novel smoothness term is designed to suppress noisy matches. Experiment results (see Fig. 2) shows that it can effectively remove mismatches caused by noise and feature descriptor ambiguity. In what follows, we first explain how to compute the feature vectors for each point in the source and target clouds, followed by the discussion on how to optimize Eq. 1.

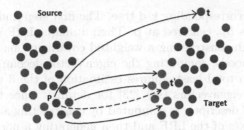

**Fig. 1.** Impact of the smoothness term. When searching for the correspondence of $\mathbf{p} \in S$, point $\mathbf{t} \in T$ may have smaller distance in the USC feature space and hence result in a mismatch. Assuming that proper matches are found for $\mathbf{p}$'s neighboring points, then the smoothness term can encourage $\mathbf{p}$ to match with $\mathbf{t}'$, which has smaller smoothness term value.

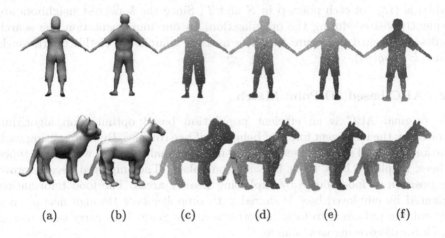

(a)          (b)          (c)          (d)          (e)          (f)

**Fig. 2.** Correspondences found under different objective functions for the woman-man (top) and tiger-horse (bottom) datasets. The source and target point clouds are sampled from meshes (b) and (a), respectively. To visualize the matching result, we color all points in the target point cloud based on their spacial coordinates (c) and points in the source point cloud using the color of their best correspondences in target (d–f). All correspondences are computed using exhaustive search, with the difference being either without using the smoothness term, i.e., $\alpha = 0$ (d), using the smoothness term with $\alpha$ gradually increased from 0 to 0.95 (e), or using the smoothness term with $\alpha$ fixed to 0.95 (f). Note that noisy matches are observed in (d), whereas the search is trapped in local minima in (f).

## 3.1   Feature Extraction and $k$ Neighbors Precomputation

To compute the USC feature vector for a given point $\mathbf{p}$ in $S$ (or $T$), we first build a k-d trees for $S$ (or $T$). A three-step procedure is then applied: spherical neighborhoods search, unique local reference frame (LRF) construction, and spherical point density analysis.

Assisted by the corresponding k-d tree, The first step finds all points within the sphere of radius $R_m$ centered at $\mathbf{p}$. Then a unique LRF is computed in the second step, through constructing a weighted covariance matrix $\mathbf{M}$ using these spherical neighborhoods, computing the eigenVector decomposition of $\mathbf{M}$, and finally performing a total least squares estimation of the 3 unit vectors of the LRF based on the eigenvectors (see [23] for details). Once the unique LRF is computed, the USC descriptor is computed by constructing a spherical grid that aligns with the 3 axes of the LRF and then generating a normalized histogram using weighted sum of each bin.

The complexity of neighborhood search, LRF construction, and point density analysis are $n \times m \times log(n)$, $n \times m$, $n(m+d)$, respectively, where $n$ is the number of points, $m$ is the average number of spherical neighborhoods, and $d$ is the number of descriptor bins. In all our experiments, we set $d = 1980$.

The k-d trees are also used to facilitate the search for the $k$ nearest neighborhoods ($\Omega_\mathbf{p}$) of each point $\mathbf{p}$ in $S$ and $T$. Since the $k$ nearest neighbors are frequently visited during the optimization, in our implementation the search results are cached for future use. The average complexity of this operation is $O(n \times k \times log(n))$.

## 3.2   ABC-based 3D Point Match

The original ABC is an efficient population based optimization algorithm inspired by the intelligent foraging behavior of bee colonies. By representing each solution as a food source, it searches the near optimal solutions with three types of bees: employed bees, scout bees and onlookers. The employed bees improve the position of food source by exploiting nearby areas. The food information exploited by employed bees is shared with onlooker bees through nectar, in a way guiding onlookers to localize better sources. Scout bees carry out random search for discovering new sources.

Different from the original ABC, which uses a single artificial bee colony to perform the optimization, our approach assigns a bee colony to each point $\mathbf{p} \in S$ and allows different colonies to communicate with each other through onlooker bees. Algorithm 1 shows the procedure of ABC-based search. The bee colony at point $\mathbf{p}$ is responsible for finding the optimal correspondence $M(\mathbf{p}) \in T$. Each candidate match is referred to as a food source and a colony maintains $c$ best food sources ($c = 4$ by default). Search is performed using $16c$ employed bees, $4c$ scout bees, and $4c$ onlookers, with each type of bees serving different roles. The employed bees optimize correspondence locally through searching among the neighbors of the existing $c$ food sources at $\mathbf{p}$. The scout bees perform global random search within the whole domain of $T$. Onlooker bees propagates good matches among neighboring points by checking the food sources at $\mathbf{p}$'s neighbors.

During the optimization, the fitness scores of different candidate matches (i.e., food sources) at point $\mathbf{p}$ are evaluated using Eq. 1. Note that, while we keep the best $c$ candidate matches at each 3D point, only the best match at each neighboring point in $\Omega_\mathbf{p}$ is used to compute the smoothness term as specified in Eq. 3. In addition, since the smoothness term can only benefit the optimization

---

**Algorithm 1.** ABC-based 3D point cloud match

---

1: set up a colony for each point in $S$;
2: randomly assign each colony $c$ food sources;
3: assign each colony $16c$ employed bees, $4c$ scout bees and $4c$ onlooker bees;
4: **repeat**
5:    **for** each point $\mathbf{p} \in S$ **do**
6:        employed bees exploit the neighbors of the $c$ food sources and update them if better ones are found;
7:        scout bees randomly exploit food sources in $T$ and replace the worst source if a better one is found;
8:        onlookers search food sources of $k$ neighbors of $\mathbf{p}$ and replace the worst source if better ones are found;
9:    **end for**
10: **until** food sources stay unchanged or a user-specified number of iterations is reached

---

at point $\mathbf{p}$ after near optimal matches are found for some of $\mathbf{p}$'s neighbors, the value of the smoothness coefficient $\alpha$ in Eq. 1 is gradually increased from 0 to the desired value throughout the optimization. This strategy allows the optimization avoid being trapped into local minima, as the case shown in Fig. 2(f).

Please also note that, both employed bees and onlookers involve searching among neighbors (either the neighbors of $\mathbf{p}$'s food sources in $T$ or the food sources at $\mathbf{p}$'s neighboring pixels in $S$). These searches are accelerated using the cached $k$ neighbors. Moreover, if the number of neighbors is larger than the number of bees, we randomly select a neighbor for each bee to exploit.

The theoretical time complexity of the above algorithm is $O(n \times t \times c(k+d))$, where $t$ is the expected number of iterations for convergence. $k+d$ is the time consumption needed for computation of geometric feature distance and smoothness term.

## 4    Experimental Results

We implemented the presented algorithm using *OpenMP* for multi-thread computation and ran it on 8-core *Intel Xeon* CPU. In addition, We based our implementation on the third-party *Point Cloud Library (PCL)* [35].

Four pairs of point clouds are used for testing. Each pair are sampled from two closely-related 3D mesh models using the point cloud processing tool *Cloud-Compare* [36]. A point cloud contains roughly $10\,K$ points. Detailed information about these dataset is listed in Table 1.

### 4.1    Importance of the Smoothness Term

Our first experiment evaluates how much impacts the smoothness term has on the correspondence results. To ensure that the results are not affected by the optimization algorithm used, here the expensive exhaustive search is performed.

**Table 1.** The experimental dataset

| Pair name | Model name | No. of points | Size | Patch radius |
|-----------|-----------|--------------|------|--------------|
| woman-man pair | woman | 10,000 | 102 | 30 |
| | man | 9,166 | 98 | 30 |
| tiger-horse pair | tiger | 7,980 | 58 | 20 |
| | horse | 8,431 | 61 | 20 |
| car-SUV pair | car | 8,392 | 64 | 20 |
| | SUV | 9,342 | 58 | 20 |
| stand-walk pair | stand | 10,000 | 43 | 13 |
| | walk | 10,000 | 41 | 13 |

As shown in Fig. 2d, without using the smoothness term (i.e., setting $\alpha = 0$ in Eq. 1), the optimal correspondences found by exhaustively searching for the best match $M(\mathbf{p}) \in T$ for each point $\mathbf{p} \in S$ independently are noisy. Close inspection shows that, for the woman-man pair (top row), the left hand of the source are mapped to the right hand of the target, and vice versa, since the two hands have similar geometric features. Other mismatches can be attributed to feature descriptor ambiguities as well.

Figure 2e further shows that these mismatches can be effectively removed through the presented smoothness term. As discussed above, once the smoothness term is introduced, the optimal match for a given point $\mathbf{p}$ depends on $\mathbf{p}$'s neighbor and hence cannot be optimized independently. Our naive solution here is to gradually increase $\alpha$ from 0 to the desired value 0.95 and under each $\alpha$ setting, we iteratively optimize each point $\mathbf{p} \in S$ in a random order until the process converges. Even though this is a computationally expansive process, it helps the search to scape from local optima. In comparison, directly setting $\alpha = 0.95$ and iteratively optimize each point $\mathbf{p} \in S$ results in suboptimal results; see Fig. 2f.

## 4.2    Effectiveness of ABC-based Optimization

The second experiment studies the effectiveness of ABC-based optimization approach. As shown in Fig. 3, the algorithm can quickly minimize both the similarity and the smoothness terms in Eq. 1, while at the same time avoid being trapped into local optima.

In addition, Fig. 4 evaluates the robustness of the proposed algorithm in handling data capturing noises. Gaussian noise of normal distribution $N(0, \sigma)$ is used to disturb point locations in both the source and the target point clouds, before the USC features are extracted. By controlling the value of $\sigma$, we obtain three noise corrupted datasets. The correspondence results (see Fig. 4) achieved by our ABC-based 3D point match algorithm are comparable with ones for noise-free inputs (see Fig. 5), even when the noise noticeably changes the object shape. This confirms the robustness of our approach in handling noise.

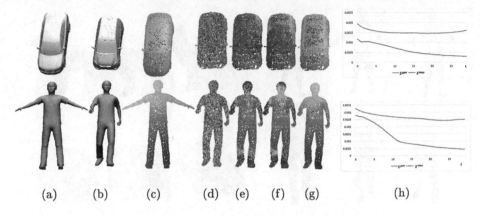

**Fig. 3.** Convergences of ABC-based point match optimization for car-SUV (top) and stand-walk (bottom) datasets. (a) and (b) are the original mesh models from which the target and source point clouds are sampled, respectively. The target point cloud is colored based on point coordinates in (c). The correspondence search results after 0, 2, 5, and 20 iterations are shown in (d–g), respectively. The convergences of the two energy terms ($E^{geo}$ and $E^{smo}$) are plotted in (h).

(a) $\sigma = 0.001\mathbf{D}$      (b) $\sigma = 0.005\mathbf{D}$      (c) $\sigma = 0.01\mathbf{D}$

**Fig. 4.** Correspondence results on the tiger-horse dataset under different noise levels. In each test, both the target (left) and the source (right) point clouds are corrupted using Gaussian noise with standard variance of $\sigma$, where $\mathbf{D}$ is the diagonal length of the input point cloud.

## 4.3   Comparison with Exhaustive Search Results

Finally, using the results obtained by iterative exhaustive search as ground truth, we evaluate the correspondences found by ABC-based optimization both visually and quantitatively. The visual comparison shown in Fig. 5 suggests that our ABC-based approach produces visually identical correspondences as the exhaustive search on all four pairs of point clouds. Table 2 further compares the objective function values obtained using the two optimization methods, as well as the computational time and space used. It shows that ABC-based optimization can obtain near optimal results using only a fraction of the computational time as the exhaustive search does.

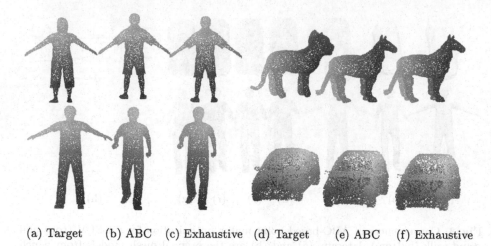

(a) Target    (b) ABC    (c) Exhaustive    (d) Target    (e) ABC    (f) Exhaustive

**Fig. 5.** Visual comparison between results obtained by our ABC-based point match with iterative exhaustive search. Given the target point clouds (a)and (d), the correspondences found by our ABC-based approach (b) and (e) and the exhaustive search (c) and (f) appears to be identical.

**Table 2.** Quantitative comparison between our ABC-based point match algorithm and the exhaustive search.

| Datasets | Objective function value | | Processing time (sec) | |
|---|---|---|---|---|
| | Exhaustive | Ours | Exhaustive | Ours |
| woman-man pair | 0.000657 | 0.000707 | 492 | 42 |
| tiger-horse pair | 0.000491 | 0.000458 | 669 | 45 |
| car-SUV pair | 0.000375 | 0.000418 | 528 | 39 |
| stand-walk pair | 0.000362 | 0.000534 | 543 | 50 |

## 5    Conclusion

A fast feature-based 3D point cloud match algorithm is presented in this paper. Through introducing a novel smoothness term to the objective function, the algorithm can effectively remove mismatches caused by noises and ambiguity of geometric-based feature descriptors. Even though the additional smoothness term makes the objective function even harder to optimize, the ABC-based optimization strategy used in our algorithm can efficiently compute the optimal solution using only a fraction of the time as the exhaustive search does.

Nevertheless, similar to other feature-based matching approaches, our algorithm also has its limitations. When the two point clouds have significant shape differences, our algorithm may not produce semantically meaningful matches. For example, due to large elastic deformation, the hands in the stand-walk dataset (bottom row of Fig. 5) are mapped to wrong regions in both our algorithm and exhaustive search (the colors of the hands in (b) and (c) are different from the ones in (a)). How to design feature descriptors that are invariant to elastic deformations and/or how to incorporate semantic-based descriptors will be investigated in the future.

# References

1. Barnes, C., Shechtman, E., Finkelstein, A., Goldman, D.: Patchmatch: a randomized correspondence algorithm for structural image editing. TOG **28**, 24 (2009)
2. Karaboga, D., Basturk, B.: A powerful and efficient algorithm for numerical function optimization: artificial bee colony (abc) algorithm. J. Global Optim. **39**, 459–471 (2007)
3. Chen, J.-H., Zheng, K.C., Shapiro, L.G.: 3D point correspondence by minimum description length in feature space. In: Daniilidis, K., Maragos, P., Paragios, N. (eds.) ECCV 2010. LNCS, vol. 6313, pp. 621–634. Springer, Heidelberg (2010). doi:10.1007/978-3-642-15558-1_45
4. Zhang, L., Snavely, N., Curless, B., Seitz, S.M.: Spacetime faces: high-resolution capture for modeling and animation. In: Deng, Z., Neumann, U. (eds.) Data-Driven 3D Facial Animation, pp. 248–276. Springer, New York (2008)
5. Blanz, V., Vetter, T.: Face recognition based on fitting a 3d morphable model. TPAMI **25**, 1063–1074 (2003)
6. Stindel, E., Briard, J., Merloz, P., Plaweski, S., Dubrana, F., Lefevre, C., Troccaz, J.: Bone morphing: 3d morphological data for total knee arthroplasty. Comput. Aided Surg. **7**, 156–168 (2002)
7. Rohr, K.: Towards model-based recognition of human movements in image sequences. CVGIP **59**, 94–115 (1994)
8. Kakadiaris, I., Metaxas, D.: Model-based estimation of 3d human motion. TPAMI **22**, 1453–1459 (2000)
9. Hu, W., Hu, M., Zhou, X., Tan, T., Lou, J., Maybank, S.: Principal axis-based correspondence between multiple cameras for people tracking. TPAMI **28**, 663–671 (2006)
10. Turk, G., O'brien, J.F.: Shape transformation using variational implicit functions. In: ACM SIGGRAPH, 13. ACM (2005)
11. Rusu, R.B., Marton, Z.C., Blodow, N., Dolha, M., Beetz, M.: Towards 3d point cloud based object maps for household environments. Robot. Autonom. Syst. **56**, 927–941 (2008)
12. Javed, O., Shah, M.: Tracking and object classification for automated surveillance. In: Heyden, A., Sparr, G., Nielsen, M., Johansen, P. (eds.) ECCV 2002. LNCS, vol. 2353, pp. 343–357. Springer, Heidelberg (2002). doi:10.1007/3-540-47979-1_23
13. Chui, H., Rangarajan, A.: A new point matching algorithm for non-rigid registration. CVIU **89**, 114–141 (2003)
14. Feldmar, J., Malandain, G., Declerck, J., Ayache, N.: Extension of the icp algorithm to non-rigid intensity-based registration of 3d volumes. In: Proceedings of the Workshop on Mathematical Methods in Biomedical Image Analysis, pp. 84–93. IEEE (1996)
15. Chui, H., Rangarajan, A.: A new algorithm for non-rigid point matching. In: CVPR, vol. 2, pp. 44–51. IEEE (2000)
16. Van Kaick, O., Zhang, H., Hamarneh, G., Cohen-Or, D.: A survey on shape correspondence. In: Computer Graphics Forum, vol. 30, pp. 1681–1707. Wiley Online Library (2011)

17. Tam, G.K., Cheng, Z.Q., Lai, Y.K., Langbein, F.C., Liu, Y., Marshall, D., Martin, R.R., Sun, X.F., Rosin, P.L.: Registration of 3d point clouds and meshes: a survey from rigid to nonrigid. IEEE Trans. Vis. Comput. Graph. **19**, 1199–1217 (2013)
18. Bendels, G.H., Schnabel, R., Klein, R.: Detail-preserving surface inpainting. In: VAST, pp. 41–48 (2005)
19. Sharf, A., Alexa, M., Cohen-Or, D.: Context-based surface completion. TOG **23**, 878–887 (2004)
20. Huang, Q.X., Adams, B., Wicke, M., Guibas, L.J.: Non-rigid registration under isometric deformations. Comput. Graph. Forum **27**, 1449–1457 (2008)
21. Alexandre, L.A.: 3d descriptors for object and category recognition: a comparative evaluation. In: IROS Workshop on Color-Depth Camera Fusion in Robotics, vol. 1(7) (2012)
22. Tangelder, J.W., Veltkamp, R.C.: A survey of content based 3d shape retrieval methods. Multimedia Tools Appl. **39**, 441–471 (2008)
23. Tombari, F., Salti, S., Stefano, L.: Unique signatures of histograms for local surface description. In: Daniilidis, K., Maragos, P., Paragios, N. (eds.) ECCV 2010. LNCS, vol. 6313, pp. 356–369. Springer, Heidelberg (2010). doi:10.1007/978-3-642-15558-1_26
24. Rusu, R.B., Blodow, N., Marton, Z.C., Beetz, M.: Aligning point cloud views using persistent feature histograms. In: IROS, pp. 3384–3391. IEEE (2008)
25. Rusu, R.B., Blodow, N., Beetz, M.: Fast point feature histograms (fpfh) for 3d registration. In: ICRA, pp. 3212–3217. IEEE (2009)
26. Fang, Y., Xie, J., Dai, G., Wang, M., Zhu, F., Xu, T., Wong, E.: 3d deep shape descriptor. In: CVPR, pp. 2319–2328 (2015)
27. Tombari, F., Salti, S., Di Stefano, L.: Unique shape context for 3d data description. In: Proceedings of the ACM Workshop on 3D Object Retrieval, pp. 57–62. ACM (2010)
28. Wei, L.Y., Levoy, M.: Fast texture synthesis using tree-structured vector quantization. In: Proceedings of the Conference on Computer Graphics and Interactive Techniques, pp. 479–488. ACM Press/Addison-Wesley Publishing Co. (2000)
29. Bentley, J.L.: Multidimensional binary search trees used for associative searching. Commun. ACM **18**, 509–517 (1975)
30. Yianilos, P.N.: Data structures and algorithms for nearest neighbor search in general metric spaces. SODA **93**, 311–321 (1993)
31. Pearson, K.: Liii. on lines and planes of closest fit to systems of points in space. Lond. Edinb. Dublin Philos. Mag. J. Sci. **2**, 559–572 (1901)
32. Barnes, C., Shechtman, E., Goldman, D.B., Finkelstein, A.: The generalized patch-match correspondence algorithm. In: Daniilidis, K., Maragos, P., Paragios, N. (eds.) ECCV 2010. LNCS, vol. 6313, pp. 29–43. Springer, Heidelberg (2010). doi:10.1007/978-3-642-15558-1_3
33. Karaboga, D., Akay, B.: A comparative study of artificial bee colony algorithm. Appl. Math. Comput. **214**, 108–132 (2009)
34. Karaboga, D., Basturk, B.: On the performance of artificial bee colony (abc) algorithm. Appl. Soft Comput. **8**, 687–697 (2008)
35. Rusu, R.B., Cousins, S.: 3d is here: point cloud library (pcl). In: ICRA, pp. 1–4. IEEE (2011)
36. Cloudcompare: 3d point cloud and mesh processing software. http://www.danielgm.net/cc/. Accessed 22 Mar 2016

# Extraction of Vascular Intensity Directional Derivative on Computed Tomography Angiography

Elijah Agbayani, Baixue Jia, Graham Woolf, David Liebeskind,
and Fabien Scalzo[✉]

Neurovascular Imaging Research Core,
Department of Neurology and Computer Science, University of California,
Los Angeles (UCLA), Los Angeles, USA
fab@cs.ucla.edu

**Abstract.** Collateral flow has been shown to have positive effects in ischemic intracranial vessel disease and can compensate for moderate stenosis and even complete occlusion of a major artery. Despite this, the common method of evaluating collaterals - computed tomography angiography (CTA) - is not effective in fully visualizing collaterals, making evaluation difficult. The spatial derivative of signal intensity, in the direction of flow, computed from standard, single-phase CTA may provide hemodynamic information that can be used to grade collaterals without directly visualizing them. We present in this paper software to compute the directional derivative, as well as to map it and the signal intensity onto a color-coded surface mesh for a 3D visualization. Our approach uses precomputed centerlines to simplify the computation and interpretation. To see if the derivative provided information that was not redundant with intensity, the software was run on a set of 43 CTA cases with stenosis, where the VOI of each was segmented by a neurology expert. Whereas KS tests comparing the intensity distributions of the healthy and affected hemispheres indicated that the two were different for 93% of cases, the distributions of directional derivative values were only different for 52.5% of cases. Therefore this derivative may be used as a tool to discriminate the severity of such cases, although its effectiveness as a collateral evaluation tool remains to be seen. While surface segmentation is time-consuming, the software can otherwise process and render color-coded 3D visualizations quickly.

## 1 Introduction

In ischemic intracranial vessel disease a blood vessel in the brain becomes narrowed or occluded, obstructing flow to the region beyond that vessel. Collateral vessels can function as an alternative source of flow; normally dormant, they are recruited following the partial or complete blocking of regular paths [1]. While current understanding of collateral flow is incomplete, it is recognized as playing an important role in ischemic intracranial vessel disease. Previous studies

© Springer International Publishing AG 2016
G. Bebis et al. (Eds.): ISVC 2016, Part I, LNCS 10072, pp. 497–506, 2016.
DOI: 10.1007/978-3-319-50835-1_45

have shown a connection between good collateral flow and more favorable treatment outcomes [2]. Evaluation of collaterals may therefore be used to inform treatment decisions for stroke victims and to predict the final outcome after intervention [3].

Beyond standard CTA, current methods of collateral imaging include Digital Subtraction Angiography (DSA) and later modes of CTA such as 4-dimensional CTA. Though DSA is considered the gold standard for contrast imaging, it is invasive, time-consuming, and requires a high radiation dose [4]. Other CT modalities such as 4-dimensional CTA can be effective for collateral imaging [5], but do not enjoy the ubiquity of standard CTA.

Standard CTA serves as the quick and most common method of diagnosing acute ischemic stroke and more general vessel stenosis, and compares well against DSA in this capacity [6]. However, collateral flow receives less contrast than main arterial flow, and so does not appear as prominently. Furthermore, collateral flow is more delayed than main arterial flow, and the lack of temporal resolution from single-phase CTA can obstruct accurate evaluation of collaterals. The miniscule size of many collateral vessels and the varying routes through which they manifest [7], make effective visualization with standard, single-phase CTA difficult.

Nevertheless, we believe that the directional derivative of signal intensity, taken from standard CTA, may provide information about collateral flow. It can give insight to flow dynamics that are not immediately evident from the normal intensity visualization; it is hoped that this will lead to an effective collateral evaluation scheme based on standard CTA (although such a scheme can be extended to other CT modalities). We precompute vessel centerlines and take the derivative of intensity along these centerlines, producing an easily-interpreted scalar function - it represents how signal intensity changes along the centerline. This paper introduces post-processing software which uses this approach to compute the directional derivative from a conventional CTA intensity image.

An additional function of the software is generating a color-coded visualization for both the intensity and its directional derivative. Similarly, a previous study had color-coded the intensity in blood vessels and overlaid this on the base image [8]. We extend the idea of color-coding to 3D by mapping interior (i.e. centerline) values of intensity and directional derivative to a surface mesh of vessel walls and color-coding the result.

## 2   Methods

### 2.1   Definitions

The directional derivative is defined as the convolution of a signal intensity function (described next) and a Gaussian derivative filter. Figure 1 shows an example surface mesh and the centerlines computed from it. A centerline is the path of the vessel center as blood flows between two endpoints. The branching of vessels means that blood from one start point may flow to any of a set of endpoints, leading to a set of centerlines - one to represent each path. Therefore

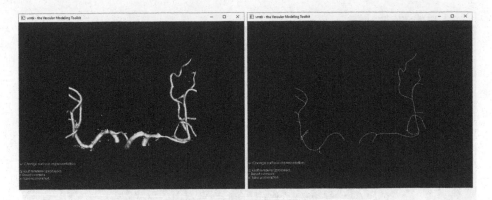

**Fig. 1.** Vessel surface mesh and computed centerlines

Fig. 2 shows that the structure from Fig. 1 is actually composed of many, largely overlapping, centerlines. An individual centerline may be isolated and the spatial location of that centerline can be cross-referenced with the raw CTA image to produce a discrete signal intensity function $I_n(x)$ for that centerline, where $n$ is the numbering of the centerline and $x$ is the arc length. The latter is the measure of distance along a centerline from its beginning. It is used identify points on the centerline, and hence to parameterize data residing in 3D space into a 1D function.

Given the (discrete) 1D Gaussian function and its first derivative:

$$g_\sigma(x) = \frac{1}{\sigma\sqrt{2\pi}}e^{-\frac{x^2}{2\sigma^2}}$$

$$\frac{dg_\sigma(x)}{dx} = \frac{x}{\sigma^3\sqrt{2\pi}}e^{-\frac{x^2}{2\sigma^2}}$$

We define the directional derivative to be:

$$D_{n,\sigma}(x) = I_n(x) \otimes \frac{dg_\sigma(x)}{dx}$$

This is in fact a 1D derivative. The direction of blood flow at a centerline point is assumed to be that of the centerline at that point, hence $I_n(x)$ captures the direction. Because we are not so interested in the direction of flow - this information is already given with the centerlines and apparent from the vessel surface - it is not specified as part of $D$.

It is desirable to view the intensity alongside its directional derivative. However, $I$ is likely to be a noisy function, so it is smoothed before being mapped onto a surface:

$$I_{n,\sigma}(x) = I_n(x) \otimes g_\sigma(x)$$

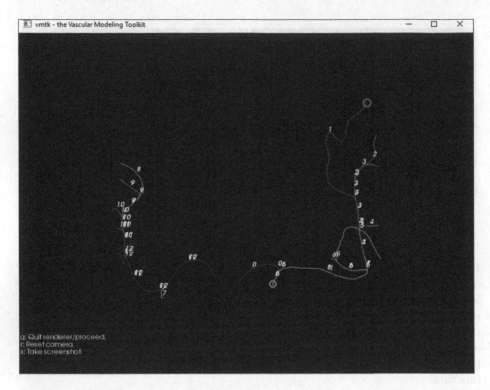

**Fig. 2.** Constitution of overlapping centerlines. The green and red circles mark the start and end respectively of centerline 1, whose intensity and directional derivative are shown in Fig. 3. (Color figure online)

In our implementation, we obtain the directional derivative by convolving the raw intensity function with the first Gaussian derivative, as opposed to convolving the smoothed intensity function with the Gaussian and then taking the derivative. The result is the same; by the properties of convolution:

$$I_n(x) \otimes \frac{dg_\sigma(x)}{dx} = \frac{d}{dx}(I_n(x) \otimes g_\sigma(x))$$

The start and end point of centerline 1 are marked in Fig. 2; using $\sigma = 3$, Fig. 3 shows the corresponding functions $I_1(x)$, $I_{1,3}(x)$, and $D_{1,3}(x)$.

## 2.2   Process Overview

The software is written in C++ and Python and makes heavy use of the Visualization Toolkit (VTK). First, from the raw CTA a surface mesh of the ROI and the corresponding centerlines are generated. Second, from the raw CTA and the centerlines the directional derivative is computed. Third, if desired, the software will map both this and the intensity onto the surface mesh. The resulting surface may be viewed by a viewer provided by the software which can highlight individual centerlines.

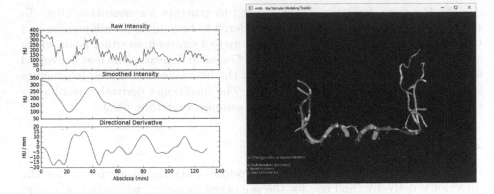

**Fig. 3.** Viewing an example end result (directional derivative).

## 2.3    Centerline Extraction

As the derivative is computed along vessel centerlines, the first step in post-processing is to identify the vessel(s) of interest and extract appropriate centerlines from the raw CTA images. Such a technique was used in our previous works [9,10]. A clinician selects a region of interest from the raw CTA image (in DICOM format) and applies an isosurface threshold to generate an initial surface mesh. This mesh is manually cleaned of artifacts (via clipping) such as unwanted bone or brain tissue before centerlines are computed off of it.

After extraction arc lengths are computed for the points on each centerline (which are represented in data as ordered sequences of points). Finally, a logical partitioning of the centerlines into branches is computed based on bifurcation points [11]. For example, two centerlines that are identical at first and then diverge would correspond to three branches: the shared segment, the segment of the first centerline after the split, and the segment of the second after the split. Each centerline can thus be decomposed as a sequence of branches. Furthermore, each point on the surface is assigned to a branch; to a first approximation, this is the branch nearest that point. The result of this step is a centerlines file with arc lengths computed and a surface file with branches computed.

## 2.4    Derivative Computation

The directional derivative is constructed using the centerlines file along with the raw CTA intensity data. A derivative is computed for each centerline. Computation for each centerline begins by generating a discrete 1D intensity function, where each function point is the arc length and intensity of a centerline point, with units of millimeters and Hounsfield units respectively. (Strictly speaking, the centerline point has no intensity, but lies within a voxel that does.) The centerline may not consist of points occuring at regular intervals with respect to arc length, so a cubic interpolation is constructed and sampled to produce $I_n(x)$. For a chosen interval $i$, e.g. 1 mm, $I_n(x)$ is defined for $x = 0, i, 2i...$, etc.

The Gaussian derivative $\frac{dg_\sigma(x)}{dx}$ is used to generate a convolution filter. To match $I_n(x)$, the horizontal axis is considered to have units of millimeters, and the derivative is sampled every millimeter up to 3 sigmas from either peak, where sigma is set at runtime. The intensity and Gaussian derivative are now convolved to produce $D_{n,\sigma}(x)$. (In a similar fashion, the base Gaussian is used to generate a convolution filter to produce $I_{n,\sigma}(x)$.) The directional derivative results are then mapped back from $D_{n,\sigma}(x)$ to each sampled centerline point.

## 2.5   Surface Visualization

After computing $D$, the software can produce a 3D visualization (one for the directional derivative and one for the smoothed intensity) where the values are color-coded and "painted" onto the vessel walls. Using the surface mesh generated earlier, the first step is to associate each point on the vessel wall to a centerline point, as wall points themselves do not have a directional derivative. The association is distance-based - a wall point is matched with the closest sampled centerline point. Branch ID's for each wall point are used to filter out centerlines that do not include that point's branch, reducing the number of distance computations made for each point. Once the exterior-to-interior mapping is complete and each wall point has the derivative value of its associated centerline point, this data is written into the surface file.

A minor final processing step exists in which the surface is divided into small rectangular patches with uniform value equal to the average of original values of points in that patch. This step is not necessary and is highly dependent on the quality of the surface mesh, i.e. how clean it is of artifacts, but the result may be easier to interpret. Regardless, the final result is a VTK surface that may be viewed through any viewer that supports the VTP format or through a special viewer in the software.

The software viewer can color-code the data. The user designates a low value to be colored red and a high value to be colored blue, with intermediate values assigned along the rainbow spectrum. Information on the distribution of directional derivative values (every 10th percentile) is provided to the user to assist with choosing the low/high thresholds. This gives the user flexibility, as using the same threshold for different cases may not be appropriate. The visualization is meant to aid the user in analysis, but care should be taken that it is not used as a substitute for further analysis. Two visualizations of the same case can differ widely depending on the choice of threshold.

The software viewer can seamlessly switch between visualizing the intensity and its directional derivative. Furthermore, the software viewer can, for each centerline, highlight the subset of the surface which corresponds to that centerline, allowing for analysis of the derivative along a certain path. To assist with this it will also display a plot of the intensity and derivative functions corresponding to the currently selected centerline. An example of this end result is shown in Fig. 4.

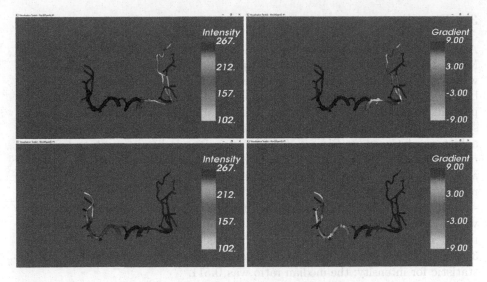

**Fig. 4.** Viewing an example end result with the software viewer; two centerline path from proximal ICA to distal MCA are highlighted. Arrow keys toggle between intensity and derivative views and cycle through centerlines.

## 2.6 Experiments

In our testing we dealt primarily with stenosis cases, i.e. cases where the vessel was not fully occluded. Given a stenotic side and normal side, we wanted to examine whether or not the directional derivative is significantly different between the two hemispheres, seperately from how the intensity differs. As a value derived in part from intensity, this derivative only has value in the information that is not redundant with intensity.

For each case in our experiment, a neurology expert selected a volume of interest that included the bilateral terminal ICA and the MCA (M1 to M3 segment). The initial intensity threshold for isosurfacing was 120, and was adjusted, by increments of 10, up if too much outside tissue was captured and down if the vessels were too thin. The skull, PCA, and most remaining outside tissue were clipped, and centerlines were computed with the proximal end of the terminal ICA as start point and the distal end of MCA branches as end points. The directional derivative was computed as detailed previously; overall 43 standard CTA cases were processed. Two-sample Kolmogorov-Smirnov tests were used to compare the distributions of intensity and derivative values between the left and right hemispheres.

We also generated the color-coded surface visualizations for each case. While not necessary for this experiment, the purpose was to verify that such visualizations could be computed in a reasonable time, and to produce a set of images for future qualitative analysis.

## 3   Results

A total of 43 CT scans were collected from patients exhibiting symptomatic MCA stenosis from Beijing Tiantan Hospital between June 2014 and June 2015, who were admitted to determine whether or not endovascular treatment should be given. The patients had average age of $54.88 \pm 12.36$ years old. 27 of the patients were male and 14 were female. 22 patients had a history of hypertension, 17 had a history of hyperlipedimia, 7 had a history of Diabetes, 1 had a history of Coronary Disease, 6 had a previous ischemic event and 21 were regular smokers. Two-sample KS tests comparing healthy hemisphere intensity and affected hemisphere intensity resulted in the rejection (alpha = 0.05) of the null hypothesis - that both hemispheres exhibit the same intensity distribution - for 40 cases (93.0%). Two-sample KS tests comparing the intensity derivative values in the healthy hemisphere against the affected hemisphere resulted in the rejection (alpha = 0.05) of the null hypothesis for 21 cases (52.5%). For all but 3 cases, the KS statistic for the directional derivative was lower than the KS statistic for intensity; the median ratio was 0.511.

The average computation time per case was 2 m 55 s (median: 3 m 6 s, min: 2 m 0 s, max: 6 m 15 s) on a Windows 10 machine running an Intel i5-5200U quad-core processor. This includes both derivative computation and surface visualization, but not centerline extraction because this was performed manually by a neurology expert. The optional patching step was also not included. Processing cases in parallel resulted in a modest reduction to 2 m 29 s per case; the software is capable of batch processing cases. However, parallel performance is not a concern as it is unlikely that clinicians would need to process many cases at once.

## 4   Discussion

Directional derivative computation from conventional CTA offers several advantages. After obtaining the centerlines, constructing the derivative and the color-coded surface visualization takes just a few minutes on a standard laptop. The derivative gives additional hemodynamic information than only intensity, and the simple approach - convolution with a Gaussian derivative - can be extended to other imaging modalities in the future. As it is the case for other modalities such as X-ray angiography [12], viewing the result on a color-coded and interactive 3D surface makes the data much easier to examine, even if just the regular intensity is being visualized.

In this experiment, the stenosis resulted in a lower intensity distribution for the side it occurred on for virtually all the cases, but otherwise did not affect the distribution of derivative values for almost half of them. This may be the result of a mild stenosis that lowers intensity but does not change the overall blood flow pattern, or collateral flow that is compensating for the stenosis; however, a more detailed and qualitative study is needed to test these hypotheses. Nevertheless, the results show that the derivative may be useful for distinguishing these cases, beyond what the intensity may indicate.

We used mostly CTA cases with no corresponding angiogram. A useful future experiment would be to take cases with both angiogram and CTA data and have a group of experts establish the collateral rating from the angiogram as the ground truth for each case. A separate group of experts would rate collaterals using the color-coded surface visualization of the directional derivative. Comparing these ratings would indicate the usefulness of this derivative for collateral evaluation. We could also consider computing the directional derivative on MRA and 3D reconstructions of DSA [13]. Linking the computed parameters with lesion growth [14,15] and hemorhagic transformation [16] are also promising directions for future research.

Currently, removing artifacts from the initial surface mesh is the most time-consuming step in the process. It is a significant downside because it requires involved interaction in an otherwise quick process, and must be done well; while the surface need not be completely free of artifacts, a poorly cleaned one will hinder the rest of the process. In our experiment particle-like artifacts (brain tissue) in and around the distal branches were especially tedious to remove. In the future, this step could be automated to reduce the time spent on this step, although certain situations may prove difficult to automate, such as when a vessel wall is joined to bone.

## 5   Conclusion

Overall, the directional derivative of signal intensity along vessel centerlines can be computed and visualized quickly leveraging common convolution filters and existing toolkits. We conclude that the use of the Visualization Toolkit (VTK) was effective in efficiently producing the derivative for a set of 43 stenosis CTA cases. Producing a satisfactory surface mesh for later steps is the primary hinderance, but has the potential to be automated. This simple approach of derivative computation and visualization has the potential to facilitate collateral evaluation without the need for invasive angiography.

**Acknowledgments.** Prof. Scalzo was partially supported by a AHA grant $16BGIA27760152$, a Spitzer grant, and received hardware donations from Gigabyte, Nvidia, and Intel.

## References

1. Tariq, N., Khatri, R.: Leptomeningeal collaterals in acute ischemic stroke. J. Vasc. Interv. Neurol. **1**, 91–95 (2008)
2. Bang, O.Y., Saver, J.L., Kim, S.J., Kim, G.M., Chung, C.S., Ovbiagele, B., Lee, K.H., Liebeskind, D.S.: Collateral flow predicts response to endovascular therapy for acute ischemic stroke. Stroke **42**, 693–699 (2011)
3. Tan, I.Y., Demchuk, A.M., Hopyan, J., Zhang, L., Gladstone, D., Wong, K., Martin, M., Symons, S.P., Fox, A.J., Aviv, R.I.: CT angiography clot burden score and collateral score: correlation with clinical and radiologic outcomes in acute middle cerebral artery infarct. AJNR Am. J. Neuroradiol. **30**, 525–531 (2009)

4. Dion, J., Gates, P., Fox, A.J., Barnett, H.J., Blom, R.J., Moulin, D.: Clinical events following neuroangiography: a prospective study. Acta. Radiol. Suppl. **369**, 29–33 (1986)
5. Frolich, A.M., Psychogios, M.N., Klotz, E., Schramm, R., Knauth, M., Schramm, P.: Antegrade flow across incomplete vessel occlusions can be distinguished from retrograde collateral flow using 4-dimensional computed tomographic angiography. Stroke **43**, 2974–2979 (2012)
6. Nguyen-Huynh, M.N., Wintermark, M., English, J., Lam, J., Vittinghoff, E., Smith, W.S., Johnston, S.C.: How accurate is CT angiography in evaluating intracranial atherosclerotic disease? Stroke **39**, 1184–1188 (2008)
7. Liebeskind, D.S.: Collateral circulation. Stroke **34**, 2279–2284 (2003)
8. Thierfelder, K.M., Havla, L., Beyer, S.E., Ertl-Wagner, B., Meinel, F.G., von Baumgarten, L., Janssen, H., Ditt, H., Reiser, M.F., Sommer, W.H.: Color-coded cerebral computed tomographic angiography: implementation of a convolution-based algorithm and first clinical evaluation in patients with acute ischemic stroke. Invest. Radiol. **50**, 361–365 (2015)
9. Leng, X., Scalzo, F., Fong, A.K., Johnson, M., Ip, H.L., Soo, Y., Leung, T., Liu, L., Feldmann, E., Wong, K.S., Liebeskind, D.S.: Computational fluid dynamics of computed tomography angiography to detect the hemodynamic impact of intracranial atherosclerotic stenosis. Neurovascular Imaging **1**, 1 (2015)
10. Nam, H.S., Scalzo, F., Leng, X., Ip, H.L., Lee, H.S., Fan, F., Chen, X., Soo, Y., Miao, Z., Liu, L., Feldmann, E., Leung, T., Wong, K.S., Liebeskind, D.S.: Hemodynamic impact of systolic blood pressure and hematocrit calculated by computational fluid dynamics in patients with intracranial atherosclerosis. J. Neuroimaging **26**, 331–338 (2016)
11. Antiga, L., Steinman, D.A.: Robust and objective decomposition and mapping of bifurcating vessels. IEEE Trans. Med. Imaging **23**, 704–713 (2004)
12. Scalzo, F., Liebeskind, D.S.: Perfusion angiography in acute ischemic stroke. Comput. Math. Methods Med. **2016**, 1–14 (2016)
13. Scalzo, F., Hao, Q., Walczak, A.M., Hu, X., Hoi, Y., Hoffmann, K.R., Liebeskind, D.S.: Computational hemodynamics in intracranial vessels reconstructed from biplane angiograms. In: Bebis, G., et al. (eds.) ISVC 2010. LNCS, vol. 6455, pp. 359–367. Springer, Heidelberg (2010). doi:10.1007/978-3-642-17277-9_37
14. Scalzo, F., Hao, Q., Alger, J.R., Hu, X., Liebeskind, D.S.: Regional prediction of tissue fate in acute ischemic stroke. Ann. Biomed. Eng. **40**, 2177–2187 (2012)
15. Stier, N., Vincent, N., Liebeskind, D., Scalzo, F.: Deep learning of tissue fate features in acute ischemic stroke. In: IEEE BIBM, pp. 1316–1321 (2015)
16. Vincent, N., Stier, N., Yu, S., Liebeskind, D.S., Wang, D.J., Scalzo, F.: Detection of hyperperfusion on arterial spin labeling using deep learning. In: IEEE BIBM, pp. 1322–1327 (2015)

# Capturing Photorealistic and Printable 3D Models Using Low-Cost Hardware

Christoph Heindl[(✉)], Sharath Chandra Akkaladevi, and Harald Bauer

Profactor GmbH, Im Stadtgut A2, 4407 Steyr-Gleink, Austria
christoph.heindl@profactor.at
http://www.profactor.at

**Abstract.** Recent advances in low cost RGB-D sensors and progress in reconstruction approaches paves way for creating real-time 3D models of people. It is equally important to enhance the visual appeal of such 3D models with textures. Most of the existing approaches use per-vertex colors, such that the color resolution is limited to mesh resolution. In this paper, we propose a feasible solution for texturing 3D models of people (3D busts) using a low-cost RGB-D sensor setup that automatically constructs the 3D geometry and textures the model in just a few minutes. Experimental evaluations evaluate the performance of the approach on synthetic and real world data against the computational time and visual appeal.

## 1 Introduction

With the availability of low-cost RGBD sensors there is growing interest in creating 3D models (3D selfies) [1,2]. Until recently it was difficult to obtain high quality 3D models of oneself. This is due to two main reasons: (a) expensive hardware setups and (b) strenuous manual post-processing steps. In this paper we present a low-cost fully automatic approach that creates high quality textured 3D models in a few minutes.

Although there exists approaches that deal with 3D reconstruction using RGB-D data, many of them do not deal with improving the visual appearance of the reconstructed model. Most of the current state-of-the-art for representing the visual appearance in such 3D reconstruction systems is still volumetric averaging of per-vertex colors, such that the color resolution is limited to mesh resolution. Mostly, these vertex colors are computed as a weighted average of the observed colors for the respective vertices [2,3]. To improve the appearance, weights based on the normals computed from the depth image are employed; to remove further artifacts, pixels close to depth discontinuities are discarded. An approach that builds seamless texture maps for uncontrolled photographs of a surface with known approximate geometry is presented in [4].

The work of [5] was among the initial contributions to improve the visual appearance of the 3D models based on a texturing framework. The authors dealt with the problem of large scale texturing in an image based reconstruction, for achieving photo-consistency over multiple images. Recently, the work

ⓒ Springer International Publishing AG 2016
G. Bebis et al. (Eds.): ISVC 2016, Part I, LNCS 10072, pp. 507–518, 2016.
DOI: 10.1007/978-3-319-50835-1_46

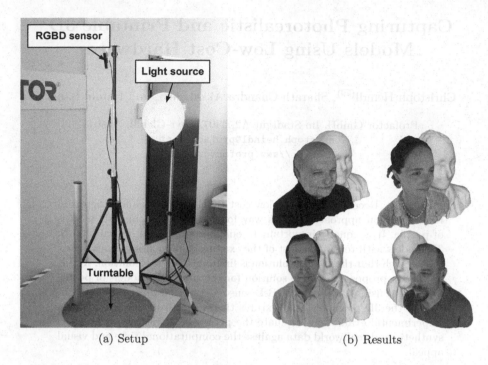

(a) Setup                                    (b) Results

**Fig. 1.** Our setup for capturing 3D bust models alongside with sample results.

in [2] presented a pipeline that allows ordinary users to capture 3D models of themselves in minutes using a single RGB-D sensor. The approach requires the users rotate themselves with the same pose for a few scans from eight different views, to obtain a super resolution scan at each of the eight key poses. The final model is generated by aligning the eight key poses in a multi-view non-rigid manner. However, the camera poses stored with registered views are error-prone when using commodity RGBD hardware. Neither the stereo calibration between depth and color sensors is exact, nor the color and depth capture is well synchronized in time. In our approach we perform a bundle adjustment (see Sect. 3) step to correct registered image poses to overcome this problem.

Another interesting approach for texturing 3D models using super key frames is proposed in [6]. The approach uses key frame based SLAM to consistently estimate the camera motion during the scan. To obtain a high-quality appearance model, the low-resolution RGB-D frames are first blurred and then fused into a super resolution key-frames. To deal with errors caused by sensor noise and optical distortions, [3] proposed an approach that optimizes camera poses in tandem with non-rigid correction functions for all images. To maximize the photometric consistency of the reconstructed mapping, all parameters are jointly optimized. However, the approach uses vertex colors for texturing the 3D mesh and has limited resolution when compared to texture maps. The authors in [7] present an approach for a static multi-texturing system to texture 3D models.

When compared to the state-of-the-art our main contributions in this paper are as follows:

– a comprehensive, visually appealing texturing framework for 3D models (3D busts)
– a low-cost single RGBD sensor hardware setup without the need for complicated calibrations
– a fully automated texture pipeline with infilling of occluded regions
– computationally attractive for real world applications (few minutes)

The paper is organized as follows: in Sect. 2 we give a brief overview of our mechanical setup and some details about geometric reconstruction. Then in Sect. 3 we present our texture framework in details. In Sect. 4 we present our results on real-world and synthetic data. Finally in Sect. 5 we conclude our paper and point towards future steps.

## 2  Setup

Our setup shown in Fig. 1a consists of three elements. An automatic turntable for the subject to stand on, a diffused light source and a commodity RGBD sensor. The scanning is ignited by having a person to stand on the turntable and press a button. A full rotation takes around 20 s to complete. During the rotation a full HD color and depth stream is recorded. We track the camera position and fuse the depth data into a global geometric model using a similar algorithm as described in [8]. Additionally, our system records the camera poses for a subsequent texture pass. Since the raw geometric model still contains holes due to occlusions we generate a watertight model using the algorithm described in [9]. Finally, we generate a flat base as we cut the model at a specific height using CSG operations [10].

## 3  Texture Pipeline

Since 3D capturing is performed by rotating a subject in front of single fixed RGBD camera and statically mounted headlights, the appearance of the object changes significantly between views. Furthermore, the turntable movement induces non-rigid body motions in the reconstruction subject.

Under such circumstances naive texturing leads to visually unpleasing results as shown in Fig. 2. The goal of our texture pipeline is the generation of a seamless textured 3D model, that is both visually appealing and ready for 3D post-processes such as 3D printing as shown in Fig. 2. In the following section we will detail our texture pipeline which can be considered an extended approach to the method proposed in [5].

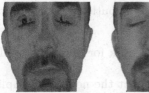   

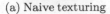

(a) Naive texturing    (b) Our method    (c) No bundle adjust-    (d) After bundle ad-
                                          ment                    justment

**Fig. 2.** Comparison between naive texturing and our method. (a) shows severe textural distortions, while (b) generates a seamless textured 3D model. Effects of performing bundle adjustment to correct registered image poses. (c) exhibits visible cuts around the mouth region, while (d) removes these artefacts.

## 3.1   Overview

Our method takes as input a triangulated watertight surface $S$ and a set of $N$ registered images $\mathcal{R} = \{\langle T_0, I_0 \rangle, ..., \langle T_N, I_N \rangle\}$ taken from varying viewpoints. Here $T_i$ denotes the i-th camera pose with respect to the surface and $I_i$ the associated image captured at the given camera position. We call a topological connected set of surface triangles with an identical registered image assigned a *chart*. The *chart boundary* is defined as the set of edges whose opposing triangles are textured from different registered images.

Given the input data our method first performs *Bundle Adjustment* to refine camera poses of all registered images for maximum color consistency. Next, in *Chart Creation* we determine which surface areas should be textured from which view. Once the assignment is determined *Color Correction* takes care of eliminating illumination differences on global and local scale. Next, *Inpainting* hallucinates colors for unseen regions. Finally, *Texture Atlas Creation* packs individual texture patches into a single texture file.

## 3.2   Bundle Adjustment

Camera poses stored with registered views are generally misaligned. This is especially true for commodity RGBD hardware where neither the stereo calibration between depth and color sensors is exact, nor the color and depth capture is well synchronized in time. Besides hardware errors, our system introduces additional accumulating positioning errors while performing frame-to-frame tracking [11]. These errors usually lead to visible texture offsets between texture chart boundaries as shown in Fig. 2((c), (d)).

Given $\mathcal{R}$ and $S$, the objective of our bundle adjustment approach is to maximize the color intensity at each vertex location between of all registered views.

$$E(\mathcal{R}, S) = \sum_{i=1}^{N} \sum_{v \in S_{vertices}} k_{v,i}(A(v) - I_i(\pi T_i^{-1} v))^2 \tag{1}$$

Here $A(v)$ denotes the average intensity at vertex $v$, $I_i(\pi T_i^{-1} v)$ is the image intensity of the vertex location projected into the i-th registered view and $k_{v,i}$ represents an indicator function whether or not the current vertex is visible in the i-th view. We minimize Eq. 1 with respect to the unknown true rigid transformations $T_i$ using an iterative Gauss-Newton non-linear least squares solver. This approach is similar in nature to the flip-flop minimization scheme proposed in [3], but extends it as we use multiple surface resolutions in order to be able to cope with larger transformations.

## 3.3   Chart Creation

Given the surface $\mathcal{S}$ and the updated set of registered images $\mathcal{R}$, the first step in chart creation is to determine the visibility of all surface triangles with respect to the registered images. We use a ray-tracing approach [12] to determine the visibility of each triangle in each view. Next, we compute a unique view label $l$ for each surface triangle. Based on [13] we rephrase the labeling task in terms of an discrete energy minimization problem of the following form

$$E(l) = \sum_{t_i \in S_{triangles}} E_{data}(t_i, l_i) + \sum_{(t_i, f_j) \in S_{edges}} (t_i, t_j, l_i, l_j) \qquad (2)$$

The data term $E_{data}$ exhibits low energy potentials for registered images in which triangles are well visible, while the smoothness terms regulates over-fragmentation of labeling in a sense that it penalizes varying labels across neighboring faces.

Inspired by [14] we use the area of the projection of surface triangles onto registered images as the inverse energy potential for the data term. This accounts for view angle, distance to surface and image resolution but ignores image sharpness. We've found that image sharpness rarely an issue with our capture setup, so we have decided not to adopt methods such as [15], who is proposing to incorporate the summed magnitude of image gradients inside the triangle's projection area as a countermeasure.

Since our setup focuses on capturing human busts it is vital to ensure that specific facial regions are textured from a single view in order to avoid generation of disfigured virtual models. This is especially true for the eye region. We therefore introduce a so called *face prior* that assigns lower costs to triangles in the eye region for a specific image. First, we select a registered view in which the face is clearly visible using [16]. Next, we use employ facial landmark estimation as proposed in [17][1] to identify the surface triangles in a specific facial region and assign those triangles a lower cost given the selected view.

We minimize $E(l)$ using iterative belief propagation [18] with an additional optimization for *Potts* model assuming piecewise constant label costs [19]. Figure 3 shows the effects of the minimization.

---

[1] Implementation based on https://github.com/cheind/dest.

(a) Data term        (b) Data and smooth-        (c) Face prior
ness term

**Fig. 3.** Effects of varying terms in chart optimization with chart borders superimposed. (a) exhibits a clear over fragmentation while (b) is much more smooth but still shows a clear defacement especially in the eye region. The face prior in (c) favors facial regions to be textured from a single view but does not enforce so as one can clearly see around the nose region.

### 3.4 Color Correction

As illustrated in Fig. 3 illumination and exposure differences across chart boundaries clearly influence the visual appearance of the textured model. These inequalities are leveled in color correction through a series of global and local correction steps.

First, we employ automatic exposure gain compensation as described in [20]. An optimal gain factor for each registered image is computed by minimizing a objective function that involves intensity differences in overlapping regions on the surface model. Since the objective function is quadratic in the unknown gain parameters, its derivative is linear and so its solution can be found by solving a sparse system of linear equations in closed form.

Next, we compute additive correction factors for all vertices using the method described in [13]. The optimal correction factors are used to modify the colors of each registered image in the area spanned by the projected triangles using barycentric triangle interpolation. The effects of global color correction is shown in Fig. 4.

Even after applying global color correction, chances are that some color seams are still visible. This usually happens either due to registration errors or non-rigid body movements (e.g. lifting of the eyebrow). We face these defects by applying Poisson image editing [21]. We restrict the editing approach to a small (usually 10–20 pixels) band around chart boundary edges. Dirichlet boundary conditions are provided by color values taken from pixel locations at band boundaries. To avoid blurring of the band region we use the band's Laplacian as guidance similar to [3,15]. See Fig. 5 for a comparison.

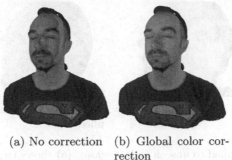

(a) No correction     (b) Global color correction

**Fig. 4.** Global color correction applied. (a) exhibits strong color discontinuities across chart boundaries, while global color correction is able to minimize these effects as shown in (b).

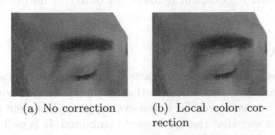

(a) No correction     (b) Local color correction

**Fig. 5.** Local color correction applied. (a) exhibits a strong visible seam in the eyebrow area, while (b) does not eliminates the effect without introducing blur.

### 3.5  Inpainting

As data capturing is performed in a single camera sweep around the subject, specific body parts remain unobserved. Unseen geometry is already filled in by Poisson surface reconstruction [9] and so we are left with task to generate artificial texture patches for unobserved regions.

First, we cluster all connected triangles without a valid registered view label $l_i$. As unseen regions might span geometric complex regions, we determine necessary geometric splits, so that the resulting segmentation is homeomorphic to a disc. We use the greedy algorithm described in [22] to determine the location of these splits. Then, for each patch we need to find a surface parametrization [23] - a mapping from surface to image domain. We use a conformal parametrization [22,24] which preserves angles locally. Once the mapping is established we solve the partial differential heat equation

$$\Delta\delta(u,v) = 0 \tag{3}$$

for the unknown function $\delta$ over the parametrized image domain. For a unique solution we provide Dirichlet boundary conditions by copying the color values at boundaries in the mapped image domain from neighboring texture charts.

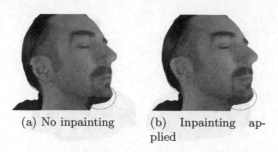

(a) No inpainting          (b)  Inpainting  applied

**Fig. 6.** Inpainting applied to unseen facial regions. (a) shows larger (chin) and smaller (ear) unseen regions, while in (b) those areas are inpainted by similar colors.

Figure 6 shows the effects on inpainting. The heat diffusion approach works well for inpainting smaller regions, but tends to get blurry by nature for larger unseen areas.

### 3.6   Texture Atlas Creation

Once the model is decomposed into charts, we create a texture atlas by copying all texture patches into a single larger atlas texture. This procedure is related to bin packing in which we search for a non-overlapping placement of (non)-convex polygons in such a way that the used space is minimal. It is well known that the packing problem is NP-hard [25, 26]. For this reason several heuristics have been proposed in computer graphics [27].

Our algorithm is based on the MAXRECT algorithm described in [27]. We additionally introduce a padding offset when packing rectangles so that enough empty space between packed charts is preserved. In order counter fight edge-bleeding, a visual artifact that stems from rescaling textures in modern rendering pipelines (e.g. mip-mapping), we fill the empty space between packed charts using similar colors from closest packed charts. We use a fast approximate discrete distance transform [28] to efficiently determine closest valid pixels to yet unfilled pixels.

## 4   Results

We validated our framework by scanning several hundred subjects during a national research event[2] (see Fig. 1b), including many challenging poses. Since validation is impossible on real world data without ground truth, we decided to additionally evaluate our pipeline using simulated data. As input we used a hand-modeled and textured bust (see Fig. 7) and simulated a 360° camera sweep around it using a virtual RGBD camera. While moving, we captured 400 RGBD frames in 1920 × 1080 perfectly synchronized in 700 mm distance from the subject. In a second sweep we turned on virtual headlights on to additionally capturing illumination effects such as shading and shadowing.

---

[2] http://www.langenachtderforschung.at.

**Fig. 7.** Hand-crafted bust used for validation purposes [29].

**Runtime:** All experiments reported have been carried out on commodity PC running an Intel Core i5-2000 CPU with an NVIDIA Geforce GTX 560 and 16 GB of RAM. The texture pipeline is written entirely in C++11. The GPU is utilized for geometric reconstruction, but the texture pipeline currently runs on a single CPU core. Table 1 reports the average runtimes for data capture, geometric and texture reconstruction for 100 models scanned.

**Table 1.** Average runtimes in seconds for each step in the pipeline.

| Algorithm | Time (s) |
|---|---|
| Data capture | 20 |
| Tracking and geometric reconstruction | 40 |
| Watertight reconstruction | 22 |
| Bundle adjustment[a] | 28 |
| Chart creation[b] | 15 |
| Color correction | 12 |
| Texture atlas creation | 8 |
| **Total** | 145 |

[a] Average number of iterations executed 20.
[b] Loopy belief propagation run for 180 iterations on average.

**Geometric:** Using the virtual RGBD data as input for the reconstruction, we are able to compare the quality of the geometric model generation aspect. As stated earlier depth data is generated using a virtual RGBD camera with perfect optics, limited resolution offset by 700 mm from the subject. The errors in geometric reconstruction are therefore stemming from imperfect camera tracking and incomplete model capture due to limited amount of viewpoints. What we find is that the mean geometric error is around 0.9 mm and standard deviation is around 0.6 mm. As expected most errors occur in regions that haven't been covered by the virtual camera such as the top of the head and under the chin as illustrated in Fig. 8.

**Photometric:** For comparing the texture quality, we captured screen shots from the input model and the reconstruction model from same viewpoints. We chose a

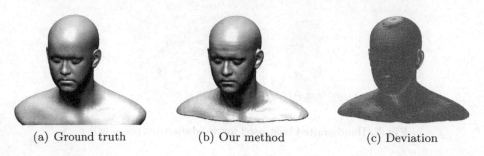

(a) Ground truth          (b) Our method          (c) Deviation

**Fig. 8.** Comparison of our reconstruction with virtual model. In (c) blue represents 0 mm deviation and red >5 mm error. (Color figure online)

variety of viewpoints from close-ups to wide shots and compared the resulting photographs for similarity using mean absolute error metric. On average the intensity deviation over all channels is 3.6 (rounded). Figure 9 shows a comparison.

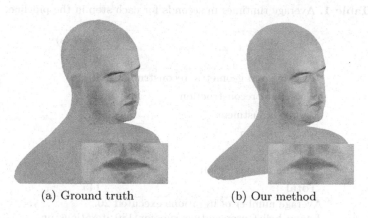

(a) Ground truth                    (b) Our method

**Fig. 9.** Comparison of our texturing with the virtual model. Both images show a wide angle view of the virtual model and a zoomed out mouth region. In (b) the mouth region appears blurrier but otherwise similar, an effect that is attributed to the limited resolution and distance of the virtual camera used to capture the data.

## 5    Conclusion and Future Work

We've shown that our method is robust for a wide variety of poses and subjects and captures high quality and detailed busts. Nevertheless we have also identified failure cases. Constraining the geometric reconstruction to rigid body motions requires that all subjects to hold significantly still on the turntable setup. We have observed that some movement is unavoidable, especially for lightweight people the acceleration of the turntable tends to induce unwanted shaking of the body. These motions can be suppressed using better hardware, however some unconscious motions such as breathing and straightening movements would probably remain. Violating the rigid body assumptions can lead to inaccurate reconstructions. In the future we would like to drop the rigid body constraint and incorporate non-rigid body methods such as [30]. Secondly, our method does not yet remove illumination effects such as shading and shadowing. Ideally we would like to perform an additional extraction step to recover the underlying albedo texture map as shown in [1,2].

**Acknowledgment.** This research is carried out within the "FTI-Projekt ProTech-Lab" project funded by the State of Upper Austria through the Strategic Economic and Research Program "Innovatives OÖ 2020".

# References

1. Ichim, A.E., Bouaziz, S., Pauly, M.: Dynamic 3D avatar creation from hand-held video input. ACM Trans. Graph. (TOG) **34**, 45 (2015)
2. Li, H., et al.: 3D self-portraits. ACM Trans. Graph. (TOG) **32**, 187 (2013)
3. Zhou, Q.Y., Koltun, V.: Color map optimization for 3D reconstruction with consumer depth cameras. ACM Trans. Graph. (TOG) **33**, 155 (2014)
4. Baumberg, A.: Blending images for texturing 3D models. In: BMVC, vol. 3, p. 5 (2002)
5. Waechter, M., Moehrle, N., Goesele, M.: Let there be color! large-scale texturing of 3D reconstructions. In: Fleet, D., Pajdla, T., Schiele, B., Tuytelaars, T. (eds.) ECCV 2014. LNCS, vol. 8693, pp. 836–850. Springer, Heidelberg (2014). doi:10.1007/978-3-319-10602-1_54
6. Maier, R., et al.: Super-resolution keyframe fusion for 3D modeling with high-quality textures. In: 2015 International Conference on 3D Vision (3DV), pp. 536–544. IEEE (2015)
7. Berjon, D., Moran, F., Garcia, N., et al.: Seamless, static multi-texturing of 3D meshes. Comput. Graph. Forum **34**, 228–238 (2015). Wiley Online Library
8. Newcombe, R.A., et al.: Kinectfusion: real-time dense surface mapping and tracking. In: 2011 10th IEEE International Symposium on Mixed and Augmented Reality (ISMAR), pp. 127–136. IEEE (2011)
9. Kazhdan, M., et al.: Poisson surface reconstruction. In: Proceedings of the Fourth Eurographics Symposium on Geometry Processing, vol. 7 (2006)
10. Requicha, A.A., Voelcker, H.B.: Constructive solid geometry (1977)
11. Rusinkiewicz, S., Levoy, M.: Efficient variants of the icp algorithm. In: Proceedings of the Third International Conference on 3-D Digital Imaging and Modeling, 2001, pp. 145–152. IEEE (2001)
12. Glassner, A.S.: An Introduction to Ray Tracing. Elsevier, Amsterdam (1989)
13. Lempitsky, V., et al.: Seamless mosaicing of image-based texture maps. In: 2007 IEEE Conference on Computer Vision and Pattern Recognition, pp. 1–6. IEEE (2007)
14. Allène, C., et al.: Seamless image-based texture atlases using multi-band blending. In: 19th International Conference on Pattern Recognition, pp. 1–4. IEEE (2008)
15. Gal, R., et al.: Seamless montage for texturing models. Comput. Graph. Forum **29**, 479–486 (2010). Wiley Online Library

16. Viola, P., Jones, M.: Rapid object detection using a boosted cascade of simple features. In: Proceedings of the 2001 IEEE Computer Society Conference on Computer Vision and Pattern Recognition, vol. 1, p. I-511. IEEE (2001)

17. Kazemi, V., Sullivan, J.: One millisecond face alignment with an ensemble of regression trees. In: Proceedings of the IEEE Conference on Computer Vision and Pattern Recognition, pp. 1867–1874 (2014)

18. Szeliski, R., et al.: A comparative study of energy minimization methods for markov random fields with smoothness-based priors. IEEE Trans. Pattern Anal. Mach. Intell. **30**, 1068–1080 (2008)

19. Felzenszwalb, P.F., Huttenlocher, D.P.: Efficient belief propagation for early vision. Int. J. Comput. Vis. **70**, 41–54 (2006)

20. Brown, M., Lowe, D.G.: Automatic panoramic image stitching using invariant features. Int. J. Comput. Vis. **74**, 59–73 (2007)

21. Pérez, P., Gangnet, M., Blake, A.: Poisson image editing. ACM Trans. Graph. (TOG) **22**, 313–318 (2003). ACM

22. Lévy, B., et al.: Least squares conformal maps for automatic texture atlas generation. ACM Trans. Graph. (TOG) **21**, 362–371 (2002). ACM

23. Heckbert, P.S.: Survey of texture mapping. IEEE Comput. Graph. Appl. **6**, 56–67 (1986)

24. Desbrun, M., Meyer, M., Alliez, P.: Intrinsic parameterizations of surface meshes. Comput. Graph. Forum **21**, 209–218 (2002). Wiley Online Library

25. Milenkovic, V.J.: Rotational polygon containment and minimum enclosure using only robust 2D constructions. Comput. Geom. **13**, 3–19 (1999)

26. Murata, H., et al.: Rectangle-packing-based module placement. In: International Conference on Computer-Aided Design, pp. 472–479. IEEE (1995)

27. Jylänki, J.: A thousand ways to pack the bin-a practical approach to two-dimensional rectangle bin packing (2010). http://clb.demon.fi/files/RectangleBinPack.pdf. Accessed

28. Borgefors, G.: Distance transformations in digital images. Comput. Vis. Graph. Image Process. **34**, 344–371 (1986)

29. McGuire, M.: Computer graphics archive (2011). http://graphics.cs.williams.edu/data

30. Li, H., et al.: Global correspondence optimization for non-rigid registration of depth scans. Comput. Graph. Forum **27**, 1421–1430 (2008). Wiley Online Library

# Improved Stereo Vision of Indoor Dense Suspended Scatterers Scenes from De-scattering Images

Chanh D. Tr. Nguyen[1], Kyeong Yong Cho[2], You Hyun Jang[3],
Kyung-Soo Kim[1], and Soohyun Kim[1(✉)]

[1] Department of Mechanical Engineering, KAIST, 291 Daehak-ro, Yuseong-gu,
Daejeon 34141, South Korea
soohyun@kaist.ac.kr
[2] USRC, KAIST, 291 Daehak-ro, Yuseong-gu, Daejeon 34141, South Korea
[3] Equipment Engineering Lab., Korea Hydro & Nuclear Power Co., 70, 1312-gil, Yuseong-daero,
Yuseong-gu, Daejeon 34141, South Korea

**Abstract.** Stereo vision is important in robotics since retrieving depth is very necessary in many robotics applications. Most of state-of-the-art stereo vision algorithms solve the problem with clear images but not the images corrupted by scattering. In this paper, we propose the stereo vision system for robot working in dense suspended scatterers environment. The imaging model of images taken in the environment under active light source based on single scattering phenomenon is analyzed. Based on that, scattering signal can be removed from images. The recovered images are then used as input image for stereo vision. The proposed method is then evaluated based on quality of stereo depth map.

## 1 Introduction

Stereo vision has been attracted significant research effort for decades knowing that the depth map is crucial in many applications such as driving assistance, automated robotics, etc. There are many cases when the system works in low visibility environment, for example, underwater robots, firefighting robots, etc. Our application is also the case, mobile robot working in nuclear power plants, which suffer from dense steam. When an accident occurs, the plant is filled with very dense steam and the robot needs to operate the plant in such an extreme environment. However, most of state-of-the-art stereo vision algorithms primarily solve the problem based on good quality images from dataset, for example Middlebury datasets [1] and focus on improving matching quality [1–3]. These methods are unable to be applied directly into the images taken in dense scattering media with active illumination. The reason is that the scene's radiance is attenuated before reaching the camera and that the scattering signal would be sensed by the cameras. Additionally, using the non-parallel artificial illumination sources generates significant backscattering signal which is spatially-varying. Thus, the intensities of the same object captured by two different cameras of the stereo vision system can be significantly different.

© Springer International Publishing AG 2016
G. Bebis et al. (Eds.): ISVC 2016, Part I, LNCS 10072, pp. 519–528, 2016.
DOI: 10.1007/978-3-319-50835-1_47

In general, the stereo algorithms can be classified in two categories, namely local and global approach. In local approach, the disparity computation at given point depends only on the intensity value within the local window. Recent advance in local methods such as support-weights window [4] or cost-volume filtering [5] can achieve good quality very efficiently. The global methods formulate the problem as global optimization problem. These problems can be solved efficiently using graph cut [6] or belief propagation [7]. These methods provide high quality results but, in practice, are rather slow.

The stereo vision in natural daylight fog scene can take advantage of developed image visibility enhancement methods. Polarization-based method enhances the haze images [8] or underwater images [9] by examining degree of polarization (DOP) from multiple images taken under different polarization states. There is a significant progress in single image dehazing based on Koschmieder's law [10] such as, Markov random fields (MRF) [11–13], dark channel prior (DCP) [14] and learning based method [15]. However, these methods cannot solve the problem of images taken under the active light. Recently, several nighttime dehazing algorithms have been developed. Zang et al. [16] utilize new imaging model to compensate light and correct color before applying DCP. Li et al. [17] incorporate a glow term into standard nighttime haze model. After the glow is decomposed from the image, DCP is employed in order to obtain the haze-free image.

Several stereo vision methods for foggy or underwater environment have been introduced. Caraffa and Tarel [18] combine photo-consistency term and atmosphere veil depth cues to formulate the problem and solve both stereo and defog by utilizing the $\alpha$-expansion algorithm. However, this method is sensitive to the nonlinear camera response and image noise. Roser et al. [19] iterates applying a conventional stereo algorithm to compute the dense depth and using depth to estimate the clear image. The method, however, does not model light scattering in stereo matching step, and does defog video frames independently, which causes error in stereo reconstruction. These studies are applicable to the images taken under uniform parallel light sources only. Negahdaripour and Sarafraz [20] use both photo-consistency and backscattering cues to estimate disparity by local matching method. The method can be applied to images corrupted by backscattering, which taken under nonhomogeneous artificial light source.

In this study, we introduce our de-scattering method from single image to remove the scattering signal of indoor images. Based on the imaging model (introduced in Sect. 2), the non-uniformity airlight in the image is easily removed and the image is transferred into standard foggy image that obeys Koschmieder's law. The resulting image, then, is processed utilizing DCP and guided image filter [21] to obtain the defogged image. Finally, defogged images from left and right cameras are the input for stereo vision. We utilize cost-volume [22] for stereo vision. Our results are compared with some other methods' results using both synthetic and real images for evaluation.

## 2   Imaging Model

Basic assumptions used in this approach:

- There is only one known illumination source in the system (Fig. 1).

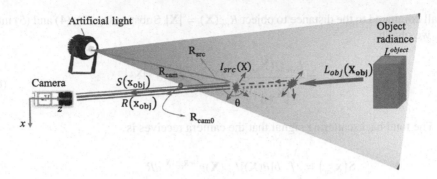

**Fig. 1.** Imaging system setup

- The source is close to the cameras (compared to the object distance); thus, the camera-illuminator baseline is small.
- The scattering is single scattering.

Let $\mathbf{X} = (X, Y, Z)$ and $\mathbf{x} = (x, y)$ are global coordinates of a point in space and its projection into image plan, respectively. The measured intensity can be modeled as a linear combination of attenuated radiance $R(\mathbf{x}_{obj})$ (attenuated fraction of object radiance $L_{obj}(\mathbf{x}_{obj})$) and scattering (or backscattering) signal $S(\mathbf{x}_{obj})$.

$$I(\mathbf{x}_{obj}) = R(\mathbf{x}_{obj}) + S(\mathbf{x}_{obj}) \tag{1}$$

Attenuated signal is

$$R(\mathbf{x}_{obj}) = L_{obj}(\mathbf{x}_{obj}) \tau(\mathbf{x}_{obj}) \tag{2}$$

where direct transmission is

$$\tau(\mathbf{x}_{obj}) = e^{-c|\mathbf{x}_{obj}|} \tag{3}$$

and $c$ and $|\mathbf{X}_{obj}|$ are attenuation coefficient of the environment and distance from object to camera, respectively. The object radiance

$$L_{obj}(\mathbf{x}_{obj}) = I_{src}(\mathbf{X}_{obj}) \rho(\mathbf{x}_{obj}) \tag{4}$$

where $\rho(\mathbf{x}_{obj})$ is object reflectance. The irradiance of a point in space that illuminated by the point light source of intensity $L_{src}$

$$I_{src}(\mathbf{X}) = \frac{L_{src} Q(\mathbf{X})}{R^2_{src}(\mathbf{X})} e^{-cR_{src}(\mathbf{X})} \tag{5}$$

where $Q(\mathbf{X})$ express the non-uniformity of the illumination source. The falloff $1/R^2_{src}(\mathbf{X})$ is caused by free space light propagation. Since baseline of illuminator-camera is very small compared to the distance to object $R_{src}(\mathbf{X}) = |\mathbf{X}|$. Substituting (3), (4) and (5) into (2), we obtain

$$R(\mathbf{x}_{obj}) = \frac{L_{src}Q(\mathbf{X}_{obj})}{\left|\mathbf{X}_{obj}\right|^2}e^{-c|\mathbf{X}_{obj}|}\rho(\mathbf{x}_{obj})e^{-c|\mathbf{X}_{obj}|} \tag{6}$$

The total backscattering signal that the camera receives is

$$S(\mathbf{x}_{obj}) = \int_{R_{cam0}}^{X_{obj}} b[\theta(\mathbf{X})]I_{src}(\mathbf{X})e^{-cR_{cam}(\mathbf{X})}dR_{cam} \tag{7}$$

where $b[\theta(\mathbf{X})]$ is phase function of backscattering. $R_{cam}(\mathbf{X})$ is the distance from a point in the line of sight (LOS) to camera and $R_{cam0}$ is the distance where the light field first intersect the LOS. Since baseline of illuminator-camera is very small compared to the distance to object, then $R_{cam0} = 0$ and $R_{cam}(\mathbf{X}) = R_{src}(\mathbf{X})$. It is also assumed that $b[\theta(\mathbf{X})] = \tilde{b}$ is constant over the field of view. Equation (7) becomes,

$$S(\mathbf{x}_{obj}) = \tilde{b}L_{src}Q(\mathbf{X}_{obj}) \int_0^{X_{obj}} \frac{e^{-cR_{cam}(\mathbf{X})}}{\left|\mathbf{X}_{obj}\right|^2}dR_{cam} \tag{8}$$

By simulation, Tribitz and Schechner [23] shown that the backscattering signal can be well approximated as

$$S(\mathbf{x}_{obj}) \approx S_\infty(\mathbf{x}_{obj})\left[1 - e^{-k|\mathbf{X}_{obj}|}\right] \tag{9}$$

where $S_\infty(\mathbf{x}_{obj}) \propto \tilde{b}L_{src}Q(\mathbf{X}_{obj})$ ([23]) denotes the saturated scattering value where $k|\mathbf{X}_{obj}| = \infty$. It is worth noting that the non-uniformity of $S_\infty(\mathbf{x}_{obj})$ is attributed to $Q(\mathbf{X}_{obj})$. Constant $k$ depends only on $c$ and $\tilde{b}$.

Substituting (6) and (9) into (1), the measured image is (see Fig. 2.)

$$I(\mathbf{x}_{obj}) = \frac{L_{src}Q(\mathbf{X}_{obj})}{\left|\mathbf{X}_{obj}\right|^2}\rho(\mathbf{x}_{obj})e^{-2c|\mathbf{X}_{obj}|} + S_\infty(\mathbf{x}_{obj})\left[1 - e^{-k|\mathbf{X}_{obj}|}\right] \tag{10}$$

**Backscattering calibration:** $S_\infty(\mathbf{x}_{obj})$ is easily obtained. Instead of taking picture when $|\mathbf{X}_{obj}| = \infty$, we take the picture of the our experimental booth (the experimental environment will be explain in Sect. 4) where $c$ is very high.

(a)                                      (b)

**Fig. 2.** Synthetic image. (a) Clear image from Middlebury dataset [24]. (b) Corrupted image by attenuation and backscattering.

## 3 Scattering Removal and Stereo Vision

### 3.1 Light Compensation

To remove the non-uniformity of backscattering, the measured image is divided by the saturated backscattering signal in order to obtain the light compensated image,

$$\hat{\mathbf{J}}(\mathbf{x}_{\text{obj}}) = \frac{L_{src}Q(\mathbf{x}_{\text{obj}})}{S_{\infty}(\mathbf{x}_{\text{obj}})|\mathbf{x}_{\text{obj}}|^2}\rho(\mathbf{x}_{\text{obj}})e^{-2c|\mathbf{x}_{\text{obj}}|} + \left[1 - e^{-k|\mathbf{x}_{\text{obj}}|}\right] \tag{11}$$

Noting that $S_{\infty}(\mathbf{x}_{\text{obj}}) \propto \tilde{b}L_{src}Q(\mathbf{X}_{\textbf{obj}})$; thus, non-uniformity of the backscattering can be removed. The (11) becomes

$$\hat{\mathbf{J}}(\mathbf{x}_{\text{obj}}) = \hat{L}_{obj}(\mathbf{x}_{\text{obj}})e^{-k|\mathbf{x}_{\text{obj}}|} + \left[1 - e^{-k|\mathbf{x}_{\text{obj}}|}\right] \tag{12}$$

where, $\hat{L}_{obj}(\mathbf{x}_{\text{obj}}) = \dfrac{L_{src}Q(\mathbf{X}_{\text{obj}})}{S_{\infty}(\mathbf{x}_{\text{obj}})|\mathbf{X}_{\text{obj}}|^2}\rho(\mathbf{x}_{\text{obj}})e^{-(2c-k)|\mathbf{x}_{\text{obj}}|} = K\dfrac{\rho(\mathbf{x}_{\text{obj}})}{|\mathbf{X}_{\text{obj}}|^2}e^{-(2c-k)|\mathbf{x}_{\text{obj}}|}$ is the compensated radiance of the object and $K$ is constant. The model in (12) is similar to Koschmieder's law with the airlight is 1. Let us denote $\tau^k(\mathbf{x}_{obj}) = e^{-k|\mathbf{x}_{\text{obj}}|}$, which is the modified direct transmission.

Noting that $\hat{L}_{obj}(\mathbf{x}_{\text{obj}})$ is neither reflectivity nor radiance of the object. It, however, is the enhanced image from the original corrupted image by strong backscattering. The value $e^{-(2c-k)|\mathbf{x}_{\text{obj}}|}$ either attenuates (when $-(2c - k) < 0$) or amplifies (when $-(2c - k) > 0$) the object radiance. However, in our experiment, those compensated radiance images are good for both viewing the scene and reconstructing depth map.

## 3.2 Fog Removal

In order to estimate patch's modified transmission $\tilde{\tau}^k(\mathbf{x}_{obj})$, we employ the well-known DCP [14], the estimation is done by:

$$\tilde{\tau}^k(\mathbf{x}_{obj}) = 1 - \min_{y \in \Omega(x)} \left( \min_c \hat{\mathbf{J}}^c(\mathbf{x}_{obj}) \right) \tag{13}$$

To refine the modified transmission, we apply guided image filter [21]. Then, the compensated radiance $\hat{L}_{obj}(\mathbf{x}_{obj})$ is easily calculated. Figure 3 shows our de-scattering result.

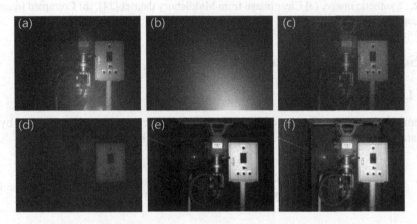

**Fig. 3.** Indoor scene de-scattering. (a) Input image. (b) Saturated backscattering signal. (c) Light compensated image. (d) Refine modified transmission. (e) De-scattering image. (f) De-scattering image from (e) with gamma correction ($\gamma = 0.6$)

## 3.3 Stereo Vison

Since, the defogging result of images taken in the dense particulates environment are very noisy, we employ cost-volume filtering [25] for stereo vision.

## 4 Results and Discussion

To demonstrate the effectiveness of the proposed method, we have tested our approach with both synthetic (from Middlebury dataset [1] and [24]) and real images. Proposed method is evaluated based on the disparity map from output of stereo vision. Our disparity map results are compared with those of two other studies. The first one is Negahdaripour and Sarafraz [20] which incorporating backscattering cue to improve the stereo matching in scattering media based on local matching method. We tuned the window size in their method to obtain the highest quality. The second study is nighttime dehazing [17]. We employed their method to obtain the haze free images before applying stereo vision. The method and parameters of the stereo vision applied to their dehazing and our de-scattering images are the same.

## 4.1  Synthetic Image

Figures 4 and 5 show the stereo vision result from synthetic images, namely, Poster and Pipes. [17] and proposed method outperforms [20] with at least 14% higher in correct matching rate. In the case of dense fog, correct matching rate of our disparity map are about 2% higher than that of [17]. For slight fogged picture, the result from us are as good as that of from [17] since the difference are under 1%.

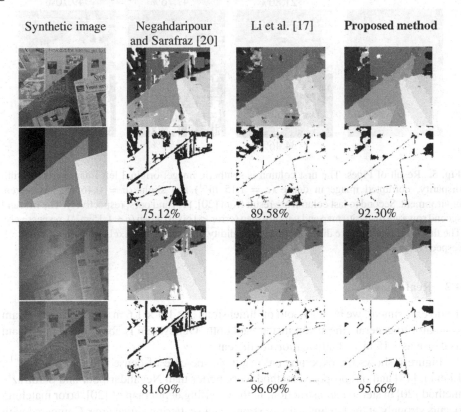

**Fig. 4.** Result of Poster. The first column is synthetic image: original left image, ground-truth disparity, corrupted image in dense (c = 1.15 m$^{-1}$) and slight (c = 0.46 m$^{-1}$) scatterers environment. Second to last column are result from [20], [17] and ours, respectively. The first and second rows are disparity map and validity map (error < 1 pixel) when (c = 1.15 m$^{-1}$), respectively. The third and last rows are disparity map and validity map (error < 1 pixel) when (c = 0.46 m$^{-1}$), respectively.

Synthetic image     Negahdaripour and     Li et al. [17]     **Proposed method**
                          Sarafraz [20]

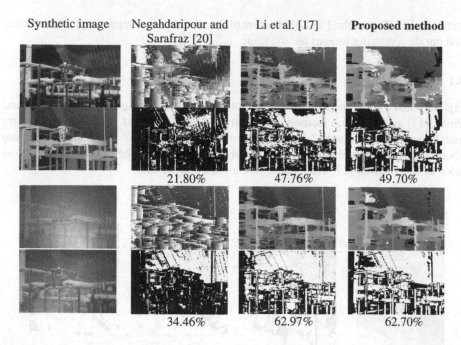

          21.80%              47.76%            49.70%


          34.46%              62.97%            62.70%

**Fig. 5.** Result of Pipes. The first column is synthetic image: original left image, ground-truth disparity, corrupted image in dense (c = 1.15 m$^{-1}$) and slight (c = 0.46 m$^{-1}$) scatterers environment. Second to last column are result from [20], [17] and ours, respectively. The first and second rows are disparity map and validity map (error < 1pixel) when (c = 1.15 m$^{-1}$), respectively. The third and last rows are disparity map and validity map (error < 1pixel) when (c = 0.46 m$^{-1}$), respectively.

## 4.2   Real Image

To do experiment, we built a booth of dimensions $3 \times 1.5 \times 1.6$ m. We utilized a steam generator to generate the steam inside the booth. Our system is able to generate steam as dense as 1.15 m$^{-1}$ of attenuation coefficient.

Figure 6 shows the experimental result. In the case of dense fog ($c = 0.77$ m$^{-1}$), Li et al. [17] and our proposed method work better than Negahdaripour and Sarafraz's method [20] in stereo reconstruction. In the resulting depth map of [20], error matching occurs strongly at the low intensity or strong backscattering signal area. Compared with Li et al. [17], both our defog and depth are better than that of them. Their method is unable to remove strong backscattering signal while our method does it better thanks to our light compensation step. This affects the matching error since stereo algorithm reply on photoconsistenness. Thus, our stereo reconstruction result better than theirs. For example, the detail of value in the last column can be preserved while that of the third column is lost. In the slight fog case, our method still work better.

Input images    Negahdaripour and    Li et al. [17]    **Proposed method**
                Sarafraz [20]

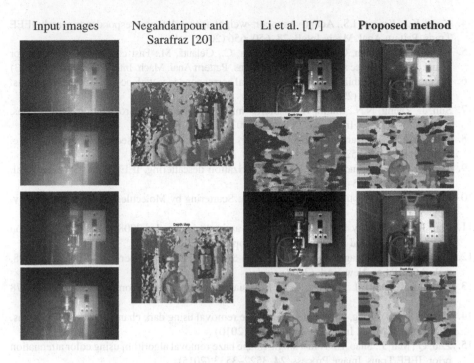

**Fig. 6.** Experiment reult. The first column is real images: left and right images in dense (c = 0.77 m$^{-1}$) and slight (c = 0.46 m$^{-1}$) steam environment. From second to last column are result from [20], [17] and our, respectively. In third and last row, the first and second row are defog of left image and depth map when (c = 0.77 m$^{-1}$), respectively. The third and last row are defog of left image and depth map when (c = 0.46 m$^{-1}$), respectively.

## 5 Conclusion

In this paper, we propose an efficient method for stereo reconstruction in scattering environment. The method utilizes the pre-calibrated light to compensate the in image that is corrupted by both attenuation and scattering. Cost-volume filtering is employed to process the de-scattering image in stereo correspondence step. It is proven that our method outperforms the other two methods. The future work may concentrate on extending to the case of non-uniform steam environment.

## References

1. Scharstein, D., Szeliski, R.: A taxonomy and evaluation of dense two-frame stereo correspondence algorithms. Int. J. Comput. Vis. **47**, 7–42 (2002)
2. Lazaros, N., Sirakoulis, G.C., Gasteratos, A.: Review of stereo vision algorithms: from software to hardware. Int. J. Optomechatronics **2**, 435–462 (2008)
3. Tippetts, B., Lee, D.J., Lillywhite, K., Archibald, J.: Review of stereo vision algorithms and their suitability for resource-limited systems. J. Real-Time Image Process. **11**, 5–25 (2013)

4. Yoon, K.J., Kweon, I.S.: Adaptive support-weight approach for correspondence search. IEEE Trans. Pattern Anal. Mach. Intell. **28**, 650–656 (2006)
5. Hosni, A., Rhemann, C., Bleyer, M., Rother, C., Gelautz, M.: Fast cost-volume filtering for visual correspondence and beyond. IEEE Trans. Pattern Anal. Mach. Intell. **35**, 504–511 (2013)
6. Kolmogorov, V., Zabih, R.: Computing visual correspondence with occlusions via graph cuts. In: ICCV, pp. 1–33 (2001)
7. Sun, J., Zheng, N.N., Shum, H.Y.: Stereo matching using belief propagation. IEEE Trans. Pattern Anal. Mach. Intell. **25**, 787–800 (2003)
8. Schechner, Y.Y., Narasimhan, S.G., Nayar, S.K.: Polarization-based vision through haze. Appl. Opt. **42**, 511–525 (2003)
9. Treibitz, T., Schechner, Y.Y.: Active polarization descattering. IEEE Trans. Pattern Anal. Mach. Intell. **31**, 385–399 (2009)
10. McCartney, E.J.: Optics of the Atmosphere: Scattering by Molecules and Particles. Wiley, New York (1976)
11. Tan, R.T.: Visibility in bad weather from a single image. In: 2008 IEEE Conference on Computer Vision and Pattern Recognition, pp. 1–8. IEEE (2008)
12. Fattal, R.: Single image dehazing. In: ACM SIGGRAPH 2008 Papers on - SIGGRAPH'08, p. 1. ACM Press, New York (2008)
13. Nishino, K., Kratz, L., Lombardi, S.: Bayesian defogging. Int. J. Comput. Vis. **98**, 263–278 (2012)
14. He, K., Sun, J., Tang, X.: Single image haze removal using dark channel prior. IEEE Trans. Pattern Anal. Mach. Intell. **33**, 2341–2353 (2010)
15. Zhu, Q., Mai, J., Shao, L.: A fast single image haze removal algorithm using color attenuation prior. IEEE Trans. Image Process. **24**, 3522–3533 (2015)
16. Zhang, J., Cao, Y., Wang, Z.: Nighttime haze removal based on a new imaging model. In: 2014 IEEE International Conference on Image Processing (ICIP), pp. 4557–4561. IEEE (2014)
17. Li, Y., Tan, R.T., Brown, M.S.: Nighttime haze removal with glow and multiple light colors. In: 2015 IEEE International Conference on Computer Vision (ICCV), pp. 226–234. IEEE (2015)
18. Caraffa, L., Tarel, J.-P.: Combining stereo and atmospheric veil depth cues for 3D reconstruction. IPSJ Trans. Comput. Vis. Appl. **6**, 1–11 (2014)
19. Roser, M., Dunbabin, M., Geiger, A.: Simultaneous underwater visibility assessment, enhancement and improved stereo. In: 2014 IEEE International Conference on Robotics and Automation, pp. 3840–3847 (2014)
20. Negahdaripour, S., Sarafraz, A.: Improved stereo matching in scattering media by incorporating a backscatter cue. IEEE Trans. Image Process. **23**, 5743–5755 (2014)
21. He, K., Sun, J., Tang, X.: Guided image filtering. IEEE Trans. Pattern Anal. Mach. Intell. **35**, 1397–1409 (2013)
22. Hosni, A., Rhemann, C., Bleyer, M., Rother, C., Gelautz, M.: Fast cost-volume filtering for visual correspondence and beyond. In: IEEE Transactions on Pattern Analysis and Machine Intelligence, pp. 504–511. IEEE (2013)
23. Treibitz, T., Schechner, Y.Y., Israel, T., Technology, I.: Instant 3D Escatter II, pp. 1861–1868 (2006)
24. Scharstein, D., Hirschmüller, H., Kitajima, Y., Krathwohl, G., Nešić, N., Wang, X., Westling, P.: High-resolution stereo datasets with subpixel-accurate ground truth. In: Jiang, X., Hornegger, J., Koch, R. (eds.) GCPR 2014. LNCS, vol. 8753, pp. 31–42. Springer International Publishing, Cham (2014). doi:10.1007/978-3-319-11752-2_3
25. Hosni, A., Rhemann, C., Bleyer, M., Rother, C., Gelautz, M.: Fast cost-volume filtering for visual correspondence and beyond. IEEE Trans. Pattern Anal. Mach. Intell. **35**, 504–511 (2013)

# Fully Automatic and Robust 3D Modeling for Range Scan Data of Complex 3D Objects

Jungjae Yim and Guoliang Fan[✉]

School of Electrical and Computer Engineering, Oklahoma State University,
Stillwater, OK 74078, USA
{jungjae,guoliang.fan}@okstate.edu

**Abstract.** 3D surface registration of two or more range scans is an important step in building a complete 3D model of an object. When the overlaps between multi-view scans are insufficient, good initial alignment is necessary that usually requires some prior assumption such as pre-defined initial camera configuration or the use of landmarks. Specifically, this paper addresses the problem of registering two or more range scans captured from complex 3D objects which have small overlaps. The proposed technique is based on the integration of a new Partial Artificial Heat Kernel Signature (PA-HKS) and a Modified Multi-view Iterative Contour Coherence (MM-ICC) algorithm. This unique combination allows us to handle multi-view range scan data with large out-of-plane rotation and with limited overlaps between every two adjacent views. The experimental results on several complex 3D objects show the effectiveness and robustness of the proposed approach.

## 1 Introduction

3D modeling has long been one of the most important research topics in the field of computer vision and pattern recognition. Recently, there are many new techniques for complex 3D object modeling [1,2]. Moreover, with recent technology advancement, many inexpensive 3D sensors [3,4] were developed, which triggers easy access to 3D depth data and allows various applications of using 3D point sets such as 3D modeling, pose estimation, and 3D object recognition. Among many, registration of the range scans to generate 3D models has drawn a great attention and many successful registration techniques have been proposed which usually require sufficient overlap across views and good camera initialization [5,6]. However, registration for partially overlapping data without any initialization still remains a challenge in this field. In this paper, we address this issue by two steps. The first is to support initial alignment of multi-view scans by using a new mesh-based feature. The second is to improve multi-view contour coherence by considering both self-occlusion and visibility of the predicted contours across views. Our goal is aimed at automatic and robust 3D registration from partial overlapping 3D point sets without any camera initialization.

The Heat kernel signature algorithm is generally applied to generate highly localized features from a 3D mesh model for pose estimation or object

© Springer International Publishing AG 2016
G. Bebis et al. (Eds.): ISVC 2016, Part I, LNCS 10072, pp. 529–541, 2016.
DOI: 10.1007/978-3-319-50835-1_48

recognition [7–9]. This technique shows a successful result exclusively on full 3D mesh data and 2.5D range data without self-occlusion. Because of self-occlusion of 3D data, the accuracy of feature extraction would deteriorate mainly due to the holes on the 3D surface. Accordingly, we develop an improved heat kernel feature in order to accommodate partially overlapped range scan data captured from different view angles. As the first step that was inspired by [7,8], we propose a new partial artificial Heat kernel signature (PA-HKS) and use it to achieve coarse alignment of the multiple range scan data. As the second step, the original Multi-view iterative contour coherence (M-ICC) algorithm [10] is enhanced by introducing an additional pruning step to remove erroneous contours, leading a modified M-ICC (MM-ICC) algorithm that is more robust and accurate. The original M-ICC algorithm requires initialization of the range scans by predefined camera configuration. In conjunction with PA-HKS based alignment, the proposed MM-ICC algorithm is able to self-initialize multi-view camera configuration to support fully automatic and robust registration and to reconstruct a detailed 3D model based on the corresponding contours from multi-view scans.

## 2    Related Work

In this section, we provide a brief overview of the background of this research, which involves two separate topics: Direct (Appearance-based) registration and Feature-based registration.

**Direct (Appearance-Based) Registration.** There have been a great deal of research on point set registration focusing on where most pixels agree. Among many, the classic iterative closest point (ICP) algorithm [5] and its variants [11] provide an effective way to register the points and reconstruct the model in a stable and effective manner. However, ICP requires good initialization and is also time consuming mainly because it has to identify the closest point pairs. The Coherence point drift (CPD) algorithm, which is another powerful method of point set registration, and the modified CPD algorithms [12] allow us to get more robust and stable outcomes in presence of noise and outliers. CPD can produce very robust results both in the rigid and non-rigid point sets. However, CPD also entails good initialization to find correct correspondences. Moreover, the M-ICC algorithm in [10] aims to perform registration based on the multi-view contour coherence. These algorithms above have proven effective and accurate under reasonable initialization. However, achieving accurate and robust registration without initialization still remains as a major challenge in point set registration.

**Feature-Based Registration.** Feature-based registration methods attempt to find corresponding features in the multiple data sets of different views and to effectively match the extracted features across views. It is a fairly recent research trend that puts an emphasis on detecting interest points on 3D mesh models. Most of the studies along this trend focus on local surface descriptors [13,14]. A multi-scale approach is commonly employed to analyze the 3D surface at consecutive scales to identify interest points at different levels [15]. A 3D extension of the 2D Harris operator was proposed that is based on the local autocorrelation of images [16,17]. The studies in [17,18] employ the Heat Kernel Signature (HKS) of a 3D mesh model. According to the geometry energy on the vertices, an interest point is selected if it remains as a local maximum of the geometry energy function within several successive scales. Therefore, it is crucial to have the distinctiveness of an interest point for a stable outcome.

Both of the two categories of point set registration reviewed above entail their own strengths and limitations. Accordingly, a number of attempts have been made to combine these two methods to alleviate the constraints and to deliver more robust and accurate outcomes [18].

# 3  Proposed Approach

The proposed algorithm consists of following two steps: *Coarse Registration* using PA-HKS and *Fine Registration* through MM-ICC. The first involves rough alignment of the multiple partial overlapping range scan based on PA-HKS extracted from each view. The second step is initialized by the first step and performs re-registration by applying via three-round contour pruning and maximizing contour coherence.

## 3.1  Coarse Registration Based PA-HK

The HKS is grounded based on the Heat kernel and this heat kernel is stable against perturbations of the shape [7]. A HKS formula is derived as $K_t = \sum_{t=0}^{\infty} exp^{\lambda_i t} \phi_i(x)^2$ where, $\lambda_i$ and $\phi_i$ are $i^{th}$ eigenvalue and eigenfunction of Laplace-Beltrami operator. This algorithm uses heat diffusion on the surface of a full 3D model to detect the highly local shape features. Heat diffusion over a longer period of time enables us to spot the summaries of a shape in large neighborhoods whereas the one with a short time period allows the observation of detailed local shape features. Therefore, through heat diffusion, we are able to compare the point signatures at different time intervals and accomplish multi-scale matching between points. The HKS algorithm operates based on the gradient of the surface; thus, it is hard to find the correct feature descriptor in the partial object surfaces under self-occlusion. So, in order to address the problem, we project the range scan data to the plane and connect the projected data with original range data using mesh. This new generated 3D volume mesh is used to apply the HKS algorithm to find the feature descriptor. Although the generated artificial 3D mesh only captures partial geometric information from the 3D model, the extracted PA-HKS features are expected to preserve some local geometric characteristics by which we can produces relatively reliable alignment between the partial surfaces observed from two adjacent views. The idea of PA-HKS is discussed in three steps as follows.

**Extracting PA-HKS Keypoints.** For each view, we generate a partial artificial 3D mesh data by projecting the range scan data to the back plane. The back and side planar surfaces of the artificial 3D mesh are added to find PA-HKS keypoints on the frontal mesh surface visible in that view. It is possible some keypoints are found along the contour between the back and side surfaces, then we move them to the front mesh surface. Thus, all PA-HKS keypoints are in the original range scan, as shown in Fig. 1(a)–(c).

**Grouping PA-HKS Keypoints.** There could be multiple local PA-HKS keypoints in the same area among the multiple range scans. In order to ensure one-to-one mapping across views, we group the keypoints by using their 3D Euclidian distance and the similarity of their PA-HKS signatures, as shown in Fig. 1(d). This will result a single local PA-HKS keypoint in those areas that have high energy and rich geometric information. Although those keypoints may not be spatially precise in terms of their locations, they offer important 3D landmarks for initial point set alignment.

**Matching PA-HKS Keypoints.** Prior to ICP-based alignment, PA-HKS features are used to initialize correspondence between two adjacent views. Given two PA-HKS feature sets from two range scans, $\mathbf{S}$ and $\mathbf{T}$, we find the correspondence pairs across two views by

$$\mathbf{t}_s = \arg \min_{\mathbf{t} \in \mathbf{T}} d(\mathbf{t}, \mathbf{s}), \forall \mathbf{s} \in \mathbf{S}, \tag{1}$$

where $d(\cdot)$ is a distance function between two PA-HKS features. To ensure robust feature matching, if $d(\mathbf{s}', \mathbf{t}_{s'})$ is larger than a threshold, we declare that $\mathbf{s}' \in \mathbf{S}$ does not have a correspondence in $\mathbf{T}$ and will not be involved in the following ICP step. After PA-HKS based correspondence initialization, we can use ICP to find the initial transformation between the two scans.

## 3.2    Fine Registration Based on MM-ICC

Wang [10] proposed a wide baseline 3D modeling algorithm (called M-ICC) that registers multi-view range scans by maximizing contour coherence between the observed and predicted contours across multiple views. A key idea in the algorithm is to remove incorrect contour points using two step pruning. Here we want to improve contour coherence by refining contour correspondences via a third pruning step. This extra pruning enables us to remove incorrect correspondences of the predicted contours according to the invisibility condition. We name the improved algorithm MM-ICC to differentiate from the original M-ICC one.

**Generating Observed $R_i$ and Predicted Range scan data $R_{i \to j}$.** A range scan $R_i$ of view $i$ provides a depth value $R_i(\mathbf{x})$ at each image pixel $\mathbf{x} = (x, y)^T \in \mathbb{R}^2$. A meshed point cloud $M_j$ is generated by range scan $R_j$ and $R_{i \to j}$ is created by projecting $M_j$ to the $i^{th}$ view. $N_i(\mathbf{x})$ is the surface normal vector of an image pixel $\mathbf{x}$ in $R_i$.

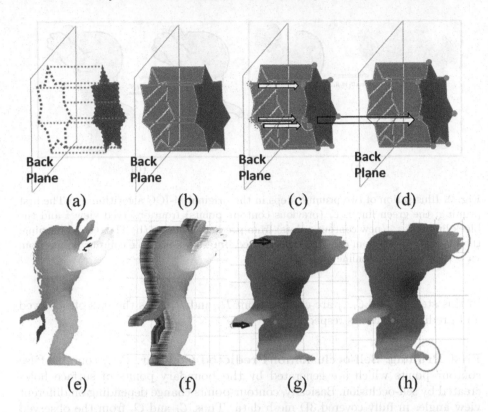

**Fig. 1.** Illustration of PA-HKS: (a) A range scan in 3D (green); (b) A partial 3D mesh created from (a); (c) PA-HKS features after shifting; (d) PA-HKS features after grouping; (e)–(h) Real object examples corresponding to (a)–(d). (Color figure online)

**Extracting Contour Points.** The observed range scan data $R_i$ has two different sets of contour points. One set is from the front contours and the other set is from the back contours. The back contours will be set as occlusion ones during the first pruning step. Given pixels belonging to the object in view $i$ as $\mathbf{X}_i$, the depth of pixels belonging to the background is set by be infinite, i.e., $R_i(\mathbf{x}) = \infty$ for $\mathbf{X} \notin \mathbf{X}_i$. The set of visible contour points $\mathcal{C}_i$ and that of occlusion contour points are distinguished by depth discontinuity of a pixel and its 8 neighboring pixels, $N_{\mathbf{x}}^8$ of range scan as follows:

$$\mathcal{C}_i = \{\mathbf{x} \in \mathbf{X}_i | \exists \mathbf{y} \in N_{\mathbf{x}}^8, R_i(\mathbf{y}) - R_i(\mathbf{x}) > \tau_1\}, \tag{2}$$

$$\mathcal{O}_i = \{\mathbf{x} \in \mathbf{X}_i | \exists \mathbf{y} \in N_{\mathbf{x}}^8, R_i(\mathbf{x}) - R_i(\mathbf{y}) > \tau_2\}, \tag{3}$$

where $\tau_1$ are $tau_2$ are two thresholds to control the quality of selected PA-HKS features. Depth discontinuity caused by connection of contours and occlusion contours indicates surface holes created by self-occlusion in the range scan data. Those surface holes can remain incorrect contour points which have to be pruned.

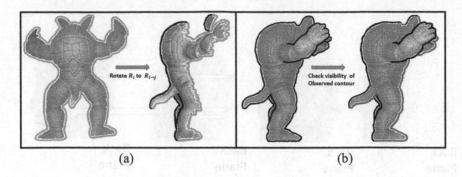

(a)                                         (b)

**Fig. 2.** Illustration of two pruning steps in the original M-ICC algorithm: (a) The first pruning: the green line is $C_i$ (previous contour points) from observed view $i$ and the black line is $C_{i \to j}$ (new contour points) from predicted view $j$. (b) The second pruning: the black line is $C_j$ from camera $j$ and the red line shows invisible contour points from view $i$. (Color figure online)

In this step, $C_i$ and $C_{i \to j}$ are created from $R_i$ and $R_{i \to j}$ as the sets of observed and predicted contours respectively.

**First Pruning: Self-occlusion of Predicted Contour.** $C_{i \to j}$ contains false contour points which are generated by the boundary points of surface holes created by self-occlusion. Basically, contour points change depending on different view angles in fully covered 3D mesh data. Thus, $C_i$ and $O_i$ from the observed view direction should not be one of the members of $C_{i \to j}$ from the predicted view direction. In Fig. 2(a), the green color line is a visible contour in previous Camera $i$ direction and the black line is a new contour in $j$ direction after rotated range scan data $R_i$. This green one should not be a valid contour in camera $j$ direction because the rotated range scan data $R_i$ does not cover the full surface of a target in camera $j$ direction. In Fig. 3(a), the square point corresponds to a contour $C_{i \to j}$ from camera view $j$ and the dot point is a contour $C_i$ from camera view $i$. If those contours are at the same 3D location, the contour should be pruned, as shown in Fig. 3(a).

$$C_{i \to j}^{(1)} = \{ \mathbf{X} \in C_{i \to j} | C_{i \to j}(\mathbf{X}) \cap (O_i(\mathbf{X}) \cup C_i(\mathbf{X}))^c \}. \tag{4}$$

**Second Pruning: Visibility of Observed Contours.** Some contour points in $C_j$ are not visible from camera location of view $i$. We prune $C_j$ based on the visibility of the corresponding contour in view $i$.

$$C_{j/i}^{(2)} = \{ \mathbf{X} \in C_j | N_j(\mathbf{X})^T \cdot (O_{i \to j} - V_j(\mathbf{X})) > 0 \}, \tag{5}$$

where $O_{i \to j}$ is the camera location of frame $i$ in camera $j$ and $V_j(\mathbf{X})$ is the back-projection operator which maps $\mathbf{X}$ in frame $j$ to its 3D location.

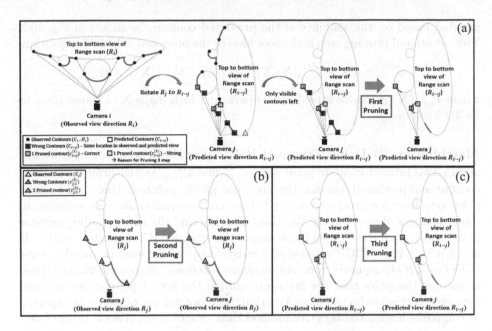

**Fig. 3.** Illustration of the three-step pruning from a top-down view where each dot represents a contour and each contour correspond to a partial surface: (a) Range Scan $R_i$, contour $C_i$ (black dots) and occlusion points $O_i$ (black dots) in camera $i$. (b) notation of Fig. 2. (c) Pruning 1: Range Scan $R_{i\rightarrow j}$, contour points $C_{i\rightarrow j}$ (square) and pruned contour points $C_{i\rightarrow j}^{(1)}$ (blue square and yellow square) in camera $j$, Some Contours(yellow square) require Third pruning. (d) Pruning 2: Range Scan($R_j$) in camera $j$ and pruned contour points ($C_{j/i}^{(2)}$) (Color figure online)

$N_j(\mathbf{x})$ is the surface normal vector of each image pixel in frame $j$. In Fig. 2(b), the black color line is a visible contour from camera $j$ direction and the red line is an invisible contour in $i$ direction. The red contour should be pruned to find the corresponding contour points only. Only black contours are left after the first and second pruning steps because the black contours have corresponding contours. In Fig. 3(b), the red triangle point presents a contour from camera $j$ and it is invisible from camera $i$. Those points do not have correspondences in camera $i$ frame thus they should be pruned.

**Third Pruning: Visibility of Predicted Contours.** As a new step introduced in this work, the third pruning is applied to the results of the first pruning which may still have incorrect contour points. Some contour points $C_{i\rightarrow j}$ generated by $R_{i\rightarrow j}$ are invisible in camera $j$. However, self-occlusion effect makes the points visible in camera $j$. Thus, these incorrect points cause errors in the matching step and obstruct accurate registration. In Fig. 3(a) and (c), although the yellow square points should not be visible in camera $j$, they are still considered as visible contours in the predicted view. Therefore, we perform the third pruning based on the visibility of the predicted contour, as shown in Fig. 3(c). This additional pruning step is the core idea of the proposed MM-ICC algorithm.

$$\mathcal{C}_{i \to j}^{(3)} = \{ \mathbf{X} \in \mathcal{C}_{i \to j}^{(1)} | N_j(\mathbf{X})^T \cdot (\mathcal{O}_{i \to j} - V_{i \to j}(\mathbf{X})) > 0 \}. \tag{6}$$

where $V_{i \to j}(\mathbf{X})$ is the back-projection operator which maps $\mathbf{X}$ in frame $R_{i \to j}$ to its 3D location.

**Matching in 3D Using Trimmed ICP.** After three pruning steps, we can obtain two pruned contour point sets, $\mathcal{C}_{j/i}^{(2)}$ and $\mathcal{C}_{j \to i}^{(3)}$ as the pruned observed contour and predicted contour. However, not all the points in those two contour point sets have a correspondence and those contour points are very sensitive to minor changes of the viewing direction. Thus, to find the corresponding contour points and match them correctly, we apply the trimmed ICP algorithm in the 3D space [19]. Trimmed ICP is based on consistent use of the least trimmed squares (LTS) to sort the square errors and minimize a certain number of smaller values. It ignores the pairs that are far apart among the set of point pairs to avoid incorrect corresponding points. Accordingly, more robust outcome is expected in comparison with the bijective method that cannot cover distant points [10].

## 4    Experimental Results

We evaluate our proposed algorithm that combines PA-HKS and MM-ICC in comparison with the original M-ICC algorithm. The results are illustrated in two parts: usefulness of PA-HKS and contribution of MM-ICC. Our 3D models are from the Standard 3D model dataset [20].

### 4.1    PA-HKS for Coarse Registration

The usefulness of PA-HKS was evaluated based on the maximum rotation deviation in angle initialization that can be corrected. In Table 1, the original M-ICC algorithm can recover only up to 60° offset in the tolerable rotation angle but fails to register the two-view range scan data beyond 60° (Fig. 4(b)). However, our proposed algorithm successfully recovers up to 90° as shown in Fig. 4(c). Successful registration results have a small angle error ($< 1°$) of angle between estimation and ground truth.

**Table 1.** Errors of recovered angles under different degrees of initial rotation deviation

| Angle deviation | 10° | 20° | 30° | 40° | 50° | 60° | 70° | 80° | 90° |
|---|---|---|---|---|---|---|---|---|---|
| M-ICC | <1 | <1 | <1 | <1 | <1 | <1 | 58 | 58 | 62 |
| **Proposed** | <1 | <1 | <1 | <1 | <1 | <1 | <1 | <1 | <1 |

(a)                                  (b)                                  (c)

**Fig. 4.** Illustration of PA-HKS based coarse registration: (a) Initialization of two range scans from the 3D Armadillo model with rotation gap 70°; (b) Registration results of the M-ICC algorithm (c) Registration results using PA-HKS for ICP.

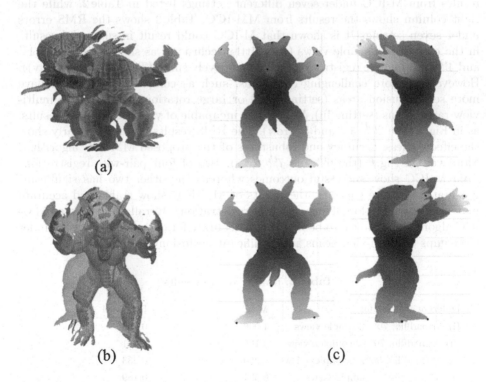

(a)

(b)                                                  (c)

**Fig. 5.** (a) Four Range scans of the armadillo in the 3D space; (b) PA-HKS features extracted from of four range scans (black dots) (c) Result of the PA-HKS based initial alignment using ICP.

Moreover, four different range scans extracted from the 3D Stanford armadillo model is used to verify the effectiveness of the proposed algorithm compared with the previous M-ICC algorithm. In Fig. 5(a), the four range scans are visualized together in the 3D space without any previously known initialization. All range scan data face to the same one camera direction in the unknown initialization setting. The proposed PA-HKS method extracted corresponding features from the partially overlapped range scan data based on Heat kernel signature(HKS) descriptor. In Fig. 4(b), the heat distribution is indicated by different colors of surface. The warm colors around the PA-HKS features indicate the high variance of the local geometry and similar distribution of feature points in the multi-view scans implies their consistency and reliability. The initial alignment result given in Fig. 4(c) confirms the usefulness of PA-HKS for coarse registration.

## 4.2   MM-ICC for Refined Registration

We compare M-ICC and MM-ICC based on the same view initialization obtained from PA-HKS based coarse registration. In Fig. 6, the left column represents the results from M-ICC under seven different settings listed in Table 2, while the right column shows the results from MM-ICC. Table 2 shows the RMS errors under seven settings It is shown that M-ICC could result in successful results in the case of two simple views (with little occlusion), as shown Fig. 6 (the $1^{st}$ and $4^{th}$ rows) where registration error is relatively small (Table 2 (setting (i,iv)). However, in more challenging conditions, such as complex views which have more self-occlusion areas (setting ii, v) or large rotation angles among multi-view range scans (setting iii), M-ICC was incapable of yielding accurate results, as in Fig. 6 (the $2^{nd}$, $3^{rd}$ and $5^{th}$ row). The RMS results in Table 2 clearly show the effectiveness, accuracy and robustness of the proposed MM-ICC algorithm. Moreover, in Fig. 6 (the $6^{th}$ and $7^{th}$ rows), two of four pair-wise registrations from M-ICC show successful outcomes whereas the other two has significant mis-match. On the contrary, the results of MM-ICC show stable and accurate matching outcomes for all four pair-wise registration. Overall, the proposed MM-ICC algorithm is proven to be robust and accurate for complex 3D objects under large gaps of multi-view scans and significant occlusion in each scan.

Table 2. RMS errors in results

| Different test setting | M-ICC | Proposed |
|---|---|---|
| (i) Armadillo, 70°, 2 simple views | 1.099 | 0.290 |
| (ii) Armadillo, 70°, 2 complex views | 3.169 | 0.281 |
| (iii) Armadillo, 90°, 2 complex views | 3.289 | 0.233 |
| (iv) Bunny, 60°, 2 simple views | 0.521 | 0.189 |
| (v) Bunny, 60°, 2 complex views | 5.116 | 0.116 |
| (vi) Bunny, 90°, 4 complex views | Ave. of 4 pairs = 1.595 | Ave. of 4 pairs = 0.206 |
| (vii) Armadillo, 90°, 4 complex views | Ave. of 4 pairs = 4.476 | Ave. of 4 pairs = 0.279 |

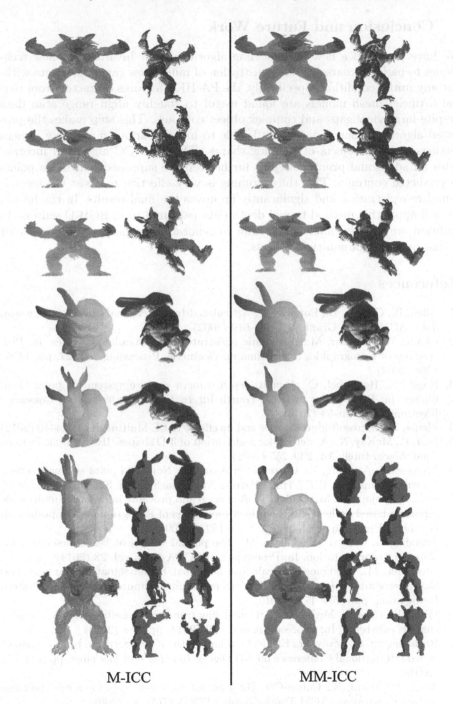

M-ICC                                   MM-ICC

**Fig. 6.** Comparison between M-ICC and MM-ICC based on two 3D models under seven settings given in Table 2. For each setting, we show the final 3D modeling result (left) and the pair-wise scan matching results of every two adjacent views (right).

# 5   Conclusion and Future Work

We have proposed a new 3D modeling algorithm that involves two new techniques to perform coarse-to-fine registration of multi-view range scan data without any initial condition. Specifically, the PA-HKS features extracted from partial artificial mesh models are found useful to roughly align range scan data despite large view gaps and complex object contours. This step makes the proposed algorithm more robust and flexible to handle various multi-view camera settings and 3D objects of complex shapes. The MM-ICC algorithm incorporates an additional pruning step to further remove supposedly invisible points in predicted contours. This third pruning is very effective to assist the second-round re-registration and significantly improves the final results. In the future, we will apply this method to real depth data captured from RGB-D sensors. In addition, we will also make an attempt to generalize the proposed approach for robust modeling of non-rigid objects.

# References

1. Allen, B., Curless, B., Popovic, Z.: Articulated body deformation from range scan data. ACM Trans. Graph. **21**, 612–619 (2002)
2. Chang, W., Zwicker, M.: Automatic registration for articulated shapes. In: Proceedings of Eurographics Symposium on Geometry Processing, vol. 27, pp. 1459–1468 (2002)
3. Rogge, S., Hentschel, C.: A multi-depth camera capture system for point cloud library. In: Proceedings of IEEE Fourth International Conference on Consumer Electronics, pp. 50–54 (2014)
4. Zhang, Z.: Microsoft kinect sensor and its effect. IEEE Multimedia **19**, 4–10 (2012)
5. Besl, P., McKay, N.: A method for registration of 3-D shapes. IEEE Trans. Pattern Anal. Mach. Intell. **14**, 239–255 (1992)
6. Myronenko, A., Song, X., Carreria-Perpinan, M.: Non-rigid point set registration: Coherent point drift. IEEE Trans. Pattern Anal. Mach. Intell. **32**, 2262–2275 (2010)
7. Sun, J., Ovsjanikov, M., Guibas, L.: A concise and provably informative multi-scale signature based on heat diffusion. In: Proceedings of Eurographics Symposium on Geometry Processing, vol. 28, pp. 1383–1392 (2009)
8. Brandao, S., Costeria, J., Veloso, M.: The partial view heat kernel descriptor for 3D object representation. In: Proceedings of ICRA 2014, vol. 28 (2014)
9. Bronstein, M., Kokkinos, I.: Scale-invariant heat kernel signatures for non-rigid shape recognition. In: 2013 IEEE Conference on Computer Vision and Pattern Recognition, pp. 1704–1711 (2010)
10. Wang, R., Choi, J., Medioni, G.: 3D modeling from wide baseline range scans using contour coherence. In: Proceedings of CVPR 2014, pp. 1–8 (2014)
11. Rusinkiewicz, S., Levoy, M.: Efficient variants of the ICP algorithm. In: Proceedings of 3rd International Conference on 3-D Digital Imaging and Modeling, pp. 145–152 (2001)
12. Aiger, D., Mitra, N., Cohen-Cor, D.: 4-points congruent sets for robust pairwise surface registration. ACM Trans. Graph. (TOG) 27(3), 85 (2008)
13. Shah, S., Bennamoun, F., Boussaid, F., El-Sallam, A.: 3D-Div: A novel local surface descriptor for feature matching and pairwise range image registration. In: 2013 IEEE International Conference on Image Processing, pp. 2934–2938 (2013)

14. Guo, Y., Sohel, F., Bennamoun, M., Lu, M., Wan, J.: TrisI: A distinctive local surface descriptor for 3D modeling and object recognition. In: 2013 International Conference on Computer Graphics Theory and Applicaitons, GRAPP 2013, pp. 86–93 (2013)
15. Tardif, C., Schafer, A., Waehnert, M., Dinse, J., Turner, R., Bazin, P.: Multi-contrast multi-scale surface registration for improved alignment of cortical areas. Neuroimage **111**, 107–122 (2015)
16. Sipiran, I., Bustos, B.: A robust 3D interest points detector based on harris operator. In: Proceedings of Eurographics Workshop on 3D Object Retrieval, pp. 7–14 (2010)
17. Dutagaci, H., Cheung, C., Godil, A.: Evaluation of 3D interest point detection techniques via human-generated ground truth. In: Proceedings of Eurographics Workshop on 3D Object Retrieval (2012)
18. Xia, R., Zhao, J., Liu, Y.: A robust feature-based registration method of multi-modal image using phase congruency and coherent point drift. In: SPIE Proceedings: Pattern Recognition and Computer Vision, vol. 8919 (2013)
19. Chetverikov, D., Svirko, D., Stepanov, D.: The trimmed iterative closest point algorithm. In: 16th International Conference on Pattern Recognition, vol. 3, pp. 1–4 (2002)
20. The stanford 3D scanning repository (Retrieved July 2015)

# ST: Advancing Autonomy for Aerial Robotics

# Real-Time Detection and Tracking of Multiple Humans from High Bird's-Eye Views in the Visual and Infrared Spectrum

Julius Kümmerle[✉], Timo Hinzmann,
Anurag Sai Vempati, and Roland Siegwart

Autonomous Systems Lab, ETH Zurich, Zurich, Switzerland
juliusku@student.ethz.ch

**Abstract.** We propose a real-time system to detect and track multiple humans from high bird's-eye views. First, we present a fast pipeline to detect humans observed from large distances by efficiently fusing information from a visual and infrared spectrum camera. The main contribution of our work is a new tracking approach. Its novelty lies in online learning of an objectness model which is used for updating a Kalman filter. We show that an adaptive objectness model outperforms a fixed model. Our system achieves a mean tracking loop time of 0.8 ms per human on a 2 GHz CPU which makes real time tracking of multiple humans possible.

## 1 Introduction

Research on fully autonomous Unmanned Aerial Vehicles (UAVs) became very popular with the development of powerful but lightweight computers and sensors. Besides the enormous popularity of multi-copters, fixed-wing UAVs are also becoming steadily more interesting mainly due to their large flight range. In a classical scenario they are used to first localize victims and then send their GPS locations to a rescue team on the ground. In this context, autonomous human tracking from fixed-wing UAVs faces several challenges. The main challenge is the flight altitude of around 50–150 m. High resolution imagery is needed to provide enough detail for accurately detecting humans. Searching small objects in large images is computationally expensive which makes the human search with real-time constraint challenging, especially on UAVs with limited computational power. For that reason, we use a long wave thermal camera (FLIR Tau 2 19 mm). In many scenes humans significantly differ in temperature from most of the background. This can be used to reduce the detection search space and thereby increase efficiency of the human detection. The main drawback of our thermal camera is the relatively low resolution of 640 × 512. We use a visual spectrum camera with a high resolution of 1600 × 1200 alongside the thermal camera to get more detail.

G. Bebis et al. (Eds.): ISVC 2016, Part I, LNCS 10072, pp. 545–556, 2016.
DOI: 10.1007/978-3-319-50835-1_49

## 2  Related Work

Object tracking is one of the big topics of computer vision and many different approaches have been developed in the last decades for which [1] gives an excellent overview. Just recently, different research groups started to use an objectness measure in trackers [2,3]. The concept of objectness is proposed by [4] and essentially aims at deciding whether an image patch contains an object or not before searching for specific object classes. Cheng et al. [5] developed an efficient algorithm for calculating an objectness measure, denoted by *BING objectness*, and thereby enabled the use of objectness in real time applications. Objectness is shown to increase accuracy when used as an additional score for tracking [2,3]. Liang et al. [3] initialize a tracker with an adaptive objectness model which is learned by an adaptive SVM [6] in the frame of the first detection. The model combines generic objectness with object specific information. The integration of the adaptive objectness model into state-of-the-art trackers is reported to outperform the original trackers in most cases [3]. Our tracker approach is also based on an adaptive objectness model. The difference to [3] lies in an ongoing online learning process to gradually transform the generic objectness model to a discriminative object specific model. The online learning framework is based on the *Passive-Aggressive* algorithm introduced in [7]. The objectness detection is integrated into a Kalman filter [8,9]. For human detection we make use of the popular Histogram of Orientated Gradients (HOG) features [10].

## 3  Approach

In the following, we describe the approach used for human detection and tracking.

### 3.1  Detection Pipeline

Human detection from heights of 50–150 m brings along many challenges. Humans only occupy few pixels of the image which makes a detailed search necessary and thereby makes the detection particularly computationally expensive. To speed up the search for humans we use the long wave infrared spectrum as additional information. Figure 1 shows an example where humans clearly stand out from the background. Compared to the corresponding visual spectrum image the infrared image shows significantly less texture. This allows us to use a simple but fast blob detector in the infrared image. At each blob we define centered bounding boxes of different sizes. These are the candidates which are given to a HOG detector. The linear SVM is trained on 2400 positive and 24000 negative human samples extracted from four infrared datasets [11–14]. The HOG detector is designed to classify patches with heights of 6–36 pixels. Compared to the original HOG detector [10] the humans are significantly smaller so we had to find new suitable parameters as described in Sect. 4.1.

(a)                                  (b)

**Fig. 1.** (a) Crop of infrared image showing humans with high contrast from background. (b) Corresponding crop of visual spectrum image.

To increase accuracy, we also use the high resolution visual spectrum image. The challenge in fusing information from multiple cameras is to find corresponding areas. Standard appearance based matching algorithms [15] can only be applied if the appearance in the images is similar. This cannot be guaranteed when using a visual and an infrared spectrum camera. Some parts of an object might show high contrast in the infrared spectrum whereas they may not be distinguishable from the background in the visual spectrum. Moreover, an object in the visual spectrum often shows significant texture which cannot be perceived in the infrared spectrum. To circumvent the problem of lacking similarity in appearance we use the assumption that the distance to the object is large compared to the baseline of the cameras.

For the theoretical case that the cameras have coincident optical centers and their principle axes are aligned the matching problem is trivially solved by finding pixels with the same projection ray.

For a vertically aligned stereo pair with parallel principle axes and no distortion, the pixel error $err_{pix}$ introduced by a non-vanishing baseline $b$ can be calculated as

$$err_{pix} = \frac{f}{l_{pix}} \cdot \frac{b}{d}, \tag{1}$$

where $f$ is the focal length, $l_{pix}$ denotes the size of a pixel and $d$ is the depth of the targeted 3D point $P$ as illustrated in Fig. 2. $f$ and $l_{pix}$ belong to the camera the error is attributed to. From this we can calculate the minimal depth $d_{min}$ of a 3D point to make a sub-pixel error w.r.t the infrared camera ($f_{ir} = 19\,\mathrm{mm}, l_{pix,ir} = 17\,\mu\mathrm{m}, b = 30\,\mathrm{mm}$)

$$d_{min} = \frac{f}{l_{pix}} \cdot b \approx 34\,\mathrm{m} \tag{2}$$

Since we target human detection at longer ranges, the error due to baseline and scene depth variations can be neglected.

For the candidates which were classified as humans in the infrared spectrum we calculate the corresponding bounding boxes in the visual spectrum image.

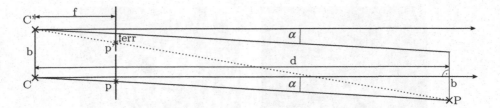

**Fig. 2.** Stereo camera pair with optical centers $C$ and $C'$. The principle axes are parallel. With the known projection $p$ of the 3D point $P$, the corresponding projection $p'$ in the other camera is approximated by assuming a vanishing baseline. The resulting error is denoted as $err$.

To compensate errors resulting from a weak stereo calibration (calibration of infrared cameras is comparably hard because of blurry imagery [16]) we extend the number of candidates in the visual spectrum image by sampling around the correspondences. As a final stage of our pipeline, we classify these candidates by another HOG detector which was trained on 3000 humans from bird's-eye views and 25000 negative samples.

### 3.2    Tracker

We perform the tracking of humans on the infrared images because in many scenes humans are more salient in the infrared than in the visual spectrum. Furthermore, we know the position of a detected person more accurately in the infrared than in the visual spectrum due to the weak camera calibration.

The key idea of our tracker approach is to use the BING algorithm [5] to rapidly generate a small number of candidates for redetecting the person in the new frame. The BING algorithm essentially is a linear SVM which approximates the SVM model and feature vector by sums of binary vectors to achieve high efficiency. A feature vector is constructed by calculating the absolute gradient field of the target region, resizing the field to $8 \times 8$ and interpreting the result as a 64D vector. Because of the resizing to $8 \times 8$ usually the model is underfitting when trained on a specific object class and therefore leads to limited usability as a single object class classifier on a large region. Therefore, we apply the BING algorithm only in a local area around the last tracker position as shown in Fig. 3(a).

Originally, the BING algorithm is used with a fixed objectness model generated by training on multiple object classes which is useful for detecting general objects. For tracking, the object is the same and might only change appearance in small ranges. Therefore, we want to learn object specific information and include it into the model. The goal of the learning process is to bias the model towards the object without completely loosing the generic objectness information which is valuable to prevent drift. We use a soft margin version of the *Passive-Aggressive* (PA) algorithm [7] to adjust the model while tracking. We define three different types of training data. *Negative* training data is generated

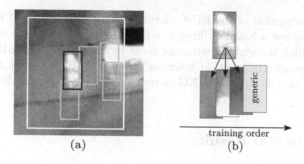

training order

(a)                                    (b)

**Fig. 3.** (a) BING candidates (gray bounding boxes) in local area (white box). The highest scoring candidate (dark bounding box) is well fitting the tracked person. (b) Training order with one object specific positive, three negatives and the generic objectness model.

by randomly sampling the neighborhood. An *object specific positive* sample is a candidate which is identified as the tracked object based on appearance and motion. We define the third type of sample as *generic positive*. The original objectness model serves as a generic positive sample. Training is only performed when an object specific positive sample is identified. We sample three negatives and train on the same object specific positive after each negative sample. After these six training rounds we train on the generic objectness model as illustrated in Fig. 3(b). This procedure ensures a balanced ratio of positives to negatives.

The identification of a good candidate is essential for the learning procedure. Since errors in the identification cannot be eliminated in practice we use a low learning rate to be more robust to false positives. Furthermore, continuous training on the generic objectness model partly compensates false updates. As mentioned before, we use an appearance model and a motion model for the identification of a positive candidate. To capture the appearance of the object we simply store positive identified patches in a FIFO storage with a capacity of five patches. To check if a candidate agrees with the stored appearance we use the $L_2$-norm of the difference of the candidate to each stored patch and check if the smallest norm is lower than a dynamic threshold. The threshold decreases with the number of successive positive identified candidates and thereby expresses the trust in the appearance model as well as in the BING model. If multiple candidates are classified as positive then we use the distance to the predicted position from the constant velocity motion model to choose a candidate. We take this uncertainty into account by weighting the learning rate of the learning algorithm by the inverse of the number of identified candidates. We have chosen this relatively simple method to compare appearance of patches since many sophisticated methods use descriptors that are not reliable on textureless and small objects as in our case. If the objects show more detail, the identifier step can be easily replaced with other methods while keeping the learning process the same.

To fuse information of the BING detector, motion model and human detection pipeline we use a Kalman filter in which the BING detector represents one update step which is weighted with the trust in the model. The BING detection is only used to update position whereas the size is updated by the detection pipeline. This speeds up the BING detection since the search is limited to a single size.

## 4    Experimental Results

For the testing of the detection pipeline and the tracker we collected a new dataset with our stereo camera pair. The videos show city scenes with a camera angle of around 45° to the horizontal so that most of the humans' front view profiles are still visible. Humans have distances in the range of 30 m–80 m to the cameras whereas the mean distance is around 50 m. This results in human heights in the infrared images of 6–36 pixels whereas the mean is around 16 pixels. In the visual spectrum humans have roughly double the pixel heights as shown in Fig. 4. Humans smaller than 12 infrared pixels often have low contrast in the infrared image and also lose the typical human shape in both the infrared and visual spectrum images. Besides the small sizes of the humans, partial occlusions and groups of humans make the dataset challenging. Furthermore, the stereo camera pair is moved and rotated which makes the tracking significantly harder.

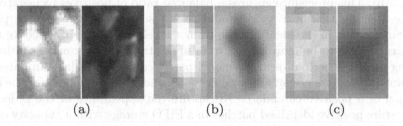

(a)                          (b)                          (c)

**Fig. 4.** Examples of humans in our dataset. (a) Humans of heights > 30 infrared pixels. (b) Human of height 15 infrared pixels. (c) Human of height < 10 infrared pixels.

### 4.1    Detection Pipeline

For the evaluation of the detection pipeline we split the detector cascade in its three stages, which are the blob detector, the HOG detector in the infrared spectrum (HOG_is) and the HOG detector in the visual spectrum (HOG_vs). We inspect the performance of the system step by step starting with only the blob detector, then adding the HOG_is stage and finally using the whole pipeline. As a performance measure we plot miss rates over false positives per image (FPPI). The evaluation is only performed on the area which is represented in both images where Fig. 5 shows the fused images.

**Fig. 5.** Image fusion of infrared and visual spectrum image. A pixel mapping based on the assumption of coincident camera centers is used. Images are undistorted and rectified.

**Blob Detector.** The main goal of the blob detector is to reduce the number of candidates for the computationally expensive classifiers in the next stages. We set the limit of blob detections to 200 to guarantee an upper bound on the runtime. On the other hand, the blob detector has to find most of the persons so that they reach the strong classifiers in the second and third stage. In other words, the miss rate should be small. The performance of the blob detector is shown in Fig. 6. We increased the thresholding spacing to make the blob detector more tolerant to intensity changes inside a blob. Therefore, increasing the threshold spacing results in detecting more low quality blobs. As we can see from Fig. 6, the performance rapidly increases for a FPPI range of 1–30 and levels out at FPPI of 40 and a miss rate of 0.2. From the high miss rates at low FPPI we see that only few humans in the infrared really appear as a homogeneous blob. Most of the humans show temperature differences e.g. warm head and legs and relative cold upper body. Some of the humans ($\approx$20%) cannot be detected by the blob detector since they show very little contrast to the background if at all. The differences in blob quality can be seen in Figs. 1 and 4. To find most of the humans and guarantee fast runtimes, we use the blob detector configuration which results in a miss rate of 20% with a FPPI of 40. The high number of false positives shows that a simple blob detector in the infrared spectrum is not a good human detector.

**Infrared HOG Detector.** The HOG_is shall reduce the number of false positives significantly. We aim at FPPI < 0.1 or preferably at FPPI < 0.01 for the final detector since each false positive detection initializes a wrong tracker. In the worst case the wrong trackers cannot be deleted quickly which results in accumulation of wrong trackers. Hence, low FPPI is an essential prerequisite for a high tracker performance. We achieved best results with the following HOG descriptor configuration: patch size $= 16 \times 32$, block size $= 8 \times 8$, block shift $= 2$,

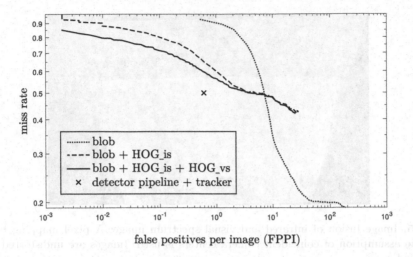

**Fig. 6.** Experimental performance results on our dataset. The detector shows significant decrease in FPPI over a wide range with each stage (see three curves). The combination of detector and tracker reduces the miss rate by 10% at same FPPI compared to the detector pipeline alone (see cross).

cell size $= 4 \times 4$ and bin number $= 9$. Two retraining rounds on hard false positives gave an improvement in miss rate of 5% at FPPI $= 0.1$. Our best performing HOG_is for FPPI of 0.01–0.1 is shown in Fig. 6. The graph shows that adding the HOG_is stage to the blob detector significantly improves performance in the low FPPI range which cannot even be reached by the blob detector. At FPPI $= 0.01$ and FPPI $= 0.1$ the miss rate is 0.87 and 0.80, respectively. The performance is in the same range as in state-of-the-art pedestrian detection of heights 30–80 pixels on visual spectrum images [17].

**Visual Spectrum HOG Detector.** The final HOG detection in the visual spectrum is expected to further reduce the FPPI at the same miss rate since some objects like warm windows or wheels might appear similar to humans in the infrared image whereas in the visual spectrum these objects clearly appear as non-humans. Since our stereo pair is not synchronized and the calibration is weak we sample multiple candidates in the visual spectrum image around the mapped detection from the infrared image. As presented in Fig. 7, the number of samples and the spacing influences the overall performance. If the sampling cannot compensate for the mapping errors the HOG_vs stage does not give any improvement. If the samples compensate for the mapping errors the performance is increased significantly by the HOG_vs stage. The best performance of the complete detection pipeline at FPPI $= 0.01$ and FPPI $= 0.1$ is reached for the setting of the HOG_is with FPPI $= 0.22$/miss rate $= 0.76$ and FPPI $= 0.45$/miss rate $= 0.68$, respectively. Figure 6 shows that with image fusion an improvement of almost 10% in miss rate in the relevant FPPI range can be achieved.

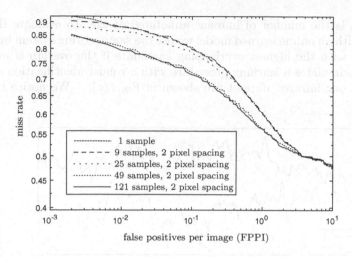

**Fig. 7.** Experimental performance results of the detector pipeline for different sampling settings in the visual spectrum. The pixel spacing is given in visual spectrum image pixels. The sampling highly influences the effectiveness of the HOG detector in the visual spectrum. With 49 samples most of the mapping errors are compensated and a reduction of up to 10% in miss rate is achieved by the classifier in the visual spectrum.

## 4.2   Tracker

As explained in Sect. 3.2 the key idea of the tracker is the adaptive BING model which is adjusted while tracking. We want to verify that learning object specific information is beneficial for tracking and outperforms a fixed model. To evaluate the performance of the BING detector independently from the rest of the tracker we perform the following experiment. First we use the original objectness model and run the BING algorithm in local areas around the annotated person positions. We take the five best candidates and check for overlaps with the ground truth human bounding box of more than 80%. The candidate with the highest overlap is used to calculate an intuitive performance score

$$s_{a,\Delta t} = \begin{cases} \frac{6-r_{a,\Delta t}}{5} & \text{if highest overlap} > 80\% \\ 0 & \text{else} \end{cases} \tag{3}$$

where $a$ denotes the annotation, $\Delta t$ is the time passed since the first frame of the annotation and $r \in [1,5]$ denotes the ranking based on the classification score of the BING detector for the candidate with the highest overlap of more than 80%. For example, if the candidate with the second highest classification score ($r = 2$) has the highest overlap with the annotation and the overlap is over 80% then the performance score is 4/5. If none of the five candidates has an overlap of more than 80% then the performance score is set to zero. The performance over all annotations is measured with the normed cumulative score

$$S_{\Delta t} = \frac{\sum_a s_{a,\Delta t}}{n_{\Delta t}}, \tag{4}$$

where $n_{\Delta t}$ is the number of humans annotated at $\Delta t$. To evaluate the BING detector with an online learned model we use the same scoring system but relearn the model with the highest overlapping candidate if the overlap is more than 80%. This simulates a learning procedure with a robust identification step. The results for our infrared dataset are shown in Fig. 8(a).    We notice that after

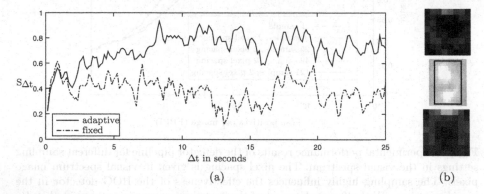

(a)                                    (b)

**Fig. 8.** (a) Performance of BING detector in the infrared spectrum with fixed and adaptive model measured with the cumulative score (see Eq. 4). The adaptive model outperforms the fixed model after few seconds. (b) Example of adaptive model (top) and fixed model (bottom) for the same tracked object (middle). The 64D model vectors (SVM weights) are represented as $8 \times 8$ patches. Bright means high and dark means low value.

a few training rounds the BING detector with an adaptive model outperforms the detector with a fixed model. The score curves show a mean difference of 0.3 which means that on average the BING detector with adaptive model needs 3 candidates less to find the tracked object than the detector with the fixed generic model. Figure 8(b) gives an example of a fixed and a learned model for a tracked human. The human clearly appears as a big blob at the top and a smaller blob at the bottom. The original BING objectness model assumes an object to have a single closed boundary which is not suitable for this example. The adaptive model shows the two blob characteristic and their size difference and thereby outperforms the fixed model.

For the evaluation of our complete detection-tracking framework we use a detection pipeline with FPPI $= 0.10$ and miss rate $= 0.72$. The complete system significantly outperforms the detection pipeline with a miss rate $= 0.50$ and FPPI $= 0.62$ as shown in Fig. 6. For the same miss rate the detector has a FPPI of 5.0 which is $8\times$ more than the FPPI of the complete system.

## 4.3    Runtime

Table 1 shows runtime results for the detector and tracker. The experiments were run on a 2.0 GHz CPU.

**Table 1.** Experimental runtime results of detector (top row) and tracker (bottom row). Detection runtime is 50× longer than tracker loop time.

| Stage | Mean runtime in ms |
|---|---|
| Blob detector | 16.3 |
| HOG_is | 22.0 |
| HOG_vs | 2.3 |
| Complete detection pipeline | 40.6 |
| BING detection | 0.17 |
| PA learning | 0.08 |
| Identification | 0.46 |
| Other | 0.10 |
| Complete tracker loop | 0.81 |

The detector pipeline is the time consuming part of the system. The HOG_is stage has to classify significantly more candidates than the HOG_vs stage which explains the difference in runtime. Usually, the detection pipeline is not used on every frame to save computational power. The efficient reduction of candidates by the BING detector results in very fast tracker loop times which enables tracking of many humans simultaneously.

## 5   Conclusion and Future Work

We introduced a simple fusion technique for infrared and visual spectrum imagery which we use in our detection pipeline. We showed from experimental results that our detection pipeline significantly improves performance by using classifiers in both the infrared and visual spectrum. For tracking humans in the infrared spectrum we proposed a novel tracking approach that is based on an adaptive objectness detector which is learned while tracking. Our experiment shows that learning biases the objectness model to a specific object and thereby leads to more meaningful candidate ranking. In future work, we want to fuse objectness proposals in both the infrared and visual spectrum to arrive at an even more reliable ranking. Furthermore, we want to combine objectness with other more sophisticated online learning algorithms and explore other methods for the identification of the tracked object. We also plan to evaluate our system on UAV datasets to determine the performance of human detection and tracking at higher altitudes and camera speeds.

**Acknowledgment.** The research leading to these results has received funding from the European Commission's Seventh Framework Programme (FP7/2007-2013) under grant agreement no. 600958 (SHERPA).

# References

1. Yilmaz, A., Javed, O., Shah, M.: Object tracking: a survey. ACM Comput. Surv. (CSUR) **38**, 13 (2006)
2. Stalder, S., Grabner, H., Gool, L.: Dynamic objectness for adaptive tracking. In: Lee, K.M., Matsushita, Y., Rehg, J.M., Hu, Z. (eds.) ACCV 2012. LNCS, vol. 7726, pp. 43–56. Springer, Heidelberg (2013). doi:10.1007/978-3-642-37431-9_4
3. Liang, P., Pang, Y., Liao, C., Mei, X., Ling, H.: Adaptive objectness for object tracking, IEEE (2015)
4. Alexe, B., Deselaers, T., Ferrari, V.: What is an object? In: 2010 IEEE Conference on Computer Vision and Pattern Recognition (CVPR), pp. 73–80. IEEE (2010)
5. Cheng, M.M., Zhang, Z., Lin, W.Y., Torr, P.: BING: binarized normed gradients for objectness estimation at 300fps. In: Proceedings of the IEEE Conference on Computer Vision and Pattern Recognition, pp. 3286–3293 (2014)
6. Yang, J., Yan, R., Hauptmann, A.G.: Adapting SVM classifiers to data with shifted distributions. In: Seventh IEEE International Conference on Data Mining Workshops (ICDMW 2007), pp. 69–76. IEEE (2007)
7. Crammer, K., Dekel, O., Keshet, J., Shalev-Shwartz, S., Singer, Y.: Online passive-aggressive algorithms. J. Mach. Learn. Res. **7**, 551–585 (2006)
8. Kalman, R.E.: A new approach to linear filtering and prediction problems. J. Basic Eng. **82**, 35–45 (1960)
9. Cuevas, E.V., Zaldivar, D., Rojas, R.: Kalman filter for vision tracking (2005)
10. Dalal, N., Triggs, B.: Histograms of oriented gradients for human detection. In: 2005 IEEE Computer Society Conference on Computer Vision and Pattern Recognition (CVPR 2005), vol. 1, pp. 886–893. IEEE (2005)
11. Wu, Z., Fuller, N., Theriault, D., Betke, M.: A thermal infrared video benchmark for visual analysis. In: Proceedings of the IEEE Conference on Computer Vision and Pattern Recognition Workshops, pp. 201–208 (2014)
12. Davis, J.W., Keck, M.A.: A two-stage template approach to person detection in thermal imagery. WACV/MOTION **5**, 364–369 (2005)
13. Davis, J.W., Sharma, V.: Background-subtraction using contour-based fusion of thermal and visible imagery. Comput. Vis. Image Underst. **106**, 162–182 (2007)
14. Vempati, A.S., Agamennoni, G., Stastny, T., Siegwart, R.: Victim detection from a fixed-wing UAV: experimental results. In: Bebis, G. (ed.) ISVC 2015. LNCS, vol. 9474, pp. 432–443. Springer, Heidelberg (2015). doi:10.1007/978-3-319-27857-5_39
15. Scharstein, D., Szeliski, R.: A taxonomy and evaluation of dense two-frame stereo correspondence algorithms. Int. J. Comput. Vis. **47**, 7–42 (2002)
16. Vidas, S., Lakemond, R., Denman, S., Fookes, C., Sridharan, S., Wark, T.: A mask-based approach for the geometric calibration of thermal-infrared cameras. IEEE Trans. Instrum. Meas. **61**, 1625–1635 (2012)
17. Dollar, P., Wojek, C., Schiele, B., Perona, P.: Pedestrian detection: an evaluation of the state of the art. IEEE Trans. Pattern Anal. Mach. Intell. **34**, 743–761 (2012)

# Combining Visual Tracking and Person Detection for Long Term Tracking on a UAV

Gustav Häger[1]([⊠]), Goutam Bhat[1], Martin Danelljan[1], Fahad Shahbaz Khan[1], Michael Felsberg[1], Piotr Rudl[2], and Patrick Doherty[2]

[1] Computer Vision Laboratory, Linköping University, Linköping, Sweden
gustav.hager@liu.se
[2] Artificial Intelligence and Integrated Computer Systems, Linköping University, Linköping, Sweden

**Abstract.** Visual object tracking performance has improved significantly in recent years. Most trackers are based on either of two paradigms: online learning of an appearance model or the use of a pre-trained object detector. Methods based on online learning provide high accuracy, but are prone to model drift. The model drift occurs when the tracker fails to correctly estimate the tracked object's position. Methods based on a detector on the other hand typically have good long-term robustness, but reduced accuracy compared to online methods.

Despite the complementarity of the aforementioned approaches, the problem of fusing them into a single framework is largely unexplored. In this paper, we propose a novel fusion between an online tracker and a pre-trained detector for tracking humans from a UAV. The system operates at real-time on a UAV platform. In addition we present a novel dataset for long-term tracking in a UAV setting, that includes scenarios that are typically not well represented in standard visual tracking datasets.

## 1 Introduction

Visual tracking is one of the classic computer vision problems, with a wide range of applications in surveillance and robotics. In a surveillance scenario, a tracking system could be used to detect when a person is moving into a prohibited area. In robotics, a real-time tracking system can be used to track the positions of objects of interest, for example to make the robot follow a specific person at a set distance. Recently a number of challenges in the visual tracking area have triggered a high pace of improvement in the area of online-tracking [1–5]. A particularly interesting class of trackers is the model-free tracker. Here *model-free* refers to the fact the tracker does not require any information beyond an initial bounding box. These methods are typically evaluated on datasets such as OTB [6], or VOT [1–3]. These datasets are composed of a large number of short videos, typically recorded using a high quality camera.

A popular robotics platform is the Unmanned Aerial Vehicle (UAV), these robots are usually equipped with a wide range of sensors, including cameras. A typical situation is that the operator instructs the UAV to follow a designated

© Springer International Publishing AG 2016
G. Bebis et al. (Eds.): ISVC 2016, Part I, LNCS 10072, pp. 557–568, 2016.
DOI: 10.1007/978-3-319-50835-1_50

**Fig. 1.** Visualization of fusion system, the detector output is blue, tracker output green and the fused result red. The combination of both tracker and detector produces a more accurate bounding box estimate than the respective inputs, as seen in the first two frames. The last two demonstrate drift correction.

person at a fixed distance without manual intervention. This requires the UAV to have the ability to track the designated target, and act on the information produced by the tracker. As the camera is fixed on the UAV the view might suddenly change when the UAV is repositioning or is impacted by wind. It is usually desired that the system can follow the designated person for an extended period of time, likely for thousands of frames rather than the few hundred common in most benchmark videos [3]. Such scenarios are problematic for the current model-free trackers, as they are prone to model drift, and will eventually lose the tracked object.

The drift problem is not present in methods based on a pre-trained object detector, as they do not update the appearance model online. The most recent methods such as deformable parts models (DPM), and convolutional neural networks (CNN) have increased the state of the art performance significantly in detection tasks [7]. Unfortunately this increase in performance demands significantly more computations. A tracking system based on general object detectors will attempt to associate each detection with a tracked object, or when no known object matches initialize a new track. A disadvantage of this type of tracker is that a single object will give a large number of detections of high confidence. For these reasons detector based methods typically give a more noisy estimate of the target bounding box.

In order for a UAV to accurately follow a designated person the tracking system must fulfill certain requirements. The object tracker should output position and size estimates that are accurate at all times, or notify the system that the estimate is not sufficiently precise to act on. The system should be robust in difficult situations such as occlusions, and unstable camera movement. Finally, in order to be practically useful it should be capable of real-time operation on the limited hardware present on a UAV. A visualization of the output from our detector, tracker and combined position estimate is present in Fig. 1.

## 1.1 Contribution

We propose an approach for fusing the output of an online model-free tracker and a pre-trained person detector for UAV based tracking of humans. The system is capable of real-time operation on a UAV platform.

Additionally we present a challenging dataset for long term tracking from a UAV. All sequences are recorded with a flying UAV, and are significantly longer than the typical tracking benchmark videos. The sequences contain long term occlusions of the entire tracked person, and background of varying complexity. Further challenging situations are long term partial occlusions, and significant change of pose of the tracked person. One sequence also includes a number of distracting events where other humans walk past the tracked person and temporarily occlude him.

## 2 Related Work

There are two common approaches to visual tracking, model free tracking using on-line learning to create a robust appearance model of the specific tracked target, or using a pre-trained detector and associating detections with a tracked target. Model free trackers such as those evaluated in the VOT challenge [1–3] require no prior information about the target, except an initial bounding box. An appearance model is created on-line by gathering additional samples while tracking. Detection based trackers on the other hand use a detector for the object or class to track, this detector is applied on each new frame. The tracking problem then becomes a matter of associating each detection with an already tracked object or initialing new objects to track. However few attempts have been made to combine the strengths of both approaches into a single system. In this paper we present such a system, for on-line tracking of humans on a micro UAV platform.

### 2.1 Visual Object Tracking

In the last few years a significant progress has been made in visual object tracking. In particular methods based on Discriminative Correlation Filters (DCF) have shown a great deal of promise, in the 2014 visual object tracking (VOT) challenge [2] the top 3 methods where DCF based. Trackers based on the DCF framework exploit the circulant structure of images and the Fourier transform to efficiently create a linear classifier. Our method is based on a combination of the winning entry in the VOT 2014 challenge [8], but rather than using the HOG features we use the lower dimensional color names suggested in [9]. The lower dimensionality of the color names descriptor allows our implementation to run at high frame rates while maintaining comparable accuracy.

### 2.2 Visual Object Detection

Methods for visual object detection, using a wide range of classifiers and feature representations exist in literature. Of particular interest is the method utilizing Histogram of Oriented gradient features proposed by Dalal [10]. Using this feature representation in a sliding window support vector machine (SVM) an efficient and robust classifier is obtained. This provides a fast detector that is suitable for real-time operation.

Other popular methods include Deformable Parts models such as the one proposed by Felsenzwalb [11] or a number of deep learning based methods [12,13]. In practice these more complex models require an order of magnitude or more of computational power beyond Dalal's method, as such they are impractical to use on a UAV with limited computational capacity, particularly when real-time operation is desired.

## 2.3  Detector and Tracker Fusion

The combination of a model-free tracker and a static detector is a conceptually simple way to improve the long term robustness of a tracking system. However combining the tracker and detector in way that maintains the accuracy of the on-line tracker while keeping the long term robustness of the detector is not trivial. A previous attempt was made in [14] were the output of both the tracker and detector where used as inputs into a Probability Hypothesis Density (PHD) filter, this approach disregards that the on-line component contains valuable appearance information from the tracked object.

Other approaches include the PN learning proposed by Kalal [15] that utilizes binary classifiers and the structural constraints of the labels. This approach is purely on-line learning based, unlike our combination of pre-trained detector and on-line learning tracker.

## 3  Active Vision Framework

Our vision framework combines the output of a pre-trained human detector with that of a model-free correlation filter based tracker. An overview of the

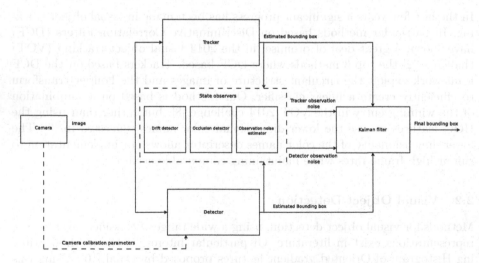

**Fig. 2.** An overview of the tracking system, the details of the tracker are described in Sect. 3.1, the detector in Sect. 3.2 and the observer components in Sect. 3.4

system is presented in Fig. 2. The complete system is composed of three main parts: an online model-free tracked based on the Discriminative correlation filter framework; A human detector trained off-line, with a static model that runs over the image in a sliding window, or is evaluated at a small region; A system that observes the performance of each subsystem in order to estimate the current reliability of each one.

### 3.1 DCF Based Online Tracker

The online tracker used is based partly on the DSST [8] and the ACT [16]. Both of these methods are based on the framework of Discriminative Correlation Filters. We use the color names representation proposed in [16], and the separate scale filter suggested in [8], where we use a gray scale feature instead of the HOG used by Danelljan et al. This is done in order to reduce the dimensionality of the translation and scale estimation filters. This reduced dimensionality (from 31 to 11 and 31 to 1 respectively) significantly reduces the computational burden while maintaining the performance.

Discriminative Correlation Filters create a classifier $h$ by specifying a desired output $y$ at a given input $x$ and minimizing the error for the classifier $h$ for the input $x$. With the commonly used approximation [8,16,17] for multidimensional features the error function becomes:

$$\epsilon = ||\sum_{l=1}^{d} h^l \star x^l - y||^2 + \lambda \sum_{l=1}^{d} ||h^l||^2 \tag{1}$$

The $\star$ denotes circular correlation, while the $\lambda$ is a small regularization factor. This optimization can be efficiently solved in the Fourier domain with the closed form solution:

$$H^l = \frac{\bar{Y} X^l}{\sum_{k=1}^{d} \bar{X}^k X^k + \lambda} \tag{2}$$

where $H, Y, X$ denotes the Fourier transform of the respective variables, and $\bar{X}$ the complex conjugate. The classifier is updated using linear interpolation for each frame yielding a compact and efficient appearance representation. Further details and derivations can be found in [8,16,17].

In a new frame a position estimate is computed from the filter response over a patch. The new position $P_{\text{trk}}$ corresponds to the pixel in the patch with the highest value.

In cases of tracker drift the model will typically be corrupted by gradually adapting to the background instead of the target. Initially this will give an offset from the true target position that gradually moves away from the correct position over time. When taking the possibility of drift into account the tracker's position estimate $P_{trk}$ could be modeled as:

$$P_{\text{trk}} = P + \mathcal{N}(b_t, \sigma_{\text{trk}}) \tag{3}$$

where the true position $P$ is perturbed by noise from $\mathcal{N}(b_t, \sigma_{\text{trk}})$ that represents the current tracker drift as a time-varying bias $b_t$, and the variance of the position estimate $\sigma_{\text{trk}}$ is approximately constant over time.

## 3.2  Person Detection

Our system uses an SVM with HOG features as image representation, as proposed by [10]. The classifier is evaluated in a sliding window manner over a scale pyramid. The scale pyramid is computed with the current target size estimate in the center. The SVM model is trained on the INRIA dataset [10], augmented with a few example frames collected by our UAV. In order to reduce the number of scales for the detection prior information of the targets size is taken into account. When no prior information about target size and position is available, the detector is run over a full scale-space pyramid of the image.

The detector outputs a large number of detections for each target, spread over a range of scales and positions. While each detection has a confidence, it is not guaranteed that the detection with the highest confidence is the correct one.

Once the detector has been evaluated over a new frame, all detections with confidence below a certain threshold are removed. For the remaining detections a weighted average is computed using a Gaussian centered on the current position estimate. This gives the detector estimate $P_{\text{det}}$ of the targets position as:

$$P_{\text{det}} = P + \mathcal{N}(0, \sigma_{\text{det}}) \tag{4}$$

Here, unlike in 3 the detector does not have a time-varying bias, as the model is not updated online. However the variance for the detector $\sigma_{\text{det}}$ is typically much larger than $\sigma_{\text{trk}}$.

## 3.3  Our Fusion Framework

We combine information from the tracker and the detector in two ways. First the position and size estimated by both the tracker and the detector is combined by a Kalman filter in order to produce a more robust measure than either one individually.

Secondly the reliability of both the model-free tracker and the detector is monitored in order to correct for tracker drift. Additionally the reliability estimates are used to update the observation noise for the Kalman filter continuously. Finally, when the tracker proves reliable for a longer period of time, a snapshot of the appearance model is stored in order to re-detect the target if it is lost.

The state vector for the Kalman filter is:

$$K_{\text{state}} = [P_x, P_y, P_w] \tag{5}$$

where $P_x, P_y$ correspond to the top-left corner of the tracked bounding box, and $P_w$ to the width of the box. As the bounding box has a fixed ratio between width and height only the width is needed to represent the bounding box size.

## 3.4  State Monitoring

The current reliability of both the detector and the tracker is estimated continuously. This is done in order to detect corruption in the on-line learning component, and to set the observation noise for both inputs into the Kalman filter.

From the proposed observation models 3 and 4, a principled approach for detecting model drift can be derived. Since the detector is unbiased but noisy, the time varying bias $b_t$ caused by the tracker drifting can be detected by comparing the position estimates over time. If the tracker maintains high confidence, but with a consistent offset in the estimated position relative to the detector, it is likely that the appearance model used by the tracker has begun to drift away from the center of the target. Due to the noisy position estimate provided by the detector it is difficult to obtain an accurate estimate of the tracker bias. Instead of producing a correct estimate of the bias, the tracker model is restarted on the current best estimated position.

A rough estimate of the tracker's confidence in the current prediction can be obtained from the height of the correlation peak. In order to correctly re-identify a lost target snapshots of the tracker model is stored periodically. The current model is considered reliable only if the score peak has been higher than some threshold $t_r$ for more than 100 consecutive frames.

Using this confidence information it is possible to detect situations when the tracked person is no longer in view for the tracker, such as occlusions. In these situations the confidence of the tracker will typically drop very low, but begin to increase as the model adapts to the occluding object. After sufficient time the confidence will be higher than typical when tracking an articulated human. At the same time the detector will consistently fail to give any detections. In such cases the system will flag for loss of target and switch into re-detection mode. When in this mode the detector scans the full image, until a reliable detection is made. Previously stored models are evaluated on the detection, if one matches sufficiently well tracking will resume.

**Kalman Filter Observation Noise.** The observation noise for the Kalman filter for both the detector and tracker is updated in each new frame. For the tracker the noise is set relative to the height of the peak. In practice only two settings for the observation noise are used: If the peak is above some threshold $T_{\text{low}}$ the observation noise is set to a low value, otherwise it is set to a high one.

For the detector it is possible to use the spread of detections to estimate the variance $\sigma_{\text{det}}$. While it is possible to use the variance directly to set the observation noise, this would discard important information gathered over time. Instead the observation noise is weighted based on how well the detections have matched with the combined estimate over a short time window.

The final detector observation noise is set according to:

$$d_n = e^{(\frac{W_{\text{match}}}{d_c})^2} \tag{6}$$

where $W_{\text{match}}$ is set high if the combined output has matched well during a short time window, and $d_c$ is the distance from the current position estimate to the current detection. The $d_c$ parameter mainly reduces the weight if the detector has very strong responses on some background object.

## 4   Dataset

We provide a dataset of four sequences for long-term UAV tracking. The sequences are recorded with the UAV flown manually, with the pilot instructed to keep the target in view. Each sequence features a different person to track. The main goal of our dataset is to capture longer sequences than is typically used in visual tracking, while representing UAV specific difficulties well. Since all sequences are recorded using a flying UAV the camera is continuously moving, with some sudden jerks as the UAV repositions. We call this new dataset 'Terra' after the lab where it was recorded. A description of the difficulties in each sequence is in Table 1.

### 4.1   Data Acquisition System

The LinkQuad is a versatile autonomous Micro Aerial Vehicle. The platform's airframe is characterized by a modular design which allows for easy reconfiguration to adopt to a variety of applications. Thanks to a compact design (below 70 cm tip-to-tip) the platform is suitable for both indoor and outdoor use.

**Fig. 3.** Example frames from some challenging situations in our dataset. From the Sitting sequence. When the tracked person sits down the deformations are severe enough that most object detectors will fail.

**Fig. 4.** The Linkquad UAV used to record our dataset. This configuration features a PointGrey camera and an Intel-NUC motherboard for running the vision system on board.

**Table 1.** An overview of the sequences included in our dataset. The first column has the sequence name, the following four columns the degree of some difficulties in each sequence. The final column the number of frames in each sequence.

|            | Occlusions            | Scale changes | Viewpoint changes | Pose change    | length |
|------------|-----------------------|---------------|-------------------|----------------|--------|
| Occlusion1 | Short full occlusion  | Significant   | Significant       | Always upright | 3610   |
| Occlusion2 | Full and partial      | Limited       | None              | Sits in chair  | 3156   |
| Sitting    | Long full occlusion   | Significant   | Minor             | Sits in chair  | 3177   |
| Walking    | Long partial occlusion| Limited       | Significant       | Always upright | 4854   |

LinkQuad is equipped with in-house designed flight control board - the LinkBoard. The LinkBoard has a modular design and this allows for adjusting the required computational power depending on mission requirements. In the full configuration, the LinkBoard weighs 30 g, has very low power consumption and has a footprint smaller than a credit card. The system is based on two ARM-Cortex micro controllers running at 72 MHz which implement the core flight functionalities.

The LinkBoard includes a three-axis accelerometer, three rate gyroscopes, and absolute and differential pressure sensors for estimation of the altitude and the air speed, respectively. The LinkBoard features a number of interfaces which allow for easy extension and integration of additional equipment.

The configuration used during the recording of the dataset was a Firefly MV FMVU-03MTC camera from Point Grey Research connected to an on board Intel NUC i5 computer. A photo of the configured LinkQuad is in Fig. 4.

### 4.2 Challenges

The sequences feature some difficulties well represented in visual tracking datasets, such as very long term partial occlusions, periodic full occlusions and jerky camera movement. One sequence has the tracked person sitting down for a period, one has multiple humans crossing each other in the image. In all sequences additional humans are present in the background. An additional difficulty is that the sequences are far longer than the ones commonly used, at 3400–4900 frames, while in most datasets sequences with more than 1000 frames are rare, and most are approximately 300–400 frames. Finally two of the sequences contain significant pose changes for the humans. A summary of each sequence is in Table 1.

Some example frames of challenging situations are presented in Fig. 3.

## 5   Experiments

We evaluate our proposed tracker and detector fusion on our own dataset. The results are reported as overlap and precision plots.

## 5.1   Evaluation Methodology

While the VOT [1–3] method of evaluating trackers provides an unbiased estimate of tracker accuracy for short term trackers, the automatic restarting present
in the toolkit makes it unsuited for evaluation of long-term trackers with an automatic recovery mechanism. Instead we use a simpler metric of computing the
bounding box overlap with the ground

We also include two short term tracker variants, the KCF [17] and the ACT
[16] tracker. For both short term trackers the implementations used are those
from the VOT 2014 challenge.

## 5.2   Results

We compare the performance of our proposed system using the tracker-detector
fusion, with two baseline variants. The results for all methods is presented in
Fig. 5. The first baseline is based only on the pre-trained detector run over the
image as described in Sect. 3.2. The best detection is used as input into the
Kalman filter in each frame. The output from the Kalman filter becomes the
bounding box estimate for each frame. The tracker only method uses the same
online learning visual tracker as the full system, but without the detector component. Resets of the tracker model are handled by observing the tracker confidence score only. Should the confidence drop to a low enough level the tracker
is restarted.

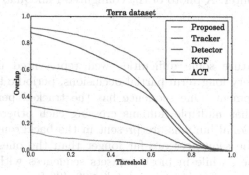

**Fig. 5.** The overlap for all frames with ground truth in the Terra dataset. The tracker-
detector fusion clearly outperforms compared methods.

Interestingly using only the online tracker with a restart heuristic in case
to low confidence yields better performance than the detection based method.
This can likely be attributed to the purely detector based method having a not-
insignificant possibility to get stuck on background objects. The KCF and ACT
methods are based only on model-free trackers, and as such are very prone to
drifting off the target and getting stuck on the background.

# 6    Conclusions and Future Work

Combining the output of a model-free tracker and a pre-trained object detector provides a significant increase in robustness for long-term tracking on UAVs. The proposed fusion method successfully combines the long-term reliability of a pre-trained detector with the precision of an online learned tracker, while maintaining real-time performance on a UAV platform. Possible future work include extending the dataset to a wider range of situations and humans, and making the system capable of tracking multiple targets at once.

**Acknowlegdements.** This work has been supported by SSF (CUAS, SymbiCloud), Wallenberg Autonomy and Software Programme (WASP) and ELLIIT.

# References

1. Kristan, M., Pflugfelder, R., Leonardis, A., Matas, J., Porikli, F., Čehovin, L., Nebehay, G., Fernandez, G., Vojir, T.: The visual object tracking VOT 2013 challenge results (2013)
2. Kristan, M.: The visual object tracking VOT2014 challenge results. In: Agapito, L., Bronstein, M.M., Rother, C. (eds.) ECCV 2014. LNCS, vol. 8926, pp. 191–217. Springer, Heidelberg (2015). doi:10.1007/978-3-319-16181-5_14
3. Kristan, M., Matas, J., Leonardis, A., Felsberg, M., Cehovin, L., Fernandez, G., Vojir, T., Hager, G., Nebehay, G., Pflugfelder, R.: The visual object tracking VOT2015 challenge results. In: The IEEE International Conference on Computer Vision (ICCV) Workshops (2015)
4. Patino, L., Ferryman, J.: Pets 2014: dataset and challenge. In: 2014 11th IEEE International Conference on Advanced Video and Signal Based Surveillance (AVSS), pp. 355–360. IEEE (2014)
5. Nawaz, T., Boyle, J., Li, L., Ferryman, J.: Tracking performance evaluation on pets 2015 challenge datasets. In: 2015 12th IEEE International Conference on Advanced Video and Signal Based Surveillance (AVSS), pp. 1–6. IEEE (2015)
6. Wu, Y., Lim, J., Yang, M.H.: Online object tracking: A benchmark. In: CVPR (2013)
7. Russakovsky, O., Deng, J., Su, H., Krause, J., Satheesh, S., Ma, S., Huang, Z., Karpathy, A., Khosla, A., Bernstein, M., et al.: Imagenet large scale visual recognition challenge. Int. J. Comput. Vis. **115**, 211–252 (2015)
8. Danelljan, M., Häger, G., Shahbaz Khan, F., Felsberg, M.: Accurate scale estimation for robust visual tracking. In: BMVC (2014)
9. Van De Weijer, J., Schmid, C., Verbeek, J., Larlus, D.: Learning color names for real-world applications. IEEE Trans. Image Process. **18**, 1512–1523 (2009)
10. Dalal, N., Triggs, B.: Histograms of oriented gradients for human detection. In: CVPR (2005)
11. Felzenszwalb, P.F., Girshick, R.B., McAllester, D., Ramanan, D.: Object detection with discriminatively trained part-based models. IEEE Trans. Pattern Anal. Mach. Intell. **32**, 1627–1645 (2010)
12. Girshick, R.: Fast R-CNN. In: Proceedings of the IEEE International Conference on Computer Vision, pp. 1440–1448 (2015)

13. Ren, S., He, K., Girshick, R., Sun, J.: Faster r-cnn: Towards real-time object detection with region proposal networks. In: Advances in Neural Information Processing Systems, pp. 91–99 (2015)
14. Danelljan, M., Khan, F.S., Felsberg, M., Granström, K., Heintz, F., Rudol, P., Wzorek, M., Kvarnström, J., Doherty, P.: A low-level active vision framework for collaborative unmanned aircraft systems. In: Agapito, L., Bronstein, M.M., Rother, C. (eds.) ECCV 2014. LNCS, vol. 8925, pp. 223–237. Springer, Heidelberg (2015). doi:10.1007/978-3-319-16178-5_15
15. Kalal, Z., Matas, J., Mikolajczyk, K.: P-N learning: Bootstrapping binary classifiers by structural constraints. In: 2010 IEEE Conference on Computer Vision and Pattern Recognition (CVPR), pp. 49–56. IEEE (2010)
16. Danelljan, M., Shahbaz Khan, F., Felsberg, M., van de Weijer, J.: Adaptive color attributes for real-time visual tracking. In: CVPR (2014)
17. Henriques, J.F., Caseiro, R., Martins, P., Batista, J.: High-speed tracking with kernelized correlation filters. IEEE Trans. Pattern Anal. Mach. Intell. 37(3), 583–596 (2015)

# Monocular Visual-Inertial SLAM for Fixed-Wing UAVs Using Sliding Window Based Nonlinear Optimization

Timo Hinzmann[1]([⊠]), Thomas Schneider[1], Marcin Dymczyk[1],
Andreas Schaffner[1], Simon Lynen[1,2], Roland Siegwart[1], and Igor Gilitschenski[1]

[1] Autonomous Systems Lab, ETH Zurich, Zurich, Switzerland
timo.hinzmann@mavt.ethz.ch
[2] Google Inc., Mountain View, USA

**Abstract.** Precise real-time information about the position and orientation of robotic platforms as well as locally consistent point-clouds are essential for control, navigation, and obstacle avoidance. For years, GPS has been the central source of navigational information in airborne applications, yet as we aim for robotic operations close to the terrain and urban environments, alternatives to GPS need to be found. Fusing data from cameras and inertial measurement units in a nonlinear recursive estimator has shown to allow precise estimation of 6-Degree-of-Freedom (DoF) motion without relying on GPS signals. While related methods have shown to work in lab conditions since several years, only recently real-world robotic applications using visual-inertial state estimation found wider adoption. Due to the computational constraints, and the required robustness and reliability, it remains a challenge to employ a visual-inertial navigation system in the field. This paper presents our tightly integrated system involving hardware and software efforts to provide an accurate visual-inertial navigation system for low-altitude fixed-wing unmanned aerial vehicles (UAVs) without relying on GPS or visual beacons. In particular, we present a sliding window based visual-inertial Simultaneous Localization and Mapping (SLAM) algorithm which provides real-time 6-DoF estimates for control. We demonstrate the performance on a small unmanned aerial vehicle and compare the estimated trajectory to a GPS based reference solution.

## 1 Introduction and Related Work

Unmanned aerial vehicles, and in particular fixed-wing UAVs, are powerful agents in scenarios where a large area needs to be scanned in a short amount of time. In recent years the interest in employing UAVs for applications such as industrial inspection, surveillance as well as agricultural monitoring has drastically increased due to the low acquisition and maintenance cost when compared to conventional aircraft. Today, GPS still remains the central source of 3-degrees of freedom (DoF) navigational information for the majority of these applications. Its limitations in certain cases, however, have motivated the exploration of alternative sources of 3-DoF signals such as ultra-sonic, laser, cameras and beacons.

© Springer International Publishing AG 2016
G. Bebis et al. (Eds.): ISVC 2016, Part I, LNCS 10072, pp. 569–581, 2016.
DOI: 10.1007/978-3-319-50835-1_51

Due to the low cost and weight of the sensor suite motion estimation based on data from cameras and inertial-measurement units (IMU) has become a common choice to obtain a metric 6-DoF estimate of the body motion in real-time. There exists a large body of robotic research focusing on probabilistic fusion of visual and inertial data over which the publications of Nerurkar et al. [1] and [2] give an excellent overview. All these approaches perform simultaneous localization and mapping by jointly minimizing errors from reprojecting triangulated 3D-landmarks and integrating the measurements from the IMU. The currently best performing algorithms employ either (nonlinear) optimization [1–3], filtering [4–8] or combinations of both [9].

Optimization based approaches potentially achieve higher accuracy due to the ability to limit linearization errors through repeated linearization of the inherently nonlinear problem. This is particularly relevant in visual-inertial navigation systems (VINS). Here the relinearization of the IMU based propagation limits errors caused by inaccurate linearization points of IMU biases. Nevertheless, solving the covariance form of the problem in a recursive estimator is a common choice due to the lower computational requirements. Only recently formulations which allow "online mapping" in inverse form have shown real-time performance [1,2]. To retain real-time calculations these algorithms approximate the problem using one of the following approaches:

- Key-frame based concepts as proposed e.g. in [1,10]. These approaches, however, require an involved marginalization strategy and the constraints imposed by integrating the IMU measurements can theoretically span an indefinite duration.
- Fixed-lag smoothing or sliding window approaches that consider time successive states within a fixed time interval in the optimization problem but *discard* measurements outside of the sliding window. Cf. discussion in e.g. [11] of how this leads to loss of information regarding the variable interaction.
- Incremental smoothing and mapping methods such as iSAM2 [12] that optimize over all robot states and landmarks, making use of all available correlations.

In this paper we combine the last two approaches such that poses and associated landmarks older than the constant smoother lag are *marginalized* to ensure a smooth pose estimate while keeping the problem size bounded. In contrast to [13], we only employ a short term sliding window in factor graph formulation. Furthermore, we use a tightly-coupled integration approach where the error originating from pre-integrated IMU measurements as well as the reprojection errors can be jointly optimized and thus all correlations within the optimization window are considered [14]. Our contributions lie in the modifications to increase robustness and to lower computational requirements which allow operation onboard a fixed-wing UAV. We furthermore discuss the hardware setup of our modular sensor pod and thereby demonstrate accurate SLAM on a platform with limited dimensions and payload capabilities.

## 2    Methodology

This section introduces the coordinate frames, states, problem statement as well as the proposed visual-inertial estimation framework.

### 2.1    Coordinate Frames

We distinguish between the camera frame $\mathcal{F}_C$, the body frame $\mathcal{F}_B$ as well as the global frame $\mathcal{F}_G$. Furthermore, the body frame $\mathcal{F}_B$ is assumed to be identical to the IMU frame $\mathcal{F}_I$ as illustrated in Fig. 1.

### 2.2    State Vector

The SLAM problem seeks to estimate the robot states $\mathbf{x}_R$ as well as the set of landmarks $\mathbf{x}_L$ with $\theta = \{\mathbf{x}_R, \mathbf{x}_L\}$. The robot state is defined as

$$\mathbf{x_R} := \left[ \mathbf{p}_B^{G^\top}, \mathbf{q}_B^{G^\top}, \mathbf{v}_B^{G^\top}, \mathbf{b}_g^\top, \mathbf{b}_a^\top \right]^\top \in \mathbb{R}^3 \times \mathbb{S}^3 \times \mathbb{R}^9 \qquad (1)$$

and comprises the robot pose and velocity in the global frame as well as the gyroscope and accelerometer biases.

### 2.3    SLAM as Maximum a Posteriori (MAP) Problem

We seek to maximize the joint probability $p(\mathbf{x}_R, \mathbf{x}_L, \mathbf{z})$ which is equivalent to minimizing the negative log-likelihood of the robot states $\mathbf{x}_R$ and set of landmarks $\mathbf{x}_L$ given the measurements $\mathbf{z}$

$$\begin{aligned} \theta^* &:= \arg\max_\theta p(\mathbf{x}_R, \mathbf{x}_L | \mathbf{z}) = \arg\max_\theta p(\mathbf{x}_R, \mathbf{x}_L, \mathbf{z}) \\ &= \arg\min_\theta \{ -\log p(\mathbf{x}_R, \mathbf{x}_L, \mathbf{z}) \} = \arg\min_\theta \{ -\mathcal{L}(\mathbf{x}_R, \mathbf{x}_L, \mathbf{z}) \}, \end{aligned} \qquad (2)$$

where $\mathcal{L}$ represents the log-likelihood function.

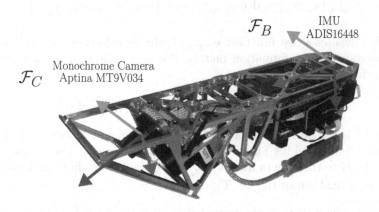

$\mathcal{F}_B$    IMU ADIS16448

Monochrome Camera
$\mathcal{F}_C$    Aptina MT9V034

**Fig. 1.** Camera and body coordinate frame of the sensor processing unit.

## 2.4 Factor Graph Formulation

The SLAM problem can be transformed into a factor graph $\mathcal{G} = \{\mathcal{F}, \theta, \mathcal{E}\}$ which is a bipartite[1] graph consisting of a set of unknown random variables to be estimated $\theta$ and a set of factors $\mathcal{F}$. In our case, the variables $\theta$ consist of the robot states $\mathbf{x}_R$ and the set of landmarks $\mathbf{x}_L$. The factors $\mathcal{F}$ are given by prior knowledge or measurements $\mathbf{z}$. The edges connect variable and factor nodes. The factor graph uses a factorization of the function $f(\theta) = \prod_i f_i(\theta_i)$ which we seek to maximize, i.e. we want to calculate

$$
\begin{aligned}
\theta^* &= \arg\max_\theta \{f(\theta)\} = \arg\min_\theta \{-\log f(\theta)\} \\
&= \arg\min_\theta \left\{ -\log \prod_i \exp\left(-\frac{1}{2}\|z_i - h_i(\theta_i)\|^2_{\Sigma_i}\right) \right\} \\
&= \arg\min_\theta \left\{ \sum_{i=1}^I \|z_i - h_i(\theta_i)\|^2_{\Sigma_i} \right\} \\
&= \arg\min_\theta \left\{ \sum_{i=1}^I \mathbf{e}_i^T \Sigma_i^{-1} \mathbf{e}_i \right\} = \arg\min_\theta \left\{ \sum_{i=1}^I \mathbf{e}_i^T W_i \mathbf{e}_i \right\},
\end{aligned}
\tag{3}
$$

where we used the fact that the measurement covariance matrix $\Sigma$ is the inverse of the information matrix $W$ and the Mahalanobis distance is defined as $\|\mathbf{e}\|^2_\Sigma := \mathbf{e}^T \Sigma^{-1} \mathbf{e}$.

**Factor and Error Term Definitions.** Only the factors and error terms are presented in this section. For the derivation of the Jacobians and information matrices we refer to [2,16,17].

*Reprojection factor.* We define the reprojection factor as

$$
f_{reproj}(\mathbf{x}_R, \mathbf{x}_L) = \mathbf{d}(\mathbf{e}_{reproj}) \propto \exp\left(-\frac{1}{2}\|\mathbf{e}_{reproj}\|^2_{\mathbf{W}^{-1}_{reproj}}\right),
\tag{4}
$$

where $\mathbf{d}(\cdot)$ denotes a cost function, $\mathbf{e}_{reproj}$ is the reprojection error and $\mathbf{W}_{reproj}$ is the corresponding information matrix. We adopt the reprojection error formulation from [17]

$$
\mathbf{e}^{i,j,k}_{reproj}(\mathbf{x}_r, \mathbf{x}_l, \mathbf{z}) = \mathbf{z}^{i,j,k} - \mathbf{h}_i(\mathbf{T}^{C_i}_{B_k} \mathbf{T}^{B_k}_G \mathbf{l}^G_j) \in \mathbb{R}^2,
\tag{5}
$$

where $\mathbf{z}^{i,j,k}$ is the observation of landmark $j$ in camera $i$ at camera frame $k$ in image coordinates and $\mathbf{h}_i(\cdot)$ is the camera projection model. The transformation from the body to the camera frames $\mathbf{T}^C_{B_k}$ was obtained by offline calibration and we assume a rigid sensor rig, i.e. $\mathbf{T}^C_{B_k} \equiv \mathbf{T}^C_B$.

---

[1] I.e. every value node is *always* connected to one or multiple factor nodes and vice versa [15].

*IMU factor.* The IMU measurements are pre-integrated and summarized in a single relative motion constraint connecting two time-consecutive poses as described in [18, 19]. The factor evaluates the residuals and Jacobians for the pose, velocity and IMU biases of the previous and current state.

## 2.5   Sliding Window Estimator (SWE)

The outline of the sliding window estimator is presented in Algorithm 1. The most relevant parts of the framework include feature extraction, landmark initialization and graph optimization: Feature tracks are generated using a Lucas-Kanade tracker with gyroscope-based feature prediction for speed-up and feature bucketing as well as two-point translation-only RANSAC outlier rejection as visualized in Fig. 2a.

**Landmark Initialization.** Only well constrained features are used as potential landmarks. We define the quality of a landmark observation by the number of observations, the minimum and maximum distance and by the angle between the incident rays:

$$d_{min} = \min(d_{min}, \|\mathbf{p}_{C_i}^G - \mathbf{p}_f^G\|_2), \ i \in [0, M)$$

$$d_{max} = \max(d_{max}, \|\mathbf{p}_{C_i}^G - \mathbf{p}_f^G\|_2), \ i \in [0, M)$$

$$\alpha_{min} = \min(\alpha_{min}, \cos^{-1}(\|\mathbf{p}_{C_i}^G - \mathbf{p}_f^G\|_2 \cdot \|\mathbf{p}_{C_j}^G - \mathbf{p}_f^G\|_2)),$$

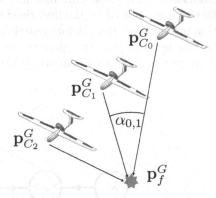

(a) The image visualizes the output of the vision front-end: Inlier feature tracks are shown in green. Tracks classified as outliers by RANSAC are visualized in red - here mainly due to the UAV's shadow violating the static feature assumption.

(b) Definition of well-constrained landmarks illustrated by the incident rays of three landmark observations. The following heuristics are used for the UAV SKATE datasets: $M_{min} = 30$, $d_{min} = 0.1\,\text{m}$, $d_{max} = 100\,\text{m}$, $\alpha_{min} = 0.5\,\text{deg}$.

**Fig. 2.** Vision front-end: Feature tracking and landmark initialization. (Color figure online)

where $i \in [0, M)$, $j \in [i+1, M)$ and $M$ represents the number of landmark observations. The basic idea as well as the used heuristics during flight are presented in Fig. 2b.

After triangulating the feature tracks the estimated landmark locations are validated by back-projecting the landmarks in the frames from which they were observed. The landmark is only inserted as a state if it lies in the visible camera cone. That is, e.g. landmarks that are triangulated behind the cameras are rejected.

**Graph Optimization.** Every factor and value node is associated with a marginalization strategy:

- Robot states: Marginalized after the graph update if the corresponding value node falls outside the sliding window.
- Landmarks: Landmark nodes are marginalized before the graph update if
  1. *opportunistic feature:* the feature track has been terminated in the previous camera frame due to the temporal condition or the feature has not been re-detected. Opportunistic features ensure that every frame is connected to *sufficient* reprojection factors.
  2. *persistent feature:* the feature has not been re-detected in the previous camera frame. Persistent features are included in the factor graph to reduce temporal drift.

A toy example of the marginalization strategy with a sliding window of $N = 4$ frames is presented in Fig. 3. In order to marginalize variable nodes the factors associated with these variables are identified and removed. The marginalized factors are replaced by the linearized factors which corresponds to a transformation into a Bayes tree. Before marginalization, the variables in the graph need to be reordered to preserve sparsity: For this purpose we use the column approximate minimum degree heuristic (COLAMD) [20]. The graph is linearized using

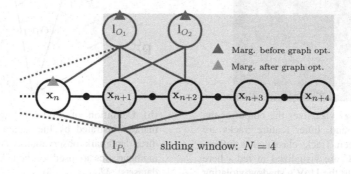

**Fig. 3.** Marginalization strategy: At step $k = n + 3$ the VI-node is propagated and the graph is augmented with the new state $\mathbf{x}_{n+4}$. Due to the temporal condition (TC) the value node $\mathbf{x}_n$ is to be marginalized. Also, the opportunistic landmark nodes $\mathbf{l}_{O_1}$ (TC) and $\mathbf{l}_{O_2}$ (not re-detected) are to be marginalized.

**Algorithm 1.** Estimator pipeline (running)

1: Extract opportunistic and persistent feature tracks:
- Lucas-Kanade feature tracker
- Gyroscope measurement integration for feature prediction
- Feature bucketing
- Two-point RANSAC outlier rejection
2: Initialize landmarks:
- Check if landmark is well constrained
- Triangulate feature tracks
- Check if triangulated landmark location is in visible camera cone
3: Add landmarks to factor graph (Fig. 4, b)
4: Detect stationary phases:
- Add velocity priors if stationary phase detected (take-off, landing)
5: Update factor graph
- Apply marginalization strategy
- Linearize and optimize factor graph
- Detect and remove outliers
6: Pre-integrate the IMU measurements and propagate the current VI-node
7: Augment the factor graph with the propagated VI-node (Fig. 4, c)
8: Add the IMU factor to the factor graph (Fig. 4, c)

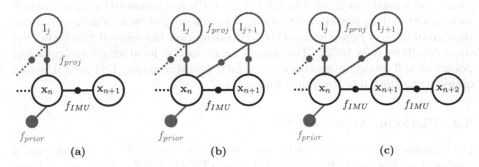

**Fig. 4.** Factor and value node insertion into the factor graph. **(a)** Initial setup at $k = n+1$. **(b)** Insertion of landmark values and reprojection factors. **(c)** Pre-integration of IMU measurements and graph augmentation.

Cholesky factorization and optimized using Levenberg-Marquardt. For marginalization and optimization of the factor graph we use the *Georgia Tech Smoothing and Mapping* (GTSAM) [21] framework.

**Estimator Initialization.** For coarse gravity alignment, the accelerometer readings $\mathbf{a}^B$ are averaged over a short static period before take-off. The calculations are performed in axis-angle notation:

$$(axis, angle)_B^G = (-W_g \times \|\bar{\mathbf{a}}^B\|, \cos^{-1}(W_g^T \|\bar{\mathbf{a}}^B\|)) \tag{6}$$

with $W_g = \begin{bmatrix} 0.0\ 0.0\ 1.0 \end{bmatrix}^T$. As noted in [14], a purely visual SLAM problem has six degrees of freedom (DoF). The visual-inertial problem has only four DoF since gravity renders two additional DoF observable (around world x- and y-axis). Based on these calculations the initial transformation $T_{B_0}^G$ is estimated and the estimator switches to the routine described in Algorithm 1.

## 3   Experimental Results

In this section we outline the hardware setup and present the results generated by the real-time visual-inertial navigation framework.

### 3.1   Sensor and Processing Unit

The sensor and processing unit used for the experiment is shown in Fig. 1: It is equipped with an Aptina MT9V034 grayscale global shutter camera which is able to record images at up to 60 fps with a resolution of $752 \times 480$ pixels. The MEMS inertial measurement unit (IMU) ADIS 16448 measures angular velocities as well as linear accelerations. The camera and IMU are integrated into an ARM-FPGA-based Visual-Inertial (VI) sensor system [22] that time-synchronizes IMU and camera on a hardware level. The Intel Atom CPU has access to the synchronized visual-inertial data stream. All components are mounted on an aluminium frame that guarantees a rigid camera-IMU transformation throughout the flight. For more details we refer to [23]. The camera intrinsics (i.e. focal length and principal point) as well as extrinsics (i.e. camera-IMU transformation $T_C^B$) are estimated offline using the calibration tool *Kalibr* [14].

### 3.2   Platform: Aurora SKATE

For demonstrating visual-inertial navigation, the sensor & processing unit is mounted on the small fixed-wing UAV SKATE. The light flying wing shown in Fig. 5 was manufactured by *Aurora*, features two independently articulated propulsion units and is controlled by an elevator control surface. Using thrust vectoring it is able to rapidly transition between vertical and horizontal flight and thus provides high agility and maneuverability. Different control modes (auto, manual) can be set by the hand-held remote control and allow for easy and safe operation of the vehicle. Note that the presented flight was performed in manual mode. The original processing unit shown in Fig. 5 is replaced by an interface specifically designed for this carrier. The interface mounts the sensor pod safely, powers it, is rigid and easily removable at the same time.

### 3.3   Simultaneous State Estimation and Sparse Map Generation

This section presents the state estimates and sparse point-cloud generated by the proposed nonlinear estimation framework based on datasets recorded by the small unmanned aerial vehicles SKATE. The test site is characterized by flat

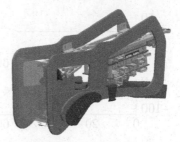

(a) SKATE by Aurora in factory configuration. The head piece contains batteries and two down-looking cameras.

(b) CAD model of sensor & processing unit as well as its power interface to SKATE. The sensors consist of an IMU and a gray-scale camera.

(c) Sensor & processing unit mounted on SKATE. The measurements from the GPS receiver are used to generate a reference trajectory.

(d) Sensor & processing unit mounted on SKATE.

**Fig. 5.** Hardware modifications made to SKATE to allow for accurate and time-synchronized visual-inertial localization and mapping.

terrain with few three-dimensional structure which makes the underlying scale estimation challenging.

Figure 6 shows the state estimates of the robot's position, velocity and IMU biases. The estimated altitude after the vehicle has landed is used as a first validation method. For this flight we registered a final altitude of around 3.1 m which demonstrates the limited translational drift. Figure 7 represents the sparse point-cloud and the estimated trajectory flown by the fixed-wing UAV. In particular take-off and landing spot show a high point density which enables automatic take-off and landing procedures. To obtain a further quantitative accuracy measurement, an error is defined as the Euclidean distance to the GPS position obtained from a uBlox LEA-6H sensor. For the complete trajectory, from take-off to landing, the RMSE amounts to 14.6 m with respect to the aligned GPS based reference trajectory. Both trajectories are shown in Fig. 8: Especially at low altitudes, the GPS measurements show large jumps due to multi-path effects while our proposed visual-inertial navigation system produces smooth estimates, including the take-off and landing phase. The runtime evaluated for the

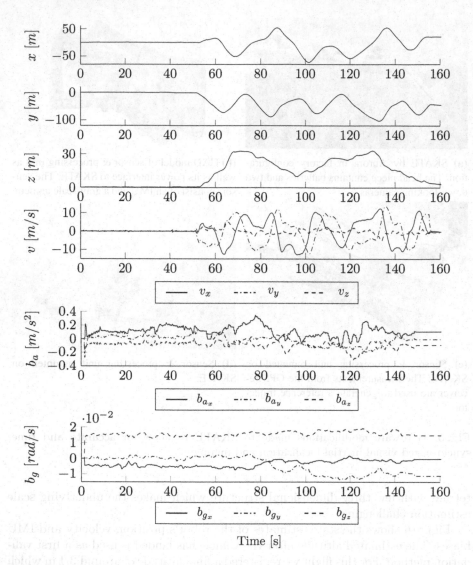

**Fig. 6.** State estimates of robot's position, velocity, accelerometer as well as gyroscope biases.

**Fig. 7.** Side-view of the generated sparse point-cloud and the estimated trajectory flown by the UAV. The right figure shows take-off and landing spot with increased point-cloud density.

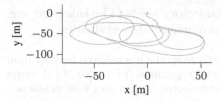

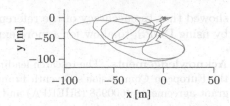

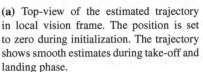

(a) Top-view of the estimated trajectory in local vision frame. The position is set to zero during initialization. The trajectory shows smooth estimates during take-off and landing phase.

(b) Top-view of the GPS trajectory in local UTM coordinates where the first GPS measurement defines the origin. Especially at low altitudes, the GPS measurements show large jumps due to multi-path effects.

**Fig. 8.** Comparison of estimated trajectory and GPS based reference trajectory.

**Table 1.** Runtime in ms for one frame.

|  | Mean [ms] | Std. dev. [ms] |
|---|---|---|
| Feature tracking* | 19.976 | 7.267 |
| Landmark initialization | 0.269 | 0.113 |
| State augmentation | 3.455 | 2.497 |
| Variable reordering (COLAMD) | 0.207 | 0.079 |
| Marginalization | 4.321 | 0.935 |
| Graph optimization | 27.370 | 17.325 |
| **Frame processing** | 42.249 | 21.805 |

*Runs in a separate thread and does not count towards total frame processing time.

SKATE mission is shown in Table 1 and was performed on an Intel(R) Core(TM) i7-4800MQ CPU @ 2.70 GHz. The profiling indicates that a camera stream of 23 Hz can be processed by the estimator in real-time.

## 4   Conclusion and Future Work

This paper presented an inverse-form visual-inertial navigation system that fuses inertial measurements and visual cues into a sliding window estimator applied to a small fixed-wing unmanned aerial vehicle. The state estimates of the robot's pose, velocity, IMU biases, and landmarks which were generated from a flight are presented and the trajectory is compared to a GPS based reference solution. The experiments showed that the locally consistent sparse point-cloud can be employed for static obstacle avoidance in terms of automatic take-off and landing for fixed-wing UAVs. Future work in the context of visual-inertial SLAM for fixed-wing UAVs will comprise further drift reduction by means of vanishing point detection, horizon tracking and loop closure. Furthermore, the experiments showed that the accuracy of the reference trajectory needs to be enhanced, e.g. by using DGPS, to allow for a more expressive quantitative evaluation.

**Acknowledgements.** The research leading to these results has received funding from the European Commission's Seventh Framework Programme (FP7/2007-2013) under grant agreement n°600958 (SHERPA) and was sponsored by Aurora Flight Sciences.

# References

1. Nerurkar, E., Wu, K., Roumeliotis, S.: C-KLAM: constrained keyframe-based localization and mapping. In: ICRA (2014)
2. Leutenegger, S., Lynen, S., Bosse, M., Siegwart, R., Furgale, P.: Keyframe-based visual-inertial odometry using nonlinear optimization. In: IJRR (2015)
3. Li, M., Mourikis, A.I.: Optimization-based estimator design for vision-aided inertial navigation. In: RSS (2013)
4. Mourikis, A.I., Roumeliotis, S.I.: A multi-state constraint Kalman filter for vision-aided inertial navigation. In: ICRA (2007)
5. Huang, G.P., Mourikis, A.I., Roumeliotis, S.I.: An observability-constrained sliding-window filter for SLAM. In: IROS (2011)
6. Hesch, J.A., Kottas, D.G., Bowman, S.L., Roumeliotis, S.I.: Camera-IMU-based localization: observability analysis and consistency improvement. In: IJRR (2014)
7. Martinelli, A.: Visual-inertial structure from motion: observability vs. minimum number of sensors. In: ICRA (2014)
8. Li, M., Kim, B.H., Mourikis, A.I.: Real-time motion tracking on a cellphone using inertial sensing and a rolling-shutter camera. In: ICRA (2013)
9. Mourikis, A.I., Roumeliotis, S.I.: A dual-layer estimator architecture for long-term localization. In: CVPRW (2008)
10. Leutenegger, S., Lynen, S., Bosse, M., Siegwart, R., Furgale, P.: Keyframe-based visual-inertial SLAM using nonlinear optimization. In: IJRR (2014)
11. Sibley, G., Matthies, L., Sukhatme, G.S.: Sliding window filter with application to planetary landing. In: JFR (2010)
12. Kaess, M., Johannsson, H., Roberts, R., Ila, V., Leonard, J., Dellaert, F.: iSAM2: incremental smoothing and mapping using the Bayes tree. In: IJRR (2012)
13. Chiu, H.P., Williams, S., Dellaert, F., Samarasekera, S., Kumar, R.: Robust vision-aided navigation using sliding-window factor graphs. In: ICRA (2013)
14. Furgale, P., Rehder, J., Siegwart, R.: Unified temporal and spatial calibration for multi-sensor systems. In: IROS (2013)
15. Grisetti, G., Kummerle, R., Stachniss, C., Burgard, W.: A tutorial on graph-based SLAM. In: ITSM
16. Leutenegger, S.: Unmanned solar airplanes. Ph.D. thesis, Dissertion, ETH Zürich, Nr. 22113 (2014)
17. Furgale, P.: Extensions to the visual odometry pipeline for the exploration of planetary surfaces. University of Toronto (2011)
18. Forster, C., Carlone, L., Dellaert, F., Scaramuzza, D.: IMU preintegration on manifold for efficient visual-inertial maximum-a-posteriori estimation. In: RSS (2015)
19. Carlone, L., Kira, Z., Beall, C., Indelman, V., Dellaert, F.: Eliminating conditionally independent sets in factor graphs: a unifying perspective based on smart factors. In: ICRA (2014)

20. Davis, T.A., Gilbert, J.R., Larimore, S.I., Ng, E.G.: A column approximate minimum degree ordering algorithm. ACM Trans. Math. Softw. **30**(3), 353–376 (2004)
21. Dellaert, F.: Factor graphs and GTSAM: a hands-on introduction. Technical report GT-RIM-CP&R-2012-002, GT RIM (2012)
22. Nikolic, J., Rehder, J., Burri, M., Gohl, P., Leutenegger, S., Furgale, P.T., Siegwart, R.: A synchronized visual-inertial sensor system with FPGA pre-processing for accurate real-time SLAM. In: ICRA (2014)
23. Oettershagen, P., Stastny, T.J., Mantel, T., Melzer, A., Rudin, K., Agamennoni, G., Alexis, K., Siegwart, R.: Long-endurance sensing and mapping using a hand-launchable solar-powered UAV. In: FSR (2015)

# Change Detection and Object Recognition Using Aerial Robots

Shehryar Khattak, Christos Papachristos, and Kostas Alexis[(⊠)]

Autonomous Robots Lab, University of Nevada, Reno, Reno, NV, USA
kalexis@unr.edu

**Abstract.** This work proposes a strategy for autonomous change detection and classification using aerial robots. For aerial robotic missions that were conducted in different spatio–temporal conditions, the pose–annotated camera data are first compared for similarity in order to identify the correspondence map among the different image sets. Then efficient feature matching techniques relying on binary descriptors are used to estimate the geometric transformations among the corresponding images, and subsequently perform image subtraction and filtering to robustly detect change. To further decrease the computational load, the known poses of the images are used to create local subsets within which similar images are expected to be found. Once change detection is accomplished, a small set of the images that present the maximum levels of change are used to classify the change by searching to recognize a list of known objects through a bag–of–features approach. The proposed algorithm is evaluated using both handheld–smartphone collected data, as well as experiments using an aerial robot.

## 1 Introduction

Aerial robotics face an unprecedented, rapid process of integration into a variety of real–life tasks and challenges. But for these systems to be able to provide their full potential, they should be able to operate robustly [1,2] and act as something much more than a position–controlled camera in the sky. In fact, the potential of aerial robots can only be exploited when advanced task–level autonomy levels are reached. As in their majority, aerial robots are utilized in inspection operations [3–8], their added value can radically increase if they become able to perform spatio–temporally varying inspection missions autonomously, identify objects in the scenery.

Motivated by this exciting potential, this work proposes a strategy for autonomous spatio–temporal detection and classification of change using aerial robots equipped with a camera and capable of pose estimation. In particular, the proposed algorithm detects change among images collected at different times, identifies the area of change and subsequently searches if a set of possible objects can be recognized within the detected image change. Figure 1 presents an instance of our experimental studies.

© Springer International Publishing AG 2016
G. Bebis et al. (Eds.): ISVC 2016, Part I, LNCS 10072, pp. 582–592, 2016.
DOI: 10.1007/978-3-319-50835-1_52

**Fig. 1.** Instance of an experiment for autonomous change detection and classification using a small aerial robot. The robot performs two spatio–temporaly varying missions, detects change on the corresponding image frames and identifies objects based on a bank of images.

Our work contributes to the body of research in the field of change detection using camera systems. The majority of the existing work focuses on detection of change in raw camera data in comparison with previous recordings [9–14], or –as an extension– on the detection of change between GPS–annotated images collected at different times [15,16]. More recent approaches employ reconstructed 3D models and identify change through comparison among those [17–19] or use object–based detection [20,21]. Within this framework, the main question to be answered is how can we establish an efficient change detection and classification strategy for aerial robotics.

The proposed approach relies on robust tests for image similarity and binary keypoints to efficiently identify the most similar image frames and estimate the geometric transformations that will allow their comparison to detect change. When knowledge of the pose of the camera (and the robot) is available, the set of images to be tested is decreased, therefore allowing faster operation. Once a small set of image frames that experienced the highest amount of change are detected, then a bag–of–features approach is employed to identify known objects based on reference images of those. The derived algorithm is detailed and experimentally verified both in handheld–smartphone experiments, as well as using an aerial robot performing an inspection mission.

The rest of the paper is structured as follows. In Sect. 2 the proposed algorithm for change detection and classification is detailed. In Sect. 3 handheld experiments are presented using a smartphone as a camera, followed by the aerial robotic tests in Sect. 4. Finally, conclusions are drawn in Sect. 5.

## 2    Proposed Approach

The proposed approach relies on two steps, that of detection and the one of object recognition through a set of reference images (classification).

### 2.1    Change Detection

The proposed change detection strategy relies on similarity calculations between two sets of images collected at different times and from different locations, computationally efficient feature extraction and feature matching employing BRISK, the corresponding estimation of geometric transformations, and optionally the robot poses –when these are available– in order to perform the necessary computations only on the subset of images that are most likely to be similar. The detailed steps of the algorithm for two, spatio–temporally varying, images sets $\mathcal{I}_A, \mathcal{I}_B$ are presented in Algorithm 1 followed by an overview of the role of each function. Note that for clarity of presentation, the algorithm is presented regarding its essential steps without showing control/flow statements (while, for, if etc.). Therefore, often the described functions act on a whole set, or set of sets, of images and variables.

---

**Algorithm 1.** Change Detection Algorithm

---

1: Acquire first set of images $\mathcal{I}_A$
2: Acquire second set of images $\mathcal{I}_B$
3: $\mathcal{I}_B \leftarrow$ SelectSubset$(\mathcal{I}_B, \mathbf{p}_A, \mathbf{p}_B, \delta_{\max}, \delta\psi_{\max})$ (optional)
4: $\mathcal{I}_{B \rightarrow A} \leftarrow$ SimilarImages$(\mathcal{I}_A, \mathcal{I}_B)$
5: $\mathcal{P}_A \leftarrow$ BRISKfeatures$(\mathcal{I}_A)$
6: $\mathcal{P}_{B \rightarrow A} \leftarrow$ BRISKfeatures$(\mathcal{I}_{B \rightarrow A})$
7: $\mathcal{F}_A \leftarrow$ ExtractFeatures$(\mathcal{I}_A, \mathcal{P}_A)$
8: $\mathcal{F}_{B \rightarrow A} \leftarrow$ ExtractFeatures$(\mathcal{I}_{B \rightarrow A}, Ps_{B \rightarrow A})$
9: $\mathcal{M}_A, \mathcal{M}_{B \rightarrow A} \leftarrow$ MatchFeatures$(\mathcal{F}_A, \mathcal{F}_{B \rightarrow A})$
10: $\mathcal{T}_{B \rightarrow A, A} \leftarrow$ GeometricTransformation$(\mathcal{M}_A, \mathcal{M}_{B \rightarrow A})$
11: $\mathcal{I}_{B \rightarrow A}^T \leftarrow$ ApplyTransformation$(\mathcal{I}_{B \rightarrow A}, \mathcal{T}_{B \rightarrow A, A})$
12: $\mathcal{I}_\Delta \leftarrow$ ImageSubtraction$(\mathcal{I}_A, \mathcal{I}_{B \rightarrow A}^T)$
13: $\mathcal{I}_\Delta \leftarrow$ RobustifyChangeDetection$(\mathcal{I}_\Delta, c)$ (optional)
14: $\mathcal{I}_\Delta', \mathcal{I}_{B \rightarrow A}' \leftarrow$ PrioritizeBasedOnChange$(\mathcal{I}_\Delta, \mathcal{I}_{B \rightarrow A})$
15: **return** $\mathcal{I}_\Delta, \mathcal{I}_\Delta', \mathcal{I}_{B \rightarrow A}$

---

**Selecting Spatially Relevant Image Subsets.** Function(s): SelectSubset. When the robot trajectories among the two spatio–temporally different missions, $\mathbf{p}_A, \mathbf{p}_B$ are available, then for each of the image frames within the first image set $\mathcal{I}_A$, a local subset $\mathcal{I}_B$ is extracted and corresponds only to the images collected from locations that are neighboring (according to a maximum distance $\delta_{\max}$ and a maximum heading difference $\delta\psi_{\max}$) assuming that the camera is fixed on the aerial robot. Extesion to cameras on pan–tilt units is straightforward. Note that for the clarity of presentation, the same symbol $\mathcal{I}_B$ is used and overloaded to refer to all matched image subsets of the initial set $\mathcal{I}_B$ that are associated to each of the frames of $\mathcal{I}_A$.

**Identifying Similar Images.** Function(s): `SimilarImages`. In order to efficiently identify the images of $\mathcal{I}_B$ that are most similar to those of $\mathcal{I}_A$, the method of calculating the two–dimensional correlation coefficient among the HSV color–normalized versions of the images of the two sets is employed. The corresponding computation takes the form:

$$r = \frac{\sum_m \sum_n (a_{mn} - \bar{a})(b_{mn} - \bar{b})}{\sqrt{\sum_m \sum_n (a_{mn} - \bar{a})^2 (\sum_m \sum_n b_{mn} - \bar{b})^2}} \tag{1}$$

where $a, b$ are the array variables of two of the HSV color–normalized images of $\mathcal{I}_A, \mathcal{I}_B$ correspondingly, and the $\bar{()}$ operator stands for the two–dimensional mean of the image array. It is noted that for implementation purposes, this operation is performed on 50%–resized versions of the collected images. The selection of the correlation coefficient was based on comparison studies between methods that judge image similarity based on the amount of common features and methods that rely on the pairwise distance between histogram calculations on the images. It was found to be more robust and very fast.

**Detecting and Matching BRISK Features.** Function(s): `BRISKfeatures`, `Extract-Feature`, `MatchFeatures`. BRISK (Binary Robust Invariant Scalable Keypoints) was employed in order to enable efficient keypoint detection. Once the process has been implemented to all the grayscale versions of the images of $\mathcal{I}_B$ that are similar to the currently processed image of $\mathcal{I}_A$ ($\mathcal{I}_{B \to A}$), feature extraction and matching takes place through the calculation of the Hamming distance.

**Estimating and Applying the Features–Based Geometric Transformation.** Function(s): `GeometricTransformation`. Given the matched keypoints, the geometric transformation from the most similar image of $\mathcal{I}_B$ to the currently processed image of $\mathcal{I}_A$ is estimated through a batch optimization process that first excludes possible outliers using the M–estimator SAmple Consensus (MSAC) algorithm. Once the geometric transformation (the total set of which is denoted as $\mathcal{T}_{B \to A, A}$) is computed, it is then applied to get the transformed images (the total set of which is denoted as $\mathcal{T}_{B \to A, A}$).

**Image Subtraction.** Function(s): `ImageSubtraction`. For each of the image frames of the sets $\mathcal{I}_A$ and $\mathcal{I}_{B \to A}^T$ image subtraction takes place to get each of the difference images of $\mathcal{I}_\Delta$, Within those images, black color indicates no change.

**Robustify Change Detection.** Function(s): `RobustifyChangeDetection`. Optionally, change detection can be robustified assuming that it has to be at least of some certain pixel–size. Each of the images of $\mathcal{I}_\Delta$ is then searched to identify patches of change that exceed a size of $c \times c$. For clarity of presentation, the result is also denoted as $\mathcal{I}_\Delta$.

**Image Prioritize Based on the Amount of Change.** Function(s): `PrioritizeBased- OnChange`. The images are prioritized based on the amount of detected change. The prioritization metric is simply the number of pixels that experience change (above a certain color–threshold). The resulting ordered set is denoted as $\mathcal{I}'_\Delta$.

## 2.2  Change Classification

Within the proposed, change classification is considered in the form of object recognition given a set of reference images. The set of reference images contains photos of the objects that could be the reason, or in general, part of the detected change. The process is described in Algorithm 2 for a set of reference frames $\mathcal{I}_R$, while description of the role of each function is further provided below.

---

**Algorithm 2.** Object Detection Algorithm

1: Acquire Reference Image $(\mathcal{I}_R)$
2: $\mathcal{I}_S \leftarrow$ `GetMostChanged`$(\mathcal{I}'_{B \rightarrow A}, N_S)$
3: $\mathcal{P}_R \leftarrow$ `SURFfeatures`$(\mathcal{I}_R)$
4: $\mathcal{P}_S \leftarrow$ `SURFfeatures`$(\mathcal{I}_S)$
5: $\mathcal{F}_R \leftarrow$ `ExtractFeatures`$(\mathcal{I}_R, \mathcal{P}_R)$
6: $\mathcal{F}_S \leftarrow$ `ExtractFeatures`$(\mathcal{I}_S, \mathcal{P}_S)$
7: $\mathcal{M}_R, \mathcal{M}_S \leftarrow$ `MatchFeatures`$(\mathcal{F}_R, \mathcal{F}_S)$
8: $\mathcal{T}_{R,S} \leftarrow$ `GeometricTransformation`$(\mathcal{M}_R, \mathcal{M}_S)$
9: $\mathcal{B} \leftarrow$ `BoundingBox`$(\mathcal{I}_R)$
10: $\mathcal{B}' \leftarrow$ `BoundingBoxTransformation`$(\mathcal{B}, \mathcal{T}_{R,S})$
11: `VisualizeResult`$(\mathcal{I}_S, \mathcal{B}')$
12: **return** $\mathcal{B}', \mathcal{M}_S$

---

**Selecting a Prioritized Image Subset.** Function(s): `GetMostChanged`. Given a desired maximum set of $N$ images, those that experience the maximum amount of change (in terms of numbers of pixels above a certain change threshold) are exported. For convenience of notation, the same variable name $\mathcal{I}'_S$ is overloaded.

**Detecting and Matching SURF Features.** Function(s): `SURFfeatures`, `ExtractFea- tures`, `MatchFeatures`. SURF (Speeded Up Robust Features) was here employed in order to enable quality yet efficient keypoint detection. Once the process has been implemented to all the grayscale versions of the images of $\mathcal{I}_S$ and to the object–reference images $\mathcal{I}_R$, feature extraction and matching takes place. Feature matching takes place through the calculation of the sum of absolute differences.

**Estimating and Applying the Features–Based Geometric Transformation.** Function(s): `GeometricTransformation`. Given the matched keypoints, the geometric transformation from $\mathcal{I}_R$ to the matched images of $\mathcal{I}_S$ is estimated through a batch optimization process using MSAC. The total set of geometric transformations from possibly detected reference images to the scene images is denoted as $\mathcal{T}_{R,S}$.

**Object Detection Visualization.** Function(s): `BoundingBox`, `BoundingBox-Transfo- rmation`, `VisualizeResult`. For the cases that a sufficient amount of matched features was found and therefore a geometric transformation was estimated, visualization takes place by creating a bounding box in the reference image, rotating it according to the relevant transformation in $\mathcal{T}_{R,S}$), and projecting it on top of the relevant frames of $\mathcal{I}_S$. In those cases, the matched features $\mathcal{M}_S$ are also shown.

The aforementioned Algorithms 1, 2 formulate an overall complete pipeline for image–based change detection and classification. This pipeline can be applied to images that are lacking pose information, while once such information exists, function `SelectSubset` ensures that limited calculations are conducted. In the following sections, both handheld and aerial robotic results are presented.

# 3   Handheld Verification

Prior to the aerial robotic evaluation of the proposed change detection strategy, a handheld study took place. This experiment was conducted using a smartphone. For the purposes of this study, the smartphone is only used for video collection, while processing takes place on a laptop computer. The experiment was conducted through a combination of body and arm motion, and the camera trajectories among the compared missions are never the same. The detailed dataset, including both raw data and processed results, can be found at [22], alongside with further results.

The employed smartphone was integrates the Sony Exmor RS IMX240 camera sensor and three tests were considered, with the first being that of scanning an office two different times. Before the second recording, a book was deployed on one of the desks and the corresponding change is detected. A reference image of the book is also used to identify it as an object in the scene. A small set of $N_S = 5$ images that experience maximum change are used for object identification and the process is terminated once the object is identified in one of them. For the problem of change detection, the results are shown in Fig. 2, while object detection is shown in Fig. 3. It is noted that only the case for one set of images is shown in this figure.

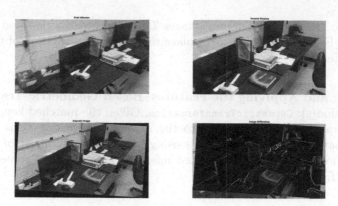

**Fig. 2.** Change detection using a smartphone observing an office. Black color indicates no change. Edges around the objects are detected as "change" due to small errors in the geometric transformation. The detailed datasets, including both raw data and processed results, can be found at [22].

## 4    Experiments Using an Aerial Robot

The employed aerial robot properties and subsystems, as well as the conducted experimental study on change detection and classification are detailed below.

### 4.1    System Overview

For the purposes of our experimental studies, a custom–built autonomous aerial robot of the hexarotor class is employed. The system is integrating the PX4 autopilot to enable robust attitude control. This low–level autopilot is then interfaced from an Intel NUC i7 computer (NUC5i7RYH) with 16 GB of RAM. For the purposes of on–board full pose estimation and mapping a monocular visual–inertial solution is deployed. The specific system integrates a 1.3 MP Color Point-Grey Chameleon3 which is interfaced via the Robot Operating System (ROS) at 60 FPS, as well as an UM–7 Inertial Measurement Unit (IMU) sampled at 200 Hz. Given the software–synchronized visual–inertial data, the Robust Visual Inertial Odometry (ROVIO) algorithm [23] is employed for robot localization and sparse mapping. Through the subsequent execution of an Extended Kalman Filter, the IMU estimates from the PX4 autopilot and the overall pose estimates from ROVIO are further fused and the system accounts for possible misalignments of the two IMUs. Figure 4 summarizes the aforementioned functionalities.

### 4.2    Change Detection Experiment

The main experimental study using the aforementioned aerial robot involves the execution of semi–manually flown (commanding on top of the on–board attitude and altitude control) trajectories within an indoors facility. The environment is

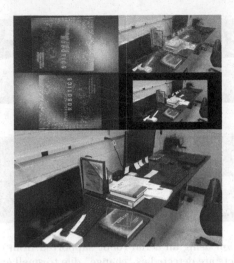

**Fig. 3.** Change classification in terms of object recognition using a bag–of–features method. The strongest features detected on the reference image (book), the scene image, the matched inliers and the polygon box showing the detected object are shown.

populated with two boxes and the robot's camera is pointed towards its direction. Two flight trajectories are recorded with the scene–difference being the deployment of a book on the top of the boxes. As the abovementioned localization pipeline enables the knowledge of the pose of the robot during each camera recording, the change detection algorithm only focuses on image frames collected from neighboring positions (no more than $\delta_{\max} = 1\,\mathrm{m}$ distance) and similar heading (no more than $\delta\psi_{\max} = 30°$ difference). The change detection and object recognition algorithms are then executed on the NUC i7 computer in near real–time fashion (processing the last new camera frame every $T_s = 0.1\,\mathrm{s}$). The relevant results are summarized in Figs. 5 and 6. It was found that although change detection worked robustly, object recognition was relatively sensitive, primarily due to the low resolution of the aerial robot camera (VGA).

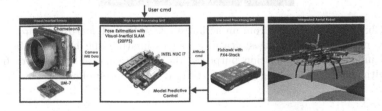

**Fig. 4.** System overview of our custom–built small aerial robot.

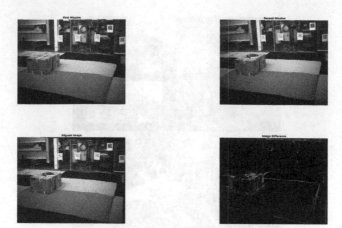

**Fig. 5.** Change detection using an aerial robot supported from onboard localization. Edges around the objects are detected as "change" due to small errors in the geometric transformation. The detailed datasets, including both raw data, robot pose information and processed results, can be found in the form of Robot Operating System (ROS) bags at [22].

**Fig. 6.** Change classification from an aerial robot. A bag–of–features approach is followed by matching the strongest features and estimating the bounding box of the matched inliers. For visualization purposes, the color image of the camera frame is shown, although for processing purposes the grayscale was employed.

## 5   Conclusions and Future Work

A strategy for change detection and classification using aerial robots was presented in this paper. The proposed method relies on efficient and robust similarity checks, benefiting from possible knowledge of the robot trajectories, fast feature matching techniques and filtering methods to robustify change detection. Subsequently, change classification is performed in the sense of object recognition using a bag–of–features approach. Experimental studies were presented using a small aerial robot equipped with a camera and capable of full pose estimation, as well as using a smartphone. Future work will aim to alleviate the sensitivity in different light conditions, integrate 3D models–based change detection and integrate the framework with autonomous path planning for inspection [4–7,24]. The relevant raw data and computed results are released in the form of an open dataset to further support scientific comparison.

# References

1. Alexis, K., Papachristos, C., Siegwart, R., Tzes, A.: Robust explicit model predictive flight control of unmanned rotorcrafts: design and experimental evaluation. In: 2014 European Control Conference (ECC), pp. 498–503 (2014)
2. Papachristos, C., Alexis, K., Tzes, A.: Dual authority thrust vectoring of a tri-tiltrotor employing model predictive control. J. Intell. Rob. Syst. **81**, 1–34 (2015)
3. Papachristos, C., Alexis, K., Carrillo, L.R.G., Tzes, A.: Distributed infrastructure inspection path planning for aerial robotics subject to time constraints. In: 2016 International Conference on Unmanned Aircraft Systems (ICUAS), pp. 406–412. IEEE (2016)
4. Bircher, A., Kamel, M., Alexis, K., Oleynikova, H., Siegwart, R.: Receding horizon "next-best-view" planner for 3d exploration. In: 2016 IEEE International Conference on Robotics and Automation (ICRA), pp. 1462–1468 (2016)
5. Bircher, A., Kamel, M., Alexis, K., Burri, M., Oettershagen, P., Omari, S., Mantel, T., Siegwart, R.: Three-dimensional coverage path planning via viewpoint resampling and tour optimization for aerial robots. Auton. Rob., 1–25 (2015)
6. Alexis, K., Papachristos, C., Siegwart, R., Tzes, A.: Uniform coverage structural inspection path-planning for micro aerial vehicles (2015)
7. Bircher, A., Alexis, K., Schwesinger, U., Omari, S., Burri, M., Siegwart, R.: An incremental sampling-based approach to inspection planning: the rapidly-exploring random tree of trees (2015)
8. Oettershagen, P., Stastny, T., Mantel, T., Melzer, A., Rudin, K., Gohl, P., Agamennoni, G., Alexis, K., Siegwart, R.: Long-endurance sensing and mapping using a hand-launchable solar-powered UAV. In: Wettergreen, D.S., Barfoot, T.D. (eds.) Field and Service Robotics. STAR, vol. 113, pp. 441–454. Springer, Heidelberg (2016). doi:10.1007/978-3-319-27702-8_29
9. Minu, S., Shetty, A.: A comparative study of image change detection algorithms in matlab. Aquatic Proc. **4**, 1366–1373 (2015)
10. Fisher, R.: Change detection in color images. In: Proceedings of 7th IEEE Conference on Computer Vision and Pattern. Citeseer (1999)
11. Lu, D., Mausel, P., Brondizio, E., Moran, E.: Change detection techniques. Int. J. Remote Sens. **25**, 2365–2401 (2004)
12. Coulter, L., Lippitt, C., Stow, D., McCreight, R.: Near real-time change detection for border monitoring. In: Proceedings from the ASPRS Annual Conference, pp. 1–5 (2011)
13. Singh, A.: Review article digital change detection techniques using remotely-sensed data. Int. J. Remote Sens. **10**, 989–1003 (1989)

14. Aach, T., Kaup, A., Mester, R.: Statistical model-based change detection in moving video. Sig. Process. **31**, 165–180 (1993)
15. Radke, R.J., Andra, S., Al-Kofahi, O., Roysam, B.: Image change detection algorithms: a systematic survey. IEEE Trans. Image Process. **14**, 294–307 (2005)
16. Lucieer, A., de Jong, S., Turner, D.: Mapping landslide displacements using structure from motion (SFM) and image correlation of multi-temporal UAV photography. Prog. Phys. Geogr. **38**, 97–116 (2013). doi:10.1177/0309133313515293
17. Wallace, L., Lucieer, A., Watson, C.: Assessing the feasibility of UAV-based lidar for high resolution forest change detection. Proc. ISPRS, Int. Archives Photogramm., Remote Sens. Spat. Inf. Sci. **38**, B7 (2012)
18. Xiao, W., Vallet, B., Paparoditis, N.: Change detection in 3D point clouds acquired by a mobile mapping system. ISPRS Ann. Photogramm., Remote Sens. Spat. Inf. Sci. **1**, 331–336 (2013)
19. Xiao, W.: Detecting changes in trees using multi-temporal airborne LiDAR point clouds. PhD thesis, Masters Thesis, University of Twente, Enschede, The Netherlands (2012)
20. Hussain, M., Chen, D., Cheng, A., Wei, H., Stanley, D.: Change detection from remotely sensed images: from pixel-based to object-based approaches. ISPRS J. Photogramm. Remote Sens. **80**, 91–106 (2013)
21. Chen, G., Hay, G.J., Carvalho, L.M., Wulder, M.A.: Object-based change detection. Int. J. Remote Sens. **33**, 4434–4457 (2012)
22. Khattak, S., Papachristos, C., Alexis, K.: Autonomous change detection using aerial robots dataset. http://changedetectiondataset.wikispaces.com/
23. Bloesch, M., Omari, S., Hutter, M., Siegwart, R.: Robust visual inertial odometry using a direct EKF-based approach. In: 2015 IEEE/RSJ International Conference on Intelligent Robots and Systems (IROS), pp. 298–304. IEEE (2015)
24. Bircher, A., Alexis, K., Burri, M., Oettershagen, P., Omari, S., Mantel, T., Siegwart, R.: Structural inspection path planning via iterative viewpoint resampling with application to aerial robotics. In: IEEE International Conference on Robotics and Automation (ICRA), pp. 6423–6430 (2015)

# Parallelized Iterative Closest Point for Autonomous Aerial Refueling

Jace Robinson, Matt Piekenbrock, Lee Burchett, Scott Nykl[✉],
Brian Woolley, and Andrew Terzuoli

Air Force Institute of Technology, Wright-Patterson, USA
scott.nykl@afit.edu

**Abstract.** The Iterative Closest Point algorithm is a widely used approach to aligning the geometry between two 3 dimensional objects. The capability of aligning two geometries in real time on low-cost hardware will enable the creation of new applications in Computer Vision and Graphics. The execution time of many modern approaches are dominated by either the $k$ nearest neighbor search ($k$NN) or the point alignment phase. This work presents an accelerated alignment variant which utilizes parallelization on a Graphics Processing Unit (GPU) of multiple $k$NN approaches augmented with a novel Delaunay Traversal to achieve real time estimates.

## 1 Introduction

Aerial refueling is an essential component in flight today, yet this capability has not yet been extended to unmanned aerial systems or remotely piloted aircraft. Autonomous aerial refueling (AAR) improves global mobility by increasing the radius of effectiveness. Enabling autonomous aerial refueling requires real time relative positioning knowledge between the tanker and the receiving aircraft. Some approaches to sensing the aircraft involve GPS technology. Our approach uses a passive sensor system, minimizing visibility to others, operates in GPS denied environments, and explicitly uses the existing hardware on the refueling tanker with no external modifications needed. Starting at the beginning of 2017, many refueling tankers will be equipped with a 3D vision system based on stereo vision technology. This vision system can be used to sense the incoming aircraft for refueling. The relative position tracking of this aircraft to the tanker is a computationally difficult problem that relies on two primary operations:

1. 3D point generation, where the 3D presence of the target aircraft is sensed through a stereo vision sensor and transformed into a set of 3D points.
2. Model alignment, where the sensed 3D point cloud is aligned to the ideal model's pose. This alignment extracts the position and orientation of the sensed point cloud relative to the optimal model thereby yielding the desired relative positioning solution.

© Springer International Publishing AG 2016
G. Bebis et al. (Eds.): ISVC 2016, Part I, LNCS 10072, pp. 593–602, 2016.
DOI: 10.1007/978-3-319-50835-1_53

The challenge of this problem is to have the solution be realizable in *real time*, in which the aforementioned two-step pipeline is completed within 200 milliseconds or less (at least five frames per second). A visual example of the scenario being discussed is given in Fig. 1. Due to their widespread availability and large throughput potential, GPUs have recently become integral to general purpose computational problems that intrinsically exhibit high amounts of parallelism [1]. The Compute Unified Device Architecture (CUDA), invented by NVIDIA, has become a mainstream parallel computing platform and programming model that allows the programmer to write the host (CPU) code and the device (GPU) code in a single source program [2]; this work presents an algorithm that is feasible for providing real time positional estimates, implemented through the CUDA programming model. The primary component of the AAR project being addressed in this work is improved alignment speed of the source (sensed) 3D point cloud to the ideal reference model's pose. Iterative Closest Point (ICP) is a well-known algorithm [3] used to compute the relative pose between two similar point clouds. Each iteration of ICP can be decomposed into two parts:

1. Finding a mapping between every point from the source cloud to its *nearest neighbor* (NN) in the reference model.
2. Computing the translational and rotational offset by minimizing the mean squared error between the aligned source cloud and the reference model.

   We introduce a GPU-based solution of ICP with a state of the art method to the mutual correspondences problem by combining the benefits of spatially-indexed *approximate nearest neighbor* (ANN) search with a novel Delaunay Traversal algorithm that converges on the exact nearest neighbor. The approach presented in this work is designed to utilize the asymptotic benefits available with spatially-indexed based approaches while exposing the parallelizable components intrinsic to the the mutual correspondences problem. Because the nearest neighbor approach has traditionally dominated the computation time in the context of ICP, and since the execution time of the other phases of the algorithm are nominal (described below), this combined approach enables real time positional estimates suitable for application contexts with strict latency requirements, such as AAR.

## 2  Related Work

Before the spatial translation and rotation information between the source and reference point clouds can be computed through ICP, a NN or ANN mapping must found for every point in the source cloud. In many serial applications, such as the Fast Library for Approximate Nearest Neighbors (FLANN) [4] and the Point Cloud Library [5], either branch-and-bound or similarity based approaches are used due to the decreased runtime complexity they offer, such as K-Dimensional Trees (*k*-d trees) [6] or Locality Sensitive Hashing (LSH) [7] techniques.

**Fig. 1.** An example reference model (aircraft2) is shown above as the solid shape. The white point cloud an initial source cloud, and the blue, yellow, orange, and red clouds are after 1, 2, 5, and 10 number of iterations respectively of the ICP algorithm.

While these methods have been shown to significantly reduce the runtime complexity of both NN and ANN searches, it is well known that direct, parallel implementations of these algorithms often lead to poor performance due to conditional computations and suboptimal memory access patterns [8]. As a result, conventional GPU-based $k$NN implementations rely on Brute Force (BF) methods parallelized on the GPU due to their intrinsic parallelism and relatively high performance gain compared to serial applications [9,10]. In the context of ICP, this is done by minimizing the Euclidean distance between point clouds through an $O(n^2)$ approach.

Although Delaunay Triangulation is a well-known algorithm that has been used in a variety of contexts outside of ICP, its use as a parallelized algorithm to the 3-dimensional $k$-nearest neighbor search problem has been limited. A heterogeneous *Single Instruction Multiple Data* (SIMD) implementation of ICP was proposed in 2012 using an octree-based approach to the nearest neighbor problem which relied on localized Delaunay Triangulation cache [11]. A similar approach using 3D Voronoi cells, the dual to the Delaunay Triangulation, was proposed in 2014 to reduce the runtime of determining all of the point correspondences, although it was not clear whether the algorithm was a parallel or serial implementation [12]. To the author's knowledge, there have been no other publications showing the utility of using Delaunay Triangulation as a preprocessed data structure in the context of either fast $k$NN searches or ICP. There were a few publications [13,14] in the context of Point Location discussing a "Jump-and-Walk" algorithm that qualitatively discusses the same idea presented by our traversal algorithm; although there was an extensive asymptotic analysis done on the complexity of such an algorithm, the algorithm itself remained undefined.

# 3    Methodology

Our approach to ICP can be separated into three major steps of preprocessing, registration, and alignment. A primary goal of this research is to reach improved registration speeds by taking advantage of preprocessed data structures.

## 3.1    Preprocessing

The vertices of a given reference model are unchanged throughout the AAR application, thus using any prior structural information known at compile-time is advantageous to maximize the runtime performance of the algorithm. The following sections summarize the $k$-d tree and Delaunay Triangulation *preprocessing* steps that enable the *exact* nearest neighbor to perform within an SIMD environment.

**$k$-d Tree Construction.** The $k$-d tree is a binary search tree (BST) in which each node represents a partitioned subspace of the $k$-dimensional space [6]. When the $k$-d tree is built, the dimension that partitions the input space is altered iteratively with each level. In this research, the tree is balanced using the standard median splitting algorithm presented in the original paper [6], unneeded dimensions are stripped from the tree, and values at the leaves are replaced with their corresponding reference model indices.

**Delaunay Triangulation.** A Delaunay Triangulation [15] maximizes the minimum angle of each triangle in the triangulation. Delaunay Triangulation is a natural solution due to the notion that the triangulation produces "nice" triangles in such a way that uniformity in execution time is empirically maximized. An additional property of the Delaunay Triangulation is that it is dual to the Voronoi tessellation, which partitions the space into regions which can be used to identify nearest neighbors. This property of the triangulation is necessary to guarantee the convergence of the Delaunay traversal to the *exact* NN. The reference model's Delaunay triangulation was computed using the QHull library and recorded as intermediary file on a per-reference point basis, where it is loaded at runtime. For every model point $i$ and for every Delaunay connected neighbor point $j$, we calculate and store:

- A unit vector in the direction from $i$ to $j$.
- Half of the Euclidean distance from $i$ to $j$. This is referred to as the midpoint for the remainder of the paper.
- The index of the target vertex $j$.

## 3.2    Registration

The registration is separated into two sub-steps, (1) $k$-d tree search and (2) Delaunay Traversal. First the $k$-d tree search gives an ANN. This result is then used as the initial guess in the Delaunay Traversal, which then produces the *exact* NN search.

**k-d Tree Search.** As the k-d tree is a binary space-partitioning data structure, the search involves separating the space into smaller, mutually exclusive subsets of space as the tree is traversed. Let $S$ represents the source point cloud, and $M$ the reference point cloud, where $s_i \in S$ and $m_j \in M$. Starting at at the root node, a single dimension of the point in the k-d tree $m_j$ is compared against the corresponding dimension of $s_i$. If $s_i \leq m_j$, traverse down the left branch to the next $m_k$ point, otherwise traverse down the right branch. These comparisons are repeated until reaching a leaf node. The value stored in the leaf node is an index corresponding to a model point (see preprocessing section) which will be used as the ANN. This process is completed for all source points in $O(n\log(n))$ steps.

In contrast to our ANN implementation, conventional k-d tree searches traverse back up the tree until the exact NN is found [6]. This NN approach increases the worst-case complexity to $O(n^2)$. The reverse-traversal often results in misaligned data access and poor memory coalescence, ultimately bottlenecking the effective bandwidth of the kernel. This performance penalty has been investigated exhaustively [16,17]. We avoid this bottleneck by transitioning to an exact NN search using a precomputed Delaunay Triangulation.

**Delaunay Traversal.** As discussed in the preprocessing section, Delaunay Triangulation, for each model point, references to neighboring model points, unit vectors to all neighbors, and the midpoints between neighbors are already precomputed. Neighbors are defined as two vertices connected by a Delaunay edge. The notation to be used is defined as $s :=$ the source point, $N :=$ number of model points, $m_i :=$ the model point with index $i$ where $0 \leq i \leq N-1$, $u_{(i,j)} :=$ the unit vector at $m_i$ pointing to neighbor $m_j$, $mp_{(i,j)} :=$ the scalar midpoint between $m_i$ and $m_j$, $D_i :=$ the vector $s - m_i$, and $Neighbors_i :=$ collection of indices of model neighbors for $m_i$.

The result of the k-d tree search will give an initial guess "close" to the exact NN. Let the current guess be represented by $m_i$ and all other model points as $m_j, i \neq j$. For each neighbor $j$ of $m_i$, $proj = dot(D_i, u_{(i,j)})$, where dot is vector dot product. If this $proj > mp_{(i,j)}$, then this shows $||D_j|| < ||D_i||$, meaning $m_j$ is a closer point. If any of the neighbors were closer, the current guess becomes $m_j$, where $m_j$ exhibits the largest difference between midpoint and projection. These computations are repeated on all neighbors for each guess until all projections are less than or equal to the midpoint, meaning the exact NN is found. Although this algorithm has a complexity of $O(n^2)$, most cases empirically converge within a miniscule number of steps, as demonstrated in the results section with Fig. 2. The algorithm is presented in more precise detail in Algorithm 1.

### 3.3 Alignment

Following the registration, the source cloud needs to be rigidly transformed onto the reference cloud. To complete this task, a rotation quaternion and

---

**Algorithm 1.** Delaunay Traversal

---

**Require:** $s :=$ Single source cloud point
**Require:** $M :=$ Collection of model cloud points
**Require:** $init :=$ Initial guess of index of model point from the $k$-d tree search
**Require:** $mp :=$ Collection of scalar midpoints among model cloud
**Require:** $u :=$ Collection of unit vectors among model cloud
**Require:** $Neighbors :=$ Collection of collections of model neighbors
 1: **function** DELAUNAYTRAVERSAL($s$, $M$, $init$, $mp$, $u$, $Neighbors$)
 2:      $i \leftarrow init$
 3:      **repeat**
 4:          $better\_neighbor \leftarrow$ FALSE
 5:          $next\_guess \leftarrow i$
 6:          $D \leftarrow s - m_i$
 7:          $max\_proj \leftarrow 0$
 8:          **for** $j$ in $Neighbors_i$ **do**
 9:              $proj \leftarrow D \cdot u_{(i,j)}$
10:              **if** $proj > mp_{(i,j)}$ **then**
11:                  $better\_neighbor \leftarrow$ TRUE
12:                  **if** $proj > max\_proj$ **then**
13:                      $next\_guess \leftarrow j$
14:                      $max\_proj \leftarrow proj - mp_{(i,j)}$
15:          $i \leftarrow next\_guess$
16:      **until** $better\_neighbor =$ FALSE
17: **return** $i$

---

translation vector are calculated and applied to the source cloud following a technique provided by Besl et al. in his 1992 paper [3] based on minimizing the alignment error. These steps, when implemented on the GPU, are much faster than the nearest neighbor search, and are therefore not the primary concern with regards to computation time.

The algorithm will repeat from the $k$-d tree search using the newly aligned source points. The average Euclidean distance between the source points and the corresponding closest points are calculated as the convergence condition. A threshold value for convergence is often determined based on the specific ICP application. In the context of AAR, when the average distance is within 10 cm of the closest point, the algorithm can be considered converged. This error metric was chosen based on previous AAR research by Werner [18].

## 4   Experimental Design

The motivation for the experiments in this research is to demonstrate the relative computation speed of the ANN and Delaunay Traversal against existing approaches on various point clouds. We standardized the position and rotation of each source point cloud prior to benchmarking. Each cloud is rotated 45° along the $x$ dimension, and then translated 1 standard deviation (positive) in each dimension.

There were four reference models used in the results section, two from the Stanford 3D Scanning repository [19], and two aircraft models to demonstrate the viability of this approach in the context of AAR. The reference models used were:

1. The Stanford Bunny (Simplified): 2,503 vertices
2. The Stanford Dragon (Simplified): 50,000 vertices
3. aircraft1 (Simplified): 18,650 vertices
4. aircraft2 (Detailed): 65,092 vertices

All performance tests were completed using a GTX 750 m GPU with compute capability 3.0. Each benchmark profile is the averaged result of 50 independent executions. All of the execution times given in Table 1 are in **milliseconds**. The normalized frequency distributions of the number of "hops" that were taken by the Delaunay traversal are shown in Fig. 2.

## 5    Results

In Table 1, the successes of the ANN $k$-d tree search and Delaunay Traversal are demonstrated. In all test cases, our algorithm outperforms the NN $k$-d tree search and brute force method. In the application of automated aerial refueling for aircraft1, the source cloud is likely within 1 k to 5 k points. In the 5 k case, the KD-ANN + Delaunay is 80 times faster than KD-NN and 10 times faster than brute force. The aircraft1 used in these tests resemble the type of reference model to be used in application, and the source point clouds produced by the stereo vision system are estimated to have between 2 k–8 k points in them; thus, these results are extremely promising towards the goal of establishing real-time positional estimates for automated aerial refueling.

Table 1 also reveals important information about the *scalability* of our approach. In the Dragon test cases, the BF and KD-NN performed particularly poor relative to the KD-ANN + Delaunay. This is due to the number of vertices in the model. When looking at the 5 k Dragon row, we can see KD-ANN + Delaunay speedups of 100 times and 40 times over the KD-NN and BF, respectively. Despite the dragon model having 30 k more points than the aircraft1, the KD-ANN + Delaunay maintained similar performance.

Figure 2 depicts the normalized frequency of the number of iterations the Delaunay Traversal requires to converge on the exact NN, over all source points. For all four models, the majority of source points converge within 15 iterations of the traversal. This low average frequency count across different models of varying sizes and distributions helps demonstrate the scalability and flexibility of the traversal to find the NN rapidly. Currently in the parallel computation process, the algorithm is only as fast as the *slowest performing thread*, so an individual NN search taking longer to converge can lead to slow downs. Future work in performance optimization can seek to take advantage of the quickly converging points (less than 15 iterations) while ignoring points which are taking longer (greater than 100 iterations), leading to further speed ups in the registration step.

**Table 1.** Below are the profiled execution times (all in milliseconds) for each of the aforementioned reference models, with varying sized source clouds (see Sect. 4. The algorithms used are the ANN $k$-d tree search as developed in this paper (KD-ANN), the Delaunay Traversal as developed in this paper (Delaunay), a full $k$-d tree search with traversal back up the tree to produce exact NN (KD-NN), and a brute force approach (BF). The performance of our approach is the sum of KD-ANN and Delaunay columns.

| Model (Number source pts) | KD-ANN + Delaunay | KD-NN | BF |
|---|---|---|---|
| Bunny (500) | 0.1144 + 0.7696 | 27.1244 | 8.1573 |
| Bunny (1,000) | 0.1039 + 1.1331 | 27.8035 | 8.8021 |
| Bunny (2,000) | 0.1170 + 1.4327 | 28.1713 | 10.6266 |
| aircraft1 (500) | 0.2506 + 5.2489 | 444.3156 | 61.0366 |
| aircraft1 (1,000) | 0.4840 + 5.2314 | 440.5676 | 60.7197 |
| aircraft1 (2,000) | 0.3852 + 6.4391 | 454.1046 | 68.3205 |
| **aircraft1 (5,000)** | **0.2651 + 10.8206** | **825.5142** | **136.4578** |
| aircraft1 (10,000) | 0.5626 + 16.3668 | 1280.4107 | 219.0711 |
| Dragon (500) | 0.8216 + 3.6488 | 435.5331 | 161.6813 |
| Dragon (1,000) | 0.9363 + 3.5139 | 429.3822 | 162.1055 |
| Dragon (2,000) | 0.6941 + 4.4726 | 432.7138 | 182.0212 |
| **Dragon (5,000)** | **0.8486 + 8.1534** | **795.7176** | **389.1141** |
| Dragon (10,000) | 1.3110 + 13.2773 | 1278.6778 | 590.9299 |
| Dragon (25,000) | 1.0765 + 25.2486 | 2841.6313 | 1371.4290 |
| aircraft2 (1,000) | 0.8471 + 10.4636 | NA | 211.9872 |
| aircraft2 (2,000) | 0.8722 + 12.9250 | NA | 237.1767 |
| aircraft2 (10,000) | 1.0405 + 33.6255 | NA | 764.9389 |

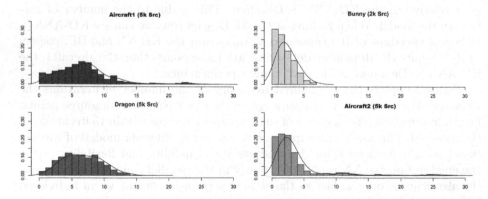

**Fig. 2.** The normalized frequency distribution of the number of iterations of the Delaunay traversal each source point required for the four models mentioned. The aircraft1 (*top left*) is given in blue, the Stanford Bunny in yellow (*top right*), the Stanford Dragon (*bottom left*) in red, and the aircraft2 (*bottom right*) is in green. (Color figure online)

# 6   Future Work

The $k$-d tree ANN implementation was exercised on a prebuilt, balanced $k$-d tree–likely the most well-cited spatial indexing structure used in $k$NN approaches. Other spatial indexing structures have been proposed that may be augmented to provide a "better guess" of the nearest neighbor compared to the traditional $k$d-tree search. Most notably R* Trees [20], Octrees [21], and Ball Trees could be explored and compared against the current $k$-d tree approach.

The use of point-to-plane algorithms, as opposed to point-to-point, have been shown to dramatically improve the convergence rate of ICP implementations [22]. However, inefficient point-to-plane algorithms that require a square root operation would most likely exceed of the "real time" requirements of AAR on a per iteration basis, although a point-to-plane metric would likely improve upon the current point-to-point error metric and theoretically decrease the number of iterations needed to ensure convergence. Particularly noisy or low-density source clouds may also benefit more from a point-to-plane implementation than larger point clouds, although in practice the structure of the reference seems to be invariant in the performance of the Delaunay traversal (as seen in Sect. 5).

Additional source point clouds gathered from non-simulated data sources of varied receiving aircrafts as they travel along their flight path to the target refueler would also provide a more accurate estimate of how applicable a Delaunay traversal ICP implementation would be to real time position estimation.

# 7   Conclusion

Parallelized ICP implementations that utilize Graphics Processing Units are capable of providing real time positioning estimates and may be indispensible to many of the challenge areas of AAR, Aerial Robotics, and Computer Vision as a whole. In this paper, we demonstrated the feasibility of ICP in real time using low-cost hardware implementations. We showed that it is possible to expose parallel characteristics of spatial indexing data structures that are often difficult to adapt to the SIMD paradigm through the CUDA architecture. We also provided a novel Delaunay Traversal and demonstrated both its efficiency and its scalability through an application context using CUDA.

**Acknowledgement.** We would like to thank our sponsor, AFRL/RQ for their support in this research.

# References

1. Owens, J.D., Houston, M., Luebke, D., Green, S., Stone, J.E., Phillips, J.C.: GPU computing. Proc. IEEE **96**, 879–899 (2008)
2. Nvidia, C.: Compute unified device architecture programming guide (2007)
3. Besl, P.J., McKay, N.D.: Method for registration of 3-D shapes. In: Robotics-DL Tentative, pp. 586–606. International Society for Optics and Photonics (1992)

4. Mount, D.M.: GTS: GNU Triangulated Surface library (2000–2004)
5. Rusu, R.B., Cousins, S.: 3D is here: point cloud library (PCL). In: ICRA. IEEE (2011)
6. Bentley, J.L.: Multidimensional binary search trees used for associative searching. Commun. ACM **18**, 509–517 (1975)
7. Indyk, P., Motwani, R.: Approximate nearest neighbors: towards removing the curse of dimensionality. In: Proceedings of the Thirtieth Annual ACM Symposium on Theory of Computing, pp. 604–613. ACM (1998)
8. Gieseke, F., Heinermann, J., Oancea, C., Igel, C.: Buffer kd trees: processing massive nearest neighbor queries on GPUs. In: Proceedings of The 31st International Conference on Machine Learning, pp. 172–180 (2014)
9. Garcia, V., Debreuve, E., Barlaud, M.: Fast k nearest neighbor search using GPU. In: IEEE Computer Society Conference on Computer Vision and Pattern Recognition Workshops, CVPRW 2008, pp. 1–6. IEEE (2008)
10. Li, S., Amenta, N.: Brute-force $k$-nearest neighbors search on the GPU. In: Amato, G., Connor, R., Falchi, F., Gennaro, C. (eds.) SISAP 2015. LNCS, vol. 9371, pp. 259–270. Springer, Heidelberg (2015). doi:10.1007/978-3-319-25087-8_25
11. Eggert, D., Dalyot, S.: Octree-based SIMD strategy for ICP registration and alignment of 3D point clouds. ISPRS Ann. Photogramm. Remote Sens. Spat. Inf. Sci. **3**, 105–110 (2012)
12. Abe, L.I., Iwao, Y., Gotoh, T., Kagei, S., Takimoto, R.Y., Tsuzuki, M., Iwasawa, T.: High-speed point cloud matching algorithm for medical volume images using 3D voronoi diagram. In: 2014 7th International Conference on Biomedical Engineering and Informatics, pp. 205–210. IEEE (2014)
13. Green, P.J., Sibson, R.: Computing dirichlet tessellations in the plane. Comput. J. **21**, 168–173 (1978)
14. Mcke, E.P., Saias, I., Zhu, B.: Fast randomized point location without preprocessing in two-and three-dimensional delaunay triangulations. Comput. Geom. **12**, 63–83 (1999)
15. Delaunay, B.: Sur la sphere vide. Izv. Akad. Nauk SSSR, Otdelenie Matematicheskii i Estestvennyka Nauk **7**, 1–2 (1934)
16. Greenspan, M., Yurick, M.: Approximate KD tree search for efficient ICP. In: Proceedings of the Fourth International Conference on 3-D Digital Imaging and Modeling, 3DIM 2003, pp. 442–448. IEEE (2003)
17. Santos, A., Teixeira, J.M., Farias, T., Teichrieb, V., Kelner, J.: Understanding the efficiency of kD-tree ray-traversal techniques over a GPGPU architecture. Int. J. Parallel Program. **40**, 331–352 (2012)
18. Werner, K.P.: Precision relative positioning for automated aerial refueling from a stereo imaging system. Technical report, DTIC Document (2015)
19. Levoy, M., Gerth, J., Curless, B., Pull, K.: The stanford 3D scanning repository (2005). http://www-graphics.stanford.edu/data/3dscanrep
20. Beckmann, N., Kriegel, H.P., Schneider, R., Seeger, B.: The r*-tree: an efficient and robust access method for points and rectangles. ACM SIGMOD Rec. **19**, 322–331 (1990). ACM
21. Meagher, D.J.: Octree encoding: a new technique for the representation, manipulation and display of arbitrary 3-D objects by computer. Electrical and Systems Engineering Department, Rensseiaer Polytechnic Institute Image Processing Laboratory (1980)
22. Low, K.L.: Linear Least-Squares Optimization for Point-to-Plane ICP Surface Registration, vol. 4. University of North Carolina, Chapel Hill (2004)

# Distributed Optimal Flocking Design
# for Multi-agent Two-Player Zero-Sum Games
# with Unknown System Dynamics
# and Disturbance

Hao Xu$^{(\boxtimes)}$ and Luis Rodolfo Garcia Carrillo

Department of Electrical and Biomedical Engineering,
University of Nevada, Reno, NV, USA
{haoxu,rodolfo}@unr.edu

**Abstract.** In this paper, distributed flocking strategies have been exploited for multi-agent two-player zero-sum games. Two main challenges are addressed, i.e. (a) handling system uncertainties and disturbances, and (b) achieving optimality. Adopting the emerging Approximate Dynamic Programming (ADP) technology, a novel distributed adaptive flocking design is proposed to optimize the multi-agent two-player zero-sum games even when the system dynamics and disturbances are unknown. First, to evaluate the multi-agent flocking performance and effects from disturbances, a novel flocking cost function is developed. Next, an innovative type of online neural network (NN) based identifier is proposed to approximate the multi-agent zero-sum game system dynamics effectively. Subsequently, another novel neural network (NN) is proposed to approximate the optimal flocking cost function by using the Hamilton-Jacobi-Isaacs (HJI) equation in a forward in time manner. Moreover, a novel additional term is designed and included into the NN update law to relax the stringent requirement of initial admissible control. Eventually, the distributed adaptive optimal flocking design is obtained by using the learnt Multi-agent zero-sum games system dynamics and approximated optimal flocking cost function. Simulation results demonstrate the effectiveness of proposed scheme.

## 1 Introduction

Flocking techniques [1, 2] are considered as promising techniques for solving the challenges of multi-agent systems (MAS) since they can collect multiple distributed interacting agents to operate as a unified group efficiently without collision. However, to reap the advantages from flocking, a proper practical distributed flocking design is urgently needed. According to the Reynolds's work [1], an efficient flocking control needs to maintain three critical rules, i.e. cohesion, separation, and alignment effectively. The authors in [2] developed a theoretical framework for the design and analysis of a distributed flocking algorithm. Recently, in [3], the authors proposed a flocking control with obstacle avoidance. Furthermore, the authors in [4] generate a distributed event-triggered hybrid flocking control for MAS.

© Springer International Publishing AG 2016
G. Bebis et al. (Eds.): ISVC 2016, Part I, LNCS 10072, pp. 603–614, 2016.
DOI: 10.1007/978-3-319-50835-1_54

However, these existing control schemes [2–4] were only maintaining the MAS stability along with satisfying the three critical flocking rules. Besides stability, optimality is much more preferred. The authors in [5] developed an optimal control for MAS to attain consensus and avoid obstacles simultaneously. However, it cannot be used to solve the optimal flocking challenges for practical MAS due to three issues, i.e., (i) with the approach in [5] it is very difficult to maintain the three important flocking rules at the same time, (ii) the practical MAS dynamics are commonly unknown beforehand due to the real-time uncertainties, and (iii) the real-time disturbances have not been considered in [5]. To overcome these deficiencies, in this paper, we propose a novel distributed adaptive optimal flocking design for practical multi-agent two-player zero-sum games in presence of uncertain system dynamics and unknown disturbances.

Firstly, to realize the three flocking rules in an optimal manner, a novel flocking cost function is proposed which includes three terms, i.e., cohesion cost function, separation cost function, and alignment cost function. Next, the distributed adaptive optimal flocking design for nonlinear multi-agent zero-sum games can be attained by minimizing the flocking cost function. Based on standard optimal control theory [6], the minimized flocking cost function can be attained by solving the Hamiltonian-Jacobi-Isaac (HJI) equation. However, the HJI equation is very difficult to be solved [6]. Inspired from computational intelligence and reinforcement learning, a novel approximate dynamic programming (ADP) technique [7] is developed to approximate the HJI equation solution. Recently, the authors in [8] proposed an iteration based ADP scheme (i.e. policy iteration and value iteration) to obtain the optimal strategies for nonlinear two-player zero-sum game. However, to find the optimal solutions, these iteration-based ADP schemes require significant large number of iterations, which is not applicable for practical nonlinear two-player zero-sum game.

To address this issue, Dierks and Jagannathan [9] introduced a time-based ADP approach to solve the optimal control of nonlinear system by using the historical information instead of iteration based data. However, most existing ADP schemes [8, 9] are not suitable for practical nonlinear multi-agent two-player zero-sum game flocking since the three flocking rules are not considered.

In this paper, we propose a novel time-based distributed adaptive optimal flocking strategy for multi-agent two-player zero-sum game by engaging the ADP technique with a novel flocking cost function which includes cohesion, separation, and alignment aspects. The main contributions of this paper include: (1) a novel flocking cost function is developed for the multi-agent two-player zero-sum game flocking problem, (2) worst case disturbances are considered in multi-agent two-player zero-sum game, (3) the need for partial system dynamics has been relaxed; and (4) closed-loop stability is demonstrated by selecting novel NN update laws.

## 2    Background

Based on [3, 4], the connection topology of multi-agent systems can be represented by using undirected graph theory [10]. Generally, the connection graph $G$ is defined as $G = \{V, E\}$, where $V = \{1, \ldots, i, \ldots, N\}$ expresses a set of vertices, $i$ denotes the $i^{th}$

agent, and the related edge set $E$ is $E \subseteq \{(i,j) : i,j \in V, i \neq j\}$. The edges indicate the potential connection links and sensing capability among the multi-agent system.

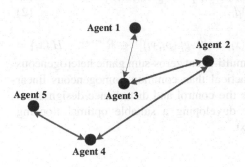

**Fig. 1.** An undirected graph for the topology of a MAS with five agents.

Next, an unweight adjacency matrix $A = [a_{ij}] \in \Re^{N \times N}, \forall i,j = 1,2,\ldots,N$, with $a_{ij}$ defined as $a_{ij} = 1$ if $(i,j) \in E$. The connection graph can be defined as linked while there is a path linking each pair of distinct vertices. Each agent in the MAS is assumed to have the equal omni-directional connection and sensing capability which denotes a mutual communication within the linked multi-agent systems. Theoretically, the adjacency matrix is symmetric, i.e. $A^T = A$, and the connection graph is undirected. An undirected communication graph topology example is demonstrated in Fig. 1.

Moreover, the degree matrix of connection graph $G$ is defined as $D = diag\{A\}$ where the diagonal element $d_{ij}$ is given as $d_{ij} = \sum_{j=1,j\neq i}^{N} a_{ij}$. Moreover, the Laplacian matrix $L = \{lp_{ij}\} \in \Re^{N \times N}, \forall i,j = 1,\ldots,N$, can be represented as $L = D - A$.

## 3   Problem Formulation

In this section, a practical heterogeneous nonlinear formulation is introduced for multi-agent zero-sum games. Moreover, to develop optimal flocking strategies, a novel cost function is developed.

### 3.1   Multi-agent Two-Player Zero-Sum Game Dynamics

In this paper, a realistic heterogeneous nonlinear system dynamics is considered to represent the MAS as

$$\dot{p}_i = v_i; \; \dot{v}_i = f_i(p_i, v_i) + g_i(p_i, v_i)u_i + h_i(p_i, v_i)d_i, \; \forall i = 1,\ldots,N \tag{1}$$

Where $p_i \in \Re^m, v_i \in \Re^m$ denotes the position and velocity of $i^{th}$ agent, respectively, $u_i \in \Re^m, d_i \in \Re^m$ represents the control input and disturbance signals, respectively, of the $i^{th}$ agent, $f_i(\bullet) \in \Re^m, g_i(\bullet) \in \Re^{m \times m}, h_i(\bullet) \in \Re^{m \times m}$ are the heterogeneous nonlinear dynamics of $i^{th}$ agent, and $N$ denotes the total number of agents.

To simplify the multi-agent zero-sum game description, we define the system state of multi-agent zero-sum game as $x_i = [p_i^T \; v_i^T]^T \in \Re^{2m}, \forall i = 1,\ldots,N$. Then, the multi-agent zero-sum game heterogeneous nonlinear system dynamics (1) can be represented as

$$\dot{x}_i = \begin{bmatrix} \dot{p}_i \\ \dot{v}_i \end{bmatrix} = \begin{bmatrix} v_i \\ f_i(p_i, v_i) \end{bmatrix} + \begin{bmatrix} 0 \\ g_i(p_i, v_i) \end{bmatrix} u_i + \begin{bmatrix} 0 \\ h_i(p_i, v_i) \end{bmatrix} d_i$$
$$= F_i(x_i) + G_i(x_i)u_i + H_i(x_i)d_i, \tag{2}$$

with $F_i(x_i) = [v_i^T \ f_i^T(p_i, v_i)]^T \in \Re^{2m}$, $G_i(x_i) = [0 \ g_i^T(p_i, v_i)]^T \in \Re^{2m \times m}$, $H_i(x_i) = [0 \ h_i^T(p_i, v_i)]^T \in \Re^{2m}$. Although the general multi-agent zeros-sum game heterogeneous nonlinear system dynamics (2) is more practical than common homogeneous linear system dynamics [3, 4], it could complicate the control and disturbance design especially for optimal flocking strategies. For developing a suitable optimal flocking scheme, a novel cost function is needed next.

## 3.2 The Novel Multi-agent Zeros-Sum Game Flocking Cost Function Setup

To attain the flocking behavior, Reynolds [1] proposed three fundamental issues, i.e. (1) Collision Avoidance (CA); (2) Velocity Matching (VM); and (3) Flock Centering (FC). Inspired from Reynolds' rules, a suitable cost function should include these necessary parts indicating the corresponding fundamental rules respectively. Therefore, a novel infinite horizon cost function for multi-agent zeros-sum game can be proposed as

$$J_i(x) = J_{CA,i}(x) + J_{VM,i}(x) + J_{FC,i}(x) - J_{DS,i}(x), \tag{3}$$

The collision avoidance (CA) part of the proposed multi-agent zeros-sum game novel cost function, i.e., $J_{CA,i}(x)$, is developed as

$$J_{CA,i}(x) = \sum_{j \in N_i} \int_t^\infty \left\{ q_{CA,ij} \left[ \psi_\alpha \left( \left\| A_{CA}x_i(\tau) - A_{CA}x_j(\tau) \right\|_\sigma \right) \right]^2 + u_i^T(\tau)R_{CA,ij}u_i(\tau) \right\} d\tau \tag{4}$$

where $A_{CA} = [I \ 0] \in \Re^{m \times 2m}$ with $I \in \Re^m$ as the identity matrix, $R_{CA,i} \in \Re^{m \times m}$ is a positive definite symmetric weighting matrix, $q_{CA,ij} > 0$ is a positive weighting scalar, and $N_i$ is the neighbor set of $i^{th}$ agent. It is important to note that $\psi_\alpha(\bullet)$ is a smooth pairwise attractive/repulsive potential function which can be utilized to avoid the collision between different agents and is defined as

$$\psi_\alpha(z) = \rho(z/d_x)\theta(z - d_\alpha) \tag{5}$$

with $d_x, d_\alpha$ representing the maximal communication distance and the desired separation distance between agents, respectively, and the bump function $\rho(y)$ and the $\theta(s)$ function are defined similar as [2]. Next, the velocity match (VM) part of the multi-agent zero-sum game cost function, i.e., $J_{VM,i}(x)$, is represented as

$$J_{VM,i}(x) = \sum_{j \in N_i} \int_t^\infty \left[ q_{VM,ij} a_{ij} \left\| A_{VM} x_i(\tau) - A_{VM} x_j(\tau) \right\|^2 + u_i^T(\tau) R_{VM,ij} u_i(\tau) \right] d\tau \quad (6)$$

where $A_{VM} = [0 \ I] \in \Re^{m \times 2m}$ with $I \in \Re^m$ is the identity matrix, $a_{ij}$ is the connection indicator between $i^{th}$ agent and its neighbor $j^{th}$ agent, $R_{VM,ij} \in \Re^{m \times m}$ is a positive definite symmetric weighting matrix, and $q_{VM,ij} > 0$ is a positive weighting scalar.

Thirdly, the flocking center (FC) part of the multi-agent zero-sum game cost function, $J_{FC,i}(x_i)$, is proposed as

$$J_{FC,i}(x) = \int_t^\infty \left[ (x_i(\tau) - x_r(\tau))^T Q_{FC,i}(x_i(\tau) - x_r(\tau)) + u_i^T(\tau) R_{FC,i} u_i(\tau) \right] d\tau \quad (7)$$

where $x_r(t) \in \Re^{2m}$ denotes the virtual flocking center of mass, and $Q_{FC,i} \in \Re^{2m \times 2m}$ and $R_{FC,i} \in \Re^{l \times l}$ are positive definite symmetric weighting matrices. Eventually, the term for disturbance signal is shown as $J_{DS,i}(x) = \int_t^\infty \left[ d_i^T(\tau) Q_{DS,i} d_i(\tau) \right] d\tau$.

where $Q_{DS,i} \in \Re^{2m \times 2m}$ is a positive definite symmetric weighting matrix used for representing the effects from disturbances. Substituting (4), (6) and (7) into (3), the novel multi-agent zero-sum game cost function for the $i^{th}$ agent can be represented as

$$J_i(x) = \sum_{j \hat{I} N_i} \int_t^\infty \left\{ \begin{array}{l} q_{CA,ij} \left[ y_a \left( \left\| A_{CA} x_i(t) - A_{CA} x_j(t) \right\|_s \right) \right]^2 + q_{VM,ij} a_{ij} \left\| A_{VM} x_i(t) - A_{VM} x_j(t) \right\|^2 \\ + u_i^T(t) R_{CA,ij} u_i(t) + u_i^T(t) R_{VM,ij} u_i(t) \end{array} \right\} dt$$

$$+ \int_t^\infty \left\{ (x_i(\tau) - x_r(\tau))^T Q_{FC,i}(x_i(\tau) - x_r(\tau)) + u_i^T(\tau) R_{u,i} u_i(\tau) \right\} d\tau - \int_t^\infty \left[ d_i^T(\tau) Q_{DS,i} d_i(\tau) \right] d\tau$$

$$(8)$$

with $R_{u,i} = \sum_{j \in N_i} (R_{CA,ij} + R_{VM,ij}) + R_{FC,i}$. The novel cost function for the entire multi-agent zero-sum game is developed as $J_{(x)} = \sum_{i=1}^N J_i(x)$. To attain the optimal flocking strategies, the HJI of multi-agent zero-sum game is needed first [6]. Based on traditional optimal control theory [6] and Lagrange Multiplier, the multi-agent zero-sum game HJI can be represented as

$$HJI(x, u) = \sum_{i=1}^N HJI_i(x, u) = \sum_{i=1}^N \left[ (x_i(\tau) - x_r(\tau))^T Q_{FC,i}(x_i(\tau) - x_r(\tau)) \right]$$

$$+ \sum_{i=1}^N \left\{ \sum_{j \in N_i} \left[ q_{VM,ij} a_{ij} \left\| A_{VM} x_i(\tau) - A_{VM} x_j(\tau) \right\|^2 + q_{CA,ij} \left[ \psi_\alpha \left( \left\| A_{CA} x_i(\tau) - A_{CA} x_j(\tau) \right\|_\sigma \right) \right]^2 \right] \right\} \quad (9)$$

$$+ \sum_{i=1}^N u_i^T(t) R_{u,i} u_i(t) - \sum_{i=1}^N d_i^T(t) Q_{DS,i} d_i(t) + \sum_{i=1}^N \left[ \frac{\partial J_i^T(x)}{\partial x_i(t)} (F_i(x_i) + G_i(x_i) u_i(t) + H(x_i) d_i(t)) \right]$$

According to optimal control theory [6], the optimal flocking strategies can be attained through $\frac{\partial H(x,u)}{\partial u_i} = 0$, $\forall i = 1, 2, \ldots, N$. Therefore,

$$u_i^*(t) = -\frac{1}{2}R_{u,i}^{-1}G_i^T(x_i)\frac{\partial J_i(x)}{\partial x_i(t)}, \quad d_i^*(t) = \frac{1}{2}Q_{DS,i}^{-1}H_i^T(x_i)\frac{\partial J_i(x)}{\partial x_i(t)}, \quad \forall i = 1, 2, \ldots, N \quad (10)$$

## 4 Distributed Adaptive Optimal Flocking Design for Multi-agent Zero-Sum Games

### 4.1 The Novel NN-Based Identifier Design

According to recent ADP literatures [8, 9], either complete or partial system dynamics of multi-agent zero-sum game (i.e. $F_i(\bullet), G_i(\bullet), H_i(\bullet), \forall i = 1, 2, \ldots, N$) are needed for solving the optimal strategies. However, in practice, the multi-agent zero-sum game system dynamics cannot be known beforehand. To relax the requirement about system dynamics, a novel online NN-based identifier is developed next.

Using the NN universal function approximation property, the MAS heterogeneous nonlinear two-player zero-sum dynamics can be represented for $i = 1, 2, \ldots, N$ as

$$F_i(x_i) = W_{F,i}^T\sigma_{F,i}(x_i) + \varepsilon_{F,i}; G_i(x_i) = W_{G,i}^T\sigma_{G,i}(x_i) + \varepsilon_{G,i}; H_i(x_i) = W_{H,i}^T\sigma_{H,i}(x_i) + \varepsilon_{H,i},$$

$$(11)$$

with $W_{F,i} \in \Re^{l_F \times 2m}, W_{G,i} \in \Re^{l_G \times 2m}, W_{H,i} \in \Re^{l_G \times 2m}, \forall i = 1, 2, \ldots, N$ denoting the ideal target NN weighs, $\sigma_{F,i}(x) \in \Re^{l_F}, \sigma_{G,i}(x) \in \Re^{l_G \times m}, \sigma_{H,i}(x) \in \Re^{l_G \times m}, \forall i = 1, 2, \ldots, N$ representing the NN activation functions, $\varepsilon_{F,i} \in \Re^{2m}, \varepsilon_{G,i} \in \Re^{2m}, \varepsilon_{H,i} \in \Re^{2m} \forall i = 1, 2, \ldots, N$ are the NN reconstruction errors respectively, and $l_F, l_G, l_H$ denote the number of neurons in NN.

Substituting (11) into (2), the multi-agent two-player zero-sum system states can be represented as

$$\dot{x}_i = F_i(x_i) + G_i(x_i)u_i + H_i(x_i)d_i \quad \forall i = 1, 2, \ldots, N$$
$$= W_{F,i}^T\sigma_{F,i}(x_i) + W_{G,i}^T\sigma_{G,i}(x_i)u_i + W_{H,i}^T\sigma_{H,i}(x_i)d_i + \varepsilon_{F,i} + \varepsilon_{G,i}u_i + \varepsilon_{H,i}d_i = W_{I,i}^T\vartheta_{I,i}(x_i)\bar{u}_i + \varepsilon_{I,i}$$

$$(12)$$

where $W_{I,i} = [W_{F,i}^T \ W_{G,i}^T \ W_{H,i}^T]^T \in \Re^{(l_F + l_G + l_H) \times 2m}$, denotes the constant NN-based identifier target weights, $\vartheta_{I,i}(x_i) = diag\{\sigma_{F,i}(x_i), \sigma_{G,i}(x_i), \sigma_{H,i}(x_i)\} \in \Re^{(l_F + l_G + l_H) \times (m+1)}$ is the corresponding activation function, $\bar{u}_i = [1 \ u_i^T \ d_i^T] \in \Re^{2m+1}$, is the augmented MAS control inputs, and $\varepsilon_{I,i} = \varepsilon_{F,i} + \varepsilon_{G,i}u_i + \varepsilon_{H,i}d_i, \forall i = 1, \ldots, N$ represents the reconstruction errors.

Moreover, the multi-agent zero-sum game system states can be estimated as

$$\dot{\hat{x}}_i = \hat{W}_{I,i}^T(t)\vartheta_{I,i}(x_i)\bar{u}_i + K_i\tilde{x}_i, \quad \forall i = 1, 2, \ldots, N \quad (13)$$

with $\hat{W}_{I,i}(t) \in \Re^{(l_F + l_G) \times 2m}, \forall i = 1, 2, \ldots, N$ as the approximated weights of the NN-based identifier, $\tilde{x}_i = x_i - \hat{x}_i \in \Re^m, \forall i = 1, \ldots, N$ represents the MAS system state estimation error, and $K_i$, $\forall i = 1, 2, \ldots, N$ is a selected identification gain for ensuring the stability of the proposed NN-based identifier.

According to Eqs. (12) and (13), the MAS state estimation error dynamics can be represented as

$$\dot{\tilde{x}}_i = \dot{x}_i - \dot{\hat{x}}_i = \tilde{W}_{I,i}^T(t) \vartheta_{I,i}(x_i) \bar{u}_i + \varepsilon_{I,i} - K_i \tilde{x}_i, \quad \forall i = 1, \ldots, N \qquad (14)$$

where $\tilde{W}_{I,i}(t) = W_{I,i} - \hat{W}_{I,i}(t)$, $\forall i = 1, \ldots, N$ denotes the NN-based identifier weight approximation error. To force the approximated weight of NN-based identifier converge close to targets, the novel update law for $\hat{W}_{I,i}(t)$, $\forall i = 1, 2, \ldots, N$ can be represented as

$$\dot{\hat{W}}_{I,i}(t) = -\alpha_{I,i} \hat{W}_{I,i}(t) + \vartheta_{I,i}(x_i) \bar{u}_i \tilde{x}_i, \quad \forall i = 1, 2, \ldots, N \qquad (15)$$

with $\alpha_{I,i}$ as tuning parameter of NN-based identifier satisfying $\alpha_{I,i} > 0, \forall i = 1, 2, \ldots, N$.

## 4.2    ADP-Based Cost Function Approximation

Using the universal approximation property of NN [11], the optimal cost function of multi-agent zero-sum game, $J_i^*(x_i)$, can be described by using a NN on a compact set $\Omega$ in the form of [11] as

$$J_i^*(x) = W_{J,i}^T \phi_{J,i}(x_i, x_{-i}) + \varepsilon_{J,i}(x_i, x_{-i}), \quad \forall i = 1, 2, \ldots, N \qquad (16)$$

Where $W_{J,i} \in \Re^L$, $\forall i = 1, 2, \ldots, N$ denotes the NN constant target weights with $L$ being the number of hidden-layer neurons, $\phi_{J,i}(x_i, x_{-i}) \in \Re^L$, $\forall i = 1, 2, \ldots, N$ represents the NN activation function with $x_i$ as the system state of $i^{th}$ agent, $x_{-i} = \{x_j\}_{j \in N_i}$ is the system state from the neighbors of $i^{th}$ agent, and $\varepsilon_{J,i}(x_i, x_{-i}) \in \Re$ denotes the NN reconstruction error. Then, substituting (16) into the HJI equation of each agent, we have

$$0 = HJI_i(x_i, u_i^*) = \bar{Q}_{1,i}(x_i) + \bar{Q}_{2,i}(x_i, x_{-i}) - \frac{1}{4} W_{J,i}^T \frac{\partial \phi_{J,i}(x_i, x_{-i})}{\partial x_i(t)} D_i(x_i) \frac{\partial \phi_{J,i}^T(x_i, x_{-i})}{\partial x_i(t)} W_{J,i}$$
$$+ \frac{1}{4} W_{J,i}^T \frac{\partial \phi_{J,i}(x_i, x_{-i})}{\partial x_i(t)} L_i(x_i) \frac{\partial \phi_{J,i}^T(x_i, x_{-i})}{\partial x_i(t)} W_{J,i} + W_{J,i}^T \frac{\partial \phi_{J,i}(x_i, x_{-i})}{\partial x_i(t)} F_i(x_i) + \varepsilon_{HJB,i}(x_i, x_{-i}), \quad \forall i = 1, \ldots, N \qquad (17)$$

with the two positive quadratic terms, $\bar{Q}_{1,i}(x_i)$, $\bar{Q}_{2,i}(x_i, x_{-i})$, defined in Eq. (9), $D_i(x_i) = G_i(x_i) R_{u,i}^{-1} G_i^T(x_i)$, $D_i(x_i) = H_i(x_i) Q_{DS,i}^{-1} H_i^T(x_i)$ and $\varepsilon_{HJB,i}(x_i, x_{-i})$, defined as

$$\varepsilon_{HJI,i}(x_i, x_{-i}) = -\frac{1}{2} W_{J,i}^T \phi_i(x_i, x_{-i}) D_i(x_i) \frac{\partial \varepsilon_i^T(x_i, x_{-i})}{\partial x_i} + \frac{1}{4} \frac{\partial \varepsilon_i(x_i, x_{-i})}{\partial x_i} D_i(x_i) \frac{\partial \varepsilon_i^T(x_i, x_{-i})}{\partial x_i} + \frac{\partial \varepsilon_i^T(x_i, x_{-i})}{\partial x_l} F_i(x_i) \qquad (18)$$

Next, the optimal cost function (17) is considered to be approximated as

$$\hat{J}_i(x) = \hat{W}_{J,i}^T(t)\phi_{J,i}(x_i, x_{-i}), \quad \forall i = 1, 2, \ldots, N \tag{19}$$

with $\hat{W}_{J,i}(t) \in \Re^L$ denoting the estimated NN weights.

Subsequently, we substitute the estimated optimal cost function of the multi-agent zero-sum game (19) into the HJI Eq. (9). The HJI equation cannot be held due to the inaccuracy of the multi-agent zero-sum game optimal cost function approximation. To quantify the inaccuracy, a residual error is defined as

$$e_{HJI,i} = \bar{Q}_{1,i}(x_i) + \bar{Q}_{2,i}(x_i, x_{-i}) + \hat{W}_{J,i}^T \frac{\partial \phi_i(x_i, x_{-i})}{\partial x_i(t)} F_i(x_i)$$

$$+ \frac{1}{4}\hat{W}_{J,i}^T \frac{\partial \phi(x_i, x_{-i})}{\partial x_i(t)} \hat{L}_i(x_i) \frac{\partial \phi_i^T(x_i, x_{-i})}{\partial x_i(t)} \hat{W}_{J,i} - \frac{1}{4}\hat{W}_{J,i}^T \frac{\partial \phi(x_i, x_{-i})}{\partial x_i(t)} \hat{D}_i(x_i) \frac{\partial \phi_i^T(x_i, x_{-i})}{\partial x_i(t)} \hat{W}_{J,i}$$

$$\tag{20}$$

where $\hat{D}_i(x_i) = \hat{G}_i(x_i)R_{u,i}^{-1}\hat{G}_i^T(x_i)$, $\hat{L}_i(x_i) = \hat{H}_i(x_i)Q_{DS,i}^{-1}\hat{H}_i^T(x_i)$ with $\hat{G}_i(x_i), \hat{H}_i(x_i)$ denotes the estimated MAS system dynamics from the identifier.

Using the normalized gradient descent algorithm and residual error (20), a novel NN update law is proposed as

$$\dot{\hat{W}}_{J,i}(t) = -\alpha_{J1,i} \frac{\hat{\omega}_i(x_i, x_{-i})e_{HJI,i}}{1 + \hat{\omega}_i^T(x_i, x_{-i})\hat{\omega}_i(x_i, x_{-i})} + \frac{\alpha_{J2,i}\hat{D}_i x_i \partial \phi_{J,i}(x_i, x_{-i})}{2\partial x_i}$$

$$- \frac{\alpha_{J2,i}\hat{L}_i x_i \partial \phi_{J,i}(x_i, x_{-i})}{2\partial x_i}, \tag{21}$$

with $\hat{\omega}_i(x_i, x_{-i}) = \frac{\partial \phi_i(x_i, x_{-i})}{\partial x_i}\left[\hat{F}_i(x_i) - \frac{1}{2}\hat{D}_i(x_i)\frac{\partial \phi_i^T(x_i, x_{-i})}{\partial x_i}\hat{W}_{J,i} + \frac{1}{2}\hat{L}_i(x_i)\frac{\partial \phi_i^T(x_i, x_{-i})}{\partial x_i}\hat{W}_{J,i}\right]$ and $\alpha_{J1,i} > 0, \alpha_{J2,i} > 0, \forall i = 1, \ldots, N$ is the NN tuning parameter.

### 4.3   ADP-Based Distributed Adaptive Optimal Flocking Control for Multi-agent Zero-Sum Game

According to the ideal optimal flocking strategies derived in (10) which is obtained by minimizing the optimal cost function defined in (9), the distributed adaptive optimal flocking strategies can be expressed as

$$u_i^*(t) = -\frac{1}{2}R_{u,i}^{-1}G_i^T(x_i)\frac{\partial \phi_i^T(x_i, x_{-i})}{\partial x_i}W_{J,i} - \frac{1}{2}R_{u,i}^{-1}G_i^T(x_i)\frac{\partial \varepsilon_i^T(x_i, x_{-i})}{\partial x_i} \quad \forall i = 1, 2, \ldots, N$$

$$d_i^*(t) = \frac{1}{2}Q_{DS,i}^{-1}H_i^T(x_i)\frac{\partial \phi_i^T(x_i, x_{-i})}{\partial x_i}W_{J,i} + \frac{1}{2}R_{u,i}^{-1}H_i^T(x_i)\frac{\partial \varepsilon_i^T(x_i, x_{-i})}{\partial x_i}$$

$$\tag{22}$$

Using the approximated optimal cost function (19) and the identified multi-agent zero-sum game system dynamics, the distributed adaptive optimal strategies can be estimated for $i = 1, 2, \ldots, N$ as

$$\hat{u}_i(t) = -\frac{1}{2}R_{u,i}^{-1}\hat{G}_i^T(x_i)\frac{\partial \phi_i^T(x_i, x_{-i})}{\partial x_i}\hat{W}_{J,i}, \; \hat{d}_i(t) = -\frac{1}{2}Q_{DS,i}^{-1}\hat{H}_i^T(x_i)\frac{\partial \phi_i^T(x_i, x_{-i})}{\partial x_i}\hat{W}_{J,i}, \quad (23)$$

## 5 Simulation Results

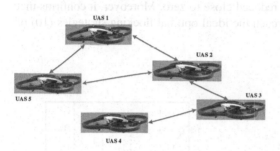

**Fig. 2.** The graph topology of five UAS

Among diverse real-time applications, a nonlinear multiple unmanned aircraft systems (multi-UAS) scenario is a good multi-agent zero-sum game example to study. The dynamics of the multi-UAS are given similar to [2]. Further, assuming that all the UAS are operated in the same height [3], then the position of each UAS can be represented in a two-dimensional space. The initial positions of UAS are generated randomly in a 100 m ×
100 m region by using the norm distribution function. Moreover, the velocities for multi-UAS are initialized as zeroes.

The simulation considers five UAS with the graph topology given as in Fig. 2. The flocking cost function weighting matrices are selected as $q_{CA,ij} = 0.5$, $q_{VM,ij} = 1$, $\forall i, j = 1, \ldots, N$, and $Q_{FC,i} = 1.5 * I^{3\times3}$, $R_{u,i} = 0.5$, $Q_{DS,i} = 1.5$, $\forall i = 1, \ldots, N$. The activation function of the NN-based identifier and involved flocking cost function approximation NN is generated as a polynomial function [9] in the form of $[x_{i,1}^2, x_{i,1}x_{i,2},$ $x_{i,1}x_{i,3}, .., x_{i,3}^2, \ldots, x_{i,1}^6, x_{i,1}^5x_{i,2}, x_{i,1}^5, x_{i,3}, .., x_{i,3}^6]^T$. Moreover, the initial NN-based identifier weights are selected randomly within $[-2, 3]$, the flocking cost function approximation NN initial weights are set to zeroes, and the tuning parameter is designed as $\alpha_{I,i} = 0.5, \alpha_{J1,i} = 0.1, \alpha_{J2,i} = 0.001$, $K_{I,i} = 3I$ $\forall i = 1, 2, \ldots, N$. Next, the simulation results demonstrate the effectiveness of proposed scheme from two aspects: (1) the flocking behavior, and (2) the optimality.

*__The Flocking Performance:__* Similar to most existing flocking control literatures [2, 3], the flocking behavior of the proposed scheme is evaluated through three aspects (i.e. cohesion, separation and alignment) by observing the trajectory of multi-UAS. For the sake of generality, we initialize the positions of five UAS randomly in a 100 m × 100 m region by using norm distribution function with the mean and variance selected as 5 and 10. As shown in Fig. 3, five UAS can follow the virtual leader (i.e. the red trajectory) successfully, avoid collisions, and achieve the velocity consensus for multi-UAS. This result indicates that the proposed scheme can deliver an acceptable flocking performance for multi-UAS.

***Optimality Evaluation:*** Similar to [9], the estimated flocking cost function and control input cannot hold the multi-agent zero-sum game HJI equation. Hence, the optimality of the proposed scheme can be achieved only while the proper design is forcing the residual error (15) of the multi-agent zero-sum game to converge close to zero. As a critical optimality evaluation parameter, the performance of the residual error needs to be evaluated. Without loss of generality, the average norm of residual error performance for a total of five UAS has been demonstrated in Fig. 4. It indicates that the proposed ADP-based distributed adaptive optimal flocking strategies ensure the entire multi-UAS system residual errors are reduced close to zero. Moreover, it confirms that the approximated control signals approach the ideal optimal flocking strategies (10) of the multi-UAS closely.

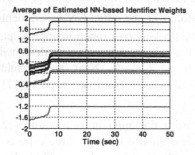

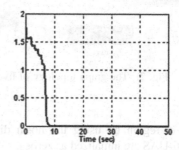

**Fig. 3.** The trajectories of five UAS (Color figure online)

**Fig. 4.** The average norm of residual error

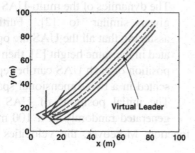

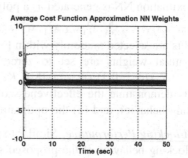

**Fig. 5.** The average estimated NN weights: (a) estimated NN-identifier weights, (b) estimated cost function approximation NN weights

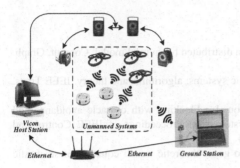

**Fig. 6.** The experiment setup.

Recalling to most existing NN and ADP literatures [8, 9], both the estimated NN-identifier weights and cost function approximation NN weights are needed to converge to the constant targets. Otherwise, the proposed scheme cannot converge to the optimal solution due to the existence of NN estimation error. Therefore, the performance of estimated NN weights for multi-UAS is analyzed. Similar to the residual error evaluation, the average estimated NN weights for all five UAS are shown in Fig. 5(a) and (b). It can be observed that both average estimated NN-identifier weights and multi-UAS cost function approximation NN weights converge consistent to constant target. According to the simulation results presented from Figs. 3, 4 and 5, the proposed design is not only maintaining the stability of multi-UAS, but also achieving the ideal optimal flocking performance closely.

Moreover, the effectiveness of proposed scheme is also demonstrated through a practical experiment in Unmanned System Laboratory at University of Nevada, Reno (UNR). The experiment setup is shown in Fig. 6. Proposed scheme can maintain the multi-agent (including unmanned ground vehicle and unmanned aircraft systems) flocking performance even in presence of uncertain system dynamics and unknown disturbances.

## 6 Conclusion

A novel ADP-based distributed adaptive optimal flocking strategy for multi-agent zero-sum games in presence of completely unknown system dynamics is proposed. First, to obtain the optimal flocking design, a novel optimal flocking cost function is developed for multi-agent zero-sum games. Subsequently, a novel NN-based identifier is proposed to relax the requirement of multi-agent zero-sum games dynamics. Then, using an ADP technique, another NN is proposed to approximate the multi-agent zero-sum game optimal flocking cost function closely. The proposed novel update law can relax the requirement of an initial stabilizing controller due to an extra term. Eventually, using the identified multi-agent zero-sum game dynamics, the distributed adaptive optimal flocking strategies are attained by utilizing the estimated optimal flocking cost function. The proposed design yields a set of forward-in-time and online control inputs which can harvest more advantages from practical applications. Simulation results verify the theoretical solution.

# References

1. Reynolds, C.W.: Flocks, herds, and schools: a distributed behavioral model. Comput. Graph. **21**, 25–34 (1986)
2. Saber, R.O.: Flocking for multi-agent dynamic systems: algorithms and theory. IEEE Trans. Autom. Control **51**, 401–420 (2006)
3. Wang, Q., Fang, H., Chen, J., Mao, Y., Dou, L.: Flocking with obstacle avoidance and connectivity maintenance in multi-agent systems. In: Proceedings of IEEE Control and Decision Conference, pp. 4009–4014 (2012)
4. Dragan, V., Morozan, R.: Global solution to game-theoretic riccati equation of stochastic control. J. Diff. Equ. **138**, 328–350 (1997)
5. Wang, J., Xin, M.: Integrated optimal formation control of multiple unmanned aerial vehicles. IEEE Trans. Control Syst. Tech. **21**, 1731–1744 (2013)
6. Lewis, F.L., Vrabie, D., Syrmos, V.L.: Optimal Control, 3rd edn. Wiley, New York (2012)
7. Bertsekas, D.P., Tsitsiklis, J.: Neuro-Dynamic Programming. Athena Scientific, CA (1996)
8. Al-Tamimi, A., Lewis, F.L., Abu-Khalaf, M.: Model-free Q-learning designs for linear discrete-time zero-sum games with application to H-infinity control. Automatica **3**, 471–481 (2007)
9. Dierks, T., Jagannathan, S.: Online optimal control of affine nonlinear discrete-time systems with unknown internal dynamics by using time-based policy update. IEEE Trans. Neural Netw. Learn. Syst. **23**, 1118–1129 (2012)
10. Diestel, R.: Graph Theory. Graduate Texts in Mathematics, vol. 184. Springer, Heidelberg (2000)
11. Jagannathan, S.: Neural Network Control of Nonlinear Discrete-Time Systems. CRC Press, FL (2006)

# Medical Imaging

# MinMax Radon Barcodes
# for Medical Image Retrieval

H.R. Tizhoosh[1](✉), Shujin Zhu[2], Hanson Lo[3], Varun Chaudhari[4],
and Tahmid Mehdi[5]

[1] KIMIA Lab, University of Waterloo, Waterloo, Canada
tizhoosh@uwaterloo.ca
[2] School of Electronic and Optical Engineering,
Nanjing University of Science and Technology, Nanjing, Jiangsu, China
[3] Cheriton School of Computer Science, University of Waterloo, Waterloo, Canada
[4] Department of Mathematics, University of Waterloo, Waterloo, Canada
[5] Centre for Computational Mathematics in Industry and Commerce,
University of Waterloo, Waterloo, Canada

**Abstract.** Content-based medical image retrieval can support diagnostic decisions by clinical experts. Examining similar images may provide clues to the expert to remove uncertainties in his/her final diagnosis. Beyond conventional feature descriptors, binary features in different ways have been recently proposed to encode the image content. A recent proposal is "Radon barcodes" that employ binarized Radon projections to tag/annotate medical images with content-based binary vectors, called barcodes. In this paper, MinMax Radon barcodes are introduced which are superior to "local thresholding" scheme suggested in the literature. Using IRMA dataset with 14,410 x-ray images from 193 different classes, the advantage of using MinMax Radon barcodes over *thresholded* Radon barcodes are demonstrated. The retrieval error for direct search drops by more than 15%. As well, SURF, as a well-established non-binary approach, and BRISK, as a recent binary method are examined to compare their results with MinMax Radon barcodes when retrieving images from IRMA dataset. The results demonstrate that MinMax Radon barcodes are faster and more accurate when applied on IRMA images.

## 1 Introduction

Searching for similar images in archives with millions of digital images is a difficult task that may be useful in many application domains. We usually search for images via "text" (or meta-data). In such cases, which appear to be the dominant mode of image retrieval in practice, all images have been tagged or annotated with some textual descriptions. Hence, the user can provide his/her own search terms such as "birds", "red car", or "tall building campus" to find images attached to these keywords. Of course, text-based image search has a very limited scope. We cannot annotate all images with proper keywords that fully describe the image content. This is sometimes due to the sheer amount

© Springer International Publishing AG 2016
G. Bebis et al. (Eds.): ISVC 2016, Part I, LNCS 10072, pp. 617–627, 2016.
DOI: 10.1007/978-3-319-50835-1_55

of manpower required to annotate a large number of images. But, more importantly, most of the time it is simply not possible to describe the content of the image with words such that there is enough discrimination between images of different categories. For example, search for a "breast ultrasound tumor" may be relatively easy even with existing text-based technologies. However, looking for a "lesion which is taller than wide and is highly spiculated" may prove to be very challenging. Apparently, domains such as medical image analysis are not profiting much from the text-based image search.

Content-based image retrieval (CBIR) has been an active research field for more than two decades. CBIR algorithms are primarily trimmed toward describing the content of the image with non-textual attributes, for instance with some type of features. If we manage to extract good features from the image, then image search becomes a classification and matching problem that works based on visual clues and not based on the text. Under *good* features we usually understand such attributes that are invariant to scale, translation, rotation, and maybe even some types of deformation. In other words, features are good if they can uniquely characterize each image category with respect to their what they contain (shape, colors, edges, textures, segments etc.).

The literature on feature extraction is rich and vast. Methods like SIFT and SURF have been successfully applied to many problems. In more recent literature, we observe a shift from traditional feature descriptors to *binary* descriptors. This shift has been mainly motivated by the tremendous increase in the size of image archives we are dealing with. Binary descriptors are compact with inherent efficiency for searching, properties that lend themselves nicely to deal with big image data.

In this paper, we focus on one of the recently introduced binary descriptors, namely Radon barcodes (Sect. 2). We introduce a new encoding scheme for Radon barcodes to binarize the projections (Sect. 4). We employ the IRMA dataset with 14,410 x-ray images with 193 classes to validate the performance of the proposed approach (Sect. 5). In order to complete the experimentations, two other established methods, namely SURF and BRISK, are for the first time tested on IRMA dataset as well to draw some more general conclusions with respect to the performance of the proposed MinMax Radon barcodes.

## 2   Background

The literature on CBIR in general, and on medical CBIR, in particular, is quite vast. Ghosh et al. [1] review online solutions for content-based medical image retrieval such as GoldMiner, FigureSearch, BioText, Yottalook, IRMA, Yale Image Finder and iMedline. Multiple surveys are available that review recent literature [2,3]. To recent approaches that have used IRMA dataset (see Sect. 5.1) belong autoencoders for image area reduction [4] and local binary patterns (LBPs) [5–7].

Although binary images (or embeddings) have been used to facilitate image retrieval in different ways [8–11], it seems that binarizing Radon projections to use them directly for CBIR tasks is a rather recent idea [12]. Capturing a 3D object is generally the main motivation for Radon transform [13]. There are many applications of Radon transform reported in literature [14–16]. Chen and Chen [17] introduced Radon composite features (RCFs) that transform binary shapes into 1D representations for feature calculation. Tabbone et al. [18] propose a histogram of the Radon transform (HRT) invariant to geometrical transformations. Dara et al. [19] generalized Radon transform to radial and spherical integration to search for 3D models of diverse shapes. Trace transform is also a generalization of Radon transform [20] for invariant features via tracing lines applied on shapes with complex texture on a uniform background for change detection.

SURF (Speeded Up Robust Features) [21] is one of the most commonly used keypoint detectors and feature descriptors for various applications. BRISK (Binary Robust Invariant Scalable Keypoints) [22], in contrast, is one of the recently introduced binary feature descriptors that appears to be one of the robust binary schemes for CBIR [23]. We use both SURF and BRISK in our experiments for comparative purposes. For the first time, we report the accuracy of these methods on IRMA dataset [24,25].

## 3   Radon Barcodes

The idea of Radon barcodes was introduced recently [12,26]. Examining an image $I$ as a 2D function $f(x,y)$, one can project $f(x,y)$ along a number of parallel projection directions $\theta$. A projection is the sum (integral) of $f(x,y)$ values along lines constituted by each angle $\theta$ to create a new image $R(\rho,\theta)$ with $\rho = x\cos\theta + y\sin\theta$. Hence, using the Dirac delta function $\delta(\cdot)$ the Radon transform can be given as

$$R(\rho,\theta) = \int_{-\infty}^{+\infty} \int_{-\infty}^{+\infty} f(x,y)\delta(\rho - x\cos\theta - y\sin\theta)dxdy. \tag{1}$$

If we binarize all projections (lines) for individual directions using a "local" threshold for that angle (as proposed in [12]), then we can assemble a barcode of all binarized projections as depicted in Fig. 1. A straightforward method to binarize the projections is to set a representative (or typical) value. This can be done by calculating the median value of all non-zero projection values as initially proposed in [12].

Algorithm 1 describes the generation of **Radon barcodes (RBC)**[1]. In order to receive same-length barcodes $Normalize(I)$ resizes all images into $R_N \times C_N$ images (i.e. $R_N = C_N = 2^n, n \in \mathbb{N}^+$).

## 4   MinMax Radon Barcodes

The thresholding method introduced in [12] to binarize Radon projections is quite simple, hence, it may lose a lot of information that could contribute to

---

[1] Matlab code taken from http://tizhoosh.uwaterloo.ca/.

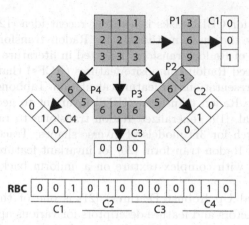

**RBC** | 0 | 0 | 1 | 0 | 1 | 0 | 0 | 0 | 0 | 0 | 1 | 0 |

C1    C2    C3    C4

**Fig. 1.** Radon barcode (RBC) according to [12] – Parallel projections (here P1 to P4) are binarized to create code fragments C1 to C4. Putting all code fragments together delivers the barcode **RBC**.

---

**Algorithm 1.** Radon Barcode (RBC) Generation [12]

---

1: Initialize Radon Barcode $\mathbf{r} \leftarrow \emptyset$
2: Initialize: angle $\theta \leftarrow 0$, $\theta_{\max} = 180$, and image size $R_N = C_N \leftarrow 32$
3: $\bar{I} = \text{Normalize}(I, R_N, C_N)$
4: Set the number of projection angles, e.g. $n_p \leftarrow 8$
5: **while** $\theta < \theta_{\max}$ **do**
6:     Get all projections $\mathbf{p}$ for $\theta$
7:     Find typical value $T_{\text{typical}} \leftarrow \text{median}_i(\mathbf{p}_i)|_{\mathbf{p}_i \neq 0}$
8:     Binarize projections: $\mathbf{b} \leftarrow \mathbf{p} \geq T_{\text{typical}}$
9:     Append the new row $\mathbf{r} \leftarrow \text{append}(\mathbf{r}, \mathbf{b})$
10:    $\theta \leftarrow \theta + \frac{\theta_{\max}}{n_p}$
11: **end while**
12: Return $\mathbf{r}$

---

the uniqueness of the barcode. For instance, employing a local threshold will not capture the general curvature of the projections. In contrast, if we examine how the projection values transit between local extrema, this may provide more expressive clues for capturing the shape characteristics of the scene/image depicted in that specific angle.

Algorithm 2 provides the general steps for generating MinMax Radon barcodes. The smoothing function (Algorithm 2, line 7) just applies a moving average to remove small peaks/valleys. We then can detect all peaks (maximums) and valleys (minimums) (Algorithm 2, line 8). Subsequently, we locate all values that are on the way to transit from min/max to max/min, respectively (Algorithm 2, lines 9–10). The projection can then be encoded by assigning corresponding values of zeros or ones (Algorithm 2, lines 11–13). These are the main differences to the Radon barcode (Algorithm 1).

---

**Algorithm 2.** MinMax Radon Barcodes

---
1: Initialize Radon Barcode $\mathbf{r} \leftarrow \emptyset$
2: Initialize: angle $\theta \leftarrow 0$, $\theta_{\max} = 180$, and image size $R_N = C_N \leftarrow 32$
3: $\bar{I} = \text{Normalize}(I, R_N, C_N)$
4: Set the number of projection angles, e.g., $n_p \leftarrow 8$
5: **while** $\theta < \theta_{\max}$ **do**
6:     Get all projections $\mathbf{p}$ for $\theta$
7:     Smooth $\mathbf{p}$: $\bar{\mathbf{p}} \leftarrow \text{Smooth}(\mathbf{p})$
8:     Find all minimums and maximums of $\bar{\mathbf{p}}$
9:     $b_{\min} \leftarrow$ Find all $\bar{\mathbf{p}}$ bins that are in a min-max interval
10:    $b_{\max} \leftarrow$ Find all $\bar{\mathbf{p}}$ bins that are in a max-min interval
11:    $\mathbf{b} \leftarrow \bar{\mathbf{p}}$
12:    Set bits: $\mathbf{b}(b_{\min}) \leftarrow 0$; $\mathbf{b}(b_{\max}) \leftarrow 1$
13:    Append the new row $\mathbf{r} \leftarrow \text{append}(\mathbf{r}, \mathbf{b})$
14:    $\theta \leftarrow \theta + \frac{\theta_{\max}}{n_p}$
15: **end while**
16: Return $\mathbf{r}$

---

Figure 2 illustrates how MinMax Radon barcodes are generated for a given angle $\theta$. The order of assignments for zeros/ones for transitions from min/max to max/min, of course, is just a convention and hence must be maintained consistently within a given application.

Figure 3 shows barcodes for three images from IRMA dataset. For each image, both barcodes are provided to examine the visual difference between Radon barcodes using local thresholding and MinMax Radon barcodes as introduced in this paper. The former appears to be a coarse encoding as the latter shows finer bit distribution.

## 5  Experiments

In this section, we first describe the IRMA dataset, the benchmark data we used. The error calculation is reviewed next. Subsequently, we report two series of experiments to validate the performance of the proposed MinMax Radon barcodes for medical image retrieval. The first series of experiments compares MinMax barcodes against the recently introduced Radon barcodes using local thresholding using $k$-NN search. The second series of experiments compare Min-Max barcodes against SURF and BRISK when hashing is used for matching.

### 5.1  Image Test Data

The Image Retrieval in Medical Applications (IRMA) database[2] is a collection of more than 14,000 x-ray images (radiographs) randomly collected from daily routine work at the Department of Diagnostic Radiology of the RWTH Aachen

---

[2] http://irma-project.org/.

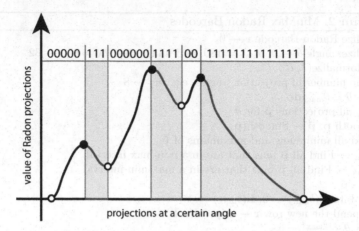

**Fig. 2.** MinMax Radon Barcodes. Projections at a certain angle are smoothed to find minimums and maximums. All bins between a minimum and a maximum are assigned 0, whereas all bins between a maximum and a minimum are assigned 1.

University[3] [24,25]. All images are classified into 193 categories (classes) and annotated with the "IRMA code" which relies on class-subclass relations to avoid ambiguities in textual classification [25,27]. The IRMA code consists of four mono-hierarchical axes with three to four digits each: the technical code T (imaging modality), the directional code D (body orientations), the anatomical code A (the body region), and the biological code B (the biological system examined). The complete IRMA code subsequently exhibits a string of 13 characters, each in $\{0, \ldots, 9; a, \ldots, z\}$:

$$TTTT\text{-}DDD\text{-}AAA\text{-}BBB. \tag{2}$$

Details of the IRMA database is described in literature [24,25,27]. IRMA dataset offers 12,677 images for training and 1,733 images for testing. Figure 4 shows some sample images from the dataset long with their IRMA code in the format TTTT-DDD-AAA-BBB.

## 5.2 Error Calculation

We used the formula provided by *ImageCLEFmed09* to compute the error between the IRMA codes of the testing images (1,733 images) and the first hit retrieved from all indexed images (12,677 images) in order to evaluate the performance of the retrieval process. We then summed up the error for all testing images. The formula is provided as follows:

$$E_{Total} = \sum_{m=1}^{1733} \sum_{j=1}^{4} \sum_{i=1}^{l_j} \frac{1}{b_{l_j,i}} \frac{1}{i} \delta(I_{l_j,i}^m, \tilde{I}_{l_j,i}^m) \tag{3}$$

---

[3] http://www.rad.rwth-aachen.de/.

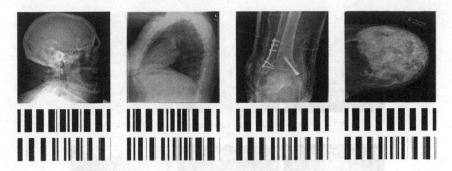

**Fig. 3.** Local Radon barcodes (top barcodes) and MinMax Radon barcodes (bottom barcodes) for four sample images from IRMA dataset. Images were resized to $64 \times 64$ and projected at 8 angles.

Here, $m$ is an indicator to each image, $j$ is an indicator to the structure of an IRMA code, and $l_j$ refers to the number of characters in each structure of an IRMA code. For example, consider the IRMA code: 1121-4a0-914-700, $l_1 = 4$, $l_2 = 3$, $l_3 = 3$ and $l_4 = 3$. Here, $i$ is an indicator to a character in a particular structure. Here, $l_{2,2}$ refers to the character "a" and $l_{4,1}$ refers to the character "7". $b_{l_j,i}$ refers to the number of branches, i.e. number of possible characters, at the position $i$ in the $l_j^{th}$ structure in an IRMA code. $I^m$ refers to the $m^{th}$ testing image and $\tilde{I}^m$ refers to its top 1 retrieved image. $\delta(I^m_{l_j,i}, \tilde{I}^m_{l_j,i})$ compares a particular position in the IRMA code of the testing image and the retrieved image. It then outputs a value in $\{0, 1\}$ according to the following rules:

$$\delta(I^m_{l_j,i}, \tilde{I}^m_{l_j,i}) = \begin{cases} 0, & I^m_{l_j,h} = \tilde{I}^m_{l_j,h} \forall h \leq i \\ 1, & I^m_{l_j,h} \neq \tilde{I}^m_{l_j,h} \exists h \leq i \end{cases} \tag{4}$$

We used the Python implementation of the above formula provided by Image-CLEFmed09 to compute the errors[4].

### 5.3   Results

We report two series of experiments in this section: First we compare the proposed MinMax Radon barcodes with the local thresholding barcodes to validate their retrieval performance. Second, we compare MinMax Radon barcodes with SURF (with non-binary features) and BRISK (with binary features). All experiments were conducted using IRMA x-ray images.

### 5.4   MinMax Versus Thresholding

We applied both types of Radon barcodes on IRMA dataset. We first used 12,677 images and indexed them with both types of barcodes. Then, we used 1,733

---

[4] http://www.imageclef.org/.

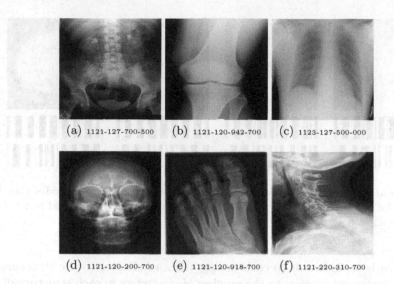

(a) 1121-127-700-500     (b) 1121-120-942-700     (c) 1123-127-500-000

(d) 1121-120-200-700     (e) 1121-120-918-700     (f) 1121-220-310-700

**Fig. 4.** Sample x-ray images with their IRMA codes TTTT-DDD-AAA-BBB.

remaining images to measure the retrieval error of each barcode type according to IRMA code error calculation (see Sect. 5.2). To measure the similarity between two given barcodes we used Hamming distance. For conducting the actual search, we used $k$-NN with $k = 1$ (no pre-classification was used). Table 1 shows the results. The retrieval error clearly drops when we use MinMax barcodes. The reduction for 8 or 16 projection angles is around 15%.

**Table 1.** Comparing MinMax barcodes with thresholding barcodes as described in [12]. Images were normalized into $32 \times 32$. Projections angles were equi-distance in $[0°, 180°)$. A total of 12,677 images were indexed. Retrievals were run for 1,733 unseen images.

|                        | 8 angles | 16 angles |
|------------------------|----------|-----------|
| Thresholding Barcodes  | 605.83   | 576.45    |
| MinMax Barcodes        | 509.24   | 489.35    |
| Error reduction        | 15.94%   | 15.11%    |

## 5.5  Barcodes Versus SURF and BRISK

In this series of experiments, we also examined SURF (as a non-binary method) and BRISK (as a binary method). To our knowledge, this is the first time that these methods are being applied on IRMA images. Using $k$-NN as before was not an option because initial experiments took considerable time as SURF and BRISK appear to be slower than barcodes. Hence, we used locality-sensitive

**Table 2.** Comparing MinMax barcodes with SURF and BRISK. Images were normalized into 32 × 32 (12,677 indexed images and 1,733 test images). LSH was used for the actual search to deliver 10 matches. The top hit was found via correlation measurement with the query image.

| Method | Total error | Failure | $\bar{t}$ (s) |
|---|---|---|---|
| SURF | 526.05 | 4.56% | 6.345 |
| BRISK | 761.96 | 1.095% | 6.805 |
| MinMax RBC | 415.75 | 0.00% | 0.537 |

hashing (LSH) [28] to hash the features/codes into patches of the search space that may contain similar images[5]. We made several tests in order to find a good configuration for each method. As well, the configuration of LSH (number of tables and key size for encoding) was subject to some trial and errors. We set the number of tables for LSH to 30 (with comparable results for 40) and the key size to a third of the feature vectors' length. We selected the top 10 results of LSH and chose the top hit based on highest correlation with the input image for each method. The results are reported in Table 2.

As apparent from the results, not only do SURF and BRISK deliver higher error rates than MinMax barcodes, but also for many cases, they fail to provide any features at all. Hence, we measured their error only for the cases they successfully located key points and extracted features. For failed cases we just incremented the number of failures.

# 6    Summary and Conclusions

In this paper, we improved Radon barcodes by introducing a new encoding scheme called MinMax Radon barcodes. Instead of local thresholding we encode the projection values for each angle of Radon transform by examining the extreme values of the projection curvature. We employed IRMA dataset with 14,410 x-ray images to validate the proposed MinMax Radon barcodes. The results confirm 15% reduction in retrieval error for IRMA images.

We also compared the proposed MinMax Radon barcodes with SURF and BRISK. Using locality-sensitive hashing (LSH), we applied SURF and BRISK, for the first time, on IRMA images. We found that MinMax Radon barcodes are both more accurate (lower error), more reliable (no failure) and faster (shorter average time $\bar{t}$) compared with SURF and BRISK for this dataset.

Radon barcodes seem to have a great potential for medical image retrieval. One question that needs to be answered is which projection angles may provide more discrimination in order to make Radon barcodes even more accurate. Other schemes for encoding Radon projections may need to be investigated as well.

---

[5] Matlab code: http://goo.gl/vFYvVJ.

# References

1. Ghosh, P., Antani, S., Long, L., Thoma, G.: Review of medical image retrieval systems and future directions. In: International Symposium on Computer-Based Medical Systems (CBMS), pp. 1–6 (2011)
2. Rajam, F., Valli, S.: A survey on content based image retrieval. Life Sci. J. **10**(2), 2475–2487 (2013)
3. Dharani, T., Aroquiaraj, I.: A survey on content based image retrieval. In: 2013 International Conference on Pattern Recognition, Informatics and Mobile Engineering (PRIME), pp. 485–490 (2013)
4. Camlica, Z., Tizhoosh, H., Khalvati, F.: Autoencoding the retrieval relevance of medical images. In: The Fifth International Conference on Image Processing Theory, Tools and Applications (IPTA) (2015)
5. Ojala, T., Pietikainen, M., Maenpaa, T.: Multiresolution gray-scale and rotation invariant texture classification with local binary patterns. IEEE Trans. Pattern Anal. Mach. Intell. **24**(7), 971–987 (2002)
6. Ahonen, T., Hadid, A., Pietikainen, M.: Face description with local binary patterns: application to face recognition. IEEE Trans. Pattern Anal. Mach. Intell. **28**(12), 2037–2041 (2006)
7. Camlica, Z., Tizhoosh, H., Khalvati, F.: Medical image classification via svm using LBP features from saliency-based folded data. In: The 14th International Conference on Machine Learning and Applications (ICMLA) (2015)
8. Tizhoosh, H.R., Khalvati, F.: Computer system and method for atlas-based consensual and consistent contouring of medical images, US Patent App. 14/344,946(2012)
9. Tizhoosh, H.R., Khalvati, F.: Method and system for binary and quasi-binary atlas-based auto-contouring of volume sets in medical images, US Patent App. 14/110,529 (2012)
10. Daugman, J.: How iris recognition works. IEEE Trans. Circuits Syst. Video Technol. **14**(1), 21–30 (2004)
11. Arvacheh, E., Tizhoosh, H.: Iris segmentation: detecting pupil, limbus and eyelids. In: IEEE International Conference on Image Processing, pp. 2453–2456 (2006)
12. Tizhoosh, H.: Barcode annotations for medical image retrieval: a preliminary investigation. In: 2015 IEEE International Conference on Image Processing (ICIP), pp. 818–822 (2015)
13. Radon, J.: Über die bestimmung von funktionen durch ihre integralwerte längs gewisser mannigfaltigkeiten. Ber. über Verh. Königlich-Sächsischen Akad. Wiss. Leipzig **69**, 262–277 (1917)
14. Zhao, W., Zhou, G., Yue, T., Yang, B., Tao, X., Huang, J., Yang, C.: Retrieval of ocean wavelength and wave direction from SAR image based on radon transform. In: IEEE International Geoscience and Remote Sensing Symposium, pp. 1513–1516 (2013)
15. Hoang, T.V., Tabbone, S.: Invariant pattern recognition using the RFM descriptor. Pattern Recogn. **45**, 271–284 (2012)
16. Jadhav, D., Holambe, R.: Feature extraction using radon and wavelet transforms with application to face recognition. Neurocomputing **72**, 1951–1959 (2009)
17. Chen, Y., Chen, Y.: Invariant description and retrieval of planar shapes using radon composite features. IEEE Trans. Signal Process. **56**(10), 4762–4771 (2008)
18. Tabbone, S., Terrades, O., Barrat, S.: Histogram of radon transform. A useful descriptor for shape retrieval. In: 19th International Conference on Pattern Recognition, ICPR 2008, pp. 1–4 (2008)

19. Daras, P., Zarpalas, D., Tzovaras, D., Strintzis, M.: Efficient 3-d model search and retrieval using generalized 3-d radon transforms. IEEE Trans. Multimedia **8**(1), 101–114 (2006)
20. Kadyrov, A., Petrou, M.: The trace transform and its applications. IEEE Trans. Pattern Anal. Mach. Intell. **23**, 811–828 (2001)
21. Bay, H., Ess, A., Tuytelaars, T., Van Gool, L.: Speeded-up robust features (surf). Comput. Vis. Image Underst. **110**, 346–359 (2008)
22. Leutenegger, S., Chli, M., Siegwart, R.: Brisk: binary robust invariant scalable keypoints. In: IEEE International Conference on Computer Vision, pp. 2548–2555 (2011)
23. Choi, S., Han, S.: New binary descriptors based on brisk sampling pattern for image retrieval. In: 2014 International Conference on Information and Communication Technology Convergence (ICTC), pp. 575–576 (2014)
24. Lehmann, T., Deselaers, T., Schubert, H., Guld, M., Thies, C., Fischer, B., Spitzer, K.: The irma code for unique classification of medical images. In: SPIE Proceedings, vol. 5033, pp. 440–451 (2003)
25. Mueller, H., Clough, P., Deselares, T., Caputo, B.: ImageCLEF - Experimental Evaluation in Visual Information Retrieval. Springer, Heidelberg (2010)
26. Tizhoosh, H., Gangeh, M., Tadayyon, H., Czarnota, G.: Tumour ROI estimation in ultrasound images via Radon barcodes in patients with locally advanced breast cancer. In: International Symposium on Biomedical Imaging (2016)
27. Lehmann, T., Deselaers, T., Schubert, H., Guld, M., Thies, C., Fischer, B., Spitzer, K.: Irma - a content-based approach to image retrieval in medical applications. In: IRMA International Conference, vol. 5033, pp. 911–912 (2006)
28. Indyk, P., Motwani, R.: Approximate nearest neighbors: towards removing the curse of dimensionality. In: Proceedings of the Thirtieth Annual ACM Symposium on Theory of Computing, pp. 604–613 (1998)

# Semantic-Based Brain MRI Image Segmentation Using Convolutional Neural Network

Yao Chou[1], Dah Jye Lee[1(✉)], and Dong Zhang[2]

[1] Electrical and Computer Engineering,
Brigham Young University, Provo, UT, USA
djlee@ee.byu.edu
[2] School of Electronics and Information Technology, Sun Yat-sen University,
Guangzhou, Guangdong, China

**Abstract.** Segmenting Magnetic Resonance images plays a critical role in radiotherapy, surgical planning and image-guided interventions. Traditional differential filter-based segmentation algorithms are predefined independently of image features and require extensive post processing. Convolutional Neural Networks (CNNs) are regarded as a powerful visual model that yields hierarchies of features learned from image data, however, its usage is limited in medical imaging field as it requires large-scale data for training. In this paper, we propose a simple binary detection algorithm to bridge CNNs and medical imaging for accurate medical image segmentation. It applies high-capacity CNNs to extract features from image data. When labeled training medical images are scarce, the proposed algorithm splits data into small regions, and labels them to boost training data size automatically. Rather than replaces classic segmentation methods, this paper presents an alternative that is unique and provides more desirable segmentation results....

## 1  Introduction

In computer vision, the goal of segmentation is to simplify and/or change the representation of an image into something that is more meaningful and easier to analyze. Image segmentation is typically used to locate objects and boundaries in image [1]. More precisely, image segmentation is the process of assigning a label to every pixel in an image such that pixels with the same label share certain common characteristics [2]. Many applications require image segmentation, such as content-based image retrieval, machine vision, medical imaging [3], object detection [4], recognition tasks [5], control systems, and video surveillance.

Computer-aided image analysis systems can enhance the diagnostic capabilities of physicians and reduce the time required for accurate diagnosis [6]. As one of the major techniques, medical image segmentation plays a significant role in clinical diagnosis. It is considered challenging because medical images often have low contrast, various types of noise, and missing or diffused boundaries [7]. Research efforts have been devoted to processing and analyzing medical images to segment meaningful information such as volume, shape, and motion

© Springer International Publishing AG 2016
G. Bebis et al. (Eds.): ISVC 2016, Part I, LNCS 10072, pp. 628–638, 2016.
DOI: 10.1007/978-3-319-50835-1_56

of organs, to detect abnormalities, and to quantify changes in follow-up studies [8]. Many image segmentation techniques are available in the literature. Some use only the gray level histogram [1] or spatial details and others use fuzzy set theoretic approaches. Most of these techniques are sensitive to noise, and thus not suitable for medical imaging. The Markov Random Field model is robust to noise, but involves a huge amount of computations [9]. Manual segmentation is an expensive, time consuming task. It is subject to manual variation and subjective judgments, which increases the possibility that different observers will reach different conclusions about the presence or absence of tumors. Even the same observer will occasionally reach different conclusions on different occasions [10]. An efficient and consistent medical image segmentation algorithm would help avoid these confusions.

Deep learning algorithms have shown remarkable results in various image processing fields for most benchmark image datasets including MNIST (classify handwritten digits) [11], CIFAR-10 (classify $32 \times 32$ color images for 10 categories) [12], CIFAR-100 (classify $32 \times 32$ color images for 100 categories) [13], STL-10 (similar to CIFAT-10 but with $96 \times 96$ images)[14], and SVHN (the street view house numbers dataset)[15], etc. Convolutional Neural Networks (CNNs), as a milestone model of deep learning, are driving advances in image analysis. CNNs not only improve the performance of whole-image classification, but also make progress on extracting features. CNNs make a prediction for every pixel and are able to take the advantage of the detailed features of an object image. Krizhevsky et al. made a significant improvement in image classification accuracy on the ImageNet large-scale visual recognition challenge (2012) [16]. Different from traditional image processing methods (e.g. SIFT [17], HOG [18], etc.), which involve a hand-crafted feature descriptor, CNNs are deep architectures for learning features. All the features are learned hierarchically from pixels to classifier, and each layer extracts features from the output of previous layers [19]. However, to obtain superior performance, CNNs usually require a large-scale training process. To collect an abundance of medical images is costly and not feasible. The training process also consumes too much time and resources to provide manually annotated training datasets.

In this paper, we propose a brand new concept on how to use CNNs for brain image segmentation with implicit features that link medical imaging to deep learning. We divide training images into regions and label them automatically to boost the size of the training dataset. A CNN learning framework is designed to capture the local structure of the ROIs and automatically learn the most relevant features.

After a brief introduction to the background, the problem formulation along with the data generation is provided in Sect. 2. In Sect. 3, we present the details of a CNN architecture. Section 4 shows the results and includes discussion. Finally, the paper is summarized and concluded with future research directions in Sect. 5.

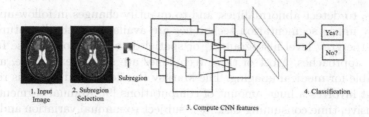

**Fig. 1.** Segmentation system overview. (1) Brain MRI input image, (2) region extraction, (3) feature computation for each region using a convolutional neural network, and (4) region classification to detect ROI pixels.

## 2 Region-Based Segmentation

Image segmentation is a process of assigning a label to every pixel in an image such that pixels with the same label share certain characteristics. Therefore, assigning pixel labels using CNNs based on the features obtained from the image data is a reasonable strategy for segmentation. The main highlight of a deep learning algorithm is that all features are learned from the image data directly. The neural network architecture has more than 60 million parameters, which makes training on GPUs a necessity. A straightforward way to improve the performance of CNNs is by increasing the size of training data. Acquiring such data is not always feasible for medical imaging. In order to take the advantage of CNNs to obtain accurate segmentation, we propose a method that can solve the limited training data problem from which CNNs generally suffer. Figure 1 presents an overview of our method. After boosting the size of training data, we perform the stochastic gradient descent (SGD) training of CNN parameters using this large dataset. The result is a customizable segmentation operation whose performance and behavior reflect the segmentation criteria learned directly from the training data. The proposed method is composed of three main steps:

1. Generate enough training data from the limited original data
2. Label data efficiently
3. Augment the dataset

### 2.1 Generate Training Data

In dealing with Magnetic Resonance Imaging (MRI) images, one of the most challenging aspect is the process of partitioning some specific cells and tissues from the rest of the image. An MRI image from our dataset is shown in Fig. 2(a). Experienced doctors segment out the tumor area (white area in the lower half) in the image manually to get the binary ground-truth segmentation as shown in Fig. 2(b) (zoomed in for clarity). In Fig. 2(b), pixels in the tumor area are set to black and pixels in the background are set to white. In order to provide enough annotated training images for CNN, a sliding window of $n \times m$ pixels is applied to extract small regions' proposals. These patches from one image sample are used for training.

## 2.2  Label Training Data

To label the patches obtained with a sliding window, the image regions tightly enclosing ROI pixels are regarded as positive examples (e.g. window c in Fig. 2(b), while the non-ROI regions, which have nothing to do with the tumor area, are treated as negative examples (window d). Regions that partially overlap the ROI are treated with a central area overlapping process. The ground-truth segmentation is also regarded as positive example if it goes through the central area of a region's proposals. Otherwise, the region is considered as negative. Figures 2(c–f) show the zoomed in areas in four boxes in Fig. 2(b).

## 2.3  Augment Positive Data

After data generation and labeling, we convert one image into a large dataset which includes around 300 positive regions and 20,000 negative regions. Because the size of the positive training set is much smaller than the negative training set, data augmentation is necessary to improve classification performance. According to the characteristics of our data, we choose 2 ways flips (horizontal and vertical) and 35 rotations ($10°$, $20°$, $30°$, ..., $340°$, $350°$). Here, we rotate the whole original image and ground truth image by different angles, then use the same algorithm mentioned above to obtain the positive patches. After this step, we increase the positive training examples from 300 to 11,400.

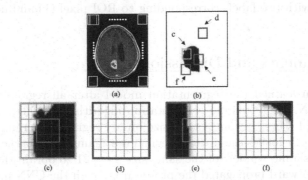

**Fig. 2.** An overview of data generation. (a) The original brain MRI image, (b) zoomed in segmentation labeled by doctors, (c) positive sample which tightly encloses the ROI pixels, (d) negative sample which is background pixels (e) positive sample which ground-truth segmentation line (the boundary) falls within the central area, (f) negative sample which the boundary does not pass through the central box.

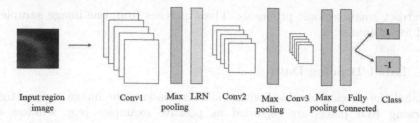

Input region    Conv1    Max    LRN    Conv2    Max    Conv3 Max    Fully    Class
image                    pooling                      pooling          pooling Connected

**Fig. 3.** Illustration of Convolutional Neural Network (CNN) architecture

## 3    CNN Architecture and Model Learning

The architecture of the CNN used in this paper is illustrated in Fig. 3. This CNN has three convolution-max pooling layers followed by a 2-way softmax output layer. The CNN is configured with Rectified Linear Units (ReLUs), as they train several times faster than their equivalents with tanh connections. This section articulates details of those layers. $21 \times 21$ patches were used as data for the CNN in this study. Patches are all gray images, and 1 channel is used for the input data. The first convolutional layer uses 96 kernels of size $5 \times 5$ with a stride of 4 pixels and padding of 2 pixels on the edges, followed by a $3 \times 3$ max pooling layer with a stride of 2. A Local Response Normalization (LRN) layer is applied after the first pooling layer. The second convolutional layer uses 128 filters of size $3 \times 3$ with a stride of 2 pixels and padding of 2 pixels on the edges. A second pooling layer has the same specification as the first one. The third convolutional layer uses 128 filters of size $3 \times 3$ with stride and padding of 1. The third pooling layer also has the same configuration as the two before it and leads to a softmax output layer with two labels corresponding to ROI pixel (1) and non-ROI pixel (−1) classes.

## 4    Experiments and Discussions

The algorithm learned the segmentation model after all regions were trained using our CNN. We tested our segmentation algorithm on different brain MRI slices. Our goal was to output a same size binary segmentation image similar to the ground-truth image the doctors segmented manually. For the test images, we applied a sliding window of the same size $21 \times 21$ to obtain the region proposals, then forward propagated the proposal through the CNN model in order to determine the class to be positive or negative. We recorded the location of each region's central pixel in the original image for constructing the binary segmentation. If the region was classified as positive, which means the center of this region is considered as a ROI pixel, the central pixel was set to 0 (black) in the segmentation output image. Otherwise, the central pixel was considered a non-ROI pixel or background and was set to 1 (white).

In clinical MRI applications, transverse plane, coronal plane, and sagittal plane are three main planes of the body used to describe the location of body parts in relation to one another. The transverse plane is a horizontal plane that divides the body into superior and inferior parts, the coronal plane is any vertical plane that divides the body into ventral and dorsal sections, and the sagittal plane is any vertical plane which divides the body into right and left halves. Scans of different plane vary significantly. We trained different models for different planes in Sect. 4.1. We also experimented with creating one general model to detect tumors in images from all three scans. Since our model is based on deep learning, this challenge is easily addressed by extending the training data set to cover all three cases, The results are shown in Sect. 4.2.

In general, a primary brain tumor has only one large lesion. It is usually associated with extensive local edema and is easy to be detected. Whereas, a secondary brain tumor usually has several very small lesions without local edema and is hard to be detected. We chose images with secondary brain tumors as our test samples to demonstrate the superiority of our method. All images chosen for study had small brain tumors, and they were not all visible in all slices. Because of the limitation of the medical image resource, in our experiments, we used the MRI images from 5 patients (A–E). The patients' information is listed in Table 1. We picked the slices in which the tumor can be seen and labeled by experienced doctors.

**Table 1.** The information of patients

| Number | Gender | Age | Occupy | Diagnosis |
| --- | --- | --- | --- | --- |
| A | F | 52 | Farmer | Brain metastases of breast carcinoma |
| B | F | 74 | Worker | Brain metastases of breast carcinoma |
| C | F | 46 | Farmer | Brain metastases of lung carcinoma |
| D | F | 28 | Farmer | Brain metastases of breast carcinoma |
| E | F | 57 | Farmer | Brain metastases of lung carcinoma |

In each SGD iteration of our training, we uniformly sample 32 positive regions and 32 negative examples to construct a minibatch of size 64. We biased the sampling towards positive regions, because they are extremely rare compared to the background or negative regions. The CNN portion of our experiments used Caffe framework [20] running on the NVIDIA Kepler series K40 GPUs. We used Matlab to produce the final segmentation results. The CNN model presented in Fig. 3 was trained using region images several times to increase its ability to automatically detect ROI pixels in any test image with a variant resolution.

## 4.1 Three Plane Models

We performed two experiments for each plane. In the first experiment (Test 1, 3 and 5), we used different slices from the same patient for training and testing. For the second experiment (Test 2, 4 and 6), we picked slices from multiple patients (excluded testing patient) for training. Table 2 shows the detail of the experiments' setup. Experiment results are shown in Figs. 4 and 5. All training images are listed in the Appendix A. To evaluate the performance, we compared our method with Otsu' method [21]. Test 1 shown in Fig. 4(a–d) used one slice for training. The algorithm was able to detect the tumor areas accurately although with some noise. Segmentation result for Test 2 shown in Fig. 4(g) is almost identical to the doctors' labeling. Result of Test 2 was better than Test 1 mostly because more slices were used for training. Results of Test 1 to 2 show the algorithm was able to effectively and accurately locate the tumor.

**Table 2.** The details of experiments' setup

|          | Transverse | | Coronal | | Sagittal | |
|----------|--------|--------|--------|--------|--------|--------|
|          | Test 1 | Test 2 | Test 3 | Test 4 | Test 5 | Test 6 |
| Training | A      | A C D  | B      | C E    | A      | B C D  |
| Testing  | A      | B      | B      | B      | A      | A      |

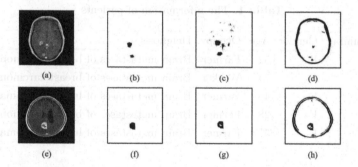

**Fig. 4.** Transverse plane segmentation. Test 1: (a) One transverse slice from patient A as the testing image, (b) ground-truth of (a), (c) our segmentation, (d) Otsu's segmentation. Test 2: (e) One transverse slice from patient B as the testing image, (g) ground-truth of (e), (g) our segmentation, (h) Otsu's segmentation.

Compared with Otsu's method, our method was able to distinguish boundary pixels of the skull from tumor pixels. However, Otsu's method failed to differential tumor area from the skull boundary. So we had to apply morphological post-processing to remove the boundary of the results for comparison ('Otsu-p') as shown in Table 3. As mentioned before, since we chose 3 × 3 central window, this would dilate the final result. For a fair comparison, we also applied a simple erosion method to our raw result, where 'Ours-1' means the erosion operation was applied once, and 'Ours-2' means the erosion operation was applied twice. The comparison performance is presented in Table 3.

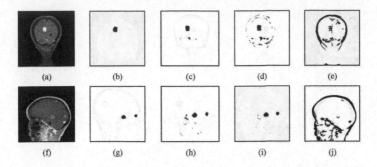

**Fig. 5.** Coronal and sagittal plane segmentations. (a) Testing image in Test 3 and 4, (b) segmentation of (a) labeled by doctors, (c) our segmentation in Test 3, (d) our segmentation in test 4, (e) Otsu's segmentation of (a), (f) testing image in Test 5 and 6, (g) segmentation of (f) labeled by doctors, (h) our segmentation in Test 5, (i) our segmentation in Test 6, (j) Otsu's segmentation of (f).

Test 3 and 4 used the same image Fig. 5(a) to test, and both can locate the tumor with high recall scores listed in Table 3. However, for Test 4, there are only two patients whose tumors could be seen in coronal plane scan. Since the training data were scarce and much different from the test image, the result of Test 4 presented in Fig. 5(d) showed some contour noise which can be removed by simple post processing techniques, e.g. 'Ours-2' boosted the precision score to 0.64 from 0.29. Tests 5 and 6 show our method has a strong response for the two tumor areas, which outperformed Otsu's method. Test 6 has better recall and precision scores than Test 5, since Test 6 took use of more training images. Better accuracy could be obtained if more training data were available.

**Table 3.** Comparison results in Test 1–6

| Methods | | | Ours | Otsu' | Otsu'-p | Ours-1 | Ours-2 |
|---|---|---|---|---|---|---|---|
| Transvers | Test 1 | Recall | **0.9640** | 0.0661 | 0.1178 | 0.8921 | 0.7587 |
| | | Precision | 0.3929 | 0.0070 | 0.0661 | 0.6060 | **0.7140** |
| | Test 2 | Recall | 0.8900 | 0.7613 | **0.9824** | 0.7945 | 0.6621 |
| | | Precision | 0.8429 | 0.1053 | 0.2945 | **0.9131** | 0.9114 |
| Coronal | Test 3 | Recall | **0.8845** | 0.5961 | 0.5961 | 0.8362 | 0.7509 |
| | | Precision | 0.6878 | 0.0530 | 0.1650 | 0.7957 | **0.8364** |
| | Test 4 | Recall | **0.9184** | 0.5961 | 0.5961 | 0.8785 | 0.8011 |
| | | Precision | 0.2940 | 0.0530 | 0.1650 | 0.5005 | **0.6423** |
| Sagittal | Test 5 | Recall | **0.9856** | 0.1150 | 0.1150 | 0.8802 | 0.6166 |
| | | Precision | 0.4901 | 0.0060 | 0.0152 | 0.7905 | **0.8355** |
| | Test 6 | Recall | **0.9984** | 0.1150 | 0.1150 | 0.9217 | 0.7252 |
| | | Precision | 0.6250 | 0.0060 | 0.0152 | 0.8266 | **0.8566** |

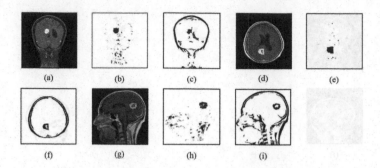

**Fig. 6.** Test 7 results, (a–c) transvers plane, (d–f) coronal plane, (g–i) sagittal plane.

**Table 4.** Comparison results in Test 7.

| Methods | | Ours | Otsu' | Otsu'-p | Ours-1 | Ours-2 |
|---|---|---|---|---|---|---|
| Transvers | Recall | **0.9910** | 0.7993 | 0.7993 | 0.9595 | 0.8815 |
| | Precision | 0.2851 | 0.0643 | 0.1764 | 0.5664 | **0.7618** |
| Coronal | Recall | **0.9955** | 0.7365 | 0.7365 | 0.9707 | 0.8734 |
| | Precision | 0.7056 | 0.0978 | 0.2288 | 0.8613 | **0.8918** |
| Sagittal | Recall | **0.7922** | 0.6442 | 0.6442 | 0.5136 | 0.3073 |
| | Precision | 0.7056 | 0.0978 | 0.2288 | 0.8613 | **0.8918** |

As shown in the Table 3, the proposed segmentation algorithm has the best recall score in every Test except Test 2. Otsu's method with post processing performed better in this case. However, its precision is pretty low. For Precision, our method with simple post processing performed the best.

From the perspective of running speed, one pass for our CNN model takes close to 1 ms. Each pass can be done individually to take the advantage of parallel processing. Whereas, the Otsu' method takes one whole second and its computation cannot be parallelized. Our method has great potential to be implemented in hardware for real time segmentation.

## 4.2 General Model

We selected one slice from each of three scans from patient B as the test image for Test 7. The general model was trained using one slice of each scan that tumor areas were visible from all other patients. The results for this experiment are listed in Fig. 6. We also compared our results with Otsu' method shown in Table 4. We observed noisier segmentation using a general model than using a specialized model, but the general model was able to segment tumor on all three planes. Table 4 shows our methods have the best recall and precision scores.

# 5   Conclusion

In this paper, we propose to use a Convolutional Neural Network for brain MRI image segmentation. We train a CNN with ROIs and non-ROIs patterns iteratively so that it is able to automatically segment tumor areas effectively. Our result is very promising. Since all features are learned from labeled data, our model is able to accurately locate the tumor areas.

Our motivation for this work is not to replace any existing well-known segmentation methods. This work proposes an interesting concept that could be improved further. Since all important information for segmentation is learned from the data labeled by the experts, our model has demonstrated its capability of mimicking the expert's segmentation style represented in the ground truth. Other segmentation methods require fine tuning the parameters manually for different applications. An advantage of the proposed method is its flexibility and potential to adapt for different applications or imaging modalities without any modifications of the algorithm. Unlike the traditional deep learning methods that require a large scale of training data, which is often not feasible for medical image applications, this algorithm requires only a small set of training images and the ground truth.

The proposed method trains the CNN model with only a couple of images. Training with more images will further improve its performance. Because our dataset size is small, starting with a pre-trained model would also improve its performance. Meanwhile, different experimental settings might change the performance, which needs to be investigated in the future.

## Appendix: A

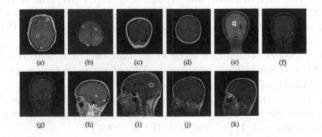

**Fig. 7.** Training images. (a) Training image in Test 1 and 2, (b–d) in Test 2, (e) in Test 3, (f–g) in Test 4, (h) training image in Test 5 and 6, (i–k) in Test 6.

## References

1. Shapiro, L.G., Stockman, G.C.: Computer Vision. Prentice Hall, Upper Saddle River (2001)

2. Barghout, L., Lee, L.: Perceptual information processing system. US Patent App. 10/618,543 (2003)
3. Pham, D.L., Xu, C., Prince, J.L.: Current methods in medical image segmentation 1. Ann. Rev. Biomed. Eng. **2**, 315–337 (2000)
4. Gould, S., Gao, T., Koller, D.: Region-based segmentation and object detection. In: Advances in Neural Information Processing Systems, pp. 655–663 (2009)
5. Zhou, Y., Wang, W., Huang, X.: FPGA design for PCANet deep learning network. In: 2015 IEEE 23rd Annual International Symposium on Field-Programmable Custom Computing Machines (FCCM), p. 232. IEEE (2015)
6. El-Dahshan, E.S.A., Mohsen, H.M., Revett, K., Salem, A.B.M.: Computer-aided diagnosis of human brain tumor through MRI: a survey and a new algorithm. Expert Syst. Appl. **41**, 5526–5545 (2014)
7. Sharma, N., Aggarwal, L.M., et al.: Automated medical image segmentation techniques. J. Med. Phys. **35**, 3 (2010)
8. Huang, X., Tsechpenakis, G.: Medical image segmentation
9. Despotović, I., Goossens, B., Philips, W.: MRI segmentation of the human brain: challenges, methods, and applications. In: Computational and Mathematical Methods in Medicine 2015 (2015)
10. Nabizadeh, N., Kubat, M.: Brain tumors detection and segmentation in MR images: Gabor wavelet vs. statistical features. Comput. Electr. Eng. **45**, 286–301 (2015)
11. Wan, L., Zeiler, M., Zhang, S., Cun, Y.L., Fergus, R.: Regularization of neural networks using dropconnect. In: Proceedings of the 30th International Conference on Machine Learning (ICML-13), pp. 1058–1066 (2013)
12. Graham, B.: Fractional max-pooling (2014). arXiv preprint arXiv:1412.6071
13. Clevert, D.A., Unterthiner, T., Hochreiter, S.: Fast and accurate deep network learning by exponential linear units (ELUs) (2015). arXiv preprint arXiv:1511.07289
14. Zhao, J., Mathieu, M., Goroshin, R., Lecun, Y.: Stacked what-where auto-encoders (2015). arXiv preprint arXiv:1506.02351
15. Lee, C.Y., Gallagher, P.W., Tu, Z.: Generalizing pooling functions in convolutional neural networks: mixed, gated, and tree (2015). arXiv preprint arXiv:1509.08985
16. Krizhevsky, A., Sutskever, I., Hinton, G.E.: Imagenet classification with deep convolutional neural networks. In: Advances in Neural Information Processing Systems, pp. 1097–1105 (2012)
17. Lowe, D.G.: Object recognition from local scale-invariant features. In: The Proceedings of the Seventh IEEE International Conference on Computer Vision, 1999, vol. 2, pp. 1150–1157. IEEE (1999)
18. Dalal, N., Triggs, B.: Histograms of oriented gradients for human detection. In: IEEE Computer Society Conference on Computer Vision and Pattern Recognition, 2005, CVPR 2005, vol. 1, pp. 886–893. IEEE (2005)
19. Razavian, A., Azizpour, H., Sullivan, J., Carlsson, S.: CNN features off-the-shelf: an astounding baseline for recognition. In: Proceedings of the IEEE Conference on Computer Vision and Pattern Recognition Workshops, pp. 806–813 (2014)
20. Jia, Y., Shelhamer, E., Donahue, J., Karayev, S., Long, J., Girshick, R., Guadarrama, S., Darrell, T.: Caffe: convolutional architecture for fast feature embedding. In: Proceedings of the ACM International Conference on Multimedia, pp. 675–678. ACM (2014)
21. Zhu, N., Wang, G., Yang, G., Dai, W.: A fast 2d otsu thresholding algorithm based on improved histogram. In: Chinese Conference on Pattern Recognition, 2009, CCPR 2009, pp. 1–5. IEEE (2009)

# SAHF: Unsupervised Texture-Based Multiscale with Multicolor Method for Retinal Vessel Delineation

Temitope Mapayi and Jules-Raymond Tapamo[✉]

School of Engineering, University of KwaZulu-Natal, Durban, South Africa
{mapayit,tapamoj}@ukzn.ac.za

**Abstract.** Automatic vessel delineation has been challenging due to complexities during the acquisition of retinal images. Although, great progress have been made in this field, it remains the subject of on-going research as there is need to further improve on the delineation of more large and thinner retinal vessels as well as the computational speed. Texture and color are promising, as they are very good features applied for object detection in computer vision. This paper presents an investigatory study on sum average Haralick feature (SAHF) using multi-scale approach over two different color spaces, CIElab and RGB, for the delineation of retinal vessels. Experimental results show that the method presented in this paper is robust for the delineation of retinal vessels having achieved fast computational speed with the maximum average accuracy of 95.67% and maximum average sensitivity of 81.12% on DRIVE database. When compared with the previous methods, the method investigated in this paper achieves higher average accuracy and sensitivity rates on DRIVE.

**Keywords:** Multicolor · Multiscale · Vessel delineation · Texture

## 1 Introduction

Retinal fundus imaging has been very useful to ophthalmologists for the medical diagnosis and progression monitoring of diabetic retinopathy (DR) [2]. Although several digital imaging modalities are used in ophthalmology, colored fundus photography remains an important retinal imaging modality due to its safety and cost-effective mode of retinal abnormalities documentation [2].

Image segmentation, which is an important step in image analysis, involves the partitioning of a digital image into multiple regions having the same attributes like intensity, texture or color [28]. It is applied for the detection of boundaries, objects or parts of images. There are several important anatomic structures in the human retina. The robust segmentation of the different anatomic structures of the retina is necessary for a reliable characterisation of healthy or diseased retina. Several automated techniques have successfully

© Springer International Publishing AG 2016
G. Bebis et al. (Eds.): ISVC 2016, Part I, LNCS 10072, pp. 639–648, 2016.
DOI: 10.1007/978-3-319-50835-1_57

been used to detect different anatomic features as well as retinopathy features in retinal images [24].

As image analysis continues to assist the ophthalmologists in achieving accurate diagnosis and efficient management of larger number of retinopathies' patients, they focus on retinal vessel morphological feature analysis such as tortuosity measurement after detecting the vessel network in the retinal images [3,10]. Retinal vessel delineation is the process of detecting vessel network in retinal images. Efficient retinal vessel delineation and vessel feature analysis are of required for the diagnosis and progress monitoring of the various retinopathies and vascular diseases.

Texture, color and shape are very good features applied for object detection in computer vision. The investigation of texture over different color spaces for object detection or recognition is very important [9,17]. This is due to the fact that color and texture are two major properties of the image required for image analysis [25], and the good performance of texture in image analysis is strongly influenced by the color representation chosen [16,19]. While most of the automatic vessel segmentation methods have often utilized the green channel of the RGB color and the grayscale of the retinal images, there is a need to further investigate the use of other color spaces for the delineation of the vessels. Since the analysis of color-texture has been important in image analysis, two different color spaces will be investigated and evaluated for the delineation of the vessels using texture information.

## 2   Related Works

The retinal vessel segmentation methods that have been proposed in the literature can be categorized into supervised and unsupervised segmentation approaches. In supervised vessel segmentation methods [12,15,20,22,23], different algorithms are used for learning the set of rules required for the retinal vessel extraction. A set of manually segmented retinal vessels, by trained and skilled personnel, is considered as the reference image. These reference images are used for the training phase of the supervised segmentation techniques. Reliable training samples used during the supervised image segmentation can be expensive or unavailable sometimes [7]. The supervised methods are also computationally expensive since training time is required. Another major drawback of the supervised vessel segmentation techniques is the high dependence of their performance on the training samples. The methods based on unsupervised segmentation [5,6,8,10,11,21], on the other hand discover and utilize the underlying patterns of blood vessels to determine whether a particular pixel of the retinal image is vessel-pixel or not. Training samples are, however, not required for the unsupervised segmentation methods.

Automated retinal vessel delineation are faced with several challenges such as the varying retinal vessel-widths, low contrast of thinner vessels and non-homogeneous illumination across the retinal images [8]. Single scale matched filter have weak responses due to large variation in the widths of the vessels.

In order to handle this limitation, several authors have introduced multi-scale filters for the segmentation of vessel networks. Martinez-Perez et al. [13] combined scale space analysis with region growing to detect the vessel network. The method, however, failed to segment the thin vessels. There are also a lot of false vessel-like structures at the border of the optic disc. A multi-scale retinal vessel segmentation method was implemented in [26]. The multi-scale line-tracking was applied for the vessel detection and morphological was applied for the post-processing. The drawback of the method proposed in [26] is its inability to segment the thin vessels. Li et al. [8] applied the multi-scale production of the matched filter (MPMF) responses as multi-scale data fusion strategy. The proposed MPMF vessel extraction scheme applied multi-scale matched filtering, scale multiplication in the image enhancement step and double thresholding in the vessel classification step. This method required 8 s to detect vessels without post-processing and required 30 s to detect vessels while combined with a post-processing phase. Although this method achieved a faster computational time without post-processing, the accuracy rate is relatively low. It is also noted that this method spent most of the time on the post-processing phase.

A multi-wavelet kernels combined with multi-scale hierarchical decomposition was proposed in [27] for the detection of retinal vessels. Vessels were enhanced using matched filtering with multi-wavelet kernels. The enhanced image was normalised using multi-scale hierarchical decomposition. A local adaptive thresholding technique based on the vessel edge information was used to generate the segmented vessels. Although good accuracy rates were obtained, this method fails to detect thin vessels. Another drawback of this method is its average computational time of 210 s (3.5 min) required to segment vessels in each retinal image. Patasius et al. [18] investigated different color spaces and affirmed the usefulness of green channel of the RGB color and hue component of HSV for the delineation of blood vessels while the S component of HSV can be applied for reflex detection. Soares et al. [22] implemented a supervised segmentation method based on two-dimensional (2-D) Gabor wavelet transform combined with Bayesian classifier for the segmentation of the retinal vessel. A feature vector comprising a multi-scale 2-D Gabor wavelet transform responses and pixel intensity was generated from the retinal images for training the classifier. Each of the pixels was further classified as vessel or non-vessel using a Bayesian classifier. Although the technique had a good performance, segmentation of thinner vessels as well as false detections around the border of the optic disc remain a challenge. Another drawback is that the method required 9 hours for the training phase and an average time of about 190 s (3 min, 10 s) to segment vessels in each retinal image.

## 3   Methods and Techniques

The segmentation of retinal vessels are faced with several challenges from the varying retinal vessel-widths to low contrast of thinner vessels and nonhomogeneous illumination across the retinal images [8]. Although existing methods have made great progress in this field, it remains the subject of on-going research as there is a need to improve further on the detection of more large and thin vessels as well as the computational speed.

Due to the non-homogeneous illumination, low contrast of thin vessels and large variation in the widths of the retinal vessels [8], this study investigates the use of sum average which is a Haralick texture feature [4] over different color spaces using unsupervised segmentation approach for the delineation of large and thin retinal vessels. This texture feature and some other Haralick [4] texture features have been applied for through supervised image segmentation in the literature [4]. While this texture feature has been applied supervised learning approach, the contribution of this work lies in the investigation of sum average Haralick feature (SAHF) using multi-scale approach over two different color spaces, CIElab and RGB in an unsupervised manner. This study further contributes by investigating SAHF using multi-scale approach over an hybrid of the two color spaces. Although, RGB is not a perceptually uniform color space, it is widely used. CIELab on the other hand is not often used. This study investigates the influence of these different color spaces on the use of SAHF in the detection of retinal vessels.

The 'L' channel of the CIELab color space and the green channel of the RGB color space of the retinal image is sharpen by applying an unsharp filter. An average filter is then applied for smoothing of the image. The image contrasts is then enhanced to improve the contrast of thin vessels in the image. A median filter with local window size $w*w$ is further applied to the enhanced image as

$$U(i,j) = H(x,y) * V^1_{w*w}(x,y) \tag{1}$$

where $U(i,j)$ is the filtered retinal image, $V^1(x,y)$ is the result obtained after an unsharp filter with mean filter has been applied, and the $H(x,y)$ is a local median filter with window size $(w \times w)$. The width of the retinal vessels can vary from very large (15 pixels) to very small (3 pixels) [8]. The window size $(15 \times 15)$ is selected based on the adequate spectrum it provides for the very large vessels. In order to achieve illumination balance across the image, an image $D(x,y)$ is computed as

$$D(x,y) = U(i,j) - V^1(x,y) \tag{2}$$

This is followed by the computation of the local adaptive threshold based on the SAHT information. Sum average feature [4] is extracted from the 'a' channel of CIELAB color space. Since the width of retinal vessels can vary from very large (15 pixels) to very small (3 pixels) [8], a multi-scale approach is applied on the SAHF information considering the pixel of interest in relationship with its spacial neighbourhood to compute a local adaptive threshold. The multi-scale thresholding approach handles the challenge of vessel width variation. The multi-scale approach applied investigates the distances $(d_i)_{i=1,...,4}$ across the four orientations (horizontal: 0°, diagonal: 45°, vertical: 90° and anti-diagonal: 135°) as it covers adequate spectrum of vessel texture information ($4 \times 4 = 16$) to compute the local threshold for each pixel of interest. The grey level co-occurrence matrix (GLCM) for the retinal fundus image is first computed (For more information on computing GLCM, see [4]).

The sum average feature over the varying distances, $d$, and orientation, $\Phi$, is computed as

$$SA = \sum_{k=0}^{2N_g-2} kP_{x+y}(k) \tag{3}$$

where $p_{x+y}(k) = \sum_{\substack{i=0 \\ i+j=k}}^{N_g-1} \sum_{j=0}^{N_g-1} p(i,j)$, $N_g$ is the number of gray scales, and $p(i,j)$ is the $(i,j)^{th}$ entry in a normalised grey level co-occurrence matrix of the retinal fundus image.

A feature matrix is computed using the multi-scale feature measurement of the sum average over the varying distances '$d$' and orientations '$\Phi$' as:

$$SA^{fmatrix} = (SA_{ij}), 1 \le i,j \le 4 \tag{4}$$

such that

$$SA_{ij} = SA_{(d_i,\Phi_j)}, 1 \le i,j \le 4 \tag{5}$$

where $\Phi_1 = 0°$, $\Phi_2 = 45°$, $\Phi_3 = 90°$ and $\Phi_4 = 135°$, and $(d_i)_{i=1,...,4}$.

The adaptive thresholding value applied for the vessel segmentation is then computed as

$$T(x,y) = \frac{\min_{1 \le i \le 4} \| \max_{1 \le j \le 4}(SA_{ij}) - \min_{1 \le j \le 4}(SA_{ij}) \|}{\max(d)} \tag{6}$$

such that $\max(d) = 4$.

The delineated vessel network is

$$S_{image}(x,y) = \begin{cases} 0, & \text{if } D(x,y) \le T(x,y) \\ 1, & \text{otherwise} \end{cases} \tag{7}$$

where $S_{image}$ represents the detected vessels obtained from 'L' channel of CIELab or the green channel of RGB.

In order to further improve the vessel detection performance rate, the combination of the detected vessels obtained from 'L' channel of CIELab and the green channel of RGB was investigated. The two different vessel networks are combined using an 'OR' operation as shown in the Eq. 8:

$$S_{image}^{L \oplus G} = S_{image}^L(x,y) \oplus S_{image}^G(x,y) \tag{8}$$

where $S_{image}^L$ is the detected vessels obtained from 'L' channel of CIELab and $S_{image}^G$ is the detected vessels obtained from green channel of RGB.

Due to the presence of false vessel-like structures, there is a need for post-processing. Mophological operator based on area opening and median filter of a

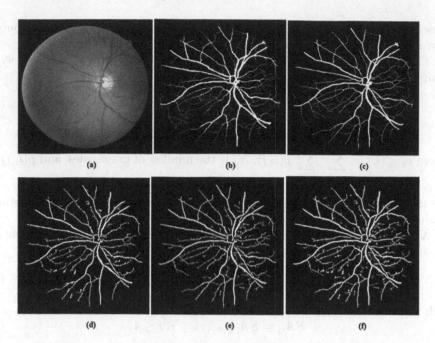

**Fig. 1.** (a) Color retinal image 4 on DRIVE (b) Ground truth of image 4 on DRIVE (c) Manual delineation of the second observer of image 4 on DRIVE (d) Result of the investigated technique based 'L' channel of CIELAB on image 4 of DRIVE (e) Result of the investigated technique based green channel of RGB on image 4 of DRIVE (f) Result of the investigated hybrid technique on image 4 of DRIVE.

moving $2 \times 2$ sliding-window are applied in the postprocessing phase to $S_{image}$ obtained from the adaptive thresholding technique and $S_{image}^{L \oplus G}$ to remove the false vessel-like structures. This is followed by subtracting the FOV mask from the result obtained after removing the false vessel-like structures to obtain the final delineated vessel networks in the circular field of view.

## 4    Experimental Results and Discussion

This experiment is conducted using matlab 2014a. The dataset utilized in this paper is the DRIVE database [1] which is publicly available. The time required to detect the vessel from the 'L' channel of CIELAB color space, green channel of RGB color space and the hybrid techniques are 2.8 s, 2.6 s and 3.7 s respectively. Figure 1 shows a color retinal image on DRIVE [1], the ground truth, the manual delineation of the second observer and the results obtained from the three different techniques investigated in this paper. Figure 2 shows two results obtained from two different images through the hybrid technique and their ground truth.

The performance measures utilized in this paper are sensitivity, specificity and accuracy measures (see Eqs. (9)–(11)). The ability of a method to detect

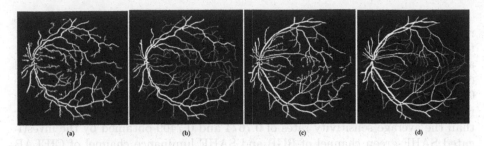

**Fig. 2.** (a) Result of the investigated hybrid technique on image 9 of DRIVE (b) Ground truth of image 9 on DRIVE (c) Result of the investigated hybrid technique on image 12 of DRIVE (d) Ground truth of image 12 on DRIVE

vessels in the retinal images is indicated using the sensitivity while the ability of a segmentation method to detect the background in retinal images is indicated using specificity. The degree to which the overall segmented retinal image conforms to an expert's ground truth is indicated using accuracy. In order to ascertain a good segmentation performance, the sensitivity, specificity and accuracy measures of a segmentation method must be high [11].

$$Sensitivity = TP/(TP + FN) \tag{9}$$

$$Specificity = TN/(TN + FP) \tag{10}$$

$$Accuracy = (TP + TN)/(TP + TN + FP + FN) \tag{11}$$

where TP, TN, FP and FN are true positive, true negative, false positive and false negative respectively.

**Table 1.** Performance of our methods in comparison with other methods on DRIVE

| Method | Average accuracy | Average sensitivity | Average specificity |
|---|---|---|---|
| Human observer [1] | 0.9473 | 0.7761 | 0.9725 |
| Staal et al. [23] | 0.9442 | 0.7345 | 0.9773 |
| Niemeijer et al. [15] | 0.9416 | 0.7145 | 0.9801 |
| Soares et al. [22] | 0.9466 | N/A | N/A |
| Marin et al. [12] | 0.9452 | N/A | N/A |
| Martinez-Perez et al. [13] | 0.9181 | 0.6389 | 0.9496 |
| Mendonca et al. [14] | 0.9463 | 0.7315 | N/A |
| Saffarzadeh et al. [21] | 0.9387 | N/A | N/A |
| Yin et al. [29] | 0.9267 | 0.6522 | 0.9710 |
| SAHF L-Channel of CIElab | **0.9567** | **0.7409** | **0.9777** |
| SAHF G-Channel of RGB | **0.9531** | **0.7674** | **0.9712** |
| SAHF-based hybrid | **0.9421** | **0.8112** | **0.9549** |

All the techniques investigated in this study achieved mean sensitivity rates ranging from 0.7409 to 0.8112 with average accuracy rates ranging from 0.9421 to 0.9567 on DRIVE database (see Table 1). The average accuracy rates of 0.9531 and 0.9567 by the SAHF green channel of RGB and SAHF luminance channel of CIELAB respectively compared favourably with the average accuracy rate 0.9421 obtained from the investigated hybrid technique. The average sensitivity rate of 0.8112 obtained from the investigated hybrid technique is, however, higher than the average sensitivity rates of 0.7674 and 0.7409 obtained by the investigated SAHF green channel of RGB and SAHF luminance channel of CIELAB respectively. This reflects the improvement in the vessel detection achieved by the hybrid technique over the individual SAHF green channel of RGB and SAHF luminance channel of CIELAB techniques.

The sensitivity and accuracy rates of all the investigated techniques compared favourably with the average sensitivity rate of 0.7145 and lower average accuracy rate of 0.9416 presented in [15]. The average sensitivity rates of all the investigated techniques compared favourably with the average sensitivity rate of 0.7345 presented in [23]. Only two average accuracy rates of 0.9531 and 0.9567 by the SAHF green channel of RGB and SAHF luminance channel of CIELAB respectively are higher than the average accuracy rate of 0.9442 presented by Staal et al. [23]. Two average accuracy rates of 0.9531 and 0.9567 by the SAHF green channel of RGB and SAHF luminance channel of CIELAB respectively are higher than the average accuracy rates 0.9452, 0.9387 and 0.9466 obtained by Marin et al. [12], Saffarzadeh et al. [21] and Soares et al. [22] respectively. Martinez-Perez et al. [13], Mendonca et al. [14] and Yin et al. [29] present lower average sensitivity rates of 0.6389, 0.7315 and 0.6522 with average accuracy rates of 0.9181, 0.9463 and 0.9267 respectively when compared with all the SAHF based methods investigated in this paper. The human observer [1] present a higher average sensitivity rate of 0.7761 than the average sensitivity rates 0.7674 and 0.7409 obtained by the investigated SAHF green channel of RGB and SAHF luminance channel of CIELAB respectively. The human observer [1], however, present a lower average sensitivity rate of 0.7761 as compared to the average sensitivity rate 0.8112 obtained by the investigated SAHF hybrid technique.

## 5   Conclusion and Future Work

This paper implemented the delineation of vessel in retinal images through sum average Haralick feature (SAHF) using multi-scale approach over two different color spaces, CIElab and RGB. This paper presented an investigation of sum average Haralick feature (SAHF) using multi-scale approach over two different color spaces, CIElab and RGB. This paper also presented a study of SAHF using multi-scale approach over an hybrid of the two color spaces. Experimental results presented in this paper show that the hybrid method for the delineation of retinal vessels made a significant improvement when compared to (SAHF) using multi-scale approach over two different color spaces, CIElab and RGB on DRIVE database. Experimental results also showed that the hybrid method and the multi-scale approach over two different color spaces, CIElab and RGB achieved higher average sensitivity and accuracy rates with faster computational time when compared with the previous methods on DRIVE. In the future, we shall consider a study on the efficient ways of characterising the delineated retinal vessels.

**Acknowledgement.** We thank DRIVE [1] for making the retinal images dataset publicly available.

# References

1. Research section, digital retinal image for vessel extraction (drive) database. Utrecht, The Netherlands, University Medical Center Utrecht, Image Sciences Institute. http://www.isi.uu.nl/Research/Databases/DRIVE
2. Abràmoff, M.D., Garvin, M.K., Sonka, M.: Retinal imaging, image analysis. IEEE Rev. Biomed. Eng. **3**, 169–208 (2010)
3. Davitt, B.V., Wallace, D.K.: Plus disease. Surv. Ophthalmol. **54**(6), 663–670 (2009)
4. Haralick, R.M., Shanmugam, K., Dinstein, I.H.: Textural features for image classification. IEEE Trans. Systems Man Cybern. **3**(6), 610–621 (1973)
5. Hoover, A., Kouznetsova, V., Goldbaum, M.: Locating blood vessels in retinal images by piecewise threshold probing of a matched filter response. IEEE Trans. Med. Imaging **19**(3), 203–210 (2000)
6. Jiang, X., Mojon, D.: Adaptive local thresholding by verification-based multi-threshold probing with application to vessel detection in retinal images. IEEE Trans. Pattern Anal. Mach. Intell. **25**(1), 131–137 (2003)
7. Li, B., Li, H.K.: Automated analysis of diabetic retinopathy images: principles, recent developments, and emerging trends. Curr. Diab. Rep. **13**(4), 453–459 (2013)
8. Li, Q., You, J., Zhang, D.: Vessel segmentation and width estimation in retinal images using multiscale production of matched filter responses. Expert Syst. Appl. **39**(9), 7600–7610 (2012)
9. Mäenpää, T., Pietikäinen, M.: Classification with color and texture: jointly or separately? Pattern Recogn. **37**(8), 1629–1640 (2004)
10. Mapayi, T., Tapamo, J.-R., Viriri, S., Adio, A.: Automatic retinal vessel detection and tortuosity measurement. Image Anal. Stereology **35**(2), 117–135 (2016)
11. Mapayi, T., Viriri, S., Tapamo, J.-R.: Comparative study of retinal vessel segmentation based on global thresholding techniques. Comput. Math. Methods Med. **2015** (2015)
12. Marín, D., Aquino, A., Gegúndez-Arias, M.E., Bravo, J.M.: A new supervised method for blood vessel segmentation in retinal images by using gray-level, moment invariants-based features. IEEE Trans. Med. Imaging **30**(1), 146–158 (2011)
13. Martínez-Pérez, M.E., Hughes, A.D., Stanton, A.V., Thom, S.A., Bharath, A.A., Parker, K.H.: Retinal blood vessel segmentation by means of scale-space analysis and region growing. In: Taylor, C., Colchester, A. (eds.) MICCAI 1999. LNCS, vol. 1679, pp. 90–97. Springer, Heidelberg (1999). doi:10.1007/10704282_10
14. Mendonca, A.M., Campilho, A.: Segmentation of retinal blood vessels by combining the detection of centerlines and morphological reconstruction. IEEE Trans. Med. Imaging **25**(9), 1200–1213 (2006)

15. Niemeijer, M., Staal, J., van Ginneken, B., Loog, M., Abramoff, M.D.: Comparative study of retinal vessel segmentation methods on a new publicly available database. In: Medical Imaging 2004, pp. 648–656. International Society for Optics and Photonics (2004)
16. Ohta, Y.-I., Kanade, T., Sakai, T.: Color information for region segmentation. Comput. Graph. Image Process. **13**(3), 222–241 (1980)
17. Palm, C.: Color texture classification by integrative co-occurrence matrices. Pattern Recogn. **37**(5), 965–976 (2004)
18. Patasius, M., Marozas, V., Jegelevicius, D., Lukoševičius, A.: Ranking of color space components for detection of blood vessels in eye fundus images. In: Sloten, J.V., Verdonck, P., Nyssen, M., Haueisen, J. (eds.) 4th European Conference of the International Federation for Medical and Biological Engineering, pp. 464–467. Springer, Heidelberg (2009)
19. Pratt, W.: Spatial transform coding of color images. IEEE Trans. Commun. Technol. **19**(6), 980–992 (1971)
20. Ricci, E., Perfetti, R.: Retinal blood vessel segmentation using line operators and support vector classification. IEEE Trans. Med. Imaging **26**(10), 1357–1365 (2007)
21. Saffarzadeh, V.M., Osareh, A., Shadgar, B.: Vessel segmentation in retinal images using multi-scale line operator, K-means clustering. J. Med. Sig. Sens. **4**(2), 122 (2014)
22. Soares, J.V., Leandro, J.J., Cesar, R.M., Jelinek, H.F., Cree, M.J.: Retinal vessel segmentation using the 2-D gabor wavelet, supervised classification. IEEE Trans. Med. Imaging **25**(9), 1214–1222 (2006)
23. Staal, J., Abràmoff, M.D., Niemeijer, M., Viergever, M.A., van Ginneken, B.: Ridge-based vessel segmentation in color images of the retina. IEEE Trans. Med. Imaging **23**(4), 501–509 (2004)
24. Tobin, K.W., Edward Chaum, V., Govindasamy, P., Karnowski, T.P.: Detection of anatomic structures in human retinal imagery. IEEE Trans. Med. Imaging **26**(12), 1729–1739 (2007)
25. Van de Wouwer, G., Scheunders, P., Livens, S., Van Dyck, D.: Wavelet correlation signatures for color texture characterization. Pattern Recogn. **32**(3), 443–451 (1999)
26. Vlachos, M., Dermatas, E.: Multi-scale retinal vessel segmentation using line tracking. Comput. Med. Imaging Graph. **34**(3), 213–227 (2010)
27. Wang, Y., Ji, G., Lin, P., Trucco, E., et al.: Retinal vessel segmentation using multiwavelet kernels and multiscale hierarchical decomposition. Pattern Recogn. **46**(8), 2117–2133 (2013)
28. Yang, Y., Huang, S.: Image segmentation by fuzzy C-means clustering algorithm with a novel penalty term. Comput. Inf. **26**(1), 17–31 (2012)
29. Yin, Y., Adel, M., Bourennane, S.: Automatic segmentation and measurement of vasculature in retinal fundus images using probabilistic formulation. Comput. Math. Methods Med. **2013** (2013)

# Unsupervised Caries Detection in Non-standardized Bitewing Dental X-Rays

D. Osterloh and S. Viriri[✉]

School of Maths, Statistics and Computer Science,
University of KwaZulu-Natal, Durban, South Africa
{209501289,viriris}@ukzn.ac.za

**Abstract.** In recent years dental image processing has become a useful tool in aiding healthcare professionals diagnose patients. Despite advances in the field, accurate diagnoses are still problematic due to the non-uniform nature of dental X-rays. This is attributed to current systems utilizing a supervised learning model for their deterministic algorithm when identifying caries. This paper presents a method for the detection of caries across a variety of non-uniform X-ray images using an unsupervised learning model. This method aims to identify potential caries hallmarks within a tooth without comparing against a set of criteria learned from a database of images. The results show the viability of an unsupervised learning approach and the effectiveness of the method when compared to the supervised approaches.

## 1 Introduction

Dental caries are one of the most prevalent diseases present in modern society, with approximately 36% of the world's population showing symptoms of caries [1]. In the past, developing countries were considered to be less at risk due to their lower consumption of sugary foods, with Africa having a far lower diagnosis rate of dental caries compared to the America [2]. Despite this, changing living conditions have increased the rate of tooth decay in African countries thus worsening the already prevalent disease. In order to keep the disease under control it is important to treat it during its early stages before advanced tooth decay occurs.

Oral healthcare professionals have a variety of diagnostic methods at their disposal which are used to diagnose dental caries in patients. Fluorescent methods, whereby a fluorescent light or laser is used to illuminate a tooth, have proven to have a higher diagnostic accuracy when detecting proximal caries [3]. For inter proximal caries, X-ray based imaging still proves to be the most effective diagnostic tool available [3].

Rad et al. [4] focused on segmentation and feature extraction for dental diagnosis purposes and used a K-mean clustering technique to distinguish teeth from gum by grouping teeth in X-rays as a single structure. The textural features along this structure's contour were stored using a gray-level co-occurrence matrix. Zhou et al. [5] used an active contour method to first divide their images

© Springer International Publishing AG 2016
G. Bebis et al. (Eds.): ISVC 2016, Part I, LNCS 10072, pp. 649–658, 2016.
DOI: 10.1007/978-3-319-50835-1_58

into regions of interest, each region comprising of a single tooth. They then used top-hat and bottom-hat filters and obtained an enhanced image by subtracting the bottom-hat of the original image from the sum of its top-hat and itself. Jain et al. [6] used integral projection for both vertical and horizontal separation of X-ray images thus resulting in the segmentation of X-rays into individual teeth. Nomir et al. [7] also implemented an integral projection approach in order to obtain segmentation into individual teeth. In order to achieve better results in images with poor contrast they first applied iterative thresholding followed by adaptive thresholding to their initial images. Their final separation lines were obtained by rotating their initial lines around a small angle and the line with the fewest points of intersection was selected. Lin et al. [8] also used an adaptation of the method presented in [7] but focused on obtaining contour information from each tooth for use in human identification.

Olivera [9] made use of a supervised learning approach and developed a set of classifiers for caries detection. Statistical, region based, textural and boundary features were obtained by using an active contour method to isolate the boundary of each tooth after segmentation. This data was then compared against the classifiers which were obtained from a learning set where the presence of caries were known. Similarities between the test image and the classifiers resulted in a positive caries diagnosis.

This paper presents an unsupervised learning approach for identifying potential dental caries in X-rays. This approach makes use of either an upper or lower jaw bitewing X-ray to detect the teeth with caries. Furthermore, the proposed approach is robust to process X-rays where there are high noise levels, or where the X-rays have imperfect exposure levels resulting in blurred or dark images.

## 2    Segmentation

### 2.1    Pre-processing

The iterative and adaptive thresholding techniques applied to the dental images require that only pixels relating to teeth, gums, jawbones and the background are present. To achieve this each image undergoes a cleanup which removes any anomalies from the image. With respect to the dataset which was used [10], this mostly involved removing digital signatures from the image which were used to inform healthcare professionals which radiograph they were viewing. Artifact cleanup primarily involved the removal of position indicating devices (PID) which were sometimes visible in the X-ray images. Once all unnecessary pixels have been removed, the image is normalized by using histogram equalization to enhance the contrast.

### 2.2    Thresholding

Due to the nature of the images being analyzed, it is unknown ahead of time what the exposure rate of the X-ray will be and as such a robust thresholding technique is required in order to differentiate tooth pixels from gum and jaw pixels. An adapted form of the method outlined in [7] forms the basis of most thresholding approaches. As such, a similar approach is used with an iterative thresholding technique followed by an adaptive thresholding technique being applied to each image. This method was originally used by Hu et al. [11] for use in an automatic segmentation method required for the segmentation of CT lung images.

**Iterative Thresholding.** In order to obtain the threshold value for the iterative thresholding stage a canny edge detector is used to obtain the general outline of the teeth in the X-ray image. A morphological dilation is then applied to these edges in order to obtain the pixels in the area assumed to be the tooth boundary. Approximately half of the pixels obtained this way will correspond to the tooth and the other half will be of the jaw bone and other background objects. The initial threshold value is calculated from the average pixel value of the assumed tooth pixels and the background pixels and subsequent thresholds are calculated as follows:

$$\mu_D^i = \frac{\sum_{(i,j)\, \in\, dental}\, f\,(i,j)}{\#dental\_pixels}, \tag{1}$$

$$\mu_B^i = \frac{\sum_{(i,j)\, \in\, dental}\, f\,(i,j)}{\#background\_pixels}, \tag{2}$$

$$T_{i+1} = \frac{\mu_B^i + \mu_D^i}{2}. \tag{3}$$

Where f(i, j) is the grayscale value of a pixel at point (i, j), $\mu_D^i$ and $\mu_D^i$ are the mean grayscale values for their respective regions and $T_i$ is the threshold value for the whole image calculated from the average values of the background and tooth pixels. This step is repeated until the iterative threshold value does not change in subsequent re-evaluations or until the process is repeated fifteen times.

**Adaptive Thresholding.** Unlike the approach used in [7], a straight implementation of adaptive thresholding did not yield the desired result of eliminating all non-tooth pixels. This was partly due to background pixels being within the allowed variance of the tooth pixels as well as some tooth pixels appearing darker than the background pixels due to cavities. In order to obtain a threshold value to eliminate all non-tooth pixels a combination of adaptive thresholding and standard thresholding was implemented. A global thresholding value was obtained by processing a sample set of 40 images. This value was obtained by first applying adaptive thresholding to each pixel in the mask to obtain an adaptive threshold value for that pixel.

The average of all adaptive threshold values was used to obtain an average threshold for each X-ray. The average of the sample set was then used to generate the global threshold value. It was determined that by using

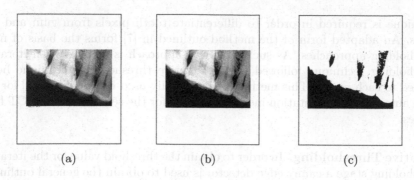

(a)          (b)          (c)

**Fig. 1.** (a) The original image; (b) The mask of the image obtained after iterative thresholding; (c) The threshold of the mask obtained from adaptive thresholding.

$AT' = 0.8 \times AT(i, j)$ the best threshold value could be obtained. This threshold was then applied to each mask in order to obtain the images used in the segmentation process as shown in Fig. 1.

## 2.3 Tooth Separation

In order to process each tooth and determine whether or not caries are present, the masked image obtained from the previous stage needs to be separated into individual teeth. Due to the nature of the X-rays being processed, the X-rays only contained teeth of the upper jaw or lower jaw but never of both regions in the same image.

**Integral Projection.** In order to separate the teeth in each image an adapted integral projection in the vertical direction was used. An initial sweep of the image was done to obtain all valleys between the mask image. Due to the system not knowing if these masks related to upper or lower jaw images, all valleys are accepted at this point, whether they correspond to gaps between the teeth or the crest between the root of the tooth. The center of each horizontal valley was then used as a spacing pixel to allow for the creation of dividing lines. These pixels are then grouped into clusters denoting potential separation points within the image. For the nature of the dataset being processed, clusters are determined as any group of blank pixels marked in the integral projection where there is not a vertical difference between subsequent points greater than 75% of the vertical height of the image nor a horizontal gap between subsequent points greater than 3.5% of the width of the image. For the size of the X-rays being analyzed clusters were classed as any group of 40 or more spacing pixels.

**Separation Lines.** In order to separate each tooth, two variations of the simple linear regression algorithm were used. The first algorithm was the standard

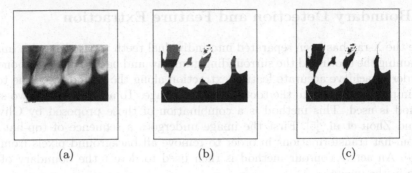

(a)                     (b)                    (c)

**Fig. 2.** (a) The original image; (b) The binary image of the mask with division valleys obtained from integral projection; (c) The threshold of the image with dividing lines.

formula defined as follows:

$$\hat{\beta} = \frac{\sum_{i=1}^{n}(x_i - \bar{x})(y_i - \bar{y})}{\sum_{i=1}^{n}(x_i - \bar{x})^2}, \tag{4}$$

$$= \frac{\sum_{i=1}^{n} x_i y_i - \frac{1}{n}\sum_{i=1}^{n} x_i \sum_{j=1}^{n} y_j}{\sum_{i=1}^{n} x_i^2 - \frac{1}{n}\left(\sum_{i=1}^{n} x_i\right)^2}, \tag{5}$$

$$= \frac{\bar{x}y - \bar{x}\bar{y}}{\bar{x}^2 - \bar{x}^2}, \tag{6}$$

$$\hat{\alpha} = \bar{y} - \hat{\beta}\bar{x}. \tag{7}$$

Where n denotes the number of points, $\hat{\beta}$ denotes the gradient of the slope and $\hat{\alpha}$ denotes the y-intercept.

The second formula was a weighted linear regression model which proved effective in generating a correct separating line in cases where cluster distribution was favored in one direction. If there was an equal distribution of points around the median then the simple linear regression model was used. If the distribution of points was greater or less than the median then the value of n in the above equation was calculated to be half the total number of points.

In order to determine which formula generated the best separating line a selective algorithm is used to determine which line intersects with the fewest pixels. This is important in the case of Fig. 1c where separation lines need to pass through tooth matter due to impacting teeth. If at least 60% of the line intercepted pixels which represented dental matter the line was not drawn as this was assumed to be a crest between the tooth. This allows the program to process dental images without knowledge of the jaw region. Each line also undergoes a rotation from $-20°$ to $20°$ in increments of $0.25°$ in order to find the best position for separation as shown in Fig. 2.

# 3  Boundary Detection and Feature Extraction

Once the X-ray has been separated into individual teeth we are left with images containing the tooth and the surrounding gum, jaw and background components. In order to achieve accurate feature extraction along the boundary of the tooth it is important to isolate the tooth from the image. To achieve this a two stage method is used. This method is a combination of those proposed by Oliveira [9] and Zhou et al. [5]. First the image undergoes a sequence of top-hat and bottom-hat transformations in order to remove all background pixels from the image. An active contour method is then used to detect the boundary of the tooth in the image.

## 3.1  Top and Bottom Hat Transformations

In order to increase the contrast of the image and isolate the brighter areas of the image where dental matter is located, a composite transformation is used as follows:

$$I_{output} = (I_{Original} + TH) - BH$$

Where $I_{output}$ is the desired output image, $I_{Original}$ is the original image obtained from the previous segmentation process, TH is the top hat transformation applied to the original image and BH is the bottom hat transformation applied to the original image.

The output is obtained through the addition and subtraction of pixel values obtained from these transformations. Any negative value is set to 0 and any number exceeding 255 is set to 255 in order to maintain the grayscale nature of the X-ray. This method more closely resembles that proposed in [5] which was used during their segmentation stage. As noted in [9], continuing to the second stage of image subtraction, wherein the initial output further undergoes top and bottom-hat transformations, will result in images of poorer quality losing all tooth definition thus making feature extraction impossible. As such only a single parse of the processing technique was used.

## 3.2  Active Contour

Experimentation with the active contour model proved to yield the best results when attempting to isolate the tooth in each image and thus obtain its boundary. After the top and bottom hat transformations carried out in the previous step each image contained a high contrast image of the tooth with some gum and jaw pixels present. Due to the nature of the previous transformation, all non-tooth pixels had a much darker contrast than the desired pixels. To eliminate these pixels from the adaptive contour a threshold was applied to the image before it was converted to binary in order to ensure accurate results. After experimentation it was determined that a threshold of 66% of the average pixel value eliminated all non-tooth pixels from the image. Once this threshold was applied and the image was converted to binary the active contour model was applied in order to find the boundary of the tooth.

## 4   Caries Detection

From experimentation, the best results for caries identification were obtained when pixels along 10–15% of the boundary were analyzed. To achieve this, the distance between the two sides of the tooth was measured and the longest distance was used as the base width. Then the boundary region was expanded inwards by 10–15% of the maximum width and all points between the inner boundary and outer boundary were analyzed.

As there is no database to compare against it is important that the information obtained from the boundary is considered relative to the image itself. Due to the top and bottom hat transformations applied in the previous stage, all potential caries are highlighted as areas of darker contrast. In order to identify these regions a threshold value is calculated. This threshold is calculated to be 45% of the lower quartile of all the pixel values found along the boundary. All pixels below this value are hallmarked as potential caries and are analyzed further by an analytical system.

In order to ensure the identified clusters are not noise within the X-ray, the size of the cluster is evaluated relative to the boundary. If the cluster is greater than or equal to 1–2% of the total boundary region it is retained as a region of interest otherwise it is discarded.

Once all dark spots have been identified as regions of interest further feature extraction is required. The area around each caries cluster is evaluated using a connectivity mask. This is done to identify the intensity of the surrounding pixels and determine whether the dark patch is a caries region or simply a dark area of the tooth as a whole. The mean pixel value of the potential caries region is compared to the mean value of the surrounding tooth pixels. If the caries region is less than 80% of the surrounding mean then the area is flagged as a caries marker.

## 5   Results and Discussion

In this section the results for both the tooth segmentation and caries identification methods are outlined and evaluated. Both processes were applied to the dataset in [10] which contained 114 grayscale X-rays of both upper and lower jaw regions. A total of 380 teeth were analyzed across all the images and were comprised of healthy teeth, teeth with fillings, teeth with varying stages of dental caries and impacted teeth. Furthermore varying degrees of exposure levels were present across the dataset resulting in dark to pale radiographs. This allowed the algorithms to be tested against a wide spectrum of dental cases.

### 5.1   Segmentation Results

As the region of the jaw is unknown, an algorithm was used that allowed for separation regardless of the angle of the molar teeth. This was done as large gaps between the roots of some molar teeth were mistaken as a separation between teeth by the system. Table 1 shows the results of the segmentation process. Correctly separated segmented teeth are defined as being any tooth that is not partially separated during the process. The instances where teeth were not properly separated arise from images with poor image quality or extremely impacted teeth. Images with teeth at the edge of the image also proved problematic as the separation algorithm could not easily find a division line.

**Table 1.** Segmentation results

|  | Upper jaw | Lower jaw |
|---|---|---|
| Total number of teeth in 114 images | 141 | 239 |
| Number of correctly separated teeth | 120 | 216 |
| **% of correctly separated teeth** | **85%** | **90%** |

Table 2 shows how these results compare to existing separation algorithms. In order to determine the effectiveness of the changes made to the segmentation process used in this paper, a comparison is made with the results obtained by Nomir and Abdel-Mottaleb [7]. To determine if the segmentation results are able to allow for accurate caries diagnosis, a comparison is also made to the results of Oliveira [9]. The findings do however show that the segmentation process outlined in this paper yields better results than two existing methods.

## 5.2   Caries Detection Results

The results of the caries detection were compared against a set of ground tooth data in which some positively identified caries were present as well as some false positive flags. Regions of interest along the boundary were hallmarked for analysis through blob detection. These regions of interest were denoted as caries hallmarks after a statistical comparison of the surrounding area was done, which took into account gradual darkening of the area as part of the radiograph intensity rates, as well as the depth of the perceived caries to the edge of the boundary. Table 3 compares the results of the caries diagnoses against the ground truth data. As the ground truth did not contain all possible caries locations this comparison is done to determine the rate at which caries are missed.

**Table 2.** Segmentation results comparison

|  | Upper jaw | Lower jaw |
|---|---|---|
| Nomir and Abdel-Mottaleb [7] | 84% | 81% |
| Oliveira [9] | 72% | 72% |
| **Our approach** | **85%** | **90%** |

**Table 3.** Caries identification results (ground truth data)

|                                               | Upper jaw | Lower jaw |
|-----------------------------------------------|-----------|-----------|
| Total number of caries in the ground truth    | 28        | 41        |
| Number of correctly identified caries         | 26        | 36        |
| **% of correctly identified caries**          | **93%**   | **88%**   |

Table 4 shows a comparison against the findings of Tracy et al. [12], who tested the diagnostic rates of dentists using the Logicon Caries Detector system, Dykstra [13], who analyzed the diagnostic rates of dentists without the aid of CAD systems and Oliveira [9], who used a supervised learning approach to developing his classification algorithm.

**Table 4.** Caries identification results comparison (upper jaw)

|                                             | Our results | Tracy | Dykstra | Oliveira |
|---------------------------------------------|-------------|-------|---------|----------|
| Percentage of correctly categorized teeth   | **96%**     | 94%   | 60%     | 98%      |
| Percentage of false positives               | **2%**      | N/A   | 20%     | N/A      |
| Percentage of missed caries                 | **2%**      | 6%    | 20%     | 2%       |

Despite the identification rate obtained by Oliveira being marginally higher than that outlined in this paper, this is partly due to the nature of the input images. The slight loss of classification accuracy is offset by the ability of the system to diagnose non-uniform input and due to the nature of the algorithm being derived from an unsupervised learning model, results obtained from images spanning a large spectrum of X-ray density levels will favour the approach outlined above.

## 5.3   Conclusion and Future Work

In this paper, an unsupervised learning approach for dental caries detection has been presented. This approach incorporates the use of several adapted and modified methods for the purpose of segmentation, as well as new analysis methods for determining the presence of caries. The proposed approach segments accurately bitewing images either top or bottom jaws into individual tooth. Furthermore, the proposed approach achieved a positive dental caries detection rate of 96%. The approach obtains a high success rate comparable to the existing techniques, and it is capable of detecting caries hallmarks relative to the boundary of the tooth. Further work analyzing both bitewing and panoramic X-rays is envisaged.

# References

1. Vos, T., Flaxman, A.D., Naghavi, M., et al.: Years lived with disability (YLDS) for 1160 sequelae of 289 diseases and injuries 1990–2010: a systematic analysis for the global burden of disease study 2010. Lancet **380**, 2163–2196 (2013)
2. da Silveira Moreira, R.: Epidemiology of Dental Caries in the World. INTECH Open Access Publisher, Rijeka (2012)
3. Fasihinia, H., Khalesi, M., et al.: Dental caries diagnostic methods. Avicenna J. Dent. Res. **2**, 1–12 (2011)
4. Rad, A.E., Rahim, M.S.M., Norouzi, A.: Digital dental x-ray image segmentation and feature extraction. Indonesian J. Electr. Eng. Comput. Sci. **11**, 3109–3114 (2013)
5. Zhou, J., Abdel-Mottaleb, M.: A content-based system for human identification based on bitewing dental x-ray images. Pattern Recogn. **38**, 2132–2142 (2005)
6. Jain, A.K., Chen, H.: Matching of dental x-ray images for human identification. Pattern Recogn. **37**, 1519–1532 (2004)
7. Nomir, O., Abdel-Mottaleb, M.: A system for human identification from x-ray dental radiographs. Pattern Recogn. **38**, 1295–1305 (2005)
8. Lin, P.L., Lai, Y.H., Huang, P.W.: Dental biometrics: human identification based on teeth and dental works in bitewing radiographs. Pattern Recogn. **45**, 934–946 (2012)
9. Oliveira, J.: Caries detection in panoramic dental x-ray images (2009)
10. Dental Clinic, Health Center (UTM): Dental x-ray (periapical) dataset (2013)
11. Hu, S., Hoffman, E.A., Reinhardt, J.M.: Automatic lung segmentation for accurate quantitation of volumetric x-ray CT images. IEEE Trans. Med. Imaging **20**, 490–498 (2001)
12. Tracy, K.D., Dykstra, B.A., et al.: Utility and effectiveness of computer-aided diagnosis of dental caries. Gen. Dent. **59**, 136–144 (2010)
13. Dykstra, B.: Interproximal caries detection: how good are we? Dent. Today **27**, 144–146 (2008)

# Vessel Detection on Cerebral Angiograms Using Convolutional Neural Networks

Yang Fu, Jiawen Fang, Benjamin Quachtran, Natia Chachkhiani, and Fabien Scalzo$^{(\boxtimes)}$

Neurovascular Imaging Research Core,
Department of Neurology and Computer Science, University of California,
Los Angeles (UCLA), Los Angeles, USA
fab@cs.ucla.edu

**Abstract.** Blood-vessel segmentation in cerebral angiograms is a valuable tool for medical diagnosis. However, manual blood-vessel segmentation is a time consuming process that requires high levels of expertise. The automatic detection of blood vessels can not only improve efficiency but also allow for the development of automatic diagnosis systems. Vessel detection can be approached as a binary classification problem, identifying each pixel as a vessel or non-vessel. In this paper, we use deep convolutional neural networks (CNNs) for vessel segmentation. The network is tested on a cerebral angiogram dataset. The results show the effectiveness of deep learning approach resulting in an accuracy of 95%.

## 1 Introduction

Cerebral angiography is the gold standard imaging technique for visualizing blood vessels in the brain. It is an X-ray image obtained through injection of contrast dye into an artery. Blood vessel segmentation is important for many clinical diagnostic tasks such as arteriosclerosis, arteriovenous malformations, vasculitis and tears in the lining of an artery. For some diagnostic tasks it is necessary to measure the vessel diameter, length, abnormal branching or bulging of the vessels. Unfortunately, manual segmentation of vessels is complex and tedious, limiting the study of large cohorts of images. Therefore, there is a need for automatic blood vessel detection systems. Automating vessel segmentation is beyond current methods due to the challenge associated with noise, bone artifacts, and significant differences in the diameter of arteries and veins.

Several different methods have been developed to segment blood vessels. The vast majority of the literature, however, focuses on retinal images since there are many public data sets available such as DRIVE, STARE, ARIA, ImageRet and Messidor [1]. The discussion of methods pertaining to vessel segmentation is largely validated and derived from this area of research. A comprehensive survey [2] described over 70 papers and proposed to classify major approaches in following areas: matched filtering [3], morphological processing [4], multi-modal

---

Yang Fu and Jiawen Fang contributed equally to this paper.

© Springer International Publishing AG 2016
G. Bebis et al. (Eds.): ISVC 2016, Part I, LNCS 10072, pp. 659–668, 2016.
DOI: 10.1007/978-3-319-50835-1_59

approach, vessel tracing/tracking [5] and pattern classification/machine Learning. Above algorithms are not specific to retinal vessels and can, in principle, be applied to other vasculatures. In practice, however, standard morphological and tracking methods do not offer satisfying results to the challenging nature of brain angiograms.

Vessel segmentation based on pattern classification and machine learning has become a very popular one in the last two decades. Recent improvements in computer hardware and interest in big data have led to advances in machine learning and one sub-field that holds immense promise for biomedical imaging applications is Deep Learning. It is now well established as an effective method of pattern recognition and has been applied to a wide variety of biomedical problems, including detection of intracranial hypertension [6], prediction of lesion growth in stroke [7], and detection of hyperperfusion in MRI [8]. These systems could provide valuable inputs to physicians in terms of computer-aided diagnosis.

Several researchers have been attempted to apply CNNs to vessel segmentation problem in retinal images using a 10-layer CNN [9] to classify each pixel as a vessel or non-vessel, or using an ensemble of 12 three layer networks [10] with randomly selected patches for each network. The use of a Conditional Random Fields(CRFs) after CNN classification seems also promising [11]. The CNNs are used for generating vessel probability maps to distinguish between vessel and the background. Afterwards CRFs are used to combine the given map and long-range interactions between pixels for final classification.

Our method is inspired by these recent works in vessel segmentation in retinal images using deep learning. The proposed solution uses deep network as a pixel classifier for vessel segmentation. In this method, the neural network is trained using raw pixels extracted from angiograms instead of extracting the feature vectors first. Each image is segmented into small patches. The central pixel is labeled either as a vessel or background. These patches are fed to the CNN as an input. The networks output layer is a binary classifier labeling the central pixel of each input patch. This paper evaluates the effectiveness of deep learning models (specifically convolutional neural networks) when applied to automatic detection of blood vessels on cerebral angiograms.

## 2    Methods

### 2.1    Dataset

The imaging dataset used in this study was collected from patients evaluated at a comprehensive stroke center and identified with symptoms of acute ischemic stroke. The use of this dataset was approved by the local Institutional Review Board (IRB). Inclusion criteria for this study included: (1) final diagnosis of acute ischemic stroke, (2) last known well time within six hours at admission, (3) Digital Subtraction Angiography (DSA) of the brain performed as part of a thrombectomy procedure. A total of 88 patients satisfied the above criteria and were included in this study. The DSA scanning was performed on a Philips

Allura Xper FD20® Biplane using a routine timed contrast-bolus passage technique. A manual injection of omnipaque 300 was performed at a dilution of 70% (30% saline) such that 10cc of contrast was administered intravenously at an approximate rate of $5\,\mathrm{cm}^3/\mathrm{s}$. The median peak voltage output of 95 Kv, IQR 86, 104. Image size were all $1024 \times 1024$ but were acquired with different field of view.

### 2.2   Pre-processing

**Patch Sampling.** For training, we exploit a set of cerebral angiograms and their corresponding manually labeled images. The dataset $\{X, Y\}$ used to train and to evaluate the predictive model is created by extracting local patches of fixed size $m \times m$ among input images with their corresponding label. Each patch is described by its raw pixel values, yielding an input vector of $s = n \times 1 \times m \times m$ dimensions. Where $n$ is number of inputs, 1 represents grayscale channel and $m$ is a patch size. Our method samples a large number of patches at random positions from all training images. The inputs to the network were normalized by subtracting the mean and diving it by standard deviation across all patches, resulting in the data having zero mean and standard deviation of one.

### 2.3   Predictive Model

Convolutional neural networks (CNNs) have been used with great success for image classification and segmentation tasks. CNNs learn relevant features from data itself, which often produces state of the art results in many applications. Since our goal is to do vessel segmentation on cerebral angiograms, we believe deep learning can provide an automated solution to detecting blood vessels.

CNNs consist of sequence of alternating convolutional and max pooling layers followed by fully connected layers. The network takes input data consisting of image samples and maps them to output class probabilities. Both feature extraction and classification parameters are optimized during the network training at each "epoch". Each epoch consists of a "feed forward" step that involves feeding inputs, followed by a "back-propagation" step that involves adjusting the network's parameters by back-propagating the error. No prior knowledge of the features has been incorporated in the model. To test the accuracy of the trained network, we provide independent X-ray images, and compare the outcomes to the values manually assigned by experts.

**Convolutional Layer.** In constructing a Neural Network, we are able to generate learnable filters that can identify features linked to an input's proper classification. Convolutional layers can consist of many filters and, when stacked together, can expand the number of detectable features used for learning. For each layer's filter, the 2D convolutional operation between filter $W$ and input image $X$ is calculated as

$$f(x, y) = \sum_{m_1=0}^{N_1} \sum_{m_2=0}^{N_2} X_{m_1, m_2} \cdot W_{x-m_1, y-m_2} \tag{1}$$

Where $m_1$ ($m_2$) is the local region of the input, which is connected to the convolution layers, and $W$ means the filters or the kernel for input of Convolution Layers. The activation function is then applied to $f(x, y)$, providing a standardized measurement of the convolutional outputs. Use of a rectifier function

$$y(z) = \max(0, z) \tag{2}$$

where $z$ is the input to the neuron, has been shown to create networks that converge faster than those utilizing sigmoidal or hyperbolic functions [12].

**Max-Pooling Layer.** The ability of CNN's to extract features can be computationally intensive due to the large number of parameters present. To combat this, max-pooling can be used to select only key values in a local region, disregarding other non-critical elements and thereby reducing the number of network parameters. The input, with dimensions $M \times N$, is divided into $\frac{M*N}{L^2}$ sub-regions, each of size $L \times L$, and from each sub-region a single maximum value is sampled. The result is a down-sampling that maintains the relative locations of the local maxima.

**Fully-Connected Layer.** Fully-connected layers operate through element-wise multiplication of a vector of input neurons $x_m$ and a filter matrix $w_{mn}$ that is summed and passed through an activation function.

$$O_n = f\left(\sum_m x_n w_{mn}\right) \tag{3}$$

where $W$ is the weight matrix, $m$ is the number of input $x$ and $n$ is the dimension of the input $x$. These dense outputs can generate meaningful probabilistic results through use of a softmax activation, shown to be an effective output stage for classification in CNN's because its ability to characterize multi-class regressions [12, 13]. The softmax activation gives a likelihood function

$$P(y_j = k | x_j) = \frac{\exp(x_j \theta_k^T)}{\sum_{k=1}^{M} \exp(x_j \theta_k^T)} \tag{4}$$

for input $x_j$ and model parameter vectors $\theta_k$ with $k$ rows. A maximum likelihood estimator is then used to predict the correct label

$$L_j = \text{argmax}_k P(y_j = k | x_j) \tag{5}$$

**Back-Propagation.** Proper weight calibration can be achieved using a feed-forward back-propagation algorithm that is able to fine-tune each filter's parameters through gradient descent of an error function $E$. For predicted labels $L_j$ and ground truths $y_j$, the categorical cross-entropy error is defined as

$$E = -\sum_j y_j \log L_j \tag{6}$$

Upon each feed-forward iteration, consisting of the layers mentioned in prior sections, the gradient of the error with respect to the layer weights is calculated using the chain rule

$$\frac{\partial E}{\partial w_{ij}} = \frac{\partial E}{\partial y_j} \frac{\partial y_j}{\partial u_j} \frac{\partial u_j}{\partial w_{ij}} \tag{7}$$

where $u_j$ and $y_j$ are the inputs and outputs of a given network layer. The weights $w_i$ are adjusted in the direction of the negative gradient, thus decreasing the error function's value.

**Neural Network Architecture.** Our overall goal is to use the predicted values from each patch to construct a full prediction image. We can use our knowledge of the patch sampling process to associate the CNN's outputs with coordinates, and reconstruct a full image. Then the entire image can be interpreted by a clinician, or used for further data-driven analysis. To quantify the error in our predictions, we use accuracy and an area under the ROC curve (AUC) approach.

The model using dilated convolutions consists of 12 total layers (Fig. 1). The network has an input layer, 3 convolutional layers, two MaxPooling layers following with two LRN layers, and two fully-connected, two drop out and an output layer. The input layer can accept varying patch sizes, and the output layer will always produce one binary output per input patch. We worked with a variety of input sizes while developing the model, but experimented primarily with smaller patches in sizes: $37 \times 37$, $29 \times 29$, $21 \times 21$.

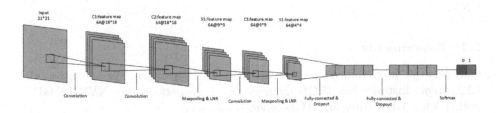

**Fig. 1.** A visual representation of the CNN model's layer architecture

Relatively smaller filters were used in every convolutional layer with sizes of $3 \times 3$ and $2 \times 2$. It has been shown that smaller filter sizes act as a good regularization technique which prevents over-fitting. The output dimensions of convolutional layer is calculated by subtracting the filter size from input size and adding 1. If the input has dimension of $n \times n$ and the filter size is of $m \times m$ then the output dimensions of convolutional layer is $(n - m + 1) \times (n - m + 1)$.

The network training is done using Stochastic Gradient Descent (SGD) and nesterov momentum. The learning rate starts at 0.1 and slows down as training proceeds stopping at 0.0001. The momentum is also updated across the epochs from 0.9 to 0.999. The produced features from convolutional layers are fed to fully connected layer where output neurons are connected to every input neuron. The final output layer is a fully connected layer with two neurons per class for vessel and non-vessel.

The input to the network is the collection of square patches extracted from training images, which has corresponding manually segmented images used for supervised learning. The odd number of pixel blocks are chosen with central pixel and surrounding region in order to classify the central pixel as vessel or non-vessel. After the training is done, the trained model is used to classify each pixel from the test image. The resulting pixel classification is used reconstruct the original image providing visual of the segmented image.

The equal amounts of positive and negative samples were used for training in order to avoid the bias. All the manually labeled blood vessels were considered positive examples and everything else as negative. Since the amount of patches extracted per image exceeded 100k, the patches were randomly sub-sampled for each image to reduce the size of training input. Positive and negative samples were shuffled before passing it to CNN.

The main hyper-parameters we had to vary were the size of the kernels, the amount of output maps of each layer, the number of neurons for fully connected layers, classification threshold, and size of the input patches. These hyper-parameters must be adjusted for different data sets, and currently there aren't standardized or codified recommendations for selecting these hyper-parameters in the Deep learning community. Hyper-parameter selection was performed using a manual approach: we compared accuracy, quality of predictive images, and computational time. Selecting parameters that create long computational times can make it difficult to reproduce results and lower the practical value of the CNN.

## 2.4   Experiments

Our network was trained on Amazon EC2 GPU instance, specifically model *g2.2xlarge*. Instance has 15 GB memory and high-performance NVIDIA GPU, with 1,536 CUDA cores and 4 GB of video memory.

All of our Deep learning experiments described use patches extracted from 2D cerebral angiography images. Our experiment was meant to examine how the predictions of our deep learning network compared with the manual annotations. We wanted to quantify how accurate a deep learning approach is, and how viable the predictive abilities are for future research and clinical applications.

For our experiments, we tried number of different sized square patches ranging from 37 × 37 to 9 × 9. Larger patches such as 29 and up, resulted in a very
low classification accuracy, which may be explained by other content and background noise in the patch, that confused the classifier. The best results were
achieved when we used inputs with a patch size of 21 × 21. We also tried different pre-processing techniques such as standard normalization, PCA and ZCA
whitening on resulting patches or no pre-processing at all before feeding it to
network (Fig. 2).

Original DSA              Groundtruth              CNN result

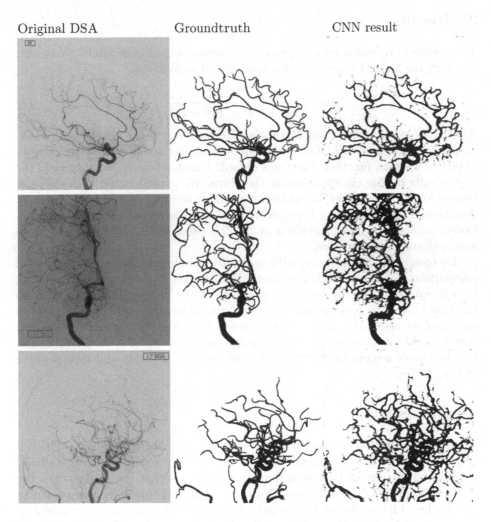

**Fig. 2.** Illustration the CNN vessel detection model on 3 images.

Samples from 88 patients were used for training and testing. These were split
into 3 groups, so that each group could be tested with a CNN trained by the other

group (3-fold validation). Each of these test patients had an existing "ground truth" image that was produced by Neurology experts. We directly compared the predictive output to the ground truth images, using accuracy and the area under ROC curve as quantitative measures of success.

We experimented with range of CNN architectures. Experiments included varying number of convolutional/max-pooling/fully connected layers, trying different numbers of neurons for fully connected layers, and changing the probabilities for drop-out layers to compare the results of each architecture.

## 3    Results

The results were evaluated using metrics in terms of area under ROC curve $auc$, accuracy $acc$ and $f1 - score$, which are defined as following:

$$acc = \frac{TP + FP}{TP + FP + TN + FN} \tag{8}$$

AUC score is calculated using Python's *sklearn* library. The classification decision for training and validation sets is made using default threshold of 0.5 probability of softmax function. The same default threshold value does not yield the best results during classification on test data. We experimented with different threshold values in order to achieve maximum $acc$ and $auc$ scores. The best results were achieved using network with dilated convolutional layers with following parameters: input patch size of $21 \times 21$, patches normalized by zero mean and unit standard deviation.

By comparing these images with manually annotated images, we obtained a comparison of accuracy using area under ROC curve. Through visual inspection, we can quantitatively analyze the accuracy of the images; this is relevant to the way imaging is used quantitatively in clinical practice. In addition, we can qualitatively assess the results; this approach is relevant to data-driven medical solutions. The $auc$ for our CNN gave an average accuracy of $95.71 \pm 2.77\%$. The best $acc$ score achieved is 0.9884, with true positive of 0.9416 and false positive of 0.0085 (Fig. 1).

## 4    Discussion

There are many advantages to Deep learning, and specifically convolutional neural networks. They are relatively fast to develop and use computationally efficient techniques. In particular, having kernel sizes that are smaller than the input layer gives CNNs a unique advantage compared to similar Deep learning approaches [14] that do not have smaller kernel sizes. The networks are modular, easy to implement in a variety of coding languages, and can be customized to do learning on a variety of input types.

The main downside is the lack of standardized hyper-parameter selection [15]. This can make it difficult to apply neural networks to new problems without manual manipulation. In the future, a more systematic approach to hyper-parameter selection could improve results. In addition, we could improve the amount of training data, as this is a consistent way to improve neural network performance [15]. Another promising improvement would be the use of 3D patches. There is already evidence of the effectiveness of 3D patches for CNNs that use spatial and temporal information [16].

Comparing the vessel segmentation results on cerebral angiograms to published papers on vessel detection in retinal images we notice few differences. We see that when applying the described architectures and approaches to vessel detection on cerebral angiograms, they yield to much lower accuracy. This can be explained by more uniform diameter of vessels in retinal images. Whereas the difference in diameter of finer vessels and larger arteries in cerebral angiograms are much more significant. These variations require much larger networks, with bigger training set to achieve desirable results. By utilizing dilated convolutions in our model we increased the classification accuracy compared to when using regular convolutional layers as described in number of other papers for retinal images.

In future experiments, it could be advantageous to use a larger training set; in this experiment, we were limited by the availability of quality data sets and computational resources. Other improvements would include training multiple networks and averaging the classification accuracy to remove the bias. One major improvement for future studies would be to have additional experts produce manual annotations that were used as ground truth. All ground truth was based on manual annotations from two experts; it is possible that the manual annotations could be closer to an actual ground truth if we averaged results from many experts.

The automatic detection of blood vessel in cerebral angiograms is one step closer to the automatic quantification of blood flow [17,18] on DSA in major arteries of the brain.

## 5   Conclusion

Overall, while convolutional neural networks can be challenging to design optimally, they have powerful predictive abilities. We conclude that the use of 12 layer convolutional neural network was computationally adequate to detect blood vessels in cerebral angiograms. Our results imply that a computationally simple CNN has great potential as an accurate method for vessel segmentation. However, there is room for improvement using more complex network architectures. This has potential to aid decision making in a clinical setting and provide clinicians with a powerful tool.

**Acknowledgments.** Prof. Scalzo was partially supported by a AHA grant $16BGIA27760152$, a Spitzer grant, and received hardware donations from Gigabyte, Nvidia, and Intel.

# References

1. Staal, J., Abramoff, M., Niemeijer, M., Viergever, M., van Ginneken, B.: Ridge based vessel segmentation in color images of the retina. IEEE Trans. Med. Imaging **23**, 501–509 (2004)
2. Fraz, M.M., Remagnino, P., Hoppe, A., Uyyanonvara, B., Rudnicka, A.R., Owen, C.G., Barman, S.A.: Blood vessel segmentation methodologies in retinal images-a survey. Comput. Methods Programs Biomed. **108**, 407–433 (2012)
3. Chaudhuri, S., Chatterjee, S., Katz, N., Nelson, M., Goldbaum, M.: Detection of blood vessels in retinal images using two-dimensional matched filters. IEEE Trans. Med. Imaging **8**, 263–269 (1989)
4. Zana, F., Klein, J.C.: Segmentation of vessel-like patterns using mathematical morphology and curvature evaluation. IEEE Trans. Image Process. **10**, 1010–1019 (2001)
5. Can, A., Shen, H., Turner, J.N., Tanenbaum, H.L., Roysam, B.: Rapid automated tracing and feature extraction from retinal fundus images using direct exploratory algorithms. IEEE Trans. Inf. Technol. Biomed. **3**, 125–138 (1999)
6. Quachtran, B., Hamilton, R., Scalzo, F.: Detection of intracranial hypertension using deep learning. In: ICPR, pp. 1–6 (2016)
7. Stier, N., Vincent, N., Liebeskind, D., Scalzo, F.: Deep learning of tissue fate features in acute ischemic stroke. In: IEEE BIBM, pp. 1316–1321 (2015)
8. Vincent, N., Stier, N., Yu, S., Liebeskind, D.S., Wang, D.J., Scalzo, F.: Detection of hyperperfusion on arterial spin labeling using deep learning. In: IEEE BIBM, pp. 1322–1327 (2015)
9. Melinščak, M., Prentašić, P., Lončarić, S.: Retinal vessel segmentation using deep neural networks. In: VISAPP (2015)
10. Maji, D., Santara, A., Mitra, P., Sheet, D.: Ensemble of deep convolutional neural networks for learning to detect retinal vessels in fundus images. arXiv preprint arxiv:1603.04833 (2016)
11. Fu, H., Xu, Y., Wong, D.W.K., Liu, J.: Retinal vessel segmentation via deep learning network and fully-connected conditional random fields. In: ISBI (2016)
12. Krizhevsky, A., Sutskever, I., Hinton, G.E.: Imagenet classification with deep convolutional neural networks. In: NIPS, pp. 1097–1105 (2012)
13. Karpathy, A., Toderici, G., Shetty, S., Leung, T., Sukthankar, R., Fei-Fei, L.: Large-scale video classification with convolutional neural networks. In: CVPR (2014)
14. Goodfellow, I., Bengio, Y., Courville, A.: Deep Learning. MIT Press (2016). http://www.deeplearningbook.org
15. Simard, P.Y., Steinkraus, D., Platt, J.C.: Best practices for convolutional neural networks applied to visual document analysis. In: ICDAR, pp. 958–963 (2003)
16. Ji, S., Xu, W., Yang, M., Yu, K.: 3D convolutional neural networks for human action recognition. IEEE TPAMI **35**, 221–231 (2013)
17. Scalzo, F., Liebeskind, D.S.: Perfusion angiography in acute ischemic stroke. Comput. Math. Methods Med. **2016**, 1–14 (2016)
18. Scalzo, F., Hao, Q., Walczak, A.M., Hu, X., Hoi, Y., Hoffmann, K.R., Liebeskind, D.S.: Computational hemodynamics in intracranial vessels reconstructed from biplane angiograms. In: Bebis, G., et al. (eds.) ISVC 2010. LNCS, vol. 6455, pp. 359–367. Springer, Heidelberg (2010). doi:10.1007/978-3-642-17277-9_37

# False Positive Reduction in Breast Mass Detection Using the Fusion of Texture and Gradient Orientation Features

Mariam Busaleh[1], Muhammad Hussain[1(✉)], Hatim A. Aboalsamh[1(✉)], Mansour Zuair[2], and George Bebis[3]

[1] Department of Computer Science, King Saud University, Riyadh, Saudi Arabia
mhussain@ksu.edu.sa, mariam.bosaleh@gmail.com
[2] Department of Computer Science, College of Computer and Information Sciences, King Saud University, Riyadh, Saudi Arabia
[3] Department of Computer Science and Engineering, University of Nevada, Reno, USA

**Abstract.** The presence of masses in mammograms is among the main indicators of breast cancer and their diagnosis is a challenging task. The one problem of Computer aided diagnosis (CAD) systems developed to assist radiologists in detecting masses is high false positive rate i.e. normal breast tissues are detected as masses. This problem can be reduced if localised texture and gradient orientation patterns in suspicious Regions Of Interest (ROIs) are captured in a robust way. Discriminative Robust Local Binary Pattern (DRLBP) and Discriminative Robust Local Ternary Pattern (DRLTP) are among the state-of-the-art best texture descriptors whereas Histogram of Oriented Gradient (HOG) is one of the best descriptor for gradient orientation patterns. To capture the discriminative micro-patterns existing in ROIs, we propose localised DRLBP-HOG and DRLTP-HOG descriptors by fusing DRLBP, DRLTP and HOG for the description of ROIs; the localisation is archived by dividing each ROI into a number of blocks (sub-images). Support Vector Machine (SVM) is used to classify mass or normal ROIs. The evaluation on DDSM, a benchmark mammograms database, revealed that localised DRLBP-HOG with 9 (3×3) blocks forms the best representation and yields an accuracy of 99.80±0.62(ACC±STD) outperforming the state-of-the-art methods.

## 1 Introduction

The statistics reported by the American Cancer Society show that 246,660 new breast cancer cases and 40,890 deaths are expected in 2016, breast cancer alone is expected to account for 29% of all new cancer cases among women [1]. According to a report by King Faisal Specialist Hospital and Research Centre in Riyadh, the number of new cancer cases in Saudi Arabia has increased by more than 25% in the past 15 years, and is expected to rise considerably in the future. At 15% of the total number of cancers, breast cancer is the most common cancer

© Springer International Publishing AG 2016
G. Bebis et al. (Eds.): ISVC 2016, Part I, LNCS 10072, pp. 669–678, 2016.
DOI: 10.1007/978-3-319-50835-1_60

type, followed by colorectal cancer with the share of 10.4% [2]. One of the main symptoms of breast cancer is the presence of masses in the breast. The studies have proven that the early detection of cancer would increase the life expectancy of the patients [1].

A mammogram is the most effective imaging modality for early breast cancer detection. However, computer aided diagnosis of masses with mammograms is a challenging task. About 95 % of the 10 % of women, whose mammogram is found to be abnormal, do not have cancer i.e. the number of false positives is high [1]. Many techniques have been proposed to overcome this problem. The efficiency and robustness of any technique depend on how effective is it in representing the micro-structures of ROIs. Recently, texture [3–7,14] and gradient orientation based [8] descriptors have been employed separately to represent ROIs and their performances indicate that both texture and gradient orientation micropatterns play important role in the discrimination of ROIs. As such, the fusion of texture and gradient orientation based descriptors can result in a more effective and robust description of ROI. Based on this idea, we propose new descriptors DRLBP-HOG and DRLTP-HOG by fusing DRLBP and DRLTP, which are stat-of-the-art best texture descriptors, and HOG, which is one of the best descriptor for gradient orientation patterns. Different micro-patterns exit at different locations in an ROI and to take into account their location is also important. We incorporate location information by dividing an ROI into a number of blocks (sub-images), thus computing localised DRLBP-HOG and DRLTP-HOG descriptors, which effectively capture the discriminative information of ROIs. For classification, we used SVM, and evaluated the proposed descriptors using DDSM, a benchmark database. Our method outperforms the state-of-the-art methods by giving an accuracy of 99.80±0.6201.

The organization of the rest of the paper is as follows. In the next section, we give an overview of the stat-of-the-art techniques for false positive reduction. In Sect. 3, the methodology has been described in detail. Section 4 presents the results and discussion. Section 5 concludes the paper with future work.

## 2    Related Work

In this section, first we present an overview of the recent work related to texture description and then we briefly review the recent methods which have been proposed for false positive reduction in mammogram based Computer Aided Diagnosis (CAD) systems for masses. We will focuss mainly on those techniques which employ different texture descriptors and gradient orientation for the representation of ROIs.

Local Binary Pattern (LBP) [9] and Local Ternary Pattern (LTP) are two state-of-the-art local texture features, which have given promising performance results in many recognition and detection problems [3]. Both LBP and LTP suffer from the problem of brightness reversal of object and background i.e., they treat differently the bright object against a dark background and dark object against a bright background. Also, they do not differentiate between local patterns having weak contrast and those with strong contrast. To overcome these issues associated with LBP and LTP, Amit at el. [10] proposed Discriminative Robust Local Binary Pattern (DRLBP) and Discriminative Robust Local Ternary Pattern (DRLTP). Both DRLBP and DRLTP incorporate texture and edge information and are robust against the problem of the brightness reversal of object and background. Also, they discriminate between weak contrast and strong contrast local patterns.

Different types of texture features have been used to describe suspicious ROIs for false positive reduction. Llad et al. [3] proposed a new approach for false positive reduction. For the description of ROIs, they used localised LBP descriptor to differentiate true masses and normal parenchyma. First, they divide each ROI into blocks, extract LBP codes from each block, compute histogram of LBP codes, and finally concatenate the histograms corresponding to all blocks to form the descriptor. They used SVM for classification. This method yielded AUC of 0.94 on DDSM database.

Employing co-occurrence matrix and optical density transformation, Shen-Chuan et al. [11] proposed two complex descriptors, which describe local texture and the discrete photometric distribution of ROIs. For discriminating abnormal ROIs from normal ones, they used stepwise linear discriminant analysis, where decision is taken by selecting and rating the individual performance of each feature. The performance of this method in terms of area under ROC (AUC) is 0.98.

Abdel-Nasser et al. [6] proposed uniform local directional pattern (ULDP) descriptor for feature extraction from ROIs. This descriptor encodes the neighborhood of a pixel in an ROI based on its edge responses and spatial information. The histogram of ULDP forms the descriptor of an ROI and characterizes breast masses as well as different tissues in the breast. With SVM as classification technique, the performance of this method on MIAS database is 0.93 in terms of AUC.

Oliveira et al. [5] addressed the problem of the discrimination of ROIs as mass and non-mass using SVM. For the description of ROIs, they employed two types of texture features: taxonomic diversity index and taxonomic distinctness. They used logarithmic non-linear contrast enhancement to improve the quality of the regions and a mean filter mask to eliminate small structures from ROIs. The performance of this method on DDSM database is 98.8 % in terms of accuracy.

Liu et al. [12] used texture features extracted employing gray level co-occurrence matrix (GLCM) and completed local binary pattern (CLBP) for the description of ROIs in their automatic mass detection method. They used support vector machine (SVM) to classify ROIs whether non-masses or masses. The performance results in this paper are given in terms of sensitivity and specificity, the results show that there is significant reduction if false positives.

Employing Gabor filters optimised with particle swarm optimization (PSO) technique for texture feature description from ROIs, Salabat et al. [13] proposed a false positive reduction method, which uses SVM for classification. This method archived an accuracy of 98.82 % on DDSM database.

Pomponiu et al. [8] proposed an approach based on histogram of oriented gradients (HOG) for decreasing mass false positives by a computer aided detection (CAD) system. After describing ROIs using HOG, they classify them to identify mass and non-mass with support vector machine (SVM).

Different texture features and gradient orientation separately have been used for the description of ROIs and have shown promising results. Employing stat-of-the-art best texture descriptors DRLBP and DRLTP and gradient orientation based features such as HOG, we propose new descriptors for ROI description, which are more effective in the discrimination of mass and non-mass tissues.

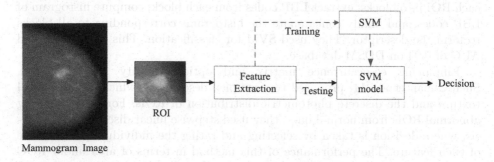

**Fig. 1.** An overview of false positive reduction method

# 3    Methodology

In computer aided diagnosis of masses in mammograms, suspicious mass regions are extracted from a mammogram; these ROIs may be true masses or normal tissues, which have been falsely identified as masses (false positives). The false positive reduction problem is to identify whether a suspicious ROI is a mass or normal tissue and it is a classification problem involving two classes (mass or normal tissue). An overview of the proposed method for false positive reduction is shown in Fig. 1. The main steps in this method are an ROI description and SVM, a classifier. Classification performance depends on how much discriminatory is the description of ROIs. We propose two techniques for ROI description in the next subsection.

## 3.1    Feature Extraction

Texture and gradient orientation patterns in a mammogram play important role in the discrimination of masses from normal parenchyma. Capturing these patterns effectively can lead to a discriminative description of ROIs, which result in small intra-class variation and large inter-class variation. In this section, we propose two descriptors which effectively encode texture and gradient orientation patterns.

LBP [9] is a local feature that is commonly used for texture description and has shown promising performance in many applications. LBP code of each pixel in an image is computed using a neighborhood (P, R), where P is the number of neighbors and R is the radius of the neighborhood. The intensities of the neighbors are converted into bits by thresholding them with the intensity value of the central pixel and a binary code is formed, which is the LBP code of the central pixel. LBP codes of all pixels are calculated and the histogram of these codes is computed, which is an LBP description of the image. There are four variants of LBP: simple LBP (LBP), uniform LBP ($LBP^u$), rotation invariant LBP ($LBP^{ri}$) and uniform rotation invariant LBP ($LBP^{uri}$). We tested all variants and found that ($LBP^u$) gives the best results among all variants of LBP. It is robust to illumination and contrast variations, but sensitive to noise, small pixel fluctuations and does not differentiate between weak and strong contrast [10]. To overcome the drawbacks of LBP, Satpathy et al. [10] proposed DRLBP. In LBP descriptor, uniform weights are given to LBP codes while binning them into the histogram irrespective of whether an LBP pattern has a weak contrast or strong contrast. To account for the contrast of an LBP pattern, an LBP code is weighted by the corresponding pixel gradient magnitude before binning into the histogram. The resulting descriptor is called Discriminative Robust Local Binary Pattern (DRLBP). It is invariant to changes of contrast and shape, and is more suitable for capturing texture patterns of breast masses, which involve changes in contrast and shape. Note that DRLBP involves gradient magnitude to weight LBP codes according to their local contrast edge micro-patterns, but does not employ gradient orientation and so it does not encode the gradient orientation patterns, which are also important for the discrimination of mass ROIs. Pomponiu et al. [8] have shown its effectiveness. We use HOG [15] to represent gradient orientation patterns.

HOG descriptor is computed as the histogram of gradient directions or edge orientations over the pixels, and thus it captures the gradient orientations patterns. It has excellent performance in many pattern recognition tasks including effective decrease in mass false positives for Computer aided diagnosis [8]. Fusing DRLBP and HOG, we compute DRLBP-HOG descriptor, which is robust in capturing texture edge micropatterns under illumination as well as contrast variations and gradient orientation patterns.

Local Ternary Pattern (LTP) is a variant of LBP, which is robust against noise. Similar to DRLBP, Discriminative Robust Local Ternary Pattern (DRLTP) descriptor is computed that is robust against illumination, contrast and shape changes [10]. Fusing DRLTP and HOG, we calculate DRLTP-HOG descriptor, which effectively represents the discriminative content of mass ROIs.

Note that DRLBP-HOG and DRLTP-HOG accumulate local edge micro-patterns and gradient orientation patterns occurring at different locations, thus giving their global distributions, which do not take into account the fine local structural detail. To determine the local distributions of DRLBP-HOG and DRLTP-HOG descriptors for capturing the final local structural detail, we

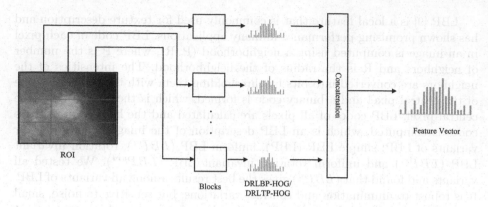

**Fig. 2.** The detail of extracting localised DRLBP-HOG and DRLTP-HOG descriptors

divide each ROI into a number of blocks, compute DRLBP-HOG and DRLTP-HOG descriptors from each block and then concatenate them to form localised DRLBP-HOG and DRLTP-HOG descriptors, Fig. 2 shows this process.

### 3.2    Classification

False positive reduction is a two class classification problem and it has been shown that for this problem, SVM outperforms other classifiers like multilayer perception (MLP)[16]. The SVM performs classification task by constructing optimal hyperplane with maximum margin in a multidimensional space that separates regions belonging to the two classes [17]. SVM is a linear classier but in general the space of DRLBP-HOG and DRLTP-HOG features is not linearly separable. The solution is kernel trick, which transforms the original space to a higher dimensional space where the original space becomes linearly separable. As the Radial Basis Function (RBF) kernel has shown promising results in mass classification, so we employ RBF kernel. SVM with RBF kernel involves two parameters: $\sigma$, the width of RBF kernel and C, the soft margin parameter. Using training data, ten-fold cross-validation, and loose and fine grid search, the optimal values of these parameters are calculated [16].

## 4    Result and Discussion

In this section we present the results and discuss them. For the validation of the proposed method, we test it using 512 ROIs taken from Digital Database for Screening Mammography (DDSM) [11] using the annotation of each case selecting the cases which are not obvious. Half of these ROIs are normal, but look like mass ROIs, some sample ROIs have been shown in Fig. 3.

The proposed method involves several parameters: $\sigma$, the width of RBF kernel, C, the soft margin parameter, the number of blocks for the division

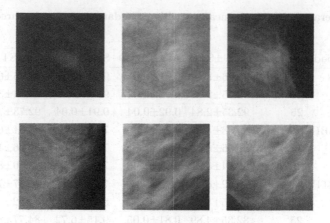

**Fig. 3.** Top Row Mass ROIs, Bottom Row Normal ROIs

of an ROI, and the number of bins in HOG. The first two parameters are related to SVM and are tuned using the method described in Sect. 2. We divided ROIs into numbers of blocks N×N, N = 3, 4 and 5 i.e. 9, 16 and 25 blocks to find the best division. For the computation of DRLBP, we used uniform LBP and found that HOG with 32 bins gives the best result. For performance evaluation, we employed ten-fold cross-validation procedure, where a dataset is divided into 10 folds of equal sizes, one fold at a time is held out for testing and the remaining folds are used to train the classifier; a performance measure is computed as an average over ten-folds along with standard deviation (STD). In this way, the system is trained with different data and is tested with different data, which has not been shown to the system during training, avoiding over-fitting. We measured the performance using common performance metrics: accuracy (ACC), area under the ROC Curve (AUC), Sensitivity (SN), and Specificity (SP).

To validate the effectiveness of DRLBP-HOG and DRLTP-HOG descriptors, we also evaluated HOG, DRLBP and DRLTP separately; the results are shown in Table 1, which indicate that 25 blocks give an overall good performance in terms of the four measures. HOG gives better result than DRLBP and DRLTP, which means that gradient orientation pattern have a dominant role in the discrimination of mass ROIs. For localised LBP-HOG, DRLBP-HOG and DRLTP-HOG descriptors, we tested 9, 16 and 25 blocks and found that 9 blocks give the best performance; the results are given in Table 2. There is significant improvement in the results, which implies that our assumption about the edge micro-patterns and gradient orientation is justified. Also, notice that LBP-HOG does not improve the results over HOG, and DRLBP-HOG yields the best performance in terms of all four metrics, especially the sensitivity is 100 %.

ROC curves illustrate the performance on a binary classification problem where classification is based on simply thresholding a set of scores at varying levels. It shows the tradeoff between sensitivity and specificity, any increase in sensitivity will be accompanied by a decrease in specificity. For the cases, whose

**Table 1.** Average performance measures with a standard deviation for three descriptors

| Method | #Blocks | ACC±STD | AUC±STD | SN±STD | SP±STD |
|--------|---------|---------|---------|--------|--------|
| HOG | 9 | 91.76±3.17 | 0.91±0.04 | 92.15±4.16 | 91.55±6.53 |
| | 16 | 92.15±2.06 | 0.92±0.03 | 90.91±4.40 | 93.33±3.36 |
| | 25 | 92.35±2.84 | 0.92±0.04 | 0.91±0.04 | 92.73±4.22 |
| DRLBP | 9 | 80.58±4.57 | 0.80±0.05 | 79.28±5.19 | 81.61±6.55 |
| | 16 | 81.56±4.35 | 0.79±0.08 | 79.95±9.04 | 81.66±11.26 |
| | 25 | 82.64±5.37 | 0.81±0.06 | 79.55±7.28 | 85.10±8.60 |
| DRLTP | 9 | 79.02±4.03 | 0.78±0.05 | 76.57±5.86 | 80.97±7.12 |
| | 16 | 82.35±4.23 | 0.81±0.07 | 82.11±6.60 | 81.62±10.05 |
| | 25 | 82.35±4.89 | 0.81±0.05 | 9.15±6.72 | 84.77±8.78 |

**Table 2.** Average performance measures with standard deviation for LBP-HOG, DRLBP-HOG and DRLTP-HOG descriptors

| Method | #Blocks | ACC±STD | AUC±STD | SN±STD | SP±STD |
|--------|---------|---------|---------|--------|--------|
| LBP+HOG | 9 | 91.57±2.93 | 0.86±0.02 | 79.76±5.44 | 95.26±±3.56 |
| DRLBP+HOG | 9 | 99.80±0.62 | 0.99±0.01 | 100±0 | 99.80±1.21 |
| DRLTP+HOG | 9 | 98.23±1.71 | 0.98±0.02 | 98.52±2.41 | 98.0847±2.72 |

**Table 3.** Comparison with state-of-the-art false positive reduction methods

| Method | Year | Dataset | ACC(%) | AUC |
|--------|------|---------|--------|-----|
| DRLBP-HOG (Proposed) | 2016 | DDSM | **99.80** | **0.99** |
| Salabat et al. [13] | 2016 | DDSM | 98.82 | 0.99 |
| Oliveira et al. [5] | 2015 | DDSM | 98.88 | |
| Salabat et al. [7] | 2015 | DDSM | 98.02 | 0.96 |
| Tai et al. [18] | 2014 | DDSM | | 0.98 |
| Hussain [4] | 2014 | DDSM | 98.93 | 0.99 |

results are shown in Table 2, ROC curves are shown in Fig. 4, which reflect the performance of the system in terms of sensitivity and specificity.

A comparison with state-of-the-art methods is given in Table 3. We made comparison with those recent methods which employ texture descriptors other than LBP and DDSM for evaluation; it shows that the proposed method (DRLBP-HOG with SVM) outperforms in false positive reduction method on average in terms of accuracy and AUC.

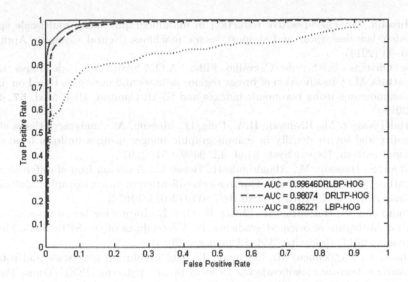

**Fig. 4.** ROC curve of the outperformance descriptors

## 5   Conclusion and Future Work

The false positive reduction problem is a challenging problem, and the effectiveness of any method addressing this problem depends on how effectively it extracts the discriminative information from an ROI. Assuming that an ROI contains texture micropatterns with varying contrast and gradient orientation patterns, we proposed two descriptors DRLBP-HOG and DRLTP-HOG by fusing DRLBP, DRLTP which capture texture patterns and HOG which encodes gradient orientation patterns. For localised distribution of these descriptors, we divided an ROI into a number of blocks. The experiments on ROIs from DDSM database revealed that DRLBP-HOG with 9 blocks and 30 bins of HOG give the best performance, which is better that those by recent method. The results corroborate our assumption and this can further be utilised to classify the mammograms based on density and also for the classification of benign and malignant masses. This is our future work.

## References

1. Siegel, R.L., Miller, K.D., Jemal, A.: Cancer statistics, 2016. CA: Cancer J. Clin. **66**, 7–30 (2016)
2. Hospital, K.F.S., Centre, R.: Breast cancer report, 15 February 2016. https://www.kfshrc.edu.sa/en/home
3. Llad, X., Oliver, A., Freixenet, J., Mart, R., Mart, J.: A textural approach for mass false positive reduction in mammography. Comput. Med. Imaging Graph. **33**(6), 415–422 (2009)

4. Hussain, M.: False-positive reduction in mammography using multiscale spatial weber law descriptor and support vector machines. Neural Comput. Appl. **25**, 83–93 (2014)
5. de Oliveira, F.S.S., de Carvalho Filho, A.O., Silva, A.C., de Paiva, A.C., Gattass, M.: Classification of breast regions as mass and non-mass based on digital mammograms using taxonomic indexes and SVM. Comput. Biol. Med. **57**, 42–53 (2015)
6. Abdel-Nasser, M., Rashwan, H.A., Puig, D., Moreno, A.: Analysis of tissue abnormality and breast density in mammographic images using a uniform local directional pattern. Expert Syst. Appl. **42**, 9499–9511 (2015)
7. Khan, S., Hussain, M., Aboalsamh, H., Bebis, G.: A comparison of different gabor feature extraction approaches for mass classification in mammography. Multimedia Tools Appl., 1–25 (2015). doi:10.1007/s11042-015-3017-3
8. Pomponiu, V., Hariharan, H., Zheng, B., Gur, D.: Improving breast mass detection using histogram of oriented gradients. In: Proceedings of the SPIE 9035, Medical Imaging 2014, Computer-Aided Diagnosis (2014)
9. Ojala, T., Pietikainen, M., Maenpaa, T.: Multiresolution gray-scale and rotation invariant texture classification with local binary patterns. IEEE Trans. Pattern Anal. Mach. Intell. **24**, 971–987 (2002)
10. Satpathy, A., Jiang, X., Eng, H.L.: LBP-based edge-texture features for object recognition. IEEE Trans. Image Process. **23**, 1953–1964 (2014)
11. Tai, S.C., Chen, Z.S., Tsai, W.T.: An automatic mass detection system in mammograms based on complex texture features. IEEE J. Biomed. Health Inform. **18**, 618–627 (2014)
12. Liu, X., Zeng, Z.: A new automatic mass detection method for breast cancer with false positive reduction. Neurocomputing **152**, 388–402 (2015)
13. Khan, S., Hussain, M., Aboalsamh, H., Mathkour, H., Bebis, G., Zakariah, M.: Optimized gabor features for mass classification in mammography. Appl. Soft Comput. **44**, 267–280 (2016)
14. Liu, X., Tang, J.: Mass classification in mammograms using selected geometry and texture features, and a new SVM-based feature selection method. IEEE Syst. J. **8**, 910–920 (2014)
15. Dalal, N., Triggs, B.: Histograms of oriented gradients for human detection. In: 2005 IEEE Computer Society Conference on Computer Vision and Pattern Recognition, CVPR 2005, vol. 1, pp. 886–893 (2005)
16. Hussain, M., Wajid, S., Elzaart, A., Berbar, M.: A comparison of SVM kernel functions for breast cancer detection. In: 2011 Eighth International Conference on Computer Graphics, Imaging and Visualization (CGIV), pp. 145–150 (2011)
17. Cristianizzi, N., Shawe-Taylor, J.: An Introduction to Support Vector Machines and Other Kernel-Based Learning Methods. Cambridge University Press, New York (2000). 204 pages
18. Tai, S.-C., Chen, Z.S., Tsai, W.T.: An automatic mass detection system in mammograms based on complex texture features. IEEE J. Biomed. Health Inform. **18**(2), 618–9627 (2014)

# Virtual Reality

# Enhancing the Communication Spectrum in Collaborative Virtual Environments

Edward Kim$^{(\boxtimes)}$ and Christopher Moritz

Department of Computing Sciences, Villanova University, Villanova, PA, USA
edward.kim@villanova.edu

**Abstract.** The importance of interpersonal and group communication has been studied and recognized for thousands of years. With recent technological advances, humans have enabled remote interaction through shared virtual spaces; however, research is still needed to develop methods for expressing many important non-verbal communication cues. Our work explores the methods for enhancing the communication spectrum in collaborative virtual environments. Our primary contribution is a machine learning framework that maps human facial data to avatars in the virtual world. We developed a synthetic training process to create labeled data to alleviate the burden of manual annotation. Additionally, we describe a collaborative virtual environment that can utilize both verbal and non-verbal cues for improved user communication and interaction. Finally, we present results demonstrating the success of our method in a sample collaborative scenario.

## 1 Introduction

Collaborative virtual environments (CVEs) are digital spaces where participants can collaborate and interact with one another. These are typically networked software platforms where the participants are represented as avatars in the virtual space. In different CVEs, users have vastly differing communication capabilities where verbal communication is the most dominant communication modality. However, only relying on verbal communication can be problematic. Research has shown that our words only account for 7% of our overall message [1], and in fact most of our communication spectrum resides in the non-verbal space. Some examples of non-verbal communication cues include facial expressions, gaze, tone of voice, and body language. Thus, for CVEs to truly emulate the entire range of human communication, the non-verbal cues need to be presented and expressed in the virtual world.

Our work explores a method of enhancing the communication spectrum in collaborative virtual environments. Our primary contribution is a framework for a flexible facial expression model that can map keypoint descriptors on a face to facial blendshape coefficients. Our model can easily be trained to map any number of keypoints to blendshapes using our described random face generator. Thus, the burden of labeling training data for alternative machine learning

© Springer International Publishing AG 2016
G. Bebis et al. (Eds.): ISVC 2016, Part I, LNCS 10072, pp. 681–690, 2016.
DOI: 10.1007/978-3-319-50835-1_61

approaches is alleviated by our approach. Additionally, we describe the methodology and tools required to build a networked CVE that utilizes both verbal and non-verbal cues for virtual collaboration. Finally, we present the quantitative and qualitative results of our method on facial expression videos, a standard expression dataset, and demonstrate the non-verbal cues in a sample CVE scenario.

## 2    Background

Collaborative virtual environments have been researched for decades, but have been increasing in functionality and expressiveness in recent years. Fabri et al. [2] has explored the use of emotionally expressive agents to engender empathy amongst the users. Their work used the Facial Action Coding System (FACS) to express facial activity in avatars [3]. Action Units (AUs) that correspond to facial muscle motion were tweaked for expressive virtual agents. The impact of gaze and avatar realism was explored by Garau et al. [4]. Tanenbaum et al. [5] provides a thorough summary of the state of non-verbal communication in virtual worlds and states that the lack of non-verbal communication in virtual worlds leads to a state of confusion for users. Others have noted that more natural perception of each other (and of autonomous actors) increases their sense of being together, and thus the overall sense of shared presence in the environment [6].

As noted by the literature, there is abundant evidence demonstrating the importance of both verbal and non-verbal communication in CVEs. Towards this goal, researchers have branched out to other fields of computing for solutions. For facial expressiveness, a significant body of work from the computer vision community exists describing how to localize keypoints on the face [7–9]. Given these keypoints, one could map (or retarget) a human face expression to a virtual avatar. For facial keypoint retargeting, some have had success with facial rigging that requires manual tweaking [10] or with commercial software and blackbox packages [11,12]. Alternative methods of facial retargeting can ease the burden on computer vision systems by leveraging hardware improvements i.e. RGB-D and depth sensors [13,14]. Distinct from many of these methods, our work does not require manual tweaking, nor time consuming manual keypoint annotation for training. We can use simple webcams instead of RGB-D cameras for wide spread compatibility and integrate these verbal and non-verbal communication in CVEs.

## 3    Methodology

For our collaborative virtual environment, we are using the Unity3D[1] game engine. Unity3D provides the necessary tools and libraries for networking, facial animation, and distribution. We obtain our 3D face models from Adobe Mixamo[2]. The models are auto-rigged with a skeleton and optionally can

---

[1] http://www.unity3d.com.
[2] http://www.mixamo.com.

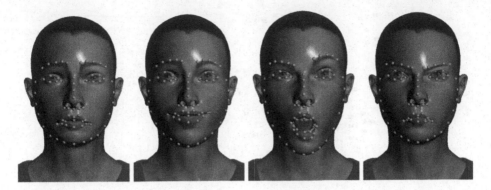

**Fig. 1.** Visualization of the 68 vertices tracked using a random face generation blend-shape script. In order to train the mapping between the blendshape coefficients and the tracked facial points, we generate 2,000 random faces and project their vertex positions to x,y pixel locations. (Color figure online)

be enhanced with 50 facial blendshapes. These blendshapes can be manually tweaked to alter the facial movements of the 3D model. Some example blend-shapes include a left and right eye blinks, cheek puff, outer eyebrow lower/raiser, mouth open, etc. The first task we describe is to build a facial expression model that can take arbitrary points on a human face and map their influence onto these 50 blendshapes. Then, we present our CVE system and describe the integration of both verbal and non-verbal cues.

### 3.1  Facial Expression Model

**Synthetic Generation of Training Data -** In a typical machine learning scenario, training a regression model requires a large amount of labeled data that can be expensive or time consuming to obtain. In the application of keypoint face localization, this is usually a very tedious task where a human annotator typically has to click on each point of the face. Existing facial position landmarks have been proposed in the literature (68 point markup from the Multi-PIE [15] dataset) which we adopt in our framework.

To alleviate the training burden, we developed a random face generator that generates a random face within a constrained range. Vertices of a face mesh that correspond to the standard 68 point markup are identified and tracked as facial blendshapes are randomly tweaked. The 3D vertex positions are projected into the 2D camera plane. We autonomously generate 2,000 faces for training a machine learning algorithm. Because the training data is synthetic, perturbations are added to the points for robustness and data augmentation purposes. Green spheres have been placed on the corresponding mesh for visualization purposes, see Fig. 1.

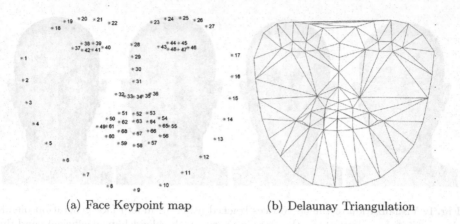

(a) Face Keypoint map          (b) Delaunay Triangulation

**Fig. 2.** A visualization of the 68 keypoints used in our method and delaunay triangulation features extracted from our faces. The features correspond to the euclidean distances between points of the triangle mesh. These distances are normalized by the face width.

**Training the Keypoint to Blendshape Model -** Our next task is to map these 68 face keypoints to avatar blendshape coefficients. This will enable any 68 point annotation on real human faces to transfer to a virtual character. We train this model using a two layer, feed forward neural network with hidden layer sigmoid activations and a linear output. We compute a delaunay triangulation of the keypoints of the face and compute the distance between triangle vertices. The input layer takes these 178 computed distances (see Fig. 2 for an illustration of the distances used as features), passes it to a fully connected layer of 20 nodes, and forwards the data to a linear output layer. In total, we train 31 separate neural networks corresponding to different parts of the face. These neural networks include networks for major muscles of the face including eye control, mouth control, an upperface/brow network, lips, cheeks, nose, etc.

**Human Face Keypoints from Video -** Given a machine learning model that maps keypoints to blendshapes, we can map human expressions to avatars. After an evaluation of several facial keypoint computer vision methods, we chose the CLM [9] framework which utilizes a constrained local neural field for landmark detection. In our experiments, it was the most robust in video annotation with variable lighting conditions, and had a relatively fast processing time (<0.3 s per frame on an Intel i7). For proper normalization, we create a common alignment for all the faces so we can more precisely detect the variations between expressions. We utilize the extended Cohn-Kanade (CK+) face database [16,17] to compute a mean face shape across the entire dataset. Each individual face is aligned to the mean shape through an affine warp of the outer 27 keypoints of the face and 4 keypoints of the nose bridge. We did not use a full 68 keypoint warp, as it could distort the facial muscle activations.

## 3.2   Other Non-verbal and Verbal Communication

**Verbal Communication -** The requirement of our CVE is to enable both verbal and non-verbal communication. Thus, we addressed the verbal communication through the standard high level API (HLAPI) multiplayer library for Unity. A user of our system can speak into a standard webcam microphone and their voice packets will be distributed to all other networked players in the CVE. The audio is played back as a 3D sound in the virtual world and an additional "speaking" indicator appears above the avatar's head when the system detects that they are talking.

**Avatar Body Transform and Head IK -** The user's head orientation is also a very important non-verbal cue that we wanted to incorporate in the CVE. The user can control their avatar's overall transformation using a keyboard and mouse. Since our avatar is fully rigged with facial blendshapes and skeleton, we can control where the avatar's head is pointing by controlling the head IK "lookAt" position. When a user moves their mouse around the screen to change their camera view, the avatar's head IK follows the camera's Z axis. This transform is then synchronized across the network. For a more immersive experience, we also enabled the Oculus Rift virtual reality headset and synchronized the sensors with the avatar transforms. The Oculus provides both positional and orientational data that is used to control the translation of the body and head IK of the avatar. We discuss some of the limitations of the Rift in our experiments and results section.

**Body Motion Capture Scripts -** Finally, we enabled a suite of motion capture animations through the Unity mecanim animation system. These are triggered animations that play when a user performs certain actions e.g. walking, talking, or can be triggered manually by the user using mapped keyboard actions. We plan to explore the Oculus Rift Touch when it becomes commercially available and plan to experiment with other technologies like the skeleton tracking system in the Microsoft Kinect.

## 4   Results

For our experiments and results, we present our data on training the keypoint to blendshape model, and visualize some of the results of the regression model on webcam video and on publically available expression datasets. We also demonstrate our integrated framework of verbal and non-verbal communication in a sample CVE.

### 4.1   Training the Keypoint to Blendshape Model

As mentioned previously, we train 31 models to control the avatar's various blendshapes (eyes, mouth, upper facial muscles, lower facial muscles, etc.).

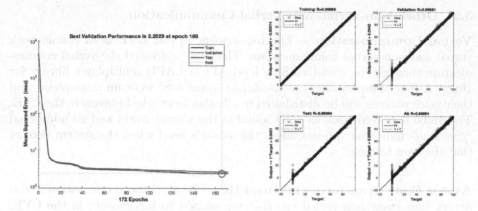

**Fig. 3.** Visualization of the training on our eye blendshape model. The model is trained with 70% of our data and validated and tested on remaining 30% of the data (15%, 15% split.) The training/validation/testing error is shown as well as a regression plot visualizing a linear fit to the data.

Each model is trained using 70% of the labeled data, and the remaining 30% is used for testing and validation. The model uses the Levenberg-Marquardt algorithm and L2 regularization to prevent overfitting. The training process runs for 1000 epochs or until a validation threshold is met. The training process is fairly quick, taking only 1–2 min to obtain each of the models. The training error and regression error can be seen in Fig. 3, which is computed from the mean squared error between the output and targets. The test triangulation distance data is transformed to have zero mean and variance of 1.

## 4.2   Extended Cohn-Kanade (CK+)

The extended Cohn-Kanade (CK+) dataset is a fairly standard and popular dataset for expression recognition that consists of 593 recordings of 123 subjects. The image sequences vary between 10 and 60 frames, but only the last frame (peak expression) has been FACS coded. Every frame has also been manually annotated with 68 facial keypoints. The dataset is primarily used for obtaining an average face for which all other faces can be affinely transformed and normalized. Additionally, we can use the data for visualization of avatar emotion. The range of emotions expressed through this database covers a wide spectrum, including happiness, sadness, surprise, disgust, etc. We extract a peak expression frame from each video sequence, resulting in 593 frames. These keypoints are processed through our model and some of the visualizations can be seen in the last row of Fig. 4.

## 4.3   Webcam Video

One of the primary goals of our work is to transfer expressions from standard webcam video to virtual characters. We captured video and utilized the CLM algorithm to analyze the frames of the video. Some results of our experiments can be seen in the first two rows of Fig. 4. Unlike the single image snapshots of the CK+ dataset, with our video we performed temporal smoothing of the resulting blendshape coefficients using a moving average of 10 image frames. This reduced some of the "jittery" effects perceived when viewing the avatar's expressions in real-time.

**Failure Cases -** There are number of failure cases in our testing that relate to the variability in the real world. The first failure case happens when our face keypoint detector fails to accurately localize the face. Most of the error occurs in the mouth region if the person greatly exaggerates an expression. This error propagates down the neural network and ultimately fails to register on the generated face. Another common failure situation are when the person expresses very slight muscle movement. Generally speaking, humans many be able to detect these subtle changes; however, our system has difficulty translating minor variances to the model.

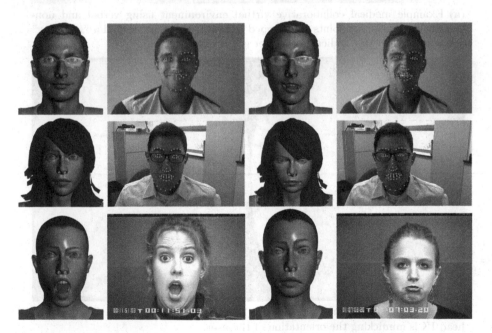

**Fig. 4.** Visualization of results of our model when mapping CLM facial keypoints to avatar blendshapes. The first two rows of the figure illustrate results on standard webcam video. The last row demonstrates the results on images from the CK+ dataset. The CK+ dataset provides manual keypoint coordinates so we did not need to perform any computer vision processes.

## 4.4    Sample CVE Scenario

We built a sample collaborative virtual environment scenario around the application of medical training and evaluation. Multiple users can join and interact with

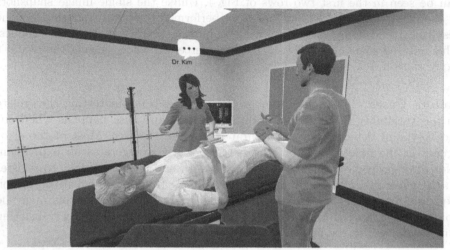

(a) Example medical collaborative virtual environment using verbal and non-verbal cues. Facial keypoints are mapped to avatar blendshapes and a "speaking" icon can be seen that indicates the user is currently talking.

(b) Example of the visualization through virtual reality headsets. The avatar's head IK is mimicking the orientation of the user.

**Fig. 5.** Example medical simulation using a collaborative virtual environment. The non-verbal cues are mapped to the virtual avatars which include facial expression blendshape data rendered from facial keypoint analysis, scripted motion capture body animation, and inverse kinematic head motion indicating where the user is looking.

each other in a shared virtual operating room. A user can verbally communicate with everyone in the room using a standard microphone, and a "speech" indicator pops up over their head to draw the participants attention, see Fig. 5(a). The audio is fully 3D, meaning that one can use stereo sound to localize the audio source in 3D space. Non-verbal cues in the CVE include playback of our facial keypoint blendshape model (current work in progress to make this run at 30 frames per second), and head joint IK to control the avatar's gaze direction. Pre-scripted body animations can be triggered by the user; however, hand tracking devices could easily be added for avatar hand IK motion. The Oculus Rift virtual reality headset has also been integrated, and the head orientation and motion mapped to the avatar's head, see Fig. 5(b). Unfortunately, the current headset occludes the face and interferes with the facial keypoint algorithm for accurate facial expression transfer. Future work will look into building a machine learning face keypoint model that can support virtual reality headsets as demonstrated by Li et al. [18].

## 5   Conclusion

In summary, we present a framework for enhancing the communication spectrum in collaborative virtual environments. Our primary contribution is a machine learning framework that maps facial keypoint data to facial blendshape coefficients. We developed a synthetic training process to create labeled data to alleviate the burden of manual annotation. Additionally, we describe a CVE built that can utilize both verbal and non-verbal cues for improved user communication and interaction. Finally, we present both quantitative and qualitative results demonstrating the success of our method in a collaborative scenario.

## References

1. Mehrabian, A.: Nonverbal Communication. Transaction Publishers, New Brunswick (1977)
2. Fabri, M., Moore, D.: The use of emotionally expressive avatars in collaborative virtual environments. In: Virtual Social Agents, vol. 88 (2005)
3. Ekman, P., Rosenberg, E.: What the Face Reveals: Basic and Applied Studies of Spontaneous Expression Using the Facial Action Coding System (FACS). Oxford University Press, New York (1997)
4. Garau, M., Slater, M., Vinayagamoorthy, V., Brogni, A., Steed, A., Sasse, M.A.: The impact of avatar realism and eye gaze control on perceived quality of communication in a shared immersive virtual environment. In: Proceedings of the SIGCHI Conference on Human Factors in Computing Systems, pp. 529–536. ACM (2003)
5. Tanenbaum, J., Seif El-Nasr, M., Nixon, M.: Nonverbal Communication in Virtual Worlds: Understanding and Designing Expressive Characters. ETC Press, Pittsburgh (2014)
6. Guye-Vuillème, A., Capin, T.K., Pandzic, S., Thalmann, N.M., Thalmann, D.: Nonverbal communication interface for collaborative virtual environments. Virtual Reality 4, 49–59 (1999)

7. Cootes, T.F., Edwards, G.J., Taylor, C.J., et al.: Active appearance models. IEEE Trans. Pattern Anal. Mach. Intell. **23**, 681–685 (2001)
8. Zhu, X., Ramanan, D.: Face detection, pose estimation, and landmark localization in the wild. In: 2012 IEEE Conference on Computer Vision and Pattern Recognition (CVPR), pp. 2879–2886. IEEE (2012)
9. Baltrusaitis, T., Robinson, P., Morency, L.P.: Constrained local neural fields for robust facial landmark detection in the wild. In: International Conference on Computer Vision Workshops, pp. 354–361 (2013)
10. Sintel: Sintel face rig (2016). https://durian.blender.org/about/
11. Mixamo: Adobe mixamo (2016). https://www.mixamo.com/faceplus
12. Faceware: Faceware technology (2016). http://facewaretech.com/products/software/
13. Realsense: Intel realsense technology (2016). https://software.intel.com/en-us/articles/realsense-overview
14. Hsieh, P.L., Ma, C., Yu, J., Li, H.: Unconstrained realtime facial performance capture. In: Proceedings of the IEEE Conference on Computer Vision and Pattern Recognition, pp. 1675–1683 (2015)
15. Gross, R., Matthews, I., Cohn, J., Kanade, T., Baker, S.: Multi-pie. Image Vis. Comput. **28**, 807–813 (2010)
16. Kanade, T., Cohn, J.F., Tian, Y.: Comprehensive database for facial expression analysis. In: IEEE Conference on Automatic Face and Gesture Recognition, pp. 46–53 (2000)
17. Lucey, P., Cohn, J., Kanade, T., Saragih, J., Ambadar, Z., Matthews, I.: The extended Cohn-Kanade dataset (CK+): a complete dataset for action unit and emotion-specified expression. In: Computer Vision and Pattern Recognition Workshops, pp. 94–101 (2010)
18. Li, H., Trutoiu, L., Olszewski, K., Wei, L., Trutna, T., Hsieh, P.L., Nicholls, A., Ma, C.: Facial performance sensing head-mounted display. ACM Trans. Graph. (TOG) **34**, 47 (2015)

# Narrative Approach to Assess Fear of Heights in Virtual Environments

Angelo D. Moro, Christian Quintero, and Wilson J. Sarmiento[✉]

Multimedia Research Group, Military Nueva Granada University, Bogotá, Colombia
{u1200569,christian.quintero,wilson.sarmiento}@unimilitar.edu.co

**Abstract.** This paper presents an approach to the detection and identification of measurable human responses to heights inside a virtual environment. Biometric data such as heart rate and movement reactions are acquired during the execution of a task within a specific framework, signal based analysis is done to validate behavioral responses and interpretation of fear. Thus, giving a better understanding of the effect and extend of these stimuli in a person on a controlled virtual scene.

## 1 Introduction

Virtual reality (VR) is being used to recreate sensory experiences to users within a simulated ambient. This corresponds to traditional approaches that often use artificial stimulation devices to excite nerve receptors in the body. However, the main objective of VR generated scenarios is to trigger the same cognitive and emotional sensations as are experienced in the real world. Since emotions are far more complex than simple sense stimuli it's necessary to measure and quantify the body's physiological responses to find a correlation between the latter and the user emotions when are induced within a Virtual Environment (VE).

Thereby directing the research towards this direction, this presents a method to recognize levels of a specific emotion such as fear of heights supported by signal processing applied to biometric inputs. The data is captured while the user is stimulated inside a VE. Unlike previous researches that focus on how a virtual environment produces a biological change in a user by different stimuli, the main contribution of this work is the narrative component to generate a suitable cognitive link that will allow to experience a more believable scene.

For testing purposes, a virtual environment was developed having in mind that to induce *fear of heights* a believable narrative was needed. The test environment simulates a moving platform that increases the elevation in three different levels while participants are instructed to follow a task in the narrative context. By focusing the central attention on the task at hand regardless of the change of altitude, triggering *fear of heights* will arouse as a natural response. The results show that the proposed approach allows to identify three levels of fear emotion in subjects without being diagnosed of *acrophobia* (fear of heights).

Thus, the next section describes the related work. Following this, the narrative approach is detailed, giving information about the method and texts given

© Springer International Publishing AG 2016
G. Bebis et al. (Eds.): ISVC 2016, Part I, LNCS 10072, pp. 691–700, 2016.
DOI: 10.1007/978-3-319-50835-1_62

to the participants. The full experiment setup is shown using a simple diagram to give notion of space with the grading scale of heights. The equipment used in the experiment is then enlisted as well as the hardware to render the virtual scene and handle the computing tasks. To finish the section, the virtual activity is detailed for each height level, giving the audio, time and special events that composed the experience. Afterwards, the signal and biometric data is exposed by showing the key components of the metrics and what statistical and signal processing techniques were used. Finally, the results are represented using matrices and then evaluated as we give the conclusions of the work.

## 2   Related Work and Background

Emotions can be used to describe one or multiple states of a person, and from a physiological perspective, the human body reflects those changes. So they can be measured and quantified at any moment. For instance, skin conductivity, sweating, pupil dilation or heart rate may have a different range of values that depend upon a situation. By capturing biometric data with specialized equipment, it's possible to quantify each emotional state. This raw data or vital signs are then processed with a computer to create a meaningful report describing how the user is currently experiencing the virtual activity.

Currently, there are several studies of how heart rate measurement is used to identify psychophysiological states of users immersed in a VE. For example, in the medical field these results are used to improve measuring devices. Considering the work done by Betella et al., they have created a system that consists of both a heart rate and a galvanic skin sensor fastened to the user while sustaining a regular breath cycle [1]. With this, they intended to validate how a non-intrusive device allows better quantification of data in daily life conditions. Other interesting research done in signal interpretation is the work of Nasoz et al. They have proposed an emotional analysis system using several algorithms based on heart rate, temperature and skin conductivity data [2].

Another notable area of research in the medicine is medical therapy. Some scenarios like the virtual reality exposure therapies (VRETs) are recreated. The patient is exposed to a particular situation inducing the desired phobia, later this may serve to identify possible treatment pathways. Creating systems for treating different types of psychiatric disorders are often built using multiple devices in VEs. For instance, to treat acrophobia, researchers placed subjects within a VE with head-mounted displays or with a computer automated virtual environment (CAVE) [3], and the outcome of the experiment was positive for both devices. Moreover, the results of analyzing vital signals have proven to be effective for treating phobias with VE [4]. Regardless of how realistic the VE are, tests done from 1995 [5,6] showed that treatments with the technology available at that time were helpful for most types of phobias.

# 3 Narrative Approach

There are three main guidelines that shape the proposed approach. The first most important is to provide a *narrative context* within the VE so the subject is able to reach an optimal level of cognitive immersion. The second is an *engaging activity*, which hooks the attention and redirects the participant's attention to a task so emotional responses are naturally triggered and can be fully studied. The third, is a *set of biometric signals* that supports recognition and analysis of these emotional responses.

In this case study the narrative context recreates a training process of an "Olympic diver". To engage the participants, the activity must be easy and have a clear purpose, for example, we use the activity "you need reach a balloon with your hand". The following text presents a short and simple story that includes the narrative context and the *engaging activity*.

> "You must think that you are Olympic diver. Part of your training is to have complete knowledge of the diving platform. For this, you need to perform an exploration activity while at same time gaining confidence to walk over it. You will have to move across the pool platform and try to reach the balloons that appear at random locations with your hands. The activity has three (3) different stages with increased height."

This particular scenario was chosen because it reflects the transition between the steady ground and altitude as height increases. Also instead of having a solid plate floor underneath, the water tends to give a positive and relaxing cognitive effect. Another key component was added to the experiment and it was to have the participants perform while standing over a physical board the entire session as shown on Fig. 1. For this, a platform was created matching the dimensions from the one depicted in the VE.

## 3.1 Experiment Design

The setup of the experiment is displayed on Fig. 1(a) and the participant can be identified wearing the equipment and VR headset on Fig. 1(b). This experiment presents an update over our previous work [7] because a wooden board is used to enhance the perception of the virtual platform.

As we said before, the scene has a total of four distinguishable height stages (including the initial level). At ground level, the participant begins with a training tutorial for introducing the avatar movement and overall feel of the environment. To have a grasp of the height, the Fig. 2(a) depicts the elevation from a third person perspective and Fig. 2(b) shows the same instant of time seen by the participant. The height reference is displayed on Fig. 2(c) where Ground level (G) stands at ($y_0 = 0$ m), first level (L1) at ($y_1 = 2$ m), second level (L2) at ($y_2 = 5$ m), third level (L3) at ($y_3 = 10$ m) and *user start position $S_p$* is displayed on the right-hand side.

First, the experiment supervisor sets a subject identification (ID) inside the log book. The characterization questionnaire is filled by the participant that

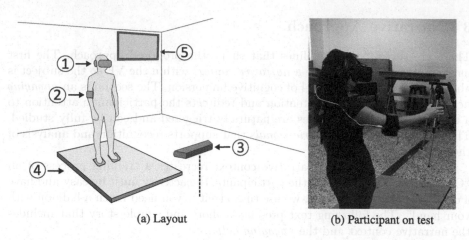

(a) Layout

(b) Participant on test

**Fig. 1.** (a) Experimental setup: (1) HMD and headphones; (2) Pulse sensor; (3) Microsoft's Kinect V1; (4) Wooden board with neutral location; (5) Display monitor. (b) Photograph of the participant taking the test standing over the platform in the room.

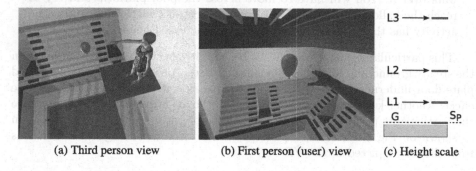

(a) Third person view

(b) First person (user) view

(c) Height scale

**Fig. 2.** Aquatic Complex VE screenshots taken at the 3rd level.

includes basic information such as age, birthdate, gender, etc., it also includes specific questions like eye sight problems or motion sickness. The user shows an explicative video with a description of and *engaging activity*. Afterwards, the supervisor helps to adjust the armband with the PPG sensor and the headset system (HMD and headphones) and the demo scene provided by Oculus is run to adjust the HMD. Also, to assure each test subject starts at the same position within the room, we used fixed feet marks. The lights are turned off and the room remains as silent as possible for the experiment to begin. The subject is instructed to stand over the platform and execute the tasks and finish the test if possible. When the session has finished, the gear is removed and the subjective evaluation questionnaire based on the work of Shari et. al [8] is completed by the participant. All logs are stored in real-time even if the experiment needs to be aborted at any given time.

The tracking devices are the Microsoft's Kinect V1 sensor and an Arduino microcontroller. The latter one has plugged a Pulse Sensor Amped (PSA) and can be described as an optical plethysmogram or photoplethysmogram (PPG). It serves as a non-invasive blood pressure measurement device [9], since it uses a conventional sensor to measure the saturation of blood underneath the dermis (skin).

In addition to this, a Head-mounted display (HMD) with generic USB headphones are used, both connected to the personal computer via universal serial bus (USB) ports. The HMD is an Oculus Rift Development Kit 2 (DK2) and runs with the software development kit (SDK) 0.8.0.0 Beta PC. The computer used is a Hewlett-Packard HP Z640 workstation with the following specifications:

- Processor: Intel(R) Xeon(R) CPU E5-26020 v3 @ 2.40 GHz
- Graphics Card: Gigabyte AMD Radeon R7 260X GPU with 1 GB GDDR5 RAM
- Memory: 32 GB DDR4 RAM (2 modules of 16 GB each one)
- Operating System (OS): Windows 10 Pro 64-bits

The *engaging activity* includes 6 balloons in the inner semicircle and 6 more in the outer semicircle, for a total of 12 objects per level. The subject starts using the left hand to reach balloons $(1, 2, 3)$ then the right hand for balloons $(4, 5, 6)$ for completing the inner balloons. This is repeated for the next semicircle of objects, please note that the idea of the outward semicircle is to push the subject to move from its "comfort" position. Only a balloon is visible in the activity. When the user reaches the first balloon it disappears and the next becomes visible. When a balloon appears on the scene, a 3D sound effect is played to give a hint of the object's location in the virtual space. It can also be triggered if the user allows the lifetime $t_f$ of the balloon to finish. For this experiment, the active time is $t_f = 10$ s. After the sequence is over, the system displays a text to inform the subject that the avatar needs to be relocated over the initial position so the platform can be elevated. The Fig. 3 shows the balloon sequences for each level, the footprints indicate the initial position.

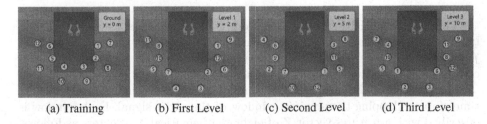

(a) Training          (b) First Level          (c) Second Level          (d) Third Level

**Fig. 3.** Balloon sequences

## 3.2   Data and Metrics

Let us now consider that if subtle body movements are detected in a person (conscious or involuntary), then emotional state changes can be registered. In our experiment, the MS Kinect motion sensor can collect up to 22 control points simultaneously labelled according to the human skeleton bones. So, by taking the world positions of these joints we are able to create a set of six (6) move vectors. The data is taken from the log file that stores the values of each of the points represented with a blue circle every $t_k = 250$ ms. As shown on Fig. 4, each vector has its origin denoted with a diamond shape [⋄] and pointing to the direction of the next joint in the hierarchy. Using a simple algebraic transformation we eliminate the component to get the inclination of the vector. For both hands and legs, an average value is calculated to obtain the four-body (**4-body**) oscillation data set.

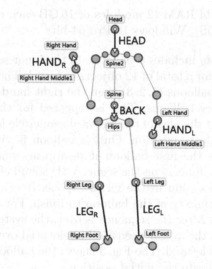

**Fig. 4.** 4-body movement vectors: **HEAD, BACK, HANDS, LEGS**.

The heart rate (HR) signal is sent from the microprocessor every $20 \pm 5$ ms, but a higher time step of 50 ms was used, thus decreasing the frequency from $f = 50$ Hz to $f_{HR} = 20$ Hz. In this way, a biometric data set is completed and is composed of the HR and 4-body movement signals.

For processing the signals, a 2 s window sequence is created with a 0.5 s time step overlapping the previous window of the entire signal. Each window is described with a features vector $Z$ of eight mathematical parameters as follows:

$$Z = \langle \bar{x}, \sigma^2, G_2, E[\sigma^2], E_s, \psi_1, \psi_2, \psi_3 \rangle \qquad (1)$$

where:

- $\bar{x} = \sum x/n_i$: the **arithmetic mean**;
- $\sigma^2 = 1/n \sum (x_i - \bar{x})^2$: is the **population variance**;
- $G_2$: is the **kurtosis**;
- $E[\sigma^2]$: is the **variance bias**;
- $E_s$: is the **energy of the signal**;
- $\psi_1$, $\psi_2$, $\psi_3$: are the **three main frequencies** of the signal after the deletion of the DC component of the **FFT**.

## 3.3   Population

Our experiment was conducted with a total of $n = 10$ participants (3 female and 7 men) with ages ranging from 17 to 29 and an average age of 22 years old. According to the results of the characterization form, 80% are right-handed and 20% of them left-handed. Only 30% of the participants don't have eyesight problems, 10% have myopia, 30% astigmatism and half of the total experience other vision problems. 4 out of 10 have already participated in a similar test while the rest 6 are not familiar with such type of virtual reality tests.

Concerning video-games skill and frequency of play, 40% declared to practice video-games sporadically, 20% played once or twice last month, 30% usually play a couple of times per week and 10% on a daily basis. Of all participants that played videogames, we needed to know their experience with first person games (like a First-Person Shooter FPS). So, the results of the poll show that 40% play 1 or 2 times a week, 20% only play a couple of times in a month and 40% rarely play. 60% considered themselves strong players, 30% average player and 10% weak players. Finally the last questions concerns the experience of 3D movies and use of glasses at home or at cinema. Half of them never experimented dizziness, 40% rarely felt dizzy while 10% sometimes felt dizzy.

Three participants didn't finished the test. The first one suffering *acrophobia* had to terminate the experiment, because the subject was unable to continue after reaching the 2nd stage. As for the two others, we encounter minor technical problems so both tests had to be ended before the end of the experiment. The application's frame rates displayed in the HMD decreased, having a negative impact on the participant, thus inducing a dizziness effect.

## 4   Results

The Fig. 5 shows comparison matrices between Bhattacharyya distances of feature vectors computed by level. The Bhattacharyya distances is a metric used in machine learning to measure between class separation. A high distance (or higher value) is an indicator of a feature vector allowing it to differentiate two class, in this case, two conditions of fear. Numbers in the figures represent each of the heights: 1 stands for the Ground Level (**L0**) and 2, 3, 4 represent **L1**, **L2** and **L3** respectively. For instance, head oscillation seen on Fig. 5(a)

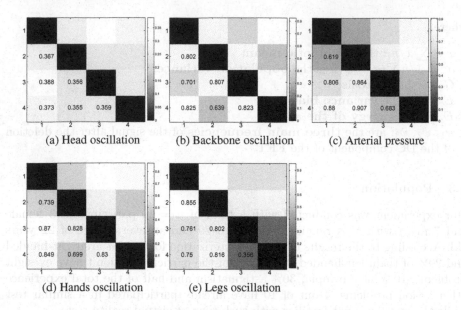

(a) Head oscillation  (b) Backbone oscillation  (c) Arterial pressure

(d) Hands oscillation  (e) Legs oscillation

**Fig. 5.** Bhattacharyya distances of dataset features.

are low, since $d_{HEAD} \in [0.355, 0.388]$. In contrast, the other bones oscillations on Fig. 5(b), (d) and (e) have achieved a high degree of differentiation, since the values don't fall below 0.6. With the exception on Fig. 5(e), where the changes from (L2) to (L3) are similar to those seen on the head oscillation. Finally, concerning the heart rate data, the results exposed on Fig. 5(c) show that there is also a high degree of separability, because the cross comparison are roughly between 0.7 and 0.9.

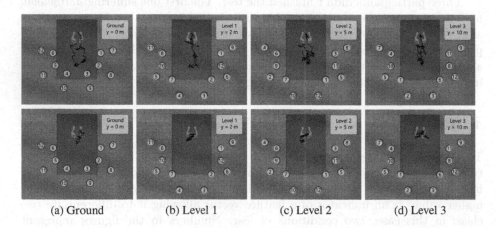

(a) Ground  (b) Level 1  (c) Level 2  (d) Level 3

**Fig. 6.** Movement paths: first row corresponds to subject #4 and second row to subject #10

Also, we noted that as the height increases, so does the degree of differentiation. For instance, taking into account hand oscillations if the distances are $d_{1-2} = 0.739$, $d_{1-3} = 0.87$ and $d_{1-4} = 0.849$, we have that $d_{1-2} < d_{1-3}$ and $d_{1-2} \sim d_{1-3}$ (but remain high enough to see a change).

Some samples of movement paths of the participants are provided in a row on Fig. 6. The motion paths describe the movement over the platform at each level allowing horizontal comparison.

## 5 Conclusions

Using the data collected and comparing the Bhattacharyya distances of the sets, the scenario provided to the user helps to see a gradual biometric changes of the participants. We can infer that the narrative context, the visuals of the scene and the implementation of the physical board used in the experiment, all play a key function in order to provide a more believable experience.

Also, when looking into the motion paths of the subjects on Fig. 6, tracing forth the movements, on overall they appear to shrink at the start position, the location where the subject must stand for the platform to move to the next level when the sequence is over. This also is in correlation with the data described above, where at low levels, the participants feel more free and relaxed, and as height increases so does the cognitive load about the fear of height. It's important to highlight that the data processed from the limb movement (hands and legs) show a better performance to express the identification of fear levels, than the sensor heart rate data.

For future works, we would like to have more study cases and develop a more complex narrative context for the identification of emotions in the fear spectrum. As well as to have a possible positive impact improving VR therapies for participants suffering a special type of phobia.

**Acknowledgments.** This research project, with identification "ID **INV-ING-2115**" has been funded by the *Vicerrectoría de Investigaciones* department of the Universidad Militar Nueva Granada.

## References

1. Betella, A., Pacheco, D., Zucca, R., Arsiwalla, X.D., Omedas, P., Lanatà, A., Mazzei, D., Tognetti, A., Greco, A., Carbonaro, N., Wagner, J., Lingenfelser, F., André, E., Rossi, D.D., Verschure, P.F.: Interpreting psychophysiological states using unobtrusive wearable sensors in virtual reality. In: The Seventh International Conference on Advances in Computer-Human Interactions, ACHI 2014, pp. 331–336 (2014)
2. Nasoz, F., Lisetti, C.L., Alvarez, K., Finkelstein, N.: Emotion recognition from physiological signals for user modeling of affect. In: User Modeling, p. 8 (2003)
3. Krijn, M., Emmelkamp, P.M.G., Biemond, R., De Ligny, C.W., Schuemie, M.J., Van Der Mast, C.A.P.G.: Treatment of acrophobia in virtual reality: the role of immersion and presence. Behav. Res. Ther. **42**, 229–239 (2004)

4. Torres, M.P.: Virtual environment usage and application procedures in phobia treatment, pp. 1–11 (2008)
5. Rothbaum, B.O., Hodges, L.F., Kooper, R., Opdyke, D., Williford, J.S., North, M.: Virtual reality graded exposure in the treatment of acrophobia: a case report. Behav. Ther. **26**, 547–554 (1995)
6. Hodges, L.F., Meyer, T.C., Rothbaum, B.O., Williford, J.S., North, M.M.: Virtual Environments for Treating the Fear of Heights Virtual Environments for Treating the Fear of Heights, pp. 1–4 (1995). Page 2 of 4
7. Gonzalez, D.S., Quintero, C., Sarmiento, W.J.: Fear levels in virtual environments, an approach to detection and experimental user stimuli sensation. In: STSIVA (2016)
8. Shari A., Steinman, B.A.T.: Cognitive processing and acrophobia: validating the heights interpretation questionnaire (2011)
9. McCarthy, B.M., O'Flynn, B., Mathewson, A.: An investigation of pulse transit time as a non-invasive blood pressure measurement method. J. Phys. Conf. Ser. **307**, 12060 (2011)

# Immersive Industrial Process Environment
# from a P&ID Diagram

Víctor H. Andaluz[1,2(✉)], Washington X. Quevedo[1],
Fernando A. Chicaiza[1], Catherine Gálvez[1], Gabriel Corrales[1],
Jorge S. Sánchez[1], Edwin P. Pruna[1], Oscar Arteaga[1],
Fabián A. Álvarez[1], and Galo Ávila[1]

[1] Universidad de las Fuerzas Armadas ESPE, Sangolquí, Ecuador
{vhandaluzl,wjquevedo,fachicaiza,clgalvez,lgcorrales,
jssanchez,eppruna,obarteaga,faalvarez,
gravila}@espe.edu.ec
[2] Universidad Técnica de Ambato, Ambato, Ecuador
victorhandaluz@uta.edu.ec

**Abstract.** This work presents the development of an interactive and intuitive three-dimensional Human Machine Interface, based on Virtual Reality, which emulates the operation of an industrial plant and contains a two-dimensional Human Machine Interface for control and monitoring a process of one or more variables, applying the concept of user immersion in the virtual environment. The application is performed by using Computer Aided Design software and a graphics engine. Furthermore, experimental results are presented and discussed to validate the proposed system applied to a real process of a plant.

**Keywords:** Industrial virtual interface · Unity · Flow control

## 1 Introduction

In industries exists a growing demand of production quality and systems performance, which increases the complexity of automation levels and structure of industrial processes at a larger scale, also, arises the need to ensure their reliability and safety; this causes the constant evolving and research of monitoring systems through the use of the latest technology, becoming their main objective to provide information on the status of the plant for the expert staff to take appropriate decisions to keep the systems in desired conditions [1–3]. Monitoring systems collect characteristic parameters of different areas of the plant in defined periods, resulting in the growth of the amount of data to be processed and evaluated according to the criteria of operation, quality and profitability [4, 5]. The monitoring and control systems are composed by a bilateral communication channel that guarantee data delivery in real time and without failures; also these systems consist of a human machine interfaces, HMI, to show the most relevant information at each level of the plant [6–8].

An industrial HMI can vary from an indicator LED to specialized equipment, *e.g.*, touchscreens which present robust features that allow them to operate under different conditions in industrial environments [1, 9, 10]. In this type of device provided to the

© Springer International Publishing AG 2016
G. Bebis et al. (Eds.): ISVC 2016, Part I, LNCS 10072, pp. 701–712, 2016.
DOI: 10.1007/978-3-319-50835-1_63

user relevant and sufficient information, including graphical representation of the process in terms of data collection from the plant locally and remotely [7, 11, 12]. From the commercial point of view there are several solutions for the implementation of HMI, generally compatible with the Windows operating system; some of the most commonly used are FactoryTalk View Site Edition, Wonderware Intouch, and many other platforms from firms such as Siemens, Schneider Electric and even National Instruments LabVIEW with the complementary Datalogging and Supervisory Control module, DSC; all are applicable in the supervision and control of various industrial processes, and presents essential and useful functionalities, for instance the management and historical of alarms, data logging, trend graphs, reporting, levels of security access for multiple users, and managing multiple servers and databases [14–17]. Nowadays it exists the interest in developing a new generation of advanced, flexible and unconventional HMI because of the increment of complexity in the processes [3, 13].

From the development of sophisticated platforms that integrate multi-modal sensors [18], CPUs with high processing capacity, cheapening hardware and evolution of graphics engines, there has been an advance in the field of Virtual Reality, VR, which has renewed the interaction between human and computer, so that the user is able to visualize, interact and be immersed in three-dimensional environments, with the possibility of enhancing the experience of the real environment with virtual information (augmented reality) [18–23]. These technological advances resulting in numerous applications related to entertainment, social communication, rehabilitation, graphic design, professional skills training as surgery processes in medicine, among others [21, 24–26]. The work of VR oriented to the industry are focused on providing solutions in different ambits, such as a system of ergonomic assessment of the activity of workers during their manual tasks [27], the training of technicians to improve skills in maintenance and assembly [18], the utilization of an intuitive checklist with gesture recognition [28], the interactive representation of a product or a manufacturing process that involve industrial robots [22], likewise, assistance solutions from operators on the operation and conditions of a process, presented in virtual scenarios similar to the plant, using commercial devices [10, 13, 29].

In this context, this paper presents the development of an interface based on VR for monitoring, control and immersion of an industrial plant, as a proposal to the Supervisory Control and Data Acquisition systems, SCADA, and/or Decentralized Control System, DCS, which are aimed to monitor the different areas that conform an industrial process. For the implementation of the industrial VR interface it is considered the Computer Aided Design, CAD, to perform 2D and 3D graphics, so they can be exported to a software of characterization and animation of objects to create an interactive application that monitors the status of one or more variables in real form, and the user perceives and distinguishes easily the components of the plant. Additionally, the performance of the implementation of the proposed industrial virtual interface associated with an industrial process.

This paper is organized in VI sections including the Introduction. Section 2 presents the problem formulation and the proposed solution; whereas in Sect. 3 the methodology to migrate from a 2D plane to a 3D VR environment is shown. The mode of operation of the proposed monitoring system is presented in Sect. 4. Then, in Sect. 5

experimental results of the implementation of the proposed system associated with a flow process are exposed; and finally the conclusions are contained in Sect. 6.

## 2 Problem Formulation

Nowadays, monitoring and control of industrial processes are based on the automation pyramid. In the third level is the level of supervision, HMI, the main objective of the HMI is to present the data information monitored, this allows real-time viewing different dynamic physical variables *e.g.*, temperature, pressure, level, flow, etc. These display interfaces are presented in 2D graphics environments, for design, reading and identification of instruments are required to have knowledge of the rules of standardization of Piping & Instrumentation Diagrams, P&ID, and experience in the use of solutions HMI; additionally a complex presentation system is required for data: processes, trends, historical, events, alarms and others; mentioned entails that users have to navigate in different windows for monitoring plant.

This paper presents a visualization system HMI and industrial monitoring, it considers on the third level of the automation pyramid virtual reality environment in Fig. 1, to provide transparency and dip the user and ease of identification of each of the

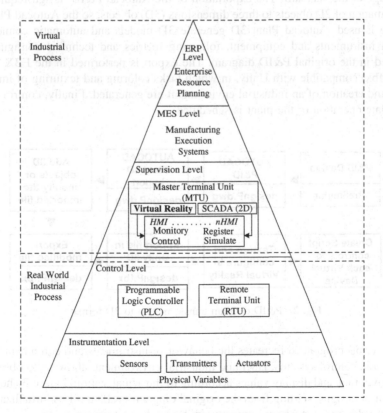

**Fig. 1.** Proposed system including in an automation pyramid.

instruments in the industrial process, allowing users to interpret and equipment variables of interest; ideally a HMI that explain itself intuitively, without superior technical training.

Proposed should allow their growth, expansion and adapt to the future needs of the process and of the plant. The usability of the application should not have trouble, should have graphical interfaces that show a basic scheme and actual process. Additionally to allowing data acquisition process, and communication at all levels (local and network management).

# 3  P&ID Diagram to 3D Transformation

The preliminary design of the P&ID diagram are the original drawings of the process, whose rules are based on standards that allow be interpreted by any operator. For the conversion of a P&ID diagram to a compatible format for Unity 3D, 5 steps shown in Fig. 2 are performed. The preliminary design includes equipment, instruments and devices that make up the field station, so the first step in converting to a 3D format is the redesign in AutoCad P&ID. (designP.dwg), which is where the designer create, modify and manages the piping and instrumentation diagrams without the need of the knowledge of the standard. The exportation of the Autocad P&ID design requires the transformation of 2D objects to three dimensions (3D) objects, so the Autocad Plant 3D software is used. Autocad Plant 3D generate 3D models and automatic connections between instruments and equipment, following metrics and technical configurations described in the original P&ID diagram. The export is performed in the FBX format (design.fbx) compatible with Unity, in which tasks coloring and texturing of imported design and creation of an industrial environment are generated. Finally, control scripts to simulate operation of the plant is scheduled.

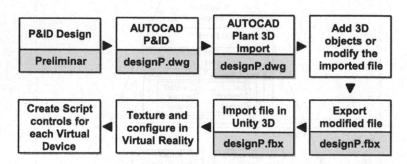

**Fig. 2.** P&ID diagram transformation to 3D format

The scripts programed recreates the behavior of instruments and equipment for the field station, control systems, HMI and industrial environment, allowing to observe its change over time and display values according to the actual station. Figure 3 shows the evolution of designs, starting from the original diagram P&ID until its virtualization in Unity, to achieve a virtual environment similar to the real process.

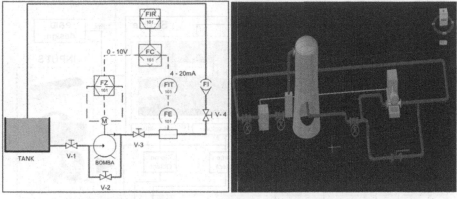

(a) Original diagram P&ID                              (b) Original 3D diagram P&ID

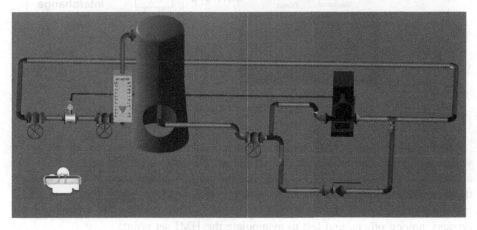

(c) 3D Model in Virtual Reality

**Fig. 3.** P&ID diagram to Unity environment transformation

## 4 Operating Scheme

In the Unity environment, the control scripts for each virtual device are programmed to response like the process behavior. For this, a scheme of operation divided into five phases intends showed in Fig. 4. In the *(i) Input Stage*, a set of devices for handling variables are proposed with haptic devices, gestural control and tracking position. The purpose of a haptic device is experiencing the forces generated by the environment, *e.g.*, adjusting a valve, the perception of force flow, liquid level detection in a tank, among others. As for the gestural control device, Leap Motion, it allows exchange of settings between the field and control center, and allows the modification of set point plant values. The head mount display (HMD) Oculus Rift, it allows immersion in a virtual environment by tracking the HMD in space, to change the viewing angle of the user according to the movements.

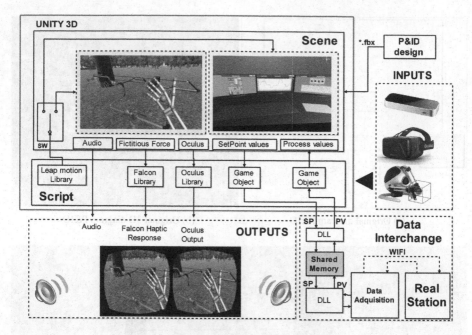

**Fig. 4.** Operating scheme

In the *(ii) Unity scenes phase*, the simulated field contains the plant simulation in virtual reality programming with each of the instruments and equipment, which work according to the diagram P&ID original and the control system used. In the other way, the control center contains a virtual environment that simulates an identical to that used in the actual plant, with historical data, access levels, data visualization summarized the process, among others, and lets to manipulate the HMI set point.

In the *(iii) data interchange phase,* set point values and process values are swap between the virtual environment and the actual process. The method of exchange of information is generated through a shared memory for updating data in real time between two programs. Shared memory allows get sensor information and display plant in Unity scenes. Similarly, the value of SP altered by the input devices in the virtual environment is modified to change the behavior of the plant and modify the physical environment at the user. Physically, the plant is located at the remote site and share information through the IEEE 802.15 standard. The software that accepts this information is open to be a specific industrial program, *e.g.*, OPC Server (KeepServer, TopServer), MATLAB, LabView, Excel, Databases, among others, with the limitation that it must have the ability to use Dynamic Link Libraries, DLL, for use shared memory [30]. Thus, the use of the virtual environment is scalable according to the data receiver software.

The *(vi) phase involves the interaction of scripts* with input devices and information exchange step, whereby each of the instruments and equipment can update the scene according to dimensions from the actual plant. Also, scripts allow you to modify values that affect the control of the plant, allowing the desired change from the virtual environment to the process values. Finally, the *(v) output phase* involves force feed-back (Novint Falcon), audio alarm and visual immersion in the virtual environment.

## 5   Results and Discussions

The industrial VR interface is based on a flow control station, which consists of a PLC Siemens S7-1200, a Touch Panel Siemens KTP600, a frequency converter, a pump, a rotameter and a transmitter of pallets Georg Fischer 8550. The operation of the process is based on the data that the PLC receives from the transmitter, which according to the control algorithm implanted in it, sends a response to the frequency converter to modify the speed of the pump and at the same time the flow circulation by the pipeline to reach the set point. The information provided to the monitoring and control of the process is performed by a data acquisition system using computer vision, which aims to acquire the measure of the pattern element (rotameter) and send it to the remote site; the structure of the full system shown in the block diagram of Fig. 5.

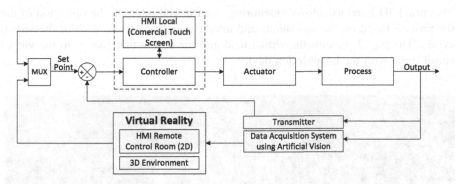

**Fig. 5.**  Block diagram of the implemented experimental system.

The results of industrial VR interface are specified as follows, a Remote 2D HMI content in a virtual control room, 3D environment of the plant in the field.

### 5.1   Remote HMI Content in a Virtual Control Room

This industrial virtual reality interface is similar to a real control room where the user can monitor and control the process flow through a 2D HMI environment, where is centralized all the variables and information of the plants. There are two functionalities that use the operator's hand with the LeapMotion gestural controller device: (a) to switch the scene to the field station environment by clicking the Field Station button and (b) change the set point variable. The Fig. 6 shows the view of the virtual HMI and the operator's hand.

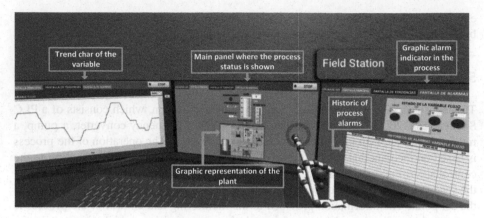

**Fig. 6.** Virtual 2D HMI in a inmmersive control center

## 5.2   3D Environment of the Plant in the Field

This virtual 3D interface allows monitoring, control and interpret the operation of the flow process based on the animations and information that present each of the virtual devices. The Fig. 7 presents the virtual field and the button that change to the virtual control room with the LeapMotion device.

**Fig. 7.** Virtual field showed

## 5.3   Experimentation

The experiment is about handling the set point variable in 3 preset positions 0–5–10 Gallons Per Minute, GPM, to check the reliability of the system by displaying instruments flow indicators in the pipeline like rotameter and flow transmitter. Figure 8 shows the picture sequence corresponding to *(a)* the set point change value to 0 GPM,

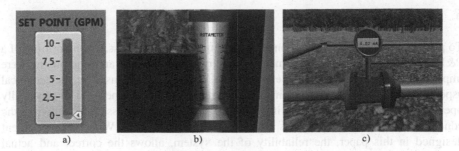

**Fig. 8.** Measure of 0 gpm

*(b)* rotameter indicator at 0 GPM and *(c)* transmitter value at 4.02 mA that means a value transmission of 0 GPM to the controller.

Figures 9 and 10 presents the image sequence of 5 and 10 GPM with set point, rotameter and flow transmitter information respectively. After the test is found that handling the set point variable in the control center generates the expected change in the field station. The experiment shows the reliability of the data in the control center and the field station, allowing the implementation of any diagram P&ID with its own control algorithm.

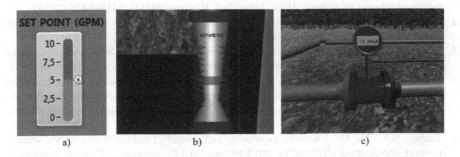

**Fig. 9.** Measure of 5 gpm

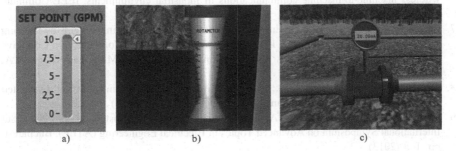

**Fig. 10.** Measure of 10 gpm

# 6 Conclusion

To provide immersion in the demonstration of an industrial process, a transforming of a P&ID diagram to a 3D environment with virtual instruments and equipment were implemented. The virtual reality environment can instruct the user on the technical aspects and operation of a plant in its actual state, and avoids the need to physically operator in the field of work -with difficult and hazards access- and allowing the educational and training proposes with saving time and costs. With the experiment designed in this paper, the reliability of the system, allows the correct and actual performance of any design P&ID to transform it into 3D.

**Acknowledgment.** The authors would like to thanks to the Consorcio Ecuatoriano para el Desarrollo de Internet Avanzado -CEDIA- for financing the project "Tele-Operación Bilateral Cooperativo de Múltiples Manipuladores Móviles – CEPRAIX-2015-05", and others Institutions like the Universidad de las Fuerzas Armadas ESPE and the Universidad Técnica de Ambato for the technical and human support to develop this paper.

# References

1. Yin, S., Ding, S.X., Xie, X., Luo, H.: A review on basic data-driven approaches for industrial process monitoring. IEEE Trans. Ind. Electron. **61**(11), 6418–6428 (2014)
2. Hou, L., Bergmann, N.W.: Novel industrial wireless sensor networks for machine condition monitoring and fault diagnosis. IEEE Trans. Instrum. Meas. **61**(10), 2787–2798 (2012)
3. Skripcak, T., Tanuska, P.: Utilisation of on-line machine learning for SCADA system alarms forecasting. In: Science and Information Conference (SAI), London, pp. 477–484 (2013)
4. Venkatasreehari, R., Chakravarthi, M.K.: Industrial pollution monitoring GUI system using internet, LabVIEW AND GSM. In: 2014 International Conference on Control, Instrumentation, Communication and Computational Technologies (ICCICCT), Kanyakumari, pp. 787–791 (2014)
5. Truong, N.V., Vu, D.L.: Remote monitoring and control of industrial process via wireless network and Android platform. In: 2012 International Conference on Control, Automation and Information Sciences (ICCAIS), Ho Chi Minh City, pp. 340–343 (2012)
6. Stenumgaard, P., Chilo, J., Ferrer-Coll, J., Angskog, P.: Challenges and conditions for wireless machine-to-machine communications in industrial environments. IEEE Commun. Mag. **51**(6), 187–192 (2013)
7. Lee, A.N., Martinez Lastra, J.L.: Enhancement of industrial monitoring systems by utilizing context awareness. In: 2013 IEEE International Multi-disciplinary Conference on Cognitive Methods in Situation Awareness and Decision Support (CogSIMA), San Diego, CA, pp. 277–284 (2013)
8. Gaj, P., Jasperneite, J., Felser, M.: Computer communication within industrial distributed environment—a survey. IEEE Trans. Ind. Inf. **9**(1), 182–189 (2013)
9. Georgescu, V.C.: Optimized SCADA systems for electrical substations. In: 2013 8th International Symposium on Advanced Topics in Electrical Engineering (ATEE), Bucharest, pp. 1–4 (2013)

10. Gorecky, D., Schmitt, M., Loskyll, M., Zühlke, D.: Human-machine-interaction in the industry 4.0 era. In: 2014 12th IEEE International Conference on Industrial Informatics (INDIN), Porto Alegre, pp. 289–294 (2014)

11. Lima, J., Moreira, J.F.P., Sousa, R.M.: Remote supervision of production processes in the food industry. In: 2015 IEEE International Conference on Industrial Engineering and Engineering Management (IEEM), Singapore, pp. 1123–1127 (2015)

12. Jamro, M., Trybus, B.: IEC 61131-3 programmable human machine interfaces for control devices. Im: 2013 6th International Conference on Human System Interactions (HSI), Sopot, pp. 48–55 (2013)

13. Posada-Carlos-Toro, J., Barandiaran, I., Oyarzun, D., Stricker, D., de Amicis, R., Pinto, E. B., Eisert, P., Döllner, J., Vallarino, I.: Visual computing as a key enabling technology for industrie 4.0 and industrial internet. IEEE Comput. Graph. Appl. **35**(2), 26–40 (2015)

14. Xiaodong, Z., Jie, Z., Ke, L.: Design and implementation of control system for beer fermentation process based on SIMATIC PLC. In: The 27th Chinese Control and Decision Conference (2015 CCDC), Qingdao, pp. 5653–5656 (2015)

15. Kumar, B., Dewal, M.L., Mukherjee, S.: Control and monitoring of MSF-RO hybrid desalination process. In: 2013 International Conference on Control, Automation, Robotics and Embedded Systems (CARE), Jabalpur, pp. 1–5 (2013)

16. Vidarte, J.D.T., Londoño, H.F.F., Vidarte, J.D.T.: A substation automation system for the ECOPETROL power plants at Cantagallo and Yariguí. In: Robotics Symposium, 2011 IEEE IX Latin American and IEEE Colombian Conference on Automatic Control and Industry Applications (LARC), Bogota, pp. 1–5 (2011)

17. Cristian, B., Constantin, O., Zoltan, E., Adina, P.V., Florica, P.: The control of an industrial process with PLC. In: 2014 International Conference on Applied and Theoretical Electricity (ICATE), Craiova, pp. 1–4 (2014)

18. Webel, S., Bockholt, U., Engelke, T., Gavish, N., Olbric, M., Preusche. C.: An augmented reality training platform for assembly and maintenance skills. In: Fraunhofer IGD, Germany, Ort Braude College, Israel. German Aerospace Center (DLR), Institute of Robotics and Mechatronics, Germany. Available online 1 November 2012

19. Cheng, T., Teizer, J.: Real-time resource location data collection and visualization technology for construction safety and activity monitoring applications School of Civil and Environmental Engineering, Georgia Institute of Technology, 790 Atlantic Drive N.W., Atlanta, GA 30332–0355, United States Accepted 16 October 2012, Available online 13 November 2012

20. Wang, X., Kim, M.J., Love, P.E.D., Kang, S.-C.: Augmented Reality in built environment: Classification and implications for future research, School of Built Environment, Curtin University, Australia Department of Housing and Interior Design, Kyung Hee University, Republic of Korea Department of Civil Engineering, National Taiwan University, Taiwan Australasian Joint Research Centre for Building Information Modelling, Australia Accepted 8 November 2012, Available online 28 February 2013

21. Empirical evidence, evaluation criteria and challenges for the effectiveness of virtual and mixed reality tools for training operators of car service maintenance

22. Lisboa, H.B., de Oliveira Santos, L.A.R., Miyashiro, E.R., Sugawara, K.J., Miyagi, P.E., Junqueira, F.: 3D Virtual Environments For Manufacturing Automation. In: 22nd International Congress of Mechanical Engineering (COBEM 2013), University of São Paulo, Brazil November 3–7, 2013, Ribeirão Preto, SP, Brazil (2013)

23. Sampaio, A.Z., Martins, O.P.: The application of virtual reality technology in the construction of bridge: the cantilever and incremental launching methods Department of Civil Engineering and Architecture, Technical University of Lisbon, Lisbon, Portugal Accepted 19 October 2013, Available online 12 November 2013

24. Evaluating virtual reality and augmented reality training for industrial maintenance and assembly tasks
25. Wang, X., Truijens, M., Hou, L., Wang, Y., Zhou, Y.: Integrating augmented reality with building information modeling: onsite construction process controlling for liquefied natural gas industry Curtin-Woodside Chair Professor for Oil, Gas & LNG Construction and Project Management & Co-Director of Australasian Joint Research Centre for BIM, Curtin University, Australia International Scholar, Department of Housing and Interior Design, Kyung Hee University, South Korea, Woodside Energy, Ltd., Australia Australasian Joint Research Centre for BIM, Curtin University, Australia Huazhong University of Science and Technology and Northeastern University, China Accepted 7 December 2013, Available online 12 February 2014
26. Chi, H.-L., Kang, S.-C., Wang, X.: Research trends and opportunities of augmented reality applications in architecture, engineering, and construction. Australasian Joint Research Centre for BIM, School of Built Environment, Curtin University, Australia; International Scholar, Department of Housing and Interior Design, Kyung Hee University, Republic of Korea. Accepted 29 December 2012, Available online 22 January 2013
27. Vignais, N., Miezal, M., Bleser, G., Mura, K., Gorecky, D., Marin, F.: Innovative system for real-time ergonomic feedback in industrial manufacturing. In: UMR CNRS 7338 Biomechanics and Bioengineering, University of Technology of Compiègne, Research Center, Dct Schweitzer Street, 60200 Compiègne, France b DFKI GmbH, German Research Center for Artificial Intelligence, Trippstadter Strasse 122, D-67663 Kaiserslautern, Germany SmartFactoryKL, Trippstadter Strasse 122, 67663 Kaiserslautern, Germany Received 24 April 2012, Accepted 26 November 2012, Available online 20 December 2012
28. Fillatreau, P., Fourquet, J.-Y., Le Bolloc'h, R., Cailhol, S., Datas, A., Puel, B.: Using virtual reality and 3D industrial numerical models for immersive interactive checklists, LGP-ENIT, INPT, Université de Toulouse, 47 Avenue d'Azereix, BP 1629, 65016 Tarbes Cedex, France, Alstom Transport, France, Received 4 September 2012, Revised 11 March 2013, Accepted 28 March 2013, Available online 24 May 2013
29. Skripcak, T., Tanuska, P., Konrad, U., Schmeisser, N.: Toward nonconventional human-machine interfaces for supervisory plant process monitoring. IEEE Trans. Hum. Mach. Syst. 43(5), 437–450 (2013)
30. Andaluz, V.H., Chicaiza, F.A., Gallardo, C., Quevedo, W.X., Varela, J., Sánchez, J.S., Arteaga, O.: Unity3D-MatLab simulator in real time for robotics applications. In: Paolis, L. T., Mongelli, A. (eds.) AVR 2016. LNCS, vol. 9768, pp. 246–263. Springer, Heidelberg (2016). doi:10.1007/978-3-319-40621-3_19

# Automatic Environment Map Construction for Mixed Reality Robotic Applications

David McFadden, Brandon Wilson, Alireza Tavakkoli$^{(\boxtimes)}$, and Donald Loffredo

University of Houston-Victoria, Victoria, USA
{McFaddendD,WilsonBJ1,TavakkoliA,LoffredoD}@uhv.edu

**Abstract.** As Virtual Reality technologies proliferate to traditional multimedia application areas, there is a need to create systemic and automated processes to establish the main building blocks of the virtual environments in support of such applications. In this paper, we propose a unified framework for procedurally creating a virtual reality replica of a remotely situated robot's physical environment. The proposed approach utilizes only robot's onboard camera and automatically generates the environment map for the final VR environment. The main contributions of this paper are in the hierarchical generation of the epirectangular panorama, the efficient diffuse filling of missing pixel values and the use of the developed virtual environment in improving telepresence for remote social robotics applications.

## 1 Introduction

With the availability of new Head Mounted Displays (HMDs) and technologies for Virtual Reality, it is natural to see an increase in applications of these technologies from gaming to remote operation of robotic agents [1]. As Virtual Reality technologies proliferate to other application areas, there is a need to create systemic and automated processes to establish the main building blocks of the virtual environments in support of such applications. Such virtual environments have applications in tele-presence [2,3] and telerobotics. This paper presents an automated pipeline utilizing a NAO humanoid robot to acquire images and to produce its surroundings as a virtual environment. The resultant virtual environment may be utilized for telepresence applications in which NAO serves as the remotely operated robotic agent for social robotics.

The first process in modeling a new environment is the acquisition of the scene and generation of the virtual environment map. Image-based environment modeling is the most low cost alternative to generating an environment map [4]. Gurrieri and Dubois developed a technique for the efficient acquisition and rendering of omnistereoscopic images based on sampling the scene with clusters of three panoramic images arranged in a controlled geometric pattern [5]. This approach utilizes a sequence of two-images, as the left and right stereoscopic views, to generate panoramas. However, in telepresenece applications in which remote

© Springer International Publishing AG 2016
G. Bebis et al. (Eds.): ISVC 2016, Part I, LNCS 10072, pp. 713–722, 2016.
DOI: 10.1007/978-3-319-50835-1_64

robotic agents are utilized, the inclusion of two cameras would unnecessarily burden the already scares on-board resources–i.e. transmission bandwidth.

DiVerdi et al. discussed the development of a system for generating the environment map using a vision-based frame-by-frame landmark tracking registration framework [6]. This framework is robust in using a gyroscope in conjunction with the camera placed on a tripod to help with the registration process. However, the system requires a burdensome setup for the image acquisition, preventing its seamless utility in tele-presence applications.

In this paper, we discuss an architecture that utilizes a humanoid robot as the telepresence system for both the acquisition of the virtual environment map and the telepresence agent in the physical environment.

## 2    Overview

Figure 1 shows an overview of the proposed pipeline. The robotic agent (in this application a NAO humanoid robot) is utilized in a social robotics application, and is located within the remote environment. The robot utilizes its camera to acquire images from the physical environment by taking overlapping photos of its surroundings in a grid pattern. The acquired images are transferred wirelessly to the main Virtual Reality engine, where the virtual environment is created, maintained, and is rendered for the remote human operator. The latitude-longitude panoramic environment map is then generated through a three-pass hierarchical pipeline. In the first pass of this process, input images are stitched together in a $3 \times 3$ lattice to form the basis input images for the second and third passes.

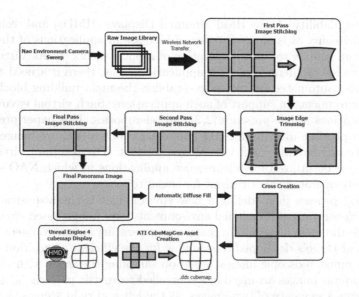

**Fig. 1.** The full pipeline used in the cubemap generation process

The second and third passes of the stitching process combine each section of the panoramic view generated from the first pass to produce the complete 360° panorama forming the basis of the final environment map. This latitude-longitude cylindrical environment map is then passed through a spherical projection to generate the cubemap diffuse texture for the final VR environment map. This cubemap is shown as the cube-cross in Fig. 1 and is used as the projected texture onto the skysphere actor within the Unreal Engine 4 (UE4).

# 3  Automated Environment Map Pipeline

This sections presents the proposed pipeline for creating the environment map of the remotely situated robot's physical surroundings. We also show the results of each stage of the proposed pipeline while discussing the benefits of each stage within the proposed pipeline.

## 3.1  The Nao Robot and Image Capture Process

This project utilizes a NAO humanoid robot by Aldebaran Inc. as the social robotic agent integrated within an immersive telerobotic environment. Images of the surrounding environment are captured through the NAO's MT9M114, 1.22 Mp camera. The camera captures single, jpeg images of the size 640 × 480 and stores them within its own on-board memory. The Nao robot is able to remotely walk around the environment and rotate its head ±119° horizontally from a forward-facing position and between 30° and 40° upwards and downwards.

The robot is controlled using Aldebaran's Choregraphe software from a remote computer, with communication via a wireless connection. The remote computer in this instance acts both as the Virtual Reality server as well as the main computational processing unit for the immersive telerobotics system.

The environment is captured through a forward and a backward direction in order to cover enough overlapping images to produce the panoramic environment map. First, the robot's body remains still while the head unit and embedded camera pan horizontally from −119° to 119° yaw. For each yaw, the robot head takes three images, once per a −8.9°, −20°, and 10° pitch angle. The robot then rotates so that the camera can capture sections of the environment that are out of range during the forward direction.

## 3.2  Efficient Hierarchical Panoramic Image Generation

Once the input images are acquired by the robot, the data is transferred to the main server for the production of the environment map. The first step in this process is to generate a panoramic view of the physical environment captured by the robot. This stage of the algorithm goes through a hierarchical process to stich the images together to produce the final panorama. The main stitching process in our implementation follows a similar process as the technique designed by Brown and Lowe [7]. However, in the original automatic stitching method, the input images are provided in a random order for processing. This requires the algorithm to find appropriate matches for the input images by utilizing SIFT features [8] and a ranking-based image registration technique to find the best candidates among the unordered images to stitch.

In order to improve the efficiency of the generation of the final panoramic view, our proposed approach utilizes a three pass hierarchical approach in conjunction with the robot's ability to control its viewpoint to relieve the main obstacle in finding candidate image matches. This hierarchical mechanism improves on both the speed and memory consumption of the overall stitching process. We can leverage this to improve on the performance of the stitching algorithm by grouping the input images into a 3 × 3 pattern of overlapping images.

In the first pass, several 3 × 3 "grids" of bordering raw images are processed, one grid at a time. Since the NAO robot has control over the orientation of the camera, we can utilize the camera rotation along its central axis (i.e. the robot head-neck joint) by a rotation vector, $\theta = [\theta_r, \theta_y, \theta_p]$ and the focal length $f$. Since the input images are taken by the rotational change in the robot camera, we can use the 3 × 3 grid of images as connected components of overlapping/matching images. The bundled adjustment [9] is then used to accurately solve for actual camera rotation and parameters jointly on pairs of images from the 3 × 3 grid.

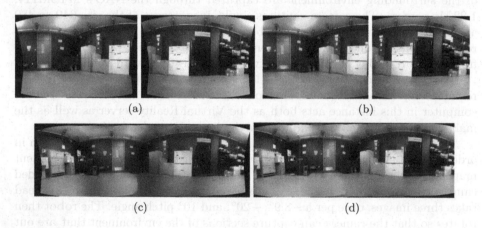

**Fig. 2.** The output of the first and second passes of the panorama stitching with (a) and without (b) rectifying the resultant image in each pass. Artifacts introduced into the results of the second pass without rectification (c) and corrected results (d).

During the feature stitching process in the first pass, the resultant images become skewed. The vertical edges become slightly concave while the horizontal edges form a convex bend, as seen in Fig. 2(a). This is due to the fact that the images are taken by camera rotation and therefore represent a spherical transformation. This representation is accurate in the top and bottom portion of the final panorama and environment map. However, the left and right portion of the panorama should represent a cylindrical transformation, and therefore these distortions produced as a result of the first pass of the stitching process introduce negative artifacts in the next pass if the images are not rectified. These artifacts can be seen in Fig. 2(c).

In order to avoid introducing the artifacts into the second pass of the stitching process, we eliminate the concave boundaries of the images produced in the first pass. In our approach, we calculate the apex of the concavity curvatures at each edge of the images produced in the first pass and remove the edges of the resultant images at these apex points, see Fig. 2(b). The trimmed images are then used in the second pass of the stitching process to produce the next level of the panorama. An example of the second pass panorama is shown in Fig. 2(d) in which the artifacts are not present and the stitched results are more clear.

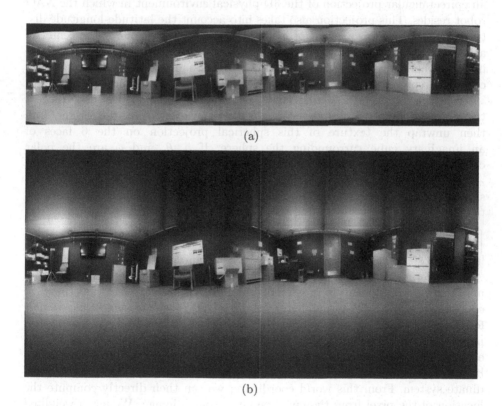

(a)

(b)

**Fig. 3.** The final panorama generated by the proposed stitching process (a) without the automatic diffuse fill, and (b) with the proposed automatic diffuse fill.

The process of finding the trimming point is rather straightforward. We first calculate the derivative of the boundary of each image on the left and right, and look for the apex point as the location where the derivative reaches zero:

$$P_y = Arg \max_x \frac{df(\cdot)}{dx} \tag{1}$$

where $f(\cdot)$ represents the concavity of the image edge and $P_y$ is the column location at the apex point of this concave curve.

Upon trimming completion, a second pass stitches the first image set into a "second" stage image set to produce the final panorama. In the last pass of the stitching process, the resulting images form the second pass are combined to create a final, full panorama picture of the original environment. Figure 3(a) shows the results of the entire process.

## 3.3   Converting Epirectangular Panorama to Cubemap

The panoramic map generated by the proposed approach in Sect. 3.2 represents an epirectangular projection of the 3D physical environment in which the NAO robot resides. This projection also takes into account the latitude-longitude distortions introduced as a result of having the camera rotate about the center of acquisition (i.e. the robot's head location). In order to utilize this panoramic image within the virtual environment in Unreal Engine 4, we need to create a cubemap representing the spherical projection of this epirectangular map.

To perform this projection and create the cubemap, we first project the epirectangular panorama onto a sphere positioned at the origin, and then unwrap the texture of this spherical projection on the 6 faces of an imaginary cube surrounding the sphere. If $\rho$, $\theta$, and $\phi$ are the polar coordinates of the sphere surface, where $\rho = 1$, $0 \leq \theta \leq \frac{\pi}{2}$ and $-\pi \leq \phi \leq \pi$, we can calculate the $u$ and $v$ coordinates of each sides of the cubemap according to the epirectangular projection equations: $[u,v]_{left} = \left[\tan(\phi), \frac{\cot(\theta)}{\cos(\phi)}\right]$, $[u,v]_{right} = \left[\tan(\phi), \frac{\cot(\theta)}{\cos(\phi-\frac{\pi}{2})}\right]$, $[u,v]_{front} = \left[\tan(\phi-\frac{\pi}{2}), \frac{\cot(\theta)}{\cos(\phi-\frac{\pi}{2})}\right]$, $[u,v]_{back} = \left[\tan(\phi-3\frac{\pi}{2}), \frac{\cot(\theta)}{\cos(\phi-3\frac{\pi}{2})}\right]$, $[u,v]_{top} = [\tan(\theta) \cdot \cos(\phi), \tan(\theta)\sin(\phi)]$, and $[u,v]_{bot} = [-\tan(\theta)\cos(\phi), -\tan(\theta)\sin(\phi)]$.

However, using these forward calculations of the UV coordinates of the cubemap texture would result in missing pixels. This is due to the fact that the $[u,v]$ coordinates above will be rounded to integer pixel values. To avoid this, we perform the backward calculation of the UV texture pixel locations to the spherical polar $[\rho, \theta, \phi]$ coordinates of the epirectangular panoramic image. We first, from each $[u,v]$ location in the final cubemap, determine to which face the pixel should be projected. This will give us the $[x,y,z]$ location of the pixel in the world coordinate system. From this world coordinate, we can then directly compute the location of the pixel from the epirectangular source image. We use a weighted average filter to interpolate the four neighboring pixel locations nearest to this calculated location within the source image to produce the color pixel values for the final cubemap location $[u,v]$. Figure 4(a) shows the results of this process.

Once the six faces of the cubemap are generated, we will need to perform post-processing on the cubemap texture to clear seams and fix the edges of the textures at the six faces of the cubemap. We utilize the technique proposed in [10,11] for the processing of the cubemap cross and for generating a High Dynamic Range (HDR) cubemap texture to be used in the virtual environment within Unreal Engine 4. We utilize a disc filter for the angular filtering and a pull

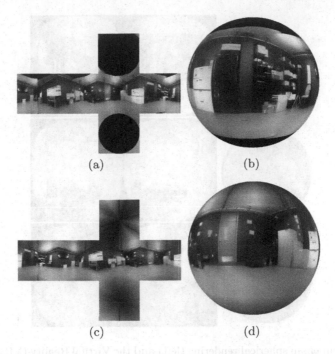

(a)                              (b)

(c)                              (d)

**Fig. 4.** The cubemap cross and spherical projection generated from the final panorama: (a–b) without the proposed diffuse fill, and (c–d) with the proposed diffuse fill.

Hermite interpolation as the edge fixup method. The spherical representation of the resulting cubemap is shown in Fig. 4(b).

### 3.4 Automatic Diffuse Fill

As shown in Fig. 4(a) and (b), the top and bottom faces of the cubemap lack pixel values. This is due to the fact that the robot's camera cannot observe and photograph the areas directly above and blow the robot's position. Therefore, pixel values for the spherical projection for the north and south poles of the projection are missing. In order to improve the quality of the cubemap, it is best to utilize a novel fill operator in which portions of the image diffuse texture of the top and bottom portions of the panoramic image spatially interpolated to replace the missing pixel values.

We further implemented the proposed diffuse fill operation in parallel to address two important issues. Firstly, traditional context sensitive fill operators process pixel values in a certain order; e.g. from bottom to top or left to right. This will make the resulting filter dependent on the direction of the applied filter, requiring additional iterations over the image to correct the artifacts. Secondly, the iterative process slows down the computation, since the iterative serial operation will have a step complexity of $O(n)$ for the work complexity of $O(n)$, where $n$ is the width/height of the image.

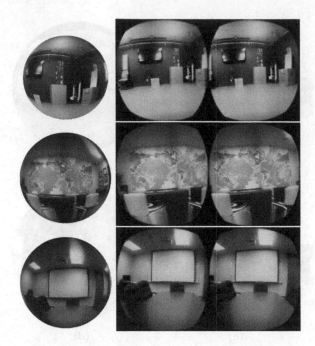

**Fig. 5.** The cubemap spherical rendering (left) and the Virtual Reality (VR) renderings (right) of three environments using Oculus Rift Head Mounted Display: Lab (top row), Office (middle row), and Conference Room (bottom row).

Our parallel implementation for each row in the section of the image missing pixel values, takes the sum of all neighboring pixels across a vertical box window. A bilateral average of pixels in this window is computed to update the value of the pixel being processed in each thread. This parallelized process calculates entire rows of pixels concurrently utilizing nVidia's CUDA. The row closest to the center of the image is calculated first, and then the further rows are calculated in a sequential fashion for all pixels missing values. Our proposed parallel diffuse fill has an asymptotic step complexity of $O(1)$ for the work complexity of $O(n)$ compared to traditional diffuse filtering operations. The resulting epirectangular panorama is shown in Fig. 3(b). Figure 4(c) and (d) show the resulting cubemap and its spherical rendering after the proposed diffuse fill is applied.

## 4    Experimental Results

The proposed technique is used to create virtual environments in Unreal Engine 4, for a social robotics experiment. The environment utilizes the cubemap generated by the proposed approach from a sequence of images acquired by the NAO robot located in a number of indoor environments. Figure 6 shows a view of the lab cubemap applied to a skysphere in the UE4 editor.

A comparison between the regular image stitching technique and our proposed approach technique with image rectification applied between each passes of the hierarchical stitching algorithm is shown in Fig. 2. By comparing Fig. 2(c)–(d) we can observe that the artifacts are eliminated and the stitched results are much more clear with the proposed rectification stage.

Figure 3 presents the epirectangular panoramic image produced by the proposed technique. In Fig. 3(a) the panorama without the application of the proposed automatic diffuse fill is shown. Since the robot can not record images of the environment directly above and below, these areas are missing from the final panoramic image. The proposed diffuse fill stage produces a seamless transition between the top and bottom areas of the panorama with the regions missing pixel values. This results in a much better final outcome as shown in Fig. 3(b).

**Fig. 6.** The environment employed as the cubemap texture for a skyshpere in UE 4.

The final cubemap as well as a spherical projection of the panorama are shown in Fig. 4. The top row shows the resulting cubemap without the application of the diffuse fill, while the bottom row shows the results with the diffuse fill algorithm applied. As it can be observed from these figures, the proposed diffuse fill technique, in conjunction with the use of angular extent filtering and the edge fixup, result in a much better quality of the final cubemap texture.

Finally, Fig. 5 shows three environments automatically generated by the proposed technique from the images captured by a NAO robot. The left column shows the sphere projection of the generated cubemap, while the right column presents the virtual environments seen through an Oculus Rift.

## 5  Conclusions and Future Work

In this paper we presented a pipeline for efficient generation of a virtual environment for remote social robotics application. The proposed approach utilizes the robot's on-board camera to produce an omnidirectional 360° virtual replica of the robot's physical surroundings. This will enable the robot's remote operators to be remotely and virtually present with the robot they are operating. The proposed method does not require manual capture of the imagery or an artist's depiction of the virtual environment. We showed photo-realistic results and efficient and speedy generation of the final virtual environment product. Our experiments show the proposed technique is robust under varying lighting conditions. Moreover, the proposed technique is demonstrated to produce quality results environments for which traditional techniques are slow or inaccurate.

In order to evaluate the impact of the proposed technique in remote robotic applications, a counterbalanced repeated-measures experimental design (same participants in each group) will be used to compare the results in two conditions (operation modes): using traditional video camera input from the robot versus using virtual reality environment. The independent variable in the study will be operation mode (2 conditions) and the measured dependent variables (3 conditions) will be task completion rate, task completion time, and self reporting survey differences. To control order effect, half of the participants will perform in the traditional video condition first and the other half of the participants will perform in the virtual reality environment condition first.

**Acknowledgements.** This material is based upon work supported in part by the U. S. Army Research Laboratory and the U. S. Department of Defense under grant numbers W911NF-15-1-0024 and W911NF-15-1-0455. This support does not necessarily imply endorsement by the DoD or the ARL.

# References

1. Bounds, M., Wilson, B., Tavakkoli, A., Loffredo, D.: An integrated architecture for telerobotics aided by immersive virtual reality. In: The 25th IEEE International Symposium on Robot and Human Interactive Communication (2016)
2. Müller, J.H., Langlotz, T., Regenbrecht, H.: PanoVC: Pervasive Telepresence using Mobile Phones (2016)
3. Uyttendaele, M., Criminisi, A., Kang, S.B., Winder, S., Szeliski, R., Hartley, R.: Image-based Interactive exploration of real-world environments. IEEE Comput. Graph. Appl. **24**, 52–63 (2004)
4. Grosh, T.: PanoAR: interactive augmentation of omni-direnctional images with consistent lighting. In: Proceedings of Mirage (2005)
5. Gurrieri, L., Dubois, E.: Efficient panoramic sampling of real-world environments for image-based stereoscopic telepresence. In: Proceedings of SPIE, vol. 8288 (2012)
6. DiVerdi, S., Wither, J., Höllerer, T.: Envisor: online environment map construction for mixed reality. In: IEEE Virtual Reality, pp. 19–25 (2008)
7. Brown, M., Lowe, D.G.: Automatic panoramic image stitching using invariant features. Int. J. Comput. Vis. **74**, 59–73 (2007)
8. Lowe, D.G.: Object recognition from local scale-invariant features. In: The Proceedings of the Seventh IEEE International Conference on Computer Vision, vol. 2, pp. 1150–1157. IEEE (1999)
9. Triggs, B., McLauchlan, P.F., Hartley, R.I., Fitzgibbon, A.W.: Bundle adjustment — a modern synthesis. In: Triggs, B., Zisserman, A., Szeliski, R. (eds.) IWVA 1999. LNCS, vol. 1883, pp. 298–372. Springer, Heidelberg (2000). doi:10.1007/3-540-44480-7_21
10. ATI 3D Application Research Group: A Cubemap Filtering and Mipchain Generation Tool (2005)
11. Isidoro, J.R., Mitchell, J.L.: Angular extent filtering with edge fixup for seamless cubemap filtering. In: ACM SIGGRAPH 2005 Sketches, SIGGRAPH 2005 (2005)

# Foveated Path Tracing

## A Literature Review and a Performance Gain Analysis

Matias Koskela(✉), Timo Viitanen, Pekka Jääskeläinen, and Jarmo Takala

Department of Pervasive Computing,
Tampere University of Technology, Tampere, Finland
matias.koskela@tut.fi

**Abstract.** Virtual Reality (VR) places demanding requirements on the rendering pipeline: the rendering is stereoscopic and the refresh rate should be as high as 95 Hz to make VR immersive. One promising technique for making the final push to meet these requirements is foveated rendering, where the rendering effort is prioritized on the areas where the user's gaze lies. This requires rapid adjustment of level of detail based on screen space coordinates. Path tracing allows this kind of changes without much extra work. However, real-time path tracing is fairly new concept. This paper is a literature review of techniques related to optimizing path tracing with foveated rendering. In addition, we provide a theoretical estimation of performance gains available and calculate that 94% of the paths could be omitted. For this reason we predict that path tracing can soon meet the demanding rendering requirements of VR.

## 1 Introduction

Not long ago it was uncommon to own a smartphone. Nowadays everyone is accessing the web wirelessly from all over the world, finding places on their vacation trips without carrying maps and connecting to their relatives with video calls. All this is done with the help of mobile devices. *Virtual Reality* (VR) and *Augmented Reality* (AR), in other words, applications that create non-existing 3D worlds and applications that lay extra content on top of the real world, are starting to introduce societal changes of similar scale.

VR and AR devices require refresh rates as high as 95 Hz and maximum latency of 20 ms from user action to last photons, caused by the action, to be sent from displays [1]. When these requirements are met, users have reported to experience immersion, that is, the feeling of being present in another world. Consequently, rendering hardware and software will have to see major improvements to keep up with these requirements.

In this paper, we present a literature review on foveated path tracing, a promising technique which exploits eye tracking to reduce the computational cost of rendering. We also present a theoretical estimate of benefits available on contemporary and future VR devices. We start by briefly covering path tracing and fields that are most essentially connected to foveated rendering in Sect. 2. Then we explain foveated rendering in Sect. 3. We conduct the theoretical performance gain estimation in Sect. 4 and conclude the paper in Sect. 5.

© Springer International Publishing AG 2016
G. Bebis et al. (Eds.): ISVC 2016, Part I, LNCS 10072, pp. 723–732, 2016.
DOI: 10.1007/978-3-319-50835-1_65

 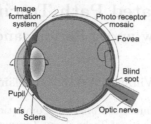 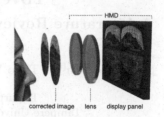

**Fig. 1.** Example of a path traced image

**Fig. 2.** Different parts of the human eye

**Fig. 3.** Barrel distortion is used when rendering VR frames (Image by Daniel Pohl, licensed under https://creativecommons. org/licenses/by/4.0/)

## 2 Background

### 2.1 Path Tracing

Path tracing is a rendering method often used for offline, photorealistic rendering. In practice, basic forward path tracing renders images by shooting virtual photons from the camera into the scene, which then rebound at random from scene objects until they hit a light source. At each rebound, the light sample is weighed by the *Bidirectional Reflectance Distribution Function* (BRDF) of the surface material. Typically many such samples are taken per pixel and averaged before the image reaches good quality: as a Monte Carlo method, path tracing has square root convergence. Path tracing naturally models visual effects such as diffuse lighting, reflections, refractions, shadows, focal blur and caustics, which are approximated with special techniques in rasterization-based rendering.

A single sample in path tracing consist of tracing multiple rays in the scene. For this reason, path tracing can be made faster with two different main strategies: firstly, ray traversal can be sped up, or secondly, the amount of rays can be reduced. Ray traversal typically means finding out closest intersection of a single ray and the 3D geometry of the scene. There have been major leaps forward with the ray traversal thanks to improved algorithm design to exploit parallel hardware resources [2–4] and thanks to algorithmic improvements [5–7]. These improvements have paved the road for the real-time ray tracing frameworks [8–10]. However, these frameworks still require high-end desktop hardware to reach real-time frame rates. In 2013 it was estimated that 8 to 16 times more computation power is needed to enable path traced games [11].

In addition to improving ray traversal throughput, there is a large literature on reducing the number of rays needed for acceptable image quality. In rough terms, importance sampling and adaptive sampling techniques aim to select the traversed rays efficiently, while reconstruction filters out noise after rendering. There is a recent survey of related techniques by Zwichker et al. [12]. The number of rays can also be reduced with *foveated rendering*, which focuses the main rendering effort around the user's gaze, measured using eye tracking equipment. In fact, the main and the only user for virtually all rendering tasks is the human eye [13] and that is why it is important to know how human eyes work.

## 2.2 Human Eye

The human eye is a complex system. In simplified terms, it consists of two main components: the image formation system and the photoreceptor mosaic. This structure is visible in Fig. 2. Photons travel through the image formation system to the photoreceptor mosaic, which sends the measured light data to the brain via the optic nerve [14].

The image formation system, like all optical systems, is not perfect, which means that the image will be somewhat blurred [14]. However, the system satisfies homogeneity and superposition, consequently, a linear system can be constructed which maps the input light density into the image projected on the photoreceptor mosaic. Thanks to this property there are accurate models of human eyes [13]. Moreover, the linearity means that there are no flaws, like inaccuracies, in the optical system, which could be used to optimize rendering.

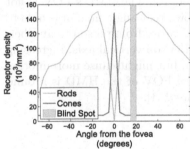

**Fig. 4.** Example of (*rod*) and (*cone*) density as a function of the angle to the center of the fovea

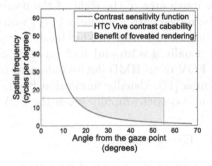

**Fig. 5.** A slice of the (*Contrast sensitivity function*), which models how much details an eye is able to resolve

On the other hand, the photoreceptor mosaic consists of more than 100 million light sensitive cells [14]. There are two types of cells: color sensitive *cones* and luminance sensitive *rods*. Cones require brighter lighting conditions to function. In contrast, rods stop working at bright lighting conditions.

The center of the human photoreceptor mosaic contains only color sensitive cones. This area is called *fovea* [14] and its size is around ten degrees. The lack of rods means that dim light sources can only be seen when viewer is not looking directly at them. More importantly, in the areas where the viewer's gaze is not fixed there are only few cones. Consequently, edges of the vision sense mostly changes in the brightness and mainly at dim lighting conditions. The distribution of the cones and rods can be seen in Fig. 4. The point where the optic nerve is attached to is called the *blind spot*, because there are no photo receptor cells in that area.

The amount of details the human eye is able to detect at certain point relative to gaze direction can be estimated with *Contrast Sensitivity Function* (CSF) visible in Fig. 5. The function has been deduced from measurements of human eyes and it is tested in user studies. It is a kind of worst case estimate for the use in computer graphics, meaning that it estimates the maximum amount of details most people are able to see [15].

Photons of a computer generated images are sent to the human eyes with various types of display devices. Conventional displays may have multiple users, making it difficult to take advantage of characteristics of a single human eye. However, there is a sub-class of displays called *head-mounted displays*, where each display has only one user.

### 2.3   Head-Mounted Displays

The idea of *Head-Mounted Displays* (HMD) is to have displays affixed to the head of the user. By tracking the head motion and rendering so that the virtual camera moves correspondingly, HMDs can produce a sense of immersion in a virtual world. Therefore, HMDs are typically used with VR and AR applications.

An important property of a HMD is its *Field Of View* (FOV), which measures how much area of the sight of the user they cover [16]. The HMD's FOV is not to be mixed with a human's FOV, which tells how great angle human is able to see without rotating his/her head. A typical FOV varies from person to another, but usually it is around 160° on horizontal and 135° on vertical axis. Increasing the FOV of an HMD device enhances immersion, but might cause more motion sickness [17]. Usually immersion begins when the FOV of the HMD is around 80° and deepens rapidly when the FOV is increased [1].

### 2.4   Eye Tracking

Eye tracking is the task of measuring what the user is currently looking at. The task can be divided into two subtasks: how to measure which direction the gaze of the user is pointing at and how to interpret the direction samples.

There are multiple ways to measure the direction of the user's gaze [18]. Typically there is some kind of a camera taking pictures of the eye. The camera may be, for example, an infrared camera combined with a bright infrared light [19]. Signal processing is used to determine which pixels correspond to different parts of the eye, e.g. the pupil, the iris and the sclera. What part of the eye is actually used in tracking depends on the camera configuration used [18]. All that is left to do is to map the tracked part's coordinates in the captured images to screen space locations on the display the user is looking at.

Coordinates in the image can be mapped to screen locations by calibrating the system at the beginning of eye tracking [18]. The user can be asked to look at different locations on the screen, and the screen space coordinates are connected to the tracking results. Another option is to accurately measure the position of the eye relative to the camera and calculate the calibration results. The main difficulty with calibrations is that they can gradually lose accuracy. For example, if a head mounted eye tracking device changes its relative orientation to the user's head, this causes drifting in the tracking results. One solution is to track the relative position of the device on the head. Another is to use multiple different eye tracking methods from different angles. When the calibration is in place, the device is able to obtain accurate estimate of gaze coordinates on the screen space. This raises the problem of interpreting the coordinates.

The other subtask of eye tracking is interpreting the gaze coordinate data. Often the application wants to know so called *fixation* points of human sight, which are the points where sight pauses to look at informative regions of interest. Rapid movements between fixations are called *saccades*. The distinction between fixations and saccades is important, because only little or no visual processing is done by the brain during saccades [20,21].

One of the easiest ways to classify tracking data to fixations and saccades is based on the velocity [20]. However, this is very vulnerable to noise in the data and the selection of parameters can change the fixation points completely [22]. The problem of noise can be overcome by looking at a window of tracking samples at once or using filtering such as Kalman filter [23].

Eye tracking enables interesting optimizations for real-time rendering tasks because rendering can concentrate on the area where the user is looking at. Some sources refer to this as *gaze-directed* or *gaze-contingent rendering* [21,24–26], but nowadays *foveated rendering* [1,27–29] seems to be more commonly used.

## 3    Foveated Rendering

Foveated rendering means that only those details are rendered which the user is actually looking at, based on eye tracking data. There is a large body of work in optimizing rasterized rendering based on gaze-direction. In contrast, foveated path tracing has not gained as much interest, maybe because path tracing, at the time of the writing, has not been widely used in real-time applications.

### 3.1    Rasterized Foveated Rendering

One approach for adding foveated rendering to an existing rendering pipeline is use the gaze direction as an input to complex fragment shaders. The shader code can then run a simplified version, if it realises that the user is not looking at the current target pixel. For example, fragment shading for the uninteresting parts can be done with fewer ambient occlusion samples [26,30]. This technique increases divergence in the shader code, but neighbouring pixels are always almost as far from the gaze point, so they usually follow the same code paths.

Significant performance gain can be achieved if the whole rendering pipeline is designed around the estimate on how much detail the eye sees in different angles to the gaze point, that is the CSF function. The gaze direction can be given as an input to the *Level of Detail* (LoD) algorithms [21]. The idea of LoD is to replace distant geometry with a simplified version that has fewer triangles. In an extreme case, a distant model with thousands of triangles might take up only a few on-screen pixels. The basic idea is straightforward, but there is a large literature on techniques to make the transition between levels of detail seamless and avoid visual artifacts. In CSF based LoD, the level of detail is based on eye-tracking data in addition to distance. This requires having multiple versions of each model in memory, rather than changing the model only once when distance to the object changes. Moreover, changing a model that covers great portion of the display area often causes flickering [31].

Another idea is to reduce the amount of samples in the screen space. In theory, perfect results could be achieved by sampling the 3D world according to the CSF. However, such resampling is difficult to map to a rasterization pipeline. Guenter et al. [27] render sections of the image at multiple resolutions. A final rendering pass blends the sections into a foveated image. This approach has the drawback that sections need to overlap. In addition, vertex and geometry shaders are re-run for each section, but the savings in rasterized and shaded pixels are enough to improve performance by a factor of 5–6.

Along with the gaze direction, also the gaze speed should be used as an input to the detail reduction algorithm. In an extreme case, Ohshima et al. [21] are not updating the image at all during saccades. A more commonly used idea is to reduce the quality more dramatically when the eye is moving [15, 27, 31].

Foveated rendering can achieve significant speedups. Guenter et al. [27] reported that a 100x speedup is possible with a FOV of 70%. Moreover, they state that increasing the display's FOV, which usually has a quadratic effect on rendering requirements, has a linear effect on foveated rendering, because the added extra display area is only adding an even lower level of quality rendering.

In summary, there are still two major difficulties with rasterization and foveated rendering: Firstly, it is hard to sample according to the CSF in screen space. Secondly, changing LoD based on gaze direction causes quick model changes all the time and, therefore, requires having multiple levels of details versions of the same model in memory.

## 3.2 Foveated Path Tracing

In contrast to fixed resolution of rasterization, in path tracing, rays are sent from screen locations. It is straightforward to distribute these rays according to the CSF. This optimization is one idea of making path tracing faster by reducing the total ray count.

There are already a few publications of techniques for foveated ray tracing. Murphy et al. [24] chose so called ray casting, which sends out only one ray per pixel, because it suited better for their test cases, where they change both the image space sampling rates and the model quality. Zhang et al. [28] use a screen-space ray tracing technique based on depth peeling the scene, but this approach is approximate and limited to simple scenes. Swafford et al. [30] test different amounts of quality reduction with foveated ray casting using multi-layer relief mapping. In fourth found paper Fujita et al. [29] call their ray tracing foveated, even though they do not utilize eye tracking and, therefore, they have the best quality always on the center of the screen. Siekawa et al. [25] reduce the rendering time of a single path traced frame from 48 min to 15 min by introducing a simulated static gaze point to their non-real-time rendering.

## 4   Theoretical Performance Gain Analysis

The motivation of this analysis is to find a lower bound on the speed up foveation can give to path tracing. CSF estimates how much details the human eye is able to resolve as a function of the angle from the gaze fixation point. The size of the detail is expressed as so called *spatial frequency* and the unit is cycles per degree (*c/deg*). That is, how many of given sized details fit into one degree of human vision. By using CSF it is possible to find out how many rays we can omit when using foveated path tracing. Approximation model of CSF can be divided into two separate parts

$$H(e, v) = M(e) \times G(v) \tag{1}$$

where $M(e)$ is a function of angle $e$ to the center of the gaze fixation point and $G(v)$ depends on the velocity $v$ of the eye rotation [15]. Increasing velocity reduces the amount of contrast human eye is able to detect. Since we are trying to find the minimum amount of quality we can omit, we set the velocity to its most pessimistic value of zero. That is, the situation when the eye is focused and seeing as much details as it can, in other words $G(0) = 1$. Taking into account that the smallest detail humans are able to resolve is ca. 60 c/deg, the equation from [15] can be simplified to

$$H(e, 0) = M(e) = \begin{cases} 60.0 & 0 \le e \le 5.79 \\ \frac{449.4}{(0.3e+1)^2} & e > 5.79 \end{cases} \tag{2}$$

First we examine performance gain on a perfect HMD device capable of showing as much details as human eyes are able to resolve. A perfect HMD device would be one capable of displaying this 60 c/deg details with the oval FOV of 160° horizontal and 135° degrees vertical. The biggest amount details need to be rendered when the user is looking at the center of the screen. For this reason, to provide lower bound estimate, we substitute the angle $e = 0$ of the Eq. 2 to the center of the perfect HMD's FOV. In that case, $e$ tells the angle from the center of the FOV. One slice of the FOV area is shown in Fig. 5.

Then we integrate the Eq. 2 over the whole area of the oval FOV. When the volume is compared to the maximum amount of resolvable details 60 c/deg on the same area, the result is that 94% of the details are unresolvable.

Another interesting case to estimate in the theoretical examination is calculating the same number for one of a contemporary consumer grade VR helmet, the HTC Vive, which is able to display details with around 15.3 c/deg [32]. We limit the Eq. 2 to this number and calculate the integral over a circular area with radius of 110°. The result is that at least 70% of the details can be omitted. The area of these omitted details is highlighted in Fig. 5. Remember that this is just one slice of the solid of revolution around the vertical axis.

The ratio of the details that could be omitted might not linearly correlate to the speed up gains possible with path tracing. However, there are many ways how details can be omitted, for example, there can be fewer paths for each pixel or paths can, e.g., use simplified lighting instead of full path tracing. The use of less samples produces higher frequency noise, but this can be reduced with more intensive filtering on areas where the user is not looking at. For example, foveated rasterized rendering can use anti-alias sampling to reduce artefacts [27].

What is the best way to reduce path tracing quality with eye-tracking is currently an open research question and therefore the ratio of extra details can be used as rough performance gain estimate. 94% performance gain is a bit better than the numbers Guenter et al. [27] found in their user studies as a number of pixels that can be reduced with rasterized rendering. Since their display is far from the perfect HMD, their pixel saving results should be lower. Moreover, since the FOV of their desktop display is smaller, the theoretical number of 70% savings on HTC Vive is a lower bound and in reality higher numbers are possible.

Path tracing a arbitrary scene might require hundreds of rays per pixel. However, a scene for adequate quality path tracing could be built so that it requires for example around 11 rays per pixel [33,34]. This can be achieved by using only simple materials or by using more complex post processing. HTC Vive has a refresh rate of 90 Hz and a resolution of $2160 \times 1200$ with 15% of the pixels invisible to the user [32]. This results in a required number of rays per second of around 2 180 MRays/s. According to the worst case estimate above, at least 70% of the rays could be omitted, which makes the requirement into 654 MRays/s. This number should be reachable with a modern high-end GPU setup [35]. In addition, the pipeline step of distortion handling [36], visualised in Fig. 3, can be greatly simplified or even avoided with path tracing. Reduced ray counts reflect savings in rendering computations and memory bandwidth usage.

## 5    Conclusions

Foveated path tracing is a promising technique for rendering VR applications. In foveated rendering the computation effort is focused mostly to screen space area where the user is looking at. With rasterized rendering this has already shown to improve performance by a factor of 5–6. However, foveated rendering is even more suited for path tracing, which is done by sending rays from screen space locations. Recently, real-time ray tracing has been made feasible on high-end hardware. Foveation could enable real-time path tracing on consumer devices, especially on hand-held mobile devices. Furthermore, typically VR and AR applications use HMD devices. Given that a HMD is specific to a single user, and covers wide field of view, the idea of foveated rendering is even more appealing.

We derived from a theoretical worst case model that foveation can omit at least 94% of rays required for the path tracing on future VR device which is capable of showing as much details as humans are able to perceive. Already on today's VR device at least 70% rays can be omitted. Moreover, thanks to reduced rendering work provided by the foveation, the very demanding rendering requirements of VR could be met today with high-end GPUs. For these reasons we believe that path tracing is a very promising choice of rendering technique in the future of VR. As a future work we are interested in building the proposed system to empirically validate the numerical estimates proposed in this paper.

**Acknowledgement.** We would like to thank anonymous reviewers for fruitful comments and Williams College and the Stanford University scanning repository for the 3D models. In addition, we are thankful to our funding sources: TUT graduate school, TEKES (project "Parallel Acceleration 3", funding decision 1134/31/2015), European Commission in the context of ARTEMIS project ALMARVI (ARTEMIS 2013 GA 621439) and industrial research fund of TUT by Tuula and Yrjö Neuvo.

# References

1. Abrash, M.: What VR could, should, and almost certainly will be within two years Steam Dev Days, Seattle (2014)
2. Wald, I., Benthin, C., Boulos, S.: Getting rid of packets - efficient SIMD single-ray traversal using multi-branching BVHs. In: Proceedings of the IEEE Symposium on Interactive Ray Tracing (2008)
3. Laine, S., Karras, T., Aila, T.: Megakernels considered harmful: wavefront path tracing on GPUs. In: Proceedings of the High-Performance Graphics (2013)
4. Garanzha, K., Premože, S., Bely, A., Galaktionov, V.: Grid-based SAH BVH construction on a GPU. Vis. Comput. **27**(6–8), 697–706 (2011)
5. Pantaleoni, J., Luebke, D.: HLBVH: hierarchical LBVH construction for real-time ray tracing of dynamic geometry. In: Proceedings of the High-Performance Graphics (2010)
6. Karras, T.: Maximizing parallelism in the construction of BVHs, octrees, and k-d trees. In: Proceedings of the High-Performance Graphics (2012)
7. Keely, S.: Reduced precision hardware for ray tracing. In: Proceedings of the High-Performance Graphics (2014)
8. Wald, I., Woop, S., Benthin, C., Johnson, G.S., Ernst, M.: Embree: a kernel framework for efficient CPU ray tracing. ACM Trans. Graph. **33**(4), 143 (2014)
9. Parker, S.G., Bigler, J., Dietrich, A., Friedrich, H., Hoberock, J., Luebke, D., McAllister, D., McGuire, M., Morley, K., Robison, A., et al.: Optix: a general purpose ray tracing engine. ACM Trans. Graph. **29**(4), 66 (2010)
10. AMD: RadeonRays SDK (2016). https://github.com/GPUOpen-LibrariesAndSDKs/RadeonRays_SDK. Accessed 6 Oct 2016
11. Bikker, J., van Schijndel, J.: The brigade renderer: a path tracer for real-time games. Int. J. Comput. Games Technol. **2013**, 1–14 (2013). https://www.hindawi.com/journals/ijcgt/2013/578269/
12. Zwicker, M., Jarosz, W., Lehtinen, J., Moon, B., Ramamoorthi, R., Rousselle, F., Sen, P., Soler, C., Yoon, S.E.: Recent advances in adaptive sampling and reconstruction for monte carlo rendering. Comput. Graph. Forum **34**(2), 667–681 (2015)
13. Deering, M.F.: A photon accurate model of the human eye. In: ACM SIGGRAPH Papers (2005)
14. Wandell, B.A.: Foundations of Vision. Sinauer Associates (1995)
15. Reddy, M.: Perceptually optimized 3D graphics. IEEE Comput. Graph. Appl. **21**(5), 68–75 (2001)

16. Bowman, D.A., Kruijff, E., LaViola Jr., J.J., Poupyrev, I.: 3D User Interfaces: Theory and Practice. Addison-Wesley, New York (2004)
17. Benko, H., Ofek, E., Zheng, F., Wilson, A.D.: Fovear: combining an optically see-through near-eye display with projector-based spatial augmented reality. In: Proceedings of the ACM Symposium on User Interface Software and Technology (2015)
18. Hua, H.: Integration of eye tracking capability into optical see-through head-mounted displays. In: Proceedings of SPIE (2001)
19. Stengel, M., Grogorick, S., Eisemann, M., Eisemann, E., Magnor, M.A.: An afford-able solution for binocular eye tracking and calibration in head-mounted displays. In: Proceedings of the ACM International Conference on Multimedia (2015)
20. Salvucci, D.D., Goldberg, J.H.: Identifying fixations and saccades in eye-tracking protocols. In: Proceedings of the Eye Tracking Research and Applications (2000)
21. Ohshima, T., Yamamoto, H., Tamura, H.: Gaze-directed adaptive rendering for interacting with virtual space. In: Proceedings of the VR Annual International Symposium (1996)
22. Shic, F., Scassellati, B., Chawarska, K.: The incomplete fixation measure. In: Proceedings of the 2008 Symposium on Eye Tracking Research and Applications (2008)
23. Ji, Q., Yang, X.: Real time visual cues extraction for monitoring driver vigilance. In: Schiele, B., Sagerer, Gerhard (eds.) ICVS 2001. LNCS, vol. 2095, pp. 107–124. Springer, Heidelberg (2001). doi:10.1007/3-540-48222-9_8
24. Murphy, H.A., Duchowski, A.T., Tyrrell, R.A.: Hybrid image/model-based gaze-contingent rendering. ACM Trans. Appl. Percept. 5(4), 22 (2009)
25. Siekawa, A., Mantiuk, S.R.: Gaze-dependent ray tracing. In: Proceedings of Central European Seminar on Computer Graphics (non-peer-reviewed) (2014)
26. Mantiuk, R., Janus, S.: Gaze-dependent ambient occlusion. In: Bebis, G., et al. (eds.) ISVC 2012. LNCS, vol. 7431, pp. 523–532. Springer, Heidelberg (2012). doi:10.1007/978-3-642-33179-4_50
27. Guenter, B., Finch, M., Drucker, S., Tan, D., Snyder, J.: Foveated 3D graphics. ACM Trans. Graph. 31(6), 164 (2012)
28. Zhang, X., Chen, W., Yang, Z., Zhu, C., Peng, Q.: A new foveation ray casting approach for real-time rendering of 3D scenes. In: Proceedings of the Computer-Aided Design and Computer Graphics (2011)
29. Fujita, M., Harada, T.: Foveated real-time ray tracing for virtual reality headset. Technical report, Light Transport Entertainment Research (2014)
30. Swafford, N.T., Iglesias-Guitian, J.A., Koniaris, C., Moon, B., Cosker, D., Mitchell, K.: User, metric, and computational evaluation of foveated rendering methods. In: Proceedings of the ACM Symposium on Applied Perception (2016)
31. Luebke, D., Hallen, B.: Perceptually driven simplification for interactive rendering. In: Proceedings of the Eurographics Workshop (2001)
32. Vlochos, A.: Advanced VR rendering Game Developers Conference, San Francisco (2015)
33. Sen, P., Darabi, S.: Implementation of random parameter filtering. Technical report (2011)
34. Lee, W.J., Shin, Y., Lee, J., Kim, J.W., Nah, J.H., Jung, S., Lee, S., Park, H.S., Han, T.D.: SGRT: A mobile GPU architecture for real-time ray tracing. In: Proceedings of the High-Performance Graphics (2013)
35. Aila, T., Laine, S., Karras, T.: Understanding the efficiency of ray traversal on GPUs-Kepler and Fermi addendum. Technical report, NVIDIA Corporation (2012)
36. Pohl, D., Johnson, G.S., Bolkart, T.: Improved pre-warping for wide angle, head mounted displays. In: Proceedings of the ACM Symposium on VR Software and Technology (2013)

# ST: Computer Vision as a Service

# OCR as a Service: An Experimental Evaluation of Google Docs OCR, Tesseract, ABBYY FineReader, and Transym

Ahmad P. Tafti[1(✉)], Ahmadreza Baghaie[2], Mehdi Assefi[3], Hamid R. Arabnia[3], Zeyun Yu[4], and Peggy Peissig[1(✉)]

[1] Biomedical Informatics Research Center, Marshfield Clinic Research Foundation, Marshfield, WI 54449, USA
{pahlavantafti.ahmad,peissig.peggy}@mcrf.mfldclin.edu
[2] Department of Electrical Engineering, University of Wisconsin-Milwaukee, Milwaukee, WI 53211, USA
[3] Department of Computer Science, University of Georgia, Athens, GA 30602, USA
[4] Department of Computer Science, University of Wisconsin-Milwaukee, Milwaukee, WI 53211, USA

**Abstract.** Optical character recognition (OCR) as a classic machine learning challenge has been a longstanding topic in a variety of applications in healthcare, education, insurance, and legal industries to convert different types of electronic documents, such as scanned documents, digital images, and PDF files into fully editable and searchable text data. The rapid generation of digital images on a daily basis prioritizes OCR as an imperative and foundational tool for data analysis. With the help of OCR systems, we have been able to save a reasonable amount of effort in creating, processing, and saving electronic documents, adapting them to different purposes. A set of different OCR platforms are now available which, aside from lending theoretical contributions to other practical fields, have demonstrated successful applications in real-world problems. In this work, several qualitative and quantitative experimental evaluations have been performed using four well-know OCR services, including Google Docs OCR, Tesseract, ABBYY FineReader, and Transym. We analyze the accuracy and reliability of the OCR packages employing a dataset including 1227 images from 15 different categories. Furthermore, we review the state-of-the-art OCR applications in healtcare informatics. The present evaluation is expected to advance OCR research, providing new insights and consideration to the research area, and assist researchers to determine which service is ideal for optical character recognition in an accurate and efficient manner.

## 1   Introduction

Optical character recognition (OCR) has been a very practical research area in many scientific disciplines, including machine learning [1–3], computer vision [4–6], natural language processing (NLP) [7–9], and biomedical informatics [10–12]. This computational technology has been utilized in converting scanned,

© Springer International Publishing AG 2016
G. Bebis et al. (Eds.): ISVC 2016, Part I, LNCS 10072, pp. 735–746, 2016.
DOI: 10.1007/978-3-319-50835-1_66

hand-written, or PDF files into an editable text format (e.g., text file or MS Word/Excel file) for further processing tasks [13,14]. OCR has contributed to significant process improvement in many different real world applications in healthcare, finance, insurance, and education. For example, in healthcare there has been a need to deal with vast amounts of patient forms (e.g., insurance forms). In order to analyze the information in such forms, it is critical to input the patient data in a standarized format into a database so it can be accessed later for analysis. Using OCR systems, we are able to automatically extract information from the forms and enter it into databases, so that every patient's data is immediately recorded. OCR really simplifies the process by turning those documents into easily editable and searchable text data. In the sense of software engineering "Software as a Service" (SaaS), as an architectural model behind the centralized computing, has emerged as a design pattern and also a delivery model in which a software could be accessed by both human-oriented and application-oriented standards [15–19]. Human users can get the SaaS system through a web browser, and an application will utilize the service using APIs (application programming interfaces).

To date, several attempts have been made to design and develop OCR services and/or packages, such as Google Docs OCR [20], Tesseract [21,22], ABBYY FineReader [23,24], Transym [25], Online OCR [26], and Free OCR [27]. Based on core functionalities, including recognition accuracy, performance, multilingual support, open-source implementation, delivery as a software development kit (SDK), high availability, and rating in the OCR community [28,29], the present contribution is mainly focused on the experimental evaluation of Google Docs OCR, Tesseract, ABBYY FineReader, and Transym. The current work is expected to provide better insights to the OCR study, and address several capabilities for possible future enhancements.

The rest of the paper is arranged as follows. The Google Docs OCR, Tesseract, ABBYY FineReader, and Transym OCR systems will be introduced in Sect. 2. In Sect. 3 we review, from an application perspective, the state-of-the-art OCR systems in healthcare informatics. Experimental validations including the dataset, testbed, and the results will be reported in Sect. 4. Section 5 provides discussion and concludes the work.

## 2   OCR Toolsets

OCR toolsets and their underlying algorithms not only focus on text and character recognition in a reliable manner, but may also address: (1) Layout analysis in which they can detect and understand different items in an image (e.g., text, tables, barcodes), (2) Support of various alphabets, including English, Greek, Persian, and etc., and (3) Support of different types of input images (e.g., TIFF, JPEG, PNG, PDF) and capabilities to export text data in different output formats. The basis of OCR methods dates back to 1914 when Goldberg designed a machine that was able to read characters and turn them into standard telegraph code [13]. With the emergence of computerized systems, many artificial intelligence researchers have tried to tackle the problem of OCR complexity to build efficient OCR systems capable of working in accurate and real-time fashion (e.g., [2,30–33]). Although there are many OCR methods and toolsets available now in the literature, here we limit the work to a comparative study of four well-known OCR toolsets namely "Google Docs OCR", "Tesseract", "ABBYY FineReader", and "Transym".

**Google Docs OCR** [20] is an easy-to-use and highly available OCR service offered by Google within the Google Drive service [34]. We can convert different types of image data into editable text data using Google Drive. Once we upload an image or a PDF file to the Google Drive, we can start the OCR conversion by right-clicking on the file to select "Open with Google Docs" item, then the image is inside a Google Doc document and the extracted text is right below the image.

**Tesseract** was originally developed by HP as an open-source OCR toolset released under the Apache License [35], available for different operating system platforms, such as Mac OS X, Linux, and Windows. Since 2006, Tesseract developments have been maintained by Google [36], and it is among one of the top OCR systems used worldwide [29]. The Tesseract algorithm, at step one, uses adaptive thresholding strategies [37] to convert the input image into a binary one. It then utilizes connected component analysis to extract character layouts in which such layouts are then turned into *blobs*, the regions in an image data that differ in some part of the properties including color or intensity, compared to surrounding pixels [36]. *Blobs* are then formed as text lines, and consequently examined for an equivalent text size which is then divided into words using fuzzy spaces [36]. Text recognition will then proceed in a two stage process. In the first stage, the algorithm tries to discover each word from the text. Then, every satisfactory word will be passed to an adaptive classifier to train the data in stage one. In the second stage, the adaptive classifier assists to discover text data in a more reliable way [36].

**ABBYY FineReader** as an advanced OCR software system has been designed and developed by an international company, namely "ABBYY" [23] to provide high level OCR services. It has been improving the main functionalities of optical character recognition for many years, providing promising results in text retrieval from digital images [28]. The underlying algorithms of ABBYY FineReader have not yet been illustrated to the research community, probably because it is a commercial software product, and the package is not available as open-source code. Researchers and developers can access the ABBYY FineReader OCR by two different ways: (1) The ABBYY FineReader SDK which is available at https://www.abbyy.com/resp/promo/ocr-sdk/, and (2) Employing a web browser to try it over the Internet at https://finereaderonline.com/en-us/Tasks/Create.

**Transym** is another OCR software package that assists research and development communities in extracting accurate information from digital documents, particularly scanned and digital images. The source code of the Transym and its underlying algorithms are not available, but it has been delivered as a SDK which provides a high level API, and it also has a software package with a light GUI (graphical user interface) which can be easily installed and used efficiently. Transym OCR package along with some sample codes are available at http:// www.transym.com/download.htm.

# 3  Applications in Healthcare Informatics

There have been limited studies surrounding the application of OCR within healthcare. Generally, the studies are divided into two major approaches: (1) Prospective data collection using forms that are specifically designed to capture hand printed data for OCR processing, and (2) Retrospective OCR data extraction using scanned historical paper documents or image forms [38]. There are several innovative examples of prospective OCR data capture at point-of-care. Titlestad [39] created a special OCR form to register new cancer patients into a large cancer registry. The OCR forms captured basic patient demographics and cancer codes. More recently OCR was introduced to capture data on anti-retroviral treatment, drug switches and tolerability for human immunodeficiency virus (HIV-1) patients [40]. This application enabled clinical staff to better manage the care of the HIV patient because the data could be tracked from visit to visit. Lee et al. [40] used OCR to minimize the transcription effort of radiologists when creating radiology reports. The Region of Interest (ROI) values (including area, mean, standard deviation, maximum and minimum) were limited to view on the computed tomography (CT) console or image analysis workstation. This image was then stored in a Picture Archiving and Communicating System (PACS). Radiologists would review the PAC images on the screen and then type the ROI measurements into a radiology report. OCR was used to automatically capture the ROI and measurements to place it on the clip board so it could be copied into the radiology report. Finally, Hawker et al. [41] used a set of cameras to capture the patient name when processing lab samples. OCR was used to interpret the patient name on incoming biological samples and then the name was compared to the laboratory information system for validity. The OCR mislabeling identification process outperformed the normal quality assurance process.

The majority of retrospective OCR studies have focused on retrieving medical data for research use. Peissig et al. [42] used OCR to extract cataract subtypes and severity from handwritten ophthalmology forms to enrich existing electronic health record data for a large genome-wide association study. This application extracted data from existing clinical forms that were not designed for OCR use with high accuracy rates. Fenz et al. [43] developed a pipeline that processed paper-based medical records using the open-source OCR engine Tesseract to extract synonyms and formal specifications of personal and medical data elements. The pipeline was applied on a large scale to health system documents and the output then used to identify representative research samples. Finally, OCR was applied to photographed printed medical records to detect diagnosis codes, medical tests and medications enabling the creation of structured personal health records. This study applied OCR to a real-world situation and addressed image quality problems and complex content by pre-processing and using multiple OCR engine synthesis [44].

## 4  Experimental Validations

To validate the accuracy, reliability, and performance of the Google Docs OCR, Tesseract, ABBYY FineReader, and Transym, several experiments on real, and also synthetic data were performed. In Sect. 4.1 we discuss the experimental setup, including the proposed dataset along with the testbed and its configurations. In Sect. 4.2 the qualitative OCR visualization results achieved from the OCR packages/services are reported. Subsequently, in Sect. 4.3 we examine the accuracy and reliability of the OCR systems, and perform a quantitative comparative study. Section 4.3 also presents and compare a set of quality attributes that the OCR systems offer to the research community.

### 4.1  Experimental Setup: The Dataset and Testbed

We have gathered 1227 images from 15 categories, including: (1) Digital Images, (2) Machine-written characters, (3) Machine-written digits, (4) Hand-written characters, (5) Hand-written digits, (6) Barcodes, (7) Black and white images, (8) Multi-oriented text strings, (9) Skewed images, (10) License plate numbers, (11) PDF files including electronic forms, (12) Digital receipts, (13) Noisy images, (14) Blurred images, and (15) Multilingual text images. Figure 1 shows an example from every category listed here. Except the PDF files (dataset No. 11), all images were taken in different resolutions using multiple formats, such as JPEG, TIFF, PNG, etc. The dataset attributes are explained in Table 1. Every dataset came up with the ground truth information including a list of the characters existing in the images. For all experiments illustrated here, we used 64-bit MS Windows 8 operating system on a personal computer with 3.00 GHz Intel Dual core CPU, 4 MB cache and 6 GB RAM. To communicate with Google Docs OCR [20], we employed Mozilla Firefox Version 48.0.1 at https://www.mozilla.org/.

### 4.2  Qualitative OCR Visualization

Using different images from the dataset illustrated in Sect. 4.1 we examined the qualitative visualization of the OCR systems. Figure 2 shows some sample results in extracting text data from digital images.

### 4.3  Comparative Study

Here, we further analyzed and compared the accuracy and reliability of the Google Docs OCR, Tesseract, ABBYY FineReader, and Transym using the dataset reported in Table 1. A detailed comparative study is reported in Table 2.

**Table 1.** Dataset attributes. First column shows the image categories. Number and type of the images is shown in the second column. CG, BW, and BWC stands for color and gray-scale, black & white, and black & white and color images respectively.

| Image category | Images | Formats |
|---|---|---|
| Digital images | 131 CG | TIFF, JPEG, GIF, PNG |
| Machine-written characters | 47 CG | TIFF, JPEG, GIF, PNG |
| Machine-written digits | 28 CG | TIFF, JPEG, GIF, PNG |
| Hand-written characters | 49 BW | TIFF, JPEG, GIF, PNG |
| Hand-written digits | 28 BW | TIFF, JPEG, GIF, PNG |
| Barcodes | 224 BWC | TIFF, JPEG, GIF, PNG |
| Black and white images | 101 BW | TIFF, JPEG, PNG |
| Multi-oriented text string | 27 CG | TIFF, JPEG, PNG |
| Skewed images | 93 CG | JPEG, PNG |
| License plate numbers | 204 CG | JPEG, PNG |
| PDF files | 14 CG | PDF |
| Digital receipts | 108 CG | JPEG, PNG |
| Noisy images | 24 CG | JPEG, PNG |
| Blurred images | 31 CG | JPEG, PNG |
| Multilingual text images | 118 CG | TIFF, JPEG, PNG |

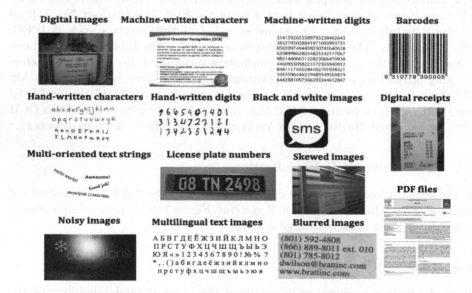

**Fig. 1.** Sample images from each category of the proposed dataset. The dataset includes 1227 digital images in 15 different categories.

| Image category | Sample image | Google Docs OCR | Tesseract | ABBYY FineReader | Transym |
|---|---|---|---|---|---|
| Digital images |  | RAE BUTLER BUILDING | RAB BUTLER BUILDING | Failed! | RAB BUTLER BUILDING |
| Machine-written characters | Explain that Stuff! | Explain that StUff | Explain that Stuff! | Explain that Stuff | Explain that Stuf f ! |
| Hand-written digits |  72104149159 0690159734 | 72104 9j8 DG90 I 597B4 | 7L/MI'1M'7 0(9401547'54 | 72104 I D 94 I 59 4 | 7LI04 I Y Db90 I 597b4 |
| License plate number |  WB 02 W 6886 | Failed! | W8 02 H 6886 | IND HB 02 H 6886 | WB02 W 6886 |
| Barcodes | | 0.1234" 56789 | 01234"56789 | 01234 5b789 | Failed! |
| Digital receipt | Total Seal $3.80 CREDIT CARD $3.80 | Total Oued 53.80 CREDIT CARD 53.80 | Total Owed 53.8) CREDIT FARO 53.8) | Total Owed 53.80 CREDIT CARD 53.80 | T...tal Uved 53. REDIT t-FRD 53 |
| Skewed images |  | Failed! | Failed! | Failed! | Failed! |
| Noisy images | | Failed! | Failed! | Failed! | Failed! |
| Blurred images |  agency agency | agency | Failed! | Failed! | ingen( y |
| Multi-oriented text | 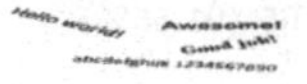 | A/ S/o ho, Awesome! abcdefghijk 1234567890 | YG//o Awesome! 3 3 abcdefghijk 1234567890 | Awesome! | Awesome! Go abcdefghijk 1234567890 |

**Fig. 2.** The qualitative visualization of the four OCR systems using some sample images from the dataset.

A comparative examination of color as well as gray-scale images, with or without applying low-level image processing tasks (e.g., contrast/brightness enhancement) is shown in Fig. 3. To calculate the accuracy for every OCR systems discussed in the current work, we divided the number of characters which correctly extracted from a dataset by the number of characters existing in the same dataset using the Eq. (1), where $n$ denotes the number of images in the dataset. Then, we calculated an average to obtain the total accuracy for each individual OCR system.

$$Accuracy = \frac{\sum_{k=1}^{n}(number of\ correctly\ extracted\ characters)}{\sum_{k=1}^{n}(number\ of\ total\ characters\ in\ the\ dataset)} \times 100 \quad (1)$$

Table 2 shows that the Google Docs OCR and ABBYY FineReader produced more promising results on the stated dataset, and the population standard deviation of accuracy obtained by those two are further consistent across the dataset. In addition to the experiments illustrated in Table 2, we divided the dataset into two parts including color and gray-scale images. Using color images, we obtained 74%, 64%, 71%, and 59% accuracy for the Google Docs OCR, Tesseract, ABBYY FineReader, and Transym respectively. After performing low-level image processing tasks including brightness and contrast enhancements, we obtained 75%,

**Table 2.** A Comparative study of the OCR systems. In this table we report analysis results obtained from 15 different image categories, examining the ability of the OCR systems to correctly extract characters from images. The percentage in the table means accuracy (Eq. 1).

| Image category | Existing characters | Extracted characters | | | |
| | | Google Docs OCR | Tesseract | ABBY FineReader | Transym |
| --- | --- | --- | --- | --- | --- |
| Digital images | 1834 | 1613 (87.95%) | 1539 (83.91%) | 1528 (83.31%) | 1463 (79.77%) |
| Machine-written characters | 703 | 569 (80.94%) | 549 (78.09%) | 574 (81.65%) | 554 (78.81%) |
| Machine-written digits | 211 | 191 (90.52%) | 193 (91.47%) | 193 (91.47%) | 194 (91.94%) |
| Hand-written characters | 2036 | 1254 (61.59%) | 984 (48.33%) | 1204 (59.14%) | 960 (47.15%) |
| Hand-written digits | 43 | 29 (67.44%) | 11 (25.58%) | 25 (58.14%) | 10 (23.26%) |
| Barcodes | 867 | 841 (97%) | 844 (97.35%) | 832 (95.96%) | 845 (97.47%) |
| Black and white images | 71 | 69 (97.19%) | 69 (97.19%) | 65 (91.55%) | 61 (85.92%) |
| Multi-oriented text strings | 106 | 68 (64.15%) | 30 (28.3%) | 75 (70.75%) | 23 (21.7%) |
| Skewed images | 96 | 38 (39.58%) | 31 (32.3%) | 36 (37.5%) | 27 (28.13%) |
| License plate numbers | 1953 | 1871 (95.8%) | 1812 (92.78%) | 1894 (96.98%) | 1732 (88.68%) |
| PDF Files | 15693 | 15409 (98.19%) | 14121 (89.98%) | 15376 (97.98%) | 14133 (90%) |
| Digital receipts | 3672 | 3256 (88.67%) | 3341 (90.99%) | 3302 (89.92%) | 3077 (83.8%) |
| Noisy images | 337 | 179 (53.12%) | 161 (47.77%) | 184 (54.6%) | 169 (50.15%) |
| Blurred images | 461 | 259 (56.18%) | 263(57.05%) | 282 (61.17%) | 277 (60.09%) |
| Multilingual text images | 3597 | 2831 (78.7%) | 2474 (68.78%) | 2799 (77.81%) | 1740 (48.37%) |
| **Standard Deviation** | | $\sigma = 18.19$ | $\sigma = 25.56$ | $\sigma = 18.02$ | $\sigma = 25.79$ |

64%, 75%, and 62% accuracy (Fig. 3). Using gray-scale images, we obtained 77%, 71%, 78%, and 68% accuracy for the Google Docs OCR, Tesseract, ABBYY FineReader, and Transym respectively. After performing low-level image processing tasks, such as brightness and contrast enhancement, we achieved 81%, 72%, 79%, and 70% accuracy (Fig. 3).

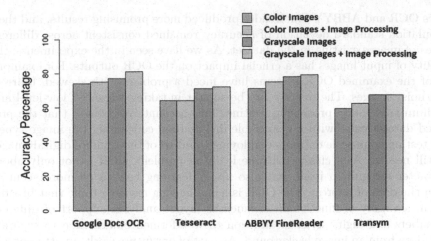

**Fig. 3.** A comparative study of the OCR systems using color and gray-scale images, with or without applying low-level image processing tasks (e.g., contrast/brightness enhancement). (Color figure online)

**Table 3.** A Comparative study of quality attributes of the OCR systems.

| Quality attribute | Google Docs OCR | Tesseract | ABBYY FineReader | Transym |
|---|---|---|---|---|
| Open-source | No | Yes | No | No |
| Available online | Yes | No | Yes | No |
| Available as a SDK | No | Yes | Yes | Yes |
| Available as a Service | Yes | Could be | No | No |
| Multilingual support | Yes | Yes | Yes | Yes |
| Free | Yes | Yes | No | No |
| Operating systems | Any | Linux, Mac OS X, Windows | Linux, Mac OS X, Windows | Windows |

Table 3 summarizes a comparative analysis of a set of quality attributes delivered by the OCR systems.

## 5   Discussion and Conclusion

We performed a qualitative and quantitative comparative study of four optical character recognition services, including Google Docs OCR, Tesseract, ABBYY FineReader, and Transym using a dataset containing 1227 images in 15 different categories. In addition to experimentally evaluating the OCR systems, we also reviewed OCR applications in the field of healthcare informatics. Based on our experimental evaluations using stated dataset, and without employing advanced image processing procedures (e.g., denoising, image registration), the Google

Docs OCR and ABBYY FineReader produced more promising results, and their population standard deviation of accuracy remained consistent across different types of images existing in the dataset. As we have seen in the experiments, the quality of input images has a crucial impact on the OCR outputs. For example, all of the examined OCR systems have faced a problem with skewed, blurred, and noisy images. The remedy can be sought in taking advanced low-level and medium-level image processing routines into account. We believe that the proposed dataset came with a reasonable distribution concerning the image types, but testing large-scale datasets employing hundred of thousand of digital images is still needed. As a classic machine learning problem, OCR is not only about character recognition itself, but also about learning how to be more accurate from the data of interest. The OCR is a challenging research topic that broadly lies in a variety of functionalities, such as layout analysis, support of different alphabets and digits style, in addition to well-formed binarisation to separate text data from an image background. As part of our future work, an attempt will be made to evaluate further OCR services using large-scale datasets, incorporating more significant statistical analysis for the accuracy and reliability. We will take advantage of advanced image processing algorithms and examine the benefit of their use towards developing more accurate and efficient optical character recognition systems.

**Acknowledgement.** The authors of the paper wish to thank Anne Nikolai at Marshfield Clinic Research Foundation for her valuable contributions in manuscript preparation. We also thank two anonymous reviewers for their useful comments on the manuscript.

# References

1. Lin, H.-Y., Hsu, C.-Y.: Optical character recognition with fast training neural network. In: 2016 IEEE International Conference on Industrial Technology (ICIT), pp. 1458–1461. IEEE (2016)
2. Patil, V.V., Sanap, R.V., Kharate, R.B.: Optical character recognition using artificial neural network. Int. J. Eng. Res. Gen. Sci. **3**(1), 7 (2015)
3. Spitsyn, V.G., Bolotova, Y.A., Phan, N.H., Bui, T.T.T.: Using a haar wavelet transform, principal component analysis and neural networks for OCR in the presence of impulse noise. Comput. Opt. **40**(2), 249–257 (2016)
4. Bunke, H., Caelli, T.: Hidden Markov Models: Applications in Computer Vision, vol. 45. World Scientific, River Edge (2001)
5. Gupta, M.R., Jacobson, N.P., Garcia, E.K.: OCR binarization and image preprocessing for searching historical documents. Pattern Recogn. **40**(2), 389–397 (2007)
6. Jadhav, P., Kelkar, P., Patil, K., Thorat, S.: Smart traffic control system using image processing (2016)
7. Afli, H., Qiu, Z., Way, A., Sheridan, P.: Using SMT for OCR error correction of historical texts. In: Proceedings of LREC-2016, Portorož, Slovenia (2016, to appear)

8. Kolak, O., Byrne, W., Resnik, P.: A generative probabilistic OCR model for NLP applications. In: Proceedings of the 2003 Conference of the North American Chapter of the Association for Computational Linguistics on Human Language Technology, vol. 1, pp. 55–62. Association for Computational Linguistics (2003)

9. Kolak, O., Resnik, P.: OCR post-processing for low density languages. In: Proceedings of the Conference on Human Language Technology and Empirical Methods in Natural Language Processing, pp. 867–874. Association for Computational Linguistics (2005)

10. Deselaers, T., Müller, H., Clough, P., Ney, H., Lehmann, T.M.: The CLEF 2005 automatic medical image annotation task. Int. J. Comput. Vis. **74**(1), 51–58 (2007)

11. Kaggal, V.C., Elayavilli, R.K., Mehrabi, S., Joshua, J.P., Sohn, S., Wang, Y., Li, D., Rastegar, M.M., Murphy, S.P., Ross, J.L., et al.: Toward a learning health-care system-knowledge delivery at the point of care empowered by big data and NLP. Biomed. Inf. Insights **8**(Suppl1), 13 (2016)

12. Pomares-Quimbaya, A., Gonzalez, R.A., Quintero, S., Muñoz, O.M., Bohórquez, W.R., García, O.M., Londoño, D.: A review of existing applications and techniques for narrative text analysis in electronic medical records (2016)

13. Herbert, H.F.: The History of OCR, Optical Character Recognition. Recognition Technologies Users Association, Manchester Center (1982)

14. Tappert, C.C., Suen, C.Y., Wakahara, T.: The state of the art in online handwriting recognition. IEEE Trans. Pattern Anal. Mach. Intell. **12**(8), 787–808 (1990)

15. Assefi, M., Liu, G., Wittie, M.P., Izurieta, C.: An experimental evaluation of apple siri and google speech recognition. In: Proccedings of the 2015 ISCA SEDE (2015)

16. Assefi, M., Wittie, M., Knight, A.: Impact of network performance on cloud speech recognition. In: 2015 24th International Conference on Computer Communication and Networks (ICCCN), pp. 1–6. IEEE (2015)

17. Hatch, R.: SaaS Architecture, Adoption and Monetization of SaaS Projects using Best Practice Service Strategy, Service Design, Service Transition, Service Operation and Continual Service Improvement Processes. Emereo Pty Ltd., London (2008)

18. Tafti, A.P., Hassannia, H., Piziak, D., Yu, Z.: SeLibCV: a service library for computer vision researchers. In: Bebis, G., et al. (eds.) ISVC 2015. LNCS, vol. 9475, pp. 542–553. Springer, Heidelberg (2015). doi:10.1007/978-3-319-27863-6_50

19. Xiaolan, X., Wenjun, W., Wang, Y., Yuchuan, W.: Software crowdsourcing for developing software-as-a-service. Front. Comput. Sci. **9**(4), 554–565 (2015)

20. Google docs (2012). http://docs.google.com

21. Tesseract OCR (2016). https://github.com/tesseract-ocr

22. Tesseract.js, a pure javascript version of the tesseract OCR engine (2016). http://tesseract.projectnaptha.com/

23. Abbyy OCR (2016). https://www.abbyy.com/

24. Abbyy OCR online (2016). https://finereaderonline.com/en-us/Tasks/Create

25. Transym (2016). http://www.transym.com/

26. Online OCR (2016). http://www.onlineocr.net/

27. Free OCR (2016). http://www.free-ocr.com/

28. Mendelson, E.: Abbyy finereader 12 professional. Technical report, PC Magazine (2014)

29. Rice, S.V., Jenkins, F.R., Nartker, T.A.: The fourth annual test of OCR accuracy. Technical report, Technical Report 95 (1995)

30. Bautista, C.M., Dy, C.A., Mañalac, M.I., Orbe, R.A., Cordel, M.: Convolutional neural network for vehicle detection in low resolution traffic videos. In: 2016 IEEE Region 10 Symposium (TENSYMP), pp. 277–281. IEEE (2016)

31. LeCun, Y., Bengio, Y., Hinton, G.: Deep learning. Nature **521**(7553), 436–444 (2015)
32. Shah, P., Karamchandani, S., Nadkar, T., Gulechha, N., Koli, K., Lad, K.: OCR-based chassis-number recognition using artificial neural networks. In: 2009 IEEE International Conference on Vehicular Electronics and Safety (ICVES), pp. 31–34. IEEE (2009)
33. Ye, Q., Doermann, D.: Text detection and recognition in imagery: a survey. IEEE Trans. Pattern Anal. Mach. Intell. **37**(7), 1480–1500 (2015)
34. Google drive (2012). http://drive.google.com
35. Apache license, version 2.0 (2004). http://www.apache.org/licenses/LICENSE-2.0
36. Smith, R.: An overview of the tesseract OCR engine (2007)
37. Bradley, D., Roth, G.: Adaptive thresholding using the integral image. J. Graph. GPU Game Tools **12**(2), 13–21 (2007)
38. Rasmussen, L.V., Peissig, P.L., McCarty, C.A., Starren, J.: Development of an optical character recognition pipeline for handwritten form fields from an electronic health record. J. Am. Med. Inf. Assoc. **19**(e1), e90–e95 (2012)
39. Titlestad, G.: Use of document image processing in cancer registration: how and why? Medinfo. MEDINFO **8**, 462 (1994)
40. Bussmann, H., Wester, C.W., Ndwapi, N., Vanderwarker, C., Gaolathe, T., Tirelo, G., Avalos, A., Moffat, H., Marlink, R.G.: Hybrid data capture for monitoring patients on highly active antiretroviral therapy (haart) in urban Botswana. Bull. World Health Org. **84**(2), 127–131 (2006)
41. Hawker, C.D., McCarthy, W., Cleveland, D., Messinger, B.L.: Invention and validation of an automated camera system that uses optical character recognition to identify patient name mislabeled samples. Clin. Chem. **60**(3), 463–470 (2014)
42. Peissig, P.L., Rasmussen, L.V., Berg, R.L., Linneman, J.G., McCarty, C.A., Waudby, C., Chen, L., Denny, J.C., Wilke, R.A., Pathak, J., et al.: Importance of multi-modal approaches to effectively identify cataract cases from electronic health records. J. Am. Med. Inform. Assoc. **19**(2), 225–234 (2012)
43. Fenz, S., Heurix, J., Neubauer, T.: Recognition and privacy preservation of paper-based health records. Stud. Health Technol. Inf. **180**, 751–755 (2012)
44. Li, X., Hu, G., Teng, X., Xie, G.: Building structured personal health records from photographs of printed medical records. In: AMIA Annual Symposium Proceedings, vol. 2015, p. 833. American Medical Informatics Association (2015)

# Animal Identification in Low Quality Camera-Trap Images Using Very Deep Convolutional Neural Networks and Confidence Thresholds

Alexander Gomez[1], German Diez[1], Augusto Salazar[1(✉)], and Angelica Diaz[2]

[1] Grupo de Investigación SISTEMIC, Facultad de Ingeniería,
Universidad de Antioquia UdeA, Calle 70 No. 52-21, Medellín, Colombia
alexander.gomezvilla@supsi.ch, augusto.salazar@udea.edu.co
[2] Instituto Alexander Von Humboldt, Calle 28A No. 15-09, Bogota D.C, Colombia

**Abstract.** Monitoring animals in the wild without disturbing them is possible using camera trapping framework. Automatic triggered cameras, which take a burst of images of animals in their habitat, produce great volumes of data, but often result in low image quality. This high volume data must be classified by a human expert. In this work a two step classification is proposed to get closer to an automatic and trustfully camera-trap classification system in low quality images. Very deep convolutional neural networks were used to distinguish images, firstly between birds and mammals, secondly between mammals sets. The method reached 97.5% and 90.35% in each task. An alleviation mode using a confidence threshold of automatic classification is proposed, allowing the system to reach 100% of performance traded with human work.

## 1 Introduction

Currently, automated camera-traps used in wildlife are small devices, fixed to a plant, rock or other structure. Camera-traps are powerful tools for wildlife scientists, whose, by using this method, can answer fundamental questions and resolve issues like: detecting rare species, delineating species, distributions, documenting predation, monitoring animal behaviour, and other vital rates [1]. Hence, it allows biologists to protect animals and their environments from extinction or man-made damage.

Camera-trapping generates a large volume of images. Therefore, it is a big challenge to process the recorded images and it is even harder, if the biologists are looking to identify all photographed species. Currently, no automatic approach is used to identify species from camera-trap images. Researchers analyse thousands or millions of photographs manually [2]. An automatic system that deals with this problem would accelerate the professionals' work, allowing them to focus on data analysis and important issues only.

Automatic classification of animal species in camera-trap images has been approached in very unrealistic or specific scenarios. A few previous works proposed solutions for this problem. Yu et al. [3] manually cropped and selected

G. Bebis et al. (Eds.): ISVC 2016, Part I, LNCS 10072, pp. 747–756, 2016.
DOI: 10.1007/978-3-319-50835-1_67

images, which contain the whole animal body. This conditioning allowed then to obtain 82% of accuracy classifying 18 animal species in their own dataset. Although Chen et al. [4] use an automatic segmentation algorithm and did not manually select images they obtained only 38.3% of accuracy. Finally Gomez et al. [5] got 88.9% in challenging scenarios without manually selecting images used high quality images with three channels.

In this work very deep convolutional neural networks are used to classify between animal species sets. Instead of classifying each image as belonging to a species a partition using a hierarchy based on biologist knowledge was used. First, all the input images are classified as birds or other. Secondly, the other cluster is classified as big mammals or small mammals, each group has several species tidied up by biologist.

Our result show that, if direct animal species classification is avoided, and the species are clustered in smart biologically inspired sets, high performance even in low quality and gray scale images is possible. Also trusting in the system prediction only when a confidence threshold is surpassed and leave hard decisions to a human expert leads to nearly perfect performance and confidence.

The rest of the paper is organized as follows. Related work is mentioned in Sect. 2. In Sect. 3 the challenges present in camera- trapping framework are described; also the methods used in the identification model are explained. Section 4 describes the experiments used to test the models. Results are presented in Sect. 5. Finally, in Sect. 6 conclusions and future work are presented.

## 2   Related Work

This section reviews previous approaches to identify species in camera-trap images. To the best of our knowledge there are only three previous approaches to identify animal species in camera-trap images. Sparse coding spatial pyramid matching (ScSPM) with a linear support vector machine was used by Yu et al. [3] to recognize 18 species of animals, reaching 82% of accuracy on their own dataset. As input to the ScSPM the photo-trap images were preprocessed by removing empty frames (images without animals), manually cropping all the animals from the images, and selecting only those images that capture the animals' whole body without distortions or noise. This procedure gave Yu et al. high performance but in unrealistic conditions.

A deep convolutional neural network (ConvNet) was used by Chen et al. [4] to classify 20 animal species in their own dataset. An important difference from [3] is that they use an automatic segmentation method (Ensemble Video Object Cut) for cropping the animals from the images and use this crops to train and test their system. Although this is a realistic classification scenario the classification model is too weak to capture class variability. Also the automatic segmentation algorithm gave Chen et al. a lot of empty images which give them a 38.31% of accuracy.

Very deep ConvNets were used by Gomez et al. [5] to classify 26 animal species in the Snapshot Serengeti dataset. Multiple versions of training and testing samples as unbalanced samples, empty frames, incomplete animal images, cropped animals and objects too far from focal distance were used. A comparison using the Chen et al. dataset showed that deeper architectures outperform shallow ones in the same dataset. Although the performance of the models of Gomez et al. showed high values in the Snapshot Serengeti dataset, said model performance in Chen et al.'s dataset was less than 60% due to a high-noisy training set. This fact reveals a lack of confidence in low quality camera-trap images.

Our approach uses very deep ConvNets as [5], but is different in two main aspects. First, unlike the Snapshot Serengeti dataset, our data contain images of animals in the south american jungle, which presents a very cluttered background, also poor illumination conditions, gray scale, and low resolution. Second, we do not directly classify animal species but animal sets proposed by biologist in order to make a trade-off between classification complexity and human effort.

# 3 Methods

In this section different situations, present in camera-trap images, that must be overcome to make species identification automatically, are described and analysed. Also, a solution based on very deep convolutional neural networks is proposed.

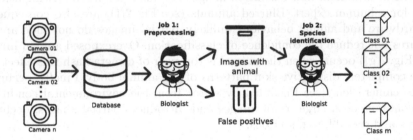

**Fig. 1.** Framework of data processing in camera-trap

## 3.1 Framework of Data Processing in Camera-Trap

The framework of data processing in camera-trap is showing in Fig. 1. All images are put in a database, which is processed in 2 ways: First (Job 1), all the images without animals (false positive) are removed. This pre-process is the most time-consuming step since typically more than 50% of the images are false positives. Then the images than contains animals are classified in species (Job 2) using the biologist knowledge to identify visually and using metadata information as hour and temperature. A few works has tried to solve Job 1. Analizing Job 2 as a computer vision problem it implies a segmentation of the animal and a classification of the segmented region. In this work only the classification part of Job 2 is solved.

The image classification problem is interpreted as an object recognition problem in which for instance a bird (see Fig. 4(b)) must be recognized. However as were said in previous works this kind of prototype images are an ideal and scarce case in camera-trap framework. Common camera-trap images are corrupted by eight possible noise conditions.

First and most common problem is partial capture of the animal (see Fig. 2(b)). This problem can confuse any automatic algorithm that learned a class appearance based in an specific feature (like head attributes or legs shape) even biologist are unable to identify some images in this condition. Background occlusion is a common feature of camera-trap images in jungle or dense forest. Unlike Snapshot Serengeti dateset where African savannah makes difficult to occlude any animal in jungle or forest is very common. Although camera-traps must be set in a clean region plants grown or animals continuously enter and exit from vegetation zones. Occlusion has the same effect of partial images and additionally introduces a lot of noise in the animal body regions.

Auto-oclussion (see Fig. 2(d)) has the same effect of partial images, complex poses that hides main features of the species are commonly found in camera-trap images. Low resolution images (see Fig. 2(e)) can be consequence of hardware selection or animal behaviour. High resolution cameras can be used but as result less cameras can be acquired. Even if the camera has high resolution animals do not always walk near the camera as is expected or the scene is too deep as African savannah. Low resolution images can make animal undistinguishable even for a human expert. Blurred animals (see Fig. 2(f)) are also consequence of hardware and animal behaviour unlikely partial images do not hide animal features but reduce the confidence of classification. Overexposed animal images (see Fig. 2(g)) occurs when the animal is too near of camera flash this effect can erase completely distinctive skin patterns of the animal body. Finally, occlusion of the camera lens (see Fig. 2(h)) by water from the environmental conditions can contaminate a large set of images and introduces partial images, occluded images and even blurred sections.

## 3.2    Alleviation Mode

In camera-trap framework biologist have a lot of responsibility in species classification task, since some species are very unlikely to appear on image (like jaguar in Colombian camera-traps). If one of this scarce species are omitted the whole region study is wrong, since this species are in extinction danger or gives a lot of biological information. Trust in an automatic classifier means take the bet of the automatic system will never incorrectly classify an image that have this scarce species.

A multinomial logistic regression gives a probability of membership to each class computed. When a new sample is processed if the probability of membership to each class is very similar the classifier, actually the model is more likely to assign it to an incorrect class [6]. In this situation is more secure to let a human expert to classify the sample. This process allow a trade-off between

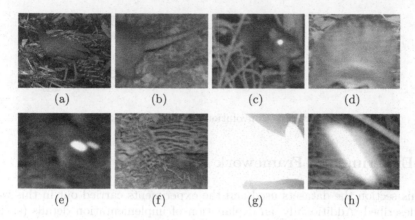

**Fig. 2.** (a) Ideal and scarce case in camera-trap framework. (b) Partial capture of the animal. (c) Background occlusion. (d) Auto-oclussion. (e) Low resolution images. (f) Blurred animal. (g) Overexposed animal (h) Occlusion of the camera lens.

human work and performance of the system and has been used previously in machine learning systems [7]

$$confidence = \mid log_{10}(Prob_A/Prob_B) \mid \qquad (1)$$

The confidence of a classification is computed using Eq. 1. Where $Prob_A$ is the probability of membership to class one and $Prob_B$ is the probability of membership to class two. If the confidence of a classification is less that a threshold level called alleviation this classification is passed to a human expert.

### 3.3 Convolutional Neural Networks

Convolutional neural networks [8] consist of stacked convolutional and pooling layers ending in a fully connected layer with a feature vector as Fig. 3 shows as output. Convolutional layers generate feature maps followed by a non-linear activation function. Pooling layers provides scale invariant capacity to the extracted features. A common topology in a ConvNet consists of many sequential stacked convolutional and pooling layers that can extract discriminative features from an input image.

A transformation that maps from low level to high level features is done in a ConvNet. The first layers contain low level features (e.g., edges and orientation) and the last layers contain high level representation features, such as wrinkles, or in the case of animals, the fur details and its discriminative patterns. An important issue in ConvNets architectures is the Depth, reason why community attempts to boost topology Depth. In this work AlexNet [9], VGGNet [10], GoogLenet [11], and ResNets [12] are used in order to probe how Depth in ConvNets impacts in camera trapping species recognition.

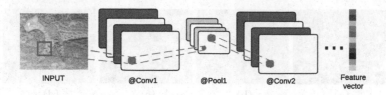

INPUT            @Conv1        @Pool1         @Conv2        Feature
                                                            vector

**Fig. 3.** Convolutional neural network

# 4    Experimental Framework

In this section the datasets used and the experiments carried out in this work, are described. Additionally, an explanation of implementation details (such as libraries and architecture parameters) is included.

## 4.1    Dataset

Our dataset is composed of 95000 images took in Colombian territory by the Von Humboldt Institute. This images are a collection of camera-trap captures taken in nine sites. The raw dataset was pre-processed by human experts cutting out the animals present on the images. Nevertheless a high percentage of the total amount of images not contain animals, but vegetation or useless information instead of identifiable animal parts. The used dataset was a subset of the original group of 95000 images where the original images were segmented only on the animal containing parts. The segmented dataset was split in two experiments. The total number of images for each experiment is 1572 for Experiment 1 and 2597 for Experiment 2. This images were split in test and train sets, as Table 2 shows. Notice the unbalanced nature of the training set in both experiments.

## 4.2    Experiments

The ideal classification task is distinguishing species, however, like previous works with similar images showed, the performance with these low-quality images is far from acceptable. In this work two experiments proposed by biologist are done. First, a separation between birds and other animals is done, since camera-trap framework is not designed for birds, however, birds appear on scene and activate camera sensors. This filter is the first step to alleviate the experts' work. Once all the birds are removed from the set the second experiment classify between two mammals sets. Further details of theses sets are shown in Table 1.

Although this separation is no per-species it gives a lot of useful information to the biologists. The second filter is an easier task for the classifier and helps the species classification task. Since the used dataset is too small and unbalanced for a successful supervised training, a data augmentation strategy was used. The training set in both experiments was augmented using images from the ImageNet dataset. Using images from the same species and testing the system only in our

**Table 1.** Mammals species sets

| Set 1 | Set 2 |
|---|---|
| Carnivora | Didelphimorphia |
| Artiodactyla | Cingulata |
| Perissodactyla | Pilosa |
| | Rodentia |
| | Lagomorpha |

**Table 2.** Training set before and after data augmentation

| Exp | Testing set | Training set class 1 | Training set class 2 | Training set using ImageNet class 1 | Training set using ImageNet class 2 |
|---|---|---|---|---|---|
| 1 | 100 | 67 | 1305 | 2193 | 2193 |
| 2 | 420 | 577 | 1600 | 1600 | 1600 |

dataset allowed us to successfully train supervised models. Table 2 summarizes the training and testing sets before and after using the Imagenet images.

In both experiments all deep architectures were used. Table 3 shows the six very deep ConvNets used in this work. They are the state of the art in object recognition. Since data augmentation puts a lot of the ImageNet images in the training set, a fine-tuning procedure did not have a significant effect on the system's performance, hence, just the multi-class logistic classifier at the end of the network was trained and the ConvNet used as black box feature extractor. This work uses multiple very deep ConvNets in order to probe how the Depth in ConvNets impacts on the camera-trapping classification problem in low quality images.

### 4.3 Metrics

A confusion matrix is used as performance evaluation in both experiments. Efficiency, recall, specificity, and precision are extracted from the confusion matrix. In alleviation experiments only efficiency is used.

**Table 3.** Architectures used in the experiments

| Label | Architecture | # layers |
|---|---|---|
| A | AlexNet | 8 |
| B | VGG Net | 16 |
| C | GoogLenet | 22 |
| D | ResNet-50 | 50 |
| E | ResNet-101 | 101 |
| F | ResNet-152 | 152 |

## 4.4  Implementation Details

All the dataset images were resized to fit in the ConvNet topologies input: AlexNet ($227 \times 227$), VGGNet ($224 \times 224$), GoogLenet ($224 \times 224$), and ResNets ($224 \times 224$). To use ConvNets as feature extractors the last full connected layer was modified to deal with 2 classes instead of 1000 Imagenet challenge classes.

All used architectures were pre-trained with the ImageNet dataset [13]. The implementation was done in the deep learning framework Caffe [14], as well as all pre-trained models that were found in the Caffe model Zoo and where performed using a Graphics processing unit Nvidia gtx 850M.

## 5  Results

In Table 4 the results are shown. Each experiment (1 or 2) is paired with a deep architecture (represented with a label listed in Table 3).

**Table 4.** Results of experiments and performance metrics

| Experiment | Efficiency [%] | Recall [%] | Precision [%] |
|------------|----------------|------------|---------------|
| 1A | 77.50 | 80.23 | 69.23 |
| 1B | 82.50 | 83.66 | 78.26 |
| 1C | 85.00 | 86.63 | 75.00 |
| 1D | 95.00 | 99.99 | 78.26 |
| 1E | **97.50** | 100 | 90.00 |
| 1F | 95.00 | 100 | 85.73 |
| 2A | 74.28 | 70.81 | 75.51 |
| 2B | 73.57 | 64.59 | 78.94 |
| 2C | 73.09 | 67.46 | 75.40 |
| 2D | 85.23 | 85.64 | 84.03 |
| 2E | **90.23** | 95.69 | 85.83 |
| 2F | 84.76 | 90.90 | 80.50 |

The results of Experiment 1 show a high efficiency using ResNet-101. This shows how successfully the deep architecture has learned the concept of "bird". Notice that the deeper architecture does not have the highest performance, however, the tendency depth versus performance is crescent till 101 layers. ResNet-101 has the best efficiency in Experiment 2, too. Although the performance is not as high as in Experiment 1, it is promising and even acceptable in the total automatic classification mode. In contrast to Experiment 1, the results from GoogleNet and VGGnet were worse than the results from AlexNet. These performance results can be enhanced using the alleviation mode.

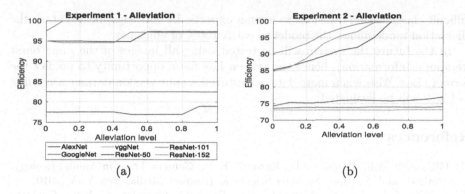

**Fig. 4.** (a) Alleviation in Experiment 1. (b) Alleviation in Experiment 2.

Figure 4 shows the results of the alleviation experiments. Alleviation level equal to 0 means total automatic system and increasing threshold means increasing the distance between probabilities of memberships to be an acceptable result. The alleviation did no show significance improvement in Experiment 1. Only one architecture (ResNet-101) reaches 100%, others did not improve or just a bit. An important observation is that only residual architectures and AlexNet improved using the alleviation. The residual architecture improved in a lower value of the alleviation. Experiment 2 showed a lot of improvement using the alleviation strategy. Residual architectures reached 100% of efficiency. Notice that the two deep residual nets reached in 0.6 and the less deeper near to this alleviation level 0.7. Similar to Experiment 1 the three less deep architectures did not show a lot of improvement using the alleviation and GoogleNet and VGGnet keep constant performance.

The alleviation mode represents how much the expert trusts in the classifier. When the expert expects high confidence in the classifier's decision and the model has high learning capacity (e.g. deeper networks) a perfect performance is reached.

## 6   Conclusions

In this paper a two step classification strategy using deep convolutional neural networks for low quality camera-trap images was proposed. Instead of directly classifying species (which previously showed low performance in this type of images) the images are classified in two steps: first birds are separated from mammals, then mammals are classified in two sets proposed by biologists. As proved in this work cluster of mammal species reduce the complexity of the classification task and still give a lot of information to the biologists. In the first classification phase the best performance was 97.5% using residual networks with 101 layers. In the second step the best performance was 90.23% also using residual networks with 101 layers. An alleviation mode is proposed to hand over difficult classification decisions to human experts. In both classification task the alleviation mode allows the model to reach 100% of efficiency.

In the future the system will be tested using all images of the same burst (temporal information), hence the system has more opportunity to predict the correct class. Also when more data is captured a split version dataset according to Fig. 2 will be evaluated.

# References

1. O'Connell, A.F., Nichols, J.D., Karanth, K.U.: Camera Traps in Animal Ecology: Methods and Analyses. Springer Science & Business Media, New York (2010)
2. Fegraus, E.H., Lin, K., Ahumada, J.A., Baru, C., Chandra, S., Youn, C.: Data acquisition and management software for camera trap data: a case study from the team network. Ecol. Inform. **6**, 345–353 (2011)
3. Yu, X., Wang, J., Kays, R., Jansen, P.A., Wang, T., Huang, T.: Automated identification of animal species in camera trap images. EURASIP J. Image Video Process. **2013**, 1–10 (2013)
4. Chen, G., Han, T.X., He, Z., Kays, R., Forrester, T.: Deep convolutional neural network based species recognition for wild animal monitoring. In: 2014 IEEE International Conference on Image Processing (ICIP), pp. 858–862. IEEE (2014)
5. Gomez, A., Salazar, A., Vargas, F.: Towards automatic wild animal monitoring: identification of animal species in camera-trap images using very deep convolutional neural networks. arXiv preprint arXiv:1603.06169 (2016)
6. Lewis, D.D., Catlett, J.: Heterogeneous uncertainty sampling for supervised learning. In: Proceedings of the Eleventh International Conference on Machine Learning, pp. 148–156 (1994)
7. Beijbom, O., Edmunds, P.J., Roelfsema, C., Smith, J., Kline, D.I., Neal, B.P., Dunlap, M.J., Moriarty, V., Fan, T.Y., Tan, C.J., et al.: Towards automated annotation of benthic survey images: variability of human experts and operational modes of automation. PloS one **10**, e0130312 (2015)
8. LeCun, Y., Bottou, L., Bengio, Y., Haffner, P.: Gradient-based learning applied to document recognition. Proc. IEEE **86**, 2278–2324 (1998)
9. Krizhevsky, A., Sutskever, I., Hinton, G.E.: Imagenet classification with deep convolutional neural networks. In: Advances in Neural Information Processing Systems, pp. 1097–1105 (2012)
10. Simonyan, K., Zisserman, A.: Very deep convolutional networks for large-scale image recognition. arXiv preprint arXiv:1409.1556 (2014)
11. Szegedy, C., Liu, W., Jia, Y., Sermanet, P., Reed, S., Anguelov, D., Erhan, D., Vanhoucke, V., Rabinovich, A.: Going deeper with convolutions. In: Proceedings of the IEEE Conference on Computer Vision and Pattern Recognition, pp. 1–9 (2015)
12. He, K., Zhang, X., Ren, S., Sun, J.: Deep residual learning for image recognition. arXiv preprint arXiv:1512.03385 (2015)
13. Russakovsky, O., Deng, J., Su, H., Krause, J., Satheesh, S., Ma, S., Huang, Z., Karpathy, A., Khosla, A., Bernstein, M., Berg, A.C., Fei-Fei, L.: ImageNet large scale visual recognition challenge. Int. J. Comput. Vis. (IJCV) **115**, 211–252 (2015)
14. Jia, Y., Shelhamer, E., Donahue, J., Karayev, S., Long, J., Girshick, R., Guadarrama, S., Darrell, T.: Caffe: convolutional architecture for fast feature embedding. arXiv preprint arXiv:1408.5093 (2014)

# A Gaussian Mixture Model Feature for Wildlife Detection

Shengzhi Du[1]([✉]), Chunling Du[2], Rishaad Abdoola[3],
and Barend Jacobus van Wyk[1]

[1] Department of Mechanical Engineering, Mechatronics and Industrial Design,
Tshwane University of Technology, Pretoria 0001, South Africa
dushengzhi@gmail.com
[2] Department of Computer Systems Engineering,
Tshwane University of Technology, Pretoria 0001, South Africa
tclchunling@gmail.com
[3] Melbourne Institute of Technology, Melbourne, Australia

**Abstract.** This paper addresses the challenge of the camouflage in the
wildlife detection. The protective coloring makes the color space distance
between the features of animal pattern and background pattern very
small. The texture information should be considered under this situation.
A reliable differential estimator for digital image data is employed. The
estimation of the first order and the second order differentials of animal
and background patterns are modelled using Gaussian mixture model
method. It is shown the animal and background have bigger distance
in Gaussian mixture models than in the color space. The mathematical
expectation and standard deviation of the Gaussian models are therefore used to build the features to represent animal and background patterns. To demonstrate the performance of the proposed features, a neural
network classifier is employed. The experiment results on wildlife scene
images show that the proposed features have high classifying capacity to
detect animals with camouflage from the background environment.

**Keywords:** Image differentials · Gaussian Mixture Model (GMM) ·
Unmanned Aerial Vehicle (UAV) · Wildlife detection · Texture
classification

## 1 Introduction

With the human footprint increasing and climate changes, there are large number of wildlife becoming endangered or threatened. Governments and natural
conserve departments are spending huge amount of time and money on developing numerous protective methods to preserve these wildlife. One of the important
tasks is regular survey focusing on detecting and estimating the distribution of
specific species. These surveys provide basic data of wild animals, such as the
size of herd, the sex ratio, number of new generated cubs. Adequate size of
population, proper sex ratio, and reasonable adult to cubs ratio are the critical

© Springer International Publishing AG 2016
G. Bebis et al. (Eds.): ISVC 2016, Part I, LNCS 10072, pp. 757–765, 2016.
DOI: 10.1007/978-3-319-50835-1_68

factors for their state of survival. To obtain these data, the animal counting and identifying are critical. To cover large areas in limited time span, unmanned aerial vehicles (UAVs) are commonly employed to capture the video of animals in wildlife scenes. Then computer vision techniques are employed to analyze the video data towards population census, herd behavior study, and individual inspection.

Counting animals always follows after isolating them from complicate background. The latter belongs to object detection [1], which becomes one of the important tasks in computer vision and pattern preconization. Feature definition and detection are the basic components of object detection. Commonly recognized object features include color [2], texture [3], spatio-temporal features [4] and so on. Object detection can be categorized to static and moving object detection. According to these two categories, many algorithms were developed and applied, such as background substraction [5], and optical flow [6], etc. These methods can be applied in different purposes, for instance, driver assistance systems, robotic systems, wheelchairs and so on. Wildlife recognition is one of the most challenging applications in object detection. Firstly, different categories of animals have different coat pattern. Even for same species they also have quite different spots on their body. Secondly, a large number of the wildlife have protective coloring, they use this color to merge themselves into the background environment, so it is difficult to detect them from videos and images. Thirdly, some animals are moving but some keep static in the same scene. All these facts bring challenges for wildlife detection.

In this paper, the Gaussian mixture model (GMM) is used to model the differential feature of digital image data for wildlife detection, which is helpful especially under the challenge of camouflage. The feature is robust against uncertainties of lightness, contrast, and even noise. The proposed feature is verified by unmanned aerial vehicle (UAV) captured image data. The feature can be used to make a distinction between species according to their appearance, and also possibly recognize individual animal using the unique spot on the body.

## 2    Related Works

Varieties of computer vision based object detection applications were developed, for example, vehicle detection [7], intention detection [8], etc. However, wildlife detection is one of the most complicate and difficult tasks on object detection, due to the camouflage blending animals into the background.

### 2.1    Animal Detection

Animal detection is one of most complicate and difficult task on object detection. A number of animal detection systems have been developed. Feature based methods are commonly used, for instance, the face recognition for animal intention detection [9]. A system was proposed for vehicle to detect moose on the road [10]. Color based methods were also developed, where different color models of animals are used to classify them. For example, a scheme to track group of fishes [11] was developed, where background substraction was applied following preprocesses to remove the light reflection and then two dimensional GMM is used for fish group tracking. In literature [12], an algorithm was developed to recognize birds, where the hue saturation value was used to obtain all possible bird pixels from input images, and then artificial neural networks and template matching methods were employed to detect birds. There are also some other methods developed for animal tracking, such as wild animal migration corridor tracking [13], animal detect based on infrared image sensor [14].

Recently, with the fast developing of unmanned aerial vehicle (UAV) technology, more and more space is provided for wildlife environment monitoring. UAV can capture video from dangerous or complicate venues where human cannot approach to obtain good viewpoint.

## 2.2  Differential Information for Digital Images

The pixel intensity variation of digital images are commonly treated by discrete neighboring operators, such as Sobel operator, Gabor wavelet filters, etc.

In fact, most of the real world objects have continuous coloring patterns, for instance the human faces, animal fur, surface of a stone, etc. An image can be considered as 'sampled' data from a continuous signal, so the differential or its approximation of the image could exist. Considering this fact, a differential estimating method for digital images was proposed [15], where the integrating method commonly used in control system theory was employed to smooth the input pixel value series, then the input of integrating terms are the estimated differentials. In the integrating method [15], to estimate the differentials of an image, each row of the image is considered as a time series. This time series is input to the integrating chain, where the output of the chain is controlled to follow the input series (pixel intensities) by minimizing the feedback error. The output series can be considered as a filtered/smoothed version of the original image data. Since the output series is generated by integrating operation, the existence of its differential is guaranteed. To consider the coloring variety in the vertical direction, the columns are input for the estimator, then the differential in vertical orientation is obtained as well. The horizontal and vertical differentials can be considered as the project of the 2-dimensional differential vector on the two Cartesian coordinate axes respectively. The differential information of an image represents the texture feature.

## 3    The Proposed Method

This research aims to propose stable features that can accommodate the challenge of the camouflage, where the coloring pattern of animals and background are usually very close. Under this situation, the texture features become important for the purpose of detecting animals from background. The differential information of the original images is used to build the pattern features towards classification. Then the distance between animals and background can be increased in the differential space, which is helpful for classification.

### 3.1    Differential Estimation

The simulation diagram of the differential estimator is shown in Fig. 1, where the only tunable parameter $z$ can be considered as a smoothing factor [15]. In this research the value of $z$ is 0.05.

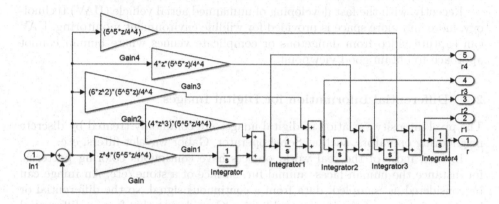

**Fig. 1.** The simulation diagram of the differential estimator [15]

In Fig. 1, the input **In1** is a row of pixels from the image, and the out **r** is controlled to follow the input **In1** by minimizing the feedback error (**In1-r**). **r** is obtained by integrating on **r1**, so **r1** is the differential of **r** the approximation of **In1**. Therefore, **r1** can be considered as the approximation of the differential of **In1**.

To demonstrate the differentials estimated by this method, an image shown in Fig. 2(a) is used as input. Figure 2(b) shows the output image of the integrating chain. Figures 2(c) and (d) are the estimated the first and second order differentials.

### 3.2    Gaussian Mixture Model for Pattern Representation

Due to the protective coloring and the uncertainties of light intensity, contrast, shadowing, etc., the coloring pattern is not reliable. Fortunately the differentials, which physically represent the variety of color intensity, are relatively robust against these uncertainties. More details and experiments on the robustness of the differential estimator can be found in the literature [15].

Figure 3 shows the color space intensity distribution of animal pattern and background pattern, where the distinguishing capacity is clearly low due to the camouflage. Neither the mean intensity nor the deviation can be used to indicate the differences between the two classes.

(a) Original image

(b) Filtered/Smoothed image

(c) The first order differential

(d) The second order differential

**Fig. 2.** The differentials of an image

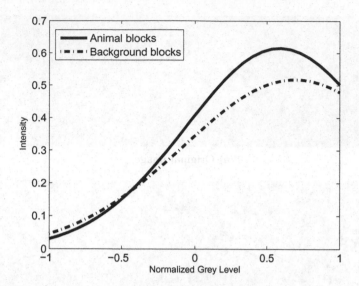

**Fig. 3.** The grey level probability distribution function

Figures 4(a) and (b) are the intensity distribution of the first order and the second order differentials respectively. It is clear that the distributions of animal blocks and background block have distinct differences. The Gaussian model parameters, i.e. the expectation $\mu$ and deviation $\delta$, can be considered as the pattern feature as shown in Eq. (1).

$$F = < \mu_1 \ \delta_1 \ \mu_2 \ \delta_2 > \tag{1}$$

where $\mu_1, \delta_1$ are the expectation and deviation of the first order differential respectively. $\mu_2$ and $\delta_2$ are the distribution parameters of the second differential.

## 4  Experiment Results

To demonstrate the performance of the proposed feature, a two layer neural network classifier is used to classify farm images captured by UAV.

Firstly, only the first order feature defined in Eq. (2) was applied. All blocks classified as background are marked in green color. As shown in Fig. 5(a), the first order differential has high distinguishing capacity for the two classes (animal and background), although there are some blocks were incorrectly recognized. Most of these blocks are just solitons (no neighboring blocks belong to the same class) which can be easily removed by morphology operations. The only concern is the blocks circled in white color, where the animal blocks were incorrectly classified to background. It is hard to remove using morphology operating, since the neighbors are also recognized as background.

$$F1 = < \mu_1 \ \delta_1 > \tag{2}$$

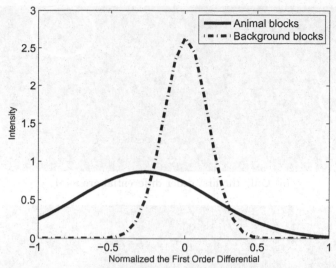

(a) The first order differential probability distribution function

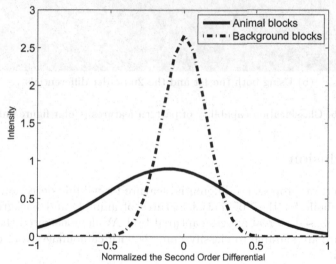

(b) The second order differential probability distribution function

**Fig. 4.** The intensity distribution in differential spaces

Figure 5(b) shows the result when both the first and the second order differentials are used. The feature is defined in Eq. (1). Clearly, the performance is improved, where most blocks contain partitions of animals were correctly detected and much fewer background blocks were considered as animals.

(a) Only the first order differential are used

(b) Using both the 1st and the 2nd order differentials

**Fig. 5.** Classification capability of pattern features (Color figure online)

## 5  Conclusion

In this paper, we proposed a differential feature for wildlife detection. Gaussian models are built for the differential features of animals and background. The experiments based on real images captured by UAV demonstrated that the proposed feature are suitable to classify animals with camouflage from complicate background.

## References

1. Zhao, Y., Shi, H., Chen, X., Li, X., Wang, C.: An overview of object detection and tracking. In: The Proceedings of IEEE International Conference on Information and Automation, pp. 280–286 (2015)
2. Gevers, T., Smeulders, A.W.: Color-based object recognition. Pattern Recogn. **32**(3), 453–464 (1999)
3. Lowe, D.G.: Object recognition from local scale-invariant features. In: The Proceedings of the Seventh IEEE International Conference on Computer vision, vol. 2, pp. 1150–1157 (1999)

4. Doll, P., Rabaud, V., Cottrell, G., Belongie, S.: Behavior recognition via sparse spatio-temporal features. In: The proceedings of IEEE International Workshop on Visual Surveillance and Performance Evaluation of Tracking and Surveillance, pp. 65–72 (2005)

5. Surendar, E., Thomas, V.M., Posonia, A. M.: Animal tracking using background subtraction on multi threshold segmentation. In: The proceedings of International Conference on Circuit, Power and Computing Technologies (ICCPCT 2016), pp. 1–6 (2016)

6. Pooya, K., Wang, J., Huang, T.: Multiple animal species detection using robust principal component analysis and large displacement optical flow. In: Proceedings of the 21st International Conference on Pattern Recognition (ICPR), Workshop on Visual Observation and Analysis of Animal and Insect Behavior (2012)

7. Tu, C.-L., Du, S.-Z.: Moving vehicle detection in dynamic traffic contexts. In: Hussain, A. (ed.) Electronics, Communications and Networks V. LNEE, vol. 382, pp. 263–269. Springer, Heidelberg (2016). doi:10.1007/978-981-10-0740-8_30

8. Nakauchi, Y., Noguchi, K., Somwong, P., Matsubara, T.: Human intention detection and activity support system for ubiquitous sensor room. J. Robot. Mechatron. **16**, 545–550 (2004)

9. Burghardt, T., Calic, J.: Analysing animal behaviour in wildlife videos using face detection and tracking. IEEE Proc. Vis. Image Signal Process. **153**(3), 305–312 (2006)

10. Mammeri, A., Zhou, D., Boukerche, A., Almulla, M.: An efficient animal detection system for smart cars using cascaded classifiers. In: The Proceedings of IEEE International Conference on Communications (ICC), pp. 1854–1859 (2014)

11. Fukunaga, T., Kubota, S., Oda, S., Iwasaki, W.: GroupTracker: video tracking system for multiple animals under severe occlusion. Comput. Biol. Chemis. **57**, 39–45 (2015)

12. Nadimpalli, U.D., Price, R.R., Hall, S.G., Bomma, P.: A comparison of image processing techniques for bird recognition. Biotechnol. Prog. **22**(1), 9–13 (2006)

13. Matuska, S., Hudec, R., Benco, M., Kamencay, P., Zachariasova, M.: A novel system for automatic detection and classification of animal. In: The Proceedings of IEEE ELEKTRO, pp. 76–80 (2014)

14. Forslund, D., Bjärkefur, J.: Night vision animal detection. In: The Proceedings of IEEE Intelligent Vehicles Symposium, pp. 737–742. IEEE (2014)

15. Du, S., Wyk, B.J., Wyk, M.A., Qi, G., Zhang, X., Tu, C.: Image representation in differential space. In: Bebis, G., et al. (eds.) ISVC 2008. LNCS, vol. 5359, pp. 624–633. Springer, Heidelberg (2008). doi:10.1007/978-3-540-89646-3_61

# Biometrics

# Age Classification from Facial Images: Is Frontalization Necessary?

A. Báez-Suárez[1,2](✉), C. Nikou[1](✉), J.A. Nolazco-Flores[2](✉),
and I.A. Kakadiaris[1](✉)

[1] Computational Biomedicine Lab, Department of Computer Science,
University of Houston, Houston, TX, USA
{cnikou,ikakadia}@central.uh.edu
[2] Department of Computer Science, ITESM Campus Monterrey, Monterrey, Mexico
basuam@gmail.com, jnolazco@itesm.mx

**Abstract.** In the majority of the methods proposed for age classification from facial images, the preprocessing steps consist of alignment and illumination correction followed by the extraction of features, which are forwarded to a classifier to estimate the age group of the person in the image. In this work, we argue that face frontalization, which is the correction of the pitch, yaw, and roll angles of the headpose in the 3D space, should be an integral part of any such algorithm as it unveils more discriminative features. Specifically, we propose a method for age classification which integrates a frontalization algorithm before feature extraction. Numerical experiments on the widely used FGnet Aging Database confirmed the importance of face frontalization achieving an average increment in accuracy of 4.43%.

## 1 Introduction

Human age classification from facial images has become an active research topic in computer vision and pattern recognition due to its applications to demographic analysis, electronic customer relationship management, and video security surveillance. Nonetheless, human age classification is challenging because of: (i) the aging process, which is complicated, irreversible and uncontrollable [1]; (ii) changes in apparent age due to facial hair (beards and mustaches) and makeup; and (iii) the difficulty in collecting complete and sufficient training data [2].

The aging process and apparent age have been modeled via geometrical and textural features which have been employed to describe the craniofacial development that occurs as a series of overlapping events in human chronological age [3]. Specifically, geometrical features consist of ratios [4] or models created from fiducial points such as active appearance models [5] and the textural features consist of filters which are able to find patterns in the skin. The most common textural features are local binary patterns (LBP) [6], Gradient Orientation Pyramid (GOP) [7], and biologically-inspired features (BIF) [8]. However, the discriminative information that is extracted using geometrical and textural features depends on the pose of the head with respect to the camera.

© Springer International Publishing AG 2016
G. Bebis et al. (Eds.): ISVC 2016, Part I, LNCS 10072, pp. 769–778, 2016.
DOI: 10.1007/978-3-319-50835-1_69

Kwon and Lobo [4] categorized facial images into three age groups: babies, young adults, and senior adults, using six ratios of distances between primary facial components (e.g., eyes, nose, mouth, chin). Geng *et al.* [9] proposed an automatic age estimation method named AGing pattErn Subspace (AGES) which, instead of taking each facial image as a single point in the aging pattern, models each aging pattern as a sequence of samples. Age estimation is then accomplished by minimizing the reconstruction error. Guo *et al.* [8] extracted biologically-inspired features which proved to be effective as they are still employed in the age estimation task. Kilinc and Akgul [10] extracted 34 ratios and textural features such as BIF [8] and LBP [6] which are fused in eight different ways, confirming that classifiers perform better if both geometric and textural features are provided. Recently, Levi and Hassner [11] developed a shallow convolutional neural network for age and gender classification. The deep-learning architecture was designed to avoid overfitting due to the limitation of training data by increasing the size of the training set using cropped versions of the training images.

Although much work has been done on the task of human age classification, most of the published work focuses on frontal images. Mirzaei and Toygar [12] studied the influence of gender on the age classification task, but their work is constrained to frontal images free of glasses, mustache, and beard. Levi and Hassner [11] also constrained their work to in-plane aligned images when feeding their convolutional neural network (CNN). Liu *et al.* [13] described two new geometrical features (CirFace and Angle) which are Gaussianly distributed along certain age ranges and are defined on frontal images. Nevertheless, current databases, such as the FGnet Aging Database [14], contain images in the wild with variations in head pose.

In this work, we present an algorithm for Frontalized fACial Image Age cLassification (FACIAL). A method that addresses the age classification task employing a frontalization technique [15] which normalizes pose, size, and alignment before the feature extraction procedure. The importance of the frontalization technique is examined in different image resolutions and in different age groups.

Our first contribution is proposing the use of a frontalization algorithm, which normalizes the facial images reducing the variation due to the position of the head and increases the classification accuracy. The second contribution is the study of BIF and GOP features for different image resolutions. Therefore, the effect of frontalization can be quantified in the presence of different features and image resolutions. Finally, new age groups are defined following the human development [16], which result in improved accuracy. A comparison with the age groups proposed in Liu *et al.* [17] justifies the proposed age grouping.

The rest of the paper is organized as follows: In Sect. 2 we introduce the overall method. In Sect. 3 we discuss important implementation details and present the experimental evaluation. In Sect. 4 we summarize our findings.

## 2    Age Classification Using Frontalized Facial Images

The steps of FACIAL are illustrated in Fig. 1. Standard pre-processing converts images from color to grayscale and, after locating the center of the eyes, the images are rotated, scaled, cropped and aligned. In our method, frontalization [15] registers a 2D facial image onto a 3D facial model where pose, size, and alignment are normalized.

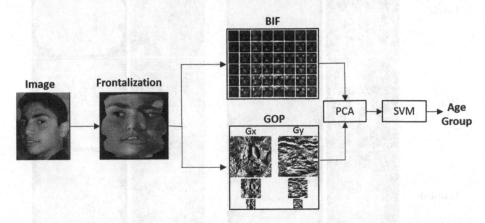

**Fig. 1.** Depiction of a block diagram of FACIAL. Facial images are pre-processed in order to have the same pose, size, and alignment. Then, features are extracted (BIF/GOP) and PCA is employed to reduce the dimensionality. Finally, the age group is determined through an SVM classifier.

In frontalization, a 3D Annotated Face Model (AFM) [18] is reconstructed from single 2D images to lift the 2D facial appearance [19] to a canonical 2D space (geometry image space) [18]. To construct the final representation, a mapping between the original image and the geometry image space is performed. It has been reported that face alignment [20] has an impact on the estimation of age. In this work, we study how frontalization improves the performance of the age classification. Representative examples of frontalized images are depicted in Fig. 2.

With regard to image resolution, there is no preferred standard size. In many works [8,20,21], an image resolution of $60 \times 60$ has been used, in Liu *et al.* [13] the image resolution is $180 \times 150$ and in Levi and Hassner [11] the image resolution is $256 \times 256$.

In this work, two features are employed: BIF [8] and GOP [7]. BIF features are derived from a feedforward model of the primate visual object recognition pathway (HMAX Model [22]). The method alternates between layers called simple (S) and complex (C) cell units. BIF features are built following the procedure in Guo *et al.* [8] and are chosen because several state-of-the-art results have been achieved [2,23–25] using these features. GOP features are insensitive to

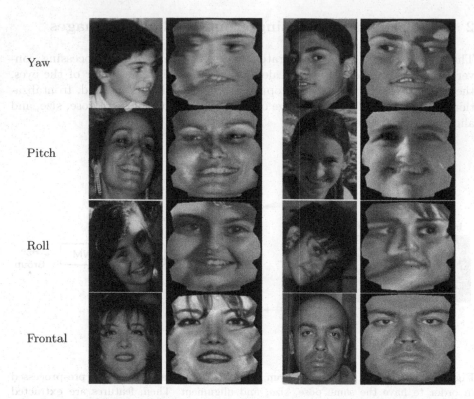

**Fig. 2.** Representative examples of non-frontalized and frontalized images under various initial head pose orientations. The first column indicates the dominant orientation of the non-frontalized image.

illumination changes and the pyramid provides robustness at different scales [7]. They are based on normalizing the gradient vector at each pixel and concatenating the results for both directions. From the work presented in Liu *et al.* [13], it is observed that frontal faces are better described using GOP features which improve the classification accuracy.

Dimensionality reduction of the feature vectors is accomplished through principal component analysis (PCA) [26]. Then, a one-versus-all multiclass support vector machine (SVM) [27] is trained to classify the features, following the age groups defined in Table 1. The overall methodology is described in Algorithm 1. The FGnet Aging Database [14] was used for testing the methodology.

An ideal definition of the age groups would follow the human craniofacial development discussed by Shu *et al.* [3]. However, there is no one-to-one correspondence between age groups and craniofacial state. Therefore, we propose to define the age groups based on the aging process defined by Armstrong [16], as aging and craniofacial development are correlated. Armstrong [16] described overlapping age groups, but in our work, non-overlapping age groups are chosen to set crisp boundaries with respect to craniofacial development.

**Table 1.** Age groups used by Liu *et al.* [17] and the age groups proposed in this paper.

| Author | Group name | Age groups | | | | | | | | | |
|---|---|---|---|---|---|---|---|---|---|---|---|
| | Liu-3 | 0–3 | 4–19 | 20–69 | - | - | - | - | - | - | - |
| | Liu-4 | 0–5 | 6–12 | 13–21 | 22–69 | - | - | - | - | - | - |
| Liu *et al.* [17] | Liu-5 | 0–4 | 5–10 | 11–15 | 16–29 | 30–69 | - | - | - | - | - |
| | Liu-6 | 0–4 | 5–9 | 10–14 | 15–29 | 30–49 | 50–69 | - | - | - | - |
| | Liu-7 | 0–4 | 5–9 | 10–14 | 15–19 | 20–25 | 26–35 | 36–69 | - | - | - |
| Proposed Groups | FACIAL-7 | 0–3 | 4–6 | 7–8 | 9–11 | 12–19 | 20–35 | 36–50 | - | - | - |
| | Liu-8 | 0–4 | 5–9 | 10–14 | 15–19 | 20–29 | 30–39 | 40–49 | 50–69 | - | - |
| Liu *et al.* [17] | Liu-9 | 0–4 | 5–9 | 10–14 | 15–19 | 20–29 | 30–35 | 36–41 | 42–49 | 50–69 | - |
| | Liu-10 | 0–4 | 5–9 | 10–14 | 15–19 | 20–29 | 30–34 | 35–39 | 40–44 | 45–49 | 50–69 |

**Algorithm 1.** Frontalized fACial Image Age cLassification (FACIAL).

**Input:** Facial Image
**Output:** Age Group Label
1: Frontalize the input image
2: Extract BIF or GOP features from the frontalized image
3: Reduce the dimensionality of the features using PCA
4: Classify the reduced features using SVM

## 3   Experimental Results

To evaluate FACIAL, we have used the publicly available FGnet Aging Database [14] which contains 1,002 color and gray-scale facial images with large variations in illumination, pose, and expression (the pictures are taken in the wild). The age range is from 0 to 69 years old with chronological aging images available for each subject as each person has between 6 to 18 facial images at different ages. It comprises 34 female and 48 male subjects for a total of 82 subjects. The proposed age groups for the FGnet Aging Database are presented in Table 2 where the number of images and the number of subjects per age group are reported.

**Table 2.** FGnet DB [14] summary.

| Age groups | #Images | #Subjects | #Images/Subject |
|---|---|---|---|
| 0–3 | 151 | 68 | 2.2 |
| 4–6 | 123 | 66 | 1.9 |
| 7–8 | 72 | 54 | 1.3 |
| 9–11 | 98 | 59 | 1.7 |
| 12–19 | 266 | 79 | 3.4 |
| 20–35 | 201 | 55 | 3.7 |
| 36–50 | 70 | 30 | 2.3 |
| 51–80 | 21 | 8 | 2.6 |

FGnet Aging Database [14] contains images with interpupillary distances (IPD) ranging from 78 to 200 pixels. For comparison purposes, we selected two image resolutions ($60 \times 60$ and $150 \times 150$) having an IPD of 32 and 80 pixels, respectively. BIF and GOP features were extracted. BIF were created with 12 scales and 8 orientations resulting in a feature dimensionality of 6,752 and 45,424 for the $60 \times 60$ and $150 \times 150$ image resolutions, respectively. GOP were built with two and three scales resulting in a feature dimensionality of 9,450 and 59,860 for the $60 \times 60$ and $150 \times 150$ image resolutions, respectively. The features are normalized to have zero-mean and unit standard deviation. Next, dimensionality reduction was performed through PCA retaining 95% of the variance. Furthermore, to determine the parameter of the SVM linear kernel classifier, a 5-fold cross-validation was applied for the cost parameter in the range of $[2^{-5}, 2^{-3}, ..., 2^{15}]$ and the area under the ROC curve was the criterion for the selection of the best model. In particular, the LibSVM library [28] was used to train the classifier. Finally, Leave-One-Person-Out (LOPO) was employed for testing and comparison.

Representative results from FACIAL are depicted in Fig. 3. The variation in pose is normalized for the frontalization technique delivering a better

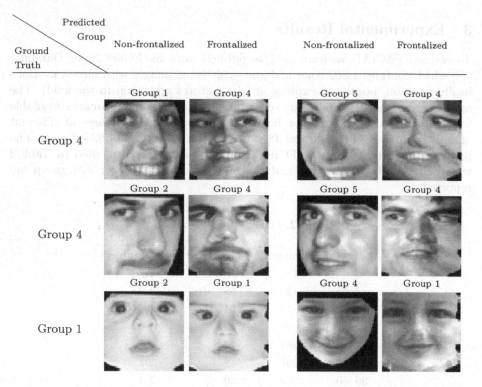

**Fig. 3.** Representative results from FACIAL applied to images from the FGnet Aging Database [14], where frontalized images are correctly classified with respect to their non-frontalized counterpart. Five age groups were considered.

**Table 3.** Classification accuracy (%) on the FGnet Aging Database using images with a resolution of $60 \times 60$ and $150 \times 150$, and the age groups proposed by Liu *et al.* [17]. Results for both BIF and GOP features are presented.

| | Size $60 \times 60$ | | | | Size $150 \times 150$ | | | |
| | Non-frontalized | | Frontalized | | Non-frontalized | | Frontalized | |
| #Groups | BIF | GOP | BIF | GOP | BIF | GOP | BIF | GOP |
|---|---|---|---|---|---|---|---|---|
| 3 | 73.65 | **74.35** | 74.85 | **75.25** | **73.75** | 73.25 | **77.54** | 77.35 |
| 4 | **61.08** | 58.78 | **65.67** | 64.07 | **62.87** | 60.68 | **66.37** | 65.57 |
| 5 | **54.49** | 50.90 | **58.88** | 57.68 | **55.69** | 52.99 | **57.39** | 55.59 |
| 6 | **53.09** | 51.10 | 52.89 | **55.09** | 52.99 | 52.79 | 56.19 | **56.99** |
| 7 | **42.22** | 39.92 | 42.51 | **43.11** | **42.81** | 41.22 | **47.21** | 47.01 |
| 8 | 39.72 | **40.42** | 40.22 | **41.82** | **41.52** | 41.12 | 45.51 | **45.71** |
| 9 | **39.92** | 39.12 | 40.02 | **41.32** | **41.12** | 40.52 | **45.01** | 44.91 |
| 10 | 38.32 | **39.12** | 39.72 | **41.62** | **40.92** | 40.22 | **45.21** | 45.11 |

classification performance. The experiments were designed to examine the impact of frontalization, image resolution, and age groups definition. The classification using the age groups proposed by Liu *et al.* [17] are considered as baseline.

Table 3 summarizes the results of age classification using the non-frontalized and frontalized images. On average, when the image resolution is $60 \times 60$ and images are frontalized, the classification accuracy increases along the different splits by 1.53% for BIF and 3.28% for GOP. When the image resolution is $150 \times 150$, the classification accuracy is increased by 3.60% for BIF and 4.43% for GOP. From both of these results, we may conclude that frontalization improves the performance in age classification. It may also be observed that the frontalized version of GOP achieves higher accuracy than the non-frontalized version. In the case of BIF features, the non-frontalized version and the frontalized version have similar performance.

Table 3 also highlights the difference in performance when the image resolution increases. On average, the classification accuracy increases along the different splits by 1.15% for BIF and 1.14% for GOP when the non-frontalized images are compared and by 3.21% for BIF and 2.29% for GOP when the frontalized images are compared. In the case of $60 \times 60$ images, the frontalized version of GOP is superior to the non-frontalized versions of BIF and GOP. On the other hand, for the $150 \times 150$ images the non-frontalized and frontalized versions of BIF are better.

Table 4 summarizes the performance achieved when the age groups are defined following the human age development based on Armstrong [16]. It is worth mentioning that to avoid imbalance in the data set, the 21 images of the last group in Table 2 were not used because the number of images in that group is very low with respect to the number of images in the other groups.

**Table 4.** Comparison of classification accuracy (%) using the Liu-7 group (1,002 images) and FACIAL-7 group (981 images).

| Groups by | Groups | Size 60 × 60 | | | | Size 150 × 150 | | | |
| | | Non-frontalized | | Frontalized | | Non-frontalized | | Frontalized | |
| | | BIF | GOP | BIF | GOP | BIF | GOP | BIF | GOP |
|---|---|---|---|---|---|---|---|---|---|
| Liu *et al.* [17] | Liu-7 | 42.22 | 39.92 | 42.51 | 43.11 | 42.81 | 41.22 | 47.21 | 47.01 |
| FACIAL | FACIAL-7 | 44.55 | 42.30 | 48.11 | 46.99 | 43.22 | 44.04 | 49.54 | 47.50 |

Table 4 also summarizes the performance when the age groups are defined following Liu *et al.* [17]. It may be observed that the proposed splitting achieves better classification results in all the configurations: non-frontalized, frontalized, 60 × 60, and 150 × 150. The average accuracy increment is 2.36% and 4.74% in images with a resolution of 60 × 60 non-frontalized and frontalized, respectively. And the average accuracy increment is 1.62% and 1.41% in images with a resolution of 150 × 50 non-frontalized and frontalized, respectively.

## 4    Conclusions

In this work, we presented a methodology for age classification which uses frontalized images. We concluded that using face frontalization before feature extraction is beneficial. The method was tested on the FGnet Aging Database [14]. As it was demonstrated, the frontalization increases the age classification accuracy in cases with different image resolution, features (BIF and GOP) and age groups. In addition, a new age grouping based on the human aging process was proposed and evaluated.

**Acknowledgments.** This work has been funded in part by the Mexican National Council for Science and Technology (CONACYT) scholarship 328083 and by the UH Hugh Roy and Lillie Cranz Cullen Endowment Fund. The authors acknowledge the use of the Maxwell/Opuntia Cluster and the support of the Center of Advanced Computing and Data Systems at the University of Houston to carry out the research presented herein. All statements of fact, opinion or conclusions contained herein are those of the authors and should not be construed as representing the official views or policies of the sponsors.

## References

1. Ling, H., Soatto, S., Ramanathan, N., Jacobs, D.: Face verification across age progression using discriminative methods. IEEE Trans. Inf. Forensics Secur. **5**, 82–91 (2010)
2. Geng, X., Yin, C., Zhou, Z.H.: Facial age estimation by learning from label distributions. IEEE Trans. Pattern Anal. Mach. Intell. **35**, 2401–2412 (2013)
3. Shu, X., Xie, G.S., Li, Z., Tang, J.: Age progression: current technologies and applications. Neurocomputing **208**, 249–261 (2016)

4. Kwon, Y., da Vitoria Lobo, N.: Age classification from facial images. In: Proceedings of IEEE Conference on Computer Vision and Pattern Recognition, Seattle, WA, pp. 762–767 (1994)
5. Cootes, T.F., Edwards, G.J., Taylor, C.J.: Active appearance models. In: Proceedings of European Conference on Computer Vision, Freiburg, Germany, vol. 2, pp. 484–498 (1998)
6. Ojala, T., Pietikäinen, M., Harwood, D.: A comparative study of texture measures with classification based on featured distributions. Pattern Recogn. **29**, 51–59 (1996)
7. Ling, H., Soatto, S., Ramanathan, N., Jacobs, D.: A study of face recognition as people age. In: Proceedings of IEEE International Conference on Computer Vision, Rio de Janeiro, Brazil, pp. 1–8 (2007)
8. Guo, G., Mu, G., Fu, Y., Huang, T.: Human age estimation using bio-inspired features. In: Proceedings of IEEE Conference on Computer Vision and Pattern Recognition, Miami, FL, pp. 112–119 (2009)
9. Geng, X., Zhou, Z.H., Smith-Miles, K.: Automatic age estimation based on facial aging patterns. IEEE Trans. Pattern Anal. Mach. Intell. **29**, 2234–2240 (2007)
10. Kilinc, M., Akgul, Y.S.: Human age estimation via geometric and textural features. In: Proceedings of International Joint Conference on Computer Vision, Imaging and Computer Graphics Theory and Applications, Rome, Italy, pp. 531–538 (2012)
11. Levi, G., Hassner, T.: Age and gender classification using convolutional neural networks. In: Proceedings of IEEE Conference on Computer Vision and Pattern Recognition Workshops, Boston, Massachusetts (2015)
12. Mirzaei, F., Toygar, O.: Facial age classification using subpattern-based approaches. In: Proceedings of International Conference on Image Processing, Computer Vision, and Pattern Recognition, Las Vegas, NV (2011)
13. Liu, K.H., Yan, S., Kuo, C.C.J.: Age group classification via structured fusion of uncertainty-driven shape features and selected surface features. In: Proceedings of IEEE Winter Conference on Applications of Computer Vision, Steamboat Springs, CO, pp. 445–452 (2014)
14. Lanitis, A.: FG-NET aging database face and gesture recognition (2012). http://grail.cs.washington.edu/aging/FGNET.zip. Accessed 21 Oct 2016
15. Kakadiaris, I.A., Toderici, G., Evangelopoulos, G., Passalis, G., Chu, D., Zhao, X., Shah, S.K., Theoharis, T.: 3D–2D face recognition with pose and illumination normalization. Computer Vision and Image Understanding (2016, in press). http://dx.doi.org/10.1016/j.cviu.2016.04.012
16. Armstrong, T.P.: The Human Odyssey: Navigating the Twelve Stages of Life. Sterling, New York (2008)
17. Liu, K.H., Yan, S., Kuo, C.C.: Age estimation via grouping and decision fusion. IEEE Trans. Inf. Forensics Secur. **10**, 2408–2423 (2015)
18. Kakadiaris, I.A., Passalis, G., Toderici, G., Murtuza, M.N., Lu, Y., Karampatziakis, N., Theoharis, T.: Three-dimensional face recognition in the presence of facial expressions: an annotated deformable model approach. IEEE Trans. Pattern Anal. Mach. Intell. **29**, 640–649 (2007)
19. Toderici, G., Passalis, G., Zafeiriou, S., Tzimiropoulos, G., Petrou, M., Theoharis, T., Kakadiaris, I.: Bidirectional relighting for 3D-aided 2D face recognition. In: Proceedings of IEEE Conference on Computer Vision and Pattern Recognition, San Francisco, CA, pp. 2721–2728 (2010)
20. Wang, H.L., Wang, J.G., Yau, W.Y., Chua, X.L., Tan, Y.P.: Effects of facial alignment for age estimation. In: Proceedings of International Conference on Control Automation Robotics Vision, Singapore, pp. 644–647 (2010)

21. Han, H., Otto, C., Liu, X., Jain, A.: Demographic estimation from face images: human vs. machine performance. IEEE Trans. Pattern Anal. Mach. Intell. **37**, 1148–1161 (2014)
22. Riesenhuber, M., Poggio, T.: Hierarchical models of object recognition in cortex. Nat. Neurosci. **2**, 1019–1025 (1999)
23. Guo, G., Wang, X.: A study on human age estimation under facial expression changes. In: Proceedings of IEEE Conference on Computer Vision and Pattern Recognition, Providence, RI, pp. 2547–2553 (2012)
24. Zhang, C., Guo, G.: Age estimation with expression changes using multiple aging subspaces. In: Proceedings of IEEE International Conference on Biometrics: Theory Applications and Systems, Washington DC, pp. 1–6 (2013)
25. Zhang, C., Guo, G.: Exploiting unlabeled ages for aging pattern analysis on a large database. In: Proceedings of IEEE Conference on Computer Vision and Pattern Recognition Workshops, Portland, OR, pp. 458–464 (2013)
26. Webb, A.: Statistical Pattern Recognition, 2nd edn. Wiley, New York (2002)
27. Boser, B.E., Guyon, I.M., Vapnik, V.N.: A training algorithm for optimal margin classifiers. In: Proceedings of Annual Workshop on Computational Learning Theory, Pittsburgh, PA, pp. 144–152 (1992)
28. Chang, C.C., Lin, C.J.: LibSVM: a library for support vector machines. ACM Trans. Intell. Syst. Technol. **2**, 1–27 (2011)

# PH-BRINT: Pooled Homomorphic Binary Rotation Invariant and Noise Tolerant Representation for Face Recognition Under Illumination Variations

Raqinah Alrabiah[1,2]([✉]), Muhammad Hussain[2],
Hatim A. Aboalsamh[2], Mansour Zuair[3], and George Bebis[4]

[1] Department of Information Technology, College of Computer,
Qassim University, Qassim, Saudi Arabia
raqinah@qu.edu.sa
[2] Department of Computer Science, King Saud University, Riyadh, Saudi Arabia
mhussain@ksu.edu.sa
[3] Department of Computer Engineering, College of Computer and Information
Sciences, King Saud University, Riyadh, Saudi Arabia
[4] Department of Computer Science and Engineering,
University of Nevada, Reno, USA

**Abstract.** Face recognition under varying illumination conditions is a challenging problem. We propose a simple and effective multiresolution approach Pooled Homomorphic Binary Rotation Invariant and Noise Tolerant (PH-BRINT) for face recognition under varying illumination conditions. First, to reduce the effect of illumination, wavelet transform based homomorphic filter is used. Then Binary Rotation Invariant and Noise Tolerant (BRINT) operators with three different scales are employed to extract multiscale local rotation invariant and illumination insensitive texture features. Finally, the discriminative information from the three scales is pooled using MAX pooling operator and localized gradient information is computed by dividing the pooled image into blocks and calculating the gradient magnitude and direction of each block. The PH-BRINT technique has been tested on a challenging face database Extended Yale B, which was captured under varying illumination conditions. The system using minimum distance classifier with L1-norm achieved an average accuracy of 86.91%, which is comparable with the state-of-the-art best illumination-invariant face recognition techniques.

**Keywords:** Face recognition · Local binary pattern · Feature extraction · Illumination invariant

## 1 Introduction

Face recognition is a complicated and challenging problem for computer vision experts. Although, the level of performance achieved so far by a lot of existing approaches has increased to a point where face recognition is assumed to be suitable and reliable for many applications, there are still various difficulties that need to be overcome to build

© Springer International Publishing AG 2016
G. Bebis et al. (Eds.): ISVC 2016, Part I, LNCS 10072, pp. 779–789, 2016.
DOI: 10.1007/978-3-319-50835-1_70

accurate and robust face recognition systems. Varying illumination conditions, differences of pose, facial expressions changes, age variations and occlusion offer challenges for face recognition. The motivation of this research is to handle illumination variations in face recognition. There has been research to overcome this aspect of face recognition, but it is still a challenge.

We propose a new approach to recognize faces under the variations of illumination. For the description of face images, we propose a new method called Pooled Homomorphic Binary Rotation Invariant and Noise Tolerant (PH-BRINT). This method uses wavelet transform based homomorphic filtering technique to mitigate the effects of illumination and uses multiscale BRINT operators, which were originally proposed for texture description [1] and are state-of-the-art best local texture feature extractors, and pooling to extract the discriminative information from face images. For classification, we used minimum distance classifier with L1-norm. The performance of the method has been evaluated using a benchmark database for illumination invariant face recognition - Extended Yale-B. The performance is comparable with the state-of-the-art methods dealing with face recognition under varying illumination.

The rest of the paper is structured as follows. Section 2 gives an overview of some state-of-the-art techniques, which have addressed the same problem. Section 3 illustrates in detail the proposed PH-BRINT approach. Section 4 discusses the implementation detail and interprets the results. Finally, Sect. 5 concludes the paper.

## 2 Related Work

In this section, first we give an overview of the recent work on illumination invariant face recognition and then give an overview of BRINT.

### 2.1 Literature Review

In the literature, there are many methods that focus on face recognition under illumination variations using texture descriptors. One such technique uses Local binary patterns (LBP) [2]. Another approach [3] uses Local Ternary Pattern (LTP), which is similar to LBP and is based on extracting local texture micro-patterns.

In the illumination-invariant approach [4], the histogram-equalized faces are divided into tiny overlapping local patches (LPs), then illumination-invariance for these LPs is accomplished by the difference of the vectors and local average illumination, and these vectors are logarithmically normalized to improve the local disparity.

Moreover, Local Directional Pattern (LDP) [5] and Local Directional Number Pattern (LDN) [6], which are based on Kirsch compass masks and generate eight directional edge images from a face image and encode the directional information to represent illumination-invariant face image. The LDP technique represents each pixel using an 8-bit binary code, assigning ones to the three bits corresponding to the three dominant numbers, and zeros to the other five bits. The second approach, LDN represents each pixel using 6-bit binary code; the first three bits encode the position of the top positive directional number and the next three bits encode the position of the top negative directional number. The generated codes from both the approaches are transformed into their corresponding decimal values to create LDP and LDN images.

Faraji et al. [7] proposed a method called adaptive homomorphic eight local directional pattern (*AH-ELDP*) for illumination invariant face recognition. This method adapts adaptive homomorphic filtering to decrease the influence of illumination from an input face image. They apply an interpolative enhancement function to stretch the filtered image, and using Kirsch compass masks, generate eight directional edge images, which are used to create an illumination-insensitive representation.

## 2.2    Binary Rotation Invariant and Noise Tolerant (BRINT) Feature

The idea of face description in our approach is based on BRINT, which was proposed for texture classification. For this reason, we give an overview of BRINT in this section.

LBP is widely used for texture description, but there are two main problems with LBP: (i) the number of LBP codes increases exponentially with the number of neighbors R in the circular neighborhood (P, R) of radius R of a pixel, and (ii) it is not robust against noise. To overcome these drawbacks of LBP, Liu et al. [1] proposed BRINT, which is computationally simple and very fast. It is robust against noise, and illumination and rotation variations. Also, it deals with a large number of scales and large circular neighborhoods efficiently.

For computing BRINT feature of a pixel, the $BRINT_{r,q}$ operator is applied on its circular neighborhood consisting of ($8q$) points located on the circle of radius $r$. The parameter $r$ defines the spatial scale of the BRINT and $q$ controls the quantization of the angular space. The interesting aspect of BRINT is that a BRINT code always consists of 8 bits regardless of the scale $r$ and the number of sampling points ($8q$).

The construction of Binary Noise Tolerant (BNT) code is shown in Fig. 1. The sampling scheme in BNT is similar to that in LBP, the points around a central pixel $x_c$ are sampled on the circle of radius $r$. The number of sampled points is a multiple of eight, thus the neighbors of the central pixel $x_c$ sampled on radius $r$ are $\underline{x}_{r,8q} = [x_{r,8q,0}, ..., x_{r,8q,8q-1}]^T$. Figure 1 shows the case with $q = 3$.

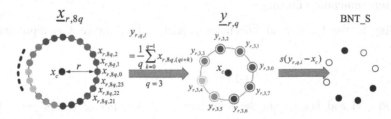

**Fig. 1.** The construction of BNT code [1]

BNT uses ABQ idea i.e. Average-Before-Quantization and converts the original grey-level values of the neighborhood into local average values $\{y_{r,8q,0}, ...., y_{r,8q,7}\}$, where

$$y_{r,q,i} = \frac{1}{q}\sum_{k=0}^{q-1} \chi_{r,8q,(qi+k)}, \quad i = 0,\ldots\ldots,7. \tag{1}$$

This averaging operation makes BNT robust against noise. After averaging, BNT applies thresholding function, which is similar to that used in LBP computation,

$$BNT\_S_{r,q} = \sum_{n=0}^{7} s(y_{r,q,n} - x_c)2^n. \tag{2}$$

The thresholding function $s(x) = 1$ if $x \geq 0$, and $s(x) = 0$ otherwise. As result, there are $2^8 = 256$ BNT binary patterns for each $(r, q)$. To make BNT rotation invariant i.e. BRINT, the following operation is applied, which is similar to the one used for rotation invariant LBP,

$$BRINT\_S_{r,q} = min\{ROR(BNT, i)|i = 0, .., 7\}. \tag{3}$$

Here $ROR(x, i)$ is a rotation function that performs $i$ times a circular bit-wise right shift on $x$ and retains only rotationally-unique patterns; in this way the number of resulted bins for each scale is 36 [8].

## 3   Pooled Homomorphic BRINT Based Face Recognition

In this section, we describe in detail our proposed system for face recognition under varying illumination conditions, the structure of the system is shown in Fig. 2. The two main components of the system are face description and classification. For classification, we used minimum distance classifier (KNN with K = 1) with $L_1$-norm [9] . For face description, we proposed a new descriptor, which is the main contribution of the paper. The construction of the descriptor involves three main operations: homomorphic filtering, generation of multiscale BRINT codes and pooling. In the following sections, give the detail of these operations.

### 3.1   Homomorphic Filtering

According to the Lambertian-reflectance model, a face image I is represented as follows

$$I(x, y) = R(x, y)L(x, y) \tag{4}$$

where $R(x, y)$ and $L(x, y)$ are the reflectance and illuminance components. $R$ is a high-frequency component and contains texture information of a face, also it embeds the detail of high frequency parts like skin, eyebrows, eyes and lips, and as such it plays the key role in recognition. On the other hand, $L$ is a low-frequency component because the illumination values of neighboring pixels in face image are similar to each other [7, 10] For illumination invariant face recognition, it is important to mitigate the effect

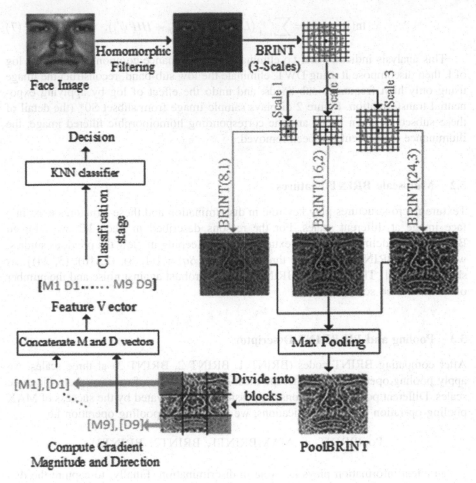

**Fig. 2.** The architecture of the PH-BRINT based face recognition

of illumination. The image I(x, y) is not separable, it can be separated using logarithmic operation as follows:

$$\ln(I(x,y)) = \ln(R(x,y)) + \ln(L(x,y)). \qquad (5)$$

The Discreet Wavelet Transform (DWT) of ln (I(x, y)) gives:

$$\mathrm{DWT}(\ln(I(x,y))) = \sum_{i=1}^{j} (LH^i\psi_v^i + HL^i\psi_h^i + HH^i\psi_d^i) + LL^J\phi^J. \qquad (6)$$

The first term on the right hand side of Eq. (6) is the high frequency component where the second term is the low frequency component. Keeping in view Eq. (5), the first term on the right hand side of Eq. (6) is the log of R i.e.

$$\ln(\mathrm{R}(x,y)) = \sum_{i=1}^{j} (LH^i \psi_v^i + HL^i \psi_h^i + HH^i \psi_d^i). \tag{7}$$

This analysis indicates that t.o eliminate the illuminance component, first take log of I, then discompose it using DWT, eliminate the low sub-band, reconstruct the image using only high frequency sub-bands, and undo the effect of log by applying exponential transformation. Figure 2 displays sample image from subset S0* (the detail of these subsets is given later), and the corresponding homomorphic filtered image, the illuminance component has been removed.

### 3.2    Multiscale BRINT Features

Texture micro-structures play key role in discrimination and these structures exist in a face image at different scales. For the reasons described in Sect. 2.2, we adopted BRINT for modeling multiscale texture patterns. Keeping in view the previous studies, we compute BRINT codes with three scales: $(r, 8q) = \{(1, 8), (2, 16), (3, 24)\}$, as shown in Fig. 1. The computed BRINT codes are robust against noise and the number of codes at each scale is same.

### 3.3    Pooling and PH-BRINT Descriptor

After computing BRINT codes (BRINT 1, BRINT 2, BRINT 3) at three scales, we apply pooling operation to extract the most discriminative information from the three scales. Different pooling operations are possible, but motivated by the success of MAX pooling operation in many applications, we apply MAX pooling operation i.e.

PoolBRINT  =  MAX(BRINT1, BRINT2, BRINT3)

Gradient information plays key role in discrimination. Finally, to capture the discrimination information keeping in view its spatial location, we divide PoolBRINT into a number of blocks, compute the gradient magnitude and direction vectors of each block and concatenate them.

## 4    Results and Discussion

In this section, we evaluate the performance of the proposed method, give comparison with the state-of-the-art methods. First, we give the detail of the Extended Yale B database as we used in our experiments, and the different parameters involved in the system and the evaluation protocol. Then we discuss the tuning of parameters and finally present the results and discuss them.

## 4.1    Evaluation Protocol

PH-BRINT approach was tested by conducting experiments on Extended Yale B face database. This database was chosen because the face images have considerable variation of illumination and is available on the Internet as a benchmark database for research purposes [11].

The Extended Yale B database contains greyscale face images of 38 subjects. The images were captured under 9 different poses and 64 illumination conditions. The frontal face images were used in the experiments for each subject. Following the protocol used in [7], the face images were classified into six subsets S0 ~ S5 according to the angle between the light source direction and the central camera axis, as shown in Table 1.

**Table 1.** The detail of Extended Yale B face database used for the evaluation of PH-BRINT method. The total number of subjects is 38.

| Set | S0 | S0* | S1 | S2 | S3 | S4 | S5 |
|---|---|---|---|---|---|---|---|
| Angle between light and camera axis | 0° | 0° | 1° ~ 12° | 13° ~ 25° | 26° ~ 50° | 51° ~ 77° | above78° |
| Images/subject | 1 | 5 | 8 | 10 | 12 | 10 | 18 |
| Total images | 38 | 190 | 301 | 380 | 449 | 380 | 676 |

The subject S0 contains 6 images per subject, out of these 6 images, one image is held out as training and the remaining 5 are used for testing. As such, the subject is partitioned into S0, consisting of one image per subject, and S0*, containing 5 images per subject. There are six possibilities of selecting one image, so there are six different versions of S0. Taking each version of S0, six experiments were performed for each of the six sub-sets S0* ~ S5. We computed accuracy as the percentage of correctly recognized faces, average accuracy over six different choices of S0 is used for performance evaluation.

## 4.2    Parameter Tuning

The system involves several parameters, the tuning of these parameters is important for best performance. The parameters of BRINT were adjusted according to the recommendation given in [1] i.e. rotation invariant version was applied with three different scales $(r, 8q) \in \{(1, 8), (2, 16), (3, 24)\}$.

Homomorphic filtering with DWT involves the level of decomposition J. Several experiments were conducted to assess the effect of the level of decompositions (J), and it was concluded that four levels i.e. J = 4 gives the best performance.

Moreover, PoolBRINT face image is divided into blocks, so the number of blocks is another parameter to be tuned for best performance. We tested eleven different options: 1, 2 × 2, 3 × 3, 4 × 4, ... until 11 × 11 with J = 4 and there is no mapping. The corresponding results are shown in Table 2. There is no significant difference between different choices, however the division 6 × 6 gives the best accuracy of

**Table 2.** Recognition accuracy with different number of blocks: 1, 2 × 2, 3 × 3, 4 × 4, until 11 × 11, where is no mapping

| Number of blocks | S0* | S1 | S2 | S3 | S4 | S5 | Average |
|---|---|---|---|---|---|---|---|
| 1 × 1 | 83.60 | 90.86 | 87.32 | 85.75 | 88.82 | 84.32 | 86.78 |
| 2 × 2 | 83.77 | 90.97 | 87.37 | 86.04 | 88.77 | 84.20 | 86.85 |
| 3 × 3 | 83.68 | 91.14 | 87.32 | 85.89 | 88.68 | 84.37 | 86.85 |
| 4 × 4 | 84.20 | 90.53 | 87.63 | 86.12 | 88.29 | 83.88 | 86.78 |
| 5 × 5 | 83.68 | 90.81 | 87.37 | 86.23 | 88.07 | 84.22 | 86.73 |
| 6 × 6 | 83.33 | 91.20 | 87.72 | 86.08 | 88.86 | 84.27 | **86.91** |
| 7 × 7 | 83.25 | 90.81 | 87.63 | 86.15 | 88.29 | 84 | 86.69 |
| 8 × 8 | 83.07 | 90.59 | 87.41 | 86.04 | 88.16 | 83.90 | 86.53 |
| 9 × 9 | 83.07 | 90.97 | 87.46 | 85.93 | 88.82 | 83.83 | 86.68 |
| 10 × 10 | 82.89 | 91.20 | 86.45 | 86.04 | 88.33 | 83.56 | 86.46 |
| 11 × 11 | 80.53 | 90.20 | 86.75 | 84.48 | 85.39 | 81.16 | 84.75 |

**Table 3.** Recognition accuracy with different mappings: uniform version (u2), rotation invariant (ri), rotation invariant uniform (riu2), and no mapping where blocks' number is 6 × 6

| Mapping type | S0* | S1 | S2 | S3 | S4 | S5 | Average |
|---|---|---|---|---|---|---|---|
| **No mapping** | 83.33 | 91.20 | 87.72 | 86.08 | 88.86 | 84.27 | **86.91** |
| u2 | 82.89 | 88.48 | 86.67 | 85.97 | 88.03 | 83.56 | 85.93 |
| ri | 80.09 | 84.33 | 84.39 | 85.23 | 86.32 | 79.44 | 83.30 |
| riu2 | 73.42 | 81.71 | 79.82 | 80.55 | 86.32 | 71.15 | 78.83 |

86.91%, so we fixed the number of blocks to 6 × 6 blocks in our next experiments to test the best type of mapping as shown in Table 3. The outcomes illustrate that the proposed simple PoolBRINT with 6 × 6 blocks gives the best accuracy.

### 4.3 Discussion of Results

In Extended Yale B database, there are six images per person with zero angle between light and camera axis, we selected one image per person at a time to form the training set S0, there were six choices for S0. For every choice of S0, taking S0* ~ S5 as testing sets, we performed experiments. The results are shown in Table 4. The PH-BRINT method achieved an average accuracy of 86.91%. The accuracy is lowest when image-6 is selected for training, whereas the accuracy is highest when image-2 is used as training image. With four levels of the variation of illumination (S1 ~ S4), the average recognition accuracy is almost same, and better than those with the other two levels S0* and S5. The reason why the system does not give good result for S0* is that this set changes during each of the experiments. Overall, the system performs well when the variation of illumination is below 78°.

**Table 4.** Recognition accuracy with differnt training images

| Training image | S0* | S1 | S2 | S3 | S4 | S5 | Average |
|---|---|---|---|---|---|---|---|
| Image1 | 86.84 | 87.38 | 95.79 | 79.29 | 88.95 | 76.33 | 85.76 |
| Image2 | 86.84 | 95.02 | 92.89 | 86.41 | 91.05 | 84.62 | 89.47 |
| Image3 | 83.16 | 88.37 | 82.37 | 88.86 | 84.21 | 88.76 | 85.96 |
| Image4 | 79.47 | 85.38 | 73.95 | 92.65 | 93.42 | 98.22 | 87.18 |
| Image5 | 83.68 | 92.69 | 98.42 | 82.85 | 94.21 | 79.88 | 88.62 |
| Image6 | 80 | 98.34 | 82.89 | 86.41 | 81.32 | 77.81 | 84.46 |
| Average | 83.33 | 91.20 | 87.72 | 86.08 | 88.86 | 84.27 | 86.91 |

## 4.4 Comparison with Exiting Methods

The performance results of recognition accuracy of our system are compared with four recently proposed techniques, which we have discussed in Sect. 2.1. The state-of-the-art systems used for comparison are LBP [2], LDP [5], LDN [6], and AH-ELDP [7]. Table 5 and Fig. 3 show the comparative results. It can be noted that PH-BRINT outperforms LBP, LDP, LDN, and AH-ELDP. It indicates that the performance of the proposed system is comparable that with the state-of-the-best algorithms.

**Table 5.** Recognition accuracy (%) of PH-BRINT and state-of-the-art methods

| Method | S0* | S1 | S2 | S3 | S4 | S5 | Average |
|---|---|---|---|---|---|---|---|
| LBP | 63.07 | 82.45 | 76.32 | 67.52 | 72.54 | 75.17 | 72.29 |
| LDP | 67.89 | 84.60 | 77.10 | 73.31 | 65.96 | 64.32 | 70.06 |
| LDN | 61.58 | 83.17 | 74.30 | 65.07 | 66.27 | 64.08 | 67.39 |
| AH-ELDP | 77.46 | 88.26 | 84.82 | 81.89 | 86.32 | 89.79 | 84.42 |
| **PH-BRINT** | **83.33** | **91.20** | **87.72** | **86.08** | **88.86** | **84.27** | **86.91** |

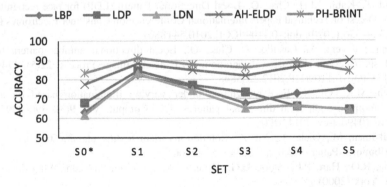

**Fig. 3.** Recognition accuracy comparison of PH-BRINT method while change training image

# 5 Conclusion

This paper proposes face-recognition system based on homomorphic filtering, multi-scale BRINT and pooling to recognize face images which suffer from variations in illumination. The homomorphic filter is used to reduce the influence of illumination. To capture the multiscale texture micro-patterns, multiscale BRINT with three scales is used. In addition, max pooling is applied to extract the most discriminative information. The experiments on the Extended Yale B database show that the proposed PH-BRINT method achieved average accuracy of 86.91%. The comparison reveals that the proposed method is comparable with the state-of-the-art techniques. The future work is to investigate alternative techniques for feature vector extraction from Pool-BRINT image and to further validate the performance of the method on other illumination invariant databases.

# References

1. Liu, L., Long, Y., Fieguth, P.W., Lao, S., Zhao, G.: BRINT: binary rotation invariant and noise tolerant texture classification. IEEE Trans. Image Process. 23(7), 3071–3084 (2014). doi:10.1109/TIP.2014.2325777
2. Ahonen, T., Hadid, A., Pietikainen, M.: Face description with local binary patterns: application to face recognition. IEEE Trans. Pattern Anal. Mach. Intell. 28(12), 2037–2041 (2006). doi:10.1109/TPAMI.2006.244
3. Tan, X., Triggs, B.: Enhanced local texture feature sets for face recognition under difficult lighting conditions. IEEE Trans. Image Process. 19(6), 1635–1650 (2010). doi:10.1109/TIP.2010.2042645
4. Shafie, A.A., Hafiz, F., Mustafah, Y.M.: Face recognition using illumination-invariant local patches. In: 2014 5th International Conference on Intelligent and Advanced Systems (ICIAS), pp. 1–6 (2014). doi:10.1109/ICIAS.2014.6869544
5. Jabid, T., Kabir, M.H., Chae, O.: Local Directional Pattern (LDP) for face recognition. In: 2010 Digest of Technical Papers International Conference on Consumer Electronics (ICCE), pp. 329–330 (2010). doi:10.1109/ICCE.2010.5418801
6. Ramirez Rivera, A., Castillo, R., Chae, O.: Local directional number pattern for face analysis: face and expression recognition. IEEE Trans. Image Process. 22(5), 1740–1752 (2013). doi:10.1109/TIP.2012.2235848
7. Faraji, M.R., Qi, X.: Face recognition under varying illumination based on adaptive homomorphic eight local directional patterns. IET Comput. Vis. 9(3), 390–399 (2015). doi:10.1049/iet-cvi.2014.0200
8. Pietikäinen, M., Ojala, T., Xu, Z.: Rotation-invariant texture classification using feature distributions. Pattern Recognit. 33, 43–52 (2000)
9. Duda, R.O., Hart, P.E., Stork, D.G.: Pattern Classification, 2nd edn. Wiley-Interscience, New York (2000)

10. Huang, Y.-S., Li, C.-Y.: An Effective Illumination Compensation Method for Face Recognition. In: Lee, K.-T., Tsai, W.-H., Liao, H.-Y.M., Chen, T., Hsieh, J.-W., Tseng, C.-C. (eds.) MMM 2011. LNCS, vol. 6523, pp. 525–535. Springer, Heidelberg (2011). doi:10.1007/978-3-642-17832-0_49
11. Georghiades, A.S., Belhumeur, P.N., Kriegman, D.J.: From few to many: illumination cone models for face recognition under variable lighting and pose. IEEE Trans. Pattern Anal. Mach. Intell. 23(6), 643–660 (2001)

# Multi-Kernel Fuzzy-Based Local Gabor Patterns for Gait Recognition

Amer G. Binsaadoon and El-Sayed M. El-Alfy[(✉)]

Information and Computer Science Department, College of Computer
Sciences and Engineering, King Fahd University of Petroleum and Minerals,
Dhahran 31261, Saudi Arabia
agbinsaadoon@gmail.com, alfy@kfupm.edu.sa

**Abstract.** This paper proposes a novel multi-kernel fuzzy-based local
Gabor binary patterns method (MFLGBP) for the purpose of gait representation and recognition. First, we construct the gait energy image
(GEI) from mean motion cycle of a gait sequence. Then, we apply Gabor
filters and encode the variations in the Gabor magnitude by using a
kernel-based fuzzy local binary pattern (KFLBP) operator. Finally, classification is performed using a support vector machine (SVM). Experiments are carried out using the benchmark CASIA B gait database. Our
proposed feature extraction method has shown promising performance
in terms of correct recognition rate as compared to other methods.

## 1 Introduction

Automatic gait recognition is an emerging technology which has recently
attracted the attention of researchers in the field of biometrics and pattern
recognition. It can have several applications in behavioral monitoring, security,
public safety and physiotherapy. Unlike other biometrics, gait-based systems can
effectively operate at a distance (10 m or more) and with low resolution videos.
Gait recognition is non-intrusive in the sense that no cooperation of persons is
required and even can operate without their knowledge. Gait can also be hard to
be disguised or concealed. However, gait recognition still has several challenges
including being affected by body conditions like injuries, illness, motion disorder,
drunkenness, variations in walking speeds, age, mood, and fatigue. Among other
factors that have impact on the gait-based recognition system performance are
environmental conditions such as walking surface, type of shoes, shadows near
feet, carried objects, clothing, and weather [1]. Thus, further investigation is
required to improve the system performance.

Gabor features have been widely utilized in many applications. Features in
Gabor domain are robust against local distortion and noise and provide a high
degree of invariance to intensity, translation, and orientation [2]. Gabor features
have been applied in some biometric applications such as face [3] and gait recognition [4,5]. Several methods have been proposed to reduce the high dimensionality
of Gabor patterns and generate more effective low-dimensionality Gabor-based
features. Local Binary Pattern (LBP) [6] operator has been incorporated with

© Springer International Publishing AG 2016
G. Bebis et al. (Eds.): ISVC 2016, Part I, LNCS 10072, pp. 790–799, 2016.
DOI: 10.1007/978-3-319-50835-1_71

Gabor patterns to encode the variations in magnitude and phase. Wenchao et al. proposed local Gabor binary pattern (LGBP) descriptors for face recognition [7]. Xie et al. [8] proposed local Gabor XOR patterns (LGXP) that utilize local XOR pattern (LXP) operator to encode Gabor phase variations in face images.

In this paper, we propose an effective multi-kernel fuzzy-based local Gabor binary patterns (MFLGBP) descriptor for robust feature extraction and gait recognition. MFLGBP encodes the Gabor magnitude variations by using our proposed kernel-based fuzzy local binary pattern (KFLBP) operator. We first construct a gait-energy image (GEI) [9] which captures the spatio-temporal characteristics of a walking person within one gait cycle. Then, the GEI image is convolved with a Gabor-filter bank of five different scales and eight different orientations. Subsequently, the KFLBP operator is applied on the resulting patterns to encode their magnitude variations.

The remaining of the paper is organized as follows. In Sect. 2, we describe our proposed descriptor in detail. The performance of the proposed method is then evaluated in Sect. 3 using the benchmark CASIA B database. Finally, we conclude the paper in Sect. 4.

## 2    Methodology

The proposed approach begins with the detection of gait period and construction of GEI image followed by the convolution with a Gabor filter bank to produce a more robust gait representation. We then apply our proposed KFLBP operator on Gabor responses to encode their magnitude variations. Figure 1 illustrates the flowchart of the proposed framework.

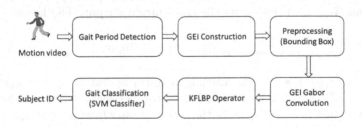

**Fig. 1.** Flowchart of the MFLGBP descriptor

### 2.1    Gait-Period Detection

To construct the GEI image, we analyze the input gait sequence of binary silhouettes to detect the gait cycle based on the algorithm suggested in [10]. The 2D dimensions aspect ratio of the moving subject's silhouette bounding box is tracked over time. The background component is then ignored by subtracting and dividing the aspect ratio mean and standard deviation, respectively. Symmetric average filter is then applied to smooth the signal. Next, autocorrelation is computed to find the peak locations using the first-order derivative of the autocorrelated signal. The distance between each pair of consecutive peaks is averaged to represent the gait period.

## 2.2   Gait-Energy Image (GEI) Construction

Given the gait cycle of a certain gait sequence, the GEI image is constructed as the average of the binary silhouettes within that cycle. Due to the variations in camera view and depth, each silhouette is first binarized, normalized into 240 × 240, and finally aligned. The GEI image is created as follows [9]:

$$G(x, y) = \frac{1}{M} \sum_{t=1}^{M} B_t(x, y); \forall x, y \tag{1}$$

where $M$ is the number of silhouettes within one gait cycle and $B_t(x, y)$ is the binary silhouette at time $t$ within the cycle sequence.

## 2.3   Gabor-Filter Bank

The GEI image is convolved with a Gabor filter bank to get a more robust Gabor-based gait representation. The Gabor filter bank has five different scales and eight different orientations. The output of convolution is given by [11]:

$$G_{v,\mu}(x, y) = G(x, y) * \psi_{v,\mu}(x, y) \tag{2}$$

where * represents convolution, $\psi_{v,\mu}(x, y)$ is a 2D Gabor wavelet kernel function at orientation $\mu = 0, 1, 2, ..., 7$ and scale $v = 0, 1, 2, 3, 4$; $G(x, y)$ is the gait-energy image; and $G_{v,\mu}(x, y)$ represents the convolution output. The kernel is defined by [11]:

$$\psi_{v,\mu}(z) = \frac{\|k_{v,\mu}\|^2}{\sigma^2} e^{-(\|k_{v,\mu}\|^2 \|z\|^2 / 2\sigma^2)} [e^{ik_{v,\mu}z} - e^{-\sigma^2/2}] \tag{3}$$

where $z = (x, y)$, $\| \bullet \|$ is the Euclidean norm operator, $k_{v,\mu} = k_v e^{i\varphi_\mu}$ with $k_v = k_{max}/\lambda^v$, $\lambda = 1.2$ is the spacing factor between Gabor wavelets in the frequency domain, $\phi_\mu = \pi\mu/8$ is the orientation where $\mu = 0, 1, 2, ..., 7$, and $k_{max} = 0.35$. Each Gabor response contains two main parts: real part, $R_{v,\mu}(x, y)$, and imaginary part, $Im_{v,\mu}(x, y)$. We utilize the magnitude of the Gabor response which is generated as follows:

$$Mag_{v,\mu}(x, y) = \sqrt{R_{v,\mu}^2(x, y) + Im_{v,\mu}^2(x, y)} \tag{4}$$

## 2.4   Local-Binary Patterns (LBP)

Basically, LBP operator describes the relationships between a central pixel, $p_c$, and its $p$ surrounding pixels which are equally spaced around the center pixel at radius, $r$. The coordinates of the $p$ neighbors are located at $(r \sin(2\pi n/p),$

$r\cos(2\pi n/p))$. Interpolation is applied when coordinates do not fit in the exact center of pixels. Neighbors with values greater than or equal to the central pixel will produce binary 1, otherwise 0. Then, the binaries have been scanned sequentially in a clockwise manner to form a micropattern which is utilized to characterize the textural properties of an image $I$. LBP operator is defined as follows:

$$LBP(p,r) = \sum_{n=0}^{p-1} s(p_n - p_c)2^n \tag{5}$$

where $s(x) = 1$ if $x \geq 0$ and $s(x) = 0$ otherwise. A histogram $h$ of length $N = 2^p$ is then constructed to describe the distribution of the generated patterns of the whole textured image $I$.

## 2.5  Fuzzy Local-Binary Patterns (FLBP)

FLBP operator was first proposed by Iakovidis et al. [12] to incorporate fuzzy logic rules into the conventional LBP operator. FLBP measures the degree of certainty that a neighbor $p_n$ is greater or smaller than a central pixel $p_c$. This is achieved by using two membership functions $m_1$ and $m_0$. Let $m_1$ measures the degree to which a neighbor $p_n$ has a greater value than $p_c$ and is defined by:

$$m_1(n) = \begin{cases} 1 & p_n \geq p_c + T \\ \frac{T+p_n-p_c}{2\cdot T} & p_c - T < p_n < p_c + T \\ 0 & p_n \leq p_c - T \end{cases} \tag{6}$$

Similarly, $m_0$ measures the degree to which a neighboring $p_n$ has a smaller value than $p_c$ and is defined by:

$$m_0(n) = \begin{cases} 0 & p_n \geq p_c + T \\ \frac{T-p_n+p_c}{2\cdot T} & p_c - T < p_n < p_c + T \\ 1 & p_n \leq p_c - T \end{cases} \tag{7}$$

where $T$ is a thresholding parameter that manages the level of fuzziness. We set $T = 5$ in our experiments.

Consequently, FLBP can generate more than one LBP code for the central pixel $p_c$. The membership functions $m_1$ and $m_0$ are used to determine the contribution of each LBP code to a single bin of the FLBP histogram as follows:

$$C(LBP) = \prod_{n=0}^{p-1} m_{s_n}(n) \tag{8}$$

where $s_n \in \{0,1\}$. The total contribution of all LBP codes is equal to the unity as follows:

$$\sum_{LBP=0}^{2^p-1} C(LBP) = 1 \tag{9}$$

Finally, FLBP histogram $h$ of size $N = 2^p$ represents the feature vector. It describes the distribution of the generated LBP binary codes of the textured image. FLBP histogram almost has no zero-valued bins and, consequently, is more informative than the conventional LBP histogram which may have bins of zero value.

## 2.6   Kernel-based FLBP (KFLBP)

We have extended the FLBP operator to increase its resistance to gray-level variations due to noise and illumination change and improve its discrimination ability. We propose a kernel-based FLBP (FLBP) operator by utilizing more than one radius $r$. Surrounding pixels are sampled over $K$ radii (kernels). It is not necessary to have the same neighbors $p$ for each radius $r$. Then, the information provided by multiple FLBP operators is combined to form the final binary code. This leads to capturing more important structural and statistical gait information. Moreover, it alleviates the effect of noise due to changes in the gray-level intensities as well as illumination variations. Figure 2 illustrates the proposed idea using an example of two kernels and eight sampling points for each kernel. Node numbers indicate the sequence of bits that form the final binary code.

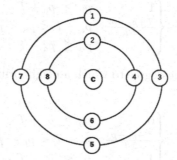

**Fig. 2.** KFLBP scheme where $K = 2$, $p_{r_1} = p_{r_2} = 4$

In contrast to FLBP, KFLBP has the same formulation with the difference of having multiple FLBP operators fused together. Each kernel has a separate operator with the same or different number of neighbors $p_{r_k}$.

$$KFLBP_{p_{r_k}, r_k} = \sum_{n=0}^{p_{r_k}-1} s(p_n^{r_k} - p_c)2^n \tag{10}$$

where $p_{r_k}$ is the number of neighbors at radius $r_k$; $p_c$ is the center pixel; $p_n^{r_k}$ is the $n^{th}$ neighbor pixel at radius $r_k$.

The output of each operator is then combined together to form the final binary code. In our experiments and for simplicity, we have chosen $K = 2$ and

$p_{r_1} = p_{r_2} = 4$. So, we have two FLBP operators at two different radii $r_1 = 1$ and $r_2 = 2$ as follows:

$$KFLBP^{K=2}_{p_{r_1}, r_1} = \sum_{n=0}^{p_{r_1}-1} s(p_n^{r_1} - p_c)2^n \tag{11}$$

$$KFLBP^{K=2}_{p_{r_2}, r_2} = \sum_{n=0}^{p_{r_2}-1} s(p_n^{r_2} - p_c)2^n \tag{12}$$

Although KFLBP preserves a lot of structural and statistical information by combining information from different kernels, KFLBP histogram $h$ size is still the same as that of the conventional FLBP and LBP histograms; in our experiments, a histogram of $N = 2^8 = 256$ bins.

## 2.7  MFLGBP Descriptors

First, GEI images are constructed as described above. Then, they are convolved with Gabor filter bank of five different scales and eight different orientations to obtain more robust and informative Gabor-based gait representation. Once the convolution process is completed, MFLGBP descriptors encode the variations in the magnitude of Gabor responses by applying the proposed KFLBP operator.

The extracted fuzzy-based local Gabor patterns from the magnitude of Gabor response at scale $v$ and orientation $\mu$ are formulated as follows:

$$MFLGBP_{v,\mu}(p_c) = \sum_{n=0}^{p-1} MFLGBP_{v,\mu}^n \cdot 2^n \tag{13}$$

where $p_c$ denotes the central pixel, $p$ is the number of neighbor pixels around $p_c$, and $MFLGBP_{v,\mu}^n$ denotes the single binary and is calculated as follows:

$$MFLGBP_{v,\mu}^n = KFLBP(Mag_{v,\mu}(p_c), Mag_{v,\mu}(p_n)) \tag{14}$$

where $Mag_{v,\mu}(\bullet)$ denotes the magnitude of Gabor response with scale $v$ and orientation $\mu$, and $p_n$ is the $n^{th}$ neighbor pixel. Our KFLBP operator is applied on the magnitude of Gabor response to generate the fuzzy-based local Gabor patterns as follows:

$$KFLBP_{v,\mu}(p_{r_k}, r_k) = \sum_{n=0}^{p_{r_k}-1} s(Mag_{v,\mu}(p_n^{r_k}) - Mag_{v,\mu}(p_c))2^n \tag{15}$$

where $p_{r_k}$ is the number of neighbors at radius $r_k$; $p_c$ is the center pixel; $p_n^{r_k}$ is the $n^{th}$ neighbor pixel at radius $r_k$.

The outputs of each operator are then combined together to form the final fuzzy-based local Gabor patterns. Again, we have chosen $K = 2$ and $p_{r_1} = p_{r_2} = 4$. So, we have two KFLBP operators at two different radii $r_1$ and $r_2$ as follows:

$$KFLBP_{v,\mu}(p_{r_1}, r_1) = \sum_{n=0}^{p_{r_1}-1} s(Mag_{v,\mu}(p_n^{r_1}) - Mag_{v,\mu}(p_c))2^n \tag{16}$$

$$KFLBP_{v,\mu}(p_{r_2}, r_2) = \sum_{n=0}^{p_{r_2}-1} s(Mag_{v,\mu}(p_n^{r_2}) - Mag_{v,\mu}(p_c))2^n \qquad (17)$$

Based on the defined MFLGBP patterns, one pattern histogram is calculated from each Gabor response and then all histograms under all scales and orientations (40 combinations in our setup) are finally concatenated to form the MFLGBP descriptors of the GEI gait image.

## 3    Experiments and Results

### 3.1    Gait Database and Experimental Setup

CASIA B gait database [13] is used to carry out all experiments. It includes 13,640 gait sequences samples among 124 subjects (93 males and 31 females). During the dataset collection, the creators have used 11 cameras to record sequences from 11 different viewing angles. Each subject has 110 video sequences generated from walking 10 times through a straight line of concrete ground as follows: 6 with normal walking, 2 while wearing a coat, and 2 while carrying a bag. Thus, the database contains $110 \times 124 = 13,640$ total sequences for all subjects. We used a setup similar to that of the authors of CASIA B database. One gallery set of normal walking of all subjects is used to train the SVM model and the three sets under different covariates are used as the probe sets: Probe Set A where subjects are normally walking, Probe Set B where subjects are carrying bags, and Probe Set C where subjects are wearing coats.

### 3.2    Performance Metric

The correct classification rate (CCR) represents the performance at rank-1, which indicates that the probe sample is matching with the only one returned candidate. Equation 18 represents the CCR percentage.

$$CCR(\%) = \frac{s_c}{s_t} * 100 \qquad (18)$$

where $s_c$ is the number of correctly identified subjects; $s_t$ is the total number of tested subjects. We adopted the closed-set identification strategy which guarantees the existence of the unknown subject within the database gallery.

### 3.3    Discussions

We evaluated the performance of the proposed MFLGBP on different walking covariates in the database in terms of CCR. We also compared the performance with several other gait recognition methods. Some methods have been applied on silhouette images in the original papers but we reimplemented and applied them on GEI images such as pyramid of Histogram of Gradient (pHOG) [14]. Tables 1, 2 and 3 report the experimental results of KFLBP and MFLGBP on CASIA B

**Table 1.** Evaluation and comparison of KFLBP and MFLGBP with other methods under normal-walking covariate

| Method | CCR(%) | | | | | | | | | | |
|---|---|---|---|---|---|---|---|---|---|---|---|
| | 0° | 18° | 36° | 54° | 72° | 90° | 108° | 126° | 144° | 162° | 180° |
| GEI [9] | 89.11 | 87.5 | 85.08 | 82.25 | 87.9 | 89.11 | 88.3 | 85.88 | 83.87 | 83.46 | 89.11 |
| GEI+pHOG [14] | 82.76 | 74.57 | 76.72 | 76.72 | 81.47 | 86.21 | 81.04 | 77.59 | 76.72 | 78.45 | 83.62 |
| GEI+PCA [15] | 83.06 | 73.38 | 75 | 72.58 | 85.08 | 84.67 | 83.46 | 83.06 | 77.41 | 75.8 | 87.09 |
| GEI+LXP [16] | 61.64 | 61.21 | 53.02 | 56.04 | 60.78 | 62.07 | 63.36 | 57.33 | 57.33 | 63.79 | 53.02 |
| GEI+LBP [17] | 56.9 | 66.81 | 60.35 | 56.9 | 68.54 | 73.28 | 68.97 | 62.5 | 61.21 | 68.97 | 57.33 |
| GEI+SLBP [18] | 68.54 | 65.52 | 61.21 | 63.79 | 68.54 | 68.97 | 65.52 | 68.54 | 66.81 | 75.43 | 66.38 |
| GEI+FLBP | 74.14 | 78.45 | 67.24 | 74.14 | 75.43 | 78.02 | 76.29 | 75.86 | 75 | 77.59 | 70.69 |
| GEI+**KFLBP** | 89.66 | 92.24 | 82.33 | 82.76 | 90.95 | 88.79 | 87.93 | 87.07 | 85.35 | 91.38 | 82.76 |
| LGBP [7] | 88.31 | 80.65 | 78.23 | 77.42 | 83.87 | 85.08 | 87.5 | 87.09 | 81.45 | 83.47 | 86.29 |
| LGXP [8] | 88.71 | 79.84 | 77.02 | 77.82 | 83.87 | 83.47 | 86.29 | 87.09 | 81.85 | 84.27 | 87.9 |
| SLGBP | 85.08 | 77.82 | 77.82 | 79.44 | 83.87 | 85.89 | 85.48 | 85.48 | 81.05 | 84.27 | 83.87 |
| FLGBP | 90.52 | 88.31 | 84.91 | 87.93 | 88.79 | 87.93 | 92.24 | 90.09 | 87.5 | 86.64 | 89.66 |
| **MFLGBP** | **94.4** | **93.54** | **92.67** | **93.54** | **93.1** | **95.69** | **96.12** | **94.4** | **92.67** | **93.54** | **95.69** |

**Table 2.** Evaluation and comparison of KFLBP and MFLGBP with other methods under carrying-bag covariate

| Method | CCR(%) | | | | | | | | | | |
|---|---|---|---|---|---|---|---|---|---|---|---|
| | 0° | 18° | 36° | 54° | 72° | 90° | 108° | 126° | 144° | 162° | 180° |
| GEI [9] | 50.8 | 42.74 | 45.56 | 41.53 | 45.16 | 41.12 | 41.12 | 37.5 | 40.72 | 46.37 | 51.2 |
| GEI+pHOG [14] | 45.26 | 30.6 | 30.6 | 24.57 | 20.26 | 22.41 | 18.54 | 21.98 | 20.26 | 35.78 | 42.67 |
| GEI+PCA [15] | 40.32 | 35.48 | 35.88 | 30.64 | 37.5 | 33.46 | 39.51 | 33.06 | 29.83 | 34.67 | 41.93 |
| GEI+LXP [16] | 26.72 | 18.54 | 15.95 | 15.95 | 9.91 | 18.54 | 18.1 | 18.1 | 8.62 | 21.55 | 20.69 |
| GEI+LBP [17] | 28.02 | 43.1 | 34.05 | 30.6 | 34.05 | 37.5 | 34.48 | 31.47 | 28.02 | 35.35 | 29.74 |
| GEI+SLBP [18] | 28.45 | 28.88 | 23.71 | 25 | 29.74 | 35.78 | 31.04 | 26.72 | 31.9 | 27.16 | 28.45 |
| GEI+FLBP | 40.85 | 43.54 | 36.91 | 33.62 | 36.72 | 40.1 | 38.9 | 31.16 | 30.16 | 40.55 | 37.35 |
| GEI+**KFLBP** | 55.17 | **53.45** | 40.09 | 37.93 | 40.52 | 42.24 | 42.67 | 31.04 | 33.62 | 46.98 | 51.72 |
| LGBP [7] | 50 | 34.68 | 36.29 | 33.87 | 33.87 | 34.68 | 33.06 | 34.68 | 41.94 | 43.95 | 48.39 |
| LGXP [8] | 48.39 | 33.87 | 34.68 | 35.48 | 29.84 | 31.45 | 31.85 | 35.48 | 39.92 | 42.74 | 47.18 |
| SLGBP | 44.35 | 29.44 | 28.23 | 24.59 | 29.03 | 30.24 | 26.61 | 31.05 | 32.66 | 33.06 | 41.53 |
| FLGBP | 54.74 | 46.55 | 42.74 | 38.79 | 49.57 | 53.45 | 46.12 | 40.95 | 38.79 | 48.71 | 46.55 |
| **MFLGBP** | **62.07** | 51.72 | **55.17** | **46.12** | **52.16** | **53.45** | **48.71** | **53.45** | **55.17** | **62.07** | **64.45** |

using CCR measure under normal walking, walking with bags, and walking with coats covariates, respectively. Comparing to other methods, MFLGBP is mostly outperforming under various viewing angles. It is obvious from the reported results that normal walking covariate achieves the best results over carrying-bag and wearing-coat covariates. This can be attributed to the level of deformation caused by the coat or the bag which cause difficulties in capturing the basic discriminative features originated from the normal walking. The performance under carrying bag is moderate because the bag is occupying a region in the middle of the human body causing deformity for that part of body during walking. However, coat causes the largest amount of deformity to the human body.

**Table 3.** Evaluation and comparison of KFLBP and MFLGBP with other methods under wearing-coat covariate

| Method | CCR(%) | | | | | | | | | | |
|---|---|---|---|---|---|---|---|---|---|---|---|
| | 0° | 18° | 36° | 54° | 72° | 90° | 108° | 126° | 144° | 162° | 180° |
| GEI [9] | 22.98 | 20.07 | 20.07 | 15.32 | 10.88 | 16.12 | 13.7 | 16.12 | 23.79 | 22.98 | 23.38 |
| GEI+pHOG [14] | 12.93 | 13.79 | 12.07 | 9.05 | 9.48 | 8.19 | 9.48 | 10.78 | 11.21 | 13.79 | 12.93 |
| GEI+PCA [15] | 17.33 | 15.72 | 18.54 | 12.5 | 19.75 | 19.35 | 18.54 | 19.07 | 24.19 | 19.75 | 16.93 |
| GEI+LXP [16] | 7.33 | 9.05 | 7.33 | 12.07 | 12.07 | 6.47 | 9.48 | 9.48 | 13.79 | 7.33 | 6.9 |
| GEI+LBP [17] | 9.91 | 9.91 | 15.95 | 18.1 | 16.38 | 15.09 | 13.79 | 17.24 | 10.78 | 10.78 | 11.21 |
| GEI+SLBP [18] | 7.33 | 12.07 | 13.79 | 11.64 | 12.07 | 13.79 | 11.64 | 13.36 | 11.21 | 12.07 | 7.33 |
| GEI+FLBP | 11.33 | 16.5 | 17.62 | 20.64 | 20.36 | 21.07 | 16.5 | 18.52 | 14.81 | 13.91 | 13.9 |
| GEI+**KFLBP** | 13.36 | 20.26 | 20.26 | 24.57 | 26.29 | 25.43 | 20.69 | 19.4 | 18.1 | 15.95 | 15.52 |
| LGBP [7] | 22.85 | 24.86 | 27.59 | 27.16 | 31.47 | 29.74 | 31.47 | 23.71 | 24.14 | 17.24 | 22.85 |
| LGXP [8] | 16.13 | 17.74 | 16.94 | 16.94 | 18.95 | 20.56 | 15.73 | 15.73 | 16.94 | 15.32 | 20.56 |
| SLGBP | 16.13 | 15.32 | 12.9 | 16.53 | 11.69 | 8.06 | 10.48 | 14.92 | 12.9 | 13.71 | 20.97 |
| FLGBP | 38.79 | 32.33 | 34.68 | 41.81 | 44.4 | 41.81 | 40.95 | **45.26** | 42.67 | 30.6 | 32.76 |
| **MFLGBP** | **40.09** | **34.68** | **40.09** | **43.54** | **47.41** | **43.97** | **47.41** | 43.97 | **43.97** | **35.41** | **40.09** |

Consequently, wearing a coat covariate is the most difficult scenario to discover and extract representative features for all tested methods.

## 4 Conclusion

A multi-kernel fuzzy-based local Gabor binary patterns (MFLGBP) is presented in this paper for gait representation and recognition. MFLGBP encodes the Gabor magnitude of gait using kernel-based fuzzy local binary pattern (KFLBP) operator. GEI spatio-temporal image of gait cycle was adopted to the human gait. GEI is convolved with a Gabor filter bank of five different scales and eight different orientations to produce Gabor-based gait representation. Then, KFLBP operator is utilized to encode the variations in the Gabor magnitude. The experimental results showed that the proposed method is outperforming existing methods under different gait covariates. We intend to investigate MFLGBP with other gait databases and using different classifiers.

**Acknowledgment.** The authors would like to thank King Fahd University of Petroleum and Minerals (KFUPM), Saudi Arabia, for the support during this work. The first author would also like to thank Hadhramout Establishment for Human Development (HEHD) for supporting him during the master degree.

## References

1. Bouchrika, I., Carter, J.N., Nixon, M.S.: Towards automated visual surveillance using gait for identity recognition and tracking across multiple non-intersecting cameras. Multimedia Tools Appl. **75**, 1201–1221 (2016)

2. Kamarainen, J.K., Kyrki, V., Kalviainen, H.: Invariance properties of Gabor filter-based features-overview and applications. IEEE Trans. Image Process. **15**, 1088–1099 (2006)
3. Liu, C., Wechsler, H.: Gabor feature based classification using the enhanced fisher linear discriminant model for face recognition. IEEE Trans. Image Process. **11**, 467–476 (2002)
4. Hu, M., Wang, Y., Zhang, Z., Wang, Y.: Combining spatial and temporal information for gait based gender classification. In: 20th International Conference on Pattern Recognition (ICPR), pp. 3679–3682 (2010)
5. Huang, D.Y., Lin, T.W., Hu, W.C., Cheng, C.H.: Gait recognition based on Gabor wavelets and modified gait energy image for human identification. J. Electron. Imaging **22**, 043039 (2013)
6. Ojala, T., Pietikainen, M., Maenpaa, T.: Multiresolution gray-scale and rotation invariant texture classification with local binary patterns. IEEE Trans. Pattern Anal. Mach. Intell. **24**, 971–987 (2002)
7. Zhang, W., Shan, S., Gao, W., Chen, X., Zhang, H.: Local Gabor binary pattern histogram sequence (LGBPHS): a novel non-statistical model for face representation and recognition. Tenth IEEE Int. Conf. Comput. Vis. (ICCV) **1**, 786–791 (2005)
8. Xie, S., Shan, S., Chen, X., Chen, J.: Fusing local patterns of Gabor magnitude and phase for face recognition. IEEE Trans. Image Process. **19**, 1349–1361 (2010)
9. Han, J., Bhanu, B.: Individual recognition using gait energy image. IEEE Trans. Pattern Anal. Mach. Intell. **28**, 316–322 (2006)
10. Wang, L., Tan, T., Ning, H., Hu, W.: Silhouette analysis-based gait recognition for human identification. IEEE Trans. Pattern Anal. Mach. Intell. **25**, 1505–1518 (2003)
11. Lades, M., Vorbruggen, J., Buhmann, J., Lange, J., von der Malsburg, C., Wurtz, R., Konen, W.: Distortion invariant object recognition in the dynamic link architecture. IEEE Trans. Comput. **42**, 300–311 (1993)
12. Iakovidis, D.K., Keramidas, E.G., Maroulis, D.: Fuzzy local binary patterns for ultrasound texture characterization. In: Campilho, A., Kamel, M. (eds.) ICIAR 2008. LNCS, vol. 5112, pp. 750–759. Springer, Heidelberg (2008). doi:10.1007/978-3-540-69812-8_74
13. Yu, S., Tan, D., Tan, T.: A framework for evaluating the effect of view angle, clothing and carrying condition on gait recognition. In: Proceedings of 18th International Conference on Pattern Recognition (ICPR), vol. 4, pp. 441–444 (2006)
14. Yang, G., Yin, Y., Park, J., Man, H.: Human gait recognition by pyramid of HOG feature on Silhouette images. In: Proceedings of SPIE Optical Pattern Recognition, vol. 8748 (2013). 87480J–87480J-6
15. Ali, H., Dargham, J., Ali, C., Moung, E.: Gait recognition using gait energy image. Int. J. Signal Process. Image Process. Pattern Recogn. **4**, 141–152 (2011)
16. Zhang, B., Shan, S., Chen, X., Gao, W.: Histogram of Gabor phase patterns (HGPP): a novel object representation approach for face recognition. IEEE Trans. Image Process. **16**, 57–68 (2007)
17. Kumar, H.P.M., Nagendraswamy, H.S.: LBP for gait recognition: a symbolic approach based on GEI plus RBL of GEI. In: International Conference on Electronics and Communication Systems (ICECS), pp. 1–5 (2014)
18. Ahonen, T., Pietikinen, M.: Soft histograms for local binary patterns. In: Proceedings of the Finnish Signal Processing Symposium (FINSIG) (2007)

# A Comparative Analysis of Deep and Shallow Features for Multimodal Face Recognition in a Novel RGB-D-IR Dataset

Tiago Freitas[1,2](✉), Pedro G. Alves[2], Cristiana Carpinteiro[2],
Joana Rodrigues[2], Margarida Fernandes[2], Marina Castro[2],
João C. Monteiro[1,2], and Jaime S. Cardoso[1,2]

[1] INESC-TEC, Porto, Portugal
vilab.biometrics@gmail.com
[2] Faculty of Engineering, University of Porto, Porto, Portugal

**Abstract.** With new trends like 3D and deep learning alternatives for face recognition becoming more popular, it becomes essential to establish a complete benchmark for the evaluation of such algorithms, in a wide variety of data sources and non-ideal scenarios. We propose a new RGB-depth-infrared (RGB-D-IR) dataset, RealFace, acquired with the novel Intel® RealSense™ collection of sensors, and characterized by multiple variations in pose, lighting and disguise. As baseline for future works, we assess the performance of multiple deep and "shallow" feature descriptors. We conclude that our dataset presents some relevant challenges and that deep feature descriptors present both higher robustness in RGB images, as well as an interesting margin for improvement in alternative sources, such as depth and IR.

## 1   Introduction

Over the past few years, the issue of face recognition has been on the spotlight of many research works in pattern recognition, due to its wide array of real-world applications. The *face* is a natural, easily acquirable, trait with a high degree of uniqueness, representing one of the main sources of information during human interaction. These marked advantages, however, fall short when images of limited quality, acquired under unconstrained environments, are presented to the system. The fact that humans perform and rely on face recognition routinely and effortlessly throughout their daily lives leads to an increased interest in replicating this process in an automated way, even when above limitations are known to frequently occur.

Whereas technological improvements in image capturing and transmitting equipment managed to attenuate most noise factors, partial face occlusions, severe illumination changes and extreme pose variations still represent genuine challenges to automated face recognition [1,2]. Approaching these issues will, therefore, be a matter of either exploring new sources of data, to compensate

G. Bebis et al. (Eds.): ISVC 2016, Part I, LNCS 10072, pp. 800–811, 2016.
DOI: 10.1007/978-3-319-50835-1_72

the more traditional alternatives in less ideal scenarios, or designing more robust algorithms, capable of encompassing such limitations.

Recently, a new trend has been observed in face recognition works, with information from the three-dimensional structure of the face being incorporated in recognition frameworks, in an attempt to grant higher robustness in scenarios such as critically low illumination, where the extraction of color information is severely limited, or extreme pose variations. In conjunction with the more traditional color images, 3D data can be used to develop more robust multimodal approaches [3].

Research in automated face recognition has also found an interesting new alternative in methodologies based on Deep Learning, such as deep Convolutional Neural Networks (CNN). These approaches have shown increased performance in a multiplicity of image recognition tasks, due to their capacity to learn abstract and invariant high-level features when compared to the more traditional application-tailored features [4].

The development of biometric recognition systems is generally limited by the shortage of large public databases acquired under real unconstrained working conditions. Database collection represents a complicated process, in which a high degree of cooperation from a large number of participants is needed. For that reason, nowadays, the number of existing public databases that can be used to evaluate the performance of biometric recognition systems in real-life acquisition conditions and making use of multiple sources of information is quite limited.

Motivated by this need and the growing interest of the research community in both 3D and deep learning strategies for face recognition, we present a new database, named RealFace, acquired using the novel Intel® RealSense™ collection of sensors. In addition to this new dataset, we also establish an experimental setup and a performance baseline using a set of more traditional tailored feature descriptors as well as some deep learning alternatives. We aim to assess the accuracy, robustness and generalization capability of such features with regards to both color and 3D information, as well as establishing a solid baseline for further research in the biometrics scientific community. Finally, we present a new CNN, trained specifically for face recognition using depth representations of the 3D structure of the face, validated both on the state-of-the-art EURECOM dataset, as well as our proposed RealFace dataset.

## 2   Related Work

Following the good results obtained in object recognition by Krizhevsky et al. [5] using deep CNNs, their use has shown promising performance in many computer vision related tasks, as they can achieve more correct assumptions about the image's local pixel dependencies. This approach showed an absolute decrease in the error rate of about 10% when compared with densely-sampled SIFT keypoint descriptors applied to the same tasks [5]. In the field of face recognition, DeepFace [4] has achieved 97.35% accuracy and FaceNet [6] from Google has achieved 99.63% recognition accuracy on the benchmark Labeled Faces in the

Wild dataset. These results surpass those achieved with "shallow" methods like
Local Binary Patterns (95.15% accuracy) [7] and SIFT [8] (93.03% accuracy),
due to the ability of deep neural networks to better handle the large amounts of
data present in such datasets, extracting and learning more high dimensional,
invariant features. This translates in increased robustness of the system to variations in occlusion, pose and illumination.

Simpler networks have also been proposed, achieving results comparable to
the state-of-the art, such as the VGG-Face network by Parkhi et al. [9]. This
network has the advantage of being one of the few pre-trained, publicly available,
deep CNNs. To the extent of our knowledge only a few approaches have made use
of this network [10,11], as of the writing of this paper. All these works conclude
that the VGG-Face can outperform more hand-crafted feature extraction methods, as it extracts highly discriminative and invariant face descriptors. This was
further noted in the recent International Challenge on Biometric Recognition
in the Wild (ICB-RW), where all the top-ranked algorithms made use of face
descriptors extracted by the VGG-Face. A more thorough exploration of deep
learning approaches in this field is deemed necessary, especially when new data
sources, such as 3D and infrared data, are being made more easily accessible.

Recent technological advances have made it feasible to deploy low-cost alternatives to the more traditional high-cost 3D scanners, such as Minolta, Inspeck,
CyberWare and 3dMD [12]. The appearance of Microsoft Kinect has opened a
wide array of opportunities to include three-dimensional information in computer vision solutions that were, otherwise, limited by the wider availability of
color images. These sensors provide two types of data: depth images and 3D
models, that can be point clouds (PC) or meshes. 3D models consist in a representation that retains all geometric information of the head. On the other hand,
depth images, or 2.5D, are bi-dimensional representations of a set of 3D points,
in which each pixel in the $XY$ plane stores the depth $z$ value. While the use
of multiple sources of information has been shown to improve performance in a
vast number of biometric recognition works [3], the potential of using a single
sensor to acquire multiple representations of the same data makes it worth to
invest on such alternatives.

A number of datasets have already been built using RGB-D sensors. Some
of these databases include the Aalborg University RGB-D Face Database, the
Florence Superface Dataset, CurtinFaces, FaceWarehouse, EURECOM Kinect
Face database, IIIT-D face database and the Labeled Infrared-Depth Face. A
more detailed state-of-the-art-review regarding these datasets is presented in
our previous work [3]. While the aforementioned datasets present a wide variety of conditions, there is still not enough available relevant public data that
uses the more recent sensors like the Kinect v2 or the Intel® RealSense™
models. Data acquired with these sensors could present useful alternatives for
the face biometrics research community. The scientific relevance of the Intel®
RealSense™ sensor is even higher considering that, to the extent of our knowledge, no publicly available dataset was built on this novel sensor. Intel® provides
two models, the SR300 (previously named F200) for short range applications,

and the R200 for long range acquisitions. Both sensors, similarly to Kinect v2, also provide IR images. Both models are based on the same technology, consisting in 3 streams that provide RGB images, stereoscopic IR and its resulting depth-map representations of 3D shape. The prospect of designing a dataset that comprises all these modalities in conjunction with simulated real-world acquisition environments would certainly result in a strong contribution to the field. With this prospect in mind, the next section will serve as a detailed presentation of our proposed RealFace multimodal face dataset, with regards to both the acquisition setup as well as its final composition.

## 3    RealFace Dataset Description

The RealFace dataset was acquired from a set of 42 volunteers, with different ethnicities, ages and genders.[1] Ages ranged from 18 to 40 years, gender distribution was 22 male and 20 female, while regarding nationality 41 were Portuguese and 1 was Venezuelan. After signing an agreement for the sole use of the images for scientific research purposes, each of these individuals carried out the acquisition protocol detailed below.

The acquisition protocol followed in the present work was designed so that the environmental conditions presented to the sensor would closely simulate a realistic set of real-world unconstrained conditions. With this in mind variations in pose (frontal, left/right profile and left/right $\pm 45°$), facial expression (neutral and open mouth), occlusions (handkerchief and glasses) and illumination (natural, artificial and darkness) were considered in the acquisition setup. All combinations of occlusion (2) and facial expression (2) were replicated for every illumination (3) and pose (5, plus an extra neutral) conditions, and acquisition was made in a sequential way so as not to render the whole process too long and tedious for the volunteers. Due to the different optimal operating ranges, the whole process was repeated for each sensor, with the distance to the sensor being varied from 0.5 m, for the SR300 model, to 1.3 m, for the R200. The full acquisition setup is depicted in Fig. 1 and the whole acquisition process took approximately 12 m per subject, resulting in a total of 72 conditions. Some representative examples are depicted in Fig. 2.

To take advantage of all data streams made available by the Intel® RealSense™ sensors, for each of the aforementioned conditions, we acquired an RGB image and its respective Point Cloud, as well as the IR images provided by the integrated sensors (two for the R200 and one for the SR300) and the corresponding depth maps. This wide array of modalities and conditions confers our dataset a high versatility regarding its possible uses within the biometrics research community. A representative example of the data obtained with the SR300 model for a single acquisition is depicted in Fig. 3.

Additionally to the multiple data sources, for each RGB/Point Cloud/IR group, a set of facial keypoints were also manually annotated, to both facilitate

---

[1] All volunteers were gathered from the students and staff community of the Faculty of Engineering of the University of Porto, Portugal).

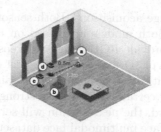

**Fig. 1.** RealFace dataset acquisition setup: (a) subject; (b) acquisition control software; (c) SR300 model and (d) R200 model.

**Fig. 2.** Representative examples of the poses, occlusion, illumination and expression variations considered for each subject during the RealFace acquisition process.

the region-of-interest (ROI) segmentation, as well as allowing the dataset to be used as a benchmark for keypoint detection in any of the presented modalities. The amount and nature of the annotated keypoints depended on the variations that characterized each image. In frontal images, both eye centers, the nose tip and both mouth corners were annotated, except for the handkerchief occlusion scenario, where both nose tip and mouth corners were not considered. In profile and rotated pictures, the closest visible eye center, the nose tip and the closest visible mouth corner were considered, as well as the visible ear lobe. The handkerchief occlusion limitations were also verified here, with no nose tip and mouth corners being considered. When hair occlusion resulted in no visible ear lobe this point was also left out from the annotation. A visual example of the manual annotation in each of these scenarios is depicted in Fig. 4.

The whole RealFace dataset will be made publicly available for research purposes. For more information regarding its availability contact the mailing author.

**Fig. 3.** Multimodal data from a single acquisition in the RealFace dataset: (a) RGB; (b) Depth-map; (c) Point-Cloud and (d) Infrared.

**Fig. 4.** Manual annotation on the RealFace dataset: (a) Frontal neutral; (b) Frontal occlusion; (c) Profile neutral and (d) Profile occlusion.

## 4 Experimental Setup for the RealSense Dataset

In this section we set an experimental setup for performance assessment in the RealFace dataset. The baseline results obtained following the setup will be presented afterwards in this section. We will cover data partitioning and region-of-interest segmentation, as well as the shallow and deep feature representations chosen for the baseline performance assessment. We start this analysis by presenting some global considerations regarding some cases we chose to leave out of the present work, but could be the focus of future endeavors on this dataset.

**Global Considerations:** We chose to work solely on frontal poses, leaving both the ±45° and the profile images out of our baseline analysis. We felt that including this kind of images would dilute the focus of the paper. The R200 model was also left out of this work due to the fact that we confirmed what it had been previously reported in literature: the quality of the depth images acquired with this model is still very low and unfit for object recognition problems [13]. Nevertheless, we propose a region-of-interest segmentation strategy for non-frontal images, and the whole setup is easily extrapolated for future work with the R200 images.

**Pre-processing:** The manually annotated keypoints were used to crop a region-of-interest (ROI) around the nose. In frontal images, a square ROI was considered, with the center corresponding to the nose tip and the side set to twice the distance between the eye centers. For ±45° variations, on the other hand, we considered a square box centered on the horizontal line passing through the nose tip, and with side corresponding from 1.5× the distance between the nose tip and the ear lobe. For the profile images a similar strategy was followed, but the side corresponded to 1× the aforementioned distance.

**Data Partitioning:** We chose images characterized by both neutral expression and artificial illumination to serve as training data for each individual. This decision is based on the fact that we want the most controlled scenarios to be used during training, and the most complicated ones be left for testing. It is intuitive to understand that training an algorithm to encompass all possible acquisition scenarios is unfeasible, when real-world applications are considered. Thus, by using the more stable images during training we aim to assess the capability of algorithms of presenting robust behaviour when more complicated challenges are presented to them. All other combinations of conditions were assessed individually during testing: illumination (natural - N; artificial - A; darkness - D), occlusion (S - scarf; G - glasses) and expression (N - neutral; OpM - open mouth).

**Shallow Features:** From an extensive list of state-of-the-art feature extraction methods for face recognition using RGB and IR images, the top performances were observed for PHOW, TPLBP and FHOG. A similar analysis was carried out for depth images, with both PHOW and FHOG presenting consistently better performances, while 3D-LBP finished the top-ranked descriptors. TPLBP (Three-Patch LBP) and 3DLBP are variants of traditional LBP. Presented in [14], 3DLBP was proposed as a variation of traditional LBP, for depth images, where depth differences are encoded in the final descriptor. In [15] TPBLP was proposed as an upgrade of traditional LBP descriptor for face identification. Here, three patches are considered to produce a single bit value for each pixel. The Felzenszwalb's HOG (FHOG) descriptor has been described in [16] as a variant of traditional HOG for object detection, where a feature pyramid is calculated for a finite number of scales, using repeated smoothing and sub-sampling. PHOW, presented in [17] consists in a variation of dense-SIFT which is applied at multiple scales and combined with VLAD (Vector of Linearly Aggregated Descriptors) encoding.

**Deep Features:** Using the pre-trained model provided by [18], we tested the VGG-Face CNN for all modalities, by extracting features from the $fc7$ layer and using them to train a logistic regression classifier, as described in the following paragraph. For depth images, we also decided to train a new CNN from scratch. To serve as training we used data from 195 subjects obtained from all the available datasets presented in Sect. 2 (except EURECOM and RealFace, which were left for performance assessment). To avoid the class unbalance caused by the high degree of heterogeneity in the original number of samples per individual, we chose to generate synthetic depth maps, by flipping and rotating the original point clouds, until a total of 1000 samples per subject were obtained. The tested architecture consisted in 5 conv-relu-conv-relu-pool blocks followed by 2 fully connected layers. All conv layers include $3 \times 3$ filters, whereas the number of filters for each block is $8 - 16 - 32 - 64$, respectively. Finally the two fully connected layers consist of 256 units each. A batch size of 256 and a logarithmically decaying learning rate from $10^{-1}$ to $10^{-6}$ were considered, for a total of 50k iterations.

**Classification:** A set of logistic regression models was trained for classification, using each of the aforementioned shallow and deep feature descriptors. The model choice was motivated by its simplicity, leaving a considerable margin for improvement for future works on the dataset, as well as the good performance that it revealed when compared to other alternatives, such as SVM and $k$-nearest neighbors. The fact that class probabilities can be easily obtained was also a ruling factor of this choice, as it facilitated the multimodal fusion process described in the next section. Decision for a single feature representation and modality is carried out by maximum probability, with regards to all possible IDs.

**Multimodal Fusion:** As referred earlier, the joint use of multiple data sources to solve the biometric recognition problem has shown improved performance in a multiplicity of recent works. To evaluate such effect in the RealFace dataset, we combine the individual logistic regression probabilities for a given ID from the RGB, depth and IR representations of a single test sample, $p_{mod}(ID|x_i)$, using a weighted-sum rule, $p(ID|x_i) = w_{RGB} \cdot p_{RGB}(ID|x_i) + w_d \cdot p_d(ID|x_i) + w_{IR} \cdot p_{IR}(ID|x_i)$, with $\sum_{mod} w_{mod} = 1$ and $w_{mod}$ optimized by grid search. Decision is then carried out by maximizing the fusion probability $p(ID|x_i)$ with regards to all possible IDs. To overcome the loss of performance in the case of RGB in darkness conditions, a new method is proposed to deal with severely low illumination conditions. For all test images, the individual mean intensity of gray-scale converted RGB image, $\mu_i$, is calculated and, depending on this value, a corrected weight for RGB-modality, $w_{RGB}^*$, is calculated, using a logistic function, $w_{RGB}^* = \frac{1}{1+e^{(-0.5(-\theta+\mu_i))}} \cdot w_{RGB}$, where $\theta$ was empirically set to 20 as it was observed to be the mean transition intensity between fair and poor illumination conditions. This adaptation allows the algorithm to self-adapt its performance, by adjusting the RGB weight to be higher in better illumination, and lower in less ideal low illumination conditions. The weight loss $w_{RGB}^* - w_{RGB}$ is then divided equally between the other modalities.

Following the experimental setup described throughout this section the baseline performance for the RealFace dataset will be presented next. Furthermore, some experiments were also carried out on the RGB-D EURECOM dataset, so as to better understand the challenges of our proposed dataset when compared with a state-of-the-art alternative.

## 5 Results and Discussion

In this section we start by giving some insight into the EURECOM dataset and the experimental setup used for performance assessment in this alternative. We then proceed with the discussion of the results obtained for each tested dataset, with regards to the specific challenges that each one poses.

### 5.1 EURECOM Dataset

**Composition:** The EURECOM dataset, acquired with the Microsfot Kinect v1 sensor, is composed by a set of well-aligned 2D, 2.5D, 3D and video data. It includes scans from 52 subjects (38 males and 14 females) from two sessions interleaved from 5 to 14 days. Each session has nine types of scans that include:

**Fig. 5.** Example RGB (a)–(g) and depth (h)–(o) images from the multiple subsets of the EURECOM dataset.

neutral face (N), open mouth (OpM), smile (S), strong illumination (LO), occlusion with sunglasses (OE), occlusion by hand (OM), occlusion by paper (OP), right face profile and left face profile. The acquisition environment is controlled in terms of luminosity, with the individuals always in a range from 0.7 to 0.9 m to the sensor. A blank background was chosen to make the processing of the data easier. An example of the 2D and 2.5D images from a single individual is presented in Fig. 5.

**Experimental Setup:** We chose to follow a setup similar to the one we proposed for the RealFace dataset. The neutral images from both sessions were, therefore, chosen for training and all other subsets were considered individually for testing. ROI segmentation was carried out using the keypoints provided by the dataset, using a methodology analogous to the one described in Sect. 4 for both RGB and depth images. Resizing was carried out to 96 × 96 and 224 × 224, for depth and RGB data respectively. These dimensions were chosen to correspond to the inputs expected by the CNNs used in this work.

## 5.2   Performance Analysis

The results for the EURECOM dataset are summarized in Table 1. In RGB images, shallow and deep features presented similar high performance for all tested conditions. PHOW with VLAD encoding was the shallow descriptor with better overall performance, and showed great versatility in image description by achieving the highest overall performance also for depth images. For such images, the overall performance drop comparatively to their RGB counterparts is clear. In this case, shallow features outperform deep features by a considerable margin. This drop in performance can be understood by the fact that only RGB images were considered during the training of the VGG-Face CNN. As there is no trivial visual similarity between the two types of images, it is logic to conclude that the filters learnt for the RGB problem are not directly applicable to depth inputs. This observation is also corroborated by the fair results presented by the proposed pre-trained CNN ($PT_{CNN}$) evaluated in the non-occlusion cases. Clearly, the learnt filters are able to achieve some discrimination, unlike the VGG-face alternative, but fail to adapt to non-ideal cases related to occlusions. When both modalities are combined, as referred in the state-of-the-art, the global

**Table 1.** Performance comparison of shallow (S) and deep (D) features on the RGB and depth modalities of the EURECOM dataset.

| | Feat/SS | RGB | | | | | | | Depth | | | | | | |
|---|---|---|---|---|---|---|---|---|---|---|---|---|---|---|---|
| | | LO | OE | OM | OP | OpM | Sm | G | LO | OE | OM | OP | OpM | Sm | G |
| S | FHOG | 100 | 96.2 | 84.6 | 63.5 | 88.5 | 98.1 | 88.5 | 89.4 | 89.4 | 23.1 | 6.7 | 87.5 | 100 | 66.0 |
| | PHOW | 99.0 | 96.2 | 100 | 97.1 | 100 | 100 | 98.7 | 98.1 | 92.3 | 52.9 | 26.0 | 89.4 | 99.1 | 76.3 |
| | LBP | 100 | 95.2 | 95.2 | 88.5 | 95.2 | 98.1 | 95.7 | – | – | – | – | – | – | – |
| | 3D-LBP | – | – | – | – | – | – | – | 90.4 | 93.3 | 12.5 | 4.8 | 89.4 | 99.1 | 64.9 |
| D | VGG-F_O | 100 | 98.1 | 95.2 | 96.2 | 100 | 100 | 98.2 | 34.6 | 12.5 | 18.3 | 13.5 | 16.4 | 38.46 | 19.1 |
| | $PT_{CNN}$ | – | – | – | – | – | – | – | 85.6 | 82.7 | 6.7 | 2.9 | 49.0 | 84.6 | 51.9 |
| MM | VGG+PHOW | 100 | 98.1 | 96.2 | 96.2 | 100 | 100 | 98.4 | | | | | | | |
| | PHOW+PHOW | 100 | 99.1 | 100 | 97.1 | 100 | 100 | 99.4 | | | | | | | |

**Table 2.** Performance comparison of shallow (S) and deep (D) features on the RGB, depth and IR modalities of the RealFace dataset.

| | Feat/SS | RGB | | | | | | | | | | |
|---|---|---|---|---|---|---|---|---|---|---|---|---|
| | | NN | NOpM | NS | NG | AOpM | AS | AG | DN | DOpM | DS | DG | G |
| S | FHOG | 54.8 | 39.3 | 26.2 | 66.7 | 96.4 | 42.9 | 90.5 | – | – | – | – | 59.5 |
| | PHOW | 42.9 | 33.3 | 14.3 | 42.9 | 100 | 54.8 | 97.6 | – | – | – | – | 55.1 |
| | LBP | 64.3 | 42.9 | 27.4 | 65.5 | 96.4 | 56.0 | 95.2 | – | – | – | – | 64.0 |
| D | VGG-F_o | 98.8 | 96.4 | 81.0 | 89.3 | 100 | 88.1 | 95.2 | – | – | – | – | 92.7 |

| | Feat/SS | Depth | | | | | | | | | | |
|---|---|---|---|---|---|---|---|---|---|---|---|---|
| | | NN | NOpM | NS | NG | AOpM | AS | AG | DN | DOpM | DS | DG | G |
| S | FHOG | 71.4 | 46.4 | 28.6 | 79.8 | 78.6 | 33.3 | 76.2 | 90.5 | 66.7 | 32.1 | 70.2 | 61.3 |
| | PHOW | 76.2 | 66.7 | 46.4 | 66.7 | 88.1 | 48.8 | 65.5 | 88.1 | 77.4 | 36.9 | 54.8 | 65.0 |
| | 3D-LBP | 54.8 | 47.6 | 26.2 | 66.7 | 76.2 | 21.4 | 61.9 | 83.3 | 60.7 | 16.7 | 57.1 | 52.1 |
| D | VGG-F_o | 17.9 | 13.1 | 6.0 | 15.5 | 11.9 | 9.5 | 14.3 | 19.1 | 9.5 | 9.5 | 15.5 | 12.9 |
| | $PT_{CNN}$ | 48.8 | 44.1 | 15.5 | 66.7 | 72.6 | 16.7 | 56.0 | 58.3 | 51.2 | 13.1 | 53.6 | 45.1 |

| Feat/SS | IR | | | | | | | | | | |
|---|---|---|---|---|---|---|---|---|---|---|---|
| | NN | NOpM | NS | NG | AOpM | AS | AG | DN | DOpM | DS | DG | G |
| FHOG | 88.1 | 75.0 | 45.2 | 89.3 | 94.1 | 53.6 | 89.3 | 95.2 | 79.8 | 44.1 | 82.1 | 76.0 |
| PHOW | 97.6 | 94.1 | 60.7 | 90.5 | 100 | 66.7 | 96.4 | 98.8 | 91.7 | 48.8 | 88.1 | 84.9 |
| LBP | 84.5 | 76.2 | 42.9 | 85.7 | 94.1 | 45.4 | 86.9 | 92.9 | 77.4 | 33.3 | 81.0 | 72.8 |
| VGG-F_o | 100 | 96.4 | 76.2 | 78.6 | 96.4 | 75.0 | 73.8 | 98.8 | 95.2 | 61.9 | 71.4 | 84.0 |

| Feat/SS | Multimodal | | | | | | | | | | |
|---|---|---|---|---|---|---|---|---|---|---|---|
| | NN | NOpM | NS | NG | AOpM | AS | AG | DN | DOpM | DS | DG | G |
| VGG+PHOW+VGG | 100 | 100 | 89.3 | 91.7 | 98.8 | 90.5 | 95.2 | 98.8 | 95.2 | 63.1 | 76.2 | 90.8 |
| VGG+PHOW+PHOW | 98.8 | 96.4 | 81.0 | 89.3 | 100 | 88.1 | 95.2 | 100 | 90.5 | 58.3 | 90.5 | 89.8 |

performance is slightly increased, although not statistically relevant due to the already very high performances obtained by the RGB modality alone.

Table 2 presents the main results obtained for the RealFace dataset. As expected from being a more challenging dataset than EURECOM, the overall performance drop is evident. In RGB images, deep features clearly present a more robust behaviour, when presented to more variable illumination and occlusion conditions. The PHOW shallow descriptor, however, keeps the highest performance for depth images, proving to be an interesting alternative for object description in this type of data. The same observations regarding the VGG-Face and our proposed CNN for depth images can be made for this dataset, with the occlusion scenarios severely compromising global performance. In the IR modality some interesting observations can also be made. First, both PHOW and the deep descriptors from VGG-Face achieve the best overall performances. While the obtained performance is still significantly lower than the observed for RGB images, it is interesting to note how the filters learnt by VGG-Face still carry some of the discriminative power to this new modality. As referred above, for depth images, the visual similarity between RGB and IR images might translate into similar responses to the pre-trained filters, thus justifying the similar observed behaviour. The improvement caused by multimodal fusion in this dataset is more clearly noted than in EURECOM. It should be considered that no darkness conditions were evaluated for the RGB modality alone and, therefore, direct comparison of multimodal performance can only be carried out with the remaining modalities.

## 6    Conclusion and Future Work

The growing interest in 3D information for face recognition, as well as the emergence of new low-cost sensors, such as the Intel RealSense, has motivated the creation of the RealFace dataset, a multimodal set of images acquired under a wide array of non-ideal conditions to be used for performance assessment in a multiplicity of applications. Even though we only assessed its use in biometric recognition, we acknowledge that its usability can extend to fields such as face alignment, gender and age prediction as well as face detection in depth and IR images. The manually annotated keypoints, as well as the defined ROI segmentation methodologies, make the performed experiments easily replicable and confer the presented performance baseline a strong starting point for further research in the community. However, the number of enrolled subjects is still not as high as desirable, and an extended version of the dataset would be an interesting line of research in the future. The inclusion of more intermediate non-frontal poses would further extend the usability of the dataset for alternative applications such as pose quantification.

Regarding the comparative analysis between deep and shallow features we observed that a few challenges are still unsolved. While the publicly available VGG-face network showed excellent performance in the RGB modality for all tested scenarios in both datasets, surpassing all alternative shallow feature alternatives, performance dropped considerably for depth images. The pre-trained CNN that we presented showed increased performance in some scenarios, but still stays below the results obtained with specific tailored features such as PHOW and FHOG. The fact that the amount of data used to train VGG-Face is considerably higher than the amount of depth data used to train our CNN may account for these observations. With the appearance of more datasets based on depth representations of faces, and the consequent growth in the amount of available data, an improved version of the proposed CNN could also be easily obtained, namely by augmenting the training dataset to better deal with the presence of occlusions.

**Acknowledgments.** This work was funded by the Project "NanoSTIMA: Macro-to-Nano Human Sensing: Towards Integrated Multimodal Health Monitoring and Analytics/NORTE–01–0145–FEDER–000016" financed by the North Portugal Regional Operational Programme (NORTE 2020), under the PORTUGAL 2020 Partnership Agreement, and through the European Regional Development Fund (ERDF), and also by Fundação para a Ciência e Tecnologia (FCT) within PhD grant number SFRH/BD/87392/2012.

# References

1. Nech, A., Kemelmacher-Shlizerman, I.: Megaface 2: 672,000 identities for face recognition (2016)
2. Monteiro, J.C., Cardoso, J.S.: A cognitively-motivated framework for partial face recognition in unconstrained scenarios. Sensors **15**, 1903–1924 (2015)
3. Monteiro, J.C., Freitas, T., Cardoso, J.S.: Multimodal hierarchical face recognition using information from 2.5 D images. U. Porto J. Eng. **2**, 39–54 (2016)
4. Taigman, Y., Yang, M., Ranzato, M., Wolf, L.: Deepface: closing the gap to human-level performance in face verification. In: The IEEE Conference on Computer Vision and Pattern Recognition (CVPR) (2014)
5. Krizhevsky, A., Sutskever, I., Hinton, G.E.: ImageNet classification with deep convolutional neural networks. In: Advances in neural information processing systems, pp. 1097–1105 (2012)
6. Schroff, F., Kalenichenko, D., Philbin, J.: FaceNet: a unified embedding for face recognition and clustering. In: Proceedings of the IEEE Conference on Computer Vision and Pattern Recognition, pp. 815–823 (2015)
7. Chen, D., Cao, X., Wen, F., Sun, J.: Blessing of dimensionality: high-dimensional feature and its efficient compression for face verification. In: The IEEE Conference on Computer Vision and Pattern Recognition (CVPR) (2013)
8. Simonyan, K., Parkhi, O.M., Vedaldi, A., Zisserman, A.: Fisher vector faces in the wild. In: British Machine Vision Conference (2013)
9. Parkhi, O.M., Vedaldi, A., Zisserman, A.: Deep face recognition. In: British Machine Vision Conference (2015)
10. Crosswhite, N., Byrne, J., Parkhi, O.M., Stauffer, C., Cao, Q., Zisserman, A.: Template adaptation for face verification and identification. CoRR abs/1603.03958 (2016)
11. El Khiyari, H., Wechsler, H., et al.: Face recognition across time lapse using convolutional neural networks. J. Inf. Secur. **7**, 141 (2016)
12. Min, R., Kose, N., Dugelay, J.L.: KinectFaceDB: a kinect database for face recognition. IEEE Trans. Syst. Man Cybern. Syst. **44**, 1534–1548 (2014)
13. Song, S., Lichtenberg, S.P., Xiao, J.: Sun RGB-D: a RGB-D scene understanding benchmark suite. In: Proceedings of the IEEE Conference on Computer Vision and Pattern Recognition, pp. 567–576 (2015)
14. Huang, Y., Wang, Y., Tan, T.: Combining statistics of geometrical and correlative features for 3d face recognition. In: BMVC, pp. 879–888. Citeseer (2006)
15. Wolf, L., Hassner, T., Taigman, Y.: Descriptor based methods in the wild. In: Workshop on Faces in 'Real-Life' Images: Detection, Alignment, and Recognition (2008)
16. Felzenszwalb, P.F., Girshick, R.B., McAllester, D., Ramanan, D.: Object detection with discriminatively trained part-based models. IEEE Trans. Pattern Anal. Mach. Intell. **32**, 1627–1645 (2010)
17. Bosch, A., Zisserman, A., Munoz, X.: Image classification using random forests and ferns. In: Proceedings of the International Conference on Computer Vision (ICCV) (2007)
18. Parkhi, O.M., Vedaldi, A., Zisserman, A.: Deep face recognition. In: Proceedings of the British Machine Vision, vol. 1, p. 6 (2015)

# ST: Visual Perception and Robotic Systems

# Automated Rebar Detection
# for Ground-Penetrating Radar

Spencer Gibb and Hung Manh La$^{(\boxtimes)}$

University of Nevada, Reno, USA
hla@unr.edu

**Abstract.** Automated rebar detection in images from ground-penetrating radar (GPR) is a challenging problem and difficult to perform in real-time as a result of relatively low contrast images and the size of the images. This paper presents a rebar localization algorithm, which can accurately locate the pixel locations of rebar within a GPR scan image. The proposed algorithm uses image classification and statistical methods to locate hyperbola signatures within the image. The proposed approach takes advantage of adaptive histogram equalization to increase the visual signature of rebar within the image despite low contrast. A Naive Bayes classifier is used to approximately locate rebar within the image with histogram of oriented gradients feature vectors. In addition, a histogram based method is applied to more precisely locate individual rebar in the image, and then the proposed methods are validated using existing GPR data and data collected during the course of the research for this paper.

## 1 Introduction

GPR has been increasingly used in applications for structural surveys since the 1980s [1]. Uses for GPR include bridge integrety inspection [1,2], metro tunnel inspection [3], beam and pillar structural inspection, as well as many others. GPR provides a visual representation of metallic objects underneath concrete surfaces, which are indicated by their hyperbolic signatures in the scan image. Prior to recent research in automated object detection using GPR, object location was done manually or using commercial software [4]. Manually locating objects in a scan can be extremely time consuming considering scans can contain hundreds of rebar depending on the size of the bridge being inspected and commercial software costs thousands of dollars in some cases; when combined with the cost of GPR itself, this can easily prevent users from successfully using the technology.

With the end goal of moving toward a fully automated solution for bridge inspection, the primary concerns with modern methods are detection accuracy and the ability to perform detection in real-time. While research is still continuing in this field, recent methods utilize support vector machines, gradient descent, and various computationally intense methods for detecting rebar [5–9]. The accuracy of some of these methods has been high, but they are typically tested on ideal cases where scan data is not representative of aged structures,

© Springer International Publishing AG 2016
G. Bebis et al. (Eds.): ISVC 2016, Part I, LNCS 10072, pp. 815–824, 2016.
DOI: 10.1007/978-3-319-50835-1_73

or simulated data, and they often have too high of a run time to be performed on site [10–12].

This paper presents a novel method for automated rebar localization that can be performed in real-time, with scans from long bridges being run in a short amount of time. The proposed method in this paper utilizes adaptive histogram equalization to eliminate difficulties caused by low contrast images with regard to the hyperbola signatures being too faint to detect. A Naive Bayes classifier, which has been shown to be sufficient for simple classification tasks [13], is used to approximately locate rebar within the image, and then a simple method developed for this paper is employed, called histogram localization. This method combines histogram maxima detection with a local search for maximum pixel intensity that can more precisely locate the vertex of the hyperbolic signature for each rebar in the image.

The remainder of the paper is organized as follows. Section 2 provides a description of the need for and application of adaptive histogram equalization. Section 3 describes the features used for the image classifier. Section 4 describes the training of the Naive Bayes classifier. Section 5 outlines the central concepts of the Naive Bayes classifier used. Section 6 details the methods used to more precisely localize the rebar within the scan image. Experimental results are provided in Sect. 7. Lastly, a conclusion is provided in Sect. 8.

## 2    Adaptive Histogram Equalization for Contrast Stretching

Due to the typically low-contrast nature of B-scan images obtained via GPR scans, it is necessary to stretch the contrast of these images prior to feature extraction, training, and classification [14]. Contrast stretching helps strengthen the accuracy of the image classifier and makes it easier for humans to verify the work of the classifier, since it is often difficult or impossible to locate objects in low contrast images. Because standard histogram equalization leads to artifacts in the images, contrast stretching is accomplished in this paper through Contrast Limited Adaptive Histogram Equalization (CLAHE) [15]. Peaks in a histogram are typically attributed to uniform regions in an image, and through the equalization process the intensity values within the image that correspond to the peaks are spread out across a wider range of intensity values. Although spreading peaks in this way is the primary use for histogram equalization, as it applies contrast stretching and compression, issues can arise when uniform regions of an image contain noise. The noise in uniform regions is then spread across the image as equalization is applied, which can lead to artifacts as the noise is overamplified throughout the image. The CLAHE algorithm presents a solution to this problem that allows adaptive histogram equalization to be performed without propagating noise across the image.

Given an image $I$, which is $M$ by $N$ pixels, histogram equalization is applied across nonoverlapping regions of the image sized $M/8$ by $N/8$ pixels, in the same manner as adaptive histogram equalization. However, the difference between the

CLAHE method and standard adaptive histogram equalization is that a clip limit is set, which prevents noise being overamplified in homogeneous regions of the image and causing artifacts. The clip limit is used to determine how much of the histogram's peak to remove prior to calculating the cumulative distribution function that is used in that region. The part of the histogram peak that is clipped can be redistributed across the bins of the histogram so that it is still present and does not incorrectly skew the cumulative distribution function of the image. When histogram equalization is applied to a GPR image with low contrast it typically leads to areas of the image being too bright or too dark. On the other hand, when CLAHE is applied, the bright areas and dark areas are less prevalent, which makes it easier to classify regions of the image because the image has more defined features.

## 3 Histogram of Oriented Gradients as Hyperbola Features

Histogram of oriented gradients (HOG) was originally described by Dalal and Triggs in 2005 as a feature descriptor used for object detection [16]. This method uses gradient orientation across an image that is split into uniform cells. HOG features are invariant to geometric transformations and illumination and can be quickly computed. As a result, HOG features have been widely used for object detection in computer vision problems since 2005 [17,18]. The steps for computing HOG features used in this paper are as follows.

Given a grayscale image $I$, the image can be globally normalized to make the feature selection process more invariant to illumination. Then first order gradients of the normalized image must be computed as

$$\nabla I_N = \begin{bmatrix} g_x \\ g_y \end{bmatrix} \tag{1}$$

where $g_x$ and $g_y$ are the normalized image gradients in the $x$ and $y$ direction respectively and $I_N$ is the normalized image. The magnitude of the normalized image is given by

$$magnitude(I_N) = \sqrt{g_x^2 + g_y^2} \tag{2}$$

and the orientation of the normalized image is given by

$$\theta = atan2(g_y, g_x) * (180/\pi) + 90. \tag{3}$$

The image is then segmented into cells. In this paper, it was empirically determined that 5 by 5 pixel cells yielded the best results throughout the training and classification processes. The training and testing image size used in this paper is 50 by 15 pixels, which means that each training and testing image is made up of 30 cells. For each of the cells, a histogram of gradient orientations is accumulated. Finally, to increase the invariance of this method to illumination, block normalization is applied. Blocks consist of several cells; 3 cell by 3 cell blocks were used in this paper. The cells are normalized within respective blocks yielding final image descriptors. The features vectors used in the training and classification methods for this paper contain 240 elements, as each image is 10 by 3 cells and 8 bins were used for the accumulation of histograms of oriented gradients.

## 4    Training

In order to train the Naive Bayes classifier used in this paper, HOG features are extracted from a set of manually selected training images, comprised of two classes: images containing hyperbolas that would indicate the presence of rebar in a GPR scan, and images that do not contain hyperbolas. Each of the selected images is manually assigned a class label for the purpose of training the classifier. The classifier in the next section uses the information from the determined HOG feature vectors for training images as a basis for a priori knowledge about each class. Infoma-

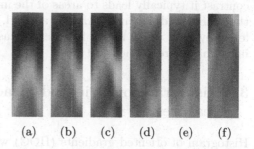

(a)    (b)    (c)    (d)    (e)    (f)

**Fig. 1.** (a)–(c) Positive samples used in the training process that contain clear hyperbolas indicating the presence of rebar; (d)–(f) Negative samples used in the training process that do not contain a hyperbola. Each of these 6 samples is 50 by 15 pixels.

tion on the number of training images and the class they belong to can be seen in Table 1. In addition, examples of training images can be seen in Fig. 1.

**Table 1.** Training data set

| Class | Class name | Number of images |
|-------|------------|------------------|
| 1 | Hyperbolas | 304 |
| 2 | Not Hyperbolas | 1800 |

## 5    Naive Bayes Classification

A Naive Bayes classifier is used in this paper that classifies new GPR images based on their computed HOG feature vectors, as well as the feature vectors from the training images. More advanced methods are not necessary since the classifier is not solely responsible for the location of rebar in a GPR scan. This classifier was chosen for its simplicity and speed.

Given a vector of HOG features $x = (x_1, ..., x_n)$, where $n$ is the number of features in the vector, Bayes' theorem states that the probability of a class given

a sample is the product of the a priori probility for that class and the probability
of the sample given the class. The Bayes model can be written as

$$p(C_k|x) = \frac{1}{Z}p(C_k)\prod_{i=1}^{n}p(x_i|C_k) \tag{4}$$

where $Z$ is a constant scaling factor that depends on the contents of the feature
vector and $C_k$ is class $k$. $Z$ will change depending on the implementation of the
Naive Bayes classifier.

The model from Eq. (4) can be used as a classifier to assign class labels to
test samples as follows

$$\hat{y} = \underset{k\in\{1,...,K\}}{\arg\max}\ p(C_k)\prod_{i=1}^{n}p(x_i|C_k) \tag{5}$$

where $\hat{y}$ is the assigned class label given a sample, which is chosen based on the
maximum probability of a class given the sample. This method, the maximum
a posteriori probability (MAP) estimate, classifies solely based on the posteriori
probability determined by the Naive Bayes classifier for each class.

Prior to using this Naive Bayes classifier, a search area is determined in the
test image. The search area is located based on a primary trait of all GPR scan
images; they all contain a significant dark region in the image where the ground
surface is. No searching should be done higher in the image than the ground
surface. Once the ground surface is located through finding large occurrences of
dark horizontal intensity values, the search window is limited again by performing edge detection on the area of the image below the ground plane. The end
of the search area is given by taking the average $y$ pixel location of each edge
pixel and searching up to that average location. This works because the edge
information shows where the general rebar location is along the $y$ axis.

Searching and classfication is performed on a sliding window starting from
just below the ground plane to the average $y$ location of edges determined previously. The distance of this classification search can be changed in cases where
bridge decks may contain rebar that is sporadically located along the $y$ axis of the
image; however, significantly expanding the search window limits the real-time
capabilities of any method including those outlined in this paper. In addition,
to limit the time it takes to apply the sliding window, odd numbered $y$ coordinates are skipped since they do not affect the accuracy of this method and only
increase its run time. At each sliding window location within the search area, if
the classifier assigns a hyperbola class label to the test image, that point is saved
for further processing to more exactly localize hyperbolas within the image.

In the previous sections, an image is first contrast stretched using adaptive
histogram equalization. Then the search area within the image is determined
using edge detection and the location of the ground plane. Next, training is
performed on previously selected images. Then classification is performed on
a sliding window, using HOG features, accross the search window within the
image.

# 6  Final Localization of Rebar

Given a set of points in the original image, $P_{IN}$, indicating where a hyperbola was detected and classified by the Naive Bayes classifier, it is necessary to more accurately localize the hyperbola. Typical methods for hyperbola localization and fitting include use of the Hough transform or RANSAC [6,7]. However, both of these methods are typically time consuming and therefore not ideal for real-time applications such as that of online automated rebar detection. The methods used in this paper provide a real-time solution, we refer to as histogram localization, that is of linear time-complexity, since it just moves through a list of pixels in each step that only increases in size as the size of the image and number of pixels increases. This method also allows for accurate rebar localization.

The points in the image are used to accumulate a histogram of their $x$ coordinates. From the accumulated histogram, local maxima are preserved while non-maxima are suppressed in order to yield a set of vertical lines indicating the locations of the most positive matches in a local area. In this paper, a 13 pixel wide area was used to choose local maxima, which were allowed during this step since they will be eliminated as they converge to the same point in following steps.

After histogram localization is performed, the pixels on each vertical line are compared against each other to find the location of the maximum intensity value. The pixel with the maximum intensity value is significant because the nature of GPR means that objects in the image with high intensity values are typically metallic and rebar is the object that is being located. Once the highest intensity pixels along each vertical line are located, another search is performed for local maxima within a 5 pixel by 5 pixel region surrounding each of the high intensity pixels.

A final maxima search allows for any location that may be too low on the rebar or that may be off center to be correctly localized, which also accounts for multiple local maxima in the previous step since these maxima typically converge to the same point. For multiple remaining maxima, the maxima closest to the top of the image can be chosen. This should be performed on a small window to ensure that correct positives are not ignored. A summary of the previously described algorithm can be seen in Algorithm 1.

# 7  Experimental Results

The methods proposed in this paper have been validated on scans from three bridges that were collected prior to the research done for this paper and provided by Geophysical Survey Systems, Inc., as well as scans from a bridge that were collected during the course of this research. All processing was done on a 5-year-old system running an i5 2500k processor. Rebar detection results can be seen in Table 2. Included in the results is the average run time for images of each bridge, accuracy, precision, and the number of rebar that were present in the GPR images of each bridge, as well as the location of each bridge. Examples of rebar localization (red squares) can be seen in Fig. 2.

---

**Algorithm 1.** PRECISE HYPERBOLA LOCALIZATION

---

**Input:** $P_{IN} = \{P_1, P_2, ..., P_n\} | P_n = (x_n, y_n)$
$s$ = starting search location
$e$ = ending search location
**Output:** $P_{OUT} = \{P_1, P_2, ..., P_3\}$

1  $x\_histogram[Image\ width]$ **for** $x \leftarrow P_{IN}[0][0]$ **to** $P_{IN}[n][0]$ **do**
2     $x\_histogram[x] \mathrel{+}= 1$

3  **for** $i \leftarrow 0$ **to** $x\_histogram\ length$ **do**
4     **if** $x\_histogram[i] > 0$ **then**
5          $maxima \leftarrow true$
6          $Maxima\_list \leftarrow [\ ]$
7          **for** $j \leftarrow i - 7$ **to** $i + 6$ **do**
8               **if** $j > -1$ *and* $j < x\_histogramlength$ **then**
9                    **if** $x\_histogram[j] > x\_histogram[i]$ **then**
10                       $maxima \leftarrow false$

11          **if** $maxima == true$ **then**
12              append $maxima$ to $Maxima\_list$

13  $x\_coords \leftarrow [\ ]$
14  $y\_coords \leftarrow [\ ]$
15  **for** $i \leftarrow 0$ **to** $Maxima\_list\ length$ **do**
16     $x \leftarrow -1$
17     $y \leftarrow -1$
18     **for** $j \leftarrow search\_start$ **to** $search\_end$ **do**
19          **if** $Image[j, Maxima\_list[i]] > x$ **then**
20               $x \leftarrow Image[j, Maxima\_list[i]]$
21               $y \leftarrow j$

22     append $x$ to $x\_coords$
23     append $y$ to $y\_coords$

24  $P_{OUT} \leftarrow [\ ]$
25  **for** $i \leftarrow 0$ **to** $x\_coords\ length$ **do**
26     $x \leftarrow x\_coords[i]$
27     $y \leftarrow y\_coords[i]$
28     $intensity \leftarrow Image[x, y]$
29     $final\_x \leftarrow -1$
30     $final\_y \leftarrow -1$
31     **for** $j \leftarrow y - 3$ **to** $y + 2$ **do**
32          **for** $k \leftarrow x - 3$ **to** $x + 2$ **do**
33               **if** $Image[j, k] > intensity$ **then**
34                    $intensity \leftarrow Image[j, k]$
35                    $final\_x \leftarrow k$
36                    $final\_y \leftarrow j$

37     append $(final\_x, final\_y)$ to $P_{OUT}$

---

**Table 2.** Automated rebar detection results.

| Bridge name | Location | Number of GPR images | Total rebar in images | Accuracy | Precision | Run time/image |
|---|---|---|---|---|---|---|
| East Helena Bridge | Helena, MT | 14 | 1055 | 99.15% | 98.22% | 32.40 s |
| Kendall Pond Road Bridge | Derry, NH | 12 | 2284 | 91.46% | 97.79% | 32.91 s |
| Ramp D | Lewiston, ME | 14 | 3699 | 92.89% | 93.787% | 55.46 s |
| Pleasant Valley Bridge | Reno, NV | 20 | 13206 | 96.67% | 99.59% | 118.32 s |

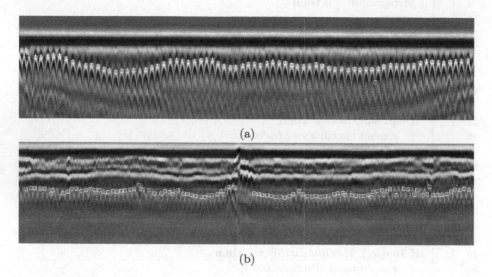

(a)

(b)

**Fig. 2.** Rebar localization results (red squares): (a) GPR image from East Helena Bridge, Helena, MT; (b) GPR image from Kendall Pond Road Bridge, Derry, NH. (Color figure online)

The results show that this method performs well on the data from the four bridges used in this paper. The accuracy of the proposed method decreases slightly in cases where adaptive histogram equalization did not affect how clear the hyperbolas are. This is the case with the photos of the Kendall Pond Road Bridge in New Hampshire, which had feint hyperbola. In addition, the classifier performs better in cases where hyperbola are clearly visually separable, as opposed to in cases where they are cluttered and appear to overlap. In cases of overlap, some rebar will not be detected. Overall, the precision of the proposed method remains high, indicating that rebar are not found in areas where none exist.

Finally, with respect to run time of the proposed method, it performs well in all cases. Increased run time is proportional to the length of the bridge. A longer bridge usually contains more rebar and therefore requires more processing.

However, all of the run times listed in this paper are short enough that they can be run as part of a fully autonomous robotic system, in real-time [19,20].

## 8  Conclusion and Future Work

This paper proposed a real-time automated rebar detection method, which combines adaptive histogram equalization, HOG features, and a Naive Bayes classifier. The proposed method works in real-time to accurately detect rebar in GPR scan images. Moreover, it has been validated through tests run on four sets of real bridge data. Future work in this area of research will include the use of this software in a fully autonomous robotic bridge inspection system. In addition, increased invariance to varying bridge conditions and further real-time capability will be researched. Fusion of GPR data with other nondestructive evaluation (NDE) sensors will be also studied for enhancing the condition assessment of the bridge deck [21,22].

**Acknowledgment.** The authors would like to thank the University of Nevada, Reno and the National Science Foundation (NSF) for their financial support to conduct this research: NSF support under grant: NSF-IIP # 1639092.

## References

1. Simi, A., Manacorda, G., Benedetto, A.: Bridge deck survey with high resolution ground penetrating radar. In: 2012 14th International Conference on Ground Penetrating Radar (GPR), pp. 489–495 (2012)
2. Krause, V., Abdel-Qader, I., Abudayyeh, O.: Detection and classification of small perturbations in GPR scans of reinforced concrete bridge decks. In: 2012 IEEE International Conference on Electro/Information Technology (EIT), pp. 1–4 (2012)
3. Hai-zhong, Y., Yu-feng, O., Hong, C.: Application of ground penetrating radar to inspect the metro tunnel. In: 2012 14th International Conference on Ground Penetrating Radar (GPR), pp. 759–763 (2012)
4. Marecos, V., Fontul, S., Antunes, M.L., Solla, M.: Assessment of a concrete prestressed runway pavement with ground penetrating radar. In: 2015 8th International Workshop on Advanced Ground Penetrating Radar (IWAGPR), pp. 1–4 (2015)
5. Shaw, M., Millard, S., Molyneaux, T., Taylor, M., Bungey, J.: Location of steel reinforcement in concrete using ground penetrating radar and neural networks. NDT E Int. **38**, 203–212 (2005). Structural Faults and Repair
6. Kaur, P., Dana, K.J., Romero, F.A., Gucunski, N.: Automated GPR rebar analysis for robotic bridge deck evaluation. IEEE Trans. Cybern. **46**, 2265–2276 (2016)
7. Al-Nuaimy, W., Huang, Y., Nakhkash, M., Fang, M., Nguyen, V., Eriksen, A.: Automatic detection of buried utilities and solid objects with GPR using neural networks and pattern recognition. J. Appl. Geophys. **43**, 157–165 (2000)
8. La, H.M., Lim, R.S., Basily, B.B., Gucunski, N., Yi, J., Maher, A., Romero, F.A., Parvardeh, H.: Mechatronic systems design for an autonomous robotic system for high-efficiency bridge deck inspection and evaluation. IEEE/ASME Trans. Mechatron. **18**, 1655–1664 (2013)

9. La, H.M., Gucunski, N., Kee, S.H., Yi, J., Senlet, T., Nguyen, L.: Autonomous robotic system for bridge deck data collection and analysis. In: 2014 IEEE/RSJ International Conference on Intelligent Robots and Systems, pp. 1950–1955 (2014)
10. Xianqi-He, Z.-Z., Guangyin-Lu, Q.-L.: Bridge management with GPR. In: 2009 International Conference on Information Management, Innovation Management and Industrial Engineering, vol. 3, pp. 325–328 (2009)
11. Pasolli, E., Melgani, F., Donelli, M.: Automatic analysis of GPR images: a pattern-recognition approach. IEEE Trans. Geosci. Remote Sens. **47**, 2206–2217 (2009)
12. Zhao, Y., Chen, J., Ge, S.: Maxwell curl equation datuming for GPR test of tunnel grouting based on kirchhoff integral solution. In: 2011 6th International Workshop on Advanced Ground Penetrating Radar (IWAGPR), pp. 1–6 (2011)
13. Shi, H., Liu, Y.: Naïve Bayes vs. support vector machine: resilience to missing data. In: Deng, H., Miao, D., Lei, J., Wang, F.L. (eds.) AICI 2011. LNCS (LNAI), vol. 7003, pp. 680–687. Springer, Heidelberg (2011). doi:10.1007/978-3-642-23887-1_86
14. Wang, Z.W., Zhou, M., Slabaugh, G.G., Zhai, J., Fang, T.: Automatic detection of bridge deck condition from ground penetrating radar images. IEEE Trans. Autom. Sci. Eng. **8**, 633–640 (2011)
15. Pizer, S.M., Amburn, E.P., Austin, J.D., Cromartie, R., Geselowitz, A., Greer, T., Romeny, B.T.H., Zimmerman, J.B.: Adaptive histogram equalization and its variations. Comput. Vis. Graph. Image Process. **39**, 355–368 (1987)
16. Dalal, N., Triggs, B.: Histograms of oriented gradients for human detection. In: 2005 IEEE Computer Society Conference on Computer Vision and Pattern Recognition (CVPR 2005), vol. 1, pp. 886–893 (2005)
17. Pang, Y., Zhang, K., Yuan, Y., Wang, K.: Distributed object detection with linear SVMs. IEEE Trans. Cybern. **44**, 2122–2133 (2014)
18. Nigam, S., Khare, M., Srivastava, R.K., Khare, A.: An effective local feature descriptor for object detection in real scenes. In: 2013 IEEE Conference on Information Communication Technologies (ICT), pp. 244–248 (2013)
19. Lim, R.S., La, H.M., Shan, Z., Sheng, W.: Developing a crack inspection robot for bridge maintenance. In: 2011 IEEE International Conference on Robotics and Automation (ICRA), pp. 6288–6293 (2011)
20. Lim, R.S., La, H.M., Sheng, W.: A robotic crack inspection and mapping system for bridge deck maintenance. IEEE Trans. Autom. Sci. Eng. **11**, 367–378 (2014)
21. La, H.M., Gucunski, N., Kee, S.H., Nguyen, L.V.: Data analysis and visualization for the bridge deck inspection and evaluation robotic system. Visual. Eng. **3**, 6 (2015)
22. La, H.M., Gucunski, N., Lee, S.H., Nguyen, L.V.: Visual and acoustic data analysis for the bridge deck inspection robotic system. In: The 31st International Symposium on Automation and Robotics in Construction and Mining (ISARC), pp. 50–57 (2014)

# Improving Visual Feature Representations by Biasing Restricted Boltzmann Machines with Gaussian Filters

Arjun Yogeswaran[✉] and Pierre Payeur

School of Electrical Engineering and Computer Science,
University of Ottawa, Ottawa, Canada
{ayoge099,ppayeur}@uottawa.ca

**Abstract.** Advances in unsupervised learning have allowed the efficient learning of feature representations from large sets of unlabeled data. This paper evaluates visual features learned through unsupervised learning, specifically comparing biasing methods using Gaussian filters on a single-layer network. Using the restricted Boltzmann machine, features emerging through training on image data are compared by classification performance on standard datasets. When Gaussian filters are convolved with adjacent hidden layer activations from a single example during training, topographies emerge where adjacent features become tuned to slightly varying stimuli. When Gaussian filters are applied to the visible nodes, images become blurrier; training on these images leads to less localized features being learned. The networks are trained and tested on the CIFAR-10, STL-10, COIL-100, and MNIST datasets. It is found that the induction of topography or simple image blurring during training produce better features as evidenced by the consistent and notable increase in classification results.

## 1 Introduction

Feature representations learned directly from unlabeled data have proven to be more effective than handcrafted features in modern visual object classification applications. Recent advances in unsupervised learning mechanisms have fueled this increased performance. An effective way to assess these methods and their properties is to test them on single-layer networks, as opposed to the commonly-used multi-layered networks used for image classification, such that the influence of network architecture is minimized and the actual performance of the learning mechanism can more easily be isolated and compared. Coates *et al.* [1] structured their comparison similarly by comparing single-layer networks and their classification performance on standard image classification datasets under a variety of parameters. That study outlined the efficacy of several single-layer techniques at learning discriminative features from raw pixel data. Modeled after that study, our current research aims to compare biasing techniques on a single layer network in order to boost image classification performance through generating better features. The properties of these features, which are more

© Springer International Publishing AG 2016
G. Bebis et al. (Eds.): ISVC 2016, Part I, LNCS 10072, pp. 825–835, 2016.
DOI: 10.1007/978-3-319-50835-1_74

difficult to interpret at higher levels in a multi-layer network, may lead to further understanding of their role in object recognition.

In unsupervised learning, Gaussian filters have been considered for inducing topography into feature representations, falling under the idea of incorporating information from neighboring regions [2]. In this work, the same application of Gaussian filters will be performed to create a topography in the network during training. Topography can provide insight into what learned features are similar or are most likely to co-occur. It also allows the grouping of those features through pooling to produce more invariant responses, thus behaving as an improved feature representation. This work will show that, even without pooling, learning features in a topography produces better results on its own than when topography is not used. Topographic independent component analysis (TICA) [3] learns features from unlabeled data and creates topography in those learned features. Kavukcuoglu et al. [4] learn invariant features across a topographic map through a technique called predictive sparse decomposition (PSD). These features are learned directly from the data and show better performances when compared to handcrafted features for object classification tasks. The topography also improves the invariance of features compared to regular PSD, with the results showing that they also form a better feature representation. Goh et al. [2] introduce 2D topography into a restricted Boltzmann machine (RBM) which learns invariant color features that vary smoothly over the hidden layer.

Downsampling has been used to provide incremental invariance to transformations and dimensionality reduction in the convolutional neural network via pooling [5] or skipping samples [6], thus increasing the discriminative capabilities of the learned features. In a sense, convolution with a low-pass filter produces the same invariance without the dimensionality reduction. That principle is used in this work, where blurring can aid in learning better features, and the Gaussian filter is used here for that purpose.

Gaussian filters provide the link between the two above-mentioned procedures, falling under the idea of combining information from neighboring regions. It is expected that sharing information between neighbors will benefit the learning of good features. Le et al. created a deep network that leveraged neighborhoods of features found using TICA en route to state-of-the-art results on a variety of object recognition benchmarks [7]. Sermanet et al. learns visual features directly from the data using sparse coding to build a deep network which achieved state-of-the-art results on a variety of pedestrian detection datasets [8]. These results show that better classification results can be achieved when learning features directly from large amounts of image data and provides suitable motivation to explore different methods of biasing unsupervised learning networks to improve feature representations.

This work characterizes the effectiveness of biasing methodologies, specifically based around the Gaussian filter, at learning discriminative features by classification performance on standard datasets. The testing datasets will be the CIFAR-10 [9], STL-10 [1], and COIL-100 [10] image classification datasets. To reduce variability when comparing techniques, an RBM [11] with fixed hyperparameters is used as a singular architecture on which they are tested.

# 2 Background

## 2.1 Restricted Boltzmann Machine

The RBM [11] is an undirected bipartite network which uses its hidden layer to represent input data from the visible layer. It is an energy-based model, and calculates the energy of the joint configuration of visible nodes and hidden nodes by (1).

$$E(v, h) = -a'v - b'h - h'Wv. \tag{1}$$

where v and h are the visible and hidden node states, respectively, a and b are the visible and hidden biases, respectively, and W are the symmetric weights connecting the hidden and visible nodes.

Equation (2) determines the probability that a binary hidden node is on, given the visible vector. To deal with image data, the visible vector is modeled using linear nodes. Equation (3) determines the visible node given the hidden vector.

$$P(h_j = 1|v) = sigmoid(b_j + \sum_i w_{ij}v_i). \tag{2}$$

$$P(v_i = v|h) = \mathcal{N}(v|a_i + \sum_j w_{ij}h_j, 1). \tag{3}$$

where $h_j$ is the $j^{th}$ hidden node, v is the visible node vector, $b_j$ is the bias of the $j^{th}$ hidden node, $a_i$ is the bias of the $i^{th}$ visible node, $w_{ij}$ is the weight connecting the $i^{th}$ visible node, $v_i$, and $h_j$, $N(\mu, \sigma^2)$ is a probability density of Gaussian distribution with mean $\mu$ and standard deviation $\sigma$. Since the image data is normalized, unit variance is used.

Training is accomplished using contrastive divergence (CD), and involves lowering the energy for preferred configurations of hidden and visible nodes, and raising the energy for undesirable configurations [11]. The training alternates between the positive phase and negative phase, where the positive phase samples the hidden state, $h^+$, and the visible state, $v^+$, from the data while the negative phase produces the reconstructions of the hidden state, $h^-$, and the visible state, $v^-$. The weight update is defined as:

$$\Delta w_{ij} = \gamma[<v_i^+ h_j^+> - <v_i^- h_j^->]. \tag{4}$$

where $\gamma$ is the learning rate, and $< . >$ is the average over a number of samples.

Sparsity has been shown to increase discriminative power and optimize RBM representation of data by forcing only a subset of nodes to represent presented data. Lee et al. [12] specify a sparsity target and add a regularization term to encourage activation with the target frequency by increasing or decreasing the bias.

## 2.2 Gaussian Filters

The purposes of the Gaussian filter in this work are conceptually varied, despite obvious similarities. In the case of the topographic RBM, the Gaussian filter incorporates information from local hidden nodes to induce a dependence thus influencing nodes to develop properties similar to its neighbors. For the purpose of image blurring, the Gaussian filter serves to soften edges such that the network learns blurrier features and perhaps helps remove noise. The effect of the sigma value, which represents the standard deviation of the Gaussian function, will also be evaluated. These filters are normalized to have a gain of 1.

# 3 Methodologies

The idea of this work is to compare the application of Gaussian filters to induce different effects during unsupervised learning of visual features in an RBM. The compared biasing methods will be: regular RBM, topography, and input blurring.

When training in a batch, the weighted sums in (2) and (3) are performed by matrix multiplication. The visible input matrix contains all of the training data to be used in the current batch, where each row represents a training pattern, or image patch in this work, and each column represents a visible node. The weight matrix contains the weights connecting each visible node to each hidden node. The hidden activation matrix is calculated by multiplying the visible matrix and the weight matrix, resulting in a matrix of activations with each row representing a pattern and each column representing a hidden node. Figure 1 shows how a Gaussian filter is applied in the hidden activation matrix and visible inputs matrix for each method.

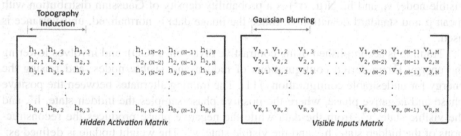

**Fig. 1.** Application of convolution, where h are hidden node activations, v are visible inputs, M is the # of visible nodes, N is the # of hidden nodes, and R is # of patterns. Gaussian filters for topography induction are applied to the hidden activation matrix (left), while the input blurring filter is applied to the visible inputs matrix (right)

## 3.1 Regular RBM

An RBM with regularization only to induce sparsity [12] is used as a control and will be compared as a baseline. This will be referred to as the regular RBM.

## 3.2    Topography

Topography is induced in the RBM by biasing the network during training. By ordering the nodes for a 1D topography, or arranging the hidden nodes in a grid for a 2D or 3D topography, neighboring nodes can be determined. Applying a Gaussian filter to hidden node activations at each example, each node incorporates information about its neighboring nodes. Applied during learning, adjacent nodes develop slightly different features that gradually vary across the grid.

Assuming batch training, a Gaussian filter is applied among adjacent hidden nodes exposed to the same pattern in the activation matrix. The positive phase activations of the hidden nodes are modified by (5) as found in [2].

$$\hat{h}_j^{(k)} = \sum_n^N h_n^{(k)+} \omega(j, n).$$ (5)

where $\hat{h}_j^{(k)}$ is the topography-induced positive activation of hidden node j at pattern k, $h_n^{(k)+}$ is the positive phase hidden activation of hidden node n at pattern k, and the neighborhood function, $\omega$, is a set of fixed neighborhood weights which controls the impact of the surroundings on each activation. $\omega$ is set to a Gaussian function. $1 \times 3$, $3 \times 3$, and $3 \times 3 \times 3$ kernels are used for the 1D, 2D, and 3D topographies, respectively.

## 3.3    Input Blurred

For input blurring, image patches are blurred using a Gaussian filter with kernel width 3 and varying sigmas, using (6), before being passed to the RBM.

$$v_i^{(k)} = \sum_{m=1}^M v_m^{(k)} \omega(i, m).$$ (6)

where $v_i^{(k)}$ is the visible node i at pattern k being blurred, $v_m^{(k)}$ is a neighboring visible node m at pattern k, and the neighborhood function, $\omega$, is the Gaussian filter.

# 4    Experimental Work

## 4.1    Preprocessing

In both training and testing, all patches are contrast normalized and whitened, as these are common techniques to reduce redundant information [1].

## 4.2    Training

CIFAR-10 is composed of real-world $32 \times 32$ colour images containing objects belonging to 10 different classes, with a total of 50,000 training images and 10,000 testing images. STL-10 is similar to CIFAR-10 with 10 classes, but contains $96 \times 96$

colour images. It contains 500 training images and 800 test images per class, plus 100,000 unlabeled images for unsupervised learning. COIL-100 contains images of 100 objects on a black background rotated 360° about the vertical axis at 5° increments, resulting in 72 images per object. Samples of CIFAR-10 and COIL-100 are shown in Fig. 2.

(a)                                          (b)

**Fig. 2.** (a) Some examples of images found in CIFAR-10, with labels of horse and boat. (b) Example object from different angles in the COIL-100 dataset

Primarily, the network is trained on random patches from the CIFAR-10 dataset. 50,000 random 8 × 8 color patches, divided into batches of 100, were used as training data. The networks were trained for 100 epochs. This dataset contains enough variation to learn a variety of features from real-world images. As an additional experiment, the network is also trained on random patches from STL-10 as well as random patches from COIL-100 to see if the same effects persisted across training datasets. Finally, the networks are also trained on the MNIST handwritten dataset [13], with the full pattern instead of patches, to determine if these techniques work in a different domain.

### 4.3    Testing

As a measure of how effective the techniques are, the networks are tested on three datasets: CIFAR-10 [9], STL-10 [1], and COIL-100 [10]. The networks are used to extract features via a rudimentary convolution procedure, and a linear classifier is trained on the resulting outputs.

The convolution procedure follows the one outlined in [1]. The training example is transformed into a set of subpatches, each of which are passed through the RBM to generate a set of feature vectors representing the entire image. Experiments in this work use a stride of 1, which means no patches are skipped over and an image of n-by-n pixels, and an input-patch size of w-by-w, produces an (n-w+1)-by-(n-w+1) representation with K features. $y_{ij}$ denotes the K-dimensional representation extracted at position (i, j). A simple pooling mechanism is implemented by dividing the image into 4 quadrants, and the feature vector is reduced from a (n-w+1)-by-(n-w+1)-by-K representation to a 2-by-2-by-K representation by summing the $y_{ij}$'s in each quadrant. A standard linear classifier is used for classification with the summed feature vectors and the associated label.

Classification accuracy is reported according to the standard testing procedure for each dataset. For CIFAR-10, the features extracted from the training set are used to train the final classifier; the reported classification accuracy is on the test set. STL-10 is divided in to 10 folds, where features extracted from a subset of examples are used for training and testing in each fold. The reported accuracy is the average test accuracy across the folds. With COIL-100, the testing procedure follows that of Mobahi *et al.* [14]. Features extracted from each object at 0, 90, 180, and 270° are used for training. The testing is conducted on all other angles. With MNIST, convolution is not used since the networks are trained on the full image.

# 5  Results and Analysis

Experiments were carried out with RBMs using the methodologies detailed earlier: Regular, 1D, 2D, and 3D topographies, and input blurred. All networks are regularized with the a sparsity of 0.01, weight decay of 0.002, and no momentum term. CIFAR-10 is used for training unless otherwise stated. An $8 \times 8$ color receptive field size was used in all tests, except with MNIST where the full grayscale image is used. Any other parameters specific to each method are outlined in the results.

In the 3D topography, to keep the same number of nodes in each dimension, a different number of total nodes than the 1D and 2D topography was chosen for comparison. The largest cube number that is smaller than the comparison number is chosen as the number of hidden nodes for the 3D topography. This amounts to 216, 343, 512, 729, 1000, and 1331 nodes for the 3D topography corresponding to 225, 400, 625, 900, 1225, and 1600 nodes for the other topographies, respectively.

Figure 3 shows the results of training a RBM after inducing a 2D topography, where each element in the $20 \times 20$ grid is a visualization of the feature that each hidden node learns. For example, a vertical feature node responds best to vertical edges, a colored feature node responds best to the displayed color, and a patterned feature node responds best to the displayed pattern. Examples of features learned by the regular and input blurred RBMs, are also shown in Fig. 3.

The regular RBM contains many localized features resembling Gabor filters, acting as very small edge detectors. The 2D topography contains smooth variations among neighboring nodes in both axes, and is made up of similar edge detectors yet they are much larger in size. The features learned by the RBM with input blurring shows more high frequency features with less localization. The topographical RBM also has more high frequency features with less localization, but they look less clean and isolated; while less pleasant to look at, it indicates a more diverse and complex set of correlations.

Primarily, the sigma parameter in the Gaussian filter will determine the impact of the biasing. The classification accuracies on CIFAR-10 of each of the techniques with varying sigma values is shown in Fig. 4 for 225 nodes and 900 nodes. The graphs show that all of the techniques outperform the regular RBM by a significant margin at peak performance. The stronger biasing of the 3D topography provides too much of a constraint among the nodes, causing them to develop poorer features and decrease performance as sigma increases. Otherwise, a larger sigma generally increases

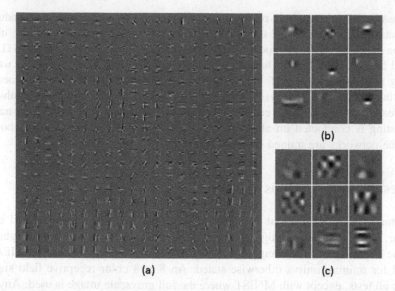

(a)    (b)    (c)

**Fig. 3.** (a) 20 × 20 grid of features produced by 2D Topography in an RBM. (b) Examples of features learned by the regular RBM. (c) Examples of features learned by the input blurred RBM (Color figure online)

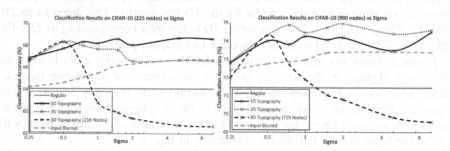

**Fig. 4.** Classification accuracy on the CIFAR-10 test set vs. Sigma for each technique at 225 hidden nodes (left) and 900 hidden nodes (right)

performance. Aside from the 3D topography, the methods are relatively robust to the sigma parameter choice, and a poor choice is still likely to produce better results than the regular RBM.

The methods and their classification accuracies on CIFAR-10 relative to the number of hidden nodes in the network are shown in Fig. 5. Within each method, the sigma with the best accuracy at 900 nodes is the representative. As expected, an increase in hidden nodes produces an increase in the quality of the feature representation thus increasing the classification accuracy. Here, the input blurring and the topographical methods show a constant improvement over the regular RBM.

The simple blurring of training images produces a surprising increase in classification accuracy, producing over a 2% increase at 225 nodes and 900 nodes. The

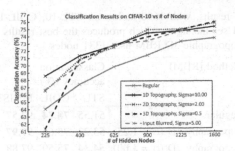

**Fig. 5.** Best parameters for each method comparing the classification accuracy on the CIFAR-10 test set vs. the number of hidden nodes

biasing to induce topography also produces better classification results than without biasing. At 225 nodes, the 1D topography's performance exceeds the regular RBM's by over 4%. At 900 nodes, the 2D topography's performance exceeds the regular RBM's by over 3%.

Training on CIFAR-10 produces image features which translate well to other visual datasets, including STL-10 and COIL-100. The classification accuracies of each method tested on various datasets, when trained on CIFAR-10 at 1600 nodes, is shown in Table 1. The sigma with the best classification accuracy on CIFAR at 1600 nodes is used, determined by evaluations between 0.0 and 2.0.

**Table 1.** Classification results, with 1600 nodes, on CIFAR-10, STL-10, and COIL-100, when trained on CIFAR-10. Uses the sigma which produces the best results on CIFAR-10 for each method. Note that the topographic 3D RBM uses 1331 nodes

| Method (RBM) | Classification accuracy (%) | | |
|---|---|---|---|
| | CIFAR | STL | COIL |
| Regular | 73.82 | 51.49 | 84.24 |
| Topography 1D ($\sigma = 1.25$) | 75.41 | 52.21 | 85.69 |
| Topography 2D ($\sigma = 1.00$) | **76.24** | 54.06 | 86.28 |
| Topography 3D ($\sigma = 0.75$) | 75.65 | **54.76** | 84.28 |
| Input Blurring ($\sigma = 1.50$) | 74.76 | 52.10 | **86.82** |

Again, each of the techniques produces a notable increase in performance over the regular RBM across all datasets; some greater than others depending on the dataset. With such a large amount of features, representational power tends to saturate and classification accuracy plateaus. Therefore, it is interesting that the techniques still produce a fixed increase in classification performance despite hidden layer size.

To evaluate representation learning on different data, Table 2 shows the results of training and testing on the same dataset for STL-10, COIL-100, and MNIST.

It can be seen that the techniques, trained on STL-10, produce similar increases relative to the regular RBM as when they are trained on CIFAR-10. STL-10 contains

**Table 2.** Classification results, with 1600 nodes, on STL-10, COIL-100, and MNIST when trained on themselves. Uses the sigma which produces the best results on CIFAR-10 for each method. Note that the topographic 3D RBM uses 1331 nodes

| Method (RBM) | Classification accuracy (%) | | |
|---|---|---|---|
| | STL | COIL | MNIST |
| Regular | 51.55 | **78.74** | 97.57 |
| Topography 1D ($\sigma$ = 1.25) | 53.22 | 75.66 | **97.97** |
| Topography 2D ($\sigma$ = 1.00) | **54.34** | 75.59 | 97.88 |
| Topography 3D ($\sigma$ = 0.75) | 54.31 | 76.06 | 97.80 |
| Input Blurring ($\sigma$ = 1.50) | 52.28 | 78.69 | 97.38 |

very similar images to CIFAR-10, including a lot of background imagery. These training samples are taken from real images, as a result, they produce similar performance. But training on a simpler dataset, such as COIL-100, produces worse results. This is likely due to the large amount of uninformative patches, since there is a lot of black space in COIL-100 due to a lack of background. These techniques actually degrade performance from the regular RBM if the dataset contains enough uninformative patches. Given the improved results on MNIST, a dataset where a 0.2% increase in accuracy is considered statistically significant [15], it is visible that the topography techniques also translate to another domain.

In general, the topographic methods perform best, and classification accuracy is boosted even without pooling, as the features themselves benefit from the shared information within the neighborhood during training. At peak sigmas, the 1D topography produces similar results to the 2D and 3D topographies. However, it is computationally simpler, since its $1 \times 3$ kernel only requires 2 neighbors. Thus, sharing a small amount of information between nodes produces a large improvement in features, and this improvement does not correlate with the number of neighbors, given that the results of the 3D topography are not much better than the others. For these reasons, the 1D topography is a better solution than the other topographic methods when training time is important. Otherwise, they are comparable in terms of accuracy.

# 6    Conclusion

This paper performed a comparison between biasing effects of Gaussian filters in the training of RBMs to evaluate their relative performance when it comes to learning good visual feature representations. The quantitative comparison was based on classification results on several image classification datasets.

Primarily, biasing to induce topography quite obviously produces better classification results than without biasing. The 1D topography provides the best balance between computational simplicity and effectiveness. The simple blurring of training images also produces a notable increase in classification accuracy.

The comparison between classification results produces tangible evidence that, despite differences in the approach, improved features can be achieved by biasing the network appropriately. The same biasing can likely be applied to improve image classification results on larger scale multi-layer networks. Overall, this work shows that the simple sharing of information between neighboring nodes, both input and hidden, during training allows the networks to consistently develop better visual feature representations.

# References

1. Coates, A., Lee, H., Ng, A.: An analysis of single-layer networks in unsupervised feature learning. In: Proceedings of International Conference on Artificial Intelligence and Statistics, pp. 215–223 (2011)
2. Goh, H., Kusmierz, L., Lim, J.-H., Thome, N., Cord, M.: Learning invariant color features with sparse topographic restricted Boltzmann machines. In: Proceedings of IEEE Conference on Image Processing, pp. 1241–1244 (2011)
3. Hyvärinen, A., Hoyer, P., Inki, M.: Topographic independent component analysis. Neural Comput. 13, 1527–1558 (2001)
4. Kavukcuoglu, K., Ranzato, M., Fergus, R., LeCun, Y.: Learning invariant features through topographic filter maps. In: Proceedings of IEEE Conference on Computer Vision and Pattern Recognition, pp. 1605–1612 (2009)
5. He, K., Zhang, X., Ren, S., Sun, J.: Spatial pyramid pooling in deep convolutional networks for visual recognition. IEEE Trans. Pattern Anal. Mach. Intell. 37, 1904–1916 (2015)
6. Simard, P., Steinkraus, D., Platt, J.: Best practices for convolutional neural networks applied to visual document analysis. In: Proceedings of International Conference on Document Analysis and Recognition, pp. 958–962 (2003)
7. Le, Q., Ranzato, M., Monga, R., Devin, M., Chen, K., Corrado, G., Dean, J., Ng, A.: Building high-level features with large scale unsupervised learning. In: Proceedings of International Conference on Machine Learning, pp. 81–88 (2012)
8. Sermanet, P., Kavukcuoglu, K., Chintala, S., LeCun, Y.: Pedestrian detection with unsupervised multi-stage feature learning. In: Proceedings of IEEE Conference on Computer Vision and Pattern Recognition, pp. 3626–3633 (2013)
9. Krizhevsky, A.: Learning multiple layers of features from tiny images. Technical report, University of Toronto (2009)
10. Nayar, S., Nene, S.A., Murase, H.: Real-time 100 object recognition system. IEEE Trans. Pattern Anal. Mach. Intell. 18, 1186–1198 (1996)
11. Hinton, G., Salakhutdinov, R.: Reducing the dimensionality of data with neural networks. Science 313, 504–507 (2006)
12. Lee, H., Ekanadham, C., Ng, A.: Sparse deep belief net model for visual area V2. In: Proceedings of Advances in Neural Information Processing Systems, pp. 873–880 (2008)
13. LeCun, Y., Bottou, L., Bengio, Y., Haffner, P.: Gradient-based learning applied to document recognition. Proc. IEEE 86, 2278–2324 (1998)
14. Mobahi, H., Collobert, R., Weston, J.: Deep learning from temporal coherence in video. In: Proceedings of International Conference on Machine Learning, pp. 737–744 (2009)
15. Larochelle, H., Bengio, S.: Classification using discriminative restricted Boltzmann machines. In: Proceedings of International Conference on Machine Learning, pp. 536–543 (2008)

# Image Fusion Quality Measure Based on a Multi-scale Approach

Jorge Martinez[1]([✉]), Silvina Pistonesi[1], María Cristina Maciel[1],
and Ana Georgina Flesia[2]

[1] Departamento de Matemática, UNS, Bahía Blanca, Argentina
martinez@uns.edu.ar, {lpistone,immaciel}@criba.edu.ar
[2] FaMAF-UNC and CIEM-CONICET, Córdoba, Argentina
flesia@famaf.unc.edu.ar

**Abstract.** In this paper, we present a general purpose and non-reference multi-scale structural similarity measure for objective quality assessment of image fusion. We aim to extend Piella's measure [1] in several ways, within a multi-scale approach, by making multiple Piella's measure image evaluations at different image scales, fusing the result into a single evaluation. The main advantage of multi-scale methods lie in its ability to capture the relevant and useful image information at different resolutions. We validated our proposal in different imaging application scenarios, particularly in a 2015 multi-exposure image fusion database that provides human subjective evaluations. Experimental results show that our approach achieves high correlation with the subjective scores provided by the database and makes a significant improvement over the previous Piella's single-scale fusion quality measure.

## 1 Introduction

Image fusion is a process which aims to integrate multiple input images into a composite image with higher visual characteristics, more suitable for purposes of human visual-level perception and computer processing. With the growing trend of employing visual information for situation assessment and decision making, it is of great interest to evaluate the quality of an image generated by fusing an arbitrary number of images into a composite image, as well as to determine parameters in the fusion process. The algorithms and measures designed for evaluating the quality of composite images must be automatic and in agreement with human quality judgments [2].

Considerable efforts have been made to develop objective performance measures for image fusion given the large variety of applications [3]. One of the problems of introducing a suited quality measure for image fusion lies in the difficulty to compare fused images with a gold standard [4]. In this scenario, non-reference measures evaluate quality giving a score that can only be correlated with human quality assessments.

This research was supported by grants from SCyT-UNS, SeCyT-UNC and CONICET, Argentina.

© Springer International Publishing AG 2016
G. Bebis et al. (Eds.): ISVC 2016, Part I, LNCS 10072, pp. 836–845, 2016.
DOI: 10.1007/978-3-319-50835-1_75

In 2003, Piella and Heijmans [1] introduced three non-reference quality image fusion measures based on the Universal Image Quality index ($Q$) [5]. These quality measures give an indication of how much of the salient information contained in each of the input images has been transferred into the fused image. These measures were tested in a large variety of imaging applications related to infrared, visual, computed tomography and resonance magnetic images, multi-focus images and with images corrupted by noise integration. It has been shown that they correlate well with subjective criteria, see [6] and references within. These three original fusion measures were developed and tested with a source sequence containing only two input images for fusion. Later, extensions of Piella's measures were proposed to determine the quality of multi-focus image fusion from several polychromatic images [7] and the quality of the output of an enhancing technique in image fusion visualization [8].

The construction of benchmark databases has also been a breakthrough in image fusion quality research. Several subjective experiments have been performed, which led to create Ma's 2015 multi-exposure image fusion database (MEF) [2], Liu's 2015 remote sensing image database [9], and Hassen's 2015 multi-exposure multi-focus image database [10]. Such databases would allow researchers to test their measures in a controlled environment against human quality scores.

The comparative study developed by Ma et al. [2] showed that Piella's measure was very limited in predicting perceived quality of MEF images, but Hassen et al. [10], in multi-exposure multifocus context, identified Piella's measure as the second most competitive measure at the time. These somehow contradictory results give indications of the difficulties that a general purpose measure may encounter.

In this paper, we propose a measure that applies the structural similarity (SSIM) quality index [11], developed for scoring quality of regular digital images, on a multiresolution decomposition of the fused image, combining the result in a weighted product that can be tuned according to the special needs of the different databases. Our measure has been designed for testing the output of the fusion of several images, checking the structure of several input and a single output on different resolutions. Experimental results, performed in different imaging application scenarios, particularly on the MEF database, show that our measure is consistent with subjective evaluations and outperforms existing objective image quality measures for general image fusion.

The rest of the paper is organized as follows: Sect. 2 gives a brief introduction of the SSIM index and several definitions of measures for two and multi-input images. Section 3 describes our proposed measure, whereas Sect. 4 provides a discussion on the experiments and results. Finally, Sect. 5 summarizes our conclusion and prospects.

## 2    Single-Scale Structural Similarity Quality Assessment

### 2.1    Structural Similarity Index

Quality scoring is all about mimicking the assessment of perceptual characteristics made by the human visual system (HVS) on the images. Structural loss is one of such characteristics, which Wang and Bovik [5] and Wang et al. [11] tried to appraise with the definition of the Universal Quality Index, the $Q$ index, first and the structural similarity (SSIM) quality index later. The SSIM quantifies the structural loss based on statistical moments.

Let $x$ and $y$ be the original and test image signals of size $M \times N$ pixels, respectively. The SSIM index can be decomposed into three different components: the first one measures the degree of linear correlation between $x$ and $y$, the second measures the similarity between the luminance of $x$ and $y$, and the third measures the similarity related to the contrast between the images [11]. This index is defined as follows:

$$\text{SSIM}(x, y) = \left( \frac{2\bar{x}\bar{y} + C_1}{\bar{x}^2 + \bar{y}^2 + C_1} \right)^{\alpha} \left( \frac{2S_x S_y + C_2}{S_x^2 + S_y^2 + C_2} \right)^{\beta} \left( \frac{S_{xy} + C_3}{S_x S_y + C_3} \right)^{\gamma}, \quad (1)$$

where $\bar{x}$ and $\bar{y}$ are the sample average values of images $x$ and $y$; $S_x$, $S_y$ and $S_{xy}$ are the sample deviations and the sample covariance, respectively. The parameters $\alpha$, $\beta$ and $\gamma$ adjust the relative importance of the three components. The constants $C_1$, $C_2$ and $C_3$ are included to avoid instability when denominators are very close to zero. In order to simplify the expression (1), Wang et al. set $\alpha = \beta = \gamma = 1$ and $C_3 = C_2/2$. This parameter set results in a specific form of the SSIM index:

$$\text{SSIM}(x, y) = \frac{(2\bar{x}\bar{y} + C_1)(2S_{xy} + C_2)}{(\bar{x}^2 + \bar{y}^2 + C_1)(S_x^2 + S_y^2 + C_3)}. \quad (2)$$

In order to evaluate the overall image quality, the local indexes SSIM are averaged using a sliding window approach. The resulting performance index takes values between $-1$ and $1$. The maximum value 1, is achieved when $x$ and $y$ are identical. The Universal Quality index proposed in [5], named $Q$ index, corresponds to a special case of SSIM index, when $C_1 = C_2 = 0$.

### 2.2    Structural Similarity Based Quality Measure for Fused Imagery

In 2003, Piella [1] used the $Q$ index, a special version of (2), to define a quality measure, named $Q_W$, for two image input fusion schemes. This measure quantifies the fused image $f$ quality obtained by fusion of the input images $x$ and $y$. It can be expressed as follows:

$$Q_W(x, y, f) = \sum_{w \in W} c(w) \left[ \lambda(w) \, \text{SSIM}(x, f|w) + (1 - \lambda(w)) \, \text{SSIM}(y, f|w) \right], \quad (3)$$

where $c(w) = \dfrac{C(w)}{\sum\limits_{w' \in W} C(w')}$, with $C(w) = \max\{s(x|w), s(y|w)\}$ and $\lambda(w) = \dfrac{s(x|w)}{s(x|w) + s(y|w)}$.

The $s(x|w)$ and $s(y|w)$ are the local saliencies of the two input images $x$ and $y$ within the window $w$, respectively. They reflect the local relevance of the source image within the window $w$, and they were defined as functions of contrast, sharpness or entropy.

In 2009, Piella [8] introduced an extended version of the weighted fusion quality measure $Q_W$ to measure the performance of a multi-image fusion process. It was defined as

$$Q_W(I, f) = \sum_{n=1}^{K} \sum_{w \in W} c(w) \lambda_n(w) \, \mathrm{SSIM}(I_n, f|w), \tag{4}$$

where $I = (I_1, \ldots, I_K)$ is the multi-valued image, whose components $I_n, n = 1, \ldots, K$ are the input images, $f$ is the fused image, $\lambda_n(w) = \frac{s(I_n|w)}{\sum_{n=1}^{K} s(I_n|w)}$ the local weight, with $s(I_n|w)$ the local salience, and $c(w) = \frac{C(w)}{\sum_{w' \in W} C(w')}$, with $C(w) = \max \{s(I_1|w), \ldots, s(I_K|w)\}$.

## 3 Proposed Multi-scale Structural Similarity Quality Measure

The performance of fusion measures is directly related to the way they measure the information sent from the input images into the fused image. The concept of information in an image is generally represented by its features that are usually two dimensional signals. Multi-scale decomposition is an appropriate way to incorporate image details into different resolutions [2,12]. Also scale-space decompositions provide a convenient representation of the local geometric structures [8]. The proposed multi-scale based image fusion measure scheme is illustrated in Fig. 1. The system iteratively applies a low-pass filter followed by a downsampling by a factor of 2. The input images are denoted as scale 1, and the highest scale in the decomposition as scale $L$, obtained after $L-1$ iterations. The overall multi-scale fusion measure is obtained by combining the measurement at different scales using the equation,

$$\mathrm{MS\text{-}Q}(I, f) = \prod_{l=1}^{L} [Q_W(I_l, f_l)]^{\beta_l}, \tag{5}$$

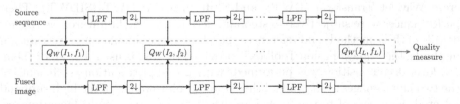

**Fig. 1.** Multi-scale image fusion measure system. LPF: low-pass filtering; 2 $\downarrow$: downsampling by a factor of 2.

**Fig. 2.** "Pepsi" image. SIDWT fused image and their structural quality maps for the scale levels $L = 1, 3$ and 5, respectively. Brightness indicates better quality.

where $I_l = (I_{l1}, \ldots, I_{lK})$ is the multi-valued image and $f_l$ is the fused image, both at scale level $l$, with $L$ the total number of scales. The parameter $\beta_l$ is the weight assigned to the $l$-th scale that adjusts the relative importance of each scale in the final formula. The measure includes the single-scale $Q_W$ in (4) as a special case $(L = 1)$. Figure 2 shows the quality maps of one fused image created from two source images by the Shift Invariant Discrete Wavelet Transform (SIDWT) method.

## 4   Experimental Results

In order to validate the proposed image fusion quality measure, we carried out three experiments. Each experiment addresses a relevant feature in our image fusion quality measure: general purpose, stable behavior and a good correlation with subjective judgments. In all of them, to compute our multi-scale measure we considered an $8 \times 8$ window size, $C_1 = C_2 = 0$, $s(\cdot|w)$ as the variance of image within window $w$, like Piella's implementation [1], a number of scales $L = 1, \ldots, 5$ and the scale weights given by $\beta_1 = 0.0448$, $\beta_2 = 0.2856$, $\beta_3 = 0.3001$, $\beta_4 = 0.2363$ and $\beta_5 = 0.1333$ [12]. These weights are normalized (sum to one) and used to calculate the exponents in (5). All parameters are inherited from previous publications to enable appropriate comparison.

### 4.1   First Experiment: General Purpose Assessment

In the first experiment, in order to test the performance of our proposed MS-Q measure as a general purpose tool, we considered different imaging application scenarios with only two input images. For this task, four prominent image fusion algorithms were evaluated: Laplacian Pyramid (LP), Ratio Pyramid (RP), Discrete Wavelet Transform (DWT), and Shift Invariant DWT (SIDWT). Their performances were subjectively tested and accepted in the literature, see [13] for details of these methods and references therein. For the simulation of these fusion methods, the "Image Fusion Toolbox", provided by [13], is used. For all of them, a 3-level decomposition was performed, with the approximation coefficients of the two input images averaged and the larger absolute values of the high subband selected. Four sets of testing image are used: "Pepsi" (two multi-focus images, e.g. camera vision), "Medical" (one computed tomography and one magnetic resonance image), "Remote" (pair of bands of a multi-band remote sensing image),

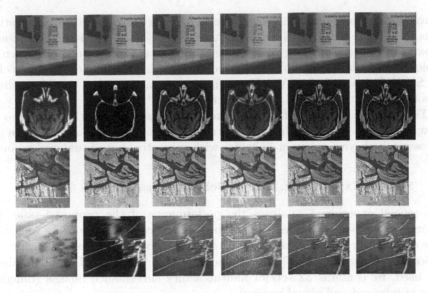

**Fig. 3.** From left to right: the pair of input images; LP, RP, DWT and SIDWT fused images, respectively.

**Table 1.** Objective evaluations of image fusion performance on different imaging application scenarios. Maximum scores by column are highlighted in bold typeface.

| Image | Size | Method | MS-Q | | |
|-------|------|--------|------|------|------|
| | | | $L = 1$ Piella's [1] | $L = 3$ | $L = 5$ |
| "Pepsi" | $(512 \times 512 \times 2)$ | LP | 0.9437 | 0.9491 | 0.9643 |
| | | RP | 0.7959 | 0.8775 | 0.9126 |
| | | DWT | 0.9350 | 0.9434 | 0.9610 |
| | | SIDWT | **0.9439** | **0.9522** | **0.9669** |
| "Medical" | $(256 \times 256 \times 2)$ | LP | **0.8089** | **0.7478** | **0.7051** |
| | | RP | 0.6319 | 0.5763 | 0.5244 |
| | | DWT | 0.7315 | 0.6733 | 0.6375 |
| | | SIDWT | 0.7780 | 0.7133 | 0.6721 |
| "Remote" | $(512 \times 512 \times 2)$ | LP | 0.8656 | **0.9061** | **0.9199** |
| | | RP | 0.8137 | 0.8744 | 0.8948 |
| | | DWT | 0.8505 | 0.8894 | 0.9080 |
| | | SIDWT | **0.8725** | 0.9058 | 0.9196 |
| "Navi" | $(512 \times 512 \times 2)$ | LP | **0.8187** | **0.7460** | **0.6856** |
| | | RP | 0.5742 | 0.5610 | 0.5312 |
| | | DWT | 0.7907 | 0.6924 | 0.6383 |
| | | SIDWT | 0.8059 | 0.7136 | 0.6574 |

"Navi" (one infra-red and one visual image, used for surveillance and navigation tasks). In Fig. 3 we show the sets of images with some of their fusion counterparts. The corresponding quantitative fusion evaluation results are given in Table 1. In this test, the multi-scales measures assign the highest values to LP and SIDWT, followed by DWT. The worst scores correspond to the RP method. This behavior is maintained on every scale.

The good performance of LP compare with the wavelets method is due to its known ability to preserve edges and to reduce ringing artifacts around them [1]. These results have a coherent behavior with subjective perceptual evaluations.

## 4.2   Second Experiment: Stable Behavior Assessment

The second experiment analyzes the performance of the proposed objective fusion measure across different inputs in the same context, according to a variance calculation. Lower variance indicates good stability of a fusion measure for a specific fusion algorithm [3]. To this purpose, the "TNO UN Camp" database was used, its contains 32 sets of multimodality surveillance images (different pairs of infra-red and visual images).

These images were fused with the same fusion methods used in the previous experiment. The numerical values reported in Table 2 evidence that the MS-Q measure for $L = 5$ is more stable in all of the fusion methods under study. This behavior is clearly confirmed in Fig. 4. The standard deviation (SD) was increased 100 times for better visual perception.

**Table 2.** The variance of fusion methods across 32 set images. The best results are highlighted in bold typeface.

| Image | Size | Method | MS-Q | | |
|---|---|---|---|---|---|
| | | | $L = 1$ Piella's [1] | $L = 3$ | $L = 5$ |
| "TNO UN Camp" | (360 × 270 × 2) | LP | 3.8104E−05 | 5.3833E−05 | **2.8654E−05** |
| | | RP | 2.3001E−05 | 1.7657E−05 | **1.6518E−05** |
| | | DWT | 2.8163E−05 | 2.4889E−05 | **1.2909E−05** |
| | | SIDWT | 2.5976E−05 | 3.4924E−05 | **1.8982E−05** |

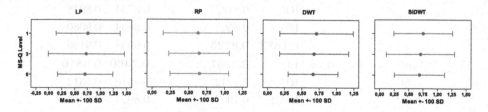

**Fig. 4.** Error bars (Mean $\pm\, 100 \times$ SD) of the fusion measures MS-Q on "TNO UN Camp".

## 4.3   Third Experiment: Good Correlation Assessment

In the third experiment, the agreement between the MS-Q measure score and the subjective evaluations provided by a benchmark database was assessed and compared with (single scale) $Q_W$ scores [8]. We used the 2015 MEF database made available by Ma et al. [2] for benchmarking purposes. It includes a subjective user study to evaluate the quality of images generated by eight MEF algorithms[1]. Figure 5 shows one source sequence example and all the corresponding fused images.

Two commonly used criteria, the Spearman Rank-Order Correlation Coefficient (SRCC) and the Kendall Rank-Order Correlation Coefficient (KRCC) are employed to analyze the level of agreement between the scores of all image fusion quality measures and the subjective evaluations. Both criteria range between $-1$ to $1$. These numbers represent perfect disagreement or agreement between quality measure and subjective opinion, respectively. The measures included in the study are Piella's measure and our MS-Q measure with two levels of decomposition, $L = 3$ and $L = 5$.

Table 3 summarizes the evaluation results of the SRCC and KRCC on the MEF database. The MS-Q has high scores in all scales, specially when the decomposition is up to the scale $L = 5$.

In this test, Piella's measure does not provide adequate predictions of the perceived quality of fused images. According to these results and the recent outcomes of Ma et al. [2], our proposed measure significantly outperforms the nine existing general purpose fusion measures, in the MEF context. The particular measure of Ma et al., designed specifically for this type of imagery, provide slightly better scores. For more details on Ma's measure see [2].

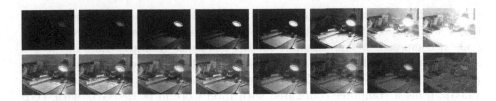

**Fig. 5.** An example of the 17 high-quality natural source image sequences (underexposed, overexposed and in between cases) of MEF database: "Lamp1". First row: some input images. Second row: fused images created by different MEF algorithms, ordered according to the Mean Subjective Ranks (MSR) and the value of our measure for $L = 5$: Mertens07 (MSR = 8.4783, MS-Q = 0.7745), Li12 (MSR = 7.7826, MS-Q = 0.7597), ShutaoLi12 (MSR = 6.8261, MS-Q = 0.7199), Li13 (MSR = 6.4348, MS-Q = 0.7384), Global Energy Weighted (MSR = 6.0870, MS-Q = 0.7041), Gu12 (MSR = 4.0870, MS-Q = 0.7745), Raman09 (MSR = 4.0435, MS-Q = 0.5964), and Local Energy Weighted (MSR = 2.378, MS-Q = 0.3933). See Ma et al. [2] for description and references of the methods.

---

[1] We used the same notation of the MEF algorithms that appears in [2].

**Table 3.** SRCC and KRCC performance evaluations of the proposed multi-scale measure against Piella's quality measure. The best correlations achieved in MEF database are highlighted in bold typeface.

| Source sequence | Size | SRCC | | | KRCC | | |
|---|---|---|---|---|---|---|---|
| | | Piella's [8] $(L = 1)$ | MS-Q $(L = 3)$ | MS-Q $(L = 5)$ | Piella's [8] $(L = 1)$ | MS-Q $(L = 3)$ | MS-Q $(L = 5)$ |
| Ballons | $(339 \times 512 \times 9)$ | 0.6429 | 0.8095 | **0.9048** | 0.4286 | 0.6429 | **0.7143** |
| Belgium house | $(384 \times 512 \times 9)$ | 0.6228 | 0.9102 | 0.9461 | 0.4728 | 0.8365 | 0.8365 |
| Lamp1 | $(384 \times 512 \times 15)$ | 0.6905 | 0.8571 | **0.9762** | 0.5000 | 0.7857 | **0.9286** |
| Candle | $(264 \times 512 \times 10)$ | 0.6667 | 0.7143 | **0.9524** | 0.5000 | 0.5714 | **0.8571** |
| Cave | $(384 \times 512 \times 4)$ | 0.5715 | 0.7619 | **0.8810** | 0.4286 | 0.5714 | **0.7143** |
| Chinese garden | $(340 \times 512 \times 3)$ | 0.5000 | 0.6667 | 0.8810 | 0.2143 | 0.5000 | 0.7143 |
| Farm house | $(341 \times 512 \times 3)$ | 0.5952 | 0.6190 | 0.6905 | 0.5000 | 0.5000 | 0.5000 |
| House | $(340 \times 512 \times 4)$ | 0.4048 | 0.7143 | **0.8810** | 0.2143 | 0.5000 | **0.7143** |
| Kluki | $(341 \times 512 \times 3)$ | 0.1190 | 0.6429 | **0.9286** | 0.0714 | 0.4286 | **0.7857** |
| Lamp2 | $(342 \times 512 \times 6)$ | 0.5952 | 0.6190 | 0.5714 | 0.2857 | 0.3571 | 0.2857 |
| Landscape | $(341 \times 512 \times 3)$ | 0.4524 | **0.6667** | **0.5238** | 0.2857 | **0.4286** | 0.3571 |
| Light house | $(340 \times 512 \times 3)$ | 0.1905 | 0.5714 | 0.5714 | 0.0714 | 0.2857 | 0.3571 |
| Madison capitol | $(384 \times 512 \times 30)$ | 0.5238 | 0.8333 | 0.7143 | 0.4286 | 0.7143 | 0.5000 |
| Memorial | $(512 \times 381 \times 16)$ | 0.7143 | 0.8095 | **0.8810** | 0.5714 | 0.6429 | **0.7143** |
| Office | $(340 \times 512 \times 6)$ | 0.4579 | 0.6506 | 0.7109 | 0.2965 | 0.4447 | 0.5189 |
| Tower | $(512 \times 341 \times 3)$ | 0.6190 | 0.8333 | 0.8571 | 0.5714 | 0.7143 | 0.7857 |
| Venice | $(341 \times 512 \times 3)$ | 0.2036 | 0.6467 | 0.8264 | 0.1091 | 0.4001 | 0.6910 |
| Average | | 0.5041 | 0.7251 | 0.8060 | 0.3499 | 0.5485 | 0.6460 |

Regarding computational costs, the proposed MS-Q measure algorithm is linear with respect to the number of pixels in the image and the level of the scale decomposition. For example, for the sequence "Lamp1" that includes a source sequence of fifteen exposure levels ($384 \times 512$ size) and eight fused images (see Fig. 5), our MS-Q (with $L = 5$) takes an overall computation time of about 14.05 s, using a computer configured with Intel Core i5 @ 1.80 GHz with 4 GB RAM, and unoptimized MATLAB code. As the number of source images in a sequence is usually different, an average time is not provided.

We conclude that the MS-Q fusion measure has a competitive quality prediction performance at a reasonable speed showing good potential for all these applications.

## 5    Conclusion and Future Work

In this paper, we presented a general purpose, non-reference multi-scale structural similarity measure for objective quality assessment of image fusion. This novel measure improves the performance of Piella's measure $Q_W$, preserving its general purpose approach, increasing its stability and its correlation with human subjective evaluation, as shown in the experimental results. The image fusion quality assessment through a multi-scale analysis provides a convenient representation of the local geometric structures and a way of incorporating more image information at different resolutions. All these features are useful tools in the image fusion process since the source images may exhibit different inherent characteristics in the application scenarios, e.g. noise presence, overexposure, underexposure, different resolutions, etc.

We will continue working on the calibration of the multi-scale image fusion approach parameters, which can potentially be employed in a much broader scope of applications, such as multi-exposure multi-focus image context [10], and remote sensing and satellite imaging [9], among others.

# References

1. Piella, G., Heijmans, H.: A new quality metric for image fusion. In: Proceedings of International Conference on Image Processing, vol. 3, pp. 173–176 (2003)
2. Ma, K., Zeng, K., Wang, Z.: Perceptual quality assessment for multi-exposure image fusion. IEEE Trans. Image Process. **24**, 3345–3356 (2015)
3. Liu, Z., Blasch, E., Xue, Z., Zhao, J., Laganière, R., Wu, W.: Objective assessment of multiresolution image fusion algorithms for context enhancement in night vision: a comparative study. IEEE Trans. Pattern Anal. Mach. Intell. **34**, 94–109 (2012)
4. Ardeshir Goshtasby, A., Nikolov, S.G.: Image fusion: advances in the state of the art. Inf. Fusion **8**, 114–118 (2007)
5. Wang, Z., Bovik, A.: A universal image quality index. IEEE Sig. Process. Lett. **9**, 81–84 (2002)
6. Petrović, V.: Subjective tests for image fusion evaluation and objective metric validation. Inf. Fusion **8**, 208–216 (2007)
7. Bueno, A.M., Alvarez Borrego, J., Acho, L., Chávez Sánchez, M.C.: Polychromatic image fusion algorithm and fusion metric for automatized microscopes. Opt. Eng. **44**, 1–7 (2005)
8. Piella, G.: Image fusion for enhanced visualization: a variational approach. Int. J. Comput. Vis. **83**, 1–11 (2009)
9. Liu, J., Huang, J., Liu, S., Li, H., Zhou, Q., Liu, J.: Human visual system consistent quality assessment for remote sensing image fusion. J. Photogrammetry Remote Sens. **105**, 79–90 (2015)
10. Hassen, R., Wang, Z., Magdy, M.A.S.: Objective quality assessment for multiexposure multifocus image fusion. IEEE Trans. Image Process. **24**, 2712–2724 (2015)
11. Wang, Z., Bovik, A.C., Sheikh, H.R., Simoncelli, E.P.: Image quality assessment: from error visibility to structural similarity. IEEE Trans. Image Process. **13**, 600–612 (2004)
12. Wang, Z., Simoncelli, E.P., Bovik, A.C.: Multi-scale structural similarity for image quality assessment. In: Proceedings of IEEE Asilomar Conference on Signals, Systems and Computers, pp. 1398–1402 (2003)
13. Rockinger, O.: Image Fusion Toolbox (1999). http://www.metapix.de/toolbox.htm/

# Vision-Based Self-contained Target Following Robot Using Bayesian Data Fusion

Andrés Echeverri Guevara, Anthony Hoak, Juan Tapiero Bernal, and Henry Medeiros(✉)

Department of Electrical and Computer Engineering, Marquette University, 1551 W. Wisconsin Ave., Milwaukee, WI 53233, USA
{andres.echeverri,anthony.hoak,juan.tapierobernal, henry.medeiros}@marquette.edu

**Abstract.** Several visual following robots have been proposed in recent years. However, many require the use of several, expensive sensors and often the majority of the image processing and other calculations are performed off-board. This paper proposes a simple and cost effective, yet robust visual following robot capable of tracking a general object with limited restrictions on target characteristics. To detect the objects, tracking-learning-detection (TLD) is used within a Bayesian framework to filter and fuse the measurements. A time-of-flight (ToF) depth camera is used to refine the distance estimates at short ranges. The algorithms are executed in real-time (approximately 30 fps) in a Jetson TK1 embedded computer. Experiments were conducted with different target objects to validate the system in scenarios including occlusions and various illumination conditions as well as to show how the data fusion between TLD and the ToF camera improves the distance estimation.

## 1 Introduction

Target tracking using mobile robotic platforms is a well-researched problem within the computer vision and robotics communities [1–7]. Object following capabilities are increasingly popular for aerial platforms and wheeled vehicles alike [8–12]. Object/target following is typically an extension of target tracking in the sense that the tracking error is used as input to a controller that changes the position of the robotic platform with respect to the target.

In this paper, an autonomous, low-cost, computationally light target following platform is presented. The platform consists of consumer grade portable hardware and uses visual information only to estimate the relative position of the robot and generate the corresponding control signals. Specifically, the platform is comprised of an iRobot Create 2 mobile robot, a Creative Senz3D camera, and an Nvidia Jetson TK1 embedded computer. The proposed system is flexible since it imposes no constraints on the shape or color of the target. This is accomplished using the tracking-learning-detection (TLD) [13] algorithm for object detection. The output of the object detection algorithm, in addition to the depth information from the 3D camera, is used as a measurement for a standard Kalman filter which effectively tracks the target through the image sequence.

© Springer International Publishing AG 2016
G. Bebis et al. (Eds.): ISVC 2016, Part I, LNCS 10072, pp. 846–857, 2016.
DOI: 10.1007/978-3-319-50835-1_76

## 2   Related Work

There has been significant interest in robotic platforms for object or pedestrian tracking and following. The design of such platforms usually involve three main elements: (1) a tracker that is flexible enough to detect and follow different types of targets, (2) an on-board computing system that is able to perform intensive computer vision operations in real-time, and (3) a robust depth estimation mechanism. We discuss each of these elements in more detail below.

Vision-based tracking algorithms for robotic platforms must be flexible such that only a limited amount of information about the target must be known a priori. They must also be robust enough so that the platform can keep track of the target under a variety of conditions. Many existing platforms rely on defining some kind of 'unique identifier' for the system to detect and track. This could be as simple as a specific color or shape [7–10,14–17] or as intricate as using known markers such as LEDs attached to the target [18]. Although a certain level of robustness can be obtained by such approaches as long as the assumptions on the appearance of the target and the background are not violated, they lack the flexibility needed to make such systems practically useful. Flexibility can be obtained by relying on discriminative trackers that can be initialized with a target appearance at time $t_0$ and then updated on-the-fly [13,19,20]. These trackers can be endowed with additional robustness by integrating them with recursive Bayesian estimation methods that can effectively limit the number of opportunities for the algorithms to make mistakes [21–24].

Regarding the availability of on-board processing capabilities, image processing is notoriously computationally expensive, especially for high resolution images. In many robotic tracking systems, image processing is performed remotely, off-board [4,8,10,12,16] due to the lack of on-board processing power. There are only a few systems that present truly autonomous vehicles that perform all the processing on-board. For example in [5] a low-cost FPGA is used to increase the efficiency and speed of the image processing algorithms. FPGA-based systems are, however, intrinsically less flexible than general computing architectures and cannot, in general, benefit from the widespread dissemination of algorithms designed for general graphics processing units (GPUs). The advent of low-power embedded architectures with integrated GPUs, such as the Nvidia Tegra TK1 SOC[1], made it possible for these highly parallel algorithms to make their way into low-cost robotic applications.

The third major issue in the design of portable target following robotic systems is the availability of appropriate depth estimation mechanisms. Depth information is vital for the platform to maneuver in three dimensions and successfully follow a target. Although estimating the distance between the target and the robotic platform based on scale variations of the target is a viable option, such approach tends to be fragile in the presence of relatively small errors in the estimated target boundaries. Alternative sensing technologies can be employed in conjunction with traditional vision-based depth estimation to mitigate this problem.

---

[1] http://www.nvidia.com/object/tegra-k1-processor.html.

Over the past few years, RGB-D sensors have been widely used for that purpose [8,25–27]. The ideal depth sensor needs to provide sufficient RGB image resolution and depth information at a feasible cost. Although structured light sensors tend to perform well in indoors applications, their performance under natural illumination suffers. Sensors based on time-of-flight (ToF) technology, although still not immune to illumination problems, tend to perform better.

Few autonomous target following systems [2,28] are flexible enough not to require 'unique identifiers', efficient enough to perform all processing and control operations on-board, and incorporate depth information for robust target following performance while using relatively low-cost consumer grade hardware. Similar systems to the one presented in this paper have been proposed, however, some make use of large robotic platforms [2], expensive sensors [28], or unreliable sensors [15], and may not be as robust as one based on a Bayesian framework [17]. Therefore a low-cost, computationally light, robust vision based control system for an autonomous vehicle is still subject of active research.

## 3   Proposed Vision-Based Target Following System

This section describes the design of the proposed platform as well as the methods used to estimate the target position and to control the robot.

### 3.1   System Description

The system is composed of the following hardware: A Creative Senz3D ToF camera that is able to capture an RGB and depth image. The camera has a depth range of approximately 1 m and generates range images at 30 fps.[2] A Jetson TK1 embedded computer is attached to the iRobot Create 2 in order to process the information collected from the camera and send control commands to the robot. See Fig. 1 for an illustration of the overall system (the cost of the components for one prototype was approximately 500 US dollars).

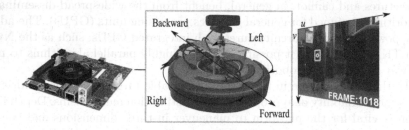

**Fig. 1.** Overall robotic platform architecture.

---

[2] Although other ToF cameras such as the classic $SR4000$ from MESA imaging, the PMD CamCube 3.0 or SoftKinetic's DS536A have ranges of up to 5 m, the low-cost and lightweight Senz3D was deemed sufficient for our purposes.

## 3.2  Target Detection

In order to measure the position of the target at each frame, the system uses a C++ implementation of TLD [29] which computes the target position in the image plane ($u$ and $v$) as well as its width and height ($w$ and $h$). TLD is used because it is a discriminative tracker and hence does not require previous information about the target, which gives the system the flexibility needed to track any object of interest. The target is initially selected by the user and variations on target appearance are learned as it is tracked.

## 3.3  System Model

The system is modeled using a linear Kalman Filter. The state vector is $\mathbf{x} = [u\ v\ z\ \dot{u}\ \dot{v}\ \dot{z}]$, where $u$, $v$ are the pixel coordinates of the object, $z$ is the distance from the sensor to the object, and $\dot{u}$, $\dot{v}$, $\dot{z}$ are the velocities in each dimension, respectively. The object tracking system is then modeled in state space form as:

$$\mathbf{x}(t) = A\mathbf{x}(t-1) + B\mathbf{u}(t) + \mathbf{w}(t) \tag{1}$$

$$\mathbf{y}(t) = C\mathbf{x}(t) + \mathbf{v}(t) \tag{2}$$

where Eq. (1) represents the system dynamics, including the state transition matrix $A$, the influence of the control action $B$ and the process noise $\mathbf{w}$, and Eq. (2) is the measurement model, which includes the observation matrix $C$ and the measurement noise $\mathbf{v}$. The process noise and measurement noise are assumed to be white, Gaussian, with variances $R_{ww}$ and $R_{vv}$, respectively. That is, $\mathbf{w} \sim \mathcal{N}(0, R_{ww})$, and $\mathbf{v} \sim \mathcal{N}(0, R_{vv})$.

The object tracking system is modeled with the following state transition and measurement matrices:

$$A = \begin{bmatrix} I_3 & I_3 \\ 0_{3\times3} & I_3 \end{bmatrix}, \quad B = \begin{bmatrix} 0_{2\times3} \\ k_1 & 0 \\ 0 & 0 \\ 0 & k_2 \end{bmatrix}, \quad C = \begin{bmatrix} I_2 & 0_{2\times2} & 0_{2\times2} \\ 0_{2\times2} & 1_{2\times1} & 0_{2\times3} \end{bmatrix} \tag{3}$$

where $I_m$ is a $m \times m$ identity matrix and $0_{m\times n}$ and $1_{m\times n}$ are $m \times n$ matrices of zeros and ones, respectively. Matrix $A$ above assumes that the target moves with a constant velocity such that $\dot{u}(t) = \dot{u}(t-1)$, $\dot{v}(t) = \dot{v}(t-1)$ and $\dot{z}(t) = \dot{z}(t-1)$ $\forall(t)$. Matrix $B$ accounts for the effect of the control action of the PID controller on the velocities of the $x$ and $z$ axes. The rotation of the robot is accomplished by controlling the displacement in the image $\Delta u$, this relationship can be considered $\theta \approx \Delta u$ since the displacement from one frame to another is small in comparison to the distance between the robot and the target (see Fig. 2). Translation is carried out by attempting to preserve the relative distance between the robot and the target at the first instant of time. The $C$ matrix indicates that the measurements available at any given time are the current $u$, $v$ coordinates of the object (the output of TLD) and $z$, the range from the robot to the object, which is obtained from both the ToF camera and TLD. Matrix $C$ is a $6 \times 4$ matrix

**Fig. 2.** Small angle approximation justification.

whose first two rows correspond to the observations of $u$ and $v$ provided by TLD and whose last two rows correspond to the distance measurements obtained by the ToF camera and by the relative scale computed using TLD. The data fusion between the TLD and ToF measurements will be covered in detail below.

### 3.4   Data Fusion Approach

There are two main purposes for fusing measurements in this system. The first is to increase the overall estimation accuracy. The second is to allow the robot to follow a target even when it goes beyond the threshold of the ToF camera. The ToF camera is able to measure depth consistently and precisely when a target is located less than 1 m away, however, it becomes very noisy and unreliable beyond this distance, generating many false measurements. A depth estimate based on relative scale changes as measured by TLD is used to compensate for these false measurements, effectively extending the operating range of the system.

The depth measurement from the ToF camera is calculated by averaging all the non-zero depth pixels inside the target bounding box (pixels whose depth cannot be estimated, such as those beyond the camera range, are read with a zero value). The height and width ($h$ and $w$) provided by TLD are used to measure the scale variations of the target and hence provide an indirect depth estimate. The scale change of the target is translated to a real distance according to

$$TLD_z = K_z \cdot \sqrt{\frac{w_{img} \times h_{img}}{w \times h}} \qquad (4)$$

where $K_z$ is a constant obtained by relating the initial depth measurement from the camera to the initial target bounding box size ($w$ and $h$) and $h_{img}$ and $w_{img}$ are the height and width of the image.

The reliability of the ToF depth measurement is determined according to the following sigmoidal relationship

$$Rvv_\zeta = 1 - \frac{1}{1 + e^{(\eta \times r_0 - \zeta)}} \qquad (5)$$

where $r_0$ is the percentage of zero elements in the target bounding box image, $\eta$ defines the slope of the function and $\zeta$ is the value where the penalization takes place. The sigmoid function allows the Kalman filter to smoothly transition between the ToF and the TLD distance measurements using the following $4 \times 4$ covariance matrix

$$R_{vv} = diag(R_{vv_u}, R_{vv_v}, Rvv_{ToF}, Rvv_{TLD}) \tag{6}$$

where $diag(.)$ represents a diagonal matrix, $R_{vv_u}$ and $R_{vv_v}$ reflect the uncertainties in the observation of $u$ and $v$ and $Rvv_{TOF}$ and $Rvv_{TLD}$ represent the distance uncertainties as computed by the ToF camera and the TLD scale and are defined as follows

$$Rvv_{TOF} = \kappa \times Rvv_\zeta \tag{7}$$

$$Rvv_{TLD} = \kappa \times (1 - Rvv_\zeta) \tag{8}$$

Hence, as $R_{vv_\zeta}$ varies, the confidence level of the system is adjusted so that more weight is given to the ToF measurements or to the TLD relative scale. $\kappa$ represents the penalization amplitude in the sigmoid function.

### 3.5 Controller Design

Independent PID controllers are used for the translational and rotational velocities of the robot. As shown in Fig. 1, the translational velocity allows the robot to drive forward or backward, and the rotational velocity turns it to the left or to the right.

The set-point for the translational controller is the initial distance between the target and the robot in the first measurement. We require this distance to be within the range of the ToF camera so that the TLD scale measurement can be properly initialized. The PID constants for the rotational controller are $Kp = 0.82$, $Ki = 0$ and $Kd = 0$. The set-point for the angular controller is the center of the image in the $x$ axis. The constants for this controller are $Kp = 0.4$, $Ki = 0$ and $Kd = 0.03$. All the controller constants were found experimentally so that the robot would show a fast yet smooth response.

In order to decouple the control actions, we implemented a simple heuristic that checks for the magnitude of the error in the set points and decides whether to move forward or to turn at each frame based on the largest error. That is, if the difference between the $u$ coordinate of the target and the corresponding set point in the center of the image is larger than the difference between the radial distance from the target to the sensor and its corresponding set point, the rotation controller is activated. Otherwise, the translation controller is activated. In order to be able to compare these distances, they are both normalized so that they range between 0 and 1.

## 4 Experimental Results

We qualitatively evaluated the ability of the system to track a given target by attaching an object (recycling bin) to another iRobot Create 2 which was manually controlled while the autonomous robot followed it successfully through a

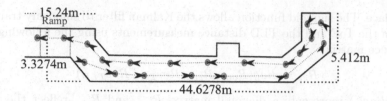

**Fig. 3.** Floor plan sketch showing the robot trajectory.

**Fig. 4.** Screen captures from the qualitative experiment illustrating the system's robustness to a variety of conditions, particularly illumination changes.

**Fig. 5.** System recovering the target object (recycling bin) after a full occlusion by another object (large trash bin).

variety of conditions. A sketch of the map illustrating the trajectory of the robot is shown in Fig. 3. As the figure shows, the system autonomously followed the target for approximately 110 m. Screen captures obtained by the robot during this experiment are shown in Fig. 4. The parameter values used for the experiments are the following: $\zeta = 12$, $\eta = 20$, $\kappa = 100$, $k_1 = k_2 = 0.01$, $R_{ww} = \text{diag}(0, 0, 0, 0.1, 0.1, 0.1)$, and $R_{vv_u} = R_{vv_v} = 0.3$.

In order to evaluate the ability of the system to recover from full occlusion while still carrying out smooth depth estimation, we tracked a target object (recycling bin) sliding across the ground so that another object (large trash bin) entirely occluded the target. As the screen captures in Fig. 5 indicate, despite abrupt variations in depth measurements caused by the occluding object, the system is able to fully recover from severe occlusions while maintaining its distance from the target.

Figure 6 demonstrates the system's ability to respond to a fast moving target at distances beyond the range of the ToF camera. Figure 7 shows quantitative results regarding this experiments. The top left graph shows the measured and the estimated pixel positions $u_{pos}$ and its set point $s_{p_u}$, which is the center of the camera field of view. The top right graph shows the reference distance from the target, $s_{p_z}$, the measured range from $TLD_z$ and $ToF_z$ as well as the fused estimate $est_z$. Finally, in the bottom plots of the figure we can see the control actions performed in order to move the robot in response to the position

**Fig. 6.** The target object (backpack) is moved backwards, quickly and beyond the ToF camera's range (>1 m), the system is able to respond smoothly, making use of $TLD_z$, and successfully follows the object.

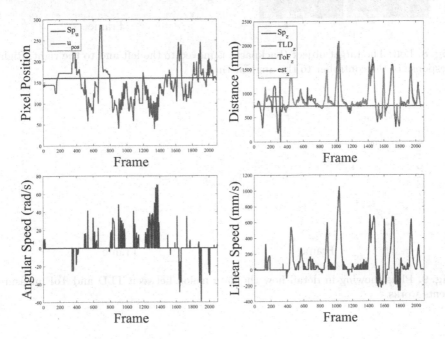

**Fig. 7.** Quantitative results corresponding to the backpack tracking experiment shown in Fig. 6. $s_{p_u} = 160$ corresponds to the center of the image in the horizontal direction, and $s_{p_z} = 750$ corresponds to the initial distance to the target in millimeters.

error estimates. As the figure indicates, the linear and angular speed controllers try to compensate for the estimated errors $u_{pos}$ and $est_z$, respectively.[3]

Figure 8 illustrates the response of the system to fast motions along the $u$ axis. As the target moves in a certain direction, the robot moves to compensate for that. As the figure shows, when the target stops moving (from around iteration 500 to 590 and 700 to 750), the robot motion quickly stabilizes with the target near the set point. Note that the small bias in position could be easily compensated by further tuning the rotation controller.

---

[3] Note that the set points $s_{p_u}$ and $s_{p_z}$ correspond to the desired target position with respect to the robot, not to the actual robot position. The controllers use the set points to move the robot so that the difference between the estimated position and the set point is minimized.

 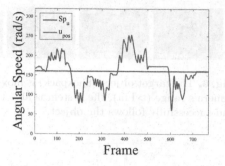

**Fig. 8.** Left: The target object (backpack) is moved to the left and to the right. Right: Response of the controller to the angular turn.

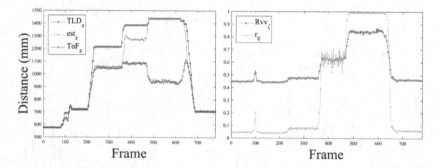

**Fig. 9.** Plots showing in detail how the data fusion between TLD and ToF measurements works.

In order to show the effects of moving the target out of the range of the ToF camera, we kept the robot static and tracked a target at different distances starting well within the ToF range and progressing towards the 1 m threshold and beyond. The results of this experiment are shown in Fig. 9. The left graph shows that when the target is within the range of the ToF sensor, the estimate relies on measurements from TLD and ToF (frames $\sim$100–200). When the target is farther than 1 m (frames $\sim$350–650), the estimated distance is based almost entirely on TLD. When the target is moved back to the starting position (frame $\sim$650) the ToF measurements are again considered in the estimate. The right plot shows that when the target is near the 1 m mark (frames $\sim$350–500), the ToF measurements are very noisy and hence relying mostly on TLD is in fact an appropriate strategy.

We validate our choice of $Rvv_\zeta$ by illustrating that the percentage of zeros in the depth image is a viable way to determine the accuracy of the ToF sensor. In other words, the error between the ToF measurements and actual distance should increase monotonically as $Rvv_\zeta$ increases. This experiment also consisted of moving the target object progressively farther away while keeping the robot static. However, this time the focus was not on the behavior near the threshold of 1 m,

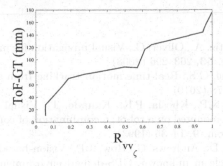

**Fig. 10.** Correlation between the distance and the level of confidence $Rvv_\zeta$.

but on the overall trend of the error as the distance increased. The graph in Fig. 10 shows that as the target moves away from the robot, the error between ToF measurements and the ground truth increases and so does $Rvv_\zeta$.

## 5 Conclusion

In this paper, an autonomous, cost effective, vision-based object following ground vehicle was proposed. The system was based on an iRobot Create 2 mobile platform, a Creative Senz3D ToF camera, and a Jetson TK1 embedded computer. Object detection was accomplished using TLD and tracking was performed by a Kalman filter. Data fusion was implemented in order to extend the operating range of the system beyond the measuring capabilities of the ToF sensor. All the processing was performed in real-time on the on-board computer. Several experiments were conducted where the system successfully followed target objects in a variety of situations, including illumination changes, full occlusions, and rapid movement at far (>1 m) distances. Quantitative experiments showed in detail how data fusion is accomplished.

Although the proposed approach is not restricted to Kalman filters and alternative recursive Bayesian methods such as Sequential Monte Carlo approaches [30] could be employed for increased robustness, one of our main objectives was to devise a lightweight method that could be used in portable embedded platforms. Hence, a Kalman filter seemed like the most effective choice.

There are several future directions to explore in this project. In the first place it would be beneficial to improve the control heuristics so that the decision between moving forward and turning would occur more seamlessly thereby reducing the chances of losing track of the target due to abrupt motions. Second, the ToF camera used in this project has a limited range and cannot be used outdoors, so a better camera would extend the use of the system. In addition, faster and more robust tracking can be accomplished simply by porting more of the software implementation to the GPU in the embedded computer. Finally, exploring data association and track management mechanisms would allow for the system to perform more robustly in more complex scenarios in which multiple similar targets move in close proximity.

# References

1. Bonin-Font, F., Ortiz, A., Oliver, G.: Visual navigation for mobile robots: a survey. J. Intell. Rob. Syst. **53**, 263–296 (2008)
2. Jung, B., Sukhatme, G.S.: Real-time motion tracking from a mobile robot. Int. J. Soc. Robot. **2**, 63–78 (2010)
3. Papanikolopoulos, N.P., Khosla, P.K., Kanade, T.: Visual tracking of a moving target by a camera mounted on a robot: a combination of control and vision. IEEE Trans. Robot. Autom. **9**, 14–35 (1993)
4. Ahrens, S., Levine, D., Andrews, G., How, J.P.: Vision-based guidance and control of a hovering vehicle in unknown, GPS-denied environments. In: IEEE International Conference on Robotics and Automation, ICRA 2009, pp. 2643–2648 (2009)
5. Fowers, S.G., Lee, D.J., Tippetts, B.J., Lillywhite, K.D., Dennis, A.W., Archibald, J.K.: Vision aided stabilization and the development of a quad-rotor micro UAV. In: International Symposium on Computational Intelligence in Robotics and Automation, CIRA 2007, pp. 143–148 (2007)
6. Kwon, H., Yoon, Y., Park, J.B., Kak, A.C.: Person tracking with a mobile robot using two uncalibrated independently moving cameras. In: Proceedings of the 2005 IEEE International Conference on Robotics and Automation, ICRA 2005, pp. 2877–2883 (2005)
7. Schlegel, C., Illmann, J., Jaberg, H., Schuster, M., Wrz, R.: Vision based person tracking with a mobile robot. In: BMVC, pp. 1–10 (1998)
8. Benavidez, P., Jamshidi, M.: Mobile robot navigation and target tracking system. In: 2011 6th International Conference on System of Systems Engineering (SoSE), pp. 299–304 (2011)
9. Hu, C., Ma, X., Dai, X.: A robust person tracking and following approach for mobile robot. In: International Conference on Mechatronics and Automation, ICMA 2007, pp. 3571–3576 (2007)
10. Kim, J., Shim, D.H.: A vision-based target tracking control system of a quadrotor by using a tablet computer. In: 2013 International Conference on Unmanned Aircraft Systems (ICUAS), pp. 1165–1172 (2013)
11. Papachristos, C., Tzoumanikas, D., Alexis, K., Tzes, A.: Autonomous robotic aerial tracking, avoidance, and seeking of a mobile human subject. In: Bebis, G., et al. (eds.) ISVC 2015. LNCS, vol. 9474, pp. 444–454. Springer, Heidelberg (2015). doi:10.1007/978-3-319-27857-5_40
12. Woods, A.C., La, H.M.: Dynamic target tracking and obstacle avoidance using a drone. In: Bebis, G., et al. (eds.) ISVC 2015. LNCS, vol. 9474, pp. 857–866. Springer, Heidelberg (2015). doi:10.1007/978-3-319-27857-5_76
13. Kalal, Z., Mikolajczyk, K., Matas, J.: Tracking-learning-detection. IEEE Trans. Pattern Anal. Mach. Intell. **34**, 1409–1422 (2012)
14. Ma, X., Hu, C., Dai, X., Qian, K.: Sensor integration for person tracking and following with mobile robot. In: IEEE/RSJ International Conference on Intelligent Robots and Systems, IROS 2008, pp. 3254–3259 (2008)
15. Clark, M., Feldpausch, D., Tewolde, G.S.: Microsoft kinect sensor for real-time color tracking robot. In: 2014 IEEE International Conference on Electro/Information Technology (EIT), pp. 416–421 (2014)
16. Teuliere, C., Eck, L., Marchand, E.: Chasing a moving target from a flying UAV. In: 2011 IEEE/RSJ International Conference on Intelligent Robots and Systems (IROS), pp. 4929–4934 (2011)

17. Guerin, F., Fabri, S.G., Bugeja, M.K.: Double exponential smoothing for predictive vision based target tracking of a wheeled mobile robot. In: 2013 IEEE 52nd Annual Conference on Decision and Control (CDC), pp. 3535–3540 (2013)
18. Wang, W.J., Chang, J.W.: Implementation of a mobile robot for people following. In: 2012 International Conference on System Science and Engineering (ICSSE), pp. 112–116 (2012)
19. Pieropan, A., Bergström, N., Ishikawa, M., Kjellström, H.: Robust 3d tracking of unknown objects. In: 2015 IEEE International Conference on Robotics and Automation (ICRA), pp. 2410–2417. IEEE (2015)
20. Babenko, B., Yang, M.H., Belongie, S.: Visual tracking with online multiple instance learning. In: IEEE Conference on Computer Vision and Pattern Recognition, CVPR 2009, pp. 983–990 (2009)
21. Rigatos, G.G.: Extended kalman and particle filtering for sensor fusion in motion control of mobile robots. Math. Comput. Simul. **81**, 590–607 (2010)
22. Dinh, T.B., Yu, Q., Medioni, G.: Co-trained generative and discriminative trackers with cascade particle filter. Comput. Vis. Image Underst. **119**, 41–56 (2014)
23. Medeiros, H., Park, J., Kak, A.: Distributed object tracking using a cluster-based kalman filter in wireless camera networks. IEEE J. Sel. Top. Sign. Proces. **2**, 448–463 (2008)
24. Medeiros, H., Holguín, G., Shin, P.J., Park, J.: A parallel histogram-based particle filter for object tracking on SIMD-based smart cameras. Comput. Vis. Image Underst. **114**, 1264–1272 (2010)
25. Yoon, Y., han Yun, W., Yoon, H., Kim, J.: Real-time visual target tracking in RGB-D data for person-following robots. In: 2014 22nd International Conference on Pattern Recognition (ICPR), pp. 2227–2232 (2014)
26. Shimura, K., Ando, Y., Yoshimi, T., Mizukawa, M.: Research on person following system based on RGB-D features by autonomous robot with multi-kinect sensor. In: 2014 IEEE/SICE International Symposium on System Integration (SII), pp. 304–309 (2014)
27. Nakamura, T.: Real-time 3-D object tracking using kinect sensor. In: 2011 IEEE International Conference on Robotics and Biomimetics (ROBIO), pp. 784–788 (2011)
28. Chen, C.H., Cheng, C., Page, D., Koschan, A., Abidi, M.: A moving object tracked by a mobile robot with real-time obstacles avoidance capacity. In: 18th International Conference on Pattern Recognition, ICPR 2006, vol. 3, pp. 1091–1094. IEEE (2006)
29. Nebehay, G.: Robust object tracking based on tracking-learning-detection. Master's thesis, TU Wien (2012)
30. Loy, G., Fletcher, L., Apostoloff, N., Zelinsky, A.: An adaptive fusion architecture for target tracking. In: Proceedings of Fifth IEEE International Conference on Automatic Face and Gesture Recognition, 2002, pp. 261–266. IEEE (2002)

# Dual Back-to-Back Kinects
# for 3-D Reconstruction

Ho Chuen Kam[1(✉)], Kin Hong Wong[1], and Baiwu Zhang[2]

[1] Department of Computer Science and Engineering,
The Chinese University of Hong Kong, Shatin, Hong Kong
hckam@cse.cuhk.edu.hk
[2] University of Toronto, Toronto, ON M5S, Canada

**Abstract.** In this paper, we investigated the use of two Kinects for
capturing the 3-D model of a large scene. Traditionally the method of
utilising one Kinect is used to slide across the area, and a full 3-D model
is obtained. However, this approach requires the scene with a significant number of prominent features and careful handling of the device.
To tackle the problem we mounted two back-to-back Kinects on top of
a robot for scanning the environment. This setup requires the knowledge of the relative pose between the two Kinects. As they do not have
a shared view, calibration using the traditional method is not possible. To solve this problem, we place a dual-face checkerboard (the front
and back patterns are the same) on top of the back-to-back Kinects,
and a planar mirror is employed to enable either Kinect to view the
same checkerboard. Such an arrangement will create a shared calibration
object between the two sensors. In such an approach, a mirror-based pose
estimation algorithm is applied to solve the problem of Kinect camera
calibration. Finally, we can merge all local object models captured by
the Kinects together to form a combined model with a larger viewing
area. Experiments using real measurements of capturing an indoor scene
were conducted to show the feasibility of our work.

## 1 Introduction

In recent years visual reality is becoming popular, and many applications are
developed for industrial and domestic use. Virtual tour in museums and tourist
attractions is one of the potential applications. This requires the capturing of
the environments and turning them into various 3-D models. With the range
cameras, images and depth information are easily aggregated to construct virtual
scenes.

A variety of 3-D range cameras are already available in the market, such
as Microsoft Kinect, etc. It is economical so that it is extensively used in 3-D
vision research. In 3-D reconstruction, normally one Kinect is employed to scan
the entire environment. KinectFusion [1,2] are examples of the renowned algorithms for capturing the virtual scene. However, this kind of one-Kinect method
suffers from some undesirable effects. As the algorithm is largely based on feature
matching among frames, it will not work on the following cases:

© Springer International Publishing AG 2016
G. Bebis et al. (Eds.): ISVC 2016, Part I, LNCS 10072, pp. 858–867, 2016.
DOI: 10.1007/978-3-319-50835-1_77

1. The Kinect twitches, i.e., translates and rotates too fast to a great extent.
2. The object surface is too plain and lack of features (e.g. plain wall).

Under these circumstances the one-Kinect algorithm fails to converge, yielding undesirable results.

In this paper, a simple and efficient way is proposed to tackle the 3-D reconstruction problem. First, two back-to-back Kinects are mounted on top of a robot, and each of them captures a point cloud. Finally, they are merged to form the whole scene. To accomplish the task, we have to find the relative locations of the cameras. However, as they share no common views, traditional algorithms for camera calibration [3] do not work. We propose putting a dual-face checkerboard (the front and back patterns are the same) on top of the two Kinects, and a planar mirror is employed to recover the images of checkerboard for the cameras. By doing so, we created a calibration object for the RGB cameras of the two Kinects without shared view.

This paper is organised as follows. The related work will be discussed at Sect. 2 and theories used are explained in Sect. 3. Synthetic and real experiments are conducted, and the results are shown in Sect. 4. Section 5 concludes our work.

## 2 Related Work

### 2.1 KinectFusion

KinectFusion [1] by Newcombe et al. is one of the notable and first of the 3-D volumetric reconstruction techniques. It totally relies on the object features for registration and calculates the correspondences by the estimation algorithm Iterative Closet Point (ICP) [4]. By using one Kinect and sliding it across a scene, a unique 3-D model is generated by the following steps:

1. Surface Extraction of 3-D object.
2. Alignment of sensor.
3. Volumetric integration to fill 3-D model.
4. Raycasting.

Although the algorithm can achieve an extraordinary accuracy, it suffers from various limitations which are unstable in some scenarios. The major working principle relies on feature matching step using ICP. Therefore it fails when the cameras move too fast, or the object it captures contains few features.

### 2.2 Pose Estimation Without a Direct View

First, the problem is coined by Sturm and Bonfort [5] in 2006. They are the first to suggest the use of a planar mirror for pose estimation. However using a mirror, the calibration object can become a virtual image of a camera viewing through the mirror. Besides, they pointed out that the motion between two consecutive virtual views is on the intersection line of two planes. This motion can be described as *fixed-axis rotation*.

Later, Kumar et al. [6] formulated a linear method to calibrate cameras using a planar mirror. This method requires five virtual views to be incorporated in the linear system, but this does not require the constraints of fixed-axis rotation.

Hesch et al. [7] put forward the use of the maximum-likelihood estimator to compute the relative poses of a camera using a planar mirror. They tried to minimise the solving system from five virtual views to three points viewed in three planes when compared to the method of Kumar et al. [6].

Later in 2010 Rodrigues et al. [8] further extended the linear method to a better closed-form solution. The mirror planes positions can be simply and unambiguously solved by a system of linear equations. The method enabled a minimum of three virtual views to converge.

In 2012 Takahashi et al. [9] introduced a new algorithm of using Perspective-3-Point (P3P) to return solutions from three virtual images. The solutions can then be computed by an orthogonality constraint, which was proven to be a significant improvement on accuracy and robustness.

In our paper, the algorithm originated from Rodrigues et al. [8] is used in the localisation of two non-overlapping Kinects.

## 3   Theory

### 3.1   Overview of Our Proposed System

To demonstrate our idea, we have built the system for capturing the scene and reconstruction. The subsequent subsections cover the details.

Two Kinects, "Master Kinect $K_1$" and "Reference Kinect $K_2$", are placed in the scene as shown in Fig. 1. They are positioned in a back-to-back manner such that their views are non-overlapping. A checkerboard is placed on the top of Kinect $K_2$. Each Kinect can capture the point clouds ($P_1$ and $P_2$) of its field of view respectively. To merge the point clouds together to form the complete scene, point cloud $P_2$ should be translated to the coordinate system of $K_1$. The pose of $K_2$ must be known to $K_1$ in order to perform this task. In addition, the

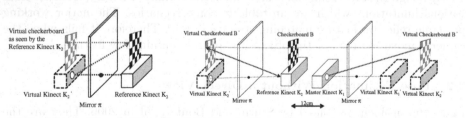

(a) Reference Kinect $K_2$ and the virtual checkerboard $B'$

(b) Master Kinect $K_1$ and the virtual checkerboard $B'$

**Fig. 1.** Overview of our proposed system

position of checkerboard is not as same as that of Kinect $K_2$ cameras. Therefore, the pose of the checkerboard with respect to the $K_2$ camera must also be known. In summary, the proposed algorithm finds out the following to recover the whole 3-D environment:

- The relative pose between $K_1$ and $K_2$.
- The relative pose between the checkerboard $B$ and the camera of $K_2$.

To achieve the tasks, we used a planar mirror to recover the calibration pattern images and the estimation is conducted by the linear methods. In the following sections, we will describe (1) the geometry of the symmetric reflection and (2) the linear method for recovering poses of the back-to-back Kinects.

### 3.2    Geometry of Mirror Reflection

The formation of the mirror image and the camera geometry are shown in this section. Theories from Rodrigues et al. [8] are summarized and presented here.

First, we define the 3-D point projection. From bringing back the points from the world coordinate to a camera coordinate, the transformation matrix $T$ is applied to the points.

$$T = \begin{pmatrix} R & t \\ \mathbf{0} & 1 \end{pmatrix} \tag{1}$$

$T$ is a $4 \times 4$ transformation matrix containing a $3 \times 3$ rotation matrix $R$ and a $3 \times 1$ translation matrix $t$.

Moreover, two parameters are needed to define the mirror $\pi$. They are the normals in unit vector $\mathbf{n}$ and the orthogonal distance $d$ from the mirror to the origin. An arbitrary point $x$ is on the plane $\pi$ if and only if:

$$\mathbf{n}^T x = d \tag{2}$$

Now we define the point projection properties. Assume $P$ is the point in the world that cannot be seen by the camera directly, and $\widehat{P}$ is the reflected point of $P$. The projection on the plane can be represented by:

$$p \sim K \begin{pmatrix} I & 0 \end{pmatrix} T \begin{pmatrix} \widehat{P} \\ 1 \end{pmatrix} \tag{3}$$

From the Fig. 2, we can establish the relationship between the 3-D point $P$ and its reflection $\widehat{P}$.

$$\widehat{P} = P + 2(d - \mathbf{n}^T P)\mathbf{n} \tag{4}$$

By simplifying it to matrix form:

$$\begin{pmatrix} \widehat{P} \\ 1 \end{pmatrix} = S \begin{pmatrix} P \\ 1 \end{pmatrix} \tag{5}$$

where $S$ is an symmetry transformation caused by mirror $\pi$.

$$S = \begin{pmatrix} 1 - 2\mathbf{n}\mathbf{n}^T & 2d\mathbf{n} \\ 0 & 1 \end{pmatrix} \tag{6}$$

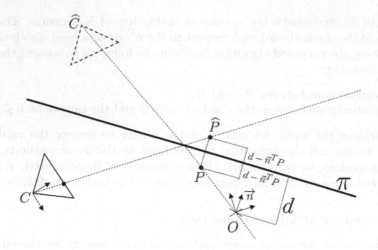

**Fig. 2.** Overview of mirror geometry. $P$ is a 3-D point and $\widehat{P}$ is its reflection.

Now we define the geometry of the reflected camera model - virtual camera. By combining Eqs. 3 and 5,

$$p \sim K \left( I\ 0 \right) TS \begin{pmatrix} P \\ 1 \end{pmatrix} \tag{7}$$

From Eq. 7, $TS$ transforms the points in world coordinates to the respective mirrored camera frame $\widehat{C}$. There is a remark from Kumar et al. [6] that the handiness changes caused by any symmetry transformation. More Importantly, the transformation from the real space camera $C$ to the virtual space camera $\widehat{C}$ is defined by $S'$ symmetry matrix,

$$S' = TST^{-1} \tag{8}$$

The transformation $S'$ is involutionary, i.e. $S'$ can also be applied to transformation from the virtual space to the real space.

### 3.3   Problem Formulation

After the reflection geometry is defined, the calibration problem can then be formulated.

Figure 3 shows the geometry of virtual cameras and mirrors. In the followings we take the virtual camera $\widehat{C}_1$ as the reference frame.

$T_{i=1..N}$ are the rigid transformations among virtual cameras. Note that Gluckman and Nayar [10] revealed that those transformation are always planar.

Let $\widehat{P}_i$ and $P_r$ be the same 3-D point expressed with respect to $\widehat{C}_i$ and $C_r$ respectively. From Eqs. 5 and 8,

$$\begin{pmatrix} P_r \\ 1 \end{pmatrix} = T_i S_i T_i^{-1} \begin{pmatrix} \widehat{P}_i \\ 1 \end{pmatrix} \tag{9}$$

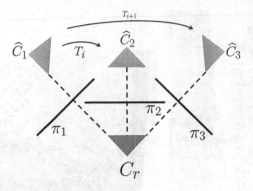

**Fig. 3.** Mirrors $\pi_i$ and virtual cameras $\widehat{C}_i$

After all, the following sets of linear constraints can then be established:

$$t_i = 2(d_1 - 2d_i cos(\frac{\theta_i}{2}))n_1 + 2d_i n_i \tag{10}$$

$$t_i^T n_1 - 2d_1 + 2cos(\frac{\theta_i}{2})d_i = 0 \tag{11}$$

$$[t_i]_x n_1 - 2sin(\frac{\theta_i}{2})w_i d_i = 0 \tag{12}$$

With more than 3 virtual views, we can form the following matrix:

$$\begin{pmatrix} B_1 & b_1 & 0 & \cdots & 0 \\ B_2 & 0 & b_2 & \cdots & 0 \\ \vdots & \vdots & \vdots & \ddots & \vdots \\ B_{N-1} & 0 & 0 & \cdots & b_{N-1} \end{pmatrix} \begin{pmatrix} n_1 \\ d_1 \\ d_2 \\ d_3 \\ \vdots \\ d_N \end{pmatrix} = 0, \tag{13}$$

$$\text{where } B_i = \begin{pmatrix} t_i^T & -2 \\ [t_i]_x & 0 \end{pmatrix}, b_i = \begin{pmatrix} 2cos(\frac{\theta_i}{2}) \\ -2sin(\frac{\theta_i}{2})w_i \end{pmatrix}$$

By applying SVD to the system, the least square solution can be obtained and hence the positions of mirror planes can then be calculated. With this information, we can further determine the symmetry matrix $S$ and locates the real camera $C_r$.

## 4    Experiments

To illustrate our idea our group had built a 160-cm-tall robot with two Kinects on the rotation platform. Figure 4a shows the robot. They are placed in a back-to-back manner, are separated by a distance of 25 cm. The back-to-back Kinect

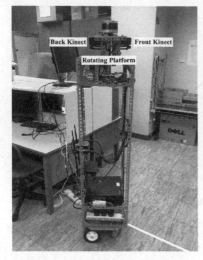 

(a) Our robot                    (b) Calibrating the Kinect by a mirror

**Fig. 4.** Using our scene capturing robot

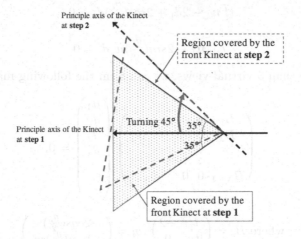

**Fig. 5.** The region captured by the front Kinect at **step 1** and **step 2**

pair is placed on a rotating platform controlled by a computer. At step 1, we first capture the front and back region by the Kinect pair. Since the Kinect can only cover a region of 70°, so we need to rotate the Kinect pair to cover a larger region. Thus we take another 3-D view at step 2 by turning the Kinect pair 45° horizontally. We repeat till step 4. So the front view $(4 \times 45° + 35° \times 2 = 250°)$ will be covered by the front Kinect. Since the back Kinect also capture the back scene with the same scope, the full 360° scene can be covered. The regions covered by the front Kinect at step 1 and step 2 are shown in Fig. 5. The final process is

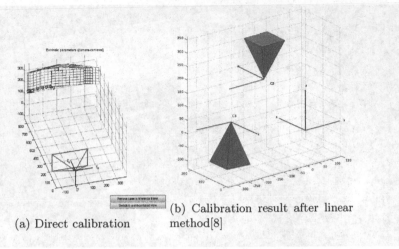

(a) Direct calibration

(b) Calibration result after linear method[8]

**Fig. 6.** Calibration results

to merge the point clouds captured at all the steps according to their relative positions (shown in Fig. 6b).

### 4.1 Calibration Using Mirror

In order to verify the algorithm, we performed experiments by manoeuvring mirrors in different key positions and capturing the images. After we had aggregated all the results, we tested and analysed them by Bouguet's Matlab camera calibration toolbox [11].

Figure 6a shows the result of direct calibration. As the calibration algorithm was not aware of the mirrors, the checkerboard patterns appeared to be far behind of them. The process was repeated with the second Kinect at the back. After we had collected all the samples, the linear method by Rodriduges et al. [8] was used to estimate the camera positions.

After the Kinects are calibrated, we applied it to our scanning robot. The rotation platform will turn so that the two Kinects can capture the whole 360-degree scene. Here shows the result of aggregation and merging of point cloud in Fig. 7. Our proposed solution successfully reconstruct an indoor environment, without the need of displacing the Kinect around the scene such as required by KinectFusion [1].

**Fig. 7.** Point cloud merging results

## 5    Conclusion

In this paper, we proposed a multiple-Kinect approach to solving the problem of 3-D scene reconstruction. Two back-to-back Kinects were mounted on top of a robot and performed scanning. The aggregated result is stable and accurate as compared to one-Kinect methods such as KinectFusion [1]. In addition, the system is easy to deploy and requires low-cost hardware only. In the future, we are confident that the complete system can be built for various virtual reality applications such as building virtual models for virtual tourism or virtual museums.

**Acknowledgement.** This work is supported by a direct grant (Project Code: 4055045) from the Faculty of Engineering of the Chinese University of Hong Kong.

## References

1. Newcombe, R.A., Izadi, S., Hilliges, O., Molyneaux, D., Kim, D., Davison, A.J., Kohi, P., Shotton, J., Hodges, S., Fitzgibbon, A.: KinectFusion: real-time dense surface mapping and tracking. In: 2011 10th IEEE International Symposium on Mixed and Augmented Reality (ISMAR), pp. 127–136. IEEE (2011)
2. Kim, S., Kim, J.: Occupancy mapping and surface reconstruction using local Gaussian processes with kinect sensors. IEEE Trans. Cybern. **43**, 1335–1346 (2013)
3. Zhang, Z.: A flexible new technique for camera calibration. IEEE Trans. Pattern Anal. Mach. Intell. **22**, 1330–1334 (2000)
4. Whelan, T., Johannsson, H., Kaess, M., Leonard, J.J., McDonald, J.: Robust real-time visual odometry for dense RGB-D mapping. In: 2013 IEEE International Conference on Robotics and Automation (ICRA), pp. 5724–5731. IEEE (2013)

5. Sturm, P., Bonfort, T.: How to compute the pose of an object without a direct view? In: Narayanan, P.J., Nayar, S.K., Shum, H.-Y. (eds.) ACCV 2006. LNCS, vol. 3852, pp. 21–31. Springer, Heidelberg (2006). doi:10.1007/11612704_3
6. Kumar, R.K., Ilie, A., Frahm, J.M., Pollefeys, M.: Simple calibration of non-overlapping cameras with a mirror. In: IEEE Conference on Computer Vision and Pattern Recognition, CVPR 2008, pp. 1–7. IEEE (2008)
7. Hesch, J.A., Mourikis, A.I., Roumeliotis, S.I.: Mirror-based extrinsic camera calibration. In: Chirikjian, G.S., Choset, H., Morales, M., Murphey, T. (eds.) Algorithmic Foundation of Robotics VIII, pp. 285–299. Springer, Heidelberg (2009)
8. Rodrigues, R., Barreto, J.P., Nunes, U.: Camera pose estimation using images of planar mirror reflections. In: Daniilidis, K., Maragos, P., Paragios, N. (eds.) ECCV 2010. LNCS, vol. 6314, pp. 382–395. Springer, Heidelberg (2010). doi:10. 1007/978-3-642-15561-1_28
9. Takahashi, K., Nobuhara, S., Matsuyama, T.: A new mirror-based extrinsic camera calibration using an orthogonality constraint. In: 2012 IEEE Conference on Computer Vision and Pattern Recognition (CVPR), pp. 1051–1058. IEEE (2012)
10. Gluckman, J., Nayar, S.K.: Catadioptric stereo using planar mirrors. Int. J. Comput. Vis. **44**, 65–79 (2001)
11. Bouguet, J.Y.: Camera calibration toolbox for Matlab (2004)

# Author Index

Printed in the United States
By Bookmasters

Printed in the United States
By Bookmasters